Better Critical Thinking Skills

Connect History builds critical thinking and writing skills through "Critical Missions" scenarios that place students in a pivotal moment in time and ask them to read and examine sources, maps, and timelines and develop a historical argument.

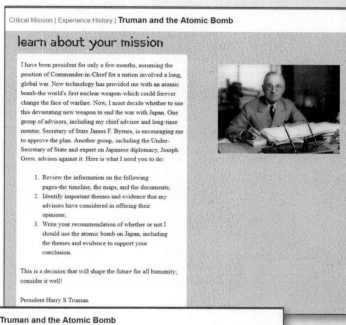

Critical Mission | Experience History | **Truman and the Atomic Bomb**

learn about your mission

I have been president for only a few months, assuming the position of Commander-in-Chief for a nation involved a long, global war. New technology has provided me with an atomic bomb-the world's first nuclear weapon-which could forever change the face of warfare. Now, I must decide whether to use this devastating new weapon to end the war with Japan. One group of advisors, including my chief advisor and long-time mentor, Secretary of State James F. Byrnes, is encouraging me to approve the plan. Another group, including the Under-Secretary of State and expert on Japanese diplomacy, Joseph Grew, advises against it. Here is what I need you to do:

1. Review the information on the following pages-the timeline, the maps, and the documents;
2. Identify important themes and evidence that my advisors have considered in offering their opinions;
3. Write your recommendation of whether or not I should use the atomic bomb on Japan, including the themes and evidence to support your conclusion.

This is a decision that will shape the future for all humanity; consider it well!

President Harry S Truman

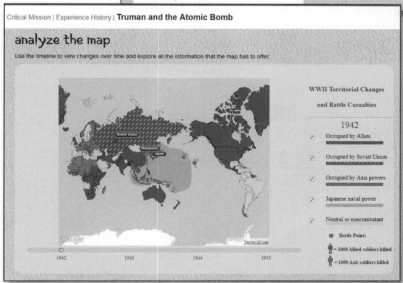

Critical Mission | Experience History | **Truman and the Atomic Bomb**

analyze the map

Use the timeline to view changes over time and explore all the information that the map has to offer.

WWII Territorial Changes

and Battle Casualties

1942

☑ Occupied by Allies

☑ Occupied by Soviet Union

☑ Occupied by Axis powers

☑ Japanese naval power

☑ Neutral or noncombatant

✸ Battle Points

🚹 = 1000 Allied soldiers killed

🚹 = 1000 Axis soldiers killed

1942   1943   1944   1945

Better Geography Skills

Embedded narrated map video learning resources in SmartBook support geographical as well as historical thinking.

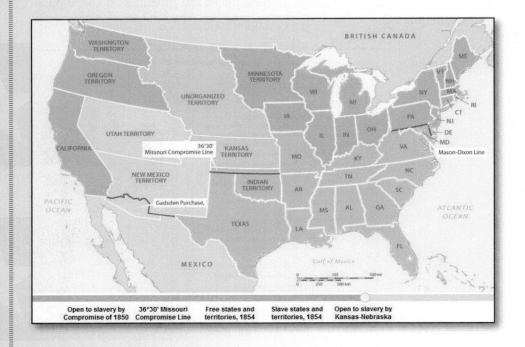

Better Grades

Connect History offers a number of powerful reports and charts to give you the information you need to easily evaluate performance and keep students on a path to success. Connect Insight—now available for both students and instructors—is a series of visual data displays that provide at-a-glance information regarding student performance. Either quick review or in-depth, these reports remove the guesswork so you can focus on what matters most.

THE UNFINISHED NATION

A Concise History of the American People

Eighth Edition

ALAN BRINKLEY
Columbia University

with Contributions from

JOHN GIGGIE
University of Alabama

ANDREW HUEBNER
University of Alabama

THE UNFINISHED NATION: A CONCISE HISTORY OF THE AMERICAN PEOPLE, EIGHTH EDITION

Published by McGraw-Hill Education, 2 Penn Plaza, New York, NY 10121. Copyright © 2016 by McGraw-Hill Education. All rights reserved. Printed in the United States of America. Previous editions © 2014, 2010, and 2008. No part of this publication may be reproduced or distributed in any form or by any means, or stored in a database or retrieval system, without the prior written consent of McGraw-Hill Education, including, but not limited to, in any network or other electronic storage or transmission, or broadcast for distance learning.

Some ancillaries, including electronic and print components, may not be available to customers outside the United States.

This book is printed on acid-free paper.

1 2 3 4 5 6 7 8 9 0 DOC/DOC 1 0 9 8 7 6 5

ISBN 978-0-07-351333-1
MHID 0-07-351333-4

Senior Vice President, Products & Markets: *Kurt L. Strand*
Vice President, General Manager, Products & Markets: *Michael Ryan*
Vice President, Content Design & Delivery: *Kimberly Meriwether David*
Managing Director: *Gina Boedeker*
Brand Manager: *Jason Seitz*
Director, Product Development: *Meghan Campbell*
Lead Product Developer: *Rhona Robbin*
Product Developer: *Cynthia Ward*
Executive Marketing Manager: *April Cole*
Marketing Manager: *Alexandra Schultz*
Executive Market Development Manager: *Stacy Ruel*

Digital Product Developer: *David Chodoff*
Director, Content Design & Delivery: *Terri Schiesl*
Program Manager: *Marianne Musni*
Content Project Managers: *Susan Trentacosti, Marianne Musni, Karen Jozefowicz*
Buyer: *Susan K. Culbertson*
Design: *David Hash*
Content Licensing Specialists: *Carrie Burger, Ann Marie Jannette*
Cover Image: © *Underwood & Underwood/Corbis;* © *Uwe Kazmaier/imageBROKER//Corbis*
Compositor: *Aptara®, Inc.*
Printer: *R. R. Donnelley*

Credits: *Frontmatter: Page ix (T):* © *Biblioteca Nacional, Madrid, Spain/Bridgeman Images; (B):* © *MPI/Getty Images; p. x: The Library of Congress; p. xi (T):* © *MPI/Hulton Archive/Getty Images; (B): Courtesy National Gallery of Art, Washington, D.C.; p. xii:* © *Walters Art Museum, Baltimore, USA/Bridgeman Images; p. xiii:* © *Saint Louis Art Museum, Missouri, USA/Gift of Bank of America/Bridgeman Images; p. xiv (T): The Library of Congress; (B):* © *Bettmann/Corbis; p. xv:* © *Granger, NYC -All Rights Reserved.; p. xvi: The Library of Congress; p. xvii:* © *Photo Reproduction by Transcendental Graphics/Getty Images; p. xix:* © *United Artists/ Photofest; p. xx:* © *Granger, NYC -All Rights Reserved.; p. xxi (T):* © *Instituto Nazionale Luce/Alinari/Getty Images; (B):* © *Popperfoto/Getty Images; p. xxiv:* © *Ian Dagnall/Alamy. Design elements: Scales:* © *Comstock/ Jupiter Images; Phonograph:* © *Burke/Triolo/Brand X Pictures/Jupiter Images; Race car:* © *George Doyle/ Stockbyte/Getty Images (RF); Wooden top:* © *Image Club; Stack of books:* © *D. Hurst/Alamy; American flag:* © *Steve Cole/Getty Images (RF); Double hemisphere map:* © *Stockbyte/Getty Images (RF)*

Library of Congress Cataloging-in-Publication Data

Brinkley, Alan.
   The unfinished nation: a concise history of the American people / Alan Brinkley, Columbia University; with contributions from John Giggie, University of Alabama; Andrew Huebner, University of Alabama. — Eighth edition.
      pages cm
   ISBN 978-0-07-351333-1 (alkaline paper) — ISBN 0-07-351333-4 (alkaline paper)
   1. United States—History. I. Giggie, John Michael, 1965- II. Huebner, Andrew. III. Title.
   E178.1.B827 2016
   973—dc23

                                                                        2015025264

The Internet addresses listed in the text were accurate at the time of publication. The inclusion of a website does not indicate an endorsement by the authors or McGraw-Hill Education, and McGraw-Hill Education does not guarantee the accuracy of the information presented at these sites.

mheducation.com/highered

ABOUT THE AUTHORS

ALAN BRINKLEY is the Allan Nevins Professor of History at Columbia University. He served as university provost at Columbia from 2003 to 2009. He is the author of *Voices of Protest: Huey Long, Father Coughlin, and the Great Depression*, which won the 1983 National Book Award; *American History: Connecting with the Past; The End of Reform: New Deal Liberalism in Recession and War; Liberalism and Its Discontents; Franklin D. Roosevelt;* and *The Publisher: Henry Luce and His American Century.* He is board chair of the National Humanities Center, board chair of the Century Foundation, and a trustee of Oxford University Press. He is also a member of the Academy of Arts and Sciences. In 1998–1999, he was the Harmsworth Professor of History at Oxford University, and in 2011–2012, the Pitt Professor at the University of Cambridge. He won the Joseph R. Levenson Memorial Teaching Award at Harvard and the Great Teacher Award at Columbia. He was educated at Princeton and Harvard.

JOHN GIGGIE is associate professor of history and African American studies at the University of Alabama. He is the author of *After Redemption: Jim Crow and the Transformation of African American Religion in the Delta, 1875–1917,* editor of *America Firsthand,* and editor of *Faith in the Market: Religion and the Rise of Commercial Culture.* He is currently preparing a book on African American religion during the Civil War. He has been honored for his teaching, most recently with a Distinguished Fellow in Teaching award from the University of Alabama. He received his PhD from Princeton University.

ANDREW HUEBNER is associate professor of history at the University of Alabama. He is the author of *The Warrior Image: Soldiers in American Culture from the Second World War to the Vietnam Era* and has written and spoken widely on the subject of war and society in the twentieth-century United States. He is currently working on a study of American families and public culture during the First World War. He received his PhD from Brown University.

BRIEF CONTENTS

3 SOCIETY AND CULTURE IN PROVINCIAL AMERICA 54

4 THE EMPIRE IN TRANSITION 83

9 JACKSONIAN AMERICA 201

10 AMERICA'S ECONOMIC REVOLUTION 225

135,000 SETS, 270,000 VOLUMES SOLD.

UNCLE TOM'S CABIN

FOR SALE HERE.

AN EDITION FOR THE MILLION, COMPLETE IN 1 Vol., PRICE 37 1/2 CENTS.
IN GERMAN, IN 1 Vol., PRICE 50 CENTS.
IN 2 Vols., CLOTH, 6 PLATES, PRICE $1.50.
SUPERB ILLUSTRATED EDITION, IN 1 Vol., WITH 153 ENGRAVINGS,
PRICES FROM $2.50 TO $5.00.

The Greatest Book of the Age.

13 THE IMPENDING CRISIS 296

14 THE CIVIL WAR 321

17 | INDUSTRIAL SUPREMACY 404

18 | THE AGE OF THE CITY 427

THE title *The Unfinished Nation* is meant to suggest several things. It is a reminder of America's exceptional diversity—of the degree to which, despite all the many efforts to build a single, uniform definition of the meaning of American nationhood, that meaning remains contested. It is a reference to the centrality of change in American history—to the ways in which the nation has continually transformed itself and continues to do so in our own time. And it is also a description of the writing of American history itself—of the ways in which historians are engaged in a continuing, ever unfinished, process of asking new questions.

Like any history, *The Unfinished Nation* is a product of its time and reflects the views of the past that historians of recent generations have developed. The writing of our nation's history—like our nation itself—changes constantly. It is not, of course, the past that changes. Rather, historians adjust their perspectives and priorities, ask different kinds of questions, and uncover and incorporate new historical evidence. There are now, as there have always been, critics of changes in historical understanding who argue that history is a collection of facts and should not be subject to "interpretation" or "revision." But historians insist that history is not simply a collection of facts. Names and dates and a record of events are only the beginning of historical understanding. Writers and readers of history interpret the evidence before them, and inevitably bring to the task their own questions, concerns, and experiences.

Our history requires us to examine the many different peoples and ideas that have shaped American society. But it also requires us to understand that the United States is a nation whose people share many things: a common political system, a connection to an integrated national (and now international) economy, and a familiarity with a powerful mass culture. To understand the American past, it is necessary to understand both the forces that divide Americans and the forces that draw them together.

It is a daunting task to attempt to convey the history of the United States in a single book, and the eighth edition of *The Unfinished Nation* has, as have all previous editions, been carefully written and edited to keep the book as concise and readable as possible.

In addition to the content and scholarship updates that are detailed on pages xxxi–xxxii, we have strengthened the pedagogical features with an eye to the details. We added a glossary of historical terms and bolded those terms within the text where significantly discussed. These terms, along with key names, places, and events, are listed at the end of chapters to help students review. All of the Consider the Source features now include concise introductions that provide context for the documents. Every Consider the Source, Debating the Past, Patterns of Popular Culture, and America in the World feature is referenced within the narrative, for a clearer indication of how the different lines of inquiry work together to create a vivid and nuanced portrait of each period. Margin notes have been reinstated as well, at the request of reviewers who missed this feature from earlier editions.

It is not only the writing of history that changes with time—the tools and technologies through which information is delivered change as well. New learning resources include:

- **McGraw-Hill Connect®**—an integrated educational platform that seamlessly joins superior content with enhanced digital tools (including SmartBook®) to deliver a personalized learning experience that provides precisely what students need—when and how they need it. New visual analytics, coupled with powerful reporting, provide immediate performance perspectives. Connect makes it easy to keep students on track.

- **SmartBook**®—an adaptive eBook that makes study time as productive and efficient as possible. It identifies and closes knowledge gaps through a continually adapting reading experience that provides personalized learning resources such as narrated map videos; key point summaries; time lines; and labeling activities at the precise moment of need. This ensures that every minute spent with SmartBook is returned to the student as the most value-added minute possible.

- **Critical Missions**—an activity within Connect History that immerses students in pivotal moments in history. As students study primary sources and maps, they advise a key historical figure on an issue of vital importance—for example, should President Truman drop the atomic bomb on Japan?

- **Primary Source Primer**—a video exercise in Connect History with multiple-choice questions. The primer teaches students the importance of primary sources and how to analyze them. This online "Introduction to Primary Sources" is designed for use at the beginning of the course, to save valuable class time.

- **Create**™—a service that allows professors to create a customized version of *The Unfinished Nation* by selecting the chapters and additional primary source documents that best fit their course, while adding their own materials if desired. Register at www.mcgrawhillcreate.com to build a complimentary review copy.

- **McGraw-Hill Campus**—a first-of-its-kind institutional service that provides faculty with true, single sign-on access to all of McGraw-Hill's course content, digital tools, and other high-quality learning resources from any learning management system (LMS). This innovative offering allows secure, deep integration and seamless access to any of our course solutions, including McGraw-Hill Connect, McGraw-Hill LearnSmart, McGraw-Hill Create, and Tegrity. McGraw-Hill Campus covers our entire content library, including eBooks, assessment tools, presentation slides, and multimedia content, among other resources. This open and unlimited service allows faculty to quickly prepare for class, create tests or quizzes, develop lecture material, integrate interactive content, and much more.

ALAN BRINKLEY

ACKNOWLEDGMENTS

WE are grateful to the many advisers and reviewers who generously offered comments, suggestions, and ideas at various stages in the development of this project. Our thanks go to:

Academic Reviewers

Tramaine Anderson, *Tarrant County College, Northeast*

Darlene Antezana, *Prince George's Community College*

Maj. Paul Belmont, *U.S. Military Academy, West Point*

Peter Belser, *Ivy Tech Community College*

Robert Bender, *Eastern New Mexico University, Roswell*

Tiffany Bergman, *Missouri Valley College*

Devan Bissonette, *Excelsior College*

Blanche Brick, *Blinn College*

Brian Cervantez, *Tarrant County College, Northwest*

Sharon Courmier, *Lamar University*

Keith D. Dickson, *Old Dominion University*

Kevin Eades, *North Central Texas College*

Angela S. Edwards, *Florence-Darlington Technical College*

Ron Enders, *Ashland Community College*

Amy Essington, *California State University, Long Beach*

Glen Findley, *Odessa College*

Brandon Franke, *Blinn College*

Mary E. Frederickson, *Miami University of Ohio*

Joy Giguere, *Ivy Tech Community College*

Howell H. Gwin Jr., *Lamar University*

Donn Hall, *Ivy Tech Community College*

Maj. Adrienne Harrison, *U.S. Military Academy, West Point*

Andrew Hollinger, *Tarrant County College, Northeast*

Volker Janssen, *California State University, Fullerton*

Brian Johnson, *Tarrant County College, South*

Philbert Martin, *San Jacinto College, South*

Linda McCabe, *Tarrant County College, Northeast*

Maureen A. McCormick, *Florida State College at Jacksonville*

Brian Craig Miller, *Emporia State University*

Amanda Lea Miracle, *Emporia State University*

Josh Montandon, *North Central Texas College*

Wesley Moody, *Florida State College*

Rebekkah Morrow, *Western Oklahoma State College*

Simone de Santiago Ramos, *North Central Texas College*

Matt Schaffer, *Florence-Darlington Technical College*

Jason Scheller, *Vernon College*

Rebecca Seaman, *Elizabeth City State University*

Dennis Spillman, *North Central Texas College*

Eddie Weller, *San Jacinto College, South*

Ann K. Wentworth, *Excelsior College*

Cody Whitaker, *Drury University*

Christina A. Wilbur, *Lamar University*

Geoffrey Willbanks, *Tyler Junior College*

Martin W. Wilson, *East Stroudsburg University*

Cary Wintz, *Texas Southern University*

Connect Board of Advisors

Michael Downs, *University of Texas–Arlington*

Jim Halverson, *Judson University*

Reid Holland, *Midlands Technical College*

Stephen Katz, *Rider University*

David Komito, *Eastern Oregon University*

Wendy Sarti, *Oakton Community College*

Linda Scherr, *Mercer County Community College*

Eloy Zarate, *Pasadena City College*

Symposium and Digiposium Attendees

Gisela Ables, *Houston Community College*

Sal Anselmo, *Delgado Community College*

Mario A. J. Bennekin, *Georgia Perimeter College*

C. J. Bibus, *Wharton County Junior College*

Olwyn M. Blouet, *Virginia State University*

Michael Botson, *Houston Community College*

Cathy Briggs, *Northwest Vista College*

Brad Cartwright, *University of Texas–El Paso*

Roger Chan, *Washington State University*

June Cheatham, *Richland College*

Keith Chu, *Bergen Community College*

Karl Clark, *Coastal Bend College*

Bernard Comeau, *Tacoma Community College*
Kevin Davis, *North Central Texas College*
Michael Downs, *Tarrant County College*
Tim Draper, *Waubonsee Community College*
Laura Dunn, *Brevard Community College*
Arthur Durand, *Metropolitan Community College*
Amy Forss, *Metropolitan Community College*
Jim Good, *Lone Star College*
R. David Goodman, *Pratt Institute*
Wendy Gunderson, *Colin County Community College*
Debbie Hargis, *Odessa College*
Jim Harper, *North Carolina Central University*
Matt Hinckley, *Eastfield College*
John Hosler, *Morgan State University*
James Jones, *Prairie View A&M University*
Philip Kaplan, *University of North Florida*
Carol A. Keller, *San Antonio College*
Greg Kelm, *Dallas Baptist University*
Michael Kinney, *Calhoun Community College*
Jennifer Lang, *Delgado Community College*
Meredith R. Martin, *Collin College*
Thomas Massey, *Cape Fear Community College*
Linda McCabe, *North Lake College*
Sandy Norman, *Florida Atlantic University*
Michelle Novak, *Houston Community College*
Jessica Patton, *Tarrant County College*
Robert Risko, *Trinity Valley Community College*
Gary Ritter, *Central Piedmont Community College*
Esther Robinson, *Lone Star College*
Geri Ryder, *Ocean County College*
Horacio Salinas, *Laredo Community College*
Linda Scherr, *Mercer County Community College*

Jeffrey Smith, *Lindenwood University*
Rachel Standish, *San Joaquin Delta College*
Connie B. Thomason, *Louisiana Delta Community College*
Roger Ward, *Colin County Community College*
Don Whatley, *Blinn College*
David White, *McHenry County College*
Geoffrey Willbanks, *Tyler Junior College*
Scott M. Williams, *Weatherford College*
Carlton Wilson, *North Carolina Central University*
Chad Wooley, *Tarrant County College*

Focus Group Participants

Simon Baatz, *John Jay College*
Manu Bhagavan, *Hunter College*
David Dzurec, *University of Scranton*
Mark Jones, *Central Connecticut State University*
Stephen Katz, *Philadelphia University*
Jessica Kovler, *John Jay College*
David Lansing, *Ocean County College*
Benjamin Lapp, *Montclair State University*
Julian Madison, *Southern Connecticut State University*
David Marshall, *Suffolk Community College*
George Monahan, *Suffolk Community College*
Tracy Musacchio, *John Jay College*
Mikal Nash, *Essex County College*
Veena Oldenburg, *Baruch College*
Edward Paulino, *John Jay College*
Craig Pilant, *County College of Morris*
Susan Schmidt Horning, *Saint John's University*
Donna Scimeca, *College of Staten Island*
Matthew Vaz, *City College of New York*
Christian Warren, *Brooklyn College*

The Unfinished Nation makes history relevant to students through a series of engaging features:

CONSIDER THE SOURCE FEATURES

In every chapter, Consider the Source features guide students through careful analysis of historical documents and prompt them to closely examine the ideas expressed, as well as the historical circumstances. Among the classic sources included are Benjamin Franklin's testimony against the Stamp Act, the Gettysburg Address, a radio address from FDR, and Ronald Reagan on the role of government. Concise introductions provide context, and concluding questions prompt students to understand, analyze, and evaluate each source.

CONSIDER THE SOURCE

BARTOLOMÉ DE LAS CASAS, "OF THE ISLAND OF HISPANIOLA" (1542)

Bartolomé de Las Casas, a Dominican friar from Spain, was an early European settler of the West Indies. He devoted much of his life to describing the culture of native peoples and chronicling the many abuses they suffered at the hands of their colonizers. This excerpt is from a letter he addressed to Spain's Prince Philip.

God has created all these numberless people to be quite the simplest, without malice or duplicity, most obedient, most faithful to their natural Lords, and to the Christians, whom they serve; the most humble, most patient, most peaceful and calm, without strife nor tumults; not wrangling, nor querulous, as free from uproar, hate and desire of revenge as any in the world . . . Among these gentle sheep, gifted by their Maker with the above qualities, the Spaniards entered as soon as they knew them, like wolves, tigers and lions which had been starving for many days, and since forty years they have done nothing else; nor do they afflict, torment, and destroy them with strange and new, and divers kinds of cruelty, never before seen, nor heard of, nor read of . . .

The Christians, with their horses and swords and lances, began to slaughter and practice strange cruelty among them. They penetrated into the country and spared neither children nor the aged, nor pregnant women, nor those in child labour, all of whom they ran through the body and lacerated, as though they were assaulting so many lambs herded in their sheepfold. They made bets as to who would slit a man in two, or cut off his head at one blow, or they opened up his bowels. They tore the babes from their mothers'

against the rocks. Others they seized by the shoulders and threw into the rivers, laughing and joking, and when they fell into the water they exclaimed: "boil body of so and so!" They spitted the bodies of other babes, together with their mothers and all who were before them, on their swords.

They made a gallows just high enough for the feet to nearly touch the ground, and by thirteens, in honor and reverence of our Redeemer and the twelve Apostles, they put wood underneath and, with fire, they burned the Indians alive.

They wrapped the bodies of others entirely in dry straw, binding them in it and setting fire to it; and so they burned them. They cut off the hands of all they wished to take alive, made them carry them fastened on to them, and said "Go and carry letters"; that is, take the news to those who have fled to the mountains.

They generally killed the lords and nobles in the following way. They made wooden gridirons of stakes, bound them upon them, and made a slow fire beneath; thus the victims gave up the spirit by degrees, emitting cries of despair in their torture.

UNDERSTAND, ANALYZE, & EVALUATE

1. How did Bartolomé de Las Casas characterize the natives? How do you think they would have responded to this description?
2. What metaphor did Las Casas use to describe the natives and where does this metaphor come from?
3. What role did Las Casas expect the Spaniards to play on Hispaniola? What

DEBATING THE PAST FEATURES

DEBATING THE PAST

THE DECISION TO DROP THE ATOMIC BOMB

There has been continuing disagreement since 1945 among historians—and many others—about how to explain and evaluate President Truman's decision to use the atomic bomb against Japan.

Truman himself, both at the time and in his 1955 memoirs, insisted that the decision was a simple and straightforward one. The alternative to using atomic weapons, he claimed, was an American invasion of mainland Japan that might have cost as many as a million American lives. That view has received considerable support from historians. Herbert Feis argued in *The Atomic Bomb and the End of World War II* (1966) that Truman made his decision on purely military grounds—to ensure a speedy American victory. David McCullough, the author of a popular biography of Truman published in 1992, also accepted Truman's own account of his actions largely uncritically, as did Alonzo L. Hamby in *Man of the People* (1995), an important scholarly study of Truman. "One consideration weighed most heavily on Truman," Hamby concluded. "The longer the war lasted, the more Americans killed."

Others have strongly disagreed. As early as 1948, British physicist P. M. S. Blackett wrote in *Fear, War, and the Bomb* that the destruction of Hiroshima and Nagasaki was "not so much the last military act of the second World War as the first major operation of the cold diplomatic war with Russia." The most important critic of Truman's decision is the historian Gar Alperovitz, the author of two influential books on the subject; *Atomic Diplomacy: Hiroshima and Potsdam* (1965) and *The Decision to Use the Atomic Bomb* (1995). Alperovitz dismissed the argument that the bomb was used to shorten the war and save lives. Japan was likely to have surrendered soon even if the bomb had not been used, he claimed. Instead, he argued, the United States used

the bomb less to influence Japan than to intimidate the Soviet Union, "to make Russia more manageable in Europe."

John W. Dower's *War Without Mercy* (1986) contributed, by implication at least, to another controversial explanation of the American decision: racism. The Japanese, many Americans came to believe during the war, were almost a subhuman species. Even many of Truman's harshest critics, however, note that it is, as Alperovitz has written, "all but impossible to find specific evidence that racism was an important factor in the decision to attack Hiroshima and Nagasaki."

The debate over the decision to drop the atomic bomb is an unusually emotional one, and it has inspired bitter professional and personal attacks on advocates of almost every position. It illustrates clearly how history has often been, and remains, a powerful force in the way societies define themselves.

UNDERSTAND, ANALYZE, & EVALUATE

1. The United States dropped two atomic bombs on Japan, one on Hiroshima and the other on Nagasaki. Was dropping the bomb on Hiroshima necessary? Was it justifiable? Do the reasons for dropping the bomb on Hiroshima apply equally to the bombing of Nagasaki?
2. How might the war in the Pacific have been different if the United States had decided not to drop the bombs?

further weakened the Japanese will to resist. Moderate Japanese leaders, who had long since concluded the war was lost, were looking to end the fighting. But they continued to face powerful opposition from military leaders. Whether the moderates could ultimately have prevailed is a question historians continue to debate. In any case, their efforts became superfluous in August 1945, when the United States made use of a terrible new weapon it had been developing throughout the war.

THE MANHATTAN PROJECT AND ATOMIC WARFARE

Reports had reached the United States in 1939 that Nazi scientists had taken the first step toward the creation of an atomic bomb: a proton-mass exploded they were successive...

Debating the Past essays introduce students to the contested quality of much of the American past, and they provide a sense of the evolving nature of historical scholarship. From examining specific differences in historical understandings of the Constitution, to exploring the causes of the Civil War and the significance of Watergate, these essays familiarize students with the interpretive character of historical understanding.

AMERICA IN THE WORLD FEATURES

America in the World essays focus on specific parallels between American history and those of other nations and demonstrate the importance of the many global influences on the American story. Topics such as the global Industrial Revolution, the abolition of slavery, and the global depression of the 1920s provide concrete examples of the connections between the history of the United States and the history of other nations.

PATTERNS OF POPULAR CULTURE FEATURES

Patterns of Popular Culture essays bring fads, crazes, hangouts, hobbies, and entertainment into the story of American history, encouraging students to expand their definition of what constitutes history and gain a new understanding of what popular culture reveals about a society.

WHAT'S NEW TO *THE UNFINISHED NATION,* EIGHTH EDITION

We have revised the narrative and the features throughout this eighth edition for clarity and currency. On a chapter-by-chapter basis, major changes include:

Chapter 1, The Collision of Cultures

- New Debating the Past: "Why Do Historians So Often Differ?"

Chapter 2, Transplantations and Borderlands

- New portrait and information about early colonist Anne Pollard.
- New illustration of the early Savannah colony.

Chapter 3, Society and Culture in Provincial America

- New map of African population density in the colonies.

Chapter 6, The Constitution and the New Republic

- New illustration of the Jeffersonian vision of an agrarian republic.

Chapter 7, The Jeffersonian Era

- New political cartoon about the effects of the Embargo Act.

Chapter 8, Varieties of American Nationalism

- New portrait and information about Sequoyah.

Chapter 9, Jacksonian America

- Additional text and chapter question on the Native American response to U.S. expansion.
- New image satirizing financial policies associated with the depression of the late 1830s.

Chapter 10, America's Economic Revolution

- New Consider the Source: "*Handbook to Lowell,* 1848."

Chapter 11, Cotton, Slavery, and the Old South

- New photograph and information about Harriet Tubman.

Chapter 12, Antebellum Culture and Reform

- New Patterns of Popular Culture: "Sentimental Novels," including a discussion of *Uncle Tom's Cabin.*
- New section—"Struggles of Radical Black Women"—on preachers Jarena Lee and Rebecca Cox Jackson.

- New text connecting Thoreau's idea of civil disobedience with later abolitionist and civil rights protests.
- New text explaining why free blacks resisted the ACS's plan for populating Liberia.
- New photograph and information about Margaret Fuller.
- New painting depicting the Mormon trek to Utah.

Chapter 13, The Impending Crisis

- Revised accounts of how the Compromise of 1850 and the Lincoln-Nebraska Act were achieved.
- New Lone Star flag picture and information on Texas's years as an independent republic.
- New photograph of a multiethnic group of California gold miners.
- New cartoon illustrating a pro-slavery argument.

Chapter 14, The Civil War

- New section—"Billy Yank and Johnny Reb"— describing the motivations and outfitting of Northern and Southern recruits at the start of the Civil War.
- Revised discussion of the North's strategy for winning the war and Lincoln's search for a commander.

Chapter 15, Reconstruction and the New South

- New Patterns of Popular Culture: "The Minstrel Show."
- Expanded discussion of plans to give land to freed slaves as a first step in Reconstruction.
- New editorial cartoon on critics' view of Reconstruction.

Chapter 16, The Conquest of the Far West

- New painting, *American Progress,* illustrating the American idea of the frontier.
- New painting of a Tejanos-run ranch in Texas.
- New painting of Little Bighorn, from a Native American artist's perspective.

Chapter 17, Industrial Supremacy

- New photograph of child laborers and information about Lewis Hine's investigative photography.

Chapter 19, From Crisis to Empire

- New Patterns of Popular Culture: "Yellow Journalism."
- Revised discussion of the factors motivating American imperialism, introducing the concept of "jingoes" and the connection to ideas about the nation's masculinity.
- Revised discussion of the range of American reactions to the Cuban rebellion and the Teller Amendment.
- New discussion of race in the context of the Philippine War.
- New editorial cartoon of Chester Arthur feeling heat of competing interest groups.
- New pro-imperialism editorial cartoon.
- New photograph and information about Populist orator Mary Lease.

Chapter 20, The Progressives

- New Consider the Source: "John Muir on the Value of Wild Places."
- New photograph and information about the suffrage pageant in Washington, D.C., on the eve of Wilson's inauguration.

Chapter 21, America and the Great War

- New Consider the Source: "Race, Gender, and World War I Posters."
- Revised discussion of European alliances and the start of World War I.
- New "Intervention" subsection with a revised discussion of what compelled Wilson to enter the war.
- Revised discussion of the American contribution to the Allies' victory.
- New descriptions of American troops and how Progressive ideas were employed in basic training.
- Reorganized and revised discussion of war casualty numbers.

Chapter 22, The New Era

- New Consider the Source: "America's Early Telephone Network."

Chapter 23, The Great Depression

- Revised discussion of Depression-era literature, and addition of Richard Wright's *Native Son*.

Chapter 24, The New Deal

- New editorial cartoon of an optimistic FDR steering the nation toward recovery.
- New photo and information on the Memorial Day Massacre.
- New photo and information on Eleanor Roosevelt's role in the New Deal.

Chapter 25, The Global Crisis, 1921–1941

- New Patterns of Popular Culture: "Orson Welles and the 'War of the Worlds.'"

Chapter 26, America in a World at War

- New Consider the Source: "The Face of the Enemy."
- New scholarship on wartime culture, including two new sections: "Home-Front Life and Culture" and "Love, Family, and Sexuality in Wartime."
- Updated war casualty numbers.

Chapter 27, The Cold War

- New information on the Rosenberg case.
- Additional information on Ellen Schrecker's *Many Are the Crimes*.
- Revised discussion of Cold War attitudes.

Chapter 28, The Affluent Society

- New Patterns of Popular Culture: "On the Road."
- Expanded explanations of postwar economic growth as well as the decline in farm prices.

Chapter 29, retitled The Turbulent Sixties

- New Patterns of Popular Culture: "The Folk-Music Revival."
- New Consider the Source: "Fannie Lou Hamer on the Struggle for Voting Rights."
- Expanded discussions of the 1964 Civil Rights Act; Malcolm X; the Cuban missile crisis.

Chapter 30, The Crisis of Authority

- Additional information on the extent of the draft and resistance; the history of gay rights; the consequences of the 1973 OPEC embargo.
- New photos showing the Native American occupation of Alcatraz; Robert Kennedy with César Chávez; Nixon in China.
- New graph on the gender income gap.

Chapter 31, From the "Age of Limits" to the Age of Reagan

- New Consider the Source: "Ronald Reagan on the Role of Government."

Chapter 32, The Age of Globalization

- Thoroughly updated and reorganized chapter and illustrations to reflect events up to press time. In addition to content changes in every section:
- New Patterns of Popular Culture: "Rap."
- New Consider the Source: "Same-Sex Marriage, 2015."
- New graph on immigration trends from 1850 to the present.
- Updated discussion of environmental catastrophes, including Deepwater Horizon.

1 THE COLLISION OF CULTURES

AMERICA BEFORE COLUMBUS
EUROPE LOOKS WESTWARD
THE ARRIVAL OF THE ENGLISH

LOOKING AHEAD

1. How did the societies of native people in the South differ from those in the North in the precontact period (before the arrival of the Europeans)?
2. What effects did the arrival of Europeans have on the native peoples of the Americas?
3. How did patterns of settlement differ among the Spanish, English, French, and Dutch immigrants to the Americas?

THE DISCOVERY OF THE AMERICAS did not begin with Christopher Columbus. It began many thousands of years earlier, when human beings first crossed into the new continents and began to people them. By the end of the fifteenth century A.D., when the first important contact with Europeans occurred, the Americas were home to millions of men and women.

These ancient civilizations had experienced many changes and many catastrophes during their long history. But it is likely that none of these experiences was as tragically transforming as the arrival of Europeans. In the first violent years of Spanish and Portuguese exploration and conquest, the impact of the new arrivals was profound. Europeans brought with them diseases (most notably smallpox) to which natives, unlike the invaders, had no immunity. The result was a great demographic catastrophe that killed millions of people, weakened existing societies, and greatly aided the Spanish and Portuguese in their rapid and devastating takeover of the existing American empires.

But the European immigrants were never able to eliminate the influence of the indigenous peoples (whom they came to call "Indians"). In their many interactions, whether beneficial or ruinous, these very different civilizations shaped one another, learned from one another, and changed one another permanently and profoundly.

AMERICA BEFORE COLUMBUS

We know relatively little about the first peoples in the Americas, but archaeologists have uncovered new evidence from artifacts that have survived over many millennia. We continue to learn more about the earliest Americans.

THE PEOPLES OF THE PRECONTACT AMERICAS

For many decades, scholars believed that all early migrations into the Americas came from humans crossing an ancient land bridge over the Bering Strait into what is now Alaska, approximately 11,000 years ago. The migrations were probably a result of the development of new stone tools—spears and other hunting implements—used to pursue the large animals that crossed between Asia and North America. All of these land-based migrants are thought to have come from a Mongolian stock related to that of modern-day Siberia. Scholars refer to these migrants as the "Clovis" people, so named for a town in New Mexico where archaeologists first discovered evidence of their tools and weapons in the 1930s.

More recent archaeological evidence suggests that not all the early migrants to the Americas came across the Bering Strait. Some migrants from Asia appear to have settled as far south as Chile and Peru even before people began moving into North America by land. These first South Americans may have come not by land but by sea, using boats.

This new evidence suggests that the early population of the Americas was more diverse and more scattered than scholars used to believe. Recent DNA evidence has identified a possible early population group that does not seem to have Asian characteristics. This suggests that thousands of years before Columbus, there may have been some migration from Europe.

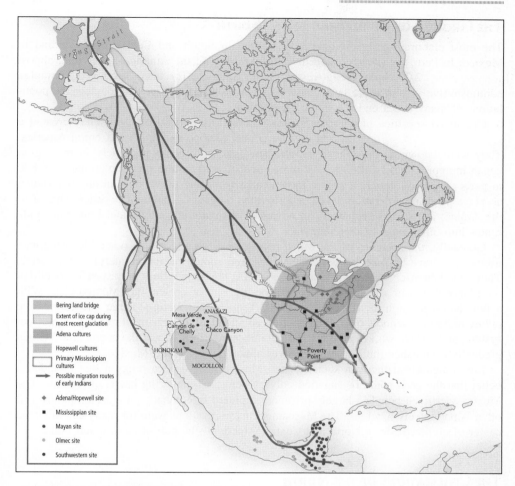

NORTH AMERICAN MIGRATIONS This map tracks some of the very early migrations into, and within, North America in the centuries preceding contact with Europe. The map shows the now-vanished land bridge between Siberia and Alaska over which thousands, perhaps millions, of migrating people passed into the Americas. It also shows the locations of some of the earliest settlements in North America. • *What role did the extended glacial field in what is now Canada play in residential patterns in the ancient American world?*

The *Archaic period* is a scholarly term for the early history of humans in America, beginning around 8000 B.C. In the first part of this period, most humans *The Archaic Period* supported themselves through hunting and gathering, using the same stone tools that earlier Americans had brought with them from Asia.

Later in the Archaic period, population groups began to expand their activities and to develop new tools, such as nets and hooks for fishing, traps for smaller animals, and baskets for gathering berries, nuts, seeds, and other plants. Still later, some groups began to farm. Farming, of course, requires people to stay in one place. In agricultural areas, the first sedentary settlements slowly began to form, creating the basis for larger civilizations.

THE GROWTH OF CIVILIZATIONS: THE SOUTH

The most elaborate early civilizations emerged in South and Central America and in Mexico. In Peru, the Incas created the largest empire in the Americas, stretching almost *The Inca in Peru* 2,000 miles along western South America. The Incas developed a complex administrative system and a large network of paved roads that welded together the populations of many tribes under a single government.

Organized societies of Mesoamericans emerged around 10,000 B.C. They created a *Mesoamerican Civilizations* civilization in what is now Mexico and much of Central America. They were known as the Olmec people. The first truly complex society in the region began in approximately 1000 B.C. A more sophisticated culture grew up around A.D. 800 in parts of Central America and in the Yucatán peninsula of Mexico, in an area known as Maya. Mayan civilization developed a written language, a numerical system similar to the Arabic, an accurate calendar, an advanced agricultural system, and important trade routes into other areas of the continents.

Gradually, the societies of the Maya region were superseded by other Mesoamerican tribes, who have become known collectively (and somewhat inaccurately) as the Aztec. They called themselves Mexica. In about A.D. 1300, the Mexica built the city of Tenochtitlán on a large island in a lake in central Mexico, the site of present-day Mexico City. With a population as high as 100,000 by 1500, Tenochtitlán featured large and impressive public buildings, schools that all male children attended, an organized military, a medical system, and a slave workforce drawn from conquered tribes. A warlike people, the Mexica gradually established their dominance over almost all of central Mexico.

Like other Mesoamerican societies, the Mexica developed a religion that included a belief that the gods could be satisfied only by being fed the living hearts of humans. The Mexica sacrificed people—largely prisoners captured in combat—on a scale unknown in other American civilizations. The Mesoamerican civilizations were for many centuries the center of civilized life in North and Central America—the hub of culture and trade.

THE CIVILIZATIONS OF THE NORTH

The peoples north of Mexico developed less elaborate but still substantial civilizations. Inhabitants of the northern regions of the continent subsisted on combinations of hunting, *Hunting, Gathering, and Fishing* gathering, and fishing. They included the Eskimo (or Inuit) of the Arctic Circle, who fished and hunted seals; big-game hunters of the northern forests, who led nomadic lives based on the pursuit of moose and caribou; tribes of the Pacific Northwest, whose principal occupation was salmon fishing and who created substantial permanent settlements along the coast; and a group of tribes spread through relatively arid regions of the Far West, who developed successful communities based on fishing, hunting small game, and gathering edible plants.

Other societies in North America were agricultural. Among the most developed were *Agricultural Societies* those in the Southwest. The people of that arid region built large irrigation systems, and they constructed towns of stone and adobe. In the Great Plains region, too, most tribes were engaged in sedentary farming (corn and other grains). They lived in large permanent settlements.

The eastern third of what is now the United States—much of it covered with forests and inhabited by the Woodland Indians—had the greatest food resources of any area of the continent. Most of the many tribes of the region engaged in farming, hunting, gathering,

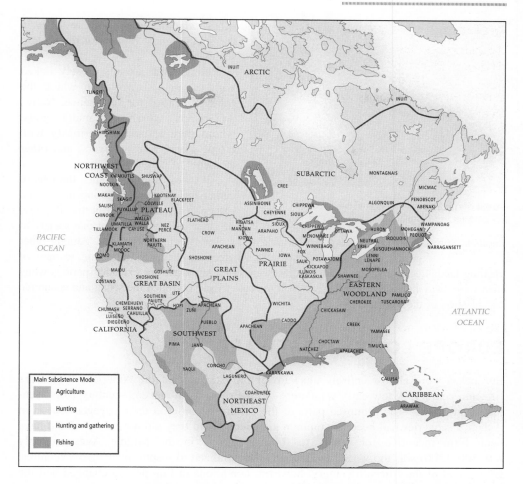

HOW THE EARLY NORTH AMERICANS LIVED This map shows the various ways in which the native tribes of North America supported themselves before the arrival of European civilization. Like most precommercial peoples, the Native Americans survived largely on the resources available in their immediate surroundings. Note, for example, the reliance on the products of the sea of the tribes along the northern coastlines of the continent, and the way in which tribes in relatively inhospitable climates in the North—where agriculture was difficult—relied on hunting large game. Most Native Americans were farmers. • *What different kinds of farming would have emerged in the very different climates of the agricultural regions shown on this map?*

and fishing simultaneously. In the South there were permanent settlements and large trading networks based on the corn and other grains grown in the rich lands of the Mississippi River valley. Cahokia, a trading center located near present-day St. Louis, had a population of 40,000 at its peak in A.D. 1200. ~~Cahokia~~

The agricultural societies of the Northeast were more mobile. Farming techniques there were designed to exploit the land quickly rather than to develop permanent settlements. Many of the tribes living east of the Mississippi River were linked together loosely by common linguistic roots. The largest of these language groups consisted of the Algonquian tribes, who lived along the Atlantic seaboard from Canada to Virginia; the Iroquois Confederacy, which was centered in what is now upstate New York; and the Muskogean

PUEBLO VILLAGE OF THE SOUTHWEST
(© C. McIntyre/PhotoLink/Getty Images)

tribes, which consisted of the tribes in the southernmost regions of the eastern seaboard.

Religion was usually closely linked with the natural world on which the tribes depended for sustenance. Native Americans worshiped many gods, whom they associated variously with crops, game, forests, rivers, and other elements of nature.

All tribes assigned women the jobs of caring for children, preparing meals, and gathering certain foods. But the allocation of other tasks varied from one society to another. Some tribal groups reserved farming tasks almost entirely for men. Among other *Gender Relations* groups, women tended the fields, whereas men engaged in hunting, warfare, or clearing land. Because women and children were often left alone for extended periods while men were away hunting or fighting, women in some tribes controlled the social and economic organization of the settlements.

EUROPE LOOKS WESTWARD

Europeans were almost entirely unaware of the existence of the Americas before the fifteenth century. A few early wanderers—Leif Eriksson, an eleventh-century Norse seaman, and others—had glimpsed parts of the eastern Atlantic on their voyages. But even if their discoveries had become common knowledge (and they did not), there would have been little incentive for others to follow. Europe in the Middle Ages (roughly A.D. 500–1500) was too weak, divided, and decentralized to inspire many great ventures. By the end of the fifteenth century, however, conditions in Europe had changed and the incentive for overseas exploration had grown.

COMMERCE AND SEA TRAVEL

Two important changes encouraged Europeans to look toward new lands. One was the significant growth in Europe's population in the fifteenth century. The Black Death, a catastrophic epidemic of the bubonic plague that began in Constantinople in 1347, had killed more than a third of the people on the Continent (according to some estimates). But a century and *European Population Growth* a half later, the population had rebounded. With that growth came a reawakening of commerce. A new merchant class was emerging to meet the rising demand for goods from abroad. As trade increased, and as advances in navigation made long-distance sea travel more feasible, interest in expanding trade grew even more quickly.

The second change was the emergence of new governments that were more united and *Strong Monarchies* powerful than the feeble political entities of the feudal past. In the western areas of Europe in particular, strong new monarchs were eager to enhance the commercial development of their nations.

In the early fourteenth century, Marco Polo and other adventurers had returned from Asia bearing exotic spices, cloths, and dyes and even more exotic tales. Europeans who craved commercial glory had dreamed above all of trade with the East. For two centuries, that trade had been limited by the difficulties of the long overland journey to the Asian courts. But in the fourteenth century, talk of finding a faster, safer sea route to East Asia began.

The Portuguese were the preeminent maritime power in the fifteenth century, largely because of Prince Henry the Navigator, who devoted much of his life to the promotion of exploration. In 1486, after Henry's death, the Portuguese explorer *Portuguese Exploration* Bartholomeu Dias rounded the southern tip of Africa (the Cape of Good Hope). In 1497–1498, Vasco da Gama proceeded all the way around the cape to India. But the Spanish, not the Portuguese, were the first to encounter the *New World,* the term Europeans applied to the ancient lands previously unknown to them.

CHRISTOPHER COLUMBUS

Christopher Columbus was born and reared in Genoa, Italy. He spent his early seafaring years in the service of the Portuguese. By the time he was a young man, he had developed great ambitions. He believed he could reach East Asia by sailing west, across the Atlantic, rather than east, around Africa. Columbus thought the world was far smaller than it actually is. He also believed that the Asian continent extended farther eastward than it actually does. Most important, he did not realize that anything lay to the west between Europe and the lands of Asia.

Columbus failed to enlist the leaders of Portugal to back his plan, so he turned instead to Spain. The marriage of Spain's two most powerful regional rulers, Ferdinand of Aragon and Isabella of Castile, had produced the strongest and most ambitious monarchy in Europe. Columbus appealed to Queen Isabella for support for his proposed westward voyage, and in 1492, she agreed. Commanding ninety men and three *Columbus's First Voyage* ships—the *Niña,* the *Pinta,* and the *Santa María*—Columbus left Spain in August 1492 and sailed west into the Atlantic. Ten weeks later, he sighted land and assumed he had reached an island off Asia. In fact, he had landed in the Bahamas. When he pushed on and encountered Cuba, he assumed he had reached China. He returned to Spain, bringing with him several captured natives as evidence of his achievement. (He called the natives "Indians" because he believed they were from the East Indies in the Pacific.)

But Columbus did not, of course, bring back news of the great khan's court in China or any samples of the fabled wealth of the Indies. And so a year later, he tried again, this time with a much larger expedition. As before, he headed into the Caribbean, discovering several other islands and leaving a small and short-lived **colony** on Hispaniola. On a third voyage, in 1498, he finally reached the mainland and cruised along the northern coast of South America. He then realized, for the first time, that he had encountered not a part of Asia but a separate continent.

Columbus ended his life in obscurity. Ultimately, he was even unable to give his name to the land he had revealed to the Europeans. That distinction went instead to a Florentine merchant, Amerigo Vespucci, who wrote a series of vivid descriptions of the lands he visited on a later expedition to the New World and helped popularize the idea that the Americas were new continents.

Partly as a result of Columbus's initiative, Spain began to devote greater resources and energy to maritime exploration. In 1513, the Spaniard Vasco de Balboa crossed the Isthmus of Panama and became the first known European to gaze westward upon the great ocean that separated America from China. Seeking access to that ocean, Ferdinand Magellan, a Portuguese

EUROPEAN EXPLORATION AND CONQUEST, 1492–1583 This map shows the many voyages of exploration to and conquest of North America launched by Europeans in the late fifteenth and sixteenth centuries. Note how Columbus and the Spanish explorers who followed him tended to move quickly into the lands of Mexico, the Caribbean, and Central and South America, while the English and French explored the northern territories of North America. • *What factors might have led these various nations to explore and colonize different areas of the New World?*

in Spanish employ, found the strait that now bears his name at the southern end of South America, struggled through the stormy narrows and into the ocean (so calm by contrast that he christened it the *Pacific*), and then proceeded to the Philippines. There Magellan died in a *Circumnavigation of the Globe* conflict with natives, but his expedition went on to complete the first known circumnavigation of the globe (1519–1522). By 1550, Spaniards had explored the coasts of North America as far north as Oregon in the west and Labrador in the east.

THE SPANISH EMPIRE

In time, Spanish explorers in the New World stopped thinking of America simply as an obstacle to their search for a route to Asia and began instead to consider it a possible source of wealth in itself. The Spanish claimed for themselves the whole of the New World, except for a large part of the east coast of South America (today's Brazil) that was reserved by a papal decree for the Portuguese.

In 1518, Hernando Cortés, who had been an unsuccessful Spanish government official in Cuba for fourteen years, led a small military expedition (about 600 men) against the Aztecs in Mexico and their powerful emperor, Montezuma, after hearing stories of great treasures there. His first assault on Tenochtitlán, the Aztec capital, failed. But Cortés and his army had unwittingly exposed the natives to smallpox, to which the natives, unlike the Europeans, had developed no immunity. The epidemic decimated the Aztec population and made it possible for the Spanish to triumph in their second attempt at conquest. Through his ruthless suppression of the surviving natives, Cortés established himself as one of the most brutal of the Spanish **conquistadores** (conquerors). Twenty years later, Francisco Pizarro conquered   *Conquistadores* the Incas in Peru and opened the way for other Spanish advances into South America.

The first Spanish settlers in America were interested only in exploiting the American stores of gold and silver, and they were fabulously successful. For 300 years, beginning in the sixteenth century, the mines of Spanish America yielded more than ten times as much gold and silver as all the rest of the world's mines combined. Before long, however, most Spanish settlers in America traveled to the New World for other reasons. Many went in hopes of profiting from agriculture. They helped establish elements of European

THE MEXICANS STRIKE BACK   In this vivid scene from the Durán Codex, Mexican artists illustrate a rare moment in which Mexican warriors gained the upper hand over the Spanish invaders. Driven back by native fighters, the Spanish have taken refuge in a room in the royal palace in Tenochtitlán while brightly attired Mexican warriors besiege them. Although the Mexicans gained a temporary advantage in this battle, the drawing illustrates one of the reasons for their inability to withstand the Spanish in the longer term. The Spanish soldiers are armed with rifles and crossbows, while the Indians carry only spears and shields. (© Biblioteca Nacional, Madrid, Spain/Bridgeman Images)

CONSIDER THE SOURCE

BARTOLOMÉ DE LAS CASAS, "OF THE ISLAND OF HISPANIOLA" (1542)

Bartolomé de Las Casas, a Dominican friar from Spain, was an early European settler of the West Indies. He devoted much of his life to describing the culture of native peoples and chronicling the many abuses they suffered at the hands of their colonizers. This excerpt is from a letter he addressed to Spain's Prince Philip.

God has created all these numberless people to be quite the simplest, without malice or duplicity, most obedient, most faithful to their natural Lords, and to the Christians, whom they serve; the most humble, most patient, most peaceful and calm, without strife nor tumults; not wrangling, nor querulous, as free from uproar, hate and desire of revenge as any in the world . . . Among these gentle sheep, gifted by their Maker with the above qualities, the Spaniards entered as soon as they knew them, like wolves, tigers and lions which had been starving for many days, and since forty years they have done nothing else; nor do they afflict, torment, and destroy them with strange and new, and divers kinds of cruelty, never before seen, nor heard of, nor read of . . .

The Christians, with their horses and swords and lances, began to slaughter and practice strange cruelty among them. They penetrated into the country and spared neither children nor the aged, nor pregnant women, nor those in child labour, all of whom they ran through the body and lacerated, as though they were assaulting so many lambs herded in their sheepfold. They made bets as to who would slit a man in two, or cut off his head at one blow: or they opened up his bowels. They tore the babes from their mothers' breast by the feet, and dashed their heads against the rocks. Others they seized by the shoulders and threw into the rivers, laughing and joking, and when they fell into the water they exclaimed: "boil body of so and so!" They spitted the bodies of other babes, together with their mothers and all who were before them, on their swords.

They made a gallows just high enough for the feet to nearly touch the ground, and by thirteens, in honor and reverence of our Redeemer and the twelve Apostles, they put wood underneath and, with fire, they burned the Indians alive.

They wrapped the bodies of others entirely in dry straw, binding them in it and setting fire to it; and so they burned them. They cut off the hands of all they wished to take alive, made them carry them fastened on to them, and said: "Go and carry letters": that is; take the news to those who have fled to the mountains.

They generally killed the lords and nobles in the following way. They made wooden gridirons of stakes, bound them upon them, and made a slow fire beneath; thus the victims gave up the spirit by degrees, emitting cries of despair in their torture.

UNDERSTAND, ANALYZE, & EVALUATE

1. How did Bartolomé de Las Casas characterize the natives? How do you think they would have responded to this description?
2. What metaphor did Las Casas use to describe the natives and where does this metaphor come from?
3. What role did Las Casas expect the Spaniards to play on Hispaniola? What did they do instead?

Source: Francis Augustus MacNutt, *Bartholomew de Las Casas: His Life, His Apostolate, and His Writings* (New York: G.P. Putnam's Sons, 1909), p. 14.

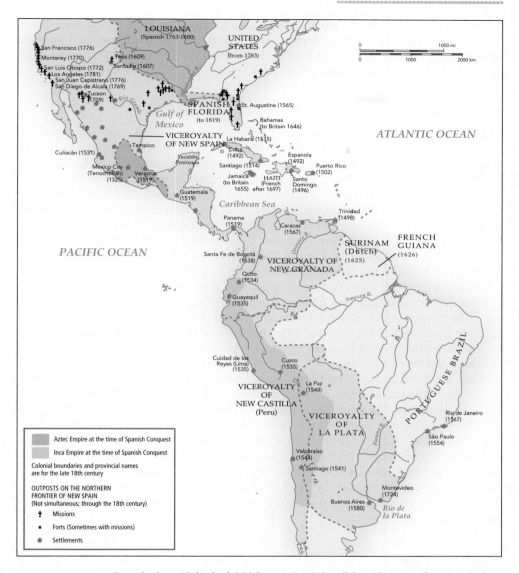

SPANISH AMERICA   From the time of Columbus's initial voyage in 1492 until the mid-nineteenth century, Spain was the dominant colonial power in the New World. From the southern regions of South America to the northern regions of the Pacific Northwest, Spain controlled one of the world's vastest empires. Note how much of the Spanish Empire was simply grafted upon the earlier empires of native peoples—the Incas in what is today Chile and Peru and the Aztecs across much of the rest of South America, Mexico, and the Southwest of what is now the United States. • *What characteristics of Spanish colonization would account for their preference for already settled regions?*

civilization permanently in America. Other Spaniards—priests, friars, and missionaries—went to America to spread the Christian religion; through their efforts, the influence of the Catholic Church ultimately extended throughout South and Central America and Mexico. One of the first friars to work in the colonies, Bartolomé de Las Casas fought for the fair treatment of native peoples by the Spanish as part of his ministry. (See "Consider the Source: Bartolomé de Las Casas, 'Of the Island of Hispaniola'").

By the end of the sixteenth century, the Spanish Empire included the Caribbean islands, Mexico, and southern North America. It also spread into South America and included what is now Chile, Argentina, and Peru. In 1580, when the Spanish and Portuguese monarchies temporarily united, Brazil came under Spanish jurisdiction as well.

NORTHERN OUTPOSTS

In 1565, the Spanish established the fort of St. Augustine in Florida, their first permanent *St. Augustine and Santa Fe* settlement in what is now the United States. But it was little more than a small military outpost. A more substantial colonizing venture began in the Southwest in 1598, when Don Juan de Oñate traveled north from Mexico with a party of 500, claimed for Spain some of the lands of the Pueblo Indians in what is now New Mexico, and began to establish a colony. Oñate granted **encomiendas** (the right to exact tribute and labor from the natives on large tracts of land) to favored Spaniards. In 1609, Spanish colonists founded Santa Fe. By 1680, there were over 2,000 Spanish colonists living among about 30,000 Pueblos. The economic heart of the colony was cattle and sheep, raised on the *ranchos* that stretched out around the small towns Spanish settlers established.

Despite widespread conversions to Catholicism, most natives (including the converts) continued to practice their own traditional religious rituals. In 1680, Spanish priests and *Popé* the colonial government tried to suppress these rituals. In response, Popé, an Indian religious leader, led an uprising that killed hundreds of European settlers, captured Santa Fe, and drove the Spanish from the region. Twelve years later, the Spanish returned and crushed a last revolt in 1696.

After the revolts, many Spanish colonists realized that they could not hope to prosper in New Mexico while in constant conflict with a native population that greatly outnumbered them. Although the Spanish intensified their efforts to assimilate the Indians, they also now permitted the Pueblos to own land. They stopped commandeering Indian labor, and they tolerated the survival of tribal religious rituals. There was significant intermarriage between Europeans and Indians. By 1750, the Spanish population had grown to about 4,000. The Pueblo population had declined (through disease, war, and migration) to about 13,000—less than half what it had been in 1680. New Mexico had by then become a reasonably stable but still weak and isolated outpost of the Spanish Empire.

BIOLOGICAL AND CULTURAL EXCHANGES

European and native cultures never entirely merged in the Spanish Empire. Nevertheless, the arrival of whites launched a process of interaction between different peoples that left no one unchanged.

That Europeans were exploring the Americas at all was a result of early contacts with the natives, from whom they had learned of the rich deposits of gold and silver. From then on, the history of the Americas became one of increasing levels of exchanges—some *Population Loss from Diseases* beneficial, others catastrophic—among different peoples and cultures. The first and perhaps most profound result of this exchange was the importation of European diseases to the New World. It would be difficult to exaggerate the consequences of the exposure of Native Americans to such illnesses as influenza, measles, typhus, and above all smallpox. Although historians have debated the question of how many people lived in the Americas before the arrival of Europeans, it is estimated that millions died. (See "Debating the Past: Why Do Historians So Often Differ?"). In some areas, native populations were virtually wiped out within a few decades of their first contact with whites. On Hispaniola, where Columbus had landed in the 1490s, the native population quickly declined from approximately 1 million to about 500. In the Maya area of Mexico, as much as 95 percent of the population perished within a few years of the natives' first contact with the Spanish. Many (although not all) of the tribes north of Mexico were spared the worst of the epidemics. But for other areas of the New World, this was a disaster at least as grave as, and in some places far worse than, the Black Death that had killed over one-third of the population of Europe two centuries before. Some Europeans, watching this biological catastrophe, saw it as evidence of God's will that they should dominate the New World—and its native population.

The decimation of native populations in the southern regions of the Americas was not only a result of exposure to infection. It was also a result of the conquistadores' deliberate policy of subjugation and extermination. Their brutality was in part a reflection of the ruthlessness with which Europeans waged war in all parts of the world. It was also a result of their conviction that the natives were "savages"—uncivilized peoples who could be treated as somehow not fully human. By the 1540s, the combined effects of European diseases and European military brutality had all but   *Population Loss from Military Brutality* destroyed the empires of Mexico and South America.

Not all aspects of the exchange were disastrous to the Indians. The Europeans introduced to the natives important new crops (among them sugar and bananas), domestic livestock (cattle, pigs, and sheep), and, perhaps most significant, the horse, which gradually became central to the lives of many natives and transformed their societies.

The exchange was at least as important (and more beneficial) to the Europeans. In both North and South America, the arriving white peoples learned from the natives new agricultural techniques appropriate to the demands of the new land. They discovered new crops—above all maize (corn), which Columbus took back to Europe from   *New World Crops* his first trip to America. Such foods as squash, pumpkins, beans, sweet potatoes, tomatoes, peppers, and potatoes all found their way into European diets.

In South America, Central America, and Mexico, Europeans and natives lived in intimate, if unequal, contact with one another. Many natives gradually came to speak Spanish or Portuguese, but they created a range of dialects fusing the European languages with elements of their own. European men outnumbered European women by at least ten to one. Intermarriage—often forcible—became frequent between Spanish immigrants and native women. Before long, the population of the colonies came to be dominated (numerically, at least) by people of mixed race, or **mestizos.**

Virtually all the enterprises of the Spanish and Portuguese colonists depended on Indian workforces. In some places, Indians were sold into slavery. More often,   *Unfree Indian labor* colonists used a coercive (or "indentured") wage system, under which Indians worked in the mines and on the plantations under duress for fixed periods. That was not, in the end, enough to meet the labor needs of the colonists. As early as 1502, European settlers began importing slaves from Africa.

AFRICA AND AMERICA

Over one-half of all the immigrants to the New World between 1500 and 1800 were Africans, virtually all of them sent to the Americas against their will. Most came from a large region below the Sahara Desert, known as Guinea.

WHY DO HISTORIANS SO OFTEN DIFFER?

Early in the twentieth century, when the professional study of history was still relatively new, many historians believed that questions about the past could be answered with the same certainty and precision that questions in more-scientific fields could be answered. By sifting through available records, using precise methods of research and analysis, and producing careful, closely argued accounts of the past, they believed they could create definitive histories that would survive without controversy. Scholars who adhered to this view believed that real knowledge can be derived only from direct, scientific observation of clear "fact." They were known as "positivists."

A vigorous debate continues to this day over whether historical research can or should be truly objective. Almost no historian any longer accepts the positivist claim that history could ever be an exact science. Disagreement about the past is, in fact, at the heart of the effort to understand history. Critics of contemporary historical scholarship often denounce the way historians are constantly revising earlier interpretations. Some denounce the act of interpretation itself. History, they claim, is "what happened," and historians should "stick to the facts."

Historians, however, continue to differ with one another both because the facts are seldom as straightforward as their critics claim and because facts by themselves mean almost nothing without an effort to assign meaning to them. Some historical facts, of course, are not in dispute. Everyone agrees, for example, that the Japanese bombed Pearl Harbor on December 7, 1941, and that

Abraham Lincoln was elected president in 1860. But many other facts are much harder to determine—among them, for example, the question of how large the American population was before the arrival of Columbus, or how many slaves resisted slavery. This sounds like a reasonably straightforward question, but it is almost impossible to answer with any certainty—because the records of slave resistance are spotty and the definition of "resistance" is a matter of considerable dispute.

Even when a set of facts is clear and straightforward, historians disagree—sometimes quite radically—over what they mean. Those disagreements can be the result of political and ideological disagreements. Some of the most vigorous debates in recent decades have been between scholars who believe that economic interests and class divisions are the key to understanding the past, and those who believe that ideas and culture are at least as important as material interests. Whites and people of color, men and women, people from the American South and people from the North, young people and older people: these and many other points of difference find their way into scholarly disagreements. Debates can also occur over differences in methodology—between those who believe that quantitative studies can answer important historical questions and those who believe that other methods come closer to the truth.

Most of all, historical interpretation changes in response to the time in which it is written. Historians may strive to be objective in their work, but no one can be entirely free from the assumptions and concerns of the present. In the 1950s, the omnipresent shadow of the Cold War had a profound effect on the way most historians viewed the past. In the 1960s, concerns about racial justice and disillusionment with the Vietnam War altered the way many historians viewed the past. Those events introduced a much more critical tone to scholarship and turned the attention of scholars away from politics and government and toward the study of society and culture.

Many areas of scholarship in recent decades are embroiled in a profound debate over whether there is such a thing as "truth." The world, some scholars argue, is simply a series of "narratives" constructed by people who view life in very different and often highly personal ways. Truth does not really exist. Everything is a product of interpretation. Not many historians embrace such radical ideas; most would agree that interpretations, to be of any value, must rest on a solid foundation of observable facts. But historians do recognize that even the most compelling facts are subject to many different interpretations and that the process of understanding the past is a forever continuing—and forever contested—process. •

UNDERSTAND, ANALYZE, & EVALUATE

1. What are some of the reasons historians so often disagree?
2. Is there ever a right or wrong in historical interpretation? What value might historical inquiry have other than reaching a right or wrong conclusion?
3. If historians so often disagree, how should a student of history approach historical content? How might disagreement expand our understanding of history?

Europeans and white Americans came to portray African society as primitive and uncivilized. But most Africans were, in fact, highly civilized peoples with well-developed economies and political systems. The residents of upper Guinea had substantial commercial contact with the Mediterranean world—trading ivory, gold,   *Trade States of West Africa* and slaves for finished goods—and, largely as a result, became early converts to Islam. After the collapse of the ancient kingdom of Ghana around A.D. 1100, they created the even larger empire of Mali, whose trading center at Timbuktu became fabled as a center of education and a meeting place of the peoples of many lands.

Farther south, Africans were more isolated from Europe and the Mediterranean and were more politically fragmented. The central social unit was the village, which usually consisted of members of an extended family group. Some groups of villages united in small kingdoms. But no large empires emerged in the south. Nevertheless, these southern societies developed extensive trade, both among themselves and, to a lesser degree, with the outside world.

African civilizations developed economies that reflected the climates and resources of their lands. In upper Guinea, fishing and rice cultivation, supplemented by the extensive trade with Mediterranean lands, were the foundation of the economy. Farther south, Africans grew wheat and other food crops, raised livestock, and fished. There were some more-nomadic tribes in the interior, who subsisted largely on hunting and gathering. But most Africans were sedentary, farming people.

As in many Indian societies in America, African families tended to be matrilineal: they traced their heredity through and inherited property from their mothers.   *Matrilineal Societies* Women played a major role, often the dominant role, in trade. In many areas, they were the principal farmers (while the men hunted, fished, and raised livestock), and everywhere,

THE ATLANTIC CONTEXT OF EARLY AMERICAN HISTORY

Most Americans understand that our nation has recently become intimately bound up with the rest of the world—that we live in what some call the "age of **globalization.**" Until recently, however, most historians have examined the nation's past in relative isolation. Among the first areas of American history to be reexamined in an international perspective is the earliest period of European settlement of the Americas. Many scholars of early American history now examine what happened in the "New World" in the context of what has become known as the "**Atlantic World.**"

The idea of an Atlantic World rests in part on the obvious connections between western Europe and the Spanish, British, French, and Dutch colonies in North and South America. All the early European civilizations of the Americas were part of a great imperial project launched by the major powers of Europe. The massive European and African immigrations to the Americas beginning in the sixteenth century, the defeat and devastation of native populations, the creation of European agricultural and urban settlements, and the imposition of imperial regulations on trade, commerce, landowning, and political life—all of these forces reveal the influence of Old World **imperialism** on the history of the New World.

But the expansion of empires is only one part of the creation of the Atlantic World. At least equally important—and closely related—is the expansion of commerce from Europe and Africa to the Americas. Although some Europeans traveled to the New World in search of religious freedom, or to escape oppression, or to search for adventure, the great majority of European immigrants were in search of economic opportunity. Not surprisingly, therefore, the European settlements in the Americas were almost from the start intimately connected to Europe through the growth of commerce between them—commerce that grew more extensive and more complex with every passing year. The commercial relationship between America and Europe was responsible not just for the growth of trade, but also for the increases in migration over time—as the demand for labor in the New World drew more and more settlers from the Old World. Commerce was also the principal reason for the rise of slavery in the Americas, and for the growth of the slave trade between European America and Africa. The Atlantic World, in other words, included not just Europe and the Americas, but Africa as well.

Religion was another force binding together the Atlantic World. The vast majority of people of European descent were Christians, and most of them maintained important religious ties to part of a hierarchical church based in Rome with close ties with the Vatican. But the Protestant faiths that predominated in North America were intimately linked to their European counterparts as well. New religious ideas and movements spread back and forth across the Atlantic with astonishing speed. Great revivals that began in Europe moved quickly to America. The "Great Awakening" of the mid-eighteenth century, for example, began in Britain and traveled to America in large part through the efforts of the English evangelist George Whitefield. American evangelists later carried religious ideas from the New World back to the Old.

The early history of European America was also closely bound up with the intellectual life of Europe. The Enlightenment—the cluster of ideas that emerged in Europe in the seventeenth and eighteenth centuries emphasizing the power of human reason—moved quickly to the Americas, producing intellectual ferment throughout the New World, but particularly in the British colonies in North America and the Caribbean. The ideas of the

British philosopher John Locke, for example, helped shape the founding of Georgia. The English Constitution, and the idea of the "rights of Englishmen," shaped the way North Americans developed their own concepts of politics. Many of the ideas that underlaid the American Revolution were products of British and continental philosophy that had traveled across the Atlantic. The reinterpretation of those ideas by Americans to help justify their drive to independence—by, among others, Thomas Paine—moved back to Europe and helped, among other things, to inspire the French Revolution. Scientific and technological knowledge—another product of the Enlightenment—traveled constantly across the Atlantic and back. Americans borrowed industrial technology from Britain. Europe acquired much of its early knowledge of electricity from experiments done in America. But the Enlightenment was only one part of the continuing intellectual connections within the Atlantic World, connections that spread artistic, scholarly, and political ideas widely through the lands bordering the ocean.

Instead of thinking of the early history of what became the United States simply as the story of the growth of thirteen small colonies along the Atlantic seaboard of North America, the idea of the Atlantic World encourages us to think of early American history as a vast pattern of exchanges and interactions—trade, migration, religious and intellectual exchange, and many other relationships—among all the societies bordering the Atlantic: western Europe, western Africa, the Caribbean, and North and South America. •

UNDERSTAND, ANALYZE, & EVALUATE

1. What is the Atlantic World?
2. What has led historians to begin studying the idea of an Atlantic World?

they managed child care and food preparation. Most tribes also divided political power by gender, with men choosing leaders to manage male affairs and women choosing parallel leaders to handle female matters.

Small elites of priests and nobles stood at the top of many African societies. Most people belonged to a large middle group of farmers, traders, crafts workers, and others. At the bottom of society were slaves—men and women, not all of them *African Slavery* African, who were put into bondage after being captured in wars, because of criminal behavior, or as a result of unpaid debts. Slaves in Africa were generally in bondage for a fixed term, and in the meantime they retained certain legal protections (including the right to marry). Children did not inherit their parents' condition of bondage.

The African slave trade long preceded European settlement in the New World. As early as the eighth century, west Africans began selling small numbers of slaves to traders from the Mediterranean and later to the Portuguese. In the sixteenth century, however, the *Sugar and the Slave Trade* market for slaves increased dramatically as a result of the growing European demand for sugarcane. The small areas of sugar cultivation in the Mediterranean could not meet the demand, and production soon spread to new areas: to the island of Madeira off the African coast, which became a Portuguese colony, and not long thereafter (still in the sixteenth century) to the Caribbean islands and Brazil. Sugar was a labor-intensive crop, and the demand for African workers in these new areas of cultivation was high. At first the slave traders were overwhelmingly Portuguese. By the seventeenth century, the Dutch had won control of most of the market. In the eighteenth century, the English dominated it. By 1700, slavery had spread well beyond its original locations in the Caribbean and South America and into the English colonies to the north. The relationship among European, African, and native peoples—however unequal—reminds us of the global context to the history of America. (See "America in the World: The Atlantic Context of Early American History.")

THE ARRIVAL OF THE ENGLISH

England's first documented contact with the New World came only five years after Spain's. In 1497, John Cabot (like Columbus, a native of Genoa) sailed to the northeastern coast of North America on an expedition sponsored by King Henry VII, in an unsuccessful search for a northwest passage through the New World to the Orient. But nearly a century passed before the English made any serious efforts to establish colonies in America.

INCENTIVES FOR COLONIZATION

Interest in **colonization** grew in part as a response to social and economic problems in sixteenth-century England. The English people suffered from frequent and costly European wars, and they suffered from almost constant religious strife within their own land. Many suffered, too, from harsh economic changes in their countryside. Because the worldwide demand for wool was growing rapidly, landowners were converting their land from fields for crops to pastures for sheep. The result was a reduction in the amount of land available *Scarce Land* for growing food. England's food supply declined at the same time that the English population was growing—from 3 million in 1485 to 4 million in 1603. To some of the English, the New World began to seem attractive because it offered something that was growing scarce in England: land.

At the same time, new merchant capitalists were prospering by selling the products of England's growing wool-cloth industry abroad. At first, most exporters did business almost entirely as individuals. In time, however, merchants formed companies, whose **charters** from the king gave them monopolies for trading in particular regions. Investors in these companies often made fantastic profits, and they were eager to expand their trade.

Central to this trading drive was the emergence of a new concept of economic life *Mercantilism* known as **mercantilism.** Mercantilism rested on the belief that one person or nation could grow rich only at the expense of another, and that a nation's economic health depended, therefore, on selling as much as possible to foreign lands and buying as little as possible from them. The principles of mercantilism spread throughout Europe in the sixteenth and seventeenth centuries. One result was the increased attractiveness of acquiring colonies, which became the source of raw materials and a market for the colonizing power's goods.

In England, the mercantilistic program thrived at first on the basis of the flourishing wool trade with the European continent, and particularly with the great cloth market in Antwerp. In the 1550s, however, that glutted market began to collapse, and English merchants had to look elsewhere for overseas trade. Some English believed colonies would solve their problems.

There were also religious motives for colonization—a result of the Protestant Reformation. Protestantism began in Germany in 1517, when Martin Luther challenged some of the basic practices and beliefs of the Roman Catholic   *Religious Motives for Colonization* Church. Luther quickly won a wide following among ordinary men and women in northern Europe. When the pope excommunicated him in 1520, Luther began leading his followers out of the Catholic Church entirely.

The Swiss theologian John Calvin went even further in rejecting the Catholic belief that human behavior could affect an individual's prospects for salvation. Calvin introduced the doctrine of predestination. God "elected" some people to be saved and condemned others to damnation; each person's destiny was determined before birth, and no one could change that predetermined fate. But those who accepted Calvin's teachings came to believe that the way they led their lives might reveal to them their chances of salvation. A wicked or useless existence would be a sign of damnation; saintliness, diligence, and success could be signs of grace. The new creed spread rapidly throughout northern Europe.

In 1529, King Henry VIII of England, angered by the refusal of the pope to grant him a divorce from his Spanish wife, broke England's ties with the Catholic Church and established himself as the head of the Christian faith in his country. This was known as the English Reformation. After Henry's death, his Catholic daughter, Queen Mary, restored England's allegiance to Rome and persecuted Protestants. But when Mary died in 1558, her half sister, Elizabeth I, became England's sovereign and once again severed the nation's connection with the Catholic Church, this time for good.

To many English people, however, the new Church of England was not reformed enough. They clamored for reforms that would "purify" the church. As a result, they became known as Puritans. The most radical Puritans, known as Separatists, were determined to   *Puritans* worship in their own independent congregations, despite English laws that required all subjects to attend regular Anglican services. Most Puritans did not wish to leave the Church of England. They wanted, rather, to simplify Anglican forms of worship and reform the leadership of the church. Like the Separatists, they grew increasingly frustrated by the refusal of political and ecclesiastical authorities to respond to their demands.

Puritan discontent grew rapidly after the death of Elizabeth, the last of the Tudors, and the accession of James I, the first of the Stuarts, in 1603. Convinced that kings ruled by divine right, James quickly antagonized the Puritans by resorting to illegal and arbitrary taxation, favoring English Catholics in the granting of charters and other favors, and supporting "high-church" forms of ceremony. By the early seventeenth century, some religious nonconformists were beginning to look for places of refuge outside the kingdom.

England's first experience with colonization came not in the New World but in neighboring Ireland. The English had long laid claim to the island, but only in the late sixteenth century did serious efforts at colonization begin. The long, brutal process by which the *Irish Colonization* English attempted to subdue the Irish created an important assumption about colonization: the belief that settlements in foreign lands must retain a rigid separation from the native populations. Unlike the Spanish in America, the English in Ireland tried to build a separate society of their own, peopled with emigrants from England itself. They would take that concept with them to the New World.

THE FRENCH AND THE DUTCH IN AMERICA

English settlers in North America encountered not only natives but also other Europeans who were, like them, driven by mercantilist ideas. There were scattered North American outposts of the Spanish Empire and, more important, there were French and Dutch settlers who were also vying for a stake in the New World.

France founded its first permanent settlement in North America at Quebec in 1608, less than a year after the English started their first at Jamestown. The colony's population grew slowly. Unlike the early English settlers, the French forged close ties with Native Americans deep inside the continent. French Jesuit missionaries established some of the first contacts between the two peoples. More important were the *coureurs de bois*— adventurous fur traders and trappers—who also penetrated far into the wilderness and developed an extensive trade that became one of the underpinnings of the French colonial *French Traders and Jesuits in Canada* economy. The French traders formed partnerships with the Indians. They often lived among the natives and married Indian women. The fur trade helped open the way for French agricultural estates (or *seigneuries*) along the St. Lawrence River and for the development of trade and military centers at Quebec and Montreal.

The Dutch, too, established a presence in North America. Holland in the early seventeenth century was one of the leading nations of the world, and its commerce moved to America in the seventeenth century. In 1609, Henry Hudson, an English explorer in the employ of *Dutch Claims* the Dutch, sailed up the river that was to be named for him in what was then New Netherland. His explorations led to a Dutch claim on the territory. The Dutch built a town on Manhattan Island named New Amsterdam. From it, Dutch trappers moved into the interior toward the Appalachian Mountains and built a profitable trade in furs.

THE FIRST ENGLISH SETTLEMENTS

The first permanent English settlement in the New World was established at Jamestown, in Virginia, in 1607. But for nearly thirty years before that, English merchants and adventurers had been engaged in a series of failed efforts to create colonies in America.

Through much of the sixteenth century, the English had harbored mixed feelings about the New World. They were intrigued by its possibilities, but they were also fearful of *English Naval Power* Spain, which remained the dominant force in America. In 1588, however, King Philip II of Spain sent one of the largest military fleets in the history of warfare—the Spanish Armada—across the English Channel to attack England itself. The smaller English fleet, taking advantage of its greater maneuverability, defeated the armada and, in a single stroke, ended Spain's domination of the Atlantic. This great shift in naval power caused English interest in colonizing the New World to grow quickly.

The pioneers of English colonization were Sir Humphrey Gilbert and his half brother Sir Walter Raleigh—both veterans of earlier colonial efforts in Ireland. In 1578, Gilbert *Gilbert and Raleigh* obtained from Queen Elizabeth a six-year patent granting him the

ROANOKE A drawing by one of the colonists in the ill-fated Roanoke expedition of 1585 became the basis for this engraving by Theodor de Bry, published in England in 1590. A small European ship approaches the island of Roanoke, at left. The wreckage of several larger vessels farther out to sea and the presence of Indian settlements on the mainland and on Roanoke itself suggest some of the perils the settlers encountered. (© The Gallery Collection/Corbis)

exclusive right "to inhabit and possess any remote and heathen lands not already in the possession of any Christian prince." Five years later, after several setbacks, he led an expedition to Newfoundland, looking for a good place to build a profitable colony. But a storm sank his ship, and he was lost at sea. The next year, Sir Walter Raleigh secured his own six-year grant from the queen and sent a small group of men on an expedition to explore the North American coast. When they returned, Raleigh named the region they had explored Virginia, in honor of Elizabeth, who was known as the "Virgin Queen."

In 1585, Raleigh recruited his cousin, Sir Richard Grenville, to lead a group of men to the island of Roanoke, off the coast of what is now North Carolina, to establish a colony. Grenville deposited the settlers on the island, destroyed an Indian village as retaliation for a minor theft, and returned to England. The following spring, with long-overdue supplies and reinforcements from England, Sir Francis Drake unexpectedly arrived in Roanoke. The dispirited colonists boarded his ships and left.

Raleigh tried again in 1587, sending an expedition to Roanoke carrying ninety-one men, seventeen women, and nine children. The settlers attempted to take up where the first group of colonists had left off. John White, the commander of the expedition, returned to England after several weeks, in search of supplies and additional settlers. Because of a war with Spain, he was unable to return to Roanoke for three *Failed Colony of Roanoke* years. When he did, in 1590, he found the island deserted, with no clue to the fate of the settlers other than the cryptic inscription "Croatoan" carved on a post.

The Roanoke disaster marked the end of Sir Walter Raleigh's involvement in English colonization of the New World. No later colonizers would receive grants of land in America as vast or undefined as those Raleigh and Gilbert had acquired. Yet the colonizing impulse remained very much alive. In the early years of the seventeenth century, a group of London merchants decided to renew the attempt at colonization in Virginia. A rival group of merchants, from the area around Plymouth, was also interested in American ventures and was sponsoring voyages of exploration farther north. In 1606, James I issued a new charter, which divided North America between the two groups. The London group got the exclusive right to colonize the south, and the Plymouth merchants received the same right in the north. Through the efforts of these and other companies, the first enduring English colonies would soon be established in North America.

CONCLUSION

The lands that Europeans eventually named the Americas were the home of many millions of people before the arrival of Columbus. Having migrated from Asia thousands of years earlier, the pre-Columbian Americans spread throughout the Western Hemisphere and eventually created great civilizations. Among the most notable of them were the Incas in Peru and the Mayas and Aztecs in Mexico. In the regions north of what was later named the Rio Grande, the human population was smaller and the civilizations were less advanced than they were farther south. Even so, North American natives created a cluster of civilizations that thrived and expanded.

In the century after European contact, these native populations suffered catastrophes that all but destroyed the civilizations they had built: brutal invasions by Spanish and Portuguese conquistadores and a series of plagues inadvertently imported by Europeans. By the middle of the sixteenth century, the Spanish and Portuguese—no longer faced with effective resistance from the native populations—had established colonial control over all of South America and much of North America.

In the parts of North America that would eventually become the United States, the European presence was for a time much less powerful. The Spanish established an important northern outpost in what is now New Mexico, a society in which Europeans and Indians lived together intimately, if unequally. On the whole, however, the North American Indians remained largely undisturbed by Europeans until English, French, and Dutch migrations began in the early seventeenth century.

KEY TERMS/PEOPLE/PLACES/EVENTS

Archaic period 3	colonization 18	mercantilism 18
Atlantic World 16	colony 7	Mesoamerica 4
Bartolomé de Las Casas 11	conquistadores 9	mestizos 13
Cahokia 5	Elizabeth I 19	Popé 12
charter 18	encomienda 12	Protestant Reformation 19
Christopher Columbus 7	globalization 16	Puritans 19
Clovis people 2	imperialism 16	Roanoke 21

RECALL AND REFLECT

1. Why were agricultural societies of the Northeast more nomadic than those of other regions?
2. What factors favored the Spanish in their conquest of native peoples?
3. How did French settlement in America differ from that of the Spanish?
4. What role did Africa play in the creation of an Atlantic World?
5. How did the English experience at colonization in Ireland affect English colonization in America?

2

TRANSPLANTATIONS AND BORDERLANDS

THE EARLY CHESAPEAKE

THE GROWTH OF NEW ENGLAND

THE RESTORATION COLONIES

BORDERLANDS AND MIDDLE GROUNDS

THE DEVELOPMENT OF EMPIRE

LOOKING AHEAD

1. How did the English colonies in the Chesapeake, New England, and mid-Atlantic differ from one another in purpose and administration?
2. How "English" were the colonies in the decades after the British settlements?
3. What did the English want from the colonies in the first century of English settlement in North America?

THE FIRST PERMANENT ENGLISH SETTLEMENTS were small, fragile communities, generally unprepared for the hardships they were to face. Seeking to improve their futures and secure a greater degree of control over their lives, the European immigrants found a world populated by Native American tribes; by colonists, explorers, and traders from Spain, France, and the Netherlands; and by immigrants from other parts of Europe and, soon, Africa. American society was from the beginning a fusion of many cultures in which disparate people and cultures coexisted often violently.

All of British North America was, in effect, a borderland during the early years of colonization. Through much of the seventeenth century, European colonies both relied on and did battle with the Indian tribes and struggled with challenges from other Europeans in their midst. Eventually, however, some areas of English settlement—most notably the growing communities along the eastern seaboard—managed to dominate their own regions, marginalizing or expelling Indians and other challengers. In these eastern colonies, the English created significant towns and cities; built political, religious, and educational institutions; and created agricultural systems of great productivity. They also developed substantial differences from one another—perhaps most notably in the growth of a slave-driven agricultural economy in the South, which had few counterparts in the North.

THE EARLY CHESAPEAKE

Once James I had issued his 1606 charters, the London Company moved quickly and decisively to launch a colonizing expedition headed for Virginia—a party of 144 men aboard three ships, the *Godspeed,* the *Discovery,* and the *Susan Constant,* which set sail for America in 1607.

COLONISTS AND NATIVES

Only 104 men survived the journey. They reached the American coast in the spring of 1607, sailed into the Chesapeake and up a river they named the James, in honor of their king. They established their colony, Jamestown, on a peninsula on the river. They chose an inland setting because they believed it would provide a measure of comfort and security.

The Jamestown settlers faced ordeals that were to a large degree of their own making. They were vulnerable to local diseases, particularly malaria, which was especially virulent along the marshy rivers they had chosen to settle. They spent more time searching for gold and other exports than growing enough food to be self-sufficient. And they could create no real community without women, who had not been recruited for the expedition.

The survival of the colonies required European immigrants to learn from local Indian tribes. This was not easy for the settlers to accept, because they believed that English civilization, with its oceangoing vessels, muskets, and other advanced weaponry, was greatly superior. Yet native agricultural techniques were far better adapted to the soil and climate of Virginia than those of English origin. The local natives were settled farmers whose villages were surrounded by neatly ordered fields. They grew a variety of crops—beans, pumpkins, vegetables, and above all maize (corn). Some of the Indian farmlands stretched over hundreds of acres and supported substantial populations.

TIME LINE

1607
Jamestown founded

1619
First African workers in Virginia

Virginia House of Burgesses meets

1620
Pilgrims found Plymouth Colony

1622
Powhatan Indians attack Virginia

1624
Dutch settle Manhattan

1630
Puritans establish Massachusetts Bay colony

1634
Maryland founded

1636
Roger Williams founds Rhode Island

1637
Anne Hutchinson expelled from Massachusetts Bay colony

Pequot War

1663
Carolina chartered

1664
English capture New Netherland

1675
King Philip's War

1676
Bacon's Rebellion

1681
Pennsylvania chartered

1686
Dominion of New England

1688
Glorious Revolution

1732
Georgia chartered

THE INDIAN VILLAGE OF SECOTON (CA. 1585), BY JOHN WHITE John White created this illustration of life among the Eastern Woodland Indians in coastal North Carolina. It shows the diversified agriculture practiced by the natives: squash, tobacco, and three varieties of corn. The hunters shown in nearby woods suggest another element of the native economy. At bottom right, Indians perform a religious ritual, which White described as "strange gestures and songs." (© Private Collection/Bridgeman Images)

The tiny English populations had no choice but to learn from the Indians. They recognized the value of corn, which was easy to cultivate and produced large yields. The English also learned the advantages of growing beans alongside corn to enrich the soil. Like the natives, the English quickly learned to combine the foods they grew and foods they hunted and fished. They built canoes like the Indians and gained the ability to navigate the local streams. They learned from the Indians how to build canoes by hollowing out a single log (dugouts) or sewing birchbark around a simple frame, sealing it with resin. Without what they learned from the natives, the early settlers would not have survived.

A few months after the first colonists arrived in Virginia, additional ships appeared with more men and supplies. By then, of the 144 men who had sailed to America only 38 were still alive, the rest killed by diseases and famine. Jamestown survived largely because of two important events. One was what they learned from the local Indians. The *John Smith* other was the leadership of Captain John Smith, who at age twenty-seven was already a famous world traveler. He imposed work and order on the community, created a shaky relationship with the natives (sometimes negotiating with the Indians, and at other times stealing food and kidnapping them).

Jamestown was a tiny colony for more than a decade. The natives were far more powerful than the English for years. Coastal Virginia had numerous tribes: the Algonquians, the Sioux, and the Iroquois. They had drawn together as part of the Powhatan   *Powhatan Confederacy* Confederacy, named after the great chief who controlled a large area near the coasts. What the English called Virginia, the natives called Tsenacommacah.

REORGANIZATION AND EXPANSION

As Jamestown struggled to survive, the London Company (now renamed the Virginia Company) was already dreaming of bigger things. In 1609, it obtained a new charter from the king, which increased its power and enlarged its territory. It offered stock in the company to planters who were willing to migrate at their own expense. And it provided free passage to Virginia for poorer people who would agree to serve the company for seven years. In the spring of 1609, two years after the first arrival of the English, a fleet of nine vessels was dispatched to Jamestown with approximately 600 people, including some women and children.

Nevertheless, disaster followed. One of the Virginia-bound ships was lost at sea in a hurricane. Another ran aground in the Bermuda islands and was unable to sail for months. Many of the new settlers succumbed to fevers before winter came. And the winter of 1609–1610 was especially severe, a period known as "starving time." By then, the   *The "Starving Time"* natives realized that the colonists were a threat to their civilization, and they blocked the English from moving inland. Barricaded in the small palisade, unable to hunt or cultivate food, the settlers lived on what they could find: "dogs, cats, rats, snakes, toadstools, horsehides," and even "the corpses of dead men," as one survivor recalled. When the migrants who had run aground in Bermuda finally arrived in Jamestown the following May, they found only about 60 emaciated people still alive. The new arrivals took the survivors onto their ship and sailed for England. But as the refugees proceeded down the James, they met an English ship coming up the river—part of a fleet bringing supplies and the colony's first governor, Lord De La Warr. The departing settlers agreed to return to Jamestown. New relief expeditions soon began to arrive, and the effort to turn a profit in Jamestown resumed.

New settlements began lining the river above and below Jamestown. The immigrants discovered a newly found crop—tobacco, which was already popular among the Spanish colonies to the south. It was already being imported to Europe. In 1612, the Jamestown planter John Rolfe began trying to cultivate the crop in Virginia. Other planters followed suit up and down the James River. Tobacco became the first profitable crop in the new colony, and its success encouraged tobacco planters to move deeper   *The Tobacco Economy* inland, intruding more and more into the native farmlands.

The emerging tobacco economy soon created a heavy demand for labor. To entice new workers to the colony, the Virginia Company established what it called the "headright system." Headrights were fifty-acre grants of land. Those who already   *The Headright System* lived in the colony received two headrights (100 acres) apiece. Each new settler received a single headright for himself or herself. This system encouraged family groups to migrate together, since the more family members who traveled to America, the more land the family would receive. In addition, anyone who paid for the passage of immigrants to Virginia would receive an extra headright for each arrival. As a result, some colonists were quickly able to assemble large plantations.

TOBACCO PLANT   This 1622 woodcut, later hand-colored, represents the tobacco plant cultivated by English settlers in Virginia in the early seventeenth century after John Rolfe introduced it to the colonists. On the right is an image of a man smoking the plant through a very large pipe. (© MPI/Getty Images)

The company also transported ironworkers and other skilled crafts workers to Virginia to diversify the economy. In 1619, it sent 100 Englishwomen to the colony to become the wives of male colonists. It also promised male colonists the full rights of Englishmen, an end to strict and arbitrary rule, and even a share in self-government. On July 30, 1619, *House of Burgesses*   delegates from the various communities met as the House of Burgesses, the first elected legislature within what was to become the United States.

A month later in 1619, Virginia established another important precedent. As John Rolfe recorded, "about the latter end of August" a Dutch ship brought in "20 and odd Negroes." At first, their status was not clear. There is some reason to believe that the colonists thought of these first Africans as servants, to be held for a term of years and then freed. *Slavery*   For a time, the use of African labor was limited. But not many years later, the African servants became more numerous and were slaves, without any possibility of freedom. It marked the first step toward the widespread enslavement of Africans within what was to become the American republic.

At the same time, Europeans began to arrive as **indentured servants**—mostly English immigrants who were also held for a time and then released. For a while, indentured servants were by far the most populous workers in Virginia and other colonies.

The European settlers in Virginia built their society also on the effective suppression of the local Indians. For two years in the 1610s, Sir Thomas Dale, De La Warr's successor as governor, commanded unrelenting assaults against the Powhatan Indians, led by (and named for) their formidable chief, Powhatan. In the process, Dale kidnapped Powhatan's young daughter Pocahontas. Several years earlier, Pocahontas had *Pocahontas* played a role in mediating differences between her people and the Europeans. But now, Powhatan refused to ransom her. Living among the English, Pocahontas gradually adapted many of their ways. She converted to Christianity and in 1614 married John Rolfe and visited England with him. There she stirred interest among many English in projects to "civilize" the Indians. She died shortly before her planned return to Virginia.

By the time of Pocahontas's marriage, Powhatan had ceased his attacks on the English in the face of overwhelming odds. But after his death several years later, his brother, Opechancanough, began secretly to plan the elimination of the English intruders. On a March morning in 1622, tribesmen called on the white settlements as if to offer goods for sale; then they suddenly attacked. Not until 347 whites of both sexes and all ages (including John Rolfe) lay dead did the Indian warriors finally retreat. And not until over twenty years later were the Powhatans finally defeated.

By then, the Virginia Company in London was defunct. In 1624, James I revoked the company's charter, and the colony came under the control of the crown, where it would remain until 1776. The colony, if not the company, had survived—but at a terrible cost. In Virginia's first seventeen years, more than 8,500 white settlers had arrived in the colony, and nearly 80 percent of them had died. Countless natives died as well, and slavery became part of the colony.

MARYLAND AND THE CALVERTS

The Maryland colony ultimately came to look much like Virginia, but its origins were very different. George Calvert, the first Lord Baltimore, envisioned *George and Cecilius Calvert* establishing a colony in America both as a great speculative venture in real estate and as a refuge for English Catholics like himself. Calvert died while he was still negotiating with the king in London for a charter to establish a colony in the Chesapeake region. But in 1632, his son Cecilius, the second Lord Baltimore, finally received the charter.

Lord Baltimore remained in England, but he named his brother, Leonard Calvert, governor of the colony. In March 1634, two ships—the *Ark* and the *Dove*—bearing Calvert along with 200 or 300 other colonists entered the Potomac River, turned into one of its eastern tributaries, and established the village of St. Mary's on a high, dry bluff. Neighboring Indians befriended the settlers and provided them with temporary shelter and with stocks of corn.

The Calverts needed to attract thousands of settlers to Maryland if their expensive colonial venture was to pay. As a result, they had to encourage the immigration of Protestants as well as their fellow English Catholics. The Calverts soon realized that Catholics would always be a minority in the colony, and so they adopted a policy of religious toleration: the 1649 "Act Concerning Religion." Nevertheless, politics in Maryland remained plagued for years by tensions, and at times violence, between the Catholic minority and the Protestant majority.

At the insistence of the first settlers, the Calverts agreed in 1635 to the calling of a representative assembly—the House of Delegates. But the proprietor retained absolute authority to distribute land as he wished; and since Lord Baltimore granted large estates to his relatives and to other English aristocrats, a distinct upper class soon established itself. By 1640, a severe labor shortage forced a modification of the land-grant procedure; and Maryland, like Virginia, adopted a headright system—a grant of 100 acres to each male settler, another 100 for his wife and each servant, and 50 for each of his children. But the great landlords of the colony's earliest years remained powerful. Like Virginia, Maryland became a center of tobacco cultivation; planters worked their land with the aid, first, of indentured servants imported from England and then, beginning late in the seventeenth century, of slaves imported from Africa.

THE GROWTH OF THE CHESAPEAKE, 1607–1750 This map shows the political forms of European settlement in the region of the Chesapeake Bay in the seventeenth and early eighteenth centuries. Note the several different kinds of colonial enterprises: the royal colony of Virginia, controlled directly by the English crown after the failure of the early commercial enterprises there; and the proprietary regions of Maryland, northern Virginia, and North Carolina, which were under the control of powerful English aristocrats. • *Did these political differences have any significant effect on the economic activities of the various Chesapeake colonies?*

BACON'S REBELLION

For more than thirty years, one man—Sir William Berkeley, the royal governor of
William Berkeley's Long Tenure Virginia—dominated the politics of the colony. He took office in 1642 at the age of thirty-six and with but one brief interruption remained in control of the government until 1677. In his first years as governor, he helped open up the interior of Virginia by sending explorers across the Blue Ridge Mountains and crushing a 1644 Indian uprising. The defeated Indians agreed to a treaty ceding to England most of the territory east of the mountains and establishing a boundary, west of which white settlement would be prohibited. But the rapid growth of the Virginia population made this agreement difficult to sustain. Between 1640 and 1660, Virginia's population rose from 8,000 to over 40,000. By 1652, English settlers had established three counties in the territory set aside by the treaty for the Indians.

In the meantime, Berkeley was expanding his own powers. By 1670, the vote for delegates to the House of Burgesses, once open to all white men, was restricted to land-owners. Elections were rare, and the same burgesses, representing the established planters of the eastern (or tidewater) region of the colony, remained in office year after year. The more recent settlers on the frontier were underrepresented.

Resentment of the power of the governor and the tidewater aristocrats grew steadily in the newly settled lands of the west (often known as the "backcountry"). In 1676, this resentment helped create a major conflict, led by Nathaniel Bacon.   *"Backcountry" Resentment* Bacon had a good farm in the West and a seat on the governor's council. But like other members of the new backcountry gentry, he resented the governor's attempts to hold the territorial line. Bacon's hostility toward Berkeley was a result of the governor's refusal to allow white settlers to move farther west. Berkeley forbid further settlement for fear of antagonizing Indians. Adding to the resentment was that Berkeley controlled the lucra-tive fur trade. Bacon wanted a piece of that trade.

The turbulence in Virginia was not just the tension between Berkeley and Bacon, both of them frontier aristocrats. It was also a result of the consequences of the indentured servant system. By the 1670s, many young men had finished their term as indentures and had found themselves without a home or any money. Many of them began moving around the colony, sometimes working, sometimes begging, sometimes stealing. They would soon become a factor in what became Bacon's rebellion.

In 1675, a major conflict erupted in the west between English settlers and natives. As the fighting escalated, Bacon and other concerned landholders demanded that the governor send the militia. When Berkeley refused, Bacon responded by offering to organize a volun-teer army of backcountry men who would do their own fighting. Berkeley rejected that offer too. Bacon ignored him and launched a series of vicious but unsuccessful pursuits of the Indian challengers. When Berkeley heard of the unauthorized military effort, he proclaimed Bacon and his men to be rebels. Bacon now turned his army against the governor and, in what became known as Bacon's Rebellion, twice led his troops east to Jamestown. The first time he won a temporary pardon from the governor; the second time, after the governor repudiated the agreement, Bacon burned much of the city and drove the governor into exile. But then Bacon died suddenly of dysentery, and Berkeley soon regained control. In 1677, the Indians reluctantly signed a new treaty that opened new lands to white settlement.

Bacon's Rebellion was part of a continuing struggle to define the Indian and white spheres of influence in Virginia. It also revealed the bitterness of the   *Consequences of Bacon's Rebellion* competition among rival white elites, and it demonstrated the potential for instability in the colony's large population of free, landless men. One result was that landed elites in both east-ern and western Virginia began to recognize a common interest in quelling social unrest from below. That was among the reasons that they turned increasingly to the African slave trade to fulfill their need for labor. African slaves, unlike white indentured servants, did not need to be released after a fixed term and hence did not threaten to become an unstable, landless class.

THE GROWTH OF NEW ENGLAND

The northern regions of British North America were slower to attract settlers than those in the south. That was in part because the Plymouth Company was never able to mount a successful colonizing expedition after receiving its charter in 1606. It did, however, sponsor other explorations. Captain John Smith, after his departure from Jamestown, made an exploratory journey for the Plymouth merchants, wrote an enthusiastic pamphlet about the lands he had seen, and called them New England.

PLYMOUTH PLANTATION

A discontented congregation of Puritan Separatists in England (unconnected to the Plymouth *Motives of English Separatists* Company) established the first enduring European settlement in New England. In 1608, a congregation of Separatists from the English hamlet of Scrooby began emigrating quietly (and illegally), a few at a time, to Leyden, Holland, where they believed they could enjoy freedom of worship. But as foreigners in Holland, they had to work at unskilled and poorly paid jobs. They also watched with alarm as their children began to adapt to Dutch society and drift away from their church. Finally, some of the Separatists decided to move again, across the Atlantic; there, they hoped to create a stable, protected community where they could spread "the gospel of the Kingdom of Christ in those remote parts of the world."

In 1620, leaders of the Scrooby group obtained permission from the Virginia Company to settle in Virginia. The "Pilgrims," as they saw themselves, sailed from Plymouth, England, *Plymouth Founded* in September 1620 on the *Mayflower*; thirty-five "saints" (Puritan Separatists) and sixty-seven "strangers" (people who were not part of the congregation) were aboard. In November, after a long and difficult voyage, they sighted land—the shore of what is now Cape Cod. That had not been their destination, but it was too late in the year to sail farther south. So the Pilgrims chose a site for their settlement in the area just north of the cape, a place John Smith had labeled "Plymouth" on a map he had drawn during his earlier exploration of New England. Because Plymouth lay outside the London Company's territory, the settlers were not bound by the company's rules. While still aboard ship, the saints in the group drew up an agreement, the Mayflower Compact, to establish a government for themselves. Then, on December 21, 1620, they stepped ashore at Plymouth Rock.

The Pilgrims' first winter was a difficult one. Half the colonists perished from malnutrition, disease, and exposure. But the colony survived, in large part because of crucial *Pilgrim-Indian Interaction* assistance from local Indians. Trade and other exchanges with the Indians were critical to the settlers and attractive to the natives. The tribes provided the colonists with furs. They also showed the settlers how to cultivate corn and how to hunt wild animals for meat. After the first autumn harvest, the settlers invited the natives to join them in a festival, the original Thanksgiving. But the relationship between the settlers and the local Indians was not a happy one for long. Thirteen years after the Pilgrims arrived, a devastating smallpox epidemic—a result of natives' exposure to Europeans carrying the disease—wiped out much of the Indian population around Plymouth.

The Pilgrims could not create rich farms on the sandy and marshy soil around Plymouth, but they developed a profitable trade in fish and furs. New colonists arrived from England, and in a decade the population reached 300. The people of Plymouth Plantation chose as their governor William Bradford, who governed successfully for many years. The Pilgrims were always poor. As late as the 1640s, they had only one plow among them. But they were, on the whole, content to be left alone to live their lives in what they considered godly ways.

THE MASSACHUSETTS BAY EXPERIMENT

Events in England encouraged other Puritans to migrate to the New World. King James I had repressed Puritans for years. When he died in 1625, his son and successor, Charles I, was even more hostile to Puritans and imprisoned many of them for their beliefs. The king dissolved Parliament in 1629 (it was not recalled until 1640), ensuring that there would be no one in a position to oppose him.

In the midst of this turmoil, a group of Puritan merchants began organizing a new colonial venture in America. They obtained a grant of land in New England for most of the area now comprising Massachusetts and New Hampshire. They acquired a charter from the king allowing them to create the Massachusetts Bay Company and to establish a colony in the New World. Some members of the Massachusetts Bay Company wanted to create a refuge in New England for Puritans. They bought out the interests of company members who preferred to stay in England, and the new owners elected a governor, John Winthrop. They then sailed for New England in 1630. With 17 ships and 1,000 people, it was the largest single migration of its kind in the seventeenth century. Winthrop carried with him the charter of the Massachusetts Bay Company, which   *Massachusetts Bay Company* meant that the colonists would be responsible to no company officials in England.

PORTRAIT OF A BOSTON WOMAN   Anne Pollard, a member of the original Winthrop expedition to Boston, was 100 years old when this portrait was painted in 1721. When she died in 1725, she left 130 direct descendants. The artist is unknown, but it is assumed to be an American working in the primitive style common in New England before the arrival of academically trained portraitists from England. (© Massachusetts Historical Society, Boston, MA, USA/Bridgeman Images)

The Massachusetts migration quickly produced several settlements. The port of Boston became the capital, but in the course of the next decade colonists established several other towns in eastern Massachusetts: Charlestown, Newtown (later renamed Cambridge), Roxbury, Dorchester, Watertown, Ipswich, Concord, Sudbury, and others.

The Massachusetts Puritans strove to lead useful, conscientious lives of thrift and hard work, and they honored material success as evidence of God's favor. Winthrop and the *Winthrop's "City upon a Hill"* other founders of Massachusetts believed they were building a holy commonwealth, a model—a "city upon a hill"—for the corrupt world to see and emulate. Colonial Massachusetts was a **theocracy,** a society in which the church was almost indistinguishable from the state. Residents had no more freedom of worship than the Puritans themselves had had in England.

Like other new settlements, the Massachusetts Bay colony had early difficulties. During the first winter (1629–1630), nearly 200 people died and many others decided to leave. But the colony soon grew and prospered. The nearby Pilgrims and neighboring Indians helped with food and advice. Incoming settlers brought needed tools and other goods. The prevalence of families in the colony helped establish a feeling of commitment to the community and a sense of order among the settlers, and it also ensured that the population would reproduce itself.

THE EXPANSION OF NEW ENGLAND

It did not take long for English settlement to begin moving outward from Massachusetts Bay. Some people migrated in search of soil more productive than the stony land around Boston. Others left because of the oppressiveness of the church-dominated government of Massachusetts.

The Connecticut River valley, about 100 miles west of Boston, began attracting English families as early as the 1630s because of its fertile lands and its isolation from Massachusetts Bay. In 1635, Thomas Hooker, a minister of Newtown (Cambridge), defied the Massachusetts government, led his congregation west, and established the town of Hartford. Four years later, the people of Hartford and of two other newly founded towns *Connecticut* nearby adopted a constitution known as the Fundamental Orders of Connecticut, which created an independent colony with a government similar to that of Massachusetts Bay but gave a larger proportion of the men the right to vote and hold office. (Women were barred from voting virtually everywhere.)

Another Connecticut colony grew up around New Haven on the Connecticut coast. Unlike Hartford, the Fundamental Articles of New Haven (1639) established a Bible-based government even stricter than that of Massachusetts Bay. New Haven remained independent until 1662, when a royal charter officially gave the Hartford colony jurisdiction over the New Haven settlements.

European settlement in what is now Rhode Island was a result of the religious and political dissent of Roger Williams, a controversial young minister who lived for a time in Salem, Massachusetts. Williams was a confirmed Separatist who argued that the Massachusetts church should abandon all allegiance to the Church of England. He also proclaimed that the land the colonists were occupying belonged to the natives. The colonial government voted to deport him, but he escaped before they could do so. During the winter of 1635–1636, he took refuge with Narragansett tribesmen; the following spring he bought a tract of land from them, and with a few followers, created the town of Providence. In 1644, after obtaining a charter from Parliament, he established a

THE GROWTH OF NEW ENGLAND, 1620–1750   The European settlement of New England, as this map reveals, traces its origins primarily to two small settlements on the Atlantic Coast. The first was the Pilgrim settlement at Plymouth, which began in 1620 and spread out through Cape Cod, southern Massachusetts, and the islands of Martha's Vineyard and Nantucket. The second, much larger settlement began in Boston in 1630 and spread rapidly through western Massachusetts, north into New Hampshire and Maine, and south into Connecticut. • *Why would the settlers of Massachusetts Bay have expanded so much more rapidly and expansively than those of Plymouth?*

government similar to that of Massachusetts but without any   *Roger Williams and Rhode Island* ties to the church. For a time, Rhode Island was the only colony in which all faiths (including Judaism) could worship without interference.

Another challenge to the established religious order in Massachusetts Bay came from Anne Hutchinson, an intelligent and charismatic woman from a substantial   *Anne Hutchinson* Boston family. She argued that many clergy were not among the "elect" and were, there-fore, entitled to no spiritual authority. Such teachings (known as the **Antinomian** heresy)

COTTON MATHER ON THE RECENT HISTORY OF NEW ENGLAND (1692)

Reviewing the history of English settlers during the seventeenth century, Puritan cleric Cotton Mather, in this excerpt from his history of New England, saw the Devil as the root of mishap and evil. He demonstrated a real mistrust of Indians and saw them as servants of the Devil.

I believe there never was a poor plantation more pursued by the wrath of the Devil than our poor New England; and that which makes our condition very much the more deplorable is that the wrath of the great God himself at the same time also presses hard upon us. It was a rousing alarm to the Devil when a great company of English Protestants and Puritans came to erect evangelical churches in a corner of the world where he had reigned without any control for many ages; and it is a vexing eye-sore to the Devil that our Lord Christ should be known and owned and preached in this howling wilderness. Wherefore he has left no stone unturned, that so he might undermine this plantation and force us out of our country.

First, the Indian Powwows used all their sorceries to molest the first planters here; but God said unto them, "Touch them not!" Then, seducing spirits came to root in this vineyard, but God so rated them off that they have not prevailed much farther than the edges of our land. After this, we have had a continual blast upon some of our principal grain, annually diminishing a vast part of our ordinary food. Herewithal, wasting sicknesses, especially burning and mortal agues, have shot the arrows of death in at our windows. Next, we have had many adversaries of our own language, who have been perpetually assaying to deprive us of those English liberties in the encouragement whereof these territories have been settled. As if this had not been enough, the Tawnies among whom we came have watered our soil with the blood of many hundreds of our inhabitants. Desolating fires also have many times laid the chief treasure of the whole province in ashes. As for losses by sea, they have been multiplied upon us; and particularly in the present French War, the whole English nation have observed that no part of the nation has proportionately had so many vessels taken as our poor New England. Besides all which, now at last the devils are (if I may so speak) in person come down upon us, with such a wrath as is justly much and will quickly be more the astonishment of the world. Alas, I may sigh over this wilderness, as Moses did over his, in Psalm 90.7, 9: "We are consumed by thine anger, and by thy wrath we are troubled: All our days are passed away in thy wrath." And I may add this unto it: the wrath of the Devil too has been troubling and spending of us all our days. . . .

Let us now make a good and a right use of the prodigious descent which the Devil in great wrath is at this day making upon our land. Upon the death of a great man once, an orator called the town together, crying out, "Concurrite cives, dilapsa cunt vestra moenia!" That is, "Come together neighbors, your town walls are fallen down!" But such is the descent of the Devil at this day upon our selves that I may truly tell you, the walls of the whole world are broken down! The usual walls of defense about mankind have such a gap made in them that the very devils are broke in upon us to seduce the souls, torment the bodies, sully the credits, and consume the estates of our neighbors, with impressions both as real and as furious as if the invisible world were becoming incarnate on purpose for the vexing of us. . . .

In as much as the devil is come down in great wrath, we had need labor, with all the care and speed we can, to divert the great wrath of Heaven from coming at the same time upon us. The God of Heaven has with long and loud admonitions been calling us to a reformation of our provoking evils as the only way to avoid that wrath of his which does not only threaten but consume us. It is because we have been deaf to those calls that we are now by a provoked God laid open to the wrath of the Devil himself.

UNDERSTAND, ANALYZE, & EVALUATE

1. According to Cotton Mather, what particular hardships did the colonists suffer?
2. What did Mather mean when he wrote that "now at last the devils [have descended] in person"?
3. What deeper explanation did Cotton Mather offer for New England's crisis? What response did he suggest?

Source: Cotton Mather, *The Wonders of the Invisible Word* (Boston, 1692), pp. 41–43, 48; cited in Richard Godbeer, *The Salem Witch Hunt: A Brief History with Documents* (Boston: Bedford St. Martin's), pp. 48–49.

were a serious threat to the spiritual authority of the established clergy. Hutchinson also challenged prevailing assumptions about the proper role of women in Puritan society. As her influence grew, and as she began to deliver open attacks on members of the clergy, the Massachusetts hierarchy mobilized to stop her. In 1637, she was convicted of heresy and sedition and was banished. With her family and some of her followers, she moved to a point on Narragansett Bay not far from Providence. Later she moved south into New York, where in 1643 she and her family died during an Indian uprising.

New Hampshire and Maine were established in 1629 by two English proprietors. But few settlers moved into these northern regions until the religious *New Hampshire and Maine* disruptions in Massachusetts Bay. In 1639, John Wheelwright, a disciple of Anne Hutchinson, led some of his fellow dissenters to Exeter, New Hampshire. Others soon followed. New Hampshire became a separate colony in 1679. Maine remained a part of Massachusetts until 1820.

SETTLERS AND NATIVES

The first white settlers in New England had generally friendly relations with the natives. Indians taught whites how to grow vital food crops such as corn, beans, pumpkins, and potatoes. European farmers also benefited from the extensive lands Indians had already cleared (and had either abandoned or sold). White traders used Indians as partners in some of their most important trading activities. Indeed, commerce with the Indians was responsible for the creation of some of the first great fortunes in British North America. Other white settlers attempted to educate the Indians in European religion and culture. Protestant missionaries converted some natives to Christianity, and a few Indians became at least partially assimilated into white society. But the great majority continued to practice their traditional faiths.

As in other areas of white settlement, however, tensions soon developed—primarily as a result of the white colonists' insatiable appetite for land and uneven respect for Indian culture and beliefs. The religious leaders of New England came to consider the tribes a threat to their hopes of creating a godly community in the New World. (See "Consider the Source: Cotton Mather on the Recent History of New England.") Gradually, the image of Indians as helpful neighbors came to be replaced by the image of Indians as "heathens" and barbarians.

King Philip's War and the Technology of Battle

In 1637, hostilities broke out between English settlers in the Connecticut Valley and the Pequot Indians of the region, a conflict (known as the Pequot War) in which the natives were almost wiped out. But the bloodiest and most prolonged encounter between whites and Indians in the seventeenth century began in 1675, a conflict that whites called King Philip's War. The Wampanoag tribe, under the leadership of a chieftain known to the *Metacomet* white settlers as King Philip and among his own people as Metacomet, rose up to resist the English. For three years, the natives terrorized a string of Massachusetts towns, killing over a thousand people. But beginning in 1676, the white settlers gradually prevailed, enlisting a group of Mohawk allies who ambushed Metacomet and killed him. Without Metacomet, the fragile alliance among the tribes collapsed, and the white settlers were soon able to crush the uprising.

The conflicts between natives and settlers were crucially affected by earlier exchanges of technology between the English and the tribes. In particular, the Indians made effective use of a relatively new European weapon that they had acquired from the English: the *Flintlock Muskets* flintlock rifle. It replaced the earlier staple of colonial musketry, the matchlock rifle, which proved too heavy, cumbersome, and inaccurate to be effective. The matchlock had to be steadied on a fixed object and ignited with a match before firing. The flintlock could be held up without support and fired without a match.

A PEQUOT VILLAGE DESTROYED An English artist drew this view of a fortified Pequot village in Connecticut surrounded by English soldiers and their allies from other tribes during the Pequot War in 1637. The invaders massacred more than 600 residents of the settlement. (The Library of Congress)

Many English settlers were slow to give up their matchlocks, but the Indians recognized the advantages of the newer rifles right away and began purchasing them in large quantities. Despite rules forbidding colonists to instruct natives on how to use and repair the weapons, the natives learned to handle the rifles, and even to repair them very effectively on their own. In King Philip's War, the very high casualties on both sides were partly a result of the use of these more advanced rifles.

Indians also used more traditional military technologies—especially the construction of forts. The Narragansett, allies of the Wampanoag in King Philip's War, built an enormous fort in the Great Swamp of Rhode Island in 1675, which became the site of one of the bloodiest battles of the war before English attackers burned it down. After that, a band of Narragansett set out to build a large stone fort, with the help of a member of the tribe who had learned masonry while working with the English. When English soldiers discovered the stone fort in 1676, after the end of King Philip's War, they killed most of its occupants and destroyed it. In the end, the technological skills of the Indians were no match for the overwhelming advantages of the English settlers in both numbers and firepower.

THE RESTORATION COLONIES

For nearly thirty years after Lord Baltimore received the charter for Maryland in 1632, no new English colonies were established in America. England was dealing with troubles of its own at home.

THE ENGLISH CIVIL WAR

After Charles I dissolved Parliament in 1629 and began ruling as an absolute monarch, he alienated a growing number of his subjects. Finally, desperately in need of money, Charles called Parliament back into session in 1640 and asked it to levy new taxes. But he antagonized the members by dismissing them twice in two years; and in 1642, members of Parliament organized a military force, sparking the English Civil War.

The conflict between the Cavaliers (the supporters of the king) and the Roundheads (the forces of Parliament, who were largely Puritans) lasted seven years. In 1649, the Roundheads defeated the king's forces and shocked all of *The Restoration of the Monarchy* Europe by beheading the monarch. The stern Roundhead leader Oliver Cromwell assumed the position of "protector." But when Cromwell died in 1658, his son and heir proved unable to maintain his authority. Two years later, Charles II, son of the executed king, returned from exile and seized the throne, in what became known as the Restoration.

Among the results of the Restoration was the resumption of colonization in America. Charles II rewarded faithful courtiers with grants of land in the New World, and in the twenty-five years of his reign he issued charters for four additional colonies: Carolina, New York, New Jersey, and Pennsylvania.

Charles II faced some of the same problems that his father had confronted, mostly because of the popular belief that he was secretly a Roman Catholic. The king supported religious toleration—which would allow Catholicism again in England, to the dismay of many Protestants. The Parliament refused to agree. Charles was prudent enough not to fight for the right of Catholics to worship openly. But he himself made a private agreement with Louis XIV of France that he would become a Catholic—which he did only on his deathbed. His son, James II, faced many of the same problems.

THE CAROLINAS

In charters issued in 1663 and 1665, Charles II awarded joint title to eight proprietors. They received a vast territory stretching south from Virginia to the Florida peninsula and west to the Pacific Ocean. Like Lord Baltimore, they received almost kingly powers over their grant, which they prudently called Carolina (a name derived from the Latin word for "Charles"). They reserved tremendous estates for themselves and distributed the rest through a headright system similar to those in Virginia and Maryland. Although committed Anglicans themselves, the proprietors guaranteed religious freedom to all Christian faiths. They also created a representative assembly. They hoped to attract settlers from the existing American colonies and to avoid the expense of financing expeditions from England.

But their initial efforts to profit from settlement in Carolina failed dismally. Anthony Ashley Cooper, however, persisted. He convinced the other proprietors to finance expeditions to Carolina from England, the first of which set sail with 300 people in the spring of 1670. The 100 people who survived the difficult voyage established a settlement at Port Royal on the Carolina coast. Ten years later, they founded a city at the junction of *Charles Town* the Ashley and Cooper Rivers, which in 1690 became the colonial capital. They called it Charles Town (it was later renamed Charleston).

With the aid of the English philosopher John Locke, Cooper (now the earl of Shaftesbury) drew up the Fundamental Constitution for Carolina in 1669. It divided the colony into counties of equal size and divided each county into equal parcels. It also established a social hierarchy with the proprietors themselves (who were to be known as "seigneurs") at the top, a local aristocracy (consisting of lesser nobles known as "landgraves" or "caciques") below them, and then ordinary settlers ("leet-men"). At the bottom of this stratified society would be poor whites, who would have few political rights, and African slaves. Proprietors, nobles, and other landholders would have a voice in the colonial parliament in proportion to the size of their landholdings.

In reality, Carolina developed along lines quite different from the carefully ordered vision of Shaftesbury and Locke. For one thing, the northern and southern regions of settlement were widely separated and socially and economically distinct from each other. The northern settlers were mainly backwoods farmers. In the South, fertile lands and the good harbor at Charles Town promoted a more prosperous economy and a more stratified, aristocratic society. Settlements grew up rapidly along the Ashley and Cooper Rivers, and colonists established a flourishing trade, particularly (beginning in the 1660s) in rice.

Southern Carolina very early developed commercial ties to the large (and overpopu-*Close Ties with the Caribbean* lated) European colony on the Caribbean island of Barbados. During the first ten years of settlement, in fact, most of the new residents in Carolina were Barbadians, some of whom established themselves as substantial landlords. African slavery had taken root on Barbados earlier than in any of the mainland colonies, and the white Caribbean migrants—tough, uncompromising profit seekers—established a similar slave-based plantation society in Carolina.

Carolina was one of the most divided English colonies in America. There were tensions between the small farmers of the Albemarle region in the north and the wealthy planters in the south. And there were conflicts between the rich Barbadians in *Carolina Divided* southern Carolina and the smaller landowners around them. After Lord Shaftesbury's death, the proprietors proved unable to establish order. In 1719, the colonists seized control of the colony from them. Ten years later, the king divided the region into two royal colonies, North Carolina and South Carolina.

New Netherland, New York, and New Jersey

In 1664, Charles II granted his brother James, the Duke of York, all the territory lying between the Connecticut and Delaware Rivers. This land, however, was also claimed by the Dutch. The growing conflict between the English and the Dutch was part of a larger commercial rivalry between the two nations throughout the world. But the English particularly rejected the Dutch presence in America, because it served as a wedge between the northern and southern English colonies and because it provided bases for Dutch smugglers evading English custom laws. And so months after James received the grant, an English fleet under the command of Richard Nicolls put in at New Amsterdam, the capital of the Dutch colony of New Netherland, and extracted a surrender from the governor, Peter Stuyvesant. Several years later, in 1673, the Dutch reconquered and briefly held their old provincial capital. But they lost it again, this time for good, in 1674.

The Duke of York renamed his territory New York. It contained not only Dutch and English but also Scandinavians, Germans, French, and a large number of Africans *New York* (imported as slaves by the Dutch West India Company), as well as members of several different Indian tribes. James wisely made no effort to impose his own Roman Catholicism on the colony. He delegated powers to a governor and a council but made no provision for representative assemblies.

Property holding and political power remained highly divided and highly unequal in New York. In addition to confirming the great Dutch "patroonships" already in existence, James granted large estates to some of his own political supporters. Power in the colony thus remained widely dispersed among wealthy English landlords, Dutch patroons, wealthy fur traders, and the duke's political appointees. By 1685, when the Duke of York ascended the English throne as James II, New York contained about four times as many people (around 30,000) as it had twenty years before.

Shortly after James received his charter, he gave a large part of the land south of New York to a pair of political allies, both Carolina proprietors, Sir John Berkeley and Sir George Carteret. Carteret named the territory New Jersey. But the *New Jersey* venture in New Jersey generated few profits, and in 1674, Berkeley sold his half interest. The colony was divided into two jurisdictions, East Jersey and West Jersey, which squabbled with each other until 1702, when the two halves of the colony were again joined. New Jersey, like New York, was a colony of enormous ethnic and religious diversity, and the weak colonial government made few efforts to impose strict control over the fragmented society. But unlike New York, New Jersey developed no important class of large landowners.

The Quaker Colonies

Pennsylvania was born out of the efforts of a dissenting English Protestant sect, the Society of Friends. They wished to find a home for their own distinctive social order. The Society began in the mid-seventeenth century under the leadership of George Fox, a Nottingham shoemaker, and Margaret Fell. Their followers came to be known as Quakers (from Fox's instruction to them to "tremble at the name of the Lord"). Unlike the Puritans, Quakers rejected the concept of predestination and original sin. All people, they believed, had divinity within themselves and needed only learn to cultivate it; all could attain salvation.

The Quakers had no formal church government and no paid clergy; in their worship they *The Quakers* spoke up one by one as the spirit moved them. Disregarding distinctions of gender and class, they addressed one another with the terms *thee* and *thou,* words commonly used in other parts of English society only in speaking to servants and social inferiors. As confirmed pacifists, they would not take part in wars. Unpopular in England, the Quakers began looking to America for asylum. A few migrated to New England or Carolina, but most Quakers wanted a colony of their own. As members of a despised sect, however, they could not get the necessary royal grant without the aid of someone influential at the court.

Fortunately for the Quaker cause, a number of wealthy and prominent men had converted to the faith. One of them was William Penn, an outspoken evangelist who had been in prison several times. Penn worked with George Fox on plans for a Quaker colony in America, and when Penn's father died in 1681, Charles II settled a large debt he had owed to the older Penn by making an enormous grant to the son of territory between New York and Maryland. At the king's insistence, the territory was to be named Pennsylvania, after Penn's late father.

Through his informative and honest advertising, Penn soon made Pennsylvania the *Pennsylvania Established* best-known and most cosmopolitan of all the English colonies in America. More than any other English colony, Pennsylvania prospered from the outset because of Penn's successful recruiting, his careful planning, and the region's mild climate and fertile soil. Penn sailed to Pennsylvania in 1682 to oversee the laying out of the city he named Philadelphia ("Brotherly Love") between the Delaware and Schuylkill Rivers.

Penn's relatively good relations with the Indians were a result in large part of his religious beliefs. Quakerism was a faith that included a refusal to participate in war or any violence and that believed that all people, whatever their background, were capable of becoming Christian. Penn worked to respect the natives and their culture. He recognized Indians' claim to the land in the province, and he was usually scrupulous in reimbursing the natives for their land. In later years, the relationships between the English residents of Pennsylvania and the natives were not always so peaceful.

By the late 1690s, some residents of Pennsylvania were beginning to resist the nearly absolute power of the proprietor. Pressure from these groups grew to the point that in 1701, shortly before he departed for England for the last time, Penn agreed to a Charter *Charter of Liberties* of Liberties for the colony. The charter established a representative assembly (consisting, alone among the English colonies, of only one house) that greatly limited the authority of the proprietor. The charter also permitted "the lower counties" of the colony to establish their own representative assembly. The three counties did so in 1703 and as a result became, in effect, a separate colony—Delaware—although until the American Revolution it continued to have the same governor as Pennsylvania.

BORDERLANDS AND MIDDLE GROUNDS

The English colonies clustered along the Atlantic seaboard of North America eventually united, expanded, and became the beginnings of a powerful nation. But in the seventeenth and early eighteenth centuries, their future was not at all clear. In those years, they were small, frail settlements surrounded by other, competing societies and settlements. The British Empire in North America was, in fact, a much smaller and weaker one than the great Spanish Empire to the south, and in many ways weaker than the enormous French Empire to the north.

The continuing contests for control of North America were most clearly visible in areas around the borders of English settlement—the Caribbean and along the northern, southern, and western borders of the coastal colonies. In the regions of *Complex Cultural Interactions* the borderlands emerged societies very different from those in the English seaboard colonies—areas described as **middle grounds,** in which diverse civilizations encountered one another and, for a time at least, shaped one another.

THE CARIBBEAN ISLANDS

The Chesapeake was the site of the first permanent English settlements in the North American continent. Throughout the first half of the seventeenth century, however, the most important destinations for English immigrants were the islands of the Caribbean and the northern way station of Bermuda. More than half of the English migrants to the New World in the early seventeenth century settled on these islands.

Before the arrival of Europeans, most of the Caribbean islands had substantial native populations. But beginning with Christopher Columbus's first visit in 1492, and accelerating after 1496, the native populations were all but wiped out by European epidemics.

The Spanish Empire claimed title to all the islands in the Caribbean, but Spain created substantial settlements only in the largest of them: Cuba, Hispaniola, and Puerto Rico. English, French, and Dutch traders began settling on some of the smaller islands early in the sixteenth century, despite the Spanish claim to them. After Spain and the Netherlands went to war in 1621 (distracting the Spanish navy and leaving the *The English Caribbean* English in the Caribbean relatively unmolested), the pace of English colonization increased. By midcentury, there were several substantial English settlements on the islands, the most important of them on Antigua, St. Kitts, Jamaica, and Barbados.

In their first years in the Caribbean, English settlers experimented unsuccessfully with tobacco and cotton. But they soon discovered that the most lucrative crop was sugar, for which there was a substantial and growing market in Europe. Sugarcane could also be distilled into rum, for which there was also a booming market abroad. Planters devoted almost all of their land to sugarcane.

Because sugar was a labor-intensive crop, English planters quickly found it necessary to import laborers. As in the Chesapeake, they began by bringing indentured *Sugar and Slavery* servants from England. But the arduous work discouraged white laborers. By midcentury, therefore, the English planters in the Caribbean (like the Spanish colonists) were relying more and more heavily on an enslaved African workforce, which soon substantially outnumbered them.

On Barbados and other islands where a flourishing sugar economy developed, the English planters were a tough, aggressive, and ambitious people. Since their livelihoods depended on their workforces, they expanded and solidified the system of African slavery there remarkably quickly. By the late seventeenth century, there were four times as many African slaves as there were white settlers.

MASTERS AND SLAVES IN THE CARIBBEAN

Fearful of slave revolts, whites in the Caribbean monitored their labor forces closely and often harshly. Planters paid little attention to the welfare of their workers. Many concluded that it was cheaper to buy new slaves periodically than to protect the well-being of those

Harsh Conditions for Slaves   they already owned, and it was not uncommon for masters literally to work their slaves to death. Few African workers survived more than a decade in the brutal Caribbean working environment—they were either sold to planters in North America or died. Even whites, who worked far less hard than did the slaves, often succumbed to the harsh climate; most died before the age of forty.

Establishing a stable society and culture was extremely difficult for people living in such harsh and even deadly conditions. White landowners in the Caribbean islands returned to England with their fortunes when they could and left their estates in the hands of overseers. Europeans in the Caribbean lacked many of the institutions that gave stability to the North American settlements: church, family, community.

Africans in the Caribbean faced much greater difficulties than did whites, but because they had no chance of leaving, they created what was in many ways a more elaborate culture than did the white settlers. They started families (although many of them were *Slave Culture and Resistance*   broken up by death or the slave trade); they sustained African religious and social traditions, and they blended them with church rituals to create their new signature expression of faith. And within the rigidly controlled world of the sugar plantations, they established patterns of resistance.

The Caribbean settlements were an important part of the Atlantic trading world in which many Americans became involved—a source of sugar and rum and a market for goods made in the mainland colonies and in England. They were the first principal source of African slaves for the mainland colonies.

THE SOUTHWEST BORDERLANDS

By the end of the seventeenth century, the Spanish had established a sophisticated and impressive empire. Their capital, Mexico City, was the most dazzling metropolis in the Americas. The Spanish residents, well over a million, enjoyed much greater prosperity than all but a few English settlers in North America.

But the principal Spanish colonies north of Mexico—Florida, Texas, New Mexico, Arizona, and California—were relatively unimportant economically to the empire. They attracted religious minorities, Catholic missionaries, and independent ranchers *Spanish Outposts in North America*   fleeing the heavy hand of imperial authority. Spanish troops defended the northern flank of the empire. But they remained weak and peripheral parts of the great empire to their south. New Mexico was the most prosperous and populous of these Spanish outposts. By the end of the eighteenth century, New Mexico had a non-Indian population of over 10,000—the largest European settlement west of the Mississippi and north of Mexico—and it was steadily expanding through the region.

The Spanish began to colonize California once they realized that other Europeans—among them English merchants and French and Russian trappers—were beginning to establish a presence in the region. Formal Spanish settlement of California began in the 1760s, when the governor of Baja California was ordered to create outposts of the empire farther north. Soon a string of missions, forts (or *presidios*), and trading communities were springing up along the Pacific Coast: beginning with San Diego and Monterey in 1769 and eventually San Francisco (1776), Los Angeles (1781), and *California*   Santa Barbara (1786). The arrival of the Spanish in California had a devastating effect on the native population, who died in great numbers from the diseases the colonists imported. As the new settlements spread, the Spanish insisted that the remaining natives convert to Catholicism. That explains the centrality of missions in almost all the major Spanish outposts in California. But the Spanish colonists were also intent on creating a prosperous agricultural economy, and they enlisted Indian laborers to help them do so. California's Indians had no choice but to accede to the demands of the Spanish, although there were frequent revolts by natives against the harsh conditions imposed on them.

The Spanish considered the greatest threat to the northern borders of their empire to be the growing ambitions of the French. In the 1680s, French explorers *French and Spanish Claims* traveled down the Mississippi Valley to the mouth of the river and claimed those lands for France in 1682. They called the territory Louisiana. Fearful of French incursions farther west, the Spanish began to fortify their claim to Texas by establishing new forts, missions, and settlements there, including San Fernando (later San Antonio) in 1731. Much of the region that is now Arizona was also becoming increasingly tied to the Spanish Empire and was governed from Santa Fe.

The Spanish colonies in the Southwest were the sparsely populated edges of the great Spanish Empire to the south—created less to increase the wealth of the empire than to defend it from threats by other European powers in the North. Nevertheless, these Spanish outposts helped create enduring societies that were very unlike those being established by the English along the Atlantic seaboard. The Spanish colonies did not displace the native populations. Rather, they enlisted them. They sought to convert them to Catholicism, to recruit them (sometimes forcibly) as agricultural workers, and to cultivate them as trading partners.

THE SOUTHEAST BORDERLANDS

The southeastern areas of what is now the United States posed a direct challenge to English ambitions in North America. After Spain claimed Florida in the 1560s, missionaries and traders began moving northward into Georgia and westward into what is now known as the Florida panhandle. Some ambitious Spaniards began to dream of expanding their empire still farther north, into what became the Carolinas and beyond. The founding of Jamestown in 1607 dampened those hopes and replaced them with *The Spanish Threat* fears. The English colonies, the Spaniards worried, could threaten their existing settlements in Florida and Georgia. As a result, the Spanish built forts in both regions to defend themselves against the increasing English presence there. Throughout the eighteenth century, the area between the Carolinas and Florida was the site of continuing tension and frequent conflict, between the Spanish and the English—and, to a lesser degree, between the Spanish and the French, who were threatening their northwestern borders with settlements in Louisiana and in what is now Alabama.

There was no formal war between England and Spain in these years, but that did not dampen the hostilities in the Southeast. English pirates continually harassed the Spanish settlements and, in 1668, actually sacked St. Augustine. The English encouraged Indians in Florida to rise up against the Spanish missions. The Spanish offered freedom to African slaves owned by English settlers in the Carolinas if they agreed to convert to Catholicism. About 100 Africans accepted the offer, and the Spanish later organized some of them into a military regiment to defend the northern border of New Spain. By the early eighteenth century, the constant fighting in the region had driven almost all the Spanish out of Florida except for settlers in St. Augustine on the Atlantic Coast and Pensacola on the Gulf Coast.

Eventually, after more than a century of conflict in the southeastern borderlands, the English prevailed—acquiring Florida in the aftermath of the Seven Years' War (known in America as the French and Indian War) and rapidly populating it with settlers from their colonies to the North. Before that point, however, protecting the southern boundary of the British Empire in North America was a continual concern to the English and contributed in crucial ways to the founding of the colony of Georgia.

THE FOUNDING OF GEORGIA

Georgia—the last English colony to be established in what would become the United States—was founded to create a military barrier against Spanish lands on the southern border of English America. It was also designed to provide a refuge for the impoverished, a place where English men and women without prospects at home could begin anew. Its founders, led by General James Oglethorpe, served as unpaid trustees of a society created to serve the needs of the British Empire.

Oglethorpe, himself a veteran of the most recent Spanish wars with England, was keenly aware of the military advantages of an English colony south of the Carolinas. Yet *Oglethorpe's Mission* his interest in settlement rested even more on his philanthropic commitments. As head of a parliamentary committee investigating English prisons, he had been appalled by the plight of honest debtors rotting in confinement. Such prisoners,

SAVANNAH IN 1734 This view of Savannah by an English artist shows the intensely orderly character of early settlement in the Georgia colony. As the colony grew, its residents gradually abandoned the plan created by Oglethorpe and his fellow trustees. (© Historic Map Works/Getty Images)

and other poor people in danger of succumbing to a similar fate, could, he believed, become the farmer-soldiers of the new colony in America.

In 1732, King George II granted Oglethorpe and his fellow trustees control of the land between the Savannah and Altamaha Rivers. Their colonization policies reflected the vital military purposes of the colony. They limited the size of landholdings to make the settlement compact and easier to defend against Spanish and Indian attacks.   *Georgia Founded* They excluded Africans, free or slave; Oglethorpe feared that slave labor would produce internal revolts and that disaffected slaves might turn to the Spanish as allies. The trustees strictly regulated trade with the Indians, again to limit the possibility of wartime insurrection. They also excluded Catholics for fear they might collude with their coreligionists in the Spanish colonies to the south.

Oglethorpe himself led the first colonial expedition to Georgia, which built a fortified town at the mouth of the Savannah River in 1733 and later constructed additional forts south of the Altamaha. In the end, only a few debtors were released from jail and sent to Georgia. Instead, the trustees brought hundreds of impoverished tradesmen and artisans from England and Scotland and many religious refugees from Switzerland and Germany. Among the immigrants was a small group of Jews. English settlers made up a lower proportion of the European population of Georgia than of any other English colony.

Oglethorpe (whom some residents of Georgia began calling "our perpetual dictator") created almost constant dissensions and conflict through his heavy-handed regulation of the colony. He also suffered military disappointments, such as a 1740 assault on the Spanish outpost at St. Augustine, Florida, which ended in failure.   *Georgia's Political Evolution* Gradually, as the threats from Spain receded, he lost his grip on the colony, which over time became more like the rest of British North America, with an elected legislature that loosened the restrictions on settlers. Georgia continued to grow more slowly than the other southern colonies, but in other ways it now developed along lines roughly similar to those of South Carolina.

MIDDLE GROUNDS

The struggle for the North American continent was not just one among competing European empires. It was also a series of contests among the many different peoples who shared the continent—the Spanish, English, French, Dutch, and other colonists, on one hand, and the many Indian tribes with whom they shared the continent, on the other.

In some parts of the British Empire—Virginia and New England, for example—English settlers quickly established their dominance, subjugating and displacing most natives until they had established societies that were dominated almost entirely by Europeans. But in other regions, the balance of power shifted for many years. Along the western borders of English settlement, in particular, Europeans and Indians lived together in regions in which neither side was able to establish clear dominance. In these middle grounds, the two populations—despite frequent conflicts—carved out ways of living together, with each side making concessions to the other. (See "Debating the Past: Native Americans and the Middle Ground.")

These were the peripheries of empires, in which the influence of formal colonial governments was at times almost invisible. European settlers, and the soldiers scattered in forts throughout these regions to protect them, were unable to displace the Indians. So they had to carve out their own relationships with the tribes. In those relationships,

Native Americans and the Middle Ground

For many generations, historians chronicling the westward movement of European settlement in North America portrayed Native Americans largely as weak and inconvenient obstacles swept aside by the inevitable progress of "civilization." Indians were presented either as murderous savages or as relatively docile allies of white people, but rarely as important actors of their own. Francis Parkman, the great nineteenth-century American historian, described Indians as a civilization "crushed" and "scorned" by the march of European powers in the New World. Many subsequent historians departed little from his assessment.

In more recent years, historians have challenged this traditional view by examining how white civilization victimized the tribes. Gary Nash's *Red, White, and Black* (1974) was one of the important modern presentations of this approach, and Ramon Guttierez's *When Jesus Came, the Corn Mothers Went* (1991) was a more recent contribution. They, and other scholars, rejected the optimistic, progressive view of white triumph over adversity and presented, instead, a picture of white brutality and futile Indian resistance, ending in defeat.

More recently, however, a new view of the relationship between the peoples of the Old and New Worlds has emerged. It sees Native Americans and Euro-Americans as uneasy partners in the shaping of a new society in which, for a time at least, both were a vital part. Richard White's influential 1991 book, *The Middle Ground,* was among the first important statements of this view.

White examined the culture of the Great Lakes region in the eighteenth century, in which Algonquian Indians created a series of complex trading and political relationships with French, English, and American settlers and travelers. In this "borderland" between the growing European settlements in the east and the still largely intact Indian civilizations farther west, a new kind of hybrid society emerged in which many cultures intermingled. James Merrell's *Into the American Woods* (1999) contributed further to this new view of collaboration by examining the world of negotiators and go-betweens along the western Pennsylvania frontier in the seventeenth and eighteenth centuries. Like White, he emphasized the complicated blend of European and Native American diplomatic rituals that allowed both groups to conduct business, make treaties, and keep the peace.

Daniel Richter extended the idea of a middle ground further in two important books: *The Ordeal of the Long-house* (1992) and *Facing East from Indian Country* (2001). Richter demonstrates that the Iroquois Confederacy was an active participant in the power relationships in the Hudson River basin; and in his later book, he tells the story of European colonization from the Native American perspective, revealing how Western myths of "first contact" such as the story of John Smith and Pocahontas look entirely different when seen through the eyes of Native Americans, who remained in many ways the more powerful of the two societies in the seventeenth century.

How did these important collaborations collapse? What happened to the middle ground? Over time, the delicate partnerships along the frontiers of white settlement gave way to the sheer numbers of Europeans (and in some places Africans) who moved westward. Joyce Chaplin's *Subject Matter* (2001) argues as well that Old World Americans at first admired the natives as a kind of natural nobility until European diseases ravaged the tribes. Their vulnerability to disease strengthened the sense of superiority among Europeans that had been a part of their view of Indians from the beginning. Jill Lepore's *The Name of War* (1998) describes how the violence of King Philip's War in seventeenth-century New England helped transform English views of the tribes. That was because of the white victory over the Indians and because of their success in turning this victory into a rationale for the moral superiority of Europeans. In fact, Europeans had used at least as much "savagery" against the natives as the natives had used against them. As the pressures of white settlement grew, as the Indian populations weakened as a result of disease and war, and as the relationship between the tribes and the European settlers grew more and more unequal, the cultural middle ground that for many decades characterized much of the contact between the Old and New Worlds gradually disappeared. By the time historians began seriously chronicling this story in the late nineteenth century, the Indian tribes had indeed become the defeated, helpless "obstacles" that they portrayed. But for generations before, the relationship between white Americans and Native Americans was much more equal than it later became. •

UNDERSTAND, ANALYZE, & EVALUATE

1. How have historians' views of Native Americans and their role in the European colonization of North America changed over time?
2. Why did the "middle ground" between Native Americans and European settlers disappear?

the Europeans found themselves obligated to adapt to tribal expectations at least as much as the Indians had to adapt to European ones.

To the Indians, the European migrants were both menacing and appealing. They feared the power of these strange European people: their guns, their rifles, their forts. But they also wanted the French and British settlers to behave like "fathers"—to help them mediate their own internal disputes, to offer them gifts, to moderate their conflicts. Europeans came from a world in which the formal institutional and military power of a nation or empire governed relationships between societies. But the natives had no understanding of the modern notion of a "nation" and thought much more in terms of ceremony and kinship. Gradually, Europeans learned to fulfill at least some of their expectations—to settle disputes among tribes, to moderate conflicts within tribes, to participate solemnly in Indian ceremonies, and to offer gifts as signs of respect.

In the seventeenth century, before many English settlers had entered the interior, the French were particularly adept at creating successful relationships with the tribes. French migrants in the interior regions of the continent were often solitary fur traders, and some of them welcomed the chance to attach themselves to—even to marry within—tribes. They also recognized the importance of treating tribal chiefs with respect and channeling gifts and tributes through them. But by the mid-eighteenth century, French influence in the interior was in decline, and British settlers gradually became the dominant European group. Eventually, the British learned the lessons that the French had long ago absorbed—that simple commands and raw force were *Elements of a Precarious Peace* ineffective in creating a workable relationship with the tribes; that they too had to learn to deal with Indian leaders through gifts and ceremonies and mediation. In large western regions—especially those around the Great Lakes—they established a precarious peace with the tribes that lasted for several decades.

But as the British (and after 1776 American) presence in the region grew, the balance of power between Europeans and natives shifted. Newer settlers had difficulty adapting to the complex rituals that the earlier migrants had developed. The stability of the relation- *The Shifting Balance of Power* ship between the Indians and whites deteriorated. By the early nineteenth century, the middle ground had collapsed, replaced by a European world in which Indians were ruthlessly subjugated and eventually removed. Nevertheless, for a considerable period of early American history the story of the relationship between whites and Indians was not simply a story of conquest and subjugation, but also—in some regions—a story of difficult but stable accommodation and tolerance.

THE DEVELOPMENT OF EMPIRE

The English colonies in America had begun as separate projects, and for the most part they grew up independent of one another and subject to only nominal control from London. But by the mid-seventeenth century, the growing commercial success of the colonial ventures was producing pressure in England for a more uniform structure to the empire.

The English government began trying to regulate colonial trade in the 1650s, when Parliament passed laws to keep Dutch ships out of the English colonies. Later, Parliament *The Navigation Acts* passed three important Navigation Acts. The first of them, in 1660, closed the colonies to all trade except that carried by English ships. The British also required that tobacco and other items be exported from the colonies only to England or to English possessions. The second act, in 1663, required that all goods sent from Europe to the colonies pass through England on the way, where they would be subject to English taxation. The third act, in 1673, imposed duties on the coastal trade among the English colonies, and it provided for the appointment of customs officials to enforce the Navigation Acts. These acts formed the legal basis of England's regulation of the colonies for a century.

THE DOMINION OF NEW ENGLAND

Before the creation of Navigation Acts, all the colonial governments except that of Virginia had operated largely independently of the crown, with governors chosen by the proprietors or by the colonists themselves and with powerful representative assemblies. Officials in London recognized that to increase their control over the colonies, they would have to increase British authority in order to enforce the new laws.

In 1675, the king created a new body, the Lords of Trade, to make recommendations *Lords of Trade* for imperial reform. In 1679, the king moved to increase his control over Massachusetts. He stripped it of its authority over New Hampshire and chartered a separate, royal colony there whose governor he would himself appoint. And in 1684, citing the colonial assembly's defiance of the Navigation Acts, he revoked the Massachusetts charter.

Charles II's brother, James II, who succeeded him to the throne in 1685, went further. He created a single Dominion of New England, which combined the government of

Massachusetts with the governments of the rest of the New England colonies and later with those of New York and New Jersey as well. He appointed a single governor, Sir Edmund Andros, to supervise the entire region from Boston. Andros's   *Sir Edmund Andros* rigid enforcement of the Navigation Acts and his brusque dismissal of the colonists' claims to the "rights of Englishmen" made him highly unpopular.

The "Glorious Revolution"

James II, unlike his father, was openly Catholic. In addition, he made powerful enemies when he appointed his fellow Catholics to high offices. The restoration of Catholicism in England led to fears that the Vatican and the pope would soon overtake the country and that the king would support him. At the same time, James II tried to control Parliament and the courts, making himself an absolute monarch. By 1688, the opposition to the king was so great that Parliament voted to force out James II, who showed no resistance to giving up the crown, aware of his grandfather's execution. He eventually left the country and spent the rest of his life in France. His daughter, Mary II, and her husband, William of Orange, of the Netherlands—both Protestants—replaced James II to reign jointly. No Catholic monarch has reigned since. This bloodless coup came to be known as the "Glorious Revolution."

When Bostonians heard of the overthrow of James II, they arrested and imprisoned the unpopular Andros. The new sovereigns in England abolished the Dominion of New England and restored separate colonial governments. In   *Dominion of New England Abolished* 1691, however, they combined Massachusetts with Plymouth and made it a single, royal colony. The new charter restored the colonial assembly, but it gave the crown the right to appoint the governor. It also replaced church membership with property ownership as the basis for voting and officeholding.

Andros had been governing New York through a lieutenant governor, Captain Francis Nicholson, who enjoyed the support of the wealthy merchants and fur traders of the province. Other, less-favored colonists had a long accumulation of grievances against Nicholson and his allies. The leader of the New York dissidents was Jacob Leisler, a German merchant. In May 1689, when news of the Glorious Revolution and the fall of Andros reached New York, Leisler raised a militia, captured the city fort, drove Nicholson into exile, and proclaimed himself the new head of government in New York. For two years, he tried in vain to stabilize his power in the colony amid fierce factional rivalry. In 1691, when William and Mary appointed a new governor, Leisler briefly resisted. He was convicted of treason and executed. Fierce rivalry between what became known as the "Leislerians" and the "anti-Leislerians" dominated the   *"Leislerians" and "Anti-Leislerians"* politics of the colony for years thereafter.

In Maryland, many people wrongly assumed that their proprietor, the Catholic Lord Baltimore, who was living in England, had sided with the Catholic James II and opposed William and Mary. So in 1689, an old opponent of the proprietor's government, the Protestant John Coode, led a revolt that drove out Lord Baltimore's officials and led to Maryland's establishment as a royal colony in 1691. The colonial assembly then established the Church of England as the colony's official religion and excluded Catholics from public office. Maryland became a proprietary colony again in 1715, after the fifth Lord Baltimore joined the Anglican Church.

The Glorious Revolution of 1688 in England touched off revolutions, mostly bloodless ones, in several colonies. Under the new king and queen, the representative assemblies that had been abolished were revived, and the scheme for colonial unification from above *The Crown's Power* was abandoned. But the Glorious Revolution in America did not stop the reorganization of the empire. The new governments that emerged in America actually increased the crown's potential authority. As the first century of English settlement in America came to its end, the colonists were becoming more a part of the imperial system than ever before.

CONCLUSION

The English colonization of North America was part of a larger effort by several European nations to expand the reach of their increasingly commercial societies. Indeed, for many years, the British Empire in America was among the smallest and weakest of the imperial ventures there, overshadowed by the French to the north and the Spanish to the south.

In the British colonies along the Atlantic seaboard, new agricultural and commercial societies gradually emerged—those in the South centered on the cultivation of tobacco and cotton and were reliant on slave labor; those in the northern colonies centered on more traditional food crops and were based mostly on free labor. Substantial trading centers emerged in such cities as Boston, New York, Philadelphia, and Charles Town, and a growing proportion of the population became prosperous and settled in these increasingly complex communities. By the early eighteenth century, English settlement had spread from northern New England (in what is now Maine) south into Georgia.

But this growing British Empire coexisted with, and often found itself in conflict with, the presence of other Europeans—most notably the Spanish and the French—in other areas of North America. In these borderlands, societies did not assume the settled, prosperous form they were taking in the Tidewater and New England. They were raw, sparsely populated settlements in which Europeans, including over time increasing numbers of English, had to learn to accommodate not only one another but also the still-substantial Indian tribes with whom they shared these interior lands. By the middle of the eighteenth century, there was a significant European presence across a broad swath of North America—from Florida to Maine, and from Texas to Mexico to California—only a relatively small part of it controlled by the British. But changes were under way within the British Empire that would soon lead to its dominance through a much larger area of North America.

KEY TERMS/PEOPLE/PLACES/EVENTS

RECALL AND REFLECT

1. Compare patterns of settlement and expansion in the Chesapeake with those in New England. What were the major differences? Were there any similarities?
2. What were the reasons for the revolts and rebellions that occurred in the colonies of Virginia, Maryland, Massachusetts, and New York between 1660 and 1700? How were these rebellions resolved?
3. How did the institution of slavery in England's Atlantic seaboard colonies differ from slavery in the Caribbean? What accounted for these differences?
4. What were the middle grounds, and how did conditions there differ from conditions in the colonies along the Atlantic seaboard?
5. How did the Glorious Revolution in England affect England's North American colonies?

3 | SOCIETY AND CULTURE IN PROVINCIAL AMERICA

THE COLONIAL POPULATION
THE COLONIAL ECONOMIES
PATTERNS OF SOCIETY
AWAKENINGS AND ENLIGHTENMENTS

LOOKING AHEAD

1. What accounted for the rapid increase in the colonial population in the seventeenth century?
2. Why did African slavery expand so rapidly in the late seventeenth century?
3. How did religion shape and influence colonial society?

MOST PEOPLE IN BOTH ENGLAND and America believed that the British colonies were outposts of the British world. And it is true that as the colonies grew and became more prosperous, they also became more English. Some of the early settlers had come to America to escape what they considered English tyranny. But by the early eighteenth century, many, perhaps most, colonists considered themselves English just as much as the men and women in England itself did.

At the same time, however, life in the colonies was diverging in many ways from England simply by the nature of the New World. The physical environment was very different—vaster and less tamed. The population was more diverse as well. The area that would become the United States was a magnet for immigrants from many lands other than England: Scotland, Ireland, the European continent, eastern Russia, and the Spanish and French Empires already established in America. English North America became as well the destination for thousands of forcibly transplanted Africans.

To the degree that the colonists emulated English society, they were becoming more and more like one another. To the degree that they were shaped by the character of their own regions, they were becoming more and more different.

THE COLONIAL POPULATION

After uncertain beginnings, the non-Indian population of English North America grew rapidly and substantially, through continued immigration and through natural increase. By the late seventeenth century, European and African immigrants outnumbered the natives along the Atlantic Coast.

A few of the early settlers were members of the English upper classes, but most were English laborers. Some came independently, such as the religious dissenters in early New England. But in the Chesapeake, at least three-fourths of the immigrants in the seventeenth century arrived as indentured servants.

INDENTURED SERVITUDE

The system of temporary (or "indentured") servitude developed out of practices in England. Young men and women bound themselves to masters for fixed terms of servitude (usually four to five years) in exchange for passage to America, food, and shelter. Their passage to America was a terrible trial of want and hunger. (See "Consider the Source: Gottlieb Mittelberger, the Passage of Indentured Servants.") Male indentures were supposed to receive clothing, tools, and occasionally land upon completion of their service. In reality, however, many left service with nothing. Most women indentures—who constituted roughly one-fourth of the total in the Chesapeake—worked as domestic servants and were expected to marry when their terms of servitude expired.

By the late seventeenth century, the indentured servant population had become one of the largest elements of the colonial population and was creating serious social problems. Some former indentures managed to establish themselves successfully as farmers, tradespeople, or artisans, and

1636
America's first college, Harvard, founded

1639
First printing press in colonies begins operation

1685
Huguenots migrate to America

1692
Salem witchcraft trials conclude

1697
Slave importations increase

1720
Cotton Mather starts smallpox inoculation

1734
Great Awakening begins
Zenger trial

1739
George Whitefield arrives in America

Great Awakening intensifies

Stono slave rebellion

1740s
Indigo production begins

CONSIDER THE SOURCE

GOTTLIEB MITTELBERGER, THE PASSAGE OF INDENTURED SERVANTS (1750)

Gottlieb Mittelberger, a German laborer, traveled to Philadelphia in 1750 and chronicled his voyage.

Both in Rotterdam and in Amsterdam the people are packed densely, like herrings so to say, in the large sea-vessels. One person receives a place of scarcely 2 feet width and 6 feet length in the bedstead, while many a ship carries four to six hundred souls; not to mention the innumerable implements, tools, provisions, water-barrels and other things which likewise occupy such space.

On account of contrary winds it takes the ships sometimes 2, 3, and 4 weeks to make the trip from Holland to . . . England. But when the wind is good, they get there in 8 days or even sooner. Everything is examined there and the custom-duties paid, whence it comes that the ships ride there 8, 10 or 14 days and even longer at anchor, till they have taken in their full cargoes. During that time every one is compelled to spend his last remaining money and to consume his little stock of provisions which had been reserved for the sea; so that most passengers, finding themselves on the ocean where they would be in greater need of them, must greatly suffer from hunger and want. Many suffer want already on the water between Holland and Old England.

When the ships have for the last time weighed their anchors near the city of Kaupp [Cowes] in Old England, the real misery begins with the long voyage. For from there the ships, unless they have good wind, must often sail 8, 9, 10 to 12 weeks before they reach Philadelphia. But even with the best wind the voyage lasts 7 weeks.

But during the voyage there is on board these ships terrible misery, stench, fumes, horror, vomiting, many kinds of sea-sickness, fever, dysentery, headache, heat, constipation, boils, scurvy, cancer, mouth rot, and the like, all of which come from old and sharply salted food and meat, also from very bad and foul water, so that many die miserably.

Add to this want of provisions, hunger, thirst, frost, heat, dampness, anxiety, want, afflictions and lamentations, together with other trouble, as . . . the lice abound so frightfully, especially on sick people, that they can be scraped off the body. The misery reaches the climax when a gale rages for 2 or 3 nights and days, so that every one believes that the ship will go to the bottom with all human beings on board. In such a visitation the people cry and pray most piteously.

Children from 1 to 7 years rarely survive the voyage. I witnessed . . . misery in no less than 32 children in our ship, all of whom were thrown into the sea. The parents grieve all the more since their children find no resting-place in the earth, but are devoured by the monsters of the sea.

That most of the people get sick is not surprising, because, in addition to all other trials and hardships, warm food is served only three times a week, the rations being very poor and very little. Such meals can hardly be eaten, on account of being so unclean. The water which is served out of the ships is often very black, thick and full of worms, so that one cannot drink it without loathing, even with the greatest thirst. Toward the end we were compelled to eat the ship's biscuit which had been spoiled long ago; though in a whole biscuit there was scarcely a piece the size of a dollar that had not been full of red worms and spiders' nests. . . .

At length, when, after a long and tedious voyage, the ships come in sight of land, so that the promontories can be seen, which the people were so eager and anxious to see, all creep from below on deck to see the land from afar and they weep for joy, and pray and sing, thanking and praising God. The sight of the land makes the people on board the ship, especially the sick and the half dead, alive again, so that their hearts leap within them; they shout and rejoice, and are content to bear their misery in patience, in the hope that they may soon reach the land in safety. But alas!

When the ships have landed at Philadelphia after their long voyage, no one is permitted to leave them except those who pay for their passage or can give good security; the others, who cannot pay, must remain on board the ships till they are purchased, and are released from the ships by their purchasers. The sick always fare the worst, for the healthy are naturally preferred and purchased first; and so the sick and wretched must often remain on board in front of the city for 2 or 3 weeks, and frequently die, whereas many a one, if he could pay his debt and were permitted to leave the ship immediately, might recover and remain alive.

The sale of human beings in the market on board the ship is carried out thus: Every day Englishmen, Dutchmen and High-German people come from the city of Philadelphia and other places, in part from a great distance, say 20, 30, or 40 hours away, and go on board the newly arrived ship that has brought and offers for sale passengers from Europe, and select among the healthy persons such as they deem suitable for their business, and bargain with them how long they will serve for their passage money, which most of them are still in debt for. When they have come to an agreement, it happens that adult persons bind themselves in writing to serve 3, 4, 5 or 6 years for the amount due by them, according to their age and strength. But very young people, from 10 to 15 years, must serve till they are 21 years old.

Many parents must sell and trade away their children like so many head of cattle; for if their children take the debt upon themselves, the parents can leave the ship free and unrestrained; but as the parents often do not know where and to what people their children are going, it often happens that such parents and children, after leaving the ship, do not see each other again for many years, perhaps no more in all their lives. . . . It often happens that whole families, husband, wife and children, are separated by being sold to different purchasers, especially when they have not paid any part of their passage money.

When a husband or wife has died at sea, when the ship has made more than half of her trip, the survivor must pay or serve not only for himself or herself but also for the deceased.

When both parents have died over halfway at sea, their children, especially when they are young and have nothing to pawn or pay, must stand for their own and their parents' passage, and serve till they are 21 years old. When one has served his or her term, he or she is entitled to a new suit of clothes at parting; and if it has been so stipulated, a man gets in addition a horse, a woman, a cow. When a serf has an opportunity to marry in this country, he or she must pay for each year which he or she would have yet to serve, 5 or 6 pounds.

UNDERSTAND, ANALYZE, & EVALUATE

1. What hardships did passengers suffer at sea? What relief could they hope for upon reaching Philadelphia?
2. Explain the different purchase agreements between passengers and masters. How did the death of a family member affect a passenger's indenture contracts?
3. What do the ordeals of indentured servants tell us about prospects in Europe? What does it tell us about the concept of liberty in the colonies?

some of the women married propertied men. Others (mostly males) found themselves without land, without employment, without families, and without prospects. As a result, there emerged in some areas, particularly in the Chesapeake, a large floating population of young single men who were a source of social unrest.

Beginning in the 1670s, a decrease in the birthrate in England and an improvement in economic conditions there reduced the pressures on laboring men and women to emigrate, and the flow of indentured servants into America declined. Those who did travel to *Growing Reliance on Slavery* America as indentures now generally avoided the southern colonies, where prospects for advancement were slim. In the Chesapeake, therefore, landowners began to rely much more heavily on African slavery as their principal source of labor.

Birth and Death

Immigration remained for a time the greatest source of population growth in the colonies. But the most important long-range factor in the increase of the colonial population was its ability to reproduce itself. Improvement in the reproduction rate began in New England and the mid-Atlantic colonies in the second half of the seventeenth century. After the 1650s, natural increase became the most important source of population growth in those *Factors in Population Growth* areas. The New England population more than quadrupled through reproduction alone in the second half of the seventeenth century. This rise was a result not only of families having large numbers of children. It was also because life expectancy in New England was unusually high.

Conditions improved much more slowly in the South. The high death rates in the Chesapeake region did not begin to decline to levels found elsewhere until the mid-eighteenth century. Throughout the seventeenth century, the average life expectancy for European men in the region was just over forty years, and for women slightly less. One in four white children died in infancy, and half died before the age of twenty. Children who survived infancy often lost one or both of their parents before reaching maturity. Widows, widowers, and orphans thus formed a substantial proportion of the white Chesapeake population. Only after settlers developed immunity to local diseases (particularly malaria) did life expectancy increase significantly. Population growth was substantial in the region, but it was largely a result of immigration.

The natural increases in the population in the seventeenth century reflected a steady improvement in the balance between men and women in the colonies. In the early years *Toward a Balanced Sex Ratio* of settlement, more than three-quarters of the white population of the Chesapeake consisted of men. And even in New England, which from the beginning had attracted more families (and thus more women) than the southern colonies, 60 percent of the inhabitants were male in 1650. Gradually, however, more women began to arrive in the colonies; and increasing birthrates contributed to shifting the sex ratio (the balance between men and women) as well. Throughout the colonial period, the population almost doubled every twenty-five years. By 1775, the non-Indian population of the colonies was over 2 million.

Medicine in the Colonies

There were very high death rates of women who bore children in the colonial era. Physicians had little or no understanding of infection and sterilization. As a result, many women and babies died from infections contracted during childbirth or surgery. Unaware of bacteria, many communities were plagued with infectious diseases transmitted by garbage or unclean water.

Because of the limited extent of medical knowledge, and the lack of regulations for any practitioners at the time, it was relatively easy for people to practice medicine, even without any professional training. The biggest beneficiaries of this were women, who established themselves in considerable numbers as midwives. Midwives   *Midwifery* assisted women in childbirth, but they also dispensed other medical advice. They were popular because they were usually friends and neighbors of the people they treated, unlike physicians, who were few and therefore not often well known to their patients. Male doctors felt threatened by the midwives and struggled continually to drive them from the field, although they did not make substantial progress in doing so until the nineteenth century.

Midwives and doctors alike practiced medicine on the basis of the prevailing assumptions of their time, most of them derived from the theory of "humoralism"   *"Humoralism"* popularized by the famous second-century Roman physician Galen. Galen argued that the human body was governed by four "humors" that were lodged in four bodily fluids: yellow bile (or "choler"), black bile ("melancholy"), blood, and phlegm. In a healthy body, the four humors existed in balance. Illness represented an imbalance and suggested the need for removing from the body the excesses of whatever fluid was causing the imbalance. That was the rationale that lay behind the principal medical techniques of the seventeenth century: purging, expulsion, and bleeding. Bleeding was practiced mostly by male physicians. Midwives favored "pukes" and laxatives. The great majority of early Americans, however, had little contact with physicians, or even midwives, and sought instead to deal with illness on their own. The assumption that treating illness was the exclusive province of trained professionals, so much a part of the twentieth century and beyond, lay far in the distance in the colonial era.

That seventeenth-century medicine rested so much on ideas produced 1,400 years before is evidence of how little support there was for the scientific method in England and America at the time. Bleeding, for example, had been in use for hundreds of years, during which time there had been no evidence at all that it helped people recover from illness; indeed, there was considerable evidence that bleeding could do great harm. But what would seem in later eras to be the simple process of testing scientific assumptions was not yet a common part of Western thought. That was one reason that the birth of the Enlightenment in the late seventeenth century—with its faith in human reason and its belief in the capacity of individuals and societies to create better lives—was important not just to politics but also to science.

WOMEN AND FAMILIES IN THE COLONIES

Because there were many more men than women in seventeenth-century America, few women remained unmarried for long. The average European woman in America married for the first time at twenty or twenty-one years of age. Because of the large   *Early Marriages* numbers of indentured servants who were forbidden to marry until their terms of service expired, premarital sexual relationships were not uncommon. Children born out of wedlock to indentured women were often taken from their mothers at a young age and were themselves bound as indentured servants.

Women in the Chesapeake could anticipate a life consumed with childbearing. The average wife experienced pregnancies every two years. Those who lived long enough bore an average of eight children apiece (up to five of whom typically died in infancy or early childhood). Since childbirth was one of the most frequent causes of female death, many women did not survive to see their children grow to maturity. Those who did, however, were often widowed, since they were usually much younger than their husbands.

LIFE IN THE AMERICAN COLONIES   This colored engraving shows the domestic life of Americans during the eighteenth century. Depicted are family members at work in their cozy surroundings. The industriousness they show was a virtue of the era. (© Bettmann/Corbis)

In New England, where many more immigrants arrived with family members and *New England and Chesapeake Families Compared*   where death rates declined more quickly, family structure was much more stable than in the Chesapeake. The sex ratio was more balanced than in the Chesapeake, so most men could expect to marry. As in the Chesapeake, women married young, began producing children early, and continued to do so well into their thirties. In contrast to their southern counterparts, however, northern children were more likely to survive, and their families were more likely to remain intact. Fewer New England women became widows, and those who did generally lost their husbands later in life.

The longer life span in New England meant that parents continued to control their children longer than did parents in the South. Few sons and daughters could choose a spouse entirely independently of their parents' wishes. Men tended to rely on their fathers for land to cultivate. Women needed dowries from their parents if they were to attract desirable husbands. Stricter parental supervision of children meant, too, that fewer women became pregnant before marriage than was the case in the South.

Puritanism placed a high value on the family, and the position of wife and mother was highly valued in Puritan culture. At the same time, however, Puritanism reinforced the idea of nearly absolute male authority. A wife was expected to devote herself almost entirely to serving the needs of her husband and the family economy.

THE BEGINNINGS OF SLAVERY IN ENGLISH AMERICA

The demand for African servants to supplement the scarce southern labor force existed almost from the first moments of settlement. For a time, however, black workers were hard to find. Not until the mid-seventeenth century, when a substantial commerce in slaves grew up between the Caribbean islands and the southern colonies, did black workers become generally available in North America. Just how slavery actually took root and spread has been a source of endless debate among historians. (See "Debating the Past: The Origins of Slavery.")

The demand for slaves in North America helped expand the transatlantic slave trade. And as slave trading grew more extensive and more sophisticated, it also *The Slave Trade* grew more horrible. Before it ended in the nineteenth century, it was responsible for the forced immigration of as many as 11 million Africans to North and South America and the Caribbean. In the flourishing slave marts on the African coast, native chieftains brought captured members of rival tribes to the ports. The terrified victims were then packed into the dark, filthy holds of ships for the horrors of the **middle passage**—the long journey to the Americas, during which the prisoners were usually kept chained in the bowels of the slave ships and supplied with only minimal food and water. Many slave traders tried to cram as many Africans as possible into their ships to ensure that enough would survive to yield a profit at journey's end. Those who died en route, and many did, were simply thrown overboard. Upon arrival in the New World, slaves were auctioned off to white landowners and transported, frightened and bewildered, to their new homes.

North America was a less important direct destination for African slaves than were such other parts of the New World as the Caribbean islands and Brazil; fewer than 5 percent of the Africans imported to the Americas arrived first in the English colonies. Through most of the seventeenth century, those blacks who were transported to what became the United States came not directly from Africa but from the West Indies. Not until the 1670s did traders start importing blacks directly from Africa to North America. Even then, the flow remained small for a time, mainly because a single group, the Royal African Company of England, monopolized the trade and kept prices high and supplies low.

A turning point in the history of the black population in North America was 1697, the year rival traders broke the Royal African Company's monopoly. With the trade now open to competition, prices fell and the number of Africans greatly increased. In 1700, about 25,000 African slaves lived in English North America. Because African Americans were so heavily concentrated in a few southern colonies, they were already beginning to outnumber whites in some areas. There were perhaps twice as many black men as black women in most areas, but in some places the African American population grew by natural increase nevertheless. By 1760, the number of Africans in the English mainland colonies had increased to *Surging Slave Population* approximately a quarter of a million, the vast majority of whom lived in the South. By then blacks had almost wholly replaced white indentured servants as the basis of the southern workforce.

For a time, the legal and social status of the African laborers remained somewhat fluid. In some areas, white and black laborers worked together on terms of relative equality. Some blacks were treated much like white hired servants, and some were freed after a fixed term of servitude. By the late seventeenth century, however, a rigid distinction emerged between blacks and whites. Gradually, the assumption *Emergence of a Race-Based System* spread that blacks would remain in service permanently and that black children would inherit their parents' bondage. White beliefs about the inferiority of Africans reinforced the growing rigidity of the system, but so did the economic advantages of the system to white slaveowners.

THE ORIGINS OF SLAVERY

The debate among historians over how and why white Americans created a system of slave labor in the seventeenth century—and how and why only African Americans should be slaves—has been an unusually lively one. At its center is a debate over whether slavery was a result of white racism, or whether racism was a result of slavery.

In 1950, Oscar and Mary Handlin published an influential article comparing slavery to other systems of "unfreedom" in the colonies. What separated slavery from other conditions of servitude, they argued, was that it was restricted to people of African descent, that it was permanent, and that it passed from one generation to the next. The unique characteristics of slavery, the Handlins argued, were part of an effort by colonial legislatures to increase the available labor force. White laborers needed an incentive to come to America; black laborers, forcibly imported from Africa, did not. The distinction between the conditions of white workers and the conditions of black workers was, therefore, based on legal and economic motives, not on racism.

Winthrop Jordan was one of a number of historians who later challenged the Handlins' thesis and argued that white racism, more than economic interests, produced African slavery. In *White Over Black* (1968) and other works, Jordan argued that Europeans had long viewed people of color as inferior beings. Those attitudes migrated with white Europeans to the New World, and white racism shaped the treatment of Africans in America from the beginning. Even without the economic incentives the Handlins described, in other words, whites would have been likely to oppress blacks in the New World.

Peter Wood's *Black Majority* (1974), a study of seventeenth-century South Carolina, was one of a number of works that moved the debate back toward social and economic conditions. Wood demonstrated that blacks and whites often worked together on relatively equal terms in the early years of settlement. But as rice cultivation expanded, it became more difficult to find white laborers willing to do the arduous work. The increase in the forcible importation of African slaves was a response to this growing demand for labor. It was also a response to fears among whites that without slavery it would be difficult to control a labor force brought to America against its will. Edmund Morgan's *American Slavery, American Freedom* (1975) argued similarly that the southern labor system was at first relatively flexible and later grew more rigid. In colonial Virginia, he claimed, white settlers did not at first intend to create a system of permanent bondage. But as the tobacco economy grew and created a high demand for cheap labor, white landowners began to feel uneasy about their reliance on a large group of dependent white workers. Such workers were difficult to recruit and control. Slavery, therefore, was less a result of racism than of the desire for whites to find a reliable and stable labor force.

Robin Blackburn's *The Making of New World Slavery* (1996) argues particularly strenuously that while race was a factor in making the enslavement of Africans easier for whites to justify to themselves, the real reasons for the emergence of slavery were hardheaded economic decisions by ambitious entrepreneurs who realized very early that a slave-labor system in the labor-intensive agricultural world of the American South and the Caribbean was more profitable than a free-labor system.

Slavery served the interests of a powerful combination of groups: planters, merchants, industrialists, and consumers. The most important reason for the creation and continuation of the system, therefore, was not racism but the pursuit of profit. Slavery was not, Blackburn concludes, an antiquated remnant of an older world. It was a recognizably modern labor system that served the needs of an emerging market economy. ●

UNDERSTAND, ANALYZE, & EVALUATE

1. What do historians say is the relationship between racism and slavery?
2. What are the economic arguments put forward by historians to explain the system of slave labor that developed in America? Do these arguments account fully for the development of slavery?

The system of permanent servitude—American slavery—became legal in the early eighteenth century when colonial assemblies began to pass **slave codes** granting white masters almost absolute authority over their slaves. Only one factor determined whether a person was subject to the slave codes: color. In the colonial societies of Spanish America, people of mixed race were granted a different (and higher) status than pure Africans. English America recognized no such distinctions.

AFRICAN SLAVE TRADE This image is from a plate from British author Amelia Opie's poem *Black Slaves in the Hold of the Slave Ship: or How to Make Sugar*, published in London in 1826. Opie's poem depicts the life of an African who was captured by slave traders and chronicles his journey to the West Indies on a slave ship and his enforced work on the sugar plantations there. Slaves were fastened and packed like cargo for the long ocean voyage. (© Universal History Archive/UG/Bridgeman Images)

IMMIGRANT GROUPS IN COLONIAL AMERICA, 1760 Even though the entire Atlantic seaboard of what is now the United States had become a series of British colonies by 1760, the population consisted of people from many nations. As this map reveals, English settlers dominated most of the regions of North America. But note the large areas of German settlement in the western Chesapeake and Pennsylvania; the swath of Dutch settlement in New York and New Jersey; the Scotch-Irish regions in the western regions of the South; and the large areas in which Africans were becoming the majority of the population, even if subjugated by the white minority. • *What aspects of the history of these colonies help explain their ethnic composition?*

CHANGING SOURCES OF EUROPEAN IMMIGRATION

The most distinctive and enduring feature of the American population was that it brought together peoples of many different races, ethnic groups, and nationalities. North America was home to a highly diverse population. The British colonies were the home to Native Americans, English immigrants, forcibly imported Africans, and a wide range of other European groups. Among the earliest European immigrants were about 300,000 French Calvinists (known as Huguenots). The Edict of Nantes of 1598 had assured them freedom of religion in France. But in 1685, the Edict was revoked, driving many   *Huguenot Refugees* Huguenots to North America. Germany had similar laws banning Protestantism, driving many Germans to America where they settled in Pennsylvania. They came to be known as the "Pennsylvania Dutch," a corruption of the German term for their nationality, *Deutsch.* Frequent wars in Europe drove many other immigrants to the American colonies.

The most numerous of the newcomers were the so-called Scotch-Irish—Scotch Presbyterians who had settled in northern Ireland (in the province of Ulster) in the early seventeenth   *Scotch-Irish* century. Most of the Scotch-Irish in America pushed out to the western edges of European settlement and occupied land without much regard for who actually claimed to own it.

There were also immigrants from Scotland itself and from southern Ireland. The Irish migrated steadily over a long period. Some abandoned their Roman Catholic religion and much of their ethnic identity after they arrived in America.

THE COLONIAL ECONOMIES

Farming, hunting, and fishing dominated almost all areas of European and African settlement in North America throughout the seventeenth and eighteenth centuries. Even so, the economies of the different regions varied markedly.

THE SOUTHERN ECONOMY

A strong European demand for tobacco enabled some planters in the Chesapeake (Maryland and Virginia) to become enormously wealthy and at times allowed the region as a whole to prosper. But throughout the seventeenth and eighteenth   *Boom-and-Bust Tobacco Economy* centuries, production of tobacco frequently exceeded demand, and as a result the price of the crop sometimes suffered severe declines. The result was a boom-and-bust cycle in the Chesapeake economy, with the first major bust occurring in 1640.

South Carolina and Georgia relied on rice production, since the low-lying coastline with its many tidal rivers made it possible to create rice paddies that could be flooded and drained. Rice cultivation was so difficult and unhealthy that white laborers generally refused to perform it. Hence planters in South Carolina and Georgia were much more dependent on slaves than were their northern counterparts. African workers were adept at rice cultivation, in part because some of them had come from rice-producing regions of west Africa and in part because they were generally more accustomed to the hot, humid climate than were Europeans. They also had a greater natural immunity to malaria. But the work was arduous and debilitating for them nevertheless.

Because of their dependence on large-scale cash crops, the southern colonies developed less of a commercial or industrial economy than the colonies of the North. The trading in tobacco and rice was handled largely by merchants based in London and, later, in the northern colonies.

"LONDON'S VIRGINIA" TOBACCO LABEL This label presents an image of tobacco designed to appeal to European consumers. Three gentlemen planters enjoy the product while a trio of faceless Africans tend the crop. (© Granger, NYC—All Rights Reserved.)

NORTHERN ECONOMIC AND TECHNOLOGICAL LIFE

In the North, as in the South, agriculture continued to dominate, but it was agriculture of a more diverse kind. In northern New England, colder weather and hard, rocky soil made it difficult for colonists to develop the kind of large-scale commercial farming system that southerners were creating. Conditions for agriculture were better in southern New England and the middle colonies, where the soil was fertile and the weather more temperate. New York, Pennsylvania, and the Connecticut River valley were the chief suppliers of wheat to much of New England and to parts of the South. Even there, however, a substantial commercial economy emerged alongside the agricultural one.

Almost every colonist engaged in a certain amount of industry at home. Occasionally these home industries provided families with surplus goods they could trade or sell. *Colonial Artisans and Entrepreneurs* Beyond these domestic efforts, craftsmen and artisans established themselves in colonial towns as cobblers, blacksmiths, riflemakers, cabinetmakers, silversmiths, and printers. In some areas, entrepreneurs harnessed water power to run small mills for grinding grain, processing cloth, or milling lumber. And in several coastal areas, large-scale shipbuilding operations began to flourish.

The first effort to establish a significant metals industry in the colonies was an iron- *Saugus Ironworks* works established in Saugus, Massachusetts, in the 1640s. The Saugus Ironworks used water power to drive a bellows, which controlled the heat in a charcoal furnace. The carbon from the burning charcoal helped remove the oxygen from the ore and thus reduced its melting temperature. As the ore melted, it trickled down into molds or was taken in the form of simple "sow bars" to a nearby forge to be shaped into iron objects such as pots and anvils. There was also a mill suitable for turning the sow bars into narrow rods that blacksmiths could cut into nails. The Saugus Ironworks was a technological success but a financial failure. It began operations in 1646; in 1668, its financial problems forced it to close its doors.

Metalworks, however, gradually became an important part of the colonial economy. The largest industrial enterprise anywhere in English North America was the ironworks of the German ironmaster Peter Hasenclever in northern New Jersey. Founded in 1764 with British capital, it employed several hundred laborers. There were other, smaller ironmaking enterprises in every northern colony, and there were ironworks as well in several of the southern colonies. Even so, these and other growing industries did not immediately become the basis for the kind of explosive industrial growth that Great Britain experienced in the late eighteenth century—in part because English parliamentary regulations such as the Iron Act of 1750 restricted metal processing in the colonies. Similar prohibitions limited the manufacture of woolens, hats, and other goods. But the biggest obstacles to industrialization in America were an inadequate labor supply, a small domestic market, and inadequate transportation facilities and energy supplies.

More important than manufacturing were industries that exploited the natural resources of the continent. By the mid-seventeenth century, the flourishing fur trade of earlier years was in decline. Taking its place were lumbering, mining, and fishing. These industries provided commodities that could be exported to England in exchange for manufactured goods. And they helped produce the most distinctive feature of the northern economy: a thriving commercial class.

THE EXTENT AND LIMITS OF TECHNOLOGY

Despite the technological progress that was occurring in the seventeenth and eighteenth centuries, much of colonial society was conspicuously lacking in even very basic technological capacities. Up to half the farmers in the colonies did not even own a plow. Substantial numbers of households lacked pots and kettles for *Persistent Colonial Poverty* cooking. And only about half the households in the colonies owned guns or rifles. The relatively low levels of ownership of these and other elementary tools was not because such things were difficult to make but because most Americans remained too poor or too isolated to be able to obtain them. Many households had few if any candles because they were unable to afford candle molds or tallow (wax) or because they had no access to commercially produced candles. In the early eighteenth century, very few farmers owned wagons. Most made do with two-wheeled carts, which were inefficient for transporting crops to market. The most commonly owned tool on American farms was the axe.

Few colonists were self-sufficient in the late seventeenth and early eighteenth centuries. A popular image of early American households is of people who grew their own food, made their own clothes, and bought little from anyone else. In fact, relatively few colonial families owned spinning wheels or looms, which suggests that most *Myth of Colonial Self-Sufficiency* people purchased whatever yarn and cloth they needed. Most farmers who grew grain took it to centralized facilities for processing. In general, people who lived in isolated or poor areas owned fewer tools and had less access to advanced technologies than did those in more populous or affluent areas.

THE RISE OF COLONIAL COMMERCE

Perhaps the most remarkable feature of colonial commerce was that it was able to survive
Obstacles to Trade   at all. American merchants faced such bewildering obstacles, and lacked so
many of the basic institutions of trade, that they managed to stay afloat only with great
difficulty and through considerable ingenuity. The colonies had almost no gold or silver,
and their paper currency was not acceptable as payment for goods from abroad. For many
years, colonial merchants had to rely on barter or on money substitutes such as beaver skins.

A second obstacle was lack of information about the supply and demand of goods and
services. Traders had no way of knowing what they would find in foreign ports; vessels
sometimes stayed at sea for years, journeying from one port to another, trading one commodity for another, attempting to find some way to turn a profit. There was also an
enormous number of small, fiercely competitive companies, which made the problem of
organizing the system of commerce even more acute.

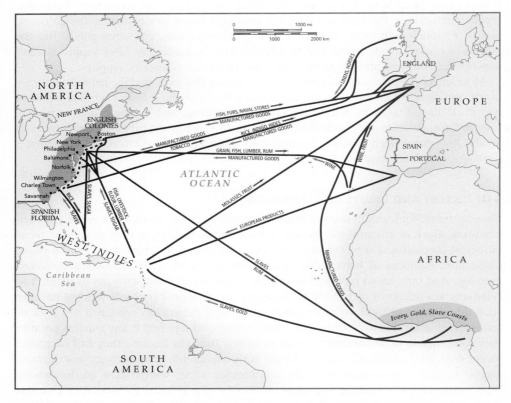

THE TRIANGULAR TRADE This map illustrates the complex pattern of trade that fueled the colonial American
economy in the seventeenth and eighteenth centuries. A simple explanation of this trade is that the American
colonies exported raw materials (agricultural products, furs, and others) to Britain and Europe and imported
manufactured goods in return. While that explanation is accurate, it is not complete, largely because the Atlantic
trade was not a simple exchange between America and Europe, but a complex network of exchanges involving the
Caribbean, Africa, and the Mediterranean. Note the important exchanges between the North American mainland
and the Caribbean islands; the important trade between the American colonies and Africa; and the wide range
of European and Mediterranean markets in which Americans were active. Not shown on this map, but also
very important to colonial commerce, was a large coastal trade among the various regions of British North
America. • *Why did the major ports of trade emerge almost entirely in the northern colonies?*

Nevertheless, commerce in the colonies survived and grew. There was elaborate trade among the colonies themselves and with the West Indies. The mainland colonies offered their Caribbean trading partners rum, agricultural products, meat, and fish. The islands offered sugar, molasses, and at times slaves in return. There was also trade with England, continental Europe, and the west coast of Africa. This commerce has often been described, somewhat inaccurately, as the **triangular trade,** suggesting a neat process by which merchants carried rum and other goods from New England to Africa, exchanged their merchandise for slaves, whom they then transported to the West Indies (hence the term *middle passage* for the dreaded journey—it was the second of the three legs of the voyage), and then exchanged the slaves for sugar and molasses, which they shipped back to New England to be distilled into rum. In reality, the so-called triangular trade in rum, slaves, and sugar was a complicated maze of highly diverse trade routes. Out of this risky trade emerged a group of adventurous entrepreneurs who by the mid-eighteenth century were beginning to constitute a distinct merchant class. The British Navigation Acts protected them from foreign competition in the colonies. They had *An Emerging Merchant Class* ready access to the market in England for such colonial products as furs, timber, and American-built ships. But they also developed markets illegally outside the British Empire—in the French, Spanish, and Dutch West Indies—where they could often get higher prices for their goods than in the British colonies.

THE RISE OF CONSUMERISM

As affluent residents of the colonies grew in number, the growing prosperity and commercialism of British America created both new appetites and new opportunities to satisfy them. The result was a growing preoccupation with the consumption of material goods.

The growth of eighteenth-century consumerism increased the class divisions in the American colonies. As the difference between the upper and lower classes became more glaring, people of means became more intent on demonstrating *Reasons for Growing Consumerism* their own membership in the upper ranks of society. The ability to purchase and display consumer goods was an important way of doing so, particularly for wealthy people in cities and towns, who did not have large estates to boast their success. But the growth of consumerism was also a product of the early stages of the Industrial Revolution. Although there was relatively little industry in America in the eighteenth century, England and Europe were making rapid advances and producing more and more affordable goods for affluent Americans to buy.

To facilitate the new consumer appetites, merchants and traders began advertising their goods in journals and newspapers. Agents of urban merchants—the ancestors of the traveling salesman—fanned out through the countryside, attempting to interest wealthy landowners and planters in the luxury goods now available to them. George and Martha Washington, for example, spent considerable time and money ordering elegant furnishings for their home at Mount Vernon, goods that were shipped to them mostly from England and Europe.

One feature of a consumer society is that things that once were considered luxuries quickly come to be seen as necessities once they are readily available. In the colonies, items that became commonplace after having once been expensive luxuries included tea, household linens, glassware, manufactured cutlery, crockery, furniture, and many other things. Another result of consumerism is the association of material goods—of the quality of a person's home and possessions and clothing, for example—with virtue and "refinement." The ideal of the cultivated "gentleman" and the gracious "lady" became increasingly powerful throughout the colonies in the eighteenth century. In part that meant striving to become educated and "refined" in speech and behavior. Americans read books *New Social Ideals of Refinement* on manners and fashion. They bought magazines about London society. And they strove to develop themselves as witty and educated conversationalists. They also commissioned portraits of themselves and their families, devoted large portions of their homes to entertainment, built shelves and cases in which they could display fashionable possessions, constructed formal gardens, and lavished attention on their wardrobes and hairstyles.

PATTERNS OF SOCIETY

Although there were sharp social distinctions in the colonies, the well-defined and deeply entrenched class system of England failed to reproduce itself in America. Aristocracies emerged, to be sure, but they tended to rely less on landownership than on control of a substantial workforce, and they were generally less secure and less powerful than their English counterparts. More than in England, white people in America faced opportunities *Social Mobility* for social mobility—both up and down. There were also new forms of community in America, and they varied greatly from one region to another.

MASTERS AND SLAVES ON THE PLANTATION

The plantation system of the American South produced one form of community. The first plantations emerged in the tobacco-growing areas of Virginia and Maryland. Some of the early planters became established aristocrats with vast estates. On the whole, however, *Realities of Plantation Life* seventeenth-century colonial plantations were rough and relatively small. In the early days in Virginia, they were little more than crude clearings where landowners and indentured servants worked side by side in conditions so harsh that death was an everyday occurrence. Most landowners lived in rough cabins or houses, with their servants or slaves nearby. The economy of the plantation was precarious. Planters could not control their markets, so even the largest plantations were constantly at risk. When prices fell, planters faced the prospect of ruin. The plantation economy created many new wealthy landowners, but it also destroyed many.

The enslaved African Americans, of course, lived very differently. On the smaller farms with only a handful of slaves, it was not always possible for a rigid separation to develop between whites and blacks. But by the early eighteenth century, over three-fourths of all *Slave Communities* slaves lived on plantations of at least ten slaves, and nearly one-half lived in communities of fifty slaves or more. In those settings, they were able to develop a society and culture of their own. Although whites seldom encouraged formal marriages among slaves, many blacks themselves developed strong and elaborate family structures. There was also a distinctive slave religion, which blended Christianity with African folklore and sacred practices, that became a central element in the emergence of an independent black culture.

Nevertheless, black society was subject to constant intrusions from and interaction with white society. Black house servants, for example, were isolated from their own community. Black women were often subject to unwanted sexual advances from owners and overseers and hence to bearing mulatto children, who were rarely recognized by their white fathers. On some plantations, black workers were treated with kindness and

AFRICAN POPULATION AS A PROPORTION OF TOTAL POPULATION, CA. 1775 This map illustrates the parts of the colonies in which slaves made up a large proportion of the population—in some areas, a majority. The slave population was smallest in the western regions of the southern colonies and in the area north of the Chesapeake, although there remained a significant African population in parts of New Jersey and New York (some slave, some free). • *What explains the dense concentration of slaves in certain areas?*

responded to their owners with genuine devotion. On others, they encountered physical brutality and occasionally even sadism, against which they were virtually powerless.

Slaves often resisted their masters, in large ways and small. The most serious example in the colonial period was the Stono Rebellion in South Carolina in 1739, *Stono Rebellion* during which about 100 slaves rose up, seized weapons, killed several whites, and attempted to escape south to Florida. The uprising was quickly crushed, and most participants were executed. A more frequent form of resistance was simply running away, but that provided no real solution either. For most, there was nowhere to go. Resistance more often took the form of subtle, and often undetected, defiance or evasion of their masters' wishes.

Most slaves, male and female, worked as field hands. But on the larger plantations that aspired to genuine self-sufficiency, some slaves learned trades and crafts: blacksmithing, carpentry, shoemaking, spinning, weaving, sewing, midwifery, and others. These skilled craftspeople were at times hired out to other planters. Some set up their own establishments in towns or cities and shared their profits with their owners. A few were able to buy their freedom.

The Puritan Community

The characteristic social unit in New England was not the isolated farm or the large plantation but the town. In the early years of colonization, each new settlement drew up a **covenant** binding all residents tightly together both religiously and socially. Colonists laid out a village, with houses and a meetinghouse arranged around a shared pasture, or "common." Thus families generally lived with their neighbors close by. They divided up the outlying fields and woodlands among the residents; the size and location of a family's field depended on the family's numbers, wealth, and social station.

THE NEW ENGLAND TOWN: SUDBURY, MASSACHUSETTS, SEVENTEENTH CENTURY Just as the plantation was a characteristic social form in the southern colonies, the town was the most common social unit in New England. This map shows the organization of Sudbury, Massachusetts, a town just west of Boston, in its early years in the seventeenth century. Note the location of the houses, which are grouped mostly together around a shared pasture (or "common") and near the church. Note, too, the outlying fields, which were divided among residents of the town, even though they were often not connected to the land on which the owners lived. The map illustrates the holdings of a single resident of Sudbury, John Goodnow, whose house was on the common, but whose lands were scattered over a number of areas of Sudbury. • *What aspects of New England life might help explain the clustering of residences at the center of the town?* (Source of data: From Sumner Chilton Powell, *Puritan Village: The Formation of a New England Town.*)

Once a town was established, residents held a yearly "town meeting" to decide important questions and to choose a group of "selectmen," who ran the town's   *Puritan Democracy*
affairs. Participation in the meeting was generally restricted to adult males who were
members of the church. Only those who could give evidence of being among the elect
assured of salvation (the "visible saints") were admitted to full church membership,
although other residents of the town were required to attend church services.

New Englanders did not adopt the English system of **primogeniture**—the passing of
all property to the firstborn son. Instead, a father divided up his land among all his sons.
His control of this inheritance gave him great power over the family. Often a son would
reach his late twenties before his father would allow him to move into his own household
and work his own land. Even then, sons would usually continue to live in close proximity to their fathers.

The early Puritan community was a tightly knit organism. But as the years passed and
the communities grew, strains and tensions began to affect this communal structure. This
was partly due to the increasing commercialization of New England society. It was also
partly due to population growth. In the first generations, fathers generally controlled
enough land to satisfy the needs of all their sons. After several generations, however, there
was often too little to go around, particularly in communities surrounded by other towns,
with no room to expand outward. The result was that in many communities, groups of
younger residents broke off and moved elsewhere to form towns of their own.

The tensions building in Puritan communities could produce bizarre and disastrous
events. One example was the widespread hysteria in the 1680s and 1690s over accusations
of witchcraft (the human exercise of satanic powers) in New England. The most famous
outbreak was in Salem, Massachusetts, where adolescent girls leveled   *Salem Witchcraft Trials*
charges of witchcraft against several West Indian servants steeped in voodoo belief and
practice. It would be difficult to overstate how the trials captured public attention. (See
"Debating the Past: The Witchcraft Trials.") Hysteria spread throughout the town, and
hundreds of people (most of them women) were accused of witchcraft. Nineteen residents
of Salem were put to death before the trials finally ended in 1692; the girls who had been
the original accusers later recanted and admitted that their story had been fabricated.

The Salem experience was not unique. Accusations of witchcraft spread through many
New England towns in the early 1690s and centered mostly on women. Research into the
background of accused witches reveals that most were middle-aged women, often widowed, with few or no children. Many accused witches were of low social position, were
often involved in domestic conflicts, had frequently been accused of other crimes, and
were considered abrasive by their neighbors. Others were women who, through inheritance
or hard work, had come into possession of substantial property of their own and thus
challenged the gender norms of the community.

The witchcraft controversies were a reflection of the highly religious character of New
England societies. New Englanders believed in the power of Satan. Belief in witchcraft
was not a marginal superstition rejected by the mainstream. It was a common feature of
Puritan religious conviction.

CITIES

In the 1770s, the two largest colonial ports—Philadelphia and New York—had populations of 28,000 and 25,000, respectively, which made them larger than most English urban
centers of their time. Boston (16,000), Charles Town (later Charleston), South Carolina

THE WITCHCRAFT TRIALS

The witchcraft trials of the 1690s—which began in Salem, Massachusetts, and spread to other areas of New England—have been the stuff of popular legend for centuries. They have also engaged the interest of generations of historians, who have tried to explain why these seventeenth-century Americans became so committed to the belief that some of their own neighbors were agents of Satan. Although there have been many explanations of the witchcraft phenomenon, some of the most important in recent decades have focused on the central place of women in the story.

Through the first half of the twentieth century, most historians dismissed the witchcraft trials as "hysteria," prompted by the intolerance and rigidity of Puritan society. This interpretation informed the most prominent popular portrayal of witchcraft in the twentieth century: Arthur Miller's play *The Crucible,* first produced in 1953, which was clearly an effort to use the Salem trials as a comment on the great anticommunist frenzy of his own era. But at almost the same time, Perry Miller, the renowned scholar of Puritanism, argued in a series of important studies that belief in witchcraft was not a product of hysteria or intolerance but a widely shared part of the religious worldview of the seventeenth century. To the Puritans, witchcraft seemed not only plausible but scientifically rational.

A new wave of interpretation of witchcraft began in the 1970s, with the publication of *Salem Possessed* (1976), by Paul Boyer and Stephen Nissenbaum. Their examination of the town records of Salem in the 1690s led them to conclude that the witchcraft controversy was a product of class tensions between the poorer, more marginal residents of one part of Salem and the wealthier, more privileged residents of another. These social tensions, which could not find easy expression on their own terms, led some poorer Salemites to lash out at their richer neighbors by charging them, or their servants, with witchcraft. A few years later, John Demos, in *Entertaining Satan* (1983), examined witchcraft accusations in a larger area of New England and similarly portrayed them as products of displaced anger about social and economic grievances that could not be expressed otherwise. Demos provided a far more complex picture of the nature of these grievances than had Boyer and Nissenbaum, but like them, he saw witchcraft as a symptom of a persistent set of social and psychological tensions.

At about the same time, however, a number of scholars were beginning to look at witchcraft through the scholarly lens of gender. Carol Karlsen's *The Devil in the Shape of a Woman* (1987) demonstrated through intensive scrutiny of records across New England that a disproportionate number of those accused of witchcraft were property-owning widows or unmarried women—in other words, women who did not fit comfortably into the normal pattern of male-dominated families. Karlsen concluded that such women were vulnerable to these accusations because they seemed threatening to people (including many women) who were accustomed to women as subordinate members of the community.

More recently, Mary Beth Norton's *In the Devil's Snare* (2002) placed the witchcraft trials in the context of other events of their time—and in particular the terrifying upheavals and dislocations that the Indian Wars of the late seventeenth century created in Puritan communities. In the face of this crisis, in which refugees from King William's War were fleeing towns destroyed by the Indians and flooding Salem and other eastern towns, fear and social instability grew. The witchcraft trials helped create a greater-than-normal readiness to connect aberrant behavior (such as the actions of unusually independent or eccentric women) to supernatural causes. The result was a wave of witchcraft accusations that ultimately led to the execution of at least twenty people. •

UNDERSTAND, ANALYZE, & EVALUATE

1. How did the Salem witchcraft trials reflect attitudes toward women and the status of women in colonial New England?
2. Why were colonial New Englanders willing to believe accusations of witchcraft about their fellow colonists?

(12,000), and Newport, Rhode Island (11,000), were also substantial communities by the standards of the day.

Colonial cities served as trading centers for the farmers of their regions and as marts for international commerce. Cities were the centers of what industry existed in the colonies. They were the locations of the most advanced schools and sophisticated cultural activities and of shops where imported goods could be bought. In addition, they were communities with urban social problems: crime, vice, pollution, traffic. Unlike smaller towns, cities needed to set up constables' offices and fire departments and develop systems for supporting the urban poor, whose numbers became especially large in times of economic crisis.

Finally, cities were places where new ideas could circulate and be discussed. There were newspapers, books, and other publications from abroad, and hence new intellectual influences. The taverns and coffeehouses of cities provided forums *Taverns and Coffeehouses* in which people could gather and debate the issues of the day. That is one reason why the Revolutionary crisis, when it began to build in the 1760s and 1770s, originated in the cities.

INEQUALITY

New England, for all its belief in community and liberty, was far from an egalitarian society. "Some must be rich and some poor," John Winthrop wrote in the early seventeenth century, and his prediction perhaps exceeded his expectations. Wealthy families and socially distinguished ones (who were usually the same people) had privileges and rights that were not available to poorer citizens. Elites were called "ladies" and "gentlemen," while people in the lower levels of society were known as "goodman" or "goodwife." The elite were given the best seats in their churches and had the greatest influence over the parish. Men had more power than women. Servants had few rights. The church itself taught that inequality reflected God's intention.

In cities, such economic stratification was significant—although, unlike in later eras, the rich were the largest sector of the population, and in Boston in the eighteenth century, the majority. That was so partly because wealthy people were most likely to move to cities and participate in commerce. In the agricultural countryside, differences in wealth were less extreme.

AWAKENINGS AND ENLIGHTENMENTS

Intellectual life in colonial America revolved around the conflict between the traditional emphasis on a personal God deeply involved in individual lives, and the new spirit of the Enlightenment, which stressed the importance of science and human reason. The old views placed a high value on a stern moral code in which intellect was less important than faith. The Enlightenment suggested that people had substantial control over their own lives and societies.

The Pattern of Religions

Religious toleration flourished in America to a degree unmatched in any European nation. Settlers in America brought with them so many different religious practices that it proved impossible to impose a single religious code on any large area.

The Church of England was established as the official faith in Virginia, Maryland, New York, the Carolinas, and Georgia. Except in Virginia and Maryland, however, the laws establishing the Church of England as the official colonial religion were largely ignored. Even in New England, where the Puritans had originally believed that they were all part of a single faith, there was a growing tendency in the eighteenth century for different congregations to affiliate with different denominations. In parts of New York and New Jersey, Dutch settlers had established their own Calvinist denomination, Dutch Reformed.

Numerous Sects   American Baptists developed a great variety of sects and shared the belief that rebaptism, usually by total immersion, was necessary when believers reached maturity. But while some Baptists remained Calvinists (believers in predestination), others came to believe in salvation by free will.

Protestants extended toleration to one another more readily than they did to Roman Catholics. New Englanders, in particular, viewed their Catholic neighbors in New France (Canada) not only as commercial and military rivals but also as dangerous agents of Rome.

Rights of Catholics   In most of the English colonies, however, Roman Catholics were too few to cause serious conflict. They were most numerous in Maryland, where they numbered 3,000. Perhaps for that reason they suffered the most persecution in that colony. After the overthrow of the original proprietors in 1691, Catholics in Maryland not only lost their political rights but also were forbidden to hold religious services except in private houses.

Jews in provincial America totaled no more than about 2,000 at any time. The largest community lived in New York City. Smaller groups settled in Newport and

Rights of Jews   Charles Town, and there were scattered Jewish families in all the colonies. Nowhere could they vote or hold office. Only in Rhode Island could they practice their religion openly.

By the beginning of the eighteenth century, some Americans were growing troubled by the apparent decline in religious piety in their society. The movement of the population westward and the wide scattering of settlements had caused many communities to lose touch with organized religion. The rise of commercial prosperity created a more secular outlook in urban areas. The progress of science and free thought caused at least some colonists to doubt traditional religious beliefs.

Concerns about weakening piety surfaced as early as the 1660s in New England, where the Puritan oligarchy warned of a decline in the power of the church. Ministers preached sermons of despair (known as **jeremiads**), deploring the signs of waning piety. By the standards of other societies or other eras, the Puritan faith remained remarkably strong. But to New Englanders, the "declension" of religious piety seemed a serious problem.

THE GREAT AWAKENING

By the early eighteenth century, similar concerns about declining piety were emerging in other regions and among members of other faiths. The result was the first great American revival: the Great Awakening.

The Great Awakening began in earnest in the 1730s and reached its climax in the 1740s. The revival had particular appeal to women (the majority of converts) and to younger sons of the third or fourth generation of settlers—those who stood to inherit the least land and who faced the most uncertain futures. The rhetoric of the revival emphasized the potential for every person to break away from the constraints of the past and start anew in his or her relationship with God. Such beliefs reflected in part the desires of many people to break away from their families or communities and start a new life.

Powerful **evangelists** from England helped spread the revival. John and Charles Wesley, the founders of Methodism, visited Georgia and other colonies in the 1730s. George Whitefield, a powerful open-air preacher from England, made several evangelizing tours through the colonies and drew tremendous crowds. But the *Wesleys, Whitefield, and Edwards* outstanding preacher of the Great Awakening was the New England Congregationalist Jonathan Edwards. From his pulpit in Northampton, Massachusetts, Edwards attacked the new doctrines of easy salvation for all. He preached anew the traditional Puritan ideas of the absolute sovereignty of God, predestination, and salvation by God's grace alone. His vivid descriptions of hell could terrify his listeners.

The Great Awakening led to the division of existing congregations (between "New Light" revivalists and "Old Light" traditionalists) and to the *"New Lights" and "Old Lights"* founding of new ones. It also affected areas of society outside the churches. Some of the revivalists denounced book learning as a hindrance to salvation. But other evangelists saw education as a means of furthering religion, and they founded or led schools for the training of New Light ministers.

THE ENLIGHTENMENT

The Great Awakening caused one great cultural upheaval in the colonies. The Enlightenment caused another, very different one. The Enlightenment was the product of scientific and intellectual discoveries in Europe in the seventeenth century—discoveries that revealed the "natural laws" that regulated the workings of nature. The new scientific *"Natural Law"* knowledge encouraged many thinkers to begin celebrating the power of human reason and to argue that rational thought, not just religious faith, could create progress and advance knowledge in the world.

In celebrating reason, the Enlightenment encouraged men and women to look to themselves and their own intellect—not just to God—for guidance as to how to live their lives and shape their societies. It helped produce a growing interest in education and a heightened concern with politics and government.

In the early seventeenth century, Enlightenment ideas in America were largely borrowed from Europe—from such thinkers as Francis Bacon and John Locke of England,

Baruch Spinoza of Amsterdam, and René Descartes of France. Later, however, such Americans as Benjamin Franklin, Thomas Paine, Thomas Jefferson, and James Madison made their own important contributions to Enlightenment thought.

LITERACY AND TECHNOLOGY

White male Americans achieved a high degree of literacy in the eighteenth century. By the time of the Revolution, well over one-half of all white men could read and write. The literacy rate for women lagged behind the rate for men until the nineteenth century. While opportunities for education beyond the primary level were scarce for men, they were almost nonexistent for women.

The large number of colonists who could read created a market for the first widely circulated publications in America other than the Bible: almanacs. By 1700, there were *Almanacs* dozens, perhaps hundreds, of almanacs circulating throughout the colonies and even in the sparsely settled lands to the west. Most families had at least one. Almanacs provided medical advice, navigational and agricultural information, practical wisdom, humor, and predictions about the future—most famously, predictions about weather patterns for the coming year, which many farmers used as the basis for decisions about crops, even though the predictions were notoriously unreliable. The most famous almanac in eighteenth-century America was *Poor Richard's Almanac,* published by Benjamin Franklin in Philadelphia.

GUIDE TO THE SEASONS Among their many purposes, almanacs sought to help farmers predict weather and plan for the demands of changing seasons. This illustration, part of a "calendar" of farming images, shows a man and a woman tending fields in July. (© American Antiquarian Society)

The wide availability of reading material in colonial America by the eighteenth century was a result of the spread of printing technology. The first printing press began operating in the colonies in 1639, and by 1695 there were more towns in America with printers than there were in England. At first, many of these presses did not get very much use. Over time, however, the rising literacy of the society created a demand for books, pamphlets, and almanacs that the presses rushed to fill.

The first newspaper in the colonies, *Publick Occurrences,* was published   *First Newspaper* in Boston in 1690 using a relatively advanced printing facility. It was the first step toward what would eventually become a large newspaper industry. One reason the Stamp Act of 1765, which imposed a tax on printed materials, created such a furor was that printing technology had by then become central to colonial life.

EDUCATION

Even before Enlightenment ideas penetrated America, colonists placed a high value on formal education. Some families tried to teach their children to read and write at home, although the heavy burden of work in most agricultural households limited the time available for schooling. In Massachusetts, a 1647 law required that every town support a school; and a modest network of public schools emerged as a result. The   *Public Schools* Quakers and other sects operated church schools, and in some communities widows or unmarried women conducted "dame schools" in their homes. In cities, some master craftsmen set up evening schools for their apprentices.

African Americans had virtually no access to education. Occasionally a master or mistress would teach slave children to read and write; but as the slave system became more firmly entrenched, strong social (and ultimately legal) sanctions developed to discourage such efforts. Indians, too, remained largely outside the white educational system—to a large degree by choice. Some white missionaries and philanthropists established schools for Native Americans and helped create a small population of Indians literate in spoken and written English.

Harvard, the first American college, was established in 1636 by Puritan theologians who wanted to create a training center for ministers. (The college was named for a Charlestown, Massachusetts, minister, John Harvard, who had left it his library and one-half of his estate.) In 1693, William and Mary College (named for the English king and queen) was established in Williamsburg, Virginia, by Anglicans. And in 1701,   *First Colleges* conservative Congregationalists, dissatisfied with the growing religious liberalism of Harvard, founded Yale (named for one of its first benefactors, Elihu Yale) in New Haven, Connecticut. Out of the Great Awakening emerged the College of New Jersey, founded in 1746 and known later as Princeton (after the town in which it was located); one of its first presidents was Jonathan Edwards. Despite the religious basis of these colleges, most of them offered curricula that included not only theology but also logic, ethics, physics, geometry, astronomy, rhetoric, Latin, Hebrew, and Greek. King's College, founded in New York City in 1754 and later renamed Columbia, was specifically devoted to the spread of secular knowledge. The Academy and College of Philadelphia, founded in 1755 and later renamed the University of Pennsylvania, was also a secular institution, established by a group of laymen under the inspiration of Benjamin Franklin.

After 1700, most colonial leaders received their entire education in America (rather than attending university in England, as had once been the case). But higher education remained available only to a few relatively affluent white men.

The Spread of Science

The clearest indication of the spreading influence of the Enlightenment in America was an increasing interest in scientific knowledge. Most of the early colleges established chairs in the natural sciences and introduced some of the advanced scientific theories of Europe, including Copernican astronomy and Newtonian physics, to their students. But the most vigorous promotion of science in these years occurred through the private efforts of amateurs *Scientific Societies* and the activities of scientific societies. Leading merchants, planters, and even theologians became corresponding members of the Royal Society of London, the leading English scientific organization. Benjamin Franklin won international fame through his experiments with electricity. Particularly notable was his 1747 theory—and his 1752 demonstration, using a kite—that lightning and electricity were the same. (Previously, most scientists had believed that there were several distinct types of electricity.) His research on the way in which electricity could be "grounded" led to the development of the lightning rod, which greatly reduced fires and other damage to buildings during thunderstorms.

The high value that influential Americans were beginning to place on scientific knowledge was clearly demonstrated by the most daring and controversial scientific experiment of the eighteenth century: inoculation against smallpox. The Puritan theologian Cotton *Cotton Mather and Vaccines* Mather had learned of experiments in England by which people had been deliberately infected with mild cases of smallpox to immunize them against the deadly disease. Despite strong opposition, he urged inoculation on his fellow Bostonians during an epidemic in the 1720s. The results confirmed the effectiveness of the technique. Other theologians took up the cause, along with many physicians. By the mid-eighteenth century, inoculation had become a common medical procedure in America.

Concepts of Law and Politics

In law and politics, as in other parts of their lives, Americans in the seventeenth and eighteenth centuries believed that they were re-creating in the New World the practices and institutions of the Old World. But as in other areas, they created something very different. Although the American legal system adopted most of the essential elements of the English system, including such ancient rights as trial by jury, significant differences developed in court procedures, punishments, and the definition of crimes. In England, for example, a printed attack on a public official, whether true or false, was considered *John Peter Zenger* libelous. At the 1734–1735 trial of the New York publisher John Peter Zenger, the courts ruled that criticisms of the government were not libelous if factually true—a verdict that removed some colonial restrictions on the freedom of the press.

More significant for the future relationship between the colonies and England were differences emerging between the American and British political systems. Because the royal government was so far away, Americans created a group of institutions of their own that gave them a large measure of self-government. In most colonies, local communities grew accustomed to running their own affairs with minimal interference from higher authorities. The colonial assemblies came to exercise many of the powers that Parliament exercised in England. Provincial governors (appointed by the king after the 1690s) had broad powers on paper, but their actual influence was limited.

The result of all this was that the provincial governments became accustomed to acting more or less independently of Parliament, and a set of assumptions and expectations about the rights of the colonists took hold in America that was not shared by policymakers in England.

The ducking stool was a common punishment for scolds in all the American colonies, save in New England.

COLONIAL PUNISHMENT American communities prescribed a wide range of punishments for misconduct and crime. Among the more common punishments were public humiliations—placing offenders in stocks, forcing them to wear badges of shame, or, as in this woodcut, binding them into a "ducking stool" and immersing them in water. (© Fotosearch/Getty Images)

These differences caused few problems before the 1760s, because the British did little to exert the authority they believed they possessed. But when, beginning in 1763, the English government began attempting to tighten its control over the American colonies, a great imperial crisis resulted.

CONCLUSION

Between the 1650s and the 1750s, the English colonies in America grew steadily in population, in the size of their economies, and in the sophistication—and diversity—of their cultures. Although most white Americans in the 1750s still believed that they were fully a part of the British Empire, they were in fact living in a world that had become very different from that of England.

Many distinct societies developed in the colonies, but the greatest distinction was between the colonies of the North and those of the South. In the North, society was dominated by relatively small family farms and by towns and cities of growing size. A thriving commercial class was developing, and with it an increasingly elaborate urban culture. In the South, there were many family farms as well. But there were also large plantations cultivating tobacco, rice, indigo (a plant used to make a dark blue dye), and cotton for export. By the late seventeenth century, these plantations were relying heavily on African workers who had been brought to the colonies forcibly as slaves. There were few significant towns and cities in the South, and little commerce other than the marketing of crops.

The colonies did, however, have much in common. Most white Americans accepted common assumptions about racial inequality. That enabled them to tolerate the enslavement of African men and women and to justify a campaign of displacement and often violence against Native Americans. Most white Americans (and, in different ways, most nonwhite Americans as well) were deeply religious. The Great Awakening, therefore, had a powerful impact throughout the colonies. And most white colonists shared a belief in certain basic principles of law and politics, which they considered embedded in the English constitution. Their interpretation of that constitution, however, was becoming increasingly different from that of the Parliament in England and was laying the groundwork for future conflict.

KEY TERMS/PEOPLE/PLACES/EVENTS

Cotton Mather 80
covenant 72
Enlightenment 76
evangelist 77
George Whitefield 77
Great Awakening 77
Huguenots 65

indentured servant 55
jeremiad 76
John and Charles Wesley 77
John Peter Zenger 80
Jonathan Edwards 77
middle passage 61
primogeniture 73

Salem witchcraft trials 73
Saugus Ironworks 66
Scotch-Irish 65
slave codes 63
Stono Rebellion 71
triangular trade 69

RECALL AND REFLECT

1. How did patterns of family life and attitudes toward women differ in the northern and southern colonies?
2. How did the lives of African slaves change over the course of the first century of slavery?
3. Who emigrated to North America in the seventeenth century, and why did they come?
4. What was the intellectual culture of colonial America, as expressed in literature, philosophy, science, education, and law?
5. How and why did life in the English colonies diverge from life in England?

4 THE EMPIRE IN TRANSITION

LOOSENING TIES
THE STRUGGLE FOR THE CONTINENT
THE NEW IMPERIALISM
STIRRINGS OF REVOLT
COOPERATION AND WAR

LOOKING AHEAD

1. How did the Seven Years' War change the balance of power in North America and throughout the world?
2. What policies did Parliament implement with regard to the colonies in the 1760s and 1770s, and why did Britain adopt these policies?
3. How did the colonists respond to Parliament's actions?

AS LATE AS THE 1750S, few Americans objected to their membership in the British Empire. The imperial system provided many benefits to the Americans, and for the most part the English government left the colonies alone. By the mid-1770s, however, the relationship between the American colonies and their British rulers had become so strained that the empire was on the verge of unraveling. And in the spring of 1775, the first shots were fired in a war that would ultimately win America its independence. How had it happened? And why so quickly?

LOOSENING TIES

In one sense, it had not happened quickly at all. Ever since the first days of English settlement, the ideas and institutions of the colonies had been diverging from those in Britain. In another sense, however, the Revolutionary crisis emerged in response to relatively sudden changes in the administration of the empire. In 1763, the English government began to enforce a series of colonial policies that brought the differences between the two societies into sharp focus.

1754

Beginning of French
and Indian War

1756

Seven Years' War begins

1760

George III becomes king

1763

Peace of Paris

Proclamation of 1763

1764

Sugar Act

1765

Stamp Act

1766

Stamp Act repealed

Declaratory Act

1767

Townshend Duties

1770

Boston Massacre

Most Townshend
Duties repealed

1771

Regulator movement
in North Carolina

1772

Committees of
correspondence
in Boston

Gaspée incident

1773

Tea Act; Boston
Tea Party

1774

Coercive Acts

First Continental
Congress in Philadelphia

1775

Battles of Lexington
and Concord

American Revolution
begins

A Decentralized Empire

In the fifty years after the Glorious Revolution, the English Parliament established a growing supremacy over the king. Under Kings George I (1714–1727) and George II (1727–1760), the prime minister and his cabinet became the nation's real executives. Because they depended politically on the great merchants and landholders of England, they were less inclined than the seventeenth-century monarchs had been to try to tighten control over the empire, which many merchants feared would disrupt the profitable commerce with the colonies. As a result, administration of the colonies remained loose, decentralized, and inefficient.

The character of royal officials in America contributed further to the looseness of the imperial system. Few governors were able men. Many, perhaps most, had used bribery to obtain their offices and continued to accept bribes once in office. Some appointees remained in England and hired substitutes to take their places in America.

The colonial assemblies, taking advantage of the weak imperial administration, had asserted their own authority to levy taxes, make appropriations, approve appointments, and pass laws. The assemblies came to look upon themselves as little parliaments, each practically as sovereign within its colony as Parliament itself was in England.

The Colonies Divided

Even so, the colonists continued to think of themselves as loyal English subjects. Many felt stronger ties to England than they did to the other American colonies. Although the colonies had slowly learned to cooperate with one another on such practical matters as intercolonial trade, road construction, and a colonial postal service, they remained reluctant to cooperate in larger ways, even when, in 1754, they faced a common threat from their old rivals, the French, and

France's Indian allies. Delegates from Pennsylvania, Maryland, New York, and New England met in Albany in that year to negotiate a treaty with the Iroquois. They *Albany Plan* tentatively approved a proposal by Benjamin Franklin to set up a "general government" to manage relations with the Indians. War with the French and Indians was already beginning when the Albany Plan was presented to the colonial assemblies. None approved it.

THE STRUGGLE FOR THE CONTINENT

The war that raged in North America through the late 1750s and early 1760s was part of a larger struggle between England and France. The British victory in that struggle, known in Europe as the Seven Years' War, confirmed England's commercial supremacy and cemented its control of the settled regions of North America. In America, the conflict, which colonists called the French and Indian War, was also the final stage in a long struggle among the three principal powers in northeastern North America: the English, the French, and the Iroquois.

New France and the Iroquois Nation

By the end of the seventeenth century, the French Empire in America was vast: the whole length of the Mississippi River and its delta (named Louisiana, after their king) and the continental interior as far west as the Rocky Mountains and as far *France's Colonial Empire* south as the Rio Grande. France claimed, in effect, the entire interior of the continent.

To secure their hold on these enormous claims, they founded a string of widely separated communities, fortresses, missions, and trading posts. Would-be feudal lords established large estates *(seigneuries)* along the banks of the St. Lawrence River. On a high bluff above the river stood the fortified city of Quebec. Montreal to the south and Sault Sainte Marie and Detroit to the west marked the northern boundaries of French settlement. On the lower Mississippi there were plantations much like those in the southern colonies of English America, worked by African slaves and owned by **Creoles** (people of European ancestry born in the Americas). New Orleans, founded in 1718 to service the French plantation economy, was soon as big as some of the larger cities of the Atlantic seaboard; Biloxi and Mobile to the east completed the string of French settlement.

Both the French and the English were aware that the battle for control of North America would be determined in part by who could best win the allegiance of native tribes. The English—with their more advanced commercial economy—could usually offer the Indians better and more plentiful goods. But the French offered tolerance. Unlike the English, the French settlers in the interior generally adjusted their own behavior to Indian patterns. French fur traders frequently married Indian women and adopted tribal ways; Jesuit missionaries interacted comfortably with the natives and converted them to Catholicism by the thousands without challenging most of their social customs. By the mid-eighteenth century, therefore, the French had better and closer relations with most of the Indians of the interior than did the English.

The most powerful native group, however, had remained aloof from both sides. The Iroquois Confederacy—five Indian nations (Mohawk, Seneca, *The Iroquois Confederacy* Cayuga, Onondaga, and Oneida) that had formed a defensive alliance in the fifteenth century—had been the most powerful native presence in the Ohio Valley since the 1640s.

The Iroquois maintained their autonomy by trading successfully with both the French and the English and astutely played them against each other.

ANGLO-FRENCH CONFLICTS

As long as peace and stability in the North American interior lasted, English and French colonists coexisted without serious difficulty. But after the Glorious Revolution in England, a complicated series of Anglo-French wars erupted in Europe and continued intermittently for nearly eighty years, creating important repercussions in America.

King William's War (1689–1697) produced only a few, indecisive clashes between the English and the French in northern New England. Queen Anne's War, which began in 1701 and continued for nearly twelve years, generated more substantial conflicts. The Treaty of Utrecht, which brought the conflict to a close in 1713, transferred substantial territory from the French to the English in North America, including Acadia (Nova Scotia) and Newfoundland. Two decades later, disputes over British trading rights in the Spanish colonies produced a conflict between England and Spain that soon grew into a much larger European war. The English colonists in America were drawn into the struggle, which they called King George's War (1744–1748). New Englanders captured the French bastion at Louisbourg on Cape Breton Island in Nova Scotia, but the peace treaty that finally ended the conflict forced them to abandon it.

In the aftermath of King George's War, relations among the English, French, and Iroquois in North America quickly deteriorated. The Iroquois (in what appears to have been a major blunder) granted trading concessions in the interior to English merchants for the first time. The French feared (probably correctly) that the English were using the concessions as a first step toward expansion into French lands. They began in 1749 to construct new fortresses in the Ohio Valley. The English responded by increasing their military forces and building fortresses of their own. The balance of power that the Iroquois had carefully maintained for so long rapidly disintegrated.

For the next five years, tensions between the English and the French increased. In the summer of 1754, the governor of Virginia sent a militia force (under the command of an inexperienced young colonel, George Washington) into the Ohio Valley to challenge *Fort Necessity* French expansion. Washington built a crude stockade (Fort Necessity) not far from France's Fort Duquesne, on the site of what is now Pittsburgh. After the Virginians staged an unsuccessful attack on a French detachment, the French countered with an assault on Fort Necessity, trapping Washington and his soldiers inside. After one-third of them died in the fighting, Washington surrendered. The clash marked the beginning of the French and Indian War.

THE GREAT WAR FOR THE EMPIRE

The French and Indian War lasted nearly nine years, and it moved through three distinct *French and Indian War* phases. The first phases—from the Fort Necessity debacle in 1754 until the expansion of the war to Europe in 1756—was primarily a local, North American conflict. The Iroquois remained largely passive in the conflict. But virtually all the other tribes were allied with the French. They launched a series of raids on western English settlements. The English colonists fought to defend themselves against those raids. By late 1755, many English settlers along the frontier had withdrawn to the east of the Allegheny Mountains to escape the hostilities.

The second phase of the struggle began in 1756, when the Seven Years' War began in Europe and beyond. (See "America in the World: The First Global War.") *Seven Years' War* The fighting now spread to the West Indies, India, and Europe itself. But the principal struggle remained the war in North America, where so far England had suffered nothing but frustration and defeat. Beginning in 1757, William Pitt, the English secretary *William Pitt* of state (and future prime minister), brought the war fully under British control. He planned military strategy, appointed commanders, and issued orders to the colonists. British commanders began forcibly enlisting colonists into the army (a practice known as **impressment**). Officers also seized supplies from local farmers and tradesmen and compelled colonists to offer shelter to British troops—all generally without compensation. The Americans resented these new impositions and firmly resisted them. By early 1758, the friction between the British authorities and the colonists was threatening to bring the war effort to a halt.

Beginning in 1758, Pitt initiated the third and final phase of the war by relaxing many of the policies that Americans had found obnoxious. He agreed to reimburse the colonists for all supplies requisitioned by the army. He returned control over recruitment to the colonial assemblies. And he dispatched large numbers of additional British troops to America. These moves turned the tide of battle in England's favor. The French had always been outnumbered by the British colonists. After 1756, moreover, the French suffered from a series of poor harvests and were unable to sustain their early military successes. By mid-1758, British regulars and colonial militias were seizing one French stronghold after another. Two brilliant English generals, Jeffrey Amherst and James Wolfe, captured the fortress at Louisbourg in July 1758; a few months later Fort Duquesne

THE SIEGE OF LOUISBOURG, 1758 The fortress of Louisbourg, on Cape Breton Island in Nova Scotia, was one of the principal French outposts in eastern Canada during the French and Indian War. It took a British fleet of 157 ships nearly two months to force the French garrison to surrender. (© Private Collection/Peter Newark American Pictures/Bridgeman Images)

THE FIRST GLOBAL WAR

The French and Indian War in North America was only a small part of a much larger conflict. Known in Europe as the Seven Years' War, it was one of the longest, most widespread, and most important wars in modern history. The war thrust Great Britain into conflicts across Europe and North America. Winston Churchill once wrote of it as the first "world war."

In North America, the war was a result of tensions along the frontiers of the British Empire. But it arose more broadly from larger conflicts among the great powers in Europe. It began in the 1750s with what historians have called a "diplomatic revolution." Well-established alliances between Britain and the Austro-Hungarian Empire and between France and Prussia collapsed, replaced by a new set of alliances setting Britain and Prussia against France and Austria. The instability that these changing alliances produced helped speed the European nations toward war.

The Austrian-British alliance collapsed because Austria suffered a series of significant defeats at the hands of the Prussians. To the British government, these failures suggested that the Austro-Hungarian Empire was now too weak to help Britain balance French power. As a result, England launched a search for new partnerships with the rising powers of northern Germany, Austria's enemies. In response, the Austrians sought an alliance with France to help protect them from the power of their former British allies. (One later result of this new alliance was the 1770 marriage of the future French king Louis XVI to the Austrian princess Marie Antoinette.) In the aftermath of these realignments, Austria sought again to defeat the Prussian-Hanover forces in Germany. In the process, Russia became concerned about the Austro-Hungarian

Empire's possible dominance in central Europe and allied itself with the British and the Prussians. These complicated realignments eventually led to the Seven Years' War, which soon spread across much of the world. The war engaged not only most of the great powers in Europe, from England to Russia, but also the emerging colonial worlds—India, West Africa, the Caribbean, and the Philippines—as the powerful British navy worked to strip France, and eventually Spain, of its valuable colonial holdings.

Like most modern conflicts, the Seven Years' War was at heart a struggle for economic power. Colonial possessions, many European nations believed, were critical to their future wealth and well worth fighting for. The war's outcome affected not only the future of America but also the distribution of power throughout much of the world. It destroyed the French navy and much of the French Empire, and it elevated Great Britain to undisputed preeminence among the colonizing powers—especially when, at the conclusion of the war, India and all of eastern North America fell firmly under English control. The war also reorganized the balance of power in Europe, with Britain now preeminent among the great powers and Prussia (later to become the core of modern Germany) rapidly rising in wealth and military power.

The Seven Years' War was not only one of the first great colonial wars but also one of the last great wars of religion, and it extended the dominance of Protestantism in Europe. In what is now Canada, the war replaced French with British rule and thus replaced Catholic with Protestant dominance. The Vatican, no longer a military power itself, had relied on the great Catholic empires—Spain, France, and Austria-Hungary—as bulwarks of its power and influence. The shift of power toward Protestant

CELEBRATING THE PEACE OF PARIS This etching shows a fireworks display in Paris on February 10, 1763, to mark the end of the Seven Years' War. (© Granger, NYC—All Rights Reserved.)

governments in Europe and North America weakened the Catholic Church and reduced its geopolitical influence.

The conclusion of the Seven Years' War strengthened Britain and Germany and weakened France. But it did not provide any lasting solution to the rivalries among the great colonial powers. In North America, a dozen years after the end of the conflict, the American Revolution—the origins of which were in many ways a direct result of the Seven Years' War—stripped the British Empire of one of its most important and valuable colonial appendages. By the time the American Revolution came to an end,

the French Revolution had sparked another lengthy period of war, culminating in the Napoleonic Wars of the early nineteenth century, which once again redrew the map of Europe and, for a while, the world. •

UNDERSTAND, ANALYZE, & EVALUATE

1. How did the Seven Years' War change the balance of power among the nations of Europe? Who gained and who lost in the war?
2. Why is the Seven Years' War described as one of the "most important wars in modern history"?

fell without a fight. The next year, at the end of a siege of Quebec, the army of General Wolfe struggled up a hidden ravine under cover of darkness, surprised the larger forces of the Marquis de Montcalm, and defeated them in a battle in which both commanders were killed. The dramatic fall of Quebec on September 13, 1759, marked the beginning of the end of the American phase of the war. A year later, in September 1760, the French army formally surrendered to Amherst in Montreal. Peace finally came in 1763, with the

Peace of Paris, by which the French ceded to Great Britain some of their West Indian islands, most of their colonies in India and Canada, and all other French territory in North America east of the Mississippi. The French then ceded New Orleans and their claims west of the Mississippi to Spain, surrendering all title to the mainland of North America.

The French and Indian War greatly expanded England's territorial claims in the New World. At the same time, the cost of the war greatly enlarged Britain's debt and substantially increased *Effects of the Conflict*   British resentment of the Americans. English leaders were contemptuous of the colonists for what they considered American military ineptitude during the war; they were angry that the colonists had made so few financial contributions to a struggle waged, they believed, largely for American benefit; they were particularly bitter that colonial merchants had been selling food and other goods to the French in the West Indies throughout the conflict. All these factors combined to persuade many English leaders that a major reorganization of the empire would be necessary. London wanted increased authority over the colonies.

The war had an equally profound effect on the American colonists. It was an experience that forced them, for the first time, to act in concert against a common foe. The 1758 return of authority to the colonial assemblies seemed to many Americans to confirm the illegitimacy of English interference in local affairs.

For the Indians of the Ohio Valley, the British victory was disastrous. Those tribes that had allied themselves with the French had earned the enmity of the victorious English. The Iroquois Confederacy, which had not allied with the French, fared only slightly better. *Consequences for Native Americans*   English officials saw the passivity of the Iroquois during the war as evidence of duplicity. In the aftermath of the peace settlement, the fragile Iroquois alliance with the British quickly unraveled. The tribes would continue to contest the English for control of the Ohio Valley for another fifty years, but were increasingly divided and increasingly outnumbered. They would seldom again be in a position to deal with their European rivals on terms of military or political equality.

THE NEW IMPERIALISM

With the treaty of 1763, England found itself truly at peace for the first time in more than fifty years. As a result, the British government could now turn its attention to the organization of its empire. Saddled with enormous debts from the many years of war, England was desperately in need of new revenues. Responsible for vast holdings in the New World, the imperial government believed it must increase its administrative capacities in America. The result was a dramatic and, for England, disastrous redefinition of the colonial relationship.

BURDENS OF EMPIRE

The experience of the French and Indian War should have suggested that increasing imperial control over the colonies would not be easy. Not only had the resistance of the colonists forced Pitt to relax his policies in 1758, but the colonial assemblies continued to defy imperial trade regulations and other British demands. But the most immediate *Britain's Staggering War Debt*   problem for London was its staggering war debt. Landlords and merchants in England were objecting strenuously to any further tax increases, and the colonial assemblies had repeatedly demonstrated their unwillingness to pay for the war effort. Many officials in England believed that only by taxing the Americans directly could the empire effectively meet its financial needs.

At this crucial moment in Anglo-American relations, the government of England was thrown into turmoil by the 1760 accession to the throne of George III. He *George the Third* brought two particularly unfortunate qualities to the position. First, he was determined to reassert the authority of the monarchy. He removed from power the relatively stable coalition of Whigs that had governed for much of the century and replaced it with a new and very unstable coalition of his own. The weak new ministries that emerged as a result each lasted in office an average of only about two years.

Second, the king had serious intellectual and psychological limitations. He suffered, apparently, from a rare mental disease that produced intermittent bouts of insanity. (Indeed, in the last years of his long reign he was, according to most accounts, unable to perform any official

THE THIRTEEN COLONIES IN 1763 This map shows the thirteen colonies at the end of the Seven Years' War. It shows the line of settlement established by the Proclamation of 1763 (the red line), as well as the extent of actual settlement in that year (the blue line). Note that in the middle colonies (North Carolina, Virginia, Maryland, and southern Pennsylvania), settlement had already reached the red line—and in one small area of western Pennsylvania moved beyond it—by the time of the Proclamation of 1763. Note also the string of forts established beyond the Proclamation line. • *How do the forts help explain the efforts of the British to restrict settlement? And how does the extent of actual settlement help explain why it was so difficult for the British to enforce their restrictions?*

functions.) Yet even when George III was lucid, which was most of the time in the 1760s and 1770s, he was painfully immature and insecure. The king's personality, therefore, contributed both to the instability and to the rigidity of the British government during these critical years.

More directly responsible for the problems that soon emerged with the colonies, *George Grenville*   however, was George Grenville, whom the king made prime minister in 1763. Grenville shared the prevailing opinion within Britain that the colonists should be compelled to pay a part of the cost of defending and administering the empire.

THE BRITISH AND THE TRIBES

With the defeat of the French, frontiersmen from the English colonies began immediately to move over the mountains and into tribal lands in the upper Ohio Valley. An alliance of Indian tribes, under the Ottawa chieftain Pontiac, struck back. Fearing that an escalation of the fighting *Proclamation of 1763*   might threaten western trade, the British government—in the Proclamation of 1763—forbade settlers to advance beyond the Appalachian Mountains.

Many Indian groups supported the Proclamation as the best bargain available to them. The Cherokee, in particular, worked actively to hasten the drawing of the boundary, hoping finally to put an end to white movements into their lands. Relations between the western tribes and the British improved for a time, partly as a result of the work of the sympathetic Indian superintendents the British appointed.

In the end, however, the Proclamation of 1763 was ineffective. White settlers continued to swarm across the boundary and to claim lands farther and farther into the Ohio Valley. The British authorities failed to enforce limits to the expansion. In 1768, new agreements with the western tribes pushed the permanent boundary farther west. But these treaties and subsequent ones also failed to stop the white advance.

BATTLES OVER TRADE AND TAXES

The Grenville ministry tried to increase its authority in the colonies in other ways as well. *Mutiny Act*   Regular British troops were stationed permanently in America, and under the Mutiny Act of 1765 the colonists were required to help provision and maintain the army. Ships of the British navy patrolled American waters to search for smugglers. The customs service was reorganized and enlarged. Royal officials were required to take up their colonial posts in person instead of sending substitutes. Colonial manufacturing was restricted so that it would not compete with rapidly expanding industries in Great Britain.

The Sugar Act of 1764 raised the duty on sugar while lowering the duty on molasses. *Sugar and Currency Acts*   It also established new vice-admiralty courts in America to try accused smugglers—thus cutting them off from sympathetic local juries. The Currency Act of 1764 required that the colonial assemblies stop issuing paper money.

At first, it was difficult for the colonists to resist these unpopular new laws. That was partly because Americans continued to harbor as many grievances against one another as they did against the authorities in London. In 1763, for example, a band of Pennsylvania frontiersmen known as the Paxton Boys descended on Philadelphia to demand tax relief and financial support for their defense against Indians. Bloodshed was averted only by concessions from the colonial assembly. In 1771, a small-scale civil war broke out in North Carolina when the *Paxton Boys and Regulators*   "Regulators," farmers of the interior, organized and armed themselves to resist high taxes. The colonial governor appointed sheriffs to enforce the levies. An army of militiamen, most of them from the eastern counties, crushed the Regulator revolt.

The unpopularity of the Grenville program helped the colonists overcome their internal conflicts and see that the policies from London were a threat to all Americans. Northern merchants would suffer from restraints on their commerce. The closing of the West to land speculation and fur trading enraged many colonists. Others were angered by the restriction of opportunities for manufacturing. Southern planters, in debt to English merchants, would be unable to ease their debts by speculating in western land. Small farmers would suffer from the abolition of paper money, which had been the source of most of their loans. Workers in towns faced the prospect of narrowing opportunities, particularly because of the restraints on manufacturing and currency. Everyone stood to suffer from increased taxes.

Most Americans soon found ways to live with the new British laws without terrible economic hardship. But their political grievances remained. Americans were accustomed to wide latitude in self-government. They believed that colonial assemblies had the sole right to control appropriations for the costs of government within the colonies. By attempting to raise extensive revenues directly from the public, the British government was challenging the basis of colonial political power.

STIRRINGS OF REVOLT

By the mid-1760s, a hardening of positions had begun in both England and America. The result was a progression of events that, more rapidly than imagined, destroyed the British Empire in America.

THE STAMP ACT CRISIS

Grenville could not have devised a better method for antagonizing and unifying the colonies than the Stamp Act of 1765. Unlike the Sugar Act of a year earlier, *The Stamp Act* which affected only a few New England merchants, the new tax fell on everyone. It levied taxes on every printed document in the colonies: newspapers, almanacs, pamphlets, deeds, wills, licenses. British officials were soon collecting more than ten times as much revenue in America as they had been before 1763. More alarming than these taxes, however, was the precedent they seemed to create. In the past, taxes and duties on colonial trade had always been designed to regulate commerce. The Stamp Act, however, was clearly an attempt by England to raise revenue from the colonies without the consent of the colonial assemblies.

Few colonists believed that they could do anything more than grumble until the Virginia House of Burgesses aroused Americans to action. Patrick Henry made a dramatic speech to the House in May 1765, concluding with a vague prediction that if present policies were not revised, George III, like earlier tyrants, might lose his head. Amid shocked cries of "Treason!" Henry introduced a set of resolutions (only some of which the assembly passed) declaring that Americans possessed the same rights as the English, especially the right to be taxed only by their *"Virginia Resolves"* own representatives; that Virginians should pay no taxes except those voted by the Virginia assembly; and that anyone advocating the right of Parliament to tax Virginians should be deemed an enemy of the colony. Henry's resolutions were printed and circulated as the "Virginia Resolves."

BENJAMIN FRANKLIN, TESTIMONY AGAINST THE STAMP ACT (1766)

In 1765 Parliament passed the first internal tax on the colonists, known as the Stamp Act. Benjamin Franklin was a colonial agent in London at the time, and as colonial opposition to the act grew, he found himself representing these views to the British government. In his testimony from Parliament he describes the role of taxes in Pennsylvania and the economic relationship between the colonies and the mother country.

Q. What is your name, and place of abode?

A. Franklin, of Philadelphia.

Q. Do the Americans pay any considerable taxes among themselves?

A. Certainly many, and very heavy taxes.

Q. What are the present taxes in Pennsylvania, laid by the laws of the colony?

A. There are taxes on all estates, real and personal; a poll tax; a tax on all offices, professions, trades, and businesses, according to their profits; an excise on all wine, rum, and other spirit; and a duty of ten pounds per head on all Negroes imported, with some other duties.

Q. For what purposes are those taxes laid?

A. For the support of the civil and military establishments of the country, and to discharge the heavy debt contracted in the last [Seven Years'] war. . . .

Q. Are not all the people very able to pay those taxes?

A. No. The frontier counties, all along the continent, have been frequently ravaged by the enemy and greatly impoverished, are able to pay very little tax. . . .

Q. Are not the colonies, from their circumstances, very able to pay the stamp duty?

A. In my opinion there is not gold and silver enough in the colonies to pay the stamp duty for one year.

Q. Don't you know that the money arising from the stamps was all to be laid out in America?

A. I know it is appropriated by the act to the American service; but it will be spent in the conquered colonies, where the soldiers are, not in the colonies that pay it.

Q. Do you think it right that America should be protected by this country and pay no part of the expense?

A. That is not the case. The colonies raised, clothed, and paid, during the last war, near 25,000 men, and spent many millions.

Q. Were you not reimbursed by Parliament?

A. We were only reimbursed what, in your opinion, we had advanced beyond our proportion, or beyond what might reasonably be expected from us; and it was a very small part of what we spent. Pennsylvania, in particular, disbursed about 500,000 pounds, and the reimbursements, in the whole, did not exceed 60,000 pounds. . . .

Q. Do you think the people of America would submit to pay the stamp duty, if it was moderated?

A. No, never, unless compelled by force of arms. . . .

Q. What was the temper of America towards Great Britain before the year 1763?

A. The best in the world. They submitted willingly to the government of the Crown, and paid, in all their courts, obedience to acts of Parliament. . . .

Q. What is your opinion of a future tax, imposed on the same principle with that of the Stamp Act? How would the Americans receive it?

A. Just as they do this. They would not pay it.

Q. Have not you heard of the resolutions of this House, and of the House of Lords, asserting the right of Parliament relating to America, including a power to tax the people there?

A. Yes, I have heard of such resolutions.

Q. What will be the opinion of the Americans on those resolutions?

A. They will think them unconstitutional and unjust.

Q. Was it an opinion in America before 1763 that the Parliament had no right to lay taxes and duties there?

A. I never heard any objection to the right of laying duties to regulate commerce; but a right to lay internal taxes was never supposed to be in Parliament, as we are not represented there.

Q. Did the Americans ever dispute the controlling power of Parliament to regulate the commerce?

A. No.

Q. Can anything less than a military force carry the Stamp Act into execution?

A. I do not see how a military force can be applied to that purpose.

Q. Why may it not?

A. Suppose a military force sent into America; they will find nobody in arms; what are they then to do? They cannot force a man to take stamps who chooses to do without them. They will not find a rebellion; they may indeed make one.

Q. If the act is not repealed, what do you think will be the consequences?

A. A total loss of the respect and affection the people of America bear to this country, and of all the commerce that depends on that respect and affection.

Q. How can the commerce be affected?

A. You will find that, if the act is not repealed, they will take very little of your manufactures in a short time.

Q. Is it in their power to do without them?

A. I think they may very well do without them.

Q. Is it their interest not to take them?

A. The goods they take from Britain are either necessaries, mere conveniences, or superfluities. The first, as cloth, etc., with a little industry they can make at home; the second they can do without till they are able to provide them among themselves; and the last, which are mere articles of fashion, purchased and consumed because of the fashion in a respected country; but will now be detested and rejected. The people have already struck off, by general agreement, the use of all goods fashionable in mourning.

Q. If the Stamp Act should be repealed, would it induce the assemblies of America to acknowledge the right of Parliament to tax them, and would they erase their resolutions [against the Stamp Act]?

A. No, never.

Q. Is there no means of obliging them to erase those resolutions?

A. None that I know of; they will never do it, unless compelled by force of arms.

Q. Is there a power on earth that can force them to erase them?

A. No power, how great so ever, can force men to change their opinions. . . .

Q. What used to be the pride of the Americans?

A. To indulge in the fashions and manufactures of Great Britain.

Q. What is now their pride?

A. To wear their old clothes over again, till they can make new ones.

UNDERSTAND, ANALYZE, & EVALUATE

1. What kind of taxes did colonists pay according to Franklin? What did the interviewer seem to think of the colonists' tax burden? What disagreements existed between Franklin and his interviewer on the purpose, legality, and feasibility of the stamp tax?

2. How did Franklin characterize the British-colonial relationship prior to 1763?

3. What colonial response to the Stamp Act and other "internal taxes" did Franklin predict? What, if anything, could Parliament do to enforce the colonists' compliance?

Source: *The Parliamentary History of England* (London, 1813), vol. XVI, pp. 138–159; in Charles Morris, *The Great Republic by the Master Historians*, vol. II (R.S. Belcher Co., 1902).

In Massachusetts at about the same time, James Otis persuaded his fellow members of the colonial assembly to call an intercolonial congress to take action against the new tax. And in October 1765, the Stamp Act Congress, as it was called, met in New York with delegates from nine colonies. In a petition to the British government, the congress denied that the colonies could rightfully be taxed except through their own provincial assemblies. Across the ocean, colonial agent Benjamin Franklin articulated such grievances before Parliament. (See "Consider the Source: Testimony against the Stamp Act.")

Meanwhile, in the summer of 1765, mobs were rising up in several colonial cities against the Stamp Act. The largest was in Boston, where men belonging to the newly organized Sons of Liberty terrorized stamp agents and burned stamps. The mob also attacked such supposedly pro-British aristocrats as the lieutenant governor, Thomas Hutchinson (who had privately opposed passage of the Stamp Act but who felt obliged to support it once it became law). Hutchinson's elegant house was pillaged and virtually destroyed.

The crisis finally subsided largely because England backed down. The authorities in London were less affected by the political protests than by economic pressure. Many New *Stamp Act Repealed* Englanders had stopped buying English goods to protest the Sugar Act of 1764, and the Stamp Act caused the boycott to spread. With pressure from English merchants, Parliament—under a new prime minister, the Marquis of Rockingham—repealed the unpopular law on March 18, 1766. To satisfy his strong and vociferous opponents, Rockingham also pushed through the Declaratory Act, which confirmed parliamentary authority over the colonies "in all cases whatsoever." But in their rejoicing over the Stamp Act repeal, most Americans paid little attention to this sweeping declaration of power.

Internal Rebellions

The conflicts with Britain were not the only uprisings emerging in the turbulent years of the 1760s. In addition to the Stamp Act crisis and other challenges to London, there were internal rebellions that had their roots in the class system in New York and New England. In the Hudson Valley in New York, great estates had grown up, in which owners had rented out their land to small farmers. The Revolutionary fervor of the time led many of these tenants to demand ownership of the land they worked. To emphasize their determination, they stopped paying rents. The rebellion soon failed, but other challenges continued. In Vermont, which still was governed by New York, insurgent farmers challenged landowners (many of them the same owners whom tenants had challenged on the Hudson) by taking up arms and demanding ownership of the land they worked. Ethan Allen (later a hero of the Revolutionary War and himself a land speculator) took up the cause of the Green Mountain farmers and accused the landowners of trying to "enslave a free people." Allen eventually succeeded in making Vermont into a separate state, which broke up some of the large estates.

The Townshend Program

When the Rockingham government's policy of appeasement met substantial opposition in England, the king dismissed the ministry and replaced it with a new government led by the aging but still powerful William Pitt, who was now Lord Chatham. Chatham had in the past been sympathetic toward American interests. Once in office, however, he was at times so incapacitated by mental illness that leadership of his administration fell to the chancellor of the exchequer, Charles Townshend.

With the Stamp Act repealed, the greatest remaining American grievance involved the Mutiny (or Quartering) Act of 1765, which required colonists to shelter and supply British troops. The colonists objected not so much to the actual burden as to being required by London to do so. The Massachusetts and New York assemblies went so far as to refuse to grant the mandated supplies to the troops.

Townshend responded in 1767 by disbanding the New York Assembly until the colonists agreed to obey the Mutiny Act. By singling out New York, he believed, he would avoid antagonizing all the colonies at once. He also imposed new taxes (known as the Townshend Duties) on various goods imported to the colonies from England—lead, paint, *Townshend Duties* paper, and tea. Townshend assumed that since these were taxes purely on "external" transactions (imports from overseas), as opposed to the internal transactions the Stamp Act had taxed, the colonists would not object. But all the colonies resented the suspension of the New York Assembly, believing it to be a threat to every colonial government. And all the colonies rejected Townshend's careful distinction between external and internal taxation.

Townshend also established a board of customs commissioners in America. The new commissioners established their headquarters in Boston. They virtually ended smuggling in Boston (although smugglers continued to carry on a busy trade in other colonial seaports). The Boston merchants—angry that the new commission was diverting the lucrative smuggling trade elsewhere—helped organize a boycott of British goods that were subject to the Townshend Duties. Merchants in Philadelphia and New York joined them in a nonimportation agreement in 1768, and later some southern *Nonimportation Agreement* merchants and planters also agreed to cooperate. Throughout the colonies, American homespun and other domestic products became suddenly fashionable.

Late in 1767, Charles Townshend died. In March 1770, the new prime minister, Lord North, hoping to end the American boycott, repealed all the Townshend Duties except the tea tax.

The Boston Massacre

Before news of the repeal reached America, an event in Massachusetts inflamed colonial opinion. The harassment of the new customs commissioners in Boston had grown so intense that the British government had placed four regiments of regular troops in the city. Many of the poorly paid British soldiers looked for jobs in their off-duty hours and thus competed with local workers. Clashes between the two groups were frequent.

On the night of March 5, 1770, a mob of dockworkers, "liberty boys," and others began pelting the sentries at the customs house with rocks and snowballs. Hastily, Captain Thomas Preston of the British regiment lined up several of his men in front of the building to protect it. There was some scuffling; one of the soldiers was knocked down; and in the midst of it all, apparently, several British soldiers fired into the crowd, killing five people.

This murky incident, almost certainly the result of panic and confusion, was quickly transformed by local resistance leaders into the "Boston *The Boston Massacre in Popular Culture* Massacre." It became the subject of such lurid (and inaccurate) accounts as the widely circulated pamphlet *Innocent Blood Crying to God from the Streets of Boston*. A famous engraving by Paul Revere portrayed the massacre as a calculated assault on a peaceful crowd. The British soldiers, tried before a jury of Bostonians, were found guilty only of manslaughter and given token punishment. But colonial pamphlets and newspapers convinced many Americans that the soldiers were guilty of official murder.

The leading figure in fomenting public outrage over the Boston Massacre was Samuel Adams. England, he argued, had become a morass of sin and corruption; only

THE BOSTON MASSACRE (1770), BY PAUL REVERE This sensationalized engraving of the conflict between British troops and Boston laborers is one of many important propaganda documents, by Revere and others, for the Patriot cause in the 1770s. Among the victims of the massacre listed by Revere was Crispus Attucks, probably the first black man to die in the struggle for American independence. (The Library of Congress)

in America did public virtue survive. In 1772, he proposed the creation of a "committee *"Committee of Correspondence"* of correspondence" in Boston to publicize the grievances against England. Other colonies followed Massachusetts's lead, and a loose interco- lonial network of political organizations was soon established that kept the spirit of dissent alive through the 1770s.

THE PHILOSOPHY OF REVOLT

Although a superficial calm settled on the colonies after the Boston Massacre, the crises of the 1760s had helped arouse enduring ideological challenges to English authority and had produced powerful instruments for publicizing colonial grievances. Gradually a political outlook gained a following in America that would ultimately serve to justify revolt.

The ideas that would support the Revolution emerged from many sources. Some were drawn from religious (particularly Puritan) sources or from the political experiences of the colonies. Others came from abroad. Most important, perhaps, were the "radical" ideas of the political opposition in Great Britain. Some were Scots, who considered the English state tyrannical. Others were embittered "country Whigs," who felt excluded from power and considered the existing system corrupt and oppressive. Drawing from some of the great philosophical minds of earlier generations—most notably John Locke—these English dissidents framed a powerful argument against their government.

Central to this emerging ideology was a new concept of what government should be. Because humans were inherently corrupt and selfish, government was necessary to protect individuals from the evil in one another. But because any government was run by corruptible leaders, the people needed safeguards against its possible abuses of power. Most people in both England and America considered the English constitution the best system ever devised to meet these necessities. By distributing power among the three elements of society—the monarchy, the aristocracy, and the common people—the English political system had ensured that no individual or group could exercise unchecked authority. Yet by the mid-seventeenth century, dissidents in both England and America had become convinced that the constitution was in danger. A single center of power—the king and his ministers—was becoming so powerful that it could not be effectively checked.

Such arguments found little sympathy in most of England. The English constitution was not a written document or a fixed set of unchangeable rules. It was a general sense of the "way things are done," and most people in England were willing to accept changes in it. Americans, by contrast, drew from their experience with colonial charters, in which the shape and powers of government were permanently inscribed on paper. They resisted the idea of a flexible, changing set of basic principles.

One basic principle, Americans believed, was the right of people to be taxed only with their own consent—a belief that gradually took shape in   *"No Taxation without Representation"* the popular slogan "No taxation without representation." Whatever the nature of a tax, it could not be levied without the consent of the colonists themselves.

This clamor about "representation" made little sense to the English. According to English constitutional theory, members of Parliament did not represent individuals or particular geographical areas. Instead, each member represented the interests of the whole nation and indeed the whole empire. The many boroughs of England that had no representative in Parliament, the whole of Ireland, and the colonies thousands of miles away—all were thus represented in the Parliament at London, even though they elected no representatives of their own. This was the theory of **"virtual" representation.** But Americans, drawing from their experiences with their town meetings and their colonial assemblies, believed in "actual" representation. Every community was entitled to its own representative, elected by the people of that community. Since the colonists had none of their own representatives in Parliament, it followed that they were not represented there. Americans believed that the colonial assemblies played the same role within the colonies as Parliament did within England. The empire, the Americans argued, was a sort of federation of commonwealths, each with its own legislative body, all tied together by loyalty to the king.

Such ideas illustrated a fundamental difference of opinion between England and America over the question of where ultimate power lay. By arguing that Parliament had the right to legislate for the empire as a whole but that only the provincial assemblies could legislate for the individual colonies, Americans were in effect arguing for a division of   *Sovereignty Debated* **sovereignty.** Parliament would be sovereign in some matters, the assemblies in others. To the British, such an argument was absurd. In any system of government there must be a single, ultimate authority. And since the empire was, in their view, a single, undivided unit, there could be only one authority within it: the English government of king and Parliament.

TAVERNS IN REVOLUTIONARY MASSACHUSETTS

In colonial Massachusetts, as in many other American colonies in the 1760s and 1770s, taverns (or "public houses," as they were often known) were crucial to the development of popular resistance to British rule. The Puritan culture of New England created some resistance to taverns, and reformers tried to regulate or close them to reduce the problems caused by "public drunkenness," "lewd behavior," and "anarchy." But as the commercial life of the colonies expanded and more people began living in towns and cities, taverns became a central institution in American social life—and eventually in its political life as well.

Taverns were appealing, of course, because they provided alcoholic drinks in a culture where the craving for alcohol—and the extent of drunkenness—was very high. But taverns had other attractions as well. They were one of the few places where people could meet and talk openly in public; indeed, many colonists considered the life of the tavern as the only vaguely democratic experience available to them. The tavern was a mostly male institution, just as politics was considered a mostly male concern. And so the fusion of male camaraderie and political discourse emerged naturally out of the tavern culture.

As the Revolutionary crisis deepened, taverns and pubs became the central meeting places for airing the ideas that fueled resistance to British policies. Educated and uneducated men alike joined in animated discussions of events. Those who could not read—and there were many—could learn about the contents of Revolutionary pamphlets from listening to tavern conversations. They could join in the discussion of the new republican ideas emerging in America by participating in tavern celebrations of, for example, the anniversaries of resistance to the Stamp Act. Those anniversaries inspired elaborate toasts in public houses throughout the colonies.

In an age before wide distribution of newspapers, taverns and tavernkeepers were important sources of information about the political and social turmoil of the time. Taverns were also the settings for political events. In 1770, for example, a report circulated through the taverns of Danvers, Massachusetts, about a local man who was continuing to sell tea despite the colonial boycott. The Sons of Liberty brought the seller to the Bell Tavern and persuaded him to sign a confession and apology before a crowd of defiant men in the public room.

Almost all politicians who wanted any real contact with the public found it necessary to visit taverns in colonial Massachusetts. Samuel Adams spent considerable time in the public houses of Boston, where he sought to encourage resistance to British rule while taking care to drink moderately so as not to erode his stature as a leader. His cousin John Adams, although somewhat more skeptical of taverns and more sensitive to the vices they encouraged, also recognized their political value. In taverns, he once said, "bastards and legislatores are frequently begotten." •

UNDERSTAND, ANALYZE, & EVALUATE

1. Why were taverns so important in educating colonists about the relationship with Britain?
2. What gathering places today serve the same purposes as taverns did in colonial America?

TAVERNS AND POLITICS The Green Dragon Tavern is where protesters planned the Boston Tea Party.

SITES OF RESISTANCE

Colonists kept the growing spirit of resistance alive in many ways, but most of all through writing and talking. Dissenting leaflets, pamphlets, and books circulated widely through the colonies. In towns and cities, men gathered in churches, schools, town squares, and, above all, taverns to discuss politics.

Taverns were also places where resistance pamphlets and leaflets could be distributed and where meetings for the planning of protests and demonstrations could be held. Massachusetts had the most elaborately developed tavern culture, which was perhaps one reason why the spirit of resistance grew more quickly there than anywhere else. (See "Patterns of Popular Culture: Taverns in Revolutionary Massachusetts.")

The apparent calm in America in the 1770s hid a growing sense of resentment about the continued enforcement of the Navigation Acts. Popular anger was visible in occasional acts of rebellion. At one point, colonists seized a British revenue ship on   *Gaspée Incident* the lower Delaware River. In 1772, angry residents of Rhode Island boarded the British schooner *Gaspée,* set it afire, and sank it.

THE TEA EXCITEMENT

The Revolutionary fervor of the 1760s intensified as a result of a new act of Parliament— one that involved the business of selling tea. In 1773, Britain's East India Company (on the verge of bankruptcy) was sitting on large stocks of tea that it could not sell in England. In an effort to save it, the government passed the Tea Act of 1773, which gave   *The Tea Act* the company the right to export its merchandise directly to the colonies without paying any of the regular taxes that were imposed on colonial merchants, who had traditionally served as the intermediaries in such transactions. With these privileges, the company could undersell American merchants and monopolize the colonial tea trade.

The act angered influential colonial merchants and, more important, revived American passions about the issue of taxation without representation. The law provided no new tax on tea. But the original Townshend duty on the commodity survived; and the East India Company was now exempt from paying it. Lord North had assumed that most colonists would welcome the new law because it would reduce the price of tea to consumers by removing the intermediaries. But resistance leaders in America argued that the law, in effect, represented an unconstitutional tax on American merchants. The colonists responded by boycotting tea.

Unlike earlier protests, most of which had involved relatively small numbers of people, the tea boycott mobilized large segments of the population. It also helped link the colonies together in a common experience of mass popular protest. Particularly important to the movement were the activities of colonial women, who led the boycott. The Daughters of *Daughters of Liberty* Liberty—a recently formed women's patriotic organization—proclaimed, "rather than Freedom, we'll part with our Tea."

In the last weeks of 1773, with strong popular support, some colonial leaders made plans to prevent the East India Company from landing its cargoes. In Philadelphia and New York, determined colonists kept the tea from leaving the company's ships, and in Charles Town, South Carolina, they stored it away in a public warehouse. In Boston, local patriots staged a spectacular drama. On the evening of December 16, 1773, three companies of fifty men each, masquerading as Mohawk Indians, went aboard three *The Boston "Tea Party"* ships, broke open the tea chests, and heaved them into the harbor. As the electrifying news of the Boston "tea party" spread, colonists in other seaports staged similar acts of resistance.

Parliament retaliated in four acts of 1774: closing the port of Boston, drastically reducing the powers of self-government in Massachusetts, permitting royal officers in America to be tried for crimes in other colonies or in England, and providing for the quartering of troops by the colonists. These Coercive Acts were more widely known in America as the "Intolerable Acts."

The Coercive Acts backfired. Far from isolating Massachusetts, they made it a martyr in the eyes of residents of other colonies and sparked new resistance up and down the coast. Colonial legislatures passed a series of resolves supporting Massachusetts. *Consequences of the Coercive Acts* Women's groups mobilized to extend the boycotts of British goods and to create substitutes for the tea, textiles, and other commodities they were shunning. In Edenton, North Carolina, fifty-one women signed an agreement in October 1774 declaring their "sincere adherence" to the anti-British resolutions of their provincial assembly and proclaiming their duty to do "every thing as far as lies in our power" to support the "publick good."

COOPERATION AND WAR

Beginning in 1765, colonial leaders developed a variety of organizations for converting popular discontent into action—organizations that in time formed the basis for an independent government.

NEW SOURCES OF AUTHORITY

The passage of authority from the royal government to the colonists themselves began on the local level. In colony after colony, local institutions responded to the resistance movement by simply seizing authority. At times, entirely new institutions emerged.

The most effective of these new groups were the committees of correspondence. Virginia established the first intercolonial committees of correspondence, which helped make possible continuous cooperation among the colonies. After the royal governor dissolved the assembly in 1774, colonists met in the Raleigh Tavern at Williamsburg, declared that the Intolerable Acts menaced the liberties of every colony, and issued a call for a Continental Congress.

Delegates from all the colonies except Georgia were present when, in September 1774, the First Continental Congress convened in Philadelphia. They made *The First Continental Congress* five major decisions. First, they rejected a plan for a colonial union under British authority. Second, they endorsed a relatively moderate statement of grievances, which addressed the king as "Most Gracious Sovereign," but which also included a demand for the repeal of all oppressive legislation passed since 1763. Third, they approved a series of resolutions recommending that military preparations be made for defense against possible attack by the British troops in Boston. Fourth, they agreed to a series of boycotts that they hoped would stop all trade with Great Britain, and they formed a "Continental Association" to see that these agreements were enforced. Fifth, the delegates agreed to meet again the following spring.

During the winter, the Parliament in London debated proposals for conciliating the colonists, and early in 1775 Lord North finally won approval for a series of measures known as the Conciliatory Propositions. Parliament proposed that the colonies would tax themselves at Parliament's demand. With this offer, Lord North hoped to separate the American moderates, whom he believed represented the views of the majority, from the extremist minority. But his offer was too little and too late. It did not reach America until after the first shots of war had been fired.

LEXINGTON AND CONCORD

For months, the farmers and townspeople of Massachusetts had been gathering arms and ammunition and preparing "minutemen" to fight on a moment's notice. The *"Minutemen"* Continental Congress had approved preparations for a defensive war, and the citizen-soldiers waited only for an aggressive move by the British regulars in Boston.

There, General Thomas Gage, commanding the British garrison, considered his army too small to do anything without reinforcements. He resisted the advice *General Thomas Gage* of less cautious officers, who assured him that the Americans would back down quickly before any show of British force. When General Gage received orders to arrest the rebel leaders Sam Adams and John Hancock, known to be in the vicinity of Lexington, he still hesitated. But when he heard that the minutemen had stored a large supply of gunpowder in Concord (eighteen miles from Boston), he decided to act. On the night of April 18, 1775, he sent a detachment of about 1,000 men out toward Lexington, hoping to surprise the colonials and seize the illegal supplies without bloodshed.

But Patriots in Boston were watching the British movements closely, and during the night two horsemen, William Dawes and Paul Revere, rode out to warn the villages and farms. When the redcoats arrived in Lexington the next day, several dozen minutemen awaited them on the town common. Shots were fired and minutemen fell; eight were killed and ten wounded. Advancing to Concord, the British discovered that the Americans had hastily removed most of the powder supply. All along the road back to Boston, the British were harassed by the gunfire of farmers hiding behind trees, rocks, and stone walls. By the end of the day, the British had lost almost three times as many men as the Americans.

The first shots—the "shots heard 'round the world," as Americans later called them—had been fired. But who had fired them first? According to one of the minutemen at Lexington, the British commander, Major Thomas Pitcairn, had shouted to the colonists on his arrival, "Disperse, ye rebels!" When they ignored him, he ordered his troops to fire. British officers and soldiers claimed that the minutemen had fired first. Whatever the truth, the rebels succeeded in circulating their account well ahead of the British version, adorning it with tales of British atrocities. The effect was to rally thousands of colonists to the rebel cause.

THE BATTLES OF LEXINGTON AND CONCORD, 1775   This map shows the fabled series of events that led to the first battle of the American Revolution. On the night of April 18, 1775, Paul Revere and William Dawes rode out from Boston to warn the outlying towns of the approach of British troops. Revere was captured just west of Lexington, but Dawes escaped and returned to Boston. The next morning, British forces moved out of Boston toward Lexington, where they met armed American minutemen on the Lexington common and exchanged fire. The British dispersed the Americans in Lexington. But they next moved on to Concord, where they encountered more armed minutemen, clashed again, and were driven back toward Boston. All along their line of march, they were harassed by riflemen. • *What impact did the Battles of Lexington and Concord (and the later Battle of Bunker Hill, also shown on this map) have on colonial sentiment toward the British?*

The War Begins   It was not immediately clear at the time that the skirmishes at Lexington and Concord were the first battles of a war. But whether people recognized it at the time or not, the War for Independence had begun.

CONCLUSION

When the French and Indian War ended in 1763, it might have seemed reasonable to expect that relations between the English colonists in America and Great Britain itself would have been cemented more firmly than ever. But in fact, the resolution of that conflict altered the imperial relationship forever, in ways that ultimately drove Americans to rebel against English rule and begin a war for independence. To the British, the lesson of the French and Indian War was that the colonies in America needed firmer control from London. The empire was now much bigger, and it needed better administration. The war had produced great debts, and the Americans—among the principal beneficiaries of the war—should help pay them. And so for more than a decade after the end of the fighting, the British tried one strategy after another to tighten control over and extract money from the colonies.

To the colonists, this effort to tighten imperial rule seemed both a betrayal of the sacrifices they had made in the war and a challenge to their long-developing assumptions about the rights of English people to rule themselves. Gradually, white Americans came to see in the British policies evidence of a conspiracy to establish tyranny in the New World. And so throughout the 1760s and 1770s, the colonists developed an ideology of resistance and defiance. By the time the first shots were fired in the American Revolution in 1775, Britain and America had come to view each other as two very different societies. Their differences, which soon appeared irreconcilable, propelled them into a war that would change the course of history for both sides.

KEY TERMS/PEOPLE/PLACES/EVENTS

Albany Plan 85
Benjamin Franklin 94
Boston Massacre 97
Boston Tea Party 102
Coercive Acts 102
committees of
    correspondence 102
Creole 85
Currency Act 92
Daughters of
    Liberty 102

First Continental
    Congress 103
Fort Necessity 86
French and Indian War 86
George Grenville 92
George III 91
impressment 87
Iroquois Confederacy 85
Mutiny Act 92
Patrick Henry 93
Paxton Boys 92

Proclamation of 1763 92
Seven Years' War 87
Sons of Liberty 96
sovereignty 99
Stamp Act 93
Sugar Act 92
Tea Act 101
Townshend Duties 97
Virginia Resolves 93
virtual representation 99
William Pitt 87

RECALL AND REFLECT

1. What Native Americans fought in the French and Indian War, and how did the war's outcome affect them? What about Native Americans who did not participate in the war?
2. How and why did the colonists' attitude toward Britain change from the time of the Seven Years' War to the beginning of the American Revolution?
3. What were the philosophical underpinnings of the colonists' revolt against Britain?
4. What did the slogan "No taxation without representation" mean, and why was it a rallying cry for the colonists?

5 THE AMERICAN REVOLUTION

THE STATES UNITED

THE WAR FOR INDEPENDENCE

WAR AND SOCIETY

THE CREATION OF STATE GOVERNMENTS

THE SEARCH FOR A NATIONAL GOVERNMENT

LOOKING AHEAD

1. What were the military strategies (both British and American) of each of the three phases of the American Revolution? How successful were these strategies during each phase?

2. How did the American Revolution become an international conflict, not just a colonial war against the British?

3. How did the new national government of the United States reflect the assumptions of republicanism?

TWO STRUGGLES OCCURRED SIMULTANEOUSLY DURING the seven years of war that began in April 1775. The first was the military conflict with Great Britain. The second was a political conflict within America.

The military conflict was, by the standards of later wars, a relatively modest one. By the standards of its own day, however, it was an unusually savage conflict, pitting not only army against army but the civilian population against a powerful external force. The shift of the war from a traditional, conventional struggle to a new kind of conflict—a revolutionary war for liberation—is what made it possible for the United States to defeat the more powerful British.

At the same time, Americans were wrestling with the great political questions that the conflict necessarily produced: first, whether to demand independence from Britain; second, how to structure the new nation they had proclaimed; and third, how to deal with questions that the Revolution had raised about slavery, the rights of Indians, the role of women, and the limits of religious tolerance in the new American society.

THE STATES UNITED

Although some Americans had long expected a military conflict with Britain, the actual beginning of hostilities in 1775 found the colonies generally unprepared for war against the world's greatest armed power.

DEFINING AMERICAN WAR AIMS

Three weeks after the Battles of Lexington and Concord, when the Second Continental Congress met in Philadelphia, delegates from every colony (except Georgia, which had not yet sent a representative) agreed to support the war. But they disagreed about its purpose. At one extreme was a group led by the Adams cousins (John and Samuel), Richard Henry Lee of Virginia, and others, who already favored independence; at the other extreme was a group led by such moderates as John Dickinson of Pennsylvania, who hoped for a quick reconciliation with Great Britain.

Most Americans believed at first that they were fighting not for independence but for a resolution of grievances against the British Empire. During the first year of fighting, however, many colonists began to change their minds. The costs of the war were so high that the original war aims began to seem too modest to justify them. Many colonists were enraged when the British began trying to recruit Indians, African slaves, and German mercenaries (the hated "Hessians") against them. When the British government blockaded colonial ports and rejected all efforts at conciliation, many colonists concluded that independence was the only remaining option.

Thomas Paine's impassioned pamphlet *Common Sense* crystallized these feelings in January 1776. Paine, who had emigrated from England less than two years before, wanted to turn the anger of Americans away from particular parliamentary measures and toward what he considered the root of the problem—the English constitution itself.

1775
Second Continental Congress

Washington commands American forces

1776
Paine's *Common Sense*

Declaration of Independence

Battle of Trenton

1777
Articles of Confederation adopted

1778
French-American alliance

British defeat at Saratoga

1781
Articles of Confederation ratified

1783
Treaty of Paris

Cornwallis surrenders at Yorktown

1784
Postwar depression begins

1786
Shays's Rebellion

1787
Northwest Ordinance

THE AMERICAN REVOLUTION

The long-standing debate over the origins of the American Revolution has tended to reflect two broad schools of interpretation. One sees the Revolution largely as a political and intellectual event; the other, as a social and economic phenomenon.

The Revolutionary generation itself portrayed the conflict as a struggle over ideals, and this interpretation prevailed through most of the nineteenth century. But in the early twentieth century, historians influenced by the reform currents of the progressive era began to identify social and economic forces that they believed had contributed to the rebellion. Carl Becker, for example, wrote in a 1909 study of New York that two questions had shaped the Revolution: "The first was the question of home rule; the second was the question . . . of who should rule at home." The colonists were not only fighting the British, but also were engaged in a kind of civil war, a contest between radicals and conservatives.

Other historians elaborated on Becker's thesis. J. Franklin Jameson, writing in 1926, argued, "Many economic desires, many social aspirations, were set free by the political struggle, many aspects of society profoundly altered by the forces thus let loose." Arthur M. Schlesinger maintained in a 1917 book that colonial merchants, motivated by their own interest in escaping the restrictive policies of British mercantilism, aroused American resistance in the 1760s and 1770s.

Beginning in the 1950s, a new generation of scholars began to reemphasize the role of ideology and de-emphasize the role of economic interests. Robert E. Brown (in 1955) and Edmund S. Morgan (in 1956) both argued that most eighteenth-century Americans shared common political principles and that the social and economic conflicts other historians had identified were not severe. The rhetoric of the Revolution, they suggested, was not propaganda but a real reflection of the ideas of the colonists. Bernard Bailyn, in *The Ideological Origins of the American Revolution* (1967), demonstrated the complex roots of the ideas behind the Revolution and argued that this carefully constructed political stance was not a disguise for economic interests but a genuine ideology, rooted in deeply held convictions about rights and power. The Revolution, he exclaimed, "was above all an ideological, constitutional, political struggle and not primarily a controversy between social groups undertaken to force changes in the organization of the society or the economy."

By the late 1960s, a new generation of historians—many influenced by the New Left—were reviving economic interpretations of the Revolution by exploring the social and economic tensions that they claimed shaped the Revolutionary struggle. Historians cited economic distress and the actions of mobs in colonial cities, the economic pressures on colonial merchants, and other changes in the character of American culture and society as critical prerequisites for the growth of the Revolutionary movement. Gary Nash, attempting to reconcile the emphasis on economic interests with the role of ideology, argued that the two things were not incompatible. "Everyone has economic interests," he claimed, "and everyone . . . has an ideology." Exploring the relationship between the two, he argued, is critical to historians'

THE BRITISH SURRENDER   This contemporary drawing depicts the formal surrender of British troops at Yorktown on October 19, 1781. Columns of American troops and a large French fleet flank the surrender ceremony, suggesting part of the reason for the British defeat. General Cornwallis, the commander of British forces in Virginia, did not himself attend the surrender. He sent a deputy in his place.   (© MPI/Hulton Archive/Getty Images)

ability to understand either. Also, as Linda Kerber and others have argued, the newer social interpretations have raised increasing interest in the experience of workers, slaves, women, Native Americans, and other groups previously considered marginal to public life as part of the explanation of the Revolutionary struggle.

Finally, Gordon Wood, in *The Radicalism of the American Revolution* (1992), revived an idea once popular and recently unfashionable: that the Revolution was a genuinely radical event that led to the breakdown of such long-standing characteristics of society

as deference, patriarchy, and traditional gender relations. Class conflict may not have caused the Revolution, he argued, but the Revolution had a profound, even radical, effect on society nevertheless.   •

UNDERSTAND, ANALYZE, & EVALUATE

1. In what way was the American Revolution an ideological struggle?
2. In what way was the American Revolution a social and economic conflict?

It was simple common sense, Paine wrote, for Americans to break completely with a political system that could inflict such brutality on its own people. *Common Sense* sold more than 100,000 copies in only a few months and helped build support for the idea of independence in the early months of 1776. (For more on the origins of the rebellion, see "Debating the Past: The American Revolution.")

THE DECLARATION OF INDEPENDENCE

In the meantime, the Continental Congress in Philadelphia was moving toward a complete break with England. At the beginning of the summer, it appointed a committee to draft a formal declaration of independence; and on July 2, 1776, it adopted a resolution: "That these *Independence Declared*   United Colonies are, and, of right, ought to be, free and independent states; that they are absolved from all allegiance to the British crown, and that all political connexion between them and the state of Great Britain is, and ought to be, totally dissolved." Two days later, on July 4, Congress approved the Declaration of Independence itself, which provided formal justifications for this resolution.

The Declaration launched a period of energetic political innovation, as one colony after another reconstituted itself as a "state." By 1781, most states had produced written constitutions for themselves. At the national level, however, the process was more uncertain. In *Articles of Confederation*   November 1777, finally, Congress adopted a plan for union, the Articles of Confederation. The document confirmed the existing weak, decentralized system.

Thomas Jefferson, a thirty-three-year-old Virginian, wrote most of the Declaration, with *Thomas Jefferson*   help from Benjamin Franklin and John Adams. The Declaration expressed concepts that had been circulating throughout the colonies over the previous few months in the form of at least ninety other, local "declarations of independence"—declarations drafted up and down the coast by town meetings, artisan and militia organizations, county officials, grand juries, Sons of Liberty, and colonial assemblies. Jefferson borrowed heavily from these texts.

The final document had two parts. In the first, the Declaration restated the familiar contract theory of John Locke: that governments were formed to protect what Jefferson called "life, liberty and the pursuit of happiness." In the second part, it listed the alleged crimes of the king, who, with the backing of Parliament, had violated his contract with the colonists and thus had forfeited all claim to their loyalty.

MOBILIZING FOR WAR

Financing the war was difficult. Congress had no authority to levy taxes on its own, and when it requisitioned money from the state governments, none contributed more than a small part of its expected share. Congress had little success borrowing from the public, since few Americans could afford to buy bonds. Instead, Congress issued paper money. Printing presses turned out enormous amounts of "Continental currency," and the states printed currencies of their own. The result, predictably, was soaring inflation, and Congress soon found that the Continental currency was virtually worthless. Ultimately, Congress financed the war mostly by borrowing from other nations.

After a first surge of patriotism in 1775, volunteer soldiers became scarce. States had to pay bounties or use a draft to recruit the needed men. At first, the militiamen remained under the control of their respective states. But Congress recognized the need for a centralized military command, and it created a Continental army with a single commander in

REVOLUTIONARY SOLDIERS   Jean Baptist de Verger, a French officer serving in America during the Revolution, kept an illustrated journal of his experiences. Here he portrays four American soldiers carrying different kinds of arms: a black infantryman with a light rifle, a musketman, a rifleman, and an artilleryman.   (© Anne S.K. Brown Military Collection, Brown University Library)

chief: George Washington. Washington, an early advocate of independence with considerable military experience, was admired, respected, and trusted by nearly all Patriots. He took command of the new army in June 1775. With the aid of foreign military experts such as the Marquis de Lafayette from France and the Baron von Steuben from Prussia, he built a force that prevailed against the mightiest power in the world. Even more important, perhaps, Washington's steadiness, courage, and dedication to his cause   *Washington Takes Command* provided the army—and the people—with a symbol of stability around which they could rally.

THE WAR FOR INDEPENDENCE

As the War for Independence began, the British seemed to have overwhelming advantages: the greatest navy and the best-equipped army in the world, the resources of an empire, a coherent structure of command. Yet the United States had advantages, too. Americans were fighting on their own ground. They were more committed to the conflict than were the British. And, beginning in 1777, they received substantial aid from abroad.

But the American victory was also a result of a series of early blunders and miscalculations by the British. It was, finally, a result of the transformation of the war—through three distinct phases—into a new kind of conflict that the British military, for all its strength, was unable to win.

THE FIRST PHASE: NEW ENGLAND

For the first year of the conflict—from the spring of 1775 to the spring of 1776—many English authorities thought that British forces were not fighting a real war, but simply quelling pockets of rebellion in the contentious area around Boston. After the redcoats

THE REVOLUTION IN THE NORTH, 1775–1776 After initial battles in and around Boston, the British forces left Massachusetts and (after a brief stay in Halifax, Canada) moved south to New York. In the meantime, American forces moved north in an effort to capture British strongholds in Montreal and Quebec, with little success. • *Why would the British have considered New York a better base than Boston?*

withdrew from Lexington and Concord in April, American forces besieged them in Boston. *Bunker Hill* In the Battle of Bunker Hill (actually fought on Breed's Hill) on June 17, 1775, the Patriots suffered severe casualties and withdrew. But they inflicted even greater losses on the enemy. The siege continued. Early in 1776, finally, the British decided that Boston was a poor place from which to fight. It was in the center of the most anti-British part of America and tactically difficult to defend because it was easily isolated and surrounded. And so, on March 17, 1776, the redcoats evacuated Boston for Halifax, Nova Scotia, with hundreds of Loyalist refugees (Americans still loyal to England and the king).

In the meantime, a band of southern Patriots, at Moore's Creek Bridge in North Carolina, crushed an uprising of Loyalists on February 27, 1776. And to the north, the Americans *Invasion of Canada* began an invasion of Canada. Generals Benedict Arnold and Richard Montgomery unsuccessfully threatened Quebec in late 1775 and early 1776 in a battle in which Montgomery was killed and Arnold was wounded.

By the spring of 1776, it had become clear to the British that the conflict was not just a local phenomenon. The American campaigns in Canada, the agitation in the South, and the growing evidence of colonial unity all suggested that England must prepare to fight a much larger conflict.

THE SECOND PHASE: THE MID-ATLANTIC REGION

During the next phase of the war, which lasted from 1776 until early 1778, the British were in a good position to win. Indeed, had it not been for a series of blunders and misfortunes, they probably would have crushed the rebellion.

The British regrouped quickly after their retreat from Boston. During the summer of 1776, hundreds of British ships and 32,000 British soldiers arrived in New York, under the command of General William Howe. He offered Congress a choice: *William Howe* surrender with royal pardon or face a battle against apparently overwhelming odds. To oppose Howe's great force, Washington could muster only about 19,000 soldiers; he had no navy at all. Even so, the Americans rejected Howe's offer. The British then pushed the Patriot forces out of Manhattan and off Long Island and drove them in slow retreat over the plains of New Jersey, across the Delaware River, and into Pennsylvania.

The British settled down for the winter in northern and central New Jersey, with an outpost of Hessians at Trenton, on the Delaware River. But Washington did not sit still. On Christmas night 1776, he daringly recrossed the icy Delaware River, surprised and scattered the Hessians, and occupied Trenton. Then he advanced to *Trenton and Princeton* Princeton and drove a force of redcoats from their base in the college there. But Washington was unable to hold either Princeton or Trenton and finally took refuge in the hills around Morristown. Still, the campaign of 1776 came to an end with the Americans having triumphed in two minor battles and with their main army still intact.

For the campaigns of 1777, the British devised a strategy to divide the United States in two. Howe would move from New York up the Hudson to Albany, while another force

THE REVOLUTION IN THE MIDDLE COLONIES, 1776–1778 These maps illustrate the major campaigns of the Revolution in the middle colonies—New York, New Jersey, and Pennsylvania—between 1776 and 1778. The large map on the left shows the two prongs of the British strategy: first, a movement of British forces south from Canada into the Hudson Valley and, second, a movement of other British forces, under General William Howe, out from New York. The strategy was designed to trap the American army between the two British movements. • *What movements of Howe helped thwart that plan?* The two smaller maps on the right show a detailed picture of some of the major battles. The upper one reveals the surprising American victory at Saratoga. The lower one shows a series of inconclusive battles between New York and Philadelphia in 1777 and 1778.

John Burgoyne   would come down from Canada to meet him. John Burgoyne, commander of the northern force, began a two-pronged attack to the south along both the Mohawk and the upper Hudson approaches to Albany. But having set the plan in motion, Howe strangely abandoned his part of it. Instead of moving north to meet Burgoyne, he went south and captured Philadelphia, hoping that his seizure of the rebel capital would bring the war to a speedy conclusion. Philadelphia fell with little resistance—and the Continental Congress moved into exile in York, Pennsylvania. After launching an unsuccessful attack against the British on October 4 at Germantown (just outside Philadelphia), Washington went into winter quarters at Valley Forge.

Howe's move to Philadelphia left Burgoyne to carry out the campaign in the north alone. He sent Colonel Barry St. Leger up the St. Lawrence River toward Lake Ontario. Burgoyne himself advanced directly down the upper Hudson Valley and easily seized Fort Ticonderoga. But Burgoyne soon experienced two staggering defeats. In one of them—at Oriskany, New York, on August 6—Patriots held off St. Leger's force of Indians and Loyalists. That allowed Benedict Arnold to close off the Mohawk Valley to St. Leger's advance. In the other battle—at Bennington, Vermont, on August 16—New England militiamen mauled a detachment that Burgoyne had sent to seek supplies. Short of materials, with all help cut off, Burgoyne fought several costly engagements and then withdrew to *Patriot Victory at Saratoga*   Saratoga, where General Horatio Gates surrounded him. On October 17, 1777, Burgoyne surrendered.

The campaign in upstate New York was not just a British defeat. It was a setback for the ambitious efforts of several Iroquois leaders. Although the Iroquois Confederacy had declared its neutrality in the Revolutionary War in 1776, some of its members allied themselves with the British, among them a Mohawk brother and sister, Joseph and Mary *Joseph and Mary Brant*   Brant. This ill-fated alliance further divided the already weakened Iroquois Confederacy, because only three of the Iroquois nations (the Mohawk, the Seneca, and the Cayuga) followed the Brants in support of the British. A year after the defeat at Oriskany, Iroquois forces joined British troops in a series of raids on white settlements in upstate New York. Patriot forces under the command of General John Sullivan harshly retaliated, wreaking such destruction on Indian settlements that large groups of Iroquois fled north into Canada to seek refuge. Many never returned.

SECURING AID FROM ABROAD

The leaders of the American effort knew that victory would not be likely without aid from abroad. Their most promising allies, they realized, were the French, who stood to gain from seeing Britain lose a crucial part of its empire. At first, France provided the United States with badly needed supplies. But they remained reluctant to formally acknowledge the new nation, despite the efforts of Benjamin Franklin in Paris to lobby for aid and diplomatic recognition. France's foreign minister, the Count de Vergennes, wanted evidence that the Americans had a real chance of winning. The British defeat at Saratoga, he believed, offered that evidence.

When the news from Saratoga arrived in London and Paris in early December 1777, a shaken Lord North made a new peace offer: complete home rule within the empire for Americans if they would quit the war. Vergennes feared the Americans might accept the *French Diplomatic Recognition*   offer and thus destroy France's opportunity to weaken Britain. Encouraged by Franklin, he agreed on February 6, 1778, to give formal recognition to the United States and to provide it with greatly expanded military assistance.

France's decision made the war an international conflict, which over the years pitted France, Spain, and the Netherlands against Great Britain. That helped reduce the resources available for the English effort in America. But France remained America's most important ally.

THE FINAL PHASE: THE SOUTH

The American victory at Saratoga and the intervention of the French transformed the war. Instead of mounting a full-scale military struggle against the American army, the British now tried to enlist the support of those elements of the American *Britain's Southern Strategy* population who were still loyal to the crown. Since Loyalist sentiment was strongest in the South, and since the English also hoped slaves would rally to their cause, the main focus of the British effort shifted there.

The new strategy failed dismally. British forces spent three years (from 1778 to 1781) moving through the South. But they had badly overestimated the extent of Loyalist sentiment. And they had underestimated the logistical problems they would face. Patriot forces could move at will throughout the region, blending in with the civilian population and

THE REVOLUTION IN THE SOUTH, 1778–1781 The final phase of the American Revolution occurred largely in the South, which the British thought would be a more receptive region for their troops. • *Why did they believe that?* This map reveals the many scattered military efforts of the British and the Americans in those years, none of them conclusive. It also shows the final chapter of the Revolution around the Chesapeake Bay and the James River. • *What errors led the British to their surrender at Yorktown?*

THE AGE OF REVOLUTIONS

The American Revolution was a result of tensions and conflicts between imperial Britain and its North American colonies. But it was also both a part, and a cause, of what historians have come to call an "age of revolutions," which spread through much of the Western world in the last decades of the eighteenth century and the first decades of the nineteenth.

The modern idea of revolution—the overturning of old systems and regimes and the creation of new ones—was to a large degree a product of the ideas of the Enlightenment. Among those ideas was the notion of popular sovereignty, articulated by, among others, the English philosopher John Locke. Locke argued that political authority did not derive from the divine right of kings or the inherited authority of aristocracies, but from the consent of the governed. A related Enlightenment idea was the concept of individual freedom, which challenged the traditional belief that governments had the right to prescribe the way people act, speak, and even think. Champions of individual freedom in the eighteenth century—among them the French philosopher Voltaire—advocated religious toleration and freedom of thought and expression. The Enlightenment also helped spread the idea of political and legal equality for all people—the end of special privileges for aristocrats and elites and the right of all citizens to participate in the formation of policies and laws. Jean-Jacques Rousseau, a Swiss-French theorist, helped define these new ideas of equality. Together, Enlightenment ideas formed the basis for challenges to existing social orders in many parts of the Western world, and eventually beyond it.

The American Revolution was the first and in many ways most influential of the Enlightenment-derived uprisings against established orders. It served as an inspiration to people in other lands who opposed unpopular regimes. In 1789, a little over a decade after the beginning of the American Revolution, dissenters rebelled in France—at first through a revolt by the national legislature against the king, and then through a series of increasingly radical challenges to established authority. The monarchy was abolished (and the king and queen publicly executed in 1793), the authority of the Catholic Church was challenged and greatly weakened, and at the peak of revolutionary chaos during the Jacobin period (1793–1794), over 40,000 suspected enemies of the revolution were executed and hundreds of thousands of others imprisoned. The radical phase of the revolution came to an end in 1799, when Napoleon Bonaparte, a young general, seized power and began to build a new French empire. But France's *ancien regime* of king and aristocracy never wholly revived.

Together, the French and American revolutions helped inspire uprisings in many other parts of the Atlantic World. In 1791, a major slave revolt began in Haiti and soon attracted over 100,000 rebels. The army of enslaved people defeated both the white settlers of the island and the French colonial armies sent to quell their rebellion. Under the leadership of Toussaint-Louverture, they began to agitate for independence, which they obtained on January 1, 1804, a few months after Toussaint's death.

The ideas of these revolutions spread next into Spanish and Portuguese colonies in the Americas, particularly among the so-called Creoles, people of European ancestry born in the Americas. In the late eighteenth century, they began to resist the continuing authority of colonial officials from Spain and Portugal and to demand a greater say in governing their own lands. When Napoleon's French armies

STORMING THE BASTILLE This painting portrays the storming of the great Parisian fortress and prison, the Bastille, on July 14, 1789. The Bastille was a despised symbol of royal tyranny to many of the French, because of the arbitrarily arrested and imprisoned people who were sent there. The July assault was designed to release the prisoners, but in fact the revolutionaries found only seven people in the vast fortress. Even so, the capture of the Bastille—which marked one of the first moments in which ordinary Frenchmen joined the Revolution—became one of the great moments in modern French history. The anniversary of the event, "Bastille Day," remains the French national holiday. (© Musee de la Ville de Paris, Musee Carnavalet, Paris, France/Bridgeman Images)

invaded Spain and Portugal in 1807, they weakened the ability of the European regimes to sustain authority over their American colonies. In the years that followed, revolutions swept through much of Latin America. Mexico became an independent nation in 1821, and provinces of Central America that had once been part of Mexico (Guatemala, El Salvador, Honduras, Nicaragua, and Costa Rica) established their independence three years later. Simón Bolívar, modeling his efforts on those of George Washington, led a great revolutionary movement that won independence for Brazil in 1822 and also helped lead revolutionary campaigns in Venezuela, Ecuador, and Peru—all of which won their independence in the 1820s. At about the same time, Greek patriots—drawing from the examples of other revolutionary nations—launched a movement to win their independence from the Ottoman Empire, which finally succeeded in 1830.

The age of revolutions left many new, independent nations in its wake. It did not, however, succeed in establishing the ideals of popular sovereignty, individual freedom, and political equality in all the nations it affected. Slavery survived in the United States and in many areas of Latin America. New forms of aristocracy and even monarchy emerged in France, Mexico, Brazil, and elsewhere. Women—many of whom had hoped the revolutionary age would win them new rights—made few legal or political gains in this era. But the ideals that the revolutionary era introduced to the Western world continued to shape the histories of nations throughout the nineteenth century and beyond. •

UNDERSTAND, ANALYZE, & EVALUATE

1. How did the American Revolution influence the French Revolution, and how were other nations affected by it?
2. What was the significance of the revolution in Haiti, and how much attention did it get in other nations?

leaving the British unable to distinguish friend from foe. The British, by contrast, suffered all the disadvantages of an army in hostile territory.

It was this phase of the conflict that made the war "revolutionary"—not only because *"Revolutionary" Phase* it introduced a new kind of warfare, but because it had the effect of mobilizing and politicizing large groups of the population. With the war expanding into previously isolated communities, and with many civilians forced to involve themselves whether they liked it or not, the political climate of the United States grew more heated than ever. And support for independence, far from being crushed, greatly increased.

In the North, the fighting settled into a stalemate. Sir Henry Clinton replaced the unsuccessful William Howe in May 1778 and moved what had been Howe's army from Philadelphia back to New York. The British troops stayed there for more than a year. In the meantime, George Rogers Clark led a Patriot expedition over the Appalachian Mountains and captured settlements in the Illinois country from the British and their Indian allies. On the whole, however, there was relatively little military activity in the North after 1778. There was, *Benedict Arnold's Betrayal* however, considerable intrigue. In the fall of 1780, American forces were shocked by the exposure of treason on the part of General Benedict Arnold. Convinced that the American cause was hopeless, Arnold conspired with British agents to betray the Patriot stronghold at West Point on the Hudson River. When the scheme was exposed and foiled, Arnold fled to the safety of the British camp, where he spent the rest of the war.

The British did have some significant military successes during this period. On December 29, 1778, they captured Savannah, Georgia. After taking the port of Charleston, South Carolina, on May 12, 1780, they advanced into the interior. Although the British were able to win conventional battles, they faced constant harrassment from such Patriot guerrillas as Thomas Sumter, Andrew Pickens, and Francis Marion, the "Swamp Fox." Penetrating to Camden, South Carolina, Lord Cornwallis (whom Clinton named British commander in the South) met and crushed a Patriot force under Horatio Gates on August 16, 1780. Congress recalled Gates, and Washington replaced him with Nathanael Greene, one of the ablest American generals of his time.

Even before Greene arrived in the South, the tide of battle had begun to turn against Cornwallis. At King's Mountain (near the North Carolina–South Carolina border) on October 7, 1780, a band of Patriot riflemen from the backwoods killed, wounded, or captured every man in a force of 1,100 New York and South Carolina Loyalists upon whom Cornwallis had depended. Once Greene arrived, he confused and exasperated Cornwallis by dividing the American forces into fast-moving contingents while avoiding open, conventional battles. One of the contingents inflicted what Cornwallis admitted was "a very unexpected and severe blow" at Cowpens on January 17, 1781. Finally, after receiving reinforcements, Greene combined all his forces and maneuvered to meet the British at Guilford Court House, North Carolina. After a hard-fought battle there on March 15, 1781, Greene was driven from the field; but Cornwallis had lost so many men that he decided to abandon the Carolina campaign. Instead, he moved north, hoping to conduct raids in the interior of Virginia. But Clinton, fearful that the southern army might be destroyed, ordered him to take up a defensive position at Yorktown.

American and French forces quickly descended on Yorktown. Washington and the *Yorktown* Count de Rochambeau marched a French-American army from New York to join the Marquis de Lafayette in Virginia, while Admiral de Grasse took a French fleet with additional troops up Chesapeake Bay to the York River. These joint operations caught Cornwallis between land and sea. After a few shows of resistance, he surrendered on October 17, 1781. Two days later, as a military band played "The World Turned Upside Down," he surrendered his whole army of more than 7,000.

Winning the Peace

Cornwallis's defeat provoked outcries in England against continuing the war. Lord North resigned as prime minister; Lord Shelburne emerged from the political wreckage to succeed him; and British emissaries appeared in France to talk informally with the American diplomats there—Benjamin Franklin, John Adams, and John Jay.

The Americans were under instructions to cooperate with France in their negotiations with England. But Vergennes insisted that France could not agree to any settlement with England until its ally Spain had achieved its principal war aim: winning back Gibraltar from the British. There was no real prospect of that happening soon, and the Americans began to fear that the alliance with France might keep them at war indefinitely. As a result, the Americans began proceeding on their own, without informing Vergennes, and soon drew up a preliminary treaty with Great Britain, which was signed on November 30, 1782. Benjamin Franklin, in the meantime, skillfully pacified Vergennes   *Franklin's Diplomacy* and avoided an immediate rift in the French-American alliance.

The final treaty, signed September 3, 1783, was, on the whole, remarkably favorable to the United States. It provided a clear-cut recognition of independence and a large, though ambiguous, cession of territory to the new nation—from the southern boundary of Canada to the northern boundary of Florida and from the Atlantic to the Mississippi. The American people had good reason to celebrate as the last of the British occupation forces embarked from New York. Dissenters around the world, too, found inspiration in news of the Revolution. (See "America in the World: The Age of Revolutions.")

WAR AND SOCIETY

Historians have long debated whether the American Revolution was a social as well as a political revolution. But whatever the intention of those who launched and fought the war, the conflict transformed American society.

Loyalists and Minorities

Estimates differ as to how many Americans remained loyal to England during the Revolution, but it is clear that there were many—at least one-fifth (and some estimate as much as one-third) of the white population. Some were officeholders in the imperial government. Others were merchants whose trade was closely tied to the imperial system. Still others were people who lived in relative isolation and had simply retained their traditional loyalties. And there were those who, expecting the British to win the war, were currying favor with the anticipated victors.

Many of these Loyalists were hounded by Patriots in their communities and harassed by legislative and judicial actions. Up to 100,000 fled the country. Those who could afford it moved to England. Others moved to Canada, establishing the first   *The Loyalists' Plight* English-speaking community in the French-speaking province of Quebec. Some returned to America after the war and gradually reentered the life of the nation.

The war weakened other groups as well. The Anglican Church, many of whose members were Loyalists, lost its status as the official religion of Virginia and Maryland. By the time the fighting ended, many Anglican parishes could no longer even afford clergymen. Also weakened were the Quakers, whose pacifism gave them widespread unpopularity.

Other Protestant denominations, however, grew stronger. Presbyterian, Congregational, and Baptist churches successfully tied themselves to the Patriot cause. Most American Catholics also supported the Patriots and won increased popularity as a result. Shortly after the peace treaty was signed, the Vatican provided the United States with its own hierarchy and, in 1789, its first bishop.

THE WAR AND SLAVERY

For some African Americans, the war meant freedom because the British enabled many escaped slaves to leave the country as a way of disrupting the American war effort. In South Carolina, for example, nearly one-third of all slaves defected during the war.

For other African Americans, the Revolution meant an increased exposure to the *Exposure to Revolutionary Ideas* concept, although seldom to the reality, of liberty. Most African Americans could not read, but few could avoid the new and exciting ideas circulating through the towns and cities and even the plantations where they lived. In several communities, slaves exposed to Revolutionary ideas engaged in open resistance to white control. In Charleston, South Carolina, for example, Thomas Jeremiah, a free black man, was executed after white authorities learned of elaborate plans for a slave uprising.

Slaveowners opposed the British efforts to emancipate their slaves, but they also feared that the Revolution itself would foment slave rebellions. Although the ideals of the Revolution produced occasional challenges to slavery by white southerners (including laws in Virginia and Maryland permitting slaveowners to free—"manumit"—their slaves if they wished), white support for slavery survived. Southern churches, some of which flirted briefly with voicing objections to the system, quickly rejected the antislavery ideas of the North and worked instead to reinforce white superiority.

In much of the North, by contrast, the combination of Revolutionary sentiment and evangelical Christian fervor helped spread antislavery sentiments widely through society. The first target was the slave trade, which was prohibited by several states (Pennsylvania, Rhode Island, and Connecticut among them). The antislavery movement next attacked state laws forbidding owners from freeing their slaves. Quakers and other antislavery activists succeeded in pressuring legislatures to allow legal emancipation in all the northern states, and even in Kentucky and Tennessee, before the end of the Revolution. The final step was emancipation of all slaves in a state. Pennsylvania was the first state, in 1780, to declare slavery illegal within its borders—again in part because of the influence of the *Gradual Emancipation in the North* fiercely antislavery Quakers. One by one, all the northern states except New York and New Jersey abolished slavery before the end of the Revolution. New York followed in 1799 and New Jersey in 1804. But northern emancipation was a gradual process in most states, despite changes in the law. A significant, although steadily dwindling, number of slaves remained in the North for several decades.

The Revolution exposed the continuing tension between the nation's commitment to liberty and its simultaneous commitment to slavery. To people in our time, and even to some people in Revolutionary times, liberty and slavery seem incompatible with each other. But to many white Americans in the eighteenth century, especially in the South, that did not seem obvious. Many white southerners believed, in fact, that enslaving Africans—whom they considered inferior and unfit for citizenship—was the best way to ensure liberty for white people. They feared that without slaves, it would be necessary to recruit a servile white workforce in the South, and that the resulting inequalities would jeopardize the survival of liberty. One of the ironies of the American Revolution was that many white Americans were fighting both to secure freedom for themselves and to pre-serve slavery for others.

NATIVE AMERICANS AND THE REVOLUTION

Indians also viewed the American Revolution with considerable uncertainty. Most tribes ultimately chose to stay out of the war. But many Indians feared that the Revolution would replace a somewhat trustworthy ruling group (the British, who had tried to limit the expan-sion of white settlement into tribal land) with one they considered generally hostile to them (the Patriots, who had spearheaded the expansion). Thus some Indians chose to join the English cause. Still others took advantage of the conflict to launch attacks of their own.

In the western Carolinas and Virginia, Cherokee led by Chief Dragging Canoe launched a series of attacks on outlying white settlements in the summer of 1776. Patriot militias responded in great force, ravaging Cherokee lands and forcing the chief and many of his followers to flee west across the Tennessee River. Those Cherokee who remained behind agreed to a new treaty by which they gave up still more land. Some Iroquois, despite the setbacks at Oriskany, continued to wage war against Americans in the West and caused widespread destruction in agricultural areas of New York and Pennsylvania. The retaliat-ing American armies inflicted heavy losses on the Indians, but the attacks continued.

In the end, the Revolution generally weakened the position of Native Americans in several ways. The Patriot victory increased white demand for western lands. Many whites resented the assistance such nations as the Mohawk had given the British and insisted on treating them as conquered people. Others drew from the   *Native American Position Weakened* Revolution a paternalistic view of the tribes. Thomas Jefferson, for example, came to view the Indians as "noble savages," uncivilized in their present state but redeemable if they were willing to adapt to the norms of white society.

The triumph of the American Patriots in the Revolution contributed to the ultimate defeat of the Indian tribes. To white Americans, independence meant, among other things, their right to move aggressively into the western lands, despite the opposition of the Indians. To the Indians, American independence was "the greatest blow that could have been dealt us," one tribal leader warned.

WOMEN'S RIGHTS AND ROLES

The long Revolutionary War had a profound effect on American women. The departure of so many men to fight in the Patriot armies left women in charge of farms and busi-nesses. Often, women handled these tasks with great success. But in other cases, inexpe-rience, inflation, the unavailability of male labor, or the threat of enemy troops led to failure. Some women whose husbands or fathers were called away to war did not have even a farm or shop to fall back on. Cities and towns had significant populations of impoverished women, who on occasion led protests against price increases, rioted, or looted food. At other times, women launched attacks on occupying British troops, whom they were required to house and feed at considerable expense.

Not all women stayed behind when the men went off to war. Some joined their male relatives in the camps of the Patriot armies. These female "camp followers" increased army morale and provided a ready source of volunteers to cook, launder, nurse, and do other nec-essary tasks. In the rough environment of the camps, traditional gender distinctions proved difficult to maintain. Considerable numbers of women became involved, at least intermit-tently, in combat. A few women even disguised themselves as men to be able to fight.

THE CORRESPONDENCE OF ABIGAIL ADAMS ON WOMEN'S RIGHTS (1776)

Between March and May 1776, Abigail Adams exchanged letters with her husband John and with Mercy Otis Warren, one of the few female political writers of the day. In these notes, the correspondents discussed the matter of women's rights in Revolutionary America.

Abigail Adams to John Adams, March 31, 1776:

I long to hear that you have declared an independancy [sic] and by the way in the new Code of Laws which I suppose it will be necessary for you to make I would desire you would Remember the Ladies, and be more generous and favourable to them than your ancestors. Do not put such unlimited power into the hands of the Husbands. Remember all men would be tyrants if they could. If particuliar care and attention is not paid to the Ladies we are determined to foment a Rebelion, and will not hold ourselves bound by any Laws in which we have no voice, or Representation.

That your Sex are Naturally Tyrannical is a Truth so thoroughly established as to admit of no dispute, but such of you as wish to be happy willingly give up the harsh title of Master for the more tender and endearing one of Friend. Why then, not put it out of the power of the vicious and the Lawless to use us with cruelty and indignity with impunity. Men of Sense in all Ages abhor those customs which treat us only as the vassals of your Sex. Regard us then as Beings placed by providence under your protection and in immitation of the Supreme Being make use of that power only for our happiness.

John Adams to Abigail Adams, April 14, 1776:
As to Declarations of Independency, be patient. Read our Privateering Laws, and our Commercial Laws. What signifies a Word.

As to your extraordinary Code of Laws, I cannot but laugh. We have been told that our Struggle has loosened the bands of Government every where. That Children and Apprentices were disobedient—that schools and Colleges were grown turbulent—that Indians slighted their Guardians and Negroes grew insolent to their Masters. But your Letter was the first Intimation that another Tribe more numerous and powerful than all the rest were grown discontented. This is rather too coarse a Compliment but you are so saucy, I wont blot it out.

Depend upon it, We know better than to repeal our Masculine systems. Altho they are in full Force, you know they are little more than Theory. We dare not exert our Power in its full Latitude. We are obliged to go fair, and softly, and in Practice you know We are the subjects. We have only the Name of Masters, and rather than give up this, which would completely subject Us to the Despotism of the Peticoat, I hope General Washington, and all our brave Heroes would fight. . . .

Abigail Adams to Mercy Otis Warren, Braintree April 27, 1776:
He is very saucy to me in return for a List of Female Grievances which I transmitted to him I think I will get you to join me in a petition to Congress. I thought it was very probable our wise Statesmen would erect a New Government and form a new code of Laws. I ventured to speak a word on behalf of our Sex, who are rather hardly dealt with by the Laws of England which gives such unlimited power to the Husband to use his wife.

I requested that our Legislators would consider our case and as all Men of Delicacy and Sentiment are adverse to Exercising the power they possess, yet as there is a natural propensity in Human Nature to domination, I thought the most generous plan was to put it out of the power of the Arbitrary and tyranick to injure us with impunity by Establishing some Laws in favour upon just and Liberal principals. I believe I even threatened fomenting a Rebellion in case we were not considered and assured him we would not hold ourselves bound by any Laws in which we had neither a voice nor representation.

In return he tells me he cannot but Laugh at my extraordinary Code of Laws. That he had heard their Struggle had loosened the bands of Government, that children and apprentices were disobedient, that Schools and Colleges had grown turbulent, that Indians slighted their Guardians, and Negroes grew insolent to their Masters. But my Letter was the first intimation that another Tribe more numerous and powerful than all the rest were grown discontented. This is rather too coarse a complement, he adds, but that I am so saucy he wont blot it out.

So I have helped the Sex abundantly, but I will tell him I have only been making trial of the Disinterestedness of his Virtue, and when weigh'd in the balance have found it wanting. It would be bad policy to grant us greater power say they since under all the disadvantages we Labour we have the ascendency over their Hearts. And charm by accepting, by submitting sway.

Abigail Adams to John Adams, May 7, 1776: I can not say that I think you very generous to the Ladies, for whilst you are proclaiming peace and good will to men, Emancipating all Nations, you insist upon retaining an absolute power over Wives. But you must remember that Arbitrary power is like most other things which are very hard, very liable to be broken and notwithstanding all your wise Laws and Maxims we have it in our power not only to free our selves but to subdue our Masters, and without violence throw both your natural and legal authority at our feet.

"Charm by accepting, by submitting sway
Yet have our Humour most when we obey."

UNDERSTAND, ANALYZE, & EVALUATE

1. What was Abigail Adams's opinion of men in power and what did she request of John Adams as they declared independence?

2. To what other social developments did John Adams compare his wife's request? What did he mean by the "Despotism of the Peticoat" (a women's undergarment)?

3. What did Abigail Adams predict in her second letter to John Adams? What do you think of her assessment of "Arbitrary power"?

Source: *The Adams Family Correspondence*, eds. L. H. Butterfield et al. (Cambridge, MA: Belknap Press of Harvard University Press, 1963), vol. I, pp. 29–31.

The emphasis on liberty and the "rights of man" led some women to begin to question their own position in society. Abigail Adams wrote to her husband, John Adams, in 1776, "In the new code of laws which I suppose it will be necessary for you to make, I desire you would remember the ladies and be more generous and favorable to them than your ancestors." (See "Consider the Source: The Correspondence of Abigail Adams on Women's Rights.") Adams was simply calling for new protections against abusive and tyrannical men. A few women, however, went further. Judith Sargent Murray, one of the leading essayists of the late eighteenth century, wrote in 1779 that women's minds were as good as those of men and that girls as well as boys therefore deserved access to education.

But little changed as a result. Under English common law, an unmarried woman had some legal rights, but a married woman had virtually no rights at all. Everything she owned and everything she earned belonged to her husband. Because she had no property rights, she could not engage in any legal transactions on her own. She could not vote. *Few Legal Rights for Women*   She had no legal authority over her children. Nor could she initiate a divorce; that, too, was a right reserved almost exclusively for men. After the Revolution, it did become easier for women to obtain divorces in a few states. Otherwise, there were few advances and some setbacks—including the loss of widows' rights to regain their dowries from their husbands' estates. The Revolution, in other words, did not really challenge, but actually confirmed and strengthened, the patriarchal legal system.

Still, the Revolution did encourage people of both sexes to reevaluate the contribution of women to the family and society. As the new republic searched for a cultural identity for itself, it attributed a higher value to the role of women as mothers. The new nation was, many Americans liked to believe, producing a new kind of citizen, steeped in the principles of liberty. Mothers had a particularly important task, therefore, in instructing their children in the virtues that the republican citizenry now was expected to possess.

THE WAR ECONOMY

The Revolution also produced important changes in the structure of the American economy. After more than a century of dependence on the British imperial system, American commerce suddenly found itself on its own. English ships no longer protected American vessels. In fact, they tried to drive them from the seas. British imperial ports were closed to American trade. But this disruption in traditional economic patterns strengthened the American economy in the long run. Enterprising merchants in New England and elsewhere began to develop new commercial networks in the Caribbean and South America. By the mid-1780s, American merchants were also developing an important trade with Asia.

When English imports to America were cut off, states desperately tried to stimulate domestic manufacturing. No great industrial expansion resulted, but there was a modest increase in production. Trade also increased substantially among the American states.

THE CREATION OF STATE GOVERNMENTS

At the same time as Americans were struggling to win their independence on the battlefield, they were also struggling to create new institutions of government to replace the British system they had repudiated.

THE ASSUMPTIONS OF REPUBLICANISM

If Americans agreed on nothing else, they agreed that their new governments would be republican. To them, **republicanism** meant a political system in which all power came from the people, rather than from some supreme authority (such as a king). The success of such a government depended on the character of its citizenry. If the population consisted of sturdy, independent property owners imbued with civic virtue, then the republic could survive. If it consisted of a few powerful aristocrats and a great mass of dependent workers, then it would be in danger. From the beginning, therefore, the ideal of the small freeholder (the independent landowner) was basic to American political ideology. Jefferson, the great champion of the independent yeoman farmer, once wrote: "Dependence begets subservience and venality, suffocates the germ of virtue, and prepares fit tools for the designs of ambition."

Another crucial part of that ideology was the concept of equality. The Declaration of Independence had given voice to the idea in its most ringing phrase: "All men are created equal." The innate talents and energies of individuals, not their positions *Rhetoric of Equality* at birth, would determine their roles in society. Some people would inevitably be wealthier and more powerful than others. But all people would have to earn their success. There might be no equality of condition, but there would be equality of opportunity.

In reality, of course, the United States was never a nation in which all citizens were independent property holders. From the beginning, there was a sizable dependent labor force, white and black. American women remained both politically and economically subordinate. Native Americans were systematically exploited and displaced. Nor was there ever full equality of opportunity. American society was more open and more fluid than that of most European nations, but the condition of a person's birth was almost always a crucial determinant of success.

Nevertheless, in embracing the assumptions of republicanism, Americans were adopting a powerful—even revolutionary—ideology, and their experiment in statecraft became a model for many other countries.

THE FIRST STATE CONSTITUTIONS

Two states—Connecticut and Rhode Island—already had governments that were republican in all but name. They simply deleted references to England and the king from their charters and adopted them as constitutions. The other eleven states, however, produced new documents.

The first and perhaps most basic decision was that the constitutions were to be written down, because Americans believed the vagueness of England's unwritten constitution had produced corruption. The second decision was that the power of the *Curbing Executive Power* executive, which Americans believed had grown too great in England, must be limited. Pennsylvania eliminated the executive altogether. Most other states inserted provisions limiting the power of governors over appointments, reducing or eliminating their right to veto bills, and preventing them from dismissing the legislature. Most important, every state forbade the governor or any other executive officer from holding a seat in the legislature, thus ensuring that, unlike in England, the executive and legislative branches of government would remain separate.

Even so, most new constitutions did not embrace direct popular rule. In Georgia and Pennsylvania, the legislature consisted of one popularly elected house. But in every other state, there were upper and lower chambers, and in most cases the upper chamber was designed to represent the "higher orders" of society. There were property requirements for voters—some modest, others substantial—in all states.

REVISING STATE GOVERNMENTS

By the late 1770s, Americans were growing concerned about the apparent instability of their new state governments. Many believed the problem was one of too much democracy. As a result, most of the states began to revise their constitutions to limit popular power. By waiting until 1780 to ratify its first constitution, Massachusetts became the first state to act on the new concerns.

Two changes in particular differentiated the Massachusetts and later constitutions from the earlier ones. The first was a change in the process of constitution *Massachusetts's Constitution* writing itself. Most of the first documents had been written by state legislatures and thus could easily be amended (or violated) by them. Massachusetts created the constitutional convention: a special assembly of the people that would meet only for the purpose of writing the constitution.

The second change was a significant strengthening of the executive. The 1780 Massachusetts constitution made the governor one of the strongest in any state. He was to be elected directly by the people; he was to have a fixed salary (in other words, he would not be dependent on the legislature each year for his wages); he would have significant appointment powers and a veto over legislation. Other states followed. Those with weak or nonexistent upper houses strengthened or created them. Most increased the powers of the governor. Pennsylvania, which had no executive at all at first, now produced a strong one. By the late 1780s, almost every state had either revised its constitution or drawn up an entirely new one in an effort to produce greater stability in government.

Toleration and Slavery

Most Americans continued to believe that religion should play some role in government, but they did not wish to give special privileges to any particular denomination. The privileges that churches had once enjoyed were now largely stripped away. In 1786, *Statute of Religious Liberty*   Virginia enacted the Statute of Religious Liberty, written by Thomas Jefferson, which called for the complete separation of church and state.

More difficult to resolve was the question of slavery. In areas where slavery was already weak—New England and Pennsylvania—it was gradually abolished. Even in the South, there were some pressures to amend or even eliminate the institution; every state but South Carolina and Georgia prohibited further importation of slaves from abroad, and South Carolina banned the slave trade during the war. Virginia passed a law encouraging the voluntary freeing of slaves.

Nevertheless, slavery survived in all of the upper and lower states. There were several reasons: racist assumptions among whites about the inferiority of blacks; the enormous economic investments many white southerners had in their slaves; and the inability of even such men as Washington and Jefferson, who had moral misgivings about slavery, to *Reasons for Slavery's Persistence*   envision any alternative to it. If slavery was abolished, what would happen to the black people in America? Few whites believed that black men and women could be integrated into American society as equals.

THE SEARCH FOR A NATIONAL GOVERNMENT

Americans were much quicker to agree on state institutions than they were on the structure of their national government. At first, most believed that the central government should remain relatively weak and that each state would be virtually a sovereign nation. It was in response to such ideas that the Articles of Confederation emerged.

The Confederation

The Articles of Confederation, which the Continental Congress had adopted in 1777, provided for a national government much like the one already in place before indepen- *Limited Power of the National Government*   dence. Congress remained the central—indeed the only—institution of national authority. Its powers expanded to give it authority to conduct wars and foreign relations and to appropriate, borrow, and issue money. But it did not have power to regulate trade, draft troops, or levy taxes directly on the people. For troops and taxes, it had to make formal requests to the state legislatures, which could—and often did—refuse them. There was no separate executive; the "president of the United States" was merely the presiding officer at the sessions of Congress. Each state had a single vote in Congress, and at least nine of the states had to approve any important measure. All thirteen state legislatures had to approve any amendment of the Articles.

During the process of ratifying the Articles of Confederation (which required approval by all thirteen states), broad disagreements over the plan became evident. The small states had insisted on equal state representation, but the larger states wanted representation to be based on population. The smaller states prevailed on that issue. More important, the states claiming western lands wished to keep them, but the rest of the states demanded that all such territory be turned over to the national government. New York and Virginia had to give up their western claims before the Articles were finally approved. They went into effect in 1781.

The Confederation, which existed from 1781 until 1789, was not a complete failure, but it was far from a success. It lacked adequate powers to deal with interstate issues or to enforce its will on the states.

DIPLOMATIC FAILURES

In the peace treaty of 1783, the British had promised to evacuate American territory; but British forces continued to occupy a string of frontier posts along the Great Lakes within the United States. Nor did the British honor their agreement to make restitution to slave-owners whose slaves the British army had confiscated. Disputes also erupted over the north-eastern boundary of the new nation and over the border between the United States and Florida. Most American trade remained within the British Empire, and Americans wanted full access to British markets; England, however, placed sharp restrictions on that access.

In 1784, Congress sent John Adams as minister to London to resolve these differences, but Adams made no headway with the English, who were   *John Adams, Ambassador to England* never sure whether he represented a single nation or thirteen different ones. Throughout the 1780s, the British government refused even to send a diplomatic minister to the American capital.

Confederation diplomats agreed to a treaty with Spain in 1786. The Spanish accepted the American interpretation of the Florida boundary. In return, the Americans recognized the Spanish possessions in North America and accepted limits on the right of United States vessels to navigate the Mississippi for twenty years. But southern states, incensed at the idea of giving up their access to the Mississippi, blocked ratification.

THE CONFEDERATION AND THE NORTHWEST

The Confederation's most important accomplishment was its resolution of controversies involving the western lands. The Confederation had to find a way to include these areas in the political structure of the new nation.

The Ordinance of 1784, based on a proposal by Thomas Jefferson, divided the western territory into ten self-governing districts, each of which could   *Ordinances of 1784 and 1785* petition Congress for statehood when its population equaled the number of free inhabitants of the smallest existing state. Then, in the Ordinance of 1785, Congress created a system for surveying and selling the western lands. The territory north of the Ohio River was to

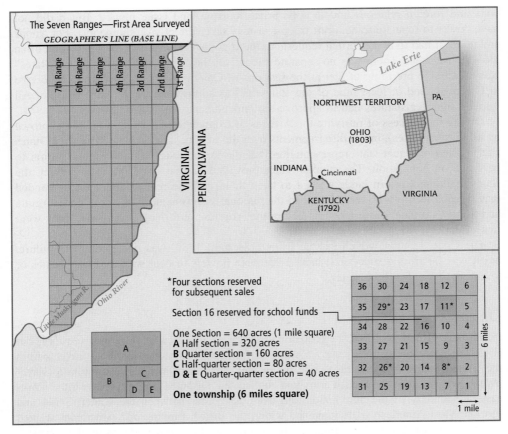

The Seven Ranges—First Area Surveyed

GEOGRAPHER'S LINE (BASE LINE)

7th Range, 6th Range, 5th Range, 4th Range, 3rd Range, 2nd Range, 1st Range

VIRGINIA
PENNSYLVANIA

Little Muskingum R. / Ohio River

Lake Erie

NORTHWEST TERRITORY
PA.

OHIO
(1803)

INDIANA   ● Cincinnati

KENTUCKY
(1792)

VIRGINIA

*Four sections reserved
for subsequent sales

Section 16 reserved for school funds

One Section = 640 acres (1 mile square)
A Half section = 320 acres
B Quarter section = 160 acres
C Half-quarter section = 80 acres
D & E Quarter-quarter section = 40 acres

One township (6 miles square)

A

B   C

D   E

36	30	24	18	12	6
35	29*	23	17	11*	5
34	28	22	16	10	4
33	27	21	15	9	3
32	26*	20	14	8*	2
31	25	19	13	7	1

6 miles

1 mile

LAND SURVEY: ORDINANCE OF 1785 In the Ordinance of 1785, the Congress established a new system for surveying and selling western lands. These maps illustrate the way in which the lands were divided in an area of Ohio. Note the highly geometrical grid pattern that the ordinance imposed on these lands. Each of the squares in the map on the left was subdivided into 36 sections, as illustrated in the map at the lower right. • *Why was this grid pattern so appealing to the planners of the western lands?*

be surveyed and marked off into neat rectangular townships, each divided into thirty-six identical sections. In every township, four sections were to be reserved by the federal government for future use or sale (a policy that helped establish the idea of "public land"). The revenue from the sale of one of these federally reserved sections was to support creation of a public school.

The precise rectangular pattern imposed on the Northwest Territory—the grid—became a model for all subsequent land policies of the federal government and for many other planning decisions in states and localities. The grid also became characteristic of the layout of many American cities. It had many advantages. It eliminated the uncertainty about property borders that earlier, more informal land systems had produced. It sped the development of western lands by making land ownership simple and understandable. But it also encouraged a dispersed form of settlement—with each farm family separated from its neighbors—that made the formation of community more difficult. Whatever its consequences, however, the 1785 Ordinance made a dramatic and indelible mark on the American landscape.

The original ordinances proved highly favorable to land speculators and less so to ordinary settlers, many of whom could not afford the price of the land. Congress compounded the problem by selling much of the best land to the Ohio and Scioto Companies before making it available to anyone else. Criticism of these policies led to the passage in 1787 of another law governing western settlement—legislation that became known as the "Northwest Ordinance." The 1787 Ordinance abandoned the ten *The Northwest Ordinance* districts established in 1784 and created a single Northwest Territory out of the lands north of the Ohio; the territory could be divided subsequently into three to five territories. It also specified a population of 60,000 as a minimum for statehood, guaranteed freedom of religion and the right to trial by jury to residents of the region, and prohibited slavery throughout the territory.

The western lands south of the Ohio River received less attention from Congress. The region that became Kentucky and Tennessee developed rapidly in the late 1770s as slave-owning territories, and in the 1780s began setting up governments and asking for statehood. The Confederation Congress was never able to resolve the conflicting claims in that region successfully.

Indians and the Western Lands

On paper, the western land policies of the Confederation brought order and stability to the process of white settlement in the Northwest. But in reality, order and stability came slowly and at great cost because much of the land was claimed by the Indians. Congress tried to resolve that problem in 1784, 1785, and 1786 by persuading Iroquois, Choctaw, Chickasaw, and Cherokee leaders to sign treaties ceding lands to the United States. But those agreements proved ineffective. In 1786, the leadership of the Iroquois Confederacy repudiated the treaty it had signed two years earlier. Other tribes had never really accepted the treaties affecting them and continued to resist white movement into their lands.

Violence between whites and Indians on the Northwest frontier reached a crescendo in the early 1790s. In 1790 and again in 1791, the Miami, led by the famed warrior Little Turtle, defeated United States forces in two major battles. Efforts to negotiate a settlement failed because of the Miami's insistence that no treaty was possible unless it forbade white settlement west of the Ohio River. Negotiations did not resume until after General Anthony Wayne led 4,000 soldiers into the Ohio Valley in 1794 and defeated *Battle of Fallen Timbers* the Indians in the Battle of Fallen Timbers.

A year later, the Miami signed the Treaty of Greenville, ceding substantial new lands to the United States in exchange for a formal acknowledgment of their claim to the territory they had managed to retain. This was the first time the new federal government recognized the sovereignty of Indian nations; in doing so, it affirmed that Indian lands could be ceded only by the tribes themselves. That hard-won assurance, however, proved a frail protection against the pressure of white expansion.

Debts, Taxes, and Daniel Shays

The postwar depression, which lasted from 1784 to 1787, increased the perennial American problem of an inadequate money supply, a burden that weighed particularly heavily on debtors. The Confederation itself had an enormous outstanding debt, accumulated during the Revolutionary War, and few means with which to pay it down. It had sold war bonds that were now due to be repaid; it owed money to its soldiers; it had substantial debts abroad. But with no power to tax, it could request money only from the states, and it received only about one-sixth of the money it asked for. The fragile new nation was faced with the grim prospect of defaulting on its obligations.

This alarming possibility brought to prominence a group of leaders who would play a crucial role in the shaping of the republic for several decades. Robert Morris, the head of the Confederation's treasury; Alexander Hamilton, his young protégé; James Madison of Virginia; and others—all called for a "continental impost," a 5 percent duty on imported goods to be levied by Congress and used to fund the debt. Many Americans, however, feared that the impost plan would concentrate too much financial power in the hands of Morris and his allies in Philadelphia. Congress failed to approve the impost in 1781 and again in 1783.

The states had war debts, too, and they generally relied on increased taxation to pay them. But poor farmers, already burdened by debt, considered such policies unfair. They demanded that the state governments issue paper currency to increase the money supply and make it easier for them to meet their obligations. Resentment was especially high among farmers in New England, who felt that the states were squeezing them to enrich already wealthy bondholders in Boston and other towns.

Throughout the late 1780s, therefore, mobs of distressed farmers rioted periodically in various parts of New England. Dissidents in the Connecticut Valley and the Berkshire Hills of Massachusetts rallied behind Daniel Shays, a former captain in the Continental army. Shays issued a set of demands that included paper money, tax relief, a moratorium on debts, and the abolition of imprisonment for debt. During the summer of 1786, the Shaysites prevented the collection of debts, private or public, and used force to keep courts from convening and sheriffs from selling confiscated property. When winter came, the rebels advanced on Springfield, hoping to seize weapons from the arsenal there. In January *Shays's Rebellion* 1787, an army of state militiamen set out from Boston, met Shays's band, and dispersed his ragged troops.

DANIEL SHAYS AND JOB SHATTUCK Shays and Shattuck were the principal leaders of the 1786 uprising of poor Massachusetts farmers demanding relief from their indebtedness. Shattuck led an insurrection in the east, which collapsed when he was captured on November 30. Shays organized the rebellion in the west, which continued until it was finally dispersed by state militia in late February 1787. The following year, state authorities pardoned Shays; even before that, the legislature responded to the rebellion by providing some relief to the impoverished farmers. This drawing is part of a hostile account of the rebellion published in 1787 in a Boston almanac.

As a military enterprise, Shays's Rebellion was a failure, although it did produce some concessions to the aggrieved farmers. Shays and his lieutenants, at first sentenced to death, were later pardoned, and Massachusetts offered the protesters some tax relief and a postponement of debt payments. But the rebellion had important consequences for the future of the United States, for it added urgency to the movement to produce a new, national constitution.

CONCLUSION

Between a small, inconclusive battle on a village green in New England in 1775 and a momentous surrender at Yorktown in 1781, the American people fought a great and terrible war against the mightiest military nation in the world. Few would have predicted in 1775 that the makeshift armies of the colonies could withstand the armies and navies of the British Empire. But a combination of luck, brilliance, determination, costly errors by the British, and timely aid from abroad allowed the Patriots, as they began to call themselves, to make full use of the advantages of fighting on their home soil and to frustrate British designs.

The war was not just a historic military event. It was also a great political one, for it propelled the colonies to unite, to organize, and to declare their independence. Having done so, they fought with even greater determination, defending now not just a set of principles, but an actual, fledgling nation. By the end of the war, they had created new governments at both the state and national level and had begun experimenting with new political forms.

The war was also important for its effects on American society—for the way it shook the existing social order; for the way it caused women to question their place in society; and for the way it spread notions of liberty and freedom throughout a society that in the past had mostly been rigidly hierarchical. Even African American slaves absorbed some of the ideas of the Revolution, although it would be many years before they would be in any position to make much use of them.

Victory in the American Revolution solved many of the problems of the new nation, but it also produced others. What should the United States do about its relations with the Indians and with its neighbors to the north and south? What should it do about the distribution of western lands? What should it do about slavery? How should it balance its commitment to liberty with its need for order? These questions bedeviled the new national government in its first years of existence.

KEY TERMS/PEOPLE/PLACES/EVENTS

Abigail Adams 123
American Patriots 121
Articles of
 Confederation 110
Battle of Fallen Timbers 129
Benedict Arnold 118
Common Sense 107
Declaration of
 Independence 110

George Washington 111
Hessians 107
John Burgoyne 114
Joseph and Mary
 Brant 114
Lord Cornwallis 118
Loyalists (Tories) 119
Northwest Ordinance 129
republicanism 124

Saratoga 114
Second Continental
 Congress 107
Shays's Rebellion 130
Thomas Jefferson 110
William Howe 113
Yorktown 118

RECALL AND REFLECT

1. What questions did the Second Continental Congress debate, and how did it answer them?
2. What was the impact of Thomas Paine's *Common Sense* on Americans' view of the war with Britain?
3. What were the ideological ideals of the new state and national governments, and how did those ideals compare with the realities of American society?
4. What was the purpose of the Articles of Confederation?
5. How did the Revolution affect the role of religion and the position of churches in American society?

6 | THE CONSTITUTION AND THE NEW REPUBLIC

FRAMING A NEW GOVERNMENT

ADOPTION AND ADAPTATION

FEDERALISTS AND REPUBLICANS

ESTABLISHING NATIONAL SOVEREIGNTY

THE DOWNFALL OF THE FEDERALISTS

LOOKING AHEAD

1. What were the most important questions debated at the Constitutional Convention of 1787, and how were they resolved?
2. What were the main tenets of the Federalist and Antifederalist arguments on ratification of the Constitution?
3. What were the origins of America's "first party system"?

BY THE LATE 1780S, MANY Americans had grown dissatisfied with the Confederation. It was, they believed, ridden with factions, unable to deal effectively with economic problems, and frighteningly powerless in the face of Shays's Rebellion. A decade earlier, Americans had deliberately avoided creating a strong national government. Now they reconsidered. In 1787, the nation produced a new constitution and a much more powerful government with three independent branches. But the adoption of the Constitution did not complete the creation of the republic, for although most Americans came to agree that the Constitution was a nearly perfect document, they often disagreed on what that document meant.

1786

Annapolis Conference

1787

Constitutional
Convention;
Constitution adopted

1787–1788

States ratify
Constitution

1789

Washington becomes
first president

Bill of Rights

French Revolution

Judiciary Act

1791

First Bank of U.S.
chartered

1792

Washington reelected

1794

Whiskey Rebellion

Jay's Treaty

1795

Pinckney's Treaty

1796

John Adams elected
president

1797

XYZ Affair

Alien and Sedition Acts

1798–1799

Quasi war with France

Virginia and Kentucky
Resolutions

1800

Jefferson elected
president

FRAMING A NEW GOVERNMENT

The Confederation Congress had become so unpopular and ineffectual by the mid-1780s that it began to lead an almost waiflike existence. In 1783, its members timidly withdrew from Philadelphia to escape army veterans demanding their back pay. They took refuge for a while in Princeton, New Jersey, then moved on to Annapolis, Maryland, and in 1785 settled in New York. Delegates were often scarce. Only with great difficulty could Congress produce a quorum to ratify the treaty with Great Britain, ending the Revolutionary War.

ADVOCATES OF REFORM

In the 1780s, some of the wealthiest and most powerful groups in the population began to clamor for a stronger national government. By 1786, such demands had grown so intense that even defenders of the existing system reluctantly agreed that the government needed strengthening at its weakest point—its lack of power to tax.

The most effective advocate of a stronger national government was Alexander Hamilton, the illegitimate son of a Scottish merchant in the West Indies, who had become a successful New York lawyer. Hamilton now called for a national convention to overhaul the Articles of Confeder-ation. He found an important ally in James Madison of Virginia, who persuaded the Virginia legislature to convene an interstate conference on commercial questions. Only five states sent delegates to the meeting, which took place at Annapolis in 1786; but the conference approved a proposal by Hamilton for a convention of special delegates from all the states to meet in Philadelphia the next year.

At first there seemed little reason to believe the Philadelphia convention would attract any more delegates than had the Annapolis meeting. Then, early in 1787, the news of Shays's Rebellion spread throughout the nation, alarming many previously apathetic leaders, including George Washington, who promptly made plans to travel to Philadelphia for the Constitutional Convention. Washington's support gave the meeting wide credibility.

A Divided Convention

Fifty-five men, representing all the states except Rhode Island, attended one or more sessions of the convention that sat in the Philadelphia State House from May to September 1787. These "Founding Fathers," as they became known much later,   *The "Founding Fathers"* were relatively young (the average age was forty-four) and well educated by the standards of their time. Most were wealthy property owners, and many feared what one of them called the "turbulence and follies" of democracy. Yet all retained the Revolutionary suspicion of concentrated power.

The convention unanimously chose Washington to preside over its sessions and then closed it to the public and the press. It then ruled that each state delegation would have a single vote and that major decisions would require not unanimity, as they did in Congress, but a simple majority. Almost all the delegates agreed that the United States needed a stronger central government. But there agreement ended.

Virginia, the most populous state, sent a well-prepared delegation to Philadelphia led by James Madison (thirty-six years old), who had devised in some detail a plan for a new "national" government. The Virginia Plan shaped the agenda of the   *Madison's Virginia Plan* convention from the moment Edmund Randolph of Virginia opened the debate by proposing that "a national government ought to be established, consisting of a supreme Legislative, Executive, and Judiciary." Even that brief description outlined a government very different from the Confederation. But the delegates were so committed to fundamental reform that they approved the resolution after only brief debate.

There was less agreement about the details of Madison's Virginia Plan. It called for a national legislature of two houses. In the lower house, states would be represented in proportion to their population. Members of the upper house were to be elected by the lower house under no rigid system of representation; thus some of the smaller states might at times have no members at all in the upper house.

The proposal aroused immediate opposition among delegates from the smaller states. William Paterson of New Jersey offered an alternative (the New   *Paterson's New Jersey Plan* Jersey Plan) that would retain the essence of the Confederacy with its one-house legislature in which all states had equal representation. It would, however, give Congress expanded powers to tax and to regulate commerce. The convention rejected Paterson's proposal, but supporters of the Virginia Plan now realized they would have to make concessions to the smaller states. They agreed to permit members of the upper house (what became the Senate) to be elected by the state legislatures.

Many questions remained unresolved. Among the most important was the question of slavery. There was no serious discussion of abolishing slavery during the convention. But other issues were debated heatedly. Would slaves be counted as part of the population in determining representation in Congress? Or would they be considered property, not entitled to representation? Delegates from the states with large slave populations wanted to have it both ways. They argued that slaves should be considered persons in determining representation but as property if the new government levied taxes on the states on the basis of population. Representatives from states where slavery had disappeared or was expected soon to disappear argued that slaves should be included in calculating taxation but not representation.

COMPROMISE

The delegates bickered for weeks. By the end of June, with both temperature and tempers rising, the convention seemed in danger of collapsing. Finally, on July 2, the convention created a "grand committee," comprised of one delegate from each state, which produced *The "Great Compromise"* a proposal that became the basis of the "Great Compromise." It called for a two-house legislature. In the lower house, the states would be represented on the basis of population; each slave would be counted as three-fifths of a free person in determining the basis for both representation and direct taxation. In the upper house, the states would be represented equally with two members apiece. On July 16, 1787, the convention voted to accept the compromise.

In the next few weeks, the convention agreed to another important compromise. To placate southern delegates, who feared the new government would interfere with slavery, the convention agreed to bar the new government from stopping the slave trade for twenty years.

Some significant issues remained unaddressed. The Constitution provided no definition of citizenship. Nor did it resolve the status of Native American tribes. Most important to *Unresolved Issues* many Americans was the absence of a list of individual rights, which would restrain the powers of the national government. Madison opposed the idea, arguing that specifying rights that were reserved to the people would, in effect, limit those rights. Others, however, feared that without such protections the national government might abuse its new authority.

THE CONSTITUTION OF 1787

Many people contributed to the creation of the American Constitution, but the most important person in the process was James Madison. Madison had devised the Virginia Plan, and he did most of the drafting of the Constitution itself. Madison's most important achievement, however, was in helping resolve two important philosophical questions: the *The Question of Sovereignty* question of sovereignty and the question of limiting power. (For historians' evolving views on the Constitution's purpose, see "Debating the Past: The Meaning of the Constitution.")

How could a national government exercise sovereignty concurrently with state governments? Where did ultimate sovereignty lie? The answer, Madison and his contemporaries decided, was that all power, at all levels of government, flowed ultimately from the people. Thus neither the federal government nor the state governments were truly sovereign. All of them derived their authority from below. The resolution of the problem of sovereignty made possible one of the distinctive features of the Constitution—its **federalism,** or division of powers between the national and state governments. The Constitution and the government it created were to be the "supreme law" of the land. At the same time, however, the Constitution left important powers in the hands of the states.

In addition to solving the question of sovereignty, the Constitution produced a distinctive solution to the problem of concentrated authority. Drawing from the ideas of the French philosopher Baron de Montesquieu, most Americans had long believed that the best way to avoid tyranny was to keep government close to the people. A large nation would breed corruption and despotism because distant rulers could not be controlled by the people.

Madison, however, helped break the grip of these assumptions by arguing that a large republic would be less likely to produce tyranny because no single group would ever be able to dominate it. The idea of many centers of power "checking one another" and preventing any single, despotic authority from emerging also helped shape the internal structure of the federal government. The Constitution's most distinctive feature was its **separation of powers** within the government, managed by a system of **checks and balances** among the legislative, executive, and judicial branches. The forces within the government would constantly compete with one another. Congress would have two chambers, each checking the other, since both would have to agree before any law could be passed. The president would have the power to veto acts of Congress. The federal courts would be protected from both the executive and the legislature, because judges would serve for life.

The "federal" structure of the government was designed to protect the United States from the kind of despotism that Americans believed had emerged in England. But it was also designed to protect the nation from another kind of despotism: the tyranny of the people. Shays's Rebellion, most of the founders believed, had been only one example of what could happen if a nation did not defend itself against the unchecked exercise of popular will. Thus in the new government, only the members   *Checks on Exercise of Popular Will* of the House of Representatives would be elected directly by the people. Senators would be chosen by state legislators. The president would be chosen by an electoral college. Federal judges would be appointed by the president and confirmed by the Senate. On September 17, 1787, thirty-nine delegates signed the Constitution.

The Constitution of 1787 was a document that established a democratic republic for white people, mostly white men. Native Americans and African Americans, the two largest population groups sharing the lands of the United States with Anglo-Americans, enjoyed virtually none of the rights and privileges offered to the white population.   *Limited Democracy* Native Americans had at least the semblance of a legal status within the nation, through treaties that assured them lands that would be theirs forever. But most of these treaties did not survive for long, and native groups found themselves driven farther and farther west without very much of the protection that the government had promised them.

Among the white leaders of the United States, there were eminent figures who believed Native Americans could in fact join the republic as citizens. Thomas Jefferson was among them, believing that they could be taught the ways of "civilization." Jefferson sought to teach the Native Americans to live as white Americans did. Efforts to teach them Anglo farming methods were based on sedentary farms that relied on men doing the farming and women caring for the home. Native Americans had no interest in such ways and preferred to retain their own traditional cultures. Their repudiation of white civilization contributed to the erosion of support among white Americans. They were not granted citizenship of the United States until the 1920s.

Far more removed from the guarantees of the Constitution were enslaved African Americans, who were given virtually none of the rights and protections that the new government provided to white people. They were not, one southern official noted, "constituent members of our society." The French-Canadian writer Hector St. John de Crèvecoeur, who after the Revolution settled in the United States, wrote a famous book in 1782 titled *Letters from an American Farmer*. In it, he posed what became a famous question: What then is the American, this new man? Crèvecoeur answered his own question by noting that "individuals of all nations" would become "melted" into a common citizenry. But he saw no room for African Americans in the new community. Indeed, among the first laws passed by the new United States under the Constitution was the Naturalization Act of 1790, which helped legalize the stream of immigrants coming into the country and allowed them to become citizens. But it defined citizenry as a status available only to white people. Even free black people were barred from inclusion.

THE MEANING OF THE CONSTITUTION

The Constitution of the United States inspired debate from the moment it was drafted. Some argue that the Constitution is a flexible document intended to evolve in response to society's evolution. Others counter that it has a fixed meaning, rooted in the "original intent" of the framers, and that to move beyond that is to deny its value.

Historians, too, disagree about why the Constitution was written and what it meant. To some scholars, the creation of the federal system was an effort to preserve the ideals of the Revolution and to create a strong national government capable of exercising real authority. To others, the Constitution was an effort to protect the economic interests of existing elites, even at the cost of betraying the principles of the Revolution. And to still others, the Constitution was designed to protect individual freedom and to limit the power of the federal government.

The first influential exponent of the heroic view of the Constitution as the culmination of the Revolution was John Fiske, whose book *The Critical Period of American History* (1888) painted a grim picture of political life under the Articles of Confederation. Many problems, including economic difficulties, the weakness and ineptitude of the national government, threats from abroad, interstate jealousies, and widespread lawlessness, beset the new nation. Fiske argued that only the timely adoption of the Constitution saved the young republic from disaster.

In *An Economic Interpretation of the Constitution of the United States* (1913), Charles A. Beard presented a powerful challenge to Fiske's view. According to Beard, the 1780s had been a "critical period" primarily for conservative business interests who feared

that the decentralized political structure of the republic imperiled their financial position. Such men, he claimed, wanted a government able to promote industry and trade, protect private property, and perhaps, most of all, make good the public debt—much of which was owed to them. The Constitution was, Beard claimed, "an economic document drawn with superb skill by men whose property interests were immediately at stake" and who won its ratification over the opposition of a majority of the people.

A series of powerful challenges to Beard's thesis emerged in the 1950s. The Constitution, many scholars now began to argue, was not an effort to preserve property but an enlightened effort to ensure stability and order. Robert E. Brown, for example, argued in 1956 that "absolutely no correlation" could be shown between the wealth of the delegates to the Constitutional Convention and their position on the Constitution. Examining the debate between the Federalists and the Antifederalists, Forrest McDonald, in *We the People* (1958), also concluded that there was no consistent relationship between wealth and property and support for the Constitution. Instead, opinion on the new system was far more likely to reflect local and regional interests. These challenges greatly weakened Beard's argument; few historians any longer accept his thesis without reservation.

In the 1960s, scholars began again to revive an economic interpretation of the Constitution—but one that differed from Beard's and nevertheless emphasized social and economic factors as motives for supporting the federal system. Jackson Turner Main argued in *The Anti-federalists* (1961) that supporters of the Constitution were

(National Archives and Records Administration)

"cosmopolitan commercialists," eager to advance the economic development of the nation; the Antifederalists, by contrast, were "agrarian localists," fearful of centralization. Gordon Wood, in *The Creation of the American Republic* (1969), suggested that the debate over the state constitutions in the 1770s and 1780s reflected profound social divisions and that those same divisions helped shape the argument over the federal Constitution. The Federalists, Wood suggested, were largely traditional aristocrats who had become deeply concerned by the instability of life under the Articles of Confederation and were particularly alarmed by the decline in popular deference toward social elites. The creation of the Constitution was part of a larger search to create a legitimate political leadership based on the existing social hierarchy; it reflected the efforts of elites to contain what they considered the excesses of democracy.

More recently, historians have continued to examine the question of "intent." Did the framers intend a strong, centralized political system; or did they intend to create a decentralized system with a heavy emphasis on individual rights? The answer, according to Jack Rakove in *Original Meanings* (1996), and

Revolutionaries (2010), is both—and many other things as well. The Constitution, he argues, was the result of a long and vigorous debate through which the views of many different groups found their way into the document. James Madison, generally known as the father of the Constitution, was a strong nationalist, as was Alexander Hamilton. They believed that only a powerful central government could preserve stability in a large nation, and they saw the Constitution as a way to protect order and property and defend the nation against the dangers of too much liberty. But if Madison and Hamilton feared too much liberty, they also feared too little. And that made them receptive to the demands of the Antifederalists for protections of individual rights, which culminated in the Bill of Rights.

The framers differed as well in their views of the proper relationship between the federal government and the state governments. Madison favored unquestioned federal supremacy, while many others, who wanted to preserve the rights of the states, saw in the federal system—and in its division of sovereignty among different levels and branches of government—a guarantee against too much national power. The Constitution is not, Rakove argues, "infinitely malleable." But neither does it have a fixed meaning that can be an inflexible guide to how we interpret it today. •

UNDERSTAND, ANALYZE, & EVALUATE

1. Is the Constitution a conservative, liberal, or radical document? Did the framers consider the Constitution something "finished" (with the exception of constitutional amendments), or did they consider it a document that would evolve in response to changes in society over time?

2. Which parts of the Constitution suggest that the framers' intent was to create a strong, centralized political system? Which parts suggest that the framers' intent was to create a decentralized system with heavy emphasis on individual rights?

Jefferson, who had briefly tried without result to give Indians a legal status within the new nation, had no such aspirations for African Americans. He was an uneasy defender of slavery, worrying about excluding "a whole race of men" from the natural rights that Jefferson himself had done much to promote. But he could never accept the idea that black men and women could attain the level of knowledge and intelligence of white people. Jefferson's long romantic relationship with a black woman, Sally Hemmings, did nothing to change his mind. Hemmings was a light-skinned woman who was a slave on Jefferson's plantation in Virginia. He lived with her after the death of his wife and fathered several of *The Hemmings Family*   her children. But his intimate relationship with the Hemmings family did not ultimately change his position on slavery. Unlike George Washington, who freed his slaves after his death, Jefferson (deeply in debt) required his heirs to sell his slaves after he died (after liberating the Hemmings family). Not until the end of the Civil War were black men and women eligible to live as citizens in the United States, and even then with only partial rights until a century later. For almost a hundred years, the United States Constitution was a document that protected white people only.

ADOPTION AND ADAPTATION

The delegates at Philadelphia had greatly exceeded their instructions from Congress and the states. Instead of making simple revisions in the Articles of Confederation, they had produced a plan for a completely different form of government. They feared that the Constitution would not be ratified under the rules of the Articles of Confederation, which required unanimous approval by the state legislatures. So the convention changed the rules, proposing that the new government would come into being when nine of the thirteen states ratified the Constitution and recommending that state conventions, not state legislatures, be called to ratify it.

FEDERALISTS AND ANTIFEDERALISTS

The Congress in New York accepted the convention's work and submitted it to the states for approval. All the state legislatures except Rhode Island elected delegates to ratifying conventions, most of which began meeting in early 1788. Even before the ratifying conventions convened, however, a great national debate on the new Constitution had begun.

Supporters of the Constitution had a number of advantages. Better organized than their opponents, they seized an appealing label for themselves: *Federalists*—a term that opponents of centralization had once used to describe themselves—thus implying that they were less committed to a "nationalist" government than in fact they were. In addition, the Federalists had the support of not only the two most eminent men in America, Franklin and Washington, but also the ablest political philosophers of their time: Alexander Hamilton, James Madison, and John Jay. Under the joint pseudonym *Publius,* these three men wrote a series of essays, widely published in newspapers throughout the nation, explaining the meaning and virtues of the Constitution. The essays were later gathered together and *The Federalist Papers*   published as a book known today as *The Federalist Papers.*

The Federalists called their critics "Antifederalists," suggesting that their rivals had *The Antifederalists*   nothing to offer except opposition. But the Antifederalists, too, led by such distinguished Revolutionary leaders as Patrick Henry and Samuel Adams, had serious and intelligent arguments. They were, they believed, the defenders of the true principles of the Revolution. They believed that the Constitution would increase taxes, weaken the states, wield dictatorial powers, favor the "well-born" over the common people, and abolish individual liberty. But their biggest complaint was that the Constitution lacked a bill of rights. Only by enumerating the natural rights of the people, they argued, could there be any certainty that those rights would be protected.

Despite the efforts of the Antifederalists, ratification proceeded quickly during the winter of 1787–1788. The Delaware convention, the first to act, ratified the Constitution unanimously, as did the New Jersey and Georgia conventions. And in June 1788, *Ratification of the Constitution* New Hampshire, the critical ninth state, ratified the document. It was now theoretically possible for the Constitution to go into effect. But a new government could not hope to succeed without Virginia and New York, the largest states, whose conventions remained closely divided. By the end of June, first Virginia and then New York consented to the Constitution by narrow margins—on the assumption that a bill of rights would be added in the form of amendments to the Constitution. North Carolina's convention adjourned without taking action, waiting to see what happened to the amendments. Rhode Island, controlled by staunch opponents of centralized government, did not even consider ratification.

COMPLETING THE STRUCTURE

The first elections under the Constitution were held in the early months of 1789. There was never any doubt about who would be the first president. George Washington had presided at the Constitutional Convention, and many who had favored ratification did so only because they expected him to preside over the new government as well. Washington received the votes of all the presidential electors. (John Adams, a leading Federalist, became vice president.) After a journey from his estate at Mount Vernon, Virginia, marked by elaborate celebrations along the way, Washington was inaugurated in New York on April 30, 1789.

GEORGE WASHINGTON AT MOUNT VERNON Washington was in his first term as president in 1790 when an anonymous folk artist painted this view of his home at Mount Vernon, Virginia. Washington appears in uniform, along with members of his family, on the lawn. After he retired from office in 1797, Washington returned happily to his plantation and spent the two years before his death in 1799 "amusing myself in agricultural and rural pursuits." He also played host to an endless stream of visitors from throughout the country and Europe.
(© Courtesy National Gallery of Art, Washington, D.C.)

The first Congress served in many ways as a continuation of the Constitutional Convention. Its most important task was drafting a bill of rights. By early 1789, even Madison had come to agree that some sort of bill of rights would be essential to legitimize the new government. On September 25, 1789, Congress approved twelve amendments, ten of which were ratified by the states by the end of 1791. These first ten amendments to the *The Bill of Rights* Constitution comprise what we know as the Bill of Rights. Nine of them placed limitations on the new government by forbidding it to infringe on certain fundamental rights: freedom of religion, speech, and the press; immunity from arbitrary arrest; trial by jury; and others.

The Bill of Rights had very specific terms; provisions for the judiciary branch were more vague. The Constitution said only: "The judicial power of the United States shall be vested in one Supreme Court, and in such inferior courts as the Congress may from time to time ordain and establish." It was left to Congress to determine the number of Supreme Court judges to be appointed and the kinds of lower courts to be organized. In the Judiciary Act of 1789, Congress provided for a Supreme Court of six members and a system of lower district courts and courts of appeal. It also gave the Supreme Court the power to make the final decision in cases involving the constitutionality of state laws.

The Constitution also said little about the organization of the executive branch. It referred indirectly to executive departments but did not specify which ones or how many there should be. The first Congress created three such departments—state, treasury, and war—and also established the offices of the attorney general and postmaster general. To *Organizing the Executive Branch* the office of secretary of the treasury, Washington appointed Alexander Hamilton of New York. For secretary of war, he chose a Massachusetts Federalist, General Henry Knox. He named Edmund Randolph of Virginia as attorney general and chose another Virginian, Thomas Jefferson, for secretary of state.

FEDERALISTS AND REPUBLICANS

The framers of the Constitution had dealt with many controversies by papering them over with a series of vague compromises; as a result, the disagreements survived to plague the new government.

At the heart of the controversies of the 1790s was the same basic difference in philosophy that had fueled the debate over the Constitution. On one side stood a powerful group who envisioned America as a genuine nation-state, with centralized authority and a complex commercial economy. On the other side stood another group whose members envisioned a more modest national government. Rather than aspire to be a highly commercial or urban nation, it should remain predominantly rural and agrarian. The centralizers became known as the Federalists and gravitated to the leadership of Alexander Hamilton. Their opponents acquired the name Republicans and admired the views of Thomas Jefferson as well as James Madison, who grew skeptical of Federalist rule.

HAMILTON AND THE FEDERALISTS

For twelve years, the Federalists retained firm control of the new government. That was in part because George Washington had always envisioned a strong national government. But the president, Washington believed, should stand above political controversies, and so he avoided personal involvement in the deliberations of Congress. As a result, the dominant figure in his administration became Alexander Hamilton. Of all the national leaders of his time, Hamilton was one of the most aristocratic in his political philosophy; he believed that a stable and effective government required an elite ruling class. Thus the new government needed the support of the wealthy and powerful; and to get that, it needed to give elites a stake in its success. Hamilton proposed, *Hamilton's "Funded" Debt Proposal* therefore, that the existing public debt be "funded": that the various certificates of indebtedness that the old Congress had issued during and after the Revolution—many of them now in the possession of wealthy speculators—be called in and exchanged for interest-bearing bonds. He also recommended that the states' Revolutionary debts be "assumed" (taken over) to cause state bondholders also to look to the central government for eventual payment. Hamilton wanted to create a permanent national debt, with new bonds being issued as old ones were paid off. He hoped to motivate the wealthy classes, who were the most likely to lend money to the government, to support perpetually the survival of that centralized state.

Hamilton also wanted to create a national bank. It would provide loans and currency to businesses, give the government a safe place for the deposit of federal funds, facilitate the collection of taxes and the disbursement of the government's expenditures, and provide a stable center to the nation's small and feeble banking system. The bank would be chartered by the federal government, but much of its capital would come from private investors.

The funding and assumption of debts would require new sources of revenue. Hamilton recommended two kinds of taxes to complement the receipts anticipated from the sales of public land. One was an excise tax on alcoholic beverages, a tax that would be most burdensome to the whiskey distillers of the backcountry, small farmers who converted part of their corn and rye crops into whiskey. The other was a tariff on imports, which Hamilton saw not only as a way to raise money but as a way to protect domestic industries from foreign competition. In his famous "Report on Manufactures" of *"Report on Manufactures"* 1791, he outlined a plan for stimulating the growth of industry and spoke glowingly of the advantages to society of a healthy manufacturing sector.

The Federalists, in short, offered more than a vision of a stable new government. They offered a vision of the sort of nation America should become—a nation with a wealthy, enlightened ruling class; a vigorous, independent commercial economy; and a thriving manufacturing sector.

ENACTING THE FEDERALIST PROGRAM

Few members of Congress objected to Hamilton's plan for funding the national debt, but many did oppose his proposal to exchange new bonds for old certificates of indebtedness on a dollar-for-dollar basis. Many of the original holders had been forced to sell during the hard times of the 1780s to speculators, who had bought them at a fraction of their face value. James Madison, now a representative from Virginia, argued for a plan by which the new bonds would be divided between the original purchasers and the speculators. But Hamilton's allies insisted that the honor of the government required a literal fulfillment of its earlier promises to pay whoever held the bonds. Congress finally passed the funding bill Hamilton wanted.

Hamilton's proposal that the federal government assume the state debts encountered greater difficulty. Its opponents argued that if the federal government took over the state debts, the states with small debts would have to pay taxes to service the states with large ones.

Massachusetts, for example, owed much more money than did Virginia. Only by striking a bargain with the Virginians were Hamilton and his supporters able to win passage of the assumption bill.

The deal involved the location of the national capital, which the Virginians wanted near them in the South. Hamilton and Jefferson met and agreed to exchange northern *Bargaining and the National Capital*   support for placing the capital in the South for Virginia's votes for the assumption bill. The bargain called for the construction of a new capital city on the banks of the Potomac River, which divided Maryland and Virginia, on land to be selected by George Washington.

Hamilton's bank bill produced the most heated debates. Madison, Jefferson, Randolph, and others argued that because the Constitution made no provision for a national bank, Congress had no authority to create one. But Congress agreed to Hamilton's bill despite these objections, and Washington signed it. The Bank of the United States began operations in 1791.

Hamilton also had his way with the excise tax, although protests from farmers later forced revisions to reduce the burden on the smaller distillers. He failed to win passage of a tariff as highly protective as he had hoped for, but the tariff law of 1792 did raise the rates somewhat.

Once enacted, Hamilton's program won the support of manufacturers, creditors, and other influential segments of the population. But others found it less appealing. Small farmers complained that they were being taxed excessively. They and others began to argue that the Federalist program served the interests of a small number of wealthy elites rather than the people at large. From these sentiments, an organized political opposition arose.

The Republican Opposition

The Constitution made no reference to political parties. Most of the framers believed that organized parties were dangerous "factions" to be avoided. Disagreement was inevitable on particular issues, but they believed that such disagreements need not and should not lead to the formation of permanent factions.

Yet not many years had passed after the ratification of the Constitution before Madison and others became convinced that Hamilton and his followers had become dangerous and self-interested. The Federalists had used the powers of their offices to reward their supporters and win additional allies. They were doing many of the same things, their opponents believed, that the corrupt British governments of the early eighteenth century had done.

Because the Federalists appeared to their critics to be creating such a menacing and tyrannical structure of power, there was no alternative but to organize a vigorous opposition. The result was the emergence of an alternative political organization, whose members called themselves "Republicans." (These first Republicans are not institutionally related to the modern Republican Party, which was created in the 1850s.) By the late 1790s, the *Formation of the First Party System*   Republicans were going to even greater lengths than the Federalists to create vehicles of partisan influence. In every state they formed committees, societies, and caucuses; Republican groups banded together to influence state and local elections. Neither side was willing to admit that it was acting as a party, nor would either concede the right of the other to exist. This institutionalized factionalism is known to historians as the "first party system."

From the beginning, the preeminent figures among the Republicans were Thomas Jefferson and James Madison. The most prominent spokesman for the cause, Jefferson

THE JEFFERSONIAN IDYLL   American artists in the early nineteenth century were drawn to tranquil rural scenes, symbolic of the Jeffersonian vision of a nation of small, independent farmers. By 1822, when Francis Alexander painted this depiction of "Ralph Wheelock's Farm," the simple agrarian republic was already being transformed by rapid economic growth. (© Courtesy National Gallery of Art, Washington, D.C.)

promoted a vision of an agrarian republic, in which most citizens would farm their own land. Jefferson did not scorn commercial or industrial activity. But he believed that the nation should be wary of too much urbanization and industrialization.

Although both parties had supporters across the country and among all classes, there were regional and economic differences. The Federalists   *Regional and Economic Differences* were most numerous in the commercial centers of the Northeast and in such southern seaports as Charleston; the Republicans were stronger in the rural areas of the South and the West. The difference in their philosophies was visible in, among other things, their reactions to the progress of the French Revolution. As that revolution grew increasingly radical in the 1790s, the Federalists expressed horror. But the Republicans applauded the democratic, antiaristocratic spirit they believed the French Revolution embodied.

When the time came for the nation's second presidential election, in 1792, both Jefferson and Hamilton urged Washington to run for a second term. The president reluctantly agreed. But while Washington had the respect of both factions, he was, in reality, more in sympathy with the Federalists than with the Republicans.

ESTABLISHING NATIONAL SOVEREIGNTY

The Federalists consolidated their position by acting effectively in managing the western territories and diplomacy.

SECURING THE WEST

Despite the Northwest Ordinance, the old Congress had largely failed to tie the outlying western areas of the country firmly to the national government. Farmers in western Massachusetts had rebelled; settlers in Vermont, Kentucky, and Tennessee had flirted with seceding from the Union. And at first, the new government under the Constitution faced similar problems.

WASHINGTON'S FAREWELL ADDRESS, *AMERICAN DAILY ADVERTISER*, SEPTEMBER 19, 1796

In this open letter to the American people, President Washington defended the young Constitution and warned against disunity among the nation's various states and political factions. Here he cautions citizens about another threat to the republic—entangling engagements abroad.

Observe good faith and justice toward all nations. Cultivate peace and harmony with all. Religion and morality enjoin this conduct. And can it be that good policy does not equally enjoin it? It will be worthy of a free, enlightened, and, at no distant period, a great nation to give to mankind the magnanimous and too novel example of a people always guided by an exalted justice and benevolence. . . .

In the execution of such a plan nothing is more essential than that permanent, inveterate antipathies against particular nations and passionate attachments for others should be excluded, and that, in place of them just and amicable feelings toward all should be cultivated. The nation which indulges toward another an habitual hatred or an habitual fondness is in some degree a slave. It is a slave to its animosity or to its affection either of which is sufficient to lead it astray from its duty and its interest. The nation prompted by ill will and resentment sometimes impels to war the government, contrary to the best calculations of policy. The government sometimes participates in the national propensity, and adopts through passion what reason would reject. . . .

So, likewise, a passionate attachment of one nation for another produces a variety of evils. Sympathy for the favorite nation, facilitating the illusion of an imaginary common interest in cases where no real common interest exists, and infusing into one the enmities of the other, betrays the former into a participation in the quarrels and wars of the latter without adequate inducement or justification. . . .

As avenues to foreign influence in innumerable ways, such attachments are particularly alarming to the truly enlightened and independent patriot. How many opportunities do they afford to tamper with domestic factions to practice the arts of seduction, to mislead public opinion, to influence or awe the public councils! Such an attachment of a small or weak toward a great and powerful nation dooms the former to be the satellite of the latter.

Against the insidious wiles of foreign influence (I conjure you to believe me, fellow citizens) the jealousy of a free people ought to be constantly awake, since history and experience prove that foreign influence is one of the most baneful foes of republican government. . . .

The great rule of conduct for us in regard to foreign nations is, in extending our commercial relation to have with them as little political connection as possible. So far as we have already formed engagements, let them be fulfilled with perfect good faith. Here let us stop.

Europe has a set of primary interests which to us have no, or a very remote, relation. Hence she must be engaged in frequent controversies, the causes of which are essentially foreign to our concerns. Hence, therefore, it must be unwise in us to implicate ourselves by artificial ties in the ordinary vicissitudes of her politics, or the ordinary combinations and collisions of her friendships or enmities.

Our detached and distant situation invites and enables us to pursue a different course. If we remain one people, under an efficient government, the period is not far off when we may defy material injury from external annoyance; when we may take such an attitude as will cause the neutrality we may at any time resolve upon to be scrupulously respected; when belligerent nations, under the impossibility of making acquisitions upon us, will not lightly hazard giving us provocation; when we may choose peace or war, as our interest, guided by justice, shall counsel.

Why forego the advantages of so peculiar a situation? Why quit our own to stand upon foreign ground? Why, by interweaving our destiny with that of any part of Europe, entangle our peace and prosperity in the toils of European ambition, rivalship, interest, humor, or caprice?

It is our true policy to steer clear of permanent alliances with any portion of the foreign world, so far, I mean, as we are now at liberty to do it. For let me not be understood as capable of patronizing infidelity to existing engagements. I hold the maxim of less applicable to public than to private affairs that honesty is always the best policy. I repeat therefore, let those engagements be observed in their genuine sense. But in my opinion it is unnecessary and would be unwise to extend them.

Taking care always to keep ourselves by suitable establishments on a respectable defensive posture, we may safely trust to temporary alliances for extraordinary emergencies.

Harmony, liberal intercourse with all nations, are recommended by policy, humanity, and interest. But even our commercial policy should hold an equal and impartial hand, neither seeking nor granting exclusive favors or preferences; . . . constantly keeping in view that it is folly in one nation to look for disinterested favors from another; that it must pay with a portion of its independence for whatever it may accept under that character; that by such acceptance it may place itself in the condition of having given equivalents for nominal favors, and yet of being reproached with ingratitude for not giving more. There can be no greater error than to expect or calculate upon real favors from nation to nation. It is an illusion which experience must cure, which a just pride ought to discard.

UNDERSTAND, ANALYZE, & EVALUATE

1. What advice did George Washington offer on foreign policy?
2. Did Washington advocate the complete isolation of the United States from Europe? Explain.
3. How did Washington characterize Europe? What circumstances of the 1790s may have inspired this assessment?

Source: www.senate.gov/artandhistory/history/minute/Washingtons_Farewell_Address.htm.

In 1794, farmers in western Pennsylvania raised a major challenge to federal authority when they refused to pay the new whiskey excise tax and began terrorizing tax collectors in the region. But the federal government did not leave settlement of the so-called Whiskey Rebellion to the authorities of Pennsylvania. At Hamilton's urging, *Whiskey Rebellion* Washington called out the militias of three states and assembled an army of nearly 15,000—and he personally led the troops into Pennsylvania. At the approach of the militiamen, the rebellion quickly collapsed.

The federal government won the allegiance of the whiskey rebels through intimidation. It secured the loyalties of other western people by accepting new states as members of the Union. The last two of the original thirteen colonies joined the Union once the Bill of Rights had been appended to the Constitution—North Carolina in 1789 and Rhode

Island in 1790. Vermont became the fourteenth state in 1791, after New York and New Hampshire agreed to give up their rights to it. Next came Kentucky, in 1792, when Virginia relinquished its claim to that region. After North Carolina ceded its western lands to the Union, Tennessee became a state in 1796.

The new government faced a greater challenge in more distant areas of the Northwest and the Southwest. The ordinances of 1784–1787, establishing the terms of white settlement in the West, had produced a series of border conflicts with native tribes. The new government inherited these tensions, which continued with few interruptions for nearly a decade.

Such clashes revealed another issue the Constitution had done little to resolve: the place of Native Americans within the new federal structure. The Constitution gave Congress power to "regulate Commerce . . . with the Indian tribes." And it bound the new government to respect treaties negotiated by the Confederation, most of which had been with the tribes. But none of this did very much to clarify the precise legal standing of Indians within the United States. The tribes received no direct representation in the *Native Americans' Ambiguous Status* new government. Above all, the Constitution did not address the major issue of land. Native Americans lived within the boundaries of the United States, yet they claimed (and the white government at times agreed) that they had some measure of sovereignty over their own land. But neither the Constitution nor common law offered any clear guide to the rights of a "nation within a nation" or to the precise nature of tribal sovereignty.

MAINTAINING NEUTRALITY

A crisis in Anglo-American relations emerged in 1793, when the revolutionary French government went to war with Great Britain. Both the president and Congress took steps to establish American neutrality in the conflict, but that neutrality was severely tested.

Early in 1794, the Royal Navy began seizing hundreds of American ships engaged in trade in the French West Indies. Hamilton was deeply concerned. War would mean an end to imports from England, and most of the revenue for maintaining his financial system came from duties on those imports. Hamilton and the Federalists did not trust the State Department, now in the hands of the ardently pro-French Edmund Randolph, to find a solution to the crisis. So they persuaded Washington to name a special commissioner—the chief justice of the Supreme Court, John Jay—to go to England and negotiate a solution. Jay was instructed to secure compensation for the recent British assaults on American shipping, to demand withdrawal of British forces from their posts on the frontier of the United States, and to negotiate a commercial treaty with Britain.

The long and complex treaty Jay negotiated in 1794 failed to achieve all these goals. But it settled the conflict with Britain, avoiding a likely war. It provided for undisputed American sovereignty over the entire Northwest and produced a reasonably satisfactory *Jay's Treaty* commercial relationship. Nevertheless, when the terms became known in America, criticism was intense. Opponents of the treaty went to great lengths to defeat it, but in the end the Senate ratified what was by then known as Jay's Treaty.

Jay's Treaty paved the way for a settlement of important American disputes with Spain. *Pinckney's Treaty* Under Pinckney's Treaty (negotiated by Thomas Pinckney and signed in 1795), Spain recognized the right of Americans to navigate the Mississippi to its mouth and to deposit goods at New Orleans for reloading on oceangoing ships; agreed to fix the northern boundary of Florida along the 31st parallel; and commanded its authorities to prevent Native Americans in Florida from launching raids north across that border. (For President Washington's views on such matters of foreign policy, see "Consider the Source: Washington's Farewell Address.")

THE DOWNFALL OF THE FEDERALISTS

Since almost everyone in the 1790s agreed that there was no place in a stable republic for organized parties, the emergence of the Republicans as a powerful and apparently permanent opposition seemed to the Federalists a grave threat to national stability. And so when international perils confronted the government in the 1790s, Hamilton and his followers moved forcefully against what they considered illegitimate dissent.

THE ELECTION OF 1796

George Washington refused to run for a third term as president in 1796. Jefferson was the obvious presidential candidate of the Republicans that year, but the Federalists faced a more difficult choice. Hamilton had created too many enemies to be a credible candidate. Vice President John Adams, who was not directly associated with any of the controversial Federalist achievements, received the party's nomination for president at a caucus of the Federalists in Congress.

The Federalists were still clearly the dominant party. But without Washington to mediate, they fell victim to fierce factional rivalries. Adams defeated Jefferson by *John Adams Elected* only three electoral votes and assumed the presidency as head of a divided party facing a powerful opposition. Jefferson became vice president by finishing second. (Not until the adoption of the Twelfth Amendment in 1804 did electors vote separately for president and vice president.)

THE QUASI WAR WITH FRANCE

American relations with Great Britain and Spain improved as a result of Jay's and Pinckney's treaties. But the nation's relations with revolutionary France quickly deteriorated. French vessels captured American ships on the high seas. The French government refused to receive Charles Cotesworth Pinckney when he arrived in Paris as the new American minister. In an effort to stabilize relations, Adams appointed a bipartisan commission to negotiate with France. When the Americans arrived in Paris in 1797, three agents of the French foreign minister, Prince Talleyrand, demanded a loan for France and a bribe for French officials before any negotiations could begin. Pinckney, a member of the commission, responded, "No! No! Not a sixpence!"

When Adams heard of the incident, he sent a message to Congress urging preparations for war. Before giving the commissioners' report to Congress, he deleted the names of the three French agents and designated them only as Messrs. X, Y, and Z. When the report was published, the "XYZ Affair," as it quickly became known, provoked *The "XYZ Affair"* widespread popular outrage at France's actions and strong popular support for the Federalists' response. For nearly two years, 1798 and 1799, the United States found itself engaged in an undeclared, **quasi war.**

Adams persuaded Congress to cut off all trade with France, to abrogate the treaties of 1778, and to authorize American vessels to capture French armed ships on the high seas.

In 1798, Congress created the Department of the Navy. The navy soon won a number of battles and captured a total of eighty-five French ships. The United States also began cooperating closely with the British. At last, the French began trying to conciliate the United States. Adams sent another commission to Paris in 1800, and the new French government (headed now by "First Consul" Napoleon Bonaparte) agreed to a treaty with the United States that canceled the old agreements of 1778 and established new commercial arrangements. As a result, the "war" came to a reasonably peaceful end.

REPRESSION AND PROTEST

The conflict with France helped the Federalists increase their majorities in Congress in 1798. They now began to consider ways to silence the Republican opposition. The result was some of the most controversial legislation in American history: the Alien and Sedition Acts.

The Alien Act placed new obstacles in the way of foreigners who wished to become American citizens. The Sedition Act allowed the government to prosecute those who engaged in "sedition" against the government. In theory, only libelous or treasonous activities were subject to prosecution; but since such activities had no clear definition, the law, in effect, gave the government authority to stifle virtually any opposition. The Republicans interpreted the new laws as part of a Federalist campaign to destroy them.

The Alien and Sedition Acts

President Adams signed the new laws but was cautious in implementing them. He did not deport any aliens, and he prevented the government from launching a broad crusade against the Republicans. But the Alien Act discouraged immigration and encouraged some foreigners already in the country to leave. And the administration used the Sedition Act to arrest and convict ten men, most of them Republican newspaper editors whose only crime had been criticism of the Federalists in government.

Republican leaders began to look for ways to reverse the Alien and Sedition Acts. Some looked to the state legislatures for help. They developed a theory to justify action by the states against the federal government in two sets of resolutions of 1798– 1799, one written (anonymously) by Jefferson and adopted by the Kentucky legislature, and the other drafted by Madison and approved by the Virginia legislature. The Virginia and Kentucky Resolutions, as they were known, used the ideas of John Locke and the Tenth Amendment to the Constitution to argue that the federal government had been formed by a "compact," or contract, among the states and possessed only certain delegated powers. Whenever a state decided that the central government had exceeded those powers, it had the right to "nullify" the appropriate laws.

Virginia and Kentucky Resolutions

The Republicans did not win wide support for the nullification idea; they did, however, succeed in elevating their dispute with the Federalists to the level of a national crisis. By the late 1790s, the entire nation was deeply and bitterly politicized. State legislatures at times resembled battlegrounds. Even the United States Congress was plagued with violent disagreements. In one celebrated incident in the chamber of the House of Representatives, Matthew Lyon, a Republican from Vermont, responded to an insult from Roger Griswold, a Federalist from Connecticut, by spitting in Griswold's eye. Griswold attacked Lyon with his cane, Lyon fought back with a pair of fire tongs, and soon the two men were wrestling on the floor.

CONGRESSIONAL BRAWLERS, 1798   This cartoon was inspired by the celebrated fight on the floor of the House of Representatives between Matthew Lyon, a Republican representative from Vermont, and Roger Griswold, a Federalist from Connecticut. Griswold (at right) attacks Lyon with his cane, and Lyon retaliates with fire tongs. Other members of Congress are portrayed enjoying the battle. (The Library of Congress)

THE "REVOLUTION" OF 1800

These bitter controversies shaped the presidential election of 1800. The presidential candidates were the same as four years earlier: Adams for the Federalists, *Election of 1800* Jefferson for the Republicans. But the campaign of 1800 was very different from the one preceding it. Adams and Jefferson themselves displayed reasonable dignity, but their supporters showed no such restraint. The Federalists accused Jefferson of being a dangerous radical whose followers were wild men who, if they should come to power, would bring on a reign of terror comparable to that of the French Revolution. The Republicans portrayed Adams as a tyrant conspiring to become king, and they accused the Federalists of plotting to impose slavery on the people. The election was close, and the crucial contest was in New York. There, Aaron Burr mobilized an organization of Revolutionary War veterans, the Tammany Society, to serve as a Republican political machine. Through Tammany's efforts, the party carried the city by a large majority, and with it the state. Jefferson was, apparently, elected.

But an unexpected complication soon jeopardized the Republican victory. The Constitution called for each elector to "vote by ballot for two persons." The expectation was that an elector would cast one vote for his party's presidential candidate and the other for his party's vice presidential candidate. To avoid a tie, the Republicans had intended that one elector would refrain from voting for the party's vice presidential candidate, Aaron Burr. But when the votes were counted, Jefferson and Burr each had 73. No candidate had a majority, and the House of Representatives had to choose between the two top candidates, Jefferson and Burr. Each state delegation would cast a single vote.

The new Congress, elected in 1800 with a Republican majority, was not to convene until after the inauguration of the president, so it was the Federalist Congress that had to decide the question. After a long deadlock, several leading Federalists concluded, following

Hamilton's advice, that Burr was too unreliable to trust with the presidency. On the thirty-sixth ballot, Jefferson was elected.

After the election of 1800, the only branch of the federal government left in Federalist hands was the judiciary. The Adams administration spent its last months in office taking *The Judiciary Act of 1801*   steps to make the party's hold on the courts secure. With the Judiciary Act of 1801, the Federalists reduced the number of Supreme Court justiceships by one but greatly increased the number of federal judgeships as a whole. Adams quickly appointed Federalists to the newly created positions. He also appointed a leading Federalist, John Marshall, to be chief justice of the Supreme Court, a position Marshall held for 34 years. Indeed, there were charges that he stayed up until midnight on his last day in office to finish signing the new judges' commissions. These officeholders became known as the "midnight appointments."

Even so, the Republicans viewed their victory as almost complete. The nation had, they believed, been saved from tyranny. The exuberance with which the victors viewed the future—and the importance they ascribed to the defeat of the Federalists—was evident in the phrase Jefferson himself later used to describe his election. He called it the "Revolution of 1800."

CONCLUSION

The Constitution of 1787 created a federal system of dispersed authority, authority divided among national and state governments and among an executive, a legislature, and a judiciary. The young nation thus sought to balance its need for an effective central government against its fear of concentrated and despotic power. The ability of the delegates to the Constitutional Convention to compromise revealed their yearning for a stable political system. The same willingness to compromise allowed the greatest challenge to the ideals of the new democracy—slavery—to survive intact.

The writing and ratifying of the Constitution settled some questions about the shape of the new nation. The first twelve years under the government created by the Constitution solved others. And yet by the year 1800, a basic disagreement about the future of the nation remained unresolved and was creating bitter divisions and conflicts within the political world. The election of Thomas Jefferson to the presidency that year opened a new chapter in the nation's public history. It also brought to a close, at least temporarily, savage political conflicts that had seemed to threaten the nation's future.

KEY TERMS/PEOPLE/PLACES/EVENTS

Alexander Hamilton 142	Great Compromise 136	Revolution of 1800 152
Alien and Sedition Acts 150	James Madison 136	separation of powers 137
Antifederalists 140	Jay's Treaty 148	*The Federalist Papers* 140
Bill of Rights 142	John Adams 141	Virginia and Kentucky
checks and balances 137	New Jersey Plan 135	Resolutions 150
Constitution 140	Pinckney's Treaty 148	Virginia Plan 135
federalism 136	quasi war 149	Whiskey Rebellion 147
Federalists 140	Republicans 144	XYZ Affair 149

RECALL AND REFLECT

1. How did the Constitution of 1787 attempt to resolve the weaknesses of the Articles of Confederation?
2. What role did *The Federalist Papers* play in the battle over ratification of the Constitution?
3. What were the main tenets of Alexander Hamilton's financial program?
4. What diplomatic crises did the United States face in the first decade of its existence, and how did the new government respond to these crises?
5. What was the "Revolution of 1800" and in what way was it a revolution?

7 | THE JEFFERSONIAN ERA

THE RISE OF CULTURAL NATIONALISM
STIRRINGS OF INDUSTRIALISM
JEFFERSON THE PRESIDENT
DOUBLING THE NATIONAL DOMAIN
EXPANSION AND WAR
THE WAR OF 1812

LOOKING AHEAD

1. How successful was Jefferson's effort to create a "republican" society dominated by sturdy, independent farmers?
2. How did the Napoleonic Wars affect the United States?
3. What events and issues led to the War of 1812?

THOMAS JEFFERSON AND HIS FOLLOWERS assumed control of the national government in 1801 as the champions of a distinctive vision of America. They favored a society of sturdy, independent farmers, happily free from the workshops, the industrial towns, and the urban mobs of Europe. They celebrated localism and republican simplicity. Above all, they proposed a federal government of sharply limited power.

Almost nothing worked out as they had planned, for during their years in power the young republic was developing in ways that made much of their vision obsolete. The American economy became steadily more diversified and complex, making the ideal of a simple, agrarian society impossible to maintain. American cultural life was dominated by a vigorous and ambitious nationalism. Jefferson himself contributed to the changes by exercising strong national authority at times and by arranging the greatest single increase in the size of the United States in its history.

THE RISE OF CULTURAL NATIONALISM

In many respects, American cultural life in the early nineteenth century reflected the Republican vision of the nation's future. Opportunities for education increased, the nation's literary and artistic life began to free itself from European influences, and American religion began to adjust to the spread of Enlightenment rationalism. In other ways, however, the new culture was posing a serious challenge to Republican ideals.

EDUCATIONAL AND LITERARY NATIONALISM

Central to the Republican vision of America was the concept of a virtuous and enlightened citizenry. Republicans believed, therefore, in the creation of a nationwide system of public schools in which all male citizens would receive free education. Such hopes were not fulfilled. Schooling remained primarily the responsibility of private institutions, most of which were open only to those who could afford to pay for them. In the South and in the mid-Atlantic states, most schools were run by religious groups. In New England, private academies were often more secular, many of them modeled on those founded by the Phillips family at Andover, Massachusetts, in 1778, and at Exeter, New Hampshire, three years later. Many were frankly aristocratic in outlook. Some educational institutions were open to the poor, but not nearly enough to accommodate everyone, and the education they offered was usually clearly inferior to that provided for more prosperous students.

Private secondary schools such as those in New England generally accepted only male students; even many public schools excluded females from the classroom. Yet the late eighteenth and early nineteenth centuries did see some important advances in education for

TIME LINE

1793
Eli Whitney invents cotton gin

1800
U.S. capital moves to Washington

1801
Second Great Awakening begins
Marshall named chief justice of Supreme Court

1803
Louisiana Purchase
Marbury v. Madison

1804–1806
Lewis and Clark expedition

1804
Jefferson reelected

1807
Embargo

1808
Madison elected president

1809
Non-Intercourse Act
Tecumseh Confederacy formed

1810
Macon's Bill No. 2

1811
Battle of Tippecanoe

1812
U.S. declares war on Great Britain
Madison reelected

1814
Hartford Convention
Treaty of Ghent

1815
Battle of New Orleans

women. As Americans began to place a higher value on the importance of the "republican mother" who would help train the new generation for citizenship, people began to ask how mothers could raise their children to be enlightened if the mothers themselves were uneducated. Such concerns helped speed the creation of female academies throughout the nation (usually for the daughters of affluent families). In 1789, Massachusetts required that its public schools serve females as well as males. Other states, although not all, soon followed.

Some women aspired to more. In 1784, Judith Sargent Murray published an essay *Judith Sargent Murray* defending the right of women to education. Women and men were equal in intellect and potential, Murray argued. Women, therefore, should have precisely the same educational opportunities as men. And they should have opportunities to earn their own livings and to establish roles in society apart from their husbands and families. Murray's ideas attracted relatively little support.

Because Jefferson and his followers liked to think of Native Americans as "noble savages" (uncivilized but not necessarily uncivilizable), they hoped that schooling the Indians in white culture would "uplift" the tribes. Missionaries and mission schools proliferated among the tribes. But there were no comparable efforts to educate enslaved African Americans.

Higher education similarly diverged from Republican ideals. The number of colleges and universities in America grew substantially, from nine at the time of the Revolution to twenty-two in 1800. None of the new schools, however, was truly public. Even universities established by state legislatures relied on private contributions and tuition fees to survive. Scarcely more than one white man in a thousand (and virtually no women, blacks, or Indians) had access to any college education, and those few who did attend universities were, almost without exception, members of prosperous, propertied families.

MEDICINE AND SCIENCE

Medicine and science were not always closely connected to each other in the early nineteenth century, but many physicians were working hard to strengthen the link. The University of Pennsylvania created the first American medical school in 1765. Most doctors, however, studied medicine by working with an established practitioner. Some American physicians believed in applying new scientific methods to medicine, but they had to struggle against age-old prejudices and superstitions. Efforts to teach anatomy, for example, encountered strong public hostility because of the dissection of cadavers that the study required. Municipal authorities had virtually no understanding of medical science and almost no idea of what to do in the face of the severe epidemics that so often swept their populations; only slowly did they respond to warnings that the lack of adequate sanitation programs was to blame for much disease.

Individual patients often had more to fear from their doctors than from their illnesses. Even the leading advocates of scientific medicine often embraced ineffective or dangerous treatments. George Washington's death in 1799 was probably less a result of the minor throat infection that had afflicted him than of his physicians' efforts to cure him by bleeding and purging.

The medical profession also used its newfound commitment to the "scientific" method to justify expanding its control over kinds of care that had traditionally been outside its domain. Most childbirths, for example, had been attended by female midwives in the *Decline of Midwifery* eighteenth century. In the early nineteenth century, physicians began to handle deliveries themselves. Among the results of that change were a narrowing of opportunities for women and a restriction of access to childbirth care for poor mothers (who could afford midwives but not physicians).

CULTURAL ASPIRATIONS OF THE NEW NATION

Many Americans dreamed of an American literary and artistic life that would rival the greatest achievements of Europe. The 1772 "Poem on the Rising Glory of America" predicted that America was destined to become the "seat of empire" and the "final stage" of civilization. Noah Webster, the Connecticut schoolmaster, lawyer, and author of widely used American spellers and dictionaries, echoed such sentiments, arguing that the American schoolboy should be educated as a nationalist. "As soon as he opens his lips," Webster wrote, "he should rehearse the history of his own country; he should lisp the praise of liberty, and of those illustrious heroes and statesmen who have wrought a revolution in her favor."

A growing number of writers began working to create a strong American literature. Among the most ambitious was the Philadelphia writer Charles *American Literature* Brockden Brown. But his fascination with horror and deviance kept him from developing a popular audience. More successful was Washington Irving of New York, whose popular folktales, recounting the adventures of such American rustics as Ichabod Crane and Rip Van Winkle, made him the widely acknowledged leader of American literary life in the early eighteenth century.

RELIGION AND REVIVALISM

By elevating ideas of individual liberty and reason, the American Revolution had weakened traditional forms of religious practice and challenged many ecclesiastical traditions. By the 1790s, only a small proportion of white Americans were members of formal churches, and ministers were complaining about the "decay of vital piety."

METHODIST CAMP MEETING, 1837 Camp (or revival) meetings were popular among some evangelical Christians in America as early as 1800. By the 1820s, there were approximately 1,000 meetings a year, most of them in the South and the West. After one such meeting in 1806, a participant wrote: "Will I ever see anything more like the day of Judgement on the side of eternity—to see the people running, yes, running from every direction to the stand, weeping, shouting, and shouting for joy.... O! Glorious day they went home singing shouting." This lithograph, dated 1837, suggests the degree to which women predominated at many revivals. (© Granger, NYC—All Rights Reserved.)

Religious traditionalists were particularly alarmed about the emergence of new, "rational" religious doctrines—theologies that reflected modern, scientific attitudes. **Deism,** which had originated among Enlightenment philosophers in France, attracted such educated Americans as Jefferson and Benjamin Franklin and by 1800 was reaching a moderately broad popular audience. Deists accepted the existence of God, but they considered Him a remote "watch-maker" who, after having created the universe, had withdrawn from direct involvement with the human race and its sins. Religious skepticism also produced the philosophies of "universalism" and "unitarianism." Disciples of these new ideas rejected the traditional Calvinist belief in predestination and the idea of the Trinity. Jesus was only a great religious teacher, they claimed, not the son of God. But religious skepticism attracted relatively few people. Most Americans clung to more traditional faiths. Beginning in 1801, traditional religion staged a dramatic comeback in a wave of revivalism known as the Second Great Awakening.

The origins of the Awakening lay in the efforts of conservative theologians to fight *The Second Great Awakening* the spread of religious rationalism and of church establishments. Presbyterians expanded their efforts on the western fringes of white settlement. Itinerant Methodist preachers traveled throughout the nation to win recruits for their new church, which soon became the fastest-growing denomination in America. Almost as successful were the Baptists, who found an especially fervent following in the South.

By the early nineteenth century, the revivalist energies of all these denominations were combining to create the greatest surge of evangelical fervor since the first Great Awakening sixty years before. In only a few years, membership in churches embracing revivalism was *Cane Ridge* mushrooming. At Cane Ridge, Kentucky, in the summer of 1801, a group of evangelical ministers presided over the nation's first "camp meeting"—an extraordinary revival that lasted several days and impressed all who saw it with its fervor and its size (some estimated that 25,000 people attended). Such events became common in subsequent years.

The basic message of the Second Great Awakening was that individuals must readmit God and Christ into their daily lives. They must embrace a fervent, active piety, and they must reject the skeptical rationalism that threatened traditional beliefs. Yet the wave of revivalism did not restore the religion of the past. Few denominations any longer accepted the idea of predestination, and the belief that people could affect their own destinies added intensity to the individual's search for salvation. The Awakening, in short, combined a more active piety with a belief in a God whose grace could be attained through faith and good works.

One of the striking features of the Awakening was the preponderance of women within *New Roles for Women* it. Female converts far outnumbered males. That may have been due in part to the movement of industrial work out of the home and into the factory. That process robbed women of one of their roles as part of a household-based economy and left many feeling isolated. Religious enthusiasm provided, among other things, access to a new range of activities—charitable societies ministering to orphans and the poor, missionary organizations, and others—in which women came to play important parts.

In some areas of the country, revival meetings were open to people of all races. From these revivals emerged a group of black preachers who became important figures within the enslaved community. Some of them translated the apparently egalitarian religious message of the Awakening—that salvation was available to all—into a similarly liberating message for blacks in the present world. Out of black revival meetings in Virginia, for example, arose an elaborate plan in 1800 (devised by Gabriel Prosser, the brother of a black preacher) for a slave rebellion and an attack on Richmond. The plan was discovered and foiled in advance by whites, but revivalism continued in subsequent years to create occasional racial unrest in the South.

The spirit of revivalism was particularly strong among Native Americans. Presbyterian and Baptist missionaries were active among the southern tribes and sparked a wave of conversions. But the most important revivalist was Handsome Lake, a *Handsome Lake* Seneca whose seemingly miraculous "rebirth" after years of alcoholism helped give him a special stature within his tribe. Handsome Lake called for a revival of traditional Indian ways, a repudiation of the individualism of white society, and a restoration of the communal quality of the Indian world. His message spread through the scattered Iroquois communities that had survived the military and political setbacks of previous decades and inspired many Indians to give up whiskey, gambling, and other destructive customs derived from white society. But Handsome Lake also encouraged Christian missionaries to become active within the tribes, and he urged Iroquois men to abandon their roles as hunters and become sedentary farmers instead. As in much of white society, Iroquois women, who had traditionally done the farming, were to move into more domestic roles.

STIRRINGS OF INDUSTRIALISM

While Americans had been engaged in a revolution to win their independence, an even more important revolution had been in progress in England: the emergence of modern industrialism. Power-driven machines were permitting manufacturing to become more rapid and extensive—with profound social and economic consequences. (See "America in the World: The Global Industrial Revolution.")

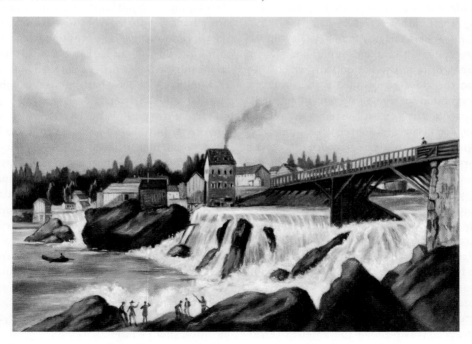

PAWTUCKET BRIDGE AND FALLS   One reason for the growth of the textile industry in New England in the early nineteenth century was that there were many sources of water power in the region to run the machinery in the factories. That was certainly the case with Slater's Mill, one of the first American textile factories. It was located in Pawtucket, Rhode Island, alongside a powerful waterfall, demonstrating the critical importance of water power to early American industry. (© Bettmann/Corbis)

THE GLOBAL INDUSTRIAL REVOLUTION

While Americans were engaged in a revolution to win their independence, they were also taking the first steps toward another great revolution—one that was already in progress in England and Europe. It was the emergence of modern industrialism. Historians differ over precisely when the **Industrial Revolution** began, but it is clear that by the end of the eighteenth century it was well under way in many parts of the world. A hundred years later, the global process of industrialization had transformed the societies of Britain, most of continental Europe, Japan, and the United States. Its social and economic consequences were complex and profound and continue to shape the nature of global society.

For Americans, the Industrial Revolution largely resulted from rapid changes in Great Britain, the nation with which they had the closest relations. Britain was the first nation to develop significant industrial capacity. The factory system took root in England in the late eighteenth century, revolutionizing the manufacture of cotton thread and cloth. One invention followed another in quick succession. Improvements in weaving drove improvements in spinning, and these changes created a demand for new devices for carding (combing and straightening the fibers for the spinner). Water, wind, and animal power continued to be important in the textile industry; but more important was the emergence of steam power—which began to proliferate after the appearance of James Watt's advanced steam engine (patented in 1769). Cumbersome and inefficient by modern standards, Watt's engine was nevertheless a major improvement over earlier "atmospheric" engines. England's textile industry

quickly became the most profitable in the world, and it helped encourage comparable advances in other fields of manufacturing as well.

Despite the efforts of the British government to prevent the export of English industrial technology, knowledge of the new machines reached other nations quickly, usually through the emigration of people who had learned the technology in British factories. America benefited the most because it received more immigrants from Great Britain than from any other country, but English technology spread quickly to the nations of continental Europe as well. Belgium was the first, developing a significant coal, iron, and armaments industry in the early nineteenth century. France—profiting from the immigration of approximately fifteen thousand British workers with advanced technological skills—had created a substantial industrial capacity in textiles and metals by the end of the 1820s, which in turn contributed to a great boom in railroad construction later in the century. German industrialization progressed rapidly after 1840, beginning with coal and iron production and then, in the 1850s, moving into large-scale railroad construction. By the late nineteenth century, Germany had created some of the world's largest industrial corporations. In Japan, the sudden intrusion of American and European traders helped spur the so-called Meiji reforms of the 1880s and 1890s, which launched a period of rapid industrialization there as well.

Industrialization changed not just the world's economies but also its societies. First in England and then in Europe, America, and Japan, social systems underwent wrenching changes. Hundreds of thousands of men and women moved from rural areas into cities to work in factories, where they experienced both the benefits and the costs of industrialization. The standard of living of the new working class, when objectively quantified, was usually significantly higher than that of the rural poor. Most of those who moved from farm to factory, in other words, experienced some improvement in nutrition and other material circumstances. But the psychological costs of being suddenly uprooted from one way of life and thrust into a fundamentally different one could outweigh the economic gains. There was little in most workers' prior experience to prepare them for the nature of industrial labor. It was disciplined, routinized work with a fixed and rigid schedule, a sharp contrast to the varying, seasonal work pattern of the rural economy. Nor were many factory workers prepared for life in the new industrial towns and expanding cities. Industrial workers experienced, too, a fundamental change in their relationship with their employers. Unlike rural landlords and local aristocrats, factory owners and managers were usually remote and inaccessible figures. The new class of industrial **capitalists,** many of them accumulating unprecedented wealth, dealt with their workers impersonally, and the result was a growing schism between the two classes— each lacking access to or understanding of the other. Working men and women throughout the globe began thinking of themselves as a distinct class, with common goals and interests. And their efforts simultaneously to adjust to their new way of life and to resist its most damaging aspects sometimes created great social turbulence. Battles between workers and employers became a characteristic feature of industrial life throughout the world.

Life in industrial nations changed at every level. Populations grew rapidly, and people began to live longer. At the same time, pollution, crime, and infectious disease (until modern sanitation systems emerged) increased greatly in industrialized cities. Around the industrial world, middle classes expanded and came, in varying degrees, to dominate the economy (although not always the culture or the politics) of their nations.

Not since the agrarian revolution thousands of years earlier, when many humans had turned from hunting to farming for sustenance, had there been an economic change of a magnitude comparable to the Industrial Revolution. Centuries of traditions, of social patterns, and of cultural and religious assumptions were challenged and often shattered. The tentative stirrings of industrial activity in the United States in the early nineteenth century, therefore, were part of a vast movement that over the course of the next century was to transform much of the globe. •

UNDERSTAND, ANALYZE, & EVALUATE

1. Why did the British government attempt to prevent the export of Britain's industrial technology?
2. What did the Industrial Revolution mean for ordinary people around the world?

TECHNOLOGY IN AMERICA

Nothing comparable to the English Industrial Revolution occurred in America in the first two decades of the nineteenth century. Yet even while Jeffersonians warned of the dangers of rapid economic change, they witnessed a series of technological advances that would ultimately help ensure that the United States, too, would be transformed. Some of these technological advances were English imports. Despite efforts by the British government to prevent the export of textile machinery or the emigration of skilled mechanics, a number of immigrants with advanced knowledge of English technology arrived in the United States, eager to introduce the new machines to America. Samuel Slater, for example, used the knowledge he had acquired before leaving England to build a spinning mill in Pawtucket, Rhode Island, for the Quaker merchant Moses Brown in 1790.

America also produced notable inventors of its own. In 1793, Eli Whitney invented a machine that performed the arduous task of removing the seeds from short-staple cotton quickly and efficiently. It was dubbed the cotton gin ("gin" was a derivative of "engine"). With the device, a single operator could clean as much cotton in a few hours as it once took a group of workers to do in a day. The results were profound. Soon cotton cultivation spread throughout the South. (Previously it had been restricted largely to the coast *The Cotton Gin and the Spread of Slavery* and the Sea Islands, the only places where long-staple cotton—easily cleaned without the cotton gin—could be grown.) Within a decade, the total cotton crop increased eightfold. African American slavery, which with the decline of tobacco production had seemed for a time to be a dwindling institution, expanded and firmly fixed itself upon the South. The large supply of domestically produced fiber also served as a strong incentive to entrepreneurs in New England and elsewhere to develop a native textile industry.

Whitney was an important figure in the history of American technology for another reason as well. He helped introduce the concept of interchangeable parts to the United States. As machines such as the cotton gin began to be widely used, it *Importance of Interchangeable Parts* became increasingly important for owners of such machines to have access to spare parts—and for the parts to be made so that they fit the machines properly. Whitney designed not only the cotton gin, but also machine tools that could manufacture its component parts to exact specifications. The U.S. government later commissioned Whitney to manufacture 1,000 muskets for the army. Each part of the gun had to be interchangeable with the equivalent part in every other gun.

Interchangeability was of great importance in the United States because of the great distances many people had to travel to reach towns or cities and the relatively limited transportation systems available to them. Interchangeable parts meant that a farmer could repair a machine himself. But the interchangeability that Whitney championed was not easy to achieve. In theory, many parts were designed to be interchangeable. In reality, the actual manufacturing of such parts was for many years not nearly precise enough. Farmers and others often had to do considerable fitting before the parts would work in their equipment. Not until later in the century would machine tools be developed to the point that they could make truly interchangeable parts.

TRANSPORTATION INNOVATIONS

One of the prerequisites for industrialization is a transportation system that allows the efficient movement of raw materials to factories and of finished goods to markets. The United States had no such system in the early years of the republic, and thus it had no domestic market extensive enough to justify large-scale production. But projects were under way that would ultimately remove the transportation obstacle.

One such project was the development of the steamboat. England had pioneered steam power, and even steam navigation, in the eighteenth century, and there had been experiments in America in the 1780s and 1790s in various forms of steam-powered transportation. A major advance emerged out of the efforts of the *Robert Fulton's Steamboat* inventor Robert Fulton and the promoter Robert R. Livingston, who made possible the launching of a steamboat large enough to carry passengers. Their *Clermont,* equipped with paddle wheels and an English-built engine, sailed up the Hudson River in the summer of 1807.

Meanwhile, what was to become known as the "turnpike era" had begun. In 1794, a corporation built a toll road running the sixty miles from Philadelphia *The "Turnpike Era"* to Lancaster, Pennsylvania, with a hard-packed surface of crushed stone that provided a good year-round surface with effective drainage (but was very expensive to construct). The Pennsylvania venture proved so successful that similar turnpikes (so named from the kind of tollgate frequently used) were laid out from other cities to neighboring towns.

The process of building the turnpikes was a difficult one. Companies had to survey their routes with many things in mind, particularly elevation. Horse-drawn vehicles had great difficulty traveling along roads with more than a five-degree incline, which required many roads to take very circuitous routes to avoid steep hills. Building roads over mountains was an almost insurmountable task, and no company was successful in doing so until governments began to participate in the financing of the projects.

COUNTRY AND CITY

Despite all these changes, America remained an overwhelmingly rural and agrarian nation. Only 3 percent of the population lived in towns of more than 8,000 in 1800. Even the nation's largest cities could not begin to compare with such European capitals as London and Paris (though Philadelphia, with 70,000 residents, New York, with 60,000, and others were becoming centers of commerce, learning, and urban culture comparable to many of the secondary cities of Europe).

People in cities and towns lived differently from the vast majority of Americans who continued to work as farmers. Among other things, urban life produced affluence, and affluent people sought increasing elegance and refinement in their homes, their grounds, and their dress. They also looked for diversions—music, theater, dancing, and, for many people, horse racing. Informal horse racing had begun as early as the 1620s, and the first formal race course in North America opened near New York City in 1665. By the early nineteenth century, it was a popular activity in most areas of the country. The crowds that gathered at horse races were an early sign of the vast appetite for popular, public entertainments that would be an enduring part of American culture. (See "Patterns of Popular Culture: Horse Racing.")

It was still possible for some to believe that this small nation might not become a complex modern society. But the forces pushing such a transformation were already at work. And Thomas Jefferson, for all his commitment to the agrarian ideal, found himself as president obliged to confront and accommodate them.

HORSE RACING

Informal horse racing began in North America almost as soon as Europeans settled the English colonies. Formal racing followed quickly. The first racetrack in North America—New Market (named for a popular racecourse in England)—was established in 1665 on Long Island, near present-day Garden City, New York. Tracks quickly developed wide appeal, and soon horse racing had spread up and down the Atlantic Coast. By the time of the American Revolution, it was popular in almost every colony and was moving as well into the newly settled areas of the Southwest. Andrew Jackson was a founder of the first racetrack in Nashville, Tennessee, in the early nineteenth century. Kentucky—whose native bluegrass was early recognized as ideal for grazing horses—had eight tracks by 1800.

Like almost everything else in the life of early America, the world of horse racing was bounded by lines of class and race. For many years, it was considered the exclusive preserve of "gentlemen," so much so that in 1674, a Virginia court fined James Bullocke, a tailor, for proposing a race, "it being contrary to Law for a Labourer to make a race, being a sport only for Gentlemen." But while white aristocrats retained control of racing, they were not the only people who participated in it. Southern planters often trained young male slaves as jockeys for their horses, just as northern horse owners employed the services of free blacks as riders. In the North and the South, African Americans eventually emerged as some of the most talented and experienced trainers of racing horses. And despite social and legal pressures, free blacks and poor whites often staged their own informal races.

Racing also began early to reflect the growing sectional rivalry between the North and South. In 1824, the Union Race Course on Long Island established an astounding $24,000 purse for a race between two famous thoroughbreds: American Eclipse (from the North) and Sir Henry (from the South). American Eclipse won two of the three heats. A southern racehorse prevailed in another such celebrated contest in 1836. These intersectional races, which drew enormous crowds and created tremendous publicity, continued into the 1850s, until the North-South rivalry began to take a more deadly form.

Horse racing remained popular after the Civil War, but two developments changed its character considerably. One was the successful effort to drive African Americans out of the sport. At least until the 1890s, black jockeys and trainers remained central to racing. At the first Kentucky Derby, in 1875, fourteen of the fifteen horses had African American riders. One black man, Isaac Murphy, won a remarkable 44 percent of all races in which he rode, including three Kentucky Derbys. Gradually, however, the same social dynamics that enforced racial segregation in so many other areas of American life penetrated racing as well. By the beginning of the twentieth century, white jockeys and organized jockey clubs had driven almost all black riders and many black trainers out of the sport.

The second change was the introduction of formalized betting. In the late nineteenth century, racetracks created betting systems to lure customers to the races. At the same time that the breeding of racehorses

OAKLAND HOUSE AND RACE COURSE This 1840 painting by Robert Brammer and August A. Von Smith portrays men and women flocking to an early race course in Louisville, Kentucky, which provided entertainment to affluent white southerners. (*Oakland House and Race Course, Louisville, 1840*. By Robert Brammer and August A. Von Smith. © Collection of The Speed Art Museum, Louisville, Kentucky. Purchase, Museum Art Fund, 56.19)

was moving into the hands of enormously wealthy families, the audience for racing was becoming increasingly working class and lower middle class. The people who now came to racetracks were mostly white men, and some white women, who were lured not by a love of horses but by the usually futile hope of quick and easy riches through gambling. •

UNDERSTAND, ANALYZE, & EVALUATE

1. Why do you think horse racing was such a popular spectator sport in early America? Why has it continued to be popular?
2. How did changes in the sport of horse racing reflect similar changes in American society at large?

JEFFERSON THE PRESIDENT

Privately, Thomas Jefferson may well have considered his victory over John Adams in 1800 to be what he later termed it: a revolution "as real . . . as that of 1776." Publicly, however, he was restrained and conciliatory, attempting to minimize the differences between the two parties and calm the passions that the bitter campaign had aroused. There was no public repudiation of Federalist policies, no true "revolution." Indeed, at times Jefferson seemed to outdo the Federalists at their own work.

THE FEDERAL CITY AND THE "PEOPLE'S PRESIDENT"

The modest character of the federal government during the Jeffersonian era was symbolized by the newly founded national capital, the city of Washington, D.C. There were many who envisioned that the uncompleted town, designed by the French architect Pierre L'Enfant, would soon emerge as the Paris of the United States.

In reality, throughout most of the nineteenth century Washington remained little more than a straggling, provincial village. Although the population increased steadily from the

3,200 counted in the 1800 census, it never rivaled that of New York, Philadelphia, or the other major cities of the nation and remained a raw, inhospitable community. Members of Congress viewed Washington not as a home but as a place to visit briefly during *Life in Washington, D.C.* sessions of the legislature. Most lived in a cluster of simple boardinghouses in the vicinity of the Capitol. It was not unusual for a member of Congress to resign his seat in the midst of a session to return home if he had an opportunity to accept the more prestigious post of member of his state legislature.

Jefferson was a wealthy planter by background, but as president he conveyed to the public an image of plain, almost crude disdain for pretension. Like an ordinary citizen, he walked to and from his inauguration at the Capitol. In the presidential mansion, which had not yet acquired the name "White House," he disregarded the courtly etiquette of his predecessors. He did not always bother to dress up, prompting the British ambassador to complain of being received by the president in clothes that were "indicative of utter slovenliness and indifference to appearances."

Yet Jefferson managed to impress most of those who knew him. He probably had a wider range of interests and accomplishments than any other major political figure in American history, with the possible exception of Benjamin Franklin. In addition to politics and diplomacy, he was an active architect, educator, inventor, farmer, and philosopher-scientist.

THOMAS JEFFERSON This 1805 portrait by the noted American painter Rembrandt Peale shows Jefferson at the beginning of his second term as president. It also conveys (through the simplicity of dress and the slightly unkempt hair) the image of democratic simplicity that Jefferson liked to project as the champion of the "common man." (© Bettmann/Corbis)

Jefferson was a shrewd and practical politician. He worked hard to exert influence as the leader of his party, giving direction to Republicans in Congress by quiet and sometimes even devious means. Although the Republicans had objected strenuously to the efforts of their Federalist predecessors to build a network of influence through patronage, Jefferson used his powers of appointment as an effective political weapon. Like Washington before him, he believed that federal offices should be filled with men loyal to the principles and policies of the administration. By the end of his second term, practically all federal jobs were held by loyal Republicans. Jefferson was a popular president and had little difficulty winning reelection against Federalist Charles C. Pinckney in 1804. Jefferson won by the overwhelming electoral majority of 162 to 14, and Republican membership of both houses of Congress increased.

Dollars and Ships

Under Washington and Adams, the Republicans believed, the government had been needlessly extravagant. Yearly federal expenditures had almost tripled between 1793 and 1800, as Hamilton had hoped. The public debt had also risen, and an extensive system of internal taxation had been erected.

The Jefferson administration moved deliberately to reverse these trends. In 1802, the president persuaded Congress to abolish all internal taxes, leaving customs duties and the sale of western lands as the only sources of revenue for the *Limiting the Federal Government* government. Meanwhile, Secretary of the Treasury Albert Gallatin drastically reduced government spending. Although Jefferson was unable entirely to retire the national debt as he had hoped, he did cut it almost in half (from $83 million to $45 million).

Jefferson also scaled down the armed forces. He reduced the already tiny army of 4,000 men to 2,500 and pared down the navy from twenty-five ships in commission to seven. Anything but the smallest of standing armies, he argued, might menace civil liberties and civilian control of government. Yet Jefferson was not a pacifist. At the same time that he was reducing the size of the army and navy, he helped establish the United States Military Academy at West Point, founded in 1802. And when trouble started brewing overseas, he began again to build up the fleet. Such trouble appeared first in the Mediterranean, off the coast of northern Africa.

For years the Barbary states of North Africa—Morocco, Algiers, Tunis, and Tripoli—had been demanding protection money, paid to avoid piracy, from all nations whose ships sailed the Mediterranean. During the 1780s and 1790s the United States, too, had agreed to treaties providing for annual tribute to the Barbary states, but Jefferson showed reluctance to continue this policy of appeasement.

In 1801, the pasha of Tripoli forced Jefferson's hand. Unhappy with American responses to his demands, he ordered the flagpole of the American *Challenging the Barbary Pirates* consulate chopped down—a symbolic declaration of war. Jefferson responded cautiously and built up American naval forces in the area over the next several years. Finally, in 1805, he agreed to terms by which the United States ended the payment of tribute to Tripoli but paid a substantial (and humiliating) ransom for the release of American prisoners.

Conflict with the Courts

Having won control of the executive and legislative branches of government, the Republicans looked with suspicion on the judiciary, which remained largely in the hands of Federalist judges. Soon after Jefferson's first inauguration, his followers in Congress launched an attack on this last preserve of the opposition. Their first step was the repeal of the Judiciary Act of 1801, thus eliminating the judgeships to which Adams had made his "midnight appointments."

The debate over the courts led to one of the most important judicial decisions in the history of the nation. Federalists had long maintained that the Supreme Court had the authority to nullify acts of Congress, and the Court itself had actually exercised the power of judicial review in 1796 when it upheld the validity of a law passed by Congress. But the Court's authority in this area would not be secure, it was clear, until it actually declared Marbury v. Madison a congressional act unconstitutional. In 1803, in the case of *Marbury v. Madison,* it did so. William Marbury, one of Adams's midnight appointments, had been named a justice of the peace in the District of Columbia. But his commission, although signed and sealed, had not been delivered to him before Adams left office. When Jefferson took office, his secretary of state, James Madison, refused to hand over the commission. Marbury asked the Supreme Court to direct Madison to perform his official duty. But the Court ruled that while Marbury had a right to his commission, the Court had no authority to order Madison to deliver it. On the surface, therefore, the decision was a victory for the administration. But of much greater importance than the relatively insignificant matter of Marbury's commission was the Court's reasoning in the decision.

The original Judiciary Act of 1789 had given the Court the power to compel executive officials to act in such matters as the delivery of commissions, and it was on that basis that Marbury had filed his suit. But the Court ruled that Congress had exceeded its authority, that the Constitution defined the powers of the judiciary, and that the legislature had no right to expand them. The relevant section of the 1789 act was, therefore, void. In seeming to deny its own authority, the Court was in fact radically enlarging it. The justices had repudiated a relatively minor power (the power to force the delivery of a commission) by asserting a vastly greater one (the power to nullify an act of Congress).

The chief justice of the United States at the time of the ruling (and until 1835) was John Marshall John Marshall. A leading Federalist and prominent Virginia lawyer, he had served John Adams as secretary of state. Ironically, it was Marshall who had failed to deliver Marbury's commission. In 1801, just before leaving office, Adams had appointed him chief justice, and almost immediately Marshall established himself as the dominant figure of the Court, shaping virtually all its most important rulings—including, of course, *Marbury v. Madison.* Through a succession of Republican presidents, he battled to give the federal government unity and strength. And in so doing, he established the judiciary as a coequal branch of government with the executive and the legislature.

DOUBLING THE NATIONAL DOMAIN

In the same year Jefferson was elected president of the United States, Napoleon Bonaparte made himself ruler of France with the title of first consul. In the year Jefferson was reelected, Napoleon named himself emperor. The two men had little in common, yet for a time they were of great assistance to each other in international politics.

JEFFERSON AND NAPOLEON

Having failed in a grandiose plan to seize India from the British Empire, Napoleon began to dream of restoring French power in the New World. The territory east of the Mississippi, which France had ceded to Great Britain in 1763, was now part of the United States, but

Napoleon hoped to regain the lands west of the Mississippi, which had belonged to Spain since the end of the Seven Years' War. In 1800, under the secret Treaty of San Ildefonso, France regained title to Louisiana, which included almost the whole of the Mississippi Valley to the west of the river. The Louisiana Territory would, Napoleon hoped, become the heart of a great French empire in America.

Jefferson was unaware at first of Napoleon's imperial ambitions in America. For a time he pursued a foreign policy that reflected his well-known admiration for France. But he began to reassess American relations with the French when he *Importance of New Orleans* heard rumors of the secret transfer of Louisiana. Particularly troubling to Jefferson was French control of New Orleans, the outlet through which the produce of the fast-growing western regions of the United States was shipped to the markets of the world.

Jefferson was even more alarmed when, in the fall of 1802, he learned that the Spanish intendant at New Orleans (who still governed the city, since the French had not yet taken formal possession of the region) had announced a disturbing new regulation. American ships sailing the Mississippi River had for many years been accustomed to depositing their cargoes in New Orleans for transfer to oceangoing vessels. The intendant now forbade the practice, even though Spain had guaranteed Americans that right in the Pinckney Treaty of 1795.

Westerners demanded that the federal government do something to reopen the river, and the president faced a dilemma. If he yielded to the frontier clamor and tried to change the policy by force, he would run the risk of a major war with France. If he ignored the westerners' demands, he would lose political support. But Jefferson envisioned another solution. He instructed Robert Livingston, the American ambassador in Paris, to negotiate

NEW ORLEANS IN 1803 Because of its location near the mouth of the Mississippi River, New Orleans was the principal port of western North America in the early nineteenth century. Through it, western farmers shipped their produce to markets in the East and Europe. This 1803 painting celebrates the American acquisition of the city from France as part of the Louisiana Purchase. (© Chicago History Museum, USA/Bridgeman Images)

for the purchase of New Orleans. Livingston, on his own authority, proposed that the French sell the United States the rest of Louisiana as well.

In the meantime, Jefferson persuaded Congress to appropriate funds for an expansion of the army and the construction of a river fleet, and he hinted that American forces might soon descend on New Orleans and that the United States might form an alliance with Great *Napoleon's Offer* Britain if the problems with France were not resolved. Perhaps in response, Napoleon suddenly decided to offer the United States the entire Louisiana Territory.

Napoleon had good reasons for the decision. His plans for an empire in America had already gone seriously awry, partly because a yellow fever epidemic had wiped out much of the French army in the New World and partly because the expeditionary force he wished to send to reinforce the troops had been icebound in a Dutch harbor through the winter of 1802–1803. By the time the harbor thawed in the spring of 1803, Napoleon was preparing for a renewed war in Europe. He would not, he realized, have the resources to secure an empire in America.

THE LOUISIANA PURCHASE

Faced with Napoleon's sudden proposal, Livingston and James Monroe, whom Jefferson had sent to Paris to assist in the negotiations, had to decide whether they should accept it even if they had no authorization to do so. But fearful that Napoleon might withdraw the offer, they decided to proceed. After some haggling over the price, Livingston and Monroe signed an agreement with Napoleon on April 30, 1803.

By the terms of the treaty, the United States was to pay a total of 80 million francs ($15 million) to the French government. The United States was also to grant certain exclusive commercial privileges to France in the port of New Orleans and to incorporate the residents of Louisiana into the Union with the same rights and privileges as other citizens. The boundaries of the purchase were not clearly defined.

In Washington, the president was both pleased and embarrassed when he received the treaty. He was pleased with the terms of the bargain; but he was uncertain about his authority to accept it, since the Constitution said nothing about the acquisition of new territory. But Jefferson's *Jefferson's Ideological Dilemma* advisers persuaded him that his treaty-making power under the Constitution would justify the purchase, and Congress promptly approved the treaty. Finally, late in 1803, General James Wilkinson, a commissioner of the United States, took formal control of the territory. Before long, the Louisiana Territory was organized on the general pattern of the Northwest Territory, with the assumption that it would be divided eventually into states. The first of these was admitted to the Union as the state of Louisiana in 1812.

EXPLORING THE WEST

Meanwhile, a series of explorations revealed the geography of the far-flung new territory to white Americans. In 1803, Jefferson helped plan an expedition that was to cross the continent to the Pacific Ocean, gather geographical information, and investigate prospects for trade with Native Americans. (See "Consider the Source: Thomas Jefferson to Meriwether Lewis, June 20, 1803.") The expedition began in May 1804. He named as its leader the twenty-nine-year-old Meriwether Lewis, a veteran of Indian wars who was skilled in the ways of the wilderness. Lewis chose as a colleague the thirty-four-year-old William Clark, *Lewis and Clark* an experienced frontiersman and soldier. Lewis and Clark, with a company of four dozen men, started up the Missouri River from St. Louis. With the Shoshone woman Sacajawea as their interpreter, they eventually crossed the Rocky Mountains, descended

EXPLORING THE LOUISIANA PURCHASE, 1804–1807 When Jefferson purchased the Louisiana Territory from France in 1803, he doubled the size of the nation. But few Americans knew what they had bought. The Lewis and Clark expedition set out in 1804 to investigate the new territory, and this map shows their route, along with that of another inveterate explorer, Zebulon Pike. Note the vast distances the two parties covered (including, in both cases, a great deal of land outside the Louisiana Purchase). Note, too, how much of this enormous territory lay outside the orbit of even these ambitious explorations. • *How did the American public react to the addition of this new territory?*

along the Snake and Columbia Rivers, and in the late autumn of 1805 camped on the Pacific Coast. In September 1806, they were back in St. Louis with elaborate records of the geography and the native civilizations they had observed along the way.

While Lewis and Clark explored, Jefferson dispatched other groups to other parts of the Louisiana Territory. Lieutenant Zebulon Montgomery Pike, twenty-six years old, led an expedition in the fall of 1805 from St. Louis into the upper Mississippi Valley. In the summer of 1806, he set out again, proceeding up the valley of the Arkansas River and into what later became Colorado. His account of his western travels helped create an enduring (and inaccurate) impression among most Americans that the land between the Missouri River and the Rockies was an uncultivatable desert.

The Burr Conspiracy

Jefferson's triumphant reelection in 1804 suggested that most of the nation approved of the new territorial acquisition. But some New England Federalists raged against it. They realized that the more new states that joined the Union, the less power their region and party would retain. In Massachusetts, a group of the most extreme Federalists, known as

CONSIDER THE SOURCE

THOMAS JEFFERSON TO MERIWETHER LEWIS, JUNE 20, 1803

In the summer of 1803, between the purchase and the incorporation of the Louisiana Territory, President Jefferson sent the following instructions to the explorer Meriwether Lewis. Here Jefferson reveals not only his own expansive curiosity, but also his administration's plans for the newly acquired lands.

To Meriwether Lewis, esquire, Captain of the 1st regiment of infantry of the United States of America: Your situation as Secretary of the President of the United States has made you acquainted with the objects of my confidential message of Jan. 18, 1803, to the legislature . . . you are appointed to carry them into execution.

Instruments for ascertaining by celestial observations the geography of the country thro' which you will pass, have already been provided. Light articles for barter, & presents among the Indians, arms for your attendants, say for from 10 to 12 men, boats, tents, & other travelling apparatus, with ammunition, medicine, surgical instruments & provisions you will have prepared with such aids as the Secretary at War can yield in his department; & from him also you will receive authority to engage among our troops, by voluntary agreement, the number of attendants above mentioned, over whom you, as their commanding officer are invested with all the powers the laws give in such a case. . . .

Your mission has been communicated to the Ministers here from France, Spain & Great Britain, and through them to their governments: and such assurances given them as to it's objects as we trust will satisfy them. The country of Louisiana having been ceded by Spain to France, the passport you have from the Minister of France, the representative of the present sovereign of the country, will be a protection with all its subjects: And that from the Minister of England

will entitle you to the friendly aid of any traders of that allegiance with whom you may happen to meet.

The object of your mission is to explore the Missouri river, & such principal stream of it, as, by it's course & communication with the waters of the Pacific Ocean, may offer the most direct & practicable water communication across this continent, for the purposes of commerce.

Beginning at the mouth of the Missouri, you will take observations of latitude & longitude, at all remarkable points on the river, & especially at the mouths of rivers, at rapids, at islands & other places & objects distinguished by such natural marks & characters of a durable kind, as that they may with certainty be recognized hereafter. . . . The interesting points of the portage between the heads of the Missouri & the water offering the best communication with the Pacific Ocean should also be fixed by observation, & the course of that water to the ocean, in the same manner as that of the Missouri.

Your observations are to be taken with great pains & accuracy, to be entered distinctly, & intelligibly for others as well as yourself, to comprehend all the elements necessary, with the aid of the usual tables, to fix the latitude and longitude of the places at which they were taken, & are to be rendered to the war office, for the purpose of having the calculations made concurrently by proper persons within the U.S. Several copies of these, as well as your other notes, should be made at leisure times & put into the care of the most trustworthy of your attendants, to guard by multiplying them, against the accidental losses to which they will be exposed. A further guard would be that one of these copies be written on the paper of the birch, as less liable to injury from damp than common paper.

The commerce which may be carried on with the people inhabiting the line you will pursue, renders a knowledge of these people important. You will therefore endeavor to make yourself acquainted, as far as a diligent pursuit of your journey shall admit, with the names of the nations & their numbers; the extent & limits of their possessions; their relations with other tribes or nations; their language, traditions, monuments; their ordinary occupations in agriculture, fishing, hunting, war, arts, & the implements for these; their food, clothing, & domestic accomodations; the diseases prevalent among them, & the remedies they use; moral & physical circumstances which distinguish them from the tribes we know; peculiarities in their laws, customs & dispositions; and articles of commerce they may need or furnish, & to what extent.

And considering the interest which every nation has in extending & strengthening the authority of reason & justice among the people around them, it will be useful to acquire what knowledge you can of the state of morality, religion & information among them, as it may better enable those who endeavor to civilize & instruct them, to adapt their measures to the existing notions & practises of those on whom they are to operate.

Other objects worthy of notice will be the soil & face of the country, it's growth & vegetable productions; especially those not of the U.S.; the animals of the country generally, & especially those not known in the U.S., the remains and accounts of any which may be deemed rare or extinct; the mineral productions of every kind; but more particularly metals, limestone, pit coal & saltpetre; salines & mineral waters, noting the temperature of the last, & such circumstances as may indicate their character. Volcanic appearances. Climate as characterized by the thermometer, by the proportion of rainy, cloudy & clear days, by lightening,

hail, snow, ice, by the access & recess of frost, by the winds prevailing at different seasons, the dates at which particular plants put forth or lose their flowers, or leaf, times of appearance of particular birds, reptiles or insects.

[. . .]

In all your intercourse with the natives treat them in the most friendly & conciliatory manner which their own conduct will admit; allay all jealousies as to the object of your journey, satisfy them of it's innocence, make them acquainted with the position, extent, character, peaceable & commercial dispositions of the U.S., of our wish to be neighborly, friendly & useful to them, & of our dispositions to a commercial intercourse with them; confer with them on the points most convenient as mutual emporiums, & the articles of most desireable interchange for them & us. If a few of their influential chiefs, within practicable distance, wish to visit us, arrange such a visit with them, and furnish them with authority to call on our officers, on their entering the U.S. to have them conveyed to this place at public expence. If any of them should wish to have some of their young people brought up with us, & taught such arts as may be useful to them, we will receive, instruct & take care of them, such a mission.

UNDERSTAND, ANALYZE, & EVALUATE

1. At the time that Jefferson wrote this letter, who held official possession of Louisiana? What European nations were present in the Louisiana Territory?
2. What do the details of this letter reveal about Jefferson's own interest in nature and science?
3. What guidance did Jefferson offer Lewis in regard to natives? What policy toward Native Americans did Jefferson seem to have in mind for the future?

Source: Gunther Barth (ed.), *The Lewis and Clark Expedition: Selections from the Journals, Arranged by Topic* (New York: Bedford St. Martin's, 1998), pp.18–22. Original manuscript in Bureau of Rolls, *Jefferson Papers*, ser. 1, vol. 9, doc. 269, reprinted in Thwaites, *Original Journals of the Lewis and Clark Expedition*, 7:247–252.

the Essex Junto, concluded that the only recourse for New England was to **secede** from the Union and form a separate "northern confederacy." If such a breakaway state were to

Threat of New England Secession   have any hope for survival, the Federalists believed, it would have to include New York and New Jersey as well as New England. But the leading Federalist in New York, Alexander Hamilton, refused to support the secessionist scheme.

Federalists in New York then turned to Hamilton's greatest political rival, Vice President Aaron Burr. Burr accepted a Federalist proposal that he become their candidate for governor

Hamilton and Burr Duel   of New York in 1804, and there were rumors that he had also agreed to support the Federalist plans for secession. Hamilton accused Burr of plotting treason and made numerous private remarks, widely reported in the press, about Burr's "despicable" character. When Burr lost the election, he blamed his defeat on Hamilton's malevolence and challenged him to a duel. Hamilton feared that refusing Burr's challenge would brand him a coward. And so, on a July morning in 1804, the two men met at Weehawken, New Jersey. Hamilton was mortally wounded; he died the next day.

Burr now had to flee New York to avoid an indictment for murder. He found new outlets for his ambitions in the West. Even before the duel, he had begun corresponding with General James Wilkinson, now governor of the Louisiana Territory. Burr and Wilkinson, it seems clear, hoped to lead an expedition that would capture Mexico from the Spanish. But there were also rumors that they wanted to separate the Southwest from the Union and create a western empire that Burr would rule. (There is little evidence that these rumors were true.)

Whether true or not, many of Burr's opponents chose to believe the rumors—including, ultimately, Jefferson himself. When Burr led a group of armed followers down the Ohio River by boat in 1806, disturbing reports flowed into Washington (the most alarming from Wilkinson, who had suddenly turned against Burr) that an attack on New Orleans was imminent. Jefferson ordered the arrest of Burr and his men as traitors. Burr was brought to Richmond for trial. But to Jefferson's chagrin, Chief Justice Marshall limited the evidence the government could present and defined the charge in such a way that the jury had little choice but to acquit. Burr soon faded from the public eye. But when he learned of the Texas revolution against Mexico years later, he said, "What was treason in me thirty years ago is patriotic now."

The Burr conspiracy was in part the story of a single man's soaring ambitions and flamboyant personality. But it also exposed the larger perils still facing the new nation. With a central government that remained deliberately weak, with ambitious political leaders willing, if necessary, to circumvent normal channels in their search for power, the legitimacy of the federal government—and indeed the existence of the United States as a stable and united nation—remained tenuous.

EXPANSION AND WAR

Two very different conflicts were taking shape in the last years of Jefferson's presidency. One was the continuing tension in Europe, which in 1803 escalated once again into a full-scale conflict (the Napoleonic Wars). As fighting between the British and the French increased, each side took steps to prevent the United States from trading with the other. The other conflict occurred in North America itself, a result of the ceaseless westward expansion of white settlement, which was colliding with a native population committed to protecting its lands from intruders. In both the North and the South, the threatened tribes mobilized to resist white encroachments. They began as well to forge connections with British forces in Canada and Spanish forces in Florida. The Indian conflict on land, therefore, became intertwined with the European conflict on the seas, and ultimately helped cause the War of 1812.

CONFLICT ON THE SEAS

In 1805, at the Battle of Trafalgar, a British fleet virtually destroyed what was left of the French navy. Because France could no longer challenge the British at sea, Napoleon now chose to pressure England in other ways. The result was what he called the Continental System, designed to close the European continent to British trade. Napoleon issued a series of decrees barring British and neutral ships touching at British ports from landing their cargoes at any European port controlled by France or its allies. The British government replied to Napoleon's decrees by establishing a blockade of the European coast. The blockade required that any goods being shipped to Napoleon's Europe be carried either in British vessels or in neutral vessels stopping at British ports—precisely what Napoleon's policies forbade.

In the early nineteenth century, the United States had developed one of the most important merchant marines in the world, one that soon controlled a large proportion of the trade between Europe and the West Indies. But the events in Europe now challenged that control, because American ships were caught between Napoleon's decrees and Britain's blockade. If they sailed directly for the European continent, they risked being captured by the British navy. If they sailed by way of a British port, they ran the risk of seizure by the French. Both of the warring powers were violating America's rights as a neutral nation. But most Americans considered the British, with their greater sea power, the worse offender—especially since British vessels frequently stopped American ships on the high seas and seized sailors off the decks, making them victims of "impressment."

IMPRESSMENT

Many British sailors called their navy—with its floggings, its low pay, and its terrible shipboard conditions—a "floating hell." Few volunteered. Most had had to be "impressed" (forced) into the service, and at every opportunity they deserted. By 1807, many of these deserters had emigrated to the United States and joined the American merchant marine or American navy. To check this loss of manpower, the British claimed the right to stop and search American merchantmen and reimpress deserters. They did not claim the right to take native-born Americans, but they did insist on the right to seize naturalized Americans born on British soil. In practice, the British navy often made no careful distinctions, impressing British deserters and native-born Americans alike.

In the summer of 1807, the British went to more provocative extremes. Sailing from Norfolk, with several alleged deserters from the British navy among the crew, the American naval frigate *Chesapeake* was hailed by the British ship *Leopard.*   Chesapeake-Leopard *Incident* When the American commander, James Barron, refused to allow the British to search the *Chesapeake,* the *Leopard* opened fire. Barron had no choice but to surrender, and a boarding party from the *Leopard* dragged four men off the American frigate.

When news of the *Chesapeake-Leopard* incident reached the United States, there was a great popular clamor for revenge. Jefferson and Madison tried to maintain the peace. Jefferson expelled all British warships from American waters to lessen the likelihood of future incidents. Then he sent instructions to his minister in England, James Monroe, to demand from the British government an end to impressment. The British government disavowed the actions of the *Leopard*'s commanding officer and recalled him; it offered compensation for those killed and wounded in the incident; and it promised to return three of the captured sailors (the fourth had been hanged). But the British cabinet refused to renounce impressment and instead reasserted its right to recover deserting seamen.

"PEACEABLE COERCION"

To prevent future incidents that might bring the nation again to the brink of war, Jefferson persuaded Congress to pass a drastic measure late in 1807. Known as the Embargo Act, *Jefferson's Embargo*   it prohibited all international trade from American ports. The **embargo** was widely evaded, but it was effective enough to create a serious depression throughout most of the nation. Hardest hit were the merchants and shipowners of the Northeast, most of them Federalists.

The presidential election of 1808 came in the midst of this embargo-induced depression. James Madison was elected president, but the Federalist candidate, Charles Pinckney again, ran much more strongly than he had in 1804. The Embargo Act was clearly a growing political liability, and Jefferson decided to back down. A few days before leaving office, he approved a bill ending his experiment with what he called "peaceable coercion."

STRUGGLING WITH THE EMBARGO   This cartoon shows a merchant being injured by the terms of the U.S. embargo, which is personified by the snapping turtle. The word *Ograbme* is "embargo" spelled backward. The embargo not only enraged American merchants but also failed to resolve the maritime tensions with the British that ultimately helped lead to war in 1812. (© Granger, NYC—All Rights Reserved.)

To replace the embargo, Congress passed the Non-Intercourse Act just before Madison took office. It reopened trade with all nations but Great Britain and France. A year later, in 1810, the Non-Intercourse Act expired and was replaced by Macon's Bill No. 2, which reopened free commercial relations with Britain and France but authorized the president to prohibit commerce with either belligerent if it should continue violating neutral shipping after the other had stopped. Napoleon, in an effort to induce the United States to reimpose the embargo against Britain, announced that France would no longer interfere with American shipping. Madison announced that an embargo against Great Britain alone would automatically go into effect early in 1811 unless Britain renounced its restrictions on American shipping.

Other Trade Acts

In time, this new, limited embargo persuaded England to repeal its blockade of Europe. But the repeal came too late to prevent war. In any case, naval policies were only part of the reason for tensions between Britain and the United States.

THE "INDIAN PROBLEM" AND THE BRITISH

Given the ruthlessness with which white settlers in North America had continued to dislodge native tribes, it was hardly surprising that Indians continued to look to England for protection. The British in Canada, for their part, had relied on the Indians as partners in the lucrative fur trade. There had been relative peace in the Northwest for over a decade after Jay's Treaty and Anthony Wayne's victory over the tribes at Fallen Timbers in 1794. But the 1807 war crisis following the *Chesapeake-Leopard* incident revived the conflict between Indians and white settlers.

The Virginia-born William Henry Harrison, already a veteran of combat against Native Americans at age twenty-six, went to Washington as the congressional delegate from the Northwest Territory in 1799. An advocate of development in the western lands, he was largely responsible for the passage in 1800 of the so-called Harrison Land Law, which enabled white settlers to acquire farms from the public domain on much easier terms than before.

William Henry Harrison

In 1801, Jefferson appointed Harrison governor of the Indiana Territory to administer the president's proposed solution to the "Indian problem." Jefferson offered the Indians a choice: they could convert themselves into settled farmers and become a part of white society, or they could migrate west of the Mississippi. In either case, they would have to give up their claims to their tribal lands in the Northwest.

Jefferson considered the assimilation policy a benign alternative to the continuing conflict between Indians and white settlers. But to the tribes, the new policy seemed terribly harsh, especially given the bludgeonlike efficiency with which Harrison set out to implement it. He used threats, bribes, trickery, and whatever other tactics he felt would help him conclude treaties. In the first decade of the nineteenth century, the number of white Americans who had settled west of the Appalachians had grown to more than 500,000—a population far larger than that of the Native Americans. The tribes would face ever-growing pressure to move out of the way of the rapidly growing white settlements.

Jefferson's Assimilation Proposal

By 1807 the United States had extracted treaty rights to eastern Michigan, southern Indiana, and most of Illinois from reluctant tribal leaders.

Meanwhile, in the Southwest, white Americans were taking millions of acres from other tribes in Georgia, Tennessee, and Mississippi. The Indians wanted desperately to resist, but the separate tribes were helpless by themselves against the power of the United States.

Yet two new factors emboldened them. One was the policy of British authorities in Canada. After the *Chesapeake* incident, they began to expect an American invasion of Canada and therefore renewed efforts to forge alliances with the Indians. A second and more important factor was the rise of two remarkable native leaders, Tenskwatawa and Tecumseh.

TECUMSEH AND THE PROPHET

Tenskwatawa was a charismatic religious leader and orator known as "the Prophet." Like

The Prophet Handsome Lake, he had experienced a mystical awakening in the process of recovering from alcoholism. Having freed himself from what he considered the evil effects of white culture, he began to speak to his people of the superior virtues of Indian civilization and the sinfulness and corruption of the white world. In the process, he inspired a religious revival that spread through numerous tribes and helped unite them. The Prophet's headquarters at the meeting of Tippecanoe Creek and the Wabash River (known as Prophetstown) became a sacred place for people of many tribes. Out of their common religious experiences, they began to consider joint military efforts as well. Tenskwatawa advocated an Indian society entirely separate from that of white Americans and a culture rooted in tribal tradition. The effort to trade with the Anglos and to borrow from their culture would, he argued, lead to the death of native ways.

Tecumseh—the chief of the Shawnees, called by his tribe "the Shooting Star"—was in many ways even more militant than his brother Tenskwatawa. "Where today are the Pequot," he thundered. "Where are . . . the other powerful tribes of our people? They have vanished before the avarice and oppression of the white man." He warned of his tribe's extermination if they did not take action against the white Americans moving into their lands.

Tecumseh understood, as few other native leaders had, that only through united action could the tribes hope to resist the steady advance of white civilization. Beginning in 1809, he set out to unite all the tribes of the Mississippi Valley into what became known as the

The Tecumseh Confederacy Tecumseh Confederacy. Together, he promised, they would halt white expansion, recover the whole Northwest, and make the Ohio River the boundary between the United States and Indian country. He maintained that Harrison and others, by negotiating treaties with individual tribes, had obtained no real title to land. The land belonged to all the tribes; none of them could rightfully cede any of it without the consent of the others. In 1811, Tecumseh left Prophetstown and traveled down the Mississippi to visit the tribes of the South and persuade them to join the alliance.

During Tecumseh's absence, Governor Harrison saw a chance to destroy the growing influence of the two Indian leaders. With 1,000 soldiers, he camped near Prophetstown, and on November 7, 1811, he provoked an armed conflict. Although the white forces suffered losses as heavy as those of the Native Americans, Harrison drove off the Indians

Battle of Tippecanoe and burned the town. The Battle of Tippecanoe (named for the creek near which it was fought) disillusioned many of the Prophet's followers, and Tecumseh returned to find the confederacy in disarray. But there were still warriors eager for combat, and by the spring of 1812 they were raiding white settlements along the frontier.

The mobilization of the tribes resulted largely from the Indians' own initiative, but Britain's agents in Canada had encouraged and helped supply the uprising. To Harrison and most white residents of the regions, there seemed only one way to make the West safe for Americans: to drive the British out of Canada and annex that province to the United States.

FLORIDA AND WAR FEVER

While white frontiersmen in the North demanded the conquest of Canada, those in the South looked to the acquisition of Spanish Florida. The territory was a continuing threat to whites in the southern United States. Enslaved people escaped across the Florida border; Indians in Florida launched frequent raids north. But white southerners also coveted Florida's network of rivers that could provide residents of the Southwest with access to valuable ports on the Gulf of Mexico.

In 1810, American settlers in West Florida (the area presently part of Mississippi and Louisiana) seized the Spanish fort at Baton Rouge and asked the federal government to annex the territory to the United States. President Madison happily agreed and then began planning to get the rest of Florida, too. The desire for Florida became yet another motivation for war with Britain. Spain was Britain's ally, and a war with England might provide an excuse for taking Spanish as well as British territory.

By 1812, therefore, war fever was raging on both the northern and southern borders of the United States. The demands of the residents of these areas found substantial support in Washington among a group of determined young congressmen who soon earned the name "War Hawks."   *"War Hawks"*

In the congressional elections of 1810, voters elected a large number of representatives of both parties eager for war with Britain. The most influential of them came from the new states in the West or from the backcountry of the old states in the South. Two of their leaders, both recently elected to the House of Representatives, were Henry Clay of Kentucky and John C. Calhoun of South Carolina, men of great intellect, magnetism, and ambition. Both were supporters of war with Great Britain.

Clay was elected Speaker of the House in 1811, and he appointed Calhoun to the crucial Committee on Foreign Affairs. Both men began agitating for the conquest of Canada. Madison still preferred peace but was losing control of Congress. On June 18, 1812, he approved a declaration of war against Britain.

THE WAR OF 1812

The British were not eager for an open conflict with the United States. Even after the Americans declared war, Britain largely ignored them for a time. But in the fall of 1812, Napoleon launched a catastrophic campaign against Russia that left his army in disarray. By late 1813, with the French Empire on its way to final defeat, Britain was able to turn its military attention to America.

BATTLES WITH THE TRIBES

In the summer of 1812, American forces invaded Canada through Detroit. They soon had to retreat back to Detroit and in August surrendered the fort there. Other invasion efforts also failed. In the meantime, Fort Dearborn (later Chicago) fell before an Indian attack.

Things went only slightly better for the United States on the seas. At first, American frigates won some spectacular victories over British warships. But by 1813, the British navy was counterattacking effectively, driving the American frigates to cover and imposing a blockade on the United States.

The United States did, however, achieve significant early military successes on the Great Lakes. First, the Americans took command of Lake Ontario, permitting them to

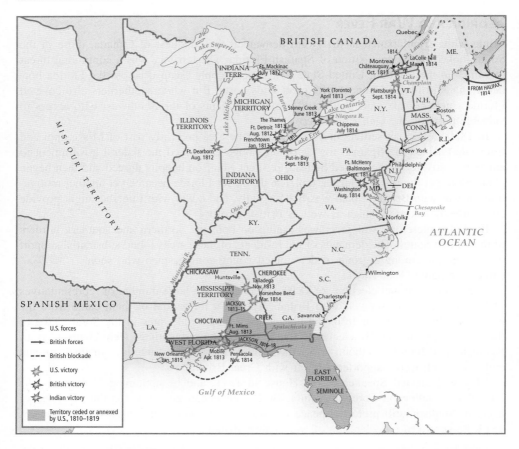

THE WAR OF 1812 This map illustrates the military maneuvers of the British and the Americans during the War of 1812. It shows all the theaters of the war, from New Orleans to southern Canada, the extended land and water battle along the Canadian border and in the Great Lakes, and the fighting around Washington and Baltimore. Note how in all these theaters there are about the same number of British and American victories. • *What finally brought this inconclusive war to an end?*

raid and burn York (now Toronto), the capital of Canada. American forces then seized control of Lake Erie, mainly through the work of the young Oliver Hazard Perry, who engaged and dispersed a British fleet at Put-in-Bay on September 10, 1813. This made possible, at last, a more successful invasion of Canada by way of Detroit. William Henry Harrison pushed up the Thames River into upper Canada and on October 5, 1813, won *Death of Tecumseh* a victory notable for the death of Tecumseh, who was serving as a brigadier general in the British army. The Battle of the Thames resulted in no lasting occupation of Canada, but it weakened and disheartened the Native Americans of the Northwest.

In the meantime, another white military leader was striking an even harder blow at Indians in the Southwest. The Creek, supplied by the Spaniards in Florida, had been attacking white settlers near the Florida border. Andrew Jackson, a wealthy Tennessee planter and a general in the state militia, set off in pursuit of the Creek. On March 27, 1814, in the Battle of Horseshoe Bend, Jackson's men took terrible revenge on the Indians, slaughtering women and children along with warriors. The tribe agreed to cede most of its lands to the United States and retreated westward. The *Defeat and Retreat of the Creek* vicious battle also won Jackson a commission as major general in the United States Army, and in that capacity he led his men farther south into Florida. On November 7, 1814, he seized the Spanish fort at Pensacola.

BATTLES WITH THE BRITISH

But the victories over the tribes did not end the war. After the surrender of Napoleon in 1814, England decided to invade the United States. A British armada *The British invasion* sailed up the Patuxent River from Chesapeake Bay and landed an army that marched to nearby Bladensburg, on the outskirts of Washington, where it dispersed a poorly trained force of American militiamen. On August 24, 1814, the British troops entered Washington and put the government to flight. Then they set fire to several public buildings, including the White House, in retaliation for the earlier American burning of the Canadian capital at York.

Leaving Washington in partial ruins, the invading army proceeded up the bay toward Baltimore. But that city, guarded by Fort McHenry, was prepared. To block the approaching fleet, the American garrison had sunk several ships in the Patapsco River (the entry to Baltimore's harbor), thus forcing the British to bombard the fort from a distance. Through the night of September 13, Francis Scott Key (a Washington lawyer on board one of the British ships to negotiate the return of prisoners) watched the bombardment. The next morning, "by the dawn's early light," he could see the flag on the fort still flying; he recorded his pride in the moment by writing a poem—"The Star-Spangled Banner." The British withdrew from Baltimore, and Key's words were soon set to the tune of an old English drinking song. (In 1931 "The Star-Spangled Banner" became the official national anthem.)

Meanwhile, American forces repelled another British invasion in northern New York. At the Battle of Plattsburgh, on September 11, 1814, they turned back a much larger British naval and land force. In the South, a formidable array of battle-hardened British veterans landed below New Orleans and prepared to advance north up the Mississippi. Awaiting the British was Andrew Jackson with a contingent of Tennesseans, Kentuckians, Creoles, blacks, pirates, and regular army troops drawn up behind earthen breastworks. On January 8, 1815, the redcoats advanced on the American fortifications, but the exposed British forces were no match for Jackson's well-protected men. After the Americans had repulsed several waves of attackers, the British finally retreated, leaving behind 700 dead, 1,400 wounded, and 500 prisoners. Jackson's losses were 8 killed and 13 wounded. Only later did news reach North America that the United States and Britain *Battle of New Orleans* had signed a peace treaty several weeks before the Battle of New Orleans.

THE REVOLT OF NEW ENGLAND

With a few notable exceptions, the military efforts of the United States between 1812 and 1815 had failed. As a result, the Republican government became increasingly unpopular. In New England, opposition both to the war and to the Republicans was so extreme that some Federalists celebrated British victories. In Congress, in the *Federalist Opposition to War* meantime, the Republicans had continual trouble with the Federalist opposition, led by a young congressman from New Hampshire named Daniel Webster.

By now the Federalists were in the minority in the country, but they were still the majority party in New England. Some of them began to dream once again of creating a separate nation. Talk of secession reached a climax in the winter of 1814–1815.

The Hartford Convention On December 15, 1814, delegates from the New England states met in Hartford, Connecticut, to discuss their grievances against the Madison administration. The would-be seceders at the Hartford Convention were outnumbered by a comparatively moderate majority. But while the convention's report only hinted at secession, it reasserted the right of nullification and proposed seven amendments to the Constitution—amendments designed to protect New England from the growing influence of the South and the West.

Because the war was going so badly, the New Englanders assumed that the Republicans would have to agree to their demands. Soon after the convention adjourned, however, the news of Jackson's victory at New Orleans reached the cities of the Northeast. A day or two later, reports of a peace treaty arrived from abroad. In the changed atmosphere, the aims of the Hartford Convention and the Federalist Party came to seem futile, irrelevant, even treasonable.

THE PEACE SETTLEMENT

Negotiations between the United States and Britain began in August 1814, when American and British diplomats met in Ghent, Belgium. John Quincy Adams, Henry Clay, and Albert Gallatin led the American delegation. Although both sides began with extravagant demands, the final treaty did little except end the fighting itself. The Americans gave up their demand for a British renunciation of impressment and for the cession of Canada to the United States. The British abandoned their call for the creation of an Indian buffer *Treaty of Ghent* state in the Northwest and made other, minor territorial concessions. The treaty was signed on Christmas Eve 1814.

Both sides had reason to accept this skimpy agreement. The British, exhausted and in debt from their prolonged conflict with Napoleon, were eager to settle the lesser dispute in North America. The Americans realized that with the defeat of Napoleon in Europe, the British would no longer have much incentive to interfere with American commerce.

Other settlements followed the Treaty of Ghent. A commercial treaty in 1815 gave Americans the right to trade freely with England and much of the British Empire. The Rush-Bagot agreement of 1817 provided for mutual disarmament on the Great Lakes; eventually (although not until 1872) the Canadian-American boundary became the longest "unguarded frontier" in the world.

For the Indian tribes east of the Mississippi, the conflict dealt another disastrous blow to their ability to resist white expansion. Tecumseh was dead. The British were gone from *Disastrous Consequences for Native Americans* the Northwest. And the intertribal alliance of Tecumseh and the Prophet had collapsed. As the end of the war spurred a new white movement westward, the Native Americans were less able than ever to defend their land.

CONCLUSION

Thomas Jefferson called his election to the presidency the "Revolution of 1800," and his supporters believed that his victory would bring a dramatic change in the character of the nation—a retreat from Hamilton's dreams of a powerful, developing nation and a return to an ideal of a simple agrarian republic.

But American society was changing rapidly, making it virtually impossible for the Jeffersonian dream to prevail. The nation's population was expanding and diversifying. Its cities were growing, and its commercial life was becoming ever more important. In 1803, Jefferson himself made one of the most important contributions to the growth of the United States: the Louisiana Purchase, which dramatically expanded the physical boundaries of the nation—and which began extending white settlement deeper into the continent. In the process, it greatly widened the battles between Europeans and Native Americans.

The growing national pride and commercial ambitions of the United States gradually created another serious conflict with Great Britain: the War of 1812, a war that was settled finally in 1814 on terms at least mildly favorable to the United States. By then, the bitter party rivalries that had characterized the first years of the republic had to some degree subsided, and the nation was poised to enter what became known, quite inaccurately, as the "era of good feelings."

KEY TERMS/PEOPLE/PLACES/EVENTS

Aaron Burr 174
Cane Ridge 158
capitalists 161
deism 158
Eli Whitney 162
embargo 176
Handsome Lake 159
Hartford Convention 182
impressment 175
Industrial Revolution 160

John Marshall 168
Judith Sargent Murray 156
Lewis and Clark 170
Marbury v. Madison 168
Noah Webster 157
Robert Fulton 163
secession 174
Second Great
  Awakening 158
Tecumseh 178

The Prophet (Tenskwatawa)
  178
War Hawks 179
War of 1812 179
Washington Irving 157
Washington, D.C. 165
William Henry Harrison 177

RECALL AND REFLECT

1. What was the impact of the Second Great Awakening on women, African Americans, and Native Americans?
2. What was the long-term significance of the *Marbury v. Madison* ruling?
3. How did Americans respond to the Louisiana Purchase?
4. What foreign entanglements and questions of foreign policy did Jefferson have to deal with during his presidency? How did these affect his political philosophy?
5. What were the consequences of the War of 1812?

8 VARIETIES OF AMERICAN NATIONALISM

STABILIZING ECONOMIC GROWTH
EXPANDING WESTWARD
THE "ERA OF GOOD FEELINGS"
SECTIONALISM AND NATIONALISM
THE REVIVAL OF OPPOSITION

LOOKING AHEAD

1. How did the economic developments and territorial expansion of this era affect American nationalism?
2. What was the "era of good feelings," and why was it given that name?
3. How did the Marshall Court seek to establish a strong national government?

LIKE A "FIRE BELL IN the night," as Thomas Jefferson said, the issue of slavery arose after the War of 1812 to threaten the unity of the nation. The debate began when the territory of Missouri applied for admission to the Union, raising the question of whether it would be a free or a slaveholding state. But the larger issue was whether the vast new western regions of the United States would ultimately align politically with the North or the South.

The Missouri crisis was significant because it was a sign of sectional crises to come. But at the time, it was also significant because it stood in such sharp contrast to the rising American nationalism of the years following the war. Whatever forces might have been working to pull the nation apart, stronger ones were acting, at least for a time, to draw it together.

STABILIZING ECONOMIC GROWTH

The end of the War of 1812 allowed the United States to resume its economic growth and territorial expansion. Yet a vigorous postwar boom led to a disastrous bust in 1819. Brief though it was, the collapse was evidence that the United States continued to lack some of the basic institutions necessary to sustain long-term growth.

THE GOVERNMENT AND ECONOMIC GROWTH

The War of 1812 produced chaos in shipping and banking, and it exposed dramatically the inadequacy of the nation's existing transportation and financial systems. The aftermath of the war, therefore, led to new efforts to strengthen national economic development.

The wartime experience underlined the need for another national bank. After the expiration of the first bank's charter, a large number of state banks had issued vast quantities of banknotes, creating a confusing variety of currency of widely differing value. It was difficult to tell what any banknote was really worth, and counterfeiting was easy. In response to these problems, Congress chartered a second Bank of the United States in 1816, much like its predecessor of 1791 but with more capital. The national bank could not forbid state banks from issuing notes, but its size and power enabled it to compel the state banks to issue only sound notes or risk being forced out of business.

Congress also acted to promote manufacturing, which the war (by cutting off imports) had already greatly stimulated. The American textile industry, in particular, had grown dramatically. Between 1807 and 1815, the total number of cotton spindles in the country increased more than fifteenfold, from 8,000 to 130,000. Before the war, the textile factories—most of them in New England—produced only yarn and thread; families

1815
U.S. treaties take western lands from Indians

1816
Second Bank of U.S.

Monroe elected president

1818
Seminole War ends

1819
Panic and depression

Dartmouth College v. Woodward; McCulloch v. Maryland

1820
Missouri Compromise

Monroe reelected

1823
Monroe Doctrine

1824
John Quincy Adams elected president

1828
Tariff of abominations

Jackson elected president

operating hand looms at home did the actual weaving of cloth. Then the Boston merchant Francis Cabot Lowell, after examining textile machinery in England, developed a power loom better *Lowell Mill* than its English counterpart. In 1813, in Waltham, Massachusetts, Lowell founded the first mill in America to carry on the processes of spinning and weaving under a single roof.

The end of the war suddenly dimmed the prospects for American industry. British ships swarmed into American ports and unloaded cargoes of manufactured goods, many priced *The Protective Tariff* below cost. In response, in 1816, protectionists in Congress passed a tariff law that effectively limited competition from abroad on a wide range of items, including cotton cloth, despite objections from agricultural interests, who stood to pay higher prices for manufactured goods.

TRANSPORTATION

The nation's most pressing economic need was a better transportation system to link the vast territories of the growing United States. An old debate resumed: should the federal government help finance roads and other "internal improvements"? The idea of using government funds to finance road building was not a new one. When Ohio entered the Union in 1803, the federal government agreed that part of the proceeds from the sale of public lands there should finance road construction. And in 1807, Congress enacted a law proposed by the Jefferson *The National Road* administration that permitted using revenues from Ohio land sales to finance a National Road from the Potomac River to the Ohio. By 1818, the highway ran as far as Wheeling, Virginia, on the Ohio River; and the Lancaster Pike, financed in part by the state of Pennsylvania, extended westward to Pittsburgh.

At the same time, steam-powered shipping was expanding rapidly. By 1816, river steamers were sailing up the Mississippi to the Ohio River and up the Ohio as far as Pittsburgh.

STEAMBOATS ON THE HUDSON Inventor Robert Fulton developed an engine that could propel a boat from Manhattan to Albany, a distance of about 150 miles, in 32 hours. His steam-powered vessels were the first to be large and reliable enough for commercial use. (Photo © Tarker/Bridgeman Images)

Steamboats were soon carrying more cargo on the Mississippi than all the earlier forms of river transport—flatboats, barges, and others—combined. They stimulated the agricultural economy of the West and the South by providing cheaper access to markets, and they enabled eastern manufacturers to send their finished goods west much more readily.

Nevertheless, serious gaps in the nation's transportation network remained, as the War of 1812 had shown. Once the British blockade had cut off Atlantic shipping, the coastal roads had become choked by the unaccustomed volume of north-south traffic. Congress passed a bill introduced by Representative John C. Calhoun that would use government funds to finance internal improvements. But President James Madison, on his last day in office, vetoed it. He believed that Congress lacked authority to fund the improvements without a constitutional amendment. For a time, state governments and private enterprise were left on their own to build the transportation network necessary for the growing American economy.

EXPANDING WESTWARD

Another reason for the rising interest in internal improvements was the dramatic westward surge of white Americans. By 1820, white settlers had pushed well beyond the Mississippi River, and the population of western regions was increasing more rapidly than the rest of the nation.

THE GREAT MIGRATION

The westward movement of the white American population was one of the most important developments of the nineteenth century. It occurred for several reasons.

One was population growth, which drove many white Americans out of the crowded East. Between 1800 and 1820, the American population nearly doubled—from 5.3 million to 9.6 million. Most Americans were still farmers, and the agricultural lands of the East were by now largely occupied or exhausted. In the South, the spread of the plantation system limited opportunities for new settlers. Another reason for westward migration *Reasons for Westward Expansion* was that the West itself was increasingly attractive to white settlers. Land there was much more plentiful than in the East. And in the aftermath of the War of 1812, the federal government continued its policy of pushing Native Americans farther and farther west, signing treaties in 1815 that took more land from the tribes. Migrants from throughout the East flocked in increasing numbers to what was then known as the Old Northwest (now part of the Midwest). Most settlers floated downstream on flatboats on the Ohio River, then left the river (often at Cincinnati) and traveled overland with wagons, handcarts, packhorses, cattle, and hogs.

WHITE SETTLERS IN THE OLD NORTHWEST

Having arrived at their new lands, most settlers built lean-tos or cabins, hewed clearings out of the forest, and planted crops of corn to supplement wild game and domestic animals. It was a rough and lonely existence. Men, women, and children worked side by side in the fields—and at times had virtually no outside contact for weeks or months.

Life in the western territories was not, however, entirely solitary or individualistic. Migrants often journeyed westward in groups and built communities with schools, churches, and stores. The labor shortage in the interior led neighbors to develop systems of mutual aid. They gathered periodically to raise a barn, clear land, or harvest crops.

Another common feature of life in the Old Northwest was mobility. Individuals and families were constantly on the move, settling for a few years in one place and then selling their land (often at a significant profit) and resettling somewhere else. When new areas for settlement opened farther to the west, it was often the people already on the western edges of white settlement—rather than those coming from the East—who flocked to them first.

The Plantation System in the Old Southwest

In the Old Southwest (later known as the Deep South), the new agricultural economy emerged along different lines. The market for cotton continued to grow, and the Old Southwest con-
The Black Belt Region   tained a broad zone where cotton could thrive. That zone became known as the Black Belt, a region of dark, productive soil in Alabama and Mississippi.

The first arrivals in the uncultivated regions of the Old Southwest were usually small farmers who made rough clearings in the forest. But wealthier planters soon followed. They bought up the cleared land, as the original settlers moved farther west. Success in the wilderness was by no means assured, even for the wealthiest settlers. Many planters managed to do little more than subsist in their new environment, and others experienced utter ruin. But some planters soon expanded small clearings into vast cotton fields. They replaced the cabins of the early pioneers with more sumptuous log dwellings and ultimately with imposing mansions. They also built up large slave workforces.

The rapid growth of the Old Northwest and Southwest resulted in the admission of
Four New States   four new states to the Union: Indiana in 1816, Mississippi in 1817, Illinois in 1818, and Alabama in 1819.

Trade and Trapping in the Far West

Not many Anglo-Americans yet knew much about the far western areas of the continent. Nevertheless, a significant trade began to develop between these western regions and the United States early in the nineteenth century, and it grew steadily for decades.

Mexico, which continued to control Texas, California, and much of the rest of the far Southwest, won its independence from Spain in 1821. Almost immediately, it opened its
Trade with Mexican Territories   northern territories to trade with the United States. American traders poured into the region and quickly displaced Indian and Mexican traders. In New Mexico, for example, the Missouri merchant William Becknell began in 1821 to offer American manufactured goods for sale, priced considerably below the inferior Mexican goods that had dominated the market in the past. Mexico effectively lost its markets in its own colony as a steady traffic of commercial wagon trains began moving back and forth along the Santa Fe Trail between Missouri and New Mexico.

Fur traders created a wholly new kind of commerce. After the War of 1812, John Jacob Astor's American Fur Company and other firms extended their operations from the Great
White Trappers in the West   Lakes area westward to the Rockies. At first, fur traders did most of their business by purchasing pelts from the Indians. But increasingly, white trappers entered the region and joined the Iroquois and other Indians in pursuit of beaver and other furs.

The trappers, or "mountain men," who began trading in the Far West were small in number. But they developed important relationships with the existing residents of the West—Indian and Mexican—and altered the character of society there. White trappers were mostly young, single men. Many of them entered into sexual relationships with Indian and Mexican women. They also recruited women as helpers in the difficult work of preparing furs and skins for trading. In some cases, though, white trappers clashed violently with the Mojave and other tribes.

In 1822, Andrew and William Ashley founded the Rocky Mountain Fur Company and recruited white trappers to move permanently into the Rockies. The Ashleys dispatched

THE RENDEZVOUS The annual rendezvous of fur trappers and traders was a major event for the lonely men who made their livelihoods gathering furs. It was also a gathering of representatives of the many cultures that mingled in the Far West, among them Anglo-Americans, Native Americans, and people of Spanish origins. (© Walters Art Museum, Baltimore, USA/Bridgeman Images)

supplies annually to their trappers in exchange for furs and skins. The arrival of the supply train became the occasion for a gathering of scores of mountain men, some of whom lived much of the year in considerable isolation. But however isolated their daily lives, these mountain men were closely bound up with the expanding market economy, an economy in which the bulk of the profits from the trade flowed to the merchants, not the trappers.

Eastern Images of the West

Americans in the East were only dimly aware of the world of the trappers. They were more aware of the explorers, many of them dispatched by the United States government. In 1819 and 1820, the War Department ordered Stephen H. Long to journey *Stephen H. Long's Expedition* up the Platte and South Platte Rivers through what is now Nebraska and eastern Colorado (where he discovered the peak that would be named for him). He then returned eastward along the Arkansas River through what is now Kansas. Long wrote an influential report on his trip, which echoed the dismissive conclusions of Zebulon Pike fifteen years before. The region "between the Missouri River and the Rocky Mountains," Long wrote, "is almost wholly unfit for cultivation, and of course uninhabitable by a people depending upon agriculture for their subsistence." On the published map of his expedition, he labeled the Great Plains the "Great American Desert."

THE "ERA OF GOOD FEELINGS"

The expansion of the economy, the growth of white settlement and trade in the West, the creation of new states—all reflected the rising spirit of nationalism that was spreading through the United States in the years following the War of 1812. That spirit found reflection for a time as well in the character of national politics.

The End of the First Party System

Ever since 1800, the presidency seemed to have been the possession of Virginians. After two terms in office, Jefferson secured the presidential nomination for his secretary of state, James Madison, and after two more terms, Madison did the same for *his* secretary of state, James

The Virginia Dynasty   Monroe. Many in the North expressed impatience with the so-called Virginia Dynasty, but the Republicans had no difficulty electing their candidate in 1816. Monroe received 183 ballots in the electoral college; his Federalist opponent, Rufus King of New York, received only 34.

Monroe entered office under what seemed to be remarkably favorable circumstances. With the decline of the Federalists, his party faced no serious opposition. And with the conclusion of the War of 1812, the nation faced no important international threats. Some American politicians had dreamed since the first days of the republic of a time in which partisan divisions and factional disputes might come to an end. In the prosperous postwar years, Monroe attempted to use his office to realize that dream.

He made that clear, above all, in the selection of his cabinet. For secretary of state, he chose former Federalist John Quincy Adams of Massachusetts, son of the second president. Jefferson, Madison, and Monroe had all served as secretary of state before becoming president; Adams, therefore, immediately became the heir apparent, suggesting that the Virginia Dynasty would soon come to an end. Speaker of the House Henry Clay declined an offer to be secretary of war, so Monroe named John C. Calhoun instead.

CELEBRATING THE NATION   Celebrations of Independence Day, like this one in New York City, became major festive events throughout the United States in the early nineteenth century, a sign of rising American nationalism. (© North Wind Picture Archives/Alamy)

Soon after his inauguration, Monroe made a goodwill tour through the country. In New England, so recently the scene of rabid Federalist discontent, he was *Monroe's Goodwill Tour* greeted everywhere with enthusiastic demonstrations. The *Columbian Centinel,* a Federalist newspaper in Boston, observed that an "era of good feelings" had arrived. And on the surface, at least, that seemed to be the case. In 1820, Monroe was reelected without opposition. For all practical purposes, the Federalist Party had ceased to exist.

John Quincy Adams and Florida

John Quincy Adams had spent much of his life in diplomatic service before becoming secretary of state. He was a committed nationalist, and he considered his most important task to be the promotion of American expansion.

His first challenge was Florida. The United States had already annexed West Florida, but that claim was in dispute. Most Americans, moreover, still believed the nation should gain possession of the entire peninsula. In 1817, Adams began negotiations with the Spanish minister, Luis de Onís, over the territory.

In the meantime, however, events in Florida were taking their own course. Andrew Jackson, now in command of American troops along the Florida frontier, had orders from Secretary of War Calhoun to "adopt the necessary measures" to stop continuing raids on American territory by Seminole Indians south of the border. Jackson used *The Seminole War* those orders as an excuse to invade Florida and seize the Spanish forts at St. Marks and Pensacola. The operation became known as the Seminole War.

Instead of condemning Jackson's raid, Adams urged the government to assume responsibility for it. The United States, he said, had the right under international law to defend itself against threats from across its borders. Jackson's raid demonstrated to the Spanish that the United States could easily take Florida by force. Adams implied that the nation might consider doing so.

Onís realized, therefore, that he had little choice but to negotiate a settlement. Under the provisions of the Adams-Onís Treaty of 1819, Spain ceded all of *Adams-Onís Treaty* Florida to the United States and gave up its claim to territory north of the 42nd parallel in the Pacific Northwest. In return, the American government gave up its claims to Texas—for a time.

The Panic of 1819

The Monroe administration had little time to revel in its diplomatic successes, for the nation was facing a serious economic crisis: the Panic of 1819. It followed a period of high foreign demand for American farm goods and thus of exceptionally high prices for American farmers. But the rising prices for farm goods stimulated a land boom in the western United States. Fueled by speculative investments, land prices soared.

The availability of easy credit to settlers and speculators—from the government (under the land acts of 1800 and 1804), from state banks and wildcat banks, even for a time from the rechartered Bank of the United States—fueled the land boom. Beginning in 1819, however, new management at the national bank began tightening credit, calling in loans, and foreclosing mortgages. This precipitated a series of failures by state banks. The result was a financial panic. Six years of depression followed.

Some Americans saw the Panic of 1819 and the widespread distress that followed as a warning that rapid economic growth and territorial expansion would destabilize the nation. But by 1820, most Americans were irrevocably committed to the idea of growth and expansion.

SECTIONALISM AND NATIONALISM

For a brief but alarming moment in 1819–1820, the increasing differences between the North and the South threatened the unity of the United States—until the Missouri Compromise averted a sectional crisis.

THE MISSOURI COMPROMISE

When Missouri applied for admission to the Union as a state in 1819, slavery was already well established there. Even so, Representative James Tallmadge Jr. of New York proposed an *Tallmadge Amendment* amendment to the Missouri statehood bill that would prohibit the further introduction of slaves into Missouri and provide for the gradual emancipation of those already there. The Tallmadge Amendment provoked a controversy that raged for the next two years.

Since the beginning of the republic, new states had come into the Union mostly in pairs, one from the North, another from the South. In 1819, there were eleven free states and eleven slave states. The admission of Missouri would upset that balance. Hence the controversy over slavery and freedom in Missouri.

Complicating the Missouri question was the admission of Maine as a new (and free) *Henry Clay's Maneuvers* state. Speaker of the House Henry Clay informed northern members that if they blocked Missouri from entering the Union as a slave state, southerners would block the admission of Maine. But ultimately the Senate agreed to combine the Maine and

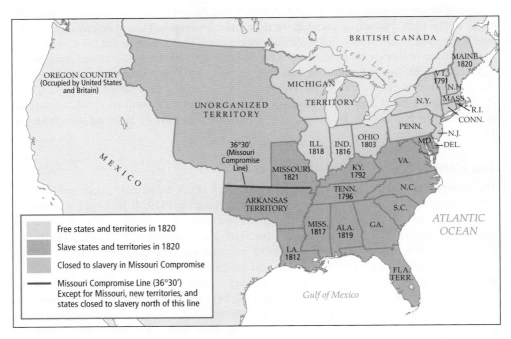

THE MISSOURI COMPROMISE, 1820 This map illustrates the way in which the Missouri Compromise proposed to settle the controversy over slavery in the new western territories of the United States. The compromise rested on the virtually simultaneous admission of Missouri and Maine to the Union, one a slave state and the other a free one. Note the red line extending beyond the southern border of Missouri, which in theory established a permanent boundary between areas in which slavery could be established and areas where it could not be. • *What precipitated the Missouri Compromise?*

Missouri proposals into a single bill. Maine would be admitted as a free state, Missouri as a slave state. Then Senator Jesse B. Thomas of Illinois proposed an amendment prohibiting slavery in the rest of the Louisiana Purchase territory north of the southern boundary of Missouri (the 36°30′ parallel). The Senate adopted the Thomas Amendment, and Speaker Clay, with great difficulty, guided the amended Maine-Missouri bill through the House.

Nationalists in both the North and South hailed this settlement—which became known as the Missouri Compromise—as the happy resolution of a danger to the Union. Former president Thomas Jefferson was less convinced that sectional harmony would last. (See "Consider the Source: Thomas Jefferson Reacts to the Missouri Compromise.")

MARSHALL AND THE COURT

John Marshall served as chief justice of the United States from 1801 to 1835. More than anyone but the framers themselves, he molded the development of the Constitution: strengthening the Supreme Court, increasing the power of the federal government, and advancing the interests of the propertied and commercial classes.

JOHN MARSHALL The imposing figure in this image is John Marshall, the most important chief justice of the Supreme Court in American history. A former secretary of state, Marshall served as chief justice from 1801 until his death in 1835 at the age of eighty. Such was the power of his intellect and personality that he dominated his fellow justices throughout that period, regardless of their previous party affiliations or legal ideologies. Marshall established the independence of the Court, gave it a reputation for nonpartisan integrity, and established its powers, which were only vaguely described by the Constitution. (© Archive Photos/Getty Images)

CONSIDER THE SOURCE

THOMAS JEFFERSON REACTS TO THE MISSOURI COMPROMISE, 1820

In this letter to Massachusetts congressman John Holmes, the former president writes of the sectional divisions supposedly resolved by the recent Missouri Compromise. Jefferson wonders how the Union will hold together amid sharp disagreements over slavery and westward expansion.

Monticello, April 22, 1820 I thank you, Dear Sir, for the copy you have been so kind as to send me of the letter to your constituents on the Missouri question. It is a perfect justification to them. I had for a long time ceased to read newspapers, or pay any attention to public affairs, confident they were in good hands, and content to be a passenger in our bark to the shore from which I am not distant. But this momentous question, like a firebell in the night, awakened and filled me with terror. I considered it at once as the knell of the Union. It is hushed, indeed, for the moment. But this is a reprieve only, not a final sentence. A geographical line, coinciding with a marked principle, moral and political, once conceived and held up to the angry passions of men, will never be obliterated; and every new irritation will mark it deeper and deeper. I can say, with conscious truth, that there is not a man on earth who would sacrifice more than I would to relieve us from this heavy reproach, in any *practicable* way.

The cession of that kind of property, for so it is misnamed, is a bagatelle which would not cost me a second thought, if, in that way, a general emancipation and *expatriation* could be effected; and gradually, and with due sacrifices, I think it might be. But as it is, we have the wolf by the ears, and we can neither hold him, nor safely let him go. Justice is in one scale, and self-preservation in the other. Of one thing I am certain, that as the passage of slaves from one state to another would not make a slave of a single human being who would not be so without it, so their diffusion over a greater surface would make them individually happier, and proportionally facilitate the accomplishment of their emancipation, by dividing the burden on a greater number of coadjutors. An abstinence too, from this act of power, would remove the jealousy excited by the undertaking of Congress to regulate the condition of the different descriptions of men composing a state. This certainly is the exclusive right of every state, which nothing in the Constitution has taken from them and given to the general government. Could Congress, for example, say that the non-freemen of Connecticut shall be freemen, or that they shall not emigrate into any other state?

I regret that I am now to die in the belief, that the useless sacrifice of themselves by the generation of '76, to acquire self-government and happiness to their country, is to be thrown away by the unwise and unworthy passions of their sons, and that my only consolation is to be, that I live not to weep over it. If they would but dispassionately weigh the blessings they will throw away against an abstract principle more likely to be effected by union than by scission, they would pause before they would perpetrate this act of suicide on themselves, and of treason against the hopes of the world. To yourself, as the faithful advocate of the Union, I tender the offering of my high esteem and respect.

1. What does Jefferson's metaphor of "a firebell in the night" suggest about his own feelings about the Missouri Compromise and its Mason-Dixon line?

2. What was Jefferson referring to when he wrote that Americans had "the wolf by the ears"? How appropriate is this metaphor in your assessment?

3. What seemed to be Jefferson's position on the powers of states and the federal government with respect to slavery?

Source: Library of Congress, *Thomas Jefferson Papers*, Series 1. General Correspondence. 1651–1827, *Thomas Jefferson to John Holmes, April 22, 1820*, http://memory.loc.gov; reproduced in Wayne Franklin (ed.), *The Selected Writings of Thomas Jefferson*, A Norton Critical Edition (New York: W.W. Norton & Company 2010), pp. 361–362.

Committed to promoting commerce, the Marshall Court staunchly defended the inviolability of contracts. In *Fletcher v. Peck* (1810), which arose out of a series of notorious land frauds in Georgia, the Court had to decide whether the Georgia legislature of 1796 could repeal the act of the previous legislature granting lands under shady circumstances to the Yazoo Land Companies. In a unanimous decision, Marshall held that a land grant was a valid contract and could not be repealed even if corruption was involved.

Dartmouth College v. Woodward (1819) further expanded the meaning of the contract clause of the Constitution. Having gained control of the New Hampshire state government, Republicans tried to revise Dartmouth College's charter to convert the private college into a state university. Daniel Webster argued the college's case. The Dartmouth charter, he insisted, was a contract, protected by the same doctrine that the Court had already upheld in *Fletcher v. Peck*. The Court ruled for Dartmouth, proclaiming that corporation charters such as the one the colonial legislature had granted the college were contracts and thus inviolable. The decision placed important restrictions on the ability of state governments to control corporations.

Dartmouth College v. Woodward

In overturning the act of the legislature and the decisions of the New Hampshire courts, the justices also implicitly claimed for themselves the right to override the decisions of state courts. But advocates of states' rights, especially in the South, continued to challenge this right. In *Cohens v. Virginia* (1821), Marshall explicitly affirmed the constitutionality of federal review of state court decisions. The states had given up part of their sovereignty in ratifying the Constitution, he explained, and their courts must submit to federal jurisdiction.

Meanwhile, in *McCulloch v. Maryland* (1819), Marshall confirmed the "implied powers" of Congress by upholding the constitutionality of the Bank of the United States. The Bank had become so unpopular in the South and the West that several of the states tried to drive branches out of business. This case presented two constitutional questions to the Supreme Court: Could Congress charter a bank? And if so, could individual states ban it or tax it? Daniel Webster, one of the Bank's attorneys, argued that establishing such an institution came within the "necessary and proper" clause of the Constitution and that the power to tax involved a "power to destroy." If the states could tax the Bank at all, they could tax it to death. Marshall adopted Webster's words in deciding for the Bank.

McCulloch v. Maryland

In the case of *Gibbons v. Ogden* (1824), the Court strengthened Congress's power to regulate interstate commerce. The state of New York had granted the steamboat company of Robert Fulton and Robert Livingston the exclusive right to carry passengers on the

Gibbons v. Ogden

Hudson River to New York City. Fulton and Livingston then gave Aaron Ogden the business of carrying passengers across the river between New York and New Jersey. But Thomas Gibbons, who had a license granted by Congress, began competing with Ogden for the ferry traffic. Ogden brought suit against him and won in the New York courts. Gibbons appealed to the Supreme Court. The most important question facing the justices was whether Congress's power to give Gibbons a license superseded the state of New York's power to grant Ogden a monopoly. Marshall claimed that the power of Congress to regulate interstate commerce (which, he said, included navigation) was "complete in itself" and might be "exercised to its utmost extent." Ogden's state-granted monopoly, therefore, was void.

The highly nationalist decisions of the Marshall Court established the primacy of the *Federal Primacy Established* federal government over the states in regulating the economy and opened the way for an increased federal role in promoting economic growth. They protected corporations and other private economic institutions from local government interference.

THE COURT AND THE TRIBES

The nationalist inclinations of the Marshall Court were visible as well in a series of decisions concerning the legal status of Indian tribes. But these decisions did not simply affirm the supremacy of the United States; they also carved out a distinctive position for Native Americans within the constitutional structure.

The first of the crucial Indian decisions was *Johnson v. McIntosh* (1823). Leaders of the Illinois and Pinakeshaw tribes had sold parcels of their land to a group of white settlers (including Johnson) but had later signed a treaty with the federal government ceding territory that included those same parcels to the United States. The government proceeded to grant homestead rights to new white settlers (among them McIntosh) on the land claimed by Johnson. The Court was asked to decide which claim had precedence. Marshall's ruling, not surprisingly, favored the United States. But in explaining it, he offered a preliminary definition of the place of Indians within the nation. The tribes had a basic right to their tribal lands, he said, that preceded all other American law. Individual American citizens could not buy or take land from the tribes; only the federal government—the supreme authority—could do that.

Even more important was the Court's 1832 decision in *Worcester v. Georgia,* in which the *Worcester v. Georgia* Court invalidated a Georgia law that attempted to regulate access by U.S. citizens to Cherokee country. Only the federal government could do that, Marshall claimed. The tribes, he explained, were sovereign entities in much the same way Georgia was a sovereign entity—"distinct political communities, having territorial boundaries within which their authority is exclusive." In defending the power of the federal government, he was also affirming, indeed expanding, the rights of the tribes to remain free from the authority of state governments.

The Marshall decisions, therefore, did what the Constitution itself had not: they defined a place for Indian tribes within the American political system. The tribes had basic property rights. They were sovereign entities not subject to the authority of state governments. But the federal government, like a "guardian" governing its "ward," had ultimate authority over tribal affairs.

THE LATIN AMERICAN REVOLUTION AND THE MONROE DOCTRINE

Just as the Supreme Court was asserting American nationalism in shaping the country's economic life, so the Monroe administration was asserting nationalism in formulating foreign policy. American diplomacy had been principally concerned with Europe. But in the 1820s, dealing with Europe forced the United States to develop a policy toward Latin America.

CHEROKEE LEADER SEQUOYAH   Sequoyah (who also used the name George Guess) was a mixed-blood Cherokee who translated his tribe's language into writing through an elaborate syllabary (equivalent to an alphabet) of his own invention, pictured here. He opposed Indian assimilation into white society and saw the preservation of the Cherokee language as a way to protect the culture of his tribe. He moved to Arkansas in the 1820s and became a chief of the western Cherokee tribes. (© Hulton Archive/Getty Images)

Americans looking southward in the years following the War of 1812 beheld a gigantic spectacle: the Spanish Empire in its death throes and a whole continent in revolt. Already the United States had developed a profitable trade with Latin America. Many believed the success of the anti-Spanish revolutions would further strengthen America's position in the region.

In 1815, the United States proclaimed neutrality in the wars between Spain and its rebellious colonies. But the United States sold ships and supplies to the revolutionaries, a clear indication that it was trying to help the revolutions. Finally, in 1822, President Monroe established diplomatic relations with five new nations—La Plata (later Argentina), Chile, Peru, Colombia, and Mexico—making the United States the first country to recognize them.

In 1823, Monroe went further and announced a policy that would ultimately be known (beginning some thirty years later) as the "Monroe Doctrine," even   *The "Monroe Doctrine"* though it was primarily the work of John Quincy Adams. "The American continents," Monroe declared, "are henceforth not to be considered as subjects for future colonization by any European powers." The United States would consider any foreign challenge to the sovereignty of existing American nations as an unfriendly act. At the same time, he proclaimed, "Our policy in regard to Europe . . . is not to interfere in the internal concerns of any of its powers."

The Monroe Doctrine emerged directly out of America's relations with Europe in the 1820s. Many Americans feared that Spain's European allies (notably France) would help Spain retake its lost empire. Even more troubling was the fear that Great Britain had designs on Cuba. Monroe and Adams wanted to keep Cuba in Spanish hands until it fell to the Americans.

The Monroe Doctrine had few immediate effects, but it was important as an expression of the growing spirit of nationalism in the United States in the 1820s. And it established the idea of the United States as the dominant power in the Western Hemisphere.

THE REVIVAL OF OPPOSITION

After 1816, the Federalist Party ceased to exist. The Republican Party became the only national political organization in America for a short time. In many ways, it now resembled the defunct Federalist Party in its commitment to economic growth and centralized government. But divisions were growing, just as they had in the late eighteenth century. By the 1820s, a two-party system was emerging once again. The mighty Republican Party split apart, and two new parties emerged. One was the Democratic Republican Party (later the Democrats), which leaned toward the old Jeffersonian vision of a decentralized nation. The Democrats opposed the federal government's growing role in the economy. The other party was the National Republican Party (later the Whigs), which leaned toward the old Federalists' belief in a centralized government. The Whigs believed in a strong national bank and a centralized economy. Both parties believed in economic growth and expansion. But they disagreed on whether the national government should oversee the economy or whether the economy should be decentralized without interference.

THE "CORRUPT BARGAIN"

Until 1820, presidential candidates were nominated by party caucuses in Congress. But in 1824, "King Caucus" was overthrown. The Republican caucus nominated William H. Crawford of Georgia, the favorite of the extreme states' rights faction of the party. But other candidates received nominations from state legislatures and won endorsements from irregular mass meetings throughout the country.

One of them was Secretary of State John Quincy Adams. But he was a man of cold and forbidding manners, with little popular appeal. Another contender was Henry Clay, the Speaker of the House. He had a devoted personal following and a definite and coherent program: the **American System,** which proposed creating a great home market for factory and farm producers by raising the protective tariff, strengthening the national bank, and financing internal improvements. Andrew Jackson, the fourth major candidate, had no significant political record—even though he was a new member of the United States Senate. But he was a military hero and had the help of shrewd political allies from his home state of Tennessee.

Jackson received more popular and electoral votes than any other candidate, but not a majority. The Twelfth Amendment to the Constitution (passed in the aftermath of the *Disputed Election* contested 1800 election) required the House of Representatives to choose among the three candidates with the largest numbers of electoral votes. Crawford was seriously ill. Clay was out of the running, but he was in a strong position to influence the result. Jackson was Clay's most dangerous political rival in the West, so Clay supported Adams, in part because Adams was an ardent nationalist and a likely supporter of the American System. With Clay's endorsement, Adams won election in the House.

The Jacksonians believed that their large popular and electoral pluralities entitled their candidate to the presidency, and they were enraged when he lost. But they grew angrier still when Adams named Clay his secretary of state. The State Department was the well-established route to the presidency, and Adams thus appeared to be naming Clay as his own successor. The outrage the Jacksonians expressed at what they called a "corrupt bargain" haunted Adams throughout his presidency.

THE SECOND PRESIDENT ADAMS

Adams proposed an ambitiously nationalist program reminiscent of Clay's American System, but Jacksonians in Congress blocked most of it. Adams also experienced diplomatic frustra- tions. He appointed delegates to an international conference that the *Diplomatic Frustrations* Venezuelan liberator Simón Bolívar had called in Panama in 1826. But Haiti was one of the participating nations, and southerners in Congress opposed the idea of white Americans mingling with the black delegates. Congress delayed approving the Panama mission so long that the American delegation did not arrive until after the conference was over.

Even more damaging to the administration was its support for a new tariff on imported goods in 1828. This measure originated with the demands of New England woolen manufacturers. But to win support from middle and western states, the administration had to accept duties on other items. In the process, it antagonized the original supporters of the bill; the benefits of protecting their manufactured goods from foreign competition now had to be weighed against the prospects of having to pay *The "Tariff of Abominations"* more for raw materials. Adams signed the bill, earning the animosity of southerners, who cursed it as the "tariff of abominations."

JACKSON TRIUMPHANT

By the time of the 1828 presidential election, the new two-party system was now in place. On one side stood the supporters of John Quincy Adams and the National Republicans. Opposing them were the followers of Andrew Jackson and the Democratic Republicans. Adams attracted the support of most of the remaining Federalists; Jackson appealed to a broad coalition that opposed the "economic aristocracy."

But issues seemed to count for little in the end, as the campaign degenerated into a war of personal invective. The Jacksonians charged that Adams had been guilty of gross waste and extravagance. Adams's supporters hurled even worse accusations at Jackson. They called him a murderer and distributed a "coffin handbill," which listed, within coffin-shaped outlines, the names of militiamen whom Jackson was said to have shot in cold blood during the War of 1812. (The men had been deserters who were legally executed after sentence by a court-martial.) And they called his wife a bigamist. Jackson had married his beloved Rachel at a time when the pair incorrectly believed her first husband had divorced her. (When Jackson's wife read of the accusations against her, she collapsed and, a few weeks later, died.)

Jackson's victory was decisive, but sectional. Adams swept virtually all of New England and showed significant strength in the mid-Atlantic region. Nevertheless, the Jacksonians considered their victory as complete and as important as Jefferson's in 1800. Once again, the forces of privilege had been driven from Washington. Once again, a champion of democracy would occupy the White House. America had entered, some Jacksonians claimed, a new era of democracy, the "era of the common man."

CONCLUSION

In the aftermath of the War of 1812, a vigorous nationalism increasingly came to characterize the political and popular culture of the United States. In all regions of the country, white men and women celebrated the achievements of the early leaders of the republic, the genius of the Constitution, and the success of the nation in withstanding serious challenges from both without and within. Party divisions faded.

But the broad nationalism of the "era of good feelings" disguised some deep divisions. Indeed, the character of American nationalism differed substantially from one region, and one group, to another. Battles continued between those who favored a strong central government committed to advancing the economic development of the nation and those who wanted a decentralization of power to open opportunity to more people. Battles continued as well over the role of slavery in American life—and in particular over the place of slavery in the new western territories. The Missouri Compromise of 1820 postponed the day of reckoning on that issue—but only for a time.

KEY TERMS/PEOPLE/PLACES/EVENTS

Adams-Onís Treaty 191
American System 198
Francis Cabot Lowell 186
Gibbons v. Ogden 195
Henry Clay 192

John Quincy Adams 191
McCulloch v. Maryland 195
Missouri Compromise 193
Monroe Doctrine 197
Panic of 1819 191

Seminole War 191
Stephen H. Long 189
Tallmadge Amendment 192
Worcester v. Georgia 196

RECALL AND REFLECT

1. How did the War of 1812 stimulate the national economy?
2. What were the reasons for the rise of sectional differences in this era? What attempts were made to resolve these differences? How successful were those attempts?
3. Why was the Monroe Doctrine proclaimed?
4. What was the significance of Andrew Jackson's victory in the election of 1828?

9 JACKSONIAN AMERICA

THE RISE OF MASS POLITICS
"OUR FEDERAL UNION"
THE REMOVAL OF THE INDIANS
JACKSON AND THE BANK WAR
THE CHANGING FACE OF AMERICAN POLITICS
POLITICS AFTER JACKSON

LOOKING AHEAD

1. How did the electorate expand during the Jacksonian era, and what were the limits of that expansion?
2. What events fed the growing tension between nationalism and states' rights, and what were the arguments on both sides of that issue?
3. What was the second party system, and how did its emergence change national politics?

MANY AMERICANS IN THE 1830s were growing apprehensive about the future of their expanding republic. Some feared that rapid growth would produce social chaos; they insisted that the country's first priority was to establish order and a clear system of authority. Others argued that the greatest danger facing the nation was the growth of inequality and privilege; they wanted to eliminate the favored status of powerful elites and make opportunity more widely available. Advocates of this latter vision seized control of the federal government in 1829 with the inauguration of Andrew Jackson.

1830

Webster and Hayne
debate

1830-1838

Indians expelled
from Southeast

1831

Anti-Mason Party holds
first convention

1832

Jackson vetoes
recharter of
Bank of U.S.

Jackson reelected

1832-1833

Nullification crisis

1833

Jackson removes
deposits from
Bank of U.S.

1835

Taney named
chief justice of
Supreme Court

1835-1842

Seminole Wars

1836

Specie circular

Van Buren
elected president

1837-1844

Panic and depression

1840

William Henry
Harrison elected
president

Independent
Treasury Act

1841

Harrison dies;
Tyler becomes
president

THE RISE OF MASS POLITICS

On March 4, 1829, thousands of Americans from all regions of the country crowded before the United States Capitol to watch the inauguration of Andrew Jackson. After the ceremonies, the crowd poured into a public reception at the White House, where, in their eagerness to shake the new president's hand, they filled the state rooms to overflowing, trampled one another, soiled the carpets, and damaged the upholstery. "It was a proud day for the people," wrote Amos Kendall, one of Jackson's closest political associates. Supreme Court Justice Joseph Story, a friend and colleague of John Marshall, remarked with disgust: "The reign of King 'Mob' seems triumphant."

In fact, the "age of Jackson" was much less a triumph of the common people than Kendall hoped and Story feared. But it did mark a transformation of American politics. Once restricted to a relatively small elite of property owners, politics now became open to virtually all the nation's white male citizens. In a political sense at least, the period had some claim to the title the Jacksonians gave it: the "era of the common man."

THE EXPANDING DEMOCRACY

What some have called the "age of Jackson" did not really bring economic equality. The distribution of wealth and property in America was little different at the end of the Jacksonian era than it had been at the start. But it did mark a transformation of American politics that widely extended to new groups the right to vote.

Until the 1820s, relatively few Americans had been permitted to vote. Most states restricted the franchise to white male property owners or taxpayers or both. But even before Jackson's election, the franchise began to expand. Change came first in Ohio and other new states of the West, which, on joining the Union, adopted constitutions that guaranteed all adult white males—not just property owners or taxpayers—the right to vote and permitted all voters the right to hold public office. Older states, concerned about the loss of their population to the West, began to drop or reduce their own property ownership or taxpaying requirements.

The wave of state reforms was generally peaceful, but in Rhode Island, democratization efforts created considerable instability. The Rhode Island constitution barred more than half the adult males in the state from voting in the 1830s. In 1840, the lawyer and activist Thomas L. Dorr and a group of his followers formed a "People's party," held a convention, drafted a new constitution, and submitted it to a popular vote. It was overwhelmingly approved, and the Dorrites began to set up a new government, with Dorr as governor. The existing legislature, however, rejected the legitimacy of Dorr's constitution. And so, in 1842, two governments were claiming power in Rhode Island. The old state government declared Dorr and his followers rebels and began to imprison them. The Dorrites, meanwhile, made an ineffectual effort to capture the state *The Dorr Rebellion* arsenal. The Dorr Rebellion, as it was known, quickly failed, but the episode helped spur the old guard to draft a new constitution that greatly expanded suffrage.

The democratization process was far from complete. In much of the South, of course, no slaves could vote. In addition, southern election laws continued to favor the planters and politicians of the older counties. Free blacks could not vote anywhere in the South and hardly anywhere in the North. In no state could women vote. Nowhere was the ballot secret, and often it was cast as a spoken vote, which meant that voters could be easily bribed or intimidated. Despite the persisting limitations, however, the number of voters increased much more rapidly than did the population as a whole.

***THE VERDICT OF THE PEOPLE* (1855), BY GEORGE CALEB BINGHAM** This scene of an election-day gathering is peopled almost entirely by white men. Women and blacks were barred from voting, but political rights expanded substantially in the 1830s and 1840s among white males. (© Saint Louis Art Museum, Missouri, USA/Gift of Bank of America/Bridgeman Images)

One of the most striking political trends of the early nineteenth century was the change in the method of choosing presidential electors. In 1800, the legislatures had chosen the presidential electors in ten states; the electors were chosen by the people in only six states. By 1828, electors were chosen by popular vote in every state but South Carolina. In the presidential election of 1824, fewer than 27 percent of adult white males had voted. Only four years later, the figure was 58 percent; and in 1840, 80 percent.

Tocqueville and *Democracy in America*

The rapid growth of the electorate—and the emergence of political parties—was among the most striking events of the early nineteenth century. As the right to vote spread widely in these years, it came to be the mark of freedom and democracy. One of the most important commentaries on this extraordinary moment in American life was a book by the French aristocrat Alexis de Tocqueville. (See "Consider the Source: Alexis de Tocqueville, *Concerning the People's Choices and the Instinctive Preferences of American Democracy*.") He spent two years in the United States in the 1830s watching the dramatic political changes in the age of Andrew Jackson. The French government had requested that he make a study of American prisons, which were thought to be more humane and effective institutions than those in Europe. But Tocqueville quickly went far beyond the study of prisons and wrote a classic study of American life, titled *Democracy in America*. Tocqueville examined not just the politics of the United States, but also the daily lives of many groups of Americans and their cultures, their associations, and their visions of democracy. In France in the early decades of the nineteenth century, the fruits of democracy were largely restricted to landowners and aristocrats. But Tocqueville recognized that traditional aristocracies were rapidly fading in America and that new elites could rise and fall no matter what their backgrounds.

Tocqueville also realized that the rising democracy of America had many limits. Democracy was a powerful, visible force in the lives of most white men. Few women could vote, although some shared the democratic ethos through their families. For many other Americans, democracy was a distant hope. Tocqueville wrote of the limits of equality and democracy:

> he first who attracts the eye, the first in enlightenment, in power and in happiness, is the white man, the European, man par excellence; below him appear the Negro and the Indian. These two unfortunate races have neither birth, nor face, nor language, nor mores in common; only their misfortunes look alike. Both occupy an equally inferior position in the country that they inhabit; both experience the effects of tyranny; and if their miseries are different, they can accuse the same author for them.

Tocqueville's book helped spread the idea of American democracy into France and other European nations. Only later did it become widely read and studied in the United States as a remarkable portrait of the emerging democracy of the United States.

The Legitimization of Party

The high level of voter participation was only partly the result of an expanded electorate. It resulted as well from growing interest in politics, a strengthening of party organization, and increasing party loyalty. Although party competition had been part of American politics almost from the beginning, acceptance of the idea of party had not. For more than thirty years, most Americans who had opinions about the nature of government considered parties evils to be avoided and thought the nation should seek a broad consensus without permanent factional lines. But in the 1820s and 1830s, those assumptions gave way to a new view that permanent, institutionalized parties were a desirable part of the political process, that they were indeed essential to democracy.

The elevation of party occurred first at the state level, most prominently in New York. There, after the War of 1812, Martin Van Buren led a dissident political faction (known as the "Bucktails") that challenged the established political elite led by the aristocratic governor, DeWitt Clinton. The Bucktails argued that Clinton's closed circle made genuine democracy impossible. They advocated institutionalized political parties in its place, based on the support of a broad public constituency. A party would need a permanent opposition, they insisted, because competition would force it to remain sensitive to the will of the people. Parties would check and balance one another in much the same way as the different branches of government did.

By the late 1820s, this new idea of party had spread beyond New York. The election of Jackson in 1828, the result of a popular movement that stood apart from the usual political elites, seemed further to legitimize it. In the 1830s, finally, a fully formed two-party system began to operate at the national level. The anti-Jackson   *The Two-Party System* forces began to call themselves the Whigs. Jackson's followers called themselves Democrats, thus giving a permanent name to what is now the nation's oldest political party.

PRESIDENT OF THE COMMON PEOPLE

Unlike Thomas Jefferson, Jackson was no democratic philosopher. The Democratic Party, much less than the old Jeffersonian Republicans, embraced no clear or uniform

ANDREW JACKSON This portrait suggests something of the fierce determination that characterized Andrew Jackson's military and political careers. Shattered by the death of his wife a few weeks after his election as president—a death he blamed (not entirely without reason) on the attacks his political opponents had leveled at her—he entered office with a steely determination to live by his own principles and give no quarter to his adversaries. (© Bettmann/Corbis)

ALEXIS DE TOCQUEVILLE, *CONCERNING THE PEOPLE'S CHOICES AND THE INSTINCTIVE PREFERENCES OF AMERICAN DEMOCRACY*

In the 1830s, the French political thinker and historian Alexis de Tocqueville devoted two years in the United States to studying the country's institutions and political culture. The result was his book *Democracy in America*. In this excerpt, Tocqueville considers the correlation between social class and political engagement.

Many people in Europe believe but do not say, or say but do not believe, that one of the great advantages of universal suffrage is that it brings men worthy of public trust into positions of leadership. The people, it is argued, may not know how to govern themselves, but they always sincerely want what is good for the state, and their instinct is unlikely to overlook men animated by the same desire and eminently capable of wielding power.

For my part, I must say that what I saw in America gives me no reason to believe that this is the case. On arriving in the United States, I was surprised to discover how common talent was among the governed and how rare in government. There is no escaping the fact that in the United States today the most outstanding men are seldom called to public office, and one is forced to acknowledge that this situation arose as democracy developed beyond all former bounds. It is clear that over the past half century the race of American statesmen has singularly shrunk in stature.

Several causes of this phenomenon may be adduced.

Whatever one does, there are limits to the degree to which people can be enlightened. Try as one might to make knowledge more accessible, improve teaching methods, and reduce the cost of acquiring learning, there is no way for people to educate themselves and develop their intelligence unless they can devote time to the effort.

How easy or hard it is for people to live without working therefore sets a necessary limit to their intellectual progress. In some countries that limit is a long way from being reached; in others not so far off. But in order for there to be no limit, the people would need to be freed of worries about their material needs, in which case they would no longer be the people. Hence it is as difficult to conceive of a society in which everyone is highly enlightened as of a state in which every citizen is wealthy; the two difficulties are related. I am perfectly willing to concede that most citizens very sincerely want what is good for their country. Taking this one step further, I would go so far as to add that in general the lower classes of society seem to me less likely than the upper classes to adulterate this desire with considerations of personal interest. What the lower classes invariably lack to one degree or another, however, is the art of judging the means to the end they sincerely wish to achieve. What a lengthy period of study and variety of ideas are necessary to form an exact idea of the character of a single man! The greatest geniuses fail at this, yet the multitude is supposed to succeed! The people never have enough time or resources to devote to the effort. They must always judge hastily and seize on whatever is most visible. That is why charlatans of every stripe are so clever at pleasing them, while more often than not their true friends fail.

What democracy lacks, moreover, is not always the capacity to choose men of merit but the desire and taste to do so.

We must not blind ourselves to the fact that democratic institutions develop the sentiment of envy in the human heart to a very high degree. This is not so much because such institutions give everyone the means to equal everyone else as because those means continually prove unavailing to those who employ them. Democratic institutions awaken and flatter the passion for equality without ever being able to satisfy it to the full. No sooner does full equality seem within the people's reach than it flies from their grasp, and its flight, as Pascal said, is eternal. The people passionately seek a good that is all the more precious because it is close enough to be familiar yet far enough away that it cannot be savored.

The chance of success spurs them on; the uncertainty of success vexes them. They struggle, they tire, they grow bitter. Anything that is beyond them in any quarter then seems an obstacle to their desires, and no form of superiority is so legitimate that the sight of it is not wearisome to their eyes.

UNDERSTAND, ANALYZE, & EVALUATE

1. What general assumption about universal suffrage did Alexis de Tocqueville want to counter?
2. What change did Tocqueville observe among American politicians since the Revolution, and how did he explain this change?
3. What relationship between social class and political understanding did Tocqueville see among Americans?

Source: *Democracy in America* by Alexis de Tocqueville, translated by Arthur Goldhammer, The Library of America, pp. 225–226. Translation copyright 2004 by Library Classics of the United States, Inc., New York.

ideological position. But Jackson himself did embrace a distinct and simple theory of democracy. Government, he said, should offer "equal protection and equal benefits" to all its white male citizens and favor no one region or class over another. In practice, that meant launching an assault on what Jackson considered the citadels of the eastern aristocracy and extending opportunities to the rising classes of the West and the South. (For historians' changing assessments of Jackson, see "Debating the Past: Jacksonian Democracy.")

Jackson's first target was the entrenched officeholders in the federal government, whom he bitterly denounced. Offices, he said, belonged to the people, not to a self-serving bureaucracy. Equally important, a large turnover in the bureaucracy would allow him to reward his own supporters with offices. One of Jackson's allies, William L. Marcy of New York, once explained, "To the victors belong the spoils"; and patronage, the process of giving out jobs as political rewards, became known as the **spoils system.** Although Jackson removed no more than one-fifth   *The Spoils System* of existing federal officeholders, his embrace of the spoils system helped cement its place in party politics.

Jackson's supporters also worked to transform the process by which presidential candidates were selected. In 1832, the president's followers staged a national convention to renominate him. Through the convention, its founders believed, power in the party would arise directly from the people rather than from such elite political institutions as the congressional caucus.

Jacksonian Democracy

To many Americans in the 1820s and 1830s, Andrew Jackson was a champion of democracy, a symbol of the spirit of anti-elitism and egalitarianism that was sweeping American life. Historians, however, have disagreed sharply not only in their assessments of Jackson himself but in their portrayal of American society in his era.

The "progressive" historians of the early twentieth century tended to see Jacksonian politics as a forebear of their own battles against economic privilege and political corruption. Frederick Jackson Turner encouraged scholars to see Jacksonianism as a protest by the frontier against the conservative aristocracy of the East. Jackson represented those who wanted to make government responsive to the will of the people rather than to the power of special interests. The culmination of this progressive interpretation of Jacksonianism was Arthur M. Schlesinger's *The Age of Jackson* (1945). Less interested in the regional basis of Jacksonianism than the disciples of Turner had been, Schlesinger argued that Jacksonian democracy was an effort "to control the power of the capitalist groups, mainly Eastern, for the benefit of non-capitalist groups, farmers and laboring men, East, West, and South." He portrayed Jacksonianism as an early version of modern reform efforts to "restrain the power of the business community."

Richard Hofstadter, in an influential 1948 essay, sharply disagreed. Jackson, he argued, was the spokesman of rising entrepreneurs—aspiring businessmen who saw the road to opportunity blocked by the monopolistic power of eastern aristocrats. The Jacksonian leaders were less sympathetic to the aspirations of those below them than they were to the destruction of obstacles to their own success. Bray Hammond, writing in 1957, argued similarly that the Jacksonian cause was "one of enterpriser against capitalist." Other historians saw Jacksonianism less as a democratic reform movement than as a nostalgic effort to restore a lost past. Marvin Meyers's *The Jacksonian Persuasion* (1957) argued that Jackson and his followers looked with misgivings on the new industrial society emerging around them and yearned instead for a restoration of the agrarian, republican virtues of an earlier time.

In the 1960s, historians began taking less interest in Jackson and his supporters and more in the social and cultural bases of American politics in the time of Jackson. Lee Benson's *The Concept of Jacksonian Democracy* (1961) used quantitative techniques to demonstrate the role of religion and ethnicity in shaping party divisions. Edward Pessen's *Jacksonian America* (1969) portrayed America in the Jacksonian era as an increasingly stratified society. This inclination to look more closely at society than at formal "Jacksonianism" continued into the late twentieth and early twenty-first centuries. Sean Wilentz, in *Chants Democratic* (1984) and in *The Rise of American Democracy* (2005), examined the rise of powerful movements among ordinary citizens who were attracted less to Jackson himself than to the notion of popular democracy.

Gradually, this attention to the nature of society has led to reassessments of Jackson himself and the nature of his regime. In *Fathers and Children* (1975), Michael Rogin portrays Jackson as a leader determined to secure the supremacy of white men in the United States. Alexander Saxton, in *The*

Rise and Fall of the White Republic (1990), makes the related argument that "Jacksonian Democracy" was explicitly a white man's democracy that rested on the subjugation of slaves, women, and Native Americans. But the portrayal of Jackson as a champion of the common people has not vanished from scholarship entirely. The most renowned postwar biographer of Jackson, Robert V. Remini, argues that, despite the flaws in his democratic vision, he was a genuine "man of the people." •

UNDERSTAND, ANALYZE, & EVALUATE

1. What was Jacksonian democracy? Was it a reform movement against conservative special interests? Was it a regional movement designed to shift power to the West? Or was it a class-based movement to elevate workers and farmers?

2. Jackson was known as a "man of the people." Which people were attracted to him?

"OUR FEDERAL UNION"

Jackson's commitment to extending power beyond entrenched elites led him to want to reduce the functions of the federal government. A concentration of power in Washington would, he believed, restrict opportunity to people with political connections. But Jackson was also strongly committed to the preservation of the Union. Thus, at the same time as he was promoting an economic program to reduce the power of the national government, he was asserting the supremacy of the Union in the face of a potent challenge. For no sooner had he entered office than his own vice president—John C. Calhoun—began to champion a controversial constitutional theory: nullification.

CALHOUN AND NULLIFICATION

Once an outspoken protectionist, Calhoun had strongly supported the tariff of 1816. But by the late 1820s, he had come to believe that the tariff was responsible for the stagnation of South Carolina's economy—even though the exhaustion of the state's farmland was the real reason for the decline. Some exasperated Carolinians were ready to consider a drastic remedy—secession.

With his future political hopes resting on how he met this challenge in his home state, Calhoun developed the theory of **nullification.** Drawing from the ideas of Madison and Jefferson and citing the Tenth Amendment to the Constitution, Calhoun argued that since the federal government was a creation of the states, the states—not the courts or Congress—were the final arbiters of the constitutionality of federal laws. If a state concluded that Congress had passed an unconstitutional law, then it could hold a special convention and declare the federal law null and void within the state. The nullification doctrine—and the idea of using it to nullify the 1828 tariff—quickly attracted broad support in South Carolina. But it did nothing to help Calhoun's standing within the new Jackson administration, in part because he had a powerful rival in Martin Van Buren.

THE RISE OF VAN BUREN

Van Buren had served briefly as governor of New York before becoming Jackson's secretary of state in 1829. He soon established himself as a member both of the official

cabinet and of the president's unofficial circle of political allies, known as the "Kitchen
The "Kitchen Cabinet"   Cabinet." And Van Buren's influence with the president grew stronger still as a result of a quarrel over etiquette that drove a wedge between Jackson
and Calhoun.

Peggy O'Neale was the attractive daughter of a Washington tavernkeeper with whom
both Andrew Jackson and his friend John H. Eaton had taken lodgings while serving as
senators from Tennessee. O'Neale was married, but rumors circulated in Washington in
the mid-1820s that she and Senator Eaton were having an affair. O'Neale's husband died
in 1828, and she and Eaton were soon married. A few weeks later, Jackson named Eaton
secretary of war and thus made the new Mrs. Eaton a cabinet wife. The rest of the administration wives, led by Mrs. Calhoun, refused to receive her. Jackson, who blamed slander-
ous gossip for the death of his own wife, was furious, and demanded that the members
of the cabinet accept her into their social world. Calhoun, under pressure from his wife,
refused. Van Buren, a widower, befriended the Eatons and thus ingratiated himself with
Jackson. By 1831, Jackson had tapped Van Buren as his preferred successor in the White
House, apparently ending Calhoun's dreams of the presidency.

THE WEBSTER-HAYNE DEBATE

In January 1830, in the midst of a routine debate over federal policy toward western lands,
a senator from Connecticut suggested that all land sales and surveys be temporarily dis-
continued. Robert Y. Hayne, a young senator from South Carolina, charged that slowing
down the growth of the West was simply a way for the East to retain its political and
economic power.

Daniel Webster, now a senator from Massachusetts, attacked Hayne (and through him
Calhoun) for what he considered an attack on the integrity of the Union—in effect, challenging Hayne to a debate not on the issues of public lands and the tariff but on the issue
States' Rights versus National Power   of states' rights versus national power. Hayne responded
with a defense of nullification. Webster then spent two full afternoons delivering what
became known as his "Second Reply to Hayne." He concluded with the ringing appeal:
"Liberty and Union, now and for ever, one and inseparable!"

Both sides waited to hear what President Jackson thought of the argument. That became
clear at the annual Democratic Party banquet in honor of Thomas Jefferson. After dinner,
guests delivered a series of toasts. The president arrived with a written text in which he
had underscored certain words: "Our Federal Union—It must be preserved." While he
spoke, he looked directly at Calhoun. The diminutive Van Buren, who stood on his chair
to see better, thought he saw Calhoun's hand shake and a trickle of wine run down his
glass as he responded to the president's toast with his own: "The Union, next to our
liberty most dear."

THE NULLIFICATION CRISIS

In 1832, the controversy over nullification finally produced a crisis when South Carolinians
responded angrily to a congressional tariff bill that offered them no relief from the 1828
tariff of abominations. Almost immediately, the legislature summoned a state convention,
which voted to nullify the tariffs of 1828 and 1832 and to forbid the collection of duties
within the state. At the same time, South Carolina elected Hayne to serve as governor
and Calhoun to replace Hayne as senator.

Jackson insisted that nullification was treason. He strengthened the federal forts in South Carolina and ordered a warship to Charleston. When Congress convened early in 1833, Jackson proposed a force bill authorizing the president to use the military to see that acts of Congress were obeyed. Violence seemed a real possibility.

Calhoun faced a predicament as he took his place in the Senate. Not a single state had come to South Carolina's support. But the timely intervention of Henry Clay, also newly elected to the Senate, averted a crisis. Clay devised a compromise by *Clay's Compromise* which the tariff would be lowered gradually so that by 1842 it would reach approximately the same level as in 1816. The compromise and the force bill were passed on the same day, March 1, 1833. Jackson signed them both. In South Carolina, the convention reassembled and repealed its nullification of the tariffs. But unwilling to allow Congress to have the last word, the convention nullified the force act—a purely symbolic act, since the tariff had already been amended. Calhoun and his followers claimed a victory for nullification, which had, they insisted, forced the revision of the tariff. But the episode taught Calhoun and his allies that no state could defy the federal government alone.

THE REMOVAL OF THE INDIANS

There had never been any doubt about Andrew Jackson's attitude toward the Indian tribes whose lands were now encircled by the eastern states and territories of the United States. He wanted them to move west. Since his early military expeditions in Florida, Jackson had harbored a deep hostility toward the Indians. In this he was little different from most white Americans.

White Attitudes toward the Tribes

In the eighteenth century, many whites had shared Thomas Jefferson's view of the Indians as "noble savages," with an inherent dignity that made civilization possible among them if they would only mimic white social, cultural, political, and economic practices. Yet by the first decades of the nineteenth century, many whites were coming to view Native Americans simply as "savages" who should be removed from all the lands east of the Mississippi. White westerners also favored removal to put an end to violence and conflict in the western areas of white settlement. Most of all, they wanted valuable land that the tribes still possessed.

Events in the Northwest added urgency to the issue of removal. In Illinois, an alliance of Sauk (or Sac) and Fox Indians under Black Hawk fought white settlers in 1831–1832 in an effort to overturn what Black Hawk considered an illegal cession of tribal lands to the United States. The Black Hawk War was notable for its viciousness. *The Black Hawk War* White forces attacked the Indians even when they attempted to surrender, pursued them as they retreated, and slaughtered many of them. The brutal war only reinforced the determination of whites to remove all the tribes to the West.

The "Five Civilized Tribes"

Even more troubling to the government in the 1830s were the remaining Indian tribes of the South, who possessed lands southerners coveted for their growing cotton empire. In western Georgia, Alabama, Mississippi, and Florida lived what were known as the "Five

BLACK HAWK AND WHIRLING THUNDER After his defeat by white settlers in Illinois in 1832, the famed Sauk warrior Black Hawk and his son, Whirling Thunder, were captured and sent on a tour by Andrew Jackson, displayed to the public as trophies of war. They showed such dignity through the ordeal that much of the white public quickly began to sympathize with them. This portrait, by John Wesley Jarvis, was painted on the tour's final stop, in New York City. Black Hawk wears the European-style suit, while Whirling Thunder wears native costume to emphasize his commitment to his tribal roots. Soon thereafter, Black Hawk returned to his tribe, wrote a celebrated autobiography, and died in 1838. (© Granger, NYC—All Rights Reserved.)

Civilized Tribes"—the Cherokee, Creek, Seminole, Chickasaw, and Choctaw. These groups had adopted various Euro-American institutions and practices, including literacy, organized government, laws, agricultural economies, and even slavery. In 1830, both the federal government and several southern states were accelerating efforts to remove the tribes to the West. That year Congress passed the Indian Removal Act, which authorized the financing of federal negotiations to relocate the southern tribes to the West. Some Indians believed removal the least disagreeable option—better, perhaps, than the prospect of destitution, white encroachment, and violence. Others fought back.

The Cherokee tried to stop Georgia from taking their lands through an appeal in the Supreme Court, and the Court's rulings in *Cherokee Nation v. Georgia* and *Worcester v. Georgia* supported the tribe's contention that the state had no authority to negotiate *Cherokee Legal Resistance* with tribal representatives. But Jackson repudiated the decisions, reportedly responding to news of the rulings with the contemptuous statement: "John Marshall has made his decision. Now let him enforce it." Then, in 1835, the United States government extracted a treaty from a minority faction of the Cherokee that ceded to Georgia the tribe's land in that state in return for $5 million and a reservation west of the Mississippi. With removal inevitable, this Cherokee "Treaty Party" reasoned, a deal for cash and land to the west was the best alternative available. But the great majority of the 17,000 Cherokee did not recognize the treaty as legitimate. Jackson sent an army of 7,000 under General Winfield Scott to round them up and drive them westward.

TRAIL OF TEARS

About 1,000 Cherokee fled to North Carolina, where eventually the federal government provided them with a small reservation in the Smoky Mountains that survives today. But

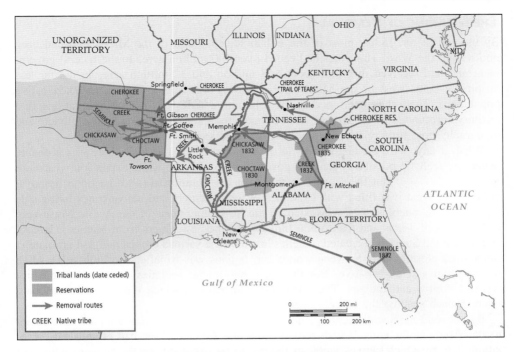

THE EXPULSION OF THE TRIBES, 1830-1835 Well before he became president, Andrew Jackson was famous for his military exploits against the tribes. Once in the White House, he ensured that few Indians would remain in the southern states of the nation, now that white settlement was increasing there. The result was a series of dramatic "removals" of Indian tribes out of their traditional lands and into new territories west of the Mississippi—mostly in Oklahoma. Note the very long distance many of these tribes had to travel. • *Why was the route of the Cherokee, shown in the upper portion of the map, known as the "Trail of Tears"?*

most of the rest made a long, forced trek to "Indian Territory," what later became Oklahoma, beginning in the winter of 1838. Thousands, perhaps a quarter or more of the émigrés, perished before reaching their unwanted destination. In the harsh new reservations, the survivors remembered the terrible journey as "The Trail Where They Cried," the Trail of Tears.

Removal

Between 1830 and 1838, virtually all the Five Civilized Tribes were forced to travel to Indian Territory. The Choctaw of Mississippi and western Alabama were the first to make the trek, beginning in 1830. The army moved out the Creek of eastern Alabama and western Georgia in 1836. A year later, the Chickasaw in northern Mississippi began their long march westward and the Cherokee, finally, a year after that.

The Seminole in Florida were able to resist removal, but even their success was limited. Like other tribes, the Seminole had agreed under pressure to a settlement by which they ceded their lands to the United States and agreed to move to Indian Territory within three years. Most did move west, but a substantial minority, under the leadership of the chieftain Osceola, balked and staged an uprising beginning in 1835 to defend their lands. (Joining the Indians in their struggle was a group of runaway black slaves, who had been living with the tribe.) Jackson sent troops to Florida, but the Seminole and their black allies were masters of guerrilla warfare in the junglelike Everglades. Finally, in 1842, the government abandoned the war. By then, many of the Seminole had been either killed or forced westward.

Seminole Wars

THE MEANING OF REMOVAL

By the end of the 1830s, most of the Indian societies east of the Mississippi had been removed to the West. The tribes had ceded over 100 million acres to the federal government and had received in return about $68 million and 32 million acres in the far less hospitable lands west of the Mississippi—territory that already had established native populations. There they lived, divided by tribe into a series of separate reservations, in a territory surrounded by a string of United States forts and in a region whose climate and topography bore little relation to anything they had known before.

What, if any, were the alternatives to the removal of the Indians? There was probably never any realistic possibility that the government could stop white expansion westward. *Alternatives to Removal* But there were, in theory at least, alternatives to the brutal removal policy. The West was filled with examples of white settlers and native tribes living side by side. In the pueblos of New Mexico, in the fur trading posts of the Pacific Northwest, and in parts of Texas and California, Indians and the newcomers from Mexico, Canada, and the United States had created societies in which the various groups mingled intimately. Sometimes close contact between whites and Indians was beneficial to both sides; often it was cruel and exploitative. But the early multiracial societies of the West did not separate whites and Indians. They demonstrated ways in which the two cultures could interact, each shaping the other.

By the mid-nineteenth century, however, white Americans had adopted a different model. Much as the early British settlers along the Atlantic Coast had established "plantations," from which natives were, in theory, to be excluded, so the western whites of later years believed that Indians could not be partners in the creation of new societies in the West. They were obstacles to be removed and, as far as possible, isolated.

JACKSON AND THE BANK WAR

Jackson was quite willing to manipulate the Indian tribes. But in other contexts, he was very reluctant to use federal authority, as shown by his 1830 veto of a congressional measure providing a subsidy to the proposed Maysville Road in Kentucky. The bill was unconstitutional, Jackson argued, because the road in question lay entirely within Kentucky and was not, therefore, a part of "interstate commerce." Jackson also thought the bill unwise because it committed the government to what he considered extravagant expenditures. A similar resistance to federal power lay behind Jackson's war against the Bank of the United States.

BIDDLE'S INSTITUTION

The Bank of the United States held a monopoly on federal deposits, provided credit to growing enterprises, issued banknotes that served as a dependable medium of exchange, and exercised a restraining effect on the less well-managed state banks. Nicholas Biddle, *Nicholas Biddle* who ran the Bank from 1823 on, had done much to put the institution on a sound and prosperous basis. Nevertheless, many Americans—among them Andrew Jackson—were determined to destroy it.

Opposition to the Bank came from two very different groups: the "soft-money" and *"Soft Money" versus "Hard Money"* "hard-money" factions. Advocates of soft money consisted largely of state bankers and their allies. They objected to the Bank because it restrained state banks from issuing notes freely. The hard-money faction believed that coin was the only safe currency, and they condemned *all* banks that issued banknotes, state or federal. The soft-money advocates believed in rapid economic growth and speculation; the hard-money forces embraced older ideas of "public virtue" and looked with suspicion on expansion and speculation. Jackson himself supported the hard-money position, and he made clear that he would not favor renewing the charter of the Bank of the United States, which was due to expire in 1836.

A Philadelphia aristocrat unaccustomed to politics, Biddle nevertheless began granting banking favors to influential men. In particular, he relied on Daniel Webster, whom he named the Bank's legal counsel and director of the Boston branch. Webster   *Bank War* helped Biddle enlist the support of Henry Clay as well. Clay, Webster, and other advisers persuaded Biddle to apply to Congress for a recharter bill in 1832, four years ahead of the expiration date. Congress passed the recharter bill; Jackson vetoed it; and the Bank's supporters in Congress failed to override the veto. The Bank question then emerged as the paramount issue of the 1832 election, just as Clay had hoped.

In 1832, Clay ran for president as the unanimous choice of the Whigs. But the "Bank War" failed to provide Clay with the winning issue he had hoped for. Jackson, with Van Buren as his running mate, won an overwhelming victory with 55 percent of the popular vote and 219 electoral votes.

The "Monster" Destroyed

Jackson was now more determined than ever to destroy the "monster." He could not legally abolish the Bank before the expiration of its charter. But he weakened it by removing the government's deposits from it. When his secretary of the treasury, believing that such an action would destabilize the financial system, refused to give the order, Jackson fired him and appointed a replacement. When the new secretary similarly procrastinated, Jackson fired him, too, and named a third: Roger B. Taney, the attorney general, a close friend and loyal ally of the president.

Taney soon began taking the government's deposits out of the Bank of the United States and putting them in a number of state banks. In response, Biddle called in loans and raised interest rates, explaining that without the government   *Government Deposits Removed* deposits the Bank's resources were stretched too thin. His actions precipitated a short recession.

As financial conditions worsened in the winter of 1833–1834, supporters of the Bank sent petitions to Washington urging its rechartering. But the Jacksonians blamed the recession on Biddle and refused. When the banker finally carried his contraction of credit too far and had to reverse himself to appease the business community, his hopes of winning a recharter of the Bank died in the process. Jackson had won a   *Jackson's Political Victory* considerable political victory. But when the Bank of the United States expired in 1836, the country was left with a fragmented and chronically unstable banking system that would plague the economy for many years.

The Taney Court

In the aftermath of the Bank War, Jackson moved against the most powerful remaining institution of economic nationalism: the Supreme Court. In 1835, when John Marshall died, the president appointed as the new chief justice his trusted ally Roger B. Taney. Taney did not bring a sharp break in constitutional interpretation, but he did help modify Marshall's vigorous nationalism.

Perhaps the clearest indication of the new judicial climate was the celebrated case of *Charles River Bridge v. Warren Bridge*   *Charles River Bridge v. Warren Bridge* of 1837. The case involved a dispute between two Massachusetts companies over the right to build a bridge across the Charles River between Boston and Cambridge. One company had a long-standing charter from the state to operate a toll bridge, a charter that the firm claimed guaranteed it a monopoly of the bridge traffic. Another company had applied to the legislature for authorization to construct a second, competing bridge that would—since it would be toll-free—greatly reduce the value of the first company's charter. The first company contended that in granting the second charter, the legislature was engaging in a breach of contract; and it noted that the Marshall Court, in the *Dartmouth College* case and other decisions, had ruled that states had no right to abrogate contracts. But now Taney supported the right of Massachusetts to award the second charter. The object of government, Taney maintained, was to promote the general happiness, an object that took precedence over the rights of property. A state, therefore, had the right to amend or abrogate a contract if such action was necessary to advance the well-being of the community. The decision reflected one of the cornerstones of the Jacksonian idea: that the key to democracy was an expansion of economic opportunity, which would not occur if older corporations could maintain monopolies.

THE CHANGING FACE OF AMERICAN POLITICS

Jackson's forceful—some people claimed tyrannical—tactics in crushing first the nullification movement and then the Bank of the United States helped galvanize a growing opposition coalition. It began as a gathering of national political leaders opposed to Jackson's use of power. Denouncing the president as "King Andrew I," they began to refer to themselves as Whigs, after the party in England that traditionally worked to limit the power of the king. With the emergence of the Whigs, the nation once again had two competing political parties. What scholars now call the "second party system" had begun its relatively brief life.

DEMOCRATS AND WHIGS

The philosophy of the Democratic Party in the 1830s bore the stamp of Andrew Jackson. The federal government, the Democrats believed, should be limited in power, except to the degree that it worked to eliminate social and economic arrangements that entrenched privilege and stifled opportunity. The rights of states should be protected except to the extent that state governments interfered with social and economic mobility. Jacksonian *Jacksonian Democrats*   Democrats celebrated "honest workers," "simple farmers," and "forthright businessmen" and contrasted them to the corrupt, monopolistic, aristocratic forces of established wealth. Democrats were more likely than Whigs to support territorial expansion, which would, they believed, widen opportunities for aspiring Americans. Among the most radical members of the party—the so-called Locofocos, mainly workingmen, small businessmen, and professionals in the Northeast—sentiment was strong for a vigorous, perhaps even violent, assault on monopoly and privilege.

In contrast, the political philosophy that became known as Whiggery favored the expansion of federal power and industrial and commercial development. Whigs *Whiggery* were cautious about westward expansion, fearful that rapid territorial growth would produce instability. And although Whigs insisted that their vision would result in increasing opportunities for all Americans, they tended to attribute particular value to the entrepreneurs and institutions that most effectively promoted economic growth.

The Whigs were strongest among the more substantial merchants and manufacturers of the Northeast, the wealthier planters of the South, and the ambitious farmers and rising commercial class of the West. The Democrats drew more support from smaller merchants and the workingmen of the Northeast; from southern planters suspicious of industrial growth; and from westerners who favored a predominantly agrarian economy. Whigs tended to be wealthier, to have more aristocratic backgrounds, and to be more commercially ambitious than the Democrats. But Whigs and Democrats alike were more interested in winning elections than in maintaining philosophical purity. And both parties made adjustments from region to region to attract the largest possible number of voters.

In New York, for example, the Whigs developed a popular following through a movement known as Anti-Masonry. The Anti-Mason Party had emerged in the *Anti-Masonry* 1820s in response to widespread resentment against the secret and exclusive, hence supposedly undemocratic, Society of Freemasons. Such resentment increased in 1826 when a former Mason, William Morgan, mysteriously disappeared from his home in Batavia, New York, shortly before he was scheduled to publish a book that would allegedly expose the secrets of Freemasonry. With help from a widespread assumption that Morgan had been abducted and murdered by vengeful Masons, Whigs seized on the Anti-Mason frenzy to launch spirited attacks on Jackson and Van Buren (both Freemasons), implying that the Democrats were connected with the antidemocratic conspiracy.

Religious and ethnic divisions also played an important role in determining the constituencies of the two parties. Irish and German Catholics tended to support the Democrats, who appeared to share their own vague aversion to commercial development and who seemed to respect their cultural values. Evangelical Protestants gravitated toward the Whigs because they associated the party with constant development and improvement. They envisioned a society progressing steadily toward unity and order, and they looked on the new immigrant communities as groups that needed to be disciplined and taught "American" ways.

The Whig Party was more successful at defining its positions and attracting a constituency than it was at uniting behind a national leader. No one person was ever able to command the loyalties of the party in the way Jackson commanded those of the Democrats. Instead, Whigs tended to divide their allegiance among the "Great Triumvirate" of Henry Clay, Daniel Webster, and John C. Calhoun.

Clay won support from many who favored internal improvements and economic development with what he called the American System. But Clay's image *The American System* as a devious political operator and his identification with the West were a liability. He ran for president three times and never won. Daniel Webster won broad support among the Whigs with his passionate speeches in defense of the Constitution and the Union; but his close connection with the Bank of the United States and the protective tariff, his reliance on rich men for financial support, and his excessive fondness for brandy prevented him from developing enough of a national constituency to win him his desired office. John C. Calhoun never considered himself a true Whig, and his identification with the nullification controversy in effect disqualified him from national leadership in any case.

Yet he sided with Clay and Webster on the issue of the national bank, and he shared with them a strong animosity toward Andrew Jackson.

The Whigs competed relatively evenly with the Democrats in congressional, state, and local races, but they managed to win only two presidential elections in the more than twenty years of their history. Their problems became particularly clear in 1836. While the Democrats united behind Andrew Jackson's personal choice for president, Martin Van

Van Buren Elected   Buren, the Whigs could not even agree on a single candidate. Instead, they ran several candidates in different regions, hoping they might separately draw enough votes from Van Buren to throw the election to the House of Representatives, where the Whigs might be better able to elect one of their candidates. In the end, however, Van Buren won easily, with 170 electoral votes to 124 for all his opponents combined.

POLITICS AFTER JACKSON

Andrew Jackson retired from public life in 1837, the most beloved political figure of his age. Martin Van Buren was less fortunate. He could not match Jackson's personal magnetism, and his administration suffered from economic difficulties that hurt both him and his party.

VAN BUREN AND THE PANIC OF 1837

Van Buren's success in the 1836 election was a result in part of a nationwide economic boom. Canal and railroad builders operated at a peak of activity.

Prices were rising, credit was plentiful, and the land business, in particular, was booming. Between 1835 and 1837, the government sold nearly 40 million acres of public land,

"THE TIMES," 1837   This savage caricature of the economic troubles besetting the United States in 1837 illustrates, among other things, popular resentment of the hard-money orthodoxies of the time. A sign on the Custom House reads: "All bonds must be paid in Specie." Next door, the bank announces: "No specie payments made here." (© Museum of the City of New York, USA/Bridgeman Images)

nearly three-fourths of it to speculators. These land sales, along with revenues the government received from the tariff of 1833, created a series of substantial federal budget surpluses and made possible a steady reduction of the national debt. From 1835 to 1837, the government for the first and only time in its history was out of debt, with a substantial surplus in the Treasury.

Congress and the administration now faced the question of what to do with the Treasury surplus. Support soon grew for returning the federal surplus to the states. An 1836 "distribution" act required the federal government to pay its surplus funds to the states each year in four quarterly installments as interest-free, unsecured loans. No one expected the "loans" to be repaid. The states spent the money quickly, mainly to promote the construction of highways, railroads, and canals. The distribution of the surplus thus gave further stimulus to the economic boom. At the same time, the withdrawal of federal funds strained the state banks in which they had been deposited by the government; the banks had to call in their own loans to make the transfer of funds to the state governments.

Congress did nothing to check the speculative fever. But Jackson feared that the government was selling land for state banknotes of questionable value. In 1836, he issued an executive order, the "specie circular." It provided that in payment for public   *Specie Circular* lands, the government would accept only gold or silver coins or currency backed by gold or silver. The specie circular produced a financial panic that began in the first months of Van Buren's presidency. Banks and businesses failed; unemployment grew; bread riots shook some of the larger cities; and prices fell, especially the price of land. Many railroad and canal projects failed; several of the debt-burdened state governments ceased to pay interest on their bonds, and a few repudiated their debts, at least temporarily. The worst depression in American history to that point, it lasted for five years, and it was a political catastrophe for Van Buren and the Democrats.

The Van Buren administration did little to fight the depression. In fact, some of the steps it took—borrowing money to pay government debts and accepting only specie for payment of taxes—may have made things worse. Other efforts failed in Congress: a "preemption" bill that would have given settlers the right to buy government land near them before it was opened for public sale, and another bill that would have lowered the price of land. Van Buren did succeed in establishing a ten-hour workday on all federal projects via a presidential order, but he had few legislative achievements.

The most important and controversial measure in the president's program was a proposal for a new financial system. Under Van Buren's plan, known as the "independent treasury" or "subtreasury" system, government funds would be   *"Independent Treasury" System* placed in an independent treasury in Washington and in subtreasuries in other cities. No private banks would have the government's money or name to use as a basis for speculation. Van Buren called a special session of Congress in 1837 to consider the proposal, but it failed in the House. In 1840, however, the administration finally succeeded in driving the measure through both houses of Congress.

THE LOG CABIN CAMPAIGN

As the campaign of 1840 approached, the Whigs realized that they would have to settle on one candidate for president. In December 1839, they held their first nominating convention. Passing over Henry Clay, they chose William Henry   *William Henry Harrison* Harrison, a renowned soldier and a popular national figure. The Democrats again nominated Van Buren.

THE PENNY PRESS

On September 3, 1833, a small newspaper appeared in New York City for the first time: the *Sun*, published by a young former apprentice from Massachusetts named Benjamin Day. Four pages long, it contained mostly trivial local news, with particular emphasis on sex, crime, and violence. It sold for a penny, launching a new age in the history of American journalism, the age of the "penny press."

Before the advent of the penny press, newspapers in America were far too expensive for most ordinary citizens to buy. But several important changes in both the business of journalism and the character of

American society paved the way for Benjamin Day and others to challenge the established press. New technologies—the steam-powered cylinder printing press, new machines for making paper, railroads and canals for distributing issues to a larger market—made it possible to publish newspapers inexpensively and to sell them widely. A rising popular literacy rate, a result, in part, of the spread of public education, created a bigger reading public.

The penny press was also a response to the changing culture of the 1820s and 1830s. The spread of an urban market economy

THE *SUN* This 1834 front page of the *Sun*, which had begun publication a year earlier, contains advertisements, human interest stories, a description of a slave auction in Charleston, South Carolina, and homespun advice: "Life is short. The poor pittance of several years is not worth being a villain for." (Collection of the New-York Historical Society)

contributed to the growth of the penny press by drawing a large population of workers, artisans, and clerks into large cities, where they became an important market for the new papers. The spirit of democracy—symbolized by the popularity of Andrew Jackson and the rising numbers of white male voters across the country—helped create an appetite for journalism that spoke to and for "the people." The *Sun* and other papers like it were committed to feeding the appetites of the people of modest means, who constituted most of their readership. "Human interest stories" helped solidify their hold on the working public.

Within six months of its first issue, the *Sun* had the largest circulation in New York—8,000 readers, more than twice the number of its nearest competitors. James Gordon Bennett's *New York Herald*, which began publication in 1835, soon surpassed the *Sun* in popularity, with its lively combination of sensationalism and local gossip and its aggressive pursuit of national and international stories. The *Herald* pioneered a "letters to the editor" column, was the first paper to have regular reviews of books and the arts, and launched the first daily sports section. By 1860, its circulation of more than 77,000 was the largest of any daily newspaper in the world.

Not all the new penny papers were as sensationalistic as the *Sun* and the *Herald*. The *New-York Tribune*, founded in 1841 by Horace Greeley, prided itself on serious reporting and commentary. As serious as the *Tribune*, but more sober and self-consciously "objective" in its reportage, was the *New York Times*, which Henry Raymond founded in 1851. "We do not mean to write as if we were in a passion—unless that shall really be the case," the *Times* huffily proclaimed in its first issue, in an obvious reference to Greeley and his impassioned reportage, "and we shall make it a point to get into a passion as rarely as possible."

The newspapers of the penny press initiated the process of turning journalism into a profession. They were the first papers to pay their reporters, and they were also the first to rely heavily on advertisements, often devoting up to half their space to paid advertising. They tended to be sensationalistic and opinionated, but they were also usually aggressive in uncovering serious and important news—in police stations, courts, jails, streets, and private homes as well as in city halls, state capitals, Washington, and the world. •

UNDERSTAND, ANALYZE, & EVALUATE

1. How were the penny press newspapers a product of the Jacksonian era?
2. Before the advent of the penny press, newspapers in America were aimed at a much narrower audience. Some published mainly business news, and others worked to advance the aims of a political party. What nationally circulated newspapers and other media today continue this tradition?

The 1840 campaign was the first in which the new and popular "penny press" carried news of the candidates to large audiences (See "Patterns of Popular Culture: The Penny Press."). Such newspapers were deliberately livelier and more sensationalist than the newspapers of the past, which had been almost entirely directed at the upper classes. The *Sun,* the first of the new breed, began publishing in 1833 and was from the beginning self-consciously egalitarian. It soon had the largest circulation in New York. Other, similar papers soon began appearing in other cities—reinforcing the increasingly democratic character of political culture and encouraging the inclination of both parties to try to appeal to ordinary voters as they planned their campaigns.

The campaign of 1840 also illustrated how fully the spirit of party competition had established itself in America. The Whigs—who had emerged as a party largely because

HARRISON AND REFORM   This hand-colored engraving was made for a brass brooch during the 1840 presidential campaign and served the same purposes that modern campaign buttons do. It conveys Harrison's presumably humble beginnings in a log cabin. In reality, Harrison was a wealthy, aristocratic man; but the unpopularity of the aristocratic airs of his opponent, President Martin Van Buren, persuaded the Whig Party that it would be good political strategy to portray Harrison as a humble "man of the people." (© David J. & Janice L. Frent Collection/Corbis)

of their opposition to Andrew Jackson's common-people democracy—presented themselves in 1840 as the party of the common people. So, of course, did the Democrats. With both parties using the same techniques of mass voter appeal, what mattered was not the philosophical purity of the party but its ability to win votes. The Whig campaign was particularly effective in portraying William Henry Harrison, a wealthy member of the frontier elite with a considerable estate, as a simple man of the people who loved log cabins and hard cider. The Democrats, already weakened by the depression, had no effective defense against such tactics. Harrison won the election with 234 electoral votes to 60 for Van Buren and with a popular majority of 53 percent.

THE FRUSTRATION OF THE WHIGS

Despite their decisive victory, the Whigs found the four years after their resounding victory frustrating and divisive. The trouble began when their appealing new president died of pneumonia just one month after taking office. Vice President John Tyler of Virginia succeeded him.

Tyler was a former Democrat who had left the party in reaction to what he considered Jackson's excessively egalitarian program; Tyler's approach to public policy still showed signs of his Democratic past. The president did agree to bills abolishing Van Buren's independent-treasury system and raising tariff rates. But he refused to support Clay's attempt to recharter the Bank of the United States, and he vetoed several internal improvement bills sponsored by Clay and other congressional Whigs. Finally, a conference of congressional Whigs voted Tyler out of the party. Every cabinet member but Webster, who was serving as secretary of state, resigned; five former Democrats took their places. When Webster, too, left the cabinet, Tyler appointed Calhoun, who had rejoined the Democratic Party, to replace him.

A new political alignment was taking shape. Tyler and a small band of conservative southern Whigs were preparing to rejoin the Democrats. Into the common   *Changes to Democratic Party* people's party of Jackson and Van Buren was arriving a faction with decidedly aristocratic political ideas, men who thought that government had an obligation to protect and even expand the institution of slavery and who believed in states' rights with almost fanatical devotion.

Whig Diplomacy

In the midst of these domestic controversies, anti-British factions in Canada launched an unsuccessful rebellion against the colonial government there in 1837. When the insurrection failed, some of the rebels took refuge near the United States border and chartered an American steamship, the *Caroline,* to ship them supplies across the   *Caroline Affair and Aroostook War* Niagara River from New York. British authorities in Canada seized the *Caroline* and burned it, killing one American in the process. Resentment in the United States grew rapidly. At the same time, tensions flared over the boundary between Canada and Maine, which had been in dispute since the treaty of 1783. In 1838, rival groups of Americans and Canadians, mostly lumberjacks, began moving into the Aroostook River region in the disputed area, precipitating a violent brawl that became known as the "Aroostook War."

Several years later, in 1841, an American ship, the *Creole,* sailed from Virginia for New Orleans with more than 100 slaves aboard. En route the slaves mutinied, seized possession of the ship, and took it to the Bahamas. British officials there declared the slaves free, and the English government refused to overrule them. Many Americans, especially southerners, were furious.

At this critical juncture, a new government eager to reduce tensions with the United States came to power in Great Britain. It sent Lord Ashburton, an admirer of America, to negotiate an agreement on the Maine boundary and other matters. The result was the Webster-Ashburton Treaty of 1842, under which the United States   *Webster-Ashburton Treaty* received slightly more than half the disputed area and agreed to a revised northern boundary as far west as the Rocky Mountains. Ashburton also eased the memory of the *Caroline* and *Creole* affairs by expressing regret and promising no future "officious interference" with American ships. Anglo-American relations improved significantly.

During the Tyler administration, the United States established its first diplomatic relations with China. In the 1844 Treaty of Wang Hya, American diplomats   *Trade with China* secured the same trading privileges as the English. In the next ten years, American trade with China steadily increased.

In their diplomatic efforts, at least, the Whigs were able to secure some important successes. But by the end of the Tyler administration, the party could look back on few other victories. And in the election of 1844, the Whigs lost the White House to James K. Polk, a Democrat with an explicit agenda of westward expansion.

CONCLUSION

The election of Andrew Jackson in 1828 reflected the emergence of a new political world. Throughout the American nation, the laws governing political participation were loosening, and the number of people permitted to vote (which eventually included most white males, but almost no one else) was increasing. Along with this expansion of the electorate was emerging a new spirit of party politics.

Jackson set out as president to entrench his party, the Democrats, in power. A fierce defender of the West and a sharp critic of what he considered the stranglehold of the aristocratic East on the nation's economic life, he sought to limit the role of the federal government in economic affairs and worked to destroy the Bank of the United States, which he considered a corrupt vehicle of aristocratic influence. And he confronted the greatest challenge yet to American unity—the nullification crisis of 1832–1833—with a strong assertion of the power and importance of the Union. These positions won him broad popularity and ensured his reelection in 1832 and the election of his designated successor, Martin Van Buren, in 1836.

But a new coalition of anti-Jacksonians, who called themselves the Whigs, launched a powerful new party that used much of the same anti-elitist rhetoric to win support for their own, much more nationalist program. Their emergence culminated in the campaign of 1840 with the election of William Henry Harrison, the first Whig president. When his death led to the accidental presidency of John Tyler, however, further realignments were set in motion.

KEY TERMS/PEOPLE/PLACES/EVENTS

Alexis de Tocqueville 204
Andrew Jackson 202
Anti-Masonry 217
Aroostook War 223
Bank War 215
Black Hawk War 211
Caroline affair 223
Daniel Webster 210
Dorr Rebellion 203
"Five Civilized Tribes" 211

Indian Removal
 Act 212
Indian Territory 213
John C. Calhoun 209
John Tyler 222
Martin Van Buren 209
Nicholas Biddle 214
nullification 209
Panic of 1837 218
Roger B. Taney 216

Seminole Wars 213
specie circular 219
spoils system 207
Trail of Tears 213
Webster-Ashburton
 Treaty 223
Webster-Hayne
 debate 210
Whigs 216
William Henry Harrison 219

RECALL AND REFLECT

1. What was Andrew Jackson's political philosophy, and how was it reflected in the policies and actions of his administration?
2. Who benefited under Jacksonian democracy? Who suffered?
3. How did Andrew Jackson change the office of the presidency?
4. Who supported and who opposed the Bank of the United States, and why? Who was right?
5. How and why did white attitudes toward Native Americans change, and how did these changes lead to the Indian Removal Act and the Trail of Tears?
6. How did Native Americans in the Southeast respond to white efforts to seize their land and remove them to the West?

10 | AMERICA'S ECONOMIC REVOLUTION

THE CHANGING AMERICAN POPULATION
TRANSPORTATION AND COMMUNICATIONS
  REVOLUTIONS
COMMERCE AND INDUSTRY
MEN AND WOMEN AT WORK
PATTERNS OF SOCIETY
THE AGRICULTURAL NORTH

LOOKING AHEAD

1. What were the factors sparking the U.S. economic revolution of the mid-nineteenth century?
2. How did the U.S. population change between 1820 and 1840, and how did the population change affect the nation's economy, society, and politics?
3. Why did America's Industrial Revolution affect the northern economy and society differently than it did the southern economy and society?

WHEN THE UNITED STATES ENTERED the War of 1812, it was still an essentially agrarian nation. There were, to be sure, some substantial cities in America and also modest but growing manufacturing, mainly in the Northeast. But the overwhelming majority of Americans were farmers and tradespeople.

By the time the Civil War began in 1861, the United States had transformed itself. Most Americans were still rural people. But even most farmers were now part of a national, and even international, market economy. Equally important, the United States was beginning to challenge the industrial nations of Europe for supremacy in manufacturing. The nation had experienced the beginning of its Industrial Revolution.

1830

Baltimore and Ohio
Railroad begins
operation

1830s

Immigration from
Ireland and Germany
begins

1834

Lowell Mills women
strike

McCormick patents
mechanical reaper

1837

Native American
Association fights
immigration

1844

Morse sends first
telegraph message

1845

Native American Party
formed

1846

Rotary press invented

1847

John Deere
manufactures
steel plows

1852

American Party
(Know-Nothings)
formed

THE CHANGING AMERICAN POPULATION

The American Industrial Revolution was a result of many factors: advances in transportation and communications, the growth of manufacturing technology, the development of new systems of business organization, and perhaps above all, population growth.

POPULATION TRENDS

Three trends characterized the American population during the **antebellum** period: rapid population increase, movement westward, and the growth of towns and cities where demand for work was expanding.

The American population, 4 million in 1790, had reached 10 million by 1820 and 17 million by 1840. Improvements in public health played a role in this growth. Epidemics declined in both frequency and intensity, and the death rate as a whole dipped. But the population increase was also a result of a high birthrate. In 1840, white women bore an average of 6.14 children each.

The African American population increased more slowly than the white population. After 1808, when the importation of slaves became illegal, the proportion of blacks to whites in the nation as a whole steadily declined. The slower increase of the black population was also a result of its comparatively high death rate. Slave mothers had large families, but life was shorter for both slaves and free blacks than for whites—a result of the enforced poverty and harsh working conditions in which virtually all African Americans lived.

Immigration, choked off by wars in Europe and economic crises in America, contributed little to the American population in the first three decades of the nineteenth century. Of the total 1830 population of nearly 13 million, the foreign-born numbered fewer than 500,000. Soon, however, immigration began to grow once again. Reduced transportation costs and increasing economic opportunities helped stimulate the immigration boom, as did deteriorating economic conditions in some areas of Europe.

Much of this new European immigration flowed into the rapidly growing cities of the Northeast. But urban growth was a result of substantial internal migration as well. As agriculture in New England and other areas grew less profitable, more and more people picked up stakes and moved—some to promising agricultural regions in the West, but many to eastern cities.

Immigration and Urban Growth, 1840–1860

The growth of cities accelerated dramatically between 1840 and 1860. The population of New York, for example, rose from 312,000 to 805,000, making it the *Rapid Urbanization* nation's largest and most commercially important city. Philadelphia's population grew over the same twenty-year period from 220,000 to 565,000; Boston's, from 93,000 to 177,000. By 1860, 26 percent of the population of the free states was living in towns (places of 2,500 people or more) or cities, up from 14 percent in 1840. The urban population of the South, by contrast, increased from 6 percent in 1840 to only 10 percent in 1860.

The booming agricultural economy of the West produced significant urban growth as well. Between 1820 and 1840, communities that had once been small villages or trading posts became major cities: St. Louis, Pittsburgh, Cincinnati, Louisville. All became centers of the growing carrying trade that connected the farmers of the Midwest with New Orleans and, through it, the cities of the Northeast. After 1830, however, an increasing proportion of this trade moved from the Mississippi River to the Great Lakes, creating such important new port cities as Buffalo, Detroit, Milwaukee, and Chicago, which gradually overtook the river ports.

Immigration from Europe swelled. Between 1840 and 1850, more than 1.5 million Europeans moved to America. In the 1850s, the number rose to 2.5 million. Almost half the residents of New York City in the 1850s were recent immigrants. In St. Louis, Chicago, and Milwaukee, the foreign-born outnumbered those of native birth. Few immigrants settled in the South.

The newcomers came from many different countries, but the overwhelming majority came from Ireland and Germany. By 1860, there were more than *Irish and German Immigrants* 1.5 million Irish-born and approximately 1 million German-born people in the United States. Most of the Irish stayed in the eastern cities where they landed and became part of the unskilled labor force. The largest single group of Irish immigrants comprised young, single women, who worked in factories or in domestic service. Germans, who—unlike the Irish—usually arrived with at least some money and often came in family groups, generally moved on to the Northwest, where they became farmers or small businessmen.

The Rise of Nativism

Many politicians, particularly Democrats, eagerly courted the support of the new arrivals. Other older citizens, however, viewed the growing foreign population with alarm. Some people argued that the immigrants were racially inferior or that they corrupted politics by selling their votes. Others complained that they were stealing jobs from the native workforce. Protestants worried that the growing Irish population would increase the power of the Catholic Church in America. Older-stock Americans feared that immigrants would become a radical force in politics. Out of these fears and prejudices emerged a number of secret societies to combat the "alien menace."

KNOW-NOTHING SOAP This illustrated advertising label for soap manufactured in Boston alludes to the Know-Nothing or nativist movement. The Indian depicted in the foreground and teepees and camp in the background symbolize the movement's prejudice against new arrivals. (The Library of Congress)

The first was the Native American Association, founded in 1837, which in 1845 became *Native American Party* the Native American Party. In 1850, it joined with other groups supporting **nativism** to form the Supreme Order of the Star-Spangled Banner, whose demands included banning Catholics or aliens from holding public office, enacting more restrictive naturalization laws, and establishing literacy tests for voting. The order adopted a strict code of secrecy, which included a secret password: "I know nothing." Ultimately, members of the movement came to be known as the "Know-Nothings."

After the 1852 elections, the Know-Nothings created a new political organization that they called the American Party. It scored an immediate and astonishing success in the *The Know-Nothings* elections of 1854. The Know-Nothings did well in Pennsylvania and New York and actually won control of the state government in Massachusetts. Outside the Northeast, however, their progress was more modest. After 1854, the strength of the Know-Nothings declined, and the party soon disappeared.

TRANSPORTATION AND COMMUNICATIONS REVOLUTIONS

Just as the Industrial Revolution required an expanding population, it also required an efficient system of transportation and communications. The first half of the nineteenth century saw dramatic changes in both.

THE CANAL AGE

From 1790 until the 1820s, the so-called turnpike era, the United States had relied largely on roads for internal transportation. But roads alone were not adequate for the nation's expanding needs. And so, in the 1820s and 1830s, Americans began to turn to other means of transportation as well.

The larger rivers became increasingly important as steamboats replaced the slow barges that had previously dominated water traffic. The new riverboats carried the corn and wheat of northwestern farmers and the cotton and tobacco of southwestern planters to New Orleans, where oceangoing ships took the cargoes on to eastern ports or abroad.

But this roundabout river-sea route satisfied neither western farmers nor eastern merchants, who wanted a way to ship goods directly to the urban markets and ports of the Atlantic Coast. New highways across the mountains provided a partial   *Advantages of Canals* solution to the problem. But the costs of hauling goods overland, although lower than before, were still too high for anything except the most compact and valuable merchandise. And so interest grew in building canals.

The job of financing canals fell largely to the states. New York was the first to act. It had the natural advantage of a good land route between the Hudson River and Lake Erie through the only break in the Appalachian chain. But the engineering tasks were still imposing. The more than 350-mile-long route was interrupted by high ridges and thick woods. After a long public debate, canal advocates prevailed, and digging began on July 4, 1817.

CANALS IN THE NORTHEAST, 1823–1860 The great success of the Erie Canal, which opened in 1825, inspired decades of energetic canal building in many areas of the United States, as this map illustrates. But none of the new canals had anything like the impact of the original Erie Canal, and thus none of New York's competitors—among them Baltimore, Philadelphia, and Boston—were able to displace it as the nation's leading commercial center.
• *What form of transportation ultimately displaced the canals?*

The Erie Canal was the greatest construction project Americans had ever undertaken. *The Erie Canal* The canal itself was basically a simple ditch forty feet wide and four feet deep, with towpaths along the banks for the horses or mules that were to draw the canal boats. But its construction involved hundreds of difficult cuts and fills to enable the canal to pass through hills and over valleys, stone aqueducts to carry it across streams, and eighty-eight locks, of heavy masonry with great wooden gates, to permit ascents and descents. Still, the Erie Canal opened in October 1825, amid elaborate ceremonies and celebrations, and traffic was soon so heavy that within about seven years, tolls had repaid the entire cost of construction. By providing a route to the Great Lakes, the canal gave New York access to Chicago and the growing markets of the West. The Erie Canal also contributed to the decline of agriculture in New England. Now that it was so much cheaper for western farmers to ship their crops east, people farming marginal land in the Northeast found themselves unable to compete.

The system of water transportation extended farther when Ohio and Indiana, inspired by the success of the Erie Canal, provided water connections between Lake Erie and the Ohio River. These canals made it possible to ship goods by inland waterways all the way from New York to New Orleans.

One of the immediate results of these new transportation routes was increased white settlement in the Northwest, because it was now easier for migrants to make the westward *Increased Westward Migration* journey and to ship their goods back to eastern markets. Much of the western produce continued to go downriver to New Orleans, but an increasing proportion went east to New York. And manufactured goods from throughout the East now moved in growing volume through New York and then to the West via the new water routes.

Rival cities along the Atlantic seaboard took alarm at New York's access to (and control over) so vast a market, largely at their expense. But they had limited success in catching up. Boston, its way to the Hudson River blocked by the Berkshire Mountains, did not even try to connect itself to the West by canal. Philadelphia, Baltimore, Richmond, and Charleston all aspired to build water routes to the Ohio Valley but never completed them. Some cities, however, saw opportunities in a different and newer means of transportation. Even before the canal age had reached its height, the era of the railroad was beginning.

THE EARLY RAILROADS

Railroads played a relatively small role in the nation's transportation system in the 1820s and 1830s, but railroad pioneers laid the groundwork in those years for the great surge of railroad building in the midcentury. Eventually, railroads became the primary transportation system for the United States, as well as critical sites of development for innovations in technology and corporate organization.

Railroads emerged from a combination of technological and entrepreneurial innovations: the invention of tracks, the creation of steam-powered locomotives, and the development of trains as public carriers of passengers and freight. By 1804, both English and American inventors had experimented with steam engines for propelling land vehicles. In 1820, John Stevens ran a locomotive and cars around a circular track on his New Jersey estate. And in 1825, the Stockton and Darlington Railroad in England became the first line to carry general traffic.

RACING ON THE RAILROAD   Peter Cooper designed and built the first steam-powered locomotives in America in 1830 for the Baltimore and Ohio Railroad. On August 28 of that year, he raced his locomotive (the "Tom Thumb") against a horse-drawn railroad car. This sketch depicts the moment when Cooper's engine overtook the horse-drawn railroad car. (© Universal Images Group/Getty Images)

American entrepreneurs quickly grew interested in the English experiment. The first company to begin actual operations was the Baltimore and Ohio, which opened a thirteen-mile stretch of track in 1830. In New York, the Mohawk and Hudson began running trains along the sixteen miles between Schenectady and *The Baltimore and Ohio* Albany in 1831. By 1836, more than a thousand miles of track had been laid in eleven states.

THE TRIUMPH OF THE RAILS

Railroads gradually supplanted canals and all other forms of transport. In 1840, the total railroad trackage of the country was under 3,000 miles. By 1860, it was over 27,000 miles, mostly in the Northeast. Railroads even crossed the Mississippi at several points by great iron bridges. Chicago eventually became the rail center of the West, securing its place as the dominant city of that region.

The emergence of the great train lines diverted traffic from the main water routes—the Erie Canal and the Mississippi River. By lessening the dependence of the West on the Mississippi, the railroads also helped weaken further the connection between the Northwest and the South.

Railroad construction required massive amounts of capital. Some came from private sources, but much of it came from government funding. State and local governments invested in railroads, but even greater assistance came from *Importance of Government Funding* the federal government in the form of public land grants. By 1860, Congress had allotted over 30 million acres to eleven states to assist railroad construction.

It would be difficult to exaggerate the impact of the rails on the American economy, on American society, even on American culture. Where railroads went, towns, ranches, and farms grew up rapidly along their routes. Areas once cut off from markets during winter found that the railroad could transport goods to and from them year-round. Most of all, the railroads cut the time of shipment and travel. In the 1830s, traveling from New York to Chicago by lake and canal took roughly three weeks. By railroad in the 1850s, the same trip took less than two days.

The railroads were much more than a fast and economically attractive form of transportation. They were also a breeding ground for technological advances, a key to the nation's economic growth, and the birthplace of the modern corporate form of organization. They became a symbol of the nation's technological prowess. To many people, railroads were the most visible sign of American advancement and greatness.

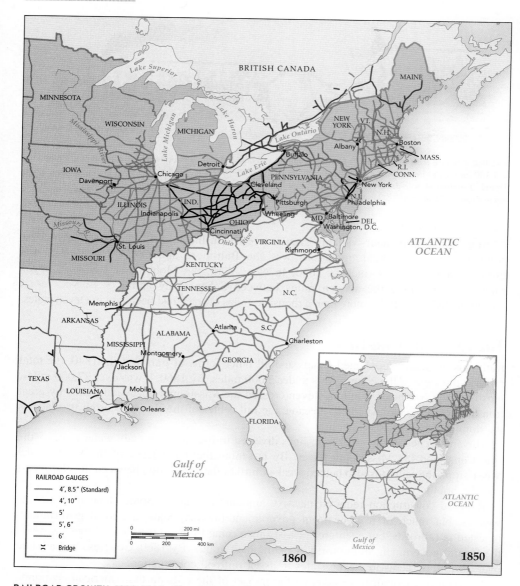

RAILROAD GROWTH, 1850–1860   These two maps illustrate the dramatic growth of American railroads in the 1850s. Note the particularly extensive increase in mileage in the upper Midwest (known at the time as the Old Northwest). Note, too, the relatively smaller increase in railroad mileage in the South. Railroads forged a close economic relationship between the upper Midwest and the Northeast and weakened the Midwest's relationship with the South. • *How did this contribute to the South's growing sense of insecurity within the Union?*

THE TELEGRAPH

What the railroad was to transportation, the telegraph was to communication—a dramatic advance over traditional methods and a symbol of national progress and technological expertise.

Before the telegraph, communication over great distances could be achieved only by direct, physical contact. That meant that virtually all long-distance communication relied on the mail, which traveled first on horseback and coach and later by railroad. There were obvious disadvantages to this system, not the least of which was the difficulty in coordinating the railroad schedules. By the 1830s, experiments with many methods of improving long-distance communication had been conducted, among them a procedure for using the sun and reflective devices to send light signals as far as 187 miles.

In 1832, Samuel F. B. Morse—a professor of art with an interest in science—began experimenting with a different system. Fascinated with the possibilities of electricity, *Morse Code* Morse set out to find a way to send signals along an electric cable. Technology did not yet permit the use of electric wiring to send reproductions of the human voice or any complex information. But Morse realized that electricity itself could serve as a communication device—that pulses of electricity could themselves become a kind of language. He experimented at first with a numerical code, in which each number would represent a word on a list available to recipients. Gradually, however, he became convinced of the need to find a more universal telegraphic "language," and he developed what became the Morse code, in which alternating long and short bursts of electric current would represent individual letters.

THE TELEGRAPH The telegraph provided rapid communication across the country—and eventually across oceans—for the first time. Samuel F. B. Morse was one of a number of inventors who helped create the telegraph, but he was the most commercially successful of the rivals. (The Library of Congress)

In 1843, Congress appropriated $30,000 for the construction of an experimental telegraph line between Baltimore and Washington; in May 1844 it was complete, and Morse succeeded in transmitting the news of James K. Polk's nomination for the presidency over the wires. By 1860, more than 50,000 miles of wire connected most parts of the country; a year later, the Pacific Telegraph, with 3,595 miles of wire, opened between New York and San Francisco. By then, nearly all the independent lines had joined in one

Western Union Telegraph Company organization, the Western Union Telegraph Company. The telegraph spread rapidly across Europe as well, and in 1866, the first transatlantic cable was laid, allowing telegraphic communication between America and Europe.

One of the first beneficiaries of the telegraph was the growing system of rails. Wires often ran alongside railroad tracks, and telegraph offices were often located in railroad stations. The telegraph allowed railroad operators to communicate directly with stations in cities, small towns, and even rural hamlets—to alert them to schedule changes and warn them about delays and breakdowns. Among other things, this new form of communication helped prevent accidents by alerting stations to problems that engineers in the past had to discover for themselves.

New Technology and Journalism

Another beneficiary of the telegraph was American journalism. The wires delivered news in a matter of hours—not days, weeks, or months, as in the past—across the country and the world. Where once the exchange of national and international news relied on the cumbersome exchange of newspapers by mail, now it was possible for papers to share their reporting. In 1846, newspaper publishers from around the nation formed the Associated Press to promote cooperative news gathering by wire.

Other technological advances spurred the development of the American press. In 1846, Richard Hoe invented the steam-powered cylinder rotary press, making it possible to print newspapers much more rapidly and cheaply than had been possible in the past. Among other things, the rotary press spurred the dramatic growth of mass-circulation newspapers.

Newspaper Circulation Growth   The *New York Sun,* the most widely circulated paper in the nation, had 8,000 readers in 1834. By 1860, its successful rival the *New York Herald*—benefiting from the speed and economies of production the rotary press made possible—had a circulation of 77,000.

COMMERCE AND INDUSTRY

By the mid-nineteenth century, the United States had developed the beginnings of a modern capitalist economy and an advanced industrial capacity. But the economy had developed along highly unequal lines—benefiting some classes and some regions far more than others.

The Expansion of Business, 1820–1840

American business grew rapidly in the 1820s and 1830s in part because of important innovations in management. Individuals or limited partnerships continued to operate most businesses, and the dominant figures were still the great merchant capitalists, who generally had sole ownership of their enterprises. In some larger businesses, however, the

Rise of Corporations   individual merchant capitalist was giving way to the corporation.

Corporations, which had the advantage of combining the resources of a large number of shareholders, began to develop particularly rapidly in the 1830s, when some legal obstacles to their formation were removed. Previously, a corporation could obtain a charter only by a special act of a state legislature; by the 1830s, states began passing general incorporation laws, under which a group could secure a charter merely by paying a fee. The laws also permitted a system of limited liability, in which individual stockholders risked losing only the value of their own investment—and not the corporation's larger losses as in the past—if the enterprise failed. These changes made possible much larger manufacturing and business enterprises.

THE EMERGENCE OF THE FACTORY

The most profound economic development in mid-nineteenth-century America was the rise of the factory. Before the War of 1812, most manufacturing took place within households or in small workshops. Later in the nineteenth century, however, New England textile manufacturers began using new water-powered machines that allowed them to bring their operations together under a single roof. This **factory system,** as it came to be known, soon penetrated the shoe industry and other industries as well.

Between 1840 and 1860, American industry experienced particularly dramatic growth. For the first time, the value of manufactured goods was roughly   *Dramatic Industrial Growth* equal to that of agricultural products. More than half of the approximately 140,000 manufacturing establishments in the country in 1860, including most of the larger enterprises, were located in the Northeast. The Northeast thus produced more than two-thirds of the manufactured goods and employed nearly three-quarters of the men and women working in manufacturing.

ADVANCES IN TECHNOLOGY

Even the most highly developed industries were still relatively immature. American cotton manufacturers, for example, produced goods of coarse grade; fine items continued to come from England. But by the 1840s, significant advances were occurring.

Among the most important was in the manufacturing of machine tools—the tools used to make machinery parts. The government supported much of the research and development of machine tools, often in connection with supplying the military. For example, a government armory in Springfield, Massachusetts, developed two important tools—the turret lathe (used for cutting screws and other metal parts)   *American-Designed Machine Tools* and the universal milling machine (which replaced the hand chiseling of complicated parts and dies)—early in the nineteenth century. The precision grinder (which became critical to, among other things, the construction of sewing machines) was designed in the 1850s to help the army produce standardized rifle parts. By the 1840s, the machine tools used in the factories of the Northeast were already better than those in most European factories.

One important result of better machine tools was that the principle of interchangeable parts spread into many industries. Eventually, interchangeability would revolutionize watch and clock making, the manufacturing of locomotives, the creation of steam engines, and the making of many farm tools. It would also help make possible bicycles, sewing machines, typewriters, cash registers, and eventually the automobile.

Industrialization was also profiting from new sources of energy. The production of coal, most of it mined around Pittsburgh in western Pennsylvania, leaped from 50,000 tons

in 1820 to 14 million tons in 1860. The new power source, which replaced wood and
Coal Production Soars water power, made it possible to locate mills away from running streams
and thus permitted the wider expansion of the industry.

The great industrial advances owed much to American inventors. In 1830, the number
American Inventors of inventions patented was 544; in 1860, it stood at 4,778. Several industries provide particularly vivid examples of how a technological innovation could produce
major economic change. In 1839, Charles Goodyear, a New England hardware merchant,
discovered a method of vulcanizing rubber (treating it to give it greater strength and
elasticity); by 1860, his process had found over 500 uses and had helped create a major
American rubber industry. In 1846, Elias Howe of Massachusetts constructed a sewing
machine; Isaac Singer made improvements on it, and the Howe-Singer machine was soon
being used in the manufacture of ready-to-wear clothing.

RISE OF THE INDUSTRIAL RULING CLASS

The merchant capitalists remained figures of importance in the 1840s. In such cities as
New York, Philadelphia, and Boston, influential mercantile groups operated shipping lines
to southern ports or dispatched fleets of trading vessels to Europe and Asia. But merchant
capitalism was declining by the middle of the century. This was partly because British
competitors were stealing much of America's export trade, but mostly because there were
greater opportunities for profit in manufacturing than in trade. That was one reason why
industries developed first in the Northeast: an affluent merchant class with the money and
the will to finance them already existed there. They supported the emerging industrial
capitalists and soon became the new aristocrats of the Northeast, with far-reaching economic and political influence.

MEN AND WOMEN AT WORK

In the 1820s and 1830s, factory labor came primarily from the native-born population.
After 1840, the growing immigrant population became the most important new source
of workers.

RECRUITING A NATIVE WORKFORCE

Recruiting a labor force was not an easy task in the early years of the factory system.
Ninety percent of the American people in the 1820s still lived and worked on farms. Many
urban residents were skilled artisans who owned and managed their own shops, and the
available unskilled workers were not numerous enough to meet industry's needs. But
dramatic improvements in agricultural production, particularly in the Midwest, meant that
each region no longer had to feed itself; it could import the food it needed. As a result,
rural people from relatively unprofitable farming areas of the East began leaving the land
to work in the factories.

Two systems of recruitment emerged to bring this new labor supply to the expanding
textile mills. One, common in the mid-Atlantic states, brought whole families from the
farm to work together in the mill. The second system, common in Massachusetts, enlisted
young women, mostly farmers' daughters in their late teens and early twenties. It was
Lowell System known as the Lowell or Waltham system, after the towns in which it first

emerged. Many of these women worked for several years, saved their wages, and then returned home to marry and raise children. Others married men they met in the factories or in town. Most eventually stopped working in the mills and took up domestic roles instead.

Labor conditions in these early years of the factory system, hard as they often were, remained significantly better than they would later become. The Lowell workers, for example, were well fed, carefully supervised, and housed in clean boardinghouses and dormitories, which the factory owners maintained. (See "Consider the Source: *Handbook to Lowell*.") Wages for the Lowell workers were relatively generous by the standards of the time. The women even published a monthly magazine, the *Lowell Offering*.

Yet even these relatively well-treated workers found the transition from farm life to factory work difficult. Forced to live among strangers in a regimented environment, many women had trouble adjusting to the nature of factory work. However uncomfortable women may have found factory work, they had few other options. Work in the mills was in many cases virtually the only alternative to returning to farms that could no longer support them.

The factory system of Lowell did not, in any case, survive for long. In the competitive textile market of the 1830s and 1840s, manufacturers found it difficult to maintain the high living standards and reasonably attractive working conditions of before. Wages declined; the hours of work lengthened; the conditions of the boardinghouses deteriorated. In 1834, mill workers in Lowell organized a union—the Factory Girls Association—which staged a strike to protest a 25 percent wage cut. Two years later, the association struck again—against a rent increase in the boardinghouses. Both strikes failed, and a recession in 1837 virtually destroyed the organization. Eight years later, the Lowell women, led by the militant Sarah Bagley, created the Female Labor Reform Association, *Sarah Bagley* which agitated for a ten-hour day and for improvements in conditions in the mills. The new association also asked state governments for legislative investigation of conditions in the mills. By then, however, the character of the factory workforce was changing again, lessening the urgency of their demands. Many mill girls were gradually moving into other occupations: teaching, domestic service, or homemaking. And textile manufacturers were turning to a less demanding labor supply: immigrants.

THE IMMIGRANT WORKFORCE

The increasing supply of immigrant workers after 1840 was a boon to manufacturers and other entrepreneurs. These new workers, because of their growing numbers and their unfamiliarity with their new country, had even less leverage than the women they displaced, and thus they often experienced far worse working conditions. Poorly paid construction gangs, made up increasingly of Irish immigrants, performed the heavy, unskilled work on turnpikes, canals, and railroads. Many of them lived in flimsy shanties, in grim conditions that endangered the health of their families (and reinforced native prejudices toward the "shanty Irish"). Irish workers began to predominate in the New England textile mills as well in the 1840s. Employers began paying piece rates rather than a daily wage and used other devices to speed up production and exploit the labor force more efficiently. The factories themselves were becoming large, noisy, unsanitary, and often dangerous places to work; the average workday was extending to twelve, often fourteen hours; and wages were declining. Women and children, whatever their skills, earned less than most men.

CONSIDER THE SOURCE

HANDBOOK TO LOWELL—1848

Strict rules governed the working life of the young women who worked in the textile mills in Lowell, Massachusetts, in the first half of the nineteenth century. Equally strict rules regulated their time away from work (what little leisure time they enjoyed) in the company-supervised boardinghouses in which they lived. The excerpts from the *Handbook to Lowell* from 1848 that follow suggest the tight supervision under which the Lowell mill girls worked and lived.

FACTORY RULES

REGULATIONS TO BE OBSERVED by all persons employed in the factories of the Hamilton Manufacturing Company. The overseers are to be always in their rooms at the starting of the mill, and not absent unnecessarily during working hours. They are to see that all those employed in their rooms are in their places in due season, and keep a correct account of their time and work. They may grant leave of absence to those employed under them, when they have spare hands to supply their places and not otherwise, except in cases of absolute necessity.

All persons in the employ of the Hamilton Manufacturing Company are to observe the regulations of the room where they are employed. They are not to be absent from their work without the consent of the overseer, except in cases of sickness, and then they are to send him word of the cause of their absence. They are to board in one of the houses of the company and give information at the counting room, where they board, when they begin, or, whenever they change their boarding place; and are to observe the regulations of their boardinghouse.

Those intending to leave the employment of the company are to give at least two weeks' notice thereof to their overseer.

All persons entering into the employment of the company are considered as engaged for twelve months, and those who leave sooner, or do not comply with all these regulations, will not be entitled to a regular discharge.

The company will not employ anyone who is habitually absent from public worship on the Sabbath, or known to be guilty of immorality.

A physician will attend once in every month at the counting-room, to vaccinate all who may need it, free of expense.

Anyone who shall take from the mills or the yard, any yarn, cloth or other article belonging to the company will be considered guilty of stealing and be liable to prosecution.

Payment will be made monthly, including board and wages. The accounts will be made up to the last Saturday but one in every month, and paid in the course of the following week.

These regulations are considered part of the contract, with which all persons entering into the employment of the Hamilton Manufacturing Company, engage to comply.

BOARDING-HOUSE RULES

REGULATIONS FOR THE BOARDING-HOUSES of the Hamilton Manufacturing Company. The tenants of the boardinghouses are not to board, or permit any part of their houses to be occupied by any person, except those in the employ of the company, without special permission.

They will be considered answerable for any improper conduct in their houses, and are not to permit their boarders to have company at unseasonable hours.

THE LOWELL MILLS Fifteen years earlier, Lowell, Massachusetts, had been a small farming village known as East Chelmsford. By the 1840s, the town had become one of the most famous manufacturing centers in America and a magnet for visitors from around the world. This painting shows female workers, who dominated the labor force in Lowell, entering the factory. (© American Textile History Museum, Lowell, Mass.)

The buildings, and yards about them, must be kept clean and in good order; and if they are injured, otherwise than from ordinary use, all necessary repairs will be made, and charged to the occupant.

The sidewalks, also, in front of the houses, must be kept clean, and free from snow, which must be removed from them immediately after it has ceased falling; if neglected, it will be removed by the company at the expense of the tenant.

It is desirable that the families of those who live in the houses, as well as the boarders, who have not had the kine pox, should be vaccinated, which will be done at the expense of the company, for such as wish it.

Some suitable chamber in the house must be reserved, and appropriated for the use of the sick, so that others may not be under the necessity of sleeping in the same room.

JOHN AVERY, Agent.

The doors must be closed at ten o'clock in the evening, and no person admitted after that time, without some reasonable excuse.

The keepers of the boarding-houses must give an account of the number, names and employment of their boarders, when required, and report the names of such as are guilty of any improper conduct, or are not in the regular habit of attending public worship.

Source: *Handbook to Lowell* (1848).

UNDERSTAND, ANALYZE, & EVALUATE

1. What do these rules suggest about the everyday lives of the mill workers?
2. What do the rules suggest about the company's attitude toward the workers? Do the rules offer any protections to the employees, or are they all geared toward benefiting the employer?
3. Why would the company enforce such strict rules? Why would the mill workers accept them?

THE FACTORY SYSTEM AND THE ARTISAN TRADITION

Factories were also displacing the trades of skilled artisans. Artisans were as much a part of the older, republican vision of America as sturdy yeoman farmers. Independent craftsmen clung to a vision of economic life that was very different from that promoted by the new capitalist class. The **artisans** embraced not just the idea of individual, acquisitive success but also a sense of a "moral community." Skilled artisans valued their independence, their stability, and their relative equality within their economic world.

Some artisans made successful transitions into small-scale industry. But others found themselves unable to compete with the new factory-made goods. In the face of this competition, skilled workers in cities such as Philadelphia, Baltimore, Boston, and New York formed societies for mutual aid. During the 1820s and 1830s, these craft societies began to combine on a citywide basis and set up central organizations known as trade unions. In 1834, delegates from six cities founded the National Trades' Union, and in 1836, printers and cordwainers (makers of high-quality shoes and boots) set up their own national craft unions.

Hostile laws and hostile courts handicapped the unions, as did the Panic of 1837 and the depression that followed. But some artisans managed to retain control over their productive lives.

FIGHTING FOR CONTROL

Industrial workers made continuous efforts to improve their lots. They tried, with little success, to persuade state legislatures to pass laws setting a maximum workday and regulating child labor. Their greatest legal victory came in Massachusetts in 1842, when the *Commonwealth v. Hunt* state supreme court, in *Commonwealth v. Hunt,* declared that unions were lawful organizations and that the strike was a lawful weapon. Other state courts gradually accepted the principles of the Massachusetts decision, but employers continued to resist.

Virtually all the early craft unions excluded women. As a result, women began establishing their own, new protective unions in the 1850s. Like the male craft unions, the female unions had little power in dealing with employers. They did, however, serve an important role as mutual aid societies for women workers.

Many factors combined to inhibit the growth of better working standards. Among the most important obstacles was the flood into the country of immigrant laborers, who were usually willing to work for lower wages than native workers. Because they were so numerous, manufacturers had little difficulty replacing disgruntled or striking workers with eager immigrants. Ethnic divisions often led workers to channel their resentments into internal bickering among one another rather than into their shared grievances. Another obstacle was the sheer strength of the industrial capitalists, who possessed not only economic but also political and social power.

PATTERNS OF SOCIETY

The Industrial Revolution was making the United States both dramatically wealthier and increasingly unequal. It was transforming social relationships at almost every level.

THE RICH AND THE POOR

The commercial and industrial growth of the United States greatly elevated the average *Income Gap Grows* income of the American people. But this increasing wealth was being distributed highly unequally. Substantial groups of the population—slaves, Indians, landless farmers, and many of the unskilled workers on the fringes of the manufacturing system—shared hardly at all in the economic growth. But even among the rest of the population, disparities of income were growing. Merchants and industrialists were accumulating enormous fortunes; and in the cities, a distinctive culture of wealth began to emerge.

CENTRAL PARK Daily carriage rides allowed the wealthy to take in fresh air while showing off their finery to their neighbors. (© Private Collection/Bridgeman Images)

In large cities, people of great wealth gathered together in neighborhoods of astonishing opulence. They founded clubs and developed elaborate social rituals. They looked increasingly for ways to display their wealth—in great mansions, showy carriages, lavish household goods, and the elegant social establishments they patronized. New York developed a particularly elaborate high society. The construction of Central Park, which began in the 1850s, was in part a result of pressure from the members of high society, who wanted an elegant setting for their daily carriage rides.

A significant population of genuinely destitute people also emerged in the growing urban centers. These people were almost entirely without resources, often *The Urban Poor* homeless, and dependent on charity or crime, or both, for survival. Substantial numbers of people actually starved to death or died of exposure. Some of these "paupers," as contemporaries called them, were recent immigrants. Some were widows and orphans, stripped of the family structures that allowed most working-class Americans to survive. Some were people suffering from alcoholism or mental illness, unable to work. Others were victims of native prejudice—barred from all but the most menial employment because of race or ethnicity. The Irish were particular victims of such prejudice.

The worst victims in the North were free blacks. Most major urban areas had significant black populations. Some of these African Americans *Harsh Life for Free Blacks* were descendants of families who had lived in the North for generations. Others were former slaves who had escaped or been released by their masters. In material terms, at least, life was not always much better for them in the North than it had been in slavery. Most had access to very menial jobs at best. In most parts of the North, blacks could not vote, attend public schools, or use any of the public services available to white residents. Even so, most African Americans preferred life in the North, however arduous, to life in the South.

SOCIAL AND GEOGRAPHICAL MOBILITY

Despite the contrasts between conspicuous wealth and poverty in antebellum America, there was relatively little overt class conflict. For one thing, life, in material terms at least, was better for most factory workers than it had been on the farms or in Europe. A significant amount of mobility within the working class also helped limit discontent. A few workers—a very small number, but enough to support the dreams of others—managed to move from poverty to riches by dint of work, ingenuity, and luck. And a much larger number of workers managed to move at least one notch up the ladder—for example, becoming in the course of a lifetime a skilled, rather than an unskilled, laborer.

More important than social mobility was geographical mobility. Some workers saved money, bought land, and moved west to farm it. But few urban workers, and even fewer poor ones, could afford to make such a move. Much more common was the movement of laborers from one industrial town to another. These migrants, often the victims of layoffs, looked for better opportunities elsewhere. Their search seldom led to marked improvement in their circumstances. The rootlessness of this large and distressed segment of the workforce made effective organization and protest difficult.

MIDDLE-CLASS LIFE

Despite the visibility of the very rich and the very poor in antebellum society, the fastest-growing group in America was the middle class. Economic development opened many *Rapidly Expanding Middle Class* more opportunities for people to own or work in shops or businesses, to engage in trade, to enter professions, and to administer organizations. In earlier times, when landownership had been the only real basis of wealth, society had been divided between those with little or no land (people Europeans generally called peasants) and a landed gentry (which in Europe usually became an inherited aristocracy). Once commerce and industry became a source of wealth, these rigid distinctions broke down; many people could become prosperous without owning land, but by providing valuable services.

Middle-class life in the antebellum years rapidly established itself as the most influential cultural form of urban America. Solid, substantial middle-class houses lined city streets, larger in size and more elaborate in design than the cramped, functional rowhouses in working-class neighborhoods—but also far less lavish than the great houses of the very rich. Middle-class people tended to own their homes, often for the first time. Workers and artisans remained mostly renters.

Middle-class women usually remained in the household, although increasingly they were also able to hire servants—usually young, unmarried immigrant women. In an age when doing the family's laundry could take an entire day, one of the aspirations of middle-class women was to escape from some of the drudgery of housework.

New household inventions altered, and greatly improved, the character of life in *Invention of Cast-Iron Stove* middle-class homes. Perhaps the most important was the invention of the cast-iron stove, which began to replace fireplaces as the principal vehicle for cooking in the 1840s. These wood- or coal-burning devices were hot, clumsy, and dirty by later standards, but compared to the inconvenience and danger of cooking on an open hearth, they seemed a great luxury. Stoves gave cooks greater control over food preparation and allowed them to cook several things at once.

Middle-class diets were changing rapidly, and not just because of the wider range of cooking that the stove made possible. The expansion and diversification of American agriculture and the ability of distant farmers to ship goods to urban markets by rail greatly increased the variety of food available in cities. Fruits and vegetables were difficult to ship over long distances in an age with little refrigeration, but families had access to a greater variety of meats, grains, and dairy products than in the past. A few wealthy households acquired iceboxes, which allowed them to keep meat and dairy products fresh for several days. Most families, however, did not yet have any refrigeration. For them, preserving food meant curing meat with salt and preserving fruits in sugar. Diets were generally much heavier and starchier than they are today, and middle-class people tended to be considerably stouter than would be considered healthy or fashionable now.

Middle-class homes came to differentiate themselves from those of workers and artisans in other ways as well. The spare, simple styles of eighteenth-century homes gave way to the much more elaborate, even baroque household styles of the Victorian era—styles increasingly characterized by crowded, even cluttered rooms, dark colors, lush fabrics, and heavy furniture and draperies. Middle-class homes also became larger. It became less common for children to share beds and for all members of a family to sleep in the same room. Parlors and dining rooms separate from the kitchen—once a luxury—became the norm among the middle class. Some urban middle-class homes had indoor plumbing and indoor toilets by the 1850s—a significant advance over outdoor wells and privies.

THE CHANGING FAMILY

The new industrializing society produced profound changes in the nature of the family. Among them was the movement of families from farms to urban areas. Sons and daughters

FAMILY TIME, 1842 This illustration for *Godey's Lady's Book*, a magazine whose audience was better-off white women, offers an idealized image of family life. The father reads to his family from a devotional text; two servants off to the side listen attentively as well. What does this image communicate about the roles of the household members? (© Archive Photos/Getty Images)

in urban households were much more likely to leave the family in search of work than they had been in the rural world. This was largely because of the shift of income-earning work out of the home. In the early decades of the nineteenth century, the family itself had been the principal unit of economic activity. Now most income earners left home each day to work in a shop, mill, or factory. A sharp distinction began to emerge between the public world of the workplace and the private world of the family. The world of the family was now dominated not by production but by housekeeping, child rearing, and other primarily domestic concerns.

There was a significant decline in the birthrate, particularly in urban areas and in middle-class families. In 1800, the average American woman could be expected to give birth to approximately seven children. By 1860, the average woman bore five children.

The "Cult of Domesticity"

The growing separation between the workplace and the home sharpened distinctions between the social roles of men and women. Those distinctions affected not only factory workers and farmers but also members of the growing middle class.

With fewer legal and political rights than men, most women remained under the virtually absolute authority of their husbands. They were seldom encouraged to pursue education above the primary level. Women students were not accepted in any college or university until 1837. For a considerable time after that, only Oberlin in Ohio offered
Mount Holyoke for Women   education to both men and women, and Mount Holyoke in Massachusetts was founded by Mary Lyon as an academy for women.

However unequal the positions of men and women in the preindustrial era, those positions had generally been defined within the context of a household in which all members played important economic roles. In the middle-class family of the new industrial society, by contrast, the husband was assumed to be the principal, usually the only, income producer. The image of women changed from one of contributors to the family economy to one of guardians of the "domestic virtues." Middle-class women learned to place a higher value on keeping a clean, comfortable, and well-appointed home; on entertaining; and on dressing elegantly and stylishly.

Within their own separate sphere, middle-class women began to develop a distinctive
Women's Separate Sphere   female culture. A "lady's" literature began to emerge. Romantic novels written for female readers focused on the private sphere that middle-class women now inhabited, as did women's magazines that focused on fashions, shopping, homemaking, and other purely domestic concerns.

This **cult of domesticity,** as some scholars have called it, provided many women greater material comfort than they had enjoyed in the past and placed a higher value on their "female virtues." At the same time, it left women increasingly detached from the public world, with fewer outlets for their interests and energies. Except for teaching and nursing, work by women outside the household gradually came to be seen as a lower-class preserve.

Working-class women continued to work in factories and mills, but under conditions far worse than those that the original, more "respectable" women workers of Lowell and Waltham had experienced. Domestic service became another frequent source of female employment.

Leisure Activities

Leisure time was scarce for all but the wealthiest Americans. Most people worked long hours, and vacations were rare. For most people, Sunday was the only respite from work, and Sundays were generally reserved for religion and rest. For many working-class and middle-class people, therefore, holidays took on a special importance,   *Importance of Holidays* as suggested by the strikingly elaborate celebrations of the Fourth of July in the nineteenth century. The celebrations were not just expressions of patriotism, but a way of enjoying one of the few nonreligious holidays from work available to most Americans.

Compared to the relentless working schedules of city residents, the erratic pattern of farmwork provided occasional relief to people in rural America. For urban people, however, leisure was something to be seized in what few free moments   *Urban Leisure Activities* they had. Men gravitated to taverns for drinking, talking, and game-playing after work. Women gathered in one another's homes for conversation and card games. For educated people, reading became one of the principal leisure activities. Newspapers and magazines proliferated rapidly, and books became staples of affluent homes.

A vigorous culture of public leisure emerged, especially in larger cities. Theaters became increasingly popular and increasingly attracted audiences that crossed class lines. Much of the popular theater of the time consisted of melodrama based on novels or American myths. Also popular were Shakespeare's plays, reworked to appeal to American audiences. Tragedies were given happy endings; comedies were interlaced with regional humor; lines were rewritten with American dialect; and scenes were abbreviated or cut so that the play could be one of several in an evening's program. So familiar were many Shakespearean plots that audiences took delight in seeing them parodied in productions such as *Julius Sneezer* and *Hamlet and Egglet.*

Minstrel shows—in which white actors wearing blackface mimicked (and ridiculed) African American culture—became increasingly popular. Public sporting events—boxing, horse racing, cockfighting (already becoming controversial), and others—often attracted considerable audiences. Baseball—not yet organized into professional leagues—was beginning to attract large crowds when played in city parks or fields. A particularly exciting event in many communities was the arrival of the circus.

Popular tastes in public spectacle tended toward the bizarre and the fantastic. Relatively few people traveled; and in the absence of film, radio, television, or even much photography, Americans hungered for visions of unusual phenomena. People going to the theater or the circus or the museum wanted to see things that amazed and even frightened them. The most celebrated provider of such experiences was the famous and unscrupulous showman P. T. Barnum, who opened the American Museum in New York in 1842—not a showcase for art or nature, but as an exhibit of "human curiosities" that included people with dwarfism, Siamese twins, magicians, and ventriloquists. Barnum was a genius in publicizing his ventures with garish posters and elaborate newspaper announcements. Later, in the 1870s, he launched the famous circus for which he is still best remembered.

Lectures were one of the most popular forms of entertainment in nineteenth-century America. Men and women flocked in enormous numbers to lyceums, churches, schools, and auditoriums to hear lecturers explain the latest advances in science, describe their visits to exotic places, provide vivid historical narratives, or rail against the evils of alcohol or slavery. Messages of social uplift and reform attracted rapt audiences, particularly among women.

P. T. BARNUM AND TOM THUMB P. T. Barnum stands next to his star Charles Stratton, whose stage name was General Tom Thumb after the fairy-tale character. Stratton joined Barnum's touring company as a child, singing, dancing, and playing roles such as Cupid and Napoleon Bonaparte. The adult Stratton and Barnum became business partners. (© Bettmann/Corbis)

THE AGRICULTURAL NORTH

Even in the rapidly urbanizing and industrializing Northeast, and more so in what nine-teenth-century Americans called the Northwest, most people remained tied to the agricultural world. But agriculture, like industry and commerce, was becoming increasingly a part of the new capitalist economy.

NORTHEASTERN AGRICULTURE

The story of agriculture in the Northeast after 1840 is one of decline and transformation. Farmers of this section of the country could no longer compete with the new and richer soil of the Northwest. In 1840, the leading wheat-growing states were New York,

Pennsylvania, Ohio, and Virginia. In 1860, they were Illinois, Indiana, Wisconsin, Ohio, and Michigan. Illinois, Ohio, and Missouri also supplanted New York, Pennsylvania, and Virginia as growers of corn. In 1840, the most important cattle-raising areas in the country were New York, Pennsylvania, and New England. By the 1850s, the leading cattle states were Illinois, Indiana, Ohio, and Iowa in the Northwest and Texas in the Southwest.

Some eastern farmers responded to these changes by moving west themselves and establishing new farms. Still others moved to mill towns and became laborers. Some farmers, however, remained on the land and turned to what was known as "truck farming"—supplying food to the growing cities. They raised vegetables or fruit and sold their produce in *"Truck Farming"* nearby towns. Supplying milk, butter, and cheese to local urban markets also attracted many farmers in central New York, southeastern Pennsylvania, and various parts of New England.

THE OLD NORTHWEST

Life was different in the states of the Old Northwest (now known as the Midwest). In the two decades before the Civil War, this section of the country experienced *Rise of Chicago* steady industrial growth, particularly in and around Cleveland (on Lake Erie) and Cincinnati, the center of meatpacking in the Ohio Valley. Farther west, Chicago was emerging as the national center of the agricultural machinery and meatpacking industries. Most of the major industrial activities of the Old Northwest either served agriculture (as in the case of farm machinery) or relied on agricultural products (as in flour milling, meatpacking, whiskey distilling, and the making of leather goods).

Some areas of the Old Northwest were not yet dominated by whites. Indians remained the most numerous inhabitants of large portions of the upper third of the Great Lakes states until after the Civil War. In those areas, hunting and fishing, along with some sedentary agriculture, remained the principal economic activities.

For the settlers who populated the lands farther south, the Old Northwest was primarily an agricultural region. Its rich lands made farming highly lucrative. Thus the typical citizen of the Old Northwest was not the industrial worker or poor, marginal farmer, but the owner of a reasonably prosperous family farm.

Industrialization, in both the United States and Europe, provided the greatest boost to agriculture. With the growth of factories and cities in the Northeast, the domestic market for farm goods increased dramatically. The growing national and worldwide demand for farm products resulted in steadily rising farm prices. For most farmers, the 1840s and early 1850s were years of increasing prosperity.

The expansion of agricultural markets also had profound effects on sectional alignments in the United States. The Old Northwest sold most of its products to the Northeast and became an important market for the products of eastern *Economic Ties between Northeast and Midwest* industry. A strong economic relationship was emerging between the two sections that was profitable to both—and that was increasing the isolation of the South within the Union.

By 1850, the growing western white population was moving into the prairie regions on both sides of the Mississippi. These farmers cleared forest lands or made use of fields the Indians had cleared many years earlier. And they developed a timber industry to make use of the remaining forests. Although wheat was the staple crop of the region, other crops—corn, potatoes, and oats—and livestock were also important.

The Old Northwest also increased production by adopting new agricultural techniques. Farmers began to cultivate new varieties of seed, notably Mediterranean wheat, which was hardier than the native type; and they imported better breeds of animals, such as hogs

CYRUS MCCORMICK'S AUTOMATIC REAPER   (© Hulton Archive/Getty Images)

and sheep from England and Spain. Most important were improved tools and farm machines. The cast-iron plow remained popular because of its replaceable parts. In 1847, John Deere established at Moline, Illinois, a factory to manufacture steel plows, which were more durable than those made of iron.

Two new machines heralded a coming revolution in grain production. The automatic *McCormick Reaper*   reaper, the invention of Cyrus H. McCormick of Virginia, took the place of sickle, cradle, and hand labor. Pulled by a team of horses, it had a row of horizontal knives on one side for cutting wheat; the wheels drove a paddle that bent the stalks over the knives, which then fell onto a moving belt and into the back of the vehicle. The reaper enabled a crew of six or seven men to harvest in a day as much wheat as fifteen men could harvest using the older methods. McCormick, who had patented his device in 1834, established a factory at Chicago in 1847. By 1860, more than 100,000 reapers were in use. Almost as important to the grain grower was the thresher—a machine that separated the grain from the wheat stalks—which appeared in large numbers after 1840. (Before that, farmers generally flailed grain by hand or used farm animals to tread it.) The Jerome I. Case factory in Racine, Wisconsin, manufactured most of the threshers. (Modern "harvesters" later combined the functions of the reaper and the thresher.)

The Old Northwest was the most self-consciously democratic section of the country. But its democracy was of a relatively conservative type—capitalistic, property-conscious, middle-class. Abraham Lincoln, an Illinois Whig, voiced the optimistic economic opinions of many of the people of his section. "I take it that it is best for all to leave each man free to acquire property as fast as he can," said Lincoln. "When one starts poor, as most do in the race of life, free society is such that he knows he can better his condition; he knows that there is no fixed condition of labor for his whole life."

RURAL LIFE

Life for farming people varied greatly from one region to another. In the more densely populated areas east of the Appalachians and in the easternmost areas of the Old Northwest, farmers made extensive use of the institutions of communities—churches, schools, stores, and taverns. As white settlement moved farther west, farmers became more isolated and had to struggle to find any occasions for contact with people outside their own families.

Religion drew farm communities together more than any other force in remote communities. Town or village churches were popular meeting places, both for services and for social events—most of them dominated by women. Even in areas with no organized churches, farm families—and women in particular—gathered in one another's homes for prayer meetings, Bible readings, and other religious activities. Weddings, baptisms, and funerals also brought communities together.

Rural Gatherings

But religion was only one of many reasons for interaction. Farm people joined together frequently to share tasks such as barn raising. Large numbers of families gathered at harvesttime to help bring in crops, husk corn, or thresh wheat. Women came together to share domestic tasks, holding "bees" in which groups of women made quilts, baked goods, preserves, and other products.

Despite the many social gatherings farm families managed to create, they had much less contact with popular culture and public life than people who lived in towns and cities. Most rural people treasured their links to the outside world—letters from relatives and friends in distant places, newspapers and magazines from cities they had never seen, catalogs advertising merchandise that their local stores never had. Yet many also valued the relative autonomy that a farm life gave them. One reason many rural Americans looked back nostalgically on country life once they moved to the city was that they sensed that in the urban world they had lost some control over the patterns of their daily lives.

CONCLUSION

Between the 1820s and the 1850s, the American economy experienced the beginnings of an industrial revolution—a change that transformed almost every area of life in fundamental ways.

The American Industrial Revolution was a result of many things: population growth, advances in transportation and communication, new technologies that spurred the development of factories and mass production, the recruiting of a large industrial labor force, and the creation of corporate bodies capable of managing large enterprises. The new economy expanded the ranks of the wealthy, helped create a large new middle class, and introduced high levels of inequality.

Culture in the industrializing areas of the North changed, too, as did the structure and behavior of the family, the role of women, and the way people used their leisure time and encountered popular culture. The changes helped widen the gap in experience and understanding between the generation of the Revolution and the generation of the mid-nineteenth century. They also helped widen the gap between North and South.

KEY TERMS/PEOPLE/PLACES/EVENTS

antebellum 226

artisan 239

Baltimore and Ohio
  Railroad 231

Commonwealth v. Hunt 240

cult of domesticity 244

Erie Canal 230

Factory Girls
  Association 237

factory system 235

Know-Nothings 228

Lowell system 236

McCormick reaper 248

Morse code 233

nativism 228

Sarah Bagley 237

Western Union Telegraph
  Company 234

RECALL AND REFLECT

1. What were the political responses to immigration in mid-nineteenth-century America? Do you see any parallels to responses to immigration today?
2. Why did the rail system supplant the canal system as the nation's major transportation network?
3. How did the industrial workforce change between the 1820s and the 1840s? What were the effects on American society of changes in the workforce?
4. How did America's Industrial Revolution and the factory system change family life and women's social and economic roles?
5. How did agriculture in the North change as a result of growing industrialization and urbanization?

11 COTTON, SLAVERY, AND THE OLD SOUTH

THE COTTON ECONOMY

SOUTHERN WHITE SOCIETY

SLAVERY: THE "PECULIAR INSTITUTION"

THE CULTURE OF SLAVERY

LOOKING AHEAD

1. How did slavery shape the southern economy and society, and how did it make the South different from the North?

2. What was the myth and what was the reality of white society in the South? Why was the myth so pervasive and widely believed?

3. How did slaves resist their enslavement? How successful were their efforts? What was the response of whites?

THE SOUTH, LIKE THE NORTH, experienced significant growth in the middle years of the nineteenth century. Southerners fanned out into the Southwest. The southern agricultural economy grew increasingly productive and prosperous. Trade in such staples as sugar, rice, tobacco, and above all cotton made the South a major force in international commerce. It also tied the South securely to the emerging capitalist world of the United States and its European trading partners.

Yet despite all these changes, the South experienced a much less fundamental transformation in these years than did the North. It had begun the nineteenth century as a primarily agricultural region; it remained overwhelmingly so in 1860. It had begun the century with few important cities and little industry; and so it remained sixty years later. In 1800, a plantation system dependent on slave labor had dominated the southern economy; by 1860, that system had only strengthened its grip on the region. As one historian has written, "The South grew, but it did not develop."

The most important economic development in the mid-nineteenth-century South was the shift of economic power from the "upper South," the original southern states along the Atlantic Coast, to the "lower South," the expanding agricultural regions in the new states of the Southwest. That shift reflected above all the growing dominance of cotton in the southern economy.

THE RISE OF KING COTTON

Much of the upper South continued to rely on the cultivation of tobacco. But the market for that crop was notoriously unstable, and tobacco rapidly exhausted the land on which it grew. By the 1830s, therefore, many farmers in the old tobacco-growing regions of Virginia, Maryland, and North Carolina were shifting to other crops, while the center of tobacco cultivation was moving westward, into the Piedmont area.

The southern regions of the coastal South—South Carolina, Georgia, and parts of Florida—continued to rely on the cultivation of rice, a more stable and lucrative crop. But rice demanded substantial irrigation and needed an exceptionally long growing season (nine months), so its cultivation remained restricted to a relatively small area. Sugar growers along the Gulf Coast similarly enjoyed a reasonably profitable market for their crop. But sugar cultivation required intensive (and debilitating) labor and a long growing time; only relatively wealthy planters could afford to grow it. In addition, producers faced major competition from the great sugar plantations of the Caribbean. Sugar cultivation, therefore, did not spread much beyond a small area in southern Louisiana and eastern Texas. Long-staple (Sea Island) cotton was another lucrative crop, but like rice and sugar, it could grow only in a limited area— the coastal regions of the Southeast.

The decline of the tobacco economy and the limits of the sugar, rice, and long-staple

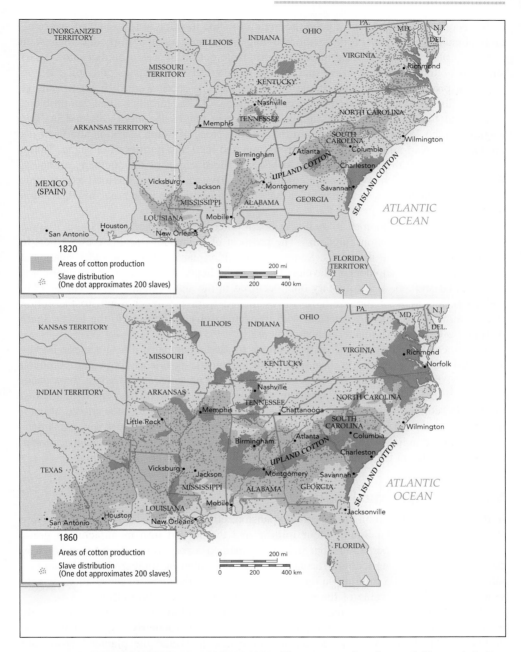

SLAVERY AND COTTON IN THE SOUTH, 1820 AND 1860   These two maps show the remarkable spread of cotton cultivation in the South in the decades before the Civil War. Both maps show the areas of cotton cultivation (the green-colored areas) as well as areas with large slave populations (the brown-dotted areas). Note how in the top map, which represents 1820, cotton production is concentrated largely in the East, with a few areas scattered among Alabama, Mississippi, Louisiana, and Tennessee. Slavery is concentrated along the Georgia and South Carolina coast, areas in which long-staple cotton was grown, with only a few other areas of highly dense slave populations. By 1860, the South had changed dramatically. Cotton production had spread throughout the lower South, from Texas to northern Florida, and slavery had moved with it. Slavery was much denser in the tobacco-growing regions of Virginia and North Carolina, which had also grown.   • *How did this economic shift affect the white South's commitment to slavery?*

cotton economies might have forced the region to shift its attention to other, nonagricul-
tural pursuits had it not been for the growing importance of a new product that soon
Short-Staple Cotton   overshadowed all else: short-staple cotton. It was a hardier and coarser
strain of cotton that could grow successfully in a variety of climates and soils. It was
harder to process than the long-staple cotton because its seeds were difficult to remove
from the fiber. But the invention of the cotton gin in 1793 had largely solved that problem.

Demand for cotton increased rapidly in Britain in the 1820s and 1830s and in New
England in the 1840s and 1850s. From the western areas of South Carolina and Georgia,
production moved into Alabama and Mississippi and then into northern Louisiana, Texas,
and Arkansas. By the 1850s, cotton had become the linchpin of the southern economy.
By the time of the Civil War, cotton constituted nearly two-thirds of the total export trade
of the United States. It was little wonder that southern politicians now proclaimed, "Cotton
is king!"

Cotton production boomed in the lower South (later known as the "Deep South"). Some
began to call it the "cotton kingdom." The prospect of tremendous profits drew settlers to
the lower South by the thousands. Some were wealthy planters from the older states, but
most were small slaveholders or slaveless farmers who hoped to move into the planter class.

A similar shift, if an involuntary one, occurred in the slave population. Between 1840
and 1860, hundreds of thousands of slaves moved from the upper South to the cotton
states—either accompanying masters who were themselves migrating to the lower South
or (more often) sold to planters already there.

This "second middle passage," as the historian Ira Berlin has called it (using a term usually
associated with the transatlantic slave trade), was a traumatic experience for perhaps a million
dislocated African Americans. Slave families were broken up and scattered across the expand-
"Second Middle Passage"   ing cotton kingdom. Marched over hundreds of rugged miles, tied
together in "coffles" (as on the earlier slave ships coming from Africa), they arrived in unfamiliar and usually forbidding territory, where they were made to construct new plantations
and work in cotton fields. The sale of slaves to the lower South became an important economic
activity for whites in the upper South, where agricultural production was declining.

Southern Trade and Industry

In the face of this booming agricultural expansion, other forms of economic activity were
slow to develop in the South. Flour milling and textile and iron manufacturing grew,
particularly in the upper South, but industry remained a relatively insignificant force in
comparison with the agricultural economy. The total value of southern textile manufactures in 1860 was $4.5 million—a threefold increase over the value of those goods twenty
years before. But the value of the exports was approximately $200 million.

The limited nonfarm commercial sector that did develop in the South was largely
intended to serve the needs of the plantation economy. Particularly important were the
brokers, or "factors," who, in the absence of banks, marketed the planters' crops and
provided them with credit. Other obstacles to economic development included the South's
inadequate transportation system. Canals were almost nonexistent; most roads were crude
and unsuitable for heavy transport; and railroads, although they expanded substantially in
the 1840s and 1850s, failed to tie the region together effectively. Despite the lack of
canals, the principal means of transportation was still water. Planters generally shipped
their crops to market along rivers or by sea; most manufacturing was in or near port towns.

The South, therefore, was becoming more and more dependent on the industrial manufacturers, merchants, and professionals of the North. Concerned by this trend, some

southerners began to advocate economic independence for the region, among them James D. B. De Bow of New Orleans, whose magazine, *De Bow's Commercial Review,* called for southern commercial expansion and economic independence from the North. Yet even *De Bow's Commercial Review* was filled with advertisements from northern manufacturing firms; and its circulation was far smaller in the South than such northern magazines as *Harper's Weekly*.

SOURCES OF SOUTHERN DIFFERENCE

An important question about antebellum southern history concerns why the region did so little to develop a larger industrial and commercial economy of its own. Why did it remain so different from the North?

Part of the reason was the great profitability of the region's agricultural system. In the Northeast, many people had turned to manufacturing as the agricultural economy of the region declined. In the South, the agricultural economy was booming, and ambitious capitalists had little incentive to look elsewhere. Another reason was that wealthy southerners had so much capital invested in land and slaves that they had little left for other investments. Some historians have also suggested that the southern climate—with its long, hot, steamy summers—was less suitable for industrial development than the climate of the North.

THE NEW ORLEANS COTTON EXCHANGE Edgar Degas, the renowned French painter, painted this scene of cotton traders examining samples in the New Orleans cotton exchange in 1873. By this time the cotton trade was producing less impressive profits than those that had made it the driving force of the booming southern economy of the 1850s. Degas's mother came from a Creole family of cotton brokers in New Orleans, and two of the artist's brothers (depicted here reading a newspaper and leaning against a window) joined the business in America. (© Musee des Beaux-Arts, Pau, France/Bridgeman Images)

But this southern failure was also due in part to a set of values distinctive to the South. Many white southerners liked to think of themselves as representatives of a special way of life. They argued that grace and refinement were more important than rapid growth and development. But appealing as this image was to southern whites, it conformed to the reality of southern society in very limited ways.

SOUTHERN WHITE SOCIETY

Only a very small minority of southern whites owned slaves. In 1860, when the white population was just above 8 million, the number of slaveholders was only 383,637. Even with all members of slaveowning families included in the figures, those living in slaveowning households still amounted to perhaps no more than one-quarter of the white population. And only a small proportion of this relatively small number of slaveowners owned slaves in substantial numbers. Yet as the cotton economy surged in the late 1850s, white supporters championed its value to southern society and argued for a ruling planter class and working slave class. (See "Consider the Source: Senator James Henry Hammond Declares, 'Cotton Is King.'")

A GEORGIA PLANTATION This map of the Hopeton Plantation in South Carolina shows both how much plantations were connected to the national and world markets and how much they tried to be self-sufficient. Note the large areas of land devoted to the growing of cotton, rice, and sugarcane, all crops for the market. • *Why would a plantation in this part of the South be so much more diversified in the market crops it raised than the cotton plantations in the Mississippi Delta?* Note also the many crops grown for the local market or for consumption by residents of the plantation—potatoes, peas, corn, and others. The top left of the map shows the distribution of living quarters, with slaves' quarters grouped together very near the owner's residence. • *Why would planters want their slaves living nearby? Why might slaves be unhappy about being so close to their owners?*

THE PLANTER CLASS

How, then, did the South come to be seen as a society dominated by wealthy slaveowning planters? In large part, it was because the planter aristocracy exercised power and influence far in excess of its numbers.

White southerners liked to compare their planter class to the old aristocracies of England and Europe, but the comparison was not a sound one. In some areas of the upper South, the great aristocrats were indeed people whose families had occupied positions of wealth and power for generations. In most of the South, however, many of the great landowners were still first-generation settlers as late as the 1850s, who had only relatively recently started to live in the comfort and luxury for which they became famous. Large areas of the South had been settled and cultivated for less than two decades at the time of the Civil War.

Nor was the world of the planter nearly as leisured and genteel as the aristocratic myth would suggest. Growing staple crops was a tough business. Planters were just as much competitive capitalists as the industrialists of the North. Even many affluent planters lived rather modestly, their wealth so heavily invested in land and slaves that there was often little left for personal comfort. And white planters, including some substantial ones, tended to move frequently as new and presumably more productive areas opened up to cultivation.

Wealthy southern whites sustained their image as aristocrats in many ways. They adopted an elaborate code of "chivalry," which obligated white men to defend their "honor," often through dueling. They tended to avoid such "coarse" occupations as trade and commerce; those who did not become planters often gravitated toward the military. The aristocratic ideal also found reflection in the definition of a special   *The Aristocratic Ideal* role for southern white women.

THE "SOUTHERN LADY"

In some respects, affluent white women in the South occupied roles very similar to those of middle-class white women in the North. Their lives generally centered in the home, where (according to the South's social ideal) they served as companions to and hostesses for their husbands and as nurturing mothers for their children. "Genteel" southern white women seldom engaged in public activities or found income-producing employment.

But the life of the "southern lady" was also very different from that of her northern counterpart. For one thing, the **cult of honor** dictated that southern white men give particular importance to the defense of women. In practice, this generally meant that white men were even more dominant and white women even   *Regional Differences in Women's Lives* more subordinate in southern culture than they were in the North. Social theorist George Fitzhugh wrote in the 1850s: "Women, like children, have but one right, and that is the right to protection. The right to protection involves the obligation to obey."

More important in determining the role of southern white women, however, was that the vast majority of them lived on farms, with little access to the "public world" and thus few opportunities to look beyond their roles as wives and mothers. For many white women, living on farms of modest size meant a fuller engagement in the economic life of the family than was typical for middle-class women in the North. These women engaged in spinning, weaving, and other production; they participated in agricultural tasks; they helped supervise the slave workforce. On the larger plantations, however, even these limited roles were often considered unsuitable for white women, and the "plantation mistress" became, in some cases, more an ornament for her husband than an active part

SENATOR JAMES HENRY HAMMOND DECLARES, "COTTON IS KING," 1858

James Henry Hammond, a U.S. senator from South Carolina, was a leading advocate for the overwhelming significance of cotton to the economy of the South and the nation. He famously made his point in 1858 in his "Cotton Is King" speech.

If we never acquire another foot of territory for the South, look at her. Eight hundred and fifty thousand square miles. As large as Great Britain, France, Austria, Prussia, and Spain. Is not that territory enough to make an empire that shall rule the world? . . . With the finest soil, the most delightful climate, whose staple productions none of those great countries can grow, we have three thousand miles of continental shore line, so indented with bays and crowded with islands, that, when their shore lines are added, we have twelve thousand miles. Through the heart of our country runs the great Mississippi, the father of waters, into whose bosom are poured thirty-six thousand miles of tributary streams; and beyond we have the desert prairie wastes, to protect us in our rear. Can you hem in such a territory as that? . . .

[. . .] Upon our muster-rolls we have a million of militia. In a defensive war, upon an emergency, every one of them would be available. At any time, the South can raise, equip, and maintain in the field, a larger army than any Power of the earth can send against her, and an army of soldiers—men brought up on horseback, with guns in their hands.

[. . .] It appears, by going to the reports of the Secretary of the Treasury, which are authentic, that last year the United States exported in round numbers $279,000,000 worth of domestic produce, excluding gold and foreign merchandise re-exported. Of this amount $158,000,000 worth is the clear produce of the South; . . .

[. . .] [W]e have nothing to do but to take off restrictions on foreign merchandise and open our ports, and the whole world will come to us to trade. They will be too glad to bring and carry for us, and we never shall dream of a war. Why the South has never yet had a just cause of war. Every time she has drawn her sword it has been on the point of honor, and that point of honor has been mainly loyalty to her sister colonies and sister States, who have ever since plundered and calumniated her.

But if there were no other reason why we should never have war, would any sane nation make war on cotton? Without firing a gun, without drawing a sword, should they make war on us we can bring the whole world to our feet. The South is perfectly competent to go on, one, two, or three years without planting a seed of cotton. I believe that if she was to plant but half her cotton for three years to come, it would be an immense advantage to her. I am not so sure but that after three total years' abstinence she would come out stronger than ever she was before and better prepared to enter afresh upon her great career of enterprise. . . . England would topple headlong and carry the whole civilized world with her, save the South. No, you dare not make war on cotton. No power on earth dares to make war upon it. Cotton *is* king.

In all social systems there must be a class to do the menial duties, to perform the drudgery of life. That is, a class requiring but a low order of intellect and but little skill. Its requisites are vigor, docility, fidelity. . . . Fortunately for the South, she found a race adapted to that purpose to her hand—a race inferior to her own, but eminently qualified in temper, in vigor, in docility, in capacity to stand the climate, to answer all her purposes. We use them for our purpose, and call them slaves. We found them slaves by the "common consent of mankind," which, according to Cicero, *"lex naturae est"*; the highest proof of what is Nature's law. We are old-fashioned at the South yet; it is a word discarded now by "ears polite." I will not characterize that class at the North by that term; but you have it; it is there; it is everywhere; it is eternal.

UNDERSTAND, ANALYZE, & EVALUATE

1. How did Hammond describe the South in comparison to the North? Compare this assessment with the experience of the South in the Civil War. How did Hammond view the South in a global context? What do you think of this assessment?
2. What justifications did Hammond offer for slavery? Describe the comparison Hammond drew between northern wage labor and southern slavery?

Source: James Henry Hammond, Speech on the Kansas-Lecompton Constitution, U.S. Senate, March 4, 1858, in *Congressional Globe*, 35th Cong., 1st Sess., Appendix, pp. 70–71; in Regina Lee Blaszczyk and Philip B. Scranton (eds.), *Major Problems in American Business History* (Boston: Houghton Mifflin Company, 2006), pp. 149–154.

of the economy or the society. Southern white women also had less access to education than their northern counterparts. The few female "academies" in the South trained women primarily to be suitable wives.

Southern white women had other special burdens as well. The southern white birthrate remained nearly 20 percent higher than that of the nation as a whole, but *Special Burdens* infant mortality in the region remained higher than elsewhere. The slave labor system also had a mixed impact on white women. It helped spare many of them from certain kinds of arduous labor, but it also damaged their relationships with their husbands. Male slaveowners had frequent forced sexual relationships with the female slaves on their plantations; the children of those unions served as a constant reminder to white women of their husbands' infidelities. Black women (and men) were obviously the most important victims of such practices, but white women suffered, too.

THE PLAIN FOLK

The typical white southerner was a yeoman farmer. Some of these "plain folk," as they became known, owned a few slaves, with whom they worked and lived more closely than did the larger planters. Some plain folk, most of whom owned their own land, devoted themselves largely to subsistence farming; others grew cotton or other crops for the market but usually could not produce enough to allow them to expand their operations or even get out of debt.

One reason was the southern educational system. For the sons of wealthy planters, the region provided ample opportunities to gain an education. In 1860, there were 260 southern colleges and universities, public and private, with 25,000 students enrolled in them. But as in the rest of the United States, universities were only within the reach of the upper class. The elementary and secondary schools of the South were not only fewer than but also inferior to those of the Northeast. The South had more than 500,000 illiterate whites, over half the nation's total. The subordination of the plain folk to the planter class raises an important question: Why did lower-class whites not oppose the aristocratic social system from which they benefited so little?

Some nonslaveowning whites did oppose the planter elite, but for the most part in limited *"Hill People"* ways and in isolated areas. These were mainly the "hill people," who lived in the Appalachian ranges east of the Mississippi, in the Ozarks to the west of the river, and in other "hill country" or "backcountry" areas. They practiced a simple form of subsistence agriculture, owned practically no slaves, and were, in most respects, unconnected to the cotton economy. Such whites frequently expressed animosity toward the planter aristocracy. Unsurprisingly, the mountain regions were the only parts of the South to resist the movement toward secession in the early 1860s. Even during the Civil War itself, many refused to support the Confederacy.

Far greater in number, however, were the nonslaveowning whites who lived in the midst of the plantation system. Many, perhaps most of them, accepted that system because they were tied to it in important ways. Small farmers depended on the local plantation aristocracy for access to cotton gins, markets for their modest crops and their livestock, and credit or other financial assistance in time of need. In many areas, moreover, the poorest resident of a county might easily be a cousin of the richest aristocrat. In the 1850s, the cotton boom allowed many small farmers to improve their economic fortunes. Some bought more land, became slaveowners, and moved into at least the fringes of plantation society. Others simply felt more secure in their positions as independent yeomen and hence were more likely to embrace the fierce regional loyalty that was spreading throughout the white South in these years.

There were other white southerners, however, who were known at the time variously as "crackers," "sand hillers," or "poor white trash." Occupying the infertile lands of the pine barrens, the red hills, and the swamps, they lived in genuine squalor. Many owned no land *Poorest Whites* and supported themselves by foraging or hunting. Others worked at times as common laborers for their neighbors. Their degradation resulted partly from dietary deficiencies and disease. Forced to resort at times to eating clay (hence the tendency of more-affluent whites to refer to them disparagingly as "clay eaters"), they suffered from pellagra, hookworm, and malaria. Planters and small farmers alike held them in contempt.

Even among these southerners—the true outcasts of white society—there was no real opposition to the plantation system or slavery. In part, this was because they were so benumbed by *Shared Sense of Racial Supremacy* poverty that they had little strength to protest. But the single greatest unifying factor among the southern white population was their perception of race. However poor and miserable white southerners might be, they could still look down on the black population of the region and feel a bond with their fellow whites and a sense of racial supremacy.

SLAVERY: THE "PECULIAR INSTITUTION"

White southerners often referred to slavery as the "peculiar institution," meaning that it was distinctive, special. And indeed it was. The South in the mid-nineteenth century was the only area in the Western world—except for Brazil, Cuba, and Puerto Rico—where slavery still existed. Slavery, more than any other single factor, isolated the South from the rest of American society and much of the world.

Within the South itself, slavery produced paradoxical results. On one hand, it isolated blacks from whites. As a result, African Americans under slavery began to develop a society and culture of their own. On the other hand, slavery created a unique bond between blacks and whites—slaves and masters—in the South. The two groups may have maintained separate spheres, but each sphere was deeply influenced by the other. In both cases, slavery profoundly affected all aspects of southern and even American society. (See "Debating the Past: The Character of Slavery.")

VARIETIES OF SLAVERY

Southern **slave codes** forbade slaves to hold property, to leave their masters' premises without permission, to be out after dark, to congregate with other slaves except   *Slave Codes* at church, to carry firearms, to testify in court against white people, or to strike a white person even in self-defense. The codes prohibited whites from teaching slaves to read or write. The laws contained no provisions to legalize slave marriages or divorces. If an owner killed a slave while punishing him, the act was generally not considered a crime. Slaves, however, faced the death penalty for killing or even resisting a white person and for inciting revolt. The codes also contained extraordinarily rigid provisions for defining a person's race. Anyone with a trace (or, often, even a rumor) of African ancestry was defined as black.

Enforcement of the codes, however, was spotty and uneven. Some slaves did acquire property, did become literate, and did assemble with other slaves. White owners themselves handled most transgressions by their slaves and inflicted widely varying punishments. In other words, despite the rigid provisions of law, there was in reality considerable difference within the slave system. Some slaves lived in almost prisonlike conditions, rigidly and harshly controlled by their masters. Many (probably most) others experienced considerable flexibility and autonomy.

The nature of the relationship between masters and slaves depended in part on the size of the plantation. White farmers with few slaves generally   *Plantation Size and Slave Experience* supervised their workers directly and often worked closely alongside them. The paternal relationship between such masters and their slaves could be warm and benevolent, or tyrannical and cruel. In general, African Americans themselves preferred to live on larger plantations, where they had a chance for a social world of their own.

Although the majority of slaveowners were small farmers, the majority of slaves lived on plantations of medium or large size, with substantial slave workforces. Thus the relationship between master and slave was much less intimate for the typical slave than for the typical slaveowner. Substantial planters often hired overseers and even assistant overseers to represent them. "Head drivers," trusted and responsible slaves often assisted by several subdrivers, acted under the overseer as foremen.

LIFE UNDER SLAVERY

Most, but not all, slaves received an adequate if rude diet, consisting mainly of cornmeal, salt pork, molasses, and, on rare occasions, fresh meat or poultry. Many slaves cultivated gardens for their own use. Their masters provided them with cheap clothing and shoes. They lived in rough cabins, called slave quarters. The plantation mistress or a doctor retained by the owner provided some medical care, but slave women themselves—as "healers," midwives, or simply as mothers—often were the more important source of medical attention.

Slaves worked hard, beginning with light tasks as children. Their workdays were longest at harvesttime. Slave women worked particularly hard. They   *Work Conditions* generally labored in the fields with the men, and they also handled cooking, cleaning, and child rearing. Many slave families were divided. Husbands and fathers often lived on neighboring plantations; at times, one spouse (usually the male) would be sold to a plantation owner far away. As a result, black women often found themselves acting in effect as single parents.

Slaves were, as a group, much less healthy than southern whites. After 1808, when the importation of slaves became illegal, the proportion of blacks to whites in the nation as a whole steadily declined as a result of the comparatively high black death rate.

THE CHARACTER OF SLAVERY

No issue in American history has produced a more spirited debate than the nature of plantation slavery. The debate began well before the Civil War, when **abolitionists** strove to expose slavery to the world as a brutal, dehumanizing institution, while southern defenders of slavery tried to depict it as a benevolent and paternalistic system. But by the late nineteenth century, with white Americans eager for sectional conciliation, most northern and southern chroniclers of slavery began to accept a romanticized and unthreatening picture of the Old South and its peculiar institution.

The first major scholarly examination of slavery was Ulrich B. Phillips's *American Negro Slavery* (1918), which portrayed slavery as an essentially benign institution in which kindly masters looked after submissive and generally contented African Americans. Phillips's apologia for slavery remained the authoritative work on the subject for nearly thirty years.

In the 1940s, challenges to Phillips began to emerge. Melville J. Herskovits disputed Phillips's contention that black Americans retained little of their African cultural inheritance. Herbert Aptheker published a chronicle of slave revolts as a way of refuting Phillips's claim that blacks were submissive and content.

A somewhat different challenge to Phillips emerged in the 1950s from historians who emphasized the brutality of the institution. Kenneth Stampp's *The Peculiar Institution* (1956) and Stanley Elkins's *Slavery* (1959) described a labor system that did serious physical and psychological damage to its victims. They portrayed slavery as something like a prison, in which men and women

had virtually no space to develop their own social and cultural lives. Elkins compared the system to Nazi concentration camps and likened the childlike "Sambo" personality of slavery to tragic distortions of character produced by the Holocaust.

In the early 1970s, an explosion of new scholarship on slavery shifted the emphasis away from the damage the system inflicted on African Americans and toward the striking success of the slaves themselves in building a culture of their own. John Blassingame in 1973 argued that "the most remarkable aspect of the whole process of enslavement is the extent to which the American-born slaves were able to retain their ancestors' culture." Herbert Gutman, in *The Black Family in Slavery and Freedom* (1976), challenged the prevailing belief that slavery had weakened and even destroyed the African American family. On the contrary, Gutman argued, the black family survived slavery with impressive strength, although with some significant differences from the prevailing form of the white family. Eugene Genovese's *Roll, Jordan, Roll* (1974) revealed how African Americans manipulated white paternalist assumptions to build a large cultural space of their own where they could develop their own family life, social traditions, and religious patterns. That same year, Robert Fogel and Stanley Engerman published the controversial *Time on the Cross,* a highly quantitative study that supported some of the claims of Gutman and Genovese about black achievement but that went much further in portraying slavery as a successful and reasonably humane (if ultimately immoral) system. Slave workers, they argued, were better treated and lived in greater

NURSING THE MASTER'S CHILD This 1855 photograph of a slave woman and master's child is documentary evidence of the complex relationships that historians of slavery have studied. (The Library of Congress)

comfort than most northern industrial workers of the same era. Their conclusions produced a storm of criticism.

Other important scholarship includes African American slave women. Elizabeth Fox-Genovese's *Within the Plantation Household* (1988) examined the lives of both white and black women on the plantation. She portrayed slave women as defined by their dual roles as members of the plantation workforce and anchors of the black family. Slave women, she argued, professed loyalty to their mistresses when forced to serve them as domestics; but their real loyalty remained to their own communities and families.

More recent studies by Walter Johnson and Ira Berlin mark an at least partial return to the "damage" approach to slavery of the 1970s. Johnson's *Soul by Soul* (2000) examines the South's largest slave market, New Orleans. For whites, he argues, purchasing slaves was a way of fulfilling the middle-class male fantasy of success and independence. For the slaves themselves, the trade was dehumanizing and destructive to black families and communities. Berlin's *Many Thousands Gone* (2000) and *Generation of Captivity* (2003)—among the most important studies of slavery in a generation—similarly emphasize the dehumanizing character of the slave market and show that, whatever white slaveowners might say, slavery was less a social system than a commodification of human beings. •

UNDERSTAND, ANALYZE, & EVALUATE

1. Why might the conclusions drawn by Robert Fogel and Stanley Engerman in *Time on the Cross* have provoked vehement criticism?

2. What might be some reasons for the resurrection of focus on the "damage" thesis of slavery, as in the works by Walter Johnson and Ira Berlin?

CLEAR STARCHING IN LOUISIANA This 1837 etching by French artist Auguste Hervieu depicts a plantation mistress verbally abusing a slave woman and child. Hervieu traveled to America with British writer and abolitionist Frances Trollope. This illustration is from Trollope's 1836 novel *The Life and Adventures of Jonathan Jefferson Whitlaw: Or, Scenes on the Mississippi,* a work that exposed the degrading effects of slavery on both slaves and slaveowners. (*The Life and Adventures of Jonathan Jefferson Whitlaw,* by Frances Trollope, 1836)

Slave mothers had large families, but the enforced poverty in which virtually all African Americans lived ensured that fewer of their children would survive to adulthood than the *High Mortality Rates* children of white parents. Even those who did survive typically died at a younger age than the average white person.

Household servants had a somewhat easier life—physically at least—than did field hands. On a small plantation, the same slaves might do both field work and housework. But on a large estate, there would generally be a separate domestic staff: nursemaids, housemaids, cooks, butlers, coachmen. These people lived close to the master and his family, eating the leftovers from the family table. Between the blacks and whites of such households, affectionate, almost familial relationships might develop. More often, however, house servants resented their isolation from their fellow slaves and the lack of privacy and increased discipline that came with living in such close proximity to the master's family. When emancipation came after the Civil War, it was often the house servants who were the first to leave the plantations of their former owners.

Female household servants were especially vulnerable to sexual abuse by their masters and *Sexual Abuse* white overseers. In addition to being subjected to unwanted sexual attention from white men, female slaves often received vindictive treatment from white women. Plantation mistresses naturally resented the sexual liaisons between their husbands and female slaves. Punishing their husbands was not usually possible, so they often punished the slaves instead—with arbitrary beatings, increased workloads, and various forms of psychological torment.

SLAVERY IN THE CITIES

The conditions of urban slavery differed significantly from those in the countryside. On the relatively isolated plantations, slaves had little contact with free blacks and lower-class whites, and masters maintained a fairly direct and effective control. In the city, however, a master often could not supervise his slaves closely and at the same time use them profitably. Even if they slept at night in carefully watched backyard barracks, they moved about during the day alone, performing errands of various kinds.

There was a considerable market in the South for common laborers, particularly since, unlike in the North, there were few European immigrants to perform menial chores. As a result, masters often hired out slaves for such tasks. Slaves on contract worked in mining and lumbering (often far from cities), but others worked on the docks and on construction sites, drove wagons, and performed other unskilled jobs in cities and towns. Slave women and children worked in the region's few textile mills. Particularly skilled workers such as blacksmiths or carpenters were also often hired out. After regular working hours, many of them fended for themselves; thus urban slaves gained numerous opportunities to mingle with free blacks and with whites. In the cities, the line between slavery and freedom was less distinct than on the plantation.

Free African Americans

Over 250,000 free African Americans lived in the slaveholding states by the start of the Civil War, more than half of them in Virginia and Maryland. In some cases, they were slaves who had somehow earned money to buy their own and their families' freedom. It was most often urban blacks, with their greater freedom of movement and activity, who could take that route. One example was Elizabeth Keckley, a slave woman *Elizabeth Keckley* who bought freedom for herself and her son with proceeds from sewing. She later became a seamstress, personal servant, and companion to Mary Todd Lincoln in the White House. But few masters had any incentive, or inclination, to give up their slaves, so this route was open to relatively few people.

Some slaves were set free by a master who had moral qualms about slavery, or by a master's will after his death—for example, the more than 400 slaves belonging to John Randolph of Roanoke, freed in 1833. From the 1830s on, *New Restrictions on Manumission* however, state laws governing slavery became stricter, in part in response to the fears Nat Turner's revolt created among white southerners. The new laws made it more difficult, and in some cases practically impossible, for owners to set free (or **manumit**) their slaves.

A few free blacks attained wealth and prominence. Some even owned slaves themselves, usually relatives whom they had bought to ensure their ultimate emancipation. In a few cities— New Orleans, Natchez, and Charleston—free black communities managed to flourish with relatively little interference from whites and with some economic stability. Most southern free blacks, however, lived in abject poverty. Yet, great as were the hardships of freedom, blacks much preferred it to slavery.

The Slave Trade

The transfer of slaves from one part of the South to another was one of the most important and terrible consequences of slavery. Sometimes slaves moved to the new cotton lands in the company of their original owners, who were migrating themselves. More often, however, the transfer occurred through the efforts of professional slave traders. The traders took slaves to such central markets as Natchez, New Orleans, Mobile, and Charleston, where purchasers bid for them. A sound young field hand could fetch a price that might vary in the 1840s and 1850s from $500 to $1,700, depending on fluctuations in the market (and the health and age of the slaves).

The domestic slave trade, essential to the growth and prosperity of the system, was one of its most horrible aspects. The trade dehumanized all who were involved in it. It separated children from parents, and parents from each other. Even families kept together by scrupulous owners might be broken up in the division of the estate after the master's death. Planters might deplore the trade, but they eased their consciences by holding the traders in contempt.

The foreign slave trade was bad or worse. Although federal law had prohibited the importation of slaves from 1808 on, some continued to be smuggled into the United States as late as the 1850s when the supply of slaves was inadequate. At the annual southern commercial conventions, planters began to discuss the legal reopening of the trade. "If it is right to buy slaves in Virginia and carry them to New Orleans," William L. Yancey asked his fellow delegates in 1858, "why is it not right to buy them in Cuba, Brazil, or Africa." The convention that year voted to repeal all the laws against slave imports, but the government never acted on their proposal.

The continued smuggling of slaves was not without resistance. In 1839, a group of 53 slaves in Cuba took charge of a ship, the *Amistad*, that was transporting them to another port in Cuba. Their goal was to sail back to their homelands in Africa. The slaves had no experience with sailing, and they tried to compel the crew to steer them across the Atlantic. Instead, the ship sailed up the Atlantic Coast until it was captured by a ship of the United States Revenue Service. Many Americans, including President Van Buren, thought the slaves should be returned to Cuba. But at the request of a group of abolitionists, former president John Quincy Adams went before the Supreme Court to argue that they should be freed. Adams argued that the foreign slave trade was illegal and thus the *Amistad* rebels could not be returned to slavery. The Court accepted his argument in 1841, and most of the former slaves were returned to Africa, with funding from American abolitionists.

THE BUSINESS OF SLAVERY The offices of slave dealers were familiar sights on the streets of pre–Civil War southern cities and towns. They provide testimony to the way in which slavery was not just a social system but a business, deeply woven into the fabric of southern economic life. (The Library of Congress)

Two years later, another group of slaves revolted on board a ship and took control of it—this time an American vessel bound from Norfolk, Virginia, to New Orleans, Louisiana—and steered it (and its 135 slaves) to the British Bahamas, where slavery was illegal and the slaves were given sanctuary. Such shipboard revolts were rare, but they were symbols of the continued effort by Africans to resist slavery.

SLAVE RESISTANCE

Slaveowners liked to argue that the slaves were generally content, "happy with their lot." But it is clear that the vast majority of southern blacks yearned for freedom and detested the peculiar institution. Evidence for that can be found, if nowhere else, in the reaction of slaves when emancipation finally came. Virtually all reacted to freedom with great joy; few chose to remain in the service of the whites who had owned them before the Civil War.

Rather than contented acceptance, the dominant response of African Americans to slavery was a complex one: a combination of adaptation and resistance. At the extremes, slavery could produce two very different reactions, each of which served as the basis for a powerful stereotype in white society. One extreme was what became known as the "Sambo"—the shuffling, grinning, head-scratching, deferential slave who acted out what he recognized as the role the white world expected of him. But the Sambo pattern of behavior was a charade put on by blacks, a façade assumed in the presence of whites. The other extreme was the slave rebel—the African American who resisted either acceptance or accommodation but remained forever rebellious.

Actual slave revolts were extremely rare, but the knowledge that they were *Slave Revolts* possible struck terror into the hearts of white southerners. In 1800, Gabriel Prosser gathered 1,000 rebellious slaves outside Richmond; but two African Americans gave away the plot, and the Virginia militia stymied the uprising before it could begin. Prosser and thirty-five others were executed. In 1822, the Charleston free black Denmark Vesey and his followers—rumored to total 9,000—made preparations for revolt; but again word leaked out and suppression and retribution followed. On a summer night in 1831, Nat Turner, a slave preacher, led a band of African Americans armed with guns and axes from house to house in Southampton County, Virginia. They killed sixty white men, women, and children before being overpowered by state and federal troops. More than a hundred blacks were executed in the aftermath.

For the most part, however, resistance to slavery took other, less violent forms. Some blacks attempted to resist by running away. A small number managed to escape to the North or to Canada, especially after sympathetic whites and free blacks began organizing secret escape routes, known as the "underground railroad," to assist them in flight. But the odds against a successful escape were very high. The hazards of distance and the slaves' ignorance of geography were serious obstacles, as were the white "slave patrols," which stopped wandering blacks on sight and demanded to see travel permits. Despite all the obstacles to success, however, blacks continued to run away from their masters in large numbers.

Perhaps the most important method of resistance was simply a pattern of everyday behavior by which blacks defied their masters. That whites so often considered *Day-to-Day Slave Resistance* blacks to be lazy and shiftless suggests one means of resistance: refusal to work hard. Some slaves stole from their masters or from neighboring whites. Others performed isolated acts of sabotage: losing or breaking tools or performing tasks improperly. In extreme cases, blacks might make themselves useless by cutting off their fingers or even committing suicide. A few turned on their masters and killed them. The extremes, however, were rare. For the most part, blacks resisted by building subtle methods of rebellion into their normal patterns of behavior.

THE CULTURE OF SLAVERY

Resistance was only part of the slave response to slavery. Another was an elaborate process of adaptation. One of the ways blacks adapted was by developing their own, separate culture, one that enabled them to sustain a sense of racial pride and unity.

SLAVE RELIGION

Almost all African Americans were Christians by the early nineteenth century. Some had converted voluntarily and others in response to coercion from their masters and Protestant missionaries who evangelized among them. Masters expected their slaves to join their denominations and worship under the supervision of white ministers. A separate slave religion was not supposed to exist. Indeed, autonomous black churches were banned by law.

Nevertheless, blacks throughout the South developed their own version of Christianity, at times incorporating into it such practices as voodoo or other polytheistic religious traditions of Africa. Or they simply bent religion to the special circumstances of bondage.

African American religion was often more emotional than its white counterpart and reflected the influence of African customs and practices. Slave prayer meetings routinely involved fervent chanting, spontaneous exclamations from the congregation, and ecstatic *Praying for Freedom* conversion experiences. Black religion was also generally more joyful and affirming than that of many white denominations. And above all, African American religion emphasized the dream of freedom and deliverance. In their prayers and songs and

HARRIET TUBMAN WITH ESCAPED SLAVES Harriet Tubman (ca. 1820–1913) was born into slavery in Maryland. In 1849, when her master died, she escaped to Philadelphia to avoid being sold out of state. Over the next ten years, she assisted first members of her own family and then up to 300 other slaves to escape from Maryland to freedom. She is shown here, on the far left, with some of the slaves she had helped free. (© Archive Photos/Getty Images)

sermons, black Christians talked and sang of the day when the Lord would "call us home," "deliver us to freedom," or "take us to the Promised Land." While whites generally chose to interpret such language merely as the expression of hopes for life after death, many blacks used the images of Christian salvation to express their own dreams of freedom in the present world.

LANGUAGE AND MUSIC

In many areas, slaves retained a language of their own. Having arrived in America speaking many different African languages, the first generations of slaves had as much difficulty communicating with one another as they did with white people. To overcome these barriers, they learned a simple, common language (known to linguists as "pidgin"). It *"Pidgin"* retained some African words, but it drew primarily, if selectively, from English. And while slave language grew more sophisticated as blacks spent more time in America, some features of this early pidgin survived in black speech for many generations.

Music was especially important in slave society. Again, the African heritage was an important influence. African music relied heavily on rhythm, and so did black music in America. Slaves often created instruments for themselves out of whatever materials were at hand. The banjo became important to slave music. But more important were voices and song.

Field workers often used songs to pass the time; since they sang them in the presence of the whites, they usually attached relatively innocuous words to them. But African Americans also created more politically challenging music in the relative privacy of their own religious services. It was there that the tradition of the spiritual emerged. *Importance of Slave Spirituals* Through the spiritual, Africans in America not only expressed their religious faith, but also lamented their bondage and expressed continuing hope for freedom.

Slave songs were rarely written down and often seemed entirely spontaneous; but much slave music was really derived from African and Caribbean traditions passed on through generations. Performers also improvised variations on songs they had heard. When the setting permitted it, African Americans danced to their music—dances very different from and much more spontaneous than the formal steps that nineteenth-century whites generally learned. They also used music to accompany another of their important cultural traditions: storytelling.

THE SLAVE FAMILY

The slave family was the other crucial institution of black culture in the South. Like religion, it suffered from legal restrictions. Nevertheless, what we now call the "nuclear family" consistently emerged as the dominant kinship model among African Americans.

Black women generally began bearing children at younger ages than most whites, often as early as fourteen or fifteen (sometimes as a result of unwanted sexual relations with their masters). Slave communities did not condemn premarital pregnancy in the way white society did, and black couples would often begin living together before marrying. It was customary, however, for couples to marry—in a ceremony involving *Slave Marriages* formal vows—soon after conceiving a child. Husbands and wives on neighboring plantations sometimes visited each other with the permission of their masters, but often such visits had to be in secret, at night. Family ties among slaves were generally no less strong than those of whites.

When marriages did not survive, it was often because of circumstances over which blacks had no control. Up to a third of all black families were broken apart by the slave trade. Extended kinship networks were strong and important and often helped compensate for the breakup of nuclear families. A slave forced suddenly to move to a new area, far from his or her family, might create fictional kinship ties and become "adopted" by a family in the new community. Even so, the impulse to maintain contact with a spouse and children remained strong long after the breakup of a family. One of the most frequent causes of flight from the plantation was a slave's desire to find a husband, wife, or child who had been sent elsewhere. After the Civil War, white and black newspapers were filled with notices from former slaves seeking to reconnect with family members separated during bondage.

However much blacks resented their lack of freedom, they often found it difficult to maintain an entirely hostile attitude toward their owners. They depended on whites for the material means of existence—food, clothing, and shelter—and they relied on them as well for security and protection. There was, in short, a paternal relationship between slave *Paternalism* and master—sometimes harsh, at other times kindly, but always important. That paternalism, in fact, became a vital instrument of white control. By creating a sense of mutual dependence, whites helped minimize though never eliminated resistance to an institution that served only the interests of the ruling race.

CONCLUSION

While the North was creating a complex and rapidly developing commercial-industrial economy, the South was expanding its agrarian economy without making many fundamental changes in the region's character. Great migrations took many southern whites, and even more African American slaves, into new agricultural areas in the Deep South, where they created a booming "cotton kingdom." The cotton economy created many great fortunes and some modest ones. It also entrenched the planter class as the dominant force within southern society—both as owners of vast numbers of slaves and as patrons, creditors, politicians, landlords, and marketers for the large number of poor whites who lived on the edge of the planter world.

The differences between the North and the South were a result of differences in natural resources, social structure, climate, and culture. Above all, they were the result of the existence within the South of an unfree labor system that prevented the kind of social fluidity that an industrializing society usually requires. Within that system, however, slaves created a vital, independent culture and religion in the face of white subjugation.

KEY TERMS/PEOPLE/PLACES/EVENTS

RECALL AND REFLECT

1. Why did cotton become the leading crop of the South?
2. Why did industry fail to develop in the South to the extent that it did in the North?
3. How did slavery function economically and socially?
4. What was the effect of slavery on white slaveowners? On slaves? On nonslaveowning whites? On free blacks?
5. Through what means did slaves maintain a distinct African American culture?

12 ANTEBELLUM CULTURE AND REFORM

THE ROMANTIC IMPULSE

REMAKING SOCIETY

THE CRUSADE AGAINST SLAVERY

LOOKING AHEAD

1. How did an American national culture of art, literature, philosophy, and communal living develop in the nineteenth century?

2. What were the issues on which social and moral reformers tried to "remake the nation"? How successful were their efforts?

3. Why did the crusade against slavery become the preeminent issue of the reform movement?

THE UNITED STATES IN THE mid-nineteenth century was growing rapidly in size, population, and economic complexity. Most Americans were excited by the new possibilities these changes produced. But many people were also painfully aware of the problems that accompanied them.

One result of these conflicting attitudes was the emergence of movements to "reform" the nation. Some reforms rested on an optimistic faith in human nature, a belief that within every individual resided a spirit that was basically good and that society should attempt to unleash. A second impulse was a desire for order and control. With their traditional values and institutions being challenged and eroded, many Americans yearned above all for stability and discipline. By the end of the 1840s, however, one issue—slavery—had come to overshadow all others. And one group of reformers—the abolitionists—had become the most influential of all.

THE ROMANTIC IMPULSE

"In the four quarters of the globe," wrote the English wit Sydney Smith in 1820, "who reads an American book? or goes to an American play? or looks at an American picture or statue?" The answer, he assumed, was obvious: no one.

American intellectuals were painfully aware of the low regard in which Europeans held their culture, and they tried to create an artistic life that would express their own nation's special virtues. At the same time, many of the nation's cultural leaders were striving for another kind of liberation, which was—ironically—largely an import from Europe: the spirit of romanticism. In literature, in philosophy, in art, even in politics and economics, American intellectuals were committing themselves to the liberation of the human spirit.

NATIONALISM AND ROMANTICISM IN AMERICAN PAINTING

Despite Sydney Smith's contemptuous question, a great many people in the United States were, in fact, looking at American paintings—and they were doing so because they believed Americans were creating important new artistic traditions of their own.

American painters sought to capture the power of nature by portraying some of the nation's most spectacular and undeveloped areas. The first great school of American painters—known as the Hudson River school—emerged in New York. Frederic Church, Thomas Cole, Thomas Doughty, Asher Durand, and others painted the spectacular vistas of the rugged and still largely untamed Hudson Valley. Like Ralph Waldo Emerson and Henry David Thoreau, whom many of the painters read and admired, they considered nature—far more than civilization—the best source of wisdom and fulfillment. In portraying the Hudson Valley, they seemed to announce that in

TIME LINE

1821
New York constructs first penitentiary

1826
Cooper's *The Last of the Mohicans*

1830
Joseph Smith publishes the Book of Mormon

1831
The *Liberator* begins publication

1833
American Antislavery Society founded

1837
Horace Mann appointed secretary of Massachusetts Board of Education

1840
Liberty Party formed

1841
Brook Farm founded

1845
Frederick Douglass's autobiography

1848
Women's rights convention at Seneca Falls, N.Y.

Oneida Community founded

1850
Hawthorne's *The Scarlet Letter*

1851
Melville's *Moby Dick*

1852
Stowe's *Uncle Tom's Cabin*

1854
Thoreau's *Walden*

1855
Whitman's *Leaves of Grass*

America, unlike in Europe, "wild nature" still existed; and that America, therefore, was a nation of greater promise than the overdeveloped lands of the Old World.

In later years, some of the Hudson River painters traveled farther west. Their enormous canvases of great natural wonders—the Yosemite Valley, Yellowstone, the Rocky Mountains—touched a passionate chord among the public. Some of the most famous of their paintings—particularly the works of Albert Bierstadt and Thomas Moran—traveled around the country attracting enormous crowds.

AN AMERICAN LITERATURE

The effort to create a distinctively American literature made considerable progress in the 1820s through the work of the first great American novelist: James Fenimore Cooper. What most distinguished his work was its evocation of the American West. Cooper had a lifelong fascination with the human relationship to nature and with the challenges (and dangers) of America's expansion westward. His most important novels—among them *The Last of the Mohicans* (1826) and *The Deerslayer* (1841)—examined the experience of rugged white frontiersmen with Indians, pioneers, violence, and the law. Cooper evoked the ideal of the independent individual with a natural inner goodness—an ideal that many Americans feared was in jeopardy.

Walt Whitman   Another, later group of American writers displayed more clearly the influence of romanticism. Walt Whitman's book of poems *Leaves of Grass* (1855) celebrated democracy, the liberation of the individual spirit, and the pleasures of the flesh. In helping free verse from traditional, restrictive conventions, he also expressed a yearning for emotional and physical release and personal fulfillment—a yearning perhaps rooted in part in his own experience as a homosexual living in a society profoundly intolerant of unconventional sexuality.

Herman Melville   Less exuberant was Herman Melville, perhaps the greatest American writer of his era. *Moby Dick,* published in 1851, is Melville's most important—although not, in his lifetime, his most popular—novel. It tells the story of Ahab, the powerful, driven captain of a whaling vessel, and his obsessive search for Moby Dick, the great white whale that had once maimed him. It is a story of courage and of the strength of human will. But it is also a tragedy of pride and revenge. In some ways it is an uncomfortable metaphor for the harsh, individualistic, achievement-driven culture of nineteenth-century America.

LITERATURE IN THE ANTEBELLUM SOUTH

The South experienced a literary flowering of its own in the mid-nineteenth century, and it produced writers and artists who were, like their northern counterparts, concerned with defining the nature of America. But white southerners tended to produce very different images of what society was and should be.

Edgar Allan Poe   The southern writer Edgar Allan Poe produced stories and poems that were primarily sad and macabre. His first book, *Tamerlane and Other Poems* (1827), received little recognition. But later works, including his most famous poem, "The Raven" (1845), established him as a major, if controversial, literary figure. Poe evoked images of individuals rising above the narrow confines of intellect and exploring the deeper—and often painful and horrifying—world of the spirit and emotions.

Other southern novelists of the 1830s (among them Nathaniel Beverley Tucker, William Alexander Caruthers, and John Pendleton Kennedy) produced historical romances and eulogies for the plantation system of the upper South. The most distinguished of the region's men of letters was William Gilmore Simms. For a time, his work expressed a broad nationalism that transcended his regional background; but by the 1840s, he too became a strong defender of southern institutions—especially slavery—against the encroachments of the North. There was, he believed, a unique quality to southern life that fell to intellectuals to defend.

One group of southern writers, however, produced works that were more broadly American. These writers from the fringes of plantation society—Augustus B. Longstreet, Joseph G. Baldwin, Johnson J. Hooper, and others—depicted the world of the backwoods south and focused on ordinary people and poor whites. Instead of romanticizing their subjects, they were deliberately and sometimes painfully realistic, seasoning their sketches with a robust, vulgar humor that was new to American literature. These southern realists established a tradition of American regional humor that was ultimately to find its most powerful voice in Mark Twain.

THE TRANSCENDENTALISTS

One of the outstanding expressions of the romantic impulse in America came from a group of New England writers and philosophers known as the **transcendentalists.** Borrowing heavily from German and English writers and philosophers, the transcendentalists promoted a theory of the individual that rested on a distinction between what they called "reason" and "understanding." Reason, as they defined it, had little to do with rationality. It was, rather, the individual's innate capacity to grasp beauty and truth by giving full expression to the instincts and emotions. Understanding, by contrast, was the use of

MARGARET FULLER As a leading transcendentalist, Fuller argued for the important relationship between the discovery of the "self" and the questioning of the prevailing gender roles of her era. In her famous feminist work *Women in the Nineteenth Century,* Fuller wrote, "Many women are considering within themselves what they need and what they have not." She encouraged her readers, especially women, to set aside conventional thinking about the role of women in society. (© Corbis)

intellect in the narrow, artificial ways imposed by society; it involved the repression of instinct and the victory of externally imposed learning. Every person's goal, therefore, should be the cultivation of "reason"—and, thus, liberation from "understanding." Each individual should strive to "transcend" the limits of the intellect and allow the emotions, the "soul," to create an "original relation to the Universe."

Transcendentalist philosophy emerged first in America among a small group of
Ralph Waldo Emerson   intellectuals centered in Concord, Massachusetts, and led by Ralph Waldo Emerson. A Unitarian minister in his youth, Emerson left the clergy in 1832 to devote himself to writing, teaching, and lecturing. In "Nature" (1836), Emerson wrote that in the quest for self-fulfillment, individuals should work for a communion with the natural world: "in the woods, we return to reason and faith. . . . Standing on the bare ground,—my head bathed by the blithe air, and uplifted into infinite space,—all mean egotism vanishes. . . . I am part and particle of God." In other essays, he was even more explicit in advocating a commitment to individuality and the full exploration of inner capacities.

Equally influential was Henry David Thoreau. Thoreau went even further in repudiating
Henry David Thoreau   the repressive forces of society, which produced, he said, "lives of quiet desperation." Each individual should work for self-realization by resisting pressures to conform to society's expectations and responding instead to his or her own instincts. Thoreau's own effort to free himself—immortalized in *Walden* (1854)—led him to build a small cabin in the Concord woods on the edge of Walden Pond, where he lived alone for two years as simply as he could, attempting to liberate himself from what he considered society's excessive interest in material comforts. In his 1849 essay "Resistance to Civil Government," he extended his critique of artificial constraints in society to government, arguing that when government required an individual to violate his or her own morality, it had no legitimate authority. The proper response was "civil disobedience," or "passive resistance"—a public refusal to obey unjust laws. It was a belief that would undergird some antislavery reforms and, much later in the mid-twentieth century, attacks on racial segregation.

THE DEFENSE OF NATURE

As Emerson's and Thoreau's tributes to nature suggest, a small but influential group of Americans in the nineteenth century feared the impact of capitalism on the integrity of the natural world. "The mountains and cataracts, which were to have made poets and painters," wrote the essayist Oliver Wendell Holmes, "have been mined for anthracite and dammed for water power."

To the transcendentalists and others, nature was not just a setting for economic activity, as many farmers, miners, and others believed. It was the source of deep, personal human
Roots of Environmentalism   inspiration—the vehicle through which individuals could best realize the truth within their own souls. Genuine spirituality, they argued, did not come from formal religion but through communion with the natural world.

In making such claims, the transcendentalists were among the first Americans to anticipate the environmental movement of the twentieth century. They had no scientific basis for their defense of the wilderness and little sense of the twentieth-century notion of the interconnectedness of species. But they did believe in, and articulate, an essential unity between humanity and nature—a spiritual unity, they believed, without which civilization would be impoverished. They looked at nature, they said, "with new eyes," and with those eyes they saw that "behind nature, throughout nature, spirit is present."

Visions of Utopia

Although transcendentalism was at its heart an individualistic philosophy, it helped spawn one of the most famous nineteenth-century experiments in communal living: Brook Farm. The dream of the Boston transcendentalist George Ripley, Brook Farm was   *Brook Farm* established in 1841 as an experimental community in West Roxbury, Massachusetts. There, according to Ripley, individuals would gather to create a new society that would permit every member to have full opportunity for self-realization. All residents would share equally in the labor of the community so that all could share as well in the leisure, which was essential for cultivation of the self. The tension between the ideal of individual freedom and the demands of a communal society, however, eventually took its toll on Brook Farm. Many residents became disenchanted and left. When a fire destroyed the central building of the community in 1847, the experiment dissolved.

Among the original residents of Brook Farm was the writer Nathaniel Hawthorne, who expressed his disillusionment with the experiment and, to some extent, with transcendental-ism in a series of novels. In *The Blithedale Romance* (1852), he wrote scathingly of Brook Farm itself. In other novels—most notably *The Scarlet Letter* (1850) and *The House of the Seven Gables* (1851)—he wrote equally passionately about the price individuals pay for cutting themselves off from society. Egotism, he claimed (in an indirect challenge to the transcendentalist faith in the self), was the "serpent" that lay at the heart of human misery.

Brook Farm was only one of many experimental communities in the years before the Civil War. The Scottish industrialist and philanthropist Robert Owen founded an experi-mental community in Indiana in 1825, which he named New Harmony. It   *New Harmony* was to be a "Village of Cooperation," in which every resident worked and lived in total equality. The community was an economic failure, but the vision that had inspired it continued to enchant some Americans. Dozens of other "Owenite" experiments were established in other locations in the ensuing years.

Redefining Gender Roles

Many of the new utopian communities were deeply concerned with the relationship between men and women. Some even experimented with radical redefinitions of gender roles.

One of the most enduring of the utopian colonies of the nineteenth century was the Oneida Community, established in 1848 in upstate New York by John Humphrey   *Oneida Community* Noyes. The Oneida "Perfectionists," as residents of the community called themselves, rejected traditional notions of family and marriage. All residents, Noyes declared, were "married" to all other residents; there were to be no permanent conjugal ties. But Oneida was not, as hor-rified critics often claimed, an experiment in unrestrained "free love." It was a place where the community carefully monitored sexual behavior, where women were protected from unwanted childbearing, and where children were raised communally, often seeing little of their own parents. The Oneidans took pride in what they considered their liberation of women from the demands of male "lust" and from the traditional restraints of family.

The Shakers, too, redefined traditional gender roles. Founded by "Mother" Ann Lee in the 1770s, the society of the Shakers survived through the twentieth century.   *Shakers* (A tiny remnant is left today.) But the Shakers attracted a particularly large following in the mid-nineteenth century and established more than twenty communities throughout the Northeast and Northwest in the 1840s. They derived their name from a unique religious ritual—in which members of a congregation would "shake" themselves free of sin while performing a loud chant and an ecstatic dance.

The most distinctive feature of Shakerism, however, was its commitment to complete celibacy—which meant, of course, that no one could be born into the faith. All Shakers had to choose it voluntarily. Shakerism attracted about 6,000 members in the 1840s, more women than men. They lived in communities where contacts between men and women were strictly limited, and they endorsed the idea of sexual equality, although women exercised the greater power.

The Shakers were not, however, motivated only by a desire to escape the burdens of traditional gender roles. They were also trying to create a society set apart from the chaos and disorder they believed had come to characterize American life. In that, they were much like other dissenting religious sects and utopian communities of their time.

THE MORMONS

Among the most important efforts to create a new and more ordered society was that of the Church of Jesus Christ of Latter-day Saints—the Mormons. Mormonism began in *Joseph Smith* upstate New York through the efforts of Joseph Smith. In 1830, when he was just twenty-four, he published a remarkable document—the Book of Mormon, named for the ancient prophet who he claimed had written it. It was, he said, a translation of a set of golden tablets he had found in the hills of New York, revealed to him by Moroni, an angel of God. The Book of Mormon told the story of two ancient civilizations in America, whose people had anticipated the coming of Christ and were rewarded when Jesus actually came to America after his resurrection. Ultimately, both civilizations collapsed because of their rejection of Christian principles. But Smith believed their history as righteous societies could serve as a model for building a new holy community in the United States.

In 1831, gathering a small group of believers around him, Smith began searching for a sanctuary for his new community of "saints," an effort that would continue unhappily for more than fifteen years. Time and again, the Latter-day Saints, as they called themselves, attempted to establish peaceful communities. Time and again, they met with persecution from their neighbors, who were suspicious of their radical religious doctrines—their claims of new prophets, new scripture, and divine authority. Opponents were also concerned by their rapid growth and their increasing political strength. Near the end of his life, Joseph Smith introduced the practice of polygamy (giving a man the right to take several wives), which became public knowledge after Smith's death. From then on, polygamy became a central target of anti-Mormon opposition.

Driven from their original settlements in Independence, Missouri, and Kirtland, Ohio, the Mormons founded a new town in Illinois that they named Nauvoo. In the early 1840s, it became an imposing and economically successful community. In 1844, however, bitter enemies of Joseph Smith published an inflammatory attack on him. Smith ordered his followers to destroy the offending press, and he was subsequently arrested and imprisoned in nearby Carthage. There, an angry mob attacked the jail and fatally shot him. The Mormons soon abandoned Nauvoo and, under the leadership of Smith's successor, Brigham Young, traveled—12,000 strong, in one of the largest single group migrations in American history—across the Great Plains and the Rocky Mountains. They established *Salt Lake City* several communities in Utah, including the present Salt Lake City, where, finally, the Mormons were able to create a lasting settlement.

Like other experiments in social organization of the era, Mormonism reflected a belief in human perfectibility. God had once been a man, the church taught, and thus every man or woman could aspire to move continuously closer to God. Within a highly developed

MORMONS HEADING WEST   This lithograph by William Henry Jackson imagines the physical challenges that Mormon pioneers faced in their journey to Utah in 1850. Many of the men are shown pulling their families and possessions on handcarts. (Private Collection/© Peter Newark American Pictures/Bridgeman Images)

and centrally directed ecclesiastical structure, Mormons created a haven for people demoralized by the disorder and uncertainty of the secular world. The original Mormons were white men and women, many of whom felt displaced in their rapidly changing society—economically marginalized by the material growth and social progress of their era. In the new religion, they found a strong and animating faith. In the society it created, they found security and order.

REMAKING SOCIETY

The reform impulse also helped create new movements to remake mainstream society—movements in which, to a striking degree, women formed both the rank and file and the leadership. By the 1830s, such movements had become organized reform societies.

REVIVALISM, MORALITY, AND ORDER

The philosophy of reform arose in part from the optimistic vision of those, such as the transcendentalists, who preached the divinity of the individual. Another source was Protestant revivalism—the movement that had begun with the Second Great Awakening early in the century and had, by the 1820s, evolved into a powerful force for social reform.

The New Light evangelicals embraced the optimistic belief that every individual was capable of salvation through his or her own efforts. Partly as a result, revivalism soon became not only a means of personal salvation but also an effort to reform the larger society. In particular, revivalism produced a crusade against personal immorality.

THE DRUNKARD'S PROGRESS   This 1846 lithograph by Nathaniel Currier shows what temperance advocates argued was the inevitable consequence of alcohol consumption. Beginning with an apparently innocent "glass with a friend," the young man rises step by step to the summit of drunken revelry, then declines to desperation and suicide while his abandoned wife and child grieve. (The Library of Congress)

Evangelical Protestantism greatly strengthened the crusade against drunkenness. No social vice, **temperance** advocates argued, was more responsible for crime, disorder, and poverty than the excessive use of alcohol. Women complained that men spent money their families needed on alcohol and that drunken husbands often beat and abused their wives. Temperance also appealed to those who were alarmed by immigration; drunkenness, many nativists believed, was responsible for violence and disorder in immigrant communities. By 1840, temperance had become a major national movement, with powerful organizations and more than a million followers who had signed a formal pledge to forgo hard liquor.

HEALTH, SCIENCE, AND PHRENOLOGY

For some Americans, the search for individual and social perfection led to an interest in new theories of health and knowledge. In the nineteenth century, more than half of those who contracted cholera—a severe bacterial infection of the intestines, usually contracted from contaminated food or water—died. Nearly a quarter of the population of New Orleans in 1833 perished from the disease. Many cities established health boards to try to find ways to prevent epidemics. But the medical profession of the time, not yet aware of the nature of bacterial infections, had no answers.

Instead, many Americans turned to nonscientific theories for improving health. Affluent men and especially women flocked to health spas for the celebrated "water cure" (known to modern scientists as hydrotherapy), which purported to improve health through immersing people in hot or cold baths or wrapping them in wet sheets. Other people adopted *New Dietary Theories*   new dietary theories. Sylvester Graham, a Connecticut-born Presbyterian minister and committed reformer, won many followers with his prescriptions for eating fruits, vegetables, and bread made from coarsely ground flour—a prescription not unlike some dietary theories today—and for avoiding meat. (The graham cracker is made from a kind of flour named for him.)

Perhaps strangest of all to modern sensibilities was the widespread belief in the new "science" of phrenology, which appeared first in Germany and became popular in the United States beginning in the 1830s through the efforts of Orson and Lorenzo Fowler, publishers of the *Phrenology Almanac.* Phrenologists argued that the shape of *Phrenology* an individual's skull was an important indicator of his or her character and intelligence. They made elaborate measurements of bumps and indentations to calculate the size (and, they claimed, the strength) of different areas of the brain. Phrenology seemed to provide a way of measuring an individual's fitness for various positions in life and to promise an end to the arbitrary process by which people matched their talents to occupations and responsibilities. The theory is now universally believed to have no scientific value at all.

MEDICAL SCIENCE

In an age of rapid technological and scientific advances, medicine sometimes seemed to lag behind. In part, that was because of the character of the medical profession, which— in the absence of any significant regulation—attracted many poorly educated people and many quacks. Efforts to regulate the profession were beaten back in the 1830s and 1840s by those who considered the licensing of physicians to be a form of undemocratic monopoly. The prestige of the profession, therefore, remained low.

The biggest problem facing American medicine, however, was the absence of basic knowledge about disease. The great medical achievement of the eighteenth century—the development of a vaccination against smallpox by Edward Jenner—came from no broad theory of infection but from a brilliant adaptation of folk practices among country people. The development of anesthetics in the nineteenth century came not from medical doctors at first, but from a New England dentist, William Morton, who was looking for ways to help his patients endure the extraction of teeth. Beginning in 1844, *Experiments with Anesthesia* Morton began experimenting with sulfuric ether. John Warren, a Boston surgeon, soon began using ether to sedate surgical patients. Even these advances met with stiff resistance from some traditional physicians, who mistrusted innovation and experimentation.

In the absence of any broad acceptance of scientific methods and experimental practice in medicine, it was very difficult for even the most talented doctors to make progress in treating disease. Even so, halting progress toward the discovery of the germ theory did occur in antebellum America. In 1843, the Boston essayist, poet, and *Progress in Germ Theory* physician Oliver Wendell Holmes published a study of large numbers of cases of "puerperal fever" (septicemia in children) and concluded that the disease could be transmitted from one person to another. This discovery of contagion met with a storm of criticism but was later vindicated by the clinical success of the Hungarian physician Ignaz Semmelweis, who noticed that infection seemed to be spread by medical students who had been working with diseased corpses. Once he began requiring students to wash their hands and disinfect their instruments, the infections virtually disappeared.

EDUCATION

One of the most important reform movements of the mid-nineteenth century was the effort to produce a system of universal public education. As of 1830, no state had such a system. Soon after that, however, interest in public education began growing rapidly.

The greatest of the educational reformers was Horace Mann, the first secretary of the Massachusetts Board of Education, which was established in 1837. To Mann and his followers, education was the only way to preserve democracy, for an educated electorate was essential to the workings of a free political system. Mann reorganized the Massachusetts *Horace Mann and Public Schools* school system, lengthened the academic year (to six months), doubled teachers' salaries, broadened the curriculum, and introduced new methods of professional training for teachers. Other states followed by building new schools, creating teachers' colleges, and offering many children access to education for the first time. By the 1850s, the principle (although not yet the reality) of tax-supported elementary schools was established in every state.

The quality of public education continued to vary widely. In some places—Massachusetts, for example—educators were generally capable men and women, often highly trained. In other areas, however, barely literate teachers and severely limited funding hindered education. Among the highly dispersed population of the West, many children had no access to *Uneven Public Education* schools at all. In the South, all African Americans were barred from education, and only about a third of all white children of school age were actually enrolled in schools in 1860. In the North, 72 percent were enrolled, but even there, many students attended classes only briefly and casually.

Among the goals of educational reformers was to teach children the social values of thrift, order, discipline, punctuality, and respect for authority. Horace Mann, for example, spoke of the role of public schools in extending democracy and expanding individual opportunity. But he spoke, too, of their role in creating social order: "Train up a child in the way he should go, and when he is old he will not depart from it."

The interest in education contributed to the growing movement to educate American Indians. Some reformers believed that Indians could be "civilized" if only they could be taught the ways of the white world. Efforts by missionaries and others to educate Indians and encourage them to assimilate were particularly prominent in such areas of the Far West as Oregon, where conflicts with the natives had not yet become acute. Nevertheless, the great majority of Native Americans remained outside the reach of white educational reform.

Despite limitations and inequities, the achievements of the school reformers were *Soaring Literacy Rates* impressive. By the beginning of the Civil War, the United States had one of the highest literacy rates of any nation in the world: 94 percent of the population of the North, and 83 percent of the white population of the South.

REHABILITATION

The belief in the potential of the individual also sparked the creation of new institutions to help the disabled—institutions that formed part of a great network of charitable activities known as the Benevolent Empire. Among them was the Perkins School for the Blind in Boston. Nothing better exemplified the romantic reform spirit of the era than the conviction of those who founded Perkins. They believed that even society's supposedly most disadvantaged members could be helped to discover their own inner strength and wisdom.

Similar impulses produced another powerful movement of reform: the creation of "asylums" for criminals and those who were mentally ill. In advocating prison and hospital reform, Americans were reacting against one of society's most glaring ills: antiquated jails and mental institutions whose inmates lived in almost inhuman conditions. Beginning in the 1820s, many states built new penitentiaries and mental asylums.

New York built the first penitentiary at Auburn in 1821. In Massachusetts, *Dorothea Dix* the reformer Dorothea Dix began a national movement for new methods of treating individuals with mental illness.

New forms of prison discipline were designed to reform and rehabilitate criminals. Solitary confinement and the imposition of silence on work crews (both instituted in Pennsylvania and New York in the 1820s) were meant to give prisoners opportunities to meditate on their wrongdoings and develop "penitence" (hence the name "penitentiary").

Some of the same impulses that produced asylums underlay the emergence of a new "reform" approach to the problems of Native Americans: the idea of the reservation. For several decades, the dominant thrust of the United States' policy toward the Indians had been relocation—getting the tribes out of the way of white *Reservation Concept Born* civilization. But among some whites, there had also been another intent: to move the Indians to a place where they would be allowed to develop to a point at which assimilation might be possible.

It was a small step from the idea of relocation to the idea of the reservation. Just as prisons, asylums, and orphanages would provide society with an opportunity to train and uplift misfits and unfortunates within white society, so the reservations might provide a way to undertake what one official called "the great work of regenerating the Indian race." These optimistic goals failed to meet the expectations of the reformers.

THE RISE OF FEMINISM

Many women who became involved in reform movements in the 1820s and 1830s came to resent the social and legal restrictions that limited their participation. Out of their concerns emerged the first American feminist movement. Sarah and Angelina Grimké, sisters who became active and outspoken abolitionists, ignored claims by men that their activism was inappropriate to their gender. "Men and women were created equal," they argued. "They are both moral and accountable beings, *Leaders of the American Feminist Movement* and whatever is right for man to do, is right for women to do." Other reformers— Catharine Beecher, Harriet Beecher Stowe (her sister), Lucretia Mott, Elizabeth Cady Stanton, Susan B. Anthony, and Dorothea Dix—similarly pressed at the boundaries of "acceptable" female behavior.

In 1840, American female delegates arrived at a world antislavery convention in London, only to be turned away by the men who controlled the proceedings. Angered at the rejection, several of the delegates became convinced that their first duty as reformers should now be to elevate the status of women. Over the next several years, Mott, Stanton, and others began drawing pointed parallels between the plight of women and the plight of slaves; and in 1848, in Seneca Falls, New York, they organized a *Seneca Falls Convention* convention to discuss the question of women's rights. Out of the meeting came the Declaration of Sentiments and Resolutions, which stated that "all men and women are created equal," and that women no less than men are endowed with certain inalienable rights. (See "Consider the Source: Declaration of Sentiments and Resolutions, Seneca Falls, New York, 1848.") In demanding the right to vote, they launched a movement for woman suffrage that would survive until the battle was finally won in 1920.

Many of the women involved in these feminist efforts were Quakers. Quakerism had long embraced the ideal of sexual equality and had tolerated, indeed encouraged, the emergence of women as preachers and community leaders. Of the women who drafted the Declaration of Sentiments, all but Elizabeth Cady Stanton were Quakers.

DECLARATION OF SENTIMENTS AND RESOLUTIONS, SENECA FALLS, NEW YORK, 1848

On July 19 and 20, 1848, leaders of the women's rights movement gathered in Seneca Falls, New York, to host a national conversation about "the social, civil, and religious conditions and rights of women." They outlined their grievances and goals in the Declaration of Sentiments and Resolutions, which helped shape a national reform movement.

When, in the course of human events, it becomes necessary for one portion of the family of man to assume among the people of the earth a position different from that which they have hitherto occupied, but one to which the laws of nature and of nature's God entitle them, a decent respect to the opinions of mankind requires that they should declare the causes that impel them to such a course.

We hold these truths to be self-evident: that all men and women are created equal; that they are endowed by their Creator with certain inalienable rights; that among these are life, liberty, and the pursuit of happiness; that to secure these rights governments are instituted, deriving their just powers from the consent of the governed. Whenever any form of government becomes destructive of these ends, it is the right of those who suffer from it to refuse allegiance to it, and to insist upon the institution of a new government, laying its foundation on such principles, and organizing its powers in such form, as to them shall seem most likely to effect their safety and happiness. Prudence, indeed, will dictate that governments long established should not be changed for light and transient causes; and accordingly all experience hath shown that mankind are more disposed to suffer, while evils are sufferable, than to right themselves by abolishing the forms to which they are accustomed. But when a long train of abuses and usurpations, pursuing invariably

the same object, evinces a design to reduce them under absolute despotism, it is their duty to throw off such government, and to provide new guards for their future security. Such has been the patient sufferance of the women under this government, and such is now the necessity which constrains them to demand the equal station to which they are entitled. The history of mankind is a history of repeated injuries and usurpations on the part of man toward woman, having in direct object the establishment of an absolute tyranny over her. To prove this, let facts be submitted to a candid world.

He has never permitted her to exercise her inalienable right to the elective franchise. He has compelled her to submit to laws, in the formation of which she had no voice. He has withheld from her rights which are given to the most ignorant and degraded men—both natives and foreigners.

Having deprived her of this first right of a citizen, the elective franchise, thereby leaving her without representation in the halls of legislation, he has oppressed her on all sides. He has made her, if married, in the eye of the law, civilly dead.

He has taken from her all right in property, even to the wages she earns.

He has made her, morally, an irresponsible being, as she can commit many crimes with impunity, provided they be done in the presence of her husband. In the covenant of marriage, she is compelled to promise obedience to her husband, he becoming, to all intents and purposes, her master—the law giving him power to deprive her of her liberty, and to administer chastisement.

He has so framed the laws of divorce, as to what shall be the proper causes, and in case of separation, to whom the guardianship of the children shall be given, as to be wholly regardless of the happiness of women—the law, in all cases, going upon a false supposition of the supremacy of man, and giving all power into his hands.

After depriving her of all rights as a married woman, if single, and the owner of property, he has taxed her to support a government which recognizes her only when her property can be made profitable to it.

He has monopolized nearly all the profitable employments, and from those she is permitted to follow, she receives but a scanty remuneration. He closes against her all the avenues to wealth and distinction which he considers most honorable to himself. As a teacher of theology, medicine, or law, she is not known.

He has denied her the facilities for obtaining a thorough education, all colleges being closed against her.

He allows her in church, as well as state, but a subordinate position, claiming apostolic authority for her exclusion from the ministry, and, with some exceptions, from any public participation in the affairs of the church.

He has created a false public sentiment by giving to the world a different code of morals for men and women, by which moral delinquencies which exclude women from society, are not only tolerated, but deemed of little account in man.

He has usurped the prerogative of Jehovah himself, claiming it as his right to assign for her a sphere of action, when that belongs to her conscience and to her God.

He has endeavored, in every way that he could, to destroy her confidence in her own powers, to lessen her self-respect, and to make her willing to lead a dependent and abject life.

Now, in view of this entire disfranchisement of one-half the people of this country, their social and religious degradation—in view of the unjust laws above mentioned, and because women do feel themselves aggrieved, oppressed, and fraudulently deprived of their most sacred rights, we insist that they have immediate admission to all the rights and privileges which belong to them as citizens of the United States.

UNDERSTAND, ANALYZE, & EVALUATE

1. What central claim about the relationship of men and women lies at the heart of this declaration? What evidence did the authors produce to support their claim?
2. With what demand did the authors conclude their resolution? How would you have reacted to this text?

Source: Elizabeth Cady Stanton, *A History of Woman Suffrage*, vol. 1 (Rochester, N.Y.: Fowler and Wells, 1889), pp. 70–71.

Feminists benefited greatly from their association with other reform movements, most notably abolitionism, but they also suffered as a result. The demands of women were usually assigned a secondary position to what many considered the far greater issue of the rights of slaves.

STRUGGLES OF RADICAL BLACK WOMEN

While black women like Sojourner Truth campaigned publicly for women's civil rights, others attempted to reform society from within their religious traditions. Like white clerics, black preachers in African American churches widely banned female congregants from becoming ordained and obtaining a license to preach and often required them to seek special permission to serve as class and prayer leaders. Indeed, no black denomination formally recognized a woman as a cleric until the African Methodist Episcopal Church ordained Julia Foote in 1895. Still, black women sought to preach throughout the colonial

and antebellum eras. Among the first was Jarena Lee, born free in 1783 in Cape May,
Jarena Lee   New Jersey. As a twenty-one-year-old woman then living in Philadelphia, she
preached in public with such verve and passion that she earned an invitation from Rev.
Richard Allen to speak at his church. Yet few other ministers welcomed her, which Lee
struggled to understand theologically. As she argued in 1833, "If the man may preach,
because the Savior died for him, why not the women, seeing he died for her also? Is he
not a whole Savior, instead of a half one, as those who hold it wrong for a woman to
preach, would seem to make it appear? Did not Mary *first* preach the risen Savior? Then
did not Mary, a woman, preach the gospel?"

A more radical contemporary of Lee's was Rebecca Cox Jackson. Growing up a free
Rebecca Cox Jackson   woman in Philadelphia during the early 1800s, she lived much of her
life with her brother, Joseph Cox, an African Methodist Episcopal minister. Following
instructions given to her by a heavenly spirit in 1830, Jackson began to host prayer meetings that quickly surged in popularity. She stirred controversy by tossing aside convention
and inviting men and women to worship side-by-side. She earned a temporary reprieve,
however, after a visit by Rev. Morris Brown, who succeeded Rev. Richard Allen as bishop
of the African Methodist Episcopal Church. Brown came to one of Jackson's meetings
with the idea of silencing her, but left thoroughly impressed by her preaching and ordered
that she be left alone. In 1833 Jackson embarked on a preaching tour outside Philadelphia
but met with new and greater resistance. Her insistence on her right to preach, open refusal
to join a church, and radical views on sexuality that included celibacy within marriage
angered area clerics and, Jackson claimed, motivated some to assault her. Eventually she
broke ranks with the free black church movement and joined a Shaker group in Watervliet,
New York. In 1851 she returned to Philadelphia and founded a Shaker community composed mainly of black women.

Lee and Jackson rejected the limitations placed on their preaching because of their
gender. Like other black women, they found confirmation for their efforts not in any
church rule or clerical pronouncement but rather through their personal interpretation of
the Bible and, more important, an unflagging conviction that God had called them to
preach. Though denied official recognition as preachers, they still touched the lives of
many and represented a vital dimension to the religious lives of northern blacks.

THE CRUSADE AGAINST SLAVERY

The antislavery movement was not new to the mid-nineteenth century. Nor was it primarily a domestic crusade. Indeed, the struggle to end slavery took root in countries around
the world. (See "America in the World: The Abolition of Slavery.") But not until 1830
in America did the antislavery movement begin to gather the force that would ultimately
enable it to overshadow virtually all other efforts at social reform.

EARLY OPPOSITION TO SLAVERY

In the early years of the nineteenth century, those who opposed slavery were, for the most
part, a calm and genteel lot, expressing moral disapproval but doing little else. To the
extent that there was an organized antislavery movement, it centered on the effort to
resettle American blacks in Africa or the Caribbean. In 1817, a group of prominent white
Virginians organized the American Colonization Society (ACS), which proposed a gradual

freeing of slaves, with masters receiving compensation. The liberated black men and women would then be transported out of the country and helped establish a new society of their own. The ACS received some private funding, some funding from Congress, and some funding from the legislatures of Virginia and Maryland. And it successfully arranged to have several groups of blacks transported out of the United States to the west coast of Africa, where in 1830 they established the nation of Liberia. (In 1846, Liberia   *Liberia* became an independent black republic, with its capital, Monrovia, named for the American president who had presided over the initial settlement.)

But the ACS was in the end a negligible force. There were far too many blacks in America in the nineteenth century to be transported to Africa by any conceivable program. And the ACS met resistance, in any case, from blacks themselves, many of whom were now three or more generations removed from Africa and, despite their loathing of slavery, had no wish to emigrate. They viewed themselves as entitled to fair treatment as Americans.

GARRISON AND ABOLITIONISM

In 1830, with slavery spreading ideology rapidly in the South and the antislavery movement seemingly on the verge of collapse, a new figure emerged: William Lloyd Garrison. Born in Massachusetts in 1805, Garrison was in the 1820s an assistant to the New Jersey Quaker Benjamin Lundy, who published the leading antislavery newspaper of the time. Garrison grew impatient with his employer's moderate tone, so in 1831 he returned to Boston to found his own newspaper, the *Liberator.*

Garrison's philosophy was so simple that it was genuinely revolutionary. Opponents of slavery, he said, should not talk about the evil influence of slavery on white society but rather the damage the system did to slaves. And they should, therefore, reject "gradualism" and demand the immediate abolition of slavery and the extension of all the rights of American citizenship to both slaves and free African Americans. Garrison   *Garrison's Antislavery Argument* wrote in a relentless, uncompromising tone. "I am aware," he wrote in the very first issue of the *Liberator,* "that many object to the severity of my language; but is there not cause for severity? I will be as harsh as truth, and as uncompromising as justice. . . . I am in earnest— I will not equivocate—I will not excuse—I will not retreat a single inch—and I will be heard."

Garrison soon attracted a large group of followers throughout the North, enough to enable him to found the New England Antislavery Society in 1832 and, a year later, after a convention in Philadelphia, the American Antislavery Society.

BLACK ABOLITIONISTS

Abolitionism had a particular appeal to the free black population of the North. These free blacks typically lived in conditions of poverty and oppression that were at times worse than those of their slave counterparts in the South. For all their problems, however, northern blacks were fiercely proud of their freedom and sensitive to the plight of those members of their race who remained in bondage. Many in the 1830s came to support Garrison. But they also rallied to leaders of their own.

Among the earliest black abolitionists was David Walker, who preceded even Garrison in publicly calling for an uncompromising opposition to slavery on moral   *David Walker* grounds. In 1829, Walker, a free black man who had moved from North Carolina to Boston, published a harsh pamphlet—*An Appeal to the Coloured Citizens of the World*—that described slavery as a sin that would draw divine punishment if not abolished. "America

THE ABOLITION OF SLAVERY

The United States formally abolished slavery through the Thirteenth Amendment of the Constitution in 1865, in the aftermath of the Civil War. But the effort to abolish slavery did not begin or end in North America. Emancipation in the United States was part of a worldwide antislavery movement that began in the late eighteenth century and continued through the end of the nineteenth.

The end of slavery, like the end of monarchies and established aristocracies, was one of the ideals of the Enlightenment, which inspired new concepts of individual freedom and political equality. As Enlightenment ideas spread throughout the Western world in the seventeenth and eighteenth centuries, people on both sides of the Atlantic began to examine slavery anew. Some Enlightenment thinkers, including some of the founders of the American republic, believed that freedom was appropriate for white people but not for people of color. But others came to believe that all human beings had an equal claim to liberty, and their views became the basis for an escalating series of antislavery movements.

Opponents of slavery first targeted the slave trade—the vast commerce in human beings that had grown up in the seventeenth

ANTISLAVERY MESSAGE The image of an enslaved man praying to God was popular in both British and American antislavery circles. It began as the seal of the Committee for the Abolition of the Slave Trade, a British abolitionist group formed in 1787, accompanied by the quote, "Am I not a man and a brother?" This example is embroidered on cloth; the image was also disseminated on medallions, jewelry, plates, tea caddies, tokens, and **snuffboxes.** (© Wilberforce House, Hull City Museums and Art Galleries, UK/Bridgeman Images)

and eighteenth centuries and had come to involve large parts of Europe, Africa, the Caribbean, and North and South America. In the aftermath of the revolutions in America, France, and Haiti, the attack on the slave trade quickly gained momentum. Its central figure was the English reformer William Wilberforce, who spent years attacking Britain's connection with the slave trade on moral and religious grounds. After the Haitian Revolution, Wilberforce and other antislavery activists denounced slavery on the grounds that its continuation would create more slave revolts. In 1807, he persuaded Parliament to pass a law ending the slave trade within the entire British Empire. The British example foreshadowed many other nations to make the slave trade illegal as well: the United States in 1808, France in 1814, Holland in 1817, Spain in 1845. Trading in slaves persisted within countries and colonies where slavery remained legal (including the United States), and some illegal slave trading continued throughout the Atlantic World. But the international sale of slaves steadily declined after 1807. The last known shipment of slaves across the Atlantic—from Africa to Cuba—occurred in 1867.

Ending the slave trade was a great deal easier than ending slavery itself, in which many people had major investments and on which much agriculture, commerce, and industry depended. But pressure to abolish slavery grew steadily throughout the nineteenth century, with Wilberforce once more helping to lead the international outcry against the institution. In Haiti, the slave revolts that began in 1791 eventually abolished not only slavery but also French rule. In some parts of South America, slavery came to an end with the overthrow of Spanish rule in the 1820s. Simón Bolívar, the great leader of Latin American independence, considered abolishing slavery an important part of his mission, freeing those who joined his armies and insisting on constitutional prohibitions of slavery in several of the constitutions he helped frame. In 1833, the British parliament passed a law abolishing slavery throughout the British Empire and compensated slave-owners for freeing their slaves. France abolished slavery in its empire, after years of agitation from abolitionists, in 1848. In the Caribbean, Spain followed Britain in slowly eliminating slavery from its colonies. Puerto Rico abolished slavery in 1873; and Cuba became the last colony in the Caribbean to end slavery, in 1886, in the face of increasing slave resistance and the declining profitability of slave-based plantations. Brazil was the last nation in the Americas, ending the system in 1888. The Brazilian military began to turn against slavery after the valiant participation of slaves in Brazil's war with Paraguay in the late 1860s; eventually, educated Brazilians began to oppose the system too, arguing that it obstructed economic and social progress.

In the United States, the power of world opinion—and the example of Wilberforce's movement in England—became an important influence on the abolitionist movement as it gained strength in the 1820s and 1830s. American abolitionism, in turn, helped reinforce the movements abroad. Frederick Douglass, the former American slave turned abolitionist, became a major figure in the international antislavery movement and was a much-admired and much-sought-after speaker in England and Europe in the 1840s and 1850s. No other nation paid such a terrible price for abolishing slavery as did the United States during its Civil War, but American emancipation was nevertheless a part of a worldwide movement toward emancipation.   •

UNDERSTAND, ANALYZE, & EVALUATE

1. Why did opponents of slavery focus first on ending the slave trade, rather than abolishing slavery itself? Why was ending the slave trade easier than ending slavery?
2. How do William Wilberforce's arguments against slavery compare with those of the abolitionists in the United States?

FUGITIVE SLAVE LAW CONVENTION Abolitionists gathered in Cazenovia, New York, in August 1850 to consider how to respond to the law recently passed by Congress requiring northern states to return fugitive slaves to their owners. Frederick Douglass is seated just to the left of the table in this photograph of some of the participants. The gathering was unusual among abolitionist gatherings in including substantial numbers of African Americans. (Digital image courtesy of the Getty's Open Content Program)

is more our country than it is the whites'—we have enriched it with our blood and tears." He urged slaves to "kill [their masters] or be killed."

Most black critics of slavery were somewhat less violent in their rhetoric but equally uncompromising in their commitment to abolition. Sojourner Truth, a freed black woman, emerged as a powerful and eloquent spokeswoman for the abolition of slavery in the *Sojourner Truth and Frederick Douglass* 1830s. The greatest African American abolitionist of all—and one of the most electrifying orators of his time, black or white—was Frederick Douglass. Born a slave in Maryland, Douglass escaped to Massachusetts in 1838, became an outspoken leader of antislavery sentiment, and spent two years lecturing in England. On his return to the United States in 1847, Douglass purchased his freedom from his Maryland owner and founded an antislavery newspaper, the *North Star,* in Rochester, New York. He achieved wide renown as well for his autobiography, *Narrative of the Life of Frederick Douglass* (1845), in which he presented a damning picture of slavery. Douglass demanded not only freedom but also full social and economic equality for blacks.

"What, to the American slave, is your 4th of July?" Douglass harshly asked in an Independence Day speech in Rochester, New York, in 1854. "I answer: a day that reveals to him, more than all other days in the year, the gross injustice and cruelty to which he is the constant victim. . . . There is not a nation on earth guilty of practices, more shocking and bloody, than are the people of these United States at this very hour."

Black abolitionists had been active for years before Douglass emerged as a leader of their cause. They held their first national convention in 1830. But with Douglass's leadership, they became a more influential force than any other African American. They began, too, to forge an alliance with white antislavery leaders such as Garrison.

ANTI-ABOLITIONISM

The rise of abolitionism provoked a powerful opposition. Almost all white southerners, of course, were bitterly hostile to the movement. But even in the North, abolitionists were a small, dissenting minority. Some whites feared that abolitionism would produce a destructive civil war. Others feared that it would lead to a great influx of free blacks into the North and displace white workers.

The result of such fears was an escalating wave of violence. A mob in Philadelphia attacked the abolitionist headquarters there in 1834, burned it to the ground, and began a bloody race riot. Another mob seized Garrison on the streets of Boston in 1835 and threatened to hang him. He was saved from death only by being locked *Violent Reprisals* in jail. Elijah Lovejoy, the editor of an abolitionist newspaper in Alton, Illinois, was victimized repeatedly and finally killed when he tried to defend his printing press from attack.

That so many men and women continued to embrace abolitionism in the face of such vicious opposition suggests that abolitionists were not people who took their political commitments lightly. They were strong-willed, passionate crusaders who displayed not only enormous courage and moral strength but, at times, a fervency that many of their contemporaries found deeply disturbing. The mobs were only the most violent expression of a hostility to abolitionism that many, perhaps most, other white Americans shared.

ABOLITIONISM DIVIDED

By the mid-1830s, the unity of the abolitionist crusade began to crack. One reason was the violence of the anti-abolitionists, which persuaded some members of the abolition movement that a more moderate approach was necessary. Another reason was the growing radicalism of William Lloyd Garrison, who shocked even many *Radicals and Moderates* of his own allies (including Frederick Douglass) by attacking not only slavery but the government itself. The Constitution, he said, was "a covenant with death and an agreement with hell." In 1840, Garrison precipitated a formal division within the American Antislavery Society by insisting that women be permitted to participate in the movement on terms of full equality. He continued after 1840 to arouse controversy with new and even more radical stands: an extreme pacifism that rejected even defensive wars; opposition to all forms of coercion—not just slavery, but prisons and asylums; and finally, in 1843, a call for northern disunion from the South.

From 1840 on, therefore, abolitionism moved in many channels and spoke with many different voices. The radical and uncompromising Garrisonians remained influential. But so were others who operated in more moderate ways, arguing that abolition could be accomplished only as the result of a long, patient, peaceful struggle. They appealed to the conscience of the slaveholders; and when that produced no results, they turned to political action, seeking to induce the northern states and the federal government to aid the cause. They joined the Garrisonians in helping runaway slaves find refuge in the North or in Canada through the underground railroad.

SENTIMENTAL NOVELS

"America is now wholly given over to a damned mob of scribbling women," Nathaniel Hawthorne complained in 1855, "and I should have no chance of success while the public taste is occupied with their trash." Hawthorne, one of the leading novelists of his time, was complaining about the most popular form of fiction in mid-nineteenth-century America—not his own dark and serious works, but the "sentimental novel," a genre of literature written and read mostly by middle-class women.

In an age when affluent women occupied primarily domestic roles, and in which finding a favorable marriage was the most important thing many women could do to secure or improve their lots in life, the sentimental novel gave voice to both female hopes and female anxieties. The plots of sentimental novels were usually filled with character-improving problems and domestic trials, but most of them ended with the heroine securely and happily married. They were phenomenally successful, many of them selling more than 100,000 copies each—far more than almost any other books of the time.

Sentimental heroines were almost always beautiful and endowed with specifically female qualities—"all the virtues," one novelist wrote, "that are founded in the sensibility of the heart: Pity, the attribute of angels, and friendship, the balm of life, delight to dwell in the female breast." Women were highly sensitive creatures, the sentimental writers believed, incapable of disguising their feelings, and subject to fainting, mysterious illnesses, trances, and, of course, tears—things rarely expected of men. But they were also capable of a kind of nurturing love and natural sincerity that was hard to find in the predominantly male public world. In Susan Warner's *The Wide, Wide World* (1850), for example, the heroine, a young girl named Ellen Montgomery, finds herself suddenly thrust into the "wide, wide world" of male competition after her father loses his fortune. She is unable to adapt to this world, but she is saved in the end when she is taken in by wealthy relatives, who will undoubtedly prepare her for a successful marriage. They restore to her the security and comfort to which she had been born and without which she seemed unable to thrive.

Sentimental novels accepted uncritically the popular assumptions about women's special needs and desires, and they offered stirring tales of how women satisfied them. But sentimental novels were not limited to romanticized images of female fulfillment through protection and marriage. They hinted as well at the increasing role of women in reform movements. Many such books portrayed women dealing with social and moral problems—and using their highly developed female sensibilities to help other women escape from their troubles. Women were particularly suitable for such reform work, the writers implied, because they were specially gifted at helping and nurturing others.

The most famous sentimental novelist of the nineteenth century was Harriet Beecher Stowe. Most of her books—*The Minister's Wooing, My Wife and I, We and Our Neighbors,* and others—portrayed the travails and ultimate triumphs of women as they became wives, mothers, and hostesses. But Stowe was and remains best known for her 1852 antislavery novel,

135,000 SETS, 270,000 VOLUMES SOLD.

UNCLE TOM'S CABIN

FOR SALE HERE.

AN EDITION FOR THE MILLION, COMPLETE IN 1 Vol., PRICE 37 1-2 CENTS.
" " IN GERMAN, IN 1 Vol., PRICE 50 CENTS.
" " IN 2 Vols., CLOTH, 6 PLATES, PRICE $1.50.
SUPERB ILLUSTRATED EDITION, IN 1 Vol., WITH 153 ENGRAVINGS,
PRICES FROM $2.50 TO $5.00.

The Greatest Book of the Age.

UNCLE TOM'S CABIN *Uncle Tom's Cabin* did much to inflame public opinion in both the North and the South in the last years before the Civil War. When Abraham Lincoln was introduced to Stowe once in the White House, he reportedly said to her: "So you are the little lady that has brought this great war." At the time, however, Stowe was equally well known as one of the most successful American writers of sentimental novels. (© Bettmann/Corbis)

Uncle Tom's Cabin, one of the most influential books ever published in America. As a story about slavery, and about an aging black man—Uncle Tom—who is unfailingly submissive to his white masters, it is in many ways very different from her other novels. But *Uncle Tom's Cabin* is a sentimental novel, too. Stowe's critique of slavery is based on her belief in the importance of domestic values and family security. Slavery's violation of those values, and its denial of that security, is what made it so abhorrent to her. The simple, decent Uncle Tom faces many of the same dilemmas that the female heroines of other sentimental novels encounter in their struggles to find security and tranquillity in their lives.

Another way in which women were emerging from their domestic sphere was in becoming consumers of the expanding products of America's industrializing economy. The female characters in sentimental novels searched not just for love, security, and social justice; they also searched for luxury and for the pleasure of buying some favored item. Susan Warner illustrated this aspect of the culture of the sentimental novel—and the desires of the women who read them—in *The Wide, Wide World,* in her description of the young Ellen Montgomery in an elegant bookstore, buying a Bible: "Such beautiful Bibles she had never seen; she pored in ecstasy over their varieties of type and binding, and was very evidently in love with them all." •

UNDERSTAND, ANALYZE, & EVALUATE

1. How did the lives of the heroines of the sentimental novels compare with the lives of real women of the nineteenth century? What made them so popular?
2. How did the sentimental novels encourage women's participation in public life? Did the novels reinforce prevailing attitudes toward women or broaden the perception of women's "proper role"?
3. *Uncle Tom's Cabin* is probably one of the best-known works of American fiction. Why was this novel so much more powerful than other sentimental novels? Why has it endured?

The abolitionists also helped fund the legal battle over the Spanish slave vessel, *Amistad.* After the Supreme Court (in *Prigg v. Pennsylvania,* 1842) ruled   **The Amistad Case** that states need not aid in enforcing the 1793 law requiring the return of fugitive slaves to their owners, abolitionists won passage in several northern states of "personal liberty laws," which forbade state officials to assist in the capture and return of runaways. The antislavery societies also petitioned Congress to abolish slavery in places where the federal government had jurisdiction—in the territories and in the District of Columbia—and to prohibit the interstate slave trade.

Antislavery sentiment underlay the formation in 1840 of the Liberty Party, which ran Kentucky antislavery leader James G. Birney for president. But this party and its successors never campaigned for outright abolition. They stood instead for "Free Soil," for keeping slavery out of the territories. Some Free-Soilers were concerned about the welfare of blacks; others were people who cared nothing about slavery but simply wanted to keep the West a country for whites. But the Free-Soil position would ultimately do what abolitionism never could: attract the support of large numbers of the white population of the North.

The slow progress of abolitionism drove some critics of slavery to embrace more drastic measures. A few began to advocate violence. A group of prominent abolitionists in New England, for example, funneled money and arms to John Brown for his bloody uprisings in Kansas and Virginia. Others attempted to arouse public anger through propaganda.

The most powerful of all abolitionist propaganda was Harriet Beecher Stowe's novel *Uncle Tom's Cabin,* published as a book in 1852. It sold more than 300,000 copies within a year of publication and was reissued again and again. It succeeded in bringing the mes-

Uncle Tom's Cabin   sage of abolitionism to an enormous new audience—not only those who read the book but also those who watched countless theater companies reenact it across the nation. An unconfirmed statement by Lincoln to Stowe has been widely publicized: "Is this the little woman who made the great war?" Reviled throughout the South, Stowe became a hero to many in the North. And in both regions, her novel helped inflame sectional tensions to a new level of passion.

Stowe's novel emerged not just out of abolitionist politics but also a popular tradition of sentimental novels written by, and largely for, women. (See "Patterns of Popular Culture: Sentimental Novels.") Stowe artfully integrated the emotional conventions of the sentimental novel with the political ideas of the abolitionist movement, and to sensational effect. Her novel, by embedding the antislavery message within a familiar literary form in which women were the key protagonists serving to improve society, brought that message to an enormous new audience.

Even divided, abolitionism remained a powerful influence on the life of the nation. Only a relatively small number of people before the Civil War ever accepted the abolitionist position that slavery must be entirely eliminated in a single stroke. But the crusade that Garrison had launched, and that thousands of committed men and women kept alive for three decades, was a constant, visible reminder of how deeply the institution of slavery was dividing America.

CONCLUSION

The rapidly changing society of antebellum America encouraged interest in a wide range of reforms. Writers, artists, intellectuals, and others drew heavily from new European notions of personal liberation and fulfillment—a set of ideas often known as romanticism. But they also strove to create a truly American culture. The literary and artistic life of the nation expressed the rising interest in personal liberation—in giving individuals the freedom to explore their own souls and to find in nature a full expression of their divinity. It also called attention to some of the nation's glaring social problems.

Reformers, too, made use of the romantic belief in the divinity of the individual. They flocked to religious revivals, worked on behalf of such "moral" reforms as temperance, supported education, and articulated some of the first statements of modern feminism. And in the North, they rallied against slavery. Out of this growing antislavery movement emerged a new and powerful phenomenon: abolitionism, which insisted on immediate emancipation of slaves. The abolitionist movement galvanized much of the North and contributed greatly to the growing schism between North and South.

KEY TERMS/PEOPLE/PLACES/EVENTS

Dorothea Dix 283	Jarena Lee 286	Seneca Falls Convention 283
Elizabeth Cady Stanton 283	Joseph Smith 278	Shakers 277
Frederick Douglass 290	Liberia 287	Sojourner Truth 290
Harriet Beecher Stowe 283	Lucretia Mott 283	Susan B. Anthony 283
Henry David Thoreau 276	Nathaniel Hawthorne 277	temperance 280
Herman Melville 274	Oneida "Perfectionists" 277	transcendentalism 275
Horace Mann 282	Ralph Waldo Emerson 276	Walt Whitman 274
Hudson River school 273	Rebecca Cox Jackson 286	William Lloyd Garrison 287

RECALL AND REFLECT

1. What is "romanticism" and how was it expressed in American literature and art?
2. How did religion affect reform movements, and what was the effect of these movements on religion?
3. What were the aims of the women's movement of the nineteenth century? How successful were women in achieving these goals?
4. What arguments and strategies did the abolitionists use in their struggle to end slavery? Who opposed them and why?

13 | THE IMPENDING CRISIS

LOOKING WESTWARD
EXPANSION AND WAR
THE SECTIONAL DEBATE
THE CRISES OF THE 1850s

LOOKING AHEAD

1. How did the annexation of western territories intensify the conflict over slavery and lead to deeper divisions between the North and the South?

2. What compromises attempted to resolve the conflicts over the expansion of slavery into new territories? To what degree were these compromises successful? Why did they eventually fail to resolve the differences between the North and the South?

3. What were the major arguments for and against slavery and its expansion into new territories?

UNTIL THE 1840s, THE TENSIONS between the North and the South remained relatively contained. Had no new sectional issues arisen, it is possible that the two sections might have resolved their differences peaceably over time. But new issues did arise. From the North came the strident and increasingly powerful abolitionist movement. From the South came a newly militant defense of slavery and the way of life it supported. And from the West, most significantly, emerged a series of controversies that would ultimately tear the fragile Union apart.

LOOKING WESTWARD

More than a million square miles of new territory came under the control of the United States during the 1840s. By the end of the decade, the nation possessed all the territory of the present-day United States except Alaska, Hawaii, and a few relatively small areas acquired later through border adjustments. Many factors accounted for this great new wave of expansion, but one of the most important was an ideology known as "**Manifest Destiny.**"

Manifest Destiny

Manifest Destiny reflected both the growing pride that characterized American nationalism in the mid-nineteenth century and the idealistic vision of social perfection that fueled so much of the reform energy of the time. It rested on the idea that America was destined—by God and by history—to expand its boundaries over a vast area.

By the 1840s, publicized by the rise of inexpensive newspapers dubbed "penny press," the idea of Manifest Destiny had spread throughout the nation. Some advocates of Manifest Destiny envisioned a vast new "empire of liberty" that would include Canada, Mexico, Caribbean and Pacific islands, and ultimately (for the most ardent believers) much of the rest of the world. Countering such bombast were politicians such as Henry Clay and others, who warned that territorial expansion would reopen the painful controversy over slavery. Their voices, however, could not compete with the enthusiasm over expansion in the 1840s, which began with the issues of Texas and Oregon.

Americans in Texas

Twice in the 1820s, the United States had offered to purchase Texas from the Republic of Mexico. Mexico indignantly refused and instead enacted a colonization law that

TIME LINE

1836
Texas declares independence from Mexico

1844
Polk elected president

1846
Oregon boundary dispute settled

U.S. declares war on Mexico

Wilmot Proviso

1848
Treaty of Guadalupe Hidalgo

Taylor elected president

California gold rush begins

1850
Compromise of 1850

Taylor dies; Fillmore becomes president

1852
Pierce elected president

1853
Gadsden Purchase

1854
Kansas-Nebraska Act

Republican Party formed

1855–1856
"Bleeding Kansas"

1856
Buchanan elected president

1857
Dred Scott decision

1858
Lecompton constitution defeated

1859
John Brown raids Harpers Ferry

1860
Lincoln elected president

offered cheap land and a four-year exemption from taxes to any American willing to move into Texas. Thousands of Americans flocked into the region, the great majority of them white southerners and their slaves, intent on establishing cotton plantations. By 1830, there were about 7,000 Americans living in Texas, more than twice the number of Mexicans there.

Stephen F. Austin Most of the settlers came to Texas through the efforts of American intermediaries, who received sizable land grants from Mexico in return for bringing new residents into the region. The most successful was Stephen F. Austin, a young immigrant from Missouri who established the first legal American settlement in Texas in 1822. Austin and others created centers of power in the region that competed with the Mexican government. Not surprisingly, in 1830 the Mexican government barred any further American immigration into the region. But Americans kept flowing into Texas anyway.

Santa Anna Seizes Power Friction between the American settlers and the Mexican government was already growing in the mid-1830s when instability in Mexico itself drove General Antonio López de Santa Anna to seize power as a dictator. He increased the powers of the Mexican government at the expense of the state governments, a measure that Texans from the United States assumed was aimed specifically at them. Sporadic fighting between Americans and Mexicans in Texas erupted in 1835. In 1836, the American settlers defiantly proclaimed their independence from Mexico.

The Alamo Santa Anna led a large army into Texas, where the American settlers were divided into several squabbling factions. Mexican forces annihilated an American garrison at the Alamo mission in San Antonio after a famous, if futile, defense by a group of Texas "patriots" that included, among others, the renowned frontiersman and former Tennessee congressman Davy Crockett. Another garrison at Goliad suffered substantially the same fate. By the end of 1836, the rebellion appeared to have collapsed.

But General Sam Houston managed to keep a small force together. And on April 21, 1836, at the Battle of San Jacinto, he defeated the Mexican army and took Santa Anna prisoner. Santa Anna, under pressure from his captors, signed a treaty giving Texas independence.

Status of Tejanos A number of Mexican residents of Texas (*Tejanos*) had fought with the Americans in the revolution. But soon after Texas won its independence, their

THE LONE STAR FLAG Texas was an independent republic for nine years. The tattered banner pictured here was one of the republic's original flags. (© Granger, NYC—All Rights Reserved.)

positions grew difficult. The Americans did not trust them, feared that they were agents of the Mexican government, and in effect drove many of them out of the new republic. Most of those who stayed had to settle for a politically and economically subordinate status.

One of the first acts of the new president of Texas, Sam Houston, was to send a delegation to Washington with an offer to join the Union. But President Jackson, fearing that adding a large new slave state to the Union would increase sectional tensions, blocked annexation and even delayed recognizing the new republic until 1837.

Spurned by the United States, Texas cast out on its own. England and France, concerned about the surging power of the United States, saw Texas as a possible check on its growth and began forging ties with the new republic. At that point, President Tyler persuaded Texas to apply for statehood again in 1844. But northern senators, fearing the admission of a new slave state, defeated it.

Oregon

Control of what was known as "Oregon country," in the Pacific Northwest, was also a major political issue in the 1840s. Both Britain and the United States claimed sovereignty in the region. Unable to resolve their conflicting claims diplomatically, they agreed in an 1818 treaty to allow citizens of each country equal access to the territory. *Joint Occupation* This "joint occupation" continued for twenty years.

At the time of the treaty neither Britain nor the United States had established much of a presence in Oregon country. White settlement in the region consisted largely of scattered American and Canadian fur trading posts. But American interest in Oregon grew substantially in the 1820s and 1830s.

By the mid-1840s, white Americans substantially outnumbered the British in Oregon. They had also devastated much of the Indian population, in part through a measles epidemic that spread through the Cayuse Indians. American settlements were sprouting up along the Pacific Coast, and the new settlers were urging the United States government to take possession of the disputed Oregon country.

The Westward Migration

The migrations into Texas and Oregon were part of a larger movement that took hundreds of thousands of white and black Americans into the far western regions of the continent between 1840 and 1860. The largest number of migrants were from the Old Northwest. Most were relatively young people who had traveled in family groups. Few were wealthy, but many were relatively prosperous. Poor people who could not afford the trip on their own usually had to join other families or groups as laborers—men as farm or ranch hands; women as domestic servants, teachers, or, in some cases, prostitutes. Groups heading for areas where mining or lumbering was the principal economic activity consisted mostly of men. Those heading for farming regions traveled mainly as families.

Migrants generally gathered in one of several major depots in Iowa and Missouri (Independence, St. Joseph, or Council Bluffs), joined a wagon train led by hired guides, and set off with their belongings piled in covered wagons, livestock trailing behind. The major route west was the 2,000-mile Oregon Trail, which stretched from *The Oregon Trail* Independence across the Great Plains and through the South Pass of the Rocky Mountains. From there, migrants moved north into Oregon or south (along the California Trail) to the northern California coast. Other migrations moved along the Santa Fe Trail, southwest from Independence into New Mexico.

However they traveled, overland migrants faced an arduous journey. Most lasted five or six months (from May to November), and travelers always felt the pressure to get through the Rockies before the snows began, often not an easy task given the very slow pace of most wagon trains. To save their horses for pulling the wagons, they walked most of the way. Diseases, including cholera, decimated and slowed many groups traveling west. The women, who did the cooking and washing at the end of the day, generally worked harder than the men, who usually rested when the caravan halted.

Despite the traditional image of westward migrants as rugged individualists, most travelers found the journey a communal experience. That was partly because many

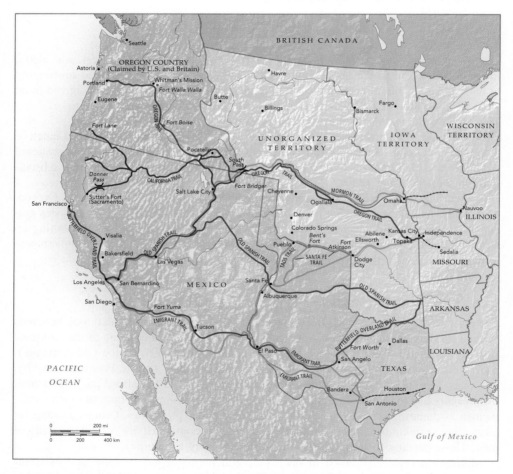

WESTERN TRAILS IN 1860 As settlers began the long process of exploring and establishing farms and businesses in the West, major trails began to develop to facilitate travel and trade between the region and the more thickly settled areas to the east. Note how many of the trails led to California and how few of them led into any of the far northern regions of United States territory. Note, too, the important towns and cities that grew up along these trails. • *What forms of transportation later performed the functions that these trails performed prior to the Civil War?*

expeditions consisted of groups of friends, neighbors, or relatives who had decided to pull up stakes and move west together. And it was also because of the intensity of the journey. It was a rare expedition in which there were not some internal conflicts before the trip was over; but those who made the journey successfully generally learned the value of cooperation.

Only a few expeditions experienced Indian attacks. In the twenty years before the Civil War, fewer than 400 migrants (slightly more than one-tenth of 1 percent) died in conflicts with the tribes. In fact, Indians were usually more helpful than dangerous to the white migrants. They often served as guides, and they traded horses, clothing, and fresh food with the travelers.

EXPANSION AND WAR

The growing number of white Americans in the lands west of the Mississippi put great pressure on the government in Washington to annex Texas, Oregon, and other territory. And in the 1840s, these expansionist pressures helped push the United States into war.

THE DEMOCRATS AND EXPANSION

In preparing for the election of 1844, the two leading candidates—Henry Clay of the Whig Party and Martin Van Buren of the Democratic Party—both tried to avoid taking a stand on the controversial annexation of Texas. Sentiment for expansion was mild within the Whig Party, and Clay had no difficulty securing the nomination despite his noncommittal position. But many southern Democrats strongly supported annexation, and the party passed over Van Buren to nominate James K. Polk, who shared their enthusiasm.

Polk had represented Tennessee in the House of Representatives for fourteen years, four of them as Speaker, and had subsequently served as governor. But by 1844, he had been out of public office for three years. What made his victory possible was his support for the position, expressed in the Democratic platform, "that the re-occupation of Oregon and the re-annexation of Texas at the earliest practicable period are great American measures." By combining the Oregon and Texas questions, the Democrats hoped *Polk Elected* to appeal to both northern and southern expansionists—and they did. Polk carried the election, 170 electoral votes to 105.

Polk entered office with a clear set of goals and with plans for attaining them. John Tyler accomplished the first of Polk's ambitions for him in the last days of his own presidency. Interpreting the election returns as a mandate for the annexation of Texas, the outgoing president won congressional approval for it in February 1845. That December, Texas became a state.

Polk himself resolved the Oregon question. The British minister in Washington brusquely rejected a compromise that would establish the United *Compromise over Oregon* States–Canadian border at the 49th parallel. Incensed, Polk again asserted the American claim to all of Oregon. There was loose talk of war on both sides of the Atlantic—talk that in the United States often took the form of the bellicose slogan "Fifty-four forty or fight!" (a reference to where the Americans hoped to draw the northern boundary of their part of Oregon). But neither country really wanted war. Finally, the British government accepted Polk's original proposal to divide the territory at the 49th parallel. On June 15, 1846, the Senate approved a treaty that fixed the boundary there.

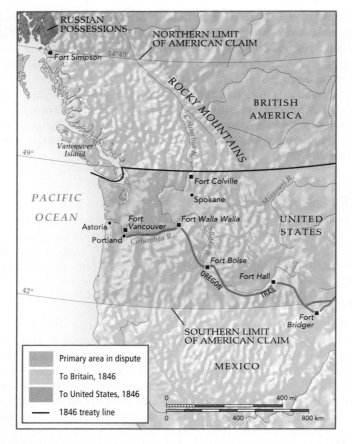

THE OREGON BOUNDARY, 1846   One of the last major boundary disputes between the United States and Great Britain involved the territory known as Oregon—the large region on the Pacific Coast north of California (which in 1846 was still part of Mexico). For years, America and Britain had overlapping claims on the territory. The British claimed land as far south as the present state of Oregon, while the Americans claimed land extending well into what is now Canada. Tensions over the Oregon border at times rose to the point that many Americans were demanding war, some using the slogan "Fifty-four forty or fight!" referring to the latitude of the northernmost point of the American claim.   •   *How did President James K. Polk defuse the crisis?*

THE SOUTHWEST AND CALIFORNIA

One of the reasons the Senate and the president had agreed so readily to the British offer to settle the Oregon question was that their attention was turning to new tensions emerging in the Southwest. As soon as the United States admitted Texas to statehood in 1845, the Mexican government broke diplomatic relations with Washington. Mexican–American relations grew still worse when a dispute developed over the boundary between Texas *Texas Boundary Disputed*   and Mexico. Texans claimed the Rio Grande as their western and southern border. Mexico, although still not conceding the loss of Texas, argued nevertheless that the border had always been the Nueces River, to the north of the Rio Grande. Polk accepted the Texas claim, and in the summer of 1845 he sent a small army under General Zachary Taylor to Texas to protect the new state against a possible Mexican invasion.

Part of the area in dispute was New Mexico, whose Spanish and Indian residents lived in a multiracial society that by the 1840s had endured for nearly a century and a half. In the 1820s, the Mexican government had invited American traders into the *New Mexico* region, hoping to speed development of the province. But New Mexico, like Texas, soon became more American than Mexican, particularly after a flourishing commerce developed between Santa Fe and Independence, Missouri.

Americans were also increasing their interest in California. In this vast region lived members of several western Indian tribes and perhaps 7,000 Mexicans. Gradually, however, white Americans began to arrive: first maritime traders and captains of Pacific whaling ships, who stopped to barter goods or buy supplies; then merchants, who established stores, imported goods, and developed a profitable trade with the Mexicans *California* and Indians; and finally pioneering farmers, who entered California from the east and settled in the Sacramento Valley. Some of these new settlers began to dream of bringing California into the United States.

President Polk soon came to share their dream and committed himself to acquiring both New Mexico and California for the United States. At the same time that he dispatched the troops under Taylor to Texas, he sent secret instructions to the commander of the Pacific naval squadron to seize the California ports if Mexico declared war. Representatives of the president quietly informed Americans in California that the United States would respond sympathetically to a revolt against Mexican authority there.

THE MEXICAN WAR

Having appeared to prepare for war, Polk turned to diplomacy by dispatching a special minister to try to buy off the Mexicans. But Mexican leaders rejected the American offer to purchase the disputed territories. On January 13, 1846, as soon as he heard the news, Polk ordered Taylor's army in Texas to move across the Nueces River, where *War Declared* it had been stationed, to the Rio Grande. For months, the Mexicans refused to fight. But finally, according to disputed American accounts, some Mexican troops crossed the Rio Grande and attacked a unit of American soldiers. On May 13, 1846, Congress declared war by votes of 40 to 2 in the Senate and 174 to 14 in the House.

Whig critics charged that Polk had deliberately maneuvered the country into the conflict and had staged the border incident that had precipitated the declaration. Many opponents also claimed that Polk had settled for less than he should have because he was preoccupied with Mexico. Opposition intensified as the war continued and as the public became aware of the rising casualties and expense.

Victory did not come as quickly as Polk had hoped. The president ordered Taylor to cross the Rio Grande, seize parts of northeastern Mexico, beginning with the city of Monterrey, and then march on to Mexico City itself. Taylor captured Monterrey in September 1846, but he let the Mexican garrison evacuate without pursuit. Polk now began to fear that Taylor lacked the tactical skill for the planned advance against Mexico City. He also feared that, if successful, Taylor would become a powerful political rival (as, in fact, he did).

In the meantime, Polk ordered other offensives against New Mexico and California. In the summer of 1846, a small army under Colonel Stephen W. Kearny captured Santa Fe with no opposition. He then proceeded to California, where he joined a conflict already in progress that was being staged jointly by American settlers, a well-armed exploring party led by John C. Frémont, and the American navy: the so-called Bear Flag Revolt. Kearny *Bear Flag Revolt*

THE MEXICAN WAR, 1846–1848 Shortly after the settlement of the Oregon border dispute with Britain, the United States entered a war with Mexico over another contested border. This map shows the movement of Mexican and American troops during the fighting, which extended from the area around Santa Fe south to Mexico City and west to the coast of California. Note the American use of its naval forces to facilitate a successful assault on Mexico City, and others on the coast of California. Note, too, how unsuccessful the Mexican forces were in their battles with the United States. Mexico won only one battle—a relatively minor one at San Pasqual near San Diego—in the war. • *How did President Polk deal with the popular clamor for the United States to annex much of present-day Mexico?*

brought the disparate American forces together under his command, and by the autumn of 1846 he had completed the conquest of California.

But Mexico still refused to concede defeat. At this point, Polk and General Winfield Scott, the commanding general of the army and its finest soldier, launched a bold new campaign. Scott assembled an army at Tampico, which the navy transported down the Mexican coast to Veracruz. With an army that never numbered more than 14,000, Scott advanced 260 miles along the Mexican National Highway toward Mexico City, kept American casualties low, and never lost a battle before finally seizing the Mexican capital. A new Mexican government took power and announced its willingness to negotiate a peace treaty.

President Polk continued to encourage those who demanded that the United States annex much of Mexico itself. At the same time, he was growing anxious to get the war finished quickly. Polk sent a special presidential envoy, Nicholas Trist, to negotiate a settlement. On February 2, 1848, he reached agreement with the new Mexican government *Treaty of Guadalupe Hidalgo* on the Treaty of Guadalupe Hidalgo, by which Mexico agreed to cede California and New Mexico to the United States and acknowledge the Rio Grande as the boundary of Texas. In return, the United States promised to assume any financial

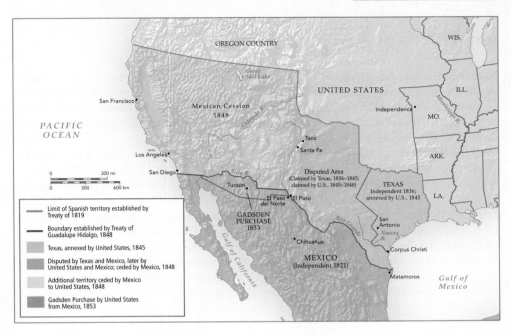

SOUTHWESTERN EXPANSION, 1845–1853 The annexation of much of what is now Texas in 1845, the much larger territorial gains won in the Mexican War in 1848, and the purchase of additional land from Mexico in 1853 completed the present continental border of the United States. • *What great event shortly after the Mexican War contributed to a rapid settlement of California by migrants from the eastern United States?*

claims its new citizens had against Mexico and to pay the Mexicans $15 million. Trist had obtained most of Polk's original demands, but he had not satisfied the new, more expansive dreams of acquiring additional territory in Mexico itself. Polk angrily claimed that Trist had violated his instructions, but he soon realized that he had no choice but to accept the treaty to silence a bitter battle growing between ardent expansionists demanding the annexation of "All Mexico!" and antislavery leaders charging that the expansionists were conspiring to extend slavery to new realms. The president submitted the Trist treaty to the Senate, which approved it by a vote of 38 to 14.

THE SECTIONAL DEBATE

James Polk tried to be a president whose policies transcended sectional divisions. But conciliating the sections was becoming an ever more difficult task, and Polk gradually earned the enmity of northerners and westerners alike, who believed his policies favored the South at their expense.

SLAVERY AND THE TERRITORIES

In August 1846, while the Mexican War had been still in progress, Polk had asked Congress to appropriate $2 million for purchasing peace with Mexico. Immediately arising was the question of whether slavery would be allowed in any newly acquired territory.

CONSIDER THE SOURCE

WILMOT PROVISO, AUGUST 8, 1846

To counter rising tensions over the question of whether territory acquired from Mexico would be slave or free, Representative David Wilmot of Pennsylvania spearheaded an effort to ban slavery from that territory forever. His amendment passed the House twice but failed in the Senate, because of heated opposition from northern pro-slavery politicians.

Provided, that, as an express and fundamental condition to the acquisition of any territory from the Republic of Mexico by the United States, by virtue of any treaty which may be negotiated between them, and to the use by the Executive of the moneys herein appropriated, neither slavery nor involuntary servitude shall ever exist in any part of said territory, except for crime, whereof the party shall first be duly convicted.

UNDERSTAND, ANALYZE, & EVALUATE

1. What condition did the proviso impose on future territory?
2. Why did this simple provision prove so controversial? What were its consequences?
3. Do you recognize the last two lines of the provision? Where do they later reappear?

Representative David Wilmot of Pennsylvania, an antislavery Democrat, introduced an amendment to the appropriation bill prohibiting slavery in any territory acquired from *Wilmot Proviso* Mexico. The so-called Wilmot Proviso passed the House but failed in the Senate. (See "Consider the Source: Wilmot Proviso, August 8, 1846.") Southern militants contended that all Americans had equal rights in the new territories, including the right to move their slaves (which they considered property) into them.

As the sectional debate intensified, President Polk supported a proposal to extend the Missouri Compromise line through the new territories to the Pacific Coast, banning slavery north of the line and permitting it south of the line. Others supported a plan, originally known as "squatter sovereignty" and later by the more dignified phrase "**popular sovereignty**," that would allow the people of each territory to decide the status of slavery there. The debate over these various proposals dragged on for many months.

The presidential campaign of 1848 dampened the controversy for a time as both Democrats and Whigs tried to avoid the slavery question. When Polk, in poor health, declined to run again, the Democrats nominated Lewis Cass of Michigan, a dull, aging party regular. The Whigs nominated General Zachary Taylor of Louisiana, hero of the Mexican War but a man with no political experience. Opponents of slavery found the choice of candidates unsatisfying, and out of their discontent emerged the new Free-Soil Party, whose candidate was former president Martin Van Buren.

Taylor won a narrow victory. But while Van Buren failed to carry a single state, he polled an impressive 291,000 votes (10 percent of the total), and the Free-Soilers elected *Free-Soil Party* ten members to Congress. The emergence of the Free-Soil Party as an important political force signaled the inability of the existing parties to contain the political passions slavery was creating. It was also an early sign of the coming collapse of the second party system in the 1850s.

The California Gold Rush

By the time Taylor took office, the pressure to resolve the question of slavery in the far western territories had become more urgent as a result of dramatic events in California. In January 1848, a foreman working in a sawmill owned by John Sutter (one of California's leading ranchers) found traces of gold in the foothills of the Sierra Nevada. Within months, news of the discovery had spread throughout the nation and much of the world. Almost immediately, hundreds of thousands of people began flocking to California in a frantic search for gold.

The atmosphere in California at the peak of the gold rush was one of almost crazed excitement and greed. Most migrants to the Far West prepared carefully before making the journey. But the California migrants (known as "Forty-niners") threw   *"Forty-niners"* caution to the winds, abandoning farms, jobs, homes, and families, piling onto ships and flooding the overland trails. The overwhelming majority of the Forty-niners (perhaps 95 percent) were white men, and the society they created in California was unusually fluid and volatile because of the almost total absence of white women, children, or families.

The gold rush also attracted some of the first Chinese migrants to the western United States. News of the discoveries created great excitement in China,   *Chinese Migrants* particularly in impoverished areas. It was, of course, extremely difficult for a poor Chinese peasant to get to America; but many young, adventurous people (mostly men) decided to go anyway—in the belief that they could quickly become rich and then return to China.

LOOKING FOR GOLD   Finding gold in California was not, for the most part, a task for lone prospectors. More common were teams of people who together built elaborate mining technologies. (© Granger, NYC—All Rights Reserved.)

Emigration brokers loaned many migrants money for passage to California, which the migrants were to pay off out of their earnings there.

The gold rush produced a serious labor shortage in California, as many male workers left their jobs and flocked to the gold fields. That created opportunities for many people who needed work (including Chinese immigrants). It also led to a frenzied exploitation *Indians Exploited*   of Indians that resembled slavery in all but name. A new state law permitted the arrest of "loitering" or orphaned Indians and their assignment to a term of "indentured" labor.

The gold rush was of critical importance to the growth of California, but not for the reasons most of the migrants hoped. There was substantial gold in the hills of the Sierra Nevada, and many people got rich from it. But only a tiny fraction of the Forty-niners ever found gold. Some disappointed migrants returned home after a while. But many stayed in California and swelled both the agricultural and urban populations of the territory. By 1856, for example, San Francisco—whose population had been 1,000 before the gold rush—was the home of over 50,000 people. By the early 1850s, California, which had always had a diverse population, had become even more heterogeneous. The gold rush had attracted not just white Americans but also Europeans, Chinese, South Americans, Mexicans, free blacks, and slaves who accompanied southern migrants. Conflicts over gold intersected with racial and ethnic tensions to make the territory an unusually turbulent place.

Rising Sectional Tensions

Zachary Taylor believed statehood could become the solution to the issue of slavery in the territories. As long as the new lands remained territories, the federal government was responsible for deciding the fate of slavery within them. But once they became states, he thought, their own governments would be able to settle the slavery question. At Taylor's urging, California quickly adopted a constitution that prohibited slavery, and in December 1849 Taylor asked Congress to admit California as a free state.

Congress balked, in part because of several other controversies concerning slavery that were complicating the debate. One was the effort of antislavery forces to abolish *Factors in Statehood Debate*   slavery in the District of Columbia. Another was the emergence of personal liberty laws in northern states, which barred courts and police officers from returning runaway slaves to their owners in defiance of the Constitution's Fugitive Slave Clause. But the biggest obstacle to the president's program was the white South's fear that new free states would be added to the northern majority. The number of free and slave states was equal in 1849—fifteen each. The admission of California would upset the balance; and New Mexico, Oregon, and Utah—all candidates for statehood—might upset it further.

Even many otherwise moderate southern leaders now began to talk about secession from the Union. In the North, every state legislature but one adopted a resolution demanding the prohibition of slavery in the territories.

The Compromise of 1850

Faced with this mounting crisis, moderates and unionists spent the winter of 1849–1850 *Clay's Compromise Debated*   trying to frame a great compromise. The aging Henry Clay, who was spearheading the effort, believed that no compromise could last unless it settled all

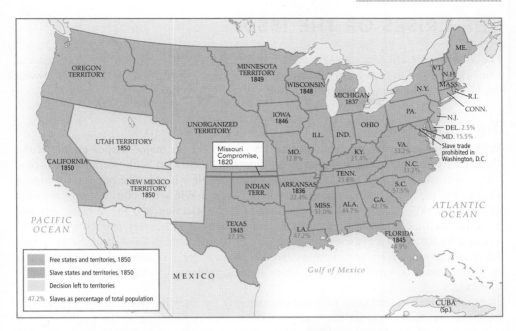

SLAVE AND FREE TERRITORIES UNDER THE COMPROMISE OF 1850   The acquisition of vast new western lands raised the question of the status of slavery in new territories organized for statehood by the United States. Tension between the North and the South on this question led in 1850 to a great compromise, forged in Congress, to settle this dispute. The compromise allowed California to join the Union as a free state and introduced the concept of "popular sovereignty" for other new territories. • *How well did the Compromise of 1850 work?*

the issues in dispute. As a result, he took several measures that had been proposed separately, combined them into a single piece of legislation, and presented it to the Senate on January 29, 1850. Among the bill's provisions were the admission of California as a free state; the formation of territorial governments in the rest of the lands acquired from Mexico, without restrictions on slavery; the abolition of the slave trade, but not slavery itself, in the District of Columbia; and a new and more effective fugitive slave law. These resolutions launched a debate that raged for seven months.

Finally in midyear, the climate for compromise improved. President Taylor suddenly died, and Vice President Millard Fillmore of New York took his place. Fillmore, who understood the important of flexibility, supported the compromise and persuaded northern Whigs to do so as well. Where the Old Guard's omnibus bill had failed, Stephen A. Douglas, a Democratic senator from Illinois, proposed breaking up the   *Stephen A. Douglas* bill. Thus representatives of different sections could support those elements of the compromise they liked and oppose those they did not. Douglas also gained support with complicated backroom deals linking the compromise to such nonideological matters as the sale of government bonds and the construction of railroads. As a result of his efforts, by mid-September Congress had enacted all the components of the compromise.

The Compromise of 1850 was a victory of individual self-interest. Still, members of Congress hailed the measure as a triumph of statesmanship; and Millard Fillmore, signing it, called it a just settlement of the sectional problem, "in its character final and irrevocable."

THE CRISES OF THE 1850s

For a few years after its passage, the Compromise of 1850 seemed to work. Sectional conflict appeared to fade amid booming prosperity and growth. But the tensions between the North and the South never really disappeared.

THE UNEASY TRUCE

With the run-up to the presidential election of 1852, both major parties endorsed the Compromise of 1850 and nominated candidates unidentified with sectional passions. *Franklin Pierce Elected* The Democrats chose the obscure New Hampshire politician Franklin Pierce, and the Whigs chose the military hero General Winfield Scott. But the sectional question quickly became a divisive influence in the election and the Whigs were the principal victims. They suffered massive defections from antislavery members who were angered by the party's evasiveness on the issue. Many of them flocked to the Free-Soil Party, whose antislavery presidential candidate, John P. Hale, repudiated the Compromise of 1850. The divisions among the Whigs helped produce a victory for the Democrats in 1852.

Franklin Pierce attempted to maintain harmony by avoiding divisive issues, particularly slavery. But it was an impossible task. Northern opposition to the Fugitive Slave Act intensified quickly after 1850. Mobs formed in some northern cities to prevent *Defiance of Fugitive Slave Act* enforcement of the fugitive slave law, and several northern states also passed their own laws barring the deportation of fugitive slaves. White southerners watched with growing anger and alarm as the one element of the Compromise of 1850 that they had considered a victory seemed to become meaningless in the face of northern defiance.

"YOUNG AMERICA"

One of the ways Franklin Pierce hoped to dampen sectional controversy was through his support of a movement in the Democratic Party known as "Young America." Its adherents saw the expansion of American democracy throughout the world as a way to divert attention from the controversies over slavery. The great liberal and nationalist revolutions of 1848 in Europe stirred them to dream of a republican Europe with governments based on the model of the United States. They dreamed as well of acquiring new territories in the Western Hemisphere.

But efforts to extend the nation's domain could not avoid becoming entangled with the sectional crisis. Pierce had been pursuing diplomatic attempts to buy Cuba from Spain (efforts begun in 1848 by Polk). In 1854, however, a group of Pierce's envoys sent him a private document from Ostend, Belgium, making a case for seizing Cuba by force. When *Ostend Manifesto* the Ostend Manifesto, as it became known, was leaked to the public, antislavery northerners charged the administration with conspiring to bring a new slave state into the Union.

The South, for its part, opposed all efforts to acquire new territory that would not support a slave system. The kingdom of Hawaii agreed to join the United States in 1854, but the treaty died in the Senate because it contained a clause prohibiting slavery in the islands. A powerful movement to annex Canada to the United States similarly foundered, at least in part because of slavery.

Slavery, Railroads, and the West

What fully revived the sectional crisis, however, was the same issue that had produced it in the first place: slavery in the territories. By the 1850s, the line of substantial white settlement had moved beyond the boundaries of Missouri, Iowa, and what is now Minnesota into a great expanse of plains, which many white Americans had once believed was unfit for cultivation. Now it was becoming apparent that large sections of this region were, in fact, suitable for farming. In the states of the Old Northwest, prospective settlers urged the government to open the area to them, provide territorial governments, and dislodge local Indians to make room for white settlers. There was relatively little opposition from any segment of white society to this proposed violation of Indian rights. But the interest in further settlement raised two issues that did prove highly controversial and that gradually became entwined with each other: railroads and slavery.

As the nation expanded westward, broad support began to emerge for building a transcontinental railroad. The problem was where to place it—and in particular, where to locate the railroad's eastern terminus, where the line could connect with the existing rail network east of the Mississippi. Northerners favored Chicago, while southerners supported St. Louis, Memphis, or New Orleans. The transcontinental   *Transcontinental Railroad and Slavery* railroad had also become part of the struggle between the North and the South.

Pierce's secretary of war, Jefferson Davis of Mississippi, removed one obstacle to a southern route. Surveys indicated that a railroad with a southern terminus would have to pass through an area in Mexican territory. But in 1853, Davis sent James   *Gadsden Purchase* Gadsden, a southern railroad builder, to Mexico, where he persuaded the Mexican government to accept $10 million in exchange for a strip of land that today comprises parts of Arizona and New Mexico. The so-called Gadsden Purchase only accentuated the sectional rivalry as it added more slave territory.

The Kansas–Nebraska Controversy

The momentum for an intercontinental railroad continued to build, but the first great barrier was the debate over where to put it. The acknowledged leader of northwestern Democrats and senator from Illinois, Stephen A. Douglas, wanted the transcontinental railroad to run north through his state, but he also recognized, as many did, that a northern route through the territories would run mostly through dense Indian populations. As a result, he introduced a bill in January 1854 to organize (and thus open to white settlement and railroads) a huge new territory, known as Nebraska, west of Iowa and Missouri from the still unorganized territory of the Louisiana Purchase.

Douglas knew the South would oppose his bill because organized territories over time become states, and the proposed territory was north of the Missouri Compromise line (36°3′) and hence closed to slavery since 1820. Initially, Douglas attempted to appease southerners by including a provision that territorial legislatures would decide the status of slavery. In theory, the region could choose to open itself to slavery, effectively repealing the Missouri Compromise. When southern Democrats demanded more, Douglas also agreed to divide the area into two territories—Nebraska and Kansas—instead of one. The new, second territory (Kansas) was thought more likely to become a slave state. In its final form, the measure was known as the Kansas-Nebraska Act. President Pierce   *Kansas-Nebraska Act* supported the bill, and after a strenuous debate, it became law in May 1854 with the unanimous support of the South and the partial support of northern Democrats.

No piece of legislation in American history produced so many immediate, sweeping, and ominous political consequences. It divided and destroyed the Whig Party. It divided the northern Democrats (many of whom were appalled at the repeal of the Missouri Compromise) and drove many of them from the party. Most important, it spurred the creation of a new party that was frankly sectional in composition and creed. People in both major parties who opposed Douglas's bill began to call themselves Anti-Nebraska Democrats and Anti-Nebraska Whigs. In 1854, they formed a new organization and named *Republican Party Founded* it the Republican Party, and it instantly became a major force in American politics. In the elections of that year, the Republicans won enough seats in Congress to permit them, in combination with allies among the Know-Nothings, to organize the House of Representatives.

"Bleeding Kansas"

White settlers began moving into Kansas almost immediately after the passage of the Kansas-Nebraska Act. In the spring of 1855, elections were held for a territorial legislature. There were only about 1,500 legal voters in Kansas by then, but thousands of Missourians, some traveling in armed bands into Kansas, swelled the vote to over 6,000. As a result, pro-slavery forces elected a majority to the legislature, which immediately legalized slavery. Outraged free-staters elected their own delegates to a constitutional convention, which met at Topeka and adopted a constitution excluding slavery. They then chose their own governor and legislature and petitioned Congress for statehood. President Pierce denounced them as traitors and threw the full support of the federal government behind the pro-slavery territorial legislature. A few months later, a pro-slavery federal marshal assembled a large posse, consisting mostly of Missourians, to arrest the free-state leaders, who had set up their headquarters in Lawrence. The posse sacked the town, burned the "governor's" house, and destroyed several printing presses. Retribution came quickly.

Among the most fervent abolitionists in Kansas was John Brown, a grim, fiercely committed *John Brown* zealot who had moved to Kansas to fight to make it a free state. After the events in Lawrence, he gathered six followers (including four of his sons) and in one night murdered five pro-slavery settlers. This terrible episode, known as the Pottawatomie Massacre, led to more civil strife in Kansas including more armed bands engaged in guerrilla warfare with some more interested in land claims or loot than slavery. Northerners and southerners alike came to believe that the events in Kansas illustrated (and were caused by) the aggressive designs of the rival section. "Bleeding Kansas" became a powerful symbol of the sectional controversy.

Another symbol soon appeared, in the United States Senate. In May 1856, Charles Sumner of Massachusetts, a strong antislavery leader, rose to give a speech titled "The Crime Against Kansas." In it he gave particular attention to Senator Andrew P. Butler of South Carolina, an outspoken defender of slavery. The South Carolinian was, Sumner claimed, the "Don Quixote" of slavery, having "chosen a mistress . . . who, though ugly to others, is always lovely to him, though polluted in the sight of the world, is chaste in his sight . . . the harlot slavery."

The pointedly sexual references and the general viciousness of the speech enraged Butler's nephew, Preston Brooks, a member of the House of Representatives from South Carolina. Several days after the speech, Brooks approached Sumner at his desk in the Senate chamber during a recess, raised a heavy cane, and began beating him repeatedly *Sumner Caned* on the head and shoulders. Sumner, trapped in his chair, rose in agony with

JOHN BROWN   Even in this formal photographic portrait (taken in 1859, the last year of his life), John Brown conveys the fierce sense of righteousness that fueled his extraordinary activities in the fight against slavery. (The Library of Congress)

such strength that he tore the desk from the bolts holding it to the floor. Then he collapsed, bleeding and unconscious. So severe were his injuries that he was unable to return to the Senate for four years. Throughout the North, he became a hero—a martyr to the barbarism of the South. In the South, Preston Brooks became a hero, too. Censured by the House, he resigned his seat, returned to South Carolina, and stood successfully for reelection.

The Free-Soil Ideology

What had happened to produce such deep hostility between the two sections? In part, the tensions were reflections of the two sections' differing economic and territorial interests. But they were also reflections of a hardening of ideas in both the North and the South.

In the North, assumptions about the proper structure of society came to center on the belief in "free soil" and "free labor." Most white northerners   *"Free Soil" and "Free Labor"* came to believe that the existence of slavery was dangerous not because of what it did to blacks but because of what it threatened to do to whites. At the heart of American democracy, they argued, was the right of all citizens to own property, to control their own labor, and to have access to opportunities for advancement.

According to this vision, the South was the antithesis of democracy—a closed, static society, in which slavery preserved an entrenched aristocracy. While the North was growing and prospering, the South was stagnating, rejecting the values of individualism and progress. The South, northern free-laborites further maintained, was engaged in a conspiracy to extend slavery throughout the nation and thus to destroy the openness of northern capitalism and replace it with the closed, aristocratic system of the South. The only solution to this "slave power conspiracy" was to fight the spread of slavery and extend the   *"Slave Power Conspiracy"* nation's democratic (i.e., free-labor) ideals to all sections of the country.

This ideology, which lay at the heart of the new Republican Party, also strengthened the commitment of Republicans to the Union. Since the idea of continued growth and progress was central to the free-labor vision, the prospect of dismemberment of the nation was to the Republicans unthinkable.

The Pro-Slavery Argument

In the meantime, in the South a very different ideology was emerging. It was a result of many things: the Nat Turner uprising in 1831, which terrified southern whites; the expansion of the cotton economy into the Deep South, which made slavery unprecedentedly lucrative; and the growth of the Garrisonian abolitionist movement, with its strident attacks on southern society. The popularity of Harriet Beecher Stowe's *Uncle Tom's Cabin* was perhaps the most glaring evidence of the power of those attacks, but other abolitionist writings had been antagonizing white southerners for years.

In response to these pressures, a number of white southerners produced a new intellectual defense of slavery. Professor Thomas R. Dew of the College of William and Mary helped begin that effort in 1832. Twenty years later, apologists for slavery summarized their views in an anthology that gave their ideology its name: *The Pro-Slavery Argument.* John C. Calhoun stated the essence of the case in 1837: Slavery was "a good—a positive good." It was good for the slaves because they enjoyed better conditions than industrial workers in the North, good for southern society because it was the only way the two races

SLAVERY AS IT EXISTS IN AMERICA.

PRO-SLAVERY CARTOON   This illustration was published by a Boston press in 1850, in the wake of the English abolitionist George Thompson's speaking tour of New York and New England. A second half of the cartoon, not shown here, portrays a dismal scene of factory life in England. This image is meant to show how much happier and better-off American slaves are by comparison. One of the northern gentlemen observing this scene asks, "Is it possible that we of the North have been so deceived by false Reports? Why did we not visit the South before we caused this trouble between the North and South?"   (The Library of Congress) could live together in peace, and good for the entire country because the southern economy, based on slavery, was the key to the prosperity of the nation.

Above all, southern apologists argued, slavery was good because it served as the basis for the southern way of life—a way of life superior to any other in the United States, perhaps in the world. White southerners looking at the North saw a spirit of greed, debauchery, and destructiveness. "The masses of the North are venal, corrupt, covetous, mean and selfish," wrote one southerner. Others wrote with horror of the factory system and the crowded, pestilential cities filled with unruly immigrants. But the South, they believed, was a stable, orderly society, free from the feuds between capital and labor plaguing the North. It protected the welfare of its workers. And it allowed the aristocracy to enjoy a refined and accomplished cultural life. It was, in short, an ideal social order in which all elements of the population were secure and content.

The defense of slavery rested, too, on increasingly elaborate arguments about the biological inferiority of African Americans, who were, white southerners claimed, inherently unfit to take care of themselves, let alone exercise the rights of citizenship.

BUCHANAN AND DEPRESSION

In this unpromising climate, the presidential campaign of 1856 began. Democratic Party leaders wanted a candidate who, unlike President Pierce, was not closely associated with the explosive question of "Bleeding Kansas." They chose James Buchanan of Pennsylvania, who as minister to England had been safely out of the country during the recent controversies. The Republicans, participating in their first presidential contest, endorsed a Whiggish program of internal improvements, thus combining the idealism of antislavery with the economic aspirations of the North. The Republicans nominated John C. Frémont, who had made a national reputation as an explorer of the Far West and who had no political record. The Native American, or Know-Nothing, Party was beginning to break apart, but it nominated former president Millard Fillmore, who also received the endorsement of a small remnant of the Whig Party.

After a heated, even frenzied campaign, Buchanan won a narrow victory over Frémont and Fillmore. Whether because of age and physical infirmities or because of a more fundamental weakness of character, he became a painfully timid and indecisive president at a critical moment in history. In the year Buchanan took office, a   *James Buchanan Elected* financial panic struck the country, followed by a depression that lasted several years. In the North, the depression strengthened the Republican Party because distressed manufacturers, workers, and farmers came to believe that the hard times were the result of the unsound policies of southern-controlled, pro-slavery Democratic administrations. They expressed their frustrations by moving into an alliance with antislavery elements and thus into the Republican Party.

THE *DRED SCOTT* DECISION

On March 6, 1857, the Supreme Court of the United States projected itself into the sectional controversy with one of the most controversial and notorious decisions in its history—*Dred Scott v. Sandford.* Dred Scott was a Missouri slave, once owned by an army surgeon who had taken Scott with him into Illinois and Wisconsin, where slavery was forbidden. In 1846, after the surgeon died, Scott sued his master's widow for freedom on the grounds that his residence in free territory had liberated him from slavery.

The claim was well grounded in Missouri law, and in 1850 the circuit court in which Scott filed the suit declared him free. By now, John Sanford, the brother of the surgeon's widow, was claiming ownership of Scott, and he appealed the circuit court ruling to the state supreme court, which reversed the earlier decision. When Scott appealed to the federal courts, Sanford's attorneys claimed that Scott had no standing to sue because he was not a citizen.

The Supreme Court (which misspelled Sanford's name in its decision) was so divided that it was unable to issue a single ruling on the case. The thrust of the various rulings, however, was a stunning defeat for the antislavery movement. Chief Justice Roger Taney, *Taney's Pro-Slavery Decision*   who wrote one of the majority opinions, declared that Scott could not bring a suit in the federal courts because he was not a citizen. Blacks had no claim to citizenship, Taney argued. Slaves were property, and the Fifth Amendment prohibited Congress from taking property without "due process of law." Consequently, Taney concluded, Congress possessed no authority to pass a law depriving persons of their slave property in the territories. The Missouri Compromise, therefore, had always been unconstitutional.

The ruling did nothing to challenge the right of an individual state to prohibit slavery within its borders, but the statement that the federal government was powerless to act on the issue was a drastic and startling one. Southern whites were elated: the highest tribunal in the land had sanctioned parts of the most extreme southern argument. In the North, the decision produced widespread dismay. The decision, the *New York Tribune* wrote, "is entitled to just so much moral weight as would be the judgment of a majority of those congregated in any Washington bar-room." Republicans threatened that when they won control of the national government, they would reverse the decision—by "packing" the Court with new members.

Deadlock over Kansas

President Buchanan timidly endorsed the *Dred Scott* decision. At the same time, he tried to resolve the controversy over Kansas by supporting its admission to the Union as a slave state. In response, the pro-slavery territorial legislature called an election for delegates to a constitutional convention. The free-state residents refused to participate, claiming that the legislature had discriminated against them in drawing district lines. As a result, the pro-slavery forces won control of the convention, which met in 1857 at Lecompton, framed a constitution legalizing slavery, and refused to give voters a chance to reject it. When an election for a new territorial legislature was called, the antislavery groups turned out in force and won a majority. The new antislavery legislature promptly submitted the Lecompton constitution to the voters, who rejected it by more than 10,000 votes.

Both sides had resorted to fraud and violence, but it was clear nevertheless that a majority of the people of Kansas opposed slavery. Buchanan, however, pressured Congress to admit Kansas under the pro-slavery Lecompton constitution. Stephen A. Douglas and other northern and western Democrats refused to support the president's proposal, which died in the House of Representatives. Finally, in April 1858, Congress approved a compromise: The Lecompton constitution would be submitted to the voters of Kansas again. If it was approved, Kansas would be admitted to the Union; if it was rejected, statehood *Lecompton Constitution Rejected*   would be postponed. Again, Kansas voters decisively rejected the Lecompton constitution. Not until the closing months of Buchanan's administration in 1861 did Kansas enter the Union—as a free state.

THE EMERGENCE OF LINCOLN

Given the gravity of the sectional crisis, the congressional elections of 1858 took on a special importance. Of particular note was the United States Senate contest in Illinois, which pitted Stephen A. Douglas, the most prominent northern Democrat, against Abraham Lincoln, who was largely unknown outside Illinois.

Lincoln was a successful lawyer who had long been involved in state politics. He had served several terms in the Illinois legislature and one undistinguished term in Congress. But he was not a national figure like Douglas, and so he tried to increase his visibility by engaging Douglas in a series of debates. The Lincoln–Douglas *Lincoln–Douglas Debates* debates attracted enormous crowds and received wide attention.

At the heart of the debates was a basic difference on the issue of slavery. Douglas appeared to have no moral position on the issue, Lincoln claimed. He stated that Douglas did not care whether slavery was "voted up, or voted down." Lincoln's opposition to slavery was more fundamental. If the nation could accept that blacks were not entitled to basic human rights, he argued, then it could accept that other groups—immigrant laborers, for example—could be deprived of rights, too. And if slavery were to extend into the western territories, he argued, opportunities for poor white laborers to better their lots there would be lost. The nation's future, Lincoln argued (reflecting the central idea of the Republican Party), rested on the spread of free labor.

Lincoln believed slavery was morally wrong, but he was not an abolitionist. That was in part because he could not envision an easy alternative to slavery in the areas where it already existed. He shared the prevailing view among northern whites that the black race was not prepared to live on equal terms with whites. But even while Lincoln accepted the inferiority of black people, he continued to believe that they were entitled to basic rights. "I have no purpose to introduce political and social equality between the white and the black races . . . But I hold that . . . there is no reason in the world why the negro is not entitled to all the natural rights enumerated in the Declaration of Independence, the right to life, liberty, and the pursuit of happiness. I hold that he is as much entitled to these as the white man." Lincoln and his party would "arrest the further spread" of slavery. They would not directly challenge it where it already existed but would trust that the institution would gradually die out there of its own accord.

Douglas's popular sovereignty position satisfied his followers sufficiently to produce a Democratic majority in the state legislature, which returned him to the Senate but aroused little enthusiasm. Lincoln, by contrast, lost the election but emerged with a growing following both in and beyond the state. And outside Illinois, the elections went heavily against the Democrats. The party retained control of the Senate but lost its majority in the House, with the result that the congressional sessions of 1858 and 1859 were bitterly deadlocked.

JOHN BROWN'S RAID

The battles in Congress, however, were almost entirely overshadowed by an event that enraged and horrified the South. In the fall of 1859, John Brown, the antislavery radical whose bloody actions in Kansas had inflamed the crisis there, staged an even more dramatic episode, this time in the South itself. With private encouragement and financial aid from some prominent abolitionists, he made elaborate plans to seize a mountain fortress in Virginia from which, he believed, he could foment a slave insurrection in the South. On October 16, he and a group of eighteen followers attacked and seized control of a United

Harpers Ferry   States arsenal in Harpers Ferry, Virginia. But the slave uprising Brown hoped to inspire did not occur, and he quickly found himself besieged in the arsenal by citizens, local militia companies, and, before long, United States troops under the command of Robert E. Lee. After ten of his men were killed, Brown surrendered. He was promptly tried in a Virginia court for treason and sentenced to death. He and six of his followers were hanged.

No other single event did more than the Harpers Ferry raid to convince white southerners that they could not live safely in the Union. Many southerners believed (incorrectly) that John Brown's raid had the support of the Republican Party, and it suggested to them that the North was now committed to producing a slave insurrection.

THE ELECTION OF LINCOLN

As the presidential election of 1860 approached, the Democratic Party was torn apart by a battle between southerners, who demanded a strong endorsement of slavery, and westerners, who supported the idea of popular sovereignty. When the party convention met in April in Charleston, South Carolina, and endorsed popular sovereignty, delegates from

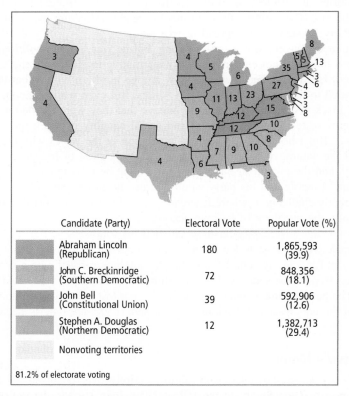

Candidate (Party)	Electoral Vote	Popular Vote (%)
Abraham Lincoln (Republican)	180	1,865,593 (39.9)
John C. Breckinridge (Southern Democratic)	72	848,356 (18.1)
John Bell (Constitutional Union)	39	592,906 (12.6)
Stephen A. Douglas (Northern Democratic)	12	1,382,713 (29.4)
Nonvoting territories		

81.2% of electorate voting

THE ELECTION OF 1860   The stark sectional divisions that helped produce the Civil War were clearly visible in the results of the 1860 presidential election. Abraham Lincoln, the antislavery Republican candidate, won virtually all the free states. Stephen Douglas, a northern Democrat with no strong position on the issue of slavery, won two of the border states, and John Bell, a supporter of both slavery and union, won others. John Breckinridge, a strong pro-slavery southern Democrat, carried the entire Deep South. Lincoln won under 40 percent of the popular vote but, because of the four-way division in the race, managed to win a clear majority of the electoral vote. • *What impact did the election of Lincoln have on the sectional crisis?*

eight states in the lower South walked out. The remaining delegates could not agree on a presidential candidate and finally adjourned after agreeing to meet again in Baltimore. The decimated convention at Baltimore nominated Stephen Douglas for   *Democrats Divided* president. In the meantime, disenchanted southern Democrats met in Richmond and nominated John C. Breckinridge of Kentucky.

The Republican leaders, in the meantime, were trying to broaden their appeal in the North. The platform endorsed such traditional Whig measures as a high tariff, internal improvements, a homestead bill, and a Pacific railroad to be built with federal financial assistance. It supported the right of each state to decide the status of slavery within its borders. But it also insisted that neither Congress nor territorial legislatures could legalize slavery in the territories. The Republican convention chose Abraham Lincoln as the party's presidential nominee. Lincoln was appealing because of his growing reputation for eloquence, because of his firm but moderate position on slavery, and because his relative obscurity ensured that he would have none of the drawbacks of other, more prominent (and therefore more controversial) Republicans.

In the November election, Lincoln won the presidency with a majority of the electoral votes but only about two-fifths of the fragmented popular vote. The Republicans, moreover, failed to win a majority in Congress. Even so, the election of Lincoln   *Lincoln Elected* became the final signal to many white southerners that their position in the Union was hopeless. And within a few weeks of Lincoln's victory, the process of disunion began— a process that would quickly lead to a prolonged and bloody war.

CONCLUSION

In the decades following the War of 1812, a vigorous nationalism pervaded much of American life, helping smooth over the growing differences among the very distinct societies emerging in the United States. During the 1850s, however, the forces that had worked to hold the nation together in the past fell victim to new and much more divisive pressures.

Driving the sectional tensions of the 1850s was a battle over national policy toward the place of slavery within the western territories. Should slavery be permitted in the new states? And who should decide? There were strenuous efforts to craft compromises and solutions to this dilemma: the Compromise of 1850, the Kansas-Nebraska Act of 1854, and others. But despite these efforts, positions on slavery continued to harden in both the North and the South. Bitter battles in the territory of Kansas over whether to permit slavery there; growing agitation by abolitionists in the North and pro-slavery advocates in the South; the Supreme Court's controversial *Dred Scott* decision in 1857; the popularity of *Uncle Tom's Cabin* throughout the decade; and the emergence of a new political party— the Republican Party—openly and centrally opposed to slavery: all worked to destroy the hopes for compromise and push the South toward secession.

In 1860, all pretense of common sentiment collapsed when no political party presented a presidential candidate capable of attracting national support. The Republicans nominated Abraham Lincoln of Illinois, a little-known politician recognized for his eloquent condemnations of slavery in a Senate race two years earlier. The Democratic Party split apart, with its northern and southern wings each nominating different candidates. Lincoln won the election easily, but with less than 40 percent of the popular vote. And almost immediately after his victory, the states of the South began preparing to secede from the Union.

KEY TERMS/PEOPLE/PLACES/EVENTS

Abraham Lincoln 317
Antonio López de Santa
  Anna 291
Charles Sumner 312
Compromise of 1850 309
Dred Scott decision 315
"Forty-niners" 307
Free-Soil Party 306
Gadsden Purchase 311

Harpers Ferry 318
James K. Polk 301
John Brown 317
Kansas-Nebraska
  Act 311
Manifest Destiny 297
Oregon Trail 299
popular sovereignty 306
Sam Houston 298

Stephen A. Douglas 309
Stephen F. Austin 298
Tejanos 298
The Alamo 291
Treaty of Guadalupe
  Hidalgo 304
Wilmot Proviso 306
"Young America" 310
Zachary Taylor 302

RECALL AND REFLECT

1. How were the boundary disputes over Oregon and Texas resolved? Why were the resolutions in the two cases so different?
2. How did Polk's decisions and actions as president intensify the sectional conflict?
3. What was the issue at stake in "Bleeding Kansas," and how did events in Kansas reflect the growing sectional division between the North and the South?
4. What was the *Dred Scott* decision? What was the decision's impact on the sectional crisis?
5. How did the growing sectional crisis affect the nation's major political parties?

14 | THE CIVIL WAR

THE SECESSION CRISIS
THE MOBILIZATION OF THE NORTH
THE MOBILIZATION OF THE SOUTH
STRATEGY AND DIPLOMACY
CAMPAIGNS AND BATTLES

LOOKING AHEAD

1. How did the North's mobilization for war differ from mobilization in the South? What accounts for these differences?
2. What were the differences between the impact of the war in the North and the South?
3. What were the military strategies employed by the North and the South from the opening clashes in 1861 through the Union victory in 1865, and how did these strategies differ?

BY THE END OF 1860, the cords that had bound the Union together had snapped. The second party system had collapsed, replaced by one that accentuated rather than muted regional controversy. The federal government was no longer a remote, unthreatening presence; the need to resolve the status of the territories had made it necessary for Washington to deal directly with sectional issues. The election of 1860 brought these tensions to a head and precipitated the most terrible war in the nation's history.

THE SECESSION CRISIS

Almost as soon as news of Abraham Lincoln's election reached the South, militant leaders began to demand an end to the Union.

THE WITHDRAWAL OF THE SOUTH

South Carolina, long the hotbed of southern separatism, seceded first, on December 20, 1860. By the time Lincoln took office, six other southern states—Mississippi (January 9, 1861), Florida (January 10), Alabama (January 11), Georgia (January 19), Louisiana (January 26), and Texas (February 1)—had withdrawn from the Union. In February 1861, representatives of the seven seceded states met at Montgomery, Alabama, and formed a new nation—the Confederate States of America. Two months earlier, President James Buchanan told Congress that no state had the right to secede from the Union but that the federal government had no authority to stop a state if it did.

The seceding states immediately seized the federal property within their boundaries. But they did not at first have sufficient military power to seize two fortified offshore military installations: Fort Sumter, in the harbor of Charleston, South Carolina, garrisoned by a small force under Major Robert Anderson; and Fort Pickens, in Pensacola, Florida. Buchanan refused to yield Fort Sumter when South Carolina demanded it. Instead, in January 1861, he ordered an unarmed merchant ship to proceed to Fort Sumter with additional troops and supplies. Confederate guns turned it back. Still, neither section was yet ready to concede that war had begun. And in Washington, efforts began once more to forge a compromise.

THE FAILURE OF COMPROMISE

Gradually, the compromise efforts came together around a proposal from John J. Crittenden of Kentucky. Known as the Crittenden Compromise, it proposed reestablishing the Missouri Compromise line and extending it westward to the Pacific. Slavery would be prohibited north of the line and permitted south of it. Southerners in the Senate seemed willing to accept the plan. But the compromise would have required the Republicans to abandon their most fundamental position—that slavery not be allowed to expand—and they rejected it. Whether the failure to compromise and find common ground between Northern and Southern politicians triggered the Civil War has been a topic of debate among historians for generations. (See "Debating the Past: The Causes of the Civil War.")

When Abraham Lincoln arrived in Washington, talk of secession, and possible war, filled the air. In his inaugural address, Lincoln insisted that acts of force or violence to support secession were insurrectionary and that the government would "hold, occupy, and possess" federal property in the seceded states—a clear reference to Fort Sumter.

But Fort Sumter was running short of supplies. So Lincoln sent a relief expedition to the fort and informed the South Carolina authorities that he would send no troops or munitions unless the supply ships met with resistance. The new Confederate government ordered General P. G. T. Beauregard, commander of Confederate forces at *Bombardment and War* Charleston, to take the fort. When Anderson refused to give up, the Confederates bombarded it for two days. On April 14, 1861, Anderson surrendered. The Civil War had begun.

Almost immediately, four more slave states seceded from the Union and joined the Confederacy: Virginia (April 17), Arkansas (May 6), Tennessee (May 7), and North Carolina (May 20). The four remaining slave states, Maryland, Delaware, Kentucky, and Missouri—under heavy political pressure from Washington—remained in the Union.

THE OPPOSING SIDES

All the important material advantages for waging war lay with the North, most notably an advanced industrial system able by 1862 to manufacture almost all the North's own war materials. The South had almost no industry at all.

In addition, the North had a much better transportation system, with more and better railroads than did the South. During the war, the already inferior Confederate railroad system steadily deteriorated and by early 1864 had almost collapsed.

But the South also had advantages. The Southern armies were, for the most part, fighting a defensive war on familiar land with local support. The Northern armies, on the other hand, were fighting mostly within the South amid hostile local populations; they had to maintain long lines of communication. The commitment of the white population of the South to the war was, with limited exceptions, clear and firm throughout much of the early years of fighting. In the North, opinion was more divided, and support remained shaky until very near the end. A major Southern victory at any one of several crucial moments might have proved decisive in breaking the North's will to continue the struggle. Finally, the dependence of the English and French textile industries on American cotton inclined many leaders in those countries to favor the Confederacy; and Southerners hoped, with some reason, that one or both might intervene on their behalf.

BILLY YANK AND JOHNNY REB

The vast majority of Civil War soldiers were volunteers. Recruiters for the Union often pulled in groups of men from the same town or ethnic group. There were entire companies and even regiments of Irish Americans, German Americans, Italian Americans, or, later,

THE CAUSES OF THE CIVIL WAR

Abraham Lincoln, in his 1865 inaugural address, looked back at the terrible war that was now nearing its end and said, "All knew [that slavery] was somehow the cause of the war." Few historians dispute that. But disagreement has been sharp over whether slavery was the only, or even the principal, cause of the war.

The debate began even before the war itself. In 1858, Senator William H. Seward of New York took note of the two competing explanations of the sectional tensions that were then inflaming the nation. On one side, he said, stood those who believed the conflicts to be "accidental, unnecessary, the work of interested or fanatical agitators." Opposing them stood those (among them Seward himself) who believed there to be "an irrepressible conflict between opposing and enduring forces."

The "irrepressible conflict" argument dominated historical discussion of the war from the 1860s to the 1920s. War was inevitable, some historians claimed, because there was no room for compromise on the central issue of slavery. Others deemphasized slavery and pointed to the economic differences between the agrarian South and the industrializing North. Charles and Mary Beard, for example, wrote in 1927 of the "inherent antagonisms" between the interests of planters and those of industrialists. Still others cited social and cultural differences as the source of an irrepressible conflict. Slavery, the historian Allan Nevins argued, was only one factor that was making residents of the North and South "separate peoples." Fundamental differences in

"assumptions, tastes, and cultural aim" made it virtually impossible for the two societies to live together in peace.

More recent proponents of irrepressible-conflict arguments similarly emphasize culture and ideology but define the concerns of the North and the South in different terms. Eric Foner, writing in 1970, argued that the moral concerns of abolitionists and the economic concerns of industrialists were less important in explaining northern hostility to the South than was the broad-based "free-labor" ideology of the region. Northerners opposed slavery because they feared it might spread into their own region or into the West and threaten the position of free white laborers.

Other historians have argued that the war was not inevitable, beginning with a group of scholars in the 1920s known as the "revisionists." James G. Randall and Avery Craven were the two leading proponents of the view that the differences between the North and the South were not so great as to require a war, that only a "blundering generation" of leaders caused the conflict. Michael Holt revived the revisionist argument in a 1978 book, in which he, too, emphasized the partisan ambitions of politicians. Holt was, along with Paul Kleppner, Joel Silbey, and William Gienapp, one of the creators of an "ethnocultural" interpretation of the war, which emphasized the collapse of the party system and the role of temperance and nativism, which was central to the coming of the conflict. •

1. Some arguments regarding the Civil War as inevitable focus on economic differences between the North and the South. What were these differences and how might they have led—inevitably—to war?

2. Some revisionist scholars attribute the Civil War to a "blundering generation" of political leaders. Who were these leaders and what blunders did they make? Could better decisions have avoided war?

African Americans. Initially, these soldiers and their officers were haphazardly trained and unprepared for battle. Many officers jokingly referred to their troops as armed mobs.

Because individual states outfitted their soldiers at the outset of the war, Union uniforms were at first far from uniform, ranging from the dark blue jackets and light blue pants of the regular army to dark blue and red "Zouave" uniforms based on the French colonial regiments in Algeria. In the war's first major battle some Union regiments wore gray uniforms, which led to tragic mixups with Confederate troops. "Federals" did not consistently wear blue uniforms until 1862, when the federal government provided them along with shoes, weapons, cartridge boxes, knapsacks, blankets, canteens, and other basic supplies.

Northerners generally saw themselves fighting to restore the Union and preserve the American democratic experiment. They questioned how the nation might endure if parts of it could secede at every undesirable election result. Most white Northerners understood that divisions over slavery had caused the Civil War, but they did not fight, at first, to abolish it. Later, when it became clear that abolishing slavery would help end the rebellion, emancipation joined reunion as a war aim. (In contrast, black Northerners immediately

SENDING THE BOYS OFF TO WAR In Thomas Nast's painting *The Departure of the Seventh Regiment to the War*, Union troops parade down Broadway in April 1861, shortly before departing for what most people thought would be a short war. (© Granger, NYC—All Rights Reserved.)

understood the war to be a struggle for emancipation.) Otherwise, beyond the timeless motivations of comradeship, honor, and adventure shared by soldiers in many wars, Union troops generally fought to sustain "the best government on earth."[1]

Like his Union counterpart, the average Confederate soldier rarely had proper military training and tended to serve with comrades from the same area. When on the march, fully provisioned Southern soldiers carried an ammunition cartridge box on their belts, a rolled-up blanket, a haversack, a tin cup, frying pan, and cloth-covered canteen. Many Confederate soldiers supplied their own shotguns, hunting rifles, or ancient flintlock muskets, and cavalrymen often provided their own horses. Regiments wore different uniforms, and even after the Confederacy adopted gray, the government was never able to clothe every soldier. Meals were meager, with soldiers on both sides subsisting on dried vegetables, salt pork and beef, coffee, and tough crackers known as hardtack.

Southerners saw themselves as the protectors of sacred American values. They defended the right of states to secede if they found the federal government oppressive, just as the colonies had claimed the right to declare independence from an oppressive Britain in the Revolutionary War. And they interpreted their defense of slavery as a defense of individual property rights in general. Indeed, slavery was at the heart of the rights Confederates sought to protect and of the life and economy they fought to preserve. Confederate vice president Alexander Stephens called slavery the "cornerstone" of the Confederacy. Outraged at the thought of living under an antislavery president, secessionists relished independence. "Thank God!" wrote one Mississippian the summer after secession. "We have a country at last . . . to live for, to pray for, to fight for, and if necessary, to die for."[2]

Beyond these abstract motivations, however, many rebels fought to protect their homes and families from the invading Yankees.

THE MOBILIZATION OF THE NORTH

In the North, the war produced considerable discord, frustration, and suffering. But it also produced prosperity and economic growth. With the South now gone from Congress, the Republican Party enjoyed almost unchallenged supremacy. During the war, it enacted an aggressively nationalistic program to promote economic development.

ECONOMIC NATIONALISM

Two 1862 acts assisted the rapid development of the West. The Homestead Act permitted any citizen or prospective citizen to purchase 160 acres of public land for a small fee after *Homestead and Morrill Acts* living on it for five years. The Morrill Act transferred substantial public acreage to the state governments, which could now sell the land and use the proceeds to finance public education. This act led to the creation of many new state colleges and universities, the so-called land-grant institutions. Congress also passed a series of tariff bills that by the end of the war had raised duties to the highest level in the nation's history—a great boon to domestic industries eager for protection from foreign competition, but a hardship for many farmers and other consumers. Without the seceding states to block their legislation, Congress bent to the political will of the Northern and western factions.

---

1 James McPherson, *Battle Cry of Freedom: The Civil War Era* (New York: Oxford UP, 1988), p. 309.
2 McPherson, *Battle Cry of Freedom*, p. 310.

Congress also moved to spur completion of a transcontinental railroad. It created two new federally chartered corporations: the Union Pacific Railroad Company, which was to build westward from Omaha, and the Central Pacific, which was to build eastward from California. The two projects were to meet in the middle and complete the link, which they did in 1869 at Promontory Point, Utah.

The National Bank Acts of 1863–1864 created a new national banking system. Existing or newly formed banks could join the system if they had enough capital *National Bank Acts* and were willing to invest one-third of it in government securities. In return, they could issue United States Treasury notes as currency. This eliminated much (although not all) of the chaos and uncertainty surrounding the nation's currency.

More difficult was financing the war itself. The government tried to do so in three ways: levying taxes, issuing paper currency, and borrowing. Congress levied new taxes on almost all goods and services and in 1861 levied an income tax for the first time. But taxation raised only a small proportion needed to fight the war, and strong popular resistance prevented the government from raising the rates.

At least equally controversial was the printing of paper currency, or "**greenbacks.**" The new currency was backed not by gold or silver but (as today) simply by the good faith and credit of the government. The value of the greenbacks fluctuated according to the fortunes of the Northern armies. Early in 1864, with the war effort bogged down, a greenback dollar was worth only 39 percent of a gold dollar. But at the close of the war, with confidence high, it was worth 67 percent of a gold dollar.

By far the largest source of financing for the war was loans. The Treasury persuaded ordinary citizens to buy over $400 million worth of bonds. Yet public bond purchases constituted only a small part of the government's borrowing, which in the end totaled $2.6 billion, most of it from banks and large financial interests.

Raising the Union Armies

At the beginning of 1861, the regular army of the United States consisted of only 16,000 troops, many of them stationed in the West. So the Union, like the Confederacy, had to raise its army mostly from scratch. Lincoln called for an increase of 23,000 in the regular army, but the bulk of the fighting, he knew, would have to be done by volunteers in state militias. When Congress convened in July 1861, it authorized enlisting 500,000 volunteers for three-year (as opposed to the customary three-month) terms.

This voluntary system of recruitment produced adequate forces only briefly, during the first flush of enthusiasm for the war. By March 1863, Congress was forced to *The Draft* pass a national draft law. Virtually all young adult males were eligible to be drafted, although a man could escape service by hiring someone to go in his place or by paying the government a fee of $300.

To many who were accustomed to a remote and inactive national government, **conscription** was strange and threatening. Opposition to the draft law was widespread, particularly among laborers, immigrants, and Democrats opposed to the war (known as "Peace Democrats" or "Copperheads" by their opponents). Occasionally opposition to the draft erupted into violence such as when demonstrators rioted in New York City for four days in July 1863, after the first names were selected for conscription. *New York City Draft Riots* More than 100 people died. Irish workers were at the center of violence. They were angry because black strikebreakers had been used against them in a recent longshoremen's strike. They blamed African Americans generally for the war, which they thought was being fought for the benefit of slaves. The rioters lynched several African Americans and burned down black homes, businesses, and even an orphanage, leaving more than 100 dead. Only the arrival of federal troops direct from the Battle of Gettysburg halted the violence.

WARTIME POLITICS

When Abraham Lincoln arrived in Washington, many Republicans considered him a *Presidential War Powers* minor prairie politician who would be easily controlled by the real leaders of his party. But Lincoln was not cowed by the distinguished figures around him. The new president understood his own (and his party's) weaknesses, and he assembled a cabinet representing every faction of the Republican Party and every segment of Northern opinion. He moved boldly to use the war powers of the presidency, blithely ignoring inconvenient parts of the Constitution because, he said, it would be foolish to lose the whole by being afraid to disregard a part.

And so he sent troops into battle without asking Congress for a declaration of war, arguing that the conflict was a domestic insurrection. He increased the size of the regular army without receiving legislative authority to do so. And he unilaterally proclaimed a naval blockade of the South.

Lincoln's greatest political problem was the widespread popular opposition to the war in the North. Lincoln ordered military arrests of civilian dissenters and suspended the right of habeas corpus (the right of an arrested person to receive a speedy trial). At first, Lincoln used these methods only in sensitive areas such as the border states; but by 1862, he proclaimed that all persons who discouraged enlistments or engaged in disloyal practices were subject to martial law.

Repression was not the only tool the North used to strengthen support for the war. In addition to arresting "disloyal" Northerners, Lincoln's administration used new tools of persuasion to build popular opinion in favor of the war. In addition to pro-war pamphlets, posters, speeches, and songs, the war mobilized a significant corps of photographers—organized by the renowned Mathew Brady, one of the first important photographers in American history— to take pictures of the war. The photographs that resulted from this effort—new to warfare— were among the grimmest ever made to that point, many of them displaying the vast numbers of dead on the Civil War battlefields. For some Northerners, the images of death contributed to a revulsion for the war. But for most they gave evidence of the level of sacrifice that had been made for the preservation of the Union and thus spurred the nation on to victory. (Southerners used similar propaganda in the Confederacy, although less effectively.)

By the time of the 1864 election, the North was in political turmoil. The Republicans had suffered heavy losses in the midterm elections of 1862, and in response party leaders tried to create a broad coalition of all the groups that supported the war. They called the new organization the Union Party, but it was, in reality, little more than the Republican Party and a small faction of War Democrats. They nominated Lincoln for a second term and Andrew Johnson of Tennessee, a War Democrat who had opposed his state's decision to secede, for the vice presidency.

The Democrats nominated George B. McClellan, a celebrated former Union general. *George B. McClellan* The party adopted a platform denouncing the war and calling for a truce. McClellan repudiated that demand, but the Democrats were clearly the peace party in the campaign, trying to profit from growing war weariness. For a time, Lincoln's prospects for reelection seemed doubtful.

At this crucial moment, however, several Northern military victories, particularly the capture of Atlanta, Georgia, early in September 1864, rejuvenated Northern morale and boosted Republican prospects. With the overwhelming support of Union troops, Lincoln won reelection comfortably, with 212 electoral votes to McClellan's 21.

THE POLITICS OF EMANCIPATION

Despite their surface unity in supporting the war and their general agreement on most economic matters, the Republicans disagreed sharply with one another on the issue of slavery. "Radical Republicans"—led in Congress by such men as Representative Thaddeus Stevens of Pennsylvania and Senators Charles Sumner of Massachusetts and Benjamin Wade of Ohio—wanted to use the war to abolish slavery immediately and completely. "Conservative Republicans" favored a more cautious policy—in part to placate the slave states that remained, precariously, within the Union.

Nevertheless, momentum began to gather behind emancipation early in the war. In 1861, Congress passed the **Confiscation Act,** which declared that all slaves   *Confiscation Act* used for "insurrectionary" purposes (that is, in support of the Confederate military effort) would be considered freed. Subsequent laws in the spring of 1862 abolished slavery in the District of Columbia and the western territories and provided for the compensation of owners. In July 1862, Radicals pushed through Congress the second Confiscation Act, which declared free the slaves of persons supporting the insurrection and authorized the president to employ African Americans as soldiers.

As the war progressed, many in the North slowly accepted emancipation as a central war aim; nothing less, they believed, would justify the enormous sacrifices the struggle had required. As a result, the Radicals gained increasing influence within the Republican Party—a development that did not go unnoticed by the president, who decided to seize the leadership of the rising antislavery sentiment himself.

On September 22, 1862, after the Union victory at the Battle of Antietam, the president announced his intention to use his war powers to issue an executive order freeing all slaves in the Confederacy. And on January 1, 1863, he formally signed the Emancipation Proclamation, which declared forever free the slaves inside the   *The Emancipation Proclamation* Confederacy. The proclamation did not apply to the Union slave states; nor did it affect those parts of the Confederacy already under Union control (Tennessee, western Virginia, and southern Louisiana). It applied, in short, only to slaves over whom the Union had no control. Still, the document was of great importance. It clearly and irrevocably established that the war was being fought not only to preserve the Union but also to eliminate slavery. Eventually, as federal armies occupied much of the South, the proclamation became a practical reality and led directly to the freeing of thousands of slaves.

Even in areas not directly affected by the proclamation, the antislavery impulse gained strength. The U.S. government's tentative measures against slavery were not, at first, a major factor in the liberation of slaves. Instead, the war helped African Americans liberate themselves, and they did so in increasing numbers as the war progressed. Many slaves were taken from their plantations and put to work as workers building defenses and other chores. Once transported to the front, many of them found ways to escape across Northern lines, where they were treated as "contraband"—goods seized from people who had no right to them. They could not be returned to their masters. By 1862, the Union army often penetrated deep into the Confederacy. Almost everywhere they went, escaped slaves flocked to join them by the thousands, often whole families. Some of them joined the

Union army, others simply stayed with the troops until they could find their way to free states. When the Union captured New Orleans and much of southern Louisiana, slaves refused to work for their former masters, even though the Union occupiers had not made any provisions for liberating African Americans.

By the end of the war, two Union slave states (Maryland and Missouri) and three Confederate states occupied by Union forces (Tennessee, Arkansas, and Louisiana) had abolished slavery. In 1865, Congress finally approved and the states ratified the *The Thirteenth Amendment* Thirteenth Amendment, which abolished slavery in all parts of the United States. After more than two centuries, legalized slavery finally ceased to exist in the United States.

AFRICAN AMERICANS AND THE UNION CAUSE

About 186,000 emancipated blacks served as soldiers, sailors, and laborers for the Union forces. Yet in the first months of the war, African Americans were largely excluded from the military. A few black regiments eventually took shape in some of the Union-occupied areas of the Confederacy. But once Lincoln issued the Emancipation Proclamation, black enlistment increased rapidly and the Union military began actively to recruit African American soldiers and sailors in both the North and, where possible, the South.

Some of these men were organized into fighting units, of which the best known was probably the Fifty-fourth Massachusetts Infantry, which (like most black regiments) had a white commander: Robert Gould Shaw, a member of an aristocratic Boston family.

Most black soldiers, however, were assigned menial tasks behind the lines, such as digging trenches and transporting water. Even though many fewer blacks than whites died in combat, the African American mortality rate was actually higher than the rate for white soldiers because so many black soldiers died of diseases contracted while working long, arduous hours in unsanitary conditions. Conditions for blacks and whites were unequal in

AFRICAN AMERICAN TROOPS   Although most of the black soldiers who enlisted in the Union army performed noncombat jobs behind the lines, some black combat regiments—members of one of which are pictured here— fought with great success and valor in critical battles. (The Library of Congress)

other ways as well. Until 1869, black soldiers were paid a third less than were white soldiers. But however dangerous, onerous, or menial the tasks that black soldiers were given, most of them felt enormous pride in their service—pride they retained throughout their lives, and often through the lives of their descendants. Many moved from the army into politics and other forms of leadership (in both the North and, after the war, the Reconstruction South). Black fighting men captured by the Confederates were sent back to their masters (if they were escaped slaves) or executed. In 1864, Confederate soldiers killed over 260 black Union soldiers after capturing them in Tennessee.

Women, Nursing, and the War

Thrust into new and often unfamiliar roles by the war, women took over positions vacated by men as teachers, salesclerks, office workers, mill and factory hands, and above all nursing. The United States Sanitary Commission, an organization   *U.S. Sanitary Commission* of civilian volunteers, mobilized large numbers of female nurses to serve in field hospitals. By the end of the war, women were the dominant force in nursing.

Female nurses encountered considerable resistance from male doctors, many of whom thought it inappropriate for women to take care of male strangers. The Sanitary Commission countered such arguments by presenting nursing in domestic terms: as a profession that made use of the same maternal, nurturing roles women played as wives and mothers.

Some women came to see the war as an opportunity to win support for their own goals. Elizabeth Cady Stanton and Susan B. Anthony together founded the Women's National Loyal League in 1863 and worked simultaneously for the abolition of slavery and the awarding of suffrage to women.

THE MOBILIZATION OF THE SOUTH

Early in February 1861, representatives of the seven seceding states met at Montgomery, Alabama, to create a new Southern nation. When Virginia seceded several months later, the leaders of the Confederacy moved to Richmond.

There were, of course, important differences between the new Confederate nation and the nation it had left. But there were also significant similarities.

The Confederate Government

The Confederate constitution was almost identical to the Constitution of the United States, with several significant exceptions. It explicitly acknowledged the sovereignty of the individual states (although not the right of secession). And it specifically sanctioned slavery and made its abolition (even by one of the states) practically impossible.

The constitutional convention at Montgomery named a provisional president and vice president: Jefferson Davis of Mississippi and Alexander H. Stephens of   *Jefferson Davis* Georgia, who were later elected by the general public, without opposition, for six-year terms. Davis had been a moderate secessionist before the war. Stephens had argued against secession. The Confederate government, like the Union government, was dominated throughout the war by men of the political center.

Davis was a reasonably able administrator and encountered little interference from the generally tame members of his unstable cabinet. But he rarely provided genuinely national leadership, spending too much time on routine items. Unlike Lincoln, he displayed a punctiliousness about legal and constitutional requirements.

Although there were no formal political parties in the Confederacy, its politics were fiercely divided nevertheless. Some white Southerners opposed secession and war altogether. Most white Southerners supported the war, but as in the North, many were openly critical of the government and the military, particularly as the tide of battle turned against the South.

States' rights had become such a cult among many white Southerners that they resisted *States' Rights within the Confederacy* virtually all efforts to exert national authority, even those necessary to win the war. States' rights enthusiasts obstructed conscription and restricted Davis's ability to impose martial law and suspend habeas corpus. Governors such as Joseph Brown of Georgia and Zebulon M. Vance of North Carolina tried at times to keep their own troops apart from the Confederate forces.

But the national government was not impotent. It experimented, successfully for a time, with a "food draft," which permitted soldiers to feed themselves by seizing crops from farms in their path. The Confederacy also seized control of the railroads and shipping; it impressed slaves to work as laborers on military projects and imposed regulations on industry; it limited corporate profits. States' rights sentiment was a significant handicap, but the South nevertheless took important steps in the direction of centralization.

Money and Manpower

Financing the Confederate war effort was a monumental task. The Confederate congress tried at first to requisition funds from the individual states; but the states were as reluctant to tax their citizens as the congress was. In 1863, therefore, the congress enacted an income tax. But taxation produced only about 1 percent of the government's total income. Borrowing was not much more successful. The Confederate government issued bonds in such vast amounts that the public lost faith in them, and efforts to borrow money in Europe, using cotton as collateral, fared no better.

As a result, the Confederacy had to pay for the war through the least stable, most destructive form of financing: paper currency, which it began issuing in 1861. By 1864, the Confederacy had issued the staggering total of $1.5 billion in paper money. The result *Inflation* was a disastrous inflation—a 9,000 percent increase in prices in the course of the war (in contrast to 80 percent in the North).

Like the United States, the Confederacy first raised armies by calling for volunteers. And as in the North, by the end of 1861 voluntary enlistments were declining. In April *Conscription Act* 1862, therefore, the congress enacted the Conscription Act, which subjected all white males between the ages of eighteen and thirty-five to military service for three years. As in the North, a draftee could avoid service if he furnished a substitute. But since the price of substitutes was high, the provision aroused such opposition from poorer whites that it was repealed in 1863.

Even so, conscription worked for a time, in part because enthusiasm for the war was intense and widespread among white men in most of the South. At the end of 1862, about 500,000 soldiers were in the Confederate army, not including the many slave men and women recruited by the military to perform such services as cooking, laundry, and manual labor. Small numbers of slaves and free blacks enlisted in the Confederate army, and a few participated in combat.

After 1862, however, conscription began producing fewer men, and by 1864 the Confederate government faced a critical manpower shortage. The South was suffering from intense war weariness, and many Southerners had concluded that defeat was inevitable. Nothing could attract or retain an adequate army any longer. *Troop Shortage* In a frantic final attempt to raise men, the congress authorized the conscription of 300,000 slaves, but the war ended before the government could attempt this incongruous experiment.

ECONOMIC AND SOCIAL EFFECTS OF THE WAR

The war cut off Southern planters and producers from Northern markets, and a Union blockade of Confederate ports made the sale of cotton overseas much more difficult. In the North, production of all goods increased during the war; in the South, it declined by more than a third. Above all, the fighting itself wreaked havoc on the Southern landscape, destroying farmland, towns, cities, and railroads. As the war continued, the shortages, the inflation, and the carnage created increasing instability in Southern society. Resistance to conscription, food impressment, and taxation increased throughout the Confederacy, as did hoarding and black-market commerce.

Some recreational pursuits found new popularity. Baseball emerged as a favorite pastime for Confederate and Union troops alike, who set up makeshift games within their ranks to relieve the pressures of the war. At the same time, civilians in northern cities flocked to cheer on local teams in the newly founded National Association of Base Ball Players. (See "Patterns of Popular Culture: Baseball and the Civil War.")

The war forced many women (and some men) to perform untraditional, nondomestic tasks during the conflict. Because the war decimated the male   *New Roles for Southern Women* population, women soon outnumbered men in most Southern states by significant margins. The result was a large number of unmarried or widowed women who had no choice but to find employment.

Even before emancipation, the war had far-reaching effects on the lives of slaves. Confederate leaders enforced slave codes with particular severity. Even so, many slaves— especially those near the front—escaped their masters and crossed Union lines.

STRATEGY AND DIPLOMACY

The military initiative in the Civil War lay mainly with the North, since it needed to destroy the Confederacy as quickly as possible. Southerners needed only to survive; however, survival required diplomatic recognition from other nations, especially Great Britain, and the financial and military aid that would accompany it. Lincoln and his diplomatic corps worked tirelessly to keep foreign powers and their resources out of the Confederacy while the Union navy blockaded Southern ports.

THE COMMANDERS

The most important Union military leader was Abraham Lincoln. He ultimately succeeded as commander in chief because he recognized the North's material advantages, and he realized that the proper objective of his armies was to destroy the Confederate armies' ability to fight. Despite his missteps and inexperience, the North was fortunate to have Lincoln, but the president struggled to find a general as well suited for his task as Lincoln was for his.

BASEBALL AND THE CIVIL WAR

Long before the great urban stadiums, the lights, the cameras, and the multimillion-dollar salaries, baseball was the most popular game in America. During the Civil War, it was a treasured pastime for soldiers and for thousands of men (and some women) behind the lines, in both the North and the South.

The legend that baseball was invented by Abner Doubleday—who probably never even saw the game—was created by Albert G. Spalding, a patriotic sporting-goods manufacturer eager to prove that the game had purely American origins. In fact, baseball was derived from a variety of earlier games, especially the English pastimes of cricket and rounders. American baseball took its own distinctive form beginning in the 1840s, when Alexander Cartwright, a shipping clerk, formed the New York Knickerbockers, laid out a diamond-shaped field with four bases, and declared that batters with three strikes were out and that teams with three outs were retired.

Cartwright moved west in search of gold in 1849, settling finally in Hawaii, where he introduced the game to Americans in the Pacific. But the game did not languish in his absence. Henry Chadwick, an English-born journalist, spent much of the 1850s popularizing the game and regularizing its rules. By 1860, baseball was being played by college students and Irish workers, by urban elites and provincial farmers, by people of all classes and ethnic groups from New England to Louisiana. Students at Vassar College formed "ladies" teams in the 1860s, and in Philadelphia, free black men formed the Pythians, the first of what was to become a great network of African American

baseball teams. From the beginning, they were barred from playing against most white teams.

When young men marched off to war in 1861, some took their bats and balls with them. Almost from the start of the fighting, soldiers in both armies took advantage of idle moments to lay out baseball diamonds and organize games. Games on battlefields were sometimes interrupted by gunfire and cannon fire. "It is astonishing how indifferent a person can become to danger," a soldier wrote home to Ohio in 1862. "The report of musketry is heard but a very little distance from us, . . . yet over there on the other side of the road is most of our company, playing Bat Ball." After a skirmish in Texas, another Union soldier lamented that, in addition to casualties, his company had lost "the only baseball in Alexandria, Texas." Far from discouraging baseball, military commanders—and the United States Sanitary Commission, the Union army's medical arm—actively encouraged the game during the war. It would, they believed, help keep up the soldiers' morale.

Away from the battlefield, baseball continued to flourish. In New York City, games between local teams drew crowds of ten thousand to twenty thousand. The National Association of Base Ball Players, founded in 1859, had recruited ninety-one clubs in ten Northern states by 1865; a North Western Association of Baseball Players, organized in Chicago in 1865, indicated that the game was becoming well established in the West as well. In Brooklyn, William Cammeyer drained a skating pond on his property, built a board fence around it, and created the first enclosed baseball field in

America—the Union Grounds. He charged ten cents for admission. The professionalization of the game had begun.

Despite all the commercialization and spectacle that came to be associated with baseball in the years after the Civil War, the game remained for many Americans what it was to millions of young men fighting in the most savage war in the nation's history—an American passion that at times, even if briefly, erased the barriers dividing groups from one another. "Officers and men forget, for a time, the differences in rank," a Massachusetts private wrote in 1863, "and indulge in the invigorating sport with a schoolboy's ardor." •

UNDERSTAND, ANALYZE, & EVALUATE

1. How could a competitive game of baseball erase "the barriers dividing groups from one another"?
2. Baseball during the Civil War crossed the lines of cultural differences between the North and the South. Does baseball today—professional or amateur—continue to cross lines of cultural differences?

From 1861 to 1864, Lincoln tried repeatedly to find a chief of staff capable of orchestrating the Union war effort. He turned first to General Winfield Scott, the ailing 74-year-old hero of the Mexican War who had already contributed strategic advice to the president, but Scott was no longer physically capable of leading an army. Lincoln then appointed the young George B. McClellan, the commander of the Union forces in the East, the Army of the Potomac. Unfortunately, the proud and overly cautious McClellan seemed too slow to act for Lincoln's tastes. Lincoln returned McClellan to his previous command in March 1862. For most of the rest of the year, Lincoln had no chief of staff at all. When he eventually appointed General Henry W. Halleck to the post, he found him ineffectual as well. Not until March 1864 did Lincoln finally find a general he trusted to command the war effort: Ulysses S. Grant, who shared Lincoln's belief in unremitting *Ulysses S. Grant* combat and in making enemy armies and resources the target of military efforts.

Lincoln's handling of the war effort faced constant scrutiny from the Committee on the Conduct of the War, a joint investigative committee of the two houses of Congress. Established in December 1861 and chaired by Senator Benjamin E. Wade of Ohio, the committee complained constantly of the inadequate ruthlessness of Northern generals, which Radicals on the committee attributed (largely inaccurately) to a secret sympathy among the officers for slavery. The committee's efforts often seriously interfered with the conduct of the war.

Southern military leadership centered on President Davis, a trained soldier who nonetheless failed to create an effective central command system. Early in 1862, Davis named General Robert E. Lee as his principal military adviser. But in fact, Davis had no intention of sharing control of strategy with anyone. After a few months, Lee left Richmond to command forces in the field, and for the next two years, Davis planned strategy alone. In February 1864, he named General Braxton Bragg as a military adviser, but Bragg never provided much more than technical advice.

At lower levels of command, men of markedly similar backgrounds controlled the war in both the North and the South. Many of the professional officers on both sides were graduates of the United States Military Academy at West Point and the United States Naval Academy at Annapolis. Amateur officers played an important role in both armies as commanders of volunteer regiments. In both the North and the South, such men were usually economic or social leaders in their communities who rounded up troops to lead. Sometimes this system produced officers of real ability; more often it did not.

GRANT (LEFT) AND LEE Of the Union general, an observer said: "He habitually wears an expression as if he had determined to drive his head through a brick wall, and was about to do it." It was an apt metaphor for Grant's military philosophy, which relied on constant, unrelenting assault. The Confederate general, in contrast, was known for his dignified and disciplined demeanor. He became a symbol to white Southerners of the "Lost Cause." (Grant: The Library of Congress; Lee: © Bettmann/Corbis)

The Role of Sea Power

The Union had an overwhelming advantage in naval power. It played two important roles
Union Blockade in the war: enforcing a blockade of the Southern coast and assisting the Union armies in field operations.

The blockade, which began in the first weeks of the war, kept most oceangoing ships out of Confederate ports, but for a time small blockade runners continued to slip through. Gradually, however, federal forces tightened the blockade by seizing the Confederate ports themselves. The last important port in Confederate hands—Wilmington, North Carolina—fell to the Union early in 1865.

The Confederates made a bold attempt to break the blockade with an ironclad warship, constructed by plating with iron a former United States frigate, the *Merrimac.* On March 8, 1862, the refitted *Merrimac,* renamed the *Virginia,* left Norfolk to attack a blockading squadron of wooden ships at nearby Hampton Roads. It destroyed two of the ships and scattered the rest. But the Union government had already built ironclads of its own, including the *Monitor,* which arrived only a few hours after the *Virginia*'s   Monitor *versus* Merrimac dramatic foray. The next day, it met the *Virginia* in battle. Neither vessel was able to sink the other, but the *Monitor* put an end to the *Virginia*'s raids and preserved the blockade.

The Union navy was particularly important in the western theater of the war, where the major rivers were navigable by large vessels. The navy transported supplies and troops and joined in attacking Confederate strong points. The South had no significant navy of its own and could defend against the Union gunboats only with ineffective fixed land fortifications.

Europe and the Disunited States

Judah P. Benjamin, the Confederate secretary of state for most of the war, was an intelligent but undynamic man who attended mostly to routine administrative tasks. William Seward, his counterpart in Washington, gradually became one of the outstanding American secretaries of state. He had invaluable assistance from Charles Francis Adams, the American minister to London. This gap between the diplomatic skills of the Union and the Confederacy was a decisive factor in the war.

At the beginning of the conflict, the sympathies of the ruling classes of England and France lay largely with the Confederacy, partly because the   *Arguments for Supporting Each Side* two nations imported much Southern cotton; but it was also because they were eager to weaken the United States, an increasingly powerful rival to them in world commerce. France was unwilling to take sides in the conflict unless England did so first. And in England, the government was reluctant to act because there was powerful popular support for the Union—particularly from the large and influential English antislavery movement. After Lincoln issued the Emancipation Proclamation, antislavery groups worked particularly avidly for the Union. Southern leaders hoped to counter the strength of the British antislavery forces by arguing that access to Southern cotton was vital to the English and French textile industries. But English manufacturers had a surplus of both raw cotton and finished goods on hand in 1861 and could withstand a temporary loss of access to American cotton. Later, as the supply began to diminish, both England and France managed to keep at least some of their mills open by importing cotton from Egypt, India, and elsewhere. Equally important, even the 500,000 English textile workers thrown out of jobs as a result of mill closings continued to support the North. In the end, therefore, no European nation offered diplomatic recognition, financial support, or military aid to the Confederacy. No nation wanted to antagonize the United States unless the Confederacy seemed likely to win, and the South never came close enough to victory to convince its potential allies to support it. In the end, the Confederacy was on its own.

Even so, tension, and on occasion near hostilities, continued between the United States and Britain. The Union government was angry when Great Britain, France, and other nations declared themselves neutral early in the war, thus implying that the two sides to the conflict had equal stature. Leaders in Washington insisted that the conflict was simply a domestic insurrection, not a war between two legitimate governments.

A more serious crisis, the so-called *Trent* affair, began in late 1861. Two Confederate diplomats, James M. Mason and John Slidell, had slipped through the then-   *The* Trent *Affair* ineffective Union blockade to Havana, Cuba, where they boarded an English steamer, the *Trent,* for England. Waiting in Cuban waters was the American frigate *San Jacinto,* commanded by the impetuous Charles Wilkes. Acting without authorization, Wilkes stopped the

British vessel, arrested the diplomats, and carried them in triumph to Boston. The British government demanded the release of the prisoners, reparations, and an apology. Lincoln and Seward were aware that Wilkes had violated maritime law. They were unwilling to risk war with England, and they eventually released the diplomats with an indirect apology.

CAMPAIGNS AND BATTLES

In the absence of direct intervention by the European powers, the two contestants in North America were left to resolve the conflict between themselves. They did so in four long *Staggering Casualties* years of bloody combat. More than 618,000 Americans died in the course of the Civil War, far more than the 112,000 who perished in World War I or the 405,000 who died in World War II. There were nearly 2,000 deaths for every 100,000 of population during the Civil War. In World War I, the comparable figure was only 109, and in World War II the comparable figure was 241. In some respects, the Civil War was the bloodiest war in modern times.

THE TECHNOLOGY OF WAR

Much of what happened on the battlefield in the Civil War was a result of new technologies that transformed the nature of combat.

The most obvious change was the nature of the armaments. Among the most important was the introduction of repeating weapons. Samuel Colt had patented a repeating pistol (the revolver) in 1835, but more important for military purposes was the repeating rifle, introduced in 1860 by Oliver Winchester. Also significant were greatly improved cannons and artillery, a result of earlier advances in iron and steel technology.

These new armaments made it impossibly deadly to fight battles as they had been fought for centuries, with lines of infantry soldiers standing erect in the field firing volleys at their opponents until one side withdrew. Soldiers quickly learned that the proper position for combat was staying low to the ground and behind cover. For the first time in the *Deadlier Weaponry* history of organized warfare, therefore, infantry did not fight in formation, and the battlefields became more chaotic places. Gradually, the deadliness of the new weapons encouraged armies on both sides to spend a great deal of time building elaborate fortifications and trenches to protect themselves from enemy fire. The sieges of Vicksburg and Petersburg, the defense of Richmond, and many other military events all produced the construction of vast fortifications around both cities and attacking armies. (They were the predecessors to the vast network of trenches of World War I.)

Other weapons technologies were less central to the fighting of the war, but important nevertheless. The relatively new technology of hot-air balloons was employed intermittently to provide a view of enemy formations in the field. The ironclad ships—and even torpedoes and submarine technology, which made fleeting appearances in the 1860s—suggested the dramatic changes that would soon overtake naval warfare.

Critical to the conduct of the war, however, were two other relatively new technologies: the railroad and the telegraph. The railroad was particularly important in mobilizing millions of soldiers and transferring them to the front. Transporting such enormous numbers *Military Importance of Railroads* of soldiers, and the supplies necessary to sustain them, by foot or by horse and wagon would have been almost impossible. But, ironically, railroads also limited the mobility of the armies. Commanders were forced to organize their campaigns at least in part around the location of the railroads rather than on the basis of the best topography or most direct land route to a destination. The dependence on the rails—and the resulting necessity of concentrating huge numbers of men in a few places—also encouraged commanders to prefer great battles with large armies rather than smaller engagements with fewer troops.

The impact of the telegraph on the war was limited both by the scarcity of qualified telegraph operators and by the difficulty of bringing telegraph wires into the fields where battles were being fought. Things improved somewhat after the new U.S. Military Telegraph Corps, headed by Thomas Scott and Andrew Carnegie, trained and employed over 1,200 operators. Gradually, too, both the Union and Confederate armies learned to string telegraph wires along the routes of their troops, so that field commanders were able to stay in close touch with one another during battles.

THE OPENING CLASHES, 1861

The Union and the Confederacy fought their first major battle of the war in northern Virginia. A Union army of over 30,000 men under General Irvin McDowell was stationed just outside Washington. About thirty miles away, at Manassas, sat a slightly smaller Confederate army commanded by General P. G. T. Beauregard. If the Northern army could destroy the Southern one, Union leaders believed, the war might end at once. In mid-July, McDowell marched his inexperienced troops toward Manassas. Beauregard moved his troops behind Bull Run, a small stream north of Manassas, and called for reinforcements, which reached him the day before the battle.

On July 21, in the First Battle of Bull Run, or First Battle of   *First Battle of Bull Run* Manassas, McDowell almost succeeded in dispersing the Confederate forces. But the Southerners managed to fight off a last strong Union assault. The Confederates then began a savage counterattack. The Union troops suddenly panicked, broke ranks, and retreated chaotically. McDowell was unable to reorganize them, and he had to order a retreat to Washington—a disorderly withdrawal complicated by the presence along the route of many civilians, who had ridden down from the capital, picnic baskets in hand, to watch the battle from nearby hills. The Confederates, as disorganized by victory as the Union forces were by defeat, did not pursue. The battle was a severe blow to Union morale and to the president's confidence in his officers.

Elsewhere, Union forces achieved some small but significant victories in 1861. A Union force under General George B. McClellan moved east from Ohio into western Virginia. By the end of 1861, it had "liberated" the antisecession   *West Virginia Established* mountain people of the region, who created their own state government loyal to the Union; the state was admitted to the Union as West Virginia in 1863.

THE WESTERN THEATER

After the battle at Bull Run, military operations in the East settled into a long and frustrating stalemate. The first decisive operations occurred in the western theater in 1862. Here Union forces were trying to seize control of the southern part of the Mississippi River from both the north and south, moving down the river from Kentucky and up from the Gulf of Mexico toward New Orleans.

In April, a Union squadron commanded by Flag Officer David G. Farragut smashed past weak Confederate forts near the mouth of the Mississippi and from there sailed up

THE WAR IN THE WEST, 1861–1863 While the Union armies in Virginia were meeting with repeated frustrations, the Union armies in the West were scoring notable successes in the first two years of the war. This map shows a series of Union drives in the western Confederacy. Flag Officer David Farragut's ironclads led to the capture of New Orleans—a critical Confederate port—in April 1862, while forces farther north under the command of Ulysses S. Grant drove the Confederate army out of Kentucky and western Tennessee. These battles culminated in the Union victory at Shiloh, which led to Union control of the upper Mississippi River. • *Why was control of the Mississippi so important to both sides?*

to New Orleans. The city was virtually defenseless because the Confederate high com-
New Orleans Seized   mand had expected the attack to come from the north. The surrender of
New Orleans on April 25, 1862, was an important turning point in the war. From then
on, the mouth of the Mississippi was closed to Confederate trade, and the South's largest
city and most important banking center was in Union hands.

Farther north in the western theater, Confederate troops under General Albert Sidney
Johnston were stretched out in a long defensive line around two forts in Tennessee, Fort
Henry and Fort Donelson. Early in 1862, Ulysses S. Grant attacked Fort Henry, whose
defenders, awed by the ironclad riverboats accompanying the Union army, surrendered
with almost no resistance. Grant then moved both his naval and ground forces to Fort
Donelson, where the Confederates put up a stronger fight but finally, on February 16, had
to surrender. Grant thus gained control of river communications and forced Confederate
troops out of Kentucky and half of Tennessee.

With about 40,000 men, Grant now advanced south along the Tennessee River. At Shiloh, Tennessee, he met a force almost equal to his own, commanded by Albert *Shiloh* Sidney Johnston and P. G. T. Beauregard. The result was the Battle of Shiloh, April 6–7, 1862. In the first day's fighting (during which Johnston was killed), the Southerners drove Grant back to the river. But the next day, reinforced by 25,000 fresh troops, Grant recovered the lost ground and forced Beauregard to withdraw. After the narrow Union victory at Shiloh, Northern forces occupied Corinth, Mississippi, and took control of the Mississippi River as far south as Memphis.

General Braxton Bragg, now in command of the Confederate army in the West, gathered his forces at Chattanooga, in eastern Tennessee, where he faced a Union army trying to capture the city. The two armies maneuvered for advantage inconclusively in northern Tennessee and southern Kentucky for several months until December 31–January 2, when they finally clashed in the Battle of Murfreesboro, or Stone's River. Bragg was forced to withdraw to the South in defeat.

By the end of 1862, Union forces had made considerable progress in the West. But the heart of the war remained in the East.

THE VIRGINIA FRONT, 1862

During the winter of 1861–1862, George B. McClellan, commander of the Army of the Potomac, concentrated on training his army of 150,000 men near Washington. Finally, he designed a spring campaign to capture the Confederate capital at Richmond. But instead of heading overland directly, McClellan chose a complicated route that he thought would circumvent the Confederate defenses. The navy would carry his troops down the Potomac to a peninsula east of Richmond, between the York and James Rivers; the army would approach the city from there in what became known as the Peninsular campaign.

McClellan set off with 100,000 men, reluctantly leaving 30,000 members of his army behind, under General Irvin McDowell, to protect Washington. McClellan eventually persuaded Lincoln to send him the additional men. But before the president could do so, a Confederate army under General Thomas J. ("Stonewall") Jackson *"Stonewall" Jackson* staged a rapid march north through the Shenandoah Valley, as if preparing to cross the Potomac and attack Washington. Lincoln postponed sending reinforcements to McClellan, retaining McDowell's corps to head off Jackson. In the Valley campaign of May 4–June 9, 1862, Jackson defeated two separate Union forces and slipped away before McDowell could catch him.

Meanwhile, McClellan was fighting Confederate troops under General Joseph E. Johnston outside Richmond in the two-day Battle of Fair Oaks, or Seven Pines (May 31–June 1), and holding his ground. Johnston, badly wounded, was replaced by Robert E. Lee, who then recalled Stonewall Jackson from the Shenandoah *Robert E. Lee* Valley. With a combined force of 85,000 to face McClellan's 100,000, Lee launched a new offensive, known as the Battle of the Seven Days (June 25–July 1), in an effort to cut McClellan off from his base on the York River. But McClellan fought his way across the peninsula and set up a new base on the James.

McClellan was now only twenty-five miles from Richmond and in a good position to renew the campaign. But despite continuing pressure from Lincoln, he did not advance. Hoping to force a new offensive against Richmond along the direct overland route he had always preferred, Lincoln finally ordered the army to move back to northern Virginia and join up with a smaller force under General John Pope. As the Army of the Potomac left

July 1861–July 1862

August–December 1862

1863

THE VIRGINIA THEATER, 1861-1863   Much of the fighting during the first two years of the Civil War took place in what became known as the Virginia theater—although the campaigns in this region eventually extended north into Maryland and Pennsylvania. The Union hoped for a quick victory over the newly created Confederate army. But as these maps show, the Southern forces consistently thwarted such hopes. The map at top left shows the battles of 1861 and the first half of 1862, almost all of them won by the Confederates. The map at lower left shows the last months of 1862, during which the Southerners again defeated the Union in most of their engagements—although Northern forces drove the Confederates back from Maryland in September. The map on the right shows the troop movements that led to the climactic battle of Gettysburg in 1863. • *Why were the Union forces unable to profit more from material advantages during these first years of the war?*

the peninsula by water, Lee moved north with the Army of Northern Virginia to strike Pope before McClellan could join him. Pope was as rash as McClellan was cautious, and he attacked the approaching Confederates without waiting for the arrival of all of McClellan's troops. In the Second Battle of Bull Run, or Manassas (August 29–30), Lee threw back the assault and routed Pope's army, which fled to Washington. With hopes for an overland campaign against Richmond now in disarray, Lincoln removed Pope from command and put McClellan back in charge of all the federal forces in the region.

Lee soon went on the offensive again, heading north through western Maryland, and McClellan moved out to meet him. McClellan had the good luck to get a copy of Lee's orders, which revealed that a part of the Confederate army, under Stonewall Jackson, had separated from the rest to attack Harpers Ferry. But instead of attacking quickly before the Confederates could recombine, McClellan stalled, again giving Lee time to pull most of his forces back together behind Antietam Creek, near the town of Sharpsburg.   *Antietam* There, on September 17, McClellan's 87,000-man army repeatedly attacked Lee's force of 50,000, with staggering casualties on both sides. Late in the day, just as the Confederate line seemed ready to break, the last of Jackson's troops arrived from Harpers Ferry to reinforce it. McClellan might have broken through with one more assault. Instead, he allowed Lee to retreat into Virginia. Technically, Antietam was a Union victory; but in reality, McClellan had squandered an opportunity to destroy much of the Confederate army. In November, Lincoln finally removed McClellan from command for good.

McClellan's replacement, General Ambrose E. Burnside, was a short-lived mediocrity. He tried to move toward Richmond by crossing the Rappahannock River at Fredericksburg. There, on December 13, he launched a series of attacks against Lee, all of them bloody, all of them hopeless. After losing a large part of his army, he withdrew to the north bank of the Rappahannock. He was relieved at his own request. The year 1862 ended, therefore, with a series of frustrations for the Union.

THE PROGRESS OF THE WAR

Why did the Union—with its much greater population, its much larger population, and its much better transportation and technology than the Confederacy—make so little progress in the first two years of the war? Had there been a decisive and dramatic victory by either side early in the war—for example, a major victory by the Union at the First Battle of Bull Run—the conflict might have ended quickly by destroying the Confederacy's morale. But no such decisive victory occurred in the first two years of the war.

Many Northerners blamed the military stalemate on timid or incompetent Union generals, and there was some truth to that view. But the more important reason for the drawn-out conflict was that it was not a war of traditional tactics and military strategy. It was, even if the leaders of both sides were not yet fully aware of it, a war of attrition, and the Confederacy could survive only if the Union quit fighting. Winning or losing battles here and there would not determine the outcome of the war. What would bring the war to a conclusion was the steady destruction of the resources that were necessary for victory. More than two bloody years of fighting were still to come. But those last years were a testimony to the slow, steady deterioration of the Confederacy's ability to maintain the war, and the consistent growth of the resources that allowed the Union armies to grow steadily stronger.

1863: YEAR OF DECISION

At the beginning of 1863, General Joseph Hooker was commanding the still-formidable Army of the Potomac, which remained north of the Rappahannock, opposite Fredericksburg. Taking part of his army, Hooker crossed the river above Fredericksburg and moved toward the town and Lee's army. But at the last minute, he drew back to a defensive position in a desolate area of brush and scrub trees known as the Wilderness. Lee divided his forces for a dual

THE SIEGE OF VICKSBURG, MAY–JULY 1863 In the spring of 1863, Grant began a campaign to win control of the final piece of the Mississippi River still controlled by the Confederacy. To do that required capturing the Southern stronghold at Vicksburg—a well-defended city sitting above the river. Vicksburg's main defenses were to the north, so Grant boldly moved men and supplies around the city and attacked it from the south. Eventually, he cut off the city's access to the outside world, and after a six-week siege, its residents finally surrendered. • *What impact did the combined victories at Vicksburg and Gettysburg have on Northern commitment to the war?*

Chancellorsville assault on the Union army. In the Battle of Chancellorsville, May 1–5, Stonewall Jackson attacked the Union right and Lee himself charged the front. Hooker barely managed to escape with his army. Lee had frustrated Union objectives, but he had not destroyed the Union army. And his ablest officer, Jackson, was fatally wounded in the course of the battle.

While the Union forces were suffering repeated frustrations in the East, they were winning some important victories in the West. In the spring of 1863, Ulysses S. Grant

was driving at Vicksburg on the Mississippi River. Vicksburg was well protected   *Vicksburg*
on land and had good artillery coverage of the river itself. But in May, Grant boldly
moved men and supplies—over land and by water—to an area south of the city, where
the terrain was reasonably good. He then attacked Vicksburg from the rear. Six weeks
later, on July 4, Vicksburg—whose residents were by then starving as a result of the
prolonged siege—surrendered. At almost the same time, the other Confederate strongpoint
on the river, Port Hudson, Louisiana, also surrendered to a Union force that had moved
north from New Orleans. With the achievement of one of the Union's basic military
aims—control of the whole length of the Mississippi—the Confederacy was split in two,
with Louisiana, Arkansas, and Texas cut off from the other seceded states. The victories
on the Mississippi were one of the great turning points of the war.

During the siege of Vicksburg, Lee proposed an invasion of Pennsylvania, which
would, he argued, divert Union troops north. Further, he argued, if he could win a major
victory on Northern soil, England and France might come to the Confederacy's aid. The
war-weary North might even quit the war before Vicksburg fell.

In June 1863, Lee moved up the Shenandoah Valley into Maryland and then entered
Pennsylvania. The Union Army of the Potomac, commanded first by Hooker and then
(after June 28) by General George C. Meade, moved north, too. The two armies finally
encountered each other at the small town of Gettysburg, Pennsylvania. There, on July 1–3,
1863, they fought the most celebrated battle of the war.

Meade's army established a strong, well-protected position on the hills south of the
town. Lee attacked, but his first assault on the Union forces on Cemetery Ridge failed.

GETTYSBURG, JULY 1–3, 1863   Gettysburg was the most important single battle of the Civil War. Had Confederate
forces prevailed at Gettysburg, the future course of the war might well have been very different. The map on the left shows
the distribution of Union and Confederate forces at the beginning of the battle, July 1, after Lee had driven the Northern
forces south of town. The map on the right reveals the pattern of the attacks on July 2 and 3. Note, in particular, Pickett's
bold and costly charge, whose failure on July 3 was the turning point in the battle and, some chroniclers have argued, the
war. • *Why did Robert E. Lee believe that an invasion of Pennsylvania would advance the Confederate cause?*

CONSIDER THE SOURCE

THE GETTYSBURG ADDRESS, NOVEMBER 19, 1863

Lincoln gave this speech on the occasion of the dedication of the Soldiers' National Cemetery in Gettysburg, Pennsylvania, four months after the famous battle.

Four score and seven years ago our fathers brought forth on this continent, a new nation, conceived in Liberty, and dedicated to the proposition that all men are created equal.

Now we are engaged in a great civil war, testing whether that nation, or any nation so conceived and so dedicated, can long endure. We are met on a great battlefield of that war. We have come to dedicate a portion of that field, as a final resting place for those who here gave their lives that that nation might live. It is altogether fitting and proper that we should do this.

But, in a larger sense, we can not dedicate—we can not consecrate—we can not hallow—this ground. The brave men, living and dead, who struggled here, have consecrated it, far above our poor power to add or detract. The world will little note, nor long remember what we say here, but it can never forget what they did here. It is for us the living, rather, to be dedicated here to the unfinished work which they who fought here have thus far so nobly advanced. It is rather for us to be here dedicated to the great task remaining before us—that from these honored dead we take increased devotion to that cause for which they gave the last full measure of devotion—that we here highly resolve that these dead shall not have died in vain—that this nation, under God, shall have a new birth of freedom—and that government of the people, by the people, for the people, shall not perish from the earth.

UNDERSTAND, ANALYZE, & EVALUATE

1. What purpose did Lincoln ascribe to the Civil War in the first two sentences of his speech?
2. Why did Lincoln state that he and his audience could not dedicate the battlefield?
3. What significance did Lincoln ascribe to the Battle of Gettysburg in the last sentence of this speech?
4. Why do you think this address endeared President Lincoln to many of his contemporaries and so many Americans since?

Source: Michael P. Johnson (ed.), *Abraham Lincoln, Slavery, and the Civil War: Selected Writings and Speeches* (Boston: Bedford St. Martin's, 2010), p. 263.

A day later, he ordered a second, larger effort. In what is remembered as Pickett's Charge, a force of 15,000 Confederate soldiers advanced for almost a mile across open country while being swept by Union fire. Only about 5,000 made it up the ridge, and this remnant finally had to surrender or retreat. By now, Lee had lost nearly a third of his army. On July 4, the same day as the surrender of Vicksburg, Lee withdrew from Gettysburg. The retreat was another major turning point in the war. Never again were the weakened Confederate forces able seriously to threaten Northern territory. Months later Lincoln visited the battlefield site and delivered one of the most famous speeches in American history. (See "Consider the Source: The Gettysburg Address.")

Gettysburg

Before the end of the year, there was one more important turning point, this time in Tennessee. After occupying Chattanooga on September 9, Union forces under General

William Rosecrans began an unwise pursuit of Bragg's retreating Confederate forces. The two armies engaged in western Georgia, in the Battle of Chickamauga (September 19–20). Union forces could not break the Confederate lines and retreated back to Chattanooga.

Bragg now began a siege of Chattanooga itself, seizing the heights nearby and cutting off fresh supplies to the Union forces. Grant came to the rescue. In the *Battle of Chattanooga* Battle of Chattanooga (November 23–25), the reinforced Union army drove the Confederates back into Georgia. Union forces had now achieved a second important objective: control of the Tennessee River.

THE LAST STAGE, 1864–1865

By the beginning of 1864, President Lincoln had appointed General Ulysses S. Grant as chief of all the Union armies. Grant, like Lincoln, believed in using the North's great advantage in troops and material resources to overwhelm the South. He planned two great offensives for 1864. In Virginia, the Army of the Potomac would advance toward Richmond and force Lee into a decisive battle. In Georgia, the western army, under General William T. Sherman, would advance east toward Atlanta and destroy the remaining Confederate force, now under the command of Joseph E. Johnston.

The northern campaign began when the Army of the Potomac, 115,000 strong, plunged into the rough, wooded Wilderness area of northwestern Virginia in pursuit of Lee's 75,000-man army. After avoiding an engagement for several weeks, Lee turned Grant back in the

VIRGINIA CAMPAIGNS, 1864–1865 From the Confederate defeat at (and retreat from) Gettysburg until the end of the war, most of the eastern fighting took place in Virginia. By now, Ulysses S. Grant was commander of all Union forces and had taken over the Army of the Potomac. Although Confederate forces won a number of important battles during the Virginia campaign, the Union army grew steadily stronger and the Southern forces steadily weaker. Grant believed that the Union strategy should reflect the North's greatest advantage: its superiority in men and equipment. • *What effect did this decision have on the level of casualties?*

Battle of the Wilderness (May 5–7). Without stopping to rest or reorganize, Grant resumed *Grant's Northern Campaign* his march toward Richmond and met Lee again in the bloody Battle of Spotsylvania Court House (May 8–21) in which 12,000 Union troops and a large, but unknown, number of Confederates fell. Grant kept moving, but victory continued to elude him. Lee kept his army between Grant and the Confederate capital and on June 1–3 repulsed the Union forces again, just northeast of Richmond, at Cold Harbor.

Grant now moved his army east of Richmond and headed south toward the railroad center at Petersburg. If he could seize Petersburg, he could cut off the capital's communications with the rest of the Confederacy. But Petersburg had strong defenses; and once Lee came to the city's relief, the assault became a prolonged siege.

In Georgia, meanwhile, Sherman was facing less ferocious resistance. With 90,000 men, he confronted Confederate forces of 60,000 under Johnston. As Sherman advanced, Johnston tried to delay him by maneuvering. The two armies fought only one real battle—Kennesaw Mountain, northwest of Atlanta, on June 27—where Johnston scored an impressive victory. Even so, he was unable to stop the Union advance toward Atlanta, prompting Davis to replace *Atlanta Taken* him with General John B. Hood. Sherman took the city on September 2 and burned it.

Hood now tried unsuccessfully to draw Sherman out of Atlanta by moving back up through Tennessee and threatening an invasion of the North. Sherman sent Union troops

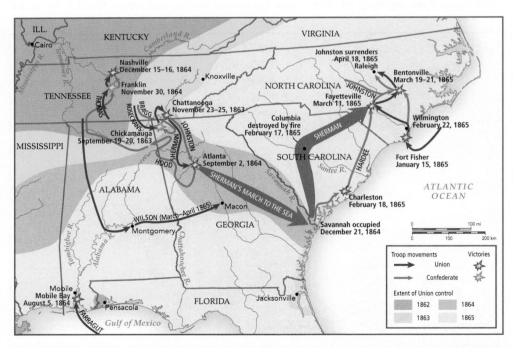

SHERMAN'S MARCH TO THE SEA, 1864–1865   While Grant was wearing Lee down in Virginia, General William Tecumseh Sherman was moving east across Georgia. After a series of battles in Tennessee and northwest Georgia, Sherman captured Atlanta and then marched unimpeded to Savannah, on the Georgia coast—deliberately devastating the towns and plantations through which his troops marched. Note that after capturing Savannah by Christmas 1864, Sherman began moving north through the Carolinas. A few days after Lee surrendered to Grant at Appomattox, Confederate forces farther south surrendered to Sherman. • *What did Sherman believe his devastating March to the Sea would accomplish?*

to reinforce Nashville. In the Battle of Nashville on December 15–16, 1864, Northern forces practically destroyed what was left of Hood's army.

Meanwhile, Sherman had left Atlanta to begin his soon-to-be-famous "March to the Sea." Living off the land, destroying supplies it could not use,   *Sherman's "March to the Sea"* his army cut a sixty-mile-wide swath of desolation across Georgia. Sherman sought not only to deprive the Confederate army of war materials and railroad communications. He was also determined to break the will of the Southern people by burning towns and plantations along his route. By December 20, he had reached Savannah, which surrendered two days later. Early in 1865, Sherman continued his destructive march, moving northward through South Carolina. He was virtually unopposed until he was well inside North Carolina, where a small force under Johnston could do no more than cause a brief delay.

In April 1865, Grant's Army of the Potomac—still engaged in the prolonged siege at Petersburg—finally captured a vital railroad junction southwest of the town. Without rail access to the South, and plagued by heavy casualties and massive desertions, Lee informed the Confederate government that he could no longer defend Richmond. Within hours, Jefferson Davis, his cabinet, and as much of the white population as could find transportation fled. That night, mobs roamed the city, setting devastating fires. And the next morning, Northern forces entered the Confederate capital. With them was Abraham Lincoln, who walked through the streets of the burned-out city surrounded by black men and women cheering him as the "Messiah" and "Father Abraham." In one particularly stirring moment, the president turned to a former slave kneeling on the street before him and said: "Don't kneel to me. . . . You must kneel to God only, and thank Him for the liberty you will enjoy hereafter."

With the remnant of his army, now about 25,000 men, Lee began moving west in the forlorn hope of finding a way around the Union forces so that he could move south and link up with Johnston in North Carolina. But the Union army pursued him and blocked his escape route. Lee finally recognized that further bloodshed was futile. He arranged to meet Grant at a private home in the small town of Appomattox Court House, Virginia,   *Appomattox Court House* where on April 9 he surrendered what was left of his forces. Nine days later, near Durham, North Carolina, Johnston surrendered to Sherman. The long war was now effectively over. Jefferson Davis was finally captured in Georgia. A few Southern diehards continued to fight, but even their resistance collapsed before long. General George Meade's shout, "It's all over," described in simple terms one of the most momentous events in the nation's history.

The war ensured the permanence of the Union, but many other issues remained far from settled. What would happen to the freedmen (the term used for slaves who were now liberated)? Could the South and the North reconcile? Would the massive industrial growth in the North during the Civil War spread to the South, or would the South remain an agrarian region with much less wealth than in the North? The end of the war was the beginning of more than a generation of struggle to determine the legacy of the Civil War.

CONCLUSION

The American Civil War began with high hopes and high ideals on both sides. In the North and the South alike, thousands of men enthusiastically enlisted in local regiments and went off to war. Four years later, over 600,000 of them were dead and many more maimed and traumatized for life. A fight for "principles" and "ideals"—a fight few people had thought would last more than a few months—had become one of the longest wars, and by far the bloodiest war, in American history, before or since.

During the first two years of fighting, the Confederate forces seemed to have all the advantages. They were fighting on their own soil. Their troops seemed more committed to the cause than those of the North. Their commanders were exceptionally talented, while Union forces were, for a time, erratically led. Gradually, however, the Union's advantages began to assert themselves. The North had a stabler political system led by one of the greatest leaders in the nation's history. It had a much larger population, a far more developed industrial economy, superior financial institutions, and a better railroad system. By the middle of 1863, the tide of the war had shifted; over the next two years, Union forces gradually wore down the Confederate armies before finally triumphing in 1865.

The war strengthened the North's economy, giving a spur to industry and railroad development. It greatly weakened the South's by destroying millions of dollars of property and depleting the region's young male population. Southerners had gone to war in part because of their fears of growing Northern dominance. Ironically, the war itself confirmed and strengthened that dominance.

But most of all, the Civil War was a victory for millions of African American slaves. The war produced Abraham Lincoln's epochal Emancipation Proclamation and, later, the Thirteenth Amendment to the Constitution, which abolished slavery altogether. It also encouraged hundreds of thousands of slaves literally to free themselves, to desert their masters and seek refuge behind Union lines—at times to fight in the Union armies. The future of the freed slaves was not to be an easy one, but three and a half million people who had once lived in bondage emerged from the war as free men and women.

KEY TERMS/PEOPLE/PLACES/EVENTS

Alexander H. Stephens 331	First Battle of Bull Run 339	Robert E. Lee 341
Antietam 343	Fort Sumter 322	Shiloh 341
Appomattox Court	George B. McClellan 341	Thirteenth Amendment 330
House 349	Gettysburg 346	Thomas J. ("Stonewall")
Confederate States of	greenbacks 327	Jackson 341
America 322	Homestead Act 326	Ulysses S. Grant 347
conscription 327	Jefferson Davis 331	U.S. Sanitary Commission
Emancipation Proclamation	March to the Sea 349	331
329	Morrill Act 326	William T. Sherman 347

RECALL AND REFLECT

1. Assess the advantages of the North and those of the South at the beginning of the Civil War. How did the advantages of each side change over the course of the war?
2. How did the Confederate government differ from the federal government of the United States?
3. How did the war affect the lives of women in the North and in the South?
4. Compare Lincoln and Davis as heads of government and commanders in chief.
5. Why did Lincoln issue the Emancipation Proclamation, and what were its effects?

15 RECONSTRUCTION AND THE NEW SOUTH

THE PROBLEMS OF PEACEMAKING
RADICAL RECONSTRUCTION
THE SOUTH IN RECONSTRUCTION
THE GRANT ADMINISTRATION
THE ABANDONMENT OF RECONSTRUCTION
THE NEW SOUTH

LOOKING AHEAD

1. What were the various plans for Reconstruction proposed by Lincoln, Johnson, and Congress? Which plan was enacted and why?
2. What were the effects of Reconstruction for blacks and whites in the South?
3. What were the political achievements and failures of the Grant administration?

FEW PERIODS IN THE HISTORY of the United States have produced as much bitterness or created such enduring controversy as the era of Reconstruction—the years following the Civil War during which Americans attempted to reunite their shattered nation. To many white Southerners, Reconstruction was a vicious and destructive experience—a period when vindictive Northerners inflicted humiliation and revenge on the defeated South. Northern defenders of Reconstruction, in contrast, argued that their policies were the only way to prevent unrepentant Confederates from restoring Southern society to what it had been before the war.

To most African Americans at the time, and to many people of all races since, Reconstruction was notable for other reasons. Neither a vicious tyranny, as white Southerners charged, nor a thoroughgoing reform, as many Northerners hoped, it was instead an important first step in the effort to secure civil rights and economic power for the former slaves. Reconstruction did not provide African Americans with either the enduring legal protections or the material resources to ensure anything like real equality. Most black men and women still had little formal power to overturn their oppression for many decades.

And yet for all its shortcomings, Reconstruction did help African Americans create new institutions and some important legal precedents that helped them survive and that ultimately, well into the twentieth century, became the basis of later efforts to win greater freedom and equality.

1863

Lincoln announces
Reconstruction plan

1864

Lincoln vetoes
Wade-Davis Bill

1865

Confederacy surrenders

Lincoln assassinated;
Johnson is president

Freedmen's Bureau

Joint Committee on
Reconstruction

1866

Republicans gain in
congressional elections

1867

Congressional
Reconstruction begins

1868

Johnson impeached and
acquitted

14th Amendment
ratified

Grant elected president

1869

Congress passes 15th
Amendment

1872

Grant reelected

1873

Panic and depression

1877

Hayes wins disputed
election

Compromise of 1877
ends Reconstruction

1883

Supreme Court
upholds segregation

1890s

Jim Crow laws in South

1895

Atlanta Compromise

1896

Plessy v. Ferguson

THE PROBLEMS OF PEACEMAKING

Although it was clear in 1865 that the war was almost over, the path to actual peace was not yet clear. Abraham Lincoln could not negotiate a treaty with the defeated government; he continued to insist that the Confederacy had no legal right to exist. Yet neither could he simply readmit the Southern states into the Union.

THE AFTERMATH OF WAR AND EMANCIPATION

The South after the Civil War was a desolate place. Towns had been gutted, plantations burned, fields neglected, bridges and railroads destroyed. Many white Southerners—stripped of their slaves through emancipation and of capital invested in now worthless Confederate bonds and currency—had almost no personal property. More than 258,000 Confederate soldiers had died in the war, and thousands more returned home wounded or sick. Some white Southerners faced starvation and homelessness.

If the physical conditions were bad for Southern whites, they were far worse for Southern blacks—the three and a half million men and women now emerging from bondage. As soon as the war ended, hundreds of thousands of them left their plantations in search of a new life in freedom. But most had nowhere to go, and few had any possessions except the clothes they wore.

COMPETING NOTIONS OF FREEDOM

For blacks and whites alike, Reconstruction became a struggle to define the meaning of the war and, above all, the meaning of freedom. But the former slaves and the defeated whites had very different conceptions of what freedom meant.

For most white Southerners, freedom meant the ability to control their own

RICHMOND, 1865 By the time Union forces captured Richmond in early 1865, the Confederate capital had been under siege for months and much of the city lay in ruins, as this photograph reveals. On April 4, President Lincoln, accompanied by his son Tad, visited Richmond. As he walked through the streets of the shattered city, hundreds of former slaves emerged from the rubble to watch him pass. "No triumphal march of a conqueror could have equalled in moral sublimity the humble manner in which he entered Richmond," a black soldier serving with the Union army wrote. "It was a great deliverer among the delivered. No wonder tears came to his eyes." (The Library of Congress)

destinies without interference from the North or the federal government. And in the immediate aftermath of the war, this meant trying to restore their society to its antebellum form. When these white Southerners fought for what they considered freedom, they were fighting above all to preserve local and regional autonomy and white supremacy.

For African Americans, freedom meant independence from white control. In the wake of advancing Union armies, millions of black Southerners sought to secure that freedom with economic opportunity, which for many meant landownership. An African American man in Charleston told a Northern reporter, "Gib us our own land and we take care ourselves."[1] For a short while during the war, Union generals and federal officials cooperated, awarding confiscated land to the former slaves who had worked it.

Early in the war, when Union forces occupied the Sea Islands of South Carolina, the islands' white property owners fled to the mainland, and 10,000 former slaves seized control of the vacated land. Later in the war, a delegation of freed slaves approached General William Sherman for outright possession of the land. Sherman acceded. He issued Special Field Order No. 15 on January 16, 1865, granting former Confederate land in   *Special Field Order No. 15* coastal Georgia and South Carolina (including the Sea Islands) to the region's ex-slaves. Within five months, nearly 400,000 acres had been distributed to 40,000 freed people.

In the war's immediate aftermath, the federal government attempted to help ex-slaves forge independent lives by establishing the Bureau of Refugees, Freedmen, and Abandoned Lands, which Congress authorized in March 1865. The Freedmen's Bureau,   *Freedmen's Bureau*

---

1 Foner, *Reconstruction*, p. 104.

as it became known, helped feed, clothe, educate, and provide medical care for ex-slaves. It also settled land disputes and set labor contracts between freedmen and white property owners. Headed by General Oliver O. Howard, the Freedman's Bureau operated on a shoestring budget with fewer than 1,000 agents, some of whom were corrupt, yet it still emerged as a key federal institution shaping black and white life in the South after the war.

The Freedmen's Bureau, for a while at least, also supported the redistribution of land, overseeing the allocation of 850,000 acres of confiscated land to former slaves. General Howard instructed his agents in his famous "Circular 13" to lease the land in 40-acre plots to former slaves with the intention of eventually selling it to them. A small number of freedmen

Land Redistribution   purchased land outright under the Southern Homestead Act of 1866 that Howard had championed; the act made 46 million acres of public land for sale in 160-acre plots in Alabama, Arkansas, Florida, Louisiana, and Mississippi. (The law was repealed before many ex-slaves were able to take advantage of it.) Some of Howard's officials and other army personnel secured mules for freed people as well, fulfilling the common wisdom that 40 acres and a mule were the building block of any stable household. The Bureau also settled land disputes and set labor contracts between freedmen and white property owners.

PLANS FOR RECONSTRUCTION

Political control of Reconstruction rested in the hands of the Republicans, who were deeply divided in their approach to the issue. Conservatives within the party insisted that the South accept abolition, but they proposed few other conditions for the readmission of

The Radical Republicans   the seceded states. The Radicals, led by Representative Thaddeus Stevens of Pennsylvania and Senator Charles Sumner of Massachusetts, urged a much harsher course, including disenfranchising large numbers of Southern whites, protecting black civil rights, confiscating the property of wealthy whites who had aided the Confederacy, and distributing the land among the freedmen. Republican Moderates rejected the most stringent demands of the Radicals but supported extracting at least some concessions from the South on black rights.

President Lincoln favored a lenient Reconstruction policy, believing that Southern Unionists (mostly former Whigs) could become the nucleus of new, loyal state governments in the South. Lincoln announced his Reconstruction plan in December 1863, more than a year before the war ended. It offered a general amnesty to white Southerners—other than high officials of the Confederacy—who would pledge an oath of loyalty to the government and accept the abolition of slavery. When 10 percent of a state's total number of voters in 1860 took the oath, those loyal voters could set up a state government. Lincoln also proposed extending suffrage to African Americans who were educated, owned property, or had served in the Union army. Three Southern states—Louisiana, Arkansas, and Tennessee, all under Union occupation—reestablished loyal governments under the Lincoln formula in 1864.

Outraged at the mildness of Lincoln's program, the Radical Republicans refused to admit representatives from the three "reconstructed" states to Congress. In July 1864, they

Wade-Davis Bill   pushed their own plan through Congress: the Wade-Davis Bill. Named for Senator Benjamin Wade of Ohio and Representative Henry Davis of Maryland, it called for the president to appoint a provisional governor for each conquered state. When a majority of the white males of a state pledged their allegiance to the Union, the governor could summon a state constitutional convention, whose delegates were to be elected by voters who had never borne arms against the United States. The new state constitutions would be required to abolish slavery, disenfranchise Confederate civil and military leaders, and repudiate debts accumulated by the state governments during the war. Only then would Congress readmit the states to the Union. Like the president's proposal, the Wade-Davis Bill left the question of political rights for blacks up to the states.

Congress passed the bill a few days before it adjourned in 1864, but Lincoln disposed of it with a pocket veto that enraged the Radical leaders, forcing the pragmatic Lincoln to recognize he would have to accept at least some of the Radical demands. The debate between Congress and Lincoln over the proper course of Reconstruction and its purpose and objectives was one that scholars would soon pick up. Indeed, beginning in the latter stages of Reconstruction, historians struggled to make sense of its meaning to America. They continue to do so today. (See "Debating the Past: Reconstruction.")

THE DEATH OF LINCOLN

What plan the president might have produced no one can say. On the night of April 14, 1865, Lincoln and his wife attended a play at Ford's Theater in *Lincoln's Assassination* Washington. John Wilkes Booth, an actor fervently committed to the Southern cause, entered the presidential box from the rear and shot Lincoln in the head. Early the next morning, the president died.

ABRAHAM LINCOLN This haunting photograph of Abraham Lincoln, showing clearly the weariness and aging that four years as a war president had created, was taken in Washington only four days before his assassination in 1865. (The Library of Congress)

RECONSTRUCTION

Debate over the nature of Reconstruction has been unusually intense. Indeed, few issues in American history have raised such deep and enduring passions.

Beginning in the late nineteenth century and continuing well into the twentieth, a relatively uniform and highly critical view of Reconstruction prevailed among historians. William A. Dunning's *Reconstruction, Political and Economic* (1907) was the principal scholarly expression of this view. Dunning portrayed Reconstruction as a corrupt and oppressive outrage imposed on a prostrate South by a vindictive group of Northern Republican Radicals. Unscrupulous carpetbaggers flooded the South and plundered the region. Ignorant and unfit African Americans were thrust into political offices. Reconstruction governments were awash in corruption and compiled enormous levels of debt. The Dunning interpretation dominated several generations of historical scholarship and helped shape such popular images

of Reconstruction as those in the novel and film *Gone with the Wind*.

W. E. B. Du Bois, the great African American scholar, offered one of the first alternative views in *Black Reconstruction* (1935). To Du Bois, Reconstruction was an effort by freed blacks (and their white allies) to create a more democratic society in the South, and it was responsible for many valuable social innovations. In the early 1960s, John Hope Franklin and Kenneth Stampp, building on a generation of work by other scholars, published new histories of Reconstruction that also radically revised the Dunning interpretation. Reconstruction, they argued, was a genuine, if inadequate, effort to solve the problem of race in the South. Congressional Radicals were not saints, but they were genuinely concerned with protecting the rights of former slaves. Reconstruction had brought important, if temporary, progress to the South and had created no more corruption there than was evident

A FREEDMEN'S BUREAU SCHOOL African American students and teachers stand outside a school for former slaves, one of many run by the Freedmen's Bureau throughout the defeated Confederacy in the first years after the war. (© Corbis)

in the North at the same time. What was tragic about Reconstruction, the revisionists claimed, was not what it did to Southern whites but what it failed to do for Southern blacks. It was, in the end, too weak and too short-lived to guarantee African Americans genuine equality.

In more recent years, some historians have begun to question the assessment of the first revisionists that, in the end, Reconstruction accomplished relatively little. Leon Litwack argued in *Been in the Storm So Long* (1979) that former slaves used the protections Reconstruction offered them to carve out a certain level of independence for themselves within Southern society: strengthening churches, reuniting families, and resisting the efforts of white planters to revive the gang labor system.

Eric Foner's *Reconstruction: America's Unfinished Revolution* (1988) and *Forever Free* (2005) also emphasized how far African Americans moved toward freedom and independence in a short time and how important they were in shaping the execution of Reconstruction policies. Reconstruction, he argues, "can only be judged a failure" as an effort to secure "blacks' rights as citizens and free laborers." But it "closed off even more oppressive alternatives.... The post-Reconstruction labor system embodied neither a return to the closely supervised gang labor of antebellum days, nor the complete dispossession and immobilization of the black labor force and coercive apprenticeship systems envisioned by white Southerners in 1865 and 1866.... The doors of economic opportunity that had opened could never be completely closed." •

UNDERSTAND, ANALYZE, & EVALUATE

1. What are the popular interpretations of Reconstruction today? Do romanticized ideals of a benighted Old South, as seen in *Gone with the Wind*, still persist?

2. A new view of Reconstruction began to emerge in the 1960s, the end of the civil rights movement. Why do you think the civil rights movement might have encouraged historians and others to reexamine Reconstruction?

The circumstances of Lincoln's death earned him immediate martyrdom. They also produced something close to hysteria throughout the North, especially because it quickly became clear that Booth had been the leader of a conspiracy. One of his associates shot and wounded Secretary of State William H. Seward on the night of the assassination, and another abandoned at the last moment a plan to murder Vice President Andrew Johnson. Booth himself escaped on horseback into the Maryland countryside, where, on April 26, he was cornered by Union troops and shot to death in a blazing barn. Eight other people were convicted by a military tribunal of participating in the conspiracy. Four were hanged.

To many Northerners, however, the murder of the president seemed evidence of an even darker conspiracy—one masterminded and directed by the unrepentant leaders of the defeated South to challenge the very authority of the nation's elected officials. Militant Republicans exploited such suspicions relentlessly in the ensuing months.

JOHNSON AND "RESTORATION"

Leadership of the Moderates and Conservatives fell immediately to Lincoln's successor, Andrew Johnson of Tennessee. A Democrat until he had joined the Union ticket in 1864, he became president at a time of growing partisan passions.

Johnson revealed his plan for Reconstruction—or "Restoration," as he preferred to call *Johnson's Reconstruction Plan* it—soon after he took office and implemented it during the summer of 1865 when Congress was in recess. Like Lincoln, he offered some form of amnesty to Southerners who would take an oath of allegiance. In most other respects, however, his plan resembled the Wade-Davis Bill. The new president appointed a provisional governor in each state and charged him with inviting qualified voters to elect delegates to a constitutional convention. To win readmission to Congress, a state had to revoke its ordinance of secession, abolish slavery and ratify the Thirteenth Amendment, and repudiate Confederate and state war debts.

By the end of 1865, all the seceded states had formed new governments—some under Lincoln's plan, others under Johnson's—and awaited congressional approval of them. But Radicals in Congress vowed not to recognize the Johnson governments, for, by now, Northern opinion had become more hostile toward the South. Delegates to the Southern conventions had angered much of the North by their apparent reluctance to abolish slavery and by their refusal to grant suffrage to any blacks. Southern states had also seemed to defy the North by electing prominent Confederate leaders to represent them in Congress, such as Alexander Stephens of Georgia, the former vice president of the Confederacy.

RADICAL RECONSTRUCTION

Reconstruction under Johnson's plan—often known as "presidential Reconstruction"—continued only until Congress reconvened in December 1865. At that point, Congress refused to seat the representatives of the "restored" states and created a new Joint Committee on Reconstruction to frame a policy of its own. The period of "congressional," or "Radical," Reconstruction had begun.

THE BLACK CODES

Meanwhile, events in the South were driving Northern opinion in still more radical directions. Throughout the South in 1865 and early 1866, state legislatures enacted sets of laws known as the **Black Codes,** which authorized local officials to apprehend unemployed blacks, fine them for vagrancy, and hire them out to private employers to satisfy the fines. Some codes forbade blacks to own or lease farms or to take any jobs other than as plantation workers or domestic servants, jobs formerly held by slaves. Former slaves raised an alarm immediately and called for swift intervention by the federal troops and for new legislation to protect them. (See "Consider the Source: Southern Blacks Ask for Help.")

Congress first responded to the Black Codes by passing an act extending the life and expanding the powers of the Freedmen's Bureau so that it could nullify work agreements forced on freedmen under the Black Codes. Then, in April 1866, Congress passed the first *Johnson's Vetoes* Civil Rights Act, which declared blacks to be fully fledged citizens of the United States and gave the federal government power to intervene in state affairs to protect the rights of citizens. Johnson vetoed both bills, but Congress overrode him on each of them.

THE FOURTEENTH AMENDMENT

In April 1866, the Joint Committee on Reconstruction proposed the Fourteenth Amendment to the Constitution. Congress approved it in early summer and sent it to the states for ratification. It offered the first constitutional definition of American citizenship. Everyone born in the United States, and everyone naturalized, was automatically a citizen and entitled to all the "privileges and immunities" guaranteed by   *Citizenship for African Americans* the Constitution, including equal protection of the laws by both the state and national governments. There could be no other requirements for citizenship. The amendment also imposed penalties on states that denied suffrage to any adult male inhabitants. (Supporters of woman suffrage were dismayed by the addition of the word *male* to the amendment.) Finally, it prohibited former members of Congress or other former federal officials who had aided the Confederacy from holding any state or federal office unless two-thirds of Congress voted to pardon them.

Congressional Radicals offered to readmit to the Union any state whose legislature ratified the Fourteenth Amendment. Only Tennessee did so. All the other former Confederate states, along with Delaware and Kentucky, refused, leaving the amendment temporarily without the necessary approval of three-fourths of the states.

But by now, the Radicals were growing more confident and determined. Bloody race riots in New Orleans and other Southern cities were among the events that strengthened their hand. In the 1866 congressional elections, Johnson actively campaigned for Conservative candidates, but he did his own cause more harm than good with his intemperate speeches. The voters returned an overwhelming majority of Republicans, most of them Radicals, to Congress. In the Senate, there were now 42 Republicans to 11 Democrats; in the House, 143 Republicans to 49 Democrats. Congressional Republicans were now strong enough to enact a plan of their own even over the president's objections.

THE CONGRESSIONAL PLAN

The Radicals passed three Reconstruction bills early in 1867 and overrode Johnson's vetoes of all of them. These bills finally established, nearly two years after the end of the war, a coherent plan for Reconstruction.

Under the congressional plan, Tennessee, which had ratified the Fourteenth Amendment, was promptly readmitted. But Congress rejected the Lincoln–Johnson governments of the other ten Confederate states and, instead, combined those states into five military districts. A military commander governed each district and had orders to register qualified voters (defined as all adult black males and those white males who had not participated in the rebellion). Once registered, voters would elect conventions to prepare new state constitutions, which had to include provisions for black suffrage. Once voters ratified the new constitutions, they could elect state governments. Congress had to approve a state's constitution, and the state legislature had to ratify the Fourteenth Amendment. Once enough states ratified the amendment to make it part of the Constitution, the former Confederate states could be restored to the Union.

By 1868, seven of the ten remaining former Confederate states had fulfilled these conditions and were readmitted to the Union. Conservative whites held up the return of Virginia and Texas until 1869 and Mississippi until 1870. By then, Congress had added an additional requirement for readmission—ratification of another   *Fifteenth Amendment* constitutional amendment, the Fifteenth, which forbade the states and the federal government to deny suffrage to any citizen on account of "race, color, or previous condition of servitude." Ratification by the states was completed in 1870.

To stop Johnson from interfering with their plans, the congressional Radicals passed two remarkable laws of dubious constitutionality in 1867. One, the Tenure of Office Act,

CONSIDER THE SOURCE

SOUTHERN BLACKS ASK FOR HELP, 1865

Even before the war ended, groups of former slaves gathered in conventions to petition the federal government for steady support for black civil rights, including the use of the U.S. Army to subdue unrepentant ex-Confederates. In this example, African Americans from Virginia publicly air their hopes and fears only three months after Appomattox.

We, the undersigned members of a Convention of colored citizens of the State of Virginia, would respectfully represent that, although we have been held as slaves, and denied all recognition as a constituent of your nationality for almost the entire period of the duration of your Government, and that by your *permission* we have been denied either home or country, and deprived of the dearest rights of human nature; yet when you and our immediate oppressors met in deadly conflict upon the field of battle—the one to destroy and the other to save your Government and nationality, we, with scarce an exception, in our inmost souls espoused your cause, and watched, and prayed, and waited, and labored for your success. . . .

When the contest waxed long, and the result hung doubtfully, you appealed to us for help, and how well we answered is written in the rosters of the two hundred thousand colored troops now enrolled in your Service; and as to our undying devotion to your cause, let the uniform acclamation of escaped prisoners, "whenever we saw a black face we felt sure of a friend," answer.

Well, the war is over, the rebellion is "put down," and we are *declared* free! Four fifths of our enemies are paroled or amnestied, and the other fifth are being pardoned, and the President has, in his efforts at the reconstruction of the civil government of the States, late in rebellion, left us entirely at the mercy of these subjugated but unconverted rebels, in *everything* save the privilege of bringing us, our wives and little ones, to the auction block. *We know* these men—know them well—and we assure you that, with the majority of them, loyalty is only "lip deep," and that their professions of loyalty are used as a cover to the cherished design of getting restored to their former relations with the Federal Government, and then, by all sorts of "unfriendly legislation," to render the freedom you have given us more Intolerable than the slavery they intended for us.

We warn you in time that our only safety is in keeping them under Governors of the *military persuasion* until you have so amended the Federal Constitution that it will prohibit the States from making any distinction between citizens on account of race or color. In one word, the only salvation for us besides the power of the Government, is in the *possession of the ballot*. Give us this, and we will protect ourselves. . . . But, 'tis said we are ignorant. Admit it. Yet who denies we *know* a traitor from a loyal man, a gentleman from a rowdy, a friend from an enemy? . . . All we ask is an *equal chance* with the white *traitors* varnished and japanned with the oath of amnesty. Can you deny us this and still keep faith with us? . . .

We are "sheep in the midst of wolves," and nothing but the military arm of the Government prevents us and all the *truly* loyal white men from being driven from the land of our birth. Do not then, we beseech you, give to one of these "wayward sisters" the rights they abandoned and forfeited when they rebelled until you have secured our rights by the aforementioned amendment to the Constitution.

UNDERSTAND, ANALYZE, & EVALUATE

1. What did the authors of this petition emphasize in the first two paragraphs, and why did they feel this was important?
2. Why did the authors emphasize that they had been "declared" free? What dangers to their prospect of freedom did they observe?
3. What federal legal responses did they propose? Can you recognize these suggestions in the constitutional changes that came with Reconstruction?

Source: "Proceedings of the Convention of the Colored People of Virginia, Held in the City of Alexandria, August 2, 3, 4, 5, 1865" (Alexandria, Va., 1865), in W. L. Fleming (ed.), *Documentary History of Reconstruction* (Cleveland, Ohio, 1906), vol. 1, pp. 195–196; located in "Southern Blacks Ask for Help (1865)," in Thomas A. Bailey and David M. Kennedy (eds.), *The American Spirit*, vol. 1, 7th ed. (Lexington, Mass., 1991), pp. 466–467.

forbade the president to remove civil officials, including members of his own cabinet, without the consent of the Senate. The principal purpose of the law was to protect the job of Secretary of War Edwin M. Stanton, who was cooperating *Limits on Presidential Powers* with the Radicals. The other law, the Command of the Army Act, prohibited the president from issuing military orders except through the commanding general of the army (General Grant), who could not be relieved or assigned elsewhere without the consent of the Senate.

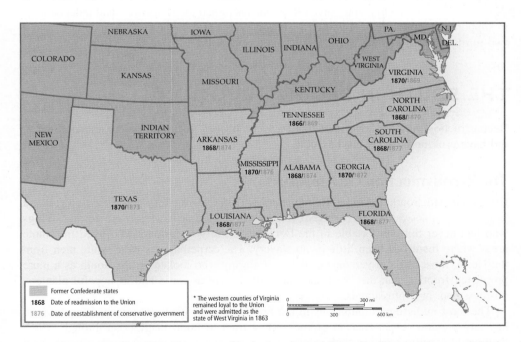

RECONSTRUCTION, 1866–1877 This map provides the date when each former Confederate state was readmitted by presidential order to the Union, as well as the date when a traditional white conservative elite took office as a majority in each state—an event white Southerners liked to call "redemption." • *What had to happen for a state to be readmitted to the Union? What had to happen before a state could experience "redemption"?*

The congressional Radicals also took action to stop the Supreme Court from interfering with their plans. In 1866, the Court had declared in the case of *Ex parte Milligan* that military tribunals were unconstitutional in places where civil courts were functioning. Radicals in Congress immediately proposed several bills that would require two-thirds of the justices to support any decision overruling a law of Congress, would deny the Court jurisdiction in Reconstruction cases, would reduce its membership to three, and would even abolish it. The justices apparently took notice. Over the next two years, the Court refused to accept jurisdiction in any cases involving Reconstruction.

THE IMPEACHMENT OF ANDREW JOHNSON

President Johnson had long since ceased to be a serious obstacle to the passage of Radical legislation, but he was still the official charged with administering the Reconstruction programs. As such, the Radicals believed, he remained a major impediment to their plans. Early in 1867, they began looking for a way to remove him from office, and a search for grounds for **impeachment** began. Republicans found it, they believed, when Johnson dismissed Secretary of War Stanton despite Congress's refusal to agree. Elated Radicals in the House quickly impeached the president and sent the case to the Senate for trial.

The trial lasted throughout April and May 1868. The Radicals put heavy pressure on all the Republican senators, but the Moderates vacillated. On the first three charges to *Johnson Acquitted* come to a vote, seven Republicans joined the Democrats and independents to support acquittal. The vote was 35 to 19, one vote short of the constitutionally required two-thirds majority. After that, the Radicals dropped the impeachment effort.

THE SOUTH IN RECONSTRUCTION

Reconstruction may not have immediately accomplished what its framers intended, but it did have profound effects on the South.

THE RECONSTRUCTION GOVERNMENTS

Critics labeled Southern white Republicans with the derogatory terms *scalawags* and *"Scalawags" and "Carpetbaggers"* carpetbaggers. Many of the scalawags were former Whigs who had never felt comfortable in the Democratic Party or farmers who lived in remote areas where there had been little or no slavery. The carpetbaggers were white men from the North, most of them veterans of the Union army who looked on the South as a more promising frontier than the West and had settled there at war's end as hopeful planters, businessmen, or professionals.

The most numerous Republicans in the South were the black freedmen, few of whom had any previous experience in politics. They tried to build institutions through which they could learn to exercise their power. In several states, African American voters held their own conventions to chart their future course. Their newfound religious independence from white churches also helped give them unity and self-confidence.

African Americans played significant roles in the politics of the Reconstruction South. They served as delegates to the constitutional conventions and held public

THE "STRONG" GOVERNMENT 1869—1877.

CRITICS' VIEW OF RECONSTRUCTION This Reconstruction-era cartoon expresses the view held by Southern white Democrats that they were being oppressed by Northern Republicans. President Grant (whose hat bears Abraham Lincoln's initials) rides in comfort in a giant carpetbag, guarded by bayonet-wielding soldiers, as the South staggers under the burden in chains. Evidence of military occupation is in the scarred background.

offices of practically every kind. Between 1869 and 1901, twenty blacks served in the United States House of Representatives, two in the Senate. Blacks served, too, in state legislatures and in various other state offices. Southern whites   *Freedmen in Politics* complained loudly about "Negro rule," but in the South as a whole, the percentage of black officeholders was small—and always far lower than the percentage of blacks in the population.

The record of the Reconstruction governments is mixed. Critics at the time and later denounced them for corruption and financial extravagance, and there is some truth to both charges. But the corruption in the South, real as it was, was hardly unique to the Reconstruction governments. Corruption had been rife in some antebellum and Confederate governments, and it was at least as rampant in the Northern states. And the large state expenditures of the Reconstruction years were huge only in comparison with the meager budgets of the antebellum era. They represented an effort to provide the South with desperately needed services that antebellum governments had never provided.

EDUCATION

Perhaps the most important accomplishment of the Reconstruction governments was a dramatic improvement in Southern education. Much of the impetus for educational reform in the South came from outside groups—the Freedmen's Bureau, Northern private philanthropic organizations, the many Northern white women who traveled to the South to teach in freedmen's schools—and from African Americans themselves. Over the opposition of many Southern whites, who feared that education would give blacks "false notions of equality," these reformers established a large network of schools for former slaves—4,000 schools by 1870, staffed by 9,000 teachers (half of them black), teaching 200,000 students. In the 1870s, Reconstruction governments began to build a comprehensive public school system. By 1876, more than half of all white children and about 40 percent of all black children were attending schools in the South (although almost all such schools were racially segregated). Several black "academies," offering more advanced education, also began operating. Gradually, these academies grew into an important network of black colleges and universities.

LANDOWNERSHIP AND TENANCY

The most ambitious goal of the Freedmen's Bureau, and of some Republican Radicals *Land Reform Thwarted* in Congress, was to reform landownership in the South. The effort failed. By June 1865, the bureau had settled nearly 10,000 black families on their own land—most of it drawn from abandoned plantations in areas occupied by the Union armies. By the end of that year, however, Southern plantation owners were returning and demanding the restoration of their property. President Johnson supported their demands, and the government eventually returned most of the confiscated lands to their original white owners.

Even so, the distribution of landownership in the South changed considerably in the postwar years. Among whites, there was a striking decline in landownership, from 80 percent before the war to 67 percent by the end of Reconstruction. Some whites lost their land because of unpaid debt or increased taxes; others left the marginal lands they had owned to move to more fertile areas, where they rented. Among blacks, during the same period, the proportion of landowners rose from virtually none to more than 20 percent.

Still, most blacks, and a growing minority of whites, did not own their own land during Reconstruction and, instead, worked for others in one form or another. Many black agricultural laborers—perhaps 25 percent of the total—simply worked for wages. Most, however, became tenants of white landowners—that is, they worked their own plots of land and paid their landlords either a fixed rent or a share of their crops (hence the term **sharecropping**). As tenants and sharecroppers, blacks enjoyed at least a physical independence from their landlords and had the sense of working their own land, even if in most cases they could never hope to buy it. But tenantry also benefited landlords in some ways, relieving them of the cost of purchasing slaves and of responsibility for the physical well-being of their workers.

INCOMES AND CREDIT

In some respects, the postwar years were a period of remarkable economic progress for African Americans in the South. The per capita income of blacks (when the material benefits of slavery are counted as income) rose 46 percent between 1857 and 1879, while the per capita income of whites declined 35 percent. African Americans were also able to work less than they had under slavery. Women and children were less likely to labor in the fields, and adult men tended to work shorter days. In all, the black labor force worked about one-third fewer hours during Reconstruction than it had been compelled to work under slavery—a reduction that brought the working schedule of blacks roughly into accord with that of white farm laborers.

But other developments limited these gains. While the black share of profits was increasing, the total profits of Southern agriculture were declining. Nor did the income redistribution of the postwar years lift many blacks out of poverty. *Persistent Black Poverty* Black per capita income rose from about one-quarter of white per capita income (which was itself low) to about one-half in the first few years after the war. After this initial increase, however, it rose hardly at all.

Blacks and poor whites alike found themselves virtually imprisoned by the **crop-lien system.** Few of the traditional institutions of credit in the South—the *The Crop-Lien System* "factors" and banks—returned after the war. In their stead emerged a new credit system, centered in large part on local country stores—some of them owned by planters, others owned by independent merchants. Blacks and whites, landowners and tenants—all depended on these stores. And since farmers did not have the same steady cash flow as other workers, customers usually had to rely on credit from these merchants to purchase what they needed. Most local stores had no competition and thus could set interest rates as high as 50 or 60 percent. Farmers had to give the merchants a lien (or claim) on their crops as collateral for the loans (thus the term *crop-lien system*). Farmers who suffered a few bad years in a row, as many did, could become trapped in a cycle of debt from which they could never escape.

As a result of this burdensome credit system, some blacks who had acquired land during the early years of Reconstruction, and many poor whites who had owned land for years, gradually lost it as they fell into debt. Southern farmers also became almost wholly dependent on cash crops—and most of all on cotton—because only such marketable commodities seemed to offer any possibility of escape from debt. The relentless planting of cotton ultimately contributed to soil exhaustion, which undermined the Southern agricultural economy over time.

THE AFRICAN AMERICAN FAMILY IN FREEDOM

A major reason for the rapid departure of so many blacks from plantations was the desire to find lost relatives and reunite families. Thousands of African Americans *Families Reunited* wandered through the South looking for husbands, wives, children, or other relatives from whom they had been separated. Former slaves rushed to have their marriages, previously without legal standing, sanctified by church and law.

Within the black family, the definition of male and female roles quickly came to resemble that within white families. Many women and children at first ceased working in the fields. Such work, they believed, was a badge of slavery. Instead, many women restricted themselves largely to domestic tasks. Still, economic necessity often compelled black women to engage in income-producing activities: working as domestic servants, taking in laundry, even helping their husbands in the fields. By the end of Reconstruction, half of all black women over the age of sixteen were working for wages.

LABORING OVER LAUNDRY One of the most common occupations of women recently emancipated from slavery was taking in laundry from white families who no longer had enslaved servants. This photograph illustrates how arduous a task laundry was. (The Library of Congress)

THE GRANT ADMINISTRATION

American voters in 1868 yearned for a strong, stable figure to guide them through the troubled years of Reconstruction. They turned trustingly to General Ulysses S. Grant.

THE SOLDIER PRESIDENT

Grant could have had the nomination of either party in 1868. But believing that Republican Reconstruction policies were more popular in the North, he accepted the Republican nomination. The Democrats nominated former governor Horatio Seymour of New York. *Grant Elected*   The campaign was a bitter one, and Grant's triumph was surprisingly narrow. Without the 500,000 new black Republican voters in the South, he would have had a minority of the popular vote.

Grant entered the White House with no political experience, and his performance was clumsy and ineffectual from the start. Except for Hamilton Fish, whom Grant appointed secretary of state, most members of the cabinet were ill equipped for their tasks. Grant relied chiefly on established party leaders—the group most ardently devoted to patronage, and his administration used the spoils system even more blatantly than most of its predecessors. Grant also alienated the many Northerners who were growing disillusioned with the Radical Reconstruction policies, which the president continued to support. Some

Republicans suspected, correctly, that there was also corruption in the Grant administration itself.

By the end of Grant's first term, therefore, members of a substantial faction of the party—who referred to themselves as Liberal Republicans—had come to oppose what they called "Grantism." In 1872, hoping to prevent Grant's reelection, they bolted the party and nominated their own presidential candidate: Horace Greeley,   *Opposition from Liberal Republicans* veteran editor and publisher of the *New York Tribune*. The Democrats, somewhat reluctantly, named Greeley their candidate as well, hoping that the alliance with the Liberals would enable them to defeat Grant. But the effort was in vain. Grant won a substantial victory, polling 286 electoral votes to Greeley's 66.

THE GRANT SCANDALS

During the 1872 campaign, the first of a series of political scandals came to light that would plague Grant and the Republicans for the next four years. It involved the French-owned Crédit Mobilier construction company, which had helped build the Union Pacific Railroad. The heads of Crédit Mobilier had used their positions as Union Pacific stockholders to steer large fraudulent contracts to their construction company, thus bilking the Union Pacific of millions. To prevent investigations, the directors had given Crédit Mobilier stock to key members of Congress. But in 1872, Congress conducted an investigation, which revealed that some highly placed Republicans—including Schuyler Colfax, now Grant's vice president—had accepted stock.

One dreary episode followed another in Grant's second term. Benjamin H. Bristow, Grant's third Treasury secretary, discovered that some of his officials and a group of distillers operating as a "whiskey ring" were cheating the government   *The "Whiskey Ring"* out of taxes by filing false reports. Then a House investigation revealed that William W. Belknap, secretary of war, had accepted bribes to retain an Indian-post trader in office (the so-called Indian ring). Other, lesser scandals also added to the growing impression that "Grantism" had brought rampant corruption to government.

THE GREENBACK QUESTION

Compounding Grant's problems was a financial crisis, known as the Panic of 1873. It began with the failure of a leading investment banking firm, Jay Cooke   *The Panic of 1873* and Company, which had invested too heavily in postwar railroad building. There had been panics before—in 1819, 1837, and 1857—but this was the worst one yet.

Debtors now pressured the government to redeem federal war bonds with greenbacks, which would increase the amount of money in circulation. But Grant and most Republicans wanted a "sound" currency—based solidly on gold reserves—which would favor the interests of banks and other creditors. There was approximately $356 million in paper currency issued during the Civil War that was still in circulation. In 1873, the Treasury issued more in response to the panic. But in 1875, Republican leaders in Congress passed the Specie Resumption Act, which provided that after January 1, 1879, greenback dollars would be redeemed by the government and replaced with new certificates, firmly pegged to the price of gold. The law satisfied creditors, who had worried that debts would be repaid in paper currency of uncertain value. But "resumption" made things more difficult for debtors, because the gold-based money supply could not easily expand.

In 1875, the "Greenbackers" formed their own political organization: the National
National Greenback Party   Greenback Party. It failed to gain widespread support, but the
money issue was to remain one of the most controversial and enduring issues in
late-nineteenth-century American politics.

Republican Diplomacy

The Johnson and Grant administrations achieved their greatest successes in foreign affairs
as a result of the work not of the presidents themselves but of two outstanding secretaries
of state: William H. Seward and Hamilton Fish.

An ardent expansionist, Seward acted with as much daring as the demands of
Reconstruction politics and the Republican hatred of President Johnson would permit.
He accepted a Russian offer to buy Alaska for $7.2 million, despite criticism from
Seward's Purchase of Alaska   many who derided the purchase as "Seward's Folly." In 1867,
Seward also engineered the American annexation of the tiny Midway Islands, west
of Hawaii.

Hamilton Fish's first major challenge was resolving the long-standing controversy over
the American claims that Britain had violated neutrality laws during the Civil War by
permitting English shipyards to build ships (among them the *Alabama*) for the Confederacy.
American demands that England pay for the damage these vessels had caused became
Hamilton Fish and the "Alabama Claims"   known as the "*Alabama* claims." In 1871, after a number of failed efforts, Fish forged an agreement, the Treaty of Washington, which provided
for international arbitration.

THE ABANDONMENT OF RECONSTRUCTION

As the North grew increasingly preoccupied with its own political and economic problems,
interest in Reconstruction began to wane. By the time Grant left office, Democrats had
taken back seven of the governments of the former Confederate states. For three other
states—South Carolina, Louisiana, and Florida—the end of Reconstruction had to wait
for the withdrawal of the last federal troops in 1877.

The Southern States "Redeemed"

In the states where whites constituted a majority—the states of the upper South—
overthrowing Republican control was relatively simple. By 1872, all but a handful of
Southern whites had regained suffrage. Now a clear majority, they needed only to organize
and elect their candidates.

In other states, where blacks were a majority or where the populations of the two races
were almost equal, whites used outright intimidation and violence to undermine the
Ku Klux Klan   Reconstruction regimes. Secret societies—the Ku Klux Klan, the Knights of
the White Camellia, and others—used terrorism to frighten or physically bar blacks from
voting. Paramilitary organizations—the Red Shirts and White Leagues—armed themselves
to "police" elections and worked to force all white males to join the Democratic Party.
Strongest of all, however, was the simple weapon of economic pressure. Some planters
refused to rent land to Republican blacks; storekeepers refused to extend them credit;
employers refused to give them work.

The Republican Congress responded to this wave of repression with the Enforcement Acts of 1870 and 1871 (better known as the Ku Klux Klan Acts), which *Enforcement Acts* prohibited states from discriminating against voters on the basis of race and gave the national government the authority to prosecute crimes by individuals under federal law. The laws also authorized the president to use federal troops to protect civil rights—a provision President Grant used in 1871 in nine counties of South Carolina. The Enforcement Acts, although seldom enforced, discouraged Klan violence, which declined by 1872.

Waning Northern Commitment

But this Northern commitment to civil rights did not last long. After the adoption of the Fifteenth Amendment in 1870, some reformers convinced themselves that their long campaign on behalf of black people was now over, that with the *Flagging Interest in Civil Rights* vote blacks ought to be able to take care of themselves. Former Radical leaders such as Charles Sumner and Horace Greeley now began calling themselves Liberals, cooperating with the Democrats, and even denouncing what they viewed as black-and-carpetbag misgovernment. Within the South itself, many white Republicans now moved into the Democratic Party as voters threw out Republican politicians whom they blamed for the financial crisis.

The Panic of 1873 further undermined support for Reconstruction. In the congressional elections of 1874, the Democrats won control of the House of Representatives for the first time since 1861. To appeal to southern white voters, Grant even reduced the use of military force to prop up the Republican regimes in the South.

The Compromise of 1877

Grant had hoped to run for another term in 1876, but most Republican leaders—shaken by recent Democratic successes and scandals by the White House—resisted. Instead, they settled on Rutherford B. Hayes, three-time governor of Ohio and a champion of civil service reform. The Democrats united behind Samuel J. Tilden, the reform governor of New York, who had been instrumental in overthrowing the corrupt Tweed Ring of New York City's Tammany Hall.

Although the campaign was a bitter one, few differences of principle distinguished the candidates from one another. The election produced an apparent Democratic victory. Tilden carried the South and several large Northern states, and his popular *Disputed Election* margin over Hayes was nearly 300,000 votes. But disputed returns from Louisiana, South Carolina, Florida, and Oregon, whose electoral votes totaled 20, threw the election in doubt. Hayes could still win if he managed to receive all 20 disputed votes.

The Constitution had established no method to determine the validity of disputed returns. The decision clearly lay with Congress, but it was not obvious with which house or through what method. (The Senate was Republican, and the House was *Victory for Hayes* Democratic.) Members of each party naturally supported a solution that would yield them the victory. Finally, late in January 1877, Congress tried to break the deadlock by creating a special electoral commission composed of five senators, five representatives, and five justices of the Supreme Court. The congressional delegation consisted of five Republicans and five Democrats. The Court delegation would include two Republicans, two Democrats, and the only independent, Justice David Davis. But when the Illinois legislature elected Davis to the United States Senate, the justice resigned from the

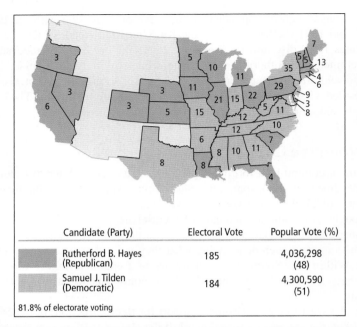

Candidate (Party)	Electoral Vote	Popular Vote (%)
Rutherford B. Hayes (Republican)	185	4,036,298 (48)
Samuel J. Tilden (Democratic)	184	4,300,590 (51)

81.8% of electorate voting

THE ELECTION OF 1876 The election of 1876 was one of the most controversial in American history. As in the elections of 1824, 1888, and 2000, the winner of the popular vote—Samuel J. Tilden—was not the winner of the electoral vote, which he lost by one vote. The final decision as to who would be president was not made until the day before the official inauguration in March. • *How did the Republicans turn this apparent defeat into a victory?*

commission. His seat went instead to a Republican justice. The commission voted along straight party lines, 8 to 7, awarding every disputed vote to Hayes.

Behind this seemingly partisan victory, however, lay a series of elaborate and sneaky compromises among leaders of both parties. When a Democratic filibuster threatened to derail the electoral commission's report, Republican Senate leaders met secretly with Southern Democratic leaders. As the price of their cooperation, the Southern Democrats exacted several pledges from the Republicans: the appointment of at least one Southerner to the Hayes cabinet, control of federal patronage in their areas, generous internal improvements, federal aid for the Texas and Pacific Railroad, and most important, withdrawal of the remaining federal troops from the South.

In his inaugural address, Hayes announced that the South's most pressing need was the restoration of "wise, honest, and peaceful local self-government," and he soon withdrew the troops and let white Democrats take over the remaining Southern state governments. *Federal Troops Withdrawn* That produced charges that he was paying off the South for acquiescing in his election—charges that were not wholly untrue. The outcome of the election created such bitterness that not even Hayes's promise to serve only one term could mollify his critics.

The president and his party hoped to build up a "new Republican" organization in the South committed to modest support for black rights. Although many white Southern leaders sympathized with Republican economic policies, resentment of Reconstruction was so deep that supporting the party became politically impossible. The "solid" Democratic South, which would survive until the mid-twentieth century, was taking shape.

The Legacy of Reconstruction

Reconstruction made important contributions to the efforts of former slaves to achieve dignity and equality in American life. There was a significant redistribution of income and a more limited but not unimportant redistribution of landownership. Perhaps most important, African Americans themselves managed to carve out a society and culture of their own and to create or strengthen their own institutions.

Reconstruction was not as disastrous for Southern white elites as most believed at the time. Within little more than a decade after a devastating war, the white South had regained control of its own institutions and, to a great extent, restored its traditional ruling class to power. The federal government imposed no drastic economic reforms on the region and, indeed, few lasting political changes of any kind other than the abolition of slavery.

Reconstruction was notable, finally, for its limitations. For in those years, the United States failed in its first serious effort to resolve its oldest and deepest social problem—the problem of race. The experience so disillusioned white Americans that it would be nearly a century before they would try again to combat racial injustice.

Given the odds confronting them, however, African Americans had reason for considerable pride in the gains they were able to make during Reconstruction. And future generations would be grateful for the two great charters of freedom—the Fourteenth and Fifteenth Amendments to the Constitution—which, although widely ignored at the time, would one day serve as the basis for a "Second Reconstruction" that would renew the drive to bring freedom to all Americans.

THE NEW SOUTH

The Compromise of 1877 was supposed to be the first step toward developing a stable, permanent Republican Party in the South. In that respect at least, it failed. In the years following the end of Reconstruction, white southerners established the Democratic Party as the only viable political organization for the region's whites. Even so, the South did change in some of the ways the framers of the Compromise had hoped.

The "Redeemers"

Many white southerners rejoiced at the restoration of what they liked to call "home rule." But in reality, political power in the region was soon more restricted than at any time since the Civil War. Once again, most of the South fell under the control of a powerful, conservative oligarchy, whose members were known variously as the "Redeemers" or the "Bourbons."

"Home Rule"

In some places, this post-Reconstruction ruling class was much the same as the ruling class of the antebellum period. In Alabama, for example, the old planter elite retained much of its former power. In other areas, however, the Redeemers constituted a genuinely new ruling class of merchants, industrialists, railroad developers, and financiers. Some of them were former planters, some of them northern immigrants, some of them ambitious, upwardly mobile white southerners from the region's lower social tiers. They combined a defense of "home rule" and social conservatism with a commitment to economic development.

The various Bourbon governments of the New South behaved in many respects quite similarly. Virtually all the new Democratic regimes lowered taxes, reduced spending, and drastically diminished state services. One state after another eliminated or reduced its support for public school systems.

INDUSTRIALIZATION AND THE NEW SOUTH

Many white southern leaders in the post-Reconstruction era hoped to see their region develop a vigorous industrial economy, a "New South." Henry Grady, editor of the *Atlanta Constitution,* and other New South advocates seldom challenged white supremacy, but they did promote the virtues of thrift, industry, and progress—qualities that prewar southerners had often denounced in northern society.

Southern industry did expand dramatically in the years after Reconstruction, most visibly in textile manufacturing. In the past, southern planters had usually shipped their cotton to manufacturers in the North or in Europe. Now textile factories appeared in the *Textiles, Tobacco, and Iron*   South itself—many of them drawn to the region from New England by the abundance of water power, the ready supply of cheap labor, the low taxes, and the accommodating conservative governments. The tobacco processing industry similarly established an important foothold in the region. In the lower South, and particularly in Birmingham, Alabama, the iron (and, later, steel) industry grew rapidly.

Railroad development also increased substantially in the post-Reconstruction years. Between 1880 and 1890, trackage in the South more than doubled. And in 1886, the South changed the gauge (width) of its trackage to correspond with the standards of the North. *Substantial Railroad Development*   No longer would it be necessary for cargoes heading into the South to be transferred from one train to another at the borders of the region.

Yet southern industry developed within strict limits, and its effects on the region were never even remotely comparable to the effects of industrialization on the North. The southern share of national manufacturing doubled in the last twenty years of the century, but it was still only 10 percent of the total. Similarly, the region's per capita income increased 21 percent in the same period, but average income in the South was still only 40 percent of that in the North; in 1860 it had been more than 60 percent. And even in those industries where development had been most rapid—textiles, iron, railroads—much of the capital had come from, and many of the profits thus flowed to, the North.

The growth of southern industry required the region to recruit a substantial industrial workforce for the first time. From the beginning, a high percentage of the factory workers were women. Heavy male casualties in the Civil War had helped create a large population of unmarried women who desperately needed employment. Hours were long (often as much as twelve hours a day), and wages were far below the northern equivalent; indeed, one of the greatest attractions of the South to industrialists was that employers were able *Worker Exploitation*   to pay workers there as little as one-half of what northern workers received. Life in most mill towns was rigidly controlled by the owners and managers of the factories, who rigorously suppressed attempts at protest or union organization. Company stores sold goods to workers at inflated prices and issued credit at exorbitant rates (much as country stores did in agrarian areas), and mill owners ensured that no competing merchants were able to establish themselves in the community.

Some industries, such as textiles, offered virtually no opportunities to African American workers. Others—tobacco, iron, and lumber, for example—did provide some employment

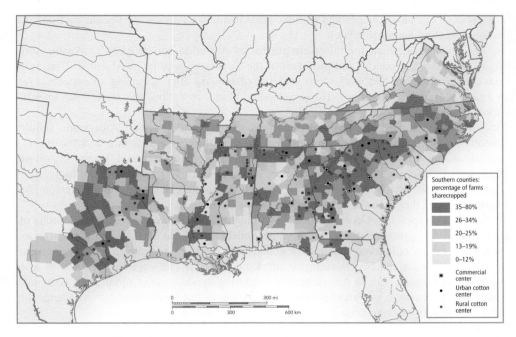

THE CROP-LIEN SYSTEM IN 1880   In the years after the Civil War, more and more southern farmers—white and black—became tenants or sharecroppers on land owned by others. This map shows the percentage of farms that were within the so-called crop-lien system, the system by which people worked their lands for someone else, who had a claim (or "lien") on a part of the farmers' crops. Note the high density of sharecropping and tenant farming in the most fertile areas of the Deep South, the same areas where slaveholding had been most dominant before the Civil War.   •   *How did the crop-lien system contribute to the shift in southern agriculture toward one-crop farming?*

for blacks. Some mill towns, therefore, were places where the black and white cultures came into close contact, increasing the determination of white leaders to take additional measures to protect white supremacy.

TENANTS AND SHARECROPPERS

The most important economic problem in the post-Reconstruction South was the impoverished state of agriculture. The 1870s and 1880s saw an acceleration of   *Growth of Tenantry* the process that had begun in the immediate postwar years: the imposition of systems of tenantry and debt peonage on much of the region; the reliance on a few cash crops rather than on a diversified agricultural system; and increasing absentee ownership of valuable farmlands. During Reconstruction, perhaps a third or more of the farmers in the South were tenants; by 1900, the figure had increased to 70 percent.

AFRICAN AMERICANS AND THE NEW SOUTH

The "New South creed" was not the property of whites alone. Many African Americans were attracted to the vision of progress and self-improvement as well. Some former slaves (and, as the decades passed, their offspring) succeeded in elevating themselves into the middle class, acquired property, established small businesses, or entered professions. Believing strongly that education was vital to the future of their people, they expanded the network of black colleges and institutes that had taken root during Reconstruction into an important educational system.

The chief spokesman for this commitment to education was Booker T. Washington, *Booker T. Washington* founder and president of the Tuskegee Institute in Alabama. Born into slavery, Washington had worked his way out of poverty after acquiring an education (at Virginia's Hampton Institute). He urged other blacks to follow the same road to self-improvement.

Washington's message was both cautious and hopeful. African Americans should attend school, learn skills, and establish a solid footing in agriculture and the trades. Industrial, not classical, education should be their goal. Blacks should, moreover, refine their speech, improve their dress, and adopt habits of thrift and personal cleanliness; they should, in short, adopt the standards of the white middle class. Only thus, Washington claimed, could they win the respect of the white population.

In a famous speech in Georgia in 1895, Washington outlined a controversial philosophy of *Atlanta Compromise* race relations that became widely known as the Atlanta Compromise. Blacks, he said, should forgo agitation for political rights and concentrate on self-improvement and preparation for equality. Washington offered a powerful challenge to those whites who wanted to discourage African Americans from acquiring an education or winning any economic gains. But his message was also intended to assure whites that blacks would not challenge the emerging system of segregation.

THE BIRTH OF JIM CROW

Few white southerners had ever accepted the idea of racial equality. That the former slaves acquired any legal and political rights at all after emancipation was in large part the result of their own efforts and crucial federal support. That outside support all but vanished after 1877, when federal troops withdrew and the Supreme Court stripped the Fourteenth and Fifteenth Amendments of much of their significance. In the so-called civil rights cases of 1883, the Court ruled that the Fourteenth Amendment prohibited state governments from discriminating against people because of race but did not restrict private organizations or individuals from doing so. Popular culture reflected these frightening political developments. The rise of minstrel shows—slapstick dramatic representations of black culture—typically embodied racist ideas. "Corked-up" whites (or whites using heavy makeup to appear black) grossly caricatured African American culture as silly, unintelligent, sensual, and immoral. Late in the 1800s, however, blacks founded their own minstrel shows in part to modify these stereotypes, though with only modest success. (See "Patterns of Popular Culture: The Minstrel Show.")

Eventually, the Court also validated state legislation that institutionalized the separa-*Plessy v. Ferguson* tion of the races. In *Plessy v. Ferguson* (1896), a case involving a Louisiana law that required segregated seating on railroads, the Court held that separate accommodations did not deprive blacks of equal rights if the accommodations were equal. In *Cumming v. County Board of Education* (1899), the Court ruled that communities could establish schools for whites only, even if there were no comparable schools for blacks.

Even before these dubious decisions, white southerners were working to separate the races to the greatest extent possible, and were particularly determined to strip African Americans of the right to vote. In some states, disenfranchisement had begun almost as soon as Reconstruction ended. But in other areas, black voting continued for some time after Reconstruction—largely because conservative whites believed they could control the black electorate and use it to beat back the attempts of poor white farmers to take control of the Democratic Party.

In the 1890s, however, franchise restrictions became much more rigid. During those years, some small white farmers began to demand complete black *Black Disenfranchisement* disenfranchisement—because they objected to the black vote being used against them by the Bourbons. At the same time, many members of the conservative elite began to doubt their ability to influence black voters and fear that poor whites might unite politically with poor blacks to challenge them.

In devising laws to disenfranchise black males, the southern states had to find ways to evade the Fifteenth Amendment, which prohibited states from denying anyone the right to vote because of race. Two devices emerged before 1900 to accomplish this goal: the poll tax, or some form of property qualification (few blacks were prosperous enough to meet such requirements); and the "literacy" or "understanding" test, which required voters to demonstrate an ability to read and to interpret the Constitution. Even those African Americans who could read had a hard time passing the difficult test white officials gave them, which often required them to interpret an arcane part of the Constitution to the satisfaction of a white elected official. (The laws affected poor white voters as well as blacks.) By the late 1890s, the black vote had decreased by 62 percent, the white vote by 26 percent.

Laws restricting the franchise and segregating schools were only part of a network of state and local statutes—collectively known as the Jim Crow laws—that by *Jim Crow Laws* the first years of the twentieth century had institutionalized an elaborate system of racial hierarchy reaching into almost every area of southern life. Blacks and whites could not ride together in the same railroad cars, sit in the same waiting rooms, use the same washrooms, eat in the same restaurants, or sit in the same theaters. Blacks had no access to many public parks, beaches, or picnic areas; they could not be patients in many hospitals. Much of the new legal structure did no more than confirm what had already been widespread social practice in the South. But the Jim Crow laws also stripped blacks of many of the modest social, economic, and political gains they had made in the late nineteenth century.

More than legal efforts were involved in this process. The 1890s witnessed a dramatic increase in white violence against blacks, which, along with the Jim Crow laws, served to inhibit black agitation for equal rights. The worst such violence—lynching of blacks by white mobs—reached appalling levels. In the nation as a whole in the 1890s, there was an average of 187 lynchings each year, more than 80 percent of them in the South. The vast majority of victims were black. Those who participated in lynchings often saw their actions as a legitimate form of law enforcement, and some victims of lynchings had in fact committed crimes. But lynchings were also a means by which whites controlled the black population through terror and intimidation.

The rise of lynchings shocked the conscience of many white Americans in a way that other forms of racial injustice did not. In 1892, Ida B. Wells, a committed *Ida B. Wells* black journalist, published a series of impassioned articles after the lynching of three of her hometown friends in Memphis, Tennessee; her articles launched what became an international antilynching movement. The movement gradually attracted substantial support from whites in both the North and the South (particularly from white women). Its goal was a federal antilynching law, which would allow the national government to do what state and local governments in the South were generally unwilling to do: punish those responsible for lynchings.

THE MINSTREL SHOW

The minstrel show was one of the most popular forms of entertainment in America in the second half of the nineteenth century. It was also a testament to the high awareness of race (and the high level of racism) in American society both before and after the Civil War. Minstrel performers were mostly white, usually disguised as black. But African American performers also formed their own minstrel shows and transformed them into vehicles for training black entertainers and developing new forms of music and dance.

Before and during the Civil War, when minstrel shows consisted almost entirely of white performers, performers blackened their faces with cork and presented grotesque stereotypes of the slave culture of the American South. Among the most popular of the stumbling, ridiculously ignorant characters invented for these shows were such figures as "Zip Coon" and "Jim Crow" (whose name later resurfaced as a label for late-nineteenth-century segregation laws). A typical minstrel show presented a group of seventeen or more men seated in a semicircle facing the audience. The man in the center ran the show, played the straight man for the jokes of others, and led the music—lively

MINSTRELSY AT HIGH TIDE The Primrose & West minstrel troupe—a lavish and expensive entertainment that drew large crowds in the 1800s—was one of many companies to offer this brand of entertainment to eager audiences all over the country. Although minstrelsy began with white musicians performing in blackface, the popularity of real African American minstrels encouraged the impresarios of the troupe to include groups of white and black performers alike. (The Library of Congress)

dances and sentimental ballads played on banjos, castanets, and other instruments and sung by soloists or the entire group.

After the Civil War, white minstrels began to expand their repertoire. Drawing from the famous and successful freak shows of P. T. Barnum and other entertainment entrepreneurs, some began to include Siamese twins, bearded ladies, and even a supposedly 8-foot 2-inch "Chinese giant" in their shows. They also incorporated sex, both by including women in some shows and, even more popularly, by recruiting female impersonators. One of the most successful minstrel performers of the 1870s was Francis Leon, who delighted crowds with his female portrayal of a flamboyant "prima donna."

One reason white minstrels began to move in these new directions was that they were now facing competition from black performers, who could provide more-authentic versions of black music, dance, and humor. They usually brought more talent to the task than white performers. The Georgia Minstrels, organized in 1865, was one of the first all-black minstrel troupes, and it had great success in attracting white audiences in the Northeast for several years. By the 1870s, touring African American minstrel groups were numerous. The black minstrels used many of the conventions of the white shows. There were dances, music, comic routines, and sentimental recitations. Some black performers even chalked their faces to make themselves look as dark as the white blackface performers with whom they were competing. Black minstrels sometimes denounced slavery (at least indirectly) and did not often speak demeaningly of the capacities of their race. But they could not entirely escape caricaturing African American life as they struggled to meet the expectations of their white audiences.

The black minstrel shows had few openly political aims. They did help develop some important forms of African American entertainment and transform them into a part of the national culture. Black minstrels introduced new forms of dance, derived from the informal traditions of slavery and black community life. They showed the "buck and wing," the "stop time," and the "Virginia essence," which established the foundations for the tap and jazz dancing of the early twentieth century. They also improvised musically and began experimenting with forms that over time contributed to the growth of ragtime, jazz, and rhythm and blues.

Eventually, black minstrelsy—like its white counterpart—evolved into other forms of theater, including the beginnings of serious black drama. At Ambrose Park in Brooklyn in the 1890s, for example, the celebrated black comedian Sam Lucas (a veteran of the minstrel circuit) starred in the play *Darkest America,* which one black newspaper later described as a "delineation of Negro life, carrying the race through all their historical phases from the plantation, into reconstruction days and finally painting our people as they are today, cultured and accomplished in the social graces, [holding] the mirror faithfully up to nature."

But interest in the minstrel show did not die altogether. In 1927, Hollywood released *The Jazz Singer,* the first feature film with sound. It was about the career of a white minstrel performer, and its star was one of the most popular singers of the twentieth century: Al Jolson, whose career had begun on the blackface minstrel circuit years before. •

UNDERSTAND, ANALYZE, & EVALUATE

1. How did minstrel shows performed by white minstrels reinforce prevailing attitudes toward African Americans?
2. Minstrel shows performed by black minstrels often conformed to existing stereotypes of African Americans. Why?
3. Can you think of any popular entertainments today that carry remnants of the minstrel shows of the nineteenth century?

A LYNCH MOB, 1893 A large, almost festive crowd gathers to watch the lynching of a black man accused of the murder of a three-year-old white girl. Lynchings remained frequent in the South until as late as the 1930s, but they reached their peak in the 1890s and the first years of the twentieth century. Lynchings such as this one—publicized well in advance and attracting whole families who traveled great distances to see them—were relatively infrequent. Most lynchings were the work of smaller groups, operating with less visibility. (The Library of Congress)

But the substantial southern white opposition to lynchings stood as an exception to the general white support for suppression of African Americans. Indeed, just as in the antebellum period, the shared commitment to white supremacy helped dilute class animosities between poorer whites and the Bourbon oligarchies. Economic issues tended to play a secondary role to race in southern politics, distracting people from the glaring social inequalities that afflicted blacks and whites alike.

CONCLUSION

Reconstruction was a profoundly important moment in American history. Despite the bitter political battles in Washington and throughout the South, culminating in the unsuccessful effort to remove President Andrew Johnson from office, the most important result of the effort to reunite the nation after its long and bloody war was a reshaping of the lives of ordinary people in all regions.

In the North, Reconstruction solidified the power of the Republican Party. The rapid expansion of the northern economy accelerated, drawing more and more of its residents into a burgeoning commercial world.

In the South, Reconstruction fundamentally rearranged the relationship between white and black citizens. African Americans initially participated actively and effectively in southern politics. After a few years of widespread black voting and significant black officeholding, however, the forces of white supremacy shoved most African Americans to the margins of the southern political world, where they would mostly remain until the 1960s.

In other ways, however, the lives of southern blacks changed dramatically and permanently. Overwhelmingly, they left the plantations. Some sought work in towns and cities. Others left the region altogether. But the great majority began farming on small farms of their own—not as landowners, except in rare cases, but as tenants and sharecroppers on land owned by whites. The result was a form of economic bondage, driven by debt, only scarcely less oppressive than the legal bondage of slavery. Within this system, however, African Americans managed to carve out a much larger sphere of social and cultural activity than they had ever been able to create under slavery. Black churches proliferated in great numbers. African American schools and printing presses emerged in some communities, and black colleges began to operate in the region. Some former slaves owned businesses and flourished.

Strenuous efforts by "New South" advocates to advance industry and commerce in the region produced impressive results in a few areas. But the South on the whole remained what it had always been: a largely rural society with a sharply defined class structure. It also maintained a deep commitment among its white citizens to the subordination of African Americans—a commitment solidified in the 1890s and the early twentieth century when white southerners erected an elaborate legal system of segregation (the Jim Crow laws). Tragically, the promise of the great Reconstruction amendments to the Constitution—the Fourteenth and Fifteenth—remained largely unfulfilled in the South as the century drew to its close.

KEY TERMS/PEOPLE/PLACES/EVENTS

Andrew Johnson 357
Atlanta Compromise 374
Black Codes 358
Booker T. Washington 374
carpetbagger 362
Compromise of 1877 369
crop-lien system 365
Enforcement Acts 369
Fourteenth Amendment 358

Fifteenth Amendment 359
Freedmen's Bureau 353
Ida B. Wells 375
impeachment 362
Jim Crow laws 375
Ku Klux Klan 368
New South 372
Panic of 1873 367
Plessy v. Ferguson 374

Radical Republicans 354
Reconstruction 354
Redeemers 371
scalawag 362
sharecropping 364
Thaddeus Stevens 354
Wade-Davis Bill 354
William H. Seward 368

RECALL AND REFLECT

1. What were the principal questions facing the nation at the end of the Civil War?
2. What were the achievements of Reconstruction? Where did it fail and why?
3. What new problems arose in the South as the North's interest in Reconstruction waned?
4. What was the Compromise of 1877, and how did it affect Reconstruction?
5. How did the New South differ from the South before the Civil War?

16

THE CONQUEST OF THE FAR WEST

THE SOCIETIES OF THE FAR WEST
THE CHANGING WESTERN ECONOMY
THE ROMANCE OF THE WEST
THE DISPERSAL OF THE TRIBES
THE RISE AND DECLINE OF THE WESTERN FARMER

LOOKING AHEAD

1. What various ethnic and racial groups populated the American West, and how were the cultural characteristics of these groups reflected in the West?

2. How did the arrival and settlement of substantial numbers of Anglo-Americans transform the society and economy of the West?

3. What role did the federal government play in shaping the development of the West?

BY THE MID-1840s, WHITE AMERICAN migrants, along with many others, from the eastern regions of the nation had settled in the West in substantial numbers. Farmers, ranchers, and miners all found opportunity in the western lands. By the end of the Civil War, the West had become legendary in the eastern states. No longer the Great American Desert, it was now widely viewed as the "frontier": an empty land awaiting settlement and civilization; a place of wealth, adventure, opportunity, and untrammeled individualism.

In fact, the real West of the mid-nineteenth century bore little resemblance to its popular image. It was a diverse land, with many different regions, climates, and stores of natural resources. And it was extensively populated. The English-speaking migrants of the late nineteenth century did not find an empty, desolate land. They found Indians, Mexicans, African Americans, French and British Canadians, Asians, and others, some of whose families had been living in the West for generations.

THE SOCIETIES OF THE FAR WEST

The Far West was in fact a composite of many lands. It contained both the most arid regions and some of the wettest and lushest areas of the United States. It contained the flattest plains and the highest mountains. It also contained many peoples.

THE WESTERN TRIBES

The Indian tribes made up the largest and most important western population group before the great white migration. Some were members of eastern tribes who had been forcibly resettled west of the Mississippi. But most were members of indigenous tribes whose roots stretched back generations.

More than 300,000 Indians (among them the Serrano, Chumash, Pomo, Maidu, Yurok, and Chinook) had lived on the Pacific Coast before the arrival of Spanish settlers. They supported themselves through a combination of fishing, foraging, and simple agriculture. The Pueblos of the Southwest had long lived largely as farmers and had established permanent settlements there.

The most widespread Indian groups in the West were the Plains Indians. They were, in fact, made up of many different tribal and language groups. Some lived more or less sedentary lives as farmers, but many subsisted largely through hunting buffalo. Riding small but powerful horses, the tribes moved through the grasslands following the herds, constructing tepees as temporary dwellings. The buffalo, or bison, provided the economic basis for the Plains Indians' way of life. The flesh of the large animal was their principal source of food, and its skin supplied materials for clothing, shoes, tepees, blankets, robes, and utensils. "Buffalo chips"—dried manure—provided fuel; buffalo bones became knives and arrow tips; buffalo tendons formed the strings of bows.

TIME LINE

1862
Homestead Act

1865–1867
Sioux Wars

1869
Transcontinental railroad completed

1873
Barbed wire invented

1874
Black Hills gold rush

1876
Battle of the Little Bighorn

1877
Desert Land Act

1882
Chinese Exclusion Act

1885
Twain's *Huckleberry Finn*

1887
Dawes Act

1889
Oklahoma opened to white settlement

1890
Battle of Wounded Knee

1893
Turner thesis

The Plains warriors proved to be the most formidable foes the white settlers had encountered. But the tribes were usually unable to unite against white aggression. At times, tribal warriors even faced white forces who were being assisted by guides and even fighters from rival tribes. Some tribes, however, were able to overcome their divisions and cooperate effectively. By the mid-nineteenth century, for example, the Sioux, Arapaho, *Plains Warriors' Vulnerabilities* and Cheyenne had forged a powerful alliance that dominated the northern plains. That proved no protection, however, against the greatest danger to the tribes: ecological and economic decline. Indians were highly vulnerable to eastern infectious diseases, such as the smallpox epidemics that decimated the Pawnee in Nebraska in the 1840s. And the tribes were, of course, at a considerable disadvantage in any long-term battle with an economically and industrially advanced people.

HISPANIC NEW MEXICO

For centuries, much of the Far West had been part of the Spanish Empire and, later, the Mexican Republic. When the United States acquired its new lands there in the 1840s, it also acquired many Mexican residents.

In New Mexico, the centers of Spanish-speaking society were farming and trading communities established in the seventeenth century. Descendants of the original Spanish settlers (and more recent migrants from Mexico) engaged primarily in cattle and sheep ranching. When the United States acquired title to New Mexico in the aftermath of the Mexican War, General Stephen Kearny—who had commanded the American troops in the region—tried to establish a territorial government out of the approximately 1,000 Anglo-Americans in the region, ignoring the more than 50,000 Hispanics. There were widespread fears among Hispanics and Indians that the new American rulers would confiscate their lands. In 1847, before the new government had established itself, Taos Indians *Taos Indian Rebellion* rebelled, killing the new governor and other Anglo-American officials before being subdued by United States Army forces. New Mexico remained under military rule for three years, until the United States finally organized a territorial government there in 1850. The United States Army finally broke the power of the Navajo, Apache, and other tribes in the region. The defeat of the tribes led to substantial Hispanic migration into other areas of the Southwest and as far north as Colorado.

The Anglo-American presence in the Southwest grew rapidly once the railroads penetrated the region in the 1880s and early 1890s. With the railroads came extensive new ranching, farming, and mining. This expansion of economic activity attracted a new wave of Mexican immigrants, who moved across the border in search of work. The English-speaking proprietors of the new enterprises, however, commonly restricted most Mexicans to the lowest-paying and least stable jobs.

HISPANIC CALIFORNIA AND TEXAS

In California, Spanish settlement began in the eighteenth century with a string of Catholic missions along the Pacific Coast. The missionaries and the soldiers who accompanied them gathered most of the coastal Indians into their communities, some forcibly and others by persuasion. In the 1830s, after the new Mexican government began reducing the power of the church, the mission society largely collapsed. In its place emerged a secular Mexican aristocracy, which controlled a chain of large estates in the fertile lands west of the Sierra mountains. For them, the acquisition of California by the United States was

***TEJANO RANCHERS, 1877,* BY JAMES WALKER** The Spanish term *Tejano* or *Texano* refers to Texans of Mexican descent. The mounted rancher has roped a white mustang; a saddle is ready nearby. Small independent ranches were well established in south Texas before large Anglo-American enterprises moved in. (Private Collection/ © Peter Newark Pictures/Bridgeman Images)

disastrous. So vast were the numbers of English-speaking immigrants that the *californios* (as the Hispanic residents of the region were known) had little power   *Plight of* Californios to resist the onslaught. English-speaking prospectors organized to exclude them, sometimes violently, from the mines during the gold rush. Many *californios* also lost their lands—either through corrupt business deals or through outright seizure.

Increasingly, Mexicans and Mexican Americans became part of the lower end of the state's working class, clustered in *barrios* in Los Angeles or elsewhere or laboring as migrant farmworkers. Even small Hispanic landowners who managed to hang on to their farms found themselves unable to raise livestock, as once-communal grazing lands fell under the control of powerful Anglo ranchers.

A similar pattern occurred in Texas after it joined the United States. Many Mexican landowners lost their land—some as a result of fraud and coercion, others   *Mexicans in Texas* because even the most substantial Mexican ranchers could not compete with the emerging Anglo-American ranching kingdoms. In 1859, angry Mexicans, led by the rancher Juan Cortina, raided the jail in Brownsville and freed all the Mexican prisoners inside. But such resistance had little long-term effect. As in California, Mexicans in southern Texas became an increasingly impoverished working class, relegated largely to unskilled farm or industrial labor.

THE CHINESE MIGRATION

At the same time that ambitious or impoverished Europeans were crossing the Atlantic in search of opportunities in the New World, many Chinese were crossing the Pacific in hopes of better lives. Not all came to the United States. Many Chinese—some   *"Coolies"* as "coolies" (indentured servants whose condition was close to slavery)—moved to Hawaii, Australia, Latin America, South Africa, and even the Caribbean.

A CHINESE FAMILY IN SAN FRANCISCO This portrait of Chun Duck Chin and his seven-year-old son Chun Jan Yut was taken in a studio in San Francisco in the 1870s. Both father and son appear to have dressed up for the occasion, in traditional Chinese garb, and the studio—which likely took many such portraits of Chinese families—provided a formal Chinese backdrop. The son is holding what appears to be a chicken, perhaps to impress relatives in China with the family's prosperity. (National Archives and Records Administration)

A few Chinese traveled to the American West even before the gold rush, but after 1848 the flow increased dramatically. By 1880, more than 200,000 Chinese had settled in the United States. Almost all came as free laborers. For a time, white Americans welcomed the Chinese as a conscientious, hardworking people. Very quickly, however, white opinion turned hostile—in part because the Chinese were so industrious and successful that some white Americans began considering them rivals.

In the early 1850s, large numbers of Chinese immigrants joined the hunt for gold. Many of them were well-organized, hardworking prospectors, and for a time some enjoyed considerable success. But opportunities for the Chinese to prosper in the mines were fleeting. In 1852, the California legislature began trying to exclude the Chinese from gold mining by enacting a "foreign miners" tax. Gradually, the effect of the discriminatory laws, the hostility of white miners, and the declining profitability of the surface mines drove most Chinese out of prospecting.

As mining declined as a source of wealth and jobs for the Chinese, railroad employment grew. Beginning in 1865, over 12,000 Chinese found work building the transcontinental railroad, forming 90 percent of the labor force of the Central Pacific.   *Railroad Workers* The company preferred them to white laborers because they worked hard, made few demands, and accepted relatively low wages.

Work on the Central Pacific was arduous and often dangerous. In the winter, many Chinese tunneled into snowbanks at night to create warm sleeping areas for themselves, even though such tunnels frequently collapsed, suffocating those inside. In the spring of 1866, 5,000 Chinese railroad workers rebelled against the terrible conditions and went on strike to demand higher wages and a shorter workday. The company isolated them, surrounded them with strikebreakers, and starved them into submission.

In 1869, the transcontinental railroad was completed, and thousands of Chinese lost their jobs. Some moved into agricultural work, usually in menial positions. Increasingly, however, the Chinese flocked to cities. By far the largest single Chinese community was in San Francisco. Much of community life there, and in other "Chinatowns" throughout the West, revolved around organizations, somewhat like   *"Chinatowns"* benevolent societies, that filled many of the roles that political machines often served in immigrant communities in eastern cities. Often led by prominent merchants (in San Francisco, the leading merchants—known as the "Six Companies"—often worked together to advance their interests in the city and state), these organizations became, in effect, employment brokers, unions, arbitrators of disputes, defenders against outside persecution, and dispensers of social services. They also organized elaborate festivals and celebrations that were a conspicuous and important part of life in Chinatowns.

Other Chinese organizations were secret societies, known as "tongs." Some of the tongs were violent criminal organizations, involved in the opium trade and prostitution. Few people outside the Chinese communities were aware of their existence, except when rival tongs engaged in violent conflict (or "tong wars").

In San Francisco and other western cities, the Chinese usually occupied the lower rungs of the employment ladder. Many worked as common laborers, servants, and unskilled factory hands. Some established their own small businesses, especially laundries. There were few commercial laundries in China, but they could be started in America with very little capital and required only limited command of English. By the 1890s, Chinese constituted over two-thirds of all the laundry workers in California.

During the earliest Chinese migrations to California, virtually all the relatively small number of women who made the journey did so because they had been sold into prostitution. As late as 1880, nearly half the Chinese women in California were   *Chinese Families* prostitutes. Gradually, however, the number of Chinese women increased, and Chinese men in America became more likely to seek companionship in families.

Anti-Chinese Sentiments

As Chinese communities grew larger and more visible, anti-Chinese sentiment among white residents intensified. Anti-Chinese activities, some of them bloody, reflected the resentment of many white workers toward Chinese laborers for accepting lower wages. As the political value of attacking the Chinese grew in California, the Democratic Party took up the call. So did the Workingmen's Party of California—founded in 1878 by Denis Kearney, an Irish immigrant—which gained significant power in the state largely because of its hostility to the Chinese. By the mid-1880s, anti-Chinese agitation and violence had spread up and down the Pacific Coast and into other areas of the West.

Chinese Exclusion Act   In 1882, Congress responded to the political pressure and the growing racial violence by passing the Chinese Exclusion Act, which banned Chinese immigration into the United States for ten years and barred Chinese already in the country from becoming naturalized citizens. Congress renewed the law for another ten years in 1892 and made it permanent in 1902. It had a dramatic effect on the Chinese population, which declined by more than 40 percent in the forty years after the act's passage.

MIGRATION FROM THE EAST

The scale of post–Civil War white migration to the American West dwarfed everything that had preceded it. In previous decades, the settlers had come in thousands. Now they came in millions. Most of the new settlers were from the established Anglo-American societies of the eastern United States, but substantial numbers—over 2 million between 1870 and 1900—were foreign-born immigrants from Europe: Scandinavians, Germans, Irish, Russians, Czechs, and others.

They came to the West for many reasons. Settlers were attracted by gold and silver deposits, by the short-grass pasture for cattle and sheep, and ultimately by the rich sod of the plains and the meadowlands of the mountains. The completion of the great transcontinental railroad line in 1869, and the construction of the many subsidiary lines that spidered out from it, encouraged rapid settlement. So did the land policies of the federal *Homestead Act*   government. The Homestead Act of 1862 permitted settlers to buy plots of 160 acres for a small fee if they occupied the land they purchased for five years and improved it.

Supporters of the Homestead Act believed it would create new markets and new outposts of commercial agriculture for the nation's growing economy. But a unit of 160 acres, while ample in much of the East, was too small for the grazing and grain farming of the Great Plains. Eventually, the federal government provided some relief. The Timber Culture Act (1873) permitted homesteaders to receive grants of 160 additional acres if they planted 40 acres of trees on them. The Desert Land Act (1877) allowed claimants to buy 640 acres at $1.25 an acre, provided they irrigated part of their holdings within three years. These and other laws ultimately made it possible for individuals to acquire as much as 1,280 acres of land at little cost.

Political organization followed on the hard heels of settlement. By the mid-1860s, territorial *New Western States*   governments were in operation in the new provinces of Nevada, Colorado, Dakota, Arizona, Idaho, Montana, and Wyoming. Statehood rapidly followed. Nevada became a state in 1864, Nebraska in 1867, and Colorado in 1876. In 1889, North and South Dakota, Montana, and Washington won admission; Wyoming and Idaho entered the next year. Congress denied Utah statehood until its Mormon leaders convinced the government in 1896 that polygamy (the practice of men taking several wives) had been abandoned. At the turn of the century, only Arizona, New Mexico, and Oklahoma remained outside the Union.

THE CHANGING WESTERN ECONOMY

The great wave of Anglo-American and European settlement transformed the economy of the Far West and tied the region firmly to the growing industrial economy of the East.

Labor in the West

As commercial activity increased, many farmers, ranchers, and miners found it necessary to recruit a paid labor force—not an easy task given the small labor pool compared to that found in established cities. This labor shortage led to higher wages for some workers than were typical in the East. But working conditions were often treacherous, and job security was almost nonexistent. Once a railroad was built, a crop harvested, a herd sent to market, a mine played out, hundreds and even thousands of workers could find themselves suddenly unemployed.

The western working class was highly multiracial. English-speaking whites worked alongside African Americans and immigrants from southern and *Multiracial Working Class* eastern Europe, as they did in the East. Even more, they worked with Chinese, Filipinos, Mexicans, and Indians. But the workforce was highly stratified along racial lines. In almost every area of the western economy, white workers (whatever their ethnicity) occupied the upper tiers of employment: management and skilled labor. The lower tiers—unskilled work in the mines, on the railroads, or in agriculture—were filled overwhelmingly by nonwhites.

The western economy was, however, no more a single entity than the economy of the East. In the late nineteenth century, the region produced three major industries, each with distinctive history and characteristics: mining, ranching, and commercial farming.

The Arrival of the Miners

The first economic boom in the Far West was the result of mining. The mining boom began around 1860 and flourished until the 1890s. Then it abruptly declined.

At first it was news of a gold or silver strike that would start a stampede. The California gold rush of 1849 was the first and most famous gold rush. But it was followed by others. Individual prospectors would pan for gold, extracting the first shallow deposits of ore largely by hand, a method known as placer mining. After these surface deposits dwindled, corporations moved in to engage in lode or quartz mining, which dug deeper beneath the surface. Then, as those deposits dwindled, commercial mining declined, and ranchers and farmers moved in and established a more permanent economy.

The first great mineral strikes (other than the California gold rush) occurred just before the Civil War. In 1858, gold was discovered in the Pike's Peak district of what would soon be the territory of Colorado; the following year, 50,000 prospectors stormed in. Denver and other mining camps blossomed into "cities" overnight. Almost as rapidly as they had developed, the booms ended. Later, the discovery of silver near Leadville supplied a new source of mineral wealth.

While the Colorado rush of 1859 was still in progress, news of another strike drew miners to Nevada. Gold had been found in the Washoe district. Even more plentiful and more valuable was the silver found in the great Comstock Lode (first *Comstock Lode* discovered in 1858 by Henry Comstock) and other Washoe veins. The first prospectors to reach the Washoe fields came from California, and from the beginning, Californians dominated the settlement and development of Nevada. A remote desert without railroad transportation, the territory produced no supplies of its own, and everything had to be shipped from California to Virginia City, Carson City, and other roaring camp towns. When the first placer (or surface) deposits ran out, Californian and eastern capitalists bought the claims of the pioneer prospectors and began to use the more difficult process of quartz mining, which enabled them to retrieve silver from deeper veins. For a few years, these outside owners reaped tremendous profits: from 1860 to 1880, the Nevada lodes yielded bullion worth $306 million. After that, the mines quickly played out.

The next important mineral discoveries came in 1874, when gold was found in the Black Hills of southwestern Dakota Territory. Prospectors swarmed into the remote area. Like the others, the boom flared for a time, until surface resources faded and corporations took over—above all, the enormous Homestake Mining Company—and came to dominate the fields. The Dakotas, like other boom areas of the mineral empire, ultimately developed a largely agricultural economy.

The gold and silver discoveries generated the most popular excitement. But less glamorous natural resources proved more important to western development. The great Anaconda copper mine, launched by William Clark in 1881, marked the beginning of an industry that would remain important to Montana for many decades. In other areas, mining operations had significant success with lead, tin, quartz, and zinc.

Men greatly outnumbered women in the mining towns, and younger men in particular *Gender Disparity* had difficulty finding female companions of comparable age. Those women who did gravitate to the new communities often came with their husbands. Single women, or women whose husbands were earning no money, did work for wages at times, as cooks, laundresses, and tavernkeepers. And in the sexually imbalanced mining communities, there was always a ready market for prostitutes.

The thousands of people who flocked to the mining towns in search of quick wealth and failed to find it often remained as wage laborers in corporate mines after the boom period, working in almost uniformly terrible conditions. In the 1870s, one worker in every thirty was disabled in the mines, and one in every eighty was killed. That rate fell later in the nineteenth century, but mining remained one of the most dangerous and arduous working environments in the United States.

The Cattle Kingdom

A second important element of the changing economy of the Far West was cattle ranching. The open range—the vast grasslands of the public domain—provided a huge area on the Great Plains where cattle raisers could graze their herds.

The western cattle industry was Mexican and Texan by ancestry. Long before citizens *Mexican Roots* of the United States entered the Southwest, Mexican ranchers had developed the techniques and equipment that the cattlemen and cowboys of the Great Plains later employed: branding, roundups, roping, and the gear of the herders—their lariats, saddles, leather chaps, and spurs. Americans in Texas, with the largest herds of cattle in the country, adopted these methods and carried them to the northernmost ranges of the cattle kingdom. From Texas, too, came the small, muscular horses (broncos and mustangs) that enabled cowboys to control the herds.

At the end of the Civil War, an estimated 5 million cattle roamed the Texas ranges. Eastern markets offered good prices for steers. The challenge facing the cattle industry lay in getting the animals from the range to the railroad centers. Early in 1866, some Texas cattle ranchers began driving their combined herds, up to 260,000 steers, north to Sedalia, Missouri, on the Missouri Pacific Railroad. The caravan suffered heavy losses. But the drive proved that cattle could be driven to distant markets and pastured along the trail. This earliest of the **long drives** established the first, tentative link between the isolated cattle breeders of west Texas and the booming urban markets of the East.

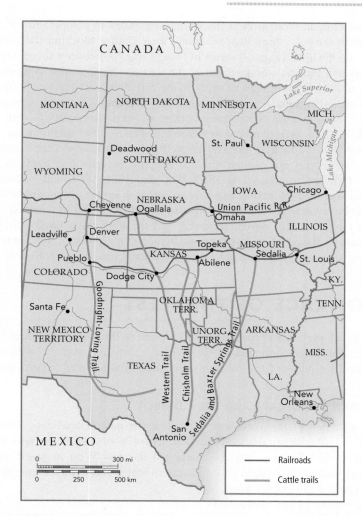

THE CATTLE KINGDOM, ca. 1866-1887   Cattle ranching and cattle drives are among the most romanticized features of the nineteenth-century West. But they were also hardheaded businesses, made possible by the growing eastern market for beef and the availability of reasonably inexpensive transportation—thanks to the dense network of trails and railroads—to take cattle to the urban markets.   • *Why was the open range necessary for the great cattle drives, and what eventually ended the cattle trails?*

Market facilities soon grew up at Abilene, Kansas, on the Kansas Pacific Railroad, and for years the town reigned as the railhead of the cattle kingdom. But by the mid-1870s, agricultural development in western Kansas had eaten away at the open-range land. Cattlemen had to develop other trails and other market outlets. As the railroads reached farther west, other locations began to rival Abilene as major centers of stock herding: Dodge City and Wichita in Kansas, Ogallala and Sidney in Nebraska, Cheyenne and Laramie in Wyoming, and Miles City and Glendive in Montana.

There had always been an element of risk and speculation in the open-range cattle business. Rustlers and Indians frequently seized large numbers of animals. But as the settlement of the plains increased, new forms of competition arose. Sheep breeders from

California and Oregon brought their flocks onto the range to compete for grass. Farmers ("nesters") from the East threw fences around their claims, blocking trails and breaking *"Range Wars"* up the open range. A series of "range wars"—between sheepmen and cattlemen, ranchers and farmers—erupted out of the tensions among these competing groups.

Accounts of the lofty profits to be made in the cattle business tempted eastern, English, and Scottish capital to the plains. Increasingly, the structure of the cattle economy became *Decline of the Open-Range Industry* corporate; in one year, twenty corporations with a combined capital of $12 million were chartered in Wyoming. The result of this frenzied, speculative expansion was that the ranges, already shrunk by the railroads and the farmers, became overstocked. There was not enough grass to support the crowding herds or sustain the long drives. Two severe winters, in 1885–1886 and 1886–1887, and a searing summer between them scorched the plains. Streams and grass dried up. Hundreds of thousands of cattle died. Princely ranches and costly investments disappeared in a season.

The open-range industry never recovered, and the long drive finally disappeared for good. Railroads displaced the trail as the route to market for livestock. But some established cattle ranches survived, grew, and prospered, eventually producing more beef than ever.

THE ROMANCE OF THE WEST

The rapidly developing West occupied a special place in the Anglo-American imagination. Many white Americans continued to consider it a romantic place, a wilderness where individuals could experience true freedom. But such thinking was more fiction than fact.

THE WESTERN LANDSCAPE AND THE COWBOY

Part of the attraction of the West was its spectacular natural landscape. Painters of the *"Rocky Mountain School"* new "Rocky Mountain school"—of whom the best known were Albert Bierstadt and Thomas Moran—celebrated the new West in grandiose canvases, some of which toured the eastern and midwestern states and attracted enormous crowds, eager for a vision of the Great West.

Gradually, paintings and photographs inspired a growing wave of tourism among people eager to see the natural wonders of the region. In the 1880s and 1890s, resort hotels began to spring up near some of the region's most spectacular landscapes.

Even more appealing was the rugged, free-spirited lifestyle that many Americans associated with the West. Many nineteenth-century Americans came especially to idealize the figure of the cowboy. Western novels such as Owen Wister's *The Virginian* (1902) roman-*Cowboys in Fiction* ticized the cowboy's supposed freedom from traditional social constraints, his affinity with nature, even his supposed propensity for violence. Wister's character— one of the most enduring in popular American literature—was a semi-educated man whose natural decency, courage, and compassion made him a powerful symbol of the supposed virtues of the "frontier." But *The Virginian* was only the most famous example of a type of literature that soon swept throughout the United States. Novels and stories glorified the West and the lives of cowboys in particular, in boys' magazines, pulp novels, theater, and serious literature.

Among the reasons for the widespread admiration of the cowboy were the remarkably popular Wild West shows that traveled throughout the United States and Europe. Most successful were the shows of Buffalo Bill Cody, a former Pony Express rider, Indian fighter, and hero of popular dime novels for children. Cody's Wild West show, which spawned dozens of imitators, exploited his own fame and romanticized the life of the cowboy through reenactments of Indian battles and displays of horsemanship and riflery (many of them by the famous sharpshooter Annie Oakley). Buffalo Bill and his imitators confirmed the popular image of the West as a place of romance and glamour and helped keep that image alive for later generations.

THE IDEA OF THE FRONTIER

It was not simply the particular character of the new West that resonated in the nation's imagination. It was also that many Americans considered it the last natural frontier. Since the earliest moments of European settlement in America, the image of uncharted territory to the west had always comforted and inspired those who dreamed of starting life anew.

Mark Twain gave voice to this romantic vision of the frontier in a *Mark Twain* series of novels and memoirs. In *The Adventures of Tom Sawyer* (1876) and *The Adventures of Huckleberry Finn* (1885), he produced characters who repudiated the constraints of organized society and attempted to escape into a more natural world. (For Huck Finn, the vehicle of escape was a small raft on the Mississippi.) This yearning for freedom reflected a larger vision of the West as the last refuge from the constraints of civilization.

AMERICAN PROGRESS, 1872   The Brooklyn artist John Gast painted this image of hardy settlers marching toward the frontier for western travel guides. The goddess of progress, holding a schoolbook and telegraph line, leads the way. Native Americans, buffalo, and a bear are pushed off to the margins by the pioneers' approach. (The Library of Congress)

THE FRONTIER AND THE WEST

The emergence of the history of the American West as an important field of scholarship can be traced to a paper Frederick Jackson Turner delivered to the American Historical Association in 1893: "The Significance of the Frontier in American History." Turner stated his thesis simply. The settlement of the West by white Americans—"the existence of an area of free land, its continuous recession, and the advance of American settlement westward"—was the central story of the nation's history. The process of westward expansion had transformed a desolate and savage land into modern civilization and had continually renewed American ideas of democracy and individualism.

In the first half of the twentieth century, virtually everyone who wrote about the West echoed at least part of Turner's argument. Ray Allen Billington's *Westward Expansion* (1949) was almost wholly consistent with the Turnerian model. In *The Great Plains* (1931) and *The Great Frontier* (1952), Walter Prescott Webb similarly emphasized the bravery and ingenuity of white settlers in the Southwest.

Serious efforts to displace the Turner thesis as the explanation of western American history began after World War II. In *Virgin Land* (1950), Henry Nash Smith examined many of the same heroic images of the West that Turner and his disciples had presented; but he treated those images less as descriptions of reality than as myths. Earl Pomeroy challenged Turner's notion of the West as a place of individualism, innovation, and democratic renewal. "Conservatism, inheritance, and continuity bulked at least as large," he claimed. Howard Lamar, in *Dakota Territory, 1861–1889* (1956) and *The Far Southwest*

(1966), emphasized the highly diverse character of the West.

The western historians who emerged since the late 1970s launched an even more emphatic attack on the Turner thesis and the idea of the "frontier." "New western historians" such as Richard White, Patricia Nelson Limerick, William Cronon, Donald Worster, Peggy Pascoe, and many others challenged the Turnerians on a number of points.

Turner saw the nineteenth-century West as "free land" awaiting the expansion of Anglo-American settlement and American democracy. The more recent western historians reject the concept of an empty "frontier," emphasizing instead the elaborate and highly developed civilizations that already existed in the region. White, English-speaking Americans, they have argued, did not so much "settle" the West as conquer it. And they continued to share the region not only with the Indians and Hispanics who preceded them there, but also with African Americans, Asians, Latin Americans, and others who flowed into the West at the same time they did.

The Turnerian West was a place of heroism, triumph, and above all progress, dominated by the feats of brave white men. The West that the new western historians describe was a less triumphant (and less masculine) place in which bravery and success coexisted with oppression, greed, and failure; in which decaying ghost towns, bleak Indian reservations, impoverished barrios, and ecologically devastated landscapes have been as characteristic of western development as great ranches, rich farms, and prosperous cities.

To Turner and his disciples, the nineteenth-century West was a place where rugged individualism flourished and replenished American democracy. The newer scholars point out that the region was inextricably tied to a national and international capitalist economy. Westerners depended on government-subsidized railroads for access to markets, federal troops for protection from Indians, and (later) government-funded dams and canals for irrigating their fields and sustaining their towns.

And while Turner defined the West as a process—a process of settlement that came to an end with the "closing of the frontier" in the late nineteenth century—the newer historians see the West as a region. Its distinctive history did not end in 1890 but continues into our own time. •

UNDERSTAND, ANALYZE, & EVALUATE

1. How and why did the portrayal of the West by the newer western historians differ from the West that Turner described?
2. Why did the newer western historians challenge Turner's views, and why has their depiction of the west, in turn, provoked such controversy?

One of the most beloved and successful artists of the nineteenth century was Frederic Remington, a painter and sculptor whose works came to represent the *Frederic Remington* romance of the West. He portrayed the cowboy as a natural aristocrat, much like Wister's *The Virginian,* living in a natural world in which all the normal supporting structures of "civilization" were missing.

Theodore Roosevelt also contributed to the romanticizing of the West. He traveled to the Dakota badlands in the mid-1880s to recover from the sudden death of his young wife. In the 1890s, he published a four-volume history, *The Winning of the West,* with a heroic account of the spread of white civilization into the frontier.

Perhaps the most influential statement of the romantic vision of the frontier came from the young historian Frederick Jackson Turner, in a memorable paper he delivered as a thirty-two-year-old in Chicago in 1893 titled "The Significance of the Frontier in American History." In it he boldly claimed that the experience of western expansion had stimulated individualism, nationalism, and democracy; kept opportunities for advancement alive; and made Americans the distinctive people that they were. "Now," Turner concluded portentously, "the frontier has gone and with its going has closed the first period of American history." The **Turner thesis** was widely accepted by his contemporaries, but later historians have *Turner Thesis* challenged it. (See "Debating the Past: The Frontier and the West.")

In accepting the idea of the "passing of the frontier," many Americans were acknowledging the end of one of their most cherished myths. As long as it had been possible for them to see the West as an empty, open land, it was possible to believe that there were constantly revitalizing opportunities in American life. But by the end of the nineteenth century, there was a vague and ominous sense of opportunities foreclosed.

THE DISPERSAL OF THE TRIBES

Having imagined the West as a "virgin land" awaiting civilization by white people, many Americans tried to force the region to match their image of it. That meant, above all, ensuring that the Indian tribes would not be obstacles to the spread of white society.

WHITE TRIBAL POLICIES

The traditional policy of the federal government was to regard the tribes simultaneously as independent nations (with which the United States could negotiate treaties) and as wards of the president (who would exercise paternalistic authority over the Indians). The concept of Indian sovereignty had supported the government's attempt before 1860 to erect a permanent frontier between whites and Indians. But the belief in tribal sovereignty and the treaties or agreements with the Indians were not strong enough to withstand the desire of white settlers for more and more Indian lands.

By the early 1850s, the government created a new reservations policy known as *"Concentration" Policy* "concentration." In 1851, the government assigned each tribe its own defined reservation, confirmed by individual treaties—treaties often illegitimately negotiated with unauthorized Indian "representatives" chosen by whites, people known sarcastically as "treaty chiefs." The new arrangement had many benefits for whites and few for the Indians. It divided the tribes from one another and made them easier to control. It allowed the government to force tribes into scattered locations and to take over the most desirable lands for white settlement. But concentration did not survive as the basis of Indian policy for long.

In 1867, Congress established the Indian Peace Commission, composed of both soldiers and civilians, to recommend a new and presumably permanent Indian policy. The commission recommended that the government move all the Plains tribes into two large reservations—one in Indian Territory (Oklahoma), the other in the Dakotas. At a series of meetings with the tribes, government agents cajoled, bribed, and tricked their representatives into agreeing to treaties establishing the new reservations.

But this "solution" worked little better than previous ones for Indians. Part of the problem was the corrupt or incompetent agents of the Bureau of Indian Affairs who

HELD UP BY BUFFALO Once among the most numerous creatures in North America, the buffalo almost became extinct as a result of indiscriminate slaughter by white settlers and travelers, who often fired at herds from moving trains simply for the sport of it. (Private Collection/© Peter Newark American Pictures/Bridgeman Images)

administered the reservations. But the problem was also exacerbated by the relentless slaughter of buffalo herds by whites that destroyed the tribes' way of life. After the Civil War, professional and amateur hunters—even casual visitors shooting from passing trains—swarmed over the plains, slaughtering the huge animals. Some Indian tribes (notably the Blackfeet) also began killing large numbers of buffalo *Buffalo Herds Decimated* to sell in the booming new market for their hides and meat. In 1865, there had been at least 15 million buffalo; a decade later, fewer than 1,000 of the great beasts survived. By destroying the buffalo herds, whites were destroying the Indians' source of food and supplies and their ability to resist white advance.

THE INDIAN WARS

Whites and Indians fought incessantly from the 1850s to the 1880s, as Indians struggled against the growing threats to their civilizations. Indian warriors attacked wagon trains, stagecoaches, and isolated ranches, often in retaliation for earlier attacks on them by whites. As the United States Army became more deeply involved in the fighting, the tribes began to focus more of their attacks on white soldiers.

At times, this small-scale fighting escalated. During the Civil War, the eastern Sioux in Minnesota, cramped on a small reservation and exploited by corrupt white agents, suddenly rebelled. Led by Little Crow, they killed more than 700 whites before being subdued. Thirty-eight of the Indians were hanged, and the tribe was exiled to the Dakotas.

At the same time, fighting flared up in eastern Colorado, where the Arapaho and Cheyenne were coming into conflict with white miners settling in the region. Bands of Indians attacked stagecoach lines and settlements in an effort to regain territory they had lost. In response to these incidents, whites called up a large territorial militia. The governor urged all friendly Indians to congregate at army posts for protection before the army began its campaign. One Arapaho and Cheyenne band under Black Kettle, apparently in response to the invitation, camped near Fort Lyon on Sand Creek in November 1864. Some members of the party were warriors, but Black Kettle believed he was under official protection and exhibited no hostile intention. Nevertheless, Colonel J. M. Chivington led a volunteer militia force—largely consisting of unemployed miners, many of whom were apparently drunk—to the unsuspecting camp and massacred 133 people, 105 of them women and children. Black Kettle himself escaped the Sand Creek massacre. But four years later, in 1868, he and Cheyenne soldiers went to war with the whites. The Indians *George A. Custer* were caught on the Washita River, near the Texas border, by Colonel George A. Custer. White troops killed the chief and his people.

At the end of the Civil War, white troops stepped up their wars against the western Indians on several fronts. The most serious and sustained conflict was in Montana, where the army was attempting to build a road, the Bozeman Trail, to connect Fort Laramie, Wyoming, to the new mining centers. The western Sioux resented this intrusion into the heart of their buffalo range. Led by one of their great chiefs, Red Cloud, they so harried the soldiers and the construction party that the road could not be used.

But it was not only the United States military that harassed the tribes. It was also unofficial violence by white vigilantes who engaged in what became known as "Indian hunting." Sometimes the killing was in response to Indian raids on white *"Indian Hunting"* communities. But considerable numbers of whites were committed to the goal of literal "elimination" of the tribes whatever their behavior, a goal that rested on the belief in the essential inhumanity of Indians and the impossibility of white coexistence with them. In

BATTLE OF THE LITTLE BIGHORN: AN INDIAN VIEW This 1898 watercolor by one of the Sioux participants portrays the aftermath of the cattle. The corpses of Custer (at left, in a yellow buckskin) and his men cover the ground. Standing at center are Sitting Bull, Rain-in-the-Face, Crazy Horse, and Kicking Bear (the artist). At lower right, Indian women begin preparations for a ceremony to honor the returning warriors, shown on horseback. (© Granger, NYC—All Rights Reserved.)

California, civilians killed close to 5,000 Indians between 1850 and 1880—one of many factors (disease and poverty being the more important) that reduced the Indian population of the state from 150,000 before the Civil War to 30,000 in 1870.

The treaties negotiated in 1867 brought a temporary lull to many of the conflicts. But new forces soon shattered the peace again. In the early 1870s, more waves of white settlers, mostly miners, began to penetrate the lands in Dakota Territory supposedly guaranteed to the tribes in 1867. Indian resistance flared anew. In the northern plains, the Sioux rose up in 1875 and left their reservation. When white officials ordered them to return, bands of warriors gathered in Montana and united under two great leaders: Crazy Horse and Sitting Bull. Three army columns set out to round them up and force them back onto the reservation. With the expedition, as colonel of the famous Seventh Cavalry, was the colorful and controversial George A. Custer. At the *Battle of the Little Bighorn* Battle of the Little Bighorn in southern Montana in 1876, an unprecedentedly large army, perhaps 2,500 tribal warriors, surprised Custer and part of his regiment, surrounded them, and killed every soldier.

But the Indians did not have the political organization or the supplies to keep their troops united. Soon the warriors drifted off in bands to elude pursuit or search for food, and the army ran them down and returned them to Dakota. The power of the Sioux quickly collapsed. They accepted defeat and life on reservations.

One of the most dramatic episodes in Indian history occurred in Idaho in 1877. The Nez Percé were a small and relatively peaceful tribe, some of whose members had managed to live unmolested in Oregon into the 1870s without ever signing a treaty with the United States. But under pressure from white settlers, the U.S. government forced them to move onto a reservation. With no realistic prospect of resisting, the Indians began the journey to the reservation; but on the way, several younger Indians, drunk and angry, killed four white settlers.

The leader of the band, Chief Joseph, persuaded his followers to flee from the inevitable retribution. American troops pursued and attacked them, only to be   *Chief Joseph* driven off in a battle at White Bird Canyon. After that, the Nez Percé scattered in several directions and became part of a remarkable chase. Joseph moved with 200 warriors and 350 women, children, and old people in an effort to reach Canada. Pursued by four columns of American soldiers, the Indians covered 1,321 miles in seventy-five days, repelling or evading the army time and again. They were finally caught just short of the Canadian boundary. Some escaped and slipped across the border; but Joseph and most of his followers, weary and discouraged, finally gave up. "Hear me, my chiefs," Joseph said after meeting with the American general Nelson Miles, "I am tired. My heart is sick and sad. From where the sun now stands, I will fight no more forever."

The last Indians to maintain organized resistance against the whites were the Chiricahua Apache. The two ablest chiefs of this fierce tribe were Mangas Colorados and Cochise. Mangas was murdered during the Civil War by white soldiers who tricked him into surrendering. In 1872 Cochise agreed to peace in exchange for a reservation that included some of the tribe's traditional land. But Cochise died in 1874, and his successor, Geronimo,   *Geronimo* fought on for more than a decade longer, establishing bases in the mountains of Arizona and Mexico and leading warriors in intermittent raids against white outposts. With each raid, however, the number of warring Apache dwindled, as some warriors died and others drifted away to the reservation. By 1886, Geronimo's band consisted of only about 30 people, including women and children, while his white pursuers numbered perhaps 10,000. Geronimo recognized the odds and surrendered.

The Apache Wars, the most violent of all the Indian conflicts, produced brutality on both sides. But it was the whites who committed the most flagrant atrocities. That did not end with the conclusion of the Apache Wars. Another tragic encounter occurred in 1890 as a result of a religious revival among the Sioux—a revival that itself symbolized the catastrophic effects of the white assaults on Indian civilization. As other tribes had done in trying times in the past, many of these Indians turned to a prophet who led them in a religious revival.

This time the prophet was Wovoka, a Paiute who inspired a fervent spiritual awakening that began in Nevada and spread quickly to the plains. Wovoka predicted the imminent coming of a messiah. The new revival's most conspicuous feature was a mass, emotional "Ghost Dance," which inspired ecstatic, mystical visions—including images   *"Ghost Dance"* of the retreat of white people from the plains and a restoration of the great buffalo herds. White agents on the Sioux reservation, bewildered and fearful, warned the army that dances might be the prelude to hostilities.

On December 29, 1890, the Seventh Cavalry tried to round up a group of about 350 cold and starving Sioux at Wounded Knee, South Dakota. Fighting broke out in which about 40 white soldiers and up to 200 Indians died. An Indian may   *Wounded Knee Massacre* have fired the first shot, but the battle soon turned into a one-sided massacre, as the white soldiers turned their new machine guns on the Indians and mowed them down in the snow.

THE DAWES ACT

Even before the Ghost Dance and the Wounded Knee tragedies, the federal government had moved to destroy forever the tribal structure that was the cornerstone of Indian culture. Reversing its policy of nearly fifty years, Congress abolished the practice by which tribes owned reservation lands communally. The new policy required Indians to become landowners and farmers, to abandon their collective society and culture and become part of white civilization. Some supporters of the new policy believed they were acting for the good of the Indians, whom they considered a "vanishing race" in need of rescue by and assimilation into white society.

The Dawes Severalty Act of 1887 provided for the gradual elimination of most tribal ownership of land and the allotment of tracts to individual owners: 160 acres to the head of a family, 80 acres to a single adult or orphan, 40 acres to each dependent child. Adult owners were given United States citizenship, but unlike other citizens, they could not gain full title to their property for twenty-five years (supposedly to prevent them from selling the land to speculators).

In applying the Dawes Act, the Bureau of Indian Affairs relentlessly promoted the idea of assimilation that lay behind it. Not only did agents of the bureau try to move Indian families onto their own plots of land, they also took many Indian children away from their families and sent them to boarding schools run by whites. They moved as well to stop Indian religious rituals and encouraged the spread of Christianity and the creation of Christian churches on the reservations.

Few Indians were prepared for this wrenching change. In any case, white administration of the Dawes Act was so corrupt and inept that ultimately the government simply abandoned most efforts to enforce it. Much of the reservation land, therefore, was never distributed to individual owners.

THE RISE AND DECLINE OF THE WESTERN FARMER

The arrival of the miners, the empire building of the cattle ranchers, the dispersal of the Indian tribes—all served as a prelude to the decisive phase of white settlement of the Far West. Even before the Civil War, farmers had begun moving into the plains region, challenging the dominance of the ranchers and the Indians. By the 1870s, what was once a trickle had become a deluge. Western journalists and visitors alike told tall tales of money to be had for the taking: the region's healthy climate, pure water, fertile soil, and nutrient-rich grasses, they crowed, made industries like cattle ranching into can't-miss investment opportunities. (See "Consider the Source: Walter Baron Von Richthofen, *Cattle Raising on the Plains in North America*.") And they came. Farmers poured into the plains and beyond, enclosed land that had once been hunting territory for Indians and open range for cattle, and established a new agricultural region.

For a time in the late 1870s and early 1880s, the new western farmers flourished, enjoying the fruits of an agricultural economic boom. Beginning in the mid-1880s, however, the boom turned to bust, and the western agricultural economy began a long, steady decline.

FARMING ON THE PLAINS

Many factors combined to produce the surge of post–Civil War western agricultural settlement, but the most important was the railroads. Before the war, the Great Plains had been accessible only through a difficult journey by wagon. But beginning in the 1860s, a great new network of railroad lines made huge areas of settlement accessible for the first time.

The building of the transcontinental train line—completed in 1869 when the two lines met at Promontory Point, Utah—was a dramatic and monumental achievement. But the construction of subsidiary lines in the following years proved of greater importance to the West. State governments, imitating Washington, subsidized railroad development by offering direct financial aid, favorable loans, and more than 50 million acres of land (on top of the 130 million acres the federal government had already provided). Although built and operated by private corporations, the railroads were in many respects public projects.

The railroad companies also actively promoted settlement. The companies set rates so low for settlers that almost anyone could afford the trip west. And they *Cheap Rail Rates* sold much of their land at very low prices and with liberal credit to prospective settlers.

Contributing further to the great surge of white agricultural expansion was a pronounced but temporary change in the climate of the Great Plains. For several years in succession, beginning in the 1870s, rainfall in the plains states was well above average. White Americans now rejected the old idea that the region was the "Great American Desert."

But even under the most favorable conditions, farming on the plains presented special problems. First was the problem of fencing. Farmers had to enclose their land, but materials for traditional wood or stone fences were unavailable. In the mid-1870s, however, two Illinois farmers, Joseph H. Glidden and I. L. Ellwood, solved this problem by developing and marketing barbed wire, which became standard equipment on the plains and revolutionized fencing practices all over the world.

The second problem was water. Water was scarce even when rainfall was above average. After 1887, a series of dry seasons began, and lands that had been fertile *Scarce Water* now returned to semidesert. Some farmers dealt with the problem by using deep wells pumped by steel windmills, by turning to "dryland farming" (a system of tillage designed to conserve moisture in the soil by covering it with a dust blanket), or by planting drought-resistant crops. In many areas of the plains, however, only large-scale irrigation could save the endangered farms. But irrigation projects of the necessary magnitude required government assistance, and neither the federal nor the state governments were prepared to fund the projects.

Most of the people who moved into the region had previously been farmers in the Midwest, the East, or Europe. In the booming years of the early 1880s, with land values rising, the new farmers had no problem obtaining extensive and easy credit. But the arid years of the late 1880s—during which crop prices fell while production became more expensive—changed the farmers' prospects. Tens of thousands of farmers could not pay their debts and were forced to abandon their farms. There was, in effect, a *Reverse Migration* reverse migration: white settlers moving back east, sometimes turning once-flourishing western communities into desolate ghost towns. Those who remained continued to suffer from falling prices (for example, wheat, which had sold for $1.60 a bushel at the end of the Civil War, dropped to 49 cents in the 1890s) and persistent indebtedness.

COMMERCIAL AGRICULTURE

By the late nineteenth century, the sturdy, independent farmer of popular myth was being replaced by the commercial farmer—attempting to do in the agricultural economy what industrialists were doing in the manufacturing economy. Commercial farmers specialized in cash crops that were sold in national or world markets. They did not often make their own household supplies or grow their own food but bought them from merchants. This kind of farming, when it was successful, raised farmers' living standards. But it also made

WALTER BARON VON RICHTHOFEN, *CATTLE RAISING ON THE PLAINS IN NORTH AMERICA*, 1885

Boosters of the West's lucrative economy were plentiful. Walter Baron Von Richthofen, an immigrant and scion of an aristocratic German Austrian family, lauded cattle ranching as a western industry that begged for investors eager to make easy money.

The immense profits which have been universally realized in the Western cattle business for the past, and which will be increased in the future, owing to the more economical methods pursued, so long as ranges can be purchased at present prices, may seem incredible to many of my readers, who, no doubt, have considered the stories of the fortunes realized as myths. Yet it is true that many men who started only a few years ago with comparatively few cattle, are now wealthy, and, in some cases, millionaires. They certainly did not find the gold upon the prairies, nor did they have any source of revenue beyond the increase of their cattle. The agencies producing this immense wealth are very natural and apparent.

The climate of the West is the healthiest on the earth; the pure, high mountain air and dry atmosphere are the natural remedies, or rather preventives, against sickness among cattle in general, and against all epidemic diseases in particular; for "nowhere in the Western states do we find any traces of pleuro-pneumonia, foot or mouth, and such like contagious diseases."

The pure, clear water of the mountain rivers affords to cattle another health preserver, and the fine nutritious and bountiful grasses, and in winter the naturally cured hay, furnish to them the healthiest natural food.

Formerly these pastures cost nothing, and at present only a trifle . . . so that the interest on the investment in purchasing land is of little importance in the estimate of the cost of keeping a herd. In fact, ownership of land is now indispensable for a herd-owner. This land in less than ten years will be a considerable factor in the profits of the cattle business, as the value of pastures will constantly-increase.

The principal cost of raising cattle is only the herding and watching the cattle by herders, without any cost for sheltering or feeding. In time even these expenses will be reduced, as now already herds are kept in large fenced ranges, and many of the herders are dispensed with.

The losses of cattle, as shown by statistics, are larger among Eastern and European herds, which are sheltered in stables and fed the whole year round, than among the shelterless herds of the West. The losses in the West . . . are practically reduced by long experience to a certain percentage, which enables the stockmen to calculate infallibly the profits and losses of their business.

This annual loss is found to average 2 to 3 per cent. We may safely put the loss in the extreme Northern states at about 3 per cent, and in the more Southern and temperate districts at 2 or less per cent. The annual cost of herding the cattle . . . is about $.70 per head; adding the other expenses, such as taxes, loss of interest on the purchase-money of land, etc., we find that the entire annual expense is less than $1.50 per head.

Now let me illustrate the profits realized from one Texas cow, worth $30.00. In ten years she will have eight calves, which, if they are all steers, will have produced at the end of fourteen years $320, or a profit of $272.00. The cow herself still remains, and is worth about her original cost for the butcher. These figures are made without reference to any increase in the value of cattle or beef, and without reference to any improvement of the stock by crossing it with better blood. . . .

Ten years ago an Irish servant-girl wanted money due her, amounting to $150, from a cattle-raiser who lived in Montana. Cattle had been dull, and he could not dispose of any of his herd, but agreed to her to brand fifteen cows in her name, give her the increase, and carry them with his herd, free of cost, until she was ready to sell, he to have the first privilege of purchase. She accepted, held on to her purchase, and last May sold out her master for $25,000.

Source: Walter Baron Von Richthofen, *Cattle Raising on the Plains of North America* (1885; repr., Norman: University of Oklahoma Press, 1964), pp. 70–73, 80; located in Marilynn S. Johnson (ed.), *Violence in the West: The Johnson County Range War and the Ludlow Massacre: A Brief History with Documents* (Boston: Bedford St. Martin's, 2009), pp. 37–39.

UNDERSTAND, ANALYZE, & EVALUATE

1. How did Von Richthofen describe the land and natural resources for cattle ranching in the North American plains? Why did Von Richthofen stress the importance of landownership?
2. Does Von Richthofen strike you as a cautious businessman? What might explain the confidence he showed in his projections?
3. Why do you think the author concluded with the example of the Irish servant girl?

them dependent on bankers and interest rates, railroads and freight rates, national and European markets, world supply and demand. And unlike the capitalists of the industrial order, they could not regulate their production or influence the prices of what they sold.

Between 1865 and 1900, farm output increased dramatically, not only in the United States but in Brazil, Argentina, Canada, Australia, New Zealand, Russia, and elsewhere. Beginning in the 1880s, worldwide overproduction led to a drop in *Worldwide Overproduction* prices for most agricultural goods and hence to great economic distress for many of the more than 6 million American farm families. By the 1890s, 27 percent of the farms in the country were mortgaged; by 1910, 33 percent. In 1880, 25 percent of all farms had been operated by tenants; by 1910, the proportion had grown to 37 percent. Commercial farming made some people fabulously wealthy. But the farm economy as a whole was suffering a significant decline relative to the rest of the nation.

THE FARMERS' GRIEVANCES

American farmers were painfully aware that something was wrong. But few people yet understood the implications of national and world overproduction. Instead, they concentrated their attention and anger on more immediate, more comprehensible—and no less real—problems: inequitable freight rates, high interest charges, and an inadequate currency.

The farmers' first and most burning grievance was against the railroads. In many cases, the railroads charged higher rates for farm goods than for other goods, and higher rates in the South and West than in the Northeast. Railroads also controlled elevator and warehouse facilities in buying centers and charged arbitrary storage rates.

Farmers also resented the institutions controlling credit—banks, loan companies, insurance corporations. Since sources of credit in the West and South were few, farmers had to take loans on whatever terms they could get, often at interest rates ranging from 10 to 25 percent. Many farmers had to pay these loans back in years when prices were dropping and currency was becoming scarce. As a result, expansion of the currency became an increasingly important issue to farmers.

A third grievance concerned prices. A farmer could plant a large crop at a moment when its price was high and find that by the time of the harvest the price had declined. Farmers' fortunes rose and fell in response to unpredictable forces. But many farmers became convinced (often with some reason) that "intermediaries"—speculators, bankers, regional and local agents—were conspiring with one another to fix prices so as to benefit themselves at the growers' expense. Many farmers also came to believe (again, not entirely without reason) that manufacturers in the East were colluding to keep the prices of farm goods low and the prices of industrial goods high. Although farmers sold their crops in a competitive world market, they bought manufactured goods in a domestic market protected by tariffs and dominated by trusts and corporations.

THE AGRARIAN MALAISE

These economic difficulties helped produce social and cultural resentments. Among them was the isolation of farm life. Farm families in some parts of the country were virtually cut off from the outside world. During the winter months, the loneliness and boredom could *Reasons for Discontent*   become nearly unbearable. Many farmers lacked access to adequate education for their children. They had few or no proper medical facilities. There were few organized recreational or cultural activities. Older farmers felt the sting of watching their children leave the farm for the city. They felt the humiliation of being ridiculed as "hayseeds" by the new urban culture that was coming to dominate American life.

This sense of isolation and obsolescence led to a growing malaise among many farmers, a discontent that helped create a great national political movement in the 1890s. It found reflection, too, in some of the literature that emerged from rural America. Writers in the late nineteenth century might romanticize the rugged life of the cowboy and the western miner. For the farmers, however, the image of the agricultural world was different. Hamlin Garland, for example, reflected the growing disillusionment in a series of novels and short stories. In the introduction to his novel *Jason Edwards* (1891), he wrote that in the past, the agrarian frontier had seemed to be "the Golden West, the land of wealth and freedom and happiness." Now, however, the bright promise had faded. The trials of rural life were crushing the human spirit. "So this is the reality of the dream!" a character in *Jason Edwards* exclaims, "A shanty on a barren plain, hot and lone as a desert. My God!" Once, sturdy yeoman farmers had viewed themselves as the backbone of American life. Now they were becoming painfully aware that their position was declining in relation to the rising urban-industrial society to the east.

CONCLUSION

To many Americans in the late nineteenth century, the West seemed an untamed "frontier" in which hardy pioneers were creating a new society. The reality of the West in these years, however, was very different from this enduring image. White Americans moved into the vast regions west of the Mississippi at a remarkable rate in the years after the Civil War, and many of them indeed settled in lands far from any civilization they had ever known. But the West was not an empty place. It contained a large population of Indians, with whom the white settlers sometimes lived uneasily and with whom they sometimes battled; but almost always in the end, the Indians were pushed aside and (with help from the federal government) relocated onto lands whites did not want. There were significant numbers of Mexicans in some areas, small populations of Asians in others, and African Americans moving in from the South in search of land and freedom. The West was no barren frontier but a place of many cultures.

The West was also closely and increasingly tied to the emerging capitalist-industrial economy of the East. The miners who flooded into California, Colorado, Nevada, the Dakotas, and elsewhere were responding to the demand in the East for gold and silver, but even more for iron ore, copper, lead, zinc, and quartz. Cattle and sheep ranchers produced meat, wool, and leather for eastern consumers and manufacturers. Farmers grew crops for sale in national and international commodities markets. The West certainly looked different from the East. But the growth of the West was very much a part of the growth of the rest of the nation. And the culture of the West, despite the romantic images of pioneering individuals embraced by easterners and westerners alike, was at its heart as much a culture of economic growth and capitalist ambition as was that of the rest of the nation.

KEY TERMS/PEOPLE/PLACES/EVENTS

Californios 383
Chief Joseph 397
Chinese Exclusion
  Act 386
concentration policy 394
coolies 383
Dawes Severalty Act 398

Frederick Jackson
  Turner 393
Frederic Remington 393
George A. Custer 395
Geronimo 397
Homestead Act 386
Little Bighorn 396

long drive 388
Mark Twain 391
Plains Indians 381
range wars 390
Rocky Mountain school 390
Turner thesis 393
Wounded Knee 397

RECALL AND REFLECT

1. How did the ethnic, racial, and cultural prejudice affect western society?
2. What were the three major industries involved in the development of the West, and how did these industries transform the western economy?
3. What was the romantic image of the West, and how was this image expressed in art, literature, and popular culture?
4. How did actions and policies of the federal government affect the fate of Indians in the West?

17 INDUSTRIAL SUPREMACY

SOURCES OF INDUSTRIAL GROWTH
CAPITALIST CONSERVATISM AND ITS CRITICS
THE ORDEAL OF THE WORKER

LOOKING AHEAD

1. What factors drove America's industrial expansion in the late nineteenth and early twentieth centuries?

2. Who were the critics of America's new industrial economy, what were their criticisms, and what solutions did they propose?

3. How did the conditions and characteristics of the workforce change during this period of rapid industrialization?

"TWENTY-FIVE YEARS AFTER THE DEATH of Lincoln, America had become, in the quantity and value of her products, the leading manufacturing nation of the world. What England had accomplished in a hundred years, the United States had achieved in half the time." So boasted the historians Charles and Mary Beard in the 1920s, expressing the amazement many Americans felt when they considered the remarkable expansion of their industrial economy in the late nineteenth century.

In fact, America's rise to industrial supremacy was not as sudden as such observers suggested. The nation had been building a manufacturing economy since early in the nineteenth century. But Americans were clearly correct in observing that the accomplishments of the last three decades of the nineteenth century overshadowed all the earlier progress.

The remarkable growth did much to increase the wealth and improve the lives of many Americans. But such benefits were very unequally shared. While industrial titans and a growing middle class were enjoying a prosperity without precedent in the nation's history, workers, farmers, and others were experiencing an often painful ordeal that slowly edged the United States toward a great economic and political crisis.

SOURCES OF INDUSTRIAL GROWTH

Many factors contributed to the growth of American industry: abundant raw materials, a large and growing labor supply, a surge in technological innovation, the emergence of a talented and often ruthless group of entrepreneurs, a federal government eager to assist the growth of business, and an expanding domestic market for the products of manufacturing.

INDUSTRIAL TECHNOLOGIES

The rapid emergence of new technologies, together with the discovery of new materials and productive processes, was one of the principal sources of late-nineteenth-century industrial growth. Some of the most important innovations were in communications. In 1866, Cyrus W. Field laid a transatlantic telegraph cable to Europe. During the next decade, Alexander Graham Bell developed the first telephone with commercial capacity. By 1900, there were 1.35 million telephones, and by 1920, 13.3 million. And the Italian inventor Guglielmo Marconi was taking the first steps toward the development of radio in the 1890s; the technology he developed quickly found its way to the United States. Other inventions that speeded the pace of business organization were the typewriter (by Christopher L. Sholes in 1868), the cash register (by James Ritty in 1879), and the calculating, or adding, machine (by William S. Burroughs in 1891).

Among the most revolutionary innovations was the introduction in the 1870s of electricity as a source of light and power. The pioneers of electric lighting included Charles F. Brush, who devised the arc lamp for street illumination, and Thomas A. Edison, who invented the incandescent lamp (or lightbulb). Edison and others designed improved generators and built large power plants to furnish electricity to

TIME LINE

1859
First oil well drilled

1866
National Labor Union founded
First transatlantic cable

1870
Rockefeller founds Standard Oil

1873
Carnegie Steel founded
Economic panic

1876
Bell invents telephone

1877
Nationwide railroad strike

1879
Edison invents electric lightbulb

1881
American Federation of Labor founded

1886
Haymarket bombing

1888
Bellamy's *Looking Backward*

1892
Homestead steel strike

1893
Depression begins

1894
Pullman strike

1901
Carnegie publishes *The Gospel of Wealth*

1903
Wright brothers' airplane flight

1914
Ford introduces factory assembly lines

whole cities. By the turn of the century, electric power was becoming commonplace in street railway systems, in the elevators of urban skyscrapers, in factories, and increasingly in offices and homes.

Particularly important to trade and industry was the development of new high-efficiency steam engines capable of powering larger ships at faster speeds than ever before. The new high-speed freighters, for example, made it cheaper for Britain to buy wheat grown in Canada and the United States than to grow it at home. The introduction of refrigerated ships in the 1870s made it possible to transport meat from North America, and even Australia and Asia, to Europe.

THE TECHNOLOGY OF IRON AND STEEL PRODUCTION

Iron production had developed slowly in the United States through most of the nineteenth century, mostly driven by the demand for iron rails; steel production had developed hardly at all by the end of the Civil War. In the 1870s and 1880s, however, iron production soared as railroads added 40,000 new miles of track, and steel production made great strides toward its eventual dominance in the metals industry.

An Englishman, Henry Bessemer, and an American, William Kelly, developed, almost simultaneously, a process for converting iron into the much more durable and versatile steel. (The process, which took Bessemer's name, consisted of blowing air through molten iron to burn out the impurities and create a much stronger metal.) The Bessemer process also relied on the discovery by the British metallurgist Robert Mushet that ingredients could be added during the conversion process to give steel additional strength. In 1868, the New Jersey ironmaster Abram S. Hewitt introduced from Europe another method of making steel—the open-hearth process. These techniques made possible the production of steel in great quantities and large dimensions, for use in the manufacture of locomotives, rails, and girders for the construction of tall buildings.

The steel industry emerged first in western Pennsylvania and eastern Ohio, partly because iron ore could be found there in abundance. It was also because the new forms of steel production created a demand for new kinds of fuel—and particularly for the anthracite (or hard) coal that was plentiful in Pennsylvania. Later, new techniques made it possible to use bituminous (or soft) coal, also easily mined in western Pennsylvania. As a result, Pittsburgh quickly became the center of the steel world. But the industry was growing fast and new sources of ore soon emerged. The upper peninsula of Michigan, the Mesabi Range in Minnesota, and the area around Birmingham, Alabama, became important ore-producing locales and new centers of steel production grew up near them: Cleveland, Detroit, Chicago, and Birmingham, among others.

Until the Civil War, iron and steel furnaces were mostly made of stone and usually built against the side of a hill to reduce construction demands. By the 1870s, however, furnaces were redesigned as cylindrical iron shells lined with brick. These massive new furnaces were 75 feet tall and higher and could produce over 500 tons a week.

As the steel industry spread, new transportation systems emerged to serve it. Steel production in the Great Lakes region produced steam freighters that could carry ore on the lakes. Shippers used new steam engines to speed the unloading of ore. The demand for vessels capable of transporting oil and the development of new and more powerful steam engines led to the design of larger and heavier freighters.

There was an even closer relationship between the emerging steel companies and the railroads. Steel manufacturers provided rails and parts for cars; railroads were both markets

PIONEER OIL RUN, 1865 The American oil industry emerged first in western Pennsylvania, where speculators built makeshift facilities almost overnight. An oil field on the other side of the hill depicted here had been producing 600 barrels a day, and the wells quickly spilled over the hill and down the slope shown in the photograph. (The Library of Congress)

for and transporters of manufactured steel. But the relationship soon became more intimate than that. The Pennsylvania Railroad, for example, actually created the *Steel and Railroads* Pennsylvania Steel Company.

The steel industry's need for lubrication for its machines helped create another important new industry in the late nineteenth century—oil. (Not until later did oil become important primarily for its potential as a fuel.) The existence of petroleum reserves in western Pennsylvania had been common knowledge for some time. The Pennsylvania businessman George Bissell showed that the substance could be burned in lamps and that it could also yield such products as paraffin, naphtha, and lubricating oil. Bissell raised money to begin drilling; and in 1859, Edwin L. Drake, one of Bissell's employees, established the first oil well near Titusville, Pennsylvania, which soon produced 500 barrels of oil a month. Demand for petroleum grew quickly, and promoters soon developed other oil fields in Pennsylvania, Ohio, and West Virginia.

THE AUTOMOBILE AND THE AIRPLANE

Among the most important technological innovations was the invention of the automobile. Two technologies led to its development. First was the creation of gasoline (or petrol), the product of an extraction process developed in the late nineteenth century in the United States by which lubricating oil and fuel oil were removed separately from crude oil. The second technology was the development of a self-contained engine. As early as the 1870s, designers in France, Germany, and Austria had begun to develop an "internal combustion engine," which used the expanding power of burning gas to drive pistons. A German, Nicolaus August Otto, created a gas-powered "four-stroke" engine in the mid-1860s, which was a precursor to automobile engines. But he did not develop a way to untether it from gas lines to be used portably in machines. One of Otto's former employees, Gottfried Daimler, later perfected an engine that could be used in automobiles.

Henry Ford   The American automobile industry developed rapidly in the aftermath of these European breakthroughs. Charles and Frank Duryea built the first gasoline-driven motor vehicle in America in 1893. Three years later, Henry Ford produced the first of the famous cars that would bear his name. In 1895, there were only four automobiles on the American highways. By 1917, there were nearly 5 million.

The search for a means of human flight, as old as civilization, had been almost entirely futile until the late nineteenth century, when engineers, scientists, and tinkerers in both the United States and Europe began to experiment with a wide range of aeronautic devices. Balloonists began to consider ways to make dirigibles useful vehicles of transportation. Others experimented with kites and gliders.

The Wright Brothers   Two brothers in Ohio, Wilbur and Orville Wright, began to construct a glider in 1899 that could be propelled through the air by an internal combustion engine. Four years later, Orville made a celebrated test flight near Kitty Hawk, North Carolina, in which an airplane took off by itself and traveled 120 feet in 12 seconds under its own power before settling back to earth. By the fall of 1904, the Wright brothers had improved the plane to the point where they were able to fly over 23 miles, and in the following year they began to take a few passengers on their flights with them.

Although the first working airplane was built in the United States, aviation technology was slow to gain a foothold in America. Most of the early progress in airplane design occurred in France, where there was substantial government funding for research and development. The U.S. government created the National Advisory Committee on Aeronautics in 1915, twelve years after the Wright brothers' flight, and American airplanes became a significant presence in Europe during World War I. But the prospects for commercial flight seemed dim until the 1920s, when Charles Lindbergh's famous solo flight from New York to Paris electrified the nation and the world.

RESEARCH AND DEVELOPMENT

New industrial technologies persuaded many businesses to build their own research operations. The corporate research-and-development (R&D) laboratories coincided with a decline in government support for research, helping corporations attract skilled researchers. It also decentralized the sources of research funding and ensured that inquiry would move in many directions, and not just along paths determined by the government.

A rift began to emerge between scientists and engineers. Engineers—both inside and outside of universities—became increasingly tied up with the R&D agendas of corporations. Many scientists continued to scorn this "commercialization" of knowledge and preferred to stick to basic research that had no immediate practical applications. But many American scientists were more closely connected to practical challenges than were their European counterparts, and some joined engineers in corporate R&D laboratories, which over time began to sponsor both practical and basic research.

THE SCIENCE OF PRODUCTION

Central to the growth of the automobile and other industries were changes in the techniques of production. By the turn of the century, many industrialists were embracing the

WOMEN ON THE ASSEMBLY LINE This photograph, from 1902, shows women at work on the lock and drill department assembly line at the National Cash Register Company in Dayton, Ohio. (© Everett Collection Historical/Alamy)

new principles of "scientific management," often known as "Taylorism" after *"Taylorism"* its leading theoretician, Frederick Winslow Taylor. Taylor and his many admirers argued that scientific management made human labor compatible with the demands of the machine age. He persuaded employers to take control of the workplace. Taylor also urged employers to reorganize the production process by subdividing tasks. This sped up production and made workers more interchangeable, thus diminishing a manager's dependence on any particular employee. If properly managed by trained experts, he claimed, workers using modern machines could perform simple tasks at much greater speed, greatly increasing productive efficiency.

The most important change in industrial technology was the emergence of mass production and, along with it, the moving assembly line, which Henry Ford *Assembly Line* introduced in his automobile plants in 1914. The assembly line was a particular place— a factory through which automobiles moved as they were assembled by workers who specialized in particular tasks. It was also a concept. The concept stressed the complete interchangeability of parts. General Motors adopted the same philosophy. Automobile production relied on other technologies, too, in particular the intensive use of electricity— to drive the assembly line, to light the factories, and to run the critical ventilating systems that kept dust from interfering with the machines. The revolutionary assembly-line technique enabled Ford to raise wages and reduce hours while cutting the base price of his Model T from $950 in 1914 to $290 in 1929. It became a standard for many other industries.

RAILROAD EXPANSION AND THE CORPORATION

The principal agent of industrial development in the late nineteenth century was still the expansion of the railroads. Railroads gave industrialists access to distant markets and remote sources of raw materials. They were America's biggest investors, stimulating economic growth through their own enormous expenditures on construction and equipment and sale of their vast tracks of land.

Total railroad trackage increased from 30,000 miles in 1860 to 193,000 in 1900. *Importance of Government Subsidies* Subsidies from federal, state, and local governments (along with foreign loans and investments) were vital to this expansion. Equally important was the emergence of great railroad "combinations" (mergers), many of them dominated by one or two individuals. The achievements (and excesses) of these tycoons—Cornelius Vanderbilt, James J. Hill, Collis P. Huntington, and others—became symbols to much of the nation of concentrated economic power. But railroad development was less significant for the individual barons it created than for its contribution to the growth of a new institution: the modern corporation.

There had been various forms of corporations in America since colonial times, but the modern corporation emerged as a major force only after the Civil War. By then, railroad magnates and other industrialists realized that their great ventures could not be financed by any single person.

Under the laws of incorporation passed in many states in the 1830s and 1840s, business organizations could raise money by selling stock to members of the public; after the Civil War, one industry after another began doing so. What made these stocks appealing was that investors now had only "limited liability"—they risked only the amount of their

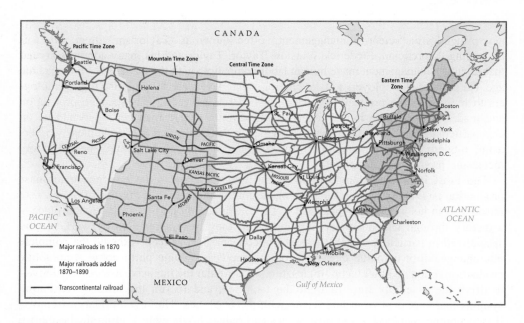

RAILROADS, 1870–1890 This map illustrates the rapid expansion of railroads in the late nineteenth century. In 1870, there was already a dense network of rail lines in the Northeast and Midwest, illustrated here by the green lines. The red lines show the further expansion of rail coverage between 1870 and 1890, much of it in the South and the areas west of the Mississippi River. • *Why were railroads so essential to the nation's economic growth in these years?*

investments and were not liable for any debts the corporation might accumulate beyond that point. The ability to sell stock to a broad public made it possible for entrepreneurs to gather vast sums of capital and undertake great projects with manageable financial risk.

The Pennsylvania and other railroads were among the first to adopt the new corporate form of organization. But incorporation quickly spread beyond the railroad industry. Andrew Carnegie, a Scottish immigrant, worked his way up from modest beginnings and, in 1873, opened his own steelworks in Pittsburgh. Soon he dominated the industry. With his associate Henry Clay Frick, he bought up coal mines and   *Carnegie, Frick, and Morgan* leased part of the Mesabi iron range in Minnesota, operated a fleet of ore ships on the Great Lakes, and acquired railroads. He financed his vast undertakings not only out of his own profits but also out of the sale of stock. Then, in 1901, he sold out for $450 million to the banker J. Pierpont Morgan, who merged the Carnegie interests with others to create the giant United States Steel Corporation—a $14 billion enterprise that controlled almost two-thirds of the nation's steel production.

Other industries developed similarly. Gustavus Swift forged a relatively small meatpacking company into a great national corporation. Isaac Singer patented a sewing machine in 1851 and created I. M. Singer and Company—one of the first modern manufacturing corporations.

Large, national business enterprises needed systematic administrative structures. As a result, corporate leaders introduced managerial techniques that relied on the systematic division of responsibilities. Companies built carefully designed hierarchies of control, strict cost-accounting procedures, and a new breed of business executives: the "middle managers," who formed a layer of command between workers and owners. Efficient administrative capabilities helped make possible another major feature of the modern corporation: consolidation.

Businessmen created large consolidated organizations primarily through two methods. **Horizontal integration** combined a number of firms engaged in the same enterprise into a single corporation such as the consolidation of many different railroad lines into one company. Through **vertical integration,** a company took over all the different businesses on which it relied for its primary function, for example, Carnegie Steel, which came to control not only steel mills but also mines, railroads, and other enterprises.

The most celebrated corporate empire of the late nineteenth century was John D. Rockefeller's Standard Oil. Shortly after the Civil War, Rockefeller   *Rockefeller's Standard Oil* launched a refining company in Cleveland and immediately began trying to eliminate his competition. Allying himself with other wealthy capitalists, he formed the Standard Oil Company of Ohio in 1870, which in a few years had acquired twenty of the twenty-five refineries in Cleveland, as well as plants in Pittsburgh, Philadelphia, New York, and Baltimore.

So far, Rockefeller had expanded only horizontally—buying many refineries. But soon he began expanding vertically as well. He built his own barrel factories, terminal ware-houses, and pipelines. Standard Oil owned its own freight cars and developed its own marketing organization. By the 1880s, Rockefeller had established such dominance within the petroleum industry that to much of the nation he served as a leading symbol of monopoly.

Rockefeller and other industrialists saw consolidation as a way to cope with what they believed was the greatest curse of the modern economy: "cutthroat competition." Most businessmen claimed to believe in free enterprise and a competitive marketplace, but in fact they feared that substantial competition could spell instability and ruin for all.

As the movement toward consolidation accelerated, new vehicles emerged to facilitate it. The railroads began with so-called pool arrangements—informal agreements among various companies to stabilize rates and divide markets (arrangements that would, in later years, be known as cartels). But the pool arrangements were too weak and could not ensure cost stability.

Trusts The failure of the pools led to new techniques of consolidation. The next effort to stabilize prices was the creation of the "trust"—pioneered by Standard Oil in the early 1880s and the banker J. P. Morgan. Under a trust agreement, stockholders in individual corporations transferred their stocks to a small group of trustees in exchange for shares in the trust itself. Owners of trust certificates often had no direct control over the decisions of the trustees; they simply received a share of the profits of the combination. The trustees themselves, on the other hand, might literally own only a few companies but could exercise effective control over many.

In 1889, the state of New Jersey helped produce a third form of consolidation by changing its laws of incorporation to permit companies to buy up rivals. Other states soon followed. Once actual corporate mergers were permitted, the original trusts became unnecessary. Rockefeller, for example, quickly relocated Standard Oil to New Jersey and created *Holding Companies* what became known as a "holding company"—a central corporate body that would buy up the stock of various members of the Standard Oil trust and establish direct, formal ownership of them.

By the end of the nineteenth century, 1 percent of the corporations in America were able to control more than 33 percent of the manufacturing. A system of economic orga-*Concentration of Power* nization was emerging that lodged enormous power in the hands of very few men—the great bankers of New York such as Morgan, industrial titans such as Rockefeller (who himself gained control of a major bank), and others.

The industrial giants of the era clearly contributed to substantial economic growth. They were also creating the basis for one of the greatest public controversies of their era: a raging debate over concentrated economic and political power that continued well into the twentieth century.

CAPITALIST CONSERVATISM AND ITS CRITICS

The inequality of the roaring capitalism of the late nineteenth century was not without its critics. Farmers, workers, middle-class businessmen, and many others considered the new capitalism to be a threat to their own destinies. But the industrial titans built a powerful defense for the new corporate economy.

SURVIVAL OF THE FITTEST

The new rationale for capitalism was based on the belief of individualism—an ideology *Ideology of Individualism* that would remain at the heart of American conservatism for many decades. Wealthy capitalists defended their wealth by saying that they had earned their wealth and power through their own hard work and their acquisitiveness and thrift. Those who failed had only themselves to blame—a result of ignorance, stupidity, or laziness.

Conservative social theories helped support the belief that through "survival of the fittest" wealthy capitalists deserved their success. Among them was the theory of **Social Darwinism.** Darwin's theories argued that the fittest forms of life survived over thousands of years because of their biological fitness. Social Darwinism argued that individuals rose or fell in society because of their innate "fitness." (Darwin himself, along with most scientists, debunked Social Darwinism, but many Americans embraced it nevertheless.) The English philosopher and biologist Herbert Spencer introduced the theory of Social Darwinism in his book *Principles of Biology* (1864). Society, he argued, benefited from the elimination of the unfit and the survival of the strong and talented. William Graham Sumner, a sociologist at Yale, borrowed from Spencer's theory and created a theory of his own in his famous 1906 book *Folkways*. Those who failed, he argued in a 1913 essay, were unfit for success: "Before the tribunal of nature a man has no more right to life than a rattlesnake; he has no more right to liberty than any wild beast; his right to pursuit of happiness is nothing but a license to maintain the struggle for existence." Wealthy corporate leaders were attracted to the ideas of Spencer and Sumner. Their success confirmed their own virtues and "fitness."

Capitalists argued that they earned their wealth through the honest, all-American virtues of competition and the free market. But critics of the industrial and financial titans claimed that they earned their wealth not because of the innate fitness of those who succeeded, but because they replaced the natural workings of the marketplace by building great monopolies that would protect them from competition.

THE GOSPEL OF WEALTH

Some businessmen attempted to temper the harsh philosophy of Social Darwinism with a gentler, if in some ways equally self-serving, idea: the "**gospel of wealth.**" People of great wealth, they argued, had not only great power but also a great responsibility to use their riches to advance social progress. Elaborating on this creed in his 1889 article "The Gospel of Wealth," and elaborated on in the 1901 book of the same title, Andrew Carnegie wrote that people of wealth should consider all revenues in excess of their own needs to be "trust funds" used for the good of the community. (See "Consider the Source: Andrew Carnegie Explains "The Gospel of Wealth."") Carnegie was only one of many industrialists who devoted large parts of their fortunes to philanthropic works.

The idea of private wealth as a public blessing existed alongside another popular concept: the notion of great wealth as something available to all. Russell H. Conwell, a Baptist minister, became one of the most prominent spokesmen for the idea by delivering one lecture, "Acres of Diamonds," more than 6,000 times between 1880 and 1900. Conwell told a series of stories, which he claimed were true, of individuals who had found opportunities for extraordinary wealth in their own backyards. (One such story involved a modest farmer who discovered a vast diamond mine in his own fields.) Most of the millionaires in the country, Conwell claimed (inaccurately), had begun on the lowest rung of the economic ladder and had worked their way to success.

But the most famous promoter of the success story was Horatio Alger. He was originally a minister in a small town in Massachusetts but was driven from his *Horatio Alger* pulpit as a result of sexual scandals. He moved to New York, where he wrote over 100 celebrated novels—all of them tributes to social mobility and the ability of Americans to rise from "rags to riches." (See "Patterns of Popular Culture: The Novels of Horatio Alger.")

If Alger's rags-to-riches tales captured the aspiration of many men, Louisa May Alcott's enormously popular novels helped give voice to the often unstated *Louisa May Alcott* ambitions of many women. Alcott was the daughter of a noted New England reformer,

ANDREW CARNEGIE EXPLAINS "THE GOSPEL OF WEALTH," 1889

Writing for a general audience in the literary and culture magazine *The North American Review*, billionaire Andrew Carnegie made one of the industrial age's most famous arguments about the inherent justness of the unequal distribution of economic power and wealth.

The problem of our age is the proper administration of wealth, that the ties of brotherhood may still bind together the rich and poor in harmonious relationship. The conditions of human life have not only been changed, but revolutionized, within the past few hundred years. In former days there was little difference between the dwelling, dress, food, and environment of the chief and those of his retainers. The Indians are today where civilized man then was. . . . The contrast between the palace of the millionaire and the cottage of the laborer with us to-day measures the change which has come with civilization. This change, however, is not to be deplored, but welcomed as highly beneficial. It is well, nay, essential, for the progress of the race that the houses of some should be homes for all that is highest and best in literature and the arts,—and for all the refinements of civilization, rather than that none should be so. Much better this great irregularity than universal squalor. . . . The "good old times" were not good old times. Neither master nor servant was as well situated then as to-day. A relapse to old conditions would be disastrous to both—not the least so to him who serves—and would sweep away civilization with it. But whether the change be for good or ill, it is upon us, beyond our power to alter, and, therefore, to be accepted and made the best of. It is a waste of time to criticize the inevitable.

It is easy to see how the change has come. . . . In the manufacture of products we have the whole story. . . . To-day the world obtains commodities of excellent quality at prices which even the preceding generation would have deemed incredible. The poor enjoy what the rich could not before afford. What were the luxuries have become the necessaries of life. The laborer has now more comforts than the farmer had a few generations ago. The farmer has more luxuries than the landlord had, and is more richly clad and better housed. The landlord has books and pictures rarer and appointments more artistic than the king could then obtain.

The price we pay for this salutary change is, no doubt, great. . . . Under the law of competition, the employer of thousands is forced into the strictest economies, among which the rates paid to labor figure prominently, and often there is friction between the employer and the employed, between capital and labor, between rich and poor. Human society loses homogeneity.

The price which society pays for the law of competition, like the price it pays for cheap comforts and luxuries, is also great; but the advantages of this law are also greater still than its cost—for it is to this law that we owe our wonderful material development, which brings improved conditions in its train. But, whether the law be benign or not, we must say of it, as we say of the change in the conditions of men to which we have referred: It is here; we cannot evade it; no substitutes for it have been found; and while the law may be sometimes hard for the individual, it is best for the race, because it insures the survival of the fittest in every department.

What is the proper mode of administering wealth after the laws upon which civilization is founded have thrown it into the hands of the few? . . .

There remains . . . only one mode of using great fortunes; in this we have the true antidote for the temporary unequal distribution of wealth, the reconciliation of the rich and the poor—a reign of harmony. . . . It is founded upon the present most intense Individualism, and the race is prepared to put it in practice by degrees whenever it pleases. Under its sway we shall have an ideal State, in which the surplus wealth of the few will become, in the best sense, the property of the many, because administered for the common good; and this wealth, passing through the hands of the few, can be made a much more potent force for the elevation of our race than if distributed in small sums to the people themselves. Even the poorest can be made to see this, and to agree that great sums gathered by some of their fellow-citizens and spent for public purposes, from which the masses reap the principal benefit, are more valuable to them than if scattered among themselves in trifling amounts through the course of many years. . . .

Poor and restricted are our opportunities in this life, narrow our horizon, our best work most imperfect; but rich men should be thankful for one inestimable boon. They have it in their power during their lives to busy themselves in organizing benefactions from which the masses of their fellows will derive lasting advantage, and thus dignify their own lives. The highest life is probably to be reached, not by such imitation of the life of Christ as Count Tolstoi gives us, but, while animated by Christ's spirit, by recognizing the changed conditions of this age, and adopting modes of expressing this spirit suitable to the changed conditions under which we live, still laboring for the good of our fellows, which was the essence of his life and teaching, but laboring in a different manner.

This, then, is held to be the duty of the man of wealth: To set an example of modest, unostentatious living, shunning display or extravagance; to provide moderately for the legitimate wants of those dependent upon him; and, after doing so, to consider all surplus revenues which come to him simply as trust funds, which he is called upon to administer, and strictly bound as a matter of duty to administer in the manner which, in his judgment, is best calculated to produce the most beneficial results for the community—the man of wealth thus becoming the mere trustee and agent for his poorer brethren, bringing to their service his superior wisdom, experience, and ability to administer, doing for them better than they would or could do for themselves. . . .

[T]he best means of benefiting the community is to place within its reach the ladders upon which the aspiring can rise—free libraries, parks, and means of recreation, by which men are helped in body and mind; works of art, certain to give pleasure and improve the public taste; and public institutions of various kinds, which will improve the general condition of the people; in this manner returning their surplus wealth to the mass of their fellows in the forms best calculated to do them lasting good.

Thus is the problem of rich and poor to be solved. The laws of accumulation will be left free, the laws of distribution free. Individualism will continue, but the millionaire will be but a trustee for the poor, intrusted for a season with a great part of the increased wealth of the community, but administering it for the community far better than it could or would have done for itself. . . .

Such, in my opinion, is the true gospel concerning wealth, obedience to which is destined some day to solve the problem of the rich and the poor, and to bring "Peace on earth, among men good will."

UNDERSTAND, ANALYZE, & EVALUATE

1. What did Carnegie think of the inequality of wealth in industrial America? What were the wealthy supposed to do in this inequality of wealth, and what role did Andrew Carnegie envision for the poor?
2. What was the price of this new inequality?

Source: Andrew Carnegie, "Wealth," *North American Review* (1889), located in: Michael P. Johnson, *Reading the American Past: Selected Historical Documents, vol. 2: From 1865*, 5th ed. (Boston: Bedford St. Martin's, 2012), pp. 52–55.

THE NOVELS OF HORATIO ALGER

A young boy, perhaps an orphan, makes his way through life on the rough streets of the city by selling newspapers or peddling matches. One day, his energy and determination catch the eye of a wealthy man, who gives him a chance to improve himself. Through honesty, charm, hard work, and aggressiveness, the boy rises in the world to become a successful man.

That, in a nutshell, is the story that Horatio Alger presented to his vast public in novel after novel—over 100 of them in all—for over forty years. During his lifetime, Americans bought millions of copies of his novels. After his death in 1899, his books (and others written in his name) continued to sell at an astonishing rate. Even today, when the books themselves are largely forgotten, the name Horatio Alger has come to represent the idea of individual advancement through (in a phrase Alger coined) "pluck and luck."

Alger was born in 1832 into a middle-class New England family, attended Harvard, and spent a short time as a Unitarian minister. In the mid-1850s, he turned to writing stories and books, and he continued to do so for the rest of his life. His most famous novel, *Ragged Dick*, was published in 1868. Almost all of his books were fables of a young man's rise "from rags to riches." The purpose of his writing, he claimed, was twofold. He wanted to "exert a salutary influence upon the class of whom [he] was writing, by setting before them inspiring examples of what energy, ambition, and an honest purpose may achieve." He also wanted to show his largely middle-class readers "the life and experiences of the friendless and vagrant children to be found in all our cities."

Most Americans of the late nineteenth and early twentieth centuries were attracted to Alger's stories because the stories helped them believe in one of the most cherished national myths: that with willpower and hard work, individuals could rise in the world. That belief was all the more important in the late nineteenth century when large-scale corporate industrialization was making it increasingly difficult for individuals to control their own fates.

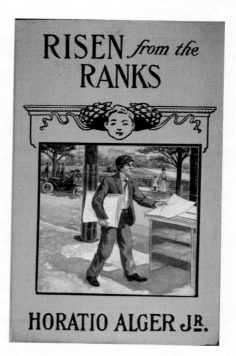

A NEWSBOY'S STORY Alger's novels were even more popular after his death in 1899 than they had been in his lifetime. This reprint of one of his many rags-to-riches stories—about a New York newsboy's rise to wealth and success—was typical of his work. (© Granger, NYC—All Rights Reserved.)

Alger placed great emphasis on the moral qualities of his heroes; their success was a reward for their virtue. But many of his readers ignored the moral message and clung simply to the image of sudden and dramatic success. After the author's death, his publishers abridged many of Alger's works, eliminating the parts of his stories where the heroes do good deeds and focusing solely on the success of Alger's heroes in rising in the world.

Alger himself had very mixed feelings about the new industrial order he described. His books were meant to reveal not just the opportunities for advancement it sometimes created, but also its cruelty. That was one reason that in almost all his books, his heroes triumphed not just because of their own virtues or efforts, but because of some amazing stroke of luck. To Alger, at least, the modern age did not guarantee success through hard work alone; there had to be some providential assistance as well. Over time, however, Alger's admirers ignored his own misgivings

about industrialism and portrayed his books purely as celebrations of (and justifications for) laissez-faire capitalism and the accumulation of wealth.

An example of the transformation of Alger into a symbol of individual achievement is the Horatio Alger Award, established in 1947 by the American Schools and Colleges Association to honor "living individuals who by their own efforts [have] pulled themselves up by their bootstraps in the American tradition." Among its recipients have been Presidents Dwight D. Eisenhower and Ronald Reagan, evangelist Billy Graham, and Supreme Court Justice Clarence Thomas. •

UNDERSTAND, ANALYZE, & EVALUATE

1. How do Alger's novels both defend industrial capitalism and criticize it?
2. According to the essay, Alger placed great emphasis on the moral qualities of his heroes, but his publishers later eliminated that aspect of the novels. Why?

but her family nevertheless experienced considerable hardship. After serving as a nurse in the Civil War and writing a series of popular adventure novels (under a pen name, A. M. Barnard, that disguised her gender), she became a major literary figure with the publication of *Little Women* in 1869 and two sequels over the next twenty years. The main character in these novels, Jo March, struggles to build a life for herself that is not defined by conventional women's roles and ambitions. She spurns a conventional marriage and eventually weds a professor who appears to support her literary ambitions. "Girls write to ask who the little women marry, as if that was the only end and aim of a woman's life," Alcott wrote a friend. "I won't marry Jo to Laurie [the attractive, wealthy neighbor who proposes to her] to please any one." Alcott's female characters, in some ways like Alger's male ones, are remarkable for their independence and drive. Jo March is willful, rebellious, stubborn, ambitious, and often selfish—far from the posed, romantic, submissive women in most popular sentimental novels of Alcott's time aimed at female audiences.

ALTERNATIVE VISIONS

Alongside the celebrations of competition and the justifications for great wealth stood a group of alternative philosophies, challenging the corporate ethos and, at times, capitalism itself.

One such philosophy came from the sociologist Lester Frank Ward. In *Dynamic Sociology* (1883) and other books, he argued that civilization was not governed by natural selection but by human intelligence, which could shape society as it wished. In contrast to

"MODERN COLOSSUS OF (RAIL) ROADS"   Cornelius Vanderbilt, known as the "Commodore," accumulated one of America's great fortunes by consolidating several large railroad companies in the 1860s. His name became a synonym not only for enormous wealth but also (in the eyes of many Americans) for excessive corporate power—as suggested in this cartoon, showing him standing astride his empire and manipulating its parts. (© Niday Picture Library/Alamy)

Sumner, who believed that state intervention to remodel the environment was futile, Ward thought that an active government engaged in positive planning was society's best hope.

Other Americans adopted more-radical approaches to reform. Some dissenters found a home in the Socialist Labor Party, founded in the 1870s and led for many years by Daniel De Leon, an immigrant from the West Indies. Although De Leon attracted a following in the industrial cities, the party never became a major political force and never polled more than 82,000 votes. A dissident faction of De Leon's party, eager to forge stronger ties with organized labor, broke away and in 1901 formed the more enduring American Socialist Party.   *American Socialist Party*

Other radicals gained a wider following. Among them was the California writer and activist Henry George. His angrily eloquent *Progress and Poverty,* published in 1879,   *Henry George* became one of the best-selling nonfiction works in American publishing history. George blamed social problems on the ability of a few monopolists to grow wealthy as a result of rising land values. An increase in the value of land, he claimed, was not a result of any effort by the owner, but an "unearned increment," produced by the growth of society around the land. Such profits were rightfully the property of the community. And so George proposed a "single tax" on land, to replace all other taxes, which would return the increment to the people. The tax, he argued, would destroy monopolies, distribute wealth more equally, and eliminate poverty.

Rivaling George in popularity was Edward Bellamy, whose utopian novel *Looking Backward,* published in 1888, sold more than 1 million copies. It described   *Edward Bellamy* the experiences of a young Bostonian who went into a hypnotic sleep in 1887 and awoke in the year 2000 to find a new social order in which want, politics, and vice were unknown. The new society had emerged through a peaceful, evolutionary process: the large trusts of the late nineteenth century had continued to grow in size and to combine with one another until ultimately they formed a single, great trust, controlled by the government, which distributed the abundance of the industrial economy equally among all the people. "Fraternal cooperation" had replaced competition. Class divisions had disappeared. Bellamy labeled the philosophy behind this vision "nationalism."

THE PROBLEMS OF MONOPOLY

Relatively few Americans shared the views of those who questioned capitalism itself. But as time went on, a growing number of people were becoming deeply concerned about the growth of **monopoly.**

By the end of the century, a wide range of groups had begun to assail monopoly and economic concentration. In the absence of competition, they argued, monopolistic industries could charge whatever prices they wished. Railroads, in particular, charged very high rates along some routes because they knew their customers had no choice but to pay them. Beginning in 1873, the economy fluctuated erratically, producing severe recessions every five or six years, each worse than the last.

THE ORDEAL OF THE WORKER

Most workers in the late nineteenth century experienced a real rise in their standard of living. But they did so at the cost of arduous and often dangerous working conditions, diminishing control over their own work, and a growing sense of powerlessness.

THE IMMIGRANT WORKFORCE

The industrial workforce expanded dramatically in the late nineteenth century as a result of massive migration into industrial cities. Rural Americans continued to flow into factory towns and cities—people disillusioned with or bankrupted by life on the farm. There was also a great wave of immigration from abroad (primarily from Europe, but also from Asia, Canada, Mexico, and other areas) in the decades following the Civil War—an influx greater than that of any previous era. The 25 million immigrants who arrived in the United States between 1865 and 1915 were more than four times the number who had arrived in the previous fifty years.

In the 1870s and 1880s, most of the immigrants came from England, Ireland, and northern Europe. By the end of the century, however, the major sources of immigrants had shifted, with large numbers of southern and eastern Europeans (Italians, Poles, Russians, Greeks, Slavs, and others) moving into the country and into the industrial workforce.

The new immigrants came to America in part to escape poverty and oppression in their homelands. But they were also attracted by expectations of new opportunities. Railroads lured immigrants into their western landholdings by distributing misleading advertisements overseas. Industrial employers actively recruited immigrant workers under the Labor Contract Law, which—until its repeal in 1885—permitted them to pay for the passage of workers in advance and deduct the amount later from their wages. Even after the repeal of the law, employers continued to encourage the immigration of unskilled laborers, often with the assistance of foreign-born labor brokers, such as the Greek and Italian *padrones,* who recruited work gangs of their fellow nationals.

The arrival of these new groups heightened ethnic tensions within the working class. *Job Competition* Low-paid Poles, Greeks, and French Canadians began to displace higher-paid British and Irish workers in the textile factories of New England. Italians, Slavs, and Poles emerged as a major source of labor for the mining industry. Chinese and Mexicans competed with Anglo-Americans and African Americans in mining, farmwork, and factory labor in California, Colorado, and Texas.

WAGES AND WORKING CONDITIONS

At the turn of the century, the average income of the American worker was $400 to $500 a year—below the $600 figure that many believed was required to maintain a reasonable level of comfort. Nor did workers have much job security. All were vulnerable to the boom-and-bust cycle of the industrial economy and the instability caused by technological advances. Even those who kept their jobs could find their wages suddenly and substantially cut in hard times. Few workers, in other words, were ever very far from poverty.

Many first-generation workers, accustomed to the patterns of agrarian life, had trouble adjusting to the nature of modern industrial labor: routine, repetitive tasks on a strict and monotonous schedule. Skilled artisans, whose once-valued tasks were now performed by machines, found the new system impersonal and demeaning. Most factory laborers worked ten hours a day, six days a week; in the steel industry they worked twelve hours a day. Industrial accidents were frequent.

The decreasing need for skilled work in factories induced many employers to increase the use of women and children, whom they could hire for lower wages than adult males. By 1900, 20 percent of all manufacturing workers were women. Women labored in all areas of industry, even in some of the most arduous jobs. Most women, however, worked in a few industries where unskilled and semiskilled machine labor (as opposed to heavy manual labor) prevailed. The textile industry remained the largest single industrial employer of women. (Domestic service, though, remained the most common female occupation overall.) Women worked for wages well below the minimum necessary for survival (and well below the wages paid to men working the same jobs).

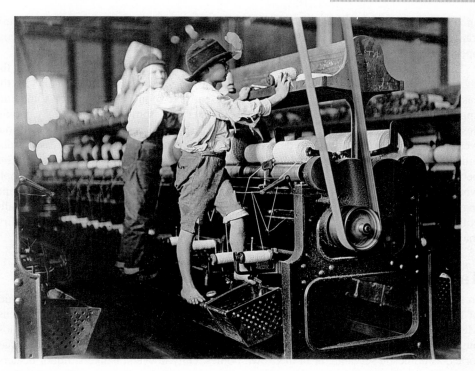

SPINDLE BOYS Young boys, some of them barefoot, clamber among the great textile machines in a Georgia cotton mill, mending broken threads and replacing empty bobbins. Many of them were the children or siblings of women who worked in the plant. The photograph is by Lewis Hine, who traveled around the country documenting abuses for the National Child Labor Committee. (© Bettmann/Corbis)

At least 1.7 million children under sixteen years of age were employed in factories and fields; 10 percent of all girls aged ten to fifteen, and 20 percent of all boys, held jobs. Under public pressure, thirty-eight states passed child labor laws in the late *Child Labor* nineteenth century. But 60 percent of child workers were employed in agriculture, which was typically exempt from the laws. For children employed in factories, the laws merely set a minimum age of twelve years and a maximum workday of ten hours, standards that employers often ignored in any case.

EMERGING UNIONIZATION

Laborers attempted to fight back against such conditions by creating national unions. By the end of the century, however, their efforts had met with little success.

There had been craft unions in America, representing small groups of skilled workers, since well before the Civil War. But most unions could not hope to exert significant power in the economy. And during the turbulent recession years of the 1870s, unions faced the additional problem of widespread public hostility. When labor disputes with employers turned bitter and violent, as they occasionally did, much of the public instinctively blamed the workers for the trouble, rarely the employers. Particularly alarming to middle-class Americans was the emergence of the "Molly Maguires," *Molly Maguires* an Irish secret society, in the anthracite coal region of western Pennsylvania. This militant labor organization sometimes used violence and even murder in its battle with coal operators.

Excitement over the Molly Maguires paled beside the near hysteria that gripped the *Railroad Strike of 1877* country during the railroad strike of 1877, which began when the eastern railroads announced a 10 percent wage cut and soon expanded into something approaching a class war. Strikers disrupted rail service from Baltimore to St. Louis, destroyed equipment, and rioted in the streets of Pittsburgh and other cities. State militias were called out, and in July President Hayes ordered federal troops to suppress the disorders. In Baltimore, eleven demonstrators died and forty were wounded in a conflict between workers and militiamen. In Philadelphia, the state militia killed twenty people when the troops opened fire on thousands of workers and their families who were attempting to block the railroad crossings. In all, over 100 people died before the strike finally collapsed several weeks after it had begun. The great railroad strike was America's first major national labor conflict.

THE KNIGHTS OF LABOR

In the first major effort to create a genuinely national labor organization, the Noble Order of the Knights of Labor was founded in 1869 under the leadership of Uriah S. Stephens. Membership was open to all who "toiled," a definition that included all workers, most business and professional people, and virtually all women—whether they worked in factories, as domestic servants, or in their own homes. Only lawyers, bankers, liquor dealers, and professional gamblers were excluded. The Knights of Labor championed an eight-hour workday and the abolition of child labor, but they were more interested in long-range reform of the economy. The Knights hoped to replace the "wage system" with a new "cooperative system," in which workers would themselves control their workplaces.

For several years, the Knights remained a secret fraternal organization. But in the late 1870s, under the leadership of Terence V. Powderly, the order moved into the open and entered a period of spectacular expansion. By 1886, it claimed a total membership of over 700,000. Local unions or assemblies associated with the Knights launched a series of railroad and other strikes in the 1880s in defiance of Powderly's wishes. Their failures to win any meaningful concessions helped discredit the organization. By 1890, membership of the Knights had shrunk to 100,000. A few years later, the organization disappeared altogether.

THE AMERICAN FEDERATION OF LABOR

Even before the Knights began to decline, a rival association appeared. In 1881, representatives of a number of craft unions formed the Federation of Organized Trade and Labor Unions of the United States and Canada. Five years later, this body took the name it has borne ever since, the American Federation of Labor (AFL).

Rejecting the Knights' idea of one big union for everybody, the federation was an association of essentially autonomous craft unions that represented mainly skilled workers. *Samuel Gompers* Samuel Gompers, the powerful leader of the AFL, concentrated on labor's immediate objectives: wages, hours, and working conditions. As one of its first objectives, the AFL demanded a national eight-hour workday and called for a general strike if the goal was not achieved by May 1, 1886. On that day, strikes and demonstrations for a shorter workday took place all over the country.

In Chicago, a center of labor and radical strength, a strike was already in progress at the McCormick Harvester Company. City police had been harassing the strikers, and labor and radical leaders called a protest meeting at Haymarket Square on May 1. *Haymarket Bombing* When the police ordered the crowd to disperse, someone threw a bomb that killed seven policemen and injured sixty-seven others. The police, who had killed four strikers the day before, fired into the crowd and killed four more people. Conservative, property-conscious Americans—frightened and outraged—demanded retribution. Chicago officials finally rounded up eight anarchists and charged them with murder, on the grounds that their statements had incited whoever had hurled the bomb. All eight scapegoats were found guilty after a remarkably injudicious trial. Seven were sentenced to death. One of them committed suicide, four were executed, and two had their sentences commuted to life imprisonment.

To most middle-class Americans, the Haymarket bombing was an alarming symbol of social chaos and radicalism. "Anarchism" now became in the public mind a code word for terrorism and violence, even though most anarchists were relatively peaceful. For the next thirty years, the specter of anarchism remained one of the most frightening concepts in the American imagination. Business owners exploited it to smear labor leaders and disrupt their activities. It became a constant obstacle to the goals of the AFL and other labor organizations, and it did particular damage to the Knights of Labor. However much they tried to distance themselves from radicals, labor leaders were always vulnerable to accusations of anarchism, as the violent strikes of the 1890s occasionally illustrated.

THE HOMESTEAD STRIKE

The Amalgamated Association of Iron and Steel Workers was the most powerful trade union in the country in the late 1800s. Its members were skilled workers, in great demand by employers, and they had long been able to exercise significant power in the workplace. In the mid-1880s, however, demand for skilled workers declined as new production methods changed the steelmaking process. In the streamlined Carnegie system, which was coming to dominate the steel industry, the union was able to maintain a foothold in only one of the corporation's three major factories—the Homestead plant near Pittsburgh.

By 1890, Carnegie and his chief lieutenant, Henry Clay Frick, had decided that the Amalgamated "had to go." Over the next two years, they repeatedly cut wages at Homestead. At first, the union acquiesced, aware that it was not strong enough to wage a successful strike. But in 1892, when the company stopped even discussing its decisions with the union and gave it two days to accept another wage cut, the Amalgamated called for a strike.

Frick abruptly shut down the plant and called in 300 guards from the Pinkerton Detective Agency, well known as strikebreakers, to enable the company to hire *Pinkertons* nonunion workers. They approached the plant by river, on barges, on July 6, 1892. The strikers poured gasoline on the water, set it on fire, and then met the Pinkertons at the docks with guns and dynamite. After several hours of fighting, which killed three guards and ten strikers and injured many others, the Pinkertons surrendered and were escorted roughly out of town.

But the workers' victory was temporary. The governor of Pennsylvania, at the company's request, sent the state's entire National Guard contingent, some 8,000 men, to

Homestead. Production resumed, with strikebreakers now protected by troops. And public opinion turned against the strikers when a radical made an attempt to assassinate Frick. Slowly, workers drifted back to their jobs, and finally—four months after the strike began—the Amalgamated surrendered. By 1900, every major steel plant in the Northeast had broken with the Amalgamated. Its membership shrank from a high of 24,000 in 1891 (two-thirds of all eligible steelworkers) to fewer than 7,000 a decade later.

THE PULLMAN STRIKE

A dispute of greater magnitude, if less violence, was the Pullman strike in 1894. The Pullman Palace Car Company manufactured railroad sleeping and parlor cars at a plant near Chicago. There the company constructed a 600-acre town, Pullman, and rented its trim, orderly houses to the employees. George M. Pullman, owner of the company, saw the town as a model—a solution to the problems of industrial workers. But many residents chafed at the regimentation (and the high rents). In the winter of 1893–1894, the Pullman Company slashed wages by about 25 percent, citing its own declining revenues in the depression, without reducing the rent it charged its employees. Workers went on strike and persuaded the militant American Railway Union, led by Eugene V. Debs, to support

Eugene V. Debs and the Railway Union   them by refusing to handle Pullman cars and equipment. Within a few days, thousands of railroad workers in twenty-seven states and territories were on strike, and transportation from Chicago to the Pacific Coast shut down.

Unlike most elected politicians, the governor of Illinois, John Peter Altgeld, was a man with demonstrated sympathies for workers and their grievances. He refused to call out the militia to protect employers. Infuriated, railroad operators bypassed Altgeld and asked the federal government to send regular army troops to Illinois, using the pretext that the strike was preventing the movement of mail on the trains. In July 1894, President Grover Cleveland ordered 2,000 troops to the Chicago area. A federal court issued an injunction forbidding the union to continue the strike. When Debs and his associates defied it, they were arrested and imprisoned. With federal troops protecting the hiring of new workers and with the union leaders in a federal jail, the strike quickly collapsed.

SOURCES OF LABOR WEAKNESS

In the last decades of the nineteenth century, labor made few real gains despite militant organizing efforts. Industrial wages rose hardly at all. To be sure, labor leaders won a few legislative victories—the abolition of the Contract Labor Law, the establishment of an eight-hour day for government employees, compensation for some workers injured on the job, and others. But many such laws were not enforced. Widespread strikes and pro-tests, and many other working-class forms of resistance, large and small, led to few enduring gains. The end of the century found most workers with less political power and less control of the workplace than they had had forty years before.

Workers failed to make greater gains for many reasons. The principal labor organiza-tions represented only a small percentage of the industrial workforce; the AFL, the most important, blatantly excluded unskilled workers and most women, blacks, and recent immigrants. Divisions within the workforce, such as tensions among different ethnic and racial groups, contributed further to union weakness.

Another source of labor weakness was the shifting nature of the workforce. Many immigrant workers came to America intending to earn some money and then return home.

The assumption that they had no long-range future in the country tamed their enthusiasm to organize. Other workers were in constant motion, moving from one job to another, one town to another, seldom in a single place long enough to establish any institutional ties or exert any real power.

Above all, perhaps, workers made few gains in the late nineteenth century because they faced corporate organizations of vast wealth and power, which were generally determined to crush any efforts by workers to challenge their prerogatives. And as the Homestead and Pullman strikes suggest, the corporations usually had the support of local, state, and federal authorities, who were willing to send in troops to "preserve order" and crush labor uprisings on demand.

Despite the creation of new labor unions and a wave of strikes and protests, workers in the late nineteenth century failed on the whole to create successful organizations or to protect their interests. In the battle for power within the emerging industrial economy, almost all the advantages seemed to lie with capital.

CONCLUSION

In the four decades after the Civil War, the United States propelled itself into the forefront of the industrializing nations of the world. Large areas of the nation remained overwhelmingly rural, to be sure. But even so, America's economy, and along with it the nation's society and culture, was being profoundly transformed.

New technologies, new forms of corporate management, and new supplies of labor helped make possible the rapid growth of the nation's industries and the construction of its railroads. The factory system contributed to the growth of the nation's cities. Immigration provided a steady supply of new workers for the growing industrial economy. The result was a steady increase in national wealth, rising living standards for much of the population, and the creation of great new fortunes.

But industrialization did not spread its fruits evenly. Large areas of the country, most notably the South, and large groups in the population, most notably minorities, women, and recent immigrants, profited relatively little from economic growth. Industrial workers experienced arduous conditions of labor. Small merchants and manufacturers found themselves overmatched by great new combinations.

Industrialists strove to create a rationale for their power and to persuade the public that everyone had something to gain from it. But many Americans remained skeptical of modern capitalism, and some—workers struggling to form unions, reformers denouncing trusts, socialists envisioning a new world, and many others—created broad and powerful critiques of the new economic order. Industrialization brought both progress and pain to late-nineteenth-century America. Controversies over its effects defined the era and would continue to define the first decades of the twentieth century.

KEY TERMS/PEOPLE/PLACES/EVENTS

American Federation of
  Labor 422
American Socialist
  Party 419

Andrew Carnegie 411
Edward Bellamy 419
Eugene V. Debs 424
gospel of wealth 413

Haymarket bombing 423
Henry Clay Frick 411
Henry Ford 408
Henry George 419

RECALL AND REFLECT

1. Who were some of the business and industrial titans of the late nineteenth century, and what did they contribute to America's industrial growth?
2. What changes took place in corporate organization in the late nineteenth century, and how did these changes affect the nation's economy?
3. What was the gospel of wealth?
4. How did Social Darwinism attempt to justify the social consequences of industrial capitalism?
5. How did workers respond to the expansion of industrialization and the new industrial economy?

18 THE AGE OF THE CITY

THE NEW URBAN GROWTH
THE URBAN LANDSCAPE
STRAINS OF URBAN LIFE
THE RISE OF MASS CONSUMPTION
LEISURE IN THE CONSUMER SOCIETY
HIGH CULTURE IN THE URBAN AGE

LOOKING AHEAD

1. What were some of the problems that resulted from rapid urbanization, and how did urban governments respond to these problems?
2. How did the sources of immigration to America shift in the late nineteenth century, and what was the native response to the change?
3. How did the rise of mass consumption affect leisure and entertainment?

THE FACE OF AMERICAN SOCIETY was transformed in countless ways by the growth of industry and commerce. But no change was more profound than the growing size and influence of cities. Having begun its life as a primarily agrarian republic, the United States in the late nineteenth century was becoming an urban nation.

THE NEW URBAN GROWTH

Although the great movement of people to the city was not unique to the United States, Americans found urbanization particularly jarring. The urban population increased sevenfold in the half century after the Civil War. And in 1920, the census revealed that for the first time, a majority of the American people lived in "urban" areas—defined as communities of 2,500 people or more.

Natural increase accounted for only a small part of the urban growth. Families in cities experienced a high rate of infant mortality, a declining fertility rate, and a high death rate from disease. It was immigration, rather, that expanded the urban population so dramatically.

THE MIGRATIONS

In the late nineteenth century, Americans left the declining agricultural regions of the East at a dramatic rate. Some moved to the newly developing farmlands of the West. But almost as many moved to the growing cities of the East and the Midwest.

Among those leaving rural America for industrial cities in the 1880s were black men and women trying to escape the poverty, debt, violence, and oppression they faced in the rural South. They were also seeking new opportunities in cities. Factory jobs for African Americans were rare and professional opportunities almost nonexistent. Urban blacks tended to work in service occupations as cooks, janitors, domestic servants, and so on. Because many such jobs were considered women's work, black women often outnumbered black men in the cities.

The most important source of urban population growth, however, was the great number of new immigrants from abroad—part of a larger pattern of mobility around the world. (See "America in the World: Global Migrations.") Some came from Canada, Latin America, and—particularly on the West Coast—China and Japan. But the greatest number came from Europe. After 1880, the flow of new arrivals began to include large numbers of people from southern and eastern Europe. By the 1890s, more than half of all immigrants came from these regions.

In earlier years, most new immigrants from Europe (particularly Germans and Scandinavians) had arrived with at least some money and education. Most of them arrived at one of the major port cities on the Atlantic Coast (the greatest number landing at New York's immigrant depot at Castle Garden) and then headed west. But the new immigrants of the late nineteenth century generally lacked the capital to buy farmland and lacked the education to establish themselves in professions. So, like similarly poor Irish immigrants before the Civil War, they settled overwhelmingly in industrial cities, where they worked largely in unskilled jobs.

The Ethnic City

By 1890, most of the population of the major cities consisted of immigrants: 87 percent of the population in Chicago, 80 percent in New York, 84 percent in Milwaukee and

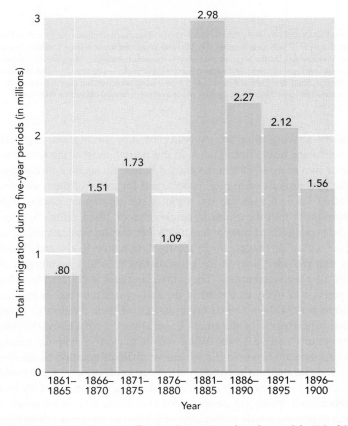

TOTAL IMMIGRATION, 1861–1900 Over 10 million immigrants from abroad entered the United States in the last forty years of the nineteenth century, with particularly high numbers arriving in the 1880s and 1890s. This chart shows the pattern of immigration in five-year intervals. • *What external events might help explain some of the rises and falls in the rates of immigration in these years?*

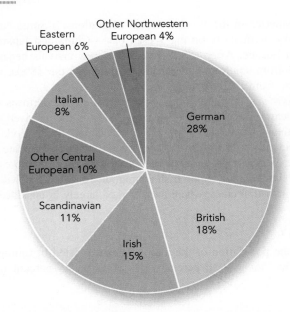

SOURCES OF IMMIGRATION FROM EUROPE, 1860–1900   This pie chart shows the sources of European immigration in the late nineteenth century. The largest number of immigrants continued to come from traditional sources (Britain, Ireland, Germany, Scandinavia), but the beginnings of what in the early twentieth century would become a major influx of immigrants from new sources—southern and eastern Europe in particular—are already visible here. Immigration from other sources—Mexico, South and Central America, and Asia—was also significant during this period.   •   *Why would these newer sources of European and other kinds of immigration create controversy among older-stock Americans?*

Detroit. Equally striking was the diversity of new immigrant populations. In other countries experiencing heavy immigration in this period, most of the new arrivals were coming from one or two sources. But in the United States, no single national group dominated.

Most of the new arrivals were rural people, and for many of them the adjustment to city life was painful. To help ease the transition, some immigrant groups formed close-knit ethnic communities within the cities, in neighborhoods often called "immigrant ghettoes." Ethnic neighborhoods offered newcomers much that was familiar, including newspapers and theaters in their native languages, stores selling their native foods, and church and fraternal organizations that provided links to their national pasts. Many immigrants also maintained close ties with their native countries. They stayed in touch with relatives who had remained behind, and perhaps as many as a third in the early years returned to their homelands after a relatively short time. Others helped bring the rest of their families to America.

The cultural cohesiveness of the ethnic communities clearly eased the pain of separation from the immigrants' native lands. What role it played in helping immigrants become absorbed into American economic life is a more difficult question to answer. Some ethnic groups (Jews and Germans, in particular) advanced economically more rapidly than others *Importance of Ethnic Ties*   (for example, the Irish). One explanation is that by huddling together in ethnic neighborhoods, immigrant groups tended to reinforce the cultural values of their previous societies. When those values were particularly well suited to economic advancement—for example, the high value Jews placed on education—ethnic identification may have helped members of a group improve their lots. When other values predominated—maintaining community solidarity, strengthening family ties, preserving order—economic progress could be less rapid.

But other factors were at least as important in determining how well immigrants fared. Immigrants who aroused strong racial prejudice among native-born whites found it very difficult to advance, whatever their talents. Those white immigrants who arrived with a valuable skill or with some capital did better than those who did not. And over time, those who lived in cities where people of their own nationality came to predominate—for example, the Irish in New York and Boston or the Germans in Milwaukee—gained an advantage as they learned to exert their political power.

Assimilation and Exclusion

Despite the many differences among the various immigrant communities, virtually all groups had certain things in common. Most immigrants shared the experience of living in cities. Most were young; the majority of newcomers were between fifteen and forty-five years old. And in most communities of the foreign-born, ethnic ties had to compete against the desire for assimilation.

Many of the new arrivals had come with romantic visions of the New World. And however disillusioning they might have found their first contact with the United States, they usually retained the dream of becoming true "Americans." Second-generation immigrants were especially likely to attempt to break with the old ways. Young women, in particular, sometimes rebelled against parents who tried to arrange (or prevent) marriages or who opposed women entering the workplace.

Old-stock Americans encouraged or demanded assimilation in countless ways. Public schools taught children in English, and employers often insisted that workers speak English on the job. Most nonethnic stores sold mainly American products, forcing immigrants to adapt their diets, clothing, and lifestyles to American norms. Church leaders were often native-born Americans or more assimilated immigrants *Pressure to Assimilate* who encouraged their parishioners to adopt American ways. Some even embraced reforms to make their religion more compatible with the norms of the new country. Reform Judaism, imported from Germany in the late nineteenth century, was an effort by American Jewish leaders (as it had been by German ones) to make their faith less "foreign" to the dominant culture.

The vast numbers of new immigrants, and the way many of them created distinctive communities, provoked fear and resentment among some native-born Americans in much the same way that earlier arrivals had done. In 1887, Henry Bowers, a self-educated lawyer, founded the American Protective Association, a group committed to stopping immigration. By 1894, membership in the organization reportedly reached 500,000, with chapters throughout the Northeast and Midwest. That same year, five Harvard alumni in Boston founded a more genteel organization—the Immigration *Attempts to Limit Immigration* Restriction League. They proposed screening immigrants through literacy tests and other standards, to separate the "desirable" from the "undesirable."

The government responded to popular concern about immigration even earlier. In 1882, Congress excluded the Chinese, denied entry to "undesirables"—convicts, paupers, the mentally incompetent—and placed a tax of 50 cents on each person admitted. Later legislation of the 1890s enlarged the list of those barred from immigrating.

But these laws kept out only a small number of aliens, and more ambitious restriction proposals made little progress in Congress, for immigration provided a cheap and plentiful labor supply to the rapidly growing economy. Many argued that America's industrial (and indeed agricultural) development would be impossible without it.

GLOBAL MIGRATIONS

The great waves of immigration that transformed American society in the nineteenth and early twentieth centuries were not unique to the United States. They were part of a great, global movement of peoples—unprecedented in history—that affected every continent in the world and that has continued to this day. These great migrations were the product of two related forces: population growth and industrialization.

The population of Europe grew faster in the second half of the nineteenth century than ever before and ever since—almost doubling between 1850 and the beginning of World War I. The population growth was a result of growing economies able to support more people and of more efficient and productive agriculture that helped end debilitating famines. But the rapid growth nevertheless strained the resources of many parts of Europe and affected, in particular, rural people, who were now too numerous to live off the available land. Many decided to move to other parts of the world where land was more plentiful.

At the same time, industrialization drew millions of people out of the countryside and into cities—sometimes into cities in their own countries but often to industrial cities in other, more economically advanced nations. Historians of migration speak of "push" factors (pressures on people to leave their homes) and "pull" factors (the lure of new lands) in explaining population movements. The "push" for many nineteenth-century migrants was poverty and inadequate land at home; for others it was political and religious oppression. The "pull" was the availability of land or industrial jobs in other regions or lands—and, for some, the prospect of greater freedom abroad. Faster, cheaper, and easier transportation—railroads, steamships, and much later, airplanes—also aided large-scale immigration.

From 1800 to the start of World War I, 50 million Europeans migrated to new lands overseas—people from almost all areas of Europe, but in the later years of the century (when migration reached its peak) mostly from poor rural areas in southern and eastern Europe. Italy, Russia, and Poland were among the biggest sources of late-nineteenth-century migrants. Almost two-thirds of these immigrants came to the United States. But nearly 20 million Europeans migrated to other lands. Migrants from England and

(Private Collection/© Peter Newark American Pictures/Bridgeman Images)

Ireland (among others) moved in large numbers to those areas of the British Empire with vast, seemingly open lands: Canada, Australia, New Zealand, and South Africa. Large numbers of Italians moved to Argentina and other parts of South America. Many migrants moved to open land in these countries and established themselves as farmers, using the new mechanical farming devices made possible by industrialization. In many places—Australia, New Zealand, Argentina, South Africa, and the United States—immigrants evicted the native residents of their territories and created societies of their own. Many others settled in the industrial cities that were growing up in all these regions and formed distinctive ethnic and national communities within them.

But it was not only Europeans who were transplanting themselves in these years. Tremendous numbers of poor people left Asia, Africa, and the Pacific Islands in search of better lives. Most of them could not afford the journey abroad on their own. They moved instead as indentured servants (in much the same way many English migrants moved to America in the seventeenth century), agreeing to a term of servitude in their new land in exchange for food, shelter, and transportation. Recruiters of indentured servants fanned out across China, Japan, areas of Africa and the Pacific Islands, and above all, India. French and British recruiters brought hundreds of thousands of Indian migrants to work in plantations in their own Asian and African colonies. Chinese laborers were recruited to work on plantations in Cuba and Hawaii; mines in Malaya, Peru, South Africa, and Australia; and railroad projects in Canada, Peru, and the United States. African indentured servants moved in large numbers to the Caribbean, and Pacific Islanders tended to move to other islands or to Australia.

The immigration of European peoples to new lands was largely voluntary and brought most migrants to the United States, where indentured servitude was illegal (although sometimes imposed on workers through labor contracts). But the migration of non-European peoples often involved an important element of coercion and brought relatively small numbers of people to the United States. This non-European migration was a function of the growth of European empires, and it was made possible by the imperial system—by its labor recruiters, by its naval resources, by its law, and by its economic needs. Together, these various forms of migration produced one of the greatest population movements in the history of the world and transformed not just the United States but much of the globe. •

UNDERSTAND, ANALYZE, & EVALUATE

1. What were some of the "push" and "pull" factors that motivated the migration of both Europeans and non-Europeans?
2. Why did more Europeans than non-Europeans migrate to the United States?

THE URBAN LANDSCAPE

The city was a place of remarkable contrasts. It had homes of almost unimaginable size and grandeur and hovels of indescribable squalor. It had conveniences unknown to earlier generations and problems that seemed beyond the capacity of society to solve.

THE CREATION OF PUBLIC SPACE

There were a few early American cities that were planned from the beginning—Philadelphia and Washington most prominently. By the mid-nineteenth century, reformers, planners, architects, and others began to call for more ordered visions of many other cities.

Among the most important urban innovations of the mid-nineteenth century were great city parks, which reflected the desire of urban leaders to provide an antidote to the congestion of the city landscape. Parks, they argued, would allow city residents a healthy, restorative escape from the strains of urban life by reacquainting them with the natural world. This notion of the park as refuge was most effectively promoted by the landscape designers Frederick Law Olmsted and Calvert Vaux, who together in the late 1850s *Central Park* designed New York's Central Park. They deliberately created a public space that would look as little like the city as possible. Instead of the ordered, formal spaces common in some European cities, they created a space that seemed entirely natural. Central Park was from the start one of the most popular and admired public spaces in the world.

At the same time that cities were creating great parks, they were also creating great public buildings: libraries, art galleries, natural history museums, theaters, and concert and opera halls. New York's Metropolitan Museum of Art was the largest and best known of many great museums taking shape in the late nineteenth century, but giant museums grew up quickly in Boston, Philadelphia, Chicago, and other places. In one city after another, new and lavish public libraries appeared, as if to confirm the city's role as a center of learning and knowledge.

Wealthy residents were the principal force behind the creation of the great art museums, concert halls, opera houses, and, at times, even parks. As their own material and social aspirations grew, they wanted the public life of the city to provide them with amenities to match their expectations. Becoming an important patron of a major cultural institution was an especially effective route to social distinction.

As both the size and aspirations of great cities increased, urban leaders launched monumental projects to remake them. Some cities began to clear away older neighborhoods and streets and create grand, monumental avenues lined with new and more impressive buildings. A particularly important event in inspiring such efforts was the 1893 Columbian Exposition in Chicago, a world's fair constructed to honor the 400th anniversary of Columbus's first voyage to America. At the center of the wildly popular exposition was a cluster of neoclassical buildings—the "Great White City"—arranged symmetrically around a formal lagoon. *"City Beautiful" Movement* It became the inspiration for the "city beautiful" movement, led by the architect of the Great White City, Daniel Burnham. The movement strove to impose a similar order and symmetry on the disordered life of cities around the country. Only rarely, however, were planners able to overcome the obstacles of private landowners and complicated urban politics to realize more than a small portion of their dreams.

The effort to remake the city did not focus only on redesigning existing landscapes. It occasionally led to the creation of entirely new ones. In one of the largest public works projects ever undertaken in America to that point, the city of Boston gradually filled in a large area of marshy tidal land in the late 1880s to create the neighborhood known as "Back *"Back Bay"* Bay." Boston was not alone. Chicago reclaimed large areas from Lake Michigan and at one point raised the street level for the entire city to help avoid the problems the marshy land created. In New York and other cities, the response to limited space was not so much to create new land as to annex adjacent territory. A great wave of annexations expanded the boundaries of many American cities in the 1890s and beyond, most notably New York City's 1898 annexation of Brooklyn, which was itself a large and important city.

A TENEMENT LAUNDRY   This woman, shown here with some of her children, was typical of many working-class mothers who found income-producing activities they could pursue in the home (in this case, laundry).
(© Bettmann/Corbis)

THE SEARCH FOR HOUSING

One of the greatest urban problems was to provide housing for the thousands of new residents pouring into the cities every day. For the prosperous, housing was seldom a worry. The availability of cheap labor reduced the cost of building and permitted anyone with even a moderate income to afford a house. Some of the richest urban residents lived in palatial mansions located in exclusive neighborhoods in the heart of the city—Fifth Avenue in New York, Back Bay and Beacon Hill in Boston, Society Hill in Philadelphia, Lake Shore Drive in Chicago, Nob Hill in San Francisco, and many others.

Many of the moderately well-to-do city dwellers took advantage of less expensive land on the edges of cities and settled in new suburbs, linked to the downtowns by   *New Suburbs* trains or streetcars. Chicago in the 1870s, for example, connected nearly 100 residential suburbs to the downtown by railroad. Real estate developers worked to create suburban communities that would appeal to many city dwellers' nostalgia for the countryside, promoting them with lawns, trees, and houses designed to look manorial.

Most urban residents, however, could not afford either to own a house in the city or to move to the suburbs. Instead, they stayed in the city centers and rented. Landlords tried to squeeze as many rent-paying residents as possible into the smallest available space. In Manhattan, for example, the average population density in 1894 was 143 people per acre—a rate far higher than that of any other American or European city then or since. In the cities of the South—Charleston, New Orleans, Richmond—poor African Americans lived in crumbling former slave quarters. In Boston, immigrants moved into cheap three-story wooden houses ("triple-deckers"). In Baltimore and Philadelphia, the new arrivals crowded into narrow brick row houses. And in New York and many other cities, they lived in tenements.

Tenements   The word *tenement* had originally referred simply to a multiple-family rental building, but by the late nineteenth century it had become a term for slum dwellings only. The first tenements, built in 1850, had been hailed as a great improvement in housing for the poor. But most were, in fact, miserable places, with many windowless rooms and *Jacob Riis*   little or no plumbing or heating. Jacob Riis, a Danish immigrant and New York newspaper photographer, shocked many middle-class Americans with his sensational (and, some claimed, sensationalized) descriptions and pictures of tenement life in his 1890 book *How the Other Half Lives.* But the solution reformers often adopted was simply to raze slum dwellings without building any new housing to replace them.

Urban Technologies: Transportation and Construction

Urban growth posed monumental transportation challenges. Sheer numbers of people mandated the development of mass transportation. Streetcars drawn on tracks by horses had been introduced into some cities even before the Civil War. But the horsecars were not fast enough, so many communities developed new forms of mass transit. In 1870, New York opened its first elevated railway, whose noisy, steam-powered trains moved rapidly above the city streets on massive iron structures. New York, Chicago, San Francisco, Boston, and other cities also experimented with cable cars, towed by continuously moving underground cables. Richmond, Virginia, introduced the first electric trolley line in 1888, and in 1897, Boston opened the first American subway. At the same time, cities were developing new techniques of road and bridge building. One of the great technological marvels of the 1880s was the completion of the Brooklyn Bridge in New York—a dramatic steel-cable suspension span designed by John A. Roebling.

Cities grew upward as well as outward. In Chicago, the 1884 construction of the first modern "skyscraper"—by later standards a relatively modest ten-story building—launched a new era in urban architecture. Critical to the creation of the skyscraper was a new technology of construction, which emerged as a result of several related developments. New kinds of steel girders could support much greater tension than the metals of the past. The invention and development of the passenger elevator made much taller buildings possible. And the search for ways to protect cities from the ravages of great fires, which caused such terrible destruction in wood-frame cities of the late nineteenth century, led to steel-frame construction that, among other things, made cities more fireproof. Once the technology existed to permit the construction of tall buildings, there were few obstacles to building taller and taller *Skyscrapers*   structures. The early Chicago skyscrapers paved the way for some of the great construction achievements later in the twentieth century: the Chrysler Building and the Empire State Building in New York, the LaSalle Building in Chicago, and ultimately the vast numbers of steel and glass skyscrapers of post-1945 cities around the world.

STRAINS OF URBAN LIFE

Increasing urban congestion and the absence of adequate public services produced serious hazards. Crime, fire, disease, and indigence all placed strains on the capacities of metropolitan institutions, and both governments and private agencies were for a time poorly equipped to respond.

FIRE AND DISEASE

In one major city after another, fires destroyed large downtown areas. Chicago and Boston suffered "great fires" in 1871, and other cities experienced similar disasters. The terrible experience of the great fires encouraged the construction of fireproof buildings and the development of professional fire departments. They also forced cities to rebuild at a time when new technological and architectural innovations were available. Some of the high-rise downtowns of American cities arose out of the rubble of great fires.

An even greater hazard than fire was disease, especially in poor neighborhoods with inadequate sanitation facilities. An epidemic that began in a poor neighborhood could (and often did) spread easily into other neighborhoods as well. Few municipal officials recognized the relationship of improper sewage disposal and water contamination to such epidemic diseases as typhoid fever and cholera; many cities lacked adequate systems for disposing of human waste until well into the twentieth century. Flush toilets and sewer systems began to appear in the 1870s, but they could not solve the problem as long as sewage continued to flow into open ditches or streams, polluting cities' water supplies.

ENVIRONMENTAL DEGRADATION

Modern notions of environmental science were unknown to most Americans in these years. But the environmental degradation of many American cities was a visible and disturbing fact of life. The frequency of great fires, the dangers of disease, the crowding of working-class neighborhoods—all exemplified the environmental costs of industrialization and rapid urbanization.

Poor disposal of human and industrial waste was common in almost all large cities. The presence of domestic animals—horses, cows, pigs, and other animals—also contributed to the contamination of drinking water and other environmental problems.

Air quality in many cities was poor as well. Few Americans had the severe problems that London experienced in the late nineteenth century with its seemingly perpetual "fogs" created by the burning of soft coal. But air pollution from factories and from stoves and furnaces in offices, homes, and other buildings was constant and at times severe. The incidence of respiratory infection and related diseases was much higher in cities than it was in rural areas, and it accelerated rapidly in the late nineteenth century.

By the early twentieth century, reformers, actively crusading to improve the environmental conditions of cities, were beginning to achieve some notable successes. By 1910, most large American cities had constructed sewage disposal systems, often at great cost, to protect the drinking water of their inhabitants and to prevent the great bacterial plagues that impure water had helped create in the past—such as the yellow fever epidemic in Memphis that killed 5,000 people.

In 1912, the federal government created the Public Health Service, which was charged with preventing such occupational diseases as tuberculosis, anemia, and *Public Health Service* carbon dioxide poisoning, which were common in the garment industry and other trades. It attempted to create common health standards for all factories; but since the agency had few powers of enforcement, it had limited impact. The creation of the Occupational Safety and Health Administration in 1970, which gave government the authority to require employers to create safe and healthy workplaces, was a legacy of the Public Health Service's early work.

URBAN POVERTY, CRIME, AND VIOLENCE

Above all, perhaps, urban expansion spawned widespread and often desperate poverty. Public agencies and private philanthropic organizations offered some relief. But they were generally poorly funded and, in any case, dominated by middle-class people who believed that too much assistance would breed dependency. Most tried to restrict aid to the "deserving poor"—those who truly could not help themselves. Charitable organizations conducted elaborate "investigations" to separate the "deserving" from the "undeserving." Other charitable societies—for example, the Salvation Army, which began operating in America in 1879—concentrated more on religious revivalism than on relief of the homeless and hungry.

Middle-class people grew particularly alarmed over the rising number of poor children in the cities, some of them orphans or runaways. They attracted greater attention from reformers than any other group—although that attention produced no lasting solutions to their problems.

Poverty and crowding bred crime and violence. The American murder rate rose rapidly in the late nineteenth century, from 25 murders for every million people in 1880 to over 100 by the end of the century. That reflected in part a very high level of violence in some nonurban areas: the American South, where lynching and homicide were particularly high, and the West, where the rootlessness and instability of new communities (cow towns, mining camps, and the like) created much violence. But the big cities *Factors in Rising Crime Rate* contributed their share to the increase as well. Native-born Americans liked to believe that crime was a result of the violent proclivities of immigrant groups, and they cited the rise of gangs and criminal organizations in various ethnic communities. But native-born Americans in the cities were as likely to commit crimes as immigrants. The rising crime rates encouraged many cities to develop larger and more professional police forces. But police forces themselves could spawn corruption and brutality.

Some members of the middle class, fearful of urban insurrections, felt the need for even more substantial forms of protection. Urban National Guard groups built imposing armories on the outskirts of affluent neighborhoods and stored large supplies of weapons and ammunition in preparation for uprisings that, in fact, virtually never occurred.

The city was a place of strong allure and great excitement. Yet it was also a place of alienating impersonality and, to some, of degradation and exploitation. Theodore Dreiser's *Dreiser's Urban Novel* novel *Sister Carrie* (1900) exposed one troubling aspect of urban life: the plight of single women (like Dreiser's heroine, Carrie) who found themselves without any means of support. Carrie first took an exhausting and ill-paying job in a Chicago shoe factory, then drifted into a life of "sin," exploited by predatory men.

THE MACHINE AND THE BOSS

Newly arrived immigrants were much in need of institutions to help them adjust to American urban life. For many residents of the inner cities, the principal source of assistance was the political "machine."

The urban machine owed its existence to the power vacuum that the chaotic growth of cities had created and to the potential voting power of large immigrant communities. *Function of the "Urban Boss"* Out of that combination emerged the "urban bosses." The principal function of the political boss was simple: to win votes for his organization. That

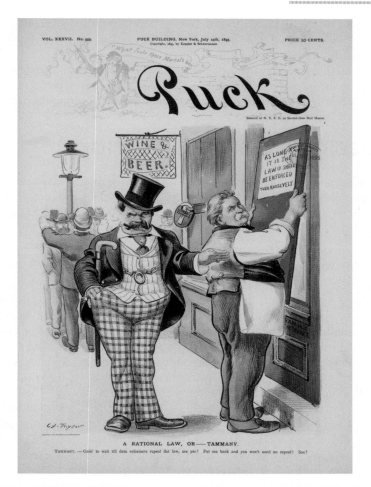

PUCK MAGAZINE *Puck* was the first successful humor magazine published in the United States. Issues were published from 1871 to 1918. It offered political cartoons, caricatures, and satire on the issues of the day. This cover shows a beer and wine seller shuttering his store by order of the government. The Tammany man indicates that the merchant will be able to operate without penalty in exchange for his support. (The Library of Congress)

meant winning the loyalty of his constituents. To do so, a boss might provide them with occasional relief—a basket of groceries or a bag of coal. He might step in to save those arrested for petty crimes from jail. When he could, he found work for the unemployed. Above all, he rewarded many of his followers with patronage: with jobs in city government or in the police (which the machine's elected officials often controlled); with jobs building or operating the new transit systems; and with opportunities to rise in the political organization itself.

Machines were also vehicles for making money. Politicians enriched themselves and their allies through various forms of graft and corruption. A politician might discover in advance where a new road or streetcar line was to be built, buy land near it, and sell it at a profit when property values rose as a result of the construction. There was also covert graft. Officials received kickbacks from contractors in exchange for contracts to build public projects, and they sold franchises for the operation of public utilities. The most famously

corrupt city boss was William M. Tweed, boss of New York City's Tammany Hall in the
"Boss" Tweed and Tammany Hall   1860s and 1870s, whose extravagant use of public funds and
kickbacks landed him in jail in 1872.

The urban machine was not without competition. Reform groups frequently mobilized
public outrage at the corruption of the bosses and often succeeded in driving machine politicians from office. But the reform organizations typically lacked the permanence of the machine.

THE RISE OF MASS CONSUMPTION

In the last decades of the nineteenth century, a distinctive middle-class culture began to
exert influence over the whole of American life. Other groups in society advanced less
rapidly, or not at all, but the rise of the new urban consumer culture began to shape a
new image of the nation.

PATTERNS OF INCOME AND CONSUMPTION

Incomes rose for almost everyone in the industrial era, although highly unevenly. One
result of the new economy was the creation of vast fortunes, but perhaps the most impor-
Growth of Middle Class   tant result for society as a whole was the growth and increasing prosperity of the middle class. Clerks, accountants, middle managers, and other "white-collar"
workers saw their salaries rise by an average of a third between 1890 and 1910. Doctors,
lawyers, and other professionals experienced a particularly dramatic increase in both the
prestige and the profitability of their professions. Working-class incomes rose in those
years as well, although from a much lower base and more slowly. The iron and steel
industries saw workers' hourly wages increase by a third between 1890 and 1910; but
industries with large female workforces—shoes, textiles, and paper—saw more modest
increases, as did almost all industries in the South. Wages for African Americans,
Mexicans, and Asians also rose more slowly than those for white workers.

Rising incomes created new markets for consumer goods, which were now available
New Consumerism   to a mass market for the first time, as a result of technological innovations
and new merchandising techniques. An example of such changes was the emergence of
ready-made clothing. In the early nineteenth century, most Americans had made their own
clothing. The invention of the sewing machine and the Civil War demand for uniforms
spurred the manufacture of clothing and helped create an enormous industry devoted to
producing ready-made garments. By the end of the century, almost all Americans bought
their clothing from stores. Partly as a result, much larger numbers of people became
concerned with personal style. Interest in women's fashion, for example, had once been
a luxury reserved for the relatively affluent. Now middle-class and even working-class
women could strive to develop a distinctive style of dress.

Buying and preparing food also became a critical part of the new **consumerism.** The
development and mass production of tin cans in the 1880s created a large new industry
devoted to packaging and selling canned food and condensed milk. Refrigerated railroad
cars made it possible for perishable foods to be transported over long distances without
spoiling. Artificially frozen ice enabled many households to afford iceboxes. The changes
brought improved diets and better health. Life expectancy rose six years in the first two
decades of the twentieth century.

DEPARTMENT STORES Department stores often created "events" to help promote sales of their many wares. Here, Strawbridge and Clothier department store creates a stir on Market Street in Philadelphia in 1907. (© Corbis)

CHAIN STORES, MAIL-ORDER HOUSES, AND DEPARTMENT STORES

Changes in marketing also altered the way Americans bought goods. New "chain stores" could usually offer a wider array of goods at lower prices than the small local stores with which they competed. The Atlantic and Pacific Tea Company (the A&P) began a national network of grocery stores in the 1870s. F. W. Woolworth built a chain of dry goods stores. Sears and Roebuck established a large market for its mail-order merchandise by distributing an enormous catalog each year.

In larger cities, the emergence of great department stores helped make shopping more alluring and glamorous. Marshall Field in Chicago created one of the first American department stores—a place deliberately designed to produce a sense of *Department Stores* wonder and excitement. Similar stores emerged in New York, Brooklyn, Boston, Philadelphia, and other cities. (For the philosophy of one of the leading department store innovators, see "Consider the Source: John Wanamaker, the Four Cardinal Points of the Department Store.")

WOMEN AS CONSUMERS

The rise of mass consumption had particularly dramatic effects on American women. Women's clothing styles changed much more rapidly than men's, which encouraged more frequent purchases. Women generally bought and prepared food for their families, so the availability of new food products changed not only how people ate but also how women shopped and cooked.

The consumer economy produced new employment opportunities for women as salesclerks and waitresses. And it spawned the creation of a new movement in which women

JOHN WANAMAKER, THE FOUR CARDINAL POINTS OF THE DEPARTMENT STORE, 1874

The Philadelphia merchant John Wanamaker was one of the most successful and innovative businessmen of his day. A pioneer of the department store, Wanamaker ran this advertisement explaining the policies and benefits for consumers of his new commercial venue.

FOUR CARDINAL POINTS

By which we will hereafter steer our craft

FULL GUARANTEE   CASH PAYMENT

ONE PRICE   CASH RETURNED

Explanation and Elaboration of the New Plan

FIRST POINT—"CASH"—Houses doing a credit business must provide for losses on bad debts, interest on long-standing accounts, capital locked up, etc. To bear such losses themselves would drive them out of business. Therefore a per cent is added to the price of each article sold to cover this leakage, and cash buyers, whether they know it or not, really pay the bad debts and the interest on the long credits of the other customers. Under the cash payment system one pays only for what he gets, and contributes nothing to a "Sinking Fund."

By this radical change we shall lose some of our customers, no doubt, but we will gain ten where we lose one, the advantages being so great to all who can avail themselves of them. So we say CASH THROUGHOUT. Bring money for Clothing and we will supply it at prices possible under no other plan.

SECOND POINT—"ONE PRICE"—The fairness of this feature of our plan all will praise. It is simply treating all alike—exacting nothing from indisposition to bargain or ignorance, and, at the same time, conceding all that shrewdness on the shrewdest customer's part could possibly extort, because the "One Price"

which we mark on our goods shall invariably be Not the "First" Price, but the Last and Lowest Price.

Not the "Top" Price, but the Very Bottom Price.

THIRD POINT—"FULL GUARANTEE"— A printed guarantee, bearing the signature of our firm will accompany each garment as a warrantee. This binds us in every sense, and will be honored as quickly as a good draft of the Government of the United States. This is a sample of the full guarantee, and tells its own story—Guarantee.

WE HEREBY GUARANTEE

First—That the prices of our goods shall be as low as the same quality of material and manufacture are sold anywhere in the United States.

Second—That prices are precisely the same to everybody for same quality, on same day of purchase.

Third—That the quality of goods is as represented on printed labels.

Fourth—That the full amount of cash paid will be refunded, if customers find the articles unsatisfactory, and return them unworn and uninjured within ten days of date of purchase.

FOURTH POINT—"CASH RETURNED"— This is simply a concession on our part to our customers, to secure them full confidence in dealing for goods they know very little about, and we thus prevent any occasion for dissatisfaction from any and every cause whatsoever. If the garment is not exactly what you thought, if your taste changes, if the "home folks" prefer another color or another shape, if you find you can buy the same material and style elsewhere for less money, if you conclude you don't need it after you get home, if the season changes suddenly and you wish you had not bought it, bring it back unworn and uninjured, and the full amount of money you paid will be returned on the spot. What more can we do for our customers than this, when we make our clothing so that they can draw the money value with it equally as well as with a check on the banks?

The ADVANTAGES incident to a system having for its cardinal points these which we have now explained, are simply innumerable. Saving of time and temper, perfect security, absence of all huckstering, etc., etc.

But above all this . . .

All of these "By-ways" lead direct to CHEAPNESS; and this without lowering the quality or style of our celebrated make of MEN'S AND BOY'S CLOTHING.

UNDERSTAND, ANALYZE, & EVALUATE

1. What were the benefits of Wanamaker's four cardinal points for consumers? What were the benefits for Wanamaker? Judging by Wanamaker's new way of doing business, what must business practices and customer service have looked like before?
2. Why might these assurances have been particularly important for a large department store? Why might it have been essential for the urban consumer market?

Source: *Golden Book of the Wanamaker Stores, Jubilee Year, 1861–1911* (Philadelphia: John Wanamaker, 1911), pp. 152–154. This advertisement was originally published in 1874. Located in Regina Lee Blaszczyk and Philip B. Scranton (eds.), *Major Problems in American Business History* (Boston: Houghton Mifflin Company, 2006), pp. 298–299.

played a vital role: the consumer protection movement. The National Consumers League (NCL), formed in the 1890s under the leadership of Florence *National Consumers League* Kelley, attempted to mobilize the power of women as consumers to force retailers and manufacturers to improve wages and working conditions. The NCL encouraged women to buy only products with the League's "white label," which indicated that the product was made under fair working conditions.

LEISURE IN THE CONSUMER SOCIETY

Closely related to the rise of consumption was a growing interest in leisure time. Members of the urban middle and professional classes had large blocks of time during which they were not at work—evenings, weekends, even paid vacations. Working hours in many factories declined, from an average of nearly seventy hours a week in 1860 to under sixty in 1900. Even farmers found that the mechanization of agriculture gave them more free time. As many people's lives became more compartmentalized, with clear distinctions between work and leisure, many Americans began to search for new forms of recreation and entertainment.

REDEFINING LEISURE

In earlier eras, relatively few Americans had considered leisure a valuable thing. Many equated it with laziness. In the late nineteenth century, however, the beginnings of a redefinition of leisure appeared. The economist Simon Patten articulated this new view of leisure in *The Theory of Prosperity* (1902), *The New Basis of Civilization* (1910), and other works. He challenged the centuries-old assumption that the normal condition of civilization was a scarcity of goods. In earlier times, Patten argued, fear of scarcity had caused people to place a high value on thrift, self-denial, and restraint. But in modern industrial societies, new economies could create enough wealth to satisfy not just the needs but also the desires of all.

As Americans became more accustomed to leisure as a normal part of life, they began to look for new experiences and entertainments. Mass entertainment occasionally bridged differences of class, race, and gender. But it could also be sharply divided. Saloons and some sporting events tended to be male preserves. Shopping and going to tea rooms and luncheonettes were more characteristic of female leisure. Theaters, pubs, and clubs were often specific to particular ethnic communities or particular work groups. When the classes did meet in public spaces—as they did, for example, in city parks—there was often considerable conflict over what constituted appropriate public behavior. Elites in New York City, for example, tried to prohibit anything but quiet, "genteel" activities in Central Park, while working-class people wanted to use the public spaces for sports and entertainments.

SPECTATOR SPORTS

Among the most important responses to the search for entertainment was the rise of *Baseball* organized spectator sports, especially baseball. A game much like baseball—known as "rounders" and derived from cricket—had enjoyed limited popularity in Great Britain in the early nineteenth century. Versions of the game began to appear in America in the early 1830s. By the end of the Civil War, interest in the game had grown rapidly.

THE AMERICAN NATIONAL GAME   Long before the modern major leagues began, local baseball clubs were active throughout much of the United States, establishing the game as the "national pastime." This print of a "grand match for the championship" depicts an 1866 game at Elysian Fields, a popular park just across the river from New York City in Hoboken, New Jersey. (© Photo Reproduction by Transcendental Graphics/Getty Images)

More than 200 amateur or semiprofessional teams and clubs existed, many of which joined a national association and proclaimed a set of standard rules. As the game grew in popularity, it offered opportunities for profit. The first salaried team, the Cincinnati Red Stockings, was formed in 1869. Other cities fielded professional teams, and in 1876 the teams banded together in the National League. A rival league, the American Association, appeared and collapsed, but in 1901 the American League emerged to replace it. And in 1903, the first modern World Series was played, in which the American League's Boston Red Sox beat the National League's Pittsburgh Pirates. By then, baseball had become an important business and a national preoccupation.

Baseball had great appeal to working-class males. The second most popular game, football, appealed at first to a more elite segment of the male population, in part because it originated in colleges and universities. The first intercollegiate football game in America occurred between Princeton and Rutgers in 1869. Early intercollegiate football bore only an indirect relation to the modern game; it was more similar to present-day rugby. By the late 1870s, however, the game was becoming standardized and was taking on the outlines of its modern form.

Basketball was invented in 1891 in Springfield, Massachusetts, by Dr. James A. Naismith, a Canadian working as an athletic director for a local college.   *Basketball Invented*   Boxing, which had long been a disreputable activity concentrated primarily among the urban lower classes, became by the 1880s a more popular and, in some places, more reputable sport.

Participation in the major sports was almost exclusively the province of men, but several sports emerged in which women became involved. Golf and tennis both attracted more and more relatively wealthy men and women. Bicycling and croquet also enjoyed widespread popularity in the 1890s among women as well as men. Women's colleges introduced their students to more strenuous sports as well—track, crew, swimming, and (beginning in the late 1890s) basketball.

MUSIC, THEATER, AND MOVIES

Other forms of popular entertainment also developed in the cities. Many ethnic communities maintained their own theaters, which presented plays in the languages of the immigrant communities. Urban theaters in the heart of the cities attracted a much broader audience. They introduced new and distinctively American entertainment forms: the musical comedy, which evolved gradually from the comic operettas of Europe; and vaudeville, a   *Vaudeville*   form of theater adapted from French models, which remained the most popular urban entertainment into the first decades of the twentieth century. It consisted of a variety of acts (musicians, comedians, magicians, jugglers, and others) and was, at least in the beginning, inexpensive to produce. As the economic potential of vaudeville grew, some promoters— most prominently Florenz Ziegfeld of New York—staged much more elaborate spectacles.

Vaudeville was also one of the few entertainment media open to black performers, who brought to it elements of the minstrel shows they had earlier developed for black audiences in the late nineteenth century. Some minstrel singers (including the most famous, Al Jolson) were white performers wearing heavy makeup (or "blackface"), but most were black. Entertainers of both races performed music based on the gospel and folk tunes of the plantation and on the jazz and ragtime of black urban communities. Performers of both races also tailored their acts to prevailing white prejudices, ridiculing African Americans by acting out demeaning stereotypes.

American popular entertainment was transformed with the emergence of motion picture shows. Thomas Edison and others had created the technology underpinning the motion picture in the 1880s. Soon after that, short films became available to individual viewers watching peepshows in pool halls, penny arcades, and amusement parks. Soon, larger projectors made it possible to display the images on big screens, which permitted substantial audiences to see films in theaters. By 1900, Americans were becoming attracted *Silent Films* in large numbers to these early movies—usually plotless films of trains or waterfalls or other spectacles. The director D. W. Griffith carried the motion picture into a new era with his silent epics—*The Birth of a Nation* (1915), *Intolerance* (1916), and others—which introduced serious (if notoriously racist) plots and elaborate productions to filmmaking. Motion pictures were the first truly mass entertainment medium.

PATTERNS OF PUBLIC AND PRIVATE LEISURE

Particularly striking about popular entertainment in the late nineteenth and early twentieth centuries was its public quality. Many Americans spent their leisure time in places where they would find not only entertainment but also other people. Thousands of working-class New Yorkers spent evenings in dance halls, vaudeville houses, and concert halls. More affluent New Yorkers enjoyed afternoons in Central Park, where a principal attraction was seeing other people (and being seen by them). Moviegoers were attracted not just by the movies themselves but also by the energy of the audiences at lavish new "movie palaces," just as sports fans were drawn by the crowds as well as by the games.

Perhaps the most striking example of popular public entertainment in the early twen-*Coney Island* tieth century was Coney Island, the famous and self-consciously fabulous amusement park and resort on a popular beach in Brooklyn. Luna Park, the greatest of the Coney Island attractions, opened in 1903 and provided rides, stunts, and lavish reproductions of exotic places and spectacular adventures: Japanese gardens, Venetian canals with gondoliers, a Chinese theater, a simulated trip to the moon, and reenactments of such disasters as burning buildings and earthquakes. A year later, a competing company opened Dreamland, which tried to outdo even Luna Park with a 375-foot tower, a three-ring circus, chariot races, and a Lilliputian village from *Gulliver's Travels.* The popularity of Coney Island in these years was phenomenal. Thousands of people flocked to the large resort hotels that lined the beaches. Many thousands more made day trips out from the city by train and (after 1920) subway. In 1904, the average daily attendance at Luna Park alone was 90,000 people.

Most people found Coney Island appealing in part because it provided an escape from the genteel standards that governed so much of American life at the time. In the amusement parks of Coney Island, decorum was often forgotten, and people delighted in finding themselves in situations that in any other setting would have seemed embarrassing or improper: women's skirts blown above their heads with hot air; people pummeled with water and rubber paddles by clowns; hints of sexual freedom as strangers were forced to come into physical contact with one another on rides and amusements.

Not all popular entertainment, however, involved public events. Many Americans *Dime Novels* amused themselves privately by reading novels and poetry. The so-called dime novels, cheaply bound and widely circulated, became popular after the Civil War, with detective stories, tales of the Wild West, sagas of scientific adventure, and novels of "moral uplift." Publishers also distributed sentimental novels of romance, which developed a large audience among women, as did books about animals and about young children growing up. Louisa May Alcott's *Little Women,* most of whose readers were female, sold more than 2 million copies.

THE TECHNOLOGIES OF MASS COMMUNICATION

American journalism experienced dramatic change in the decades following the Civil War. Between 1870 and 1910, the circulation of daily newspapers increased nearly ninefold (from under 3 million to more than 24 million), a rate three times as great as the rate of population increase. And while standards varied widely from one paper to another, American journalism was developing the beginnings of a professional identity. Salaries of reporters increased; many newspapers began separating the reporting of news from the expression of opinion; and newspapers themselves became important businesses.

This transformation was to a large degree a result of new technologies of communication. The emergence of national press services, for example, was a product of the telegraph, which made it possible to supply papers with news and features from around the nation and the world. By the turn of the century, important newspaper chains had emerged as well, linked together by their own internal wire services. The most powerful was owned by William Randolph Hearst, who by 1914 controlled   *William Randolph Hearst* nine newspapers and two magazines. New printing technologies were making possible more elaborate layouts, the publication of color pictures, and, by the end of the century, the printing of photographs. These advances not only helped publishers make their own stories more vivid; they also made it possible for them to attract more advertisers.

THE TELEPHONE

The most important new technology of communication in the late nineteenth century was the telephone, which Alexander Graham Bell had first demonstrated in 1876. In its first years, the telephone was a relatively impractical tool. Those who subscribed to telephone service had to have direct wire links to everyone else they wished to call. In 1878, the first "switchboard" opened in New Haven, Connecticut, opening the way for more practical uses of the telephone. Once there was a switchboard, a telephone subscriber needed only a line to the central telephone office from which connections could be made to any other subscriber. A new occupation—the "telephone operator"—was born. The Bell System, which controlled all American telephone service, hired young white women to work as operators, hoping that a pleasant female voice would make the experience of using the telephone (and the inconvenience of the frequent technological problems that accompanied it) less irritating to customers. Telephone signals were very weak at first, and callers could seldom reach anyone more than a few miles away. In an effort to increase the range of telephones, engineers created the "repeater," which periodically strengthened the signal as it moved over distances. By 1914, the repeaters had improved to the point that it was now practical to envision a transcontinental line.

In its early years, the telephone was an almost entirely commercial instrument. Of the nearly 7,400 telephone customers in the New York–New Jersey area in 1891, 6,000 were businesses and organizations. Even the residential telephones tended to belong to doctors or business managers.

The growing reach of the telephone in the early years of the twentieth century made the Bell System (formally named American Telephone and Telegraph, or   *The Bell System* AT&T) one of the most powerful corporations in America and a genuine monopoly.

Central to its success was an early decision by executives that the company would exclusively build and own all telephone instruments and then lease them to subscribers. That made it possible for AT&T to control both the equipment and the telephone service itself, and to exclude any competitors in either field. It also gave AT&T effective control over the local telephone companies allied with it and made the nation's telephone system into an effective cartel.

HIGH CULTURE IN THE URBAN AGE

In addition to the important changes in popular culture that accompanied the rise of cities and industry, there were profound changes in the realm of "high culture." The distinction between "highbrow" and "lowbrow" culture was largely new to the industrial era. In the early nineteenth century, most cultural activities had targeted people of all classes. By the late nineteenth century, however, elites were developing a cultural and intellectual life quite separate from the popular amusements of the urban masses.

LITERATURE AND ART IN URBAN AMERICA

One of the strongest impulses in American literature was the effort to recreate urban *Literary Realism* social reality. This trend toward realism found an early voice in Stephen Crane, who—although perhaps best known for his novel of the Civil War, *The Red Badge of Courage* (1895)—created a sensation in 1893 when he published *Maggie: A Girl of the Streets,* a grim picture of urban poverty and slum life. Theodore Dreiser, Frank Norris, and Upton Sinclair were similarly drawn to social issues as themes. Kate Chopin, a southern writer who explored the oppressive features of traditional marriage, encountered widespread public abuse after the publication of her shocking 1899 novel, *The Awakening,* which described a young wife and mother who abandoned her family in search of personal fulfillment. William Dean Howells, in *The Rise of Silas Lapham* and other works, described what he considered the shallowness and corruption in ordinary American lifestyles.

American art through most of the nineteenth century had been overshadowed by that of Europe. By 1900, however, a number of American artists broke from Old World traditions and experimented with new styles. Winslow Homer brought a distinctive approach to his paintings of New England maritime life and other American subjects. James McNeil Whistler was one of the first Western artists to introduce Asian themes into American and European art.

By the first years of the new century, some American artists were turning decisively away from the traditional academic style (a style perhaps most identified in America by the brilliant portraitist John Singer Sargent). Members of the so-called Ashcan school *Ashcan School* produced work startling in its naturalism and stark in its portrayal of the social realities of the era. John Sloan portrayed the dreariness of American urban slums; George Bellows caught the vigor and violence of his time in paintings and drawings of prizefights; Edward Hopper explored the starkness and loneliness of the modern city. The Ashcan artists were also among the first Americans to appreciate expressionism and abstraction; and they showed their interest in new forms in 1913, when they helped stage *Armory Show* the famous "Armory Show" in New York City, which displayed works of the French postimpressionists and of some American moderns.

DEMPSEY AND FIRPO The artist George Bellows began painting fight scenes in the first years of the twentieth century, when boxing appealed primarily to working-class audiences. By 1924, when he painted this moment from a famous prizefight, boxing had become one of the most popular sports in America. (© Whitney Museum of American Art, New York, USA/Bridgeman Images)

THE IMPACT OF DARWINISM

One of the most profound intellectual developments in the late nineteenth century was the widespread acceptance of the theory of evolution, associated most prominently with the English naturalist Charles Darwin. Darwin argued that the human species had evolved from earlier forms of life through a process of "natural selection." History, Darwin suggested, was not the working out of a divine plan. It was a natural process dominated by the fiercest or luckiest competitors.

The theory of evolution met widespread resistance at first from educators, theologians, and even many scientists. By the end of the century, however, the evolutionists had converted most members of the urban professional and educated classes. Even many middle-class Protestant religious leaders had accepted the doctrine, making significant alterations in theology to accommodate it. The rise of Darwinism, however,   *Divisions over Darwinism* contributed to something unseen by most urban Americans at the time: a deep schism between the new, cosmopolitan culture of the city and the more traditional, provincial culture of some rural areas. Thus the late nineteenth century saw not only the rise of a liberal Protestantism in tune with new scientific discoveries but also the beginning of an organized Protestant fundamentalism.

Darwinism helped spawn other new intellectual currents. There was the Social Darwinism of William Graham Sumner and others, which industrialists used so enthusiastically to justify their favored position in American life. But there were also more sophisticated philosophies, among them a doctrine that became known as "pragmatism."

William James, a Harvard psychologist (and brother of the novelist Henry James), was the most prominent publicist of the new theory, although earlier intellectuals such as Charles S. Peirce and later ones such as John Dewey were also important to its develop-
"Pragmatism"   ment and dissemination. According to the pragmatists, modern society should rely for guidance not on inherited ideals and moral principles but on the test of scientific inquiry. No idea or institution (not even religious faith) was valid, they claimed, unless it "worked," unless it stood the test of experience.

A similar concern for scientific inquiry was influencing the social sciences. Sociologists such as Edward A. Ross and Lester Frank Ward urged applying the scientific method to the solution of social and political problems. Historians such as Frederick Jackson Turner and Charles Beard argued that economic factors more than spiritual ideals had been the governing force in historical development. John Dewey proposed a new approach to education that placed less emphasis on the rote learning of traditional knowledge and more on flexible, democratic schooling.

The implications of Darwinism also promoted the growth of anthropology and encouraged some scholars to begin examining other cultures in new ways. Some white Americans began to look at Indian society, for example, as a coherent culture with its own norms and values that were worthy of respect and preservation, even though they were different from those of white society.

TOWARD UNIVERSAL SCHOOLING

The growing demand for specialized skills and scientific knowledge naturally created a growing, and changing, demand for education. The late nineteenth century, therefore, was a time of rapid expansion and reform of American schools and universities.

Free public primary and secondary education spread rapidly. By 1900, compulsory school attendance laws existed in thirty-one states and territories. Education was still far from universal. Rural areas lagged far behind urban-industrial ones in funding public education. In the South, many African Americans had no access to schools at all. But for many white men and women, educational opportunities were expanding rapidly.

Educational reformers tried to extend educational opportunities to the Indian tribes as well, in an effort to "civilize" them and help them adapt to white society. In the 1870s, reformers recruited small groups of Indians to attend Hampton Institute (a primarily black college). In 1879, they organized the Carlisle Indian Industrial School in Pennsylvania. Like many black colleges, Carlisle emphasized practical "industrial" education. Ultimately, however, these reform efforts failed, in part because they were unpopular with their intended beneficiaries.

UNIVERSITIES AND THE GROWTH OF SCIENCE AND TECHNOLOGY

Colleges and universities also proliferated rapidly in the late nineteenth century. The Morrill Land Grant Act of 1862, by which the federal government had donated public land to states for the establishment of colleges, led to the creation of sixty-nine "land-grant" institutions in the last decades of the century—among them the state university systems of California, Illinois, Minnesota, and Wisconsin. Other universities, including Chicago, Columbia, Harvard, Northwestern, Princeton, Syracuse, and Yale, benefited from millions of dollars contributed by business and financial titans such as Rockefeller and Carnegie. Other philanthropists founded new universities or reorganized older ones to perpetuate their family names—for example, Vanderbilt, Johns Hopkins, Cornell, Duke, Tulane, and Stanford.

These and other universities played a vital role in the economic development of the United States in the late nineteenth century and beyond. The land-grant institutions were specifically mandated to advance knowledge in "agriculture   *Higher Education and the Economy* and mechanics." From the beginning, therefore, they were committed not just to abstract knowledge but to making discoveries that would be of practical use to farmers and manufacturers. As they evolved into great state universities, they retained that tradition and became the source of many of the great discoveries that helped American industry and commerce advance. Private universities emerged that served many of the same purposes: the Massachusetts Institute of Technology, founded in 1865, soon became the nation's premier engineering school; Johns Hopkins University in Baltimore, founded in 1876, did much to advance medical scholarship, as did the Rockefeller Institute for Medical Research in New York (later Rockefeller University) and the Carnegie Institution. By the early twentieth century, older and more traditional universities were beginning to form relationships with the private sector and the government, doing research that did not just advance knowledge for its own sake but that was directly applicable to practical problems of the time.

MEDICAL SCIENCE

Both the culture of and the scientific basis for medical care were changing rapidly in the early twentieth century. Most doctors were beginning to accept the new medical assumption that there were underlying causes to particular symptoms—that a symptom was not itself a disease. They were also beginning to make use of new or improved technologies—the X-ray, improved microscopes, and other diagnostic devices—that made it possible to classify, and distinguish among, different diseases. Laboratory tests could now identify infections such as typhoid and dysentery. These technologies were a critical first step toward the effective treatment of diseases. At about the same time, pharmaceutical research began to produce some important new medicines. Aspirin was first synthesized in 1899. Other researchers experimented with chemicals that might destroy diseases in the blood, an effort that eventually led to the various forms of chemotherapy that are still widely used in treating cancer. In 1906, an American surgeon, G. W. Crile, became the first physician to use blood transfusion in treatment, which revolutionized surgery. In the past, patients often lost so much blood during operations that extensive surgery could be fatal for that reason alone. With transfusions, it became possible to conduct much longer and more elaborate operations.

The widespread acceptance by the end of the nineteenth century of the germ theory of disease had important implications. Physicians quickly discovered that   *Germ Theory Accepted* exposure to germs did not by itself necessarily cause disease, and they began looking for the other factors that determined who got sick and who did not. Among the factors they eventually discovered were general health, previous medical history, diet and nutrition, and eventually genetic predisposition. The awareness of the importance of infection in spreading disease also encouraged doctors to sterilize their instruments, use surgical gloves, and otherwise purify the medical environment.

By the early twentieth century, American physicians and surgeons were generally recognized as among the best in the world, and American medical education   *Declining Mortality* was beginning to attract students from many other countries. These improvements in medical knowledge and training, along with improvements in sanitation and public health, did much to reduce infection and mortality in most American communities.

EDUCATION FOR WOMEN

The post–Civil War era saw an important expansion of educational opportunities for women, although such opportunities continued to lag far behind those available to men and were almost entirely denied to black women.

Most public high schools accepted women readily, but opportunities for higher education were fewer. At the end of the Civil War, only three American colleges were coeducational. After the war, many of the land-grant colleges and universities in the Midwest and such private universities as Cornell and Wesleyan began to admit women along with men. But coeducation was less crucial to women's education in this period than was the creation of a network of women's colleges. Mount Holyoke in central Massachusetts had begun its life in 1836 as a "seminary" for women; it became a full-fledged college in the 1880s, at about the same time that entirely new female institutions were emerging: Vassar, Wellesley, Smith, Bryn Mawr, Wells, and Goucher. A few of the larger private universities created separate colleges for women on their campuses (Barnard at Columbia and Radcliffe at Harvard, for example).

The female college was part of an important phenomenon in the history of modern American women: the emergence of distinctive women's communities outside the family. Most faculty members and many administrators were women (usually unmarried). And college life produced a spirit of sorority and commitment among educated women that had important effects in later years. Most female college graduates ultimately married, but they married at a more advanced age than their noncollege counterparts. A significant minority, perhaps over 25 percent, did not marry at all, but devoted themselves to careers. The growth of female higher education clearly became for some women a liberating experience, persuading them that they had roles other than those of wives and mothers to perform in their rapidly changing urban-industrial society.

CONCLUSION

The extraordinary growth of American cities in the last decades of the nineteenth century led to both great achievements and enormous problems. Cities became centers of learning, art, and commerce and produced great advances in technology, transportation, architecture, and communications. They provided their residents—and their many visitors—with varied and dazzling experiences, so much so that people increasingly left the countryside to move to the city.

But cities were also places of congestion, filth, disease, and corruption. With populations expanding too rapidly for services to keep up, most American cities in this era struggled with makeshift techniques to solve the basic problems of providing water, disposing of sewage, building roads, running public transportation, fighting fire, stopping crime, and preventing or curing disease. City governments, many of them dominated by political machines and ruled by party bosses, were often models of inefficiency and corruption—although in their informal way they also provided substantial services to the working-class and immigrant constituencies who needed them most. Yet they also managed to oversee great public projects: the building of parks, museums, opera houses, and theaters, usually in partnership with private developers.

The city brought together races, ethnic groups, and classes of extraordinary variety—from the families of great wealth that the new industrial age was creating to the vast working class, much of it consisting of immigrants, who crowded into densely packed neighborhoods divided by nationality. The city also spawned temples of consumerism: shops, boutiques, and, above all, the great department stores. And it created forums for public recreation and entertainment: parks, theaters, athletic fields, amusement parks, and, later, movie palaces.

Urban life created anxiety among those who lived within the cities and among those who observed them from afar. But in fact, American cities adapted reasonably successfully over time to the great demands their growth made of them and learned to govern themselves if not entirely honestly and efficiently, at least enough to allow them to survive and grow.

KEY TERMS/PEOPLE/PLACES/EVENTS

Armory Show 448
Ashcan school 448
city beautiful
  movement 434
Coney Island 446
consumerism 440
Darwinism 449

Jacob Riis 436
Kate Chopin 448
National Consumers
  League 443
Public Health Service 437
Tammany Hall 440
tenements 436

Theodore Dreiser 438
vaudeville 445
William James 450
William M. Tweed 440
William Randolph
  Hearst 447

RECALL AND REFLECT

1. What groups of people were most likely to move to the cities of late-nineteenth-century America, and why?
2. What was the relationship between immigration and urbanization in the late nineteenth century?
3. How did the new consumer economy affect roles and expectations for women?
4. What was Darwinism, and what was its impact on American intellectual life?

19 FROM CRISIS TO EMPIRE

THE POLITICS OF EQUILIBRIUM

THE AGRARIAN REVOLT

THE CRISIS OF THE 1890s

STIRRINGS OF IMPERIALISM

WAR WITH SPAIN

THE REPUBLIC AS EMPIRE

LOOKING AHEAD

1. What were the major social and economic problems that beset the United States in the late nineteenth century, and how did the two major political parties respond to these problems?

2. What was Populism, what were its goals, and to what degree were these goals achieved?

3. How did the United States become an imperial power?

THE UNITED STATES APPROACHED the end of the nineteenth century as a fundamentally different nation from what it had been at the beginning of the Civil War. With rapid change came cascading social and political problems—problems that the weak and conservative governments of the time showed little inclination or ability to address.

A catastrophic economic depression that began in 1893 created devastating hardship for millions of Americans. Farmers responded by creating an agrarian political movement known as Populism. American workers, facing massive unemployment, staged large and occasionally violent strikes. Not since the Civil War had American politics been so polarized and impassioned. The election of 1896, which pitted the agrarian hero William Jennings Bryan against the solid conservative William McKinley, was dramatic but anticlimactic. Supported by the mighty Republican Party and many eastern groups who looked with suspicion and unease at the agricultural demands coming from the West, McKinley easily triumphed.

McKinley did little in his first term in office to resolve the problems and grievances of his time, but the economy revived nevertheless. Having largely ignored the depression, however, McKinley focused on another great national cause: the plight of Cuba in its war with Spain. In the spring of 1898, the United States declared war on Spain and entered the conflict in Cuba—a brief but bloody war that ended with an American victory four months later.

The conflict had begun as a way to support Cuban independence from the Spanish, but a group of fervent and influential imperialists worked to convert the war into an occasion for acquiring overseas possessions. Despite a powerful anti-imperialist movement, the acquisition of the former Spanish colonies proceeded—only to draw Americans into yet another imperial war, this one in the Philippines, where the Americans, not the Spanish, were the targets of local enmity.

THE POLITICS OF EQUILIBRIUM

The enormous social and economic changes of the late nineteenth century strained not only the nation's traditional social arrangements but its political institutions as well. Searching for stability and social justice, Americans looked to the government for leadership. Yet that government during much of this period was ill equipped to confront these new challenges. As a result, problems and grievances festered and grew.

THE PARTY SYSTEM

The most striking feature of late-nineteenth-century politics was the stability of the party system. From the end of Reconstruction until the late 1890s, the electorate was divided almost evenly between the Republicans and the Democrats. Sixteen states were solidly and consistently Republican, and fourteen states (most in the South) were solidly and consistently Democratic. Only a handful of states were usually in doubt, and they generally decided the results of national elections, often on the basis of voter turnout. The Republican Party captured the presidency in all but two of the elections of the era, but in the five presidential elections beginning in 1876, the average popular-vote margin separating the Democratic and Republican candidates was 1.5 percent. The congressional

TIME LINE

1867
National Grange founded

1876
Hayes elected president

1880
Garfield elected president

1881
Garfield assassinated; Arthur becomes president

1884
Cleveland elected president

1887
Interstate Commerce Act

U.S. gains base at Pearl Harbor

1888
Benjamin Harrison elected president

1890
Sherman Antitrust Act

Sherman Silver Purchase Act

McKinley Tariff

1892
Cleveland elected president again

People's Party formed

1893
Revolution in Hawaii

Economic depression begins

Sherman Silver Purchase Act repealed

1894
Coxey's Army marches on Washington, D.C.

1896
McKinley elected president

1898
War with Spain

Treaty of Paris

U.S. annexes Hawaii, Puerto Rico, Philippines

1898–1902
Philippines revolt

1899
Open Door notes

1900
Boxer Rebellion

McKinley reelected

1901
Platt Amendment

balance was similarly stable, with the Republicans generally controlling the Senate and the Democrats generally controlling the House.

Despite the relatively modest differences, most eligible Americans had strong loyalties *High Voter Turnout* to their chosen party. Voter turnout in presidential elections between 1860 and 1900 averaged over 78 percent of all eligible voters. Large groups of potential voters were disenfranchised in these years: women in most states and almost all blacks and many poor whites in the South. But for adult white males, there were few restrictions on voting.

What explains this extraordinary loyalty to the two political parties? It was not that the parties took distinct positions on important public issues. They did so rarely. *Reasons for Party Loyalties* Party loyalties reflected other factors. Region was perhaps the most important. To white southerners, loyalty to the Democratic Party—the vehicle by which they had triumphed over Reconstruction and preserved white supremacy— was a matter of unquestioned faith. Republican loyalties were equally intense in the North. To many, the party of Lincoln remained a bulwark against slavery and treason.

Religious and ethnic differences also shaped party loyalties. The Democratic Party attracted most of the Catholic voters, recent immigrants, and poorer workers. The Republican Party appealed to northern Protestants, citizens of old stock, and much of the middle class. Among the few substantive issues on which the parties took clearly different stands were immigration matters. Republicans tended to support immigration restriction and to favor temperance legislation, which many believed would help discipline immigrant communities. Catholics and immigrants viewed such proposals as assaults on them and their cultures, and the Democratic Party followed their lead.

Party identification, then, was usually more a reflection of cultural inclinations than a calculation of economic interest. Individuals might affiliate with a party because their parents had done so or because it was the party of their region, their church, or their ethnic group.

THE NATIONAL GOVERNMENT

One reason the parties avoided most substantive issues was that the federal government did relatively little. The government in Washington was responsible for delivering the mail, maintaining a military, conducting foreign policy, and collecting tariffs and taxes. It had few other responsibilities and few institutions capable of undertaking additional responsibilities even if it had chosen to do so.

There was one significant exception. From the end of the Civil War to the early twentieth century, the federal government administered a system of annual pensions for retired Union Civil War veterans and their widows. At its peak, this pension system was making payments *First Pension System* to a majority of the male citizens (black and white) of the North and to many women as well. Some reformers hoped to make the system permanent and universal, others found it corrupt and expensive. When the Civil War generation died out, the pension system died with it.

In most other respects, the United States in the late nineteenth century was a society without a modern national government. The most powerful institutions were the two political parties (and the bosses and machines that dominated them) and the federal courts.

PRESIDENTS AND PATRONAGE

Presidents in the late nineteenth century had great symbolic importance, but they were unable to do very much except distribute government appointments. A new president and his tiny staff had to make almost 100,000 appointments.

It sometimes proved impossible for a president to avoid factional conflict, as the presidency of Rutherford B. Hayes demonstrated. By the end of his term, two groups—the Stalwarts, led by Roscoe Conkling of New York, and the Half-Breeds,   *Stalwarts and Half-Breeds* captained by James G. Blaine of Maine—were competing for control of the Republican Party. Rhetorically, the Stalwarts favored traditional, professional machine politics, while the Half-Breeds favored reform. In fact, both groups were mainly interested in a larger share of patronage. Hayes tried to satisfy both and ended up satisfying neither.

The battle over patronage overshadowed all else during Hayes's unhappy presidency. His one important, substantive initiative—an effort to create a civil service system—attracted no support from either party. And his early announcement that he would not seek reelection only weakened him further.

The Republicans managed to retain the presidency in 1880 in part because they agreed on a ticket that included a Stalwart and a Half-Breed. They nominated James A. Garfield, a veteran congressman from Ohio and a Half-Breed, for president and Chester A. Arthur of New York, a Stalwart, for vice president. The Democrats nominated General Winfield Scott Hancock, a minor Civil War commander with no national following. Benefiting from the end of the recession of 1879, Garfield won a decisive electoral victory, although his popular-vote margin was thin.

GETTING HOT ENOUGH FOR HIM.

PRESIDENT CHESTER A. ARTHUR   Although originally a Stalwart, Arthur attempted to reform the spoils system. In this *Puck* cartoon, he is catching heat from a variety of Republican factions, including the Stalwarts and Half-Breeds. (The Library of Congress)

Garfield began his presidency by defying the Stalwarts and supporting civil service reform. He soon found himself embroiled in an ugly public quarrel with Conkling and the Stalwarts. The dispute was never resolved. On July 2, 1881, only four months after *Garfield Assassinated* his inauguration, Garfield was shot twice while standing in the Washington railroad station by an apparently deranged gunman (and unsuccessful office seeker) who shouted, "I am a Stalwart and Arthur is president now!" Garfield lingered for nearly three months but finally died.

Garfield's successor, Chester A. Arthur, had spent his political lifetime as a devoted, skilled, and open spoilsman and a close ally of the New York political boss Roscoe Conkling. But on becoming president, he tried—like Hayes and Garfield before him—to follow an independent course and even to promote reform. To the dismay of the Stalwarts, Arthur kept most of Garfield's appointees in office and supported civil service reform. In *Pendleton Act* 1883, Congress passed the first national civil service measure, the Pendleton Act, which required that some federal jobs be filled by competitive written examinations rather than by patronage. Relatively few offices fell under civil service at first, but its reach steadily widened.

CLEVELAND, HARRISON, AND THE TARIFF

In the unsavory election of 1884, the Republican candidate for president was Senator James G. Blaine of Maine—known to his admirers as the "Plumed Knight" but to many others as a symbol of seamy party politics. A group of disgruntled "liberal Republicans," known by their critics as the "mugwumps," announced that they would bolt the party and support an honest Democrat. Rising to the bait, the Democrats nominated Grover Cleveland, the reform governor of New York.

In a campaign filled with personal invective, what may have decided the election was the last-minute introduction of a religious controversy. Shortly before the election, a delegation of Protestant ministers called on Blaine in New York City; their spokesman, Dr. Samuel Burchard, referred to the Democrats as the party of "rum, Romanism, and rebellion." Blaine was slow to repudiate Burchard's indiscretion, and Democrats quickly *Cleveland Elected* spread the news that Blaine had tolerated a slander on the Catholic Church. Cleveland's narrow victory probably resulted from an unusually heavy Catholic vote for the Democrats in New York.

Grover Cleveland was respected, if not often liked, for his stern and righteous opposition to politicians, grafters, pressure groups, and Tammany Hall. He embodied an era in which few Americans believed the federal government could, or should, do very much. Cleveland had always doubted the wisdom of protective tariffs (taxes on imported goods designed to protect domestic producers). The existing high rates, he believed, were responsible for the annual surplus in federal revenues, which was tempting Congress to pass "reckless" and "extravagant" legislation, which he frequently vetoed. In December 1887, therefore, he asked Congress to reduce the tariff rates. Democrats in the House approved a tariff reduction, but Senate Republicans defiantly passed a bill of their own, actually raising the rates. The resulting deadlock made the tariff an issue in the election of 1888.

The Democrats renominated Cleveland and supported tariff reductions. Endorsing protection, Republicans settled on former senator Benjamin Harrison of Indiana, who was obscure but respectable (and the grandson of President William Henry Harrison). It was *Harrison Elected* one of the most corrupt elections in American history. Cleveland won the popular vote by 100,000, but Harrison won an electoral majority of 233 to 168.

New Public Issues

Benjamin Harrison's record as president was little more substantial than that of his grandfather, who had died a month after taking office. Harrison had few visible convictions, and he made no effort to influence Congress. And yet during Harrison's passive administration, public opinion was beginning to force the government to confront some of the pressing social and economic issues of the day, most notably the power of trusts.

By the mid-1880s, fifteen western and southern states had adopted laws prohibiting combinations that restrained competition. But corporations found it easy to escape limitations by incorporating in states, such as New Jersey and Delaware, that offered them special privileges. If antitrust legislation was to be effective, its supporters believed, it would have to come from the national government. In July 1890, both houses of Congress passed the Sherman Antitrust Act, almost without dissent. For over a   *Sherman Antitrust Act* decade after its passage, the Sherman Act—indifferently enforced and steadily weakened by the courts—had no impact. As of 1901, the Justice Department had instituted many antitrust suits against unions, but only fourteen against business combinations.

The Republicans were more interested in the issue they believed had won them the 1888 election: the tariff. Representative William McKinley of Ohio and Senator Nelson W. Aldrich of Rhode Island drafted the highest protective measure ever proposed to Congress. Known as the McKinley Tariff, it became law in October 1890. But Republican leaders   *McKinley Tariff* apparently misinterpreted public sentiment. Many voters saw the high tariff as a way to enrich producers and starve consumers. The party suffered a stunning reversal in the 1890 congressional election. The Republicans' substantial Senate majority was slashed to 8; in the House, the party retained only 86 of the 332 seats, losing its majority in that chamber. Nor were the Republicans able to recover over the next two years. In the presidential election of 1892, Benjamin Harrison once again supported protection; Grover Cleveland, renominated by the Democrats, once again opposed it. A new third party, the People's Party, with James B. Weaver as its candidate, advocated substantial economic reform. Cleveland won 277 electoral votes to Harrison's 145 and had a popular margin of 380,000. Weaver ran far behind.

The policies of Cleveland's second term were much like those of his first. Again, he supported a tariff reduction, which the House approved but the Senate weakened. Cleveland denounced the result but allowed it to become law as the Wilson-Gorman Tariff.

Public pressure had been growing since the 1880s for other reforms, among them regulation of the railroads. Farm organizations in the Midwest (most notably the Grangers) had persuaded several state legislatures to pass regulatory legislation in the early 1870s. But in 1886, the Supreme Court—in *Wabash, St. Louis, and Pacific Railway Co. v. Illinois,* known as the *Wabash* case—ruled one of the Granger Laws in Illinois unconstitutional. According to the Court, the law was an attempt to control interstate commerce and thus infringed on the exclusive power of Congress. Later, the courts limited the powers of the states to regulate commerce even within their own boundaries.

Effective railroad regulation, it was now clear, could come only from the federal government. Congress responded to public pressure in 1887 with the   *Interstate Commerce Act* Interstate Commerce Act, which banned discrimination in rates between long and short hauls, required that railroads publish their rate schedules and file them with the government, and declared that all interstate rail rates must be "reasonable and just." A five-person agency, the Interstate Commerce Commission (ICC) was to administer the act. But it had to rely on the courts to enforce its rulings. For almost twenty years after its passage, the Interstate Commerce Act—which was, like the Sherman Act, haphazardly enforced and narrowly interpreted by the courts—had little practical effect.

THE AGRARIAN REVOLT

No group watched the performance of the federal government in the 1880s with greater dismay than American farmers. They helped produce the Populist upheaval—one of the most powerful movements of political protest in American history.

THE GRANGERS

Farmers had been making efforts to organize politically for several decades before the 1880s. The first major farm organization was the National Grange of the Patrons of Husbandry, founded in 1867. From it emerged a network of local organizations that tried to teach new scientific agricultural techniques to their members. When the depression of 1873 caused a sharp decline in farm prices, membership rapidly increased and the direction of the organization changed. Granges in the Midwest began to organize marketing cooperatives and to promote political action to curb monopolistic practices by railroads and warehouses. At their peak, Grange supporters controlled the legislatures in most of the midwestern states. The result was the Granger Laws of the early 1870s, by which many states imposed strict regulations on railroad rates and practices. But the destruction of the new regulations by the courts, combined with the political inexperience of many Grange leaders and the return of prosperity in the late 1870s, produced a dramatic decline in the power of the association.

THE FARMERS' ALLIANCES

As early as 1875, farmers in parts of the South were banding together in so-called Farmers' Alliances just as the Granges were weakening. By 1880, the Southern Alliance had more than 4 million members; a comparable Northwestern Alliance was taking root in the plains states and the Midwest, largely replacing the Grange.

Like the Granges, the Alliances formed cooperatives and other marketing mechanisms. They established stores, banks, processing plants, and other facilities to free their members from dependence on the hated "furnishing merchants" who kept so many farmers in debt. Some Alliance leaders, however, saw the movement in larger terms: as an effort to build a society in which economic competition might give way to cooperation. Alliance lecturers traveled throughout rural areas, lambasting the concentrated power of great corporations and financial institutions.

Although the Alliances quickly became far more widespread than the Granges had ever been, they suffered from similar problems. Their cooperatives did not always work well, partly because of mismanagement and partly because of the strength of opposing market forces. These economic frustrations helped push the movement into a new phase at the end of the 1880s: the creation of a national political organization.

In 1889, the Southern and Northwestern Alliances agreed to a loose merger. The next year the Alliances held a national convention at Ocala, Florida, and issued the so-called *Ocala Demands* Ocala Demands, which were, in effect, a party platform. In the 1890 off-year elections, candidates supported by the Alliances won partial or complete control of the legislatures in twelve states. They also won six governorships, three seats in the U.S. Senate, and approximately fifty in the U.S. House of Representatives. Many of the successful Alliance candidates were Democrats who had benefited—often passively—from

MARY E. LEASE The fiery Populist orator Mary E. Lease was a fixture on the Alliance lecture circuit in the 1890s. She made some 160 speeches in 1890 alone. Her critics called her the "Kansas Pythoness," but she was popular among farmers with her denunciations of banks, railroads, and "middlemen," and her famous advice to "raise less corn and more hell." (© Corbis)

Alliance endorsements. But dissident farmers drew enough encouragement from the results to contemplate further political action.

Alliance leaders discussed plans for a third party at meetings in Cincinnati in May 1891 and St. Louis in February 1892. Then, in July 1892, 1,300 exultant delegates poured into Omaha, Nebraska, to proclaim the creation of the new party, approve an official set of principles, and nominate candidates for the presidency and vice   *People's Party Established* presidency. The new organization's official name was the People's Party, but the movement was more commonly referred to as **Populism.**

The election of 1892 demonstrated the potential power of the new movement. The Populist presidential candidate—James B. Weaver of Iowa, a former Greenbacker—polled more than 1 million votes. Nearly 1,500 Populist candidates won election to seats in state legislatures. The party elected three governors, five senators, and ten congressmen. It could also claim the support of many Republicans and Democrats in Congress who had been elected by appealing to Populist sentiment.

THE POPULIST CONSTITUENCY

Already, however, there were signs of the limits of Populist strength. Populism had great appeal to farmers, particularly to small farmers with little long-range economic security. But Populism failed to move much beyond that group. Its leaders made energetic efforts to include labor within the coalition by courting the Knights of Labor and adding a labor plank to its platform. But Populism never attracted significant labor support, in part because the economic interests of labor and the interests of farmers were often at odds.

In the South, white Populists struggled with the question of whether to accept African Americans into the party. There was an important black component to the movement—a network of "Colored Alliances" that by 1890 numbered over 1.25 million members. But most white Populists accepted the assistance of African Americans only as long as it was clear that whites would remain indisputably in control. When southern conservatives began to attack the Populists for undermining white supremacy, the interracial character of the movement quickly faded.

POPULIST IDEAS

The Populists spelled out their program first in the Ocala Demands of 1890 and then, more clearly, in the Omaha platform of 1892. They proposed a system of "subtreasuries," a network of government-owned warehouses where farmers could deposit their crops, to allow them to borrow money from the government at low rates of interest until the price *The Populists' Reform Program* of their goods went up. In addition, the Populists called for the abolition of national banks (which they believed were dangerous institutions of concentrated power), the end of absentee ownership of land, the direct election of United States senators (which would weaken the power of conservative state legislatures), and other devices to improve the ability of the people to influence the political process. They called as well for regulation and (after 1892) government ownership of railroads, telephones, and telegraphs. And they demanded a system of government-operated postal savings banks, a graduated income tax, the inflation of the currency, and, later, the remonetization of silver.

Some Populists were anti-Semitic, anti-intellectual, anti-eastern, and antiurban. But bigotry was not the dominant force behind Populism. It was, rather, a serious and usually responsible effort to find solutions to real problems. Populists emphatically rejected the laissez-faire orthodoxies of their time, including the idea that the rights of ownership are absolute, and in fact called on the federal government to promote a dramatic redistribution of wealth and power. In short, the Populists raised one of the most overt and powerful challenges of the era to the direction in which American industrial capitalism was moving.

THE CRISIS OF THE 1890s

The agrarian protest was only one of many indications of the national political crisis emerging in the 1890s. There was a severe depression, widespread labor unrest and violence, and the continuing failure of either major party to respond to the growing distress. Grover Cleveland, who took office for the second time just as the economy was collapsing, remained convinced that any government action would be a violation of principle.

The Panic of 1893

The Panic of 1893 launched the most severe depression the nation had ever experienced. It began in March 1893, when the Philadelphia and Reading Railroad, unable to meet payments on loans, declared bankruptcy. Two months later, the National Cordage Company failed as well. Together, these two corporate failures triggered a stock market collapse. And since many of the major New York banks were heavy investors in the market, a wave of bank failures soon began. That caused a contraction of credit, which meant that many of the new, aggressive, and loan-dependent businesses soon went bankrupt.

The depression reflected, among other things, the degree to which all parts of the American economy were now interconnected. And it showed how dependent the economy was on the health of the railroads, which remained the nation's most powerful corporate and financial institutions. When the railroads suffered, as they did beginning in 1893, everyone suffered.

Once the panic began, it spread with startling speed. Within six months, more than 8,000 businesses, 156 railroads, and 400 banks failed. Already low agricultural prices tumbled further. Up to 1 million workers, 20 percent of the labor force, lost their jobs. The depression was unprecedented not only in its severity but also in its persistence. Although conditions improved slightly beginning in 1895, prosperity did not fully return until 1901.

The depression produced widespread social unrest, especially among the enormous numbers of unemployed workers. In 1894, Jacob S. Coxey, an Ohio businessman and Populist, began advocating a massive public works program to create jobs for the unemployed.

COXEY'S ARMY Jacob S. Coxey leads his "army" of unemployed men through the town of Allegheny, Pennsylvania, in 1894, en route to Washington, where he hoped to pressure Congress to approve his plans for a massive public works program to put people back to work. (© Photo by Fotosearch/Getty Images)

When it became clear that Congress was ignoring his proposals, Coxey organized a march *"Coxey's Army"* of the unemployed (known as "Coxey's Army") to Washington, D.C., to present his demands to the government. Congress continued to ignore them.

To many middle-class Americans, the labor turmoil of the time—the Homestead and Pullman strikes, for example (see Chapter 17)—was a sign of a dangerous instability, even perhaps a revolution. Labor radicalism—some of it real, more of it imagined by the frightened middle class—heightened the general sense of crisis among the public.

THE SILVER QUESTION

The financial panic weakened the government's monetary system. President Cleveland believed that the instability of the currency was the primary cause of the depression. The "money question," therefore, became one of the burning issues of the era.

The debate centered on what would form the basis of the dollar, what would lie behind it and give it value. Today, the value of the dollar rests on little more than public confidence in the government. But in the nineteenth century, many people believed that currency was worthless if there was not something concrete behind it—precious metal (specie), which holders of paper money could collect if they presented their currency to a bank or to the Treasury.

During most of its existence as a nation, the United States had recognized two metals— gold and silver—as a basis for the dollar, a system known as "bimetallism." In the 1870s, however, that had changed. The official ratio of the value of silver to the value of gold for purposes of creating currency (the "mint ratio") was 16 to 1: sixteen ounces of silver equaled one ounce of gold. But the actual commercial value of silver (the "market ratio") was much higher than that. Owners of silver could get more by selling it for manufacture into jewelry and other objects than they could by taking it to the mint for conversion into coins. So they stopped taking it to the mint, and the mint stopped coining silver.

In 1873, Congress passed a law that seemed simply to recognize the existing situation by officially discontinuing silver coinage. Few objected at the time. But later in the 1870s, the market value of silver fell well below the official mint ratio of 16 to 1. Silver was suddenly available for coinage again, and it soon became clear that Congress had foreclosed a potential method of expanding the currency. Before long, many Americans concluded that a conspiracy of big bankers had been responsible for the "demonetization" of silver and referred to the law as the "Crime of '73."

Two groups of Americans were especially determined to undo the Crime of '73. One consisted of the silver-mine owners, now understandably eager to have the government take their surplus silver and pay them much more than the market price. The other group consisted of discontented farmers, who wanted an increase in the quantity of money—an inflation of the currency—as a means of raising the prices of farm products and easing payment of the farmers' debts. The inflationists demanded that the government return at once to the "free and *"Free Silver" Advocates* unlimited coinage of silver" at the old ratio of 16 to 1. Congress responded weakly to these demands with the Sherman Silver Purchase Act of 1890, which required the government to purchase silver and pay for it in gold. But the government allowed only existing silver coinage. It did not allow any newly minted silver money.

At the same time, the nation's gold reserves were steadily dropping. President Cleveland believed that the chief cause of the weakening gold reserves was the Sherman Silver Purchase Act. Early in his second administration, therefore, Congress responded to his request and repealed the Sherman Act—although only after a bitter and divisive battle that helped create a split in the Democratic Party.

"A CROSS OF GOLD"

Republicans, watching the failure of the Democrats to deal effectively with the depression, were confident of success in 1896. Party leaders, led by the Ohio boss Marcus A. Hanna, settled on former congressman William McKinley, author of the 1890   *McKinley Nominated* tariff act and now governor of Ohio, as the party's presidential candidate. The tariff, they believed, should be the key issue in the campaign. But they also opposed the free coinage of silver, except by agreement with the leading commercial nations (which everyone realized was unlikely). Thirty-four delegates from the mountain and plains states walked out of the convention in protest and joined the Democratic Party.

BEARING THE CROSS OF GOLD   The cartoonist Grant Hamilton created this image of William Jennings Bryan shortly after he made his famous "Cross of Gold" speech at the Democratic National Convention, which subsequently nominated him for president. The cartoon highlights two of the most powerful images in Bryan's speech—a "crown of thorns" and a "cross of gold," both biblical references and both designed to represent the oppression that the gold standard imposed on working people. (© Granger, NYC—All Rights Reserved.)

The Democratic Convention of 1896 was unusually tumultuous. Southern and western delegates, eager for a way to compete with the Populists, were determined to seize control of the party from conservative easterners, incorporate some Populist demands—among them free silver—into the Democratic platform, and nominate a pro-silver candidate.

Defenders of the gold standard seemed to dominate the debate, until William Jennings Bryan, a handsome, thirty-six-year-old congressman from Nebraska, mounted the podium to address the convention. His great voice echoed through the hall as he delivered what became one of the *Bryan's "Cross of Gold" Speech* most famous political speeches in American history. The closing passage sent his audience into something close to a frenzy: "Having behind us the producing masses of this nation and the world, supported by the commercial interests, the laboring interests and the toilers everywhere, we will answer their demand for a gold standard by saying to them: 'You shall not press down upon the brow of labor this crown of thorns; you shall not crucify mankind upon a cross of gold.'" It became known as the "Cross of Gold" speech.

In the glow of Bryan's speech, the convention voted to adopt a pro-silver platform. And the following day, Bryan (as he had eagerly and not entirely secretly hoped) was nominated for president on the fifth ballot.

The choice of Bryan and the Democratic platform created a quandary for the Populists. They had expected both major parties to adopt conservative programs and nominate conservative candidates, leaving the Populists to represent the growing forces of protest. But now the Democrats had stolen much of their thunder. The Populists faced the choice of naming their own candidate and splitting the protest vote or endorsing Bryan and losing their identity as a party. Many Populists argued that "fusion" with the Democrats would destroy their party. But the majority concluded that there was no viable alternative. Amid considerable acrimony, the convention voted to nominate Bryan as the Populist candidate.

THE CONSERVATIVE VICTORY

The campaign of 1896 produced panic among conservatives. The business and financial community, frightened beyond reason at the prospect of a Bryan victory, contributed lavishly to the Republican campaign. From his home in Canton, Ohio, McKinley conducted a traditional "front-porch" campaign by receiving pilgrimages of the Republican faithful, organized and paid for by Hanna.

Bryan showed no such restraint. He became the first presidential candidate in American history to stump every section of the country systematically. He traveled 18,000 miles and addressed an estimated 5 million people.

On election day, McKinley polled 271 electoral votes to Bryan's 176 and received 51.1 percent of the popular vote to Bryan's 47.7. Bryan carried the areas of the South and West where miners or struggling staple farmers predominated. The Democratic program, like that of the Populists, had been too narrow to win a national election.

For the Populists and their allies, the election results were a disaster. They had gambled *End of the People's Party* everything on their fusion with the Democratic Party and lost. Within months of the election, the People's Party began to dissolve.

McKINLEY AND RECOVERY

The administration of William McKinley saw a return to relative calm. One reason was the exhaustion of dissent. Another reason was the shrewd character of the McKinley administration itself, committed as it was to reassuring stability. Most important, however, was the gradual easing of the economic crisis, a development that undercut many of those who were agitating for change.

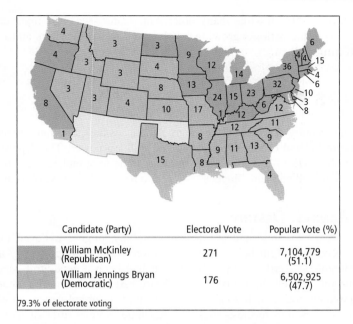

Candidate (Party)	Electoral Vote	Popular Vote (%)
William McKinley (Republican)	271	7,104,779 (51.1)
William Jennings Bryan (Democratic)	176	6,502,925 (47.7)

79.3% of electorate voting

THE ELECTION OF 1896 The results of the presidential election of 1896 are, as this map shows, striking for the regional differentiation they reveal. William McKinley won the election by a comfortable if not enormous margin, but his victory was not broad-based. He carried all the states of the Northeast and the industrial Midwest, along with California and Oregon, but virtually nothing else. Bryan carried the entire South and almost all of the agrarian West. • *What campaign issues in 1896 helped account for the regional character of the results?*

McKinley and his allies committed themselves fully to only one issue: the need for higher tariff rates. Within weeks of his inauguration, the administration won approval of the Dingley Tariff, raising duties to the highest point in American history. The administration dealt more gingerly with the explosive silver question (an issue that McKinley himself had never considered very important). He sent a commission to Europe to explore the possibility of a silver agreement with Great Britain and France. As he and everyone else anticipated, the effort produced nothing. The Republicans then enacted the Currency, or *Gold Standard Act* Gold Standard, Act of 1900, which confirmed the nation's commitment to the gold standard.

And so the "battle of the standards" ended in victory for the forces of conservatism. Economic developments at the time seemed to vindicate the Republicans. Prosperity began to return in 1898. Foreign crop failures drove farm prices upward, and American business entered another cycle of expansion. Prosperity and the gold standard, it seemed, were closely allied.

But while the free-silver movement had failed, it had raised an important question for the American economy. In the quarter century before 1900, the countries of the Western world had experienced a spectacular growth in productive facilities and population. Yet the supply of money had not kept pace with economic progress. Had it not been for a dramatic increase in the gold supply in the late 1890s (a result of new techniques for extracting gold from low-content ores and the discovery of huge new gold deposits in Alaska, South Africa, and Australia), Populist predictions of financial disaster might in fact have proved correct. In 1898, two and a half times as much gold was produced as in 1890, and the currency supply was soon inflated far beyond anything Bryan and the free-silver forces had anticipated.

By then, however, Bryan—like many other Americans—was becoming engaged with another major issue: the nation's growing involvement in world affairs and its increasing flirtation with **imperialism.**

STIRRINGS OF IMPERIALISM

As the nineteenth century drew to a close, many Americans hoped to translate the era's great industrial feats into global economic, political, and military power. The depression of 1893 further pushed observers to call for greater overseas trade to stimulate the economy. These expansionists—some called them "**jingoes**"—hoped to resume the course of Manifest Destiny.

THE NEW MANIFEST DESTINY

In addition to their economic and political motivations, jingoes believed that domestic tensions in the country might be resolved by a more robust foreign policy and stronger American nationalistic spirit—or even by war. It had been a generation since the Civil War, and some jingoes felt the nation's masculinity had withered in the meantime. Mass industrial wage labor, the same line of reasoning went, had turned American workers from independent producers into faceless cogs in a machine. Some critics of woman suffrage thought it threatened to feminize and weaken the traditional male preserve of politics. Waves of immigration and wars of labor had divided the country. A more stout assertion of power abroad, jingoes hoped, might restore American vitality and unity.

Expansionists were also driven by competitive impulses. Americans were well aware of the imperialist fever that was raging through Europe, leading the major powers to partition much of Africa among themselves and to turn eager eyes on the Far East and the Chinese Empire. (See "America in the World: Imperialism.") Some Americans feared that their nation would soon be left out of all these potential markets. Scholars and others found a philosophic justification for expansionism in Charles Darwin's theories. They contended that nations or "races," like biological species, struggled constantly for existence and that only the fittest could survive. For strong nations to dominate weak ones was, therefore, in accordance with the laws of nature.

The most effective apostle of imperialism was Alfred Thayer Mahan, a captain and, later, admiral in the United States Navy. Mahan's thesis, presented in *The Influence of* *Sea Power and Colonies* *Sea Power upon History* (1890) and other works, was simple: countries with sea power were the great nations of history. Effective sea power required, among other things, colonies. Mahan believed that the United States should, at the least, acquire defensive bases in the Caribbean and the Pacific and take possession of Hawaii and other Pacific islands. He feared that the United States did not have a large enough navy to play the great role he envisioned. But during the 1870s and 1880s, the government launched a shipbuilding program that by 1898 had moved the United States to fifth place among the world's naval powers, and by 1900 to third place.

HAWAII AND SAMOA

The islands of Hawaii in the mid-Pacific had been an important way station for American ships in the China trade since the early nineteenth century. By the 1880s, officers of the expanding United States Navy were looking covetously at Pearl Harbor on the island of

Oahu as a possible permanent base for U.S. ships. The growing number of Americans who had taken up residence on the islands also pressed for an increased American presence in Hawaii.

Settled by Polynesian people beginning in about 1500 B.C., Hawaii had developed an agricultural and fishing society in which different islands (and different communities on the same islands), each with its own chieftain, lived more or less self-sufficiently. When the first Americans arrived in Hawaii in the 1790s on merchant ships from New England, there were perhaps half a million people living there. Battles among rival communities were frequent, as ambitious chieftains tried to consolidate power over their neighbors. *First Sugar Plantation* In 1810, after a series of such battles, King Kamehameha I established his dominance, welcomed American traders, and helped them develop a thriving trade between Hawaii and China. But Americans soon wanted more than trade. Missionaries began settling there in the early nineteenth century; and in the 1830s, William Hooper, a Boston trader, became the first of many Americans to buy land and establish a sugar plantation on the islands.

The arrival of these merchants, missionaries, and planters was devastating to traditional Hawaiian society. The newcomers inadvertently brought infectious diseases to which the Hawaiians, like the American Indians before them, were tragically vulnerable. By the mid-nineteenth century, more than half the native population had died. The Americans brought other incursions as well. Missionaries worked to replace native religion with Christianity. Other white settlers introduced liquor, firearms, and a commercial economy, all of which eroded the traditional character of Hawaiian society. By the 1840s, American planters had spread throughout the islands; and an American settler, G. P. Judd, had become prime minister of Hawaii under King Kamehameha III, who had agreed to establish a constitutional monarchy. Judd governed Hawaii for over a decade.

In 1887, the United States negotiated a treaty with Hawaii that permitted it to open a naval base at Pearl Harbor. By then, growing sugar for export to America had become the basis of the Hawaiian economy—as a result of an 1875 agreement allowing Hawaiian sugar to enter the United States duty-free. The American-dominated sugar plantation system displaced native Hawaiians from their lands and relied heavily on Asian immigrants, whom the Americans considered more reliable and more docile than the natives.

Native Hawaiians did not accept their subordination without protest. In 1891, they elevated a powerful nationalist to the throne: Queen Liliuokalani, who *Queen Liliuokalani* set out to challenge the growing American control of the islands. But she remained in power only two years. In 1890, the United States had eliminated the exemption from American tariffs in Hawaiian sugar trade. The result was devastating to the economy of the islands, and American planters concluded that the only way for them to recover was to become part of the United States (and, hence, exempt from its tariffs). In 1893, they staged a revolution and called on the United States for protection. After the American minister ordered marines from a warship in Honolulu harbor to go ashore to aid the American rebels, the queen yielded her authority.

A provisional government, dominated by Americans, immediately sent a delegation to Washington to negotiate a treaty of annexation. Debate over the treaty *Hawaii Annexed* continued until 1898, when Congress finally approved the agreement.

Three thousand miles south of Hawaii, the Samoan islands had also long served as a way station for American ships in the Pacific trade. As American commerce with Asia increased, business groups in the United States regarded Samoa with new interest, and the American navy began eyeing the Samoan harbor at Pago Pago. In 1878, the Hayes administration extracted a treaty from Samoan leaders for an American naval station at Pago Pago.

IMPERIALISM

Empires were not, of course, new to the nineteenth century, when the United States acquired its first overseas colonies. They had existed since the early moments of recorded history, and they have continued into our own time.

But in the second half of the nineteenth century, the construction of empires took on a new form, and the word *imperialism* emerged for the first time to describe it. In many places, European powers now created colonies not by sending large numbers of migrants to settle and populate new lands, but instead by creating military, political, and business structures that allowed them to dominate and profit from the existing populations. This new imperialism changed the character of the colonizing nations, enriching them greatly and producing new classes of people whose lives were shaped by the demands of imperial business and administration. It changed the character of colonized societies even more, drawing them into the vast nexus of global industrial capitalism and introducing Western customs, institutions, and technologies to the subject peoples.

As the popularity of empire grew in the West, efforts to justify it grew as well. Champions of imperialism argued that the acquisition of colonies was essential for the health, even the survival, of their own industrializing nations. Colonies were sources of raw materials vital to industrial production; they were markets for manufactured goods; and they were suppliers of cheap labor. Defenders of empire also argued that imperialism was good for the colonized people. Many saw colonization as an opportunity to export Christianity to "heathen" lands, and new missionary movements emerged in Europe and America in response. More secular apologists argued that imperialism

helped bring colonized people into the modern world.

The invention of steamships, railroads, telegraphs, and other modern vehicles of transportation and communication; the construction of canals (particularly the Suez Canal, completed in 1869, and the Panama Canal, completed in 1914); the creation of new military technologies (repeating rifles, machine guns, and modern artillery)—all contributed to the ability of Western nations to reach, conquer, and control distant lands.

The greatest imperial power of the nineteenth century was Great Britain. By 1800, despite its recent loss of the colonies that became the United States, it already possessed vast territory in North America, the Caribbean, and the Pacific. In the second half of the nineteenth century, Britain greatly expanded its empire. Its most important acquisition was India, one of the largest and most populous countries in the world and a nation in which Great Britain had long exerted informal authority. In 1857, when native Indians revolted against British influence, British forces brutally crushed the rebellion and established formal colonial control over India. British officials, backed by substantial military power, now governed India through a large civil service staffed mostly by people from England and Scotland but with some Indians serving in minor positions. The British invested heavily in railroads, telegraphs, canals, harbors, and agricultural improvements, to enhance the economic opportunities available to them. They created schools for Indian children in an effort to draw them into British culture and make them supporters of the imperial system.

The British also extended their empire into Africa and other parts of Asia. The great imperial champion Cecil Rhodes expanded a small existing British colony at

THE BRITISH RAJ The Drum Corps of the Royal Fusiliers in India poses here for a formal portrait, taken in 1877. Although the drummers are British, an Indian associate is included at top left. This blending of the dominant British with subordinate Indians was characteristic of the administration of the British Empire in India—a government known as the "raj," from the Indian word for "rule." (© Photo by Time Life Pictures/Mansell/Getty Images)

Capetown into a substantial colony that included much of what is now South Africa. In 1895, he added new British territories to the north, which he named Rhodesia (and which today are Zimbabwe and Zambia). Others spread British authority into Kenya, Uganda, Nigeria, and much of Egypt. British imperialists also extended the empire into East Asia, with the acquisition of Singapore, Hong Kong, Burma, and Malaya; and they built a substantial presence—although not formal colonial rule—in China.

Other European states, watching the vast expansion of the British Empire, quickly jumped into the race for colonies. France created colonies in Indochina (Vietnam and Laos), Algeria, west Africa, and Madagascar. Belgium moved into the Congo in west Africa. Germany established colonies in the Cameroons, Tanganyika, and other parts of Africa, and in the Pacific islands north of Australia. Dutch, Italian, Portuguese, Spanish, Russian, and Japanese imperialists created colonies as well in Africa, Asia, and the Pacific—driven both by a calculation of

their own commercial interests and by the frenzied competition that had developed among rival imperial powers. In 1898, the United States was drawn into the imperial race, in part inadvertently as an unanticipated result of the Spanish-American War. But the drive to acquire colonies resulted as well from the deliberate efforts of home-grown proponents of empire (among them Theodore Roosevelt), who believed that in the modern industrial-imperial world, a nation without colonies would have difficulty remaining, or becoming, a true great power. •

UNDERSTAND, ANALYZE, & EVALUATE

1. What motivated the European nations' drive for empire in the late nineteenth century?

2. Why was Great Britain so successful in acquiring its vast empire?

3. How do the imperial efforts and ambitions of the United States at the end of the nineteenth century compare with those of European powers?

Great Britain and Germany were also interested in the islands, and they, too, secured treaty rights from the native princes. For the next ten years, the three powers jockeyed for *Samoa Divided*   dominance in Samoa, finally agreeing to create a tripartite protectorate over Samoa, with the native chiefs exercising only nominal authority. The three-way arrangement failed to halt the rivalries of its members, and in 1899, the United States and Germany divided the islands between them, compensating Britain with territories elsewhere in the Pacific. The United States retained the harbor at Pago Pago.

WAR WITH SPAIN

Imperial ambitions had thus begun to stir within the United States well before the late 1890s. But a war with Spain in 1898 turned those stirrings into overt expansionism.

CONTROVERSY OVER CUBA

Spain's once-formidable empire had grown rickety, but still included two prized island possessions: Cuba, ninety miles off the shores of Florida, and the Philippines, in Asia. As in many imperial holdings, the native peoples in these regions objected to the presence of European colonizers and occasionally waged insurrections. One rebellion in Cuba had ended in 1878 with Spanish rule intact. Nominal Cuban control over the economy followed, but the depression of the 1890s led Spain to withdraw even that privilege. In 1895 *Cuban Revolt*   Cuban revolutionaries mounted a new insurrection, led by the revolutionary poet José Martí and military heroes of the earlier wars of liberation.

The rebellion soon attracted the sympathies of people in the United States. Popular newspapers reported horrific atrocities committed by the Spanish against Cuban rebels and civilians. The Spanish governor since 1896, General Valeriano Weyler, was rounding up Cubans in detention camps to isolate rebels in the countryside, and then destroying agriculture to starve them out. These policies of "the Butcher" led to the deaths of tens of thousands of Cuban civilians. The conflict also imperiled the American-owned sugar plantations in Cuba and regional commerce more broadly. And ever since the articulation of the Monroe Doctrine in 1823, Americans had dreamed of ridding North and South America of European colonizers. Some hoped to replace the Spanish with a heavy American presence in the region, while others, including William Jennings Bryan and other prominent Democrats and members of Congress, wished only to liberate Cuba and leave it to the Cubans.

The conflict in Cuba came at a particularly opportune moment for the publishers of some American newspapers: Joseph Pulitzer with his *New York World* and William Randolph Hearst with his *New York Journal*. In the 1890s, Hearst and Pulitzer were engaged in a ruthless circulation war, and they both sent batteries of reporters and illustrators to Cuba with orders to provide accounts of Spanish atrocities. This sort of sensationalist reporting was known as **yellow journalism**. (See "Patterns of Popular Culture: Yellow Journalism.")

Although President Cleveland worried about the potential disruptions of American trade, he did not intervene. Nor, at first, did his successor, William McKinley. Both men shared the commercial and humanitarian concerns, but sought to avoid war with a European power. An irritated Theodore Roosevelt, the assistant secretary of the navy, excoriated President McKinley for his un-masculine weakness, charging that he had "no more backbone than a chocolate éclair."

The situation changed in early 1898. In January pro-Spanish Cubans rioted in Havana against the idea of a free Cuba, or *Cuba libre*, which the two American political parties had at least rhetorically supported even as successive U.S. administrations remained neutral. Thus the riots carried anti-American undertones, and President McKinley, under pressure from the popular media after unfulfilled promises from Spain, sent the U.S.S. *Maine* to Havana harbor to protect American citizens. On February 15, 1898, *The* Maine the ship exploded, killing 266 Americans. Although later investigations revealed it likely an accident, most Americans, egged on by the jingoistic press, blamed the Spanish.

For all the earlier arguments about humanity, commerce, and geopolitical strategy, the destruction of the *Maine* challenged American honor. A Democrat in the House voted for war "to defend the honor and maintain the dignity of this republic"; a Republican sought "peace with honor." On April 25, Congress passed a resolution calling for war against the Spanish. It included the Teller Amendment, named for Democratic senator *Teller Amendment* Henry T. Teller from Colorado, which swore off any intentions to occupy, possess, or control Cuba after a future victory against the Spanish.

"A Splendid Little War"

The American ambassador to England, John Hay, called the ensuing Spanish-American conflict "a splendid little war," an opinion that most Americans—with the exception of many of the enlisted men who fought in it—seemed to share. Declared in April, it was over in August, in part because Cuban rebels had already greatly weakened the Spanish resistance, making the American intervention in many respects little more than a "mopping-up" exercise. Only 460 Americans were killed in battle or died of wounds, although some 5,200 others perished of disease: malaria, dysentery, and typhoid, among others. Casualties among Cuban insurgents, who continued to bear the brunt of the fighting, were much higher.

The American war effort was not without difficulties. United States soldiers faced serious supply problems: a shortage of modern rifles and ammunition, uniforms too heavy for the warm Caribbean weather, inadequate medical services, and skimpy, almost indigestible food. The regular army numbered only 28,000 troops and officers, most of whom had experience in quelling Indian outbreaks but none in larger-scale warfare. That meant that, as in the Civil War, the United States had to rely heavily on National Guard units, organized by local communities and commanded for the most part by local leaders without military experience.

A significant proportion of the American invasion force consisted of black soldiers. Some were volunteer troops put together by African American communities. Others were members of the four black regiments in the regular army, who had been stationed on the frontier to defend white settlements against Indians and were now transferred east to fight in Cuba. As the black soldiers traveled through the South toward the training camps, some resisted the rigid segregation to which they were subjected. African American soldiers in Georgia deliberately made use of a "whites only" park; in Florida, they beat a soda-fountain operator for refusing to *Racial Tensions in the Military* serve them; in Tampa, white provocations and black retaliation led to a nightlong riot that left thirty wounded.

Racial tensions continued in Cuba. African Americans played crucial roles in some of the important battles of the war (including the famous charge at San Juan Hill) and won many medals. Nearly half the Cuban insurgents fighting with the Americans were themselves black,

YELLOW JOURNALISM

Joseph Pulitzer was a successful newspaper publisher in St. Louis, Missouri, when he traveled to New York City in 1883 to buy a struggling paper, the *New York World*. "There is room in this great and growing city," he wrote in one of his first editorials, "for a journal that is not only cheap, but bright, not only bright but large, not only large but truly democratic . . . that will serve and battle for the people with earnest sincerity." Within a year, the *World*'s daily circulation had soared from 10,000 to over 60,000. By 1886, it had reached 250,000 and was making enormous profits.

The success of Pulitzer's *World* marked the birth of what came to be known as "yellow journalism," a phrase that reportedly derived from a character in one of the *World*'s comic strips: "the Yellow Kid." Color printing in newspapers was relatively new, and yellow was the most difficult color to print; so in the beginning, the term *yellow journalism* was a comment on the new technological possibilities that Pulitzer was so eagerly embracing. Eventually, however, it came to refer to a sensationalist style of reporting and writing that spread quickly through urban America and changed the character of newspapers forever.

Sensationalism was not new to journalism in the late nineteenth century, of course. Political scandal sheets had been publishing lurid stories since before the American Revolution. But the yellow journalism of the 1880s and 1890s took the search for a mass audience to new levels. The *World* created one of the first Sunday editions, with lavishly colored special sections, comics, and illustrated features. It expanded coverage of sports, fashion,

literature, and theater. It pioneered large, glaring, overheated headlines that captured the eyes of people who were passing newsstands. It published exposés of political corruption. It made considerable efforts to bring drama and energy to its coverage of crime. It tried to involve readers directly in its stories (as when a *World* campaign helped raise $300,000 to build a base for the Statue of Liberty, with much of the money coming in donations of five or ten cents from working-class readers). And it introduced a self-consciously populist style of writing that appealed to working-class readers. "The American people want something terse, forcible, picturesque, striking," Pulitzer said. His reporters wrote short, forceful sentences. They did not shy away from expressing sympathy or outrage. And they were not always constrained by the truth.

Pulitzer very quickly produced imitators, the most important of them the California publisher William Randolph Hearst, who in 1895 bought the *New York Journal,* cut its price to one cent (Pulitzer quickly followed suit), copied many of the *World*'s techniques, and within a year raised its circulation to 400,000. Hearst soon made the *Journal* the largest-circulation paper in the country— selling more than a million copies a day. Pulitzer, whose own circulation was not far behind, accused him of "pandering to the worst tastes of the prurient and the horror-loving" and "dealing in bogus news." But the *World* wasted no time before imitating the *Journal*. The competition between these two great "yellow" journals soon drove both to new levels of sensationalism. Their success drove newspapers in other cities around the nation to copy their techniques.

The civil war in Cuba in the 1890s gave both papers their best opportunities yet for combining sensational reporting with shameless appeals to patriotism and moral outrage. They avidly published exaggerated reports of Spanish atrocities toward the Cuban rebels, fanning popular anger toward Spain. When the American battleship *Maine* mysteriously exploded in Havana harbor in 1898, both papers (without any evidence) immediately blamed Spanish authorities. The *Journal* offered a $50,000 reward for information leading to the conviction of those responsible for the explosion, and it crowded all other stories off its front page ("There is no other news," Hearst told his editors) to make room for such screaming headlines as THE WHOLE COUNTRY THRILLS WITH WAR FEVER and HAVANA POPULACE INSULTS THE MEMORY OF THE *MAINE* VICTIMS. In the three days following the *Maine* explosion, the *Journal* sold more than 3 million copies, a new world's record for newspaper circulation.

In the aftermath of the *Maine* episode, the more conservative press launched a spirited attack on yellow journalism. That was partly in response to Hearst's boast that the conflict in Cuba was "the *Journal*'s war." He sent a cable to one of his reporters in Cuba saying: "You furnish the pictures, and I'll furnish the war." Growing numbers of critics tried to discourage yellow journalism, which "respectable" editors both deplored and feared. Some schools, libraries, and clubs began to banish the papers from their premises. But the techniques the "yellow" press pioneered in the 1890s helped map the way for a tradition of colorful, popular journalism—later embodied in "tabloids," some elements of which eventually found their way into television news—that has endured into the present day. •

UNDERSTAND, ANALYZE, & EVALUATE

1. Did Pulitzer's *World,* Hearst's *Journal,* and their imitators report the news or manufacture it?
2. How did the "yellow" press influence the public's perception of the Spanish-American War?
3. How does television news continue the tradition of "yellow" journalism? In what other mass media do you see the style and techniques pioneered by the "yellow" press?

AFRICAN AMERICAN CAVALRY Substantial numbers of African Americans fought in the United States Army during the Spanish-American War. Although confined to all-black units, they engaged in combat alongside white units and fought bravely and effectively. This photograph shows a troop of African American cavalry in formation in Cuba. It is meant to be viewed through a stereoscope, which would create a single three-dimensional image. (© Corbis)

including one of the leading insurgent generals, Antonio Maceo. The sight of black Cuban soldiers fighting alongside whites as equals gave African Americans a stronger sense of the injustice of their own position.

SEIZING THE PHILIPPINES

By an accident of history, the assistant secretary of the navy during the Cuban revolution was Theodore Roosevelt, an ardent Anglophile eager to see the United States join the British and other nations as imperial powers. Roosevelt was, in fact, a relatively minor figure in the Navy Department, but he was determined to expand his power. British friends had persuaded him that the war in Cuba gave the United States a rare opportunity to expand the American empire. Roosevelt responded by sending the Navy's Pacific fleet to the Philippines, with orders to attack as soon as America declared war. On May 1, 1898, Commodore George Dewey led the fleet into Manila harbor, quickly destroyed the aging Spanish fleet, and forced the Spanish government to surrender Manila with hardly a shot fired. He became the first American hero of the war.

THE BATTLE FOR CUBA

Cuba remained the principal focus of American military efforts. At first, the American commanders planned a long period of training before actually sending troops into combat. But when a Spanish fleet under Admiral Pascual Cervera slipped past the American navy into Santiago harbor on the southern coast of Cuba, plans changed quickly. The American Atlantic fleet quickly bottled Cervera up in the harbor. And the U.S. Army's commanding general, Nelson A. Miles, hastily altered his strategy and left Tampa in June with a force of 17,000 to attack Santiago.

General William R. Shafter, the American commander, moved toward Santiago, which he planned to surround and capture. On the way he met and defeated Spanish forces at Las Guasimos and, a week later, in two simultaneous battles, El Caney and San Juan Hill. At the center of the fighting (and on the front pages of the newspapers) during many of *The Rough Riders* these engagements was a cavalry unit known as the Rough Riders. Nominally commanded by General Leonard Wood, its real leader was Colonel Theodore Roosevelt, who had resigned from the Navy Department to get into the war and who had struggled with an almost desperate fury to get his regiment into the fighting. His passion to join the war undoubtedly reflected the decision of his beloved father, Theodore Roosevelt Sr., not to fight in the Civil War, a source of private shame within the family that his son sought to erase.

Roosevelt rapidly emerged as a hero of the conflict. His fame rested in large part on his role in leading a bold, if perhaps reckless, charge up Kettle Hill (a minor part of the larger battle for the adjacent San Juan Hill) directly into the face of Spanish guns. Roosevelt himself emerged unscathed, but nearly a hundred of his soldiers were killed or wounded. He remembered the battle as "the great day of my life."

Although Shafter was now in position to assault Santiago, his army was so weakened by sickness that he feared he might have to abandon his position. But unknown to the Americans, the Spanish government had by now decided that Santiago was lost and had ordered Cervera to evacuate. On July 3, Cervera tried to escape the harbor. The waiting American squadron destroyed his entire fleet. On July 16, the commander of Spanish ground forces in Santiago surrendered. At about the same time, an American army landed

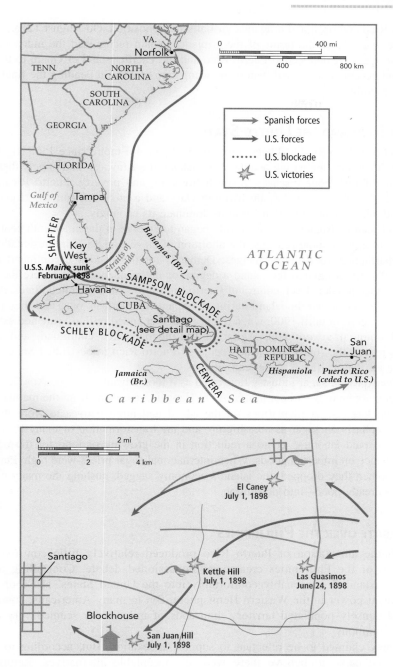

THE SPANISH-AMERICAN WAR IN CUBA, 1898 The military conflict between the United States and Spain in Cuba was a brief affair. The Cuban rebels and an American naval blockade had already brought the Spanish to the brink of defeat. The arrival of American troops was simply the final blow. In the space of about a week, U.S. troops won four decisive battles in the area around Santiago in southeast Cuba—one of them (the Battle of Kettle Hill) the scene of Theodore Roosevelt's famous charge up the adjacent San Juan Hill. This map shows the extent of the American naval blockade, the path of American troops from Florida to Cuba, and the location of the actual fighting. • *What were the implications of the war in Cuba for Puerto Rico?*

in Puerto Rico and occupied it against virtually no opposition. On August 12, an armistice ended the war. Under the terms of the armistice, Spain recognized the independence of *Puerto Rico Occupied*   Cuba, ceded Puerto Rico and the Pacific island of Guam to the United States, and accepted continued American occupation of Manila pending the final disposition of the Philippines.

Puerto Rico and the United States

The island of Puerto Rico had been a part of the Spanish Empire since 1508. By the early seventeenth century, the native people of the island, the Arawaks, had largely disappeared as a result of infectious diseases, Spanish brutality, and poverty. Puerto Rican society developed, therefore, with a Spanish ruling class and a large African workforce for the coffee and sugar plantations that came to dominate its economy.

Puerto Rican resistance to Spanish rule began to emerge in the nineteenth century. The resistance prompted some reforms: the abolition of slavery in 1873, representation in the Spanish parliament, and other changes. Demands for independence continued to grow, and in 1898, Spain granted the island a degree of independence. But before the changes had any chance to take effect, control of Puerto Rico shifted to the United States. American military forces occupied the island during the Spanish-American War, and they remained *Foraker Act*   in control until 1900, when the Foraker Act ended military rule and established a formal colonial government. Agitation for independence continued, and in 1917, Congress passed the Jones Act, which declared Puerto Rico to be United States territory and made all Puerto Ricans American citizens.

The Puerto Rican sugar industry flourished as it took advantage of the American market that was now open to it without tariffs. As in Hawaii, Americans from the mainland began establishing large sugar plantations on the island and hired natives to work them. The growing emphasis on sugar as a cash crop, and the transformation of many Puerto Rican farmers into paid laborers, led to a reduction in the growing of food for the island and greater reliance on imported goods. When international sugar prices were high, Puerto Rico did well. When they dropped, the island's economy sagged, pushing the many plantation workers—already poor—into destitution.

The Debate over the Philippines

Although the annexation of Puerto Rico produced relatively little controversy, the annexation of the Philippines created an impassioned debate. Controlling a nearby Caribbean island fit reasonably comfortably into the United States' sense of itself as the dominant power in the Western Hemisphere. But to many Americans, controlling a large and densely populated territory thousands of miles away seemed very different and more ominous.

McKinley claimed to be reluctant to support annexation. But, according to his own accounts, he came to believe there were no acceptable alternatives. Returning the *The Philippines Question*   Philippines to Spain would be "cowardly and dishonorable," he claimed. Turning them over to another imperialist power (France, Germany, or Britain) would be "bad business and discreditable." Granting them independence would be irresponsible because the Filipinos were "unfit for self government." The only solution was "to take them all and to educate the Filipinos, and uplift and Christianize them, and by God's grace do the very best we could by them."

MEASURING UNCLE SAM FOR A NEW SUIT In this *Puck* cartoon, President McKinley is favorably depicted as a tailor, meaning his client for a suit is large enough to accommodate the new possessions the United States obtained in the aftermath of the Spanish-American War. The stripes on Uncle Sam's pants bear the names of earlier, less controversial acquisitions, such as the Louisiana Purchase. (The Library of Congress)

The Treaty of Paris, signed in December 1898, confirmed the terms of the armistice and brought a formal end to the war. American negotiators had startled the Spanish by demanding that they also cede the Philippines to the United States, but an American offer of $20 million for the islands softened their resistance. They accepted all the American terms.

In the United States Senate, however, resistance was fierce. During debate over ratification of the treaty, a powerful anti-imperialist movement arose to oppose acquisition of the Philippines. The anti-imperialists included some of the *Anti-Imperialist League* nation's wealthiest and most powerful figures: Andrew Carnegie, Mark Twain, Samuel Gompers, Senator John Sherman, and others. Some anti-imperialists believed that imperialism was immoral, a repudiation of America's commitment to human freedom. Others feared "polluting" the American population by introducing "inferior" Asian races into it. Industrial workers feared being undercut by a flood of cheap laborers from the new colonies. Conservatives worried about the large standing army and entangling foreign alliances that they believed imperialism would require and that they feared would threaten American liberties. Sugar growers and other anti-imperialists feared unwelcome competition from the new territories. The Anti-Imperialist League, established late in 1898 by upper-class Bostonians, New Yorkers, and others to fight against annexation, waged a vigorous campaign against ratification of the Paris treaty (See "Consider the Source: Platform of the Anti-Imperialist League.").

But favoring ratification was an equally varied group. There were the exuberant imperialists such as Theodore Roosevelt, who saw the acquisition of empire as a way to reinvigorate the nation. Some businessmen saw opportunities to dominate the Asian trade. Most Republicans saw partisan advantages in acquiring valuable new territories through a war fought and won by a Republican administration. Perhaps the *Arguments for Annexation* strongest argument in favor of annexation, however, was that the United States already possessed the islands.

CONSIDER THE SOURCE

PLATFORM OF THE AMERICAN ANTI-IMPERIALIST LEAGUE, 1899

As part of their campaign against the annexation of the Philippines by the United States, members of the Anti-Imperialist League circulated this party platform. Here they argue that American political ideals are not compatible with imperialist actions.

We hold that the policy known as imperialism is hostile to liberty and tends toward militarism, an evil from which it has been our glory to be free. We regret that it has become necessary in the land of Washington and Lincoln to reaffirm that all men, of whatever race or color, are entitled to life, liberty, and the pursuit of happiness. We maintain that governments derive their just powers from the consent of the governed. We insist that the subjugation of any people is "criminal aggression" and open disloyalty to the distinctive principles of our Government.

We earnestly condemn the policy of the present National Administration in the Philippines. It seeks to extinguish the spirit of 1776 in those islands. We deplore the sacrifice of our soldiers and sailors, whose bravery deserves admiration even in an unjust war. We denounce the slaughter of the Filipinos as a needless horror. We protest against the extension of American sovereignty by Spanish methods.

We demand the immediate cessation of the war against liberty, begun by Spain and continued by us. We urge that Congress be promptly convened to announce to the Filipinos our purpose to concede to them the independence for which they have so long fought and which of right is theirs.

The United States have always protested against the doctrine of international law which permits the subjugation of the weak by the strong. A self-governing state cannot accept sovereignty over an unwilling people. The United States cannot act upon the ancient heresy that might makes right.

Imperialists assume that with the destruction of self-government in the Philippines by American hands, all opposition here will cease. This is a grievous error. Much as we abhor the war of "criminal aggression" in the Philippines, greatly as we regret that the blood of the Filipinos is on American hands, we more deeply resent the betrayal of American institutions at home. The real firing line is not in the suburbs of Manila. The foe is of our own household. The attempt of 1861 was to divide the country. That of 1899 is to destroy its fundamental principles and noblest ideals.

Whether the ruthless slaughter of the Filipinos shall end next month or next year is but an incident in a contest that must go on until the Declaration of Independence and the Constitution of the United States are rescued from the hands of their betrayers. Those who dispute about standards of value while the Republic is undermined will be listened to as little as those who would wrangle about the small economies of the household while the house is on fire. The training of a great people for a century, the aspiration for liberty of a vast immigration are forces that will hurl aside those who in the delirium of conquest seek to destroy the character of our institutions.

We deny that the obligation of all citizens to support their Government in times of grave national peril applies to the present situation. If an Administration may with impunity ignore the issues upon which it was chosen, deliberately create a condition of war anywhere on the face of the globe, debauch the civil service for spoils to promote the adventure, organize a truth-suppressing censorship and demand of all citizens a suspension of judgment and their unanimous support while it chooses to continue the fighting, representative government itself is imperiled.

We propose to contribute to the defeat of any person or party that stands for the forcible subjugation of any people. We shall oppose for reelection all who in the White House or in Congress betray American liberty in pursuit of un-American gains. We still hope that both of our great political parties will support and defend the Declaration of Independence in the closing campaign of the century.

Source: "Platform of the American Anti-Imperialist League," in *Speeches, Correspondence, ard Political Papers of Carl Schurz*, vol. 6, ed. Frederick Bancroft (New York: G.P. Putnam's Sons, 1913), p. 77, note 1.

UNDERSTAND, ANALYZE, & EVALUATE

1. On what grounds did the Anti-Imperialist League oppose U.S. expansion, and where were these principles ratified?
2. What were the costs of imperial expansion for the United States and what losses were Filipinos to incur?
3. How did the prospect of an American empire affect the nation's democratic principles?

When anti-imperialists warned of the danger of acquiring heavily populated territories whose people might have to become citizens, the jingoes had a ready answer: the nation's long-standing policies toward Indians—treating them as dependents rather than as citizens—had created a precedent for annexing land without absorbing people.

The fate of the treaty remained in doubt for weeks, until it received the unexpected support of William Jennings Bryan, a fervent anti-imperialist. He backed ratification because he hoped to move the issue out of the Senate and make it the subject of a national referendum in 1900, when he expected to be the Democratic presidential candidate again. Bryan persuaded a number of anti-imperialist Democrats to support the treaty so as to set up the 1900 debate. The Senate ratified it finally on February 6, 1899.

But Bryan miscalculated. If the election of 1900 was in fact a referendum on the Philippines, as Bryan expected, it proved beyond a doubt that the nation *Election of 1900* had decided in favor of imperialism. Once again Bryan ran against McKinley; and once again McKinley won—even more decisively than in 1896. It was not only the issue of the colonies, however, that ensured McKinley's victory. The Republicans benefited from growing prosperity—and also from the colorful personality of their vice presidential candidate, Theodore Roosevelt, the hero of San Juan Hill.

THE REPUBLIC AS EMPIRE

The new American empire was small by the standards of the great imperial powers of Europe. But it embroiled the United States in the politics of both Europe and the Far East in ways the nation had always tried to avoid in the past. It also drew Americans into a brutal war in the Philippines.

GOVERNING THE COLONIES

Three American dependencies—Hawaii, Alaska, and Puerto Rico—presented relatively few problems. They received territorial status (and their residents American citizenship) relatively quickly: Hawaii in 1900, Alaska in 1912, and Puerto Rico in 1917. The navy took control of the Pacific islands of Guam and Tutuila. The United States simply left alone some of the smallest, least populated Pacific islands now under its control. Cuba was a thornier problem. American military forces, commanded by General Leonard Wood, remained there until 1902 to prepare the island for independence. Americans built roads, schools, and hospitals; reorganized the legal, financial, and administrative systems; and introduced medical and sanitation reforms. But the United States also laid the basis for years of American economic domination of the island.

When Cuba drew up a constitution that made no reference to the United States, *Platt Amendment* Congress responded by passing the Platt Amendment in 1901 and pressuring Cuba into incorporating its terms into its constitution. The Platt Amendment barred Cuba from making treaties with other nations; gave the United States the right to intervene in Cuba to preserve independence, life, and property; and required Cuba to permit American naval stations on its territory. The amendment left Cuba with only nominal political independence.

American capital made the new nation an American economic appendage as well. American investors poured into Cuba, buying up plantations, factories, railroads, and refineries. Resistance to "Yankee imperialism" produced intermittent revolts against the Cuban government—revolts that at times prompted U.S. military intervention. American troops occupied the island from 1906 to 1909 after one such rebellion; they returned again in 1912 to suppress a revolt by black plantation workers. As in Puerto Rico and Hawaii, sugar production—spurred by access to the American market—increasingly dominated the island's economy and subjected it to the same cycle of booms and busts that plagued other sugar-producing appendages of the United States economy.

THE PHILIPPINE WAR

Like other imperial powers, the United States soon discovered that subjugating another people was not an easy task. The American experience in the Philippines began with a long and bloody war.

The conflict in the Philippines is the least remembered of all American wars. It was also one of the longest. It lasted from 1898 to 1902, and it was one of the most vicious. It involved 200,000 American troops and resulted in 4,300 American deaths. The number of Filipinos killed in the conflict has long been a matter of dispute, but it seems likely that at least 50,000 natives (and perhaps many more) died. The American occupiers faced brutal guerrilla tactics in the Philippines, and they soon found themselves drawn into the same pattern of brutality that had outraged so many Americans when Weyler had used them in the Caribbean.

The Filipinos had rebelled against Spanish rule before 1898, and as soon as they realized the Americans had come to stay, they rebelled against them as well. Ably led by *Emilio Aguinaldo* Emilio Aguinaldo, who claimed to head the legitimate government of the nation, Filipinos harried the American army of occupation from island to island for more than three years. At first, American commanders believed the rebels had only a small popular following. But by early 1900, General Arthur MacArthur, an American commander in the islands (and father of General Douglas MacArthur), was writing: "I have been reluctantly compelled to believe that the Filipino masses are loyal to Aguinaldo and the government which he heads."

To MacArthur and others, that realization was not a reason to moderate American tactics or conciliate the rebels, but rather to adopt much more severe measures. Gradually, the American military effort became more systematically vicious and brutal. Captured Filipino

THE AMERICAN SOUTH PACIFIC EMPIRE, 1900   Except for Puerto Rico, all of the colonial acquisitions of the United States in the wake of the Spanish-American War occurred in the Pacific. The new attraction of imperialism persuaded the United States to annex Hawaii in 1898. The war itself gave America control of the Philippines, Guam, and other, smaller Spanish possessions in the Pacific. When added to the small, scattered islands that the United States had acquired as naval bases earlier in the nineteenth century, these new possessions gave the nation a far-flung Pacific empire, even if one whose total territory and population remained small by the standards of the other great empires of the age.   •   *What was the reaction in the United States to the acquisition of this new empire?*

guerrillas were treated not as prisoners of war but as murderers. Many were summarily executed. On some islands, entire communities were evacuated—the residents forced into concentration camps while American troops destroyed their villages. A spirit of savagery grew among some American soldiers, who came to view the Filipinos as almost subhuman and, at times, seemed to take pleasure in arbitrarily killing them.

The racial undertones of the war—American soldiers called the Filipinos "niggers"— were particularly grating for African American troops serving in segregated units. They were hardly unaware that at home, southern states and lynch mobs were in the process of disenfranchising and terrorizing black people. Some noticed a resemblance between the attitude of the American military and government toward the Filipino natives and popular attitudes toward African Americans and Native Americans.

By 1902, reports of the brutality and of the American casualties had soured the American public on the war. But by then, the rebellion had largely exhausted itself and the occupiers had established control over most of the islands. The key to their victory was the March 1901 capture of Aguinaldo, who later signed a document urging his followers to stop fighting and declared his own allegiance to the United States. Fighting continued intermittently until as late as 1906, but American possession of the Philippines was now secure. In the summer of 1901, the military transferred authority over the islands

to William Howard Taft, who became their first civilian governor and gave the Filipinos broad local autonomy. The Americans also built roads, schools, bridges, and sewers; instituted major administrative and financial reforms; and established a public health sys-
Gradual Shift to Self-Rule   tem. Filipino self-rule gradually increased, and on July 4, 1946, the islands finally gained their independence.

THE OPEN DOOR

The American acquisition of the Philippines increased the already strong U.S. interest in Asia. Americans were particularly concerned about the future of China, which provided a tempting target for exploitation by stronger countries. By 1900, England, France, Germany, Russia, and Japan were beginning to carve up China among themselves, pressuring the Chinese government for "concessions" that gave them effective control over various regions of China. In some cases, they simply seized Chinese territory and claimed it as their own. Many Americans feared that the process would soon cut them out of the China trade altogether.

Eager for a way to advance American interests in China without risking war, McKinley issued a statement in September 1898 saying the United States wanted access to China but no special advantages there. "Asking only the open door for ourselves, we are ready to accord the open door to others." The next year, Secretary of State John Hay translated those words into policy when he addressed identical messages—which
Hay's "Open Door Notes"   became known as the "Open Door notes"—to England, Germany, Russia, France, Japan, and Italy. He asked that each nation with a "sphere of influence" in China allow other nations to trade freely and equally in its sphere. The principles Hay outlined would allow the United States to trade freely with China without fear of interference.

Europe and Japan received the **Open Door** proposals coolly. Russia openly rejected them; the other powers claimed to accept them in principle but to be unable to act unless all the other powers agreed. Hay refused to consider this a rebuff. He boldly announced that all the powers had accepted the principles of the Open Door in "final and definitive" form and that the United States expected them to observe those principles.

No sooner had the diplomatic maneuvering over the Open Door ended than the Boxers, a secret Chinese martial-arts society with highly nationalist convictions (and a somewhat mystical vision of their invulnerability to bullets), launched a revolt against foreigners in
Boxer Rebellion   China. The Boxer Rebellion spread widely across eastern China, attacking Westerners wherever they could find them—including many Christian missionaries. But the climax of the revolt was a siege of the entire Western foreign diplomatic corps, which took refuge in the British embassy in Peking. The imperial powers (including the United States) sent an international expeditionary force into China to rescue the diplomats. In August 1900, it fought its way into the city and broke the siege.

The Boxer Rebellion became an important event for the role of the United States in China. McKinley and Hay had agreed to American participation in quelling the Boxer Rebellion in order to secure a voice in the settlement of the uprising and prevent the partition of China by the European powers. Hay now won support for his Open Door approach from England and Germany and induced the other participating powers to accept compensation from the Chinese for the damages the Boxer Rebellion had caused. Chinese territorial integrity survived at least in name, and the United States retained access to its lucrative China trade.

A MODERN MILITARY SYSTEM

The war with Spain had revealed glaring deficiencies in the American military system. Had the United States been fighting a more powerful foe, disaster might have resulted. After the war, McKinley appointed Elihu Root, an able corporate lawyer in New York, as secretary of war to supervise a major overhaul of the armed forces.

Root's reforms enlarged the regular army from 25,000 to a maximum of 100,000. They established federal army standards for the National Guard, ensuring that never again would the nation fight a war with volunteer regiments trained and equipped differently than those in the regular army. They sparked the creation of a system of officer training schools, including the Army Staff College (later the Command and General Staff School) at Fort Leavenworth, Kansas, and the Army War College in Washington. And in 1903, a general staff (named the Joint Chiefs of Staff) was established to act as military advisers to the secretary of war. As a result of the new reforms, the United States entered the twentieth century with something resembling a modern military system.

CONCLUSION

For nearly three decades after the end of Reconstruction, American politics remained locked in a rigid stalemate. The electorate was almost evenly divided, and the two major parties differed on only a few issues. A series of unimposing if respectable presidents presided over this political system as unwitting symbols of its stability and passivity.

Beneath the calm surface of national politics, however, social issues were creating deep tensions: battles between employers and workers, growing resentment among American farmers facing declining prosperity, outrage at what many voters considered corruption in government and excessive power in the hands of corporate titans. When a great depression began in 1893, these social tensions exploded.

The most visible sign of the challenge to the political stalemate was the Populist movement, an uprising of American farmers demanding far-reaching changes in politics and the economy. In 1892, they created their own political party, the People's Party, which for a few years showed impressive strength. But in the climactic election of 1896, in which the Populist hero William Jennings Bryan became the presidential nominee of both the Democratic Party and the People's Party, the Republicans won a substantial victory— and, in the process, helped create a great electoral realignment that left the Republicans with a clear majority for the next three decades.

The crises of the 1890s helped spur the United States' growing involvement in the world. In 1898, the United States intervened in a colonial war between Spain and Cuba, won a quick and easy military victory, and signed a treaty with Spain that ceded significant territory to the Americans. A vigorous anti-imperialist movement failed to stop the imperial drive. But taking the colonies proved easier than holding them. In the Philippines, American forces became bogged down in a brutal four-year war with Filipino rebels. The conflict soured much of the American public, and the annexation of colonies in 1898 proved to be both the beginning and the end of American territorial expansion.

KEY TERMS/PEOPLE/PLACES/EVENTS

Benjamin Harrison 458

Boxer Rebellion 484

Chester A. Arthur 457

Coxey's Army 464

Farmers' Alliances 460

Free silver 464

Grangers 460

Grover Cleveland 458

Half-Breeds 457

imperialism 468

Interstate Commerce
 Act 459

James A. Garfield 457

jingoes 468

Open Door 484

Panic of 1893 463

Populism 461

Puerto Rico 484

Queen Liliuokalani 469

Rutherford B. Hayes 457

Sherman Antitrust Act 459

Spanish-American
 War 478

Stalwarts 457

William Jennings Bryan 481

William McKinley 459

yellow journalism 472

RECALL AND REFLECT

1. How and why did the federal government attempt to regulate interstate commerce in the late nineteenth century?
2. What efforts did farmers undertake to deal with the economic problems they faced in the late nineteenth century?
3. What was the "silver question"? Why was it so important to so many Americans? How did the major political parties deal with this question?
4. How did the Spanish-American War change America's relationship to the rest of the world?
5. What were the main arguments of those who supported U.S. imperialism and those who opposed the nation's imperial ambitions and efforts?

20 | THE PROGRESSIVES

THE PROGRESSIVE IMPULSE

WOMEN AND REFORM

THE ASSAULT ON THE PARTIES

SOURCES OF PROGRESSIVE REFORM

CRUSADES FOR SOCIAL ORDER AND REFORM

THEODORE ROOSEVELT AND THE MODERN
   PRESIDENCY

THE TROUBLED SUCCESSION

WOODROW WILSON AND THE NEW FREEDOM

LOOKING AHEAD

1. What role did women and women's organizations play in the reforms of the progressive era? How did progressive era reforms affect women?

2. What changes to politics and government did progressive reformers advocate at the local, state, and federal levels? How did government change as a result of their reform efforts?

3. How did Woodrow Wilson's progressivism differ from that of Theodore Roosevelt? In what ways was it similar to Roosevelt's?

WELL BEFORE THE END OF the nineteenth century, many Americans had become convinced that rapid industrialization and urbanization had created a growing crisis. The nation's most pressing need, they claimed, was to impose order and justice on a society that seemed to be approaching chaos. By the early years of the twentieth century, this outlook had acquired a name: progressivism.

Not even those who called themselves progressives could agree on what the term meant, for it was a phenomenon of great scope and diversity. But despite or perhaps because of its great diversity, the progressive movement generated a remarkable wave of political and social innovation. From the late nineteenth century until at least the end of World War I, progressive reformers brought into public debate such issues as the role of women in society, racial equality, the rights of labor, and the impact of immigration and cultural diversity.

Progressivism began as a series of local movements and encompassed many different efforts to improve the working of society. Slowly but steadily, these efforts became national efforts. Ultimately it was the presidency, not the Congress, that became the most important vehicle of national reform—first under the dynamic leadership of Theodore Roosevelt and then under the disciplined, moralistic guidance of Woodrow Wilson. By the time America entered World War I in 1917, the federal government—which had exercised limited powers prior to the twentieth century—had greatly expanded its role in American life.

THE PROGRESSIVE IMPULSE

Progressives believed, as their name implies, in the idea of progress. They were optimistic that society was capable of improvement and that continued growth and advancement were the nation's destiny. But progressives believed, too, that growth and progress could not continue to occur recklessly, as they had in the late nineteenth century. The "natural laws" of the marketplace, and the doctrines of laissez-faire and Social Darwinism that dominated those laws, were not sufficient. Direct, purposeful human intervention was essential to ordering and bettering society. These ideas percolated in the United States as well as many other industrializing parts of the world. (See "America in the World: Social Democracy.")

Progressives did not always agree on the form their interventions should take, and the result was a variety of reform impulses. One powerful impulse was the spirit of "antimonopoly," the fear of concentrated power and the urge to limit and disperse authority and wealth. Another progressive impulse was a belief in the importance of social cohesion: the belief that individuals are part of a great web of social relationships, that each person's welfare is dependent on the welfare of society as a whole. Still another impulse was a deep faith in knowledge—in the possibilities of applying to society the principles of natural and social sciences. Most progressives believed, too, that a modernized government could—and must—play an important role in the process of improving and stabilizing society.

THE MUCKRAKERS AND THE SOCIAL GOSPEL

Among the first people to articulate the new spirit of national reform were crusading journalists who began to direct public attention toward social, economic, and political injustices. Known as the **muckrakers,** after Theodore Roosevelt accused them of raking up muck through their writings, they were committed to exposing scandal, corruption, and injustice.

Their first major targets were the trusts and, particularly, the railroads, which the muckrakers considered powerful and deeply corrupt. Exposés of the great corporate organizations began to appear as early as the 1860s, when Charles Francis Adams Jr. and others uncovered corruption among the railroad barons. Decades later, journalist Ida Tarbell produced a scorching study of the Standard Oil trust. By the turn of the century, many muckrakers were turning their attention to government and particularly to the urban political machines. Among the most influential was Lincoln Steffens, a reporter for *McClure's* magazine. His portraits of "machine government" and "boss rule" in cities, written in a tone of studied moral outrage, helped arouse sentiment for urban political reform. By presenting social problems to the public with indignation and moral fervor, they helped inspire other Americans to take action.

Growing outrage at social and economic injustice committed many reformers to the pursuit of **social justice.** (*Social justice* is a term widely used around the world to promote a kind of justice that goes beyond the individual but, instead, seeks justice for whole

THE BOSSES OF THE SENATE (1889), BY JOSEPH KEPPLER   Keppler was a popular political cartoonist of the late nineteenth century who shared the growing concern about the power of the trusts—portrayed here as bloated, almost reptilian figures standing menacingly over the members of the U.S. Senate, to whose chamber the "people's entrance" is "closed."

SOCIAL DEMOCRACY

Enormous energy, enthusiasm, and organization drove the reform efforts in America in the late nineteenth and early twentieth centuries, much of it a result of social crises and political movements in the United States. But the "age of reform," as some have called it, was not an American phenomenon alone. It was part of a wave of social experimentation that was occurring throughout much of the industrial world. "Progressivism" in other countries influenced the social movements in the United States. American reform, in turn, had significant influence elsewhere as well.

Several industrializing nations adopted the term *progressivism* for their efforts—not only the United States, but also England, Germany, and France. But the term that most broadly defined the new reform energies was *social democracy*. Social democrats in many countries shared a belief in the betterment of society through the accumulation of knowledge. They favored improving the social condition of all people through reforms of the economy and government programs of social protection. And they believed that these goals could be achieved through peaceful political change, rather than through radicalism or revolution. Political parties committed to these goals emerged in several countries: the Labour Party in Britain, social democratic parties in various European nations, and the short-lived Progressive Party in the United States. Intellectuals, academics, and government officials across the world shared the knowledge they were accumulating and observed one another's social programs. American reformers at the turn of the century spent much time visiting Germany, France, Britain, Belgium, and the Netherlands, observing the reforms in progress there; and Europeans, in turn, visited

the United States. Reformers from both America and Europe were also fascinated by the advanced social experiments in Australia and, especially, New Zealand—which the American reformer Henry Demarest Lloyd once called "the political brain of the modern world." But New Zealand's dramatic experiments in factory regulation, woman suffrage, old-age pensions, progressive taxation, and labor arbitration gradually found counterparts in many other nations as well. William Allen White, a progressive journalist from Kansas, said of this time: "We were parts of one another, in the United States and Europe. Something was welding us into one

THE PARIS EXPO, A PROGRESSIVE SYMBOL The Paris Expositions of 1889 and 1900, symbolized by the Eiffel Tower and enormous globe, drew progressive experts as well as tourists with the vision of progress through industrial innovation. During the Expos, an international group of progressives held meetings to share ideas for bettering society. (© Archives Charmet/Bridgeman Images)

social and economic whole with local political variations . . . [all] fighting a common cause."

Social democracy—or, as it was sometimes called in the United States and elsewhere, social justice or the social gospel—was responsible for many public programs. Germany began a system of social insurance for its citizens in the 1880s while simultaneously undertaking a massive study of society that produced over 140 volumes of "social investigation" of almost every aspect of the nation's life. French reformers pressed in the 1890s for factory regulation, assistance to the elderly, and progressive taxation. Britain pioneered the settlement houses in working-class areas of London—a movement that soon spread to the United States—and, like the United States, witnessed growing challenges to the power of monopolies at both the local and national levels.

In many countries, social democrats felt pressure from the rising worldwide labor movement and from the rise of socialist parties in many industrial countries as well. Strikes, sometimes violent, were common in France, Germany, Britain, and the United States in the late nineteenth century. The more militant workers became, the more unions seemed to grow. Social democrats did not always welcome the rise of militant labor movements, but they took them seriously and used them to support their own efforts at reform.

The politics of social democracy represented a great shift in the character of public life all over the industrial world. Instead of battles over the privileges of aristocrats or the power of monarchs, reformers now focused on the social problems of ordinary people and attempted to improve their lot. "The politics of the future are social politics," the British reformer Joseph Chamberlain said in the 1880s, referring to efforts to deal with the problems of ordinary citizens. That belief was fueling progressive efforts across the world in the years that Americans have come to call the "progressive era." •

UNDERSTAND, ANALYZE, & EVALUATE

1. What is social democracy? How does it differ from socialism?
2. What progressive era reforms in American social and political life can be seen in other nations as well?

groups or even societies. Advocates of social justice are likely to believe in a more egalitarian society.) That impulse helped create the rise of what became known as the "Social Gospel," the effort to make faith into a tool of social reform. The Social Gospel movement was chiefly concerned with redeeming the nation's cities.

The Salvation Army, which began in England but soon spread to the United States, was one example of the fusion of religion with reform. A Christian social welfare organization with a vaguely military structure, it had recruited 3,000 "officers" and 20,000 "privates" by 1900 and was offering both material aid and spiritual service to the urban poor. In addition, many ministers, priests, and rabbis left traditional parish work to serve in the troubled cities. Charles Sheldon's book *In His Steps* (1898), the story of a young minister who abandoned a comfortable post to work among the needy, sold more than 15 million copies. The Social Gospel was never the dominant element in the movement for urban reform. But the engagement of religion with reform helped bring to progressivism a powerful moral commitment to redeem the lives of even the least favored citizens.

THE SETTLEMENT HOUSE MOVEMENT

An element of much progressive thought was the belief in the influence of the environment on individual development. Nothing produced greater distress, many urban reformers believed, than crowded immigrant neighborhoods. One response to the problems of such communities, borrowed from England, was the "settlement house." The most famous was *Jane Addams and Hull House* Hull House, which opened in 1889 in Chicago as a result of the efforts of the social worker Jane Addams. It became a model for more than 400 similar institutions throughout the nation. Staffed by members of the educated middle class, settlement houses sought to help immigrant families adapt to the language and customs of their new country.

Young college women (mostly unmarried) were important participants in the settlement house movement. Working in a settlement house, a protected site that served mostly women, was consistent with the widespread assumption that women needed to be sheltered from difficult environments. The clean and well-tended buildings that settlement houses created were not only a model for immigrant women, but an appropriate site for elite women as well.

The settlement houses also helped create another important institution of reform: the profession of social work. A growing number of programs for the professional training of social workers began to appear in the nation's leading universities, partly in response to the activities of the settlement houses.

The Allure of Expertise

As the emergence of the social work profession suggests, progressives involved in humanitarian efforts placed a high value on knowledge and expertise. Even nonscientific problems, they believed, could be analyzed and solved scientifically. Many reformers came to believe that only enlightened experts and well-designed bureaucracies could create the stability and order America needed.

Some even spoke of the creation of a new civilization, in which the expertise of scientists and engineers could be brought to bear on the problems of the economy and society. The social scientist Thorstein Veblen, for example, proposed a new economic system in which power would reside in the hands of highly trained engineers. Only they, he argued, could fully understand the "machine process" by which modern society must be governed.

The Professions

The late nineteenth century saw a dramatic expansion in the number of Americans engaged in administrative and professional tasks. Industries needed managers, technicians, and accountants as well as workers. Cities required commercial, medical, legal, and educational services. New technology required scientists and engineers, who, in turn, required institutions and instructors to train them. By the turn of the century, those performing these services had come to constitute a distinct social group—what some historians have called a "new middle class."

By the early twentieth century, millions within this new middle class were building organizations and establishing standards to secure their position in society. Most of all, they created the modern, organized professions. The idea of professionalism had been a frail one in America even as late as 1880, but as the demand for professional services increased, so did the pressures for reform.

Among the first to respond was the medical profession. In 1901, doctors who consid-
American Medical Association ered themselves trained professionals reorganized the American Medical Association (AMA) into a national professional society. By 1920, nearly two-thirds

of all American doctors were members. The AMA quickly called for strict, scientific standards for admission to the practice of medicine. State governments responded by passing new laws requiring the licensing of all physicians. By 1900, medical education at a few medical schools—notably Johns Hopkins in Baltimore (founded in 1893)—compared favorably with those in the leading institutions of Europe.

By 1916, lawyers in all forty-eight states had established professional bar associations. The nation's law schools accordingly expanded greatly. Businessmen supported the creation of schools of business administration and set up their own national organizations: the National Association of Manufacturers in 1895 and *National Association of Manufacturers* the United States Chamber of Commerce in 1912. Farmers responded to the new order by forming, through the National Farm Bureau Federation, a network of agricultural organizations designed to spread scientific farming methods.

The professions removed the untrained and incompetent. But the admission requirements also protected those already in the professions from excessive competition and lent prestige and status to the professional level. Some professions used their entrance requirements to exclude African Americans, women, immigrants, and other "undesirables" from their ranks. Others used them simply to keep the numbers down, to ensure that demand would remain high.

WOMEN AND THE PROFESSIONS

American women found themselves excluded from most of the emerging professions. But a substantial number of middle-class women—particularly those emerging from the new women's colleges and from the coeducational state universities—entered professional careers nevertheless.

A few women managed to establish themselves as physicians, lawyers, engineers, scientists, and corporate managers. Most, however, turned by necessity to those professional outlets that society considered suitable for women: settlement houses, social work, and, most important, teaching. Indeed, in the late nineteenth century, perhaps 90 percent of all professional women were teachers. For educated black women, in particular, the existence of segregated schools in the South created a substantial market for African American teachers.

Women also dominated other professional activities. Nursing had become primarily a women's field during and after the Civil War. By the early twentieth century, it was adopting professional standards. And many women entered academia—often earning advanced degrees at such predominantly male institutions as the University of Chicago, MIT, or Columbia, and then finding professional opportunities in the new and expanding women's colleges.

WOMEN AND REFORM

The prominence of women in reform movements is one of the most striking features of progressivism. In many states in the early twentieth century, women could not vote. They almost never held public office. They had footholds in only a few (and usually primarily female) professions and lived in a culture in which most people, male and female, believed that women were not suited for the public world. What, then, explains the prominent role so many women played in the reform activities of the period?

The "New Woman"

The phenomenon of the "new woman" was a product of social and economic changes in both the private and public spheres. By the end of the nineteenth century, almost all income-producing activity had moved out of the home and into the factory or the office. At the same time, many women were having fewer children, and their children were beginning school at earlier ages and spending more time there. For wives and mothers who did not work for wages, the home was less of an all-consuming place. Hence, more and more women began looking for activities outside the home.

Some educated women shunned marriage entirely, believing that only by remaining single could they play the roles they envisioned in the public world. Single women were among the most prominent reformers of the time. Some of these women lived alone. Others lived with other women, often in long-term relationships—some of them secretly romantic—that were known at the time as "Boston marriages." The divorce rate also rose rapidly in the late nineteenth century, from one divorce for every twenty-one marriages in 1880 to one in nine by 1916; women initiated the majority of divorces.

The Clubwomen

Among the most visible signs of the increasing public roles of women in the late nineteenth and early twentieth centuries were women's clubs, which proliferated rapidly beginning in the 1880s and 1890s and became the vanguard of many important reforms.

The women's clubs began largely as cultural organizations to provide middle- and upper-class women with an outlet for their intellectual energies. In 1892, when women formed the General Federation of Women's Clubs, there were more than 100,000 members in nearly 500 clubs. By 1917, there were over 1 million members.

Much of what the clubs did was uncontroversial: planting trees; supporting schools, libraries, and settlement houses; building hospitals and parks. But clubwomen were also an important force in winning passage of state (and ultimately federal) laws that regulated the conditions of woman and child labor. They pushed government to inspect workplaces, regulate the food and drug industries, reform policies toward the Indian tribes, apply new standards to urban housing, and, perhaps most notably, outlaw the manufacture and sale *Clubwomen's Causes* of alcohol. Women's clubs were instrumental in pressuring state legislatures in most states to provide "mothers' pensions" to widowed or abandoned mothers with small children—a system that ultimately became absorbed into the Social Security system. In 1912, they convinced Congress to establish the Children's Bureau in the Labor Department, an agency directed to develop policies to protect children.

In many of these efforts, the clubwomen formed alliances with other women's groups, such as the Women's Trade Union League (WTUL), founded in 1903 by female union members and upper-class reformers and committed to persuading women to join unions. In addition to working on behalf of protective legislation for women, WTUL members held public meetings on behalf of female workers, raised money to support strikes, marched on picket lines, and bailed striking women out of jail.

Black women occasionally joined clubs dominated by whites. But most clubs excluded blacks, and so African Americans formed clubs of their own. Some of them affiliated with the General Federation, but most became part of the independent National Association of Colored Women. Some black clubs also took positions on issues of particular concern to African Americans, such as lynching and aspects of segregation.

SUFFRAGE PAGEANT On March 3, 1913—the day before Woodrow Wilson's presidential inauguration—more than 5,000 supporters of woman suffrage staged a parade in Washington, D.C., that overshadowed Wilson's arrival in the capital. Crowds estimated at over half a million watched the parade; some of the onlookers attacked the marchers. In this photograph from the event, suffragist Florence Noyce poses as Liberty in front of the U.S. Treasury Building. (The Library of Congress)

WOMAN SUFFRAGE

Perhaps the largest single reform movement of the progressive era, indeed one of the largest in American history, was the fight for woman suffrage.

Throughout the late nineteenth century, many suffrage advocates argued that "natural rights" entitled them to the same rights as men—including, first and foremost, the right to vote. Elizabeth Cady Stanton, for example, wrote in 1892 of woman as "the arbiter of her own destiny . . . if we are to consider her as a citizen, as a member of a great nation, she must have the same rights as all other members." This was an argument that challenged the views of the many men and women who believed that society required a distinctive female "sphere," in which women would serve first and foremost as wives and mothers. A powerful antisuffrage movement emerged, dominated by men but with the active support of many women. To these critics, woman suffrage seemed a radical demand.

In the first years of the twentieth century, suffragists were becoming better organized and more politically sophisticated than their opponents. Under the leadership of Anna Howard Shaw, a Boston social worker, and Carrie Chapman Catt, a journalist from Iowa, membership in the National American Woman Suffrage Association (NAWSA) grew from about 13,000 in 1893 to over 2 million in 1917. The movement gained strength because many of its most prominent leaders began to justify suffrage in "safer," less threatening ways. Suffrage, some supporters began to argue, would not challenge the "separate sphere" in which women resided. Instead, they claimed that because women occupied a distinct sphere—because as mothers and wives and homemakers they had special experiences and special sensitivities to bring to public life—woman suffrage would make an important contribution to politics.

In particular, many suffragists argued that enfranchising women would help the temperance movement, by giving its largest group of supporters a political voice. Some suffrage advocates claimed that once women had the vote, war would become a thing of the past, since women would—by their calming, maternal influence—help curb the belligerence of men.

The principal triumphs of the suffrage movement began in 1910, when Washington became the first state in fourteen years to extend suffrage to women. California followed a year later, and four other western states in 1912. In 1913, Illinois became the first state east of the Mississippi to embrace woman suffrage. And in 1917 and 1918, New York and Michigan—two of the most populous states in the Union—gave women the vote. By 1919, thirty-nine states had granted women the right to vote in at least some elections; fifteen had allowed them full participation. In 1920, finally, suffragists won *Nineteenth Amendment* ratification of the Nineteenth Amendment, which guaranteed voting rights to women throughout the nation.

To some feminists, however, the victory seemed less than complete. Alice Paul, head *Alice Paul* of the militant National Woman's Party (founded in 1916), never accepted the relatively conservative "separate sphere" justification for suffrage. She argued that the Nineteenth Amendment alone would not be sufficient to protect women's rights. Women needed more: a constitutional amendment that would provide full, legal protection for their rights and would prohibit all discrimination on the basis of gender. But Alice Paul's argument found limited favor even among many of the most important leaders of the recently triumphant suffrage crusade.

THE ASSAULT ON THE PARTIES

Sooner or later, most progressive goals required the involvement of government. Only government, reformers agreed, could effectively counter the many powerful private interests that threatened the nation. But American government at the dawn of the new century was poorly adapted to meet progressive demands. Before progressives could reform *Reforming Government* society effectively, they would have to reform government itself. Many reformers believed the first step must be an assault on the dominant role the political parties played in the life of the state.

EARLY ATTACKS

Attacks on party dominance had been frequent in the late nineteenth century. Greenbackism and Populism, for example, had been efforts to break the hammerlock with which the Republicans and Democrats controlled public life. The Independent Republicans (or mugwumps) had attempted to challenge the grip of partisanship.

The early assaults enjoyed some success. In the 1880s and 1890s, for example, most states adopted the secret ballot. Prior to that, the political parties themselves had printed ballots (or "tickets"), with the names of the party's candidates, and no others. They distributed the tickets to their supporters, who then simply went to the polls to deposit them *New Secret Ballot* in the ballot boxes. The old system had made it possible for bosses to monitor the voting behavior of their constituents. The new secret ballot—printed by the government and distributed at the polls to be filled out and deposited in secret—helped chip away at the power of the parties over the voters.

Municipal Reform

Many progressives believed the impact of party rule was most damaging in the cities. Municipal government therefore became the first target of those working for political reform. The muckrakers were especially successful in arousing public outrage at corruption and incompetence in city politics. They struck a responsive chord among a powerful group of urban middle-class progressives, who set out to destroy the power of city bosses and their entrenched political organizations.

One of the first major successes in municipal reform came in Galveston, Texas, where the old city government proved completely unable to deal with the effects of a destructive hurricane in 1900. Capitalizing on public dismay, reformers won approval of a new city charter that replaced the mayor and council with an elected, nonpartisan commission. In 1907, Des Moines, Iowa, adopted its own version of the commission plan, and other cities soon followed.

Another approach to municipal reform was the city manager plan, by which elected officials hired an outside expert—often a professionally trained business manager or engineer—to take charge of the government. The city manager would presumably remain *City-Manager Plan* untainted by the corrupting influence of politics. By the end of the progressive era, almost 400 cities were operating under commissions, and another 45 employed city managers.

In most urban areas, reformers had to settle for lesser victories. Some cities made the election of mayors nonpartisan (so that the parties could not choose the candidates) or moved them to years when no presidential or congressional races were in progress (to reduce the influence of the large turnouts that party organizations produced). Reformers tried to make city councilors run at large, to limit the influence of ward leaders and district bosses. They tried to strengthen the power of the mayor at the expense of the city council, on the assumption that reformers were more likely to succeed in getting a sympathetic mayor elected than they were to win control of the entire council.

Statehouse Progressivism

Other progressives turned to state government as an agent for reform. They looked with particular scorn on state legislatures, whose ill-paid, relatively undistinguished members, they believed, were generally incompetent, often corrupt, and totally controlled by party bosses. Reformers began looking for ways to circumvent the boss-controlled legislatures by increasing the power of the electorate. A big victory came in 1913, when the states ratified a constitutional amendment—the seventeenth—that transferred the right to elect U.S. senators from the state legislatures to ordinary voters.

Two other important changes were proposed by Populists in the 1890s: the initiative and the referendum. The initiative allowed reformers to circumvent *Initiative and Referendum* state legislatures by submitting new legislation directly to the voters in general elections. The referendum provided a method by which actions of the legislature could be returned to the electorate for approval. By 1918, more than twenty states had enacted one or both of these reforms.

The direct primary and the recall were other efforts to limit the power of party and improve the quality of elected officials. The primary election was *Direct Primary and Recall* an attempt to remove the selection of candidates from the bosses and give it to the people. In the South, it was also an effort to limit black voting—since primary voting, many white southerners believed, would be easier to control than general elections. The recall gave voters the right to remove a public official from office at a special election, which could be called after a sufficient number of citizens had signed a petition. By 1915, every state in the nation had instituted primary elections for at least some offices. The recall encountered more strenuous opposition, but a few states (such as California) adopted it as well.

The most celebrated state-level reformer was Robert M. La Follette of Wisconsin. Elected *Robert La Follette* governor in 1900, he helped turn his state into what reformers across the nation described as a "laboratory of progressivism." Under his leadership, Wisconsin progressives won approval of direct primaries, initiatives, and referendums. They regulated railroads and utilities. They passed laws to regulate the workplace and provide compensation for laborers injured on the job. They instituted graduated taxes on inherited fortunes, and they nearly doubled state levies on railroads and other corporate interests.

PARTIES AND INTEREST GROUPS

The reformers did not, of course, eliminate parties from American political life. But they did contribute to a decline in party influence. Evidence of their impact came from, among other things, the decline in voter turnout. In the late nineteenth century, up to 81 percent of eligible voters routinely turned out for national elections. In the early twentieth century, the figure declined markedly. In the presidential election of 1900, 73 percent of the electorate voted. By 1912, turnout had declined to about 59 percent. Never again has voter turnout reached as high as 70 percent.

Why did voter turnout decline in these years? The secret ballot was one reason. Party bosses had less ability to get voters to the polls. Illiterate voters had trouble reading the new ballots. Party bosses lost much of their authority and were unable to mobilize voters as successfully as they had in the past. But perhaps the most important *Decline of Party Influence* reason for the decline of party rule (and voter turnout) was that other power centers were beginning to replace them. They have become known as "interest groups." Beginning late in the nineteenth century and accelerating rapidly in the twentieth century, new organizations emerged outside the party system: professional organizations, trade associations representing businesses and industries, labor organizations, farm lobbies, and many others. Social workers, the settlement house movements, women's clubs, and others learned to operate as interest groups to advance their demands without relying on parties.

SOURCES OF PROGRESSIVE REFORM

Middle-class reformers, most of them from the East, dominated the public image and much of the substance of progressivism in the late nineteenth and early twentieth centuries. But they were not alone in seeking to improve social conditions. Working-class Americans, African Americans, westerners, and even party bosses played crucial roles in advancing some of the important reforms of the era. (For historians' changing views on who the progressives were and what motivated them, see "Debating the Past: Progressivism.")

Labor, the Machine, and Reform

Although the American Federation of Labor, and its leader Samuel Gompers, remained largely aloof from many of the reform efforts of the time, some unions nevertheless played important roles in reform battles. Between 1911 and 1913, thanks to political pressure from labor groups such as the newly formed Union Labor Party, California passed a child labor law, a workmen's compensation law, and a limitation on working hours for women. Union pressures contributed to the passage of similar laws in many other states as well.

Party bosses sometimes allowed their machines to become vehicles of social reform. One example was New York's Tammany Hall, the nation's oldest and most notorious city machine. Its astute leader, Charles Francis Murphy, began in the early years of the twentieth century to fuse the techniques of boss rule with some of the concerns of social reformers. Tammany at times used its political power on behalf of legislation to improve working conditions, protect child laborers, and eliminate the worst abuses of the industrial economy.

In 1911, a terrible fire swept through the factory of the Triangle Shirtwaist Company in New York; 146 workers, most of them women, died. Many of them *Triangle Shirtwaist Fire* had been trapped inside the burning building because management had locked the emergency exits to prevent malingering. For the next three years, a state commission studied the disaster and the conditions of factories generally. In 1914, the commission issued a series of reports calling for major reforms in the conditions of modern labor. The report itself was a classic progressive document—based on the testimony of experts and filled

VICTIMS OF THE TRIANGLE SHIRTWAIST FIRE, 1911   In this bleak photograph, victims of the fire in the Triangle Shirtwaist Company are laid out on the sidewalk of the building, as police and passersby look up at the scene of the blaze. This tragedy galvanized New York legislators into passing laws to protect workers. (© Granger, NYC—All Rights Reserved.)

PROGRESSIVISM

Until the early 1950s, most historians seemed to agree on the central characteristics of early-twentieth-century progressivism. It was just what many progressives themselves had said it was: a movement by the people to curb the power of special interests. More specifically, it was a protest by an aroused citizenry against the excessive power of urban bosses, corporate moguls, and corrupt elected officials.

In 1951, the historian George Mowry began challenging these assumptions by examining progressives in California and describing them as a small, privileged elite of business and professional figures: people who considered themselves the natural leaders of society and who were trying to recover their fading influence from the new capitalist institutions that had displaced them. Progressivism was not, in other words, a popular democratic movement but the effort of a displaced elite to restore its authority. Richard Hofstadter expanded on this idea in *The Age of Reform* (1955) by describing reformers as people afflicted by "status anxiety"—fading elites suffering not from economic but from psychological discontent.

The Mowry-Hofstadter argument soon encountered a range of challenges. Gabriel Kolko, in *The Triumph of Conservatism* (1963), rejected both the older "democratic" view of progressivism and the newer status-anxiety view. Progressive reform, he argued, was not an effort to protect the people from the corporations; it was, rather, a vehicle through which corporate leaders used the government to protect themselves from competition.

A more moderate reinterpretation came from historians embracing what would later be called the "organizational" approach to twentieth-century American history. Samuel Hays, in *The Response to Industrialism* (1957), and Robert Wiebe, in *The Search for Order* (1967), portrayed progressivism as a broad effort by businessmen, professionals, and other middle-class people to bring order and efficiency to political and economic life. In the new industrial society, economic power was increasingly concentrated in large national organizations, while social and political life remained centered primarily in local communities. Progressivism, Wiebe argued, was the effort of a "new middle class"—a class tied to the emerging national economy—to stabilize and enhance its position in society by bringing those two worlds together.

In the 1970s and 1980s, much of the scholarship on progressivism focused on discovering new groups among whom "progressive" ideas and efforts flourished. Historians found evidence of progressivism in the rising movement by consumers to define their interests; in the growth of reform movements among African Americans; in the changing nature of urban political machines; and in the political activism of working people and labor organizations.

Other scholars attempted to identify progressivism with broad changes in the structure and culture of politics. Richard McCormick, writing in 1981, argued that the crucial change in the progressive era was the decline of political parties and the corresponding rise of interest groups working for particular social and economic goals.

At the same time, many historians have focused on the role of women (and the vast network of voluntary associations they created in shaping and promoting progressive reform). Some progressive battles, historians such as Kathryn Sklar, Ruth Rosen, Elaine Tyler May, and Linda Gordon have argued, were part of an effort by women to protect their interests within the domestic sphere in the face of jarring challenges from the new industrial world. This protective urge drew women reformers to such issues as temperance, divorce, prostitution, and the regulation of female and child labor. Other women worked to expand their own roles in the public world, particularly through their support of suffrage. The gendered interests of women reformers are, many historians insist, critical to an understanding of progressivism.

More recently, a number of historians have sought to place progressivism in a broader context. Daniel Rodgers's *Atlantic Crossings* (1998) is an important study of how European reformers shaped the goals of many American progressives. Both Michael McGerr, in *A Fierce Discontent* (2003), and Alan Dawley, in *Changing the World* (2003), see progressivism as a fundamentally moral project—McGerr, as an effort by the middle class to create order and stability, and Dawley, as an effort by groups on the left to attack social injustice. Progressivism, they argue, was not just a political movement but also an effort to remake society and reshape social relations. •

UNDERSTAND, ANALYZE, & EVALUATE

1. What is the gendered view of progressive reform advanced by historians?
2. Was progressivism a "people's" movement?

with statistics and technical data. When its recommendations reached the New York legislature, its most effective supporters were two Tammany Democrats from working-class backgrounds: Senator Robert F. Wagner and Assemblyman Alfred E. Smith. With the support of Murphy and the backing of other Tammany legislators, they helped pass a series of pioneering labor laws that imposed strict regulations on factory owners and established effective mechanisms for enforcement.

WESTERN PROGRESSIVES

The American West produced some of the most notable progressive leaders of the time: Hiram Johnson of California, George Norris of Nebraska, William Borah of Idaho, and others—almost all of whom spent at least some of their political careers in the United States Senate. For western states, the most important vehicle of reform was the federal government, which exercised a kind of authority in the West that it had never possessed in the East. Disputes over water, for example, almost always involved rivers and streams that crossed state lines. More significant, perhaps, the federal government exercised enormous power over the lands and resources of the western states and provided substantial subsidies to the region in the form of land grants and support for railroad and water projects. Huge areas of the West remained (and still remain) public lands, controlled by Washington. Much of the growth of the West was (and continues to be) a result of federally funded dams, water projects, and other infrastructure undertakings.

AFRICAN AMERICANS AND REFORM

Most white progressives paid little attention to race. But among African Americans themselves, the progressive era produced significant challenges to existing racial norms.

African Americans faced greater obstacles than any other group in seeking reform. So it was not surprising, perhaps, that so many African Americans embraced the message of Booker T. Washington in the late nineteenth century. Washington encouraged black men and women to work for immediate self-improvement rather than long-range social change. By the beginning of the twentieth century, however, a powerful challenge to the philosophy of Washington was emerging. The chief spokesperson for this new approach was W. E. B. Du Bois, a sociologist and historian and one of the first African Americans to receive a degree from Harvard.

In *The Souls of Black Folk* (1903), Du Bois launched an open attack on the philosophy of Washington, accusing him of encouraging white efforts to sustain segregation and of limiting the aspirations of his race. Rather than content themselves with education at trade and agricultural schools, Du Bois encouraged talented blacks to accept nothing less than a full university education and aspire to the professions. They should, above all, fight for their civil rights, not simply wait for them to be granted as a reward for patient striving. In 1905, Du Bois and a group of his supporters met at Niagara Falls—on the Canadian side of the border because no hotel on the American side of the falls would have them— and launched what became known as the Niagara Movement. Four years later, they joined with sympathetic white progressives to form the National Association for the Advancement *NAACP Founded* of Colored People (NAACP). In the years that followed, the new organization worked for equal rights.

Among the many issues that engaged the NAACP and other African American organizations was lynching in the South. The most determined opponents of lynching were southern women, and the most effective crusader was a black woman, Ida B. Wells-Barnett, *Ida B. Wells-Barnett* who worked both on her own (at great personal risk) and with such organizations as the National Association of Colored Women and the Women's Convention of the National Baptist Church to try to expose lynching and challenge segregation.

THE CRISIS W. E. B. Du Bois founded *The Crisis*, the magazine of the NAACP, in 1910. Its object was to "show the danger of race prejudice, particularly as manifested today toward colored people." This photograph shows the magazine's office. (© Underwood & Underwood/Corbis)

CRUSADES FOR SOCIAL ORDER AND REFORM

Many reformers crusaded on behalf of what they considered moral issues—working to eliminate alcohol, curb prostitution, limit divorce, and restrict immigration.

THE TEMPERANCE CRUSADE

Many progressives considered the elimination of alcohol from American life a necessary step in restoring order to society. Scarce wages vanished as male workers spent hours in saloons. Drunkenness spawned violence, and occasionally murder, within urban families. Many working-class wives and mothers hoped through temperance to reform male behavior and thus improve women's lives. Employers, too, regarded alcohol as an impediment to industrial efficiency; workers often missed time on the job because of drunkenness or came to the factory intoxicated. Critics of economic privilege denounced the liquor industry as one of the nation's most sinister trusts. And political reformers, who (correctly) looked on the saloon as one of the central institutions of the urban machine, saw an attack on drinking as part of an attack on the bosses. Out of such sentiments emerged the temperance movement.

There had been a major temperance movement before the Civil War, mobilizing large numbers of people in a crusade with strong evangelical overtones. In 1873, the movement developed new strength. Temperance advocates formed the Women's Christian Temperance Union (WCTU), which was led after 1879 by Frances Willard. By 1911, it had 245,000 *WCTU* members and had become the single largest women's organization in American history to that point. In 1893, the Anti-Saloon League joined the temperance movement and, along with the WCTU, began to press for the legal abolition of saloons. Gradually, that demand grew to include the complete prohibition of the sale and manufacture of alcoholic beverages.

Pressure for prohibition grew steadily through the first decades of the new century. By 1916, nineteen states had passed prohibition laws. America's entry into World *Prohibition* War I, which made the use of grain for alcohol seem wasteful and unnecessary, provided the last push to the advocates of prohibition. In 1917, with the support of rural fundamentalists who opposed alcohol on moral and religious grounds, progressive advocates of prohibition steered through Congress a constitutional amendment. Two years later, after ratification by every state in the nation except Connecticut and Rhode Island (with large populations of Catholic immigrants opposed to prohibition), the Eighteenth Amendment became law, to take effect in January 1920.

IMMIGRATION RESTRICTION

Virtually all reformers agreed that the growing immigrant population had created social problems, but there was wide disagreement on how best to respond. Some progressives believed that the proper approach was to help the new residents adapt to American society. Others argued that the only solution was to limit the flow of new arrivals.

In the first decades of the century, pressure grew to close the nation's gates. New scholarly theories argued that the introduction of immigrants into American society was polluting the nation's racial stock. One of these theories, **eugenics,** began as the science of altering the reproductive processes of plants and animals to produce new hybrids or breeds. But in the late nineteenth century, eugenicists spread the spurious belief that human inequalities were hereditary and that immigration was contributing to the multiplication of the unfit. A special federal commission of "experts," chaired by Senator William

P. Dillingham of Vermont, issued a study filled with statistics and scholarly testimony. It argued that the newer immigrant groups—largely southern and eastern Europeans—had proved themselves less assimilable than earlier immigrants. Immigration, the report implied, should be restricted by nationality. Even many people who rejected these racial arguments supported limiting immigration as a way to solve such urban problems as overcrowding, unemployment, strained social services, and social unrest.

The combination of these concerns gradually won the support of some of the nation's leading progressives to limit immigration—among them former president Theodore Roosevelt. Powerful opponents—employers who saw immigration as a source of cheap labor, immigrants themselves, and their political representatives—managed to block the restriction movement for a time. But by the beginning of World War I, which itself effectively blocked immigration temporarily, the nativist tide was gaining strength.

THE DREAM OF SOCIALISM

Although never a force to rival or even seriously threaten the two major parties, **socialism** gained considerable strength during the early years of the twentieth century. In the election of 1900, the Socialist Party of America attracted the support of fewer than 100,000 voters;
Eugene V. Debs   in 1912, its durable leader and perennial presidential candidate, Eugene V. Debs, received nearly 1 million ballots. Strongest in urban immigrant communities, particularly among Germans and Jews, it also attracted the loyalties of a substantial number of Protestant farmers in the South and the Midwest.

Virtually all socialists agreed on the need for basic structural changes in the economy, but they differed widely on the extent of those changes and the tactics necessary to achieve them. Some socialists endorsed the radical goals of European Marxists (a complete end to capitalism and private property); others envisioned more moderate reform that would allow small-scale private enterprise to survive but would nationalize major industries. Some believed in working for reform through electoral politics; others favored militant direct action. Among the militants was the radical labor union the Industrial Workers of the World
IWW ("Wobblies")   (IWW), known to opponents as the "Wobblies." Under the leadership of William ("Big Bill") Haywood, the IWW advocated a single union for all workers and was one of the few labor organizations to champion the cause of unskilled workers. The Wobblies were widely believed to have been responsible for dynamiting railroad lines and power stations and committing other acts of terror in the first years of the twentieth century.

Moderate socialists who advocated peaceful change through political struggle dominated the Socialist Party. They emphasized a gradual education of the public to the need for change and patient efforts within the system to enact it. But the party refused to support the nation's war effort in World War I. The growing wave of antiradicalism during the war subjected the socialists to enormous harassment and persecution, contributing to socialism's decline.

DECENTRALIZATION AND REGULATION

Most progressives retained faith in the possibilities of reform within a capitalist system. Rather than nationalize basic industries, many reformers hoped to restore the economy to a more human scale. They argued that the federal government should work to break up the largest combinations and enforce a balance between the need for bigness and the need for competition. This viewpoint came to be identified particularly closely with Louis D.
Louis Brandeis   Brandeis, a brilliant lawyer and, later, justice of the Supreme Court, who

wrote widely (most notably in his 1913 book *Other People's Money*) about the "curse of bigness." Brandeis insisted that government must regulate competition in such a way as to ensure that large combinations did not emerge.

Other progressives were less enthusiastic about the virtues of competition. More important to them was efficiency. Government, they argued, should not fight "bigness" but rather should guard against abuses of power by large institutions. It should distinguish between "good trusts" and "bad trusts." Since economic consolidation was destined to remain a permanent feature of American society, continuing oversight by a strong, modernized government was essential. Thus, many progressives believed that government should play a more active role in regulating and planning economic life. One of those who came to endorse that position (although not fully until after 1910) was Theodore Roosevelt, who once said: "We should enter upon a course of supervision, control, and regulation of those great corporations." Roosevelt became, for a time, the most powerful symbol of the reform impulse at the national level.

THEODORE ROOSEVELT AND THE MODERN PRESIDENCY

To a generation of progressive reformers, Theodore Roosevelt was more than an admired public figure; he was an idol. No president before, and few since, attracted such attention and devotion. Yet for all his popularity among reformers, Roosevelt was in many respects decidedly conservative. He earned his extraordinary popularity less because of the extent of the reforms he championed than because he brought to his office a broad conception of its powers. He invested the presidency with something of its modern status as the center of national political life.

THE ACCIDENTAL PRESIDENT

When President William McKinley was assassinated in September 1901, Roosevelt, forty-two years old at the time, became the youngest man ever to assume the presidency. "I told William McKinley that it was a mistake to nominate that wild man at Philadelphia," party boss Mark Hanna was reported to have exclaimed. "Now look, that damned cowboy is President of the United States!"

As president, Roosevelt rarely openly rebelled against the leaders of his party. He became, rather, a champion of cautious, moderate change. Reform, he believed, was a vehicle less for remaking American society than for protecting it against more radical challenges.

Roosevelt allied himself with those progressives who urged regulation (but not destruction) of the trusts. At the heart of his policy was to give the   *Roosevelt's Vision of Federal Power* government the power to investigate corporations and publicize the results.

Although Roosevelt was not a trustbuster at heart, he made a few highly publicized efforts to break up combinations. In 1902, he ordered the Justice Department to invoke the Sherman Antitrust Act against a great new railroad monopoly in the Northwest, the Northern Securities Company, a $400 million enterprise pieced together by J. P. Morgan and others. Roosevelt filed more than forty additional antitrust suits during   *Antitrust Suits* the remainder of his presidency, but he made no serious commitment to reverse the prevailing trend toward economic concentration.

When a bitter 1902 strike by the United Mine Workers endangered coal supplies for the coming winter, Roosevelt asked both the operators and the miners to accept impartial federal

BOYS IN THE MINES These young boys, covered in grime and no more than twelve years old, pose for Lewis Hine outside the coal mine in Pennsylvania where they worked as "breaker boys," crawling into newly blasted areas and breaking up the loose coal. The rugged conditions in the mines were one cause of the great strike of 1902, in which Theodore Roosevelt intervened. (The Library of Congress)

arbitration. When the mine owners balked, Roosevelt threatened to send federal troops to seize the mines. The operators finally relented. Arbitrators awarded the strikers a 10 percent wage increase and a nine-hour day, although no recognition of their union—less than the miners had wanted but more than they would likely have won without Roosevelt's intervention.

The "Square Deal"

During the 1904 campaign for the presidency, Roosevelt boasted that he had worked in the anthracite coal strike to provide everyone with a "square deal." One of his first targets after winning the election was the powerful railroad industry. The Interstate Commerce Act of 1887, establishing the Interstate Commerce Commission (ICC), had been an early effort to *Hepburn Act* regulate the industry, but over the years, the courts had sharply limited its influence. The Hepburn Railroad Regulation Act of 1906 sought to restore some regulatory authority to the government by giving the ICC the power to oversee railroad rates.

Roosevelt also pressured Congress to enact the Pure Food and Drug Act, which *Pure Food and Drug Act* restricted the sale of dangerous or ineffective medicines. *The Jungle,* a powerful novel published by Upton Sinclair in 1906, included appalling descriptions of conditions in the meatpacking industry. Roosevelt pushed for passage of the Meat Inspection Act, which helped eliminate many diseases once transmitted in impure meat. Starting in 1907, he proposed even more stringent reforms: an eight-hour day for workers, broader compensation for victims of industrial accidents, inheritance and income taxes, and regulation of the stock market. Conservative opposition blocked much of his agenda, widening the gulf between the president and the conservative wing of his party.

ROOSEVELT AND THE ENVIRONMENT

Roosevelt's aggressive policies on behalf of conservation contributed to that gulf. Using executive powers, he restricted private development on millions of acres of undeveloped government land—most of it in the West—by adding them to the previously modest national forest system. When conservatives in Congress restricted his authority over public lands in 1907, Roosevelt and his chief forester, Gifford Pinchot, seized all the forests and many of the water power sites still in the public domain before the bill became law.

Roosevelt was the first president to take an active interest in the new and struggling American conservation movement. In the early twentieth century, many people who considered themselves **conservationists**—including Pinchot, the first director of the U.S. Forest Service (which he helped create)—promoted policies to protect land for carefully managed development.

Roosevelt also supported public reclamation and irrigation projects. In 1902, the president backed the National Reclamation Act, which provided federal funds for the construction of dams, reservoirs, and canals in the West—projects that would open new lands for cultivation and (years later) provide cheap electric power.

Despite his sympathy with Pinchot's vision of conservation, Roosevelt also shared some of the concerns of the naturalists—those committed to protecting the natural beauty of the land and the health of its wildlife from human intrusion. Early in his presidency, Roosevelt spent four days camping in the Sierras with John Muir, the nation's leading preservationist and the founder of the Sierra Club. Roosevelt also added significantly to the still-young National Park System, whose purpose was to protect public land from exploitation or development. (For Muir's views on the system, see "Consider the Source: John Muir on the Value of Wild Places.")

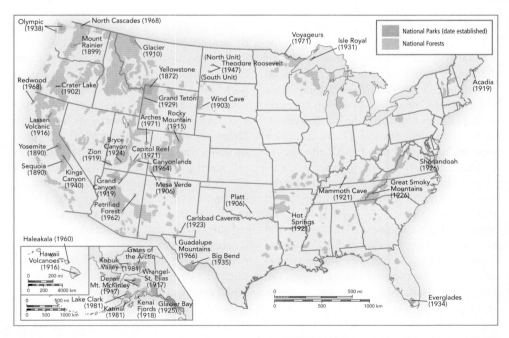

ESTABLISHMENT OF NATIONAL PARKS AND FORESTS This map illustrates the steady growth throughout the late nineteenth and twentieth centuries of the systems of national parks and national forests in the United States. Although Theodore Roosevelt is widely and correctly remembered as a great champion of national parks and forests, the greatest expansions of these systems occurred after his presidency. Note, for example, how many new areas were added in the 1920s. • *What is the difference between national parks and national forests?*

JOHN MUIR ON THE VALUE OF WILD PLACES, 1901

John Muir is often called the "father of the national parks" for his role as advocate on behalf of legislation to designate certain wilderness areas as off-limits for commercial development. In this excerpt from his book *Our National Parks,* he argues for the restorative benefits of visiting unspoiled nature.

The tendency nowadays to wander in wildernesses is delightful to see. Thousands of tired, nerve-shaken, over-civilized people are beginning to find out that going to the mountains is going home; that wildness is a necessity; and that mountain parks and reservations are useful not only as fountains of timber and irrigating rivers, but as fountains of life. Awakening from the stupefying effects of the vice of over-industry and the deadly apathy of luxury, they are trying as best they can to mix and enrich their own little ongoings with those of Nature, and to get rid of rust and disease. Briskly venturing and roaming, some are washing off sins and cobweb cares of the devil's spinning in all-day storms on mountains; sauntering in rosiny pinewoods or in gentian meadows, brushing through chaparral, bending down and parting sweet, flowery sprays; tracing rivers to their sources, getting in touch with the nerves of Mother Earth; jumping from rock to rock, feeling the life of them, learning the songs of them, panting in whole-souled exercise, and rejoicing in deep, long-drawn breaths of pure wildness. This is fine and natural and full of promise. So also is the growing interest in the care and preservation of forests and wild places in general, and in the half wild parks and gardens of towns. . . .

When, like a merchant taking a list of his goods, we take stock of our wildness, we are glad to see how much of even the most destructible kind is still unspoiled.

Looking at our continent as scenery when it was all wild, lying between beautiful seas, the starry sky above it, the starry rocks beneath it, to compare its sides, the East and the West, would be like comparing the sides of a rainbow. But it is no longer equally beautiful. . . . [T]he continent's outer beauty is fast passing away, especially the plant part of it, the most destructible and most universally charming of all.

Only thirty years ago, the great Central Valley of California, five hundred miles long and fifty miles wide, was one bed of golden and purple flowers. Now it is ploughed and pastured out of existence, gone forever,—scarce a memory of it left in fence corners and along the bluffs of the streams. . . . The same fate, sooner or later, is awaiting them all, unless awakening public opinion comes forward to stop it. . . .

The Grand Cañon Reserve of Arizona, of nearly two million acres, or the most interesting part of it, as well as the Rainier region, should be made into a national park, on account of their supreme grandeur and beauty. . . . No matter how far you have wandered hitherto, or how many famous gorges and valleys you have seen, this one, the Grand Cañon of the Colorado, will seem as novel to you, as unearthly in the color and grandeur and quantity of its architecture, as if you had found it after death, on some other star; so incomparably lovely and grand and supreme is it above all the other cañons in our fire-moulded, earthquake-shaken, rain-washed, wave-washed, river and glacier sculptured world.

UNDERSTAND, ANALYZE, & EVALUATE

1. What benefits does Muir describe as a result of spending time in the "wilderness"?

What maladies does Muir believe the "wilderness" will correct? How do his arguments reflect the economic and social history of his time?

2. What is Muir's purpose? Is he attempting primarily to instruct or to persuade? How does that purpose affect the tone of the writing?

Source: Library of Congress, Materials from the General Collection and Rare Book and Special Collections Division of the Library of Congress.

The contending views of the early conservation movement came to a head beginning in 1906 in a controversy over the Hetch Hetchy Valley in Yosemite   *Fight over Hetch Hetchy* National Park—a spectacular high-walled valley popular with naturalists. But many residents of San Francisco worried about finding enough water to serve their growing population. They saw Hetch Hetchy as an ideal place for a dam, which would create a large reservoir for the city.

In 1906, San Francisco suffered a devastating earthquake and fire. Widespread sympathy for the city strengthened the case for the dam, and Roosevelt turned the decision over to Pinchot, who approved its construction.

For over a decade, a battle raged between naturalists and the advocates of the dam, a battle that consumed the energies of John Muir for the rest of his life and that eventually, many believed, led him to an early death. To Pinchot, the needs of the city were more important than the claims of preservation. Muir helped place a referendum question on the ballot in 1908, certain that the residents of the city would oppose the project. Instead, San Franciscans approved the dam by a huge margin. Construction of the dam finally began after World War I.

This setback for the naturalists was not, however, a total defeat. The fight against Hetch Hetchy helped mobilize a new coalition of people committed to preservation of wilderness.

Panic and Retirement

Despite the flurry of reforms Roosevelt was able to enact, the government still had relatively little control over the industrial economy. That became clear in 1907, when a serious panic and recession began. Conservatives blamed Roosevelt's "mad" economic policies for the disaster. And while the president naturally (and correctly) disagreed, he nevertheless acted quickly to reassure business leaders that he would not interfere with their recovery efforts.

The financier J. P. Morgan helped construct a pool of the assets of several important New York banks to prop up shaky financial institutions. The key to the arrangement, Morgan told the president, was a purchase by U.S. Steel of the shares of the Tennessee Coal and Iron Company, currently held by a threatened New York bank. Morgan insisted that he needed assurances that the purchase would not prompt antitrust action. Roosevelt tacitly agreed, and the Morgan plan proceeded. Whether or not as a result, the panic soon subsided.

Roosevelt loved being president, and many people assumed that he would run for reelection in 1908, despite the long-standing tradition of presidents serving no more than two terms. But the Panic of 1907 and Roosevelt's reform efforts so alienated conservatives in his own party that he might have had difficulty winning the Republican nomination. In 1904, moreover, he had made a public promise to step down four years later. And so in 1909, Roosevelt, fifty years old, retired from public life—briefly.

THE TROUBLED SUCCESSION

William Howard Taft, who assumed the presidency in 1909, had been Theodore
William Howard Taft   Roosevelt's most trusted lieutenant and his handpicked successor;
progressive reformers believed him to be one of their own. But Taft was also a
restrained and moderate jurist, a man with a punctilious regard for legal process;
conservatives expected him to abandon Roosevelt's aggressive use of presidential
powers. By seeming acceptable to almost everyone, Taft easily won election to the
White House in 1908 over William Jennings Bryan, running for the Democrats for
the third time.

Four years later, however, Taft would leave office the most decisively defeated president of the twentieth century, his party deeply divided and the government in the hands
of a Democratic administration for the first time in twenty years.

TAFT AND THE PROGRESSIVES

Taft's first problem arose in the opening months of the new administration, when he called
Congress into special session to lower protective tariff rates, an old progressive demand.
But the president made no effort to overcome the opposition of the congressional Old
Guard, arguing that to do so would violate the constitutional doctrine of separation of
powers. The result was the feeble Payne-Aldrich Tariff, which reduced tariff rates scarcely
at all.

A sensational controversy that broke out late in 1909 helped destroy Taft's popularity
with reformers for good. Many progressives had been unhappy when Taft replaced
Roosevelt's secretary of the interior, James R. Garfield, an aggressive conservationist,
with Richard A. Ballinger, a conservative corporate lawyer. Suspicion of Ballinger grew
when he attempted to invalidate Roosevelt's removal of nearly 1 million acres of forests
and mineral reserves from private development.

In the midst of this mounting concern, Louis Glavis, an Interior Department investiga-
tor, charged Ballinger with having once connived to turn over valuable public coal lands
in Alaska to a private syndicate for personal profit. Glavis took the evidence to Gifford
Ballinger–Pinchot Dispute   Pinchot, still director of the U.S. Forest Service and a critic of
Ballinger's policies. Pinchot took the charges to the president. Taft investigated them and
decided they were groundless. Unsatisfied, Pinchot leaked the story to the press and asked
Congress to investigate the scandal. The president discharged him for insubordination,
and the congressional committee appointed to study the controversy, dominated by Old
Guard Republicans, exonerated Ballinger. But progressives throughout the country supported Pinchot. The controversy aroused as much public passion as any dispute of its time.
By the time it was over, Taft had alienated the supporters of Roosevelt completely—and,
it seemed, irrevocably.

THE RETURN OF ROOSEVELT

During most of these controversies, Theodore Roosevelt was out of the country on a long
hunting safari in Africa and an extended tour of Europe. To the American public, however,
Roosevelt remained a formidable presence. His return to New York in the spring of 1910
was a major public event. Roosevelt insisted that he had no plans to reenter politics, but
within a month he announced that he would embark on a national speaking tour before

ROOSEVELT AT OSAWATOMIE Roosevelt's speech at Osawatomie, Kansas, in 1910 was the most radical of his career and openly marked his break with the Taft administration and the Republican leadership. "The essence of any struggle for liberty," he told his largely conservative audience, "has always been, and must always be to take from some one man or class of men the right to enjoy power, or wealth, or position or immunity, which has not been earned by service to his or their fellows." (© Granger, NYC—All Rights Reserved.)

the end of the summer. Furious with Taft, he was becoming convinced that he alone was capable of reuniting the Republican Party.

The real signal of Roosevelt's decision to assume leadership of Republican reformers came in a speech he gave on September 1, 1910, in Osawatomie, Kansas. In it he outlined a set of principles, which he labeled the "New Nationalism," that made *"New Nationalism"* clear he had moved a considerable way from the cautious conservatism of the years of his presidency. He argued that social justice was possible only through a strong federal government whose executive acted as the "steward of the public welfare." He supported graduated income and inheritance taxes, workers' compensation for industrial accidents, regulation of the labor of women and children, tariff revision, and firmer regulation of corporations.

SPREADING INSURGENCY

The congressional elections of 1910 provided further evidence of how far the progressive revolt had spread. In primary elections, conservative Republicans suffered defeat after defeat, while almost all the progressive incumbents were reelected. In the general election, the Democrats won control of the House of Representatives for the first time in sixteen years and gained strength in the Senate. But Roosevelt still denied any presidential ambitions and claimed that his real purpose was to pressure Taft to return to progressive policies. Two events, however, changed his mind. The first, on October 27, 1911, was the announcement by the administration of a suit against U.S. Steel, which charged, among other things, that the 1907 acquisition of the Tennessee Coal and Iron Company had been illegal. Roosevelt had approved that acquisition in the midst of the 1907 panic, and he was enraged by the implication that he had acted improperly.

Roosevelt was still reluctant to become a candidate for president because Senator Robert La Follette, the great Wisconsin progressive, had been working since 1911 to secure the presidential nomination for himself. But La Follette's candidacy stumbled in February 1912 when, exhausted and distraught over the illness of a daughter, he appeared to suffer a nervous breakdown during a speech in Philadelphia. Roosevelt announced his candidacy on February 22.

ROOSEVELT VERSUS TAFT

For all practical purposes, the campaign for the Republican nomination had now become a battle between Roosevelt and Taft. Roosevelt scored overwhelming victories in all thirteen presidential primaries. Taft, however, remained the choice of most party leaders, who controlled the nominating process.

The battle for the nomination at the Chicago convention revolved around an unusually large number of contested delegates: 254 in all. Roosevelt needed fewer than half the disputed seats to clinch the nomination. But the Republican National Committee, controlled by the Old Guard, awarded all but 19 of them to Taft. At a rally the night before the convention opened, Roosevelt addressed 5,000 cheering supporters. "We stand at Armageddon," he told the roaring crowd, "and we battle for the Lord." The next day, he led his supporters out of the convention, and out of the party. The convention then quietly nominated Taft on the first ballot.

Roosevelt summoned his supporters back to Chicago in August for another convention, this one to launch the new Progressive Party and to nominate himself as its presidential can-
"Bull Moose" Party   didate. Roosevelt approached the battle feeling, as he put it, "fit as a bull moose" (thus giving his new party an enduring nickname). But Roosevelt was also aware that his cause was almost hopeless, partly because many of the insurgents who had supported him during the primaries refused to follow him out of the Republican Party. It was also because of the man the Democrats had nominated for president.

WOODROW WILSON AND THE NEW FREEDOM

The 1912 presidential contest was not simply one between conservatives and reformers. It was also one between two brands of progressivism. And it matched the two most important national leaders of the early twentieth century in an unequal contest.

WOODROW WILSON

Reform sentiment had been gaining strength within the Democratic Party as well as the Republican Party in the first years of the century. At the June 1912 Democratic Convention in Baltimore, Champ Clark, the conservative Speaker of the House, was unable to assemble the two-thirds majority necessary for nomination because of progressive opposition. Finally, on the forty-sixth ballot, Woodrow Wilson, the governor of New Jersey and the only genuinely progressive candidate in the race, emerged as the party's nominee.

Wilson had been a professor of political science at Princeton until 1902, when he was named president of the university. Elected governor of New Jersey in 1910, he quickly earned a national reputation for winning passage of progressive legislation. As a presidential candidate in 1912, Wilson presented a progressive program that came to be called the "New Freedom." Roosevelt's New Nationalism supported economic concentration and using government to regulate and control it. *Wilson's "New Freedom"* Wilson seemed to side with those who (like Louis Brandeis) believed that bigness was both unjust and inefficient, that the proper response to monopoly was not to regulate it but to destroy it.

The 1912 presidential campaign was an anticlimax. Taft, resigned to defeat, barely campaigned. Roosevelt campaigned energetically (until a gunshot wound from a would-be assassin forced him to the sidelines during the last weeks before the election), but he

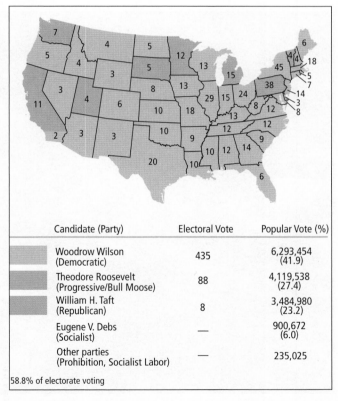

Candidate (Party)	Electoral Vote	Popular Vote (%)
Woodrow Wilson (Democratic)	435	6,293,454 (41.9)
Theodore Roosevelt (Progressive/Bull Moose)	88	4,119,538 (27.4)
William H. Taft (Republican)	8	3,484,980 (23.2)
Eugene V. Debs (Socialist)	—	900,672 (6.0)
Other parties (Prohibition, Socialist Labor)	—	235,025

58.8% of electorate voting

THE ELECTION OF 1912 The election of 1912 was one of the most unusual in American history because of the dramatic schism within the Republican Party. Two Republican presidents—William Howard Taft, the incumbent, and Theodore Roosevelt, his predecessor—ran against each other, opening the way for a victory by the Democratic candidate, Woodrow Wilson, who won with only 42 percent of the popular vote. A fourth candidate, the socialist Eugene V. Debs, received a significant 6 percent of the vote. • *What events caused the schism between Taft and Roosevelt?*

failed to draw any significant number of Democratic progressives away from Wilson. In November, Roosevelt and Taft split the Republican vote; Wilson held on to most Democrats and won. He received only 42 percent of the popular vote, compared with 27 percent for Roosevelt, 23 percent for Taft, and 6 percent for the socialist Eugene Debs. But in the electoral college, Wilson won 435 of the 531 votes.

THE SCHOLAR AS PRESIDENT

Wilson was a bold and forceful president. He exerted firm control over his cabinet, and he delegated real authority only to those who were loyal to him. His most powerful adviser, Colonel Edward M. House, was an intelligent and ambitious Texan who held no office and whose only claim to authority was his personal intimacy with the president.

In legislative matters, Wilson skillfully welded together a coalition that would support his goals. Democratic majorities in both houses of Congress made his task easier. Wilson's first triumph as president was the fulfillment of an old Democratic (and

WOODROW WILSON Woodrow Wilson, the 28th President of the United States, was a Virginian (the first southerner to be elected president since before the Civil War), a professor of political science and later president of Princeton University, governor of New Jersey, and a progressive. His election to the presidency brought the first Democrat to the White House since 1896. (The Library of Congress)

progressive) goal: a substantial lowering of the protective tariff. The Underwood-Simmons Tariff provided cuts significant enough, progressives believed, to introduce real competition into American markets and thus to help break the power of trusts. To make up for the loss of revenue under the new tariff, Congress *Lowering the Tariff* approved a graduated income tax, which the recently adopted Sixteenth Amendment to the Constitution now permitted. This first modern income tax imposed a 1 percent tax on individuals and corporations earning more than $4,000 a year, with rates ranging up to 6 percent on incomes over $500,000 annually.

Wilson held Congress in session through the summer to work on a major reform of the American banking system: the Federal Reserve Act, which *Banking System Reform* Congress passed and the president signed on December 23, 1913. It created twelve regional banks, each to be owned and controlled by the individual banks of its district. The regional Federal Reserve banks would hold a certain percentage of the assets of their member banks in reserve; they would use those reserves to support loans to private banks at an interest (or "discount") rate that the Federal Reserve system would set; they would issue a new type of paper currency—Federal Reserve notes—that would become the nation's basic medium of trade and would be backed by the government. Most important, they would be able to shift funds quickly to troubled areas—to meet increased demands for credit or to protect imperiled banks. Supervising and regulating the entire system was a national Federal Reserve Board, whose members were appointed by the president.

In 1914, turning to the central issue of his 1912 campaign, Wilson proposed two measures to deal with the problem of monopoly, which took shape as the *Corporate Oversight* Federal Trade Commission Act and the Clayton Antitrust Act. The Federal Trade Commission Act created a regulatory agency that would help businesses determine in advance whether their actions would be acceptable to the government. The agency would also have authority to launch prosecutions against "unfair trade practices," and it would have wide power to investigate corporate behavior. Wilson signed the Federal Trade Commission Bill happily, but he seemed to lose interest in the Clayton Antitrust Bill, which proposed stronger measures to break up trusts. Wilson did little to protect it from conservative assaults, which greatly weakened it.

RETREAT AND ADVANCE

By the fall of 1914, Wilson believed that the New Freedom program was essentially complete and that agitation for reform would now subside. He refused to support the movement for national woman suffrage. Deferring to southern Democrats, he condoned the reimposition of segregation in the agencies of the federal government (in contrast to Roosevelt, who had ordered the elimination of many such barriers). When congressional progressives attempted to enlist his support for new reform legislation, Wilson dismissed their proposals as unconstitutional or unnecessary.

The congressional elections of 1914, however, shattered the president's complacency. Democrats suffered major losses in Congress, and voters who in 1912 had supported the Progressive Party began returning to the Republicans. Wilson realized he would not be able to rely on a divided opposition when he ran for reelection in 1916. By the end of 1915, therefore, Wilson had begun to support a second flurry of reforms. In January 1916, he appointed Louis Brandeis to the Supreme Court, making him not only the first Jew but also the most advanced progressive to serve there. Later, Wilson supported a measure to make it easier for farmers to receive credit, and another measure creating a system of workers' compensation for federal employees.

In 1916, Wilson supported the Keating-Owen Act, which prohibited the shipment of goods produced by underage children across state lines, thus giving an expanded *Child-Labor Laws* importance to the constitutional clause assigning Congress the task of regulating interstate commerce. The president similarly supported measures that used federal taxing authority as a vehicle for legislating social change. After the Court struck down Keating-Owen, a new law attempted to achieve the same goal by imposing a heavy tax on the products of child labor. (The Court later struck down that law too.) The Smith-Lever Act of 1914 offered matching federal grants to support agricultural extension education. Over time, these innovative uses of government overcame most of the constitutional objections and became the foundation of a long-term growth in federal power over the economy.

CONCLUSION

The powerful surge of reform efforts in the last years of the nineteenth century and the first years of the twentieth century caused many Americans to identify themselves as "progressives." That label meant many different things to many different people, but at its core was a belief that human effort and government action could improve society. By the early twentieth century, progressivism had become a powerful, transformative force in American life.

This great surge of reform eventually reached the federal government and national politics, as progressives came to believe that success required the engagement of the federal government. Two national leaders, Theodore Roosevelt and Woodrow Wilson, contributed to a period of national reform that made the government in Washington a great center of power for the first time since the Civil War—a position it has never relinquished. Progressivism did not solve the nation's problems, but it gave movements, organizations, and governments new tools to deal with them.

KEY TERMS/PEOPLE/PLACES/EVENTS

Alice Paul 496
Bull Moose Party 512
conservationists 507
eugenics 503
Hetch Hetchy 509
Hull House 492
Ida B. Wells-Barnett 502
IWW ("Wobblies") 504
Jane Addams 492
John Muir 507
Louis Brandeis 504

muckrakers 489
NAACP 502
New Freedom 513
New Nationalism 511
Nineteenth Amendment 496
progressivism 488
prohibition 503
Robert La Follette 498
Social Gospel 491
socialism 504
social justice 489

Theodore Roosevelt 505
Triangle Shirtwaist
  Company fire 499
W. E. B. Du Bois 502
William Howard
  Taft 510
Women's Christian
  Temperance Union
  (WCTU) 503
Woodrow Wilson 513

RECALL AND REFLECT

1. What "moral" crusades did progressives undertake in their efforts to reform the social order?
2. How did W. E. B. Du Bois's philosophy on race relations differ from that of Booker T. Washington?
3. What were some of the approaches progressives used to challenge the power and influence of capitalist corporate America?
4. What was the difference between Theodore Roosevelt's "New Nationalism" and Woodrow Wilson's "New Freedom"?

21 | AMERICA AND THE GREAT WAR

THE "BIG STICK": AMERICA AND THE WORLD,
1901–1917

THE ROAD TO WAR

"OVER THERE"

THE SEARCH FOR A NEW WORLD ORDER

A SOCIETY IN TURMOIL

LOOKING AHEAD

1. What were the most important events that led up to the United States declaring war on Germany?

2. How did U.S. participation in the Great War affect the nation's economy and society, both during the war and after the conflict ended?

3. Why did the Great War fail to become the "war to end all wars"?

THE "GREAT WAR," AS IT was known to a generation unaware that a greater war would soon follow, began quietly in August 1914 when Austria-Hungary invaded the tiny Balkan nation of Serbia. Within weeks, however, the conflict had grown into a conflagration engaging the armies of most of the major nations of Europe. Americans looked on with horror as the war became what many people claimed was the most savage in history. It dragged on, brutally and inconclusively, for over four years. Most Americans also believed at first that the conflict had little to do with them. They were wrong. After nearly three years of attempting to affect the outcome of the conflict without becoming embroiled in it, the United States formally entered the war in April 1917.

THE "BIG STICK": AMERICA AND THE WORLD, 1901–1917

To most of the American public, foreign affairs remained largely remote in the early twentieth century. But to Theodore Roosevelt and later presidents, that remoteness made foreign affairs appealing. Overseas, the president could act with less regard for Congress and the courts.

ROOSEVELT AND "CIVILIZATION"

Theodore Roosevelt believed in using American power in the world (a conviction he once alluded to by citing the proverb, "Speak softly, and carry a big stick"). But he had two different standards for using that power.

Roosevelt believed that an important distinction existed between the "civilized" and "uncivilized" nations of the world. "Civilized" nations, as he defined them, were predominantly white and Anglo-Saxon or Teutonic; "uncivilized" nations were generally nonwhite, Latin, or Slavic. Civilized nations were also, by Roosevelt's definition, producers of industrial goods. Uncivilized nations were suppliers of raw materials and markets for industrial products. Roosevelt believed that a civilized society had the right and duty to intervene in the affairs of "backward nations" to preserve order and stability—for the sake of both nations. That belief, the obligation of a "civilized" nation to, in effect, police the world, was one important reason for Roosevelt's early support of the development of American sea power. By 1906, the American navy had attained a size and strength surpassed only by that of Great Britain.

TIME LINE

1914
World War I begins

Panama Canal opened

1915
U.S. troops in Haiti

Lusitania torpedoed

Wilson supports preparedness

1916
Wilson reelected

U.S. troops in Mexico

1917
German unrestricted submarine warfare

U.S. enters World War I

Selective Service Act

War Industries Board created

1918
Sedition Act

Wilson's Fourteen Points

Armistice ends war

Paris Peace Conference

1919
Senate rejects Treaty of Versailles

Race riots in Chicago and other cities

Steel strike and other labor actions

1920
Palmer raids and Red Scare

Harding elected president

1927
Sacco and Vanzetti executed

THE WORLD'S CONSTABLE.

"THE NEW DIPLOMACY" This 1904 drawing by the famous *Puck* cartoonist Louis Dalrymple conveys the new image of America as a great power that Theodore Roosevelt hoped to convey. Roosevelt polices the world by dealing with "less civilized" people on the left using the "big stick" and with "civilized" nations on the right by using diplomacy. (© Granger, NYC—All Rights Reserved.)

Protecting the "Open Door" in Asia

In 1904, the Japanese staged a surprise attack on the Russian fleet at Port Arthur in southern Manchuria, a province of China that both Russia and Japan hoped to control. Roosevelt, hoping to prevent either nation from becoming dominant there, agreed to mediate an end to the conflict. Russia, faring badly in the war, had no choice but to agree. At a peace conference in Portsmouth, New Hampshire, in 1905, Roosevelt pressured the embattled Russians to accept Japan's territorial gains. The Japanese agreed to cease the fighting and expand no farther. At the same time, Roosevelt negotiated a secret agreement with the Japanese to ensure that the United States could continue to trade freely in the region. Roosevelt received the Nobel Peace Prize in 1906 for his mediation of what became the Treaty of Portsmouth.

In the years that followed, relations between the United States and Japan steadily deteriorated. Japan, by then the preeminent naval power in the Pacific, began to exclude American trade from many of the territories it controlled. Roosevelt took no direct action against Japan, but to be sure the Japanese government recognized the power of the United States, he sent sixteen battleships of the new American navy (known as the "Great White *"Great White Fleet"* Fleet" because the ships were temporarily painted white for the voyage) on an unprecedented journey around the world that included a call on Japan.

The Iron-Fisted Neighbor

Roosevelt took a particular interest in Latin America. Embarking on a series of ventures in the Caribbean and South America, he established a pattern of American intervention in the region that would outlive his presidency.

In 1902, the government of Venezuela began to renege on debts to European bankers. Naval forces of Britain, Italy, and Germany blockaded the Venezuelan coast in response. Then German ships began to bombard a Venezuelan port. Amid rumors that Germany planned to establish a permanent base in the region, Roosevelt used the threat of American naval power to pressure the German navy to withdraw.

The incident helped persuade Roosevelt that European intrusions into Latin America could result not only from aggression but also from instability or irresponsibility (such as defaulting on debts) within the Latin American nations themselves. As a result, in 1904 he announced what came to be known as the "Roosevelt Corollary" to the Monroe *"Roosevelt Corollary"* Doctrine. The United States, he claimed, had the right not only to oppose European intervention in the Western Hemisphere but also to intervene in the domestic affairs of its neighbors if those neighbors proved unable to maintain order and national sovereignty on their own.

The immediate motivation for the Roosevelt Corollary, and the first opportunity for using it, was a crisis in the Dominican Republic. A revolution had toppled its corrupt and bankrupt government in 1903, but the new regime proved no better able than the old to make good on the country's $22 million in debts to European nations. Using the rationale provided by the Roosevelt Corollary, Roosevelt established, in effect, an American receivership, assuming control of Dominican customs and distributing 45 percent of the revenues to the Dominicans and the rest to foreign creditors. This arrangement lasted, in one form or another, for more than three decades.

THE PANAMA CANAL

The most celebrated foreign policy accomplishment of Roosevelt's presidency was the construction of the Panama Canal, which linked the Atlantic and the Pacific by creating a channel through Central America. At first, Roosevelt and many others favored a route across Nicaragua, which would permit a sea-level canal requiring no locks. But they soon turned instead to the narrow Isthmus of Panama (then part of Colombia), the site of an earlier failed effort by a French company to construct a channel. Although the Panama route was not at sea level, it was shorter than the one in Nicaragua, and construction was already about 40 percent complete. The French then lowered the price for its holdings, and the United States opted for Panama.

Roosevelt dispatched John Hay, his secretary of state, to negotiate an agreement with Colombian diplomats that would allow construction to begin without delay. Under heavy American pressure, the Colombian chargé d'affaires, Tomás Herrán, unwisely signed an agreement giving the United States perpetual rights to a six-mile-wide "Canal Zone" across Colombia; in return, the United States would pay Colombia $10 million and an annual rental of $250,000. The outraged Colombian senate refused to ratify the treaty. Colombia then sent a new representative to Washington with instructions to demand at least $20 million from the Americans plus a share of the payment to the French.

Roosevelt was furious and began to look for ways to circumvent the Colombian government. Philippe Bunau-Varilla, chief engineer of the French canal project, was a ready ally. In 1903, with the support of the United States, he helped organize and finance a revolution in Panama. Roosevelt landed troops from the U.S.S. *Nashville* there to "maintain order." Their presence prevented Colombian forces from suppressing the rebellion, and three days later Roosevelt recognized Panama as an independent nation. The new Panamanian government quickly agreed to the terms the Colombian senate had rejected. Work on the canal proceeded rapidly, and it opened in 1914.

THE UNITED STATES AND LATIN AMERICA, 1895–1941   Except for Puerto Rico, the Virgin Islands, and the Canal Zone, the United States had no formal possessions in Latin America and the Caribbean in the late nineteenth century and the first half of the twentieth. But as this map reveals, the United States exercised considerable influence—both political and economic, augmented at times by military intervention—in these regions throughout this period. Note the particularly intrusive presence of the United States in the affairs of Cuba, Haiti, and the Dominican Republic—as well as the canal-related interventions in Colombia and Panama. • *What were the reasons for American intervention in Latin America?*

TAFT AND "DOLLAR DIPLOMACY"

Like his predecessor, William Howard Taft worked to advance the nation's economic interests in Latin America. But he showed little interest in Roosevelt's larger vision of world stability. Instead, Taft's secretary of state, Philander C. Knox, worked aggressively to extend American investments into less-developed regions. Critics called his policies **Dollar Diplomacy.**

The policy was particularly visible in the Caribbean. When a revolution broke out in *Nicaragua Occupied* Nicaragua in 1909, the administration quickly sided with the insurgents and sent American troops into the country to seize the customs houses. As soon as peace was restored, Knox encouraged American bankers to offer substantial loans to the new government, thus increasing Washington's financial leverage over the country. When the new pro-American government faced an insurrection less than two years later, Taft again landed American troops in Nicaragua, this time to protect the existing regime. The troops remained there for more than a decade.

DIPLOMACY AND MORALITY

Woodrow Wilson entered the presidency with relatively little interest or experience in international affairs. Yet he faced international challenges of a scope and gravity unmatched by those of any president before him. In many respects, he continued—and even strengthened—the Roosevelt–Taft approach to foreign policy.

Having already seized control of the finances of the Dominican Republic in 1905, the United States established a military government there in 1916. The military occupation lasted eight years. In Haiti, Wilson landed marines in 1915 to *Interventions in the Caribbean* quell a revolution during which a mob had murdered an unpopular president. American military forces remained in the country until 1934, and American officers drafted the new Haitian constitution adopted in 1918. When Wilson began to fear that the Danish West Indies might be about to fall into the hands of Germany, he bought the colony from Denmark and renamed it the Virgin Islands. Concerned about the possibility of European influence in Nicaragua, he signed a treaty with that country's government allowing for intervention to protect American interests.

Closer to the American border, the corrupt dictator Porfirio Díaz had long permitted American businessmen to establish an enormous economic presence in Mexico. In 1910, however, Díaz was overthrown by the popular leader Francisco *Regime Changes in Mexico* Madero, who promised democratic reform and seemed hostile to American businesses in Mexico. The United States quietly encouraged a reactionary general, Victoriano Huerta, to depose Madero early in 1913. But when the new government murdered Madero, Woodrow Wilson announced that he would never recognize Huerta's "government of butchers."

Wilson hoped that by refusing to recognize Huerta he could help topple the regime and bring to power the constitutionalists, now led by Venustiano Carranza. But Huerta, with the support of American business interests, established a full military dictatorship in October 1913; a few months later, one of his army officers briefly arrested several American sailors from the U.S.S. *Dolphin* who had gone ashore in *Veracruz Incident* Tampico. The men were immediately released, but the American admiral demanded a twenty-one-gun salute as a public display of penance. The Mexicans refused. Wilson used the incident as a pretext for seizing the Mexican port of Veracruz.

Wilson had envisioned a bloodless action, but in a clash with Mexican troops, the Americans killed 126 of the defenders and suffered 19 casualties. His show of force, however, had helped strengthen the position of the Carranza faction, which captured Mexico City in August 1914 and forced Huerta to flee the country. At last, it seemed, the crisis might be over.

But Wilson reacted angrily when Carranza, whom he had previously supported, refused to accept American guidelines for the creation of a new government, and he briefly considered throwing his support to still another aspirant to leadership: Carranza's erstwhile lieutenant Pancho Villa, now staking his own claim to power. When Villa's *Pancho Villa* military position deteriorated, however, Wilson abandoned him and granted preliminary recognition to Carranza. Villa, angry at what he considered an American betrayal, retaliated in early 1916 by shooting sixteen American mining engineers in northern Mexico and seventeen more Americans across the border in Columbus, New Mexico.

Wilson ordered General John J. Pershing to lead an American expeditionary force across the Mexican border in unsuccessful pursuit of Villa. They did engage in two ugly skirmishes with Carranza's army, in which forty Mexicans and twelve Americans died. But before a fuller war could erupt, Wilson quietly withdrew American *Pershing Expedition* troops from Mexico and, in March 1917, finally granted formal recognition to the Carranza regime. By now, however, Wilson's attention was turning to a far greater international crisis.

THE ROAD TO WAR

By 1914, the European nations had created an unusually precarious international system. It careened into war very quickly on the basis of what seemed to be a minor series of provocations.

THE COLLAPSE OF THE EUROPEAN PEACE

The major powers of Europe were organized by 1914 in two great, competing alliances. The "Triple Entente" linked Britain, France, and Russia. The "Triple Alliance" united Germany, the Austro-Hungarian Empire, and Italy.

The conflict emerged most directly out of a controversy involving nationalist movements within the Austro-Hungarian Empire. On June 28, 1914, Archduke Franz Ferdinand, heir to the throne of the tottering empire, was assassinated while paying a state visit to Sarajevo, the capital of Bosnia, then a province of Austria-Hungary. Slavic nationalists wished to annex Bosnia to neighboring Serbia. The killer of the archduke and his wife Sophie was a Serbian nationalist.

Austria immediately blamed Serbia for the murders and issued impossible ultimatums. Russia, Serbia's Slavic ally and a seeker of greater influence in the Balkans, mobilized its armies along the border with Austria-Hungary. The Germans, faced with that provocation against their ally and concerned about a two-front war against Russia and France, declared war against both. Germany's subsequent assault on France ran through neutral Belgium, prompting Britain to declare war on Germany.

The coalitions soon changed in name and membership. On one side were the Central Powers: Germany and Austria-Hungary, joined in the fall by the Ottoman Empire. On the *Allies and Central Powers* other side were the Allies, made up of Britain, France, and Russia. Hoping to seize territory from the Central Powers, Italy and Japan soon threw in their lot with the Allies.

As these changes suggest, the alliance system did not necessarily *bind* nations to act as they did. Leaders made the decision for war based on their own interests and ambitions, on the assumption that national self-defense required it, and on the erroneous belief that their objectives could be met quickly. What the alliance system did was provide a framework within which the choices for war were made. As tragic as those choices seem in retrospect, no one expected or wanted the ghastly world war that followed.

WILSON'S NEUTRALITY

Wilson called on his fellow citizens in 1914 to remain "impartial in thought as well as deed." But that was impossible. Most Americans sympathized with Britain. Lurid reports of German atrocities in Belgium and France, sometimes (but not always) exaggerated by British propagandists, strengthened the hostility of many Americans toward Germany.

Economic realities also made it impossible for the United States to deal with the belligerents on equal terms. The British had imposed a naval blockade on Germany to prevent munitions and supplies from reaching the enemy. As a neutral, the United States had the right, in theory, to trade with Germany, but the British blockade made that impossible. A truly neutral response to the blockade would have been to stop trading with Britain as well. But while the United States could survive an interruption of its relatively modest trade with the Central Powers, it could not easily weather a break in its much more extensive trade with the Allies. So America tacitly accepted the blockade of Germany and continued trading with Britain. By 1915, the United States had   *Continued Trade with Britain* gradually transformed itself from a neutral power into the arsenal of the Allies.

The Germans, in the meantime, were resorting to a new and, in American eyes, barbaric tactic: submarine warfare. Unable to challenge British domination on   *Sinking of* **Lusitania** the ocean's surface, the Germans announced early in 1915 that they would sink enemy vessels on sight. Months later, on May 7, a German submarine (or U-boat, a name derived from the German *Unterseeboot*) sank the British passenger liner *Lusitania* without warning, causing the deaths of 1,198 people, 128 of them Americans. The ship was carrying both passengers and munitions, but most Americans considered the attack an unprovoked act on civilians.

Wilson angrily demanded that Germany promise not to repeat such outrages, and the Germans reluctantly agreed. But early in 1916, in response to an announcement that the Allies were now arming merchant ships to sink submarines, Germany proclaimed that it would fire on such vessels without warning. A few weeks later, it attacked the unarmed French steamer *Sussex,* injuring several American passengers. Again, Wilson demanded that Germany abandon its "unlawful" tactics; again, the German government relented.

PREPAREDNESS VERSUS PACIFISM

Despite the president's increasing bellicosity in 1916, he was still far from ready to commit the United States to war. One obstacle was American domestic politics.

The question of whether America should make military and economic preparations for war sparked a heated debate between pacifists and interventionists. Wilson at first denounced the idea of an American military buildup as needless and provocative. In the fall of 1915, however, he endorsed an ambitious proposal by American military leaders for a large and rapid increase in the nation's armed forces.

Still, the peace faction wielded considerable political strength, as became clear at the Democratic National Convention in the summer of 1916. The convention became especially enthusiastic when the keynote speaker punctuated his list of the president's diplomatic achievements with the chant, "What did we do? What did we do? . . . We didn't go to war! We didn't go to war!" That speech helped produce one of the most prominent slogans of Wilson's reelection campaign: "He kept us out of war." During the campaign, Wilson did nothing to discourage those who argued that the Republican candidate, the progressive New York governor Charles Evans Hughes, was more likely than he to lead the nation into war. Wilson ultimately won reelection by fewer than 600,000 popular votes and only 23 electoral votes. But he was uncomfortable about a slogan that had aided his victory. "Any little German lieutenant," he said of the U-boat situation, "can put us into the war at any time by some calculated outrage."

INTERVENTION

Wilson was right—but it was the German leadership that provoked him. In January 1917 Germany made a desperate gamble, declaring unrestricted submarine warfare against all maritime traffic in the hopes of defeating the Allies before Wilson could mobilize an army. Meanwhile, the German foreign secretary Arthur Zimmermann   *Zimmermann Telegram* sent a telegram to the German ambassador in Mexico instructing him to offer the Mexicans a deal: if they would join a military alliance, Germany would help Mexico take back

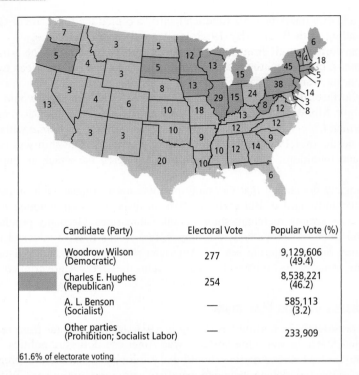

Candidate (Party)	Electoral Vote	Popular Vote (%)
Woodrow Wilson (Democratic)	277	9,129,606 (49.4)
Charles E. Hughes (Republican)	254	8,538,221 (46.2)
A. L. Benson (Socialist)	—	585,113 (3.2)
Other parties (Prohibition; Socialist Labor)	—	233,909

61.6% of electorate voting

THE ELECTION OF 1916 Woodrow Wilson had good reason to be concerned about his reelection prospects in 1916. He had won only about 42 percent of the vote in 1912, and the Republican Party—which had been divided four years earlier—was now reunited around the popular Charles Evans Hughes. In the end, Wilson won a narrow victory over Hughes with just under 50 percent of the vote and an even narrower margin in the electoral college. Note the striking regional character of his victory. • *How did Wilson use the war in Europe to bolster his election prospects?*

territory in the present states of Texas, New Mexico, and Arizona. By March, when Wilson released the intercepted and decoded telegram—and after three United States ships were torpedoed by U-boats—war with Germany seemed imminent.

Although German crimes on the seas, the offer to Mexico, and the threats to American commerce provided the immediate causes for war, Wilson had broader purposes in mind as well. The president hoped that American intervention, by earning him a seat at the postwar negotiating table, would usher in a new era. In the place of militarism, secret alliances, violence, and autocracy would come democracy, freedom of travel and commerce, open diplomacy, and self-determination.

President Wilson articulated this vision on the rainy evening of April 2, 1917, when he asked Congress for a declaration of war. German U-boat warfare had claimed American *Wilson's War Message* lives and treasure. The country's honor could not tolerate such affronts. But aware of divisions in public opinion, Wilson sought to invest the moment with higher meaning. The war would make the world "safe for democracy" and safeguard "the rights of mankind." America would not fight for material gain or territory, the president said, but to guarantee a future of free trade, self-governance, peace, and justice. Opposition to the war would not be tolerated. "If there should be disloyalty," he warned, "it will be dealt with a firm hand of repression."

Wilson's view carried the session, but dissenters spoke up. Some midwesterners and southerners saw corporate profits, not honor, at stake in the Atlantic. A few pacifists, including the first woman elected to Congress, Jeannette Rankin, a Republican from Montana, argued that no war was worth the costs. Still others argued the United States should stay out of Europe's affairs. When the declaration of war finally passed on April 6, six senators and fifty representatives voted against it.

"OVER THERE"

European armies on both sides of the conflict were decimated and exhausted by the time of Woodrow Wilson's declaration of war. The Allies looked desperately to the United States for help in breaking the stalemate.

MOBILIZING THE MILITARY

By the spring of 1917, Great Britain was suffering such vast losses from German submarines that its ability to receive vital supplies from across the Atlantic was in jeopardy. Within weeks of joining the war, the United States had begun to alter the balance. A fleet of American destroyers aided the British navy in attacking the U-boats and planting anti-submarine mines in the North Sea. The results were dramatic. Sinkings of Allied ships had totaled nearly 900,000 tons in the month of April 1917; the figure dropped to 350,000 by December 1917 and to 112,000 by October 1918.

Many Americans had hoped that providing naval assistance alone would be enough to end the war, but it quickly became clear that a major commitment of American ground forces would be necessary as well. Britain and France had few remaining reserves. After the Bolshevik Revolution in November 1917, a new communist *Bolshevik Revolution* government, led by V. I. Lenin, negotiated a hasty and costly peace between Russia and the Central Powers. That freed German troops to fight on the western front.

The United States did not have a large enough standing army to provide the necessary ground forces in 1917. Even amid recruitment efforts (see "Consider the Source: Race, Gender, and World War I Posters"), enlistments proved inadequate. Only a national draft could provide the needed men. Despite protests, Wilson won passage of the Selective Service Act in mid-May. From a prewar total of 121,000 enlisted soldiers, the army *Selective Service Act* grew to more than 4 million, 2 million of whom went to France. Draftees comprised 72 percent of all American soldiers in the war—a far higher percentage than on either side of the Civil War.

The typical American soldier (or doughboy) in the Great War was a white, single, poorly educated draftee in his early twenties. Women were barred from regular military *The Doughboy* service, but could sign up for things like nursing, clerical work, and telephone operation. As many as 400,000 African Americans joined the military, the vast majority conscripted. But this was a strict Jim Crow army. Units were segregated, white officers were in charge, and blacks generally performed menial labor. Yet two combat divisions, the Ninety-Second and Ninety-Third, were composed entirely of African American soldiers.

In training camps around the country, selectees learned how to be soldiers. They marched and drilled and practiced maneuvers. In case they weren't sure what *Basic Training* they were fighting for, every backpack contained a copy of Wilson's war message. For the huge number of foreign-born soldiers—approaching 20 percent of the wartime army, speaking forty-six different languages—military service acted as a tool of assimilation, to

RACE, GENDER, AND WORLD WAR I POSTERS

Much can be learned about a society's values from how it handles the mobilization of the home front during wartime. Nations typically clarify the terms of citizenship and service—asking some people to fight, and some to stay home and support the effort in other ways. As part of the broad national campaign to mobilize public opinion and service during World War I, American officials disseminated the two posters reproduced here. One urged enlistment, the other the purchase of war bonds.

UNDERSTAND, ANALYZE, & EVALUATE

1. How do the posters use images of women or the home to encourage either enlistment or financial support for the war?

2. What do these posters say about contemporary understandings of gender roles? What did the state and society expect from men? What did they expect from women?

3. Like almost all recruiting posters of World War I, these two depict white people—despite the fact that many African Americans and ethnic minorities served as well. What does that say about mainstream attitudes toward race and ethnicity during World War I?

(The Library of Congress)

(The Library of Congress)

AMERICA IN WORLD WAR I: THE WESTERN FRONT, 1918   These maps show the principal battles in which the United States participated in the last year of World War I. The small map on the upper right helps locate the area of conflict within the larger European landscape. The larger map at left shows the long, snaking red line of the western front in France—stretching from the border between France and southwest Germany all the way to the northeast border between Belgium and France. Along that vast line, the two sides had been engaged in murderous, inconclusive warfare for over three years by the time the Americans arrived. Beginning in the spring and summer of 1918, bolstered by reinforcements from the United States, the Allies began to win a series of important victories that finally enabled them to begin pushing the Germans back. American troops, as this map makes clear, were decisive along the southern part of the front. • *At what point did the Germans begin to consider putting an end to the war?*

the delight of nativists. The draftees received moral instruction as well. Progressives in the government, as well as thousands of American parents, worried about the sexual purity of the soldier. One social hygiene poster implored the soldier to "Remember—the folks at home. Go back to them physically fit and morally clean. Don't allow a whore to smirch your record."

THE YANKS ARE COMING

The United States had sent the first units of the American Expeditionary Forces (AEF) to France in June 1917 under the leadership of General John J. Pershing, but American soldiers weren't heavily implicated in the fighting until the next year. In March 1918, the Germans launched nimble thrusts into the Allied defenses. Under the French commander of Allied forces, Ferdinand Foch, Pershing's troops halted the German offensive at Cantigny and Château-Thierry. Then the American Second Division, including a brigade of marines, lost 9,800 casualties in a savage but successful fight to drive the Germans from Belleau Wood, a place that would live on in Marine Corps lore. In July the Germans attacked again, and at the Second Battle of the Marne, the Allies fought together to repulse them. Over the course of that summer, the influx of American divisions helped the Allies push the German army back roughly to its original position.

By September, with American troops plentiful and the Germans depleted, the Allies prepared to advance toward Germany. Pershing withdrew many of his divisions to the Americans' own sector on the southern edge of the front. From that position, the dough-boys took the Saint-Mihiel salient, a bulge into Allied lines that the Germans had held for years. Foch then ordered Pershing's divisions to their place in the war's final Allied *The Meuse-Argonne Offensive*   push, the Meuse-Argonne offensive. Beginning on September 26, more than a million American doughboys—the great majority of them seeing combat for the first time—advanced against the Germans, while to the northwest the British and French undertook coordinated campaigns. The Germans sagged but held, and something like trench warfare set in again. September and October were terrible months for the Americans, with 27,000 men killed. "Those of us who still lived," wrote one doughboy, "who were able to move, in body if not in spirit, wanted to drop to our knees and implore God to stop this horrible slaughter of mankind."

By November the Germans had been worn down, their civilian population suffering from an increasingly effective blockade, their soldiers captured by the hundreds of thou-sands, their U-boats more or less neutralized by a convoy system, and their rear harassed *Armistice*   by airplane bombardment. Facing invasion, the Germans sought an armistice. Early on the morning of November 11, 1918, while men along the front were still dying, representatives of the warring parties signed an armistice in a railway car in the French forest. The four-year "war to end all wars" shuddered to a close.

THE NEW TECHNOLOGY OF WARFARE

World War I was a proving ground for a range of new military technologies. The trench *Trench Warfare*   warfare that characterized the conflict was a result of the enormous destruc-tive power of newly improved machine guns and higher-powered artillery. It was no longer feasible to send troops out into an open field. The new weaponry would slaugh-ter them in an instant. Trenches sheltered troops while allowing limited, and usually inconclusive, fighting. But technology overtook the trenches, too, as mobile weapons— tanks and flamethrowers—proved capable of piercing entrenched positions. Most terrible of all, perhaps, new chemical weapons—poisonous mustard gas, which required troops to carry gas masks at all times—made it possible to attack entrenched soldiers without direct combat.

The new forms of technological warfare required elaborate maintenance. Faster machine guns needed more ammunition. Motorized vehicles required fuel, spare parts, and mechan-ics capable of servicing them. The logistical difficulties of supply became a major factor in planning tactics and strategy. Late in the war, when the Allied armies were advancing toward Germany, they frequently had to stop for days at a time to wait for their equipment to catch up with them.

World War I was the first conflict in which airplanes played a significant role. The planes themselves were relatively simple and not very maneuverable; but antiaircraft tech-nology was not yet highly developed either, so their effectiveness was still significant. Planes began to be constructed to serve various functions: bombers, fighters (planes that would engage in "dogfights" with other planes), and reconaissance aircraft.

The most "modern" part of the military during World War I was the navy. Battleships emerged that made use of new technologies such as turbine propulsion, hydraulic gun controls, electric light and power, wireless telegraphy, and advanced navigational aids. Submarines, which had made a brief appearance in the American Civil War, now became

LIFE IN THE TRENCHES For most British, French, German, and, to a lesser extent, American troops in France, the most debilitating part of World War I was the misery of life in the trenches. Some young men lived in these cold, wet, muddy dugouts for months, even years, surrounded by filth, sharing their space with vermin, eating mostly rotten food. Occasional attacks to try to dislodge the enemy from its trenches usually ended in failure and became the scenes of terrible slaughter. (National Archives and Records Administration)

significant weapons (as the German U-boat campaign in 1915 and 1916 made clear). The new submarines were driven by diesel engines that were more compact than steam engines and used fuel that was less explosive than that of gasoline engines.

The new technologies were responsible for the war's truly stunning statistics of death. Russia lost 1.8 million soldiers; Germany, 2 million; France, 1.4 million; *Appalling Casualties* the British Empire, 1 million; Austria-Hungary, 1.5 million; Italy, 460,000. Something like 5 million civilians died under the stress of war—by violence or slower means—though the exact number is hard to know. The United States lost 116,000 soldiers, about half of those in combat, the others to disease. Some perished in the 1918 influenza pandemic that ultimately claimed an estimated 50 to 100 million lives worldwide.

Although only in the war briefly, the Americans had played a significant role in the victory. Their casualty rates in the periods of intense fighting approximated or exceeded those of their Allies. The prospect of more doughboys arriving in the future surely affected the German leadership's capitulation in 1918. The British, Russian, and French contributions, of course, dwarfed the American one in sheer numbers. But Wilson's army had acquitted itself well enough to earn him a seat at the negotiating table—one of his ambitions all along.

ORGANIZING THE ECONOMY FOR WAR

By the time the war ended, the federal government had appropriated $32 billion for war expenses—a staggering sum at the time. The entire federal budget had seldom exceeded $1 billion before 1915, and as recently as 1910 the nation's entire gross national product had been only $35 billion. To raise the money, the government relied on two devices. First, it launched a major drive to solicit loans from the American people by selling *"Liberty Bonds"* "Liberty Bonds" to the public. By 1920, the sale of bonds, accompanied by elaborate patriotic appeals, had produced $23 billion. At the same time, new taxes were bringing in an additional sum of nearly $10 billion—some of it coming from levies on the "excess profits" of corporations but much of it coming from new, steeply graduated income and inheritance taxes that ultimately rose as high as 70 percent in some brackets.

An even greater challenge was to organize the economy to meet war needs. In 1916, Wilson established the Council of National Defense, composed of members of his cabinet, and the Civilian Advisory Commission, which set up local defense councils in every state and locality. But this early administrative structure soon proved completely unworkable, and members of the council urged a more centralized approach. The administrative structure that slowly emerged was dominated by a series of "war boards," one to oversee the railroads, one to supervise fuel supplies (largely coal), another to handle food (a board that elevated to prominence the brilliant young engineer and business executive Herbert Hoover). The boards generally succeeded in meeting essential war needs without paralyzing the domestic economy.

The War Industries Board (WIB) was created in July 1917 to coordinate government *War Industries Board* purchases of military supplies. Casually organized at first, it stumbled badly until March 1918, when Wilson restructured it and placed it under the control of the Wall Street financier Bernard Baruch. Baruch decided which factories would convert to the production of which war materials, and he set prices for the goods they produced. When materials were scarce, Baruch decided to whom they should go. When corporations were competing for government contracts, he chose among them.

Baruch viewed himself, openly and explicitly, as a partner of business; and within the WIB, businessmen themselves—the so-called dollar-a-year men, who took paid leave from their corporate jobs and worked for the government for a token salary—supervised the affairs of the private economy.

The National War Labor Board, established in April 1918, served as the final mediator of labor disputes. It pressured industry to grant important concessions to workers: an

WOMEN INDUSTRIAL WORKERS   In World War II, such women were often called "Rosie the Riveter." Their presence in these previously all-male work environments was no less startling to Americans during World War I. These women are shown working with acetylene torches to bevel armor plate for tanks. The photographer was Margaret Bourke-White, who herself broke gender boundaries as the first female photojournalist for *Life* magazine and the first female war correspondent. (Photo by Margaret Bourke-White/© The LIFE Picture Collection/Getty Images)

eight-hour day, the maintenance of minimal living standards, equal pay for women doing equal work, recognition of the right of unions to organize and bargain collectively. In return, it insisted that workers forgo strikes and that employers not engage in lockouts.

The Search for Social Unity

Government leaders were painfully aware that public sentiment about the war was sharply divided. The most conspicuous official effort to support the war was a vast propaganda campaign orchestrated by the Committee on Public Information (CPI),   *Wartime Propaganda* under the direction of the progressive journalist George Creel. The CPI supervised the distribution of over 75 million pieces of printed material and controlled much of the information available for newspapers and magazines. Creel encouraged journalists to exercise "self-censorship" when reporting war news, and most complied by covering the war largely as the government wished. By 1918, government-distributed posters and films were offering lurid (and exaggerated) portrayals of the savagery of the Germans. In this climate, songwriters and other artists produced popular works that heavily favored the war. (See "Patterns of Popular Culture: George M. Cohan, 'Over There,' 1917.")

The government also began efforts to suppress dissent. CPI-financed advertisements in magazines implored citizens to report to the authorities any evidence among their neighbors of disloyalty, pessimism, or yearning for peace. The Espionage Act of 1917 gave the government new tools with which to combat spying, sabotage, or obstruction of the war effort (crimes that were often broadly defined). The Sabotage Act and the Sedition Act,

George M. Cohan, "Over There," 1917

Music was one of the richest forms of American popular culture in the early twentieth century, much of it emanating from New York City companies in a neighborhood known as Tin Pan Alley. Lyricists and composers, eager to peddle their sheet music widely, had long captured popular attitudes toward the issues of their day. In 1915, with men dying in the Great War at a staggering rate, songwriters churned out such antimilitarist numbers as "I Didn't Raise My Boy to Be a Soldier" and "Don't Take My Darling Boy Away!"

In April 1917, however, President Wilson's demand for unanimity changed Tin Pan Alley's tune. Songs now demonized Kaiser Wilhelm II, the emperor of Germany, glorified the American *doughboy* (a term dating to the mid-nineteenth century but of mysterious origins) and sentimentalized the home-front family. Other tunes became anthems of American confidence and strength, none more so than George M. Cohan's "Over There." Even before that hit—which became the best-known song of the war—Cohan was a leading figure in the American entertainment industry, a prolific creator and performer of Broadway productions, and the composer of hundreds of original songs, including classics such as "Yankee Doodle Boy."

Written just after Wilson's war address of April 2, "Over There" offered a jaunty soundtrack for American intervention. It was sung on the home front and in basic training; doughboys in France found it in songbooks issued by various civilian agencies. "Over There" represented a prominent strain in public culture of 1917—deeply patriotic, optimistic, and sentimental—even as many Americans worried quietly about what this new war would mean for them and their families.

Johnnie, get your gun,
Get your gun, get your gun,
Take it on the run,
On the run, on the run.
Hear them calling, you and me,
Every son of liberty.
Hurry right away,
No delay, no delay,
Make your daddy glad
To have had such a lad.
Tell your sweetheart not to pine,
To be proud her boy's in line.

Chorus
Over there, over there
Send the word, send the word over there
That the Yanks are coming,
The Yanks are coming,
The drums rum-tumming
Ev'rywhere.
So prepare, say a pray'r,
Send the word, send the word to beware.
We'll be over, we're coming over,
And we won't come back till it's over
Over there.
Johnnie get your gun,
Get your gun, get your gun,
Johnnie show the Hun
Who's a son of a gun.
Hoist the flag and let her fly,
Yankee Doodle do or die.

Pack your little kit,
Show your grit, do your bit.
Yankee Doodle fill the ranks,
From the towns and the tanks.
Make your mother proud of you,
And the old Red, White and Blue. •

(repeat chorus twice)

Source: George M. Cohan, "Over There" (public domain).

UNDERSTAND, ANALYZE, & EVALUATE

1. How did this song seek to motivate young men to join the army? What image of war did this song convey?
2. What relationship between the United States and Europe did the chorus imply?

both passed in 1918, expanded the meaning of the Espionage Act to make illegal *any* public expression of opposition to the war; in practice, they *Espionage and Sedition Acts* allowed officials to prosecute anyone who criticized the president or the government.

The most frequent targets of the new legislation were anticapitalist groups such as the Socialist Party and the Industrial Workers of the World (IWW). Many Americans had favored the repression of socialists and radicals even before the war; the wartime policies now made it possible to move against them with full legal sanction. Eugene V. Debs, the humane leader of the Socialist Party and an opponent of the war, was sentenced to ten years in prison in 1918. (A pardon by President Warren G. Harding ultimately won his release in 1921.) Big Bill Haywood and members of the IWW were energetically prosecuted. Only by fleeing to the Soviet Union did Haywood avoid imprisonment. In all, more than 1,500 people were arrested in 1918 for the crime of criticizing the government or the war.

State and local governments, corporations, universities, and private citizens contributed as well to the climate of repression. A cluster of citizens' groups emerged to mobilize "respectable" members of communities to root out disloyalty. The greatest target of abuse was the German American community. Most German Americans supported the American war effort once it began, but public opinion still turned bitterly hostile. A campaign to purge society of all things German quickly gathered speed, at times assuming ludicrous forms. Performances of German music were frequently banned. German foods such as sauerkraut and bratwurst were renamed "liberty cabbage" and "liberty sausage." German books were removed from library shelves. Courses in the German language were dropped from school curricula. Germans were routinely fired from jobs in war industries, lest they "sabotage" important tasks.

THE SEARCH FOR A NEW WORLD ORDER

Woodrow Wilson had led the nation into war promising a just and stable peace at its conclusion. Even before the armistice, he was preparing to lead the fight for what he considered a democratic postwar settlement.

THE FOURTEEN POINTS

On January 8, 1918, Wilson appeared before Congress to present the principles for which he believed the nation was fighting. He grouped the war aims under fourteen headings, widely known as the "Fourteen Points." They fell into three broad categories. First, Wilson's proposals contained a series of eight specific recommendations for adjusting postwar boundaries and establishing new nations to replace the defunct Austro-Hungarian and Ottoman Empires. Second, five general principles would govern international conduct *Wilson's International Vision* in the future: freedom of the seas, open covenants instead of secret treaties, reductions in armaments, free trade, and impartial mediation of colonial claims. Finally, there was a proposal for a "League of Nations" that would help implement these new principles and territorial adjustments and resolve future controversies.

Wilson's international vision ultimately enchanted not only much of his own generation (in both America and Europe) but also members of generations to come. It reflected his belief that the world was as capable of just and efficient government as were individual nations—that once the international community accepted certain basic principles of conduct and constructed modern institutions to implement them, the world could live in peace.

Despite Wilson's confidence, leaders of the Allied powers were preparing to resist him even before the armistice was signed. Britain and France, in particular, were in no mood for a benign and generous peace. At the same time, Wilson was encountering problems at home. In 1918, with the war almost over, Wilson unwisely tied support of his peace plans to the election of Democrats to Congress in November. Days later, the Republicans captured majorities in both houses. Domestic economic troubles, more than international issues, had been the most important factor in the voting; but the results damaged his ability to claim broad popular support for his peace plans. Wilson further antagonized the Republicans when he refused to appoint any important member of their party to the negotiating team that would attend the peace conference in Paris.

THE PARIS PEACE CONFERENCE

When Wilson entered Paris on December 13, 1918, he was greeted, some claimed, by the largest crowd in the history of France. The peace conference itself, however, proved less satisfying.

The principal figures in the negotiations were the leaders of the victorious Allied nations: President Wilson, as well as David Lloyd George, the prime minister of Great Britain; Georges Clemenceau, the prime minister of France; and Vittorio Orlando, the prime minister of Italy.

From the beginning, the atmosphere of idealism Wilson had sought to create competed with his counterparts' national self-interest, thirst for revenge, and fears of the unstable *Negotiating the Peace* situation in eastern Europe and the threat of communism. Russia, whose new Bolshevik government was still fighting anti-Bolshevik counterrevolutionaries, was unrepresented in Paris; but the radical threat it seemed to pose to Western governments was never far from the minds of the delegates.

In this tense and often vindictive atmosphere, Wilson was unable to win approval of many of his broad principles or to prevent the other allies from imposing punitive reparations on Germany. Wilson did manage to win some important victories in Paris in setting boundaries and dealing with former colonies. But his most visible triumph, and the one most important to him, was the creation of a permanent international organization to oversee world affairs and prevent future wars. On January 25, 1919, the Allies voted to *The League of Nations* accept the "covenant" of the League of Nations.

THE RATIFICATION BATTLE

Wilson presented the Treaty of Versailles (so named for the palace outside Paris where the agreement was signed) to the Senate on July 10, 1919. But members of that chamber had many objections. Some—the so-called irreconcilables—believed that America should remain free of binding foreign entanglements. But many other opponents were principally concerned with constructing a winning issue for the Republicans in 1920. Most notable of these was Senator Henry Cabot Lodge of Massachusetts, the powerful *Henry Cabot Lodge* chair of the Foreign Relations Committee, who loathed the president and used every possible tactic to obstruct the treaty.

Public sentiment clearly favored ratification, so at first Lodge could do little more than play for time. Gradually, however, his opposition to the treaty crystallized into a series of "reservations"—amendments to the League covenant further limiting American obligations to the organization. Wilson might still have won approval at this point if he had agreed to some relatively minor changes in the language of the treaty. But the president refused to yield.

When he realized the Senate would not budge, Wilson decided to appeal to the public and embarked on a grueling, cross-country speaking tour to arouse public support for the treaty. For more than three weeks, he traveled over 8,000 miles by train, speaking as often as four times a day, resting hardly at all. Finally, he reached the end of his strength. After speaking at Pueblo, Colorado, on September 25, 1919, he collapsed with severe headaches.

Canceling the rest of his itinerary, he rushed back to Washington, where, a few days later, he suffered a major stroke. For two weeks, he was close to death; for six weeks more, he was so seriously ill that he was virtually unable to conduct public business. His wife and his doctor formed an almost impenetrable barrier around him, shielding the president from any official pressures that might impede his recovery.

Wilson ultimately recovered enough to resume a limited official schedule, but he was essentially an invalid for the remaining eighteen months of his presidency. His condition only intensified what had already been his strong tendency to view public issues in moral terms and to resist any attempts at compromise. When the Foreign Relations Committee finally sent the treaty to the Senate, recommending nearly fifty *League Membership Rejected* amendments and reservations, Wilson refused to consider any of them. The effort to win ratification failed.

In the aftermath of this defeat, Wilson became convinced that the 1920 national election would serve as a "solemn referendum" on the League. By now, however, public interest in the peace process had begun to fade as a series of other crises claimed attention.

A SOCIETY IN TURMOIL

Even during the Paris Peace Conference, many Americans were concerned less about international matters than about turbulent events at home. Some of this unease was a legacy of the almost-hysterical social atmosphere of the war years; some of it was a response to issues that surfaced after the armistice.

THE UNSTABLE ECONOMY

The war ended sooner than almost anyone had anticipated. Without warning, without planning, the nation lurched into the difficult task of economic reconversion. At first, the boom continued, but accompanied by raging inflation. Through most of 1919 and 1920, prices rose at an average of more than 15 percent a year. Finally, late in 1920, the economic bubble burst as inflation began killing the market for consumer *Postwar Recession* goods. Between 1920 and 1921, the gross national product declined nearly 10 percent; 100,000 businesses went bankrupt; and nearly 5 million Americans lost their jobs.

Well before this severe recession began, labor unrest increased dramatically. The raging inflation of 1919 wiped out the modest wage gains workers had achieved during the war; *Labor Unrest* many laborers were worried about job security as veterans returned to the workforce; arduous working conditions continued to be a source of discontent. Employers aggravated the resentment by using the end of the war to rescind benefits they had been forced to concede to workers in 1917 and 1918—most notably, recognition of unions. The year 1919, therefore, saw an unprecedented strike wave. In January, a walkout by shipyard workers in Seattle, Washington, evolved into a general strike that brought the entire city to a virtual standstill. In September, the Boston police force struck to demand recognition of its union. With its police off the job, Boston erupted in violence and looting. Governor Calvin Coolidge called in the National Guard to restore order and attracted national acclaim by declaring, "There is no right to strike against the public safety."

Coolidge's statement tapped into a broad middle-class hostility to unions and strikes. That hostility played a part in defeating the greatest strike of 1919: a steel strike that began in September, when 350,000 steelworkers in several Midwestern cities demanded an eight-hour day and union recognition. The long and bitter steel strike climaxed in a riot in Gary, Indiana, in which eighteen strikers were killed. Steel executives managed to keep most plants running with nonunion labor, and public opinion was so hostile to the strikers that the American Federation of Labor timidly repudiated the strike. By January, the strike—like most of the others in 1919—had collapsed.

THE DEMANDS OF AFRICAN AMERICANS

Black World War I veterans (400,000 of them) came home in 1919 and marched down the main streets of cities with other returning troops. And then in New York and elsewhere

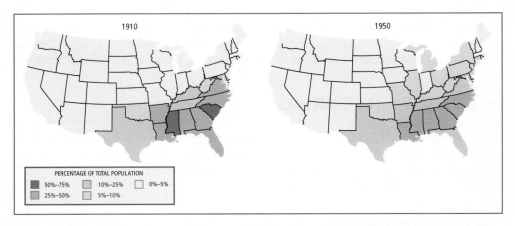

AFRICAN AMERICAN MIGRATION, 1910–1950 Two great waves of migration produced a dramatic redistribution of the African American population in the first half of the twentieth century—one around the time of World War I, the other during and after World War II. The map on the left shows the almost exclusive concentration of African Americans in the South as late as 1910. The map on the right shows both the tremendous increase in black populations in northern states by 1950, and the relative decline of black populations in parts of the South. Note in particular the changes in Mississippi and South Carolina. • *Why did the wars produce such significant migration out of the South?*

they marched again through the streets of black neighborhoods such as Harlem, led by jazz bands and cheered by thousands of African Americans. They believed that the glory of black heroism in the war would make it impossible for white society ever again to treat African Americans as second-class citizens.

As it turned out, the fact that black soldiers had fought in the war had almost no impact at all on white attitudes. But it profoundly affected black attitudes, accentuated African American bitterness, and increased the determination to fight for civil rights. During the war, nearly half a million blacks had migrated from the rural South to industrial cities (often enticed by northern "labor agents," who offered free transportation) in search of the factory jobs the war was rapidly generating. This was the beginning of what became known as the Great Migration. Suddenly, large black communities arose in northern   *Great Migration* cities, part of the broader twentieth-century transformation of the black population from a generally southern rural one to a northern urban one.

By 1919, the racial climate had become savage and murderous. In the South, lynchings suddenly increased; more than seventy blacks, some of them war veterans, died at the hands of white mobs in 1919 alone. In the North, black factory workers faced widespread layoffs as returning white veterans displaced them from their jobs. And as whites became convinced that black workers with lower wage demands were hurting them economically, animosity grew rapidly.

Wartime riots in East St. Louis and elsewhere were a prelude to a summer of much worse racial violence in 1919. In Chicago, a black teenager swimming in   *Chicago Race Riot* Lake Michigan on a hot July day happened to drift toward a white beach. Whites onshore allegedly stoned him unconscious; he sank and drowned. Angry African Americans gathered in crowds and marched into white neighborhoods to retaliate; whites formed even larger crowds and roamed into mostly black neighborhoods. For more than a week, Chicago was virtually at war. In the end, 38 people had died—15 whites and 23 blacks— and 537 were injured; over 1,000 people were left homeless. The Chicago riot was the worst but not the only racial violence during the so-called red summer of 1919; in all, 120 people died in such racial outbreaks in little more than three months.

Racially motivated urban riots were not new. But the 1919 riots were different in one respect: they did not just involve white people attacking blacks, but also blacks fighting back. The NAACP signaled this change by urging blacks not just to demand government protection but also to defend themselves. The poet Claude McKay, one of the major figures of what would soon be known as the Harlem Renaissance, wrote a poem after the Chicago riot called "If We Must Die":

> Like men we'll face the murderous cowardly pack.
> Pressed to the wall, dying, but fighting back.

At the same time, a black Jamaican, Marcus Garvey, began to attract a wide following in the United States with his ideology of black nationalism.   *Marcus Garvey and Black Nationalism* Garvey encouraged African Americans to reject assimilation into white society and to develop pride in their own race and culture. His Universal Negro Improvement Association (UNIA) launched a chain of black-owned grocery stores and pressed for the creation of other black businesses. Eventually, Garvey began urging his supporters to leave America and return to Africa, where they could create a new society of their own. In the early 1920s, the Garvey movement experienced explosive growth for a time, but it began to decline after Garvey was indicted in 1923 on charges of business fraud. He was deported to Jamaica two years later. But the allure of black nationalism survived in black culture long after Garvey was gone.

THE RED SCARE

Many Americans regarded the industrial warfare and racial violence of 1919 as frightening omens of instability and radicalism. After the Russian Revolution of November 1917, communism was no longer simply a theory, but the basis of an important regime. Concerns about the communist threat grew in 1919 when the Bolshevik government announced the formation of the Communist International (or Comintern), whose purpose was to export revolution around the world.

In America, meanwhile, there was, in addition to the great number of imagined radicals, a modest number of real ones. These small groups of radicals were presumably responsible for a series of bombings in the spring of 1919. In April, the post office intercepted several dozen parcels addressed to leading businessmen and politicians that were triggered to explode when opened. Two months later, eight bombs exploded in eight cities within minutes of one another, suggesting a nationwide conspiracy.

The combination of strikes and the Comintern announcement produced what became known as the **Red Scare.** Nearly thirty states enacted new peacetime sedition laws imposing harsh penalties on promoters of revolution. Spontaneous acts of violence against supposed radicals occurred in some communities, and universities and other institutions tried to expel radicals from their midst. But the greatest agent of the Red Scare was the federal government. On New Year's Day, 1920, Attorney General A. Mitchell Palmer and his *Palmer Raids* ambitious young assistant, J. Edgar Hoover, orchestrated a series of raids on alleged radical centers throughout the country and arrested more than 6,000 people. Most of those arrested were ultimately released, but about 500 who were not American citizens were summarily deported. Later in 1920, a bomb exploded on Wall Street, killing thirty-eight people. No one was ever convicted of this bombing.

The ferocity of the Red Scare gradually abated, but its effects lingered well into the 1920s. In May 1920, two Italian immigrants, Nicola Sacco and Bartolomeo Vanzetti, were charged with the murder of a paymaster in South Braintree, Massachusetts. The case against them was weak and suffused with nativist prejudices and fears; but because both men were confessed anarchists, they faced a widespread public presumption of guilt. They were convicted and eventually sentenced to death. Over the next several years, public *Sacco and Vanzetti* support for Sacco and Vanzetti grew to formidable proportions. But on August 23, 1927, amid widespread protests in the United States and around the world, Sacco and Vanzetti, still proclaiming their innocence, died in the electric chair.

REFUTING THE RED SCARE

An unexpected result of postwar turmoil was the emergence of a vigorous defense of civil liberties that not only discredited the Red Scare, but also helped give new force to the Bill of Rights. The heavy-handed actions of the federal government after the war created a powerful backlash. It destroyed the career of A. Mitchell Palmer. It almost nipped in the bud the ascent of J. Edgar Hoover. It damaged the Democratic Party. And it led to an organization committed to protecting civil liberties: the National Civil Liberties Bureau, launched in 1917, which in 1920 was renamed the American Civil Liberties Union (ACLU) and which remains a prominent institution today. At the same time, members of the Supreme Court—most notably Justices Oliver Wendell Holmes and Louis Brandeis—gradually moved to defend unpopular speech. The clash of "fighting faiths," Holmes wrote in a dissent in 1920, was best resolved "by free trade in ideas—that the best test of truth is . . . the competition of the market." This and other dissents eventually became law as other justices committed themselves to a robust defense of speech, however unpopular.

THE RETREAT FROM IDEALISM

On August 26, 1920, the Nineteenth Amendment, guaranteeing women the right to vote, became part of the Constitution. To the suffrage movement, this was the culmination of nearly a century of struggle. To many progressives, it seemed to promise new support for reform. Yet the Nineteenth Amendment marked not the beginning of a new era of progressive reform but the end of an earlier one.

Economic problems, labor unrest, racial tensions, and the intensity of the antiradicalism they helped create—all combined in the years immediately   *Disillusionment and Reaction* following the war to produce a general sense of disillusionment. That became particularly apparent in the election of 1920. Woodrow Wilson hoped the campaign would be a referendum on the League of Nations, and the Democratic candidates, Governor James M. Cox of Ohio and Assistant Secretary of the Navy Franklin D. Roosevelt, dutifully tried to keep Wilson's ideals alive. The Republican presidential nominee, Warren Gamaliel Harding, an obscure Ohio senator, offered a different vision. He embraced no soaring ideals, only a vague promise of a return, as he later phrased it, to "normalcy." Harding won in a landslide, with 61 percent of the popular vote and victories in every state outside the South. The party made major gains in Congress as well. To many Americans it seemed that, for better or worse, a new age had begun.

CONCLUSION

Presidents Roosevelt, Taft, and Wilson contributed to a continuation, and indeed an expansion, of America's active role in international affairs, in part as an effort to abet the growth of American capitalism and in part as an attempt to impose American ideas of morality and democracy on other parts of the world. Similar mixtures of ideals and self-interest soon guided the United States into a great world war.

For a time after the outbreak of war in Europe in 1914, most Americans—President Wilson among them—wanted nothing so much as to stay out of the conflict. But as the war dragged on and the tactics of Britain and Germany began to impinge on American trade and access to the seas, the United States found itself drawn into the conflict. In April 1917, Congress agreed to the president's request that the United States enter the war as an ally of Britain, France, and Russia.

Within a few months of the arrival of American troops in Europe, Germany agreed to an armistice and the war ended. American casualties, although not inconsiderable, were negligible compared to the millions suffered by the European combatants.

Wilson's bold and idealistic dream of a peace based on international cooperation suffered a painful death. The Treaty of Versailles, which he helped draft, contained a provision for a League of Nations, which Wilson believed could transform the international order. But the League quickly became controversial in the United States; and despite strenuous efforts by the president—efforts that hastened his own physical collapse—the treaty was defeated in the Senate. In the aftermath of that traumatic battle, the American people turned away from Wilson and his ideals and prepared for a very different era.

The social experience of the war in the United States was, on the whole, dismaying to reformers. Although the war enhanced some reform efforts—most notably prohibition and woman suffrage—it also introduced an atmosphere of intolerance and repression into American life. The aftermath of the war was even more disheartening to progressives, because of both a brief but highly destabilizing recession and a wave of repression directed against labor, radicals, African Americans, and immigrants.

KEY TERMS/PEOPLE/PLACES/EVENTS

Allies 524
Central Powers 524
Dollar Diplomacy 522
General John J. Pershing 523
Great Migration 539
Henry Cabot Lodge 537
League of Nations 536

Lusitania 525
Marcus Garvey 539
Nicola Sacco and
  Bartolomeo Vanzetti 540
Palmer Raids 540
Panama Canal 521
Pancho Villa 523

Red Scare 540
Roosevelt Corollary 521
Selective Service Act 527
The Fourteen Points 535
trench warfare 530
War Industries Board 532
Zimmermann Telegram 525

RECALL AND REFLECT

1. Who opposed U.S. involvement in World War I and why?
2. How did the Wilson administration mobilize the nation for war?
3. What effect did the war have on race relations in the United States?
4. What were some of the ways that U.S. participation in the Great War changed American society?
5. Why did the battle over ratification of the Treaty of Versailles come to an impasse? Why did the Senate ultimately reject the treaty? What was the significance of that rejection?

22

THE NEW ERA

THE NEW ECONOMY
THE NEW CULTURE
A CONFLICT OF CULTURES
REPUBLICAN GOVERNMENT

LOOKING AHEAD

1. How did the technological innovations of the early twentieth century affect industry and American social life of the 1920s?
2. What were some of the cultural conflicts of the 1920s, and what caused them?
3. Is the term the *New Era* a fitting description of the 1920s?

IN POPULAR CULTURE, THE 1920s are often remembered as an era of affluence, conservatism, and cultural frivolity. In reality, however, the decade was a time of significant, even dramatic social, economic, and political change. The American economy not only enjoyed spectacular growth but also developed new forms of organization. Many Americans reshaped themselves to reflect the increasingly urban, industrial, consumer-oriented society of the United States. And American government experimented with new approaches to public policy. That was why contemporaries liked to refer to the 1920s as the "New Era"—an age in which America was becoming a modern nation.

At the same time, however, the decade saw the rise of a series of spirited, and at times effective, rebellions against the transformations in American life. The intense cultural conflicts that characterized the 1920s showed that much of American society remained unreconciled to the modernizing currents of the New Era.

1920

Prohibition begins

Harding elected
president

1922

Lewis's *Babbitt*

1923

Harding dies; Coolidge
becomes president

Harding administration
scandals revealed

1924

National Origins
Act passed

Coolidge elected
president

Ku Klux Klan
membership peaks

1925

Fitzgerald's *The
Great Gatsby*

Scopes trial

1927

First sound motion
picture, *The Jazz Singer*

1928

Hoover elected
president

THE NEW ECONOMY

After the recession of 1921–1922, the United
States began a period of almost uninterrupted
prosperity and economic expansion. Less
visible at the time, but equally significant,
was the survival (and even the growth) of
inequalities and imbalances.

TECHNOLOGY, ORGANIZATION, AND ECONOMIC GROWTH

No one could deny the remarkable feats of
the American economy in the 1920s. The
nation's manufacturing output rose by more
than 60 percent. Per capita income grew by
a third. Inflation was negligible. A mild
recession in 1923 briefly interrupted the
pattern of growth; but when it subsided
early in 1924, the economy expanded with
even greater vigor.

The economic boom was a result of many
things, but one of the most important was
technology. As a result of the development
of the assembly line and other innovations,
automobiles now became one of the most
important industries in the nation, stimulating growth in such related industries as steel,
rubber, and glass, tool companies, oil corporations, and road construction. The increased
mobility that the automobile made possible
increased the demand for suburban housing,
fueling a boom in the construction industry.

Radio contributed as well to the economic
growth. Early radio had been able to broadcast little besides pulses, which meant that
radio communication could occur only
through the Morse code. But with the discovery of the theory of modulation, pioneered by the Canadian scientist Reginald
Fessenden, it became possible to transmit
speech and music. Many people built their
own radio sets at home for very little money,
benefiting from the discovery that inexpensive crystals could receive signals over long
distances (but not very well over short ones).
These "shortwave" radios, which allowed

individual owners to establish contact with one another, marked the beginning of what later became known as "ham radio." Once commercial broadcasting began, families flocked to buy more conventional radio sets powered by reliable vacuum tubes and capable of receiving high-quality signals over short and medium distances. By 1925, there were 2 million sets in American homes, and by the end of the 1920s, almost every family had one.

Commercial aviation developed slowly in the 1920s, beginning with the use of planes to deliver mail. On the whole, airplanes remained curiosities and sources of *Commercial Aviation* entertainment. But technological advances—the development of the radial engine and the creation of pressurized cabins—laid the groundwork for the great increase in commercial travel in the 1930s and beyond. Electronics, home appliances, plastics and synthetic fibers (such as nylon), aluminum, magnesium, oil, electric power, and other industries fueled by technological advances—all grew dramatically. Telephones continued to proliferate. By the late 1930s, there were approximately 25 million telephones in the United States, roughly one for every six people. (See "Consider the Source: America's Early Telephone Network.")

The seeds of future technological breakthroughs were also visible. In both England and America, scientists and engineers were working to transform primitive calculating machines into devices capable of performing more complicated tasks. By the early *Early Computing* 1930s, researchers at MIT, led by Vannevar Bush, had created an instrument capable of performing a variety of complicated tasks—the first analog computer. A few years later, Howard Aiken, with financial assistance from Harvard and MIT, built a much more complex computer with memory, capable of multiplying eleven-digit numbers in three seconds.

Genetic research had begun in Austria in the mid-nineteenth century through the work of Gregor Mendel, a Catholic monk who performed experiments on the *Genetic Research* hybridization of vegetables in his monastery garden. His findings attracted little attention during his lifetime, but in the early twentieth century they were discovered by several investigators and helped shape modern genetic research. Among the American pioneers was Thomas Hunt Morgan of Columbia University and, later, Cal Tech, whose experiments with fruit flies revealed how several genes could be transmitted together. He also revealed the way in which genes were arranged along the chromosome. His work helped open the path to understanding how genes could recombine—a critical discovery that led to more advanced experiments in hybridization and genetics.

Large sectors of American business accelerated their drive toward national organization and consolidation. Certain industries—notably those dependent on large-scale mass production, such as steel and automobiles—seemed to move naturally toward concentrating production in a few large firms. Other industries—less dependent on technology and less susceptible to great economies of scale—proved more resistant to consolidation.

The strenuous efforts by industrialists throughout the economy to find ways to curb competition reflected a strong fear of overcapacity. Even in the booming 1920s, industrialists remembered how too-rapid expansion and overproduction had helped produce recessions in 1893, 1907, and 1920. The great unrealized dream of the New Era was to find a way to stabilize the economy so that such collapses would never occur again.

WORKERS IN AN AGE OF CAPITAL

Despite the remarkable economic growth, more than two-thirds of the American people in 1929 lived at no better than what one major study described as the "minimum comfort level." Half of those were at or below the level of "subsistence and poverty."

AMERICA'S EARLY TELEPHONE NETWORK

Alexander Graham Bell received a patent for the invention of the telephone in 1876. By 1914, telephone exchanges linked more than 70,000 places and 8 million subscribers in the United States. This map, part of an advertisement for the American Telephone and Telegraph Company, shows the extent of telephone coverage that year.

What the Telephone Map Shows

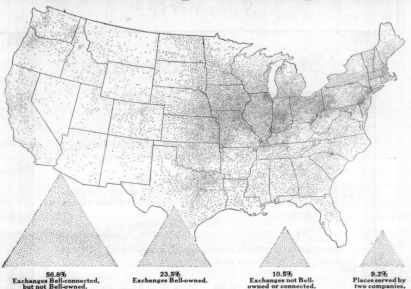

| 56.8% Exchanges Bell-connected, but not Bell-owned. | 23.5% Exchanges Bell-owned. | 10.5% Exchanges not Bell-owned or connected. | 9.2% Places served by two companies. |

EVERY dot on the map marks a town where there is a telephone exchange, the same sized dot being used for a large city as for a small village. Some of these exchanges are owned by the Associated Bell companies and some by independent companies. Where joined together in one system they meet the needs of each community and, with their suburban lines, reach 70,000 places and over 8,000,000 subscribers.

The pyramids show that only a minority of the exchanges are Bell-owned, and that the greater majority of the exchanges are owned by independent companies and connected with the Bell System.

At comparatively few points are there two telephone companies, and there are comparatively few exchanges, chiefly rural, which do not have outside connections.

The recent agreement between the Attorney General of the United States and the Bell System will facilitate connections between all telephone subscribers regardless of who owns the exchanges.

Over 8,000 different telephone companies have already connected their exchanges to provide universal service for the whole country.

AMERICAN TELEPHONE AND TELEGRAPH COMPANY

AND ASSOCIATED COMPANIES

One Policy   **One System**   *Universal Service*

For our Mutual Advantage mention Popular Electricity and Modern Mechanics when writing to Advertisers.

(*Popular Electricity and Modern Mechanics*, September, 19, 1914).

UNDERSTAND, ANALYZE, & EVALUATE

1. In what area of the United States was the concentration of telephone exchanges the heaviest? Why do you think there were more exchanges in this part of the country than in other areas?
2. The text accompanying the map explains that the same-sized dots are used for large cities as for small villages. Would the use of different-sized dots to indicate larger cities or smaller towns make the map more representative of U.S. telephone usage in 1914?
3. This map is part of an advertisement produced by the American Telephone and Telegraph Company. How does that fact influence a reading of the information provided in the map and accompanying text?

American labor experienced both the successes and the failures of the 1920s. On the one hand, most workers saw their standard of living rise during the decade. Some employers adopted paternalistic techniques that came to be known as **welfare capitalism.**

THE STEAMFITTER Lewis Hine was among the first American photographers to recognize his craft as an art. In this carefully posed photograph from the mid-1920s, Hine made a point that many other artists were making in other media: the rise of the machine could serve human beings, but might also bend them to its own needs.
(© New York Public Library, USA/Bridgeman Images)

Henry Ford, for example, shortened the workweek, raised wages, and instituted paid vacations. By 1926, nearly 3 million industrial workers were eligible for at least modest pensions upon retirement. When labor grievances surfaced despite these efforts, workers could voice them through the so-called company unions that emerged in many industries—workers' councils and shop committees, organized by the corporations themselves. But welfare capitalism, in the end, gave workers no real control over their own fates. Company unions were feeble vehicles. And welfare capitalism survived only as long as industry prospered. After 1929, with the economy in crisis, the entire system collapsed.

Welfare capitalism affected only a relatively small number of firms in any case. Most laborers worked for employers who were interested primarily in keeping their labor costs low. Workers as a whole, therefore, received wage increases that were proportionally far below the growth of the economy. At the end of the decade, the average annual income of a worker remained below $1,500, when $1,800 was considered necessary to maintain a minimally decent standard of living. Only by relying on the combined earnings of several family members could many working-class families make ends meet.

The New Era was a bleak time for labor organization, in part because many unions themselves were relatively conservative and failed to adapt to the realities of the modern economy. The American Federation of Labor (AFL), led after Samuel Gompers's death by the cautious William Green, sought peaceful cooperation with employers and remained wedded to the concept of the craft union. In the meantime, the rapidly rising number of unskilled industrial workers received little attention from the craft unions.

But whatever the unions' weaknesses, the strength of the corporations was the principal reason for the absence of effective labor organization in the 1920s. After the turmoil of 1919, corporate leaders worked hard to spread the doctrine that a crucial element of democratic capitalism was the protection of the "open shop" (a shop in which no worker could be required to join a union). The crusade for the open shop, euphemistically titled *"American Plan"* the "American Plan," became a pretext for a harsh campaign of union-busting. As a result, union membership fell from more than 5 million in 1920 to under 3 million in 1929.

WOMEN AND MINORITIES IN THE WORKFORCE

A growing proportion of the workforce consisted of women, who were concentrated in what have since become known as "pink-collar" jobs—low-paying service occupations. Large numbers of women worked as secretaries, salesclerks, and telephone operators and in other nonmanual service capacities. Because technically such positions were not industrial jobs, the AFL and other labor organizations were uninterested in organizing these workers. Similarly, the half-million African Americans who had migrated from the rural South into the cities during the Great Migration after 1914 had few opportunities for union representation. The skilled crafts represented in the AFL usually excluded black workers. Partly as a result of that exclusion, most blacks worked in jobs in which the AFL took no interest at all—as janitors, dishwashers, garbage collectors, and domestics and in other service capacities. A. Philip Randolph's *Brotherhood of Sleeping Car Porters* Brotherhood of Sleeping Car Porters was one of the few important unions dominated and led by African Americans.

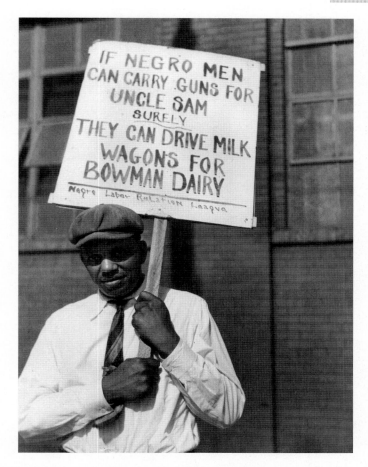

AFRICAN AMERICAN WORKER PROTESTING The frail union movement among African Americans in the 1920s, led by A. Philip Randolph and others, slowly built up a constituency within the black working class. Here, an aspiring dairy worker draws attention to the unjust treatment of African American men who had demonstrated their patriotism during the war. (© Photo by John Vachon/Anthony Potter Collection/Getty Images)

In the West and the Southwest, the ranks of the unskilled included considerable numbers of Asians and Hispanics. In the wake of the Chinese Exclusion Acts, Japanese immigrants increasingly replaced the Chinese in menial jobs in California. They worked on railroads, construction sites, farms, and in many other low-paying workplaces. Some Japanese managed to escape the ranks of the unskilled by forming their own small businesses or setting themselves up as truck farmers; and many of the Issei (Japanese immigrants) and *Issei and Nisei* Nisei (their American-born children) enjoyed significant economic success—so much so that California passed laws in 1913 and 1920 to make it more difficult for them to buy land. Other Asians—most notably Filipinos—also swelled the unskilled workforce and generated considerable hostility. Anti-Filipino riots in California beginning in 1929 helped produce legislation in 1934 virtually eliminating immigration from the Philippines.

Mexican immigrants formed a major part of the unskilled workforce throughout the Southwest and California. Nearly half a million Mexicans entered the United States in the 1920s. Most lived in California, Texas, Arizona, and New Mexico; and by 1930, most lived in cities. Large

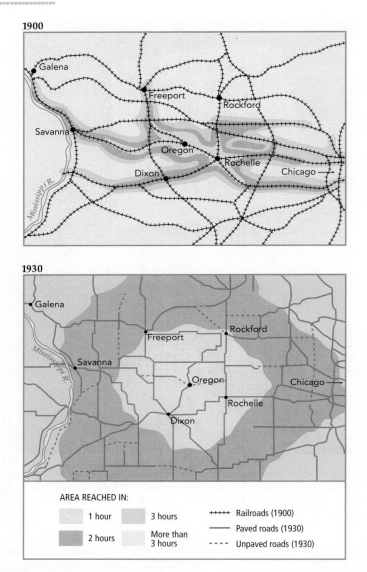

1900

1930

AREA REACHED IN:

1 hour   3 hours   ╈╈╈ Railroads (1900)

                                  —— Paved roads (1930)

2 hours   More than 3 hours   ----- Unpaved roads (1930)

BREAKING DOWN RURAL ISOLATION: THE EXPANSION OF TRAVEL HORIZONS IN OREGON, ILLINOIS
This map uses the small town of Oregon, Illinois—west of Chicago—to illustrate the way in which first railroads and then automobiles reduced the isolation of rural areas in the early decades of the twentieth century. The gold and purple areas of the two maps show the territory that residents of Oregon could reach within two hours. Note how small that area was in 1900 and how much larger it was in 1930, by which time an area of over 100 square miles had become easily accessible to the town. Note, too, the significant network of paved roads in the region by 1930, few of which had existed in 1900. • *Why did automobiles do so much more than railroads to expand the travel horizons of small towns?*

Mexican barrios grew up in Los Angeles, El Paso, San Antonio, Denver, and many other urban
Rising Mexican Immigration   centers. Some of the residents found work locally in factories and
shops; others traveled to mines or did migratory labor on farms but returned to the cities between
jobs. Mexican workers, too, faced hostility and discrimination from the Anglo population of
the region, but there were few efforts actually to exclude them. Employers in the relatively
underpopulated West needed this ready pool of low-paid and unorganized workers.

AGRICULTURAL TECHNOLOGY AND THE PLIGHT OF THE FARMER

Like industry, American agriculture in the 1920s embraced new technologies. The number of tractors on American farms quadrupled during the 1920s, especially after they began to be powered by internal combustion engines (like automobiles) rather than by the cumbersome steam engines of the past. They helped open 35 million new acres to cultivation. Increasingly sophisticated combines and harvesters proliferated, making it possible to produce more crops with fewer workers.

Agricultural researchers worked on other innovations: the invention of hybrid corn (made possible by advances in genetic research), which became available to farmers in 1921 but was not grown in great quantities for a decade or more; and the creation of chemical fertilizers and pesticides, which also had limited use in the 1920s but proliferated quickly in the 1930s and 1940s.

The new technologies greatly increased agricultural productivity, but the demand for agricultural goods was not rising as fast as production. As a result,   *Declining Food Prices* there were substantial surpluses, a disastrous decline in food prices, and a severe drop in farmers' incomes beginning early in the 1920s. More than 3 million people left agriculture altogether in the course of the decade. Of those who remained, many lost ownership of their lands and had to rent instead from banks or other landlords.

In response, some farmers began to demand relief in the form of government price supports. One price-raising scheme in particular came to dominate agrarian demands: the idea of "parity." Parity was a complicated formula for setting an adequate price for   *Parity* farm goods and ensuring that farmers would earn back at least their production costs no matter how the national or world agricultural market might fluctuate. Champions of parity urged high tariffs against foreign agricultural goods and a government commitment to buy surplus domestic crops at parity and sell them abroad.

The legislative expression of the demand for parity was the McNary-Haugen Bill, which required the government to support prices at parity for grain, cotton, tobacco, and rice. It was introduced repeatedly between 1924 and 1928. In 1926 and again in 1928, Congress approved the bill. President Calvin Coolidge vetoed it both times.

THE NEW CULTURE

The urban and consumer-oriented culture of the 1920s helped Americans in all regions live their lives and perceive their world in increasingly similar ways. That same culture exposed them to a new set of values. But different segments of American society experienced the new culture in different ways.

CONSUMERISM AND COMMUNICATIONS

The United States of the 1920s was a consumer society. More people than ever before could buy items not just because of need but also for convenience and pleasure. Middle-class families purchased electric refrigerators, washing machines, and vacuum cleaners. People wore wristwatches and smoked cigarettes. Women purchased cosmetics and mass-produced fashions. Above all, Americans bought automobiles. By the end of the decade, there were more than 30 million cars on American roads.

No group was more attuned to the emergence of consumerism (or more responsible for creating it) than the advertising industry. In the 1920s, partly as a   *Advertising Industry* result of techniques pioneered by wartime propaganda, advertising came of age. Publicists

THE CINEMA

There is probably no cultural or commercial product more closely identified with the United States than motion pictures—or, as they are known in much of the world, the cinema. Although the technology of cinema emerged from the work of inventors in England and France as well as the United States, the production and distribution of films has been dominated by Americans almost from the start. The United States was the first nation to create a film "industry," and it did so at a scale vaster than that of any other country. With 700 feature films a year in the 1920s, Hollywood produced ten times as many movies as any other nation; and even then, its films were dominating not only the huge American market but much of the world's market as well. Seventy percent of the films seen in France, 80 percent of those seen in Latin America, and 95 percent of the movies viewed in Canada and Great Britain were produced in the United States in the 1920s. As early as the 1930s, the penetration of other nations by American movies was already troubling many governments. The Soviet Union responded to the popularity of Walt Disney's Mickey Mouse cartoons by inventing a cartoon hero of its own—a porcupine, designed to entertain in a way consistent with socialist values and not the capitalist ones that they believed Hollywood conveyed. During World War II, American films were banned in occupied France (prompting some antifascist dissidents to screen such American films as Frank Capra's *Mr. Smith Goes to Washington* in protest).

American dominance was a result in part of World War I and its aftermath, which debilitated European filmmaking just as movies were vigorously growing in the United States. By 1915, the United States had gained complete control of its own vast market and had so saturated it with movie theaters that by the end of World War I, half the theaters of the world were in America. Two decades later, after an extraordinary expansion of theaters in other nations, the United States continued to have over 40 percent of the world's cinemas. And while the spread of theaters through other areas of the world helped launch film industries in many other countries, it also increased the market (and the appetite) for American films and strengthened American supremacy in their production. "The sun, it now appears," the *Saturday Evening Post* commented in the mid-1920s, "never sets on the British Empire and the American motion picture." Movies were then, and perhaps remain still, America's most influential cultural export. Even American popular music, which has enormous global reach, faces more significant local competition than American movies do in most parts of the world.

Despite this American dominance, however, filmmaking has flourished—and continues to flourish—in many countries around the world. India's fabled "Bollywood," for example, produces an enormous number of movies for its domestic market—almost as many as the American industry creates—although few of them are widely exported. This global cinema has had a significant impact on American filmmaking. The small British film industry had a strong early influence on American movies, partly because of the quality and originality of British films and partly because of the emigration of talented actors, directors, and screenwriters generation of highly individualistic directors in the United States. Asian cinema—especially the thriving film industry in Hong Kong with its gritty realism—helped lead to some of the powerfully violent American films of the 1980s and beyond, as well as the genre of martial-arts films that has become popular around the world. German, Italian, Swedish, Dutch, Japanese, Spanish, Australian, and Indian filmmakers also had enormous influence on Hollywood—and over time perhaps even greater influence on the large and growing "independent film" movement in the United States.

In recent decades, as new technologies and new styles have transformed films around the world, the American movie industry has continued to dominate global cinema. But national boundaries no longer adequately describe moviemaking in the twenty-first century. It is becoming as truly global as other commercial ventures. "American" films today are often produced abroad, often have non-American directors and actors, and are often paid for with international financing. Hollywood still dominates worldwide filmmaking, but Hollywood itself is now an increasingly global community. •

VALENTINO The popularity of the film star Rudolph Valentino among American women was one of the most striking cultural phenomena of the 1920s. Valentino was slight and delicate, not at all like the conventional image of "manliness." But he developed an enormous following among women, in part—as this poster is obviously intended to suggest—by baring his body on screen. Valentino was Italian, which made him seem somehow strange and foreign to many older-stock Americans, and he was almost always cast in exotic roles, never as an American. His sudden death in 1926 (at the age of 31) created enormous outpourings of grief among many American women. (© United Artists/Photofest)

UNDERSTAND, ANALYZE, & EVALUATE

1. Did American movies, as the Soviet Union claimed in the 1930s, promote capitalism?
2. Why has the American movie industry continued to dominate global cinema?

to the United States. The great Alfred Hitchcock, for example, made his first films in London before moving to Hollywood, where he spent the rest of his long career. After World War II, French "new wave" cinema helped spawn a new

no longer simply conveyed information; they sought to identify products with a particular lifestyle. They also encouraged the public to absorb the values of promotion and salesmanship and to admire those who were effective "boosters" and publicists. One of the most successful books of the 1920s was *The Man Nobody Knows,* by the advertising executive Bruce Barton. It portrayed Jesus as not only a religious prophet but also a "super salesman." Barton's message, one sensitive to the new spirit of the consumer culture, was that Jesus had been concerned with living a full and rewarding life in this world and that twentieth-century men and women should do the same.

The advertising industry made good use of new vehicles of communication. Newspapers were absorbed into national chains. Mass-circulation magazines attracted broad national audiences. Movies in the 1920s became an ever more popular and powerful form of mass communication. Over 100 million people saw films in 1930, as compared to 40 million in 1922. The addition of sound to motion pictures—beginning in 1927 with the first

The Jazz Singer feature-length "talkie," *The Jazz Singer* starring Al Jolson—greatly enhanced film's appeal. A series of scandals in the early 1920s led to the creation of the new Motion Picture Association, which imposed much tighter controls over the content of films. The result was safer, more conventionally acceptable films, which may in fact have broadened the appeal of movies generally. (See "America in the World: The Cinema.")

An equally important communications vehicle was the radio. The first commercial radio station in America, KDKA in Pittsburgh, began broadcasting in 1920, and the first national radio network, the National Broadcasting Company, was formed in 1927. That same year, Congress passed the Radio Act, which created a Federal Radio Commission to regulate the public airwaves used by private companies. (In 1935, it became the Federal Communications Commission, which survives today.)

WOMEN IN THE NEW ERA

College-educated women were no longer pioneers in the 1920s. There were now two and even three generations of graduates of women's or coeducational colleges and universities, and some were making their presence felt in professional areas that in the past women had rarely penetrated. The "new professional woman" was a vivid and widely publicized figure in the 1920s. In reality, however, most employed women were still nonprofessional, lower-class workers. Middle-class women, in the meantime, remained largely in the home.

Yet the 1920s constituted a new era for middle-class women nonetheless. In particular, the decade saw a redefinition of motherhood. Shortly after World War I, John B. Watson and other behavioralists began to challenge the long-held assumption that women had an

Motherhood Redefined instinctive capacity for motherhood. Maternal affection was not, they claimed, sufficient preparation for child rearing. Instead, mothers should rely on the advice and assistance of experts and professionals: doctors, nurses, and trained educators.

For many middle-class women, these changes devalued what had been an important and consuming activity. Many attempted to compensate through what are often called "companionate marriages," which elevated the importance of compatibility and love between partners. Some women now openly considered their sexual relationships with their husbands not simply as a means of procreation, as earlier generations had been taught, but as important and pleasurable experiences in their own right, the culmination of romantic love.

One result of the new era for women was growing interest in birth control. The pioneer

Margaret Sanger of the American birth-control movement, Margaret Sanger, began her career as a promoter of the diaphragm and other birth-control devices out of a concern for working-class women; she believed that large families contributed to poverty and distress in poor communities. By the 1920s, she was becoming more effective in persuading middle-class women to see the benefits of birth control. Nevertheless, some birth-control devices remained illegal in many states (and abortion remained illegal nearly everywhere).

To the consternation of many longtime women reformers and progressive suffragists, some women concluded that in the New Era it was no longer necessary to maintain a rigid, Victorian female "respectability." They could smoke, drink, dance, wear seductive

THE FLAPPER By the mid-1920s, the flapper—the young woman who challenged traditional expectations—had become not only a social type but a movement in fashion as well. Here, Catherine Dear is shown posing in a "beach costume," a fashion a long way from the rigid "respectability" of Victorian-age styles. (©Bettmann/Corbis)

clothes and makeup, and attend lively parties. Those assumptions were reflected in the emergence of the "flapper"—the modern woman whose liberated lifestyle found *"Flappers"* expression in dress, hairstyle, speech, and behavior. The flapper lifestyle had a particular impact on urban lower-middle-class and working-class single women, who were filling new jobs in industry and the service sector. At night, such women flocked to clubs and dance halls in search of excitement and companionship. Many more affluent women soon began to copy the flapper style.

Despite all the changes, most women remained highly dependent on men and relatively powerless when men exploited that dependence. The National Woman's Party, under the leadership of Alice Paul, attempted to fight that powerlessness through its campaign for the Equal Rights Amendment, although it found little support in Congress. Responding to the suffrage victory, women organized the League of Women Voters and the women's auxiliaries of both the Democratic and Republican Parties. Female-dominated consumer groups grew rapidly and increased the range and energy of their efforts.

Women activists won a brief triumph in 1921 when they helped secure passage of the Sheppard-Towner Act, which provided federal funds to states to establish prenatal and child health-care programs. From the start, however, the act produced controversy. Alice Paul and her supporters opposed the measure, complaining that it classified all women as mothers. More important, the American Medical Association fought Sheppard-Towner, warning that it would introduce untrained outsiders into the health-care field. In 1929, no longer worried about women voting as a bloc, Congress terminated the program.

THE DISENCHANTED

The generation that lived through (and in many cases fought in) the Great War quickly came to see the conflict as a useless waste of lives lost for no purpose. For many young people in the 1920s, disenchantment with the war contributed to a growing disenchantment with the United States. The newly prosperous and consumer-driven era they encountered seemed meaningless and vulgar to many artists and intellectuals in particular. As a result, they came to view their own culture with contempt. Rather than trying to influence and reform their society, they isolated themselves from it and embarked on a restless search *The "Lost Generation"* for personal fulfillment. The American writer Gertrude Stein once referred to the young Americans emerging from World War I as a "Lost Generation."

Many artists and intellectuals coming of age in the 1920s experienced that fundamental disenchantment with modern America, reflected in a series of savage critiques of *Modern Society Critiqued* modern society by a wide range of writers, some of whom were known as the "debunkers." Among them was the Baltimore journalist H. L. Mencken, who delighted in ridiculing religion, politics, the arts, even democracy itself. Sinclair Lewis published a series of savage novels—*Main Street* (1920), *Babbitt* (1922), *Arrowsmith* (1925), and others—in which he lashed out at one aspect of modern bourgeois society after another. Intellectuals of the 1920s claimed to reject the "success ethic" they believed dominated American life. The novelist F. Scott Fitzgerald, for example, attacked the American obsession with material success in *The Great Gatsby* (1925). The roster of important American writers active in the 1920s may have no equal in any other period. It included Fitzgerald, Lewis, Ernest Hemingway, Thomas Wolfe, John Dos Passos, Ezra Pound, T. S. Eliot, Gertrude Stein, Edna Ferber, William Faulkner, and Eugene O'Neill and a remarkable group of African American artists. In New York City, a new generation of black intellectuals created a flourishing artistic life widely described as the "Harlem *"Harlem Renaissance"* Renaissance." The Harlem poets, novelists, and artists drew heavily from their African roots in an effort to prove the richness of their own racial heritage and assert resistance against white racism and stereotyping. The ethos was captured in a single sentence by the poet Langston Hughes: "I am a Negro—and beautiful." Other black writers in Harlem and elsewhere—James Weldon Johnson, Countee Cullen, Zora Neale Hurston, Claude McKay, Alain Locke—as well as black artists and musicians helped establish a thriving and at times highly politicized culture.

A CONFLICT OF CULTURES

The modern, secular culture of the 1920s did not go unchallenged. It grew up alongside an older, more traditional culture, with which it continually and often bitterly competed.

PROHIBITION

When the prohibition of the sale and manufacture of alcohol went into effect in January 1920, it had the support of most members of the middle class and most of those who considered themselves progressives. Within a year, however, it had become clear that the *Failure of Prohibition* "noble experiment," as its defenders called it, was not working well. At first, prohibition did substantially reduce drinking in most parts of the country. But it also produced conspicuous and growing violations. Before long, it was almost as easy to acquire illegal alcohol in many parts of the country as it had once been to acquire legal alcohol. And since an enormous, lucrative industry was now barred to legitimate businessmen, organized crime took it over.

Many middle-class progressives who had originally supported prohibition soon soured on the experiment. But a large constituency of provincial, largely rural Protestant Americans continued vehemently to defend it. To them, prohibition represented the effort of an older

America to protect traditional notions of morality. Drinking, which they associated with the modern city and Catholic immigrants, became a symbol of the new culture they believed was displacing them.

As the decade proceeded, opponents of prohibition (or "wets") gained steadily in influence. Not until 1933, however, when the Great Depression added weight to their appeals, were they finally able to challenge the "drys" effectively and win repeal of the Eighteenth Amendment.

NATIVISM AND THE KLAN

Agitation for a curb on foreign immigration had begun in the nineteenth century and, as with prohibition, had gathered strength in the years before the war largely because of the support of middle-class progressives. In the years immediately following the war, as immigration's association with radicalism intensified and migration from Europe resumed, popular sentiment on behalf of restriction grew rapidly.

In 1921, Congress passed an emergency immigration act, establishing a quota system by which annual immigration from any country could not exceed 3 percent of the number of persons of that nationality who had been in the United States in 1910. The new law cut immigration from 800,000 to 300,000 in any single year, but the nativists remained unsatisfied. The National Origins Act of 1924 banned immigration from *National Origins Act of 1924* East Asia entirely and reduced the quota for Europeans from 3 to 2 percent. The quota would be based, moreover, not on the 1910 statistics but on the census of 1890, a year in which there had been far fewer southern and eastern Europeans in the country. What new immigration there was, in other words, would heavily favor northwestern Europeans. Five years later, a further restriction set a rigid limit of 150,000 immigrants a year. In the years that followed, immigration officials seldom permitted even half that number actually to enter the country.

To defenders of an older, more provincial America, the growth of large communities of foreign peoples, alien in speech, habits, and values, came to seem a direct threat to their own embattled way of life. Among other things, this provincial nativism helped instigate the rebirth of the Ku Klux Klan as a major force in American society. The first Klan, founded during Reconstruction, had died in the 1870s. But in 1915, a new group of white southerners met on Stone Mountain near Atlanta and established *Rise of the New Klan* a modern version of the society. Nativist passions had swelled in Georgia and elsewhere in response to the case of Leo Frank, a Jewish factory manager in Atlanta convicted in 1914 (on very flimsy evidence) of murdering a female employee; a mob stormed Frank's jail and lynched him. The premiere (also in Atlanta) of D. W. Griffith's film *The Birth of a Nation,* which glorified the early Klan, also helped inspire white southerners to form a new one.

At first the new Klan, like the old, was largely concerned with intimidating blacks. After World War I, however, concern about blacks gradually became secondary to concern about Catholics, Jews, and foreigners. At that point, membership in the Klan expanded rapidly and dramatically, not just in the small towns and rural areas of the South but in industrial cities in the North and Midwest as well. By 1924, there were reportedly 4 million members, including many women, organized in separate, parallel units. The largest state Klan was not in the South but in Indiana. Beginning in 1925, a series of scandals involving the organization's leaders precipitated a slow but steady decline in the Klan's influence.

Most Klan units (or "klaverns") tried to present their members as patriots and defenders of morality, and some did nothing more menacing than stage occasional parades and rallies. Often, however, the Klan also operated as a brutal, even violent, opponent of "alien" groups. Klansmen systematically terrorized blacks, Jews, Catholics, and foreigners. At times, they engaged in public whipping, tarring and feathering, arson, and lynching. What the Klan feared, however, was not simply "foreign" or "racially impure" groups, but anyone who posed a challenge to traditional values.

Religious Fundamentalism

Another cultural controversy of the 1920s involved the place of religion in contemporary society. By 1921, American Protestantism was already divided into two warring camps. On one side stood the modernists: mostly urban, middle-class people who were attempting to adapt religion to the teachings of modern science and to the realities of their modern, secular society. *Fundamentalists and Modernists* On the other side stood the fundamentalists: provincial, largely (although far from exclusively) rural men and women fighting to preserve traditional faith and to maintain the centrality of religion in American life. The fundamentalists insisted the Bible was to be interpreted literally. Above all, they opposed the teachings of Charles Darwin, whose theory of evolution had openly challenged the biblical story of the Creation.

By the mid-1920s, to the great alarm of modernists, fundamentalist demands to forbid the teaching of evolution in public schools were gaining political strength in some states. In Tennessee in March 1925, the legislature adopted a measure making it illegal for any public school teacher "to teach any theory that denies the story of the divine creation of man as taught in the Bible."

The Tennessee law caught the attention of the fledgling American Civil Liberties Union (ACLU), founded in 1917 to defend pacifists, radicals, and conscientious objectors during World War I. The ACLU offered free counsel to any Tennessee educator willing to defy the law and become the defendant in a test case. A twenty-four-year-old biology teacher *Scopes Trial* in the town of Dayton, John T. Scopes, agreed to have himself arrested. And when the ACLU decided to send the famous attorney Clarence Darrow to defend Scopes, the aging William Jennings Bryan (now an important fundamentalist spokesman) announced that he would travel to Dayton to assist the prosecution. Journalists from across the country flocked to Tennessee to cover the trial. Scopes had, of course, clearly and deliberately violated the law; and a verdict of guilty was a foregone conclusion, especially when the judge refused to permit "expert" testimony by evolution scholars. Scopes was fined $100, and the case was ultimately dismissed in a higher court because of a technicality. Nevertheless, Darrow scored an important victory for the modernists by calling Bryan himself to the stand to testify as an "expert on the Bible." In the course of the cross-examination, which was broadcast by radio to much of the nation, Darrow made Bryan's defense of biblical truths appear stubborn and foolish and finally maneuvered Bryan into admitting the possibility that not all religious dogma was subject to only one interpretation.

The Scopes trial put fundamentalists on the defensive. It discouraged many of them from participating openly in politics. But it did not resolve the conflict between fundamentalists and modernists, which continued to smolder.

The Democrats' Ordeal

The anguish of provincial Americans attempting to defend an embattled way of life proved particularly troubling to the Democratic Party during the 1920s. More than the

Republicans, the Democrats consisted of a diverse coalition of interest groups, including prohibitionists, Klansmen, and fundamentalists on one side and Catholics, urban workers, and immigrants on the other.

At the 1924 Democratic National Convention in New York City, a bitter conflict broke out over the platform when the party's urban wing attempted to win approval of planks calling for the repeal of prohibition and a denunciation of the Klan. Both planks narrowly failed. (The effort to condemn the Klan by name failed by one vote out of 1,085.) Even more damaging to the party was a deadlock in the balloting for a presidential candidate. Urban Democrats supported Alfred E. Smith, the Irish Catholic governor *Divided Democrats* of New York; rural Democrats backed William McAdoo, Woodrow Wilson's Treasury secretary, who had skillfully positioned himself to win the support of southern and western delegates suspicious of modern urban life but whose reputation had been tarnished by a series of scandals resulting from his work as an attorney for an unsavory oil tycoon. For 103 ballots, the convention dragged on, with Smith supporters chanting "No oil on Al," until finally both Smith and McAdoo withdrew. The party settled on a compromise: the corporate lawyer John W. Davis, who lost decisively to Calvin Coolidge.

A similar schism plagued the Democrats again in 1928, when Al Smith finally secured his party's nomination for president. He was not, however, able to unite his divided party— in part because of widespread anti-Catholic sentiment, especially in the South. He was the first Democrat since the Civil War not to carry the entire South. Elsewhere, he carried no states at all except Massachusetts and Rhode Island. Smith's opponent, and the victor in the presidential election, was a man who perhaps more than any other personified the modern, prosperous, middle-class society of the New Era: Herbert Hoover.

REPUBLICAN GOVERNMENT

For twelve years, beginning in 1921, both the presidency and the Congress rested in the hands of the Republican Party. For most of those years, the federal government enjoyed a warm and supportive relationship with the American business community. Yet the government of the New Era was more than the passive, pliant instrument that critics often described. It attempted to serve in many respects as an agent of economic change.

HARDING AND COOLIDGE

Nothing seemed more clearly to illustrate the unadventurous nature of 1920s politics than the characters of the two men who served as president during most of the decade: Warren G. Harding and Calvin Coolidge.

Harding, who was elected to the presidency in 1920, was an undistinguished senator from Ohio. He had received the Republican presidential nomination as a result of an agreement among leaders of his party, who considered him, as one noted, a "good second-rater." Harding appointed distinguished men to some important *Warren Harding* cabinet offices, and he attempted to stabilize the nation's troubled foreign policy. But he seemed baffled by his responsibilities, as if he recognized his own unfitness. "I am a man of limited talents from a small town," he reportedly told friends on one occasion. "I don't seem to grasp that I am President." Harding's intellectual limits were compounded by personal weaknesses: his penchant for gambling, illegal alcohol, and attractive women.

Harding lacked the strength to abandon the party hacks who had helped create his political success. One of them, Ohio party boss Harry Daugherty, he appointed attorney general. Another, New Mexico senator Albert B. Fall, he made secretary of the interior. Members of the so-called Ohio Gang filled important offices throughout the administration. Unknown to the public, Daugherty, Fall, and others were engaged in fraud and corruption.

Teapot Dome Scandal   The most spectacular scandal involved the rich naval oil reserves at Teapot Dome, Wyoming, and Elk Hills, California. At the urging of Fall, Harding transferred control of those reserves from the Navy Department to the Interior Department. Fall then secretly leased them to two wealthy businessmen and received in return nearly half a million dollars in "loans" to ease his private financial troubles. Fall was ultimately convicted of bribery and sentenced to a year in prison; Harry Daugherty barely avoided a similar fate for his part in another scandal.

In the summer of 1923, only months before Senate investigations and press revelations brought the scandals to light, a tired and depressed Harding left Washington for a speaking tour in the West. In Seattle late in July, he complained of severe pain, which his doctors wrongly diagnosed as food poisoning. A few days later, in San Francisco, he died. He had suffered two major heart attacks.

In many ways, Calvin Coolidge, who succeeded Harding in the presidency, was utterly different from his predecessor. Where Harding was genial, garrulous, and debauched, Coolidge was dour, silent, even puritanical. In other ways, however, Harding and Coolidge were similar figures. Both took essentially passive approaches to their office.

Elected governor of Massachusetts in 1919, Coolidge had won national attention with *Calvin Coolidge*   his tough, if laconic, response to the Boston police strike that year. That was enough to make him his party's vice presidential nominee in 1920. Three years later, after Harding's death, he took the oath of office from his father, a justice of the peace, by the light of a kerosene lamp.

If anything, Coolidge was even less active as president than Harding, partly as a result of his conviction that government should interfere as little as possible in the life of the nation. In 1924, he received his party's presidential nomination virtually unopposed. Running against John W. Davis, he won a comfortable victory: 54 percent of the popular vote and 382 of the 531 electoral votes. Coolidge probably could have won renomination and reelection in 1928. Instead, in characteristically understated fashion, he walked into a press room one day and handed each reporter a slip of paper containing a single sentence: "I do not choose to run for president in 1928."

GOVERNMENT AND BUSINESS

However passive the New Era presidents may have been, much of the federal government worked effectively and efficiently during the 1920s to adapt public policy to the widely accepted goal of the time: helping business and industry to operate with maximum efficiency and productivity. The close relationship between the private sector and the federal government forged during World War I continued. Secretary of the Treasury Andrew Mellon, a *Sharp Tax Reductions*   wealthy steel and aluminum tycoon, worked to achieve substantial reductions in taxes on corporate profits, personal incomes, and inheritances. Largely because of his efforts, Congress cut them all by more than half. Mellon also worked closely with President Coolidge after 1924 on a series of measures to trim dramatically the already modest federal budget, even managing to retire half the nation's World War I debt.

The most prominent member of the cabinet was Commerce Secretary Herbert Hoover. During his eight years in the Commerce Department, Hoover constantly encouraged voluntary cooperation in the private sector as the best avenue to stability. But the idea of voluntarism did not require that the government remain passive; on the contrary, public institutions, Hoover believed, had a duty to play an active role in creating the new, cooperative order. Above all, Hoover became the champion of the concept of business "associationalism"—a concept that envisioned the creation of national organizations of businessmen in particular industries. Through these trade associations, *"Associationalism"* private entrepreneurs could, Hoover believed, study and stabilize their industries and promote efficiency in production and marketing.

Many progressives derived encouragement from the election of Herbert Hoover to the presidency in 1928. Hoover easily defeated Al Smith, the Democratic *Herbert Hoover* candidate. And he entered office promising bold new efforts to solve the nation's remaining economic problems. But Hoover had few opportunities to prove himself. Less than a year after his inauguration, the nation plunged into the severest and most prolonged economic crisis in its history—a crisis that brought many of the optimistic assumptions of the New Era crashing down and launched the nation into a period of unprecedented social innovation and reform.

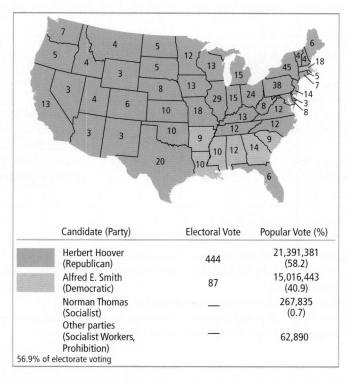

Candidate (Party)	Electoral Vote	Popular Vote (%)
Herbert Hoover (Republican)	444	21,391,381 (58.2)
Alfred E. Smith (Democratic)	87	15,016,443 (40.9)
Norman Thomas (Socialist)	—	267,835 (0.7)
Other parties (Socialist Workers, Prohibition)	—	62,890

56.9% of electorate voting

THE ELECTION OF 1928 The election of 1928 was highly one-sided. Herbert Hoover won over 58 percent of the popular vote to Alfred Smith's 41 percent. Smith carried only Massachusetts, Rhode Island, and some traditionally Democratic states in the South. • *Why did Smith do so poorly even in some parts of the South?*

CONCLUSION

The remarkable prosperity of the 1920s shaped much of what exuberant contemporaries liked to call the "New Era." In the years after World War I, America built a vibrant and extensive national culture. Its middle class moved increasingly into the embrace of the growing consumer culture. Politics were reorganized around the needs of a booming, interdependent industrial economy—rejecting many of the reform crusades of the previous generation but also creating new institutions to help promote economic growth and stability.

Beneath the glittering surface of the New Era, however, were great controversies and injustices. Although the prosperity of the 1920s was more widely spread than at any time in the nation's industrial history, more than half the population failed to achieve any real benefits from the growth. A new, optimistic, secular culture attracted millions of urban middle-class people. But many other Americans looked at it with alarm and fought against it with great fervor. The unprepossessing conservative presidents of the era suggested a time of stability, but in fact few eras in modern American history have seen so much political and cultural conflict.

The 1920s ended in a catastrophic economic crash that has colored the image of those years ever since. The crises of the 1930s should not obscure the real achievements of the New Era economy. Neither, however, should the prosperity of the 1920s obscure the inequity and instability in those years that helped produce the difficult years to come.

KEY TERMS/PEOPLE/PLACES/EVENTS

American Plan 548
Brotherhood of Sleeping
 Car Porters 548
Calvin Coolidge 560
flappers 555
Harlem Renaissance 556
Herbert Hoover 561

Issei 549
Ku Klux Klan 557
Langston Hughes 556
Lost Generation 556
Margaret Sanger 554
National Origins Act
 of 1924 557

Nisei 549
parity 551
Scopes trial 558
Teapot Dome 560
The Jazz Singer 554
Warren Harding 559
welfare capitalism 547

RECALL AND REFLECT

1. What was the impact of the automobile on American life?
2. How did labor fare during the 1920s? What particular problems did female, black, immigrant, and unskilled laborers face?
3. How did religion respond to the consumer culture of the 1920s?
4. What was the myth and what was the reality of the new professional woman of the 1920s?
5. What was the nature and extent of the nativism of the 1920s?

23 THE GREAT DEPRESSION

THE COMING OF THE DEPRESSION
THE AMERICAN PEOPLE IN HARD TIMES
THE DEPRESSION AND AMERICAN CULTURE
THE ORDEAL OF HERBERT HOOVER

LOOKING AHEAD

1. What were some of the causes of the Great Depression? What made it so severe, and why did it last so long?
2. What was the impact of the Depression on farmers, minorities, and women?
3. How did President Hoover and his administration try to deal with the Depression? What was the result of those efforts?

"WE IN AMERICA TODAY," Herbert Hoover proclaimed in August 1928, "are nearer to the final triumph over poverty than ever before in the history of any land." Only fifteen months later, those words would return to haunt him, as the nation plunged into the severest and most prolonged economic depression in its history—a depression that continued in one form or another for a full decade, not only in the United States but throughout much of the world.

THE COMING OF THE DEPRESSION

The sudden financial collapse in 1929 came as an especially severe shock because it followed so closely an era that appeared to offer economic miracles—miracles that seemed especially evident in the remarkable performance of the stock market.

In February 1928, stock prices began a steady ascent that continued, with only a few temporary lapses, for a year and a half. Between May 1928 and September 1929, the average price of stocks rose over 40 percent. Trading mushroomed from 2 or 3 million shares a day to over 5 million, and at times to as many as 10 or 12 million. In short, a widespread speculative fever grew steadily more intense, particularly once brokerage firms began encouraging the mania by offering absurdly easy credit to those buying stocks.

THE GREAT CRASH

In the autumn of 1929, the market began to fall apart. On October 29, "Black Tuesday," after a week of growing instability, all efforts to save the market failed. Sixteen million shares of stock were traded; the industrial index dropped 43 points (or nearly 10 percent), wiping out all the gains of the previous year; stocks in many companies became virtually worthless. Within a month, stocks had lost half their September value, and despite occasional, short-lived rallies, they continued to decline for several years after that.

Popular folklore has established the stock market crash as the beginning, and even the cause, of the Great Depression. Although October 1929 might have been the most visible early sign of the crisis, the Depression had earlier beginnings and other causes.

CAUSES OF THE DEPRESSION

Economists and historians have argued for decades about the causes of the Great Depression. But most agree on several things. They agree, first, that what is remarkable about the crisis is not that it occurred but that it was so severe and that it lasted so long, which most observers agree—even if they agree on little else—was the result of several factors.

One was a lack of diversification in the American economy in the 1920s. Prosperity had depended excessively on a few basic industries, notably construction and automobiles, which in the late 1920s began to decline. Expenditures on *Weaknesses in the U.S. Economy* construction fell from $11 billion in 1926 to under $9 billion in 1929. Automobile sales fell by more than a third in the first nine months of 1929. Newer industries were emerging to take up the slack—among them petroleum, chemicals, electronics, and plastics—but none had yet developed enough strength to compensate for this decline.

A second important factor was the maldistribution of purchasing power and, as a result, a weakness in consumer demand. As industrial and agricultural production increased, the proportion of the profits going to potential consumers was too small to create an adequate market for the goods the economy was producing. Even in 1929, after nearly a decade of economic growth, more than half the families in America lived on the edge of or below the minimum subsistence level.

A third major problem was the credit structure of the economy. Farmers were deeply in debt, and crop prices were too low to allow them to pay off what they owed. Small banks were in constant trouble as their customers defaulted on loans; large banks were in trouble, too. Although most American bankers were very conservative, some of the nation's biggest banks were investing recklessly in the stock market or making unwise loans. When the market crashed and the loans went bad, some banks failed and others made the crisis worse by contracting already scarce credit and calling in loans that borrowers could not pay.

A fourth factor was America's position in international trade. Late in the 1920s, European demand for American goods began to decline, partly because *Global Factors* European industry and agriculture were becoming more productive and partly because some European nations were having financial difficulties of their own. But it was also because the European economy was being destabilized by the international debt structure that had emerged in the aftermath of World War I.

This debt structure, therefore, was a fifth factor contributing to the Depression. When the war came to an end in 1918, all the European nations that had been allied with the United States owed large sums of money to American banks, sums much too large to be repaid out of their shattered economies, which is partly why the Allies had insisted on reparation payments from Germany and Austria. Reparations, they believed, would provide them with a way to pay off their own debts. But Germany and Austria were no more able to pay the reparations than the Allies were able to pay their debts.

The American government refused to forgive or reduce the debts. Instead, American banks began making large loans to European governments, which used them to pay off their earlier loans. Thus debts (and reparations) were being paid only by piling up new and greater debts. At the same time, American protective tariffs were making it difficult for Europeans to sell their goods in American markets. Without any source of foreign exchange with which to repay their loans, they began to default. The collapse of the international credit structure was one of the reasons the Depression spread to Europe after 1931. (See "America in the World: The Global Depression.")

THE GLOBAL DEPRESSION

The Great Depression began in the United States. But it did not end there. The American economy was the largest in the world, and its collapse sent shock waves across the globe. By 1931, the American depression had become a world depression, with important implications for the course of global history.

The origins of the worldwide depression lay in the pattern of debts that had emerged during and after World War I, when the United States loaned billions of dollars to European nations. In 1931, with American banks staggering and in many cases collapsing, large banks in New York began desperately calling in their loans from Germany and Austria. That precipitated the collapse of one of Austria's largest banks, which in turn created panic through much of central Europe. The economic collapse in Germany and Austria meant that those nations could not continue paying reparations to Britain and France (required by the Treaty of Versailles of 1919), which meant in turn that Britain and France could not continue paying off their loans to the United States. This spreading financial crisis was accompanied by a dramatic contraction of international trade, precipitated in part by the Hawley-Smoot Tariff in the United States, which established the highest import duties in history and stifled much global commerce. Depressed agricultural prices—a result of worldwide overproduction—also contributed to the downturn. By 1932, worldwide industrial production had declined by more than one-third, and world trade had plummeted by nearly two-thirds. By 1933, 30 million people in industrial nations were unemployed, five times the number of four years before.

But the Depression was not confined to industrial nations. Imperialism and

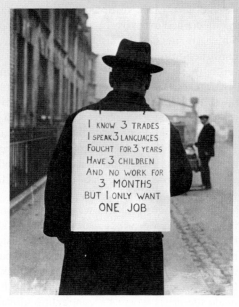

LOOKING FOR WORK IN LONDON, 1935 An unemployed London man wears a sign that seems designed to convince passersby that he is an educated, respectable person despite his present circumstances. (©Hulton Archive/Getty Images)

industrialization had drawn almost all regions of the world into the international industrial economy. Colonies and nations in Africa, Asia, and South America—critically dependent on exporting raw materials and agricultural goods to industrial countries—experienced a collapse in demand for their products and thus rising levels of poverty and unemployment. Some nations—among them the Soviet Union and China—remained relatively unconnected to the global economy and suffered relatively little from the Great Depression. But in most parts of the world, the Depression caused tremendous social and economic hardship.

It also created political turmoil. Among the countries hardest hit by the Depression was Germany, where industrial production declined by 50 percent and unemployment reached 35 percent in the early 1930s. The desperate economic conditions there contributed greatly to the rise of the Nazi Party and its leader, Adolf Hitler, who became chancellor in 1933. Japan suffered as well, dependent as it was on world trade to sustain its growing industrial economy and purchase essential commodities for its needs at home. And in Japan, as in Germany, economic troubles produced political turmoil and aided the rise of a new militaristic regime. In Italy, the fascist government of Benito Mussolini, which had first taken power in the 1920s, also saw militarization and territorial expansion as a way out of economic difficulties.

In other nations, governments sought solutions to the Depression through reform of their domestic economies. The most prominent example was the New Deal in the United States. But there were important experiments in other nations as well. Among the most common responses to the Depression around the world was substantial government investment in public works, such as roads, bridges, dams, public buildings, and other large projects. Among the nations that adopted this approach—in addition to the United States—were Britain, France, Germany, Italy, and the Soviet Union. Another response was the expansion of government-funded relief for the unemployed. All the industrial countries of the world experimented with various forms of relief, often borrowing ideas from one another in the process. And the Depression helped create new approaches to economics,

in the face of the apparent failure of classical models of economic behavior to explain, or provide solutions to, the crisis. The great British economist John Maynard Keynes revolutionized economic thought in much of the world. His 1936 book *The General Theory of Employment, Interest, and Money*, despite its bland title, created a sensation by arguing that the Depression was a result not of declining production but of inadequate consumer demand. Governments, he said, could stimulate their economies by increasing the money supply and creating investment—through a combination of lowering interest rates and public spending. Keynesianism, as Keynes's theories became known, began to have an impact in the United States in 1938, and in much of the rest of the world in subsequent years.

The Great Depression was an important turning point not only in American history but also in the history of the twentieth-century world. It transformed ideas of public policy and economics in many nations. It toppled old regimes and created new ones. And perhaps above all, it was a major factor in the coming of World War II. •

UNDERSTAND, ANALYZE, & EVALUATE

1. How did the 1919 Treaty of Versailles and the Hawley-Smoot Tariff contribute to the global depression of the 1930s?
2. How did the governments of European nations respond to the Depression?
3. What effect did the global depression have on economic theory? Why was Keynes's economic theory so revolutionary?

PROGRESS OF THE DEPRESSION

The stock market crash of 1929 did not so much cause the Depression, then, as help trigger a chain of events that exposed larger weaknesses in the American economy. During the next three years, the crisis grew steadily worse.

The most serious problem at first was the collapse of much of the banking system. Between 1930 and 1933, over 9,000 American banks either went bankrupt or closed their doors to avoid bankruptcy. Partly as a result of these banking closures, the nation's money supply shrank by perhaps a third or more between 1930 and 1933, which caused a decline in purchasing power and thus deflation. Manufacturers and merchants began reducing prices, cutting back on production, and laying off workers. Some economists argue that a severe depression could have been avoided if the Federal Reserve system had acted responsibly. But late in 1931, in a misguided effort to build international confidence in the dollar, it raised interest rates, which contracted the money supply even further.

The American gross national product plummeted from over $104 billion in 1929 to $76.4 billion in 1932—a 25 percent decline in three years. By 1932, according to the relatively crude estimates of the time, 25 percent of the American workforce was unemployed. (Some argue that the figure was even higher.) For the rest of the decade, unemployment averaged nearly 20 percent, never dropping below 15 percent. Up to another one-third of the workforce was "underemployed"—experiencing major reductions in wages, hours, or both.

THE AMERICAN PEOPLE IN HARD TIMES

Someone asked the British economist John Maynard Keynes in the 1930s whether he was aware of any historical era comparable to the Great Depression. "Yes," Keynes replied. "It was called the Dark Ages, and it lasted 400 years." The Depression did not last 400 years. It did, however, bring unprecedented economic despair to the United States and much of the Western world.

THE HUNGRY   Hundreds of men wait to be fed outside the Municipal Lodging House in New York City.
(© Bettmann/Corbis)

UNEMPLOYMENT AND RELIEF

In the industrial Northeast and Midwest, cities were virtually paralyzed by unemployment. Cleveland, Ohio, for example, had an unemployment rate of 50 percent in 1932; Akron, 60 percent; Toledo, 80 percent. Unemployed workers walked through the streets day after day looking for jobs that did not exist. An increasing number of families turned to state and local public relief systems, just to be able to eat. But those systems, which in the 1920s had served only a small number of indigents, were totally unequipped to handle the heavy new demands. In many cities, therefore, relief simply collapsed. Private charities attempted to supplement the public relief efforts, but the problem was far beyond their capabilities as well.

In rural areas, conditions were in many ways worse. Farm income declined by 60 percent between 1929 and 1932. A third of all American farmers lost their land. In addition, a large area of agricultural settlement in the Great Plains suffered from a catastrophic natural disaster: one of the worst droughts in the history of the nation. Beginning in 1930, the region that came to be known as the "Dust Bowl," which stretched north from Texas into the Dakotas, experienced a steady decline *"Dust Bowl"* in rainfall and an accompanying increase in heat. The drought continued for a decade, turning what had once been fertile farm regions into virtual deserts. Severe winds blew dust across the eastern United States.

Many farmers, like many urban unemployed, left their homes in search of work. In the South, in particular, many dispossessed farmers—black and white—simply wandered from town to town, hoping to find jobs or handouts. Hundreds of thousands of families from the Dust Bowl (often known collectively as "Okies," though not all came from *"Okies"* Oklahoma) traveled to California and other states, where they found conditions little better than those they had left. Many worked as agricultural migrants, traveling from farm to farm, picking fruit and other crops at starvation wages.

DUST STORM, SOUTHWEST PLAINS, 1937   The dust storms of the 1930s were a terrifying experience for all who lived through them. Resembling a black wall sweeping in from the western horizon, such a storm engulfed farms and towns alike, blotting out the light of the sun and covering everything with a fine dirt. (© Bettmann/Corbis)

AFRICAN AMERICANS AND THE DEPRESSION

Most African Americans had not shared very much in the prosperity of the previous decade. But they did share in the hardships of the Great Depression.

As the Depression began, over half of all black Americans still lived in the South. Most were farmers. The collapse of prices for cotton and other staple crops left some with no income at all. Many left the land altogether—either by choice or because they had been evicted by landlords who no longer found sharecropping profitable. Some migrated to southern cities. But there, unemployed whites believed they had first claim to what work there was, and some now began to take positions as janitors, street cleaners, and domestic servants, displacing the African Americans who formerly occupied those jobs. By 1932, over half the blacks in the South were unemployed.

Unsurprisingly, therefore, many black southerners—perhaps 400,000 in all—left the South in the 1930s and journeyed to the cities of the North. But conditions there were little better. In New York, black unemployment was nearly 50 percent. In other cities, it was higher. Two million African Americans—half the total black population of the country—were on some form of relief by 1932.

Traditional patterns of segregation and disenfranchisement in the South survived the Depression largely unchallenged. But a few particularly notorious examples of racism did attract the attention of the nation. The most celebrated was the Scottsboro case. In *Scottsboro Case* March 1931, nine black teenagers were taken off a freight train in northern Alabama (in a small town near Scottsboro) and were arrested for vagrancy and disorder. Later, two white women who had also been riding the train accused them of rape. In fact, there was overwhelming evidence, medical and otherwise, that the women had not been raped at all; they may have made their accusations out of fear of being arrested themselves. Nevertheless, an all-white jury in Alabama quickly convicted all nine of the "Scottsboro boys" (as they were known to both friends and foes) and sentenced eight of them to death.

The Supreme Court overturned the convictions in 1932, and a series of new trials began. The International Labor Defense, an organization associated with the Communist Party, came to the aid of the accused youths and began to publicize the case. Although the white southern juries who sat on the case never acquitted any of the defendants, all of the accused eventually gained their freedom—although the last of the Scottsboro defendants did not leave prison until 1950.

HISPANICS AND ASIANS IN DEPRESSION AMERICA

Similar patterns of discrimination confronted many Mexicans and Mexican Americans. *Hispanic Workers Targeted* The Hispanic population of the United States had been growing steadily since early in the century, largely in California and other areas of the Southwest. Chicanos (Mexican Americans) filled many of the same menial jobs there that blacks had traditionally filled in other regions. Some farmed small, marginal tracts; others became agricultural migrants. It had always been a precarious existence, and the Depression made things significantly worse. Unemployed whites in the Southwest demanded jobs held by Hispanics, jobs that whites had previously considered beneath them. Thus Mexican unemployment rose quickly to levels far higher than those for whites. Some officials arbitrarily removed Mexicans from relief rolls or simply rounded up and deported them. Perhaps half a million Chicanos left the United States for Mexico in the first years of the Depression.

There were occasional signs of organized resistance by Mexican Americans themselves, most notably in California, where some formed a union of migrant farmworkers. But harsh repression by local growers and the public authorities allied with them prevented such organizations from having much impact. As a result, many Hispanics began to migrate to cities such as Los Angeles, where they lived in poverty comparable to that of urban blacks in the South and Northeast.

For Asian Americans, too, the Depression reinforced long-standing patterns of discrimination and economic marginalization. In California, where the *Plight of Asian Americans* largest Japanese American and Chinese American populations were, educated Asians had always found it difficult, if not impossible, to move into mainstream professions. Japanese American college graduates often found themselves working in family fruit stands. For those who found jobs in the industrial or service economy, employment was precarious; like blacks and Hispanics, Asians often lost jobs to white Americans desperate for work. Japanese farmworkers, like Chicano farmworkers, suffered from the increasing competition for even these low-paying jobs with white migrants from the Great Plains.

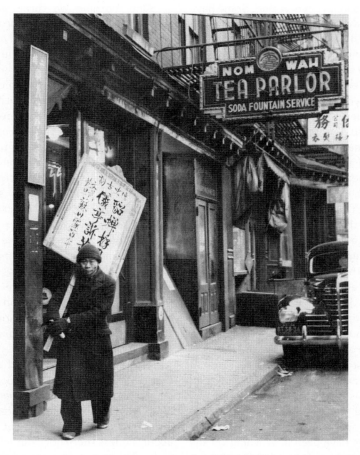

CHINATOWN, NEW YORK CITY A Chinese man carries a "sandwich board" through the streets of New York City's Chinatown bearing the latest news of the war between China and Japan, which in 1938 was well under way. Chinese Americans had the duel challenge in the 1930s of dealing both with large-scale unemployment and with continuing news of catastrophe from China, where most still had family members. (© Hulton Archive/Getty Images)

MR. TARVER REMEMBERS THE GREAT DEPRESSION

The Federal Writers' Project (FWP) was a New Deal program that employed authors and researchers during the Great Depression. Participants produced tourist guidebooks, ethnographies, oral histories, and many other kinds of documents. In 1940, an FWP writer interviewed a bank employee named Mr. Tarver.

Yes, I really went through the depression. [. . .] "There were thousands who went down during the panic—lost fortunes, homes, business, and in fact everything. Some have survived, and many never will. A great many were too old to begin building up again. In the kind of work I'm in I have been in position to know some of the devastating effects of it, and it certainly gets on your sympathy.

"I guess you would say I am recovering from it. When I say that though, I'm not boasting, but I'm deeply grateful for the good fortunes that have came my way. Then, too, I feel under everlasting obligations to some of my friends who have helped me to get where I am.

"I had not accumulated a great deal at the time of the panic, but I did have some savings and a good job. That was the trouble, my savings and my job went at the same time. Now that was real trouble. Nobody but my wife and I knew just what we did go through. [. . .]

I was making a fine salary, had a growing savings account, and a host of friends, and no serious troubles to worry about. My wife is just the smartest, thriftiest person you have ever seen. To her I owe a lot of my successes. She is fine with her needle and crocheting, and you never saw her idle. She made all her spending money that way. Even now since we have been in Washington she keeps it up. And her fruit cake! People here rave about it. She cooks an enormous amount of it every Christmas and sells it for a big profit. She can't fill all the orders she gets. She is very resourceful and right now, if I were to die and not leave her a thing, she would manage some way. One of my hobbies was gardening and it proved to be a profitable one too. This place we rented had a fine garden spot, the finest in Dublin, so every one said. I worked in it early every morning and in the afternoon after banking hours. I sold lots of vegetables, and realized a lot on them—especially the early variety that brought a good price." [. . .]

"One morning we three were at the breakfast table when the phone rang. It was one of the fellows who worked at the bank.

"Tarver, he said, 'have you heard the news?'

"'What news? No, I haven't heard any news,' said I. What's it all about?'

"Well,' he said, "hurry on down and see.'

"If you will excuse the expression, when he said that, the seat of my britches almost dropped out. I felt like it meant trouble of some kind. I had had a terrible feeling of uneasiness over the bank for some time. Banks had been closing all over the country. There had been a run on our bank some time previous to that, but we tided that over, and since then it had seemed stronger than ever.

"I hurried down and, sure enough, in front of the bank, there stood a crowd of employees, as blank expressions on their faces as I've ever seen. They were too dumbfounded to be excited even.

"The bank was closed and a notice to that effect on the door. We stood there just looking at each other until finally one said, 'Well, boys, guess we had better go on the inside and see if we can find out what it's all about. I guess there goes our jobs.'

[. . .] "Just as I was getting in the dumps about a regular job, I was notified to report at once, to act as assistant receiver for a defunct bank in Florida. They were feeling the depression there even more than we were in Georgia, and banks were closing every day.

[. . .] "Banks were still closing until it was hard to get enough receivers for them. Oh, we did work. Banks in neighboring towns were added to our work until we were liquidating six banks at one time, all in different places. I had to have another car then but was lucky to pick up a good used car almost at my own price. People had lost their cars as well as their homes, so it was no trouble to buy a good used one. Sometimes I would ride to all six of these banks in one day and when night came I would be completely given out. I couldn't stop even then, for there was scarcely a night that we didn't work."

UNDERSTAND, ANALYZE, & EVALUATE

1. Why was Mr. Tarver doubly affected by the banking crisis of the Great Depression? How did Mr. and Mrs. Tarver compensate for their losses in the job market?
2. How might the Great Depression have shaped the outlook of Mr. and Mrs. Tarver on work, leisure, and consumption for years, if not decades, to come?

Source: Mr. W. W. Tarver (White), Finance Officer in U.S. Treasury (Bank Conservator), 5001 Nebraska Ave., N.W., Washington, D.C., interviewed by Bradley. Library of Congress, *American Life Histories: Manuscripts from the Federal Writers' Project, 1936–1940.* http://memory.loc.gov/cgi-bin/query/r?ammem/wpa:@field%28DOCID+@lit%28wpa112060215%29%29.

Chinese Americans fared no better. The overwhelming majority worked, as they had for many years, in Chinese-owned laundries and restaurants. Those who moved outside the Asian community could rarely find jobs above the entry level. Chinese women, for example, might find work as stock girls in department stores but almost never as sales-clerks. Educated Chinese men and women could hope for virtually no professional opportunities outside the world of the Chinatowns.

WOMEN AND FAMILIES IN THE GREAT DEPRESSION

The economic crisis strengthened the widespread belief that a woman's proper place was in the home. Many men and women believed that with employment so scarce, what work there was should go to men and that no woman whose husband was employed should accept a job. Indeed, from 1932 until 1937, it was illegal for more than one member of a family to hold a federal civil service job.

But the widespread assumption that married women, at least, should not work outside the home did not stop them from doing so. Both single and married women worked in the 1930s because they or their families needed the money. Some women did small jobs at home or sold food or goods to make ends meet. (See "Consider the Source: Mr. Tarver Remembers the Great Depression.") By the end of the Depression, 25 percent more women were working for wages than had been doing so at the beginning, despite considerable obstacles. Professional opportunities for women declined because unemployed men began moving into professions that had previously been considered women's fields. Female industrial workers were more likely to be laid off or to *Female Wage Earners* experience wage reductions than their male counterparts. But white women also had certain advantages in the workplace. The nonprofessional jobs that women traditionally held—salesclerks, stenographers, and other service positions—were less likely to disappear than the predominantly male jobs in heavy industry.

Black women suffered massive unemployment, particularly in the South, because of a great reduction of domestic service jobs. As many as half of all black working women lost their jobs in the 1930s. Even so, at the end of the 1930s, 38 percent of black women were employed, as compared with 24 percent of white women. That was so because black women—both married and unmarried—had always been more likely to work than white women, less out of preference than out of economic necessity.

The Depression also worked to erode the strength of many family units. There was a *Declining Marriage Rate and Birthrate* decline in the divorce rate, but largely because divorce was now too expensive for some. More common was the informal breakup of families, particularly the desertion of families by unemployed men trying to escape the humiliation of being unable to earn a living. The marriage rate and the birthrate both declined for the first time since the early nineteenth century.

THE DEPRESSION AND AMERICAN CULTURE

The Great Depression was a traumatic experience for millions of Americans. Out of the crisis emerged probing criticisms of American life. But the Depression also produced powerful confirmations of more traditional values and reinforced many traditional goals. There was not one Depression culture, but many.

DEPRESSION VALUES

Prosperity and industrial growth had done much to shape American values in the 1920s. Yet even when hard times came, American social values seemed to change relatively little in response to the Depression. Instead, many people responded to hard times by redoubling their commitment to familiar ideas and goals. The Depression did not destroy the success ethic.

The survival of the ideals of work and individual responsibility was evident in many ways, not least in the reactions of those most traumatized by the Depression: people who suddenly found themselves without employment. Some expressed anger and struck out at the economic system. Many, however, seemed to blame themselves. At the same time, millions responded eagerly to reassurances that they could, through their own efforts, *Dale Carnegie* restore themselves to prosperity and success. Dale Carnegie's *How to Win Friends and Influence People* (1936), a self-help manual preaching individual initiative, was one of the best-selling books of the decade.

Yet the most popular cultural products of the 1930s diverted attention away from the Depression. And they came to Americans primarily through the two most powerful instruments of popular culture in the 1930s—radio and the movies. (For another powerful vehicle of escapist culture, see "Patterns of Popular Culture: The Golden Age of Comic Books.")

RADIO

Almost every American family had a radio in the 1930s. In cities and towns, radio consoles were as familiar a part of the furnishing of homes as tables and chairs. Even in remote rural areas without access to electricity, many families purchased radios and hooked them up to car batteries when they wished to listen.

Radio was often a community experience. Young people would place radios on their front porches and invite friends by to sit, talk, or dance. In poor urban neighborhoods, people would gather on a street or in a backyard to listen to sporting events or concerts. Within families, the radio often drew parents and children together to listen to favorite programs.

Although radio stations occasionally carried provocative programs, the staple of broadcasting was escapism, including comedies such as *Amos 'n'*   *Escapist Programming* *Andy* (with its demeaning picture of urban blacks) and adventures such as *Superman, Dick Tracy,* and *The Lone Ranger.* Radio brought a new kind of comedy to a wide audience. Jack Benny, George Burns and Gracie Allen, and other masters of elaborately timed repartee began to develop broad followings. Enormously popular, especially among women who were alone in the house during the day, were soap operas (so named because they were generally sponsored by soap companies, whose advertising was targeted at women).

Radio provided Americans with their first direct access to important public events. On-air coverage of news and sports expanded rapidly to meet the demand. Some of the most dramatic moments of the 1930s were a result of radio coverage of celebrated events: the World Series, the Academy Awards, political conventions. When the German dirigible *Hindenburg* crashed in flames in Lakehurst, New Jersey, in 1937, it   *The* Hindenburg *Crash* produced an enormous national reaction largely because of the live radio account by a broadcaster, overcome with emotion, who cried out, as he watched the terrible crash, "Oh the humanity! Oh the humanity!" The actor-director Orson Welles created another memorable event on Halloween night, 1938, when he broadcast a radio play about aliens landing in central New Jersey who had set off toward New York armed with terrible weapons. The play took the form of a news broadcast, and it created panic among some people who believed for a while that the events it described were real.

THE MOVIES

In the first years of the Depression, movie attendance dropped significantly. By the mid-1930s, however, most Americans had resumed their moviegoing habits in part because the movies (now with sound and, by the end of the decade, color) were becoming more appealing.

Hollywood continued to exercise tight control over its products in the 1930s through its resilient censor Will Hays, who ensured that most movies carried no sensational or controversial messages. The studio system—through which a few large movie companies exercised iron control over actors, writers, and directors—also worked to ensure that Hollywood films avoided controversy.

Neither the censor nor the studio system, however, could (or wished to) completely prevent films from exploring social questions. There were many serious films that portrayed the problems of the Depression—for example, King Vidor's *Our Daily Bread* (1932) and John Ford's adaptation of *The Grapes of Wrath* (1940). Gangster movies such as *Little Caesar* (1930) and *The Public Enemy* (1931) portrayed a dark, gritty, violent world with which few Americans were familiar, but their desperate stories were popular nevertheless with those engaged in their own difficult struggles.

But the most effective presentation of a social message came from the brilliant Italian-born director Frank Capra. Capra had a deep and somewhat romanticized love for his adopted country, and he translated that love into a vaguely populistic admiration for ordinary people. He contrasted the decency of small-town America   *Films of Frank Capra* and the common man with what he considered the grasping opportunism of the

THE GOLDEN AGE OF COMIC BOOKS

In the troubled years of the Great Depression (and later, World War II), many Americans sought release from their anxieties in fantasy. Movies, plays, books, radio shows, and other diversions drew people out of their own lives and into a safer or more glamorous or more exciting world. Beginning in 1938, one of the most popular forms of escape for many young Americans was the comic book.

In February 1935, Malcolm Wheeler-Nicholson founded the first comics magazine—what we now know as the "comic book"—titled *New Fun*. It was not successful, but Wheeler founded a new company, Detective Comics. He began in 1937 to design a new magazine called *Action Comics*. Wheeler ran out of money before he could publish anything, but the company continued without him. In 1938, the first issue of *Action Comics* appeared with a startling and controversial cover—a powerful man in a skintight suit lifting a car over his head. His name was Superman, and he became the most popular cartoon character of all time.

Within a year, Superman had a comic book named after him, which was selling over 1.2 million copies each issue. By 1940, there was a popular Superman radio show—introduced by a breathless announcer crying, "It's a bird! It's a plane! It's . . . Superman!" Soon, other publishers began developing new *superheroes* (a term invented by the creators of Superman) to capitalize on this growing popular appetite. In 1939, a second great comic book publisher appeared—Marvel Comics.

By the early 1940s, Superman had been joined by other superheroes: the Human Torch, the Sub-Mariner, Batman, the Flash,

and Wonder Woman, a character created in part to signal the importance of women to the war effort.

It is not hard to imagine why superheroes would be so appealing to Americans in the 1930s and 1940s—particularly to the teenage boys who were the largest single purchasers of comic books. Superman and other superheroes were idealized versions of the ideal boy—smart, good, "the perfect Boy Scout," as one fan put it. But they were also all-powerful, capable of righting wrong and preventing catastrophe. Even as the national economy faltered, comic book heroes modeled patriotic pride, resilience, and optimism. They operated with moral certainty when so much was uncertain. At a time when suffering was an ever-present reality in the world, superheroes offered a comforting escape from anxiety.

Many of the early comic book writers were young Jewish men, conscious of their outsider status in an American culture not yet wholly open to them. Almost all the characters they created had alter egos, identities they used while living within the normal world. Superman was Clark Kent, a "mild-mannered reporter." Batman was Bruce Wayne, a wealthy heir. All were part of mainstream American society, and they expressed in part the outsider's dream of assimilation. The superheroes themselves were outsiders too—but outsiders endowed with special powers and abilities unavailable to ordinary people.

In the last years of the Depression, the comic superheroes began battling the Axis powers. Marvel's Human Torch and Sub-Mariner joined forces against the German navy. Superman fought spies and saboteurs at home. Captain America, a new character created in March 1941, was a frail young man rejected by the army who, after being given a secret serum by a military doctor, became extraordinarily powerful. The cover of the first issue of *Captain America* showed the title character punching Adolf Hitler in his headquarters in Germany.

The end of the war was also the end of this first golden age of American comic books. New comic books emphasized romance, mild sexuality, and, over time, violence and cruelty. But comic books never surpassed the heights of popularity that the superhero comics attained during the Depression and World War II. •

SUPERMAN The most popular action figure in the history of comic books was Superman, whose superhuman powers were particularly appealing fantasies to Americans suffering through the Depression and, later, World War II. (© Hulton Archive/Getty Images)

UNDERSTAND, ANALYZE, & EVALUATE

1. What could comic books offer readers suffering through the crisis of the Great Depression?
2. How and why have comic book superheroes changed over time?

city and the greedy capitalist marketplace. In *Mr. Deeds Goes to Town* (1936), a simple man from a small town inherits a large fortune, moves to the city, and—not liking the greed and dishonesty he finds there—gives the money away and moves back home. In *Mr. Smith Goes to Washington* (1939), a decent man from a western state is elected to the United States Senate, refuses to join in the self-interested politics of Washington, and dramatically exposes the corruption and selfishness of his colleagues. Capra's films, incredibly popular in the 1930s, helped audiences find solace in a vision of an imagined American past—in the warmth and goodness of idealized small towns and the decency of ordinary people.

More often, however, the commercial films of the 1930s, like most radio programs, were deliberately and explicitly escapist: lavish musicals such as *Gold Diggers of 1933*, "screwball" comedies such as Capra's *It Happened One Night*, or the many films of the Marx Brothers—films designed to divert audiences from their troubles and, often, indulge their fantasies about quick and easy wealth.

The 1930s were the first years of Walt Disney's long reign as the champion of animation and children's entertainment. After producing cartoon shorts for theaters in the late 1920s, many of them starring the newly created character Mickey Mouse, Disney began to produce feature-length animated films, starting in 1937 with *Snow White*. Other enormously popular films of the 1930s were adaptations of popular novels, such as *The Wizard of Oz* and *Gone with the Wind,* both released in 1939.

A NIGHT AT THE OPERA   The antic comedy of the Marx Brothers provided a popular and welcome escape from the hardships of the Great Depression. The Marx Brothers, shown here in a poster for one of their most famous films, effectively lampooned dilemmas that many Americans faced in their ceaseless, and usually unsuccessful, efforts to find an easy route to wealth and comfort. (© Everett Collection)

Hollywood did little to challenge the conventions of popular culture on issues of gender and race. Women in movies were portrayed overwhelmingly as wives and mothers, or if not, as sexually attractive flirts. Mae West portrayed herself in a series of successful *Stereotypes in Film*   films as an overtly sexual woman manipulating men through her attractiveness. Few films included important African American characters. Most of the black men and women who did appear in movies were portrayed as servants or farmhands or entertainers.

LITERATURE AND JOURNALISM

Much literature and journalism in the 1930s dealt directly or indirectly with the tremendous disillusionment, and the increasing radicalism, of the time.

Not all literature, of course, was challenging or controversial. The most popular books and magazines of the 1930s, in fact, were as escapist and romantic as many radio shows and movies. Two of the best-selling novels of the decade were romantic sagas set in earlier eras: Margaret Mitchell's *Gone with the Wind* (1936) and Hervey Allen's *Anthony Adverse* (1933). Leading magazines focused more on fashions, stunts, scenery, and the arts than on the social conditions of the nation. The new and enor- *Life Magazine*   mously popular photographic journal *Life*, first published in 1936, had the largest readership of any publication in the United States other than *Reader's Digest*.

It devoted some attention to politics and to the economic conditions of the Depression, but it was best known for stunning photographs of sporting and theater events, natural landscapes, and impressive public projects. One of its most popular features was "*Life* Goes to a Party," which took the chatty social columns of daily newspapers and turned them into glossy photographic glimpses of the rich and famous, but also ordinary people enjoying less lavish parties.

Other Depression writing, however, was frankly and openly challenging to the dominant values of American popular culture. Some of the most *Depression-Era Fiction* significant literature offered corrosive portraits of the harshness and emptiness of American life: John Dos Passos's *U.S.A.* trilogy (1930–1936), which attacked what he considered the materialistic madness of American culture; in Richard Wright's *Native Son* (1940), the story of a young African American man broken by the system of racial oppression; Nathanael West's *Miss Lonelyhearts* (1933), the story of an advice columnist overwhelmed by the sadness he encounters in the lives of those who consult him; Jack Conroy's *The Disinherited* (1933), a harsh portrait of the lives of coal miners; and James T. Farrell's *Studs Lonigan* (1932), a portrait of a lost, hardened working-class youth. Perhaps the best-known depiction of Depression-era life is John Steinbeck's *The Grapes of Wrath* (1939). The novel's main characters are the Joad family, migrants from the Dust Bowl to California who encounter an unending string of calamities and failures. Their story offers a critique of the exploitative features of agrarian life in the West, as well as a tribute to the fortitude and heart of the community the Joads represent.

THE POPULAR FRONT AND THE LEFT

The Communist Party, a relatively small organization in the early twentieth century, flourished during the Great Depression. It had long been a harsh and unrelenting critic of American capitalism, largely hidden from the public world. But with the capitalist system's flaws exposed, the Depression brought the communists into the light. They created what came to be called the "Popular Front," a broad coalition of *Popular Front Alliances* "antifascist" groups on the left. Not all members of the Popular Front considered themselves communists, but communism was its driving force. The Popular Front presented itself as an American organization, but it was in fact largely controlled by the Soviet Union. Over time, Stalin and the Communist Party softened their attitude toward President Franklin Roosevelt (elected in 1932), hoping that he would become an ally against Nazi Germany. To that end, the Popular Front formed loose alliances with "progressive groups," and it praised even some strong anticommunists such as the labor leader John L. Lewis. In its heyday, the Popular Front did much to enhance the reputation and influence of the Communist Party. It also helped mobilize writers, artists, and intellectuals behind a critical, democratic sensibility.

The Spanish Civil War of the mid-1930s showed how the left helped give meaning and purpose to individual lives. The war in Spain pitted the forces supporting Francisco Franco (who received aid from Hitler and Mussolini and was thus allied with fascism) against the existing republican government. A substantial group of young Americans— more than 3,000 in all—formed the Abraham Lincoln Brigade and trav- *Lincoln Brigade* eled to Spain to join in what they considered a fight against the fascists. The American Communist Party was instrumental in creating the Lincoln Brigade, and directed many of its activities.

The party was active as well in organizing the unemployed in the early 1930s and staged a hunger march in Washington, D.C., in 1931. Party members were among the most effective union organizers in some industries. And the party was virtually alone among political organizations in taking a firm stand in favor of racial justice; its active defense of the Scottsboro defendants was but one example of its efforts to ally itself with the aspirations of African Americans.

The American Communist Party was not, however, the open, patriotic organization it tried to appear. It was always under the close and rigid supervision of the Soviet Union. The subordination of the party leadership to the Soviet Union was most clearly demonstrated in 1939, when Stalin signed a nonaggression pact with Nazi Germany. Moscow sent orders to the American Communist Party to abandon the Popular Front and return to its old stance of harsh criticism of American liberals. Communist Party leaders in the United States immediately obeyed—although thousands of disillusioned members left the party as a result.

The Socialist Party of America, under the leadership of Norman Thomas, also cited *The Socialist Party Message* the economic crisis as evidence of the failure of capitalism and sought vigorously to win public support for its own political program. Among other things, it attempted to mobilize support among the rural poor. The Southern Tenant Farmers Union (STFU), supported by the party and organized by a young socialist, H. L. Mitchell, attempted to create a biracial coalition of sharecroppers, tenant farmers, and others to demand economic reform. Neither the STFU nor the party itself, however, made any real progress toward establishing socialism as a major force in American politics.

Antiradicalism was a powerful force in the 1930s. Hostility toward the Communist Party, in particular, was intense at many levels of government. Congressional committees chaired by Hamilton Fish of New York and Martin Dies of Texas investigated communist influence wherever they could find (or imagine) it. White southerners tried to drive communist organizers out of the countryside, just as growers in California and elsewhere tried (unsuccessfully) to keep communists from organizing Mexican American and other workers.

At few times before (and few since) in American history did being part of the left seem *Leftist Ideas in the Arts* so respectable and even conventional among workers, intellectuals, and others. The 1930s witnessed an impressive, if temporary, widening of the ideological range of mainstream art and politics. The Roosevelt administration's New Deal, for example, sponsored artistic work through the Works Projects Administration that was frankly challenging to the capitalist norms of the 1920s. The filmmaker Pare Lorentz, with funding from New Deal agencies, made two powerful documentaries—*The Plow That Broke the Plains* (1936) and *The River* (1937)—that combined a celebration of New Deal programs with a harsh critique of the exploitation of people and the environment that industrial capitalism had produced.

Other New Deal–sponsored artists also sought to reveal the harshness of poverty and the human cost of social neglect. Notable among them were numerous documentary photographers, many of them employed by the Farm Security Administration, who traveled through rural areas recording the ravaged nature of agricultural life. They included some of the great photographers of their era—Dorothea Lange, Margaret Bourke-White, Arthur Rothstein, Russell Lee, Walker Evans, Ben Shahn, and others. Writers, too, devoted themselves to exposing social injustice, some of them working through the New Deal's Federal Writers' Project and Federal Art Project.

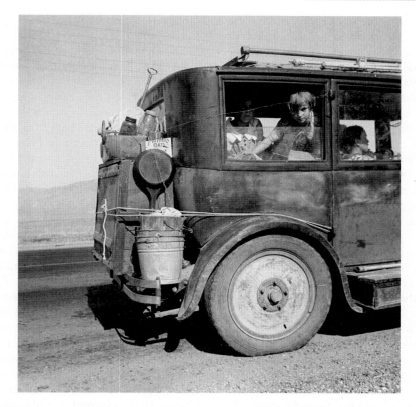

MIGRANT FAMILY   This photograph by the Great Depression photographer Dorothea Lange portrays a family of migrants leaving Texas in search of work in California. It suggests the plight of hundreds of thousands of families who fled the regions affected by drought in the 1930s—a devastation that became known as the Dust Bowl. (© Granger, NYC—All Rights Reserved.)

THE ORDEAL OF HERBERT HOOVER

Herbert Hoover began his presidency in March 1929 believing, like most Americans, that the nation faced a bright and prosperous future. For the first six months of his administration, he attempted to expand the associational policies he had advocated during his eight years as secretary of commerce. The economic crisis that began before the year was out forced Hoover to deal with a new set of problems. But for most of the rest of his term, he continued to rely on the principles that had always governed his public life.

THE HOOVER PROGRAM

Hoover first responded to the Depression by attempting to restore public confidence in the economy. "The fundamental business of this country, that is, production and distribution of commodities," he said in 1930, "is on a sound and prosperous basis." He then summoned leaders of business, labor, and agriculture to the White House and urged them to adopt a program of voluntary cooperation for recovery. He implored businessmen not to cut production or lay off workers; he talked labor leaders into forgoing demands for higher wages or better hours. But by mid-1931, economic conditions had deteriorated so much that the structure of voluntary cooperation had collapsed.

Hoover also attempted to use government spending as a tool for fighting the Depression. The president proposed to Congress an increase of $423 million—a significant sum by the standards of the time—in federal public works programs, and he encouraged state and local governments to fund public construction. But the spending was not nearly enough in the face of such devastating problems. And when economic conditions worsened, he became less willing to increase spending, worrying instead about keeping the budget balanced.

Even before the stock market crash, Hoover had begun to construct a program to assist the troubled agricultural economy. In April 1929, he proposed the Agricultural Marketing *Agricultural Marketing Act* Act, which established the first major government program to help farmers maintain prices. A federally sponsored Farm Board would make loans to national marketing cooperatives or establish corporations to buy surpluses and thus raise prices. At the same time, Hoover attempted to protect American farmers from international competition *Hawley-Smoot Tariff* by raising agricultural tariffs. The Hawley-Smoot Tariff of 1930 increased protection on seventy-five farm products. But neither the Agricultural Marketing Act nor the Hawley-Smoot Tariff ultimately helped American farmers significantly. Agricultural surpluses, combined with declining consumption, kept the farm economy in crisis.

By the spring of 1931, Herbert Hoover's political position had deteriorated considerably. In the 1930 congressional elections, Democrats won control of the House and made substantial inroads in the Senate. Many Americans blamed the president personally for the crisis and began calling the shantytowns that unemployed people established on the *"Hoovervilles"* outskirts of cities "Hoovervilles." Democrats urged the president to support more vigorous programs of relief and public spending. Hoover, instead, seized on a slight improvement in economic conditions early in 1931 as proof that his policies were working. The international financial panic of the spring of 1931 destroyed that illusion.

By the time Congress convened in December 1931, conditions had grown so desperate that Hoover supported a series of measures designed to keep endangered banks afloat and protect homeowners from foreclosure on their mortgages. Most important was a bill *The RFC* passed in January 1932 establishing the Reconstruction Finance Corporation (RFC), a government agency to provide federal loans to troubled banks, railroads, and other businesses. Unlike some earlier Hoover programs, the RFC operated on a large scale. In 1932, it had a budget of $1.5 billion for public works alone.

Nevertheless, the new agency failed to deal directly or forcefully enough with the real problems of the economy to produce any significant recovery. The RFC lent funds only to financial institutions with sufficient collateral; much of its money went to large banks and corporations. At Hoover's insistence, it helped finance only those public works projects that promised ultimately to pay for themselves (toll bridges, public housing, and others). Above all, the RFC did not have enough money to make any real impact on the Depression, and it did not even spend all the money it had.

POPULAR PROTEST

For the first several years of the Depression, most Americans were either too stunned or too confused to raise much effective protest. By the middle of 1932, however, dissident voices began to be heard.

In the summer of 1932, a group of unhappy farm owners gathered in Des Moines, Iowa, to establish a new organization: the Farmers' Holiday Association, which endorsed the withholding of farm products from the market—in effect a farmers' strike. The strike began in August in western Iowa, spread briefly to a few neighboring areas, and succeeded in blockading several markets; but in the end, it dissolved in failure.

A more celebrated protest movement emerged from American veterans. In 1924, Congress had approved the payment of a $1,000 bonus to all those who had served in World War I, the money to be paid beginning in 1945. By 1932, however, many veterans were demanding that the bonus be paid immediately. Hoover, concerned about balancing the budget, rejected their appeal. In June, more than 20,000 veterans, members of the self-proclaimed Bonus Expeditionary Force, or "Bonus Army," marched   *The "Bonus Army"* into Washington, built crude camps around the city, and promised to stay until Congress approved legislation to pay the bonus. Some of the veterans departed in July, after Congress had voted down their proposal. Many, however, remained in Washington.

CLEARING OUT THE BONUS MARCHERS   In July 1932, President Hoover ordered the Washington, D.C., police to evict the Bonus Marchers from some of the public buildings and land they had been occupying. After a series of skirmishes between police and the protesters, Hoover ordered the United States Army to complete the eviction. (© Bettmann/Corbis)

Their continued presence in Washington embarrassed President Hoover. Finally, in mid-July, he ordered police to clear the marchers out of several abandoned federal buildings in which they had been staying. A few marchers threw rocks at the police, and someone opened fire; two veterans fell dead. Hoover called the incident evidence of uncontrolled violence and radicalism, and he ordered the United States Army to assist the police in clearing out the buildings.

General Douglas MacArthur, the army chief of staff, carried out the mission himself and greatly exceeded the president's orders. He led the Third Cavalry, two infantry regiments, a machine-gun detachment, and six tanks down Pennsylvania Avenue in pursuit

Demise of the Bonus Army   of the Bonus Army. The veterans fled in terror. MacArthur followed them across the Anacostia River, where he ordered the soldiers to burn their tent city to the ground. More than 100 marchers were injured.

The incident dealt another serious blow to Hoover's already battered political standing. The "Great Engineer," the personification of the optimistic days of the 1920s, had become a symbol of the nation's failure to deal effectively with its startling reversal of fortune.

THE ELECTION OF 1932

As the 1932 presidential election approached, few people doubted the outcome. The Republican Party dutifully renominated Herbert Hoover for a second term of office, but few delegates believed he could win. The Democrats, in the meantime, gathered jubilantly in Chicago to nominate the governor of New York, Franklin Delano Roosevelt.

Roosevelt had been a well-known figure in the party for many years already. A Hudson

Franklin Delano Roosevelt   Valley aristocrat, a distant cousin of Theodore Roosevelt, and a handsome, charming young man, he progressed rapidly: from a seat in the New York State legislature to a position as assistant secretary of the navy during World War I to his party's vice presidential nomination in 1920 on the ill-fated ticket with James M. Cox. Less than a year later, he was stricken with polio. Although he never regained use of his legs (and could walk only by using crutches and braces), he built up sufficient physical strength to return to politics in 1928. When Al Smith received the Democratic nomination for president that year, Roosevelt was elected to succeed him as governor. In 1930, he easily won reelection.

Roosevelt worked no miracles in New York, but he did initiate enough programs of government assistance to be able to present himself as a more energetic and imaginative

"A New Deal"   leader than Hoover. In national politics, he avoided divisive cultural issues and emphasized the economic grievances that most Democrats shared. As a result, he was able to assemble a broad coalition within the party and win his party's nomination. In a dramatic break with tradition, he flew to Chicago to address the Democratic National Convention in person and accept the nomination. In the course of his acceptance speech, Roosevelt aroused the delegates with his ringing promise: "I pledge you, I pledge myself, to a new deal for the American people." Neither then nor in the subsequent campaign did Roosevelt give much indication of what that program would be. But Herbert Hoover's unpopularity virtually ensured Roosevelt's election.

Roosevelt won by a landslide, receiving 57.4 percent of the popular vote to Hoover's 39.7, and carried every state except Delaware, Pennsylvania, Connecticut, Vermont, New Hampshire, and Maine. Democrats won large majorities in both houses of

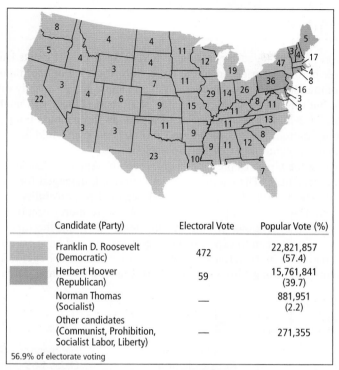

Candidate (Party)	Electoral Vote	Popular Vote (%)
Franklin D. Roosevelt (Democratic)	472	22,821,857 (57.4)
Herbert Hoover (Republican)	59	15,761,841 (39.7)
Norman Thomas (Socialist)	—	881,951 (2.2)
Other candidates (Communist, Prohibition, Socialist Labor, Liberty)	—	271,355

56.9% of electorate voting

THE ELECTION OF 1932 Like the election of 1928, the election of 1932 was exceptionally one-sided. But this time, the landslide favored the Democratic candidate, Franklin Roosevelt, who overwhelmed Herbert Hoover in all regions of the country except New England. Roosevelt obviously benefited primarily from popular disillusionment with Hoover's response to the Great Depression. • *But what characteristics of Roosevelt himself contributed to his victory?*

Congress. It was a convincing mandate, but it was not yet clear what Roosevelt intended to do with it.

THE "INTERREGNUM"

The period between the election and the inauguration (which in the early 1930s lasted more than four months) was a season of growing economic crisis. Presidents-elect traditionally do not involve themselves directly in government. But in a series of brittle exchanges with Roosevelt, Hoover tried to exact a pledge from the president-elect to maintain policies of economic orthodoxy. Roosevelt genially refused.

In February, only a month before the inauguration, a new crisis developed when the collapse of the American banking system suddenly and rapidly accelerated. *Banking Collapse* Depositors withdrew their money in panic; and one bank after another closed its doors and declared bankruptcy. Hoover again asked Roosevelt to give prompt public assurances that there would be no tinkering with the currency, no heavy borrowing, no unbalancing of the budget. Roosevelt again refused.

March 4, 1933, was, therefore, a day of both economic crisis and considerable personal bitterness. On that morning, Herbert Hoover rode glumly down Pennsylvania Avenue with a beaming, buoyant Franklin Roosevelt, who would shortly be sworn in as the thirty-second president of the United States.

CONCLUSION

The Great Depression changed many things in American life. It created unemployment on a scale never before experienced in the nation's history. It put enormous pressures on families, on communities, on state and local governments, and ultimately on Washington. The innovative but ultimately failed presidency of Herbert Hoover was unable to produce policies capable of dealing effectively with the crisis. In the nation's politics and culture, there were strong currents of radicalism and protest; and many middle-class Americans came to fear that a revolution might be approaching.

In reality, while the Great Depression shook much of American society and culture, it actually toppled very little. The capitalist system survived, damaged for a time but never truly threatened. The values of materialism and personal responsibility were shaken but never overturned. The American people in the 1930s were more receptive than they had been in the 1920s to evocations of community, generosity, and the dignity of common people. They were more open to experiments in government and business and even private lives than they had been in earlier years. But for most Americans, belief in the "American way of life" remained strong throughout the long years of economic despair.

KEY TERMS/PEOPLE/PLACES/EVENTS

Abraham Lincoln Brigade 579

Agricultural Marketing Act 582

Bonus Army 583

Dale Carnegie 574

Dust Bowl 569

Frank Capra 575

Franklin Delano Roosevelt 584

Great Depression 565

Hawley-Smoot Tariff 582

Hindenburg 575

Hoovervilles 582

John Dos Passos 579

John Steinbeck 579

Life magazine 578

Okies 569

Popular Front 579

Reconstruction Finance Corporation (RFC) 582

Richard Wright 579

Scottsboro case 570

RECALL AND REFLECT

1. Was the 1929 stock market crash the cause of the Depression? Why or why not?
2. How did farmers fare during the Depression? What environmental conditions contributed to their plight?
3. How did popular entertainment and the arts respond to the needs of Depression-era audiences?
4. What popular protests arose in response to the Depression? How successful were these protests?
5. How did Hoover's political beliefs affect his attempt to deal with the economic crisis of the Depression?

24 THE NEW DEAL

LAUNCHING THE NEW DEAL

THE NEW DEAL IN TRANSITION

THE NEW DEAL IN DISARRAY

LIMITS AND LEGACIES OF THE NEW DEAL

LOOKING AHEAD

1. What emergency measures did Franklin Delano Roosevelt (FDR) take in his first hundred days as president?

2. Who were the major critics of FDR's New Deal, and how did their criticisms influence FDR's "Second New Deal"?

3. What were the principal achievements of the Second New Deal in 1935?

DURING HIS TWELVE YEARS IN office, Franklin Roosevelt became more central to the life of the nation than any president had ever been. More important, his administration constructed a series of reforms that fundamentally altered the federal government and its relationship to society. By the end of the 1930s, the New Deal (as the Roosevelt administration's program was called) had not ended the Great Depression; only World War II did that. But it had created many of the broad outlines of the political world we know today.

LAUNCHING THE NEW DEAL

Roosevelt's first task upon taking office was to alleviate the panic that was creating the chaos in the financial system. He did so in part by force of personality and in part by rapidly constructing an ambitious and diverse program of legislation.

RESTORING CONFIDENCE

Much of Roosevelt's early success was a result of his ebullient personality. He was the first president to make regular use of the radio; and his friendly "fireside chats," during which he explained in simple terms his programs and plans to the people, helped build public confidence in the administration. But Roosevelt could not rely on image alone. On March 6, two days after taking office, he issued a proclamation closing all American banks for four days until Congress could meet in special session to consider banking reform legislation. So great was the panic about bank failures that the "bank holiday," as the president euphemistically described it, created a general sense of relief and hope.

Three days later, Roosevelt sent to Congress the Emergency Banking Act, a generally conservative bill designed primarily to protect the larger banks from being dragged down by the weakness of smaller ones. The bill provided for Treasury Department inspection of all banks before they would be allowed to reopen. It also provided federal assistance to some troubled institutions and a thorough reorganization of those banks in the greatest difficulty. Congress passed the bill within a few hours of its introduction. Whatever else the new law accomplished, it helped dispel the panic. Three-quarters of the banks in the Federal Reserve system reopened within the next three days, and $1 billion in hoarded currency and gold flowed back into them within a month. The immediate banking crisis was over.

On the morning after passage of the Emergency Banking Act, Roosevelt sent to Congress another measure—the Economy Act—designed to convince the public (and especially the business community) that the federal government was in safe, responsible hands. The act proposed to balance the federal budget by cutting the salaries of government employees and reducing pensions to veterans by as much as 15 percent. Like the banking bill, this one passed through Congress almost instantly, even though the cost cutting reduced the growth of the economy. Later that spring, Roosevelt signed the Glass-Steagall Act of June 1933, which gave the government authority to curb irresponsible speculation by banks. More important, perhaps, it established the Federal Deposit Insurance Corporation (FDIC), which guaranteed all bank deposits up to $2,500. Even if *Federal Deposit Insurance Corporation* a bank should fail, small depositors would be able to recover their money.

To restore confidence in the stock market, Congress passed the so-called Truth in Securities Act of 1933, requiring corporations issuing new securities to provide full and accurate information about them to the public. In June 1934, another act established the Securities and Exchange Commission (SEC) to police the stock market. Roosevelt also *Securities and Exchange Commission* signed a bill to legalize the manufacture and sale of beer with a 3.2 percent alcohol content— an interim measure pending the repeal of prohibition, for which a constitutional amendment (the Twenty-First) was already in process. The amendment was ratified later in 1933.

Agricultural Adjustment

These initial actions bought time for more comprehensive programs. The first was the Agricultural Adjustment Act, which Congress passed in May 1933. Under the provisions of the act, producers of seven basic commodities (wheat, cotton, corn, hogs, rice, tobacco,

THE NEW DEAL   Of the many resources at Roosevelt's disposal was the impression of his sunny personality during dark times. It conveyed to many a sense of hope and optimism. In this political cartoon from about 1934, Roosevelt is seen steering the ship of state toward economic recovery. His detractors are shown grumbling under the cloud of depression. (© Granger, NYC—All Rights Reserved.)

and dairy products) would impose production limits on their crops. The government, through the Agricultural Adjustment Administration (AAA), would then tell individual *Agricultural Adjustment Administration* farmers how much they should produce and would pay them subsidies for leaving some of their land idle. A tax on food processing (for example, the milling of wheat) would provide the funds for the new payments. Farm prices were to be subsidized up to the point of parity.

The AAA helped bring about a rise in prices for farm commodities in the years after 1933. Gross farm income increased by half in the first three years of the New Deal, and the agricultural economy as a whole emerged from the 1930s more stable and prosperous than it had been in many years. The AAA did, however, favor larger farmers over smaller ones. By distributing payments to landowners, not those who worked the land, the government allowed planters to reduce their acreage, evict tenants and sharecroppers, and fire field hands.

In January 1936, the Supreme Court struck down the crucial provisions of the AAA, arguing that the government had no constitutional authority to require farmers to limit production. But within a few weeks, the administration had secured passage of new legislation (the Soil Conservation and Domestic Allotment Act), which permitted the government to pay farmers to reduce production so as to "conserve soil," prevent erosion, and accomplish other secondary goals.

The administration launched several efforts to assist poor farmers as well. The Resettlement Administration, established in 1935, and its successor, the Farm Security *Farm Security Administration* Administration, created in 1937, provided loans to help farmers cultivating submarginal soil to relocate to better lands. But the programs moved no more than a few thousand farmers. More effective was the Rural Electrification Administration, created in 1935, which worked to make electric power available for the first time to thousands of farmers through utility cooperatives.

Industrial Recovery

Since 1931, leaders of the United States Chamber of Commerce and many others had been urging the government to adopt an antideflation program that would permit trade associations to cooperate in stabilizing prices within their industries. Existing antitrust laws clearly forbade such practices, and Herbert Hoover had refused to endorse suspension of the laws. The Roosevelt administration was more receptive. In exchange for relaxing antitrust provisions, however, New Dealers insisted on other provisions. Business leaders would have to recognize the workers' right to bargain collectively through unions and to ensure that the incomes of workers would rise along with prices. And to help create jobs and increase consumer buying power, the administration added a major program of public works spending. The result of these and many other impulses was the National Industrial Recovery Act, which Congress passed in June 1933.

At its center was a new federal agency, the National Recovery Administration (NRA), *National Recovery Administration* under the direction of the flamboyant and energetic Hugh S. Johnson. Johnson called on every business establishment in the nation to accept a temporary "blanket code": a minimum wage of between 30 and 40 cents an hour, a maximum workweek of thirty-five to forty hours, and the abolition of child labor. At the same time, Johnson negotiated another, more specific set of codes with leaders of the nation's major industries. These industrial codes set floors below which no company would lower prices or wages in its search for a competitive advantage, and they included provisions for maintaining employment and production. He quickly won agreements from almost every major industry in the country.

From the beginning, however, the NRA stumbled. The codes themselves were hastily and often poorly written. Large producers consistently dominated the *Problems of the NRA* code-writing process and ensured that the new regulations would work to their advantage and to the disadvantage of smaller firms. And the codes at times did more than simply set floors under prices; they actively and artificially raised them—sometimes to levels higher than the market could sustain.

Other NRA goals also worked against recovery. Section 7(a) of the National Industrial Recovery Act promised workers the right to form unions and engage in collective bargaining and encouraged many workers to join unions for the first time. But Section 7(a) contained no enforcement mechanisms. The Public Works Administration (PWA), established to administer the National Industrial Recovery Act's spending programs, only gradually allowed the $3.3 billion in public works funds to trickle out.

Perhaps the clearest evidence of the NRA's failure was that industrial production actually declined in the months after the agency's establishment, despite the rise in prices that the codes had helped create. The NRA failed to increase the buying power for consumers, which made the higher prices an obstacle to growth. By the spring of 1934, the NRA was besieged by criticism. That fall, Roosevelt pressured Johnson to resign and established a new board of directors to oversee the NRA.

Then in 1935, the Supreme Court intervened with a case involving alleged NRA code violations by the Schechter brothers, who operated a wholesale poultry business confined to Brooklyn, New York. The Court ruled unanimously that the Schechters were not engaged in interstate commerce (and thus not subject to federal regulation) and, further, that Congress had unconstitutionally delegated legislative power to the president to draft the NRA codes. The justices struck down the legislation establishing the agency. Roosevelt denounced the justices for their "horse-and-buggy" interpretation of the interstate commerce clause. He was rightly concerned, for the reasoning in the Schechter case threatened many other New Deal programs as well. But many New Dealers—and many others—welcomed the NRA's demise.

REGIONAL PLANNING

The AAA and the NRA largely reflected the beliefs of New Dealers who favored economic planning but wanted private interests (farmers or business leaders) to dominate the planning process. But other reformers believed that the government itself should be the chief planning agent in the economy. Their most conspicuous *Tennessee Valley Authority* success was an unprecedented experiment in regional planning: the Tennessee Valley Authority (TVA).

Progressive reformers had agitated for years for public development of the nation's water resources as a source of cheap electric power. In particular, they had urged completion of a great dam at Muscle Shoals on the Tennessee River in Alabama—a dam begun during World War I but left unfinished when the war ended. But opposition from the utilities companies had blocked further progress on the dam.

In 1932, however, one of the great utility empires—that of the electricity magnate Samuel Insull—collapsed spectacularly amid widely publicized exposés of corruption. Hostility to the

THE TENNESSEE VALLEY AUTHORITY   The Tennessee Valley Authority was one of the largest experiments in government-funded public works and regional planning in American history to that point. The federal government had helped fund many projects in its history—canals, turnpikes, railroads, bridges, dams, and others. But never before had it undertaken a project of such great scope, and never before had it maintained such close control and ownership over the public works it helped create. This map illustrates the broad reach of the TVA within the Tennessee Valley region, which spanned seven states. TVA dams throughout the region helped control floods and also provided a source of hydroelectric power, which the government sold to consumers. Note the dam near Muscle Shoals, Alabama, in the bottom left of the map. It was begun during World War I, and efforts to revive it in the 1920s helped create the momentum that produced the TVA. • *Why were progressives so eager to see the government enter the business of hydroelectric power in the 1920s?*

utilities soon grew so intense that the companies were no longer able to block the public power movement. The result was legislation, supported by the president and enacted by Congress in May 1933, creating the Tennessee Valley Authority. The TVA was authorized to complete the dam at Muscle Shoals and build other dams in the region, and to generate and sell electricity from them to the public at reasonable rates. It was also intended to promote a comprehensive redevelopment of the entire region, encouraging the growth of local industries, supervising a substantial program of reforestation, and helping farmers improve productivity.

Opposition by conservatives ultimately blocked many of the ambitious social planning projects proposed by the more visionary TVA administrators, but the Authority revitalized the region in numerous ways. It improved water transportation, virtually eliminated flooding in the region, and provided electricity to thousands who had never before had it. Throughout the country, largely because of the "yardstick" provided by the TVA's cheap production of electricity, private power rates declined. Even so, the Tennessee Valley remained a generally impoverished region despite the TVA's efforts.

THE GROWTH OF FEDERAL RELIEF

The Roosevelt administration did not consider relief to the unemployed its most important task, but it recognized the necessity of doing something to help impoverished Americans survive until the government could revive the economy to the point where relief might not be necessary. Among Roosevelt's first acts as president was the establishment of the Federal Emergency Relief Administration (FERA), which provided cash grants to states to prop up bankrupt relief agencies. To administer the program, he chose the director of the New York State relief agency, Harry Hopkins. Both Hopkins and Roosevelt had misgivings about establishing a government "dole," but they felt somewhat more comfortable with another form of government assistance: work relief. Thus when it became clear that the FERA grants were not enough, the administration established a second program: the Civil Works Administration (CWA), which put more than 4 million people to work on temporary projects between November 1933 and April 1934. Some of the projects were of lasting value, such as the construction of roads, schools, and parks; others were little more than make-work. To Hopkins, however, the important things were pumping money into the economy and providing assistance to people with nowhere else to turn.

Roosevelt's favorite relief project was the Civilian Conservation Corps (CCC). The CCC created camps in national parks and forests and in other rural   *Civilian Conservation Corps* and wilderness settings. There, young unemployed men from the cities worked in a semi-military environment on such projects as planting trees, building reservoirs, developing parks, and improving agricultural irrigation.

Mortgage relief was a pressing need for millions of farm owners and homeowners. The Farm Credit Administration, which within two years refinanced   *Mortgage Relief* one-fifth of all farm mortgages in the United States, was one response to that problem. The Frazier-Lemke Farm Bankruptcy Act of 1933 was another. It enabled some farmers to regain their land even after the foreclosure of their mortgages. Despite such efforts, however, 25 percent of all American farm owners had lost their land by 1934. Homeowners were similarly troubled, and in June 1933 the administration established the Home Owners' Loan Corporation, which by 1936 had refinanced the mortgages of more than 1 million householders. A year later, Congress established the Federal Housing Administration to insure mortgages for new construction and home repairs.

THE NEW DEAL IN TRANSITION

Seldom has an American president enjoyed such remarkable popularity as Franklin Roosevelt did during his first two years in office. But by early 1935, the New Deal faced fierce public criticism. (For reverberations of such praise and condemnation in the historical scholarship on Roosevelt, see "Debating the Past: The New Deal.") In the spring of 1935, partly in response to these growing attacks, Roosevelt launched an ambitious new program of legislation that has often been called the "Second New Deal."

THE CONSERVATIVE CRITICISM OF THE NEW DEAL

Despite his great popularity, Franklin Roosevelt had many conservative critics. Some of them detested him so bitterly that they would refuse to say his name—calling him "that man." Those critics included businessmen, financiers, wealthy families, and members of aristocratic society.

THE NEW DEAL

Contemporaries of Franklin Roosevelt debated the impact of the New Deal with ferocious intensity. Conservatives complained of a menacing tyranny of the state. Liberals celebrated the New Deal's progressive achievements. Some people on the left charged that the reforms of the 1930s were largely cosmetic and ignored the nation's fundamental problems. Although the conservative critique found relatively little scholarly expression until many years after Roosevelt's death, the liberal and left positions continued for decades to shape the way historians described the Roosevelt administration.

The dominant view from the beginning was an approving liberal interpretation, and its most important early voice was that of Arthur M. Schlesinger Jr. He argued in the three volumes of *The Age of Roosevelt* (1957–1960) that the New Deal marked a continuation of the long struggle between public power and private interests, a struggle Roosevelt had moved to a new level. Workers, farmers, consumers, and others now had much more protection than they had enjoyed in the past.

At almost the same time, however, other historians were offering more qualified assessments of the New Deal, although they remained securely within the liberal framework. Richard Hofstadter argued in 1955 that the New Deal gave American liberalism a "social-democratic tinge that had never before been present in American reform movements," but that its highly pragmatic approach lacked a central, guiding philosophy. James MacGregor Burns argued in 1956 that Roosevelt failed to make full use of his potential as a leader.

William Leuchtenburg's *Franklin D. Roosevelt and the New Deal* (1963) was the first systematic "revisionist" interpretation. Leuchtenburg challenged the views of earlier scholars who had proclaimed the New Deal a "revolution" in social policy. Leuchtenburg could muster only enough enthusiasm to call it a "halfway revolution," one that helped some previously disadvantaged groups (most notably farmers and workers) but that did little or nothing for many others (African Americans, sharecroppers, the urban poor).

Harsher criticisms soon emerged. Barton Bernstein in a 1968 essay concluded that the New Deal had saved capitalism, but at the expense of the least powerful. Ronald Radosh, Paul Conkin, and, later, Thomas Ferguson and Colin Gordon expanded on these criticisms. The New Deal, they contended, was part of the twentieth-century tradition of "corporate liberalism"—a tradition in which reform is closely wedded to the needs and interests of capitalism.

Most scholars in the 1980s and 1990s, however, seemed largely to have accepted the revised liberal view: that the New Deal was a significant and valuable chapter in the history of reform, but one that worked within rigid, occasionally crippling limits. Much of that work on the New Deal, therefore, focused on the constraints it faced. Some scholars (notably the sociologist Theda Skocpol) emphasized the issue of "state capacity"—the absence of a government bureaucracy with sufficient strength and expertise to shape or administer many programs. James T. Patterson, Barry Karl, Mark Leff, and others stressed the political constraints the New Deal encountered—the conservative inhibitions about government that remained strong in Congress and among the public. Frank Freidel, Ellis Hawley, Herbert Stein, and many others pointed as well to the ideological constraints affecting Franklin Roosevelt and his supporters—the limits of their own understanding of their time. Alan Brinkley, in *The End of Reform* (1995), described an ideological shift within New Deal liberalism that marginalized older concerns about wealth and monopoly power and replaced them with consumer-oriented Keynesianism. David Kennedy, in *Freedom from Fear* (1999), argued, by contrast, that the more aggressively anticapitalist measures of the early New Deal actually hampered recovery. Only when Roosevelt embraced the power of the market did prosperity begin to return.

The conservative attacks on the New Deal in the 2000s provided a newly powerful alternative view. A group of conservatives—among them Amity Schlaes and Burton Folsom—attacked the New Deal as a failure that created a vast bureaucracy and caused the Depression to last longer than it had to.

The phrase "New Deal liberalism" has come in the postwar era to seem synonymous with modern ideas of aggressive federal management of the economy, elaborate welfare systems, a powerful bureaucracy, and large-scale government spending. But many historians of the New Deal would argue that the modern idea of New Deal liberalism bears only a limited relationship to the ideas that New Dealers themselves embraced. •

UNDERSTAND, ANALYZE, & EVALUATE

1. How has the scholarly understanding of the New Deal changed over time?
2. Did the New Deal save capitalism? If so, how and why?

Roosevelt himself was among the most aristocratic presidents in American history. But he became the enemy of the very world that he came from. He was an alumnus of Harvard University, but the university president barely spoke to him when he went there to give a speech. He was, as many members of the American elite called him, a "traitor to his class." But even greater hatred came from conservative businessmen and financiers, who correctly accused New Dealers of imposing new regulations on the business and financial worlds. His critics were also infuriated by new taxes imposed by Roosevelt, even though high taxation reached only a few wealthy people.

The hatred of Roosevelt from conservatives took many forms. In 1935, a "whispering campaign" emerged from a New Deal effort to regulate the public utility industry. Stories circulated that the president was a drug addict, that he was insane, and that he was surrounded by psychiatrists at all times. Hamilton Fish Jr., a highly conservative member of Congress, said on the floor of the House of Representatives that "whom the gods would destroy, they make first mad."

Not all critics were as virulent in their hatred of the president. Walter Lippmann, a revered columnist, complained that Roosevelt was moving away from the nation's traditions. "We belong to a generation that has lost its way," he wrote. "Unable to develop the great truths which it inherited from the emancipators, it has returned to the heresies of absolutism, authority, and the domination of men by men." He added that the "enormous concentration of power in the hands of appointed officials . . . can lead only to waste, confusion, bureaucratic rigidity, and the loss of personal liberty." He charged that Roosevelt had become attracted to fascism and communism, instead of protecting the freedom of individuals.

Lewis Douglas, Roosevelt's first budget director, resigned in response to the president's determination to spend deficit funds to help provide relief to the unemployed. Al Smith, the former New York governor and twice the Democratic candidate, also turned against the president—partly because of jealousy, but also because he considered the New Deal much too far to the left. However, for the most part, the New Deal lacked a clear ideology and, instead, experimented in many ways, some that conservatives found offensive.

Conservative business leaders were the most committed leaders of the attack on the *Liberty League Established* New Deal. They formed a new organization called the Liberty League, led by the Du Pont family (owners of the nation's largest chemical company). Its goal was to arouse public opposition to what its members called the "dictatorial" policies of the New Deal and to what they considered its attacks on free enterprise. It was led by John Jacob Raskob (a former head of the Democratic National Committee, a former director of General Motors, and a trustee of Du Pont), who had abandoned the Democratic Party and joined the League. Within a year of its founding in 1934, there were more than 35,000 members of the League, reaching a peak of 125,000 in 1936. It also recruited college students from 345 institutions, gaining over 10,000 members. Many followers were northeastern industrialists. The League described itself as a "nonpartisan organization founded to defend the Constitution and defend the rights and liberties guaranteed by that Constitution." Its purpose was

> to teach the necessity of respect for the rights of persons and property as fundamental to every form of government . . . to teach the duty of government, to encourage and protect individual and group initiative and enterprise, to foster the right to work, earn, save and acquire property, and to preserve the ownership and lawful use of property when acquired.

The Liberty League attracted considerable attention, but it had relatively little impact on the New Deal. Its leaders tried to remain nonpartisan, even though its members were staunchly anti-Roosevelt. They became a target for the president's 1936 reelection campaign. Soon after Roosevelt's landslide victory, the League dissolved. Hatred of Roosevelt did not disappear, but there was little organized opposition after 1936.

The Populist Criticism of the New Deal

Roosevelt's critics on the far left also managed to produce alarm among some supporters of the administration. The Communist Party, the Socialist Party, and other radical and semiradical organizations were at times harshly critical of the New Deal. But like the conservatives, they failed to attract genuine mass support.

More menacing to the New Deal than either the far right or the far left was a group of dissident political movements that defied easy ideological classification. Some gained substantial public support within particular states and regions. And three men succeeded in mobilizing genuinely national followings. Dr. Francis E. Townsend, an elderly California physician, rose from obscurity to lead a movement of more than 5 million members with his plan for federal pensions for older adults. According to the Townsend *The Townsend Plan* Plan, all Americans over the age of sixty would receive monthly government pensions of $200, provided they retired (thus freeing jobs for younger, unemployed Americans) and spent the money in full each month (which would pump needed funds into the economy). By 1935, the Townsend Plan had attracted the support of many older men and women.

HUEY LONG   Few public speakers could arouse a crowd more effectively than Huey Long of Louisiana, known to many as "the Kingfish" (a nickname borrowed from a scheming character on the popular radio show *Amos 'n' Andy*). It was Long's effective use of radio, however, that contributed most directly to his spreading national popularity in the early 1930s. (© Archive Photos/Getty Images)

Father Charles E. Coughlin, a Catholic priest in the Detroit suburb of Royal Oak, Michigan, achieved even greater renown through his weekly nationally *Father Charles Coughlin* broadcast radio sermons. He proposed a series of monetary reforms—remonetization of silver, issuing of greenbacks, and nationalization of the banking system—that he insisted would restore prosperity and ensure economic justice. At first a warm supporter of Roosevelt, Coughlin had become disheartened by late 1934 by what he claimed was the president's failure to deal harshly enough with the "money powers." In the spring of 1935, he established his own political organization, the National Union for Social Justice.

Most alarming to the administration was the growing national popularity of Senator Huey P. Long of Louisiana. Long had risen to power in his home state through his *Huey Long* strident attacks on the banks, oil companies, and utilities and on the conservative political oligarchy allied with them. Elected governor in 1928, he launched an assault on his opponents so thorough and forceful that they were soon left with virtually no political power. But he also maintained the overwhelming support of the Louisiana electorate, in part because of his flamboyant personality and in part because of his solid record of conventional progressive accomplishments: building roads, schools, and hospitals; revising the tax codes; distributing free textbooks; lowering utility rates. Barred by law from succeeding himself as governor, he ran in 1930 for a seat in the United States Senate and won easily.

Long, like Coughlin, supported Franklin Roosevelt for president in 1932. But within six months of Roosevelt's inauguration, Long had broken with the president. As an alternative to the New Deal, he advocated a drastic program of wealth redistribution, a program he ultimately named the Share-Our-Wealth Plan. The government, he claimed, could end the Depression easily by using the tax system to confiscate the surplus riches of the wealthiest men and women in America and distribute these surpluses to the rest of the population. That would, he claimed, allow the government to guarantee every family a minimum "homestead" of $5,000 and an annual wage of $2,500. In 1934, Long established his own national organization: the Share-Our-Wealth Society, which soon attracted a large following through much of the nation. A poll by the Democratic National Committee in the spring of 1935 disclosed that Long might attract more than 10 percent of the vote if he ran as a third-party candidate, possibly enough to tip a close election to the Republicans.

Members of the Roosevelt administration considered dissident movements—and the broad popular discontent they represented—a genuine threat. An increasing number of advisers were warning Roosevelt that he would have to do something dramatic to counter their strength.

The "Second New Deal"

Roosevelt launched the so-called Second New Deal in the spring of 1935 in response both to growing political pressures and to the continuing economic crisis. The new proposals represented a shift in the emphasis of New Deal policy. Perhaps the most conspicuous change was in the administration's attitude toward big business. Symbolically at least, the president was now willing to attack corporate interests openly. In March, for example, he proposed to Congress an act designed to break up the great utility holding companies. The Holding Company Act of 1935 was the result, although furious lobbying by the utilities led to amendments that sharply limited its effects.

Equally alarming to affluent Americans was a series of tax reforms proposed by the president in 1935. Apparently designed to undercut the appeal of Huey Long's Share-Our-Wealth Plan, the Roosevelt proposals called for establishing the highest and most progressive peacetime tax rates in history—although the actual impact of these rates was limited.

The Supreme Court decision in 1935 to strike down the National Industrial Recovery Act also invalidated Section 7(a) of the act, which had guaranteed workers the right to organize and bargain collectively. A group of progressives in Congress, led by Senator Robert E. Wagner of New York, introduced what became the National Labor Relations Act of 1935. The new law, popularly known as the Wagner Act, provided workers with a crucial enforcement mechanism missing from the 1933 law: the National Labor Relations *National Labor Relations Board* Board (NLRB), which would have power to compel employers to recognize and bargain with legitimate unions. The president was not entirely happy with the bill, but he signed it anyway. That was largely because American workers themselves had by 1935 become so important and vigorous a force that Roosevelt realized his own political future would depend in part on responding to their demands.

Labor Militancy

The emergence of a powerful trade union movement in the 1930s occurred partly in response to government efforts to enhance the power of unions. It was also a result of the increased militancy of American workers after a lull during the 1920s. Business leaders and industrialists lost (at least temporarily) the ability to control government policies. Equally important, new and more powerful labor organizations emerged.

The American Federation of Labor (AFL) remained committed to the idea of the craft union: organizing workers on the basis of their skills. But that concept had little to offer unskilled laborers, who now constituted the bulk of the industrial workforce. During the 1930s, therefore, a newer concept of labor organization challenged the craft union ideal: industrial unionism. Advocates of this approach argued that all workers in a particular industry should be organized in a single union, regardless of what functions the workers performed. United in this way, workers would greatly increase their power.

Leaders of the AFL craft unions for the most part opposed the new concept. But industrial unionism found a number of important advocates, most prominent among them John L. Lewis, the leader of the United Mine Workers. At first, Lewis   *John Lewis and the CIO* and his allies attempted to work within the AFL, but friction between the new industrial organizations Lewis was promoting and the older craft unions grew rapidly. At the 1935 AFL convention, Lewis became embroiled in a series of angry confrontations with craft union leaders before finally walking out. A few weeks later, he created the Committee on Industrial Organization. When the AFL expelled the new committee and all the industrial unions it represented, Lewis renamed the committee the Congress of Industrial Organizations (CIO) and became its first president.

The CIO expanded the constituency of the labor movement. It was more receptive to women and to African Americans than the AFL had been, in part because CIO organizing drives targeted previously unorganized industries (textiles, laundries, tobacco factories, and others) where women and minorities constituted much of the workforce. The CIO was also more militant than the AFL. By the time of the 1936 schism, it was already engaged in major organizing battles in the automobile and steel industries.

Organizing Battles

The United Auto Workers (UAW) gradually emerged preeminent in the early and mid-1930s. But although it was gaining recruits, it was making little progress in winning recognition from the corporations. In December 1936, however, autoworkers employed a controversial and effective new technique for challenging corporate opposition: the **sit-down strike.** Employees in several General Motors plants in Detroit simply sat down inside the plants, refusing either to work or to leave, thus preventing the company from using strikebreakers. The tactic spread to other locations, and by February 1937, strikers had occupied seventeen GM plants. The strikers ignored court orders and local police efforts to force them to vacate the buildings. When Michigan's governor refused to call up the National Guard to clear out the strikers, and when the federal government also refused to intervene on behalf of employers, General Motors relented. In February 1937, it became the first major manufacturer to recognize the UAW. Other automobile companies soon did the same.

In the steel industry, the battle for unionization was less easily won. In 1936, the Steel Workers Organizing Committee (SWOC), later the United Steelworkers of America, began a major organizing drive involving thousands of workers and frequent, at times bitter, strikes. In March 1937, to the surprise of almost everyone, United States Steel, the giant of the industry, recognized the union rather than risk a costly strike. But the smaller companies (known collectively as "Little Steel") were less accommodating. On Memorial Day 1937, a group of striking workers from Republic Steel gathered with their families

THE "MEMORIAL DAY MASSACRE" The bitterness of the labor struggles of the 1930s was nowhere more evident than in Chicago in 1937, when striking workers attempting to march on a Republic Steel plant were brutally attacked by Chicago police, who used clubs, tear gas, and guns to turn away the marchers. Ten strikers were killed and many others were injured. (© Carl Linde/AP Images)

for a picnic and demonstration in south Chicago. When they attempted to march peacefully (and legally) toward the steel plant, police opened fire on them. Ten demonstrators were killed; another ninety were wounded. Despite a public outcry against the "Memorial Day Massacre," the harsh tactics of Little Steel companies succeeded. The 1937 strike failed.

But the victory of Little Steel was among the last gasps of the kind of brutal strikebreaking that had proved so effective in the past. In 1937 alone, there were 4,720 strikes— *Rapid Union Growth* over 80 percent of them settled in favor of the unions. By the end of the year, more than 8 million workers were members of unions recognized as official bargaining units by employers (as compared with 3 million in 1932). By 1941, that number had expanded to 10 million and included the workers of Little Steel, whose employers had finally recognized the SWOC.

SOCIAL SECURITY

From the first moments of the New Deal, important members of the administration had been lobbying for a system of federally sponsored social insurance for elderly people and those who were unemployed—not just for humanitarian reasons, but also to keep those groups active in the nation's economy. In 1935, Roosevelt gave public support to what became the Social Security Act, which Congress passed the same year. It established several distinct programs. For older people, there were two types of assistance. Those who were presently destitute could receive up to $15 a month in federal assistance. More important for the future, many Americans presently working were incorporated into a pension system, to which they and their employers would contribute through a payroll tax; it would provide them with an income on retirement. Pension payments would provide only $10 to $85 a month to recipients. At first, payment was not to be distributed until 1942. But public pressure pushed the payment date back to 1937. Broad categories of workers (including domestic servants and agricultural laborers) were excluded from the program. But the act was a crucial first step in building the nation's most important social program for retired Americans.

In addition, the Social Security Act created a system of unemployment insurance, which employers alone would finance. It also established a system of federal aid to people with disabilities and a program of aid to dependent children.

The framers of the Social Security Act wanted to create a system of "insurance," not "welfare." And the largest programs (old-age pensions and unemployment insurance) were in many ways similar to private insurance programs. But the act also provided considerable direct assistance based on need—to low-income aging adults, to those with disabilities, to dependent children and their mothers. These groups were widely perceived to be small and genuinely unable to support themselves. But in later generations, the programs for these groups would expand until they assumed dimensions that the planners of Social Security had not foreseen.

New Directions in Relief

Social Security was designed primarily to fulfill long-range goals. But millions of unemployed Americans had immediate needs. To help them, the Roosevelt administration established in 1935 the Works Progress Administration (WPA). Like the Civil Works Administration and other earlier efforts, the WPA established a system of work relief for the unemployed. But it was much bigger than the earlier agencies.

Under the direction of Harry Hopkins, the WPA was responsible for building or renovating 110,000 public buildings and for constructing almost 600 *Harry Hopkins and the WPA* airports, more than 500,000 miles of roads, and over 100,000 bridges. In the process, the WPA kept an average of 2.1 million workers employed and pumped needed money into the economy.

The WPA also displayed remarkable flexibility and imagination. The Federal Writers' Project of the WPA, for example, gave unemployed writers a chance to do their work and receive a government salary. The Federal Art Project, similarly, helped painters, sculptors, and others continue their careers. The Federal Music Project and the Federal Theatre Project oversaw the production of concerts and plays, creating work for unemployed musicians, actors, and directors. Other relief agencies emerged alongside the WPA. The National Youth Administration (NYA) provided work and scholarship assistance to men and women of high school and college age. The Emergency Housing Division of the Public Works Administration began federal sponsorship of public housing.

The new welfare system dealt with men and women in very different ways. For men, the government concentrated mainly on work relief—on such programs as the CCC, the CWA, and the WPA. The principal government aid to women was not work relief but cash assistance—most notably through the Aid to Dependent Children program of Social Security, which was designed largely to assist single mothers. This disparity in treatment

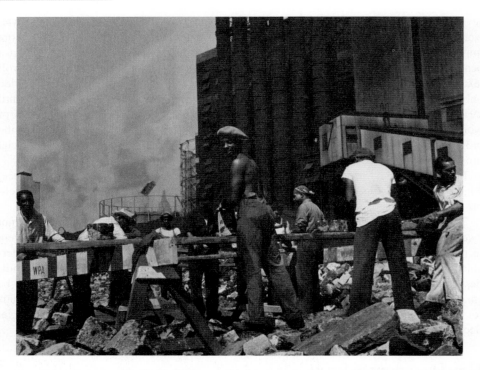

WPA WORKERS ON THE JOB The Works Progress Administration funded an enormous variety of work projects to provide jobs for unemployed individuals. The majority of WPA employees, however, worked on construction sites. (© Joseph Schwartz/Corbis)

reflected a widespread assumption that men should constitute the bulk of the paid work-force. Yet, millions of women were already employed by the 1930s.

THE 1936 "REFERENDUM"

By the middle of 1936—with the economy visibly reviving—there could be little doubt that Roosevelt would win a second term. The Republican Party nominated the moderate governor of Kansas, Alf M. Landon, who waged a relatively dull campaign. Roosevelt's dissident challengers now appeared powerless. One reason was the assassination of their most effective leader, Huey Long, in Louisiana in September 1935. Another reason was the ill-fated alliance among Father Coughlin, Dr. Townsend, and Gerald L. K. Smith (an intemperate henchman of Huey Long), who joined forces that summer to establish a new political movement—the Union Party, which nominated an undistinguished North Dakota congressman, William Lemke.

The result was the greatest landslide in American history to that point. Roosevelt polled just under 61 percent of the vote to Landon's 36 percent and carried every state except Maine and Vermont. The Democrats increased their already large majorities in both houses of Congress.

The election results demonstrated the party realignment that the New Deal had pro-duced. The Democrats now controlled a broad coalition of western and southern farmers, the urban working classes, the poor and unemployed, and white southerners, as well as

THE NEW DEAL · 603

traditional progressives and committed new liberals. New Deal aid flowing to black communities in northern cities helped pry that constituency from the Republican column. The resulting coalition constituted a substantial majority of the electorate. It would be decades before the Republican Party could again create a lasting majority coalition of its own.

THE NEW DEAL IN DISARRAY

Roosevelt emerged from the 1936 election at the zenith of his popularity. Within months, however, the New Deal was mired in serious new difficulties.

THE COURT FIGHT

The 1936 mandate, Franklin Roosevelt believed, made it possible for him to do something about the Supreme Court. No program of reform, he believed, could long survive the conservative justices, who had already struck down the NRA and the AAA.

In February 1937, Roosevelt sent a surprise message to Capitol Hill proposing an overhaul of the federal court system; included among the many provisions was one to add up to six new justices to the Supreme Court. The courts were "overworked," the president claimed, and needed additional manpower and younger blood to enable them to cope with their increasing burdens. But Roosevelt's real purpose was to give himself the opportunity to appoint new, liberal justices and change the ideological balance of the Court. (See "Consider the Source: Franklin D. Roosevelt Speaks on the Reorganization of the Judiciary.")

Conservatives were outraged at the "Court-packing plan," and even many Roosevelt supporters were disturbed by it. Still, Roosevelt might well   *Reaction to "Court-Packing Plan"* have persuaded Congress to approve at least a compromise measure had not the Supreme Court itself intervened. Of the nine justices, three reliably supported the New Deal, and four reliably opposed it. Of the remaining two, Chief Justice Charles Evans Hughes often sided with the progressives, and Associate Justice Owen J. Roberts usually voted with the conservatives. On March 29, 1937, Roberts, Hughes, and the three progressive justices voted together to uphold a state minimum-wage law—in the case of *West Coast Hotel v. Parrish*—thus reversing a 5-to-4 decision of the previous year invalidating a similar law. Two weeks later, again by a 5-to-4 margin, the Court upheld the Wagner Act, and in May it validated the Social Security Act. Whatever the reasons for the decisions, the Court's newly moderate position made the Court-packing bill seem unnecessary. Congress ultimately defeated it.

On one level, Franklin Roosevelt had achieved a victory. The Court was no longer an obstacle to New Deal reforms. But the Court-packing episode did lasting political damage to the administration. From 1937 on, southern Democrats and other conservatives voted against Roosevelt's measures much more often than they had in the past.

RETRENCHMENT AND RECESSION

By the summer of 1937, the national income—which had dropped from $82 billion in 1929 to $40 billion in 1932—had risen to nearly $72 billion. Other economic indices also showed similar advances. Roosevelt seized on these improvements as a justification for trying to balance the federal budget. Between January and August 1937,

FRANKLIN D. ROOSEVELT SPEAKS ON THE REORGANIZATION OF THE JUDICIARY

Franklin D. Roosevelt made masterful use of the radio to explain his policies to the American people and win their support and affection. On Tuesday, March 9, 1937, he went on the air to defend his controversial proposal for reforming the courts. The president couched his appeal within a broader summary of the New Deal's accomplishments.

Tonight, sitting at my desk in the White House, I make my first radio report to the people in my second term of office.

I am reminded of that evening in March, four years ago, when I made my first radio report to you. We were then in the midst of the great banking crisis.

Soon after, with the authority of the Congress, we asked the Nation to turn over all of its privately held gold, dollar for dollar, to the Government of the United States.

Today's recovery proves how right that policy was. [. . .]

In 1933 you and I knew that we must never let our economic system get completely out of joint again—that we could not afford to take the risk of another great depression.

We also became convinced that the only way to avoid a repetition of those dark days was to have a government with power to prevent and to cure the abuses and the inequalities which had thrown that system out of joint.

We then began a program of remedying those abuses and inequalities—to give balance and stability to our economic system—to make it bomb-proof against the causes of 1929.

Today we are only part-way through that program—and recovery is speeding up to a point where the dangers of 1929 are again becoming possible, not this week or month perhaps, but within a year or two.

National laws are needed to complete that program. Individual or local or state effort alone cannot protect us in 1937 any better than ten years ago.

It will take time—and plenty of time—to work out our remedies administratively even after legislation is passed. To complete our program of protection in time, therefore, we cannot delay one moment in making certain that our National Government has power to carry through.

Four years ago action did not come until the eleventh hour. It was almost too late.

If we learned anything from the depression we will not allow ourselves to run around in new circles of futile discussion and debate, always postponing the day of decision.

The American people have learned from the depression. For in the last three national elections an overwhelming majority of them voted a mandate that the Congress and the President begin the task of providing that protection—not after long years of debate, but now.

The Courts, however, have cast doubts on the ability of the elected Congress to protect us against catastrophe by meeting squarely our modern social and economic conditions.

We are at a crisis in our ability to proceed with that protection. It is a quiet crisis. There are no lines of depositors outside closed banks. But to the far-sighted it is far-reaching in its possibilities of injury to America.

I want to talk with you very simply about the need for present action in this crisis—the need to meet the unanswered challenge of one-third of a Nation ill-nourished, ill-clad, ill-housed.

Last Thursday I described the American form of Government as a three horse team provided by the Constitution to the American people so that their field might be plowed. The three horses are, of course, the three branches of government—the Congress, the Executive and the Courts. Two of the horses are pulling in unison today; the third is not. Those who have intimated that the President of the United States is trying to drive that team, overlook the simple fact that the President, as Chief Executive, is himself one of the three horses.

It is the American people themselves who are in the driver's seat.

It is the American people themselves who want the furrow plowed.

It is the American people themselves who expect the third horse to pull in unison with the other two.

[. . .] [S]ince the rise of the modern movement for social and economic progress through legislation, the Court has more and more often and more and more boldly asserted a power to veto laws passed by the Congress and State Legislatures [. . .].

In the last four years the sound rule of giving statutes the benefit of all reasonable doubt has been cast aside. The Court has been acting not as a judicial body, but as a policy-making body.

When the Congress has sought to stabilize national agriculture, to improve the conditions of labor, to safeguard business against unfair competition, to protect our national resources, and in many other ways, to serve our clearly national needs, the majority of the Court has been assuming the power to pass on the wisdom of these acts of the Congress—and to approve or disapprove the public policy written into these laws. [. . .]

We have, therefore, reached the point as a nation where we must take action to save the Constitution from the Court and the Court from itself. We must find a way to take an appeal from the Supreme Court to the Constitution itself. We want a Supreme Court which will do justice under the Constitution and not over it. In our courts we want a government of laws and not of men.

[. . .] What is my proposal? It is simply this: whenever a Judge or Justice of any Federal Court has reached the age of seventy and does not avail himself of the opportunity to retire on a pension, a new member shall be appointed by the President then in office, with the approval, as required by the Constitution, of the Senate of the United States. [. . .]

Those opposing this plan have sought to arouse prejudice and fear by crying that I am seeking to "pack" the Supreme Court and that a baneful precedent will be established.

What do they mean by the words "packing the Court"?

UNDERSTAND, ANALYZE, & EVALUATE

1. According to President Roosevelt, what had been most important for economic reform and recovery? How did he assess this recovery?
2. How were the three branches of government supposed to work, in the president's view?
3. What criticism did the president level against the courts? What solution did he offer? Was this conflict between the executive branch and the United States Supreme Court unique to the New Deal?

Source: On the Reorganization of the Judiciary, Tuesday, March 9, 1937 [35:28] WH, Fireside Chats of Franklin D. Roosevelt, Franklin D. Roosevelt Presidential Library, Hyde Park, New York.

for example, he cut the WPA in half, laying off 1.5 million relief workers. A few weeks later, the fragile boom collapsed. The index of industrial production dropped from 117 in August 1937 to 76 in May 1938. Four million additional workers lost their jobs. Economic conditions were soon almost as bad as they had been in the bleak days of 1932–1933.

The recession of 1937, known to the president's critics as the "Roosevelt recession," *Sources of the "Roosevelt Recession"* was a result of many factors. But to many observers at the time, it seemed to be a direct result of the administration's unwise decision to reduce spending. And so in April 1938, the president asked Congress for an emergency appropriation of $5 billion for public works and relief programs, and government funds soon began pouring into the economy once again. Within a few months, another tentative recovery seemed to be under way.

At about the same time, Roosevelt sent a stinging message to Congress, vehemently denouncing what he called an "unjustifiable concentration of economic power" and asking for the creation of a commission to consider major reforms in the antitrust laws. In response, Congress established the Temporary National Economic Committee (TNEC), whose members included representatives of both houses of Congress and officials from several executive agencies. Later in 1938, the administration successfully supported one of its most ambitious pieces of labor legislation, the Fair Labor Standards Act, which for the first time established a national minimum wage and a forty-hour workweek and which also placed strict limits on child labor.

Despite these achievements, however, by the end of 1938 the New Deal had essentially *End of the New Deal* come to an end. Congressional opposition now made it difficult for the president to enact any major new programs. But more important, perhaps, the threat of world crisis hung heavy in the political atmosphere, and Roosevelt was gradually growing more concerned with persuading a reluctant nation to prepare for war than with pursuing new avenues of reform.

LIMITS AND LEGACIES OF THE NEW DEAL

The New Deal made major changes in American government, some of them still controversial today. It also left important problems unaddressed.

AFRICAN AMERICANS AND THE NEW DEAL

The New Deal was not hostile to black aspirations. Eleanor Roosevelt spoke throughout the 1930s on behalf of racial justice and put continuing pressure on her husband and others in the federal government to ease discrimination against blacks. The president himself appointed a number of African Americans to significant second-level positions in his administration, creating an informal network of officeholders that became known *The "Black Cabinet"* as the "Black Cabinet." Eleanor Roosevelt, Interior Secretary Harold Ickes, and WPA Director Harry Hopkins all made efforts to ensure that New Deal relief programs did not exclude blacks. By 1935 an estimated 30 percent of all African Americans were receiving some form of government assistance, even amid persistent racial discrimination against people of color by the administrators of aid. One result was a historic change in black electoral behavior. As late as 1932, most American blacks were voting Republican, as they had been doing since the Civil War. By 1936, more than 90 percent were voting Democratic.

African Americans supported Franklin Roosevelt, but they had few illusions that the New Deal represented a major turning point in American race relations. The president was, for example, never willing to risk losing the support of southern Democrats by supporting legislation to make lynching a federal crime or to ban the poll tax, one of the most potent tools by which white southerners kept blacks from voting.

New Deal relief agencies did not challenge, and indeed reinforced, existing patterns of discrimination. The CCC established separate black camps. The NRA codes tolerated paying blacks less than whites doing the same jobs. The WPA routinely relegated African Americans and Hispanic workers to the least-skilled and lowest-paying jobs; when funding ebbed, African Americans, like women, were among the first   *Discrimination Reinforced* to be dismissed.

The New Deal was not hostile to African Americans, and it made some contributions to their progress. But it never made racial justice a significant part of its agenda.

The New Deal and the "Indian Problem"

New Deal policy toward the Indian tribes marked a significant break from earlier approaches, largely because of the efforts of the extraordinary commissioner of Indian affairs, John Collier. Collier was greatly influenced by the work of twentieth-century anthropologists who advanced the idea of cultural relativism—the theory that every culture should be accepted and respected on its own terms.

Collier wanted to reverse the pressures on Native Americans to assimilate and instead allow them to remain Indians. He effectively promoted legislation—which became the Indian Reorganization Act of 1934—that restored to   *John Collier's Advocacy* the tribes the right to own land collectively and to elect tribal governments. In the thirteen years after passage of the 1934 bill, tribal land increased by nearly 4 million acres, and Indian agricultural income increased from under $2 million in 1934 to over $49 million in 1947. Even with the redistribution of lands under the 1934 act, however, Indians continued to possess, for the most part, only territory whites did not want—much of it arid, some of it desert. And as a group, they continued to constitute the poorest segment of the population.

Women and the New Deal

Symbolically at least, the New Deal marked a breakthrough in the role of women in public life. Roosevelt appointed the first female member of the cabinet in the nation's history: Secretary of Labor Frances Perkins. He also named more than 100   *Frances Perkins* other women to positions at lower levels of the federal bureaucracy. But the administration was concerned not so much about achieving gender equality as about obtaining special protections for women.

The New Deal generally supported the widespread belief that in hard times women should withdraw from the workplace to open up more jobs for men. New Deal relief agencies offered relatively little employment for women. The Social Security program excluded domestic servants, waitresses, and other predominantly female occupations.

Repeating its handling of racial justice, the New Deal was not actively hostile to feminist aspirations, but it accepted prevailing cultural norms. There was not yet sufficient political pressure from women themselves to persuade the administration to do otherwise. Indeed, some of the most important supporters of policies that reinforced traditional gender roles (such as Social Security) were themselves women.

ELEANOR ROOSEVELT First Lady Eleanor Roosevelt was among the first women to play an important role in politics and government. She oversaw Franklin Roosevelt's political campaigns before he became president as well as developing an important career of her own working on social programs in New York. When she moved to the White House, she championed human rights issues. In this photograph she is on the way to inspect a Washington, D.C., jail that had a reputation for being overcrowded and obsolete. (© Underwood & Underwood/Corbis)

THE NEW DEAL AND THE WEST

One part of American society that did receive special attention from the New Deal was the American West. The West received more government funds per capita through relief programs than any other region.

Except for the TVA, the largest New Deal public works programs—the great dams and power stations—were mainly in the West, both because the best locations for such facilities were there and because the West had the greatest need for new sources of water and power. The Grand Coulee Dam on the Columbia River was the largest public works project in American history to that point, and it provided cheap electric power for much of the Northwest. Its construction, and that of other, smaller dams and water projects, created a basis for economic development in the region. Without this enormous public investment by the federal government, much of the economic growth that transformed the West after World War II would have been much more difficult, if not impossible, to achieve.

THE NEW DEAL, THE ECONOMY, AND POLITICS

The most frequent criticisms of the New Deal involve its failure to revive or reform the American economy. New Dealers never fully recognized the value of government spending as a vehicle for recovery. The economic boom sparked by World War II—not the New Deal—finally ended the crisis.

Nevertheless, the New Deal did have a number of important and lasting effects on the American economy. It helped elevate new groups—workers and farmers in particular—to positions from which they could at times challenge the power of the corporations. It increased the regulatory functions of the federal government in ways that helped stabilize previously troubled areas of the economy: the stock market, the banking system, and others. And the administration helped establish the basis for new forms of federal fiscal policy, which in the postwar years would give the government tools for promoting and regulating economic growth.

The New Deal also created the rudiments of the American welfare state through its many relief programs and, above all, through the Social Security system. The conservative inhibitions New Dealers brought to this task ensured that the welfare system that ultimately emerged would be limited in its impact, would reinforce some traditional patterns of gender and racial discrimination, and would be expensive and cumbersome to administer. But for all its limits, the new system marked a historic break with the nation's traditional reluctance to offer public assistance to its neediest citizens.

Finally, the New Deal had a dramatic effect on the character of American politics. It took a weak and divided Democratic Party, which had been a minority force in American politics for many decades, and turned it into a mighty coalition that would dominate national party competition for more than thirty years. It turned the attention of many voters away from some of the controversial cultural issues that had preoccupied them in the 1920s and awakened an interest in economic matters of direct importance to the lives of citizens.

CONCLUSION

From the time of Franklin Roosevelt's inauguration in 1933 to the beginning of World War II eight years later, the federal government engaged in a broad and diverse series of experiments designed to relieve the distress of unemployment and poverty; to reform the economy to prevent future crises; and to bring the Great Depression itself to an end. It had only partial success in all those efforts.

Unemployment and poverty remained high throughout the New Deal, although many federal programs provided assistance to millions of people who would otherwise have had none. The structure of the American economy remained essentially the same as it had been in earlier years, although there were by the end of the New Deal some important new regulatory agencies in Washington—and an important new role for organized labor. The New Deal failed to end the Great Depression. But some of its policies kept the Depression from getting worse; others helped alleviate the suffering of people caught in its grip; and still others pointed the way toward more effective economic policies in the future.

Perhaps the most important legacy of the New Deal was to create a sense of possibilities among many Americans. The New Deal persuaded many citizens that the fortunes of individuals need not be left entirely to chance or to the workings of an unregulated market. Many Americans, Republicans and Democrats alike, emerged from the 1930s convinced that individuals deserved some protections from the unpredictability and instability of the modern economy. The New Deal—for all its limitations—had demonstrated the value of enlisting government in the effort to provide those protections.

KEY TERMS/PEOPLE/PLACES/EVENTS

Agricultural Adjustment
  Administration (AAA) 590
Charles E. Coughlin 597
Civilian Conservation
  Corps (CCC) 593
Congress of Industrial
  Organizations (CIO) 599
Court-packing plan 603
Eleanor Roosevelt 606
Farm Security
  Administration 590
Federal Deposit Insurance
  Corporation (FDIC) 589

fireside chats 588
Frances Perkins 607
Harry P. Hopkins 601
Huey Long 597
John Collier 607
John L. Lewis 599
Liberty League 596
National Labor Relations
  Board (NLRB) 598
National Recovery
  Administration (NRA) 590
New Deal 594
Second New Deal 598

Securities and Exchange
  Commission (SEC) 589
sit-down strike 599
Social Security Act 600
Tennessee Valley Authority
  (TVA) 591
Townsend Plan 596
Works Progress
  Administration (WPA) 601

RECALL AND REFLECT

1. What New Deal programs were aimed at agricultural and industrial recovery, and what was the effect of the programs in both areas?
2. What criticisms did critics on both the right and the left level at the New Deal? How did FDR and his administration respond to these criticisms?
3. What gains did organized labor make during the 1930s?
4. What was the impact of the New Deal on women?

25 | THE GLOBAL CRISIS, 1921–1941

THE DIPLOMACY OF THE NEW ERA
ISOLATIONISM AND INTERNATIONALISM
FROM NEUTRALITY TO INTERVENTION

LOOKING AHEAD

1. What are some of the views that Americans expressed as the world crises of the 1930s expanded?
2. How did the economic crisis of the worldwide Great Depression help create new political orders in many nations?
3. What was the sequence of events between 1939 and 1941 that brought the United States into military involvement in World War II?

HENRY CABOT LODGE OF MASSACHUSETTS, Republican chair of the Senate Foreign Relations Committee, led the fight that defeated ratification of the Treaty of Versailles in 1919 and 1920. As a result, the United States declined to join the League of Nations. American foreign policy embarked instead on an independent course that for the next two decades would attempt, but ultimately fail, to expand American influence in the world without committing the United States to any lasting relationships with other nations.

Lodge was not an isolationist. He believed the United States should exert its influence internationally. But he believed, too, that the United States should remain unfettered by obligations to anyone else. He said in 1919:

> We are a great moral asset of Christian civilization. . . . How did we get there? By our own efforts. Nobody led us, nobody guided us, nobody controlled us. . . . I would keep America as she has been—not isolated, not prevent her from joining other nations for . . . great purposes—but I wish her to be master of her own fate.

In the end, the limited American internationalism of the interwar years proved insufficient to protect the interests of the United States, to create global stability, or to keep the nation from becoming involved in the most catastrophic war in human history.

THE DIPLOMACY OF THE NEW ERA

Critics in the 1920s often described American foreign policy with a single word: *isolationism*. But in reality, the United States played a more active role in world affairs in the 1920s than it had at almost any previous time in its history.

REPLACING THE LEAGUE

By the time the Harding administration took office in 1921, American membership in the League of Nations was no longer a realistic possibility. But Secretary of State Charles Evans Hughes wanted to find a replacement for the League as a guarantor of world peace and stability.

The most important effort was the Washington Conference of 1921—an attempt to prevent a destabilizing naval armaments race among the United States, Britain, and Japan. Hughes proposed a plan for dramatic reductions in the fleets of all three nations and a ten-year moratorium on the construction of large warships. To the surprise of almost everyone, the conference ultimately agreed to accept most of Hughes's terms. The Five-Power Pact of February 1922 established limits for total naval tonnage and a ratio of armaments among the signatories. For every 5 tons of American and British warships, Japan would maintain 3 and France and Italy 1.75 each.

When the French foreign minister, Aristide Briand, asked the United States in 1927 to join an alliance against Germany, Secretary of State Frank Kellogg (who had replaced Hughes in 1925) proposed instead a multilateral treaty outlawing war as an instrument of national policy. Fourteen nations signed the agreement in Paris on August 27, 1928, amid wide international acclaim. Forty-eight other nations later joined the Kellogg-Briand Pact. It contained no instruments of enforcement.

DEBTS AND DIPLOMACY

The first responsibility of diplomacy, Hughes, Kellogg, and others agreed, was to ensure that American overseas trade faced no obstacles. The Allied powers of Europe were struggling to repay $11 billion in loans they had contracted with the United States during and shortly after the war. At the same time, Germany was attempting to pay the reparations levied by the Allies. The United States stepped in with a solution.

Charles G. Dawes, an American banker who became vice president under Coolidge in 1925, negotiated an agreement in 1924 among France, Britain, Germany, and the United States. Under the Dawes Plan, American banks would provide enormous   *The Dawes Plan* loans to Germany, which would use that money to pay reparations to France and Britain; Britain and France would agree to reduce the amount of those payments and, in turn, use those funds (as well as the large loans they themselves were receiving from American banks) to repay war debts to the United States. One historian said of this circular plan, "It would have made equal sense for the U.S. to have taken the money out of one drawer in the Treasury and put it into another." The flow of funds was able to continue only by virtue of the enormous debts the European nations were acquiring to American banks and corporations. The American economic involvement in Europe continued to expand until the worldwide depression shattered the system in 1931.

During the 1920s, American military forces maintained a presence in Nicaragua, Panama, and several other countries in the region, while United States investments in Latin America more than doubled. American banks offered large loans to Latin American governments, just as in Europe; and as with the Europeans, the Latin Americans had difficulty earning the money to repay them in the face of the formidable United States tariff barrier.

HOOVER AND THE WORLD CRISIS

By 1931, the world financial crisis had produced a rising nationalism in Europe and Japan. It soon toppled some existing political leaders and replaced them with powerful, belligerent governments committed to expansion. Herbert Hoover thus confronted the beginning of a process that would ultimately lead to war.

In Latin America, Hoover tried to repair some of the damage done by earlier American policies. He made a ten-week goodwill tour through Latin America before his inauguration. Once in office, he generally abstained from intervening in the internal affairs of neighboring nations and moved to withdraw American troops from Nicaragua and Haiti. He also announced a new policy: America would grant diplomatic recognition to any sitting government in the region without questioning the means it had used to obtain power. He even repudiated the Theodore Roosevelt Corollary to the Monroe Doctrine by refusing to permit American intervention when several Latin American countries defaulted on debt obligations in October 1931.

In Europe, the administration enjoyed few successes. When Hoover's proposed moratorium on debts failed to produce financial stability, he refused to cancel all war debts to the United States as many economists advised him to do. Several European nations promptly went into default. Efforts to extend the 1921 limits on naval construction fell victim to French and British fears of German and Japanese militarism.

The ineffectiveness of American diplomacy in Europe was particularly troubling in light of the rise of **fascism,** an ideology that rejected democratic forms of government in favor of concentrated state power under a dictator. Benito Mussolini's Fascist Party had

THE SINO-JAPANESE WAR, 1931–1941

Long before Pearl Harbor, well before war broke out in Europe in 1939, the first shots of what would become World War II had been fired in the Pacific in a conflict between Japan and China.

Having lived in almost complete isolation from the world until the nineteenth century, Japan emerged from World War I as one of the world's great powers, with a proud and powerful military and growing global trade. But the Great Depression created severe economic problems for the Japanese; and as in other parts of the world, the crisis strengthened the political influence of highly nationalistic armed forces. Out of the Japanese military emerged dreams of a new empire in the Pacific. Such an empire would, its proponents believed, give the nation access to fuel, raw material, markets for its industries, as well as land for its agricultural needs and its rapidly increasing population. Such an empire, they also argued, would free Asia from its exploitation by Europe and America and would create a "new world order based on moral principles."

During World War I, Japan had taken territory and economic concessions from China and had created a particularly strong presence in the northern Chinese region of Manchuria. There, in September 1931, a group of young, militant army officers seized on a railway explosion to justify a military campaign through which they conquered the entire province. Both the United States government and the League of Nations demanded that Japan evacuate Manchuria. The Japanese ignored them and for the next six years consolidated its control over the new territory.

On July 7, 1937, Japan began a wider war when it attacked Chinese troops at the Marco Polo Bridge outside Beijing. Over the next few weeks, Japanese forces overran a large part of southern China, including most of the port cities, killing many Chinese soldiers and civilians in the process. Particularly notorious was the Japanese annihilation of many thousands of civilians in the city of Nanjing (the number has long been in dispute, but estimates range from 80,000 to over 300,000) in an event that became known in China and the West as the "Rape of Nanjing," or the Nanjing Massacre. The Chinese government fled to the mountains. As in 1931, the United States and the League of Nations protested in vain.

China was a nation in turmoil. It was engaged in a civil war of its own—between the so-called Kuomintang, a nationalist party led by Chiang Kai-shek, and the Chinese Communist Party, led by Mao Zedong; and this internal struggle weakened China's capacity to resist. But beginning in 1937, the two rivals agreed to an uneasy truce and began fighting the Japanese together, with some success—bogging the Japanese military down in a seemingly endless war and imposing great hardships on the Japanese people at home. The Japanese government and military, however, remained determined to continue the war against China, whatever the sacrifices.

One result of the costs of the war in China was a growing Japanese dependence on the United States for steel and oil to meet civilian and military needs. In July 1941, in an effort to pressure the Japanese to stop their expansion, the Roosevelt administration made it impossible for the

Japanese to continue buying American oil. Japan now faced a choice between ending its war in China or finding other sources of fuel to keep its war effort (and its civilian economy) going. Japan chose to extend the war beyond China in a search for oil. The best available sources were in the Dutch East Indies. But the only way to secure that European colony, the Japanese believed, would be to neutralize the increasingly hostile United States in Asia. Visionary military planners in Japan began advocating a daring move to immobilize the Americans in the Pacific before expanding the war elsewhere—with an attack on the American naval base at Pearl Harbor. The first blow of World War II in America, therefore, was the culmination of more than a decade of Japanese efforts to conquer China. •

UNDERSTAND, ANALYZE, & EVALUATE

1. What were the goals of the Japanese militarists in the 1930s that led to the attacks on China?
2. Why was China unable to stop Japanese aggression in the 1930s?

been in control of Italy since the early 1920s and had become increasingly nationalistic and militaristic. Still more ominous was the growing power of the National Socialist (or Nazi) Party in Germany. By the late 1920s, the Weimar Republic, the nation's government since the end of World War I, had been largely discredited by, among other things, a ruinous inflation. Adolf Hitler, the leader of the Nazis, grew rapidly in popular favor and took power in 1933. He believed in, among other things, the genetic superiority of the Aryan (German) people and in extending German territory to provide *Lebensraum* (living space) for what he called the German "master race." He displayed a pathological anti-Semitism and a passionate militarism.

Hitler and Mussolini in Europe

More immediately alarming to the Hoover administration was a major crisis in Asia—another early step toward World War II. The Japanese, suffering from an economic depression of their own, were concerned about the increasing power of the Soviet Union and

HITLER AND MUSSOLINI IN BERLIN The German and Italian dictators (shown here reviewing Nazi troops in Berlin in the mid-1930s) acted publicly as if they were equals. Privately, Hitler treated Mussolini with contempt, and Mussolini complained constantly of being a junior partner in the relationship. (© Instituto Nazionale Luce/ Alinari/Getty Images)

about the insistence of the Chinese leader Chiang Kai-shek on expanding his government's power in Manchuria, officially a part of China but over which the Japanese had maintained informal economic control since 1905. In 1931, Japan's military leaders staged what was, in effect, a coup in Tokyo. Shortly after that, a railroad explosion in southern Manchuria, *Manchuria Invaded* likely set by Japanese soldiers (and known as the "Mukden Incident"), served as a pretext for a Japanese invasion of northern Manchuria. They had conquered the region by the end of the year. Secretary of State Henry Stimson issued stern warnings to the Japanese but to no avail. Early in 1932, Japan moved farther into China, attacking the city of Shanghai and killing thousands of civilians. (For details on the ensuing war, see "America in the World: The Sino-Japanese War, 1931–1941.")

ISOLATIONISM AND INTERNATIONALISM

The administration of Franklin Roosevelt faced a dual challenge as it entered office in 1933. It had to deal with the worst economic crisis in the nation's history, and it had to deal as well with the effects of a decaying international structure.

DEPRESSION DIPLOMACY

Perhaps Roosevelt's sharpest break with the policies of his predecessor was on the question of American economic relations with Europe. Hoover had argued that only by resolving the question of war debts and reinforcing the gold standard could the American economy hope to recover. He had, therefore, agreed to participate in the World Economic Conference, to be held in London in June 1933, to attempt to resolve these issues. By the time the conference assembled, however, Roosevelt had already become convinced that the gold value of the dollar had to be allowed to fall in order for American goods to compete in world markets. Shortly after the conference convened, he released what became *FDR's "Bombshell Message"* known as the "bombshell message," repudiating the orthodox views of most of the delegates and rejecting any agreement on currency stabilization. The conference quickly dissolved.

At the same time, Roosevelt abandoned the commitments of the Hoover administration to settle the issue of war debts through international agreement. In April 1934, he signed a bill that prohibited American banks from making loans to any nation in default on its debts. The legislation ended the old, circular system by which debt payments continued only by virtue of increasing American loans. Within months, war-debt payments from every nation except Finland stopped for good.

Sixteen years after the Bolshevik Revolution of 1917, the American government still had not officially recognized the government of the Soviet Union. But a growing number of influential Americans were urging a change in policy—largely because the Soviet Union appeared to be a possible source of trade. Soviet leader Josef Stalin was hoping for American cooperation in containing Japan. In November 1933, the United States and the Soviet Union agreed to open formal diplomatic exchange. Relations with the Soviet Union, however, soon soured. American trade failed to establish a foothold in Russia, disappointing hopes in the United States. The American government did little to reassure *U.S.–Soviet Relations* the Soviets that it was interested in stopping Japanese expansion in Asia, dousing expectations in Russia. By the end of 1934, the Soviet Union and the United States were once again viewing each other with considerable mistrust.

The Roosevelt administration was also taking a new approach toward Latin America, an approach that became known as the "Good Neighbor Policy" and *"Good Neighbor Policy"* that expanded on the changes the Hoover administration had made. At an Inter-American Conference in Montevideo, Uruguay, in December 1933, Secretary of State Cordell Hull signed a formal convention declaring: "No state has the right to intervene in the internal or external affairs of another."

THE RISE OF ISOLATIONISM

With the international system of the 1920s now beyond repair, the United States faced a choice between more active efforts to stabilize the world or more energetic attempts to isolate itself from it. Most Americans unhesitatingly chose isolation. Support for **isolationism** emerged from many quarters. Some Wilsonian internationalists had grown disillusioned with the League of Nations and its inability to stop Japanese aggression in Asia. Other Americans argued that the American role in World War I was a result of Wall Street and munitions makers. An investigation by a Senate committee chaired by Senator Gerald Nye of North Dakota claimed to have produced evidence of exorbitant profiteering and tax evasion by many corporations during the war, and it suggested that bankers had pressured Wilson to intervene in the war so as to protect their loans abroad. (Few historians now lend much credence to these charges.)

Roosevelt continued to hope for at least a modest American role in maintaining world peace. In 1935, he proposed to the Senate a treaty to make the United States a member of the World Court—a largely symbolic gesture. Isolationists led by Father Coughlin and William Randolph Hearst aroused popular opposition to the agreement, and the Senate voted it down.

In the summer of 1935, Mussolini's Italy was preparing to invade Ethiopia. Fearing the invasion would provoke a new European war, American legislators tried to prevent the United States from being dragged into the conflict. The Neutrality Act *Neutrality Acts* of 1935 established a mandatory arms embargo against both sides in any military conflict and warned American citizens against traveling on the ships of warring nations. Thus, isolationists believed, the "protection of neutral rights" could not again become an excuse for American intervention in war. A 1937 law established the so-called cash-and-carry policy, by which warring nations could purchase only nonmilitary goods from the United States and could do so only by paying cash and shipping their purchases themselves.

Isolationist sentiment showed its strength again in 1936–1937 in response to the civil war in Spain. The Falangists of General Francisco Franco, a group *Spanish Civil War* somewhat like the Italian fascists, revolted in July 1936 against the existing republican government. Hitler and Mussolini supported Franco, both vocally and with weapons and supplies. Some Americans traveled to Spain to assist the republican cause, but the United States government joined with Britain and France in an agreement to offer no assistance to either side.

In the summer of 1937, Japan intensified its six-year-old assault on Manchuria and attacked China's five northern provinces. In a speech in Chicago in October 1937, Roosevelt warned that Japanese and other aggressors should be "quarantined" by the international community to prevent the contagion of war from spreading. He was deliberately vague about what such a quarantine would mean. Even so, public response to the speech was hostile, and Roosevelt drew back. On December 12, 1937, Japanese aviators bombed and sank the United States gunboat *Panay,* almost certainly deliberately, as it

THE SPANISH CIVIL WAR   Many Americans took up arms to help the republican forces fight against Franco and his army. The novelist Ernest Hemingway joined them in Spain as a reporter (and supporter of the republicans), and he spent much of his time talking with both American and Spanish troops. His novel *For Whom the Bell Tolls* was inspired by his experience in the civil war.   (Robert Capa/© International Center of Photography/Magnum Photos)

sailed the Yangtze River in China. But so reluctant was the Roosevelt administration to antagonize the isolationists that the United States eagerly seized on Japanese claims that the bombing had been an accident, accepted Japan's apologies, and overlooked the attack.

THE FAILURE OF MUNICH

In 1936, Hitler had moved the revived German army into the Rhineland, rearming an area that had been off-limits to German troops since World War I. In March 1938, German forces marched without opposition into Austria, and Hitler proclaimed a union (or *Anschluss*) between Austria, his native land, and Germany, his adopted one. Neither in America nor in most of Europe was there much more than a murmur of opposition.

Germany had by now occupied territory surrounding three sides of western Czechoslovakia, a region Hitler dreamed of annexing. In September 1938, he demanded that Czechoslovakia cede him the Sudetenland, a part of Czechoslovakia in which many ethnic Germans lived. Although Czechoslovakia was prepared to fight to stop Hitler, it needed assistance from other nations. But most Western governments, including the United States, were willing to pay almost any price to settle the crisis peacefully. On September 29, Hitler met with the leaders of France and Great Britain at Munich in an effort to resolve the crisis. The French and British agreed to accept the German demands in Czechoslovakia in return for Hitler's promise to expand no farther. Americans watched these events nervously—and the fear of war became a fixture of domestic thought and culture. (See "Patterns of Popular Culture: Orson Welles and the 'War of the Worlds.'")

The Munich agreement, which Roosevelt supported at the time, was the most prominent element of a policy that came to be known as **appeasement** and that came to be identified (not altogether fairly) with British prime minister Neville Chamberlain. Whoever was to blame, the policy was a failure. In March 1939, Hitler occupied the remaining areas of Czechoslovakia, violating the Munich agreement unashamedly. And in April, he began issuing threats against Poland.

At that point, both Britain and France assured the Polish government that they would come to its assistance in case of an invasion; they even tried, too late, to draw the Soviet Union into a mutual defense agreement. But the Soviet leader Josef Stalin, who had not even been invited to the Munich Conference, had decided he could expect no protection from the West. He signed a nonaggression pact with Hitler in August 1939, freeing the Germans, for a while, from the danger of a two-front war. Shortly after that, Hitler staged an incident on the Polish border to allow him to claim that Germany had been attacked, and on September 1, 1939, he launched a full-scale invasion of Poland.   *Invasion of Poland* Britain and France, true to their pledges, declared war on Germany two days later. World War II, already under way in Asia, had begun in Europe.

FROM NEUTRALITY TO INTERVENTION

"This nation will remain a neutral nation," the president declared shortly after the hostilities began in Europe, "but I cannot ask that every American remain neutral in thought as well." There was never any question that both he and the majority of the American people favored Britain, France, and the other Allied nations in the contest. The question was how much the United States was prepared to do to assist them.

NEUTRALITY TESTED

At the very least, Roosevelt believed, the United States should make armaments available to the Allied armies to counter the military advantage the large German munitions industry gave Hitler. In September 1939, he asked Congress to revise the Neutrality Acts and lift the arms embargo against any nation engaged in war. Congress maintained the prohibition on American ships entering war zones. But the 1939 law did permit belligerents to purchase arms on the same cash-and-carry basis that the earlier Neutrality Acts had established for the sale of nonmilitary materials.

After the German armies quickly subdued Poland, the war in Europe settled into a long, quiet lull that lasted through the winter and spring—a "phony war," some called it. But in the spring of 1940, Germany launched a massive invasion, known as the "blitzkrieg" (lightning war), to the west—first attacking Denmark and Norway, sweeping   *The Blitzkrieg* next across the Netherlands and Belgium, and driving finally deep into the heart of France. On June 10, Mussolini invaded France from the south as Hitler was attacking from the north. On June 22, France fell, and Nazi troops marched into Paris. A new French regime assembled in Vichy, largely controlled by the German occupiers; and   *Vichy Regime in France* in all of Europe, only the shattered remnants of the British and French armies—daringly rescued from the beaches of Dunkirk by a hastily organized armada of English boats, trawlers, and yachts—remained to oppose the Axis forces.

ORSON WELLES AND THE "WAR OF THE WORLDS"

On the evening of October 30, 1938, about 6 million Americans were listening to the weekly radio program *The Mercury Theatre on the Air,* produced by the actor/filmmaker Orson Welles and broadcast over the CBS network. A few minutes into the show, an announcer interrupted some dance music with a terrifying report:

> At least forty people, including six state troopers, lie dead in a field east of Grover's Mill [New Jersey], their bodies burned and distorted beyond recognition. . . . Good heavens, something's wriggling out of the shadow like a gray snake! Now it's another one and another. . . . It's large as a bear and

it glistens like black leather. But that face . . . it's indescribable! I can hardly force myself to keep looking at it.

The panicky announcer was describing the beginning of an alien invasion of earth and the appearance of Martians armed with "death rays," determined to destroy the planet. Later in the evening, an announcer claiming to be broadcasting from Times Square reported the destruction of New York City before falling dead at the microphone.

The dramatic "news bulletins" were part of a radio play by Howard Koch, loosely adapted from H. G. Wells's 1898 novel, *The War of the Worlds.* Announcers reminded the audience repeatedly throughout the broadcast that

WELLES ON THE AIR   Welles (top right) is shown here during the broadcast of the "War of the Worlds" in 1938. Although announcers told listeners throughout the broadcast that it was fiction, Welles came under intense criticism in following days for the panic it caused among many listeners. (© Bettmann/Corbis)

they were listening to a play, but many people either did not hear or did not notice the disclaimers. By the end of the hour, according to some estimates, as many as a million Americans were flying into panics, convinced that the end of the world was imminent.

Thousands of listeners in New York and New Jersey fled their homes and tried to drive along clogged highways into the hills or the countryside. In Newark, people ran from their buildings with wet towels wrapped around their faces or wearing gas masks—as if defending themselves against the chemical warfare that many remembered from the trenches in World War I. In cities across the country, people flocked into churches to pray; called police and hospitals for help; flooded the switchboards of newspapers, magazines, and radio stations desperate for information. "I never hugged my radio so closely as I did last night," one woman later explained. "I held a crucifix in my hand and prayed while looking out of my open window for falling meteors." The *New York Times* described it the next day as "a wave of mass hysteria." For weeks thereafter, Orson Welles and other producers of the show were the focus of a barrage of criticism for what many Americans believed had been a deliberate effort to create public fear. For years, sociologists and other scholars studied the episode for clues about mass behavior.

Welles and his colleagues claimed to be surprised by the reaction their show created. The broadcast proved more effective than they had expected because it touched on anxieties that ran deep in American life at the time. The show aired only a few weeks after the war fever that had preceded the Munich pact among Germany, Britain, and France; Americans already jittery about the possibility of war proved easy prey to fears of another kind of invasion. The show also tapped longer-standing anxieties about the fragility of life that afflicted many Americans during the long depression of the 1930s, and it seemed to frighten working-class people—those most vulnerable to unexpected catastrophes—in particular.

Most of all, however, the "War of the Worlds" unintentionally exploited the enormous power that radio had come to exercise in American life, and the great trust many people had developed in what they heard over the air. For many people, the broadcasts they received over the radio had become their principal, even their only, source of information about the outside world. When the actors from *The Mercury Theatre* began to use the familiar phrases and cadences of radio news announcers, it was easy for members of their audience to assume that they were hearing the truth.

Welles concluded the broadcast by describing the play as "the Mercury Theater's own radio version of dressing up in a sheet and jumping out of a bush and saying Boo! . . . So goodbye everybody, and remember, please, for the next day or so, the terrible lesson you learned tonight. The grinning, glowing, globular invader of your living room is an inhabitant of the pumpkin patch, and if your doorbell rings and there's no one there, that was no Martian . . . it's Halloween." But the real lesson of the "War of the Worlds" was the lesson of the enormous, and at times frightening, power of the medium of broadcasting. •

From *War of the Worlds* by Howard Koch. Copyright © 1938 Howard Koch.

UNDERSTAND, ANALYZE, & EVALUATE

1. Why did Welles's "War of the Worlds" broadcast create so much panic and hysteria?
2. What responsibility did Welles and his producers bear for the hysteria that followed the program? Could they have done more to prevent that hysteria and reassure their audience? If so, should they have done more?
3. Do the media today hold as much power and influence as radio did in the 1930s? Would an audience today be as likely to react with panic and hysteria to a broadcast similar to that of the "War of the Worlds"?

THE BLITZ, LONDON The German *Luftwaffe* terrorized London and other British cities in 1940–1941 and again late in the war by bombing civilian areas indiscriminately in an effort to break the spirit of the English people. The effort failed, and the fortitude of the British did much to arouse American support for their cause. St. Paul's Cathedral, largely undamaged throughout the raids, looms in the background of this photograph, as other buildings crumble under the force of German bombs. (© Daily Mail/Rex/Alamy)

On May 16, in the midst of the offensive, Roosevelt asked Congress for and quickly received an additional $1 billion for defense. That was one day after Winston Churchill, *Aid to Churchill* the new British prime minister, had sent Roosevelt the first of many long lists of requests for armaments, without which, he insisted, England could not long survive. Some Americans (including the ambassador to London, Joseph P. Kennedy) argued that the British plight was already hopeless, that any aid to the English was a wasted effort. But the president was determined to make war materials available to Britain. Roosevelt even circumvented the cash-and-carry provisions of the Neutrality Acts by giving England fifty American destroyers (most of them left over from World War I) in return for the right to build American bases on British territory in the Caribbean. He also returned to the factories a number of new airplanes purchased by the American military so that the British could buy them instead.

Roosevelt was able to take such steps in part because of a major shift in American public opinion. By July 1940, more than 66 percent of the public (according to opinion polls) believed that Germany posed a direct threat to the United States. As a result, Congress was more willing to permit expanded American assistance to the Allies. Congress was also becoming more concerned about the need for preparations for war, and in *Peacetime Draft* September it approved the Burke-Wadsworth Act, inaugurating the first peacetime military draft in American history.

But a powerful new isolationist lobby—the America First Committee, whose members included such prominent Americans as Charles Lindbergh and Senators Gerald Nye and

Burton Wheeler—joined the debate over American policy toward the war. The lobby had at least the indirect support of a large proportion of the Republican Party. Through the summer and fall of 1940, the debate was complicated by a presidential campaign.

THE CAMPAIGN OF 1940

The biggest political question of 1940 was whether Franklin Roosevelt would break with tradition and run for an unprecedented third term. The president himself did not reveal his own wishes. But by refusing to withdraw from the contest, he made it impossible for any rival Democrat to establish a claim to the nomination. And when, just before the Democratic National Convention in July, he let it be known that he would accept a "draft" from his party, the issue was virtually settled. The Democrats quickly renominated him and even reluctantly swallowed his choice for vice president: Agriculture Secretary Henry A. Wallace, a man too liberal and too controversial for the taste of many party leaders.

The Republicans nominated for president a politically inexperienced Indiana business-man, Wendell Willkie, who benefited from a powerful grassroots movement—as well as strong support from the Luce magazines—especially *Time* and *Life*. The Republicans took positions little different from Roosevelt's: they would keep the country out *FDR Reelected* of war but would extend generous assistance to the Allies. Willkie was an appealing figure and a vigorous campaigner, and he managed to evoke more public enthusiasm than any Republican candidate in decades. But Roosevelt still won decisively. He received 55 percent of the popular vote to Willkie's 45 percent, and he won 449 electoral votes to Willkie's 82.

NEUTRALITY ABANDONED

In the last months of 1940, Roosevelt began to make subtle changes in the American role in the war. Great Britain was virtually bankrupt and could no longer meet the cash-and-carry requirements imposed by the Neutrality Acts. The president therefore, *"Lend-Lease"* proposed a new system for supplying Britain: "lend-lease." It would allow the federal government not only to sell but also to lend or lease armaments to any nation deemed "pivotal to the defense of the United States." In other words, America could funnel weapons to England on the basis of no more than Britain's promise to return them when the war was over. Congress enacted the bill by wide margins in March 1941.

Attacks by German submarines had made shipping lanes in the Atlantic extremely dangerous. The British navy was losing ships more rapidly than it could replace them and was finding it difficult to transport materials across the Atlantic from America. Roosevelt argued that the western Atlantic was a neutral zone and the responsibility of the American nations. By July 1941, therefore, American ships were patrolling the ocean as far east as Iceland.

At first, Germany did little to challenge these obviously hostile American actions. By September 1941, however, the situation had changed. Nazi forces had invaded the Soviet Union in June of that year. When the Soviets did not surrender, as many had predicted they would, Roosevelt persuaded Congress to extend lend-lease privileges to them. Now American industry was providing vital assistance to Hitler's foes on two fronts, and the American navy was protecting the flow of those goods to Europe. In September, Nazi submarines began a concerted torpedo campaign against American vessels. Roosevelt ordered American ships to fire on German submarines "on sight." In October, Nazi submarines hit two American destroyers and sank one of them, the *Reuben James,* killing many

JOINT STATEMENT BY PRESIDENT ROOSEVELT AND PRIME MINISTER CHURCHILL

In August 1941, Franklin Roosevelt and Winston Churchill met aboard a British vessel off the coast of Newfoundland. The president made no military commitments, but he did join with the prime minister in releasing a document that became known as the Atlantic Charter. The two nations called for a new world order based on self-determination, economic cooperation, and antimilitarism.

The President of the United States and the Prime Minister, Mr. Churchill, representing His Majesty's Government in the United Kingdom, have met at sea. [. . .]

They have considered the dangers to world civilization arising from the policies of military domination by conquest upon which the Hitlerite government of Germany and other governments associated therewith have embarked, and have made clear the stress which their countries are respectively taking for their safety in the face of these dangers.

They have agreed upon the following joint declaration:

Joint declaration of the President of the United States of America and the Prime Minister, Mr. Churchill, representing His Majesty's Government in the United Kingdom, being met together, deem it right to make known certain common principles in the national policies of their respective countries on which they base their hopes for a better future for the world.

First, their countries seek no aggrandizement, territorial or other;

Second, they desire to see no territorial changes that do not accord with the freely expressed wishes of the peoples concerned;

Third, they respect the right of all peoples to choose the form of government under which they will live; and they wish to see sovereign rights and self-government restored to those who have been forcibly deprived of them;

Fourth, they will endeavor, with due respect for their existing obligations, to further the enjoyment by all States, great or small, victor or vanquished, of access, on equal terms, to the trade and to the raw materials of the world which are needed for their economic prosperity;

Fifth, they desire to bring about the fullest collaboration between all nations in the economic field with the objector securing, for all, improved labor standards, economic advancement and social security;

Sixth, after the final destruction of the Nazi tyranny, they hope to see established a peace which will afford to all nations the means of dwelling in safety within their own boundaries, and which will afford assurance that all the men in all the lands may live out their lives in freedom from fear and want;

Seventh, such a peace should enable all men to traverse the high seas and oceans without hindrance;

Eighth, they believe that all of the nations of the world, for realistic as well as spiritual reasons must come to the abandonment of the use of force. Since no future peace can be maintained if land, sea or air armaments continue to be employed by nations which threaten, or may threaten, aggression outside of their frontiers, they believe, pending the establishment of a wider and permanent system of general security, that the disarmament of such nations is essential. They will likewise aid and encourage all other practicable measures which will lighten for peace-loving peoples the crushing burden of armaments.

FRANKLIN D. ROOSEVELT
WINSTON S. CHURCHILL

UNDERSTAND, ANALYZE, & EVALUATE

1. What inspired this meeting between the United States and Great Britain in the Atlantic? What goals did the two nations set for future international diplomacy and the rights of nations?

2. Which mutual goals reflect the shared experience of the Great Depression? Which reflect the shared experience of World War I?

Source: The Atlantic Charter, published in Department of State Executive Agreement Series No. 236.

American sailors. Congress quickly voted to allow the United States to arm its merchant vessels and to sail all the way into belligerent ports. The United States *The Atlantic Charter* had, in effect, launched a naval war against Germany. Meanwhile, Roosevelt had met recently with Churchill to issue a statement of shared goals known as the Atlantic Charter. (See "Consider the Source: Joint Statement by President Roosevelt and Prime Minister Churchill.")

THE ROAD TO PEARL HARBOR

Japan, in the meantime, was still extending its empire in the Pacific. In September 1940, the Japanese signed the Tripartite Pact, a loose defensive alliance with Germany and Italy (although in reality, the European Axis powers never developed a very strong relationship with Japan). In July 1941, Japanese troops moved into Indochina and seized the capital of Vietnam, a colony of France. The United States, having broken Japanese codes, knew Japan's next target was to be the oil-rich Dutch East Indies; and when Tokyo failed to respond to Roosevelt's stern warnings, the president froze all Japanese assets in the United States, severely limiting Japan's ability to purchase needed American supplies.

Tokyo now faced a choice. Either it would have to repair relations with the United States to restore the flow of oil and other supplies, or it would have to find those supplies elsewhere, most notably by seizing British and Dutch possessions in *Hideki Tojo in Power* the Pacific. In October, militants in Tokyo forced the moderate prime minister out of office and replaced him with the leader of the war party, General Hideki Tojo.

By late November, the State Department had given up on the possibility of a peaceful settlement. American intelligence had decoded Japanese messages that made clear a Japanese attack was imminent. But Washington did not know where the attack would take place. Most officials continued to believe that the Japanese would not move first against American territory but against British or Dutch possessions to the south. A combination of confusion, miscalculation, and underestimation of the Japanese military caused the government to overlook indications that Japan intended a direct attack on American forces.

At 7:55 A.M. on Sunday, December 7, 1941, a wave of Japanese bombers attacked the United States naval base at Pearl Harbor in Hawaii—part of a coordinated pattern of attacks against American and British holdings in Asia. A second wave came an hour later. Within two hours, the United States lost 8 battleships, 3 cruisers, *Pearl Harbor Attacked* 4 other vessels, 188 airplanes, and several vital shore installations. More than 2,400 soldiers and sailors died, and another 1,000 were injured. The Japanese suffered only light losses.

American forces were now greatly diminished in the Pacific (although by a fortunate accident, no American aircraft carriers—the heart of the Pacific Fleet—had been at Pearl Harbor on December 7). Nevertheless, the raid on Hawaii unified the American people behind war. On December 8, after a stirring speech by the president, the Senate voted

PEARL HARBOR, DECEMBER 7, 1941 At least seven aerial torpedoes and two bombs struck the battleship USS *West Virginia* on that fateful morning. Repair workers discovered 66 bodies of *West Virginia* crewmembers. After it was restored to fighting condition, the ship reentered the war and participated in the Battles of Iwo Jima and Okinawa. (© GL Archive/Alamy)

unanimously and the House voted 388 to 1 to approve a declaration of war against Japan. Three days later, Germany and Italy, Japan's European allies, declared war on the United States; on the same day, December 11, Congress reciprocated without a dissenting vote.

CONCLUSION

American foreign policy in the years after World War I attempted something that ultimately proved impossible. Americans were determined to be a major power in the world. They were determined to extend the nation's trade broadly around the globe. And they were determined to influence other nations in ways that would be beneficial to America's, and the world's, interests. The United States was also determined to do nothing that would limit its own freedom of action. It would not join the League of Nations. It would not join the World Court. It would not form alliances with other nations. It would operate powerfully—and alone.

But ominous forces were at work in the world that would gradually push the United States into greater engagement with other nations. The economic disarray that the Great Depression created around the globe, the rise of totalitarian regimes, the expansionist ambitions of powerful new leaders—all worked to destroy the uneasy stability of the post–World War I international system. America's own interests, economic and otherwise, were now imperiled. And America's go-it-alone foreign policy seemed powerless to change the course of events.

Franklin Roosevelt tried throughout the later years of the 1930s to push the American people slowly into a greater involvement in international affairs. In particular, he tried to nudge the United States toward taking a more forceful stand against dictatorship and aggression. A powerful isolationist movement helped stymie him for a time, even after war broke out in Europe. Gradually, however, public opinion shifted toward support of the Allies (Britain, France, and the Soviet Union) and against the Axis (Germany, Italy, and Japan). The nation began to mobilize for war, to supply ships and munitions to Britain, even to engage in naval combat with German forces in the Atlantic. Finally, on December 7, 1941, the surprise Japanese attack on the American base at Pearl Harbor in Hawaii eliminated the last elements of uncertainty and drove the United States—now united behind the war effort—into the greatest and most terrible conflict in human history.

KEY TERMS/PEOPLE/PLACES/EVENTS

Adolf Hitler 615	Good Neighbor Policy 617	Neutrality Acts 617
appeasement 619	Hideki Tojo 625	Pearl Harbor 625
Atlantic Charter 624	isolationism 617	Sino-Japanese War 614
Benito Mussolini 613	Josef Stalin 616	Spanish Civil War 617
Dawes Plan 613	lend-lease 623	Vichy regime 619
fascism 613	Nazi Party 615	Winston Churchill 622

RECALL AND REFLECT

1. What diplomatic efforts and agreements of the 1920s and 1930s attempted to deal with the increasing global political crises of the era? Why were these efforts unsuccessful?
2. How did the goals of the Neutrality Acts change over the course of the 1930s? What was the reason for the change?
3. Why did Japan attack Pearl Harbor?

26

AMERICA IN A WORLD AT WAR

WAR ON TWO FRONTS
THE AMERICAN ECONOMY IN WARTIME
RACE AND ETHNICITY IN WARTIME AMERICA
ANXIETY AND AFFLUENCE IN WARTIME CULTURE
THE DEFEAT OF THE AXIS

LOOKING AHEAD

1. What was the impact of the war on the U.S. economy?
2. How was the military experience of the United States in World War II different in Europe and the Pacific?
3. How did the war affect life on the home front, especially for women, organized labor, and minorities?

THE ATTACK ON PEARL HARBOR thrust the United States into the greatest and most terrible war in the history of humanity, a war that changed the world as dramatically as any event of the twentieth century. World War II also transformed the United States in profound, if not always readily visible, ways. The war forced the American people to accept an unprecedented level of government control over their everyday lives. It transformed the roles of many women, reshaped the nation's industrial landscape, and thrust the United States into a position of global leadership that it has maintained ever since.

WAR ON TWO FRONTS

Whatever political disagreements and social tensions there may have been among the American people during World War II, there was striking unity of opinion about the conflict itself. But both unity and confidence faced severe tests in the first, troubled months of 1942.

CONTAINING THE JAPANESE

Ten hours after the strike at Pearl Harbor, Japanese airplanes attacked the American airfields at Manila in the Philippines, destroying much of America's remaining air power in the Pacific. Three days later, Guam, an American possession, fell. Wake Island and Hong Kong followed. The great British fortress of Singapore in Malaya surrendered in February 1942, the Dutch East Indies in March, and Burma in April. In the Philippines, exhausted Filipino and American troops gave up their defense of the islands on May 6. (The American commander, General Douglas MacArthur, vowed as he left, "I shall return.")

American strategists planned two broad offensives to turn the tide against the Japanese. One, under the command of MacArthur, would move north from Australia, through New Guinea, and eventually to the Philippines. The other, under Admiral Chester Nimitz, would move west from Hawaii toward major Japanese island outposts in the central Pacific. Ultimately, strategists predicted, the two offensives would come together to invade Japan itself.

The Allies achieved their first important victory in the Battle of the Coral Sea, just northeast of Australia, on May 7–8, 1942, when American forces turned back the previously unstoppable Japanese navy. An even more important turning point occurred a month later northwest of Hawaii, near the small American outpost at Midway Island. There, after an enormous four-day battle (June 3–6, 1942), the American navy, despite

TIME LINE

1942

Battle of Midway

Campaign in North Africa

Japanese Americans interned

Manhattan Project begins

CORE founded

1943

Americans capture Guadalcanal

Allied invasion of Italy

Soviet victory at Stalingrad

1944

Allies invade Normandy

Roosevelt reelected

Americans capture Philippines

1945

Roosevelt dies; Truman becomes president

Germany surrenders

U.S. drops atomic bombs on Hiroshima, Nagasaki

Japan surrenders

terrible losses, regained control of the central Pacific. The United States destroyed four Japanese aircraft carriers without losing one of its own.

The Americans took the offensive several months later in the southern Solomon Islands, to the east of New Guinea. In August 1942, American forces assaulted three of the islands: Gavutu, *Guadalcanal* Tulagi, and Guadalcanal. A struggle of terrible ferocity continued at Guadalcanal for six months, inflicting heavy losses on both sides. In the end, however, the Japanese were forced to abandon the island—and with it their last chance of launching an effective offensive to the south. The Americans, with aid from the Australians and the New Zealanders, now began the slow, arduous process of moving toward the Philippines and Japan itself.

HOLDING OFF THE GERMANS

In the European war, the United States fought in cooperation with, among others, Britain and the exiled "Free French" forces in the west, and tried also to conciliate its new ally, the Soviet Union, which was now fighting Hitler in the east. The army chief of staff, General George C. Marshall, supported a plan for a major Allied invasion of France across the English Channel in the spring of 1943, and he placed a previously little-known general, *Dwight Eisenhower* Dwight D. Eisenhower, in charge of planning the operation. The Soviet Union, which was absorbing the brunt of the German war effort, wanted the Allied invasion

WORLD WAR II IN NORTH AFRICA AND ITALY: THE ALLIED COUNTEROFFENSIVE, 1942–1943 The United States and Great Britain understood from the beginning that an invasion of France across the English Channel would eventually be necessary for a victory in the European war. In the meantime, however, they began a campaign against Axis forces in North Africa, and in the spring of 1943 they began an invasion across the Mediterranean into Italy. This map shows the points along the coast of North Africa where Allied forces landed in 1942—with American forces moving east from Morocco and Algeria and British forces moving west from Egypt. The two armies met in Tunisia and moved into Italy from there. • *Why were America and Britain reluctant to launch the cross-channel invasion in 1942 or 1943?*

to begin at the earliest possible moment. But the British wanted first to launch a series of Allied offensives around the edges of the Nazi empire—in northern Africa and southern Europe—before undertaking the invasion of France.

Roosevelt ultimately decided to support the British plan—in part because he was eager to get American forces into combat quickly and knew that a cross-channel invasion would take a long time to prepare. At the end of October 1942, the British opened a counter-offensive against General Erwin Rommel and the Nazi forces in northern Africa who were threatening the Suez Canal. In a major battle at El Alamein, they forced the Germans to retreat from Egypt. In early November, Anglo-American forces landed at Oran and Algiers in Algeria and at Casablanca in Morocco—areas under the Nazi-controlled French government at Vichy—and began moving east toward Rommel. The Germans threw the full weight of their forces in Africa against the inexperienced Americans and inflicted a serious defeat on them at the Kasserine Pass in Tunisia. General George S. Patton, however, regrouped and began an effective counteroffensive. With the help of Allied air and naval power and of British forces attacking from the east under Field Marshall Bernard Montgomery (the hero of El Alamein), the American offensive finally drove the last Germans from Africa in May 1943.

The North African campaign had tied up a large proportion of Allied resources, post- *Battle of Stalingrad* poning the planned May 1943 cross-channel invasion of France, despite angry complaints from the Soviet Union. By now, however, the threat of a Soviet collapse seemed much diminished, for during the winter of 1942–1943, the Red Army had successfully held off a major German assault at Stalingrad in southern Russia. Hitler had committed such enormous forces to the battle, and had suffered such appalling losses, that he could not continue his eastern offensive.

The Soviet successes persuaded Roosevelt to agree, in a January 1943 meeting with Churchill in Casablanca, to a British plan for an Allied invasion of Sicily. Churchill argued that the operation in Sicily might knock Italy out of the war and tie up German divisions that would otherwise be stationed in France. On the night of July 9–10, 1943, American and British armies landed in southeastern Sicily; thirty-eight days later, they had conquered the island and were moving onto the Italian mainland. In the face of these setbacks, Mussolini's government collapsed *Italy Invaded* and the dictator himself fled north toward Germany. (He was later captured by Italian insurgents and hanged.) Mussolini's successor, Pietro Badoglio, quickly committed Italy to the Allies. Germany moved eight divisions into Italy and established a powerful defensive line south of Rome. The Allied offensive, which began on September 3, 1943, got bogged down at that line. Not until May 1944 did the Allies break through the German defenses to resume their northward advance. On June 4, 1944, they captured Rome.

The invasion of Italy delayed the invasion of France by as much as a year, deeply embittering Stalin but also giving the Soviets time to begin moving toward the countries of eastern Europe.

AMERICA AND THE HOLOCAUST

In the midst of this intensive fighting, the leaders of the American government confronted one of history's great tragedies: the Nazi campaign to exterminate the Jews of Europe, which became known as the Holocaust. As early as 1942, high officials in Washington had incontrovertible evidence that Hitler's forces were rounding up Jews and others

THE *ST. LOUIS*   Many people consider the fate of the German liner *St. Louis* to be a powerful symbol of the indifference of the United States and other nations to the fate of European Jews during the Holocaust, even though its forlorn journey preceded both the beginning of World War II and the beginning of systematic extermination of Jews by the Nazi regime. The *St. Louis* carried a group of over 900 Jews fleeing from Germany in 1939, carrying exit visas of dubious legality cynically sold to them by members of Hitler's Gestapo. It became a ship without a port as it sailed from country to country—Mexico, Paraguay, Argentina, Costa Rica, and Cuba—where its passengers were refused entry time and again. Most of the passengers were hoping for a haven in the United States, but the American State Department refused to allow the ship even to dock as it sailed up the American eastern seaboard. Eventually, the *St. Louis* returned to Europe and distributed its passengers among Britain, France, Holland, and Belgium (where this photograph was taken, showing refugees smiling and waving as they prepared to disembark in Antwerp in June 1939). Less than a year later, all those nations except Britain fell under Nazi control. (© Bettmann/Corbis)

(including Poles, homosexuals, and communists) from all over Europe, transporting them to concentration camps in eastern Germany and Poland, and systematically murdering them. (The death toll would ultimately reach 6 million Jews and at least 4 million others.) News of the atrocities soon reached the public as well, and pressure began to build for an Allied effort to end the killing or at least to rescue some of the surviving Jews.

The American government consistently resisted almost all such demands. Although by *U.S. Inaction* mid-1944 Allied bombers were flying missions within a few miles of the most notorious death camp, at Auschwitz in Poland, the War Department argued that sending planes to destroy the crematoria was unfeasible. American officials also refused to destroy railroad lines leading to the camp. And the United States resisted pleas that it admit large numbers of Jewish refugees attempting to escape Europe.

More forceful action by the United States (and Britain, which was even less amenable to Jewish requests for assistance) might have saved at least some lives. That they did not take such action, it seems clear in retrospect, constituted a considerable moral failure. But policymakers justified their inaction by insisting that they needed to focus exclusively on the larger goal of winning the war. Any diversion of energy and attention to other purposes, they believed, would distract them from the overriding goal of victory.

THE AMERICAN ECONOMY IN WARTIME

Not since the Civil War had the United States been involved in so prolonged and consuming a military experience as World War II. American armed forces engaged in combat around the globe for nearly four years. American society, in the meantime, experienced changes that reached into every corner of the nation.

PROSPERITY AND THE RIGHTS OF LABOR

World War II had a profound impact on American domestic life by ending the Great Depression. By the middle of 1941, the economic problems of the 1930s—unemployment, deflation, industrial sluggishness—had vanished before the great wave of wartime industrial expansion.

The most important catalyst of the new prosperity was government spending, which after 1939 was pumping more money into the economy each year than   *Massive Government Spending* had all the New Deal relief agencies combined. In 1939, the federal budget had been $9 billion, the highest in American peacetime history. By 1945, it had risen to $100 billion. Largely as a result, the gross national product soared: from $91 billion in 1939 to $166 billion in 1945. Personal incomes in some regions grew by as much as 100 percent or more.

The West Coast, naturally, became the launching point for the war against Japan, and the government created large manufacturing facilities in California and elsewhere to serve the needs of the military. Altogether, the government made almost $40 billion worth of wartime capital investments (factories, military and transportation facilities, highways, power plants) in the West, more than in any other region. By the end of the war, the Pacific Coast had become the center of a growing American aircraft industry and an important shipbuilding center. Los Angeles, formerly a medium-sized city notable chiefly for its film industry, now became a major industrial center as well.

The war created a serious labor shortage. The armed forces took more than 16 million men and women out of the civilian workforce at the same time that the demand for labor was rising rapidly. Nevertheless, the supply of workers increased by almost 20 percent during the war—largely through the employment of many people previously considered inappropriate for the workforce: individuals who were very young or elderly, minorities, and, most important, several million women.

The war gave a substantial boost to union membership, which rose from about 10.5 million in 1941 to over 13 million in 1945. That was in part a result of labor's "maintenance-of-membership" agreement with the government,   *Union Membership Boosted* which ensured that the thousands of new workers pouring into unionized defense plants would be automatically enrolled in the unions. But the government also managed to win two important concessions from union leaders. One was the "no-strike" pledge, by which unions agreed not to stop production in wartime. Another was the so-called Little Steel formula, which set a 15 percent limit on wage increases.

Despite the no-strike pledge, nearly 15,000 work stoppages took place during the war, mostly wildcat strikes (strikes not authorized by the union leadership). When the United Mine Workers defied the government by striking in May 1943, Congress reacted by passing, over Roosevelt's veto, the Smith-Connally Act (the War Labor Disputes Act), which required that unions wait thirty days before striking and which empowered the president to seize a struck war plant. In the meantime, public animosity toward labor rose rapidly, and some states passed laws to limit union power.

STABILIZING THE BOOM AND MOBILIZING PRODUCTION

The fear of deflation, the central concern of the 1930s, gave way during the war to a fear of inflation, particularly after prices rose 25 percent in the two years before Pearl Harbor. *The Office of Price Administration*   Fighting inflation was the task of the Office of Price Administration (OPA), which helped moderate what had been a serious problem during World War I. Even so, the agency was never popular. Black-marketing and overcharging grew in proportions far beyond OPA's policing capacity.

From 1941 to 1945, the federal government spent a total of $321 billion—twice as much as it had spent in the entire 150 years of its existence as a nation to that point, and ten times as much as the cost of World War I. The national debt rose from $49 billion in 1941 to $259 billion in 1945. The government borrowed about half the revenues it needed by selling $100 billion worth of bonds. Much of the rest it raised by radically increasing income-tax rates, through the Revenue Act of 1942. To simplify collection, Congress enacted a withholding system of payroll deductions in 1943.

In January 1942, to mobilize the wartime economy, the president created the War Production Board (WPB). Throughout its troubled history, the WPB was never able to win complete control over military purchases; the army and navy often circumvented the board. Nor was it able to satisfy the complaints of small business, which charged (correctly) that most contracts went to large corporations. Gradually, the president transferred much of the WPB's authority to a new office located within the White House: the Office of War Mobilization (OWM). But the OWM was only slightly more successful than the WPB.

Despite the administrative problems, however, the war economy managed to meet almost all of the nation's critical war needs. By the beginning of 1944, American factories were, in fact, producing more than the government needed. Their output was twice that of all the Axis countries combined.

WARTIME SCIENCE AND TECHNOLOGY

More than any previous American war, World War II was a watershed for technological and scientific innovation. That was so partly because the American government poured substantial funds into research and development beginning in 1940. In that year, *Government Financing of Research*   the government created the National Defense Research Committee (which later became the Office of Scientific Research and Development). By the end of the war, the new agency had spent more than $100 million on research, more than four times the amount spent by the government on military research and development in the previous forty years.

In the first years of the war, all the technological advantages seemed to lie with the Germans and Japanese. Germany had made great advances in tanks and other mechanized armor in the 1930s, particularly during the Spanish Civil War, when it had helped arm Franco's forces. German submarine technology surpassed British and American capabilities in 1940. Japan had developed extraordinary capacity in its naval–air technology, as indicated by the successful raid on Pearl Harbor.

But Britain and America had advantages of their own. American techniques of mass production—the great automotive assembly lines in particular—were converted efficiently to military production in 1941 and 1942 and soon began producing airplanes, ships, tanks, and other armaments in much greater numbers than could the Germans and Japanese. Allied scientists and engineers moved quickly as well to improve Anglo-American aviation and naval technology, particularly submarines and tanks. By late 1942, Allied weaponry was at least as advanced as, and more plentiful than, that of the enemy. The Allies likewise enjoyed superiority in radar technology and developed effective naval mine detection systems.

Anglo-American antiaircraft technology—both on land and on sea—also improved, but never to the point where it could defeat bombing raids altogether. Germany made substantial advances in the development of rocket technology in the early years of the war and managed to launch some rocket-propelled bombs (the V1s and V2s) across the English Channel, aimed at London. The psychological effects of the rockets on the British people were considerable. But the Germans were never able to create a production technology capable of building enough such rockets to make a real difference in the balance of military power.

Beginning in 1942, British and American forces seized the advantage in the air war by producing new and powerful four-engine bombers in great numbers. At higher altitudes and with new navigation systems, they were able to conduct extensive bombing missions over Germany (and, later, Japan) with much less danger of being shot down. *Long-Range Bombing* The Allies also benefited from a radio device that sent a sonic message to airplanes to tell them when they were within 20 yards of their targets, first introduced in December 1942.

The area in which the Allies had perhaps the greatest advantage was the gathering of intelligence, much of it through Britain's top-secret Ultra project. Some of the advantages the Allies enjoyed came from the capture of German and Japanese intelligence devices. More important, however, were the efforts of cryptologists, or code breakers. Much of Germany's coded communication made use of the so-called Enigma machine, which constantly changed the coding systems it used. In the first months of the war, Polish intelligence had developed an electromechanical computer. It was called the "Bombe," and it could decipher some Enigma messages. After the fall of Poland, British scientists, led by the brilliant computer pioneer Alan Turing, took the Bombe and greatly improved it. On April 15, 1940, the new, improved high-speed Bombe deciphered a series of German messages within hours (not days, as had previously been the case). A few weeks later, it began decrypting German messages at the rate of 1,000 a day, providing the British (and, later, the Americans) with a constant flow of information about enemy operations throughout the war. British scientists working for the intelligence services, meanwhile, built the first real programmable, digital computer—the Colossus II, which became *The Colossus II* operational less than a week before the beginning of the Normandy invasion and which could decipher an enormous number of intercepted German messages almost instantly. The United States similarly developed the ability to crack a Japanese coding system.

RACE AND ETHNICITY IN WARTIME AMERICA

The war loosened many traditional barriers that had restricted the lives of minorities and women. There was so much demand for fighting men, so much demand for labor, and so much fluidity and mobility that the social and cultural barriers could not survive intact.

African Americans and the War

In the summer of 1941, A. Philip Randolph, president of the mostly African American Brotherhood of Sleeping Car Porters Union, began to insist that the *A. Philip Randolph* government require companies receiving defense contracts to integrate their workforces.

To mobilize support for the demand, Randolph planned a massive march on Washington. The threat led Roosevelt to promise to establish what became the Fair Employment Practices Commission (FEPC) to investigate discrimination against African Americans in war industries.

The need for labor in war plants greatly increased the migration of African Americans from the rural South into industrial cities. The migration improved the economic conditions *Wartime Race Riots* of many African Americans. But it also created urban tensions and occasional violence. A terrible race riot in Detroit in 1943 killed thirty-four people, twenty-five of them black.

Despite such tensions, leading black organizations redoubled their efforts to challenge segregation. The Congress of Racial Equality (CORE), organized in 1942, mobilized mass popular resistance to discrimination in a way that the older, more conservative organizations had never done. Randolph, Bayard Rustin, James Farmer, and other, younger African American leaders helped organize sit-ins and demonstrations in segregated theaters and *CORE* restaurants. CORE also organized "Freedom Rides" to desegregate buses and bus terminals. Though often unsuccessful, these efforts strengthened a culture of civil rights activism in the black community.

Pressure for change also grew within the military. The armed forces maintained their traditional practice of limiting African Americans to the most menial assignments, keeping them in segregated training camps and units, and barring them entirely from the Marine Corps and the Army Air Force. But there were signs of change. By the end of the war, the number of black servicemen had increased sevenfold, to 700,000; some training camps were being at least partially integrated. African Americans were allowed to serve on ships with white sailors, and more black units were sent into combat. The changes did not come easily. In some of the partially integrated army bases—Fort Dix, New Jersey, for example—riots broke out when black soldiers protested mistreatment and segregation.

Native Americans and the War

Approximately 25,000 Indians served in the military during World War II. Many Native Americans saw combat. Others (mostly Navajo) became military "code talkers," speak-*Navajo "Code Talkers"* ing their own language (which enemy forces would be unlikely to understand) over the radio and the telephones. The war had important effects on the Indians who served in the military. It brought them into intimate contact (often for the first time) with white society, and it awakened among some of them a taste for the material benefits of life in capitalist America that they would retain after the war. Some never returned to the reservations but chose to remain in the non-Indian world and assimilate to its ways.

The war had important effects, too, on the Native Americans who stayed on the reservations. Little war work reached the tribes. Government subsidies dwindled. Talented young people left the reservations to serve in the military or work in war production, creating workforce shortages in some tribes. The wartime emphasis on national unity undermined support for the revitalization of tribal autonomy that the Indian Reorganization Act of 1934 had launched. New pressures emerged to eliminate the reservation system and to require the tribes to assimilate into white society. The pressures were so severe that John Collier, the energetic director of the Bureau of Indian Affairs who had done so much to promote the reinvigoration of the reservations, resigned in 1945.

MEXICAN AMERICAN WAR WORKERS

Large numbers of Mexican workers entered the United States in response to wartime labor shortages on the Pacific Coast and in the Southwest. The American and Mexican governments agreed in 1942 to a program by which *braceros* (contract laborers)   Braceros Program would be admitted to the United States for a limited time. Some worked as migrant farm laborers, but many Mexicans were able for the first time to find factory jobs. They formed the second-largest group of migrants (after African Americans) to U.S. cities in the 1940s. They concentrated mainly in the West but established significant Mexican communities in Chicago, Detroit, and other industrial cities.

The sudden expansion of Mexican American neighborhoods created tensions and occasional conflict. Anglo residents of Los Angeles became alarmed at the activities of Mexican American teenagers, many of whom joined street gangs (*pachucos*). The Mexican American youths were particularly distinctive because of their style of dress. At a time when fabric had been rationed for the war effort, they wore long, loose jackets with padded shoulders, baggy pants tied at the ankles, long watch chains, broad-brimmed hats, and greased, ducktail hairstyles. The outfit was known as a "zoot suit." In June 1943,   Zoot Suits animosity toward the "zoot-suiters"—driven partly by ethnic prejudice and partly by the apparent disregard of rationing—produced a four-day riot in Los Angeles. Anglo sailors in Long Beach invaded Mexican American communities and attacked zoot-suiters. The police did little to restrain the sailors, who grabbed Hispanic teenagers, tore off and burned their clothes, cut off their ducktails, and beat them. When Mexicans tried to fight back, the police moved in and arrested them. In the aftermath of the "zoot-suit riots," Los Angeles passed a law prohibiting zoot suits.

THE INTERNMENT OF JAPANESE AMERICANS

World War II produced considerable animosity toward the Japanese. After the attack on Pearl Harbor, government propaganda and popular culture combined to create an image of the Japanese as a devious, malign, and savage people. (See "Consider the Source: The Face of the Enemy.")

This racial animosity soon extended to Americans of Japanese descent. There were not many Japanese Americans in the United States—about 127,000, most of them concentrated in a few areas in California. About one-third were unnaturalized first-generation immigrants (Issei); two-thirds were naturalized or native-born citizens of the United States (Nisei). Because they generally kept to themselves and preserved traditional Japanese cultural patterns, it was easy for Anglo Americans to imagine (wrongly) that the Japanese Americans were engaged in conspiracies on behalf of their ancestral homeland.

In February 1942, in response to pressure from military officials and political leaders on the West Coast (including California attorney general Earl Warren) and recommendations from the War Department, the president authorized the army to "intern" the Japanese Americans. More than 100,000 people (Issei and Nisei alike) were rounded up, told to dispose of their property however they could (which often meant simply abandoning it), and taken to what the government euphemistically called "relocation   *"Relocation Centers"* centers." In fact, they were facilities little different from prisons, many of them located in the western mountains and desert. A group of innocent people (many of them citizens of the United States) were forced to spend up to three years in grim, debilitating isolation, barred from lucrative employment, provided with only minimal medical care, and deprived of decent schools for their children. The Supreme Court upheld the evacuation in the 1944

THE FACE OF THE ENEMY

During World War II, illustrators used caricature, symbolism, exaggeration, and juxtaposition to mobilize public opinion and behavior. The Japanese were frequent objects of such representation. Early in the war, an artist working under the auspices of the Work Projects Administration (WPA, formerly the Works Progress Administration) produced the poster, "Salvage Scrap to Blast the Jap." The second image, Arthur Szyk's cover for *Collier's* magazine in December 1942, depicts the Japanese prime minister Hideki Tojo.

UNDERSTAND, ANALYZE, & EVALUATE

1. The Americans and Japanese are represented by different animals in the WPA poster. What do those choices suggest about how people in the United States viewed the character of the two nations?
2. What event is artist Arthur Szyk depicting in the cartoon on the *Collier's* cover? What evidence can you find in the cartoon to support your choice?

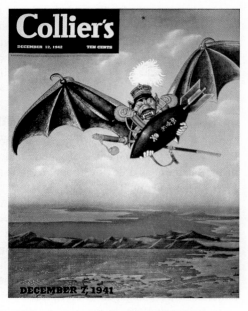

U.S. NAVY POSTER "SALVAGE SCRAP TO BLAST THE JAP" (The Library of Congress)

ARTHUR SZYK, *COLLIER'S* COVER, DECEMBER 12, 1942 (© Private Collection/Peter Newark Military Pictures/Bridgeman Images/Reproduced with the cooperation of The Arthur Szyk Society, Burlingame, CA; www.syzk.org)

Korematsu decision; and although most of the Japanese Americans were released later that year, they were unable to win any significant compensation for their   Korematsu v. U.S. losses until Congress finally acted in the late 1980s.

CHINESE AMERICANS AND THE WAR

At the same time that the war undermined the position of Japanese Americans, the American alliance with China during World War II significantly enhanced both the legal and social status of Chinese Americans. In 1943, partly to improve relations with the government of China, Congress repealed the Chinese Exclusion Act, which had barred almost all Chinese immigration since its renewal in 1892. The new quota for Chinese immigrants was minuscule (105 a year), but a substantial number of Chinese women managed to gain entry into the country through other provisions covering war brides and fiancées. Over 4,000 Chinese women entered the United States in the first three years after the war. Permanent residents of Chinese descent were finally permitted to become citizens.

Racial animosity toward the Chinese did not disappear, but it did decline—in part because government propaganda and popular culture both began presenting positive images of the Chinese (in some measure to contrast them with the Japanese) and in part because Chinese Americans (like African Americans and other previously marginal groups) began taking jobs in war plants and other booming areas suffering from labor shortages. A higher proportion of Chinese Americans (22 percent of all adult males) was drafted than that of any other national group, and the entire Chinese community in most cities worked hard and conspicuously for the war effort.

ANXIETY AND AFFLUENCE IN WARTIME CULTURE

The war created considerable anxiety in American lives. Families worried about loved ones at the front, and as the war continued, many mourned relatives who had died in combat. Women struggled to support families in the absence of husbands and fathers. Businesses and communities struggled with shortages of goods and labor. People living on the two coasts, in particular, worried about enemy invasions and sabotage.

But the abundance of the war years also created a striking buoyancy in American life. Suddenly people had money to spend again and—despite the many shortages—at least some things to spend it on. In fact, consumerism became, as it had in   *Consumerism Reborn* the 1920s, one of the most powerful forces in American culture.

HOME-FRONT LIFE AND CULTURE

As part of the consumerist resurgence of the war years, Americans spent millions of dollars and hours on entertainment and leisure. Audiences equal to about half the nation's population attended movies each week. Radio ownership increased, and pictorial magazines such as *Life* flourished. Dance halls were packed with young people drawn to the seductive music of bands. Soldiers and sailors home on leave, or awaiting shipment abroad, were special fans of the dances, which became to many of them a symbol of the life they were leaving and fighting to protect. The most popular music was the relatively new jazz form known as swing, which had emerged from the African American musical imagination. Bandleaders such as Benny Goodman and Duke Ellington were among the

most recognized figures in American popular culture, rivaling movie stars, and they sometimes hired black musicians to join their groups.

Much of what Americans read, heard, and saw during the war was managed by the
government and military. At the center of the government's propaganda effort was the
The Office of War Information   Office of War Information (OWI). The OWI issued posters, ran
magazine advertisements, and produced films. These materials urged ordinary Americans
to do their part—buy war bonds, conserve household resources, keep quiet about troop
movements.

Government and military officials, meanwhile, censored the reports that journalists
filed from the war zone. Correspondents happily refrained from printing anything that
might compromise military strategy or effectiveness—they wanted the United States to
win too, after all. But Roosevelt and others also believed that gory or depressing war news
would sap the public's will, especially in the first two years of the war. It wasn't until
September 1943 that officials allowed an image of American dead to appear in print.
Federal officials had changed their minds, deciding that slightly more graphic war coverage would awaken a public growing complacent about the sacrifices being made on
its behalf.

Hollywood films about the war—and there were hundreds of them—offered a relatively
The Celluloid War   sanitized picture of the conflict. Whether of their own volition or in
consultation with military officials, movie producers usually offered a picture of the soldier in line with journalistic reports and government propaganda. In many "platoon films,"
death came quickly and without blood and guts. Soldiers behaved courageously, missed
home, and found maturity (rather than breakdown) through combat. Blacks didn't typically
appear in these platoons—true to the reality of a Jim Crow army—but many other white
ethnic groups did. In fact, a central point of many wartime pictures, as well as OWI
propaganda posters, was that Jews, Polish Americans, Italian Americans, and other groups
largely barred by the 1924 immigration restriction had become assimilated contributors
to the American military machine.

The upshot of all this was a wartime popular culture saturated with combat imagery
but which kept some of the worst realities of war obscured. This frustrated one of the
central figures in the project of wartime information management. The beloved war correspondent Ernie Pyle, a popular and honest chronicler of the American GI before an
audience of millions, believed that no one at home had really *seen* the war. After a
Japanese sniper killed Pyle in April 1945, American soldiers found an unfinished column
in his pocket. "You didn't see him lying so grotesque and pasty beside the gravel road
in France," he wrote of the generic dead soldier. "We saw him, saw him by the multiple
thousands. That's the difference."

LOVE, FAMILY, AND SEXUALITY IN WARTIME

For men at the front, the image of home both served as a motivational symbol and helped
soften the rigors of combat. Letters and mementos from loved ones sustained the morale
of millions of service members. They dreamed of music, food, movies, and other material
comforts. Many also dreamed of women—wives and girlfriends, but also movie stars and
entertainers, who became the source of one of the most popular icons of the front: the
pinup. Sailors pasted pinups inside their lockers. Infantrymen carried them (along with
pictures of wives, mothers, and girlfriends) in their knapsacks. Fighter pilots gave their
planes female names and painted bathing beauties on their nose cones.

For the servicemen who remained in America, and for soldiers and sailors in cities far from home in particular, the company of friendly, "wholesome" women was, the military believed, critical to sustaining morale. The branches of the United Service Organization (known as USOs) recruited thousands of young women to serve as *Importance of USOs* hostesses in their clubs. They were expected to dress nicely, dance well, and chat happily with lonely men. Other women joined "dance brigades," traveling by bus to military bases for social evenings with servicemen. The "USO girls" and the members of the dance brigades were forbidden to have any contact with men except at parties at the clubs or during dances. Clearly, such regulations were often violated. The military took elaborate measures to root out gay men and lesbians from their ranks—vigilantly searching for evidence of homosexuality and unceremoniously dismissing gay people with undesirable discharges. The services quietly tolerated illicit heterosexual relationships, which they believed were temporary, natural, and, for many men, necessary.

Wartime families also experienced change. The number of women in the workforce increased by nearly 60 percent during the war, as many women replaced male industrial workers serving in the military. These new wage-earning women were likely to be married and were, on the whole, older than most who had entered the workforce in the past.

Many factory owners continued to categorize jobs by gender, reserving the most lucrative positions for men. (Female work, like male work, was also categorized by race: black women

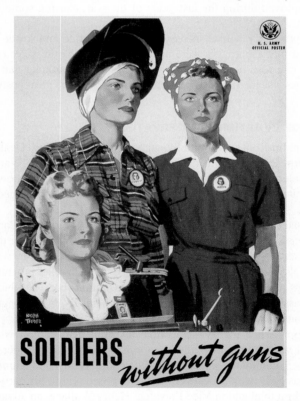

WOMEN AT WAR   Many American women enlisted in the army and navy women's corps during World War II, but an equally important contribution to the war effort was their work in factories and offices—often in jobs that would have been considered inappropriate for them in peacetime but that they were now encouraged to assume because of the absence of so many men. (The Library of Congress)

were usually assigned more menial tasks, and paid at a lower rate, than their white counterparts.) But some women began to take on heavy industrial jobs that had long been considered *"Rosie the Riveter"* "men's work." The famous wartime image of "Rosie the Riveter" symbolized the new importance of the female industrial worker. Women joined unions in substantial numbers and helped erode at least some of the prejudice, including the prejudice against mothers working, that had previously kept many of them from paid employment.

Most women workers during the war, however, were employed not in factories but in service-sector jobs. Above all, they worked for the government, whose bureaucratic needs expanded dramatically alongside its military and industrial needs. Even within the mili- *WAACs and WAVEs* tary, which enlisted substantial numbers of women as WAACs (army) and WAVEs (navy), most female work was clerical.

Many mothers whose husbands were in the military had to combine work with child care. The scarcity of child-care facilities or other community services meant that some women had no choice but to leave young children at home alone (or sometimes locked in cars in factory parking lots) or with relatives or neighbors while they worked.

Perhaps in part because of the family dislocations of the war, juvenile crime rose markedly. Young boys were arrested at increasing rates for car theft, burglary, vandalism, and vagrancy. For many children, however, the distinctive experience of the war years was not crime but work. More than a third of all teenagers between the ages of fourteen and eighteen were employed during the last years of the war, causing some reduction in high school enrollments.

The return of prosperity helped increase the marriage rate and lower the age at which people married, but many marriages were unable to survive the pressures of wartime separation. The divorce rate rose rapidly. Even so, the rise in the birthrate that accompanied the increase in marriages was the first sign of what would become the great postwar "baby boom."

The Growth of Wartime Conservatism

Late in 1943, Franklin Roosevelt publicly suggested that "Dr. New Deal," as he called it, had served its purpose and should now give way to "Dr. Win-the-War." The statement reflected the president's own genuine shift in concern: victory was now more important than reform. But it reflected, too, the political reality that had emerged during the first two years of war.

The greatest assault on New Deal reforms came from conservatives in Congress, who seized on the war as a reason to do what many had wanted to do in peacetime: dismantle many of *Conservative Assault on the New Deal* the achievements of the New Deal. They were assisted by the end of mass unemployment, which decreased the need for such relief programs as the Civilian Conservation Corps and the Works Progress Administration (both of which Congress abolished). They were assisted, too, by their own increasing numbers. In the congressional elections of 1942, Republicans gained 47 seats in the House and 10 in the Senate.

Republicans approached the 1944 election determined to exploit what they believed was resentment of wartime regimentation and unhappiness with Democratic reform. They *Democrats Drop Wallace* nominated as their candidate the young and vigorous governor of New York, Thomas E. Dewey. Roosevelt was unopposed within his party, but Democratic leaders pressured him to abandon Vice President Henry Wallace, an advanced New Dealer and hero of the CIO. Roosevelt agreed to replace him with a more moderate figure, Senator Harry S. Truman of Missouri. Truman had won acclaim as chairman of the Senate War Investigating Committee (known as the Truman Committee), which compiled an impressive record uncovering waste and corruption in wartime production.

The election revolved around domestic economic issues and, indirectly, the president's health. He was, in fact, gravely ill, suffering from, among other things, advanced arteriosclerosis. But the campaign seemed momentarily to revive him. Roosevelt made several strenuous public appearances late in October, which dispelled popular doubts about his health and ensured his reelection. He captured 53.5 percent of the popular   *Roosevelt Reelected* vote to Dewey's 46 percent, and 432 electoral votes to Dewey's 99. Democrats lost 1 seat in the Senate, gained 20 in the House, and maintained control of both.

THE DEFEAT OF THE AXIS

By the middle of 1943, America and its allies had succeeded in stopping the Axis advance in both Europe and the Pacific. In the next two years, the Allies themselves seized the offensive and launched a series of powerful drives that led the way to victory.

WORLD WAR II IN EUROPE: THE ALLIED COUNTEROFFENSIVE, 1943–1945   This map illustrates the final, climactic movements in the war in Europe—the two great offensives against Germany that began in 1943 and culminated in 1945. From the east, the armies of the Soviet Union, having halted the Germans at Stalingrad and Moscow, swept across eastern Europe toward Germany. From the west and the south, American, British, and other Allied forces moved toward Germany through Italy and—after the Normandy invasion in June 1944—through France. The two offensives met in Berlin in May 1945. Note, too, the northern routes that America and Britain used to supply the Soviet Union during the war. • *What problems did the position of the Allied forces at the end of the war help produce?*

THE EUROPEAN OFFENSIVE

By early 1944, American and British bombers were attacking German industrial installations and other targets almost around the clock, drastically cutting production and impeding transportation. A February 1945 incendiary raid on Dresden created a great firestorm that destroyed three-fourths of the previously undamaged city and killed approximately 135,000 people, almost all civilians.

An enormous offensive force had been gathering in England for two years before the spring of 1944: almost 3 million troops and perhaps the greatest array of naval vessels and armaments ever assembled in one place. On the morning of June 6, 1944 (D-Day), *D-Day* this vast invasion force moved into action. The landing came not at the narrowest part of the English Channel, where the Germans had expected and prepared for it, but along sixty miles of the Cotentin Peninsula on the coast of Normandy. While airplanes and battleships offshore bombarded the Nazi defenses, 4,000 vessels landed American, British, Canadian, and other troops and supplies on the beaches. (Three divisions of paratroopers had been dropped chaotically behind the German lines the night before.) Fighting was intense along the beach, but the superior manpower and equipment of the Allied forces gradually prevailed. Within a week, the German forces had been dislodged from virtually the entire Normandy coast.

For the next month, further progress remained slow. But in late July, in the Battle of Saint-Lô, General Omar Bradley's First Army smashed through the German lines. George S. Patton's Third Army, spearheaded by heavy tank attacks, then moved through the hole Bradley had created and began a drive into the heart of France. On August 25, Free French forces arrived in Paris and liberated the city from four years of German occupation. By mid-September the Allied armies had driven the Germans almost entirely out of France and Belgium.

THE NORMANDY INVASION This photograph, taken from a landing craft, shows American troops wading ashore and onto the Normandy beaches, where one of the decisive battles of World War II was taking shape. The invasion was launched despite threatening weather and rough seas. (© Popperfoto/Getty Images)

The great Allied drive came to a halt, however, at the Rhine River against a firm line of Nazi defenses. In mid-December, German forces struck in desperation along fifty miles of front in the Ardennes Forest. In the Battle of the Bulge (named for a *Battle of the Bulge* large bulge that appeared in the American lines as the Germans pressed forward), they drove fifty-five miles toward Antwerp before they were finally stopped at Bastogne. It was the last major battle on the western front.

While the western Allies fought their way through France, Soviet forces swept westward into central Europe and the Balkans. In late January 1945, the Russians launched a great offensive toward the Oder River, inside Germany. By early *Germany Invaded*

AUSCHWITZ, DECEMBER 1944 This photograph, taken near the end of World War II, shows a group of imprisoned children behind a barbed wire fence in one of the most notorious Nazi concentration camps. By the time this picture was taken, the Nazis had been driven out of Auschwitz and were under the control of Allied soldiers. (© Keystone/Getty Images)

spring, they were ready to launch a final assault against Berlin. General Omar Bradley, in the meantime, was pushing toward the Rhine from the west. Early in March, Bradley's forces captured the city of Cologne, on the river's west bank. The next day, they discovered and seized an undamaged bridge over the river at Remagen; Allied troops were soon pouring across the Rhine. In the following weeks, the British commander Montgomery, with a million troops, pushed into Germany in the north while Bradley's army, sweeping through central Germany, completed the encirclement of 300,000 German soldiers in the Ruhr.

The German resistance was now broken on both fronts. American forces were moving eastward faster than they had anticipated and could have beaten the Russians to Berlin and Prague. The American and British high commands decided, instead, to halt the advance along the Elbe River in central Germany to await the Russians. That decision enabled the Soviets to occupy eastern Germany and Czechoslovakia.

On April 30, with Soviet forces on the outskirts of Berlin, Adolf Hitler killed himself in his bunker in the capital. And on May 8, 1945, the remaining German forces surrendered unconditionally.

THE PACIFIC OFFENSIVE

In February 1944, American naval forces under Admiral Chester Nimitz won a series of victories in the Marshall Islands and cracked the outer perimeter of the Japanese Empire. Within a month, the navy had destroyed other vital Japanese bastions. American submarines, in the meantime, were decimating Japanese shipping and crippling Japan's domestic economy.

America's principal ally in Asia was China. To assist the Chinese forces, the army sent General Joseph W. Stilwell to help provide critical supplies to China by a land route through India and across the Himalayas. It was a brutal task, but in the fall of 1944, Stilwell's forces succeeded in constructing a road and pipelines across the mountains into China. More dangerously, the Japanese were also threatening the wartime capital of China in Chungking. Chiang Kai-shek, the Chinese premier, was reluctant to use his troops against the Japanese and seemed more concerned with attacking Chinese communists, who were also fighting the Japanese. After Stilwell left China, his successors continued to have trouble prodding Chiang to confront the Japanese.

The decisive battles of the Pacific war occurred not in China but at sea. In mid-June 1944, an enormous American armada struck the heavily fortified Mariana Islands and, after some of the bloodiest operations of the war, captured Tinian, Guam, and Saipan. On October 20, General MacArthur's troops landed on Leyte Island in the Philippines. The Japanese now employed virtually their entire fleet against the Allied invaders in three major encounters—which together constituted the decisive Battle of Leyte Gulf, the larg-

Battles of Leyte Gulf and Iwo Jima   est naval engagement in history. American forces held off the Japanese onslaught and sank four Japanese carriers, all but destroying Japan's capacity to continue a serious naval war. In February 1945, American marines seized the tiny volcanic island of Iwo Jima, just 750 miles from Tokyo, but only after the costliest battle in the history of the Marine Corps.

The battle for Okinawa, an island only 370 miles south of Japan, gave evidence of the

Okinawa   strength of the Japanese resistance in these last desperate days. Week after week, the Japanese sent kamikaze (suicide) planes against American and British ships, sacrificing

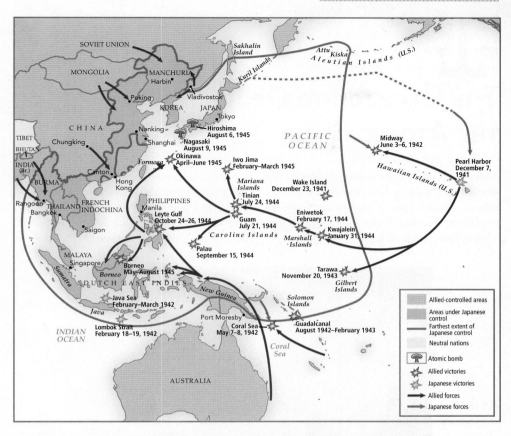

WORLD WAR II IN THE PACIFIC   This map illustrates the changing fortunes of the two combatants in the Pacific phase of World War II. The long red line stretching from Burma around to Manchuria represents the eastern boundary of the vast areas of the Pacific that had fallen under Japanese control by the summer of 1942. The blue lines illustrate the advance of American forces back into the Pacific beginning in May 1942 and accelerating in 1943 and after, which drove back the Japanese forces. The American advance was a result of two separate offensives—one in the central Pacific, under the command of Chester Nimitz, which moved west from Hawaii; and the other, under the command of Douglas MacArthur, which moved north from Australia. By the summer of 1945, American forces were approaching the Japanese mainland and were bombing Tokyo itself. The dropping of two American atomic bombs, on Hiroshima and Nagasaki, finally brought the war to an end.   • *Why did the Soviet Union enter the Pacific war in August 1945, as shown in the upper-left corner of the map?*

3,500 of them while inflicting great damage. Japanese troops on shore launched desperate nighttime attacks on the American lines. The United States and its allies suffered nearly 50,000 casualties before finally capturing Okinawa in late June 1945. Over 100,000 Japanese died in the siege.

It seemed likely that the same kind of bitter fighting would await the Americans when they invaded Japan. But there were also some signs early in 1945 that such an invasion might not be necessary. The Japanese had almost no ships or planes left with which to fight. The firebombing of Tokyo in March, in which American bombers   *Tokyo Firebombed* dropped napalm on the city and created a firestorm in which over 80,000 people died,

THE DECISION TO DROP THE ATOMIC BOMB

There has been continuing disagreement since 1945 among historians—and many others—about how to explain and evaluate President Truman's decision to use the atomic bomb against Japan.

Truman himself, both at the time and in his 1955 memoirs, insisted that the decision was a simple and straightforward one. The alternative to using atomic weapons, he claimed, was an American invasion of

NAGASAKI SURVIVORS   A Japanese woman and child look grimly at a photographer as they hold pieces of bread in the aftermath of the dropping of the second American atomic bomb—this one on Nagasaki. (© Bettmann/Corbis)

mainland Japan that might have cost as many as a million American lives. That view has received considerable support from historians. Herbert Feis argued in *The Atomic Bomb and the End of World War II* (1966) that Truman made his decision on purely military grounds—to ensure a speedy American victory. David McCullough, the author of a popular biography of Truman published in 1992, also accepted Truman's own account of his actions largely uncritically, as did Alonzo L. Hamby in *Man of the People* (1995), an important scholarly study of Truman. "One consideration weighed most heavily on Truman," Hamby concluded. "The longer the war lasted, the more Americans killed."

Others have strongly disagreed. As early as 1948, British physicist P. M. S. Blackett wrote in *Fear, War, and the Bomb* that the destruction of Hiroshima and Nagasaki was "not so much the last military act of the second World War as the first major operation of the cold diplomatic war with Russia." The most important critic of Truman's decision is the historian Gar Alperovitz, the author of two influential books on the subject: *Atomic Diplomacy: Hiroshima and Potsdam* (1965) and *The Decision to Use the Atomic Bomb* (1995). Alperovitz dismissed the argument that the bomb was used to shorten the war and save lives. Japan was likely to have surrendered soon even if the bomb had not been used, he claimed. Instead, he argued, the United States used

the bomb less to influence Japan than to intimidate the Soviet Union, "to make Russia more manageable in Europe."

John W. Dower's *War Without Mercy* (1986) contributed, by implication at least, to another controversial explanation of the American decision: racism. The Japanese, many Americans came to believe during the war, were almost a subhuman species. Even many of Truman's harshest critics, however, note that it is, as Alperovitz has written, "all but impossible to find specific evidence that racism was an important factor in the decision to attack Hiroshima and Nagasaki."

The debate over the decision to drop the atomic bomb is an unusually emotional one, and it has inspired bitter professional and personal attacks on advocates of almost every position. It illustrates clearly how history has often been, and remains, a powerful force in the way societies define themselves. •

UNDERSTAND, ANALYZE, & EVALUATE

1. The United States dropped two atomic bombs on Japan, one on Hiroshima and the other on Nagasaki. Was dropping the bomb on Hiroshima necessary? Was it justifiable? Do the reasons for dropping the bomb on Hiroshima apply equally to the bombing of Nagasaki?
2. How might the war in the Pacific have been different if the United States had decided not to drop the bombs?

further weakened the Japanese will to resist. Moderate Japanese leaders, who had long since concluded the war was lost, were looking to end the fighting. But they continued to face powerful opposition from military leaders. Whether the moderates could ultimately have prevailed is a question historians continue to debate. In any case, their efforts became superfluous in August 1945, when the United States made use of a terrible new weapon it had been developing throughout the war.

THE MANHATTAN PROJECT AND ATOMIC WARFARE

Reports had reached the United States in 1939 that Nazi scientists had taken the first step toward the creation of an atomic bomb, a weapon more powerful than any previously devised. The United States and Britain immediately began a race to develop the weapon before the Germans did.

The search for the new weapon emerged from theories developed by atomic physicists, beginning early in the century, and particularly from some of the founding ideas of modern physics developed by Albert Einstein. Einstein's famous theory of relativity had revealed that matter could be converted into a tremendous force of energy. Einstein himself, who by then had left his native Germany and was living in the United States, warned Franklin Roosevelt of German interest in atomic weapons.

By the late 1930s and early 1940s, scientists at American universities were working to catch up with the Germans. Soon after the United States entered the war, the army took over the research and named it the Manhattan Project, because it was devised in the Manhattan Engineer District Office of the Army Corps of Engineers. Over the next three years, the government secretly poured nearly $2 billion into a massive scientific and technological effort conducted at hidden laboratories in Oak Ridge, Tennessee; Los Alamos, New Mexico; Hanford, Washington; and other sites. Scientists in Oak Ridge, who were charged with finding a way to create a nuclear chain reaction that could be feasibly replicated within the confined space of a bomb, began experimenting with plutonium—a derivative of uranium first discovered by scientists at University of California–Berkeley. Plutonium proved capable of providing a practical fuel for the weapon. Scientists in Los Alamos, under the direction of J. Robert Oppenheimer, were charged with the construction of the actual atomic bomb.

By 1944, despite many unforeseen problems, the Manhattan Project scientists pushed ahead much faster than anyone had predicted. Even so, the war in Europe ended before they were ready to test the first weapon. Just before dawn on July 16, 1945, in the desert *Atomic Test in New Mexico* near Alamogordo, New Mexico, the scientists gathered to witness the first atomic explosion in history: the detonation of a plutonium-fueled bomb that scientists had named Trinity. The explosion—a blinding flash of light, perhaps brighter than any ever before seen on earth, followed by a huge, billowing mushroom cloud— created a vast crater in the barren desert. Watching the test, Oppenheimer was reminded of a passage from a Hindu scripture: "I am become death, the destroyer of worlds."

News of the explosion reached President Harry S. Truman (who had taken office in April on the death of Roosevelt) in Potsdam, Germany, where he was attending a conference of Allied leaders. He issued an ultimatum to the Japanese (signed jointly by the British), demanding that they surrender by August 3 or face utter devastation. When the Japanese failed to meet the deadline, Truman ordered the air force to use the new atomic weapons against Japan.

Controversy has continued for decades over whether Truman's decision to use the bombs was justified and what his motives were. Some have argued that the atomic attack was unnecessary—that had the United States agreed to the survival of the emperor before the bombs were used (which it ultimately did agree to after the bombings), or had it waited only a few more weeks, the Japanese would have surrendered. Others argue that nothing less than the atomic bombs could have persuaded the Japanese to surrender without a costly American invasion. (See "Debating the Past: The Decision to Drop the Atomic Bomb.")

Most of the nation's military and political leaders, however, seemed little concerned about such matters. Truman, who had not even known of the existence of the Manhattan Project until he became president, made what he apparently believed to be a simple military decision. A weapon was available that would end the war quickly; he could see no reason not to use it.

On August 6, 1945, an American B-29, the *Enola Gay,* dropped an atomic weapon on *Hiroshima Destroyed* the Japanese industrial center at Hiroshima. With a single bomb, the United States completely incinerated a four-square-mile area at the center of the previously undamaged city. More than 80,000 civilians died, according to later American estimates.

Many more suffered the crippling effects of radioactive fallout or passed those effects on to their children in the form of birth defects.

The Japanese government, stunned by the attack, was at first unable to agree on a response. Two days later, on August 8, the Soviet Union declared war on Japan. And the following day, another American plane dropped another atomic weapon—this time on the city of Nagasaki—inflicting 100,000 deaths and terrible damage on yet another unfortunate community. Finally, the emperor intervened to break the   *Second Bomb and Surrender* stalemate in the cabinet, and on August 14 the government announced that it was ready to give up. On September 2, 1945, on board the American battleship *Missouri,* anchored in Tokyo Bay, Japanese officials signed the articles of surrender.

The most destructive war in human history had come to an end, and the United States had emerged from it not only victorious but also in a position of unprecedented power, influence, and prestige. It was a victory, however, that few could greet with unambiguous joy. Fourteen million combatants had died in the struggle. As many as 50 million or more civilians may have perished, making World War II by far the deadliest war in history. The United States had suffered only light casualties in comparison with some other nations (and particularly in comparison with Russia and Germany), but the cost had still been high: more than 400,000 dead, almost 700,000 injured. And the world continued to face an uncertain future, menaced by the threat of nuclear warfare and by an emerging antagonism between the world's two strongest nations—the United States and the Soviet Union—that would darken the peace for many decades to come.

CONCLUSION

The United States played a critical, indeed decisive, role in the war against Germany and Italy. It defeated Imperial Japan in the Pacific largely alone. But America's contributions to and sacrifices in the war paled next to those of its most important allies. Britain, France, and, above all, the Soviet Union paid a staggering price—in lives, treasure, and social unity—that had no counterpart in the United States. Most American citizens in the United States experienced a booming prosperity and only modest privations during the four years of American involvement in the conflict. There were, of course, jarring social changes during the war that even prosperity could not entirely offset: shortages, restrictions, regulations, family dislocations, and, perhaps most of all, the absence of millions of men and considerable numbers of women, who went overseas to fight.

American fighting men and women, of course, had very different experiences from those of the people who remained at home. They endured tremendous hardships, substantial casualties, and much fear and loneliness. They fought effectively and bravely. They helped liberate North Africa and Italy from German occupation. And in June 1944, finally, they joined British, French, and other forces in a great and successful invasion of France. It led less than a year later to the destruction of the Nazi regime and the end of the European war. In the Pacific, Americans turned back the Japanese offensive through a series of difficult naval and land battles. Ultimately, however, it was not the American army and navy that brought the war against Japan to a close. It was the unleashing of the most destructive weapon ever created—the atomic bomb—on the people of Japan that finally persuaded the leaders of that nation to surrender.

KEY TERMS/PEOPLE/PLACES/EVENTS

A. Philip Randolph 635
Battle of the Bulge 645
braceros 637
Colossus II 635
Congress of Racial Equality
  (CORE) 636
D-Day 644
Dwight D. Eisenhower 630

Guadalcanal 630
Harry S. Truman 650
Hiroshima 650
Holocaust 631
Korematsu v. U.S. 639
Manhattan Project 650
Office of Price Administration
  (OPA) 634

Office of War Information
  (OWI) 640
Okinawa 646
relocation centers 637
Rosie the Riveter 642
United Service Organization
  (USO) 641
zoot suits 637

RECALL AND REFLECT

1. List some of the measures that the federal government took to mobilize the nation for the war effort.
2. How did advances in technology affect the course of the military conflict?
3. How did the United States contribute to the Allied victory in Europe? How important were America's allies? Which allies were most important?
4. How did the war affect U.S. society—women, workers, African Americans, Japanese Americans, and immigrants?
5. Why did the United States bomb civilians in Japan and Europe in the last years of the war?

27 | THE COLD WAR

ORIGINS OF THE COLD WAR
THE COLLAPSE OF THE PEACE
AMERICA AFTER THE WAR
THE KOREAN WAR
THE CRUSADE AGAINST SUBVERSION

LOOKING AHEAD

1. What made the growing tension between the United States and the Soviet Union evolve into the Cold War?

2. What is the theory of containment, and how did it drive U.S. foreign policy and foreign interventions in the postwar era?

3. Why did the U.S. government and the American people believe that there was a threat of internal communist subversion?

EVEN BEFORE WORLD WAR II ENDED, there were signs of tension between the United States and the Soviet Union. Once the fighting was over, those tensions grew to create what became known as the "Cold War"—a long and dangerous rivalry between the two former allies that would cast its shadow over international affairs and American domestic life for more than four decades.

The Cold War took shape gradually over a five-year period, during which the relationship between the United States and the Soviet Union deteriorated and the United States crafted a new structure for American foreign policy—known as "containment"—that sought to keep communism from expanding.

ORIGINS OF THE COLD WAR

Few issues in twentieth-century American history have aroused more debate than the origins of the Cold War. Some have claimed that Soviet duplicity and expansionism created the international tensions; others, that American provocations and global ambitions were at least equally to blame. (See "Debating the Past: The Cold War.")

SOURCES OF SOVIET–AMERICAN TENSION

At the heart of the rivalry between the United States and the Soviet Union in the 1940s—in addition to the basic ideological, economic, and political distinctions between the two societies—was a fundamental difference in the ways the great powers envisioned the postwar world. One vision, first openly outlined in the Atlantic Charter in 1941, was a world in which nations abandoned their traditional beliefs in military alliances and spheres of influence and governed their relations with one another through democratic processes, with an international organization serving as the arbiter of disputes and the protector of every nation's right of self-determination. At least in theory, that vision appealed to many Americans, including Franklin Roosevelt.

The other vision was that of the Soviet Union and, to some extent, Great Britain. Both Josef Stalin and Winston Churchill had signed the Atlantic Charter. But Churchill had always been uneasy about the implications of self-determination for Britain's own enormous empire. And the Soviet Union was determined to create a secure sphere for itself in Central and Eastern Europe as protection against possible future aggression from the West. Both Churchill and Stalin, therefore, tended to envision a postwar structure vaguely similar to the traditional European balance of power, in which the great powers would control areas of strategic interest to them. The United States, for its part, soon labored to establish and protect its own spheres of interest around the globe. When the two sides competed for influence and power in this way, the Cold War began.

WARTIME DIPLOMACY

Serious strains began to develop in the alliance with the Soviet Union in January 1943, when Roosevelt and Churchill met in Casablanca, Morocco, to discuss Allied strategy. The two leaders could not accept Stalin's most important demand—the immediate opening of a second front in Western Europe. But they tried to reassure Stalin by announcing that they would accept nothing less than the unconditional surrender of the Axis powers. They would not negotiate a separate peace with Hitler and leave the Soviets to fight on alone.

In November 1943, Roosevelt and Churchill traveled to Tehran, Iran, for their first meeting with Stalin. By now, however, Roosevelt's most effective bargaining tool— Stalin's need for American assistance against Germany—had been largely removed. The German advance against Russia had been halted; Soviet forces were now launching their own westward offensive. Nevertheless, the Tehran Conference seemed in *Tehran Conference* most respects a success. Stalin agreed to an American request that the Soviet Union enter the war in the Pacific soon after the end of hostilities in Europe. Roosevelt, in turn, promised that an Anglo-American second front would be established within six months.

On other matters, however, the origins of future disagreements were already visible. Most important was the question of Poland. Roosevelt and Churchill were willing to agree to a movement of the Soviet border westward, allowing Stalin to annex some historically Polish territory. But they differed sharply on the nature of the postwar government in the portion of Poland that would remain independent. Roosevelt and Churchill supported the claims of the Polish government-in-exile that had been functioning in London since 1940; Stalin wished to install another, pro-communist exiled government that had spent the war in Lublin, in the Soviet Union. The three leaders left the Tehran Conference with the issue unresolved.

YALTA

More than a year later, in February 1945, Roosevelt joined Churchill and Stalin again, for a peace conference in the Soviet city of Yalta. In return for Stalin's renewed promise to enter the Pacific war, Roosevelt agreed that the Soviet Union should receive some of the Pacific territory that Russia had lost in the 1904–1905 Russo-Japanese War.

The negotiators also agreed to a plan for a new international organization, one that had been hammered out during the previous summer at a conference in Washington, D.C. The new United Nations would contain a General Assembly, in which *United Nations Established* every member would be represented, and a Security Council, with permanent representatives of the five major powers (the United States, Britain, France, the Soviet Union, and China), each of which would have veto power. The Security Council would also have temporary delegates from several other nations. These agreements became the basis of the United Nations charter, drafted at a conference of fifty nations beginning April 25, 1945, in San Francisco. In sharp contrast to the American rejection of the League of Nations a generation before, the United States Senate ratified the charter in July by a vote of 80 to 2. (It was, many internationalists believed, a "second chance" to create a stable world order.)

THE COLD WAR

For more than a decade after the beginning of the Cold War, few historians saw any reason to challenge the official American interpretation of its origins. The breakdown of relations between the United States and the Soviet Union was, most agreed, a direct result of Soviet expansionism and of Stalin's violation of the wartime agreements forged at Yalta and Potsdam. The Soviet imposition of communist regimes in Eastern Europe was part of a larger ideological design to spread communism throughout the world. American policy was the logical and necessary response: a firm commitment to oppose Soviet expansionism and to keep American forces in a continual state of readiness.

Disillusionment with the official justifications for the Cold War began to find expression even in the late 1950s, when anticommunist sentiment in America remained strong and pervasive. William Appleman Williams's *The Tragedy of American Diplomacy* (1959) insisted that the Cold War was simply the most recent version of a consistent American effort in the twentieth century to preserve an "open door" for American trade in world markets. The confrontation with the Soviet Union, he argued, was less a response to Soviet aggressive designs than an expression of the American belief in the necessity of capitalist expansion.

As the Vietnam War grew larger and more unpopular in the 1960s, the scholarly critique of the Cold War quickly gained intensity. Walter LaFeber's *America, Russia, and the Cold War,* first published in 1967, maintained that America's supposedly idealistic internationalism at the close of the war was in reality an effort to ensure a postwar order shaped in the American image—with every nation open to American influence (and to American trade). That was why the United States was so apt to misinterpret Soviet policy, much of which reflected a perfectly reasonable commitment to ensure the security of the Soviet Union itself, as part of a larger aggressive design.

The revisionist interpretations of the Cold War ultimately produced a reaction of their own: what has come to be known as "postrevisionist" scholarship. The most important work in this school attempted to strike a balance between orthodoxy and revisionism and to identify areas of blame and patterns of misconceptions on both sides of the conflict. An important early statement of this approach was John Lewis Gaddis's *The United States and the Cold War, 1941–1947* (1972), which argued that "neither side can bear sole responsibility for the onset of the Cold War." Both sides had limited options, given their own political constraints and their own preconceptions. Other postrevisionist works—by Thomas G. Paterson, Melvyn Leffler, William Taubman, and others—have elaborated on ways in which the United States and the Soviet Union acted in response to genuine, if not necessarily accurate, beliefs about the intentions of the other. "The United States and the Soviet Union were doomed to be antagonists," Ernest May wrote in 1984. "There probably was never any real possibility that the post-1945 relationship could be anything but hostility verging on conflict."

Since the fall of the Soviet Union in 1991, scholars have had access to newly released Russian archives that have enriched—although not fundamentally altered—the way historians view the Cold War. John Lewis

Gaddis, in *We Now Know: Rethinking Cold War History* (1998) and *The Cold War* (2005), portrays a Cold War somewhat more dangerous than his own earlier studies, and those of many other scholars, had portrayed; and he argues that the strong anticommunist positions of Margaret Thatcher, Ronald Reagan, and Pope John Paul II had a larger impact on the weakening of the Soviet Union than was previously understood. Similarly assisted by newly released archives, Odd Arne Westad, in *The Global Cold War* (2005), roots the origins of the dangerous instability in the so-called Third World in the frequent interventions of both the Soviet Union and the United States in the Cold War era. •

UNDERSTAND, ANALYZE, & EVALUATE

1. What are the orthodox, revisionist, and postrevisionist arguments concerning the origins of the Cold War?
2. Was the Cold War inevitable?

On other issues, however, the Yalta Conference produced no real accord. Basic disagreement remained about the postwar Polish government. Stalin, whose armies now occupied Poland, had already installed a government composed of the pro-communist "Lublin" Poles. Roosevelt and Churchill insisted that the pro-Western "London" Poles must be allowed a place in the Warsaw regime. Roosevelt envisioned a government based on free, democratic elections—which both he and Stalin recognized the pro-Western forces would win. Stalin agreed only to a vague compromise by which an unspecified number of pro-Western Poles would be granted a place in the government. He said he would hold "free and unfettered elections" in Poland on an unspecified future date. They did not happen until 1989.

Dispute over Poland

Nor was there agreement about Germany. Roosevelt seemed to want a reconstructed and reunited Germany. Stalin wanted to impose heavy reparations on Germany and to ensure a permanent dismemberment of the nation. The final agreement was, like the Polish accord, vague and unstable. The decision on reparations would be referred to a future commission. The United States, Great Britain, France, and the Soviet Union would each control its own "zone of occupation" in Germany—the zones to be determined by the position of troops at the end of the war. Berlin, the German capital, was

YALTA, 1945   Churchill (*left*) and Stalin (*right*) were shocked at the physical appearance of Franklin Roosevelt (*center*) when he arrived for their critical meeting at Yalta. Roosevelt had enough energy to perform capably at the conference, but he was in fact gravely ill. Two months later, not long after he gave Congress what turned out to be an unrealistically optimistic report of the prospects for postwar peace, he died. (© Bettmann/Corbis)

already well inside the Soviet zone, but because of its symbolic importance, it would itself be divided into four occupied sectors. At an unspecified date, Germany would be reunited. As for the rest of Europe, the conference produced a murky accord on the establishment of governments "broadly representative of all democratic elements" and "responsible to the will of the people."

The Yalta accords, in other words, were less a settlement of postwar issues than a set of loose principles that sidestepped the most difficult questions. Roosevelt, Churchill, and Stalin returned home from the conference, each apparently convinced that he had signed an important agreement. But the Soviet interpretation of the accords differed so sharply from the Anglo-American interpretation that the illusion endured only briefly. In the weeks following the Yalta Conference, Roosevelt watched with growing alarm as the Soviet Union moved systematically to establish pro-communist governments in one *Soviets in Central and Eastern Europe* Central or Eastern European nation after another and as Stalin refused to make the changes in Poland that the president believed Stalin had promised. Still believing the differences could be settled, Roosevelt left Washington early in the spring for a vacation at his retreat in Warm Springs, Georgia. There, on April 12, 1945, he suffered a sudden massive stroke and died.

THE COLLAPSE OF THE PEACE

The new president, Harry S. Truman, had almost no familiarity with international issues. Nor did he share Roosevelt's apparent faith in Soviet flexibility. Truman sided with the many people inside the government who considered the Soviet Union fundamentally untrustworthy and viewed Stalin himself with suspicion and even loathing.

THE FAILURE OF POTSDAM

Truman had been in office only a few days before he decided to "get tough" with the Soviet Union. On April 23, he met with Soviet foreign minister Molotov and sharply chastised him for violations of the Yalta accords. In fact, Truman had little leverage. Russian forces already occupied Poland and much of the rest of Central and Eastern Europe. Germany was already divided among the Allies. The United States was still engaged in a war in the Pacific and was neither able nor willing to enter into a second conflict in Europe. Truman insisted that the United States should be able to get "85 percent" of what it wanted, but he was ultimately forced to settle for much less.

He conceded first on Poland. When Stalin made a few minor concessions to the pro-Western exiles, Truman recognized the Warsaw government, hoping that noncommunist forces might gradually expand their influence there. (Until the 1980s, they did not.) To settle other questions, Truman met in July at Potsdam, in Russian-occupied Germany, with Stalin and Churchill (who, after elections in Britain in the midst of the talks, was replaced as prime minister by Clement Attlee). Truman reluctantly accepted the adjustments of the Polish–German border that Stalin had long demanded; he refused, however, to permit the Russians to claim any reparations from the American, French, and British zones of Germany. This stance effectively confirmed that Germany would remain divided. The western zones ultimately united into one nation, friendly to the United States, and the Russian zone survived as another nation, with a pro-Soviet, communist government.

THE CHINA PROBLEM AND JAPAN

American hopes for an open, peaceful world "policed" by the great powers required a strong, independent China. But those hopes faced a major obstacle: the Chinese government of Chiang Kai-shek. Chiang was generally friendly to the   *Chiang versus Mao in China* United States, but his government was corrupt and incompetent, with feeble popular support. Ever since 1927, the nationalist government he headed had been engaged in a bitter rivalry with the communist armies of Mao Zedong. By 1945, Mao was in control of one-fourth of the population.

Some Americans urged the government to try to find a "third force" to support as an alternative to either Chiang or Mao. Truman, however, decided reluctantly that he had no choice but to continue supporting Chiang. For the next several years, the United States continued to pump money and weapons to Chiang, even as it was becoming clear that the cause was lost. But Truman was not prepared to intervene militarily to save the nationalist regime.

Instead, the American government began to consider an alternative to China as the strong, pro-Western force in Asia: a revived Japan. Abandoning the strict   *Support for Japan* occupation policies of the first years after the war (when General Douglas MacArthur had governed the nation), the United States lifted restrictions on industrial development and encouraged rapid economic growth in Japan. The vision of an open, united world was giving way in Asia, as it was in Europe, to an acceptance of a divided world with a strong pro-American sphere of influence.

THE CONTAINMENT DOCTRINE

By the end of 1945, a new American foreign policy was slowly emerging. It became known as **containment.** Rather than attempting to create a unified, "open" world, or to destroy communism where it already existed, the United States and its allies would work to prevent Soviet expansion.

The new doctrine emerged in part as a response to events in Europe in 1946. In Turkey, Stalin was trying to win control over the vital sea-lanes to the Mediterranean. In Greece, communist forces were threatening the pro-Western government; the British had announced they could no longer provide assistance. Faced with these challenges, Truman decided to enunciate a firm new policy. In doing so, he drew from the ideas of the American diplomat George F. Kennan, who had warned not long after the war that the only viable American response to Soviet power was "a long-term, patient but firm and vigilant containment of Russian expansive tendencies." On March 12, 1947, Truman appeared before Congress and used Kennan's warnings as the basis of what became known as the Truman Doctrine. "I believe," he argued, "that it must be the policy of the United States to   *Truman Doctrine* support free peoples who are resisting attempted subjugation by armed minorities or by outside pressures." In the same speech, he requested $400 million for aid to Greece and Turkey, which Congress quickly approved.

The American commitment ultimately helped reduce Soviet pressure on Turkey and helped the Greek government defeat the communist insurgents and, in the process, establish containment as a basis for American policy that survived for more than forty years.

THE CONSERVATIVE OPPOSITION TO CONTAINMENT

The containment doctrine attracted broad, bipartisan support for dealing with the Cold War. But not everyone believed that containment was the right way to deal with communism. Some Americans on the left believed that containment was an unnecessarily belligerent approach to the Soviet Union, that the United States could have made peace with the Russians. Wider opposition to containment came from conservative Americans, who believed that containment was too weak a response to communism—that, indeed, it was a kind of appeasement.

John Birch Society   Among the conservatives who disdained containment were members of an anticommunist organization known as the John Birch Society. Its leader was Robert Welch, a man so fearful of communism that he believed that some of the most important leaders of American government were trying to undermine the United States and collaborating with the Soviets. Welch presented his opposition in *The Blue Book of the John Birch Society,* in which he argued that much of the American government was riddled with treason. "For years," he wrote, "we have been taken steadily down the road to Communism by steps supposedly designed . . . as ways of *fighting* Communism." Instead, he argued, it was communist Americans themselves who were undermining the nation. "Both the U.S. and Soviet governments are controlled by the same furtive conspiratorial cabal of internationalists, greedy bankers, and corrupt politicians," Welch wrote. "If left unexposed, the traitors inside the U.S. government would betray the country's sovereignty to the United Nations for a collectivist New World Order, managed by a 'one-world' socialist government." Among the sources of treason, Welch claimed, was the creation of the United Nations and other international institutions. Many Americans considered the John Birch Society an extremist organization, but the belief that communism was the greatest danger facing the United States was widely supported.

The opposition to containment reached some of the highest levels of the government. John Foster Dulles, who would soon become secretary of state in the Eisenhower administration, wrote the foreign policy plank in the Republican platform in 1952. "We charge that the leaders of the Administration in power lost the peace so dearly earned by World War II," Dulles charged. "They abandoned friendly nations such as Latvia, Lithuania, Estonia, Poland, and Czechoslovakia." Containment, they argued, was a policy of weakness that had allowed the communists to take over much of the world. Instead, those who opposed containment called for what was known as "rollback." Instead of containing communism, the United States should be pushing back the borders of communism, despite the possibility of another war. President Dwight Eisenhower, however, did not share Dulles's belief in rollback, and the government abided by the containment strategy throughout the 1950s and beyond—despite the fevered opposition to what some still considered to be treason.

THE MARSHALL PLAN

An integral part of the containment policy was a proposal to aid in the economic reconstruction of Western Europe. There were many motives: humanitarian concern for the European people; a fear that Europe would remain an economic drain on the United States if it could not quickly rebuild; and a desire for a strong European market for American goods. But above all, American policymakers believed that unless something could be done to strengthen the shaky pro-American governments in Western Europe, those governments might fall under the control of the growing domestic communist parties.

In June 1947, Secretary of State George C. Marshall announced a plan to provide economic assistance to all European nations (including the Soviet Union) that would join in drafting a program for recovery. Although Russia and its Eastern satellites predictably rejected the plan, sixteen Western European nations eagerly participated. Whatever isolationist opposition there was in the United States largely vanished after a sudden coup in Czechoslovakia in February 1948, which established a Soviet-dominated communist government. In April, Congress approved the creation of the Economic Cooperation Administration, the agency that would administer the Marshall Plan, as it became known. Over the next three years, the Marshall Plan channeled $13 billion of American aid into Europe, helping to spark a substantial economic revival. By the end of 1950, European industrial production had risen 64 percent, communist strength in the member nations had declined, and opportunities for American trade had revived.

Mobilization at Home

In 1948, at the president's request, Congress approved a new military draft and revived the Selective Service System. In the meantime, the United States, having failed to reach agreement with the Soviet Union on international control of nuclear weapons, redoubled its own efforts in atomic research, elevating nuclear weaponry to a central place in its military arsenal. The Atomic Energy Commission, established in 1946, became the supervisory body charged with overseeing all nuclear research, civilian and military alike. And in 1950, the Truman administration approved the development of the new hydrogen bomb, a nuclear weapon far more powerful than those used in 1945.

The National Security Act of 1947 reshaped the nation's military and diplomatic institutions. A new Department of Defense would oversee all branches of the armed services, combining functions previously performed separately by the War and Navy Departments. A National Security Council (NSC), operating out *Creation of NSC, CIA, and Defense Department* of the White House, would govern foreign and military policy. A Central Intelligence Agency (CIA) would replace the wartime Office of Strategic Services and would be responsible for collecting information through both open and covert methods; as the Cold War continued, the CIA would also engage in secret political and military operations on behalf of American interests. The National Security Act, in other words, gave the president expanded powers with which to pursue the nation's international goals.

The Road to NATO

The United States also moved to strengthen the military capabilities of Western Europe. Convinced that a reconstructed Germany was essential to the needs of the West, Truman reached an agreement with England and France to merge the three western zones of occupation into a new West German republic (which would include the three non-Soviet sectors of Berlin, even though that city lay within the Soviet zone). Stalin responded quickly. On June 24, 1948, he imposed a tight blockade around the western sectors of Berlin. *Berlin Airlift* If Germany was to be officially divided, Stalin was implying, then the country's Western government would have to abandon the capital city in the heart of the Soviet-controlled eastern zone. Truman refused to do so. Unwilling to risk war through a military challenge to the blockade, he ordered a massive airlift to supply the city with food, fuel, and other needed goods. The airlift continued for more than ten months, transporting nearly 2.5 million tons of food and other material, keeping a city of 2 million people alive. In the spring of 1949, Stalin lifted the now ineffective blockade. And in October, the division of Germany into two nations—the Federal Republic in the west (with its new capital in Bonn) and the Democratic Republic in the East (with its capital in East Berlin)—became official.

DIVIDED EUROPE AFTER WORLD WAR II This map shows the sharp division that emerged in Europe after World War II between the area under the control of the Soviet Union and the area allied with the United States. In the east, Soviet control or influence extended into all the nations shaded brown—including the eastern half of Germany. In the west and south, the green-shaded nations were allied with the United States as members of the North Atlantic Treaty Organization (NATO). The countries shaded gold were aligned with neither of the two superpowers. The small map in the upper right shows the division of Berlin among the various occupying powers at the end of the war. Eventually, the American, British, and French sectors were combined to create West Berlin, a city governed by West Germany but entirely surrounded by communist East Germany. The airplane icons represent the airlift of supplies ordered by President Truman into the blockaded zones of West Berlin beginning in June 1948. • *How did the West prevent East Germany from absorbing West Berlin?*

The crisis in Berlin accelerated the consolidation of what was already in effect an alliance among the United States and the countries of Western Europe. On April 4, 1949, twelve nations signed an agreement establishing the North Atlantic Treaty Organization (NATO)—declaring that an armed attack against one member would be considered an attack against all. The NATO countries would, moreover, maintain a standing military force in Europe to defend against what they believed was the threat of a Soviet invasion. The formation of NATO eventually spurred the Soviet Union to create an alliance of its *Warsaw Pact*   own with the communist governments in Eastern Europe, as formalized in 1955 by the Warsaw Pact.

REEVALUATING COLD WAR POLICY

In September 1949, the Soviet Union successfully exploded its first atomic weapon. The Russian nuclear capacity came years earlier than predicted, shocking and frightening many Americans. So did the collapse of Chiang Kai-shek's nationalist government in China, which occurred with startling speed in the last months of 1949. Chiang fled with his political allies and the remnants of his army to the offshore island of Formosa (Taiwan), and the entire Chinese mainland came under the control of a   *Communist Victory in China* communist government led by Mao Zedong that many Americans believed to be an extension of the Soviet Union. The United States refused to recognize the new communist regime.

The fall of China to communism was one of the most traumatic events of the Cold War. It accelerated the fear of communism, and it persuaded many Americans that the defeat was a result of weakness, and even treason. As a result, American friends of China formed what came to be known as the China Lobby. Among its eminent leaders were members of Congress, high-level military figures, and powerful journalists. They believed that the United States had not done enough to prevent the communists from taking over mainland China. The failure persuaded many Americans that the government—particularly members of the State Department—was responsible.

In this atmosphere of escalating crisis, Truman called for a thorough review of American foreign policy. The result, a National Security Council report, issued in 1950 and commonly known as NSC-68, outlined a shift in the American position. The first statements of the containment doctrine—the writings of George Kennan, the Truman Doctrine speech—had made distinctions between areas of vital interest to the United States and areas of less importance to the nation's foreign policy. The containment doctrine also called for sharing the military burden of protecting the Western nations. But NSC-68 argued that the United States could no longer rely on other nations to take the initiative in resisting communism. It must move on its own to stop communist expansion virtually anywhere it occurred, regardless of the intrinsic strategic or economic value of the lands in question. Among other things, the report called for a major expansion of American military power, with a defense budget almost four times the previously projected figure. (See "Consider the Source: National Security Council Paper No. 68.")

AMERICA AFTER THE WAR

The crises overseas were not the only frustrations the American people encountered after the war. The nation also faced serious, if short-lived, economic difficulties in adapting to peace. And it suffered from an exceptionally heated political climate that produced a new wave of insecurity and repression.

THE PROBLEMS OF RECONVERSION

Despite widespread predictions that the end of the war would return America to depression conditions, economic growth continued after 1945. Pent-up consumer demand from workers who had accumulated substantial savings during the war helped spur the boom. So did a $6 billion tax cut. The Servicemen's Readjustment Act of 1944, better known as the GI Bill of Rights, provided housing, education, and job-training subsidies to   *GI Bill* veterans and increased spending even further.

CONSIDER THE SOURCE

NATIONAL SECURITY COUNCIL PAPER NO. 68 (NSC-68)

On April 7, 1950, foreign policy experts in the Truman administration completed a top-secret report calling for an expansion of the American commitment to containing the Soviet Union. They based that call, as outlined in the selection below, on their dim view of Soviet character and on their understanding of international power relations in the previous four decades.

Within the past thirty-five years the world has experienced two global wars of tremendous violence. It has witnessed two revolutions—the Russian and the Chinese—of extreme scope and intensity. It has also seen the collapse of five empires—the Ottoman, the Austro-Hungarian, German, Italian, and Japanese—and the drastic decline of two major imperial systems, the British and the French. During the span of one generation, the international distribution of power has been fundamentally altered. For several centuries it had proved impossible for any one nation to gain such preponderant strength that a coalition of other nations could not in time face it with greater strength. The international scene was marked by recurring periods of violence and war, but a system of sovereign and independent states was maintained, over which no state was able to achieve hegemony.

Two complex sets of factors have now basically altered this historical distribution of power. First, the defeat of Germany and Japan and the decline of the British and French Empires have interacted with the development of the United States and the Soviet Union in such a way that power has increasingly gravitated to these two centers. Second, the Soviet Union, unlike previous aspirants to hegemony, is animated by a new fanatic faith, antithetical to our own, and seeks to impose its absolute authority over the rest of the world. Conflict has, therefore, become endemic and is waged, on the part of the Soviet Union, by violent or nonviolent methods in accordance with the dictates of expediency. With the development of increasingly terrifying weapons of mass destruction, every individual faces the ever-present possibility of annihilation should the conflict enter the phase of total war. [. . .]

Our overall policy at the present time may be described as one designed to foster a world environment in which the American system can survive and flourish. It therefore rejects the concept of isolation and affirms the necessity of our positive participation in the world community.

This broad intention embraces two subsidiary policies. One is a policy which we would probably pursue even if there were no Soviet threat. It is a policy of attempting to develop a healthy international community. The other is the policy of "containing" the Soviet system. These two policies are closely interrelated and interact on one another. Nevertheless, the distinction between them is basically valid and contributes to a clearer understanding of what we are trying to do.

UNDERSTAND, ANALYZE, & EVALUATE

1. What broader historical trends did the authors of this memorandum identify as precursors to global power relations after World War II?

2. How did Memorandum NSC-68 characterize the Soviet Union? How did it characterize the goals of the United States? How does this compare to the historical record presented to you in this text?

Source: U.S. Department of State, *Foreign Relations of the United States, 1950. National Security Affairs; Foreign Economic Policy* (Washington, D.C.: U.S. Government Printing Office, 1977), I, pp. 237, 252–253, 262–263, 264, 282, 290. Located in Elizabeth Cobbs Hoffman and Jon Gjerde (eds.), *Major Problems in American History. Volume II: Since 1865* (Boston: Houghton Mifflin Company, 2002), pp. 287–288.

The GI Bill expressed the progressive hopes of many Americans who wanted to see the government do more to assist its citizens. But it also expressed some of the enduring inequalities in American life. Few GI Bill benefits were available to women, even though many women had assisted the war effort in important ways. And while the GI Bill itself did not discriminate against African Americans, its provisions giving local governments jurisdiction allowed southern states, in particular, to deny or limit benefits to black veterans.

The flood of consumer demand contributed to more than two years of inflation, during which prices rose at annual rates of 14 to 15 percent. Compounding the economic difficulties was a sharp rise in labor unrest. By the end of 1945, major strikes had occurred in the automobile, electrical, and steel industries. In April 1946, John L. Lewis led the United Mine Workers out on strike, shutting down the coal fields for forty days. Truman finally forced coal production to resume by ordering government seizure of the mines.   *Inflation and Strikes* But in the process, he pressured mine owners to grant the union most of its demands. Almost simultaneously, the nation's railroads suffered a total shutdown—the first in the nation's history—as two major unions walked out on strike. By threatening to use the army to run the trains, Truman pressured the strikers back to work after only a few days.

Reconversion was particularly difficult for the millions of women and minorities who had entered the workforce during the war. With veterans returning home, employers tended to push women, African Americans, Hispanics, and others out of the plants to make room for white males. Some war workers, particularly women, left the workforce voluntarily, out of a desire to return to their former domestic lives. But as many as 80 percent of women workers, and virtually all black and Hispanic males, wanted to continue working. The postwar inflation, the pressure of a growing high-consumption society, the rising divorce rate (which left many women responsible for their own economic well-being)—all combined to create a high demand for paid employment among women. As women workers found themselves excluded from industrial jobs, therefore, they moved increasingly into other areas of the economy (above all, the service sector).

THE FAIR DEAL REJECTED

Days after the Japanese surrender, Truman submitted to Congress a twenty-one-point domestic program outlining what he later named the "Fair Deal." It called for an expansion of Social Security benefits, the raising of the legal minimum wage from 40 to 65 cents an hour, a program to ensure full employment through aggressive use of federal spending and investment, a permanent Fair Employment Practices Act, public housing and slum clearance, long-range environmental and public works planning, and government promotion of scientific research. Weeks later he added other proposals: federal aid to education, government health insurance and prepaid medical care, funding for the St. Lawrence Seaway, and nationalization of atomic energy.

But most of Truman's programs fell victim to the same public and congressional conservatism that had crippled the last years of the New Deal. Indeed, that conservatism seemed to be intensifying, as the November 1946 congressional elections suggested. Using the simple but devastating slogan "Had Enough?" the Republican Party won control of both houses of Congress, which quickly moved to reduce government spending and chip away at New Deal reforms. Its most notable action was its assault on the Wagner Act of 1935, in the form of the Labor-Management Relations Act of 1947, better known as the Taft-Hartley Act. It made illegal the closed shop (a workplace in which no one can be hired without first being a member of a union). And although it continued to permit the creation of union shops (in which workers must join a union after being hired), it permitted states to pass "right-to-work" laws

Taft-Hartley Act   prohibiting even that. The Taft-Hartley Act also empowered the president to call for a ten-week "cooling-off" period before a strike by issuing an injunction against any work stoppage that endangered national safety or health. Outraged workers and union leaders denounced the measure as a "slave labor bill." Truman vetoed it. But both houses easily overruled him the same day. The Taft-Hartley Act did not destroy the labor movement. But it did damage weaker unions in relatively lightly organized industries such as chemicals and textiles, and it made much more difficult the organizing of workers who had never been union members at all, especially in the South and the West.

THE ELECTION OF 1948

Truman and his advisers believed that the American public was not ready to abandon the achievements of the New Deal, despite the 1946 election results. As they planned their strategy for the 1948 campaign, therefore, they hoped to appeal to enduring Democratic loyalties. Throughout 1948, Truman proposed one reform measure after another (including, on February 2, the first major civil rights bill of the century). To no one's surprise, Congress ignored or defeated them all, but the president was building campaign issues for the fall.

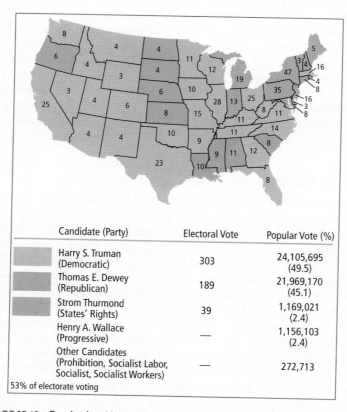

Candidate (Party)	Electoral Vote	Popular Vote (%)
Harry S. Truman (Democratic)	303	24,105,695 (49.5)
Thomas E. Dewey (Republican)	189	21,969,170 (45.1)
Strom Thurmond (States' Rights)	39	1,169,021 (2.4)
Henry A. Wallace (Progressive)	—	1,156,103 (2.4)
Other Candidates (Prohibition, Socialist Labor, Socialist, Socialist Workers)	—	272,713

53% of electorate voting

THE ELECTION OF 1948   Despite the widespread expectation that the Republican candidate, Thomas Dewey, would easily defeat Truman in 1948, the president in fact won a substantial reelection victory that year. This map shows the broad geographic reach of Truman's victory. Dewey swept most of the Northeast, but Truman dominated almost everywhere else. Strom Thurmond, the States' Rights candidate, carried four states in the South. • *What had prompted Thurmond to desert the Democratic Party and run for president on his own?*

There remained, however, the problems of Truman's personal unpopularity—the assumption among much of the electorate that he lacked stature and that his administration was weak and inept—and the deep divisions within the Democratic Party. At the Democratic National Convention that summer, two factions abandoned the party altogether. Angered by Truman's proposed civil rights bill and by the approval at the convention of a civil rights plank in the platform (engineered by Hubert Humphrey, the reform mayor of Minneapolis), some southern conservatives walked out and formed the States' Rights (Democratic or "Dixiecrat") Party, with Governor Strom Thurmond   *Divided Democratic Party* of South Carolina as its nominee. At the same time, some members of the party's left wing—contemptuous of what they considered Truman's ineffectual leadership and his excessively confrontational stance toward the Soviet Union—joined the new Progressive Party, whose candidate was Henry A. Wallace.

Many Democratic liberals who were unhappy with Truman were unwilling to leave the party. The Americans for Democratic Action (ADA), a coalition of anticommunist liberals, tried to entice Dwight D. Eisenhower, the popular war hero, to contest the nomination. Only after Eisenhower refused did liberals concede the nomination to Truman. The Republicans, in the meantime, once again nominated Governor Thomas E. Dewey of New York. Austere, dignified, and competent, he seemed to offer an unbeatable alternative to the president.

Only Truman seemed to believe he could win. As the campaign gathered momentum, he became more and more aggressive, turning the fire away from himself and toward Dewey and the "do-nothing, good-for-nothing" Republican Congress, which was, he told voters, responsible for fueling inflation and abandoning workers and common people. To dramatize his point, he called Congress into special session in July to give it a chance, he said, to enact the liberal measures the Republicans had recently written into their platform. Congress met for two weeks and, predictably, managed to pass almost nothing.

On election night, to the surprise of almost everyone, Truman won a narrow but decisive and dramatic victory: 49.5 percent of the popular vote to Dewey's   *Truman Defeats Dewey* 45.1 percent (with the two splinter parties dividing the small remainder evenly between them), and an electoral margin of 303 to 189. Democrats regained both houses of Congress by substantial margins.

THE FAIR DEAL REVIVED

Despite the Democratic victories, the Eighty-First Congress was little more hospitable to Truman's Fair Deal reform. Truman did win some important victories. Congress raised the legal minimum wage from 40 cents to 75 cents an hour. It approved an important expansion of the Social Security system, increasing benefits by 75 percent and extending them to 10 million additional people. And it passed the National Housing Act of 1949, which provided for the construction of 810,000 units of low-income housing accompanied by long-term rent subsidies.

But on other issues—national health insurance and aid to education, among them—Truman made little progress. Nor was he able to persuade Congress to accept the civil rights legislation he proposed in 1949, legislation that would make lynching a federal crime, provide federal protection of black voting rights, abolish the poll tax, and establish a new Fair Employment Practices Commission to curb discrimination in hiring. Southern Democrats filibustered to kill the bill.

Undeterred, Truman proceeded on his own to battle several forms of racial discrimination. He ordered an end to discrimination in the hiring of government employees. He began to dismantle segregation within the armed forces. And he allowed the Justice Department to become actively involved in court battles against discriminatory statutes. The Supreme Court, in the meantime, signaled its own growing awareness of the issue by ruling, in *Shelley v. Kraemer* (1948), that courts could not be used to enforce private "covenants" meant to bar blacks from residential neighborhoods.

THE NUCLEAR AGE

Looming over the many struggles of the postwar years was the image of the great and terrible mushroom clouds that had risen over Alamogordo in July 1945 and over the ruined Japanese cities of Hiroshima and Nagasaki. Americans greeted these terrible new instruments of destruction with fear and awe, but also with expectation. Postwar culture was torn between a dark image of the nuclear war that many Americans feared would result from the rivalry with the Soviet Union, and the bright image of a dazzling technological future that atomic power might help to produce.

The fear of nuclear weapons appeared widely in popular culture, but it was often dis-*Menace in Films* guised. The late 1940s and early 1950s were the heyday of *film noir,* a kind of filmmaking that originated in France and had been named for the dark lighting characteristic of the genre. American *film noir* portrayed the loneliness of individuals in an impersonal world—a staple of American culture for many decades—but also suggested the menacing character of the age, the looming possibility of vast destruction. Sometimes,

THE RED MENACE This 1949 movie poster suggests how much attention was directed to the threat of communism. The film told the story of a man and a woman who joined the Communist Party, only to become disillusioned when they watched the murder of a party member who had begun to doubt the party's principles.
(© Republic Pictures/Photofest)

popular fears addressed nuclear fear explicitly—for example, the celebrated television show of the 1950s and early 1960s, *The Twilight Zone,* which featured dramatic portrayals of the aftermath of nuclear war; or postwar comic books, which depicted powerful superheroes saving the world from destruction.

Such images resonated with the public because awareness of nuclear weapons was increasingly built into their daily lives. Schools and office buildings held regular air-raid drills to prepare people for the possibility of nuclear attack. Radio stations regularly tested the Emergency Broadcast System, which stood in readiness for war. Fallout shelters stocked with water and canned goods sprang up in public buildings and private homes. Though few Americans went about their daily lives in a state of panic, anxiety simmered below the surface.

And yet, the United States was also an exuberant nation in these years, dazzled by its own prosperity and excited by the technological innovations transforming the nation, including nuclear power. The same scientific knowledge that could destroy the world, many believed, might also lead it into a glimmering future. The *New York Times,* only days after Hiroshima, expressed its own rosy view of the nuclear future: "This new knowledge . . . can bring to this earth not death but life, not tyranny and cruelty, but a divine freedom."

That kind of optimism soon became widespread. The "secret of the atom," many Americans predicted, would bring "prosperity and a more complete life." A public opinion poll late in 1948 revealed that approximately two-thirds of those questioned believed that, "in the long run," atomic energy would "do more good than harm."   *Nuclear Power* Nuclear power plants began to spring up in many areas of the country and were welcomed as the source of cheap and unlimited electricity, their potential dangers scarcely even discussed by those who celebrated their creation.

THE KOREAN WAR

Though the Cold War started in Europe, it quickly spread to Asia. On June 24, 1950, the armies of communist North Korea swept across their southern border and invaded the pro-Western half of the Korean peninsula. Within days, they had occupied much of South Korea, including Seoul, its capital. True to the dictates of containment, the United States almost immediately committed itself to the conflict.

THE DIVIDED PENINSULA

When World War II ended, both the United States and the Soviet Union had troops in Korea fighting the Japanese; neither army was willing to leave. Instead, they divided the nation, supposedly temporarily, along the 38th parallel. The Russians finally departed in 1949, leaving behind a communist government in the north with a strong, Soviet-equipped army. The Americans left a few months later, handing control to the pro-Western government of Syngman Rhee. Anticommunist but only nominally   *Syngman Rhee* democratic, he used his relatively small military primarily to suppress internal opposition.

The relative weakness of South Korea offered a strong temptation to nationalists in the North Korean government who wanted to reunite the country, particularly after the American government implied that it did not consider Korea within its own "defense perimeter." The Soviets and Chinese did not order the invasion, but they did not try to stop it. They supported the offensive once it began.

Almost immediately, on June 27, 1950, the president ordered limited American military assistance to South Korea, and on the same day he appealed to the United Nations to intervene. The Soviet Union was boycotting the Security Council at the time (to protest the council's refusal to recognize the new communist government of China) and was thus unable to exercise its veto power. As a result, American delegates were able to win UN agreement to a resolution calling for international assistance to the Rhee government. On June 30, the United States ordered its own ground forces into Korea, and Truman appointed General Douglas MacArthur to command the UN operations there. (Several other nations provided assistance and troops, but the "UN" armies were, in fact, overwhelmingly American.)

After a surprise American invasion at Inchon in September had routed the North Korean forces from the south and sent them back across the 38th parallel, Truman gave

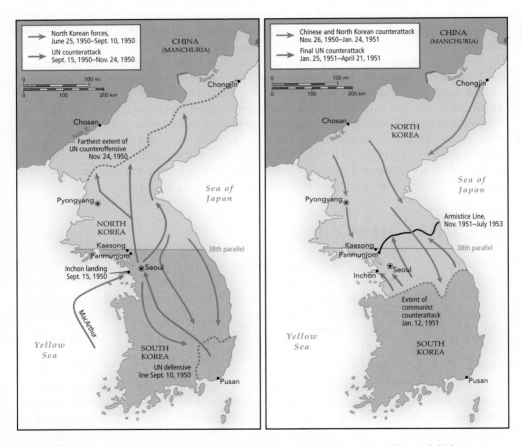

THE KOREAN WAR, 1950-1953 These two maps illustrate the changing fortunes of UN forces (which were mostly American) during the 1950–1953 Korean War. The map at the left shows the extent of the North Korean invasion of South Korea in 1950; communist forces for a time controlled all of Korea except a small area around Pusan in the southeast. On September 15, 1950, UN troops under Douglas MacArthur landed in force at Inchon and soon drove the North Koreans back across the border. MacArthur then pursued the North Koreans well into their own territory. The map at right shows the very different circumstances once the Chinese entered the war in November 1950. Chinese forces drove the UN army back below the 38th parallel and, briefly, deep into South Korea, below Seoul. The UN troops fought back to the prewar border between North and South Korea late in 1951, but the war then bogged down into a stalemate that continued for a year and a half. • *What impact did the Korean War have on American politics in the early 1950s?*

MacArthur permission to pursue the communists into their own territory. Hoping now to create "a unified, independent and democratic Korea," the president had moved beyond simple containment to an attempted rollback of communist power.

FROM INVASION TO STALEMATE

For several weeks, MacArthur's invasion of North Korea proceeded smoothly. On October 19, the capital, Pyongyang, fell to the UN forces. Victory seemed near—until the Chinese government, alarmed by the movement of American forces toward its   *China Intervenes* border, intervened. In early November, eight divisions of the Chinese army entered the war. The UN offensive stalled and then collapsed. Through December 1950, outnumbered American forces were forced into a rapid, bitter retreat in numbingly cold temperatures. Within weeks, communist forces had pushed the Americans back below the 38th parallel once again and had recaptured the South Korean capital of Seoul. By mid-January 1951 the rout had ceased; and by March the UN armies had managed to regain much of the territory they had recently lost, taking back Seoul and pushing the communists north of the 38th parallel for the second time. With that, the war turned into a protracted stalemate.

From the start, Truman had been determined to avoid a direct conflict with China, which he feared might lead to a new world war. Once China   *Truman–MacArthur Controversy* entered the war, he began seeking a negotiated solution to the struggle. But General MacArthur had ideas of his own. The United States was really fighting the Chinese, MacArthur argued. It should, therefore, attack China itself, if not through an actual invasion, then at least by bombing communist forces massing north of the Chinese border with conventional or even atomic weapons. In March 1951, he indicated his unhappiness with Truman's reluctance to invade China. In a public letter to House Republican Leader Joseph W. Martin, he concluded: "There is no substitute for victory." His position had wide popular support. Yet the release of the Martin letter struck the president as intolerable insubordination. On April 11, 1951, he relieved MacArthur of his command.

Sixty-nine percent of the American people supported MacArthur, a Gallup poll reported. When the general returned to the United States later in 1951, he was greeted with wild enthusiasm. Public criticism of Truman finally abated somewhat when a number of prominent military figures, including General Omar Bradley, publicly supported the president's decision. But substantial hostility toward Truman remained. In the meantime, the Korean stalemate continued. Negotiations between the opposing forces began at Panmunjom in July 1951, but the talks—and the war—dragged on until 1953.

LIMITED MOBILIZATION

The war in Korea produced only a limited American military commitment abroad. It also created only a limited economic mobilization at home.

Truman set up the Office of Defense Mobilization to fight inflation by holding down prices and discouraging high union wage demands. When these cautious regulatory efforts failed, the president took more drastic action. Railroad workers walked off the job in 1951, and Truman, who considered the workers' demands inflationary, ordered the government to seize control of the railroads. In 1952, during a nationwide steel strike, Truman seized the steel mills, citing his powers as commander in chief. But in a 6-to-3 decision, the Supreme Court ruled that the president had exceeded his authority, and Truman was forced to relent.

The Korean War significantly boosted economic growth by pumping new government funds into the economy at a point when many believed it was about to decline. But the war had other, less welcome effects. It came at a time of rising insecurity about America's position in the world and intensified anxiety about communism. As the long stalemate continued, producing 140,000 American dead and wounded, frustration turned to anger. The United States, which had recently won the greatest war in history, seemed unable to conclude what many Americans considered a minor border skirmish in a small country. They began to believe that something must be deeply wrong—not only in Korea but within the United States as well. Such fears contributed to the rise of the second major campaign of the century against domestic communism.

THE CRUSADE AGAINST SUBVERSION

Why did the American people develop a growing fear of internal communist subversion—a fear that by the early 1950s occasionally reached the point of hysteria? There are many possible answers but no single definitive explanation. (See "Debating the Past: McCarthyism.")

One factor was obvious: communism was not an imagined enemy. It had tangible shape, in Josef Stalin and the Soviet Union. Adding to the concern were the Korean stalemate, the "loss" of China, and the Soviet development of an atomic bomb. Searching for someone to blame, many began to believe that there was a communist conspiracy within American borders. But there were other factors as well, rooted in events in American domestic politics.

HUAC and Alger Hiss

Much of the anticommunist furor emerged out of the search by Republicans for an issue with which to attack the Democrats, and out of the efforts of the Democrats to take that issue away from them. Beginning in 1947, the House Un-American Activities Committee (HUAC) held widely publicized investigations to prove that, under Democratic rule, the government had tolerated (if not actually encouraged) communist subversion. The committee turned first to the movie industry, arguing that communists had infiltrated Hollywood and tainted American films with propaganda. Writers and producers, some of them former communists, were called to testify; and when some of them (the "Hollywood Ten") refused to answer questions about their political beliefs and those of their colleagues, they were sent to jail for contempt. Others were barred from employment in the industry when Hollywood, attempting to protect its public image, adopted a "blacklist" of those of "suspicious loyalty."

More alarming to the public was HUAC's investigation into charges of disloyalty *Alger Hiss* leveled against Alger Hiss, a former high-ranking member of the State Department. In 1948, Whittaker Chambers, a former communist agent, now a conservative editor at *Time* magazine, told the committee that Hiss had passed classified State Department documents to him in 1937 and 1938. When Hiss sued him for slander, Chambers produced microfilms of the documents (called the "pumpkin papers," because Chambers had kept them hidden in a pumpkin in his vegetable garden). Hiss could not be tried for espionage because of the statute of limitations (which protects individuals from prosecution for most crimes after seven years have passed). But largely because of the relentless efforts of Richard M. Nixon, a first-term congressman from California and a member of HUAC, Hiss was convicted of perjury and served several years in prison. The Hiss case not only discredited a prominent young diplomat, it also cast suspicion on a generation of liberal Democrats. It also transformed Nixon into a national figure and helped him win a Senate seat in 1950.

THE FEDERAL LOYALTY PROGRAM AND THE ROSENBERG CASE

Partly to protect itself against Republican attacks and partly to encourage support for the president's foreign policy initiatives, the Truman administration in 1947 initiated a widely publicized program to review the "loyalty" of federal employees. By 1951, more than 2,000 government employees had resigned under pressure and 212 had been dismissed.

The Federal Employee Loyalty Program helped launch a major assault on subversion throughout the government—and beyond. The attorney general established a widely cited list of supposedly subversive organizations. The director of the Federal Bureau of Investigation (FBI), J. Edgar Hoover, investigated and harassed alleged radicals. In 1950, Congress passed the McCarran Internal Security Act, which, among other restrictions on "subversive" activity, required that all communist organizations register with the government and publish their records. Congress easily overrode Truman's veto of the bill.

The successful Soviet detonation of an atomic bomb in 1949 suggested to some that there had been a conspiracy to pass American atomic secrets to the Russians. In 1950, Klaus Fuchs, a young British scientist, seemed to confirm those fears when he testified that he had delivered to the Russians details of the bomb's manufacture. The case ultimately moved to an obscure New York couple, Julius   *Julius and Ethel Rosenberg* and Ethel Rosenberg, members of the Communist Party. The government claimed the Rosenbergs had received secret information from Ethel's brother, a machinist on the Manhattan Project in New Mexico, and had passed it on to the Soviet Union through other agents (including Fuchs). The Rosenbergs were convicted and, on April 5, 1951, sentenced to death. After two years of appeals and public protests, they died in the electric chair on June 19, 1953. Historians now believe that Julius—but not Ethel—was guilty as charged.

All these factors—the HUAC investigations, the Hiss trial, the loyalty investigations, the McCarran Act, the Rosenberg case—combined with other concerns by the early 1950s to create a fear of communist subversion that seemed to grip the entire country. State and local governments, the judiciary, schools and universities, labor unions—all sought to purge themselves of real or imagined subversives. It was a climate that made possible the rise of an extraordinary public figure.

MCCARTHYISM

Joseph McCarthy was an undistinguished first-term Republican senator from Wisconsin until, in February 1950, in the midst of a speech in Wheeling, West Virginia, he lifted up a sheet of paper and claimed to "hold in my hand" a list of 205 known communists currently working in the American State Department. No person of comparable stature had ever made so bold a charge against the federal government. In the months to come, as McCarthy repeated and expanded on his accusations, he emerged as the nation's most prominent leader of the crusade against domestic subversion.

McCARTHYISM

The American Civil Liberties Union warned in the early 1950s, at the peak of what is now known as McCarthyism, that "the threat to civil liberties today is the most serious in the history of our country." It was expressing a view with which many Americans wholeheartedly agreed. But while there were unusually powerful challenges to freedom of speech and association in the late 1940s and early 1950s, there is wide disagreement about the causes and meaning of those challenges.

The simplest argument—and one that continues to attract scholarly support—is that the postwar Red Scare expressed real and legitimate concerns about communist subversion in the United States. William O'Neill, in *A Better World* (1982), and Richard Gid Powers, in *Not Without Honor* (1995), have both argued that anticommunism was a serious, intelligent, and patriotic movement, despite its excesses. The American Communist Party, according to this view, was an agent of Stalin and the Soviet Union within the United States, actively engaged in espionage and subversion. The effort to root communists out of public life was both understandable and justifiable—and the hysteria it sometimes produced was an unhappy but predictable by-product of an essentially rational and justifiable effort. "Anticommunism," Powers wrote, "expressed the essential American determination to stand against attacks on human freedom and foster the growth of democracy throughout the world. . . . To superimpose on this rich history the cartoon features of Joe McCarthy is to reject history for the easy comforts of moralism."

Most interpretations, however, have been less charitable. In the 1950s, in the midst of the Red Scare itself, an influential group of historians and social scientists began to portray the anticommunist fervor of their time as an expression of deep social maladjustment—an argument perhaps most closely associated with a famous essay by Richard Hofstadter, "The Paranoid Style in American Politics." There was, they argued, no logical connection between the modest power of actual communists in the United States and the hysterical form these scholars believed anticommunism was assuming. The explanation, therefore, had to lie in something other than reality, in a deeper set of social and cultural anxieties that had only an indirect connection with the political world as it existed. Extreme anticommunism, they claimed, was something close to a pathology; it expressed fear of and alienation from the modern world. A person afflicted with the "paranoid style," Hofstadter wrote,

> believes himself to be living in a world in which he is spied upon, plotted against, betrayed, and very likely destined for total ruin. He feels that his liberties have been arbitrarily and outrageously invaded. He is opposed to almost everything that has happened in American politics in the past twenty years.

Other scholars, writing not long after the decline of McCarthyism, rejected the sociocultural arguments of Hofstadter and others but shared the belief that the crusade against subversion was a distortion of normal public life. They saw the anticommunist crusade as an example of party politics run amok. Richard Freeland, in

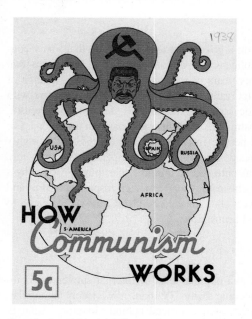

1938

HOW Communism WORKS 5¢

(Rare Book and Special Collection Division, The Library of Congress)

The Truman Doctrine and the Origins of McCarthyism (1971), argued that the Democrats began the effort to purge the government of radicals to protect themselves from attacks by the Republicans. Nelson Polsby, Robert Griffith, and others have noted how Republicans seized on the issue of communism in government in the late 1940s to reverse their nearly twenty-year exclusion from power. With each party trying to outdo the other in its effort to demonstrate its anticommunist credentials, it was hardly surprising that the crusade reached extraordinarily intense proportions.

Still other historians have emphasized the role of powerful government officials and agencies with a strong commitment to anti-communism—most notably J. Edgar Hoover and the FBI. Athan Theoharis and Kenneth

O'Reilly introduced the idea of an anticommunist bureaucracy in work published in the 1970s and 1980s. Ellen Schrecker's *Many Are the Crimes* (1998) likewise identified an interlocking cluster of official agencies committed to anticommunism and operating across many years—not just those dominated by McCarthy. Yet those agencies and individuals, she argued, whatever the sincerity of their anticommunist fervor, oversaw a period of repression that recklessly destroyed careers and lives, shattered the left, chilled dissent, and narrowed the terms of political debate.

Several scholars, finally, have presented an argument that does not so much challenge other interpretations as complement them. Anticommunist zealots were not alone to blame for the excesses of McCarthyism, they argue. It was also the fault of liberals—in politics, in academia, and, perhaps above all, in the media—who were so intimidated by the political climate, or so imprisoned within the conventions of their professions, that they found themselves unable to respond effectively to the distortions and excesses that they recognized around them. •

UNDERSTAND, ANALYZE, & EVALUATE

1. Why did the American public feel so threatened by communism? Who exploited the public's fears and why?
2. Was the public reaction to the Red Scare a logical response or disproportionate to the actual threat posed by communism?
3. How were party politics and McCarthyism connected? Do you find elements similar to McCarthyism in politics today?

Within weeks of his charges against the State Department, McCarthy leveled accusations at other agencies. After 1952, with the Republicans in control of the Senate and McCarthy now the chair of a special subcommittee, he conducted highly publicized investigations of alleged subversion in many areas of the government. McCarthy never produced conclusive evidence that any federal employee was a communist. But a growing constituency adored him nevertheless for his coarse, "fearless" assaults on a government establishment that many considered arrogant, effete, even traitorous. Republicans, in particular, rallied to his claims that the Democrats had been responsible for "twenty years of treason" and that only a change of parties could rid the country of subversion. McCarthy, in short, provided his followers with an issue into which they could channel a wide range of resentments: fear of communism, animosity toward the country's "eastern establishment," and frustrated partisan ambitions. For a time, McCarthy intimidated all but a few people from opposing him. Even the highly popular Dwight D. Eisenhower, running for president in 1952, did not speak out against him, although he disliked McCarthy's tactics and was outraged at, among other things, McCarthy's attacks on General George Marshall. Eventually his assaults against such respected figures and institutions drove McCarthy from popular favor—but not before **"McCarthyism"** came to define an era of hysterical and often unfounded accusations.

THE REPUBLICAN REVIVAL

Public frustration over the stalemate in Korea and popular fears of internal subversion combined to make 1952 a bad year for the Democratic Party. Truman, now deeply unpopular, withdrew from the presidential contest. The party united instead behind Governor Adlai E. Stevenson of Illinois. Stevenson's dignity, wit, and eloquence made him a beloved figure to many liberals and intellectuals. But those same qualities seemed only to fuel Republican charges that Stevenson lacked the strength or the will to combat communism sufficiently.

Stevenson's greatest problem, however, was the Republican candidate opposing him. Rejecting the efforts of conservatives to nominate Robert Taft or Douglas MacArthur, the Republicans turned to a man who had no previous identification with the party: General Dwight D. Eisenhower—military hero, commander of NATO, president of Columbia University—who won nomination on the first ballot. He chose as his running mate the young California senator who had gained national prominence through his crusade against Alger Hiss: Richard M. Nixon.

In the fall campaign, Eisenhower attracted support through his geniality and his statesmanlike pledges to settle the Korean conflict. Nixon (after surviving early accusations of financial improprieties, which he effectively neutralized in a famous television address, the Checkers speech) exploited the issue of domestic anticommunism by attacking the Democrats for "cowardice" and "appeasement." The response at the polls was overwhelm-*Eisenhower Elected* ing. Eisenhower won both a popular and an electoral landslide: 55 percent of the popular vote to Stevenson's 44 percent, 442 electoral votes to Stevenson's 89. Republicans gained control of both houses of Congress for the first time since 1946.

CONCLUSION

Even during World War II, when the United States and the Soviet Union were allies, it was evident to leaders in both nations that America and Russia had quite different visions of what the postwar world should look like. Very quickly after the war ended, the once fruitful relationship between the world's greatest powers quickly soured. Americans came to believe that the Soviet Union, like Hitler's Germany, harbored dangerous expansionist ambitions. Soviets came to believe that the United States was trying to protect its own dominance in the world by encircling the Soviet Union. The result of these tensions was what became known by the end of the 1940s as the Cold War.

In the early years of the Cold War, the United States constructed a series of policies designed to prevent both war and Soviet aggression. It helped rebuild the shattered economies of Western Europe through the Marshall Plan, to stabilize those nations and prevent them from becoming communist. America embraced a new foreign policy—known as containment—that committed it to keeping the Soviet Union from expanding its influence further into the world. The United States and Western Europe formed a strong and enduring alliance, NATO, to defend Europe against possible Soviet advances.

In 1950, the armed forces of communist North Korea launched an invasion of noncommunist South Korea; and to most Americans, the conflict quickly came to be seen as a test of American resolve. The Korean War was long, costly, and unpopular, with many military setbacks and frustrations. In the end, however, the United States—working through the United Nations—managed to drive the North Koreans out of South Korea and stabilize the original division of the peninsula.

The Korean War hardened American foreign policy into a much more rigidly anticommunist form. It undermined the Truman administration, and the Democratic Party, and helped strengthen conservatives and Republicans. It greatly bolstered an already powerful crusade against communists, and those believed to be communists, within the United States—a crusade often known as McCarthyism, because of the notoriety of Senator Joseph McCarthy of Wisconsin, the most celebrated leader of the effort.

America after World War II was indisputably the wealthiest and most powerful nation in the world. But in the harsh climate of the Cold War, neither wealth nor power could dispel deep anxieties and bitter divisions.

KEY TERMS/PEOPLE/PLACES/EVENTS

Alger Hiss 672
Central Intelligence Agency
  (CIA) 661
Cold War 653
containment 659
Douglas MacArthur 670
Fair Deal 665
GI Bill 663
House Un-American Activities
  Committee (HUAC) 672

John Birch Society 660
Julius and Ethel
  Rosenberg 673
Korean War 669
Mao Zedong 663
Marshall Plan 661
McCarthyism 676
North Atlantic Treaty
  Organization (NATO) 662
NSC-68 663

Syngman Rhee 669
Taft-Hartley Act 665
Truman Doctrine 659
United Nations 655
Warsaw Pact 662
Yalta Conference 657

RECALL AND REFLECT

1. How did American diplomats plan for the postwar world and settle postwar issues? How did opposing visions of the postwar world order thwart those efforts?
2. How did postwar economic problems affect American politics and society?
3. Why did the United States become involved in the war in Korea? What was the result of U.S. involvement in that war?
4. Why did the fear of communism at home reach such great proportions? What events helped fan that fear?

28 THE AFFLUENT SOCIETY

THE ECONOMIC "MIRACLE"

THE EXPLOSION OF SCIENCE AND TECHNOLOGY

PEOPLE OF PLENTY

THE OTHER AMERICA

THE RISE OF THE CIVIL RIGHTS MOVEMENT

EISENHOWER REPUBLICANISM

EISENHOWER, DULLES, AND THE COLD WAR

LOOKING AHEAD

1. Why did the U.S. economy experience such a boom in the late 1950s and early 1960s? How did this boom affect American society?

2. Who constituted the "other America," who failed to share in the economic prosperity and affluence of the postwar era? Why were they left out?

3. What was the response to the Supreme Court decision in *Brown v. Board of Education*? How did the Court's decision affect African Americans and the early civil rights movement? How did it affect white southerners?

4. What policy guided foreign affairs under Eisenhower, and how was that policy implemented around the world?

IF AMERICA EXPERIENCED A GOLDEN age in the 1950s and early 1960s, as many Americans believed at the time and many continue to believe today, it was largely a result of two developments. One was a booming national prosperity, which profoundly altered the social, economic, and even physical landscape of the United States. The other was the continuing struggle against communism, a struggle that created considerable anxiety but that also encouraged many Americans to look even more approvingly at their own society. But if these powerful forces created a widespread sense of national purpose and self-satisfaction, they also helped blind many Americans to serious problems developing at home.

THE ECONOMIC "MIRACLE"

Perhaps the most striking feature of American society in the 1950s and early 1960s was the booming economic growth that made even the heady 1920s seem pale by comparison. It was a better-balanced and more widely distributed prosperity than that of thirty years earlier. It was not, however, as universal as some Americans liked to believe.

ECONOMIC GROWTH

By 1949, despite the continuing problems of postwar reconversion, an economic expansion had begun that would continue with only brief interruptions for almost twenty years. Between 1945 and 1960, the gross national product grew by 250 percent, from $200 billion to over $500 billion. Unemployment remained at about 5 percent or lower throughout the 1950s and early 1960s. Inflation, in the meantime, hovered around 3 percent a year or less.

The causes of this growth were varied. Part of the growth came from Americans throwing off the emotional shackles of the Great Depression. Buoyed by victory in the world war, Americans again began to believe in a brighter future, and they invested in it. Government spending, which had reached new levels from fighting a world war and the Great Depression, continued to stimulate growth through public funding of schools, housing, veterans' benefits, welfare, interstate highways, and, above all, the military. Economic growth peaked during the first half of the 1950s, when military spending was highest because of the Korean War. Additionally, trade agreements after the war began to open markets for goods and services like no other time in its history. Virtually untouched by the destruction of war, U.S. manufacturing and services reaped the initial rewards of international trade.

TIME LINE

1947
Levittown construction begins

1953
Korean War ends

1954
Brown v. Board of Education
Army–McCarthy hearings

1955
Montgomery bus boycott

1956
Federal Highway Act
Eisenhower reelected
Suez crisis

1957
Sputnik launched
Kerouac's *On the Road*
Little Rock desegregation crisis

1959
Castro seizes power in Cuba

1960
U-2 incident
Eisenhower's farewell address

1961
First American in space
U.S. severs diplomatic relations with Cuba

1969
Americans land on moon

The national birthrate reversed a long pattern of decline with what is commonly called the **Baby Boom,** which began during World War II and peaked in 1957. The nation's population rose almost 20 percent in the decade, from 150 million in 1950 to 179 million in 1960, which meant increased consumer demand and expanding economic growth.

Rapid suburban expansion—a 47 percent increase in the 1950s—helped stimulate growth in several important sectors of the economy. The number of privately owned cars more than doubled in a decade. Demand for new homes helped sustain a vigorous housing industry. The construction of roads stimulated the economy as well.

The combination of post–WWII economic growth, new standards of support from government spending, and a booming population led to a renewed American vitality for the next thirty years. And while that growth was far from equally distributed, the average American in 1960 had over 20 percent more purchasing power than in 1945 and more than twice as much as during the prosperous 1920s. The American people had achieved the highest standard of living of any society in the history of the world.

The Rise of the Modern West

No region experienced more dramatic changes than the American West. Its population expanded dramatically; its cities boomed; its industrial economy flourished. By the 1960s, some parts of the West were among the most important (and populous) industrial and cultural centers of the nation.

As during World War II, much of the growth of the West was a result of federal spending and investment—on the dams, power stations, highways, and other infrastructure projects that made additional economic development possible. Military contracts continued

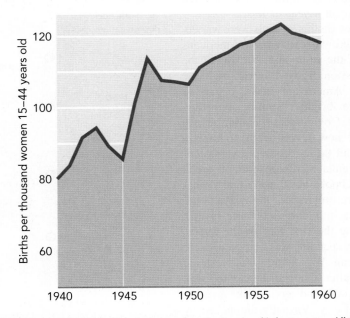

THE AMERICAN BIRTHRATE, 1940–1960 This chart shows how the American birthrate grew rapidly during and after World War II (following a long period of decline in the 1930s) to produce what became known as the "Baby Boom." At the peak of the Baby Boom, during the 1950s, the nation's population grew by 20 percent. • *What impact did the Baby Boom have on the nation's economy?*

to flow disproportionately to factories in California and Texas, many built with government funds during the war. The growing number of automobiles created new demands for petroleum and contributed to the rapid growth of oil fields in Texas and Colorado and of the metropolitan centers, among them Houston, Dallas, and Denver. State governments in the West invested heavily in their universities. The University of Texas and University of California systems, in particular, became among the nation's largest and created important centers of research. They helped attract technology-intensive industries to the region. Climate also contributed to growth in the West. Southern California, Nevada, and Arizona, in particular, attracted many migrants from the East because of their warm, dry climates. The growth of Los Angeles after World War II was a remarkable phenomenon: more than 10 percent of all new businesses in the United States between 1945 and 1950 began in Los Angeles. Its population rose by over 50 percent between 1940 and 1960.

CAPITAL AND LABOR

Booming corporations were reluctant to allow strikes to interfere with their operations; and since the most important labor unions were now so large and entrenched that they could not easily be suppressed or intimidated, leaders of large businesses made important concessions to them. By the mid-1950s, factory wages in most industries had risen substantially, to an average of $80 per week. In December 1955, the American Federation of Labor and the Congress of Industrial Organizations ended their twenty-year rivalry *AFL and CIO Merge* and merged to create the AFL-CIO, under the leadership of George Meany.

But success also bred stagnation and corruption in some union bureaucracies. In 1957, the powerful Teamsters Union became the subject of a congressional investigation, and its president, David Beck, was charged with the misappropriation of union funds.

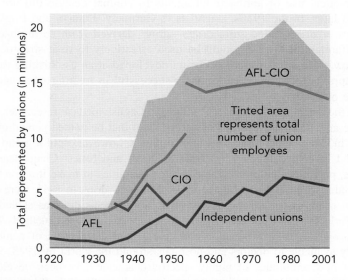

WORKERS REPRESENTED BY UNIONS, 1920–2001 This chart shows the number of workers represented by unions over an eighty-year period. Note the dramatic rise in the unionized workforce during the 1930s and 1940s, the slower but still significant rise in the 1960s and 1970s, and the steady decline that began in the 1980s. The chart, in fact, understates the decline of unionized labor in the postwar era, since it shows union membership in absolute numbers and not as a percentage of the rapidly growing workforce. • *Why did unions cease recruiting new members successfully in the 1970s, and why did they begin actually losing members in the 1980s?*

Beck ultimately stepped down to be replaced by Jimmy Hoffa, whom government investigators pursued for nearly a decade before finally winning a conviction against him in 1964 for jury tampering. The United Mine Workers, similarly, became tainted by violence and charges of corruption.

THE EXPLOSION OF SCIENCE AND TECHNOLOGY

In 1961, *Time* magazine selected as its "man of the year" not a specific person but "the American Scientist." The choice was an indication of the widespread fascination with which Americans in the age of atomic power viewed science and technology.

MEDICAL BREAKTHROUGHS

The twentieth century saw greater progress in the development of medical science than had occurred in all the centuries before it. A very large proportion of that progress occurred during and after World War II. Particularly important was the development of new antibacterial drugs capable of fighting infections that had once been all but untreatable.

To be sure, the development of antibiotics originated in the discoveries of Louis Pasteur and Jules-Francois Joubert. Working in France in the 1870s, they produced the first conclusive evidence that virulent bacterial infections could be defeated by other, more ordinary bacteria. Using their discoveries, the English physician Joseph Lister revealed the value of antiseptic solutions in preventing infection during surgery several years later.

But the practical use of antibacterial agents to combat disease did not begin until many decades later. In the 1930s, scientists in Germany, France, and England demonstrated the power of so-called sulfa drugs—drugs derived from an antibacterial agent known as sulfanilamide—which could be used effectively to treat streptococcal blood infections. New sulfa drugs were soon being developed at an astonishing rate and were frequently improved; they were enormously successful in treating what had once been a major cause of death.

In 1928, in the meantime, Alexander Fleming, an English medical researcher, accidentally discovered the antibacterial properties of an organism that he named penicillin. There was little progress in using penicillin to treat human illness, however, until a group of researchers at Oxford University, directed by Howard Florey and Ernest Chain, learned how to produce stable, potent penicillin in sizable enough quantities to make it a practical weapon against bacterial disease. The first human trials of the new drug, in 1941, were dramatically successful, but progress toward the mass availability of penicillin was stalled in England because of World War II. American laboratories further developed methods for the mass *Treatments for Bacterial Infections*   production and commercial distribution of penicillin, which became widely available to doctors and hospitals around the world by 1948. Since then, a wide range of new antibiotics of highly specific character have been developed so that bacterial infections are now among the most successfully treated of all human illnesses.

Immunization—the development of vaccines that can protect humans from contracting both bacterial and viral diseases—also progressed dramatically. The first great immunological triumph was the development of the smallpox vaccine by the English researcher Edward Jenner in the late eighteenth century. A vaccine effective against typhoid was developed by an English bacteriologist, Almroth Wright, in 1897 and was in wide use by World War I. Vaccination against tetanus became widespread just before and during World War II. Medical scientists also developed a vaccine against another major killer, tuberculosis, in the 1920s; but controversy over its safety stalled its adoption, especially in the United States, for many years. It was not widely used in the United States until after World War II, when it largely eliminated tuberculosis until a limited recurrence began in the 1990s.

Viruses are much more difficult to prevent and treat than bacterial infections, and progress toward vaccines against viral infections—except for smallpox—was relatively slow. Not until the 1930s, when scientists discovered how to grow viruses in tissue cultures, could researchers study them with any real effectiveness. Gradually, they discovered how to produce forms of a virus capable of triggering antibodies that would protect vaccinated people from contracting disease. An effective vaccine against yellow fever was developed in the late 1930s, and one against influenza—one of the great killers of the early twentieth century—appeared in 1945.

A particularly dramatic postwar triumph was the development of a vaccine against polio. In 1954, the American scientist Jonas Salk introduced an effective *Polio Vaccine* vaccine against the disease that had killed or crippled thousands of children and adults (among them Franklin Roosevelt). It was provided free to the public by the federal government beginning in 1955. After 1960, an oral vaccine developed by Albert Sabin—usually administered in a sugar cube—made widespread vaccination even easier. By the early 1960s, these vaccines had virtually eliminated polio from American life and from much of the rest of the world.

Advancements made in mass production and administration of resources expanded the use and availability of the previous decades' discoveries. As a result, both infant mortality and the death rate among young children declined significantly in the first twenty-five years after the war (although not by as much as in Western Europe). Average life expectancy in that same period rose by five years, to seventy-one. These medical advances have saved millions, but overuse of antibacterial agents and time has led to genetic mutations in once controlled diseases. These "super bugs" resist traditional medical solutions, and their defeat represents the next great challenge of the medical field.

Pesticides

Scientists also developed new kinds of chemical pesticides to protect crops from destruction by insects and to protect humans from such insect-carried diseases as typhus and *DDT* malaria. Perhaps the most famous of the new pesticides was dichlorodiphenyltrichloroethane, generally known as DDT, a compound discovered in 1939 by the Swiss chemist Paul Muller. He had discovered that although DDT seemed harmless to human beings and other mammals, it was extremely toxic to insects. American scientists learned of Muller's discovery in 1942, just as the army was grappling with the insect-borne tropical diseases—especially malaria and typhus—that threatened American soldiers.

DDT was first used on a large scale in Italy in 1943–1944 during a typhus outbreak, which it quickly helped end. Soon DDT was being sprayed in mosquito-infested areas of Pacific islands where American troops were fighting the Japanese. The incidence of malaria dropped precipitously. DDT quickly gained a reputation as a miraculous tool for controlling insects, and it undoubtedly saved thousands of lives. Only later did it become evident that DDT had long-term toxic effects on animals and humans.

Postwar Electronic Research

The 1940s and 1950s saw dramatic new developments in electronic technology. Researchers
Television in the 1940s produced the first commercially viable televisions and created a
technology that made it possible to broadcast programming over large areas. In the late
1950s, scientists at Radio Corporation of America, better known as RCA, developed color
television, which first became widely available in the early 1960s.

In 1948, Bell Labs, the research arm of AT&T, produced the first transistor, a solid-state
device capable of amplifying electrical signals that was much smaller and more efficient
than the cumbersome vacuum tubes that had powered most electronic equipment in the past.
Transistors made possible the miniaturization of many devices (radios, televisions, audio
equipment, hearing aids) and were also important in aviation, weaponry, and satellites. They
contributed as well to another major breakthrough in electronics: the development of integrated circuitry in the late 1950s.

Integrated circuits combined a number of once-separate electronic elements (transistors,
resistors, diodes, and others) and embedded them into a single, microscopically small
device. They made it possible to create increasingly complex electronic devices requiring
complicated circuitry that would have been impractical to produce through other means.
Most of all, integrated circuits helped advance the development of the computer.

Postwar Computer Technology

Prior to the 1950s, computers had been constructed mainly to perform complicated math-
ematical tasks, such as breaking military codes. In the 1950s, they began to perform
commercial functions for the first time.

The first significant computer of the 1950s was the Universal Automatic Computer (or
UNIVAC), which was developed initially for the U.S. Bureau of the Census by the
Remington Rand Company. It was able to handle both alphabetical and numerical information easily. It used tape storage and could perform calculations and other functions
much faster than its predecessor, the Electronic Numerical Integrator and Computer.
Searching for a larger market for its very expensive new device, Remington Rand arranged
UNIVAC to use a UNIVAC to predict the results of the 1952 election for CBS television
news. Analyzing early voting results, the UNIVAC accurately predicted an enormous
landslide victory for Eisenhower over Stevenson. Few Americans had ever heard of a
computer before that night, and the UNIVAC's television debut became a critical breakthrough in public awareness of computer technology.

Remington Rand had limited success in marketing the UNIVAC, but in the mid-1950s the
International Business Machines Company (IBM) introduced its first major data-processing
computers and marketed them among businesses in the United States and abroad. These early
successes, combined with the enormous amount of money IBM invested in research and
development, made the company the worldwide leader in computers for many years.

Bombs, Rockets, and Missiles

In 1952, the United States successfully detonated the first hydrogen bomb. (The Soviet
Union tested its first H-bomb a year later.) Unlike the plutonium and uranium bombs
developed during World War II, the hydrogen bomb derives its vastly greater power not
Nuclear Fusion from fission (the splitting of atoms) but fusion (the joining together of
lighter atomic elements with heavier ones).

The hydrogen bomb gave considerable impetus to a stalled scientific project in both the United States and the Soviet Union: the effort to develop unmanned rockets and missiles capable of carrying the new weapons—not suitable for delivery by airplanes—to their targets. Both nations began to put tremendous resources into their development. The United States benefited from the emigration to America of some of the German scientists who had helped develop rocketry for Germany during World War II.

In the United States, early missile research, conducted almost entirely by the air force, produced significant early successes in developing rockets capable of traveling several hundred miles. But American and Soviet leaders struggled to build longer-range missiles that were capable of traveling through space and across oceans and continents to reach distant targets: intercontinental ballistic missiles, or ICBMs. American scientists experimented   *ICBMs* in the 1950s first with the Atlas and then the Titan ICBM. Despite some early successes, the difficulty of massing sufficient stable fuel to provide the tremendous power needed to launch missiles beyond the atmosphere stymied progress. By 1958, however, scientists had created a solid fuel to replace the volatile liquid fuels of the early missiles. They had also produced miniaturized guidance systems capable of ensuring that missiles could travel to reasonably precise destinations. Within a few years, a new generation of missile capable of traveling several thousand miles, known as the Minuteman, became the basis of the American atomic weapons arsenal. American scientists also developed a nuclear missile capable of being carried and fired by submarines—the Polaris, which is launched from below the surface of the ocean by compressed air and fires its engines only once it is above the surface. A Polaris was first successfully fired from underwater in 1960.

THE SPACE PROGRAM

In the beginning, the American space program was a by-product of the rivalry with the Soviet Union. Its origins can be traced most directly to a dramatic event in 1957, when the Soviet Union announced that it had launched an earth-orbiting satellite—*Sputnik*—into outer space. The United States had yet to perform any similar feats, and the   *Sputnik* American government (and much of American society) reacted with alarm. Federal policy began encouraging (and funding) strenuous efforts to improve scientific education in the schools, to create more research laboratories, and, above all, to speed the development of America's own exploration of outer space. The United States launched its own first satellite, *Explorer I,* in January 1958.

The centerpiece of space exploration, however, soon became the manned space program, established in 1958 along with a new agency, the National Aeronautics and Space Administration (NASA). The first American space pilots, or "astronauts," quickly became revered heroes. On May 5, 1961, Alan Shepard became the first American launched into space. But his short suborbital flight came several months after a Soviet "cosmonaut," Yuri Gagarin, had made a flight in which he had actually orbited the earth. On February 2, 1962, John Glenn (later a United States senator) became the first American to orbit the globe. NASA later introduced the Gemini program, whose spacecraft could carry two astronauts at once.

These early successes led to the creation of the Apollo program, whose purpose was to land astronauts on the moon. It suffered some catastrophic setbacks, most   *Apollo Program* notably a fire in January 1967 that killed three astronauts during a training session. But on July 20, 1969, Neil Armstrong, Edwin "Buzz" Aldrin, and Michael Collins successfully traveled in a space capsule into orbit around the moon. Armstrong and Aldrin then

MOON WALK   Edwin ("Buzz") Aldrin is photographed by his fellow astronaut Neil Armstrong in July 1969, when they became the first humans to set foot on the surface of the moon.   (NASA)

detached a smaller craft from the capsule, landed on the surface of the moon, and became the first humans to walk on a celestial body other than earth. Six more lunar missions followed, the last in 1972.

Eventually, the space program became a relatively modest effort to make travel in near-space easier and more practical through the development of the "space shuttle," an airplanelike device launched by a missile but capable of both navigating in space and landing on earth, much like a conventional aircraft. The first space shuttle was success-fully launched in 1982. The explosion of one shuttle, *Challenger,* in January 1986 shortly after takeoff, killing all seven astronauts, stalled the program for two years. Missions resumed in the late 1980s, but problems remained, as illustrated by the explosion of the space shuttle *Columbia* during reentry in 2003. The space shuttle was used to launch and repair communications satellites and to insert the Hubble Space Telescope into orbit in 1990 (and to repair its flawed lens on several occasions, including in 2009). The space shuttle program officially ended in 2011.

PEOPLE OF PLENTY

Among the most striking social developments of the postwar era was the rapid extension of a middle-class lifestyle and outlook to an expanding portion of the population. The historian David Potter published an influential examination of "economic abundance and American character" in 1954. He called it *People of Plenty.* For the American middle class in the 1950s, at least, it seemed an appropriate label.

THE CONSUMER CULTURE

At the center of middle-class culture in the 1950s was a growing preoccupation with consumer goods—a result of increased prosperity, greater variety and availability of products, and the adeptness of advertisers in creating demand. It was also a result of the growth of consumer credit, which increased by 800 percent between 1945 and 1957 through the development of credit cards, revolving charge accounts, and easy-payment plans. Prosperity fueled a greater desire for such longtime consumer goods as the auto-mobile, and Detroit responded to the boom with ever-flashier styling and accessories. Consumers also responded eagerly to such new products as dishwashers, garbage dispos-als, television, and stereos.

Because consumer goods were so often marketed (and advertised) nationally, the 1950s were notable for the rapid spread of great national consumer crazes. For example, children, adolescents, and even some adults became entranced in the late 1950s with the hula hoop—a large plastic ring kept spinning around the waist. The popularity of the Walt Disney–produced children's television show *The Mickey Mouse Club* created a national demand for Mickey Mouse watches and hats and also contributed to the stunning success of Disneyland, an amusement park near Los Angeles that re-created many of the charac-ters and events of Disney entertainment programs.

THE SUBURBAN NATION

A third of the nation's population lived in suburbs by 1960—a result not only of increased affluence but of important innovations in home building, which made single-family houses affordable to millions of new people. The most famous of the suburban developers, William Levitt built low-cost, mass-produced houses in large suburban developments known as "Levittowns." These types of relatively inexpensive developments *Levittowns* popped up in New York, New Jersey, and Pennsylvania but also soon appeared through-out the country.

Why did so many Americans want to move to the suburbs? One reason was the enormous importance postwar Americans placed on family life after five years of war. Suburbs provided families with larger homes than they could find (or afford) in the cities and thus made it easier to raise larger numbers of children. The suburbs provided privacy and a sense of security from the noise and dangers of urban living. They offered space for new consumer goods—the appliances, cars, boats, outdoor furniture, and other products that many middle-class Americans craved.

Another factor motivating white Americans to move to the suburbs was race. Most suburbs were restricted to white inhabitants—both because relatively few African Americans could afford to live in them and because formal and informal barriers kept even prosperous blacks out of all but a few. In an era when the black population of most cities was rapidly growing, many white families fled to the suburbs to escape the integra-tion of urban neighborhoods and schools.

THE SUBURBAN FAMILY

For professional men (who tended to work in the city, at some distance from their homes), suburban life generally meant a rigid division between their working and personal worlds. For many middle-class women, it meant an increased isolation from the workplace. Many middle-class husbands considered it demeaning for their wives to be employed. And many women themselves shied away from the workplace when they could afford to, in part because of prevailing ideas about motherhood (popularized by such widely consulted books as Dr. Benjamin Spock's *Baby and Child Care,* first published in 1946) that advised women to stay at home with their children. Stay-at-home mothers supposedly raised healthier, more disciplined children.

Some women, however, had to balance these pressures against other, contradictory ones. As expectations of material comfort rose, many middle-class families needed a second income to maintain the standard of living they desired. As a result, the number of married women working outside the home actually increased in the postwar years. By 1960, nearly a third of all married women were part of the paid workforce.

THE BIRTH OF TELEVISION

Television was the result of a series of scientific and technological discoveries, but its impact was largely social and cultural. It quickly became perhaps the most powerful medium of mass communication in history. Experiments in broadcasting pictures (along with sound) had begun as early as the 1920s, but commercial television began only shortly after World War II. Its growth was phenomenally rapid. In 1946, there were only 17,000 sets in the country; by 1957, there were 40 million—almost as many television sets as there were families. More people had television sets, according to one report, than had refrigerators.

The television industry emerged directly out of the radio industry, and all three of the major networks—the National Broadcasting Company, the Columbia Broadcasting System, and the American Broadcasting Company—had started as radio companies. Advertising drove the television business. The need to attract advertisers determined most programming decisions; and in the early days of television, corporate sponsors often played a direct role in determining the content of programs. Many early television shows bore the names of the corporations that were paying for them: the *General Electric Theater,* the *Chrysler Theatre,* the *Camel News Caravan,* and others. Some daytime serials (known as "soap operas," because their sponsors were almost always companies making household goods targeted at women) were actually written and produced by Procter & Gamble and other companies.

By the late 1950s, television news had replaced newspapers, magazines, and radios as the nation's most important vehicle of information. Television advertising helped create a vast market for new fashions and products. Televised athletic events made college and professional sports one of the most important sources of entertainment (and one of the biggest businesses) in America by the 1970s. Television entertainment programming—almost all of it controlled by the three national networks and their corporate sponsors—replaced movies and radio as the principal source of diversion for American families.

Much of the programming of the 1950s and early 1960s created a common image of American life—an image that was predominantly white, middle class, and suburban. Television was epitomized by the popular situation comedies, featuring families in which, as the title of one of the most popular shows put it, *Father Knows Best,* and women were mothers and housewives striving to serve their children and please their husbands. Another top comedy, *I Love Lucy,* featured women in conventional roles but also tried to expand them, often in hilarious ways. *I Love Lucy* both idealized and poked fun at conventional domestic life.

LUCY AND DESI   Although the network worried that American viewers would not accept an ethnically mixed marriage (Desi was Cuban-born, Lucy was Anglo-American), *I Love Lucy* was a huge hit for CBS in the 1950s. "People identified with the Ricardos," Lucille Ball once said, "because we had the same problems they had. We just took ordinary situations and exaggerated them."   (©CBS/Photofest)

Yet television also could create conditions that could accentuate social conflict. Even those unable to share in the affluence of the era could, through television, acquire a vivid picture of how the rest of their society lived. While television was celebrating the white middle class, it was also showing glimpses of the alienation and powerlessness of groups who felt excluded from the world it portrayed. And television news conveyed with unprecedented power the social upheavals that gradually spread beginning in the late 1950s.

Travel, Outdoor Recreation, and Environmentalism

Although the idea of a paid vacation for American workers, and the connection of that idea with travel, had entered American culture beginning in the 1920s, it was not until the postwar years that vacation travel became truly widespread among middle-income Americans. The construction of the interstate highway system contributed dramatically to the growth of travel. (See Patterns of Popular Culture: "On the Road.") So did the increasing affluence of workers. Even in the 1950s, there was a healthy market for vacation vehicles—trailers and small vans. That market grew steadily larger in subsequent decades. But the urge to travel was also an expression of some of the same impulses that produced suburbs: a desire to escape the crowding and stress of densely populated areas and find a place where it was possible to experience the natural world.

ON THE ROAD

People have traveled across the Americas for thousands of years, often with considerable difficulty. Indians had to make paths over rough terrain. Immigrants from England, Scotland, Mexico, and many other places began to move from town to town often on log roads. Later, they used stones and pebbles to create new byways. Wagons and carriages often rode on bumpy or muddy surfaces. Of course, many years later more-efficient, comfortable roads were built across the American continent, a development that changed American life dramatically.

In the mid-twentieth century, automobiles traveled more slowly than they do today. But cars allowed travelers to discover interesting places and meet new people as they moved from town to town. Jack Kerouac, in his famous book *On the Road* (1957), was one of the first to capture in writing the new spirit of automobile travel. "It was drizzling and mysterious at the beginning of our journey," Kerouac wrote as he got his battered car ready. "I could see that it was all going to be one big saga of the mist. . . . We were all delighted, when we all realized we were leaving confusion and nonsense behind and performing our one and noble function of the time, *move.* And we moved!"

In the 1950s, Route 66 was one of the first highways to cross most of the United States, from the West Coast to Chicago. But Route 66 became more than a road; it became a popular symbol of a country on the move. Travelers could drive along the famous highway while listening to the hit song "(Get Your Kicks On) Route 66" on the radio. A television series called *Route 66*

depicted characters becoming involved in all sorts of drama as they traveled the storied route.

People traveling long distances, perhaps even across the continent, needed restaurants, motels, and shops, a development that encouraged the creation of fast-food chains, many of which began with drive-in restaurants where customers could be served and eat in their cars. The first drive-in restaurant, Royce Hailey's Pig Stand, opened in Dallas in 1921, followed later in the decade by the White Tower. Ray Kroc's McDonald's opened its first

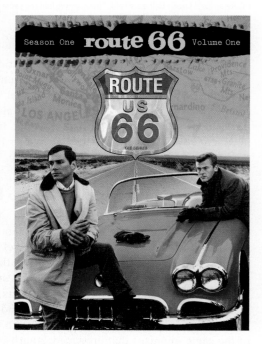

ROUTE 66 The television show *Route 66*, starring George Maharis and Martin Milner, conveyed in popular culture the optimistic energy of a driving nation. (© CBS/Photofest)

outlets in Des Plaines, Illinois, and Southern California in 1955. Five years later, there were 228 outlets. In time, with thousands of restaurants, McDonald's became the most recognizable symbol of food in the world. Large supermarket chains—catering to customers with automobiles—replaced smaller, family-owned markets in town centers. Large centers and shopping malls moved the center of retailing out of cities and into separate, sprawling complexes surrounded by large parking lots.

Eventually, with President Eisenhower's encouragement, the Federal Highway Act of 1956 provided money to build the interstate highway system. This network of highways made it possible for people to travel long distances quickly and efficiently. •

UNDERSTAND, ANALYZE, & EVALUATE

1. How did television programs like *Route 66* of the mid-1950s reflect much older American myths about the American West?
2. In what other ways than those described in this feature did the interstate highway system help the American economy?
3. What military advantages did the highway system provide?

Nowhere was this surge in travel and recreation more visible than in national parks, which underwent a long-term surge in attendance in the 1950s. People who traveled to national parks did so for many reasons—some to hike and camp, others to fish and hunt, and still others simply to see the extraordinary landscape. But whatever their motives, most visitors came in search of an experience in the wilderness. The importance of that search became clear in the early 1950s with the fight to preserve Echo Park.

Echo Park is a spectacular valley in the Dinosaur National Monument, on the border between Utah and Colorado and near the southern border of Wyoming. In the early 1950s, the federal government's Bureau of Reclamation—which encouraged irrigation, electric power, and water supplies—proposed building a dam across the Green River, which runs through Echo Valley, to create a lake for recreation and a source of *Echo Park Controversy* hydroelectric power. The American environmental movement had been relatively quiet since its searing defeat early in the century in its effort to stop a similar dam in the Hetch Hetchy Valley at Yosemite National Park. But the Echo Park proposal helped rouse it from its slumber.

In 1950, Bernard DeVoto—a well-known writer and a great champion of the American West—published an essay in the *Saturday Evening Post* titled "Shall We Let Them Ruin Our National Parks?" It had a sensational impact, arousing opposition to the Echo Valley dam from many areas of the country. The Sierra Club, relatively obscure in previous decades, sprang into action. The controversy helped elevate a new and aggressive leader, David Brower, who eventually transformed the club into one of the nation's leading environmental organizations. By the mid-1950s, a large coalition of environmentalists, naturalists, and wilderness vacationers had mobilized in opposition to the dam, and in 1956, Congress—bowing to public pressure—blocked the project and preserved Echo Park in its natural state. The controversy was a major victory for those who wished to preserve the sanctity of the national parks, and it was an important spur to the dawning environmental consciousness.

ORGANIZED SOCIETY AND ITS DETRACTORS

Large-scale organizations and bureaucracies increased their influence over American life in the postwar era, as they had been doing for many decades before. White-collar workers came to outnumber blue-collar laborers for the first time, and an increasing proportion of them worked in corporate settings with rigid hierarchical structures. Industrial workers also confronted large bureaucracies both in the workplace and in their own unions.

The debilitating impact of bureaucratic life on the individual became one of the central themes of popular and scholarly debate. William H. Whyte Jr. produced one of the most *The Organization Man* widely discussed books of the decade: *The Organization Man* (1956), which attempted to describe the special mentality of the worker in a large bureaucratic setting. Self-reliance, Whyte claimed, was losing place to conformity and the ability to "get along" and "work as a team." The sociologist David Riesman made similar observations in *The Lonely Crowd* (1950), in which he argued that the traditional "inner-directed man," who judged himself on the basis of his own values and the esteem of his family, was giving way to a new "other-directed man," more concerned with winning the approval of the larger organization or community.

Novelists, too, expressed misgivings in their work about the impersonality of modern society. Saul Bellow produced a series of novels—*The Adventures of Augie March* (1953), *Seize the Day* (1956), *Herzog* (1964), and many others—that chronicled the difficulties of American Jewish men in finding fulfillment in modern urban America. J. D. Salinger wrote in *The Catcher in the Rye* (1951) of a prep-school student, Holden Caulfield, who is unable to find any area of society—school, family, friends, city—in which he can feel secure or committed.

THE BEATS AND THE RESTLESS CULTURE OF YOUTH

The most derisive critics of bureaucracy and middle-class society were a group of young *Beat Writers* poets, writers, and artists known as the "beats" and often called "beatniks" by disapproving critics. They wrote harsh critiques of what they considered the sterility and conformity of American life, the meaninglessness of American politics, and the banality of popular culture. Jack Kerouac produced the most popular document of the Beat Generation in his novel *On the Road* (1957), an account of a cross-country automobile trip that depicts the rootless, iconoclastic lifestyle of Kerouac and his friends.

The beats were the most visible evidence of a widespread restiveness among young *"Juvenile Delinquency"* Americans in the 1950s. The phenomenon of "juvenile delinquency" attracted tremendous public attention, and in both politics and popular culture, dire warnings surfaced about the growing criminality of American youth. The 1955 film *Blackboard Jungle,* for example, was a frightening depiction of crime and violence in city schools. Scholarly studies, presidential commissions, and journalistic exposés all contributed to the sense of alarm about the spread of delinquency—although in fact, youth crime did not dramatically increase in the 1950s.

The culture of alienation that the beats so vividly represented had counterparts even in ordinary middle-class behavior: teenage rebelliousness toward parents, youthful fascination with fast cars and motorcycles, and increasing sexual activity, assisted by the greater availability of birth-control devices. The popularity of James Dean, who starred in *Rebel Without a Cause* (1955), *East of Eden* (1955), and *Giant* (1956), was a particularly vivid sign of youth culture in the 1950s. Both in the roles he played (moody, alienated teenagers and young men with a streak of self-destructive violence) and in the way he lived his own life (he died in 1955, at the age of 24, in an automobile accident), Dean became an icon of the unfocused rebelliousness of American youth in his time.

Rock 'n' Roll

One of the most important cultural developments of the 1950s was the birth of rock 'n' roll—and the enormous popularity of the greatest early rock star, Elvis Presley.   *Elvis Presley* Presley became a symbol of a youthful determination to push at the borders of the conventional and the acceptable. His sultry good looks, his self-conscious effort to dress in the vaguely rebellious style of urban gangs (motorcycle jackets and slicked-back hair, even though Presley himself was a product of the conservative rural South), and, most of all, the open sexuality of his music and his public performances—all made him wildly popular among young Americans in the 1950s. His first great hit, "Heartbreak Hotel," established him as a national phenomenon in 1956, and he remained a powerful figure in American popular culture well after his death in 1977.

Presley's music, like that of many early white rock musicians, drew heavily from black rhythm and blues traditions. Sam Phillips, a record promoter who had recorded some of the important black R&B musicians of his time, reportedly said in the early 1950s: "If I could find a white man with a Negro sound, I could make a billion dollars." Soon after that, he found Presley. But there were others as well—among them Buddy Holly and Bill Haley (whose 1955 song "Rock Around the Clock," used in the film *Blackboard Jungle,* announced the arrival of rock 'n' roll to millions of young people)—who were closely connected to African American musical traditions. Rock drew from other sources, too: from country western music (another strong influence on Presley), from gospel music, even from jazz.

ELVIS   **This photograph of the musician in performance is from very early in his career.** (© Photo by Hulton Archive/Getty Images)

The 1950s also saw African American bands and singers grow in popularity among both black and white audiences. Chuck Berry, Little Richard, B. B. King, Chubby Checker, the Temptations, the Miracles, the Supremes, and others—many of them recorded by the *Motown Records* black producer Berry Gordy, the founder and president of Motown Records in Detroit—never rivaled Presley in their popularity among white youths but did develop significant multiracial audiences of their own.

The rapid rise of rock owed a great deal to innovations in radio and television programming. By the 1950s, radio stations no longer felt obliged to present mostly live programming—especially once television took over many of the entertainment functions radio had once performed. Instead, many radio stations devoted themselves almost entirely to playing recorded music. Early in the 1950s, a new breed of radio announcers, known as "disk jockeys," or "djs" for the records they played, began to create programming aimed specifically at young fans of rock music; and when those programs became wildly successful, other stations followed suit. *American Bandstand,* which began airing in 1957, was a televised showcase for rock 'n' roll hits in which a live audience danced to recorded music. The program helped spread the popularity of rock—and made its host, Dick Clark, one of the best-known figures among young Americans.

Radio and television were important to the recording industry, of course, because they encouraged the rapidly increasing sale of records in the mid- and late 1950s, especially in the inexpensive and popular 45 rpm format—small disks that contained one song on each side. Also important were jukeboxes, which played individual songs on 45s and which proliferated in soda fountains, diners, bars, and other places where young people congregated. Sales of records increased from $182 million to $521 million between 1954 and 1960. So eager were record promoters to get their songs on the air that they routinely made secret payments to station owners and disk jockeys to encour-*Payola Scandals* age them to showcase their artists. These payments, which became known as "payola," produced a briefly sensational series of scandals when they were exposed in the late 1950s and early 1960s.

THE OTHER AMERICA

It was relatively easy for white middle-class Americans in the 1950s to believe that the world of economic growth, personal affluence, and cultural homogeneity was universal and that their values and assumptions were ones that most other Americans shared. But such beliefs were false. Large groups of Americans remained outside the circle of abundance and shared neither in the affluence of the middle class nor in many of its values.

ON THE MARGINS OF THE AFFLUENT SOCIETY

In 1962, the socialist writer Michael Harrington published a celebrated book called *The Other America,* which chronicled the continuing existence of poverty in the United States.

The great economic expansion of the postwar years reduced poverty dramatically but *The Other America* did not eliminate it. In 1960, at any given moment, more than a fifth of all American families (over 30 million people) continued to live below what the government defined as the poverty line (down from a third of all families fifteen years before). Many millions more lived just above the official poverty line, but with incomes that gave them little comfort and no security.

Most of the poor—up to 80 percent—experienced poverty intermittently and temporarily. But approximately 20 percent were people for whom poverty was a continuous, often inescapable reality. That included approximately half the nation's elderly population and a significant proportion of African Americans and Hispanics. Native Americans constituted the single poorest group in the country.

This "hard-core" poverty rebuked the popular assumption that "a rising tide lifts all boats." It was a poverty that the growing prosperity of the postwar era seemed to affect hardly at all, a poverty, as Harrington observed, that appeared "impervious to hope."

Rural Poverty

Among those on the margins of the affluent society were many rural Americans. In 1948, farmers had received 8.9 percent of the national income; in 1956, they received only 4.1 percent. In part, this decline reflected the steadily shrinking farm population; in 1956 alone, nearly 10 percent of the rural population moved into or was absorbed by cities. But it also reflected declining farm prices. Because of enormous surpluses in basic staples, prices fell 33 percent in those years, even though national income as a whole rose 50 percent at the same time. The surpluses were the result of higher yields per acre as well as increases in the amount of acreage under production, a function of the widespread use of tractors.

Sharecroppers and tenant farmers (most of them African American) continued to live at or below subsistence levels throughout the rural South—in part because of the mechanization of cotton picking after 1944, in part because of the development of synthetic fibers that reduced demand for cotton. (Two-thirds of the cotton acreage went out of production between 1930 and 1960.) Migrant farmworkers, a group concentrated especially in the West and Southwest and containing many Mexican American and Asian American workers, lived in similarly dire circumstances. In rural areas without much commercial agriculture—such as the Appalachian region in the East, where the decline of the coal economy reduced the one significant source of support for the region—whole communities lived in desperate poverty, increasingly cut off from the market economy. All these groups were vulnerable to malnutrition and even starvation.

The Inner Cities

As prospering white families moved from cities to suburbs in vast numbers, more and more inner-city neighborhoods became repositories for the poor, "ghettoes" *Growth of "Ghettoes"* from which there was no easy escape. The growth of these neighborhoods owed much to a vast migration of African Americans out of the countryside and into industrial cities. Not all these black migrants were poor, and many found in the city routes to economic progress similar to those of whites. But African Americans were substantially more likely to live in poverty than most other groups, in part because of the persistent patterns of discrimination that denied them any real opportunities.

More than 3 million black men and women moved from the South to northern cities between 1940 and 1960. Chicago, Detroit, Cleveland, New York, and other eastern and midwestern industrial cities experienced a major expansion of their black populations while many whites were leaving cities at the same time.

Similar migrations from Mexico and Puerto Rico expanded poor Hispanic neighborhoods in many American cities. Between 1940 and 1960, nearly a million Puerto Ricans moved into American cities, especially New York. Mexican workers crossed the borders into Texas and California and swelled the already substantial Latino communities of such cities as San Antonio, Houston, San Diego, and Los Angeles (which by 1960 had the largest Mexican American population of any city, approximately 500,000 people).

Inner cities filled up with poor minority residents at the same time that the unskilled industrial jobs they sought diminished. Employers were moving factories and mills from old industrial cities to new locations in suburban and rural areas, smaller cities, and even abroad—places where the costs of labor were lower. Even in the factories that remained, *Shrinking Job Opportunities* automation reduced the number of unskilled jobs. The economic opportunities that had helped earlier immigrant groups to rise up from poverty were unavailable to many of the postwar migrants. Racial discrimination in hiring, education, and housing doomed many members of these communities to continuing poverty.

THE RISE OF THE CIVIL RIGHTS MOVEMENT

After decades of skirmishes, an open battle began in the 1950s against racial segregation and discrimination, a battle that would prove to be one of the longest and most difficult social struggles of the twentieth century. White Americans ultimately played an important role in the civil rights movement. But pressure from African Americans themselves was the crucial element in raising the issue of race to prominence.

THE *BROWN* DECISION AND "MASSIVE RESISTANCE"

On May 17, 1954, the Supreme Court announced its decision in the case of *Brown v. Board of Education of Topeka.* In considering the legal segregation of a Kansas public school system, the Court rejected its own 1896 *Plessy v. Ferguson* decision, which had ruled that communities could provide African Americans with separate facilities as long *"Separate but Equal" Rejected* as the facilities were equal to those of whites. The *Brown* decision declared that segregating public schools on the basis of race was unconstitutional. The justices argued that school segregation inflicted unacceptable damage on those it affected, regardless of the relative quality of the separate schools. Chief Justice Earl Warren explained the unanimous opinion of his colleagues: "We conclude that in the field of public education the doctrine of 'separate but equal' has no place. Separate educational facilities are inherently unequal." The following year, the Court issued another decision (known as *Brown II*) to provide rules for implementing the 1954 order. It ruled that communities must work to desegregate their schools "with all deliberate speed," but it set no timetable and left specific decisions up to lower courts.

Some communities, such as Washington, D.C., complied relatively quickly and quietly. More often, however, strong local opposition (what came to be known in the South as "massive resistance") produced long delays and bitter conflicts. More than 100 southern members of Congress signed a 1956 "manifesto" denouncing the *Brown* decision and urging their constituents to defy it. Southern governors, mayors, local school boards, and nongovernmental pressure groups (including hundreds of White Citizens' Councils) all worked to obstruct desegregation. By the fall of 1957, only 684 of 3,000 affected school districts in the South had even begun to desegregate their schools.

The Eisenhower administration was not eager to join the battle over desegregation. But in September 1957, it faced a case of direct state defiance of federal authority and felt compelled to act. Federal courts had ordered the desegregation of Central High

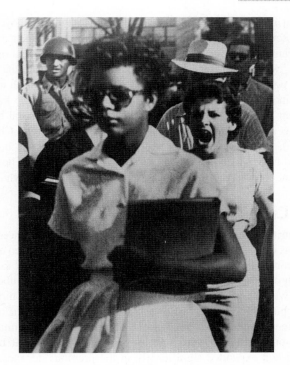

LITTLE ROCK, 1957   African American student Elizabeth Eckford passes by jeering whites on her way to Little Rock Central High School, newly integrated by federal court order. (© Everett Collection/SuperStock)

School in Little Rock, Arkansas. An angry white mob tried to stop implementation of the order by blockading the entrances to the school. Governor *Little Rock's Central High School* Orval Faubus refused to do anything to stop the obstruction. President Eisenhower finally responded by sending federal troops to Little Rock to keep the peace and ensure that the court orders would be obeyed. Only then did Central High School admit its first black students.

THE EXPANDING MOVEMENT

The *Brown* decision helped spark a growing number of popular challenges to other forms of segregation in the South. On December 1, 1955, Rosa Parks, an African *Rosa Parks* American woman, was arrested in Montgomery, Alabama, when she refused to give up her seat on a Montgomery bus to a white passenger (as required by the Jim Crow laws throughout most of the South). The arrest of this admired woman and local civil rights leader produced outrage in the city's African American community, which organized a boycott of the bus system to demand an end to segregated seating.

The boycott was almost completely effective. It put economic pressure not only on the bus company but on many Montgomery merchants, because the boycotters found it difficult to get to downtown stores and shopped instead in their own neighborhoods. Even so, the boycott might well have failed had it not been for a Supreme Court decision late in 1956, *Browder v. Gayle,* that declared segregation in public transportation to be illegal. The buses in Montgomery abandoned their discriminatory seating policies, and the boycott came to a close.

Among the most important accomplishments of the Montgomery boycott were the legitimization of a new form of racial protest and the elevation to prominence of a new figure in the civil rights movement. The man chosen to lead the boycott movement once it was launched *Martin Luther King Jr.* was a local Baptist pastor, Martin Luther King Jr., the son of a prominent Atlanta minister, a powerful orator, and a gifted leader. King's approach to black protest was based on the doctrine of nonviolent resistance to injustice, even in the face of direct attack. And he produced an approach to racial struggle that captured the moral high ground for his supporters. For the next thirteen years—as leader of the Southern Christian Leadership Conference (SCLC), an interracial group he founded shortly after the boycott—he was the most influential and most widely admired black leader in the country. The popular movement he came to represent soon spread throughout the South and the country.

CAUSES OF THE CIVIL RIGHTS MOVEMENT

Several factors contributed to the rise of African American protest in these years. The legacy of World War II was one of the most important. Millions of black women and men had served in the military or worked in war plants during the war. They had fought to end totalitarianism and the suppression of freedom abroad and now demanded basic civil liberties at home.

Another factor was the growth of an urban black middle class, which had been developing for decades but which began to flourish after the war. Much of the impetus for the civil rights movement came from the leaders of urban black communities—ministers, educators, professionals. Much of it came as well from students at black colleges and universities, which had expanded significantly in the previous decades. Men and women with education were often more aware of the obstacles to their advancement than poorer and more oppressed people.

Television and other forms of popular culture also played a role in the rising consciousness of racism. More than any previous generation, postwar blacks had constant, vivid reminders of how the white majority lived—of the world from which they were effectively excluded. Television also conveyed the activities of demonstrators to a national audience, ensuring that activism in one community would inspire similar protests in others.

Other forces mobilized many white Americans to support the movement once it began. The Cold War made racial injustice an embarrassment to Americans trying to present their nation as a model to the world. Political mobilization of northern blacks created a substantial voting bloc within the Democratic Party. Politicians from northern industrial states could not ignore their views. Labor unions with substantial black memberships also played an important part in supporting (and funding) the civil rights movement.

This great social movement emerged as one of the most powerful forces for racial change in America.

EISENHOWER REPUBLICANISM

Dwight D. Eisenhower was the least experienced politician to serve in the White House in the twentieth century. He was also among the most popular and politically successful presidents of the postwar era. At home, he pursued essentially moderate policies, avoiding most new initiatives but accepting the work of earlier reformers. Abroad, he continued and even intensified American commitments to oppose communism but also brought a measure of restraint that his successors did not always match.

"What Was Good for . . . General Motors"

The first Republican administration in twenty years staffed itself with men drawn from the same quarter as those who had staffed Republican administrations in the 1920s: the business community. But by the 1950s, many business leaders had acquired a social and political outlook very different from that of their predecessors. Above all, many of the nation's leading business executives and financiers had reconciled themselves to at least the broad outlines of the Keynesian welfare state, named after the famed Great Depression economist John Maynard Keynes and launched during the New Deal. Indeed, some corporate leaders had come to see it as something that actually benefited them—by helping maintain social order, by increasing mass purchasing power, and by stabilizing labor relations.

To his cabinet, Eisenhower appointed wealthy corporate lawyers and business executives who were unapologetic about their backgrounds. Charles Wilson, president of General Motors, assured senators considering his nomination for secretary of defense that "what was good for our country was good for General Motors, and vice versa."

Eisenhower encouraged private enterprise. He supported the private rather than public development of natural resources. To the chagrin of farmers, he lowered federal support for farm prices. He also removed the last limited wage and price controls maintained by the Truman administration, opposed the creation of new social service programs such as national health insurance, and strove constantly to reduce federal expenditures (even during the recession of 1958) and balance the budget. He ended 1960, his last full year in office, with a $1 billion budget surplus.

The Survival of the Welfare State

While the president took few new initiatives in domestic policy, he steadily resisted conservative pressure to dismantle the welfare policies of the New Deal. Indeed, during his term, he agreed to extend the Social Security system to an additional 10 million people and unemployment compensation to an additional 4 million, and he approved an increase to the minimum hourly wage from 75 cents to $1. One of the most significant legislative accomplishments of the Eisenhower administration was the Federal   *Federal Highway Act of 1956* Highway Act of 1956, which authorized $25 billion for a ten-year project that built over 40,000 miles of interstate highways—the largest public works project in American history to that point. The program was funded through a highway "trust fund," whose revenues would come from new taxes on the purchase of fuel, automobiles, trucks, and tires.

In 1956, Eisenhower ran for a second term, even though he had suffered a serious heart attack the previous year. With Adlai Stevenson opposing him once again, he won by another, even greater landslide, receiving 57.6 percent of the popular vote and 457 electoral votes to Stevenson's 73. Democrats retained control of both houses of Congress they had won back in 1954. In 1958—even during a serious recession—they increased that control by substantial margins.

The Decline of McCarthyism

The Eisenhower administration did little in its first years in office to discourage the anticommunist furor that had gripped the nation. By 1954, however, what came to be known as McCarthyism began to become increasingly unpopular.

During the first year of the Eisenhower administration, McCarthy continued to operate with impunity. But in January 1954, he attacked Secretary of the Army Robert Stevens and the armed services in general, claiming that communists had intruded into the military. At that point, the administration and influential members of Congress organized a special *Army–McCarthy Hearings* investigation of the charges, the Army–McCarthy hearings, which were among the first congressional hearings to be nationally televised. Watching McCarthy in action—bullying witnesses, hurling groundless (and often cruel) accusations, evading issues—much of the public began to see him as a villain, and even a buffoon. In December 1954, the Senate voted 67 to 22 to condemn him for "conduct unbecoming a senator." Three years later, he died—a victim, apparently, of complications arising from alcoholism. The Red Scare did not die with McCarthy, but its intensity soon began to decline.

EISENHOWER, DULLES, AND THE COLD WAR

The threat of nuclear war created a sense of high anxiety in international relations in the 1950s. But the nuclear threat also encouraged both superpowers to edge away from direct confrontations. Indeed, the attention of both the United States and the Soviet Union began to turn instead to the rapidly growing instability in the Third World.

DULLES AND "MASSIVE RETALIATION"

Secretary of State John Foster Dulles was the most important figure in the Eisenhower administration next to the president himself. He was an aristocratic corporate lawyer with a stern moral revulsion to communism. He entered office denouncing the containment policies of the Truman years as excessively passive, arguing that the United States should pursue an active program of "liberation," which would lead to a "rollback" of communist expansion. Once in power, however, he had to defer to the more moderate views of the president himself.

The most prominent of Dulles's innovations was the policy of "massive retaliation," which he announced early in 1954. The United States would, he explained, respond to communist threats to its allies not by using conventional forces in local conflicts (a policy that he claimed had led to so much frustration in Korea) but by relying on "the deterrent of massive retaliatory power" (by which he clearly meant nuclear weapons). In part, the new doctrines reflected Dulles's inclination for tense confrontations, an approach he once defined as **brinksmanship**—pushing the Soviet Union to the brink of war in order to exact concessions. But the real force behind the massive-retaliation policy was economics. With pressure growing both in and out of government for a reduction in American military expenditures, an increasing reliance on atomic weapons seemed to promise, as some advocates put it, "more bang for the buck."

FRANCE, AMERICA, AND VIETNAM

On July 27, 1953, negotiators at Panmunjom finally signed an agreement ending the hostilities in Korea. Each antagonist was to withdraw its troops a mile and a half from the existing battle line, which ran roughly along the 38th parallel—ironically, the prewar border between North and South Korea. A conference in Geneva was to consider means by which to reunite the nation peacefully—although in fact that 1954 meeting produced no agreement and left the cease-fire line in place as the apparently permanent border between the two countries into the twenty-first century.

Almost simultaneously, however, the United States was being drawn into a long, bitter struggle in Southeast Asia. Ever since 1945, France had been attempting to restore its authority over Vietnam, its one-time colony, which it had been forced to abandon to the Japanese toward the end of World War II. Opposing the French, however, were the powerful nationalist forces of Ho Chi Minh, determined to win independence *Ho Chi Minh* for their nation. Ho had hoped for American support in 1945, on the basis of the anti-colonial rhetoric of the Atlantic Charter and Franklin Roosevelt's speeches, and also because he had received support from American intelligence forces during World War II while fighting the Japanese. He was, however, not only a committed nationalist but a committed communist as well. The Truman administration ignored him and supported the French, one of America's most important Cold War allies.

By 1954, Ho was receiving aid from communist China and the Soviet Union. America, in the meantime, had been paying most of the costs of France's ineffective military campaign in Vietnam since 1950. Early in 1954, 12,000 French troops became surrounded in a disastrous siege at the village of Dien Bien Phu. Only American intervention, it was clear, could prevent the total collapse of the French military effort. Yet despite the urgings of Secretary of State Dulles, Vice President Nixon, and others, Eisenhower refused to permit direct American military intervention in Vietnam, claiming that neither Congress nor America's other allies would support such action.

Without American aid, the French defense of Dien Bien Phu finally collapsed on May 7, 1954, and France quickly abandoned Vietnam. They agreed to a settlement of the conflict at the same international conference in Geneva that was considering the Korean settlement. The Geneva accords on Vietnam of July 1954, to a participant, established a supposedly temporary division of Vietnam along the 17th parallel. The north would be governed by Ho Chi Minh, the south by a pro-Western regime. Democratic elections would be the basis for uniting the nation in 1956. The agreement marked the end of the French commitment to Vietnam and the beginning of an expanded American presence there. The United *U.S. Involvement in Vietnam* States helped establish a pro-American government in the south, headed by Ngo Dinh Diem, a member of his country's Roman Catholic minority. Because he enjoyed the full military backing of the American government, Diem acted ruthlessly at times, refusing, for example, to permit the 1956 popular elections when he realized he would lose.

COLD WAR CRISES

American foreign policy in the 1950s was challenged by both real and imagined crises in far-flung areas of the world. Among them were a series of crises in the Middle East, a region in which the United States had been little involved until after World War II.

On May 14, 1948, after years of Zionist efforts and a decision by the new United Nations, the nation of Israel proclaimed its independence. President Truman recognized the new Jewish homeland the next day. But the creation of Israel, while resolving some conflicts, created others. Palestinian Arabs, unwilling to accept being displaced *Israel Recognized* from what they considered their own country, joined with Israel's Arab neighbors and fought determinedly against the new state in 1948—the first of several Arab–Israeli wars.

Committed as the American government was to Israel, it was also concerned about the stability and friendliness of the Arab regimes in the oil-rich Middle East, where American petroleum companies had major investments. Thus the United States reacted with alarm as it watched Mohammed Mossadegh, the nationalist prime minister of Iran, begin to resist the presence of Western corporations in his nation in the early 1950s. In 1953, the

American CIA joined forces with conservative Iranian military leaders to engineer a coup *CIA-Backed Coup in Iran* that drove Mossadegh from office. To replace him, the CIA helped elevate the young shah of Iran, Mohammed Reza Pahlevi, from his position as token constitutional monarch to that of virtually absolute ruler. The shah remained closely tied to the United States for the next twenty-five years.

The U.S. State Department was less effective in influencing the nationalist government of Egypt, under the leadership of General Gamal Abdel Nasser. He began to develop a trade relationship with the Soviet Union in the early 1950s. In 1956, to punish Nasser for his friendliness toward the communists, Dulles withdrew American offers to assist in building the great Aswan Dam across the Nile. A week later, Nasser retaliated by seizing control of the Suez Canal from the British, saying that he would use the income from it to build the dam himself.

On October 29, 1956, Israeli forces attacked Egypt. The next day the British and French landed troops in the Suez to drive the Egyptians from the canal. Dulles and Eisenhower *Suez Crisis* feared that the Suez crisis would drive the Arab states toward the Soviet Union and precipitate a new world war. By refusing to support the invasion, and by joining in a United Nations denunciation of it, the United States helped pressure the French and British to withdraw and persuaded Israel to agree to a truce with Egypt.

Cold War concerns affected American relations in Latin America as well. In 1954, the *CIA in Guatemala* Eisenhower administration ordered the CIA to help topple the new, leftist government of Jacobo Arbenz Guzmán in Guatemala, a regime that Dulles (responding in part to the requests of the United Fruit Company, a major investor in Guatemala) argued was potentially communist.

No nation in the region had been more closely tied to America than Cuba. Its leader, Fulgencio Batista, had ruled as a military dictator since 1952, when American assistance *Castro in Cuba* helped him topple a more moderate government. Cuba's relatively prosperous economy had become a virtual colony of American corporations, which controlled almost all the island's natural resources and had cornered over half the vital sugar crop. American organized-crime syndicates controlled much of Havana's lucrative hotel and nightlife business. In 1957, a popular movement of resistance to the Batista regime began to gather strength under the leadership of Fidel Castro. On January 1, 1959, as Batista fled to exile in Spain, Castro marched into Havana and established a new government.

Castro soon began implementing drastic policies of land reform and expropriating foreign-owned businesses and resources. He established himself as a dictator by canceling promised elections and jailing or killing political rivals and critics. When Castro began accepting assistance from the Soviet Union in 1960, the United States cut back the "quota" by which Cuba could export sugar to America at a favored price. Early in 1961, as one of its last acts, the Eisenhower administration severed diplomatic relations with Castro. Isolated by the United States, Castro soon cemented an alliance with the Soviet Union.

THE U-2 CRISIS

Although the problems of the Third World were moving slowly toward the center of American foreign policy, the direct relationship with the Soviet Union and the effort to resist communist expansion in Europe remained the principal foreign policy concerns of the Eisenhower administration. Relations between the Soviet Union and the West soured further in 1956 in response to the Hungarian Revolution. Hungarian dissidents had launched a popular uprising in November to demand democratic reforms. Before the month was out, Soviet tanks and troops rolled into Budapest to crush the uprising and restore an orthodox, pro-Soviet regime.

THE CUBAN REVOLUTION Fidel Castro (standing at center) is shown here in the Cuban jungle in 1957 with a small group of his staff and soldiers. Two years later, Castro's forces toppled the U.S.-backed Batista government and elevated Castro to the nation's leadership, where he remained for almost fifty years. (© Bettmann/Corbis)

In November 1958, Nikita Khrushchev, who had become Soviet premier and Communist Party chief earlier that year, renewed the demands of his predecessors that the NATO powers abandon West Berlin. When the United States and its allies predictably refused, Khrushchev suggested that he and Eisenhower discuss the issue personally, both in visits to each other's countries and at a summit meeting in Paris in 1960. The United States agreed. Khrushchev's 1959 visit to America produced a cool but polite public response. Plans proceeded for the summit conference and for Eisenhower's visit to Moscow shortly thereafter. Only days before the Paris meeting, however, the Soviet Union announced that it had shot down an American U-2, a high-altitude spy plane, over Russian territory. Its pilot, Francis Gary Powers, was in captivity. Khrushchev lashed out angrily at the American incursion into Soviet airspace, breaking up the Paris summit almost before it could begin and withdrawing his invitation to Eisenhower to visit the Soviet Union.

After eight years in office, Eisenhower had failed to eliminate, and in some respects had actually increased, the tensions between the United States and the Soviet Union. Yet Eisenhower had also brought to the Cold War his own sense of the limits of American power. He had resisted military intervention in Vietnam, but he could not find a solution to Vietnam's likely slide into communism. And he had placed a measure of restraint on those who urged the creation of an enormous American military establishment. In *"Military–Industrial Complex"* his farewell address in January 1961, he warned of the "unwarranted influence" of a vast "military–industrial complex." (See "Consider the Source: Eisenhower Warns of the Military-Industrial Complex.") His caution, in both domestic and international affairs, stood in marked contrast to the attitudes of his successors, who argued that the United States must act more boldly and aggressively on behalf of its goals at home and abroad.

EISENHOWER WARNS OF THE MILITARY–INDUSTRIAL COMPLEX

In the tradition of outgoing presidents, Eisenhower delivered a "farewell address" that offered a summary of his accomplishments and vision for the future of the country. He warned of a growing "military–industrial complex" that, if left unchecked, would drive the nation's economy and politics.

Good evening, my fellow Americans. [. . .] This evening I come to you with a message of leave-taking and farewell, and to share a few final thoughts with you, my countrymen. Like every other citizen, I wish the new President, and all who will labor with him, Godspeed. I pray that the coming years will be blessed with peace and prosperity for all. [. . .]

America is today the strongest, the most influential, and most productive nation in the world. Understandably proud of this pre-eminence, we yet realize that America's leadership and prestige depend, not merely upon our unmatched material progress, riches and military strength, but on how we use our power in the interests of world peace and human betterment. [. . .]

A vital element in keeping the peace is our military establishment. Our arms must be mighty, ready for instant action, so that no potential aggressor may be tempted to risk his own destruction. Our military organization today bears little relation to that known by any of my predecessors in peacetime, or, indeed, by the fighting men of World War II or Korea. [. . .]

Now this conjunction of an immense military establishment and a large arms industry is new in the American experience. The total influence—economic, political, even spiritual—is felt in every city, every Statehouse, every office of the Federal government. We recognize the imperative need for this development. Yet we must not fail to comprehend its grave implications. Our toil, resources, and livelihood are all involved. So is the very structure of our society.

In the councils of government, we must guard against the acquisition of unwarranted influence, whether sought or unsought, by the military–industrial complex. The potential for the disastrous rise of misplaced power exists and will persist. We must never let the weight of this combination endanger our liberties or democratic processes. We should take nothing for granted. Only an alert and knowledgeable citizenry can compel the proper meshing of the huge industrial and military machinery of defense with our peaceful methods and goals, so that security and liberty may prosper together.

Akin to, and largely responsible for the sweeping changes in our industrial-military posture, has been the technological revolution during recent decades. In this revolution, research has become central, it also becomes more formalized, complex, and costly. A steadily increasing share is conducted for, by, or at the direction of, the Federal government.

Today, the solitary inventor, tinkering in his shop, has been overshadowed by task forces of scientists in laboratories and testing fields. In the same fashion, the free university, historically the fountainhead of free ideas and scientific discovery, has experienced a revolution in the conduct of research. Partly because of the huge costs involved, a government contract becomes virtually a substitute for intellectual curiosity. For every old blackboard there are now hundreds of new electronic computers. The prospect of domination of the nation's scholars by Federal employment, project allocations, and the power of money is ever present—and is gravely to be regarded.

Yet, in holding scientific research and discovery in respect, as we should, we must also be alert to the equal and opposite danger that public policy could itself become the captive of a scientific-technological elite.

It is the task of statesmanship to mold, to balance, and to integrate these and other forces, new and old, within the principles of our democratic system—ever aiming toward the supreme goals of our free society.

. . . As we peer into society's future, we—you and I, and our government—must avoid the impulse to live only for today, plundering for our own ease and convenience the precious resources of tomorrow. We cannot mortgage the material assets of our grandchildren without risking the loss also of their political and spiritual heritage. We want democracy to survive for all generations to come, not to become the insolvent phantom of tomorrow. [. . .]

Disarmament, with mutual honor and confidence, is a continuing imperative. Together we must learn how to compose differences, not with arms, but with intellect and decent purpose. Because this need is so sharp and apparent, I confess that I lay down my official responsibilities in this field with a definite sense of disappointment. As one who has witnessed the horror and the lingering sadness of war, as one who knows that another war could utterly destroy this civilization which has been so slowly and painfully built over thousands of years, I wish I could say tonight that a lasting peace is in sight. [. . .]

You and I, my fellow citizens, need to be strong in our faith that all nations, under God, will reach the goal of peace with justice. May we be ever unswerving in devotion to principle, confident but humble with power, diligent in pursuit of the Nations' great goals. [. . .]

Now, on Friday noon, I am to become a private citizen. I am proud to do so. I look forward to it.

Thank you, and good night.

UNDERSTAND, ANALYZE, & EVALUATE

1. What specifically was the military–industrial complex, and how did it support American postwar prosperity? How did it change the relationship between knowledge, industrial production, and defense?
2. What dangers for American political traditions did Eisenhower foresee? What economic dangers did he envision for future generations of Americans?

Source: Farewell address by President Dwight D. Eisenhower, January 17, 1961; Final TV Talk 1/17/61 (1), Box 38, Speech Series, Papers of Dwight D. Eisenhower as President, 1953–61, Eisenhower Library; National Archives and Records Administration [Public Domain].

CONCLUSION

The booming economic growth of the 1950s—and the anxiety over the Cold War that formed a backdrop to it—shaped the politics and the culture of the decade. For most Americans, the 1950s were years of increasing personal prosperity. Sales of private homes increased dramatically; suburbs grew precipitously; young families had children at an astounding rate—creating what came to be known as the postwar "Baby Boom." After the end of the divisive Korean War, the nation's politics entered a period of relative calm, symbolized by the genial presence in the White House of Dwight D. Eisenhower, who provided moderate and undemanding leadership through most of the decade.

The nation's culture, too, helped create a broad sense of stability and calm. Television, which emerged in the 1950s as the most powerful medium of mass culture, presented largely uncontroversial programming dominated by middle-class images and traditional values. Movies, theater, popular magazines, and newspapers all contributed to a broad sense of well-being.

But the 1950s were not, in the end, as calm and contented as the politics and popular culture of the time suggested. A powerful youth culture emerged in these years, displaying a considerable level of restiveness and even disillusionment. African Americans began to escalate their protests against segregation and inequality. The continuing existence of widespread poverty among large groups of Americans attracted increasing attention as the decade progressed. These pulsing anxieties, combined with frustration over the continuing tensions of the Cold War, produced by the late 1950s a growing sense of impatience with the calm, placid public culture of the time. That was one reason for the growing desire for action and innovation as the 1960s began.

KEY TERMS/PEOPLE/PLACES/EVENTS

AFL-CIO 681
Apollo program 685
Army–McCarthy
  hearings 700
Baby Boom 680
Beats 692
brinksmanship 700
Brown v. Board of Education
  of Topeka 696

DDT 683
Echo Park 691
Elvis Presley 693
Federal Highway Act
  of 1956 699
Fidel Castro 702
Ho Chi Minh 701
ICBMs 685
John Foster Dulles 700

Levittown(s) 687
Martin Luther
  King Jr. 698
Rosa Parks 697
Sputnik 685
The Organization Man 692
The Other America 694
U-2 crisis 702
UNIVAC 684

RECALL AND REFLECT

1. How did the economic boom of the postwar era change American lifestyles?
2. What were some of the significant scientific and technological breakthroughs, especially in medicine, chemistry, electronics, weaponry, and space exploration, of the 1950s and 1960s? How did these developments affect American life?
3. How did the increasing popularity of the automobile change the American landscape and American society?
4. How did the Cold War progress under Eisenhower?

29 THE TURBULENT SIXTIES

EXPANDING THE LIBERAL STATE
THE BATTLE FOR RACIAL EQUALITY
"FLEXIBLE RESPONSE" AND THE COLD WAR
THE AGONY OF VIETNAM
THE TRAUMAS OF 1968

LOOKING AHEAD

1. What was the domestic reform agenda of Kennedy's New Frontier, and how did Johnson's Great Society programs continue and expand on that agenda?
2. Why did the civil rights movement become increasingly assertive and militant over the course of the 1960s?
3. How did U.S. involvement in Vietnam escalate through the 1960s? What were the political and social consequences of that escalation, in both Vietnam and the United States?

BY THE LATE 1950s, a growing restlessness was bubbling beneath the apparently placid surface of American society. Ultimately, that restlessness would make the 1960s one of the most turbulent and divisive eras of the twentieth century. But at first, it contributed to a bold and confident effort by political leaders to attack social and international problems within the framework of conventional liberalism.

1960

Kennedy elected
president

1961

Freedom rides

Bay of Pigs

1962

Berlin Wall erected

Cuban missile crisis

1963

March on Washington

Kennedy assassinated;
Johnson becomes
president

1964

Civil rights
demonstrations in
Birmingham

Johnson launches war
on poverty

Civil Rights Act

Gulf of Tonkin
Resolution

Johnson elected
president

1965

Malcolm X assassinated

Voting Rights Act

U.S. troops in Vietnam

Racial violence in Watts

1967

Antiwar movement
grows

Racial violence in
Detroit

1968

Tet offensive

Martin Luther King Jr.
assassinated

Robert Kennedy
assassinated

Nixon elected president

EXPANDING THE LIBERAL STATE

Those who yearned for a more active government in the late 1950s, and who accused the Eisenhower administration of allowing the nation to "drift" in matters of social affairs, hoped for vigorous new leadership. The two men who served in the White House through most of the 1960s—John Kennedy and Lyndon Johnson—seemed for a time to embody these liberal hopes.

JOHN KENNEDY

The campaign of 1960 produced two young candidates who claimed to offer the nation active leadership. The Republican nomination went almost uncontested to Vice President Richard Nixon, who promised moderate reform. The Democrats, in the meantime, emerged from a spirited primary campaign united, although somewhat uneasily, behind John Fitzgerald Kennedy, an attractive and articulate senator from Massachusetts who had narrowly missed being the party's vice presidential candidate in 1956.

John Kennedy was the young son of the wealthy, powerful, and highly controversial Joseph P. Kennedy, former American ambassador to Britain. He premised his campaign, he said, "on the single assumption that the American people are uneasy at the present drift in our national course." But his appealing public image was at least as important as his political positions in attracting popular support. Kennedy regularly appeared on television talk shows before and during his run for president, and his appearances helped comfort the American people despite his perceived weaknesses as a presidential candidate. He overcame doubts about his youth (he turned forty-three in 1960) and religion (he was Catholic) to win with a tiny plurality of the popular vote (49.7 percent to Nixon's 49.6 percent) and only a slightly more comfortable electoral majority (303 to 219).

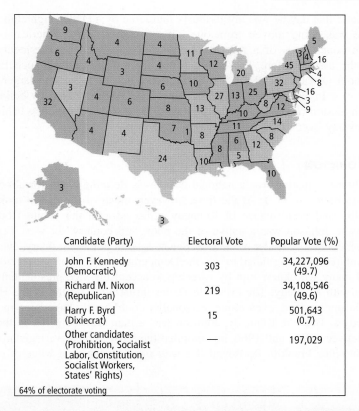

Candidate (Party)	Electoral Vote	Popular Vote (%)
John F. Kennedy (Democratic)	303	34,227,096 (49.7)
Richard M. Nixon (Republican)	219	34,108,546 (49.6)
Harry F. Byrd (Dixiecrat)	15	501,643 (0.7)
Other candidates (Prohibition, Socialist Labor, Constitution, Socialist Workers, States' Rights)	—	197,029

64% of electorate voting

THE ELECTION OF 1960 The election of 1960 was, in the popular vote at least, one of the closest in American history. John Kennedy's margin over Richard Nixon was less than one-third of 1 percent of the total national vote, but greater in the electoral college. Note the distribution of electoral strength of the two candidates. Kennedy was strong in the industrial Northeast and the largest industrial states of the Midwest, and he retained at least a portion of his party's traditional strength in the South and Southwest. But Nixon made significant inroads into the upper South, carried Florida, and swept most of the plains and mountain states. • *What was the significance of this distribution of strength to the future of the two parties?*

Kennedy had campaigned promising a set of domestic reforms he described as the "New Frontier." But his thin popular mandate and a Congress dominated by a coalition of Republicans and conservative Democrats frustrated many of his hopes. Kennedy did manage to win approval of tariff reductions his administration had negotiated, and he began to build a legislative agenda—including a call for a significant tax cut to promote economic growth.

More than any other president of the century (except perhaps the two Roosevelts and, later, Ronald Reagan), Kennedy made his own personality an integral   *Kennedy Assassination* part of his presidency and a central focus of national attention. Nothing illustrated that more clearly than the popular reaction to the tragedy of November 22, 1963. In Texas with his wife and Vice President Lyndon Johnson for a series of political appearances, as the presidential motorcade rode slowly through the streets of Dallas, shots rang out. Two bullets struck the president—one in the throat, the other in the head. He was sped to a nearby hospital, where minutes later he was pronounced dead. Lee Harvey Oswald—a young man who had spent time in the Soviet Union and, later, in Cuba—was arrested for the crime. Later that day he was mysteriously murdered by a Dallas nightclub owner, Jack Ruby, as he was being moved from one jail to another. Most Americans at the time accepted the conclusions of a federal commission appointed by President Johnson to investigate the assassination. The commission, chaired by Chief Justice Earl Warren, found that both Oswald and Ruby had acted alone, that there was no larger conspiracy. *Warren Commission*   In later years, however, many Americans came to believe that the Warren Commission report had ignored evidence of a wider conspiracy behind the murders. Controversy over the assassination continues still.

LYNDON JOHNSON

The Kennedy assassination was a national trauma—a defining event for almost everyone old enough to be aware of it. At the time, however, much of the nation took comfort in the personality and performance of Kennedy's successor in the White House, Lyndon Baines Johnson. Johnson was a native of the poor "hill country" of west Texas and had risen to become majority leader of the U.S. Senate by dint of extraordinary, even obsessive, effort and ambition. Having failed to win the Democratic nomination for president in 1960, he surprised many who knew him by agreeing to accept the vice presidential nomination on the ticket with Kennedy. The events in Dallas thrust him into the White House.

Johnson's rough-edged, even crude, personality could hardly have been more different from Kennedy's. But like Kennedy, Johnson was a man who believed in the active use of power. Between 1963 and 1966, he compiled the most impressive legislative record of any president since Franklin Roosevelt. He was aided by the tidal wave of emotion that

THE JOHNSON TREATMENT   Lyndon Johnson was legendary for his powers of persuasion—for a combination of charm and intimidation that often worked on even the most experienced politicians. He is shown here in the Oval Office meeting with his old friend Senator Richard Russell of Georgia and demonstrating one of his most powerful and unsettling techniques: moving so close to the person with whom he was talking as to be almost touching him. (Lyndon Baines Johnson Library)

followed the death of Kennedy, which helped win support for many New Frontier proposals. But Johnson also constructed a greater and more far reaching reform program of his own, one that he ultimately labeled the "Great Society." And he won *"Great Society"* approval of much of it through the same sort of skillful lobbying in Congress that had made him an effective majority leader.

Johnson's first year in office was, by necessity, dominated by the campaign for reelection. There was little doubt that he would win—particularly after the Republican Party nominated the very conservative Senator Barry Goldwater of Arizona. In the November 1964 election, the president received a larger plurality, over 61 percent, than any candidate before or since. Goldwater, with his hard-line stance against communism and government expansion, managed to carry only his home state of Arizona and five states in the Deep South. Nevertheless, the failed Goldwater campaign mobilized many right-wing activists who would propel the growth of conservative political strength for decades to come. Record Democratic majorities in both houses of Congress, many of whose members had been swept into office only because of the margin of Johnson's victory, ensured that the president would be able to fulfill many of his goals.

THE ASSAULT ON POVERTY

For the first time since the New Deal, the federal government took steps in the 1960s to create important new social welfare programs. The most important of these was Medicare, which provides federal aid to elderly individuals for medical expenses. *Medicare and Medicaid* Its enactment in 1965 came at the end of a bitter twenty-year debate between those who believed in the concept of national health assistance and those who denounced it as "socialized medicine." But Medicare pacified many critics. For one thing, it avoided the stigma of "welfare" by making Medicare benefits available to all elderly Americans, regardless of need (just as Social Security had done with pensions). That created a large middle-class constituency for the program. It also defused the opposition of the medical community by allowing doctors serving Medicare patients to practice privately and (at first) to charge their normal fees; Medicare simply shifted responsibility for paying those fees from the patient to the government. In 1966, Johnson steered to passage the Medicaid program, which extended federal medical assistance to welfare recipients and other indigent people of all ages.

Medicare and Medicaid were early steps in a much larger assault on poverty—one that Kennedy had been planning in the last months of his life and that Johnson launched only weeks after taking office. The centerpiece of this "war on poverty," as Johnson called it, was the Office of Economic Opportunity (OEO), which created an array of new educational, employment, housing, and health-care programs. But the OEO was controversial from the start, in part because of its commitment to the idea of "Community Action."

Community Action was an effort to involve members of poor communities themselves in the planning and administration of the programs designed to help *Community Action Programs* them. The Community Action programs provided jobs for many poor people and gave them valuable experience in administrative and political work. But despite its achievements, the Community Action approach proved impossible to sustain. Administrative failures damaged the program. So did the apparent excesses of a few agencies, which damaged the popular image of the Community Action programs and indeed the war on poverty as a whole.

The OEO spent nearly $3 billion during its first two years of existence, and it helped reduce poverty in some areas. But it fell far short of eliminating poverty altogether. That was in part because of the weaknesses of the programs themselves and in part because funding for them, inadequate from the beginning, dwindled as the years passed and a costly war in Southeast Asia became the nation's first priority.

Cities, Schools, and Immigration

Closely tied to the antipoverty program were federal efforts to promote the revitalization of decaying cities and to strengthen the nation's schools. The Housing Act of 1961 offered $4.9 billion in federal grants to cities for the preservation of open spaces, the development of mass-transit systems, and the subsidization of middle-income housing. In 1966, Johnson established a new cabinet agency, the Department of Housing and Urban Development (whose first secretary, Robert Weaver, was the first African American ever to serve in the cabinet). Johnson also inaugurated the Model Cities Program, which offered federal subsidies for urban redevelopment pilot programs.

Kennedy had fought for federal aid to public education, but he had failed to overcome two important obstacles. Many Americans feared that aid to education was the first step *Federal Aid to Education* toward federal control of the schools, and Catholics insisted that federal assistance must extend to parochial as well as public schools. Johnson managed to circumvent both objections with the Elementary and Secondary Education Act of 1965 and a series of subsequent measures. The bills extended aid to all types of schools and based the aid on the economic conditions of the students, not on the needs of the schools themselves.

The Johnson administration also supported the Immigration Act of 1965, one of the most important pieces of legislation of the 1960s. For decades since the 1920s, *Immigration Act of 1965* the law maintained a strict limit on the number of newcomers admitted to the country each year (170,000). But the 1965 act eliminated the "national origins" system established in the 1920s, which gave preference to immigrants from northern Europe over those from other parts of the world. It continued to restrict immigration from some parts of Latin America, but it allowed people from all parts of Europe, Asia, and Africa to enter the United States on an equal basis. By the early 1970s, the character of American immigration had changed dramatically. The numbers of immigrants grew significantly, with members of new national groups—and particularly large groups of Asians—entering the United States and transforming the character of the American population.

Legacies of the Great Society

Taken together, the Great Society reforms significantly increased federal spending. For a time, rising tax revenues from the growing economy nearly compensated for the new expenditures. In 1964, Johnson managed to win passage of the $11.5 billion tax cut that Kennedy had first proposed in 1962. The cut increased the federal deficit, but substantial economic growth over the next several years made up for much of the revenue initially lost. As Great Society programs began to multiply, however—particularly as they began to compete with the escalating costs of America's military ventures—the federal budget rapidly outpaced increases in revenues. In 1961, the federal government had spent $94.4 billion. By 1970, that sum had risen to $196.6 billion.

The high costs of the Great Society, and the failures of some of it, weakened the popularity of the federal efforts to solve social problems. But the Great Society was also responsible for some remarkable achievements. It significantly reduced hunger in America. It made medical care available to millions of elderly and poor people who would otherwise have had great difficulty affording it. It contributed to the greatest reduction in poverty in American history. In 1959, according to the most widely accepted estimates, 21 percent of the American people lived below the officially established poverty line (a level that did not survive for very long). In 1969, only 12 percent remained below that line. Much of that progress was a result of economic growth, but some of it was a direct result of Great Society programs.

THE BATTLE FOR RACIAL EQUALITY

By the early 1960s, African Americans forced issues of racial justice and equality to the forefront of American politics. While scholars debate the origins and legacies of the modern civil rights movement, none challenge how deeply it influenced the nation's history in the late twentieth century. (See "Debating the Past: The Civil Rights Movement.")

EXPANDING PROTESTS

John Kennedy was sympathetic to the cause of racial justice, but he was far from a committed crusader. Like presidents before him, he feared alienating southern voters and powerful southern Democrats in Congress. His administration hoped to contain the racial problem by enforcing existing laws and using executive orders—not proposing new legislation.

But the pressure for change was growing uncontainable even before Kennedy took office. Throughout the 1950s, African Americans in northern cities had grown increasingly active in opposing discrimination. They demanded progress in housing, jobs, and education. Protests grew in the 1960s, especially in the South. This restiveness soon spread. In February 1960, black college students in Greensboro, North Carolina, staged a sit-in at a segregated Woolworth's lunch counter; and in the following months, such demonstrations spread throughout the South, forcing many merchants to integrate their facilities. In the fall of 1960, some of those who had participated in the sit-ins formed the Student Nonviolent Coordinating Committee (SNCC)—a student branch of Martin Luther King Jr.'s Southern Christian Leadership Conference; SNCC worked to keep the spirit of resistance alive.

In 1961, an interracial group of students, working with the Congress of Racial Equality (CORE), began what they called "freedom rides." Traveling by bus   *Freedom Rides* throughout the South, they tried to force the desegregation of bus stations. They were met in some places with such savage violence on the part of some white southerners that Attorney General Robert Kennedy finally dispatched federal marshals to help keep the peace and ordered the integration of all bus and train stations.

Events in the Deep South in 1963 helped bring the growing movement to something of a climax. In April, Martin Luther King Jr. helped launch a series of nonviolent demonstrations in Birmingham, Alabama. Police Commissioner Eugene "Bull" Connor personally supervised a brutal effort to break up the peaceful marches, arresting hundreds of demonstrators and using attack dogs, tear gas, electric cattle prods, and fire hoses—at times even against small children—in full view of television cameras. Two months later,

THE CIVIL RIGHTS MOVEMENT

The civil rights movement was one of the most important events in the modern history of the United States. It helped force the dismantling of legalized segregation and disenfranchisement of African Americans and also served as a model for other groups mobilizing to demand dignity and rights. And like all important events in history, it has produced scholarship that examines the movement in a number of different ways.

The early histories of the civil rights movement remain widely accepted. They rest on a heroic narrative of moral purpose and personal courage by which great men and women inspired ordinary people to rise up and struggle for their rights. This narrative generally begins with the *Brown* decision of 1954 and the Montgomery bus boycott of 1955, continues through the civil rights campaigns of the early 1960s, and culminates in the Civil Rights Acts of 1964 and 1965. Among the central events in this narrative are the March on Washington of 1963, with Martin Luther King Jr.'s famous "I Have a Dream" speech, and the assassination of King in 1968, which has often symbolized the end of the movement and the beginning of a different, more complicated period of the black freedom struggle. The key element of these narratives is the central importance to the movement of a few great leaders, most notably King himself. Among the best examples of this narrative are Taylor Branch's powerful studies of the life and struggles of King, *Parting the Waters* (1988), *Pillar of Fire* (1998), and *At Canaan's Edge* (2006), as well as David Garrow's important study, *Bearing the Cross* (1986).

Few historians would deny the importance of King and other leaders to the successes of the civil rights movement. But a number of scholars have argued that the leader-centered narrative obscures the vital contributions of ordinary people in communities throughout the South, and the nation, to the struggle. John Dittmer's *Local People: The Struggle for Civil Rights in Mississippi* (1994) and Charles Payne's *I've Got the Light of Freedom* (1995) both examine the day-to-day work of the movement's rank and file in the early 1960s and argue that their efforts were at least as important as those of King and other leaders. The national leadership helped bring visibility to these struggles, but King and his circle were usually present only briefly, if at all, for the actual work of communities in challenging segregation. Only by understanding the local origins of the movement, these and other scholars argue, can we understand its true character.

Scholars also disagree about the time frame of the movement. Rather than beginning the story in 1954 or 1955 (as in Robert Weisbrot's excellent 1991 synthesis *Freedom Bound* or in William Chafe's remarkable 1981 local study *Civilities and Civil Rights,* which examined the Greensboro sit-ins of 1961), a number of scholars have tried to move the story into both earlier periods and later ones. Robin Kelly's *Race Rebels* (1994) emphasizes the important contributions of working-class African Americans, some of them allied for a time with the Communist Party, to the undermining of racist assumptions starting in the 1930s. These activists organized some of the earliest civil rights demonstrations—sit-ins, marches, and other efforts to challenge segregation—well before the conventional dates for the beginning of the movement. Gail O'Brien's *The Color of the Law* (1999) examines a 1946 "race riot" in Columbia, Tennessee, arguing for its importance as a signal of the early growth of African American militancy and the movement of that militancy from the streets into the legal system.

Other scholars have looked beyond the 1960s and have incorporated events outside the orbit of the formal "movement" to explain

BROWN V. BOARD OF EDUCATION This photograph, taken for an Atlanta newspaper, illustrated the long and dangerous walk that Linda Brown, one of the plaintiffs in the famous desegregation case that ultimately reached the Supreme Court, had to travel each day on her way to a segregated school in Topeka, Kansas. An all-white school was located close to her home, but to reach the black school she had to attend required a long walk and a long bus ride each day. Not only does the picture illustrate the difficulties segregation created for Linda Brown, it was also part of a broad publicity campaign launched by the supporters of the case. (Photo by Carl Iwasaki/© Time & Life Pictures/Getty Images)

the history of the civil rights struggle. A growing literature on northern, urban, and relatively radical activists has suggested that focusing too much on mainstream leaders and the celebrated efforts in the South in the 1960s diverts our view from the equally important challenges facing northern African Americans and the very different tactics and strategies that they often chose to pursue their goals. The enormous attention historians have given to the life and legacy of Malcolm X—among them Alex Haley's influential *Autobiography of Malcolm X* (1965), Michael Eric Dyson's *Making Malcolm* (1996), and Manning Marable's important biography, *Malcolm X: A Life of Reinvention* (2012)—is an example of this, as is the increasing attention scholars have given to black radicalism in the late 1960s and beyond and to such militant groups as the Black Panthers. Other literature has extended the civil rights struggle even further, into the 1980s and beyond, and has brought into focus such issues as the highly disproportionate number of African Americans sentenced to death within the criminal justice system. Randall Kennedy's

Race, Crime, and the Law (1997) is a particularly important study of this issue.

Even *Brown v. Board of Education* (1954), the great landmark of the legal challenge to segregation, has been subject to reexamination. Richard Kluger's narrative history of the *Brown* decision, *Simple Justice* (1975), is a classic statement of the traditional view of *Brown* as a triumph over injustice. But others have been less certain of the dramatic success of the ruling. James T. Patterson's *Brown v. Board of Education: A Civil Rights Milestone and Its Troubled Legacy* (2001) argues that the *Brown* decision long preceded any national consensus on the need to end segregation and that its impact was far less decisive than earlier scholars have suggested. Michael Klarman's *From Jim Crow to Civil Rights* (2004) examines the role of the Supreme Court in advancing civil rights and suggests, among other things, that the *Brown* decision may actually have retarded racial progress in the South for a time because of the enormous backlash it created. Charles Ogletree's *All Deliberate Speed* (2004) and Derrick Bell's *Silent Covenants* (2004) both argue that the Court's decision did not provide an effective enforcement mechanism for desegregation and in many other ways failed to support measures that would have made school desegregation a reality. Stephen Tuck's *We Ain't What We Ought to Be: The Black Freedom Struggle from Emancipation to Obama* (2011) concludes his bro-ad narrative of the road to racial equality by focusing on the continued activism of African Americans into the present.

As the literature on the African American freedom struggles of the twentieth century has grown, historians have begun to speak of civil rights *movements,* rather than a single, cohesive movement. •

UNDERSTAND, ANALYZE, & EVALUATE

1. If historians now speak of plural civil rights *movements,* what are these movements?
2. Why are the contributions of local grassroots workers so often over-looked, in studies of the civil rights movement as well as in accounts of other great events in American history?

Governor George Wallace stood in the doorway of the Foster Auditorium at the University of Alabama to prevent the court-ordered enrollment of several black students. Only after the arrival of federal marshals did he give way. The same night, NAACP official Medgar Evers was murdered in Mississippi. And in September, the bombing of the Sixteenth Street Baptist Church in Birmingham killed four African American children.

A NATIONAL COMMITMENT

The events in Alabama and Mississippi were a warning to the president that he could no longer avoid the issue of race. In an important television address the night of the University of Alabama confrontation, Kennedy spoke eloquently of the "moral issue" facing the nation. Days later, he introduced new legislative proposals prohibiting segregation in "public accommodations" (stores, restaurants, theaters, hotels), barring discrimination in employment, and increasing the power of the government to file suits on behalf of school integration.

To generate support for the legislation, and to dramatize the power of the growing movement, more than 200,000 demonstrators marched down the Mall in *March on Washington* Washington, D.C., in August 1963 and gathered before the Lincoln Memorial for the largest civil rights demonstration in the nation's history to that point.

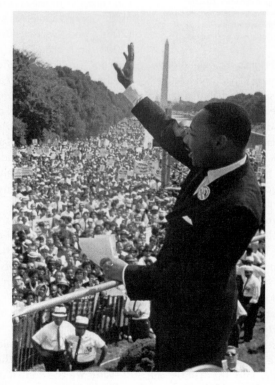

MARTIN LUTHER KING JR. IN WASHINGTON Moments after completing his memorable speech during the August 1963 March on Washington, King waves to the vast and enthusiastic crowd that had gathered in front of the Lincoln Memorial to demand "equality and jobs." (© AP Images)

Martin Luther King Jr., in one of the greatest speeches of American politics, aroused the crowd with a litany of resonant American images prefaced again and again by the phrase "I have a dream."

The assassination of President Kennedy three months later gave new impetus to civil rights legislation. The ambitious measure that Kennedy had proposed in June 1963 was stalled in the Senate after having passed through the House of Representatives with relative ease. Early in 1964, after Lyndon Johnson had applied both public   *Civil Rights Act of 1964* and private pressure, supporters of the measure finally mustered the two-thirds majority necessary to end a filibuster by southern senators; and the Senate passed the most important civil rights bill of the twentieth century.

THE BATTLE FOR VOTING RIGHTS

Having won a significant victory in one area, the civil rights movement shifted its focus to another: voting rights. During the summer of 1964, thousands of civil rights workers, black and white, northern and southern, spread throughout the South, but primarily into Mississippi, to work on behalf of black voter registration and participation. The campaign was known as "Freedom Summer," and it produced a violent   *"Freedom Summer"* response from many southern whites. Three of the first freedom workers to arrive in the South—two whites, Andrew Goodman and Michael Schwerner, and one African American, James Chaney—were murdered. Local law enforcement officials were involved in the crime.

The Freedom Summer also produced the Mississippi Freedom Democratic Party (MFDP), an integrated alternative to the regular state Democratic party organization. Under the leadership of Fannie Lou Hamer and others, the MFDP challenged the regular party's right to its seats at the Democratic National Convention that summer. (See "Consider the Source: Fannie Lou Hamer on the Struggle for Voting Rights.") President Johnson, with King's help, managed to broker a compromise by which members of the MFDP could be seated as observers, with promises of party reforms later on, while the regular party retained its official standing. Many MFDP members rejected the agreement and left the convention embittered.

A year later, in March 1965, King helped organize a major demonstration in Selma, Alabama, to press for the right of blacks to register to vote. Selma sheriff Jim Clark led local police in a vicious attack on the demonstrators, which was televised nationally. Two northern whites participating in the Selma march were murdered in the course of the effort there. The widespread national outrage that followed the events in Alabama helped push Lyndon Johnson to win passage of the Voting Rights Act of 1965, which provided federal protection to African Americans attempting to exercise their   *Selma and the Voting Rights Act* right to vote. But important as such gains were, they failed to satisfy the rapidly rising expectations of civil rights activists as the focus of the movement began to move from political to economic issues.

THE CHANGING MOVEMENT

By 1966, of African Americans 69 percent lived in metropolitan areas and 45 percent lived outside the South. Although the economic condition of most Americans was improving, in many poor urban black communities things were getting significantly worse. Indeed, more than half of all nonwhite Americans lived in poverty at the beginning of the 1960s.

FANNIE LOU HAMER ON THE STRUGGLE FOR VOTING RIGHTS

Fanny Lou Hamer shone a harsh spotlight on racial terror in her native state of Mississippi during her speech before the Credentials Committee of the Democratic National Convention in Atlantic City, New Jersey, in August 1964. With this testimony, Hamer tried—unsuccessfully—to unseat the all-white Mississippi delegation and seat members of the Mississippi Freedom Democratic Party (MFDP). Four years later, the MFDP succeeded in winning seats at the Convention.

Mr. Chairman, and to the Credentials Committee, my name is Mrs. Fannie Lou Hamer, and I live at 626 East Lafayette Street, Ruleville, Mississippi, Sunflower County, the home of Senator James O. Eastland, and Senator Stennis.

It was the 31st of August in 1962 that eighteen of us traveled twenty-six miles to the county courthouse in Indianola to try to register to become first-class citizens.

We was met in Indianola by policemen, Highway Patrolmen, and they only allowed two of us in to take the literacy test at the time. After we had taken this test and started back to Ruleville, we was held up by the City Police and the State Highway Patrolmen and carried back to Indianola where the bus driver was charged that day with driving a bus the wrong color.

After we paid the fine among us, we continued on to Ruleville, and Reverend Jeff Sunny carried me four miles in the rural area where I had worked as a timekeeper and sharecropper for eighteen years. I was met there by my children, who told me that the plantation owner was angry because I had gone down to try to register.

After they told me, my husband came, and said the plantation owner was raising Cain because I had tried to register. Before he

quit talking the plantation owner came and said, "Fannie Lou, do you know—did Pap tell you what I said?"

And I said, "Yes, sir."

He said, "Well I mean that." He said, "If you don't go down and withdraw your registration, you will have to leave." Said, "Then if you go down and withdraw," said, "you still might have to go because we are not ready for that in Mississippi."

And I addressed him and told him and said, "I didn't try to register for you. I tried to register for myself."

I had to leave that same night.

On the 10th of September 1962, sixteen bullets was fired into the home of Mr. and Mrs. Robert Tucker for me. That same night two girls were shot in Ruleville, Mississippi. Also Mr. Joe McDonald's house was shot in.

And June the 9th, 1963, I had attended a voter registration workshop; was returning back to Mississippi. Ten of us was traveling by the Continental Trailway bus. When we got to Winona, Mississippi, which is Montgomery County, four of the people got off to use the washroom, and two of the people—to use the restaurant—two of the people wanted to use the washroom.

The four people that had gone in to use the restaurant was ordered out. During this time I was on the bus. But when I looked through the window and saw they had rushed out I got off of the bus to see what had happened. And one of the ladies said, "It was a State Highway Patrolman and a Chief of Police ordered us out."

I got back on the bus and one of the persons had used the washroom got back on the bus, too.

As soon as I was seated on the bus, I saw when they began to get the five people in a highway patrolman's car. I stepped off of the bus to see what was happening and somebody screamed from the car that the five workers was in and said, "Get that one there." When I went to get in the car, when the man told me I was under arrest, he kicked me.

I was carried to the county jail and put in the booking room. They left some of the people in the booking room and began to place us in cells. I was placed in a cell with a young woman called Miss Ivesta Simpson. After I was placed in the cell I began to hear sounds of licks and screams, I could hear the sounds of licks and horrible screams. And I could hear somebody say, "Can you say, 'yes, sir,' nigger? Can you say 'yes, sir'?"

And they would say other horrible names. She would say, "Yes, I can say 'yes, sir.'"

"So, well, say it."

She said, "I don't know you well enough."

They beat her, I don't know how long. And after a while she began to pray, and asked God to have mercy on those people.

And it wasn't too long before three white men came to my cell. One of these men was a State Highway Patrolman and he asked me where I was from. I told him Ruleville and he said, "We are going to check this."

They left my cell and it wasn't too long before they came back. He said, "You are from Ruleville all right," and he used a curse word. And he said, "We are going to make you wish you was dead."

I was carried out of that cell into another cell where they had two Negro prisoners. The State Highway Patrolmen ordered the first Negro to take the blackjack.

The first Negro prisoner ordered me, by orders from the State Highway Patrolman, for me to lay down on a bunk bed on my face.

I laid on my face and the first Negro began to beat. I was beat by the first Negro until he was exhausted. I was holding my hands behind me at that time on my left side, because I suffered from polio when I was six years old.

After the first Negro had beat until he was exhausted, the State Highway Patrolman ordered the second Negro to take the blackjack.

The second Negro began to beat and I began to work my feet, and the State Highway Patrolman ordered the first Negro who had beat me to sit on my feet—to keep me from working my feet. I began to scream and one white man got up and began to beat me in my head and tell me to hush.

One white man—my dress had worked up high—he walked over and pulled my dress—I pulled my dress down and he pulled my dress back up.

I was in jail when Medgar Evers was murdered.

All of this is on account of we want to register, to become first-class citizens. And if the Freedom Democratic Party is not seated now, I question America. Is this America, the land of the free and the home of the brave, where we have to sleep with our telephones off the hooks because our lives be threatened daily, because we want to live as decent human beings, in America?

Thank you.

UNDERSTAND, ANALYZE, & EVALUATE

1. What tactics were used to prevent Hamer from registering to vote?
2. Why did the Highway Patrolmen choose black prisoners to beat Hamer?
3. When the television networks broadcast this speech, the level of public support for the Mississippi Freedom Democratic Party rose sharply. What aspects of Hamer's speech were so effective?

Source: Fannie Lou Hamer, "Testimony Before the Credentials Committee," Democratic National Convention, August 22, 1964. Copyright © 1964 by Fannie Lou Hamer. All rights reserved. Used with permission.

The great publicity of the civil rights movement in the South intensified antidiscrimination efforts in northern cities. Those cities had no Jim Crow laws but much segregation. Many African American leaders (and their white supporters), having struggled in relative obscurity in the 1940s and 1950s, began to move the battle against job discrimination to a new level. They argued that the only way for employers to prove they were not discriminating against African Americans was to demonstrate that they were hiring minorities. If necessary, they should adopt positive measures to recruit minorities. Lyndon Johnson gave his support to the concept of **affirmative action** in 1965. Over the next decade, affirmative action guidelines gradually extended to virtually all institutions doing business with or receiving funds from the federal government (including schools and universities)—and to many others as well. Discrimination based on gender also began to receive federal interest. When "sex" was added at the last minute to Title VII of the 1964 Civil Rights Act, many thought it was an attempt to kill the bill. Regardless, the result added federal authority to begin dismantling the entrenched discrimination of women in the workplace and higher education.

A symbol of the movement's new direction, and of the problems it would cause, was a major campaign in the summer of 1966 in Chicago, in which King played a prominent role. Organizers of the Chicago campaign hoped to direct national attention to housing and employment discrimination in northern industrial cities. But the Chicago campaign evoked vicious and at times violent opposition from white residents and failed to attract wide attention or support in the way events in the South had done.

URBAN VIOLENCE

Well before the Chicago campaign, the problem of urban poverty had thrust itself into national prominence when riots broke out in African American neighborhoods in major cities. There were disturbances in the summer of 1964, most notably in New York City's Harlem. The most serious race riot since the end of World War II occurred the following summer in the Watts section of Los Angeles. In the midst of a traffic arrest, a white police officer struck a protesting black bystander with his club. The incident triggered a storm of anger and a week of violence. Thirty-four people died during the uprising, which was eventually quelled by the National Guard. In the summer of 1966, forty-three additional outbreaks occurred, the most serious in Chicago and Cleveland. And in the summer of 1967, eight major disorders took place, including the largest of them all—a racial clash in Detroit in which forty-three people died.

Televised images of the violence alarmed millions of Americans and created both a new sense of urgency and a growing sense of doubt among some whites who had embraced the cause of racial justice only a few years before. A special Commission on Civil Disorders, ordered by the president in response to the riots, issued a celebrated report in the spring of 1968 recommending massive spending to eliminate the abysmal conditions of the ghettoes. To many white Americans, however, the riots exposed the need for stern measures to stop violence and lawlessness.

BLACK POWER

Disillusioned with the ideal of peaceful change through cooperation with whites, an increasing number of African Americans turned to a new approach to the racial issue: the philosophy of **black power.** Black power meant many different things. But in all its forms, it suggested a shift away from the goals of assimilation and toward increased awareness of racial distinctiveness.

Perhaps the most enduring impact of the black-power ideology was a social and psychological one: instilling racial pride in African Americans. But black power took political forms as well, and it created a deep schism within the civil rights movement. Traditional black organizations that emphasized cooperation with sympathetic whites— groups such as the NAACP, the Urban League, and King's Southern Christian Leadership Conference—now faced competition from more radical groups. The Student Nonviolent Coordinating Committee and the Congress of Racial Equality had both begun as relatively moderate interracial organizations. By the mid-1960s, however, these and other groups were calling for more radical and occasionally even violent action against white racism and were openly rejecting the approaches of older, more established black leaders.

The most radical expressions of the black-power idea came from such revolutionary organizations as the Black Panthers, based in Oakland, California, and the separatist group the Nation of Islam, which denounced whites as "devils" and appealed to African Americans to embrace the Islamic faith and work for complete racial separation. The most celebrated of the Black Muslims, as whites often termed them, was Malcolm Little, who adopted the name Malcolm X ("X" to denote his lost African *Malcolm X* surname). Malcolm X left the Nation of Islam in 1964 and founded the Muslim Mosque, Inc., which he hoped would allow him to work with other civil rights leaders. After a pilgrimage to Mecca, he returned with a new hope that racial problems could be overcome. He died in 1965 when gunmen, presumably under orders from rivals within the Nation of Islam, assassinated him. But he remained a major figure in many African American communities long after his death, attaining a stature comparable to that of Martin Luther King Jr.

"FLEXIBLE RESPONSE" AND THE COLD WAR

In international affairs as much as in domestic reform, the optimistic liberalism of the Kennedy and Johnson administrations dictated a more active and aggressive approach to dealing with the nation's problems than that of the 1950s.

DIVERSIFYING FOREIGN POLICY

The Kennedy administration entered office convinced that the United States needed to be able to counter communist aggression in more flexible ways than the atomic-weapons-oriented defense strategy of the Eisenhower years. In particular, Kennedy was unsatisfied with the nation's ability to meet communist threats in "emerging areas" of the Third World—the areas in which, Kennedy believed, the real struggle against communism would be waged in the future. He gave enthusiastic support to the expansion of the Special Forces (or "Green Berets," as they were soon known)—soldiers trained specifically to fight guerrilla conflicts and other limited wars.

Kennedy also favored expanding American influence through peaceful means. To repair the badly deteriorating relationship with Latin America, he proposed an "Alliance for Progress"—a series of projects for peaceful development and stabilization of the nations of that region. Kennedy also inaugurated the Agency for International Development

(AID) to coordinate foreign aid. And he established what became one of his most popu-
Peace Corps   lar innovations: the Peace Corps, which sent young American volunteers abroad to work in developing areas.

Among the first foreign policy ventures of the Kennedy administration was a disastrous assault on the Castro government in Cuba. The Eisenhower administration had started the project; and by the time Kennedy took office, the CIA had been working for months to
Bay of Pigs   train a small army of anti-Castro Cuban exiles. On April 17, 1961, with the approval of the new president, 2,000 of the armed exiles landed at the Bay of Pigs in Cuba, expecting first American air support and then a spontaneous uprising by the Cuban people on their behalf. They received neither. At the last minute, as it became clear that things were going badly, Kennedy withdrew the air support, fearful of involving the United States too directly in the invasion. Nor did the expected uprising occur. Instead, well-armed Castro forces easily crushed the invaders, and within two days the entire mission had collapsed.

CONFRONTATIONS WITH THE SOVIET UNION

In the grim aftermath of the Bay of Pigs, Kennedy traveled to Vienna in June 1961 for his first meeting with Soviet Premier Nikita Khrushchev. Their frosty exchange of views did little to reduce strains between the two nations—nor did Khrushchev's veiled threat of war unless the United States ceased to support a noncommunist West Berlin in the heart of East Germany.

Khrushchev was particularly unhappy about the mass exodus of residents of East Germany to the West through the easily traversed border in the center of Berlin. But he ultimately found a method short of war to stop it. Just before dawn on August 13, 1961, the East German government, complying with directives from Moscow, constructed a wall between East and West Berlin. Guards fired on those who continued to try to escape. For nearly thirty years, the Berlin Wall served as the most potent physical symbol of the conflict between the communist and noncommunist worlds.

The rising tensions culminated the following October in the most dangerous and dramatic crisis of the Cold War. During the summer of 1962, American intelligence agencies became aware of the arrival of a new wave of Soviet technicians and equip-
Cuban Missile Crisis   ment in Cuba and of military construction in progress. On October 14, aerial reconnaissance photos produced clear evidence that the Soviets were constructing sites on the island for offensive nuclear weapons. To the Soviets, placing missiles in Cuba probably seemed a reasonable—and relatively inexpensive—way to counter the presence of American missiles in Turkey (and a way to deter any future American invasion of Cuba). But to Kennedy and most other Americans, the missile sites represented an act of naked aggression by the Soviets toward the United States. Almost immediately, the president—working with a special executive committee assembled to deal with the crisis—decided that the weapons must go. On October 22, he ordered a naval and air blockade around Cuba, a "quarantine" against all offensive weapons. Preparations were under way for an American air attack on the missile sites when, late in the evening of October 26, Kennedy received a message from Khrushchev implying that the Soviet Union would remove the missile bases in exchange for an American pledge not to invade Cuba. The president agreed. And, in secret, Kennedy agreed to withdraw the
Kennedy–Khrushchev Pact   missiles from Turkey in what is now called the Kennedy–Khrushchev Pact. The resolution of the conflict was a political victory for Kennedy,

and in an effort to avoid the threat of war again, the two leaders established a Moscow–Washington hotline that created a direct link between the nuclear nations. The improved dialogue between the nuclear superpowers also paved the way for the Nuclear Test Ban Treaty of 1963, which banned atmospheric tests.

JOHNSON AND THE WORLD

Lyndon Johnson entered the presidency with little prior experience in international affairs. He was eager, therefore, not only to continue the policies of his predecessor but also to prove quickly that he, too, was a strong and forceful leader.

An internal rebellion in the Dominican Republic gave him an opportunity to do so. A 1961 assassination had toppled the repressive dictatorship of General Rafael Trujillo, and for the next four years various factions in the country had struggled for dominance. In the spring of 1965, a conservative regime began to collapse in the face of a revolt by a broad range of groups on behalf of the left-wing nationalist Juan Bosch. Arguing (without any evidence) that Bosch planned to establish a pro-Castro communist regime, Johnson dispatched 30,000 American troops to quell the disorder. Only after a conservative candidate defeated Bosch in a 1966 election were the forces withdrawn.

From Johnson's first moments in office, however, his foreign policy was almost totally dominated by the bitter civil war in Vietnam and by the expanding involvement of the United States there.

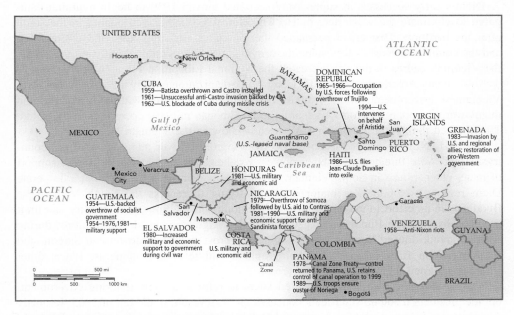

THE UNITED STATES IN LATIN AMERICA, 1954–2006 The Cold War greatly increased the readiness of the United States to intervene in the affairs of its Latin American neighbors. This map presents the many times and ways in which Washington ordered interventions in Central America, the Caribbean, and the northern nations of South America. During much of this period, the interventions were driven by Cold War concerns—by fears that communists might take over nations near the United States as they had taken over Cuba in the early 1960s. • *What other interests motivated the United States to exert influence in Latin America even after the end of the Cold War?*

THE AGONY OF VIETNAM

George Kennan, who helped devise the containment doctrine in the name of which America went to war in Vietnam, once called the conflict "the most disastrous of all America's undertakings over the whole 200 years of its history." Yet at first, the conflict in Vietnam seemed simply one more Third World struggle on the periphery of the Cold War.

AMERICA AND DIEM

Having thrown its support to the new leader of South Vietnam, Ngo Dinh Diem, in *Ngo Dinh Diem*   the aftermath of the 1954 Geneva accords, and having supported Diem in his blatant refusal to hold the elections in 1956 that the accords had required, the United States found itself drawn steadily deeper into the unstable politics of this fractious new nation.

Diem, an aristocratic Catholic from central Vietnam and an outsider in the south, was also a hard-line nationalist uncontaminated by any collaboration with the French and bent on shoring up the authority of his regime. And he was, for a time, apparently successful. With the help of the American CIA, Diem waged an effective campaign against some of the powerful religious sects and the South Vietnamese organized crime syndicate, which had challenged the authority of the central government. As a result, the United States came to regard Diem as a powerful and impressive alternative to Ho Chi Minh, his communist rival in North Vietnam. America threw military and economic aid at Diem's feet.

Diem's early successes in suppressing sects led him in 1959 to begin a similar campaign to eliminate the supporters of Ho Chi Minh who had stayed behind in the south after the partition. That effort persuaded the Vietminh—or supporters of Ho Chi Minh and the communist North—to resume the armed struggle for national unification. In 1959, the Vietminh cadres in the south created the National Liberation Front (NLF), known to *Viet Cong*   many Americans as the Viet Cong—an organization closely allied with the North Vietnamese government. In 1960, under orders from Hanoi, and with both material and manpower support from North Vietnam, the NLF began military operations in the south. This marked the beginning of what Americans know as the Vietnam War.

By 1961, NLF forces had established effective control over many areas of the countryside and were threatening Diem's power. By then, Diem was also losing the support of many other groups in South Vietnam, including his own military. In 1963, a desperate Diem regime precipitated a major crisis by trying to repress the South Vietnamese Buddhists in an effort to make Catholicism the dominant religion of the country and limit political dissent. The Buddhists staged enormous antigovernment demonstrations, during which a monk doused himself with gasoline, sat cross-legged in downtown Saigon, and set himself on fire—in view of photographers and television cameras. Later, other Buddhists burned themselves in other areas.

Alarmed American officials pressured Diem to reform his now tottering government, but the president made no significant concessions. As a result, in the fall of 1963, Kennedy gave his approval to a plot by a group of South Vietnamese generals to topple Diem. In *Diem Assassinated*   early November 1963, the generals staged the coup, assassinated Diem along with his brother Ngo Dinh Nhu (killings the United States had not wanted or expected), and established the first of a series of new governments, which were, for over three years, even less stable than the one they had overthrown. A few weeks after the coup, John Kennedy was assassinated.

FROM AID TO INTERVENTION

Lyndon Johnson inherited what was already a substantial American commitment to the survival of an anticommunist South Vietnam. During his first months in office, he expanded the American involvement in Vietnam only slightly, sending an additional 5,000 military advisers there and preparing to send 5,000 more. Then, early in August 1964, the president announced that American destroyers on patrol in international waters in the Gulf of Tonkin had been attacked by North Vietnamese torpedo boats. Later information raised serious doubts as to whether the administration reported the attacks accurately. At the time, however, virtually no one questioned Johnson's portrayal of the incident as a serious act of aggression. By a vote of 416 to 0 in the House and 88 to 2 in the Senate, Congress hurriedly passed the Gulf of Tonkin Resolution, which authorized   *Gulf of Tonkin Resolution* the president to "take all necessary measures" to protect American forces and "prevent further aggression" in Southeast Asia. The resolution became, in Johnson's view at least, an open-ended legal authorization for escalation of the conflict.

With the South Vietnamese leadership still in disarray and the communist military pressure growing stronger, more and more of the burden of opposition to the Viet Cong fell on the United States. In February 1965, after communist forces attacked an American military base at Pleiku, Johnson ordered American bombings of the north, in an attempt to destroy the depots and transportation lines responsible for the flow of North Vietnamese soldiers and supplies into South Vietnam. The bombing continued intermittently until 1972. A month later, in March 1965, two battalions of American marines landed at Da Nang in South Vietnam, bringing the total American troop strength to over 100,000.

Four months later, the president announced that American soldiers would now begin playing an active role in the conflict. By the end of the year, there were more than 180,000 American combat troops in Vietnam; in 1966, that number doubled; and by the end of 1967, over 500,000 American soldiers fought there. In the meantime, the air war intensi-fied. By the spring of 1966, more than 4,000 Americans and an unknown number of Vietnamese had been killed.

THE QUAGMIRE

Central to the American war effort in Vietnam was a strategy known as "attrition," a strategy premised on the belief that the United States could inflict more   *"Attrition" Strategy* damage on the enemy than the enemy could absorb. But the attrition strategy failed because the North Vietnamese, believing that they were fighting a war for national inde-pendence, were willing to commit many more soldiers and resources to the conflict than the United States had predicted.

The United States also failed in expecting its bombing of the north to eliminate the communists' war-making capacity. North Vietnam was not a modern industrial society, and it had relatively few of the sorts of targets against which bombing is effective. The North Vietnamese also responded to the bombing with great ingenuity. They cre-ated a network of underground tunnels, shops, and factories. The North Vietnamese also were provided substantial aid from the Soviet Union and China. They continually

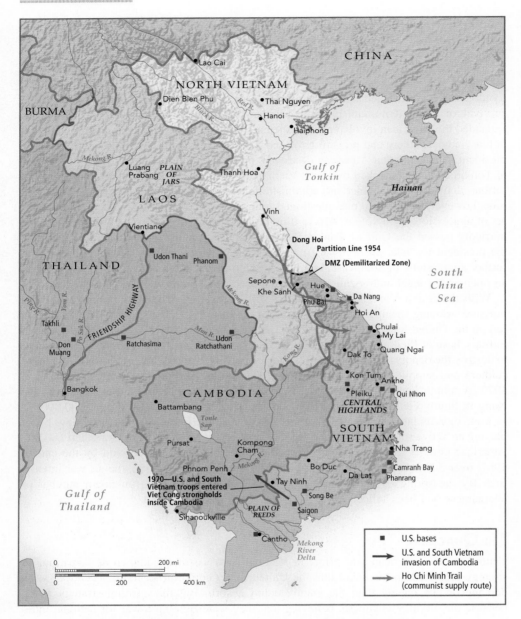

THE WAR IN VIETNAM AND INDOCHINA, 1964–1975 Much of the Vietnam War was fought in small engagements in widely scattered areas and did not conform to traditional notions of combat. But as this map shows, there were traditional battles and invasions and supply routes as well. The red arrows in the middle of the map show the general path of the Ho Chi Minh Trail, the main supply route by which North Vietnam supplied its troops and allies in the south. The blue arrow in southern South Vietnam indicates the point at which American troops invaded Cambodia in 1970. • *What is there in the geography of Indochina, as presented on this map, that helps explain the great difficulty the American military had in securing South Vietnam against communist attacks?*

moved the Ho Chi Minh Trail to make it elusive to American bombers. Far from breaking the north's resolve, the bombing seemed actually to strengthen popular commitment to the war.

Another important part of the American strategy was the "pacification" program, whose purpose was to push the Viet Cong from particular regions and then   *"Pacification" Program* "pacify" those regions by winning the "hearts and minds" of the people. Routing the Viet Cong was often possible, but the subsequent pacification was more difficult. Gradually, the pacification program gave way to a more heavy-handed relocation strategy, through which American troops uprooted villagers from their homes, sent them fleeing to refugee camps or into the cities (producing by 1967 more than 3 million refugees), and then destroyed the vacated villages and surrounding countryside. "It became necessary to destroy the village in order to save it," an American military official famously said of one such action, thus revealing the flawed assumptions of the pacification program.

As the war dragged on and victory remained elusive, some American officers and officials urged the president to expand the military efforts. But Johnson resisted—in part because he remembered the Korean War. He feared drawing China directly into the Vietnam War, and he was beginning to encounter obstacles and frustrations at home.

THE WAR AT HOME

Few Americans, and even fewer influential ones, had protested the American involvement in Vietnam as late as the end of 1965. But as the war dragged on inconclusively, political support for it began to erode.

By the end of 1967, American students opposed to the war (and to the military draft) had become a significant political force. Enormous peace marches in New York, Washington, D.C., and other cities drew broad public attention to the antiwar movement. (Music also raised awareness; see "Patterns of Popular Culture: The Folk-Music Revival.") In the meantime, a growing number of journalists, particularly reporters who had spent time in Vietnam, helped sustain the movement with their frank revelations about the brutality and apparent futility of the war.

Senator J. William Fulbright of Arkansas, chair of the Senate Foreign Relations Committee, also turned against the war and in January 1966 began to stage highly publicized and occasionally televised congressional hearings to air criticisms of it. Other members of Congress joined Fulbright in opposing Johnson's policies—including, in 1967, Robert F. Kennedy, brother of the slain president, now a senator from New York. Even within the administration, the consensus seemed to be crumbling. Robert McNamara, who had done much to help extend the initial American involvement in Vietnam, quietly left the government, disillusioned, in 1968. His successor as secretary of defense, Clark Clifford, became a quiet but powerful voice within the administration on behalf of a cautious scaling down of the commitment.

In the meantime, Johnson's commitment to fighting the war while continuing his Great Society reforms helped cause a rise in inflation, from the 2 percent level it had occupied through most of the early 1960s to 3 percent in 1967, 4 percent in 1968, and 6 percent in 1969. In August 1967, Johnson asked Congress for a tax increase to avoid even more ruinous inflation. In return, congressional conservatives demanded a $6 billion reduction in the funding for Great Society programs. The president accepted the reduction as a way to mollify congressional conservatives unnerved by economic troubles and critical of social welfare programs.

THE FOLK-MUSIC REVIVAL

Two impulses of the 1960s—the renewed interest among young people in the politics of the left, and the search for an "authentic" alternative to what many considered the artificial, consumerist culture of modern America—helped produce the revived popularity of folk music in that turbulent era. Although the harder, harsher, and more sensual music of rock 'n' roll was more visible and more popular in the 1960s, folk music more clearly expressed many of the political ideas and aspirations that were welling up in the youth culture of the time.

The folk-music tradition, like most American musical traditions, had many roots. It drew from some of the black musical traditions of the South, and from the white country music of Appalachia. And it drew most immediately from a style of music developed by musicians associated with the Communist Party's Popular Front in the 1930s. Woody Guthrie, Pete Seeger, the Weavers, and others whose music would become popular again in the 1960s began their careers singing in Popular Front and union rallies during the Great Depression. Their music, like the Popular Front itself, set out to seem entirely American, rooted in the nation's folk traditions.

Folk music remained alive in the 1940s and 1950s, but it had only a modest popular following. Pete Seeger and the Weavers continued to perform and to attract attention on college campuses. Harry Belafonte and the Kingston Trio recorded slick, pop versions of folk songs in an effort to bring them to mass audiences. In 1952, Folkway Records released the *Anthology of American Folk Music,* a collection of eighty-four performances recorded in the 1920s and 1930s that became an inspiration and an important source of

material to many younger folk musicians. Folk-music festivals—at Berkeley, Newport, and Chicago—began to proliferate beginning in 1959. And an important community of folk musicians lived and performed together in the 1950s and early 1960s in New York City's Greenwich Village.

As the politics of the 1960s became more heated, and as young people in particular became politically aroused, it was folk music that most directly reflected their new values and concerns. Peter, Paul, and Mary—although only intermittently political—became icons to much of the New Left, beginning with their 1962 recording of "If I Had a Hammer," a song first performed at Communist Party rallies in the 1940s by Pete Seeger and the Weavers. Bob Dylan, whose own politics were never wholly clear to the public, had a large impact on the 1960s left, even inadvertently providing a name to the most radical offshoot of Students for a Democratic Society (SDS), the Weathermen, who named themselves after a line from one of his songs: "You don't need a weatherman to know which way the wind blows."* Joan Baez, whose politics were no secret to anyone, was actively engaged in the antiwar movement and was arrested several times for participating in militant protests.

But it was not just the overt political messages of folk musicians that made them so important to young Americans in the 1960s. In addition, folk was a kind of music that seemed to reflect the "authenticity" the youth culture was attempting to find. In truth, neither the musicians themselves nor the young Americans attracted to them had much real connection with the traditions they were trying to evoke. The audiences

COFFEEHOUSE MUSIC The Feejon Coffee House in Manhattan was popular among young writers, poets, and others in the late 1950s, in part because it was a gathering place for folk musicians, two of whom are shown here performing at right. (© John Orris/Getty Images)

for folk music—a product of rural and working-class traditions—were overwhelmingly urban, middle-class people. But the message of folk music—that there is a "real" America rooted in values of sharing and community, hidden beneath the crass commercialism of modern culture—resonated with the yearnings of many people in the 1960s (and beyond) for an alternative to their own troubled world. When young audiences responded to Woody Guthrie's famous ballad "This Land Is Your Land," they were expressing a hope for a different America—more democratic, more honest, and more natural than the land they knew. •

UNDERSTAND, ANALYZE, & EVALUATE

1. What did folk music, with roots in the musical traditions of blacks, rural folk, and working-class people, offer that made it so appealing to and popular with urban, middle-class audiences?
2. What similarities between the 1930s and the 1960s might help explain the popularity of folk music during both those decades?
3. What musical style or form today continues the folk-music tradition of expressing a political message and reflecting the search for "authenticity"?

*Bob Dylan, "Subterranean Homesick Blues." Copyright © 1965 by Warner Bros. Music. Copyright renewed 1993 by Special Rider Music. All rights reserved. International copyright secured. Reprinted by permission.

THE TRAUMAS OF 1968

By the end of 1967, the twin crises of the war in Vietnam and the deteriorating racial situation at home had produced great social and political tensions. In the course of 1968, those tensions burst to the surface and seemed to threaten national chaos. (The year 1968 was turbulent elsewhere in the world as well; see "America in the World: 1968.")

1968

The year 1968 was one of the most turbulent in the postwar history of the United States. Much of what made it so traumatic were specifically American events—the growing controversy over the war in Vietnam, the assassinations of Martin Luther King Jr. and Robert Kennedy, racial unrest across the nation's cities, student protests on campuses throughout America. But the turmoil of 1968 was not confined to the United States. There were tremendous upheavals in many parts of the globe that year.

The most common form of turbulence around the world in 1968 was student unrest. In France, a student uprising in May far exceeded in size and ferocity anything that occurred in the United States. It attracted the support of French workers and briefly paralyzed Paris and other cities. It contributed to the downfall of the government of Charles de Gaulle a year later. In England, Ireland, Germany, Italy, the Netherlands, Mexico, Canada, Japan, and South Korea, students and other young people demonstrated in great numbers, and at times with violence, against governments, universities, and other structures of authority. Elsewhere, there was more widespread protest, as in Czechoslovakia, where hundreds of thousands of citizens took to the streets in support of what became known as "Prague Spring." It caused a demand for greater democracy and a repudiation of many of the oppressive rules and structures imposed on the nation by its Soviet-dominated communist regimes. Russian tanks rolled into the city to crush the uprising.

Many people have tried to explain why so much instability emerged in so many nations at the same time. One factor that contributed to the worldwide turbulence of 1968 was simple numbers. The postwar Baby Boom had created a very large age cohort in many nations, and by the late 1960s it was coming of age. In the industrial West, the sheer size of the new generation produced a tripling of the number of people attending colleges and universities. In fewer than twenty years it also created a heightened sense of the power of youth. The long period of postwar prosperity and relative peace in which this generation had grown up contributed to heightened expectations of what the world should offer them—and a greater level of impatience than previous generations had demonstrated with the obstacles that stood in the way of their hopes. A new global youth culture emerged that was in many ways at odds with the dominant culture of older generations. It valued nonconformity, personal freedom, and even rebellion.

A second force contributing to the widespread turbulence of 1968 was the power of global media. Satellite communication introduced in the early 1960s made it possible to transmit live news across the world. Videotape technology and the creation of lightweight portable television cameras enabled media organizations to respond to events much more quickly and flexibly than in the past. The audience for these televised images was by now global and enormous, particularly in industrial nations but even in the poorest areas of the world. Protests in one country were suddenly capable of inspiring protests in others. Demonstrators in Paris, for example, spoke openly of how campus protests in the United States in 1968—for example, the student uprising at Columbia University in New York the previous month—had helped motivate French students to rise up as well. Just as American students were protesting against what they considered antiquated, paternalistic features of their universities, French students demanded an end to the rigid, autocratic character of their own academic world.

In most parts of the world, the 1968 uprisings came and went without fundamentally altering institutions and systems. But many changes came in the wake of these protests. Universities around the globe undertook significant reforms. Religious observance in mainstream churches and synagogues in the West declined dramatically after 1968. New concepts of personal freedom gained legitimacy, helping to inspire social movements in the years that followed—among them the dramatic growth of feminism in many parts of the world and the emergence of the gay and lesbian rights movement. The events of 1968 did not produce a revolution in the United States or in most of the rest of the world, but it did help launch a period of dramatic social, cultural, and political changes that affected the peoples of many nations. •

UNDERSTAND, ANALYZE, & EVALUATE

1. What factors combined to produce the turbulence that resulted in the uprisings of 1968?
2. Did the demonstrators of 1968 succeed or fail to achieve their objectives? What were the long-term effects of the 1968 uprisings?

THE TET OFFENSIVE

On January 31, 1968, the first day of the Vietnamese New Year (Tet), communist forces launched an enormous, concerted attack on American strongholds throughout South Vietnam. A few cities, most notably Hue, fell temporarily to the communists. But what made the Tet offensive so shocking to the American people, who saw vivid reports of it on television, was the sight of communist forces in the heart of Saigon, setting off bombs, shooting down South Vietnamese officials and troops, and holding down fortified areas (including, briefly, the American embassy). The Tet offensive also suggested to the American public something of the brutality of the fighting in Vietnam. In the midst of the fighting, television cameras recorded the sight of a South Vietnamese officer shooting a captured and defenseless young Viet Cong soldier in the head in the streets of Saigon.

American forces soon dislodged the Viet Cong from most of the positions they had seized. And during the battle they had inflicted enormous casualties on the communists and permanently depleted the ranks of the NLF, forcing North Vietnamese troops to take on a much larger share of the subsequent fighting, but such accomplishments registered little with the American public who felt betrayed by an administration that had sworn the war was nearly over. Tet may have been a military victory for the United States, but it was a political defeat for the administration.

In the following weeks, opposition to the war grew substantially. Leading newspapers and magazines, television commentators, and mainstream politicians began taking public stands against the conflict. Public opposition to the war almost doubled, and Johnson's personal popularity rating had slid to 35 percent, the lowest of any president since Harry Truman.

THE POLITICAL CHALLENGE

Beginning in the summer of 1967, dissident Democrats tried to mobilize support behind an antiwar candidate who would challenge Lyndon Johnson in the 1968 primaries.

When Robert Kennedy turned them down, they recruited Senator Eugene McCarthy of Minnesota. A brilliantly orchestrated campaign by young volunteers in the New Hampshire primary produced a startling showing by McCarthy in March; he nearly defeated the president.

A few days later, Robert Kennedy entered the campaign, embittering many McCarthy supporters but bringing his own substantial strength among minorities, poor people, and workers to the antiwar cause. Polls showed the president trailing badly in the next scheduled primary, in Wisconsin. On March 31, 1968, Johnson went on television to announce a limited halt in the bombing of North Vietnam—his first major concession to the antiwar forces. And then, stunningly, he declared that he was withdrawing from the presidential contest.

Robert Kennedy quickly established himself as the champion of the Democratic primaries, winning one election after another. In the meantime, however, Vice President Hubert Humphrey, with the support of President Johnson, entered the contest and began to attract the support of party leaders and of the many delegations that were selected not by popular primaries but by state party organizations. He soon overtook Kennedy as the front-runner in the race.

ASSASSINATIONS AND POLITICS

On April 4, Martin Luther King Jr., who had traveled to Memphis, Tennessee, to lend his
Assassination of Dr. King   support to striking black sanitation workers in the city, was shot and killed while standing on the balcony of his motel. The assassin, James Earl Ray, who was captured two months later in London, had no apparent motive. Subsequent evidence suggested that he had been hired by others to do the killing, but he himself never revealed the identity of his employers.

King's tragic death produced a great outpouring of grief. Among some African Americans, it also produced anger. In the days after the assassination, major riots broke out in more than sixty American cities. Forty-three people died.

Late in the night of June 6, Robert Kennedy appeared in the ballroom of a Los Angeles hotel to acknowledge his victory in that day's California primary. As he left the ballroom after his victory statement, Sirhan Sirhan, a young Palestinian apparently enraged by pro-Israeli remarks Kennedy had recently made, emerged from a crowd and shot him in the head. Early the next morning, Kennedy died. The shock of this second tragedy in two
Assassination of Robert Kennedy   months—and only five years after the assassination of John Kennedy—cast a pall over the remainder of the presidential campaign.

When the Democrats finally gathered in Chicago in August, for a convention in which Hubert Humphrey was now the only real contender, even the most optimistic observers predicted turbulence. Inside the hall, delegates bitterly debated an antiwar plank in the party platform that both Kennedy and McCarthy supporters favored. Miles away, in a downtown park, thousands of antiwar protesters staged demonstrations. On the third night of the convention, as the delegates began their balloting on the now virtually inevitable nomination of Hubert Humphrey, demonstrators and police clashed in a bloody riot in the streets of Chicago. Hundreds of protesters were injured as police attempted to disperse them with tear gas and billy clubs. Aware that the violence was being televised to the nation, the demonstrators taunted the authorities with the chant, "The whole world is watching!" And Hubert Humphrey, who had spent years dreaming of becoming his party's candidate for president, finally got the nomination but from a badly fractured party that would make it difficult for him to manage his campaign.

THE CONSERVATIVE RESPONSE

The turbulent events of 1968 persuaded some observers that American society was in the throes of revolutionary change. In fact, however, the response of many Americans to the turmoil was to question the social changes of the prior decade and take a conservative political turn.

The most visible sign of the conservative backlash was the surprising success of the campaign of George Wallace for the presidency. Wallace had been one of the leading spokesmen for the defense of segregation when, as governor of Alabama, he had attempted to block the admission of black students to the University of Alabama in   *George Wallace* 1963. In 1968, he became a third-party candidate for president, basing his campaign on a host of conservative grievances. He denounced the forced busing of students to achieve racial integration in public schools, the proliferation of government regulations and social programs, and what he called the permissiveness of authorities toward crime, race riots, and antiwar demonstrations. There was never any serious chance that Wallace would win the election, but his standing in the polls rose at times to over 20 percent.

At the same time, a more effective effort to mobilize the conservative middle in favor of order and stability was under way within the Republican Party. Richard Nixon, whose

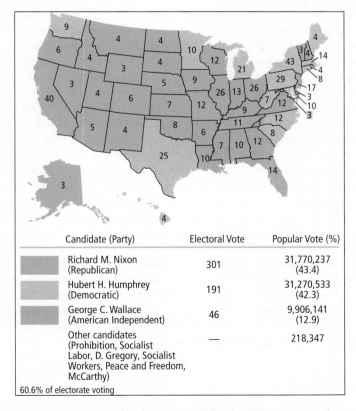

Candidate (Party)	Electoral Vote	Popular Vote (%)
Richard M. Nixon (Republican)	301	31,770,237 (43.4)
Hubert H. Humphrey (Democratic)	191	31,270,533 (42.3)
George C. Wallace (American Independent)	46	9,906,141 (12.9)
Other candidates (Prohibition, Socialist Labor, D. Gregory, Socialist Workers, Peace and Freedom, McCarthy)	—	218,347

60.6% of electorate voting

THE ELECTION OF 1968   The 1968 presidential election, which Richard Nixon won, was almost as close as the election of 1960, which he lost. Nixon might have won a more substantial victory had it not been for the independent candidacy of Governor George C. Wallace, who attracted many of the same conservative voters to whom Nixon appealed. • *How does the distribution of Democratic and Republican strength in this election compare to that in 1960?*

political career had seemed at an end after his losses in the presidential race of 1960 and *Nixon Elected* a California gubernatorial campaign two years later, reemerged as the spokesperson for what he called the "silent majority." By offering a vision of stability, law and order, government retrenchment, and "peace with honor" in Vietnam, he easily captured the nomination of his party for the presidency. And despite a last-minute surge by Humphrey, Nixon hung on to eke out a victory almost as narrow as his defeat in 1960. He received 43.4 percent of the popular vote to Humphrey's 42.3 percent (a margin of only about 500,000 votes), and 301 electoral votes to Humphrey's 191. George Wallace, who like most third-party candidates faded in the last weeks of the campaign, still managed to poll 12.9 percent of the popular vote and to carry five southern states with a total of 46 electoral ballots. Nixon had hardly won a decisive personal mandate. But the election made clear that a majority of the American electorate was more interested in restoring stability than in promoting social change.

CONCLUSION

Perhaps no decade of the twentieth century created more powerful and enduring images in America than the 1960s. It began with the election—and then the traumatic assassination—of an attractive and energetic young president, John Kennedy, who captured the imagination of millions and seemed to symbolize the rising idealism of the time. It produced a dramatic period of political innovation, led by President Lyndon Johnson, who greatly expanded the size and functions of the federal government and its responsibility for the welfare of the nation's citizens. He called it the Great Society. This time also saw the emergence of a sustained and enormously powerful civil rights movement that won a series of crucial legal victories, including two major civil rights acts that dismantled the Jim Crow system constructed in the late nineteenth and early twentieth centuries.

The spirit of dynamism and optimism that made the early 1960s so productive also helped bring to the surface problems and grievances that had no easy solutions. The civil rights movement awakened expectations of social and economic equality that laws alone could not provide. The peaceful, interracial crusade of the early 1960s gradually turned into a much more militant, confrontational, and increasingly separatist movement toward the decade's end. The idealism among white youths that began the 1960s, and played an important role in the political success of John Kennedy, evolved into an angry rebellion against many aspects of American culture and politics and produced a large upsurge of student protest that rocked the nation at the decade's end. Perhaps most of all, a small and largely unnoticed Cold War commitment to defend South Vietnam against communist aggression from the north led to a large and disastrous war that destroyed the presidency of Lyndon Johnson, sent thousands of young men and women to their deaths, and showed no signs of producing a victory. A decade that began with high hopes and soaring ideals ended with division and deep disillusionment.

KEY TERMS/PEOPLE/PLACES/EVENTS

affirmative action 720
Bay of Pigs 722
black power 720

Community Action
  programs 711
Cuban missile crisis 722

freedom rides 713
Freedom Summer 717
George Wallace 733

RECALL AND REFLECT

1. What were the political effects of John Kennedy's assassination?
2. How did increasing radicalism affect the successes and the setbacks of the civil rights movement?
3. What was the military strategy of the United States in Vietnam? What were the U.S. aims in that conflict? Why did the United States ultimately fail in Vietnam?
4. What accounted for growing opposition to the war in Vietnam?
5. What events made 1968 such a turbulent year both in the United States and elsewhere in the world? How did these events affect U.S. politics?

30 | THE CRISIS OF AUTHORITY

THE YOUTH CULTURE

THE MOBILIZATION OF MINORITIES

THE NEW FEMINISM

ENVIRONMENTALISM IN A TURBULENT
SOCIETY

NIXON, KISSINGER, AND THE VIETNAM WAR

NIXON, KISSINGER, AND THE WORLD

POLITICS AND ECONOMICS IN THE NIXON
YEARS

THE WATERGATE CRISIS

LOOKING AHEAD

1. What were some of the characteristics of the social and cultural revolutions of the 1960s and 1970s?
2. How did the U.S. strategy in Vietnam change under Nixon? What was the result of the change in strategy?
3. What was the Watergate scandal and how did it affect the presidency?

THE ELECTION OF RICHARD NIXON in 1968 was the result of more than the unpopularity of Lyndon Johnson and the Vietnam War. It was the result, too, of a broad popular reaction against what many Americans considered an assault on the foundations of their society and culture. In Richard Nixon such Americans found a man who seemed to match their mood. A product of a hardworking, middle-class family, Nixon projected an image of stern dedication to traditional values. Yet the presidency of Richard Nixon, far from returning calm and stability to American politics, coincided with, and helped produce, more years of crisis.

THE YOUTH CULTURE

Many conservatives in the 1960s and 1970s were alarmed by what they saw as a pattern of social and cultural anger by younger Americans. The protesters gave vent to two related impulses. One, emerging from the political left, was to create a great new community of "the people," which would rise up to break the traditional power of elites and force the nation to end the war, pursue racial and economic justice, and transform its political life. The other, at least equally powerful impulse was the vision of personal "liberation." It found expression in part through the efforts of many groups—African Americans, Indians, Hispanics, women, gay people, and others—to define and assert themselves and make demands on the larger society. It also found expression through the efforts of individuals to create a new culture—one that would allow them to escape from what some considered the dehumanizing pressures of the modern "technocracy."

THE NEW LEFT

Among the products of the racial crisis and the war in Vietnam was a radicalization of many American students. In the course of the 1960s, they formed what became known as the New Left. In 1962, a group of students (most of them white and many of them from the University of Michigan) gathered in Michigan to form Students for a Democratic Society (SDS), which became the most prominent organization of the New Left. Their declaration of beliefs, the Port Huron Statement, expressed their disillusionment with the society they had inherited and their determination to build a new politics. In the following years, SDS became the leading organization of student radicalism.

Since most members of the New Left were students, much of their radicalism centered for a time on issues related to the modern university. A 1964 dispute at the University

TIME LINE

1963
Friedan's *The Feminine Mystique*

1964
Free Speech Movement begins

1966
National Organization for Women formed

1968
Turmoil in universities

1969
Rock concert in Woodstock, NY

1970
Cambodian incursion
Kent State and Jackson State shootings

1971
Pentagon Papers published
Nixon imposes wage–price controls

1972
Nixon visits China
SALT I
"Christmas bombing" of North Vietnam
Watergate burglary
Nixon reelected

1973
U.S. withdraws from Vietnam
Arab oil embargo
Agnew resigns
Supreme Court decides *Roe v. Wade*

1974
Nixon resigns; Ford becomes president

1975
South Vietnam falls

DEMANDS OF THE NEW YORK HIGH SCHOOL STUDENT UNION

Like high school students across the country, young New Yorkers formed a union and demanded reform in the city's school system. Their demands from 1970 reflected the growing call among young Americans for greater control over public institutions and leaders and a new focus on the needs and aspirations of historically disadvantaged groups.

1—No suspensions, involuntary transfers, exclusion from classes, detention, harassment of students. Due process for students.

2—No cops in schools, no narcos, security guards, plain clothesmen, informers.

3—No program cards, hall checks, ID's, passes.

4—An end to commercial and general diplomas, one diploma for every student upon graduation.

5—Open admissions to colleges, a college education free for everyone who wants one.

6—Jobs and housing for every student who wants them on graduating, dropping out, or leaving home. The army is not a decent job.

7—No military recruiting in schools, no military assemblies, literature, no sending names to draft boards or recruiters. An immediate end to the draft.

8—Black and Latin departments controlled by Black and Latin students.

9—Community control of the schools and every other community facility. Students are part of the community.

10—POWER! Student control of curriculum, publications, assemblies, clubs, student government, dress, etc. The right to organize politically.

11—We support the fifteen points of the Black and Puerto Rican Citywide HS Council.

UNDERSTAND, ANALYZE, & EVALUATE

1. What might have inspired the students' demand for "due process"? What other evidence of an anti-authoritarian sentiment can you detect here?

2. How did the civil rights and the black power movements shape this Student Union? What are some of the rights movements covered in this chapter that were *not* reflected in this statement?

3. What role did the Vietnam War play for these students—what made this a possibly quite personal issue?

Source: *New York High School Free Press* (an underground newspaper), No. 8, reprinted in John Birmingham, *Our Time Is Now: Notes from the High School Underground* (New York: Praeger, 1970), p. 178.

---

of California at Berkeley over the rights of students to engage in political activities on campus—the *Free Speech Movement* the Free Speech Movement—was the first major outburst of what was to be nearly a decade of campus turmoil. The antiwar movement greatly inflamed and expanded the challenge to the universities; and beginning in 1968, campus demonstrations, riots, and building seizures became almost commonplace. At Columbia University in New York, students seized the offices of the president and others and occupied them for several days until local police forcibly ejected them. Over the next several years, hardly any major university was immune to some level of disruption. Small groups of especially dogmatic radicals—among them the "Weathermen," an offshoot of SDS—were responsible for a few cases of arson and bombing that destroyed campus buildings and claimed several lives. Protests also erupted in high schools, where students voiced similar demands for greater control over the curriculum on the subjects taught to them and over disciplinary policy. (See "Consider the Source: Demands of the New York High School Union.")

Not many people accepted the radical political philosophy of the New Left. But many supported the position of SDS and other groups on particular issues, and above all on the Vietnam War. Between 1967 and 1969, student activists organized some of the largest political demonstrations in American history to protest the war.

A related issue that helped fuel the antiwar movement was opposition to the military draft. The gradual abolition of many traditional deferments—for *Opposition to the Draft* graduate students, teachers, husbands, fathers, and others—swelled the ranks of those faced with conscription (and thus likely to oppose it). Of the almost 2 million drafted, about 7,000 draft-age Americans simply refused induction, accepting what were occasionally long terms in jail as a result. Thousands of others fled to Canada, Sweden, and elsewhere (where they were joined by deserters from the armed forces) to escape conscription.

The Counterculture

Closely related to the New Left was a new youth culture openly scornful of the values and conventions of middle-class society. The most visible characteristic of the **counterculture,** as it became known, was a change in personal styles. As if to display their contempt for conventional standards, young Americans flaunted long hair, shabby or flamboyant clothing, and a rebellious disdain for traditional speech and decorum. Also important to the counterculture was a new, more permissive view of sex and drugs.

Like the New Left, the counterculture challenged modern American society, attacking what it claimed were its banality, its hollowness, its artificiality, its isolation from nature. The most committed adherents of the counterculture—the hippies, who came to dominate the Haight-Ashbury neighborhood of San Francisco and other places, and the social dropouts, many of whom retreated to rural communes—rejected modern society altogether and attempted to find refuge in a simpler, more "natural" existence. But even those whose commitment to the counterculture was less intense shared the idea of personal fulfillment through rejecting the inhibitions and conventions of middle-class culture and giving fuller expression to personal instinct and desire.

The counterculture was only an exaggerated expression of impulses coursing through the larger society. Long hair and outlandish clothing became the badge not only of hippies and radicals but of an entire generation. The widespread use of marijuana, the freer attitudes toward sex, the iconoclastic (and often obscene) language—all spread far beyond the true devotees of the counterculture.

One of the most powerful elements of the new youth society was rock music. Its growing influence in the 1960s was a result in part of the phenomenal popularity of the Beatles, the English group whose first visit to the United States in 1964 created a remarkable sensation. For a time, most rock musicians—like most popular musicians before them—concentrated largely on uncontroversial romantic themes. By the late 1960s, however, rock had begun to reflect many of the new iconoclastic values of its time. The Beatles, for example, abandoned their once simple and seemingly innocent style for a new, experimental, even mystical approach that reflected the growing popular fascination with drugs and Eastern religions. Other groups, such as the Rolling Stones, turned even more openly

WOODSTOCK   In the summer of 1969, more than 400,000 people gathered for a music festival on a farm near Woodstock, New York. The gathering became a symbol of the youth movement of the sixties.   (© Shelly Rustin/ Black Star)

to themes of anger, frustration, and rebellion. Many popular musicians used their music to express explicit political radicalism as well—especially some of the leading folk singers of the era, such as Bob Dylan and Joan Baez. Rock's driving rhythms, its undisguised sensuality, its often harsh and angry tone—all made it an appropriate vehicle for expressing the themes of the social and political unrest of the late 1960s.

A powerful symbol of the fusion of rock music and the counterculture was the massive *Woodstock*   music festival at Woodstock, New York, in the summer of 1969, where 400,000 people gathered on a farm for nearly a week. Despite heavy rain, mud, inadequate facilities, and impossible crowding, the attendees remained peaceful and harmonious. Champions of the counterculture spoke rhapsodically at the time of how Woodstock represented the birth of a new youth culture, the "Woodstock nation." Four months later, however, another large rock concert—at the Altamont racetrack near San Francisco, featuring the Rolling Stones and attended by 300,000 people—exposed a darker side of the youth culture. Altamont became a brutal and violent event at which four people died, several accidentally or from drug overdoses but one because of injuries inflicted by members of a Hells Angels motorcycle gang, who were serving as security guards at the concert and who brutally beat and stabbed a number of people.

THE MOBILIZATION OF MINORITIES

The growth of African American protest encouraged other minorities to assert themselves and demand redress of their grievances. For Indians, Hispanic Americans, gay men and lesbians, and others, the late 1960s and 1970s were a time of growing self-expression and political activism.

SEEDS OF INDIAN MILITANCY

Few minorities had deeper or more justifiable grievances against the prevailing culture than did American Indians—or Native Americans, as they began defiantly to call themselves in the 1960s. Indians were the least prosperous, least healthy, and least stable ethnic group in the nation. And while African Americans attracted the attention (for good or for ill) of many whites, Indians for years had remained largely ignored.

For much of the postwar era, federal tribal policies tried to incorporate Indians into mainstream American society whether Indians wanted to assimilate or not. Two laws passed in 1953 established the basis of this policy, which became known *Termination Policy* as "termination." Through termination, the federal government withdrew all official recognition of the tribes as legal entities; they were no longer administratively separate from state governments and were subject to the same local jurisdictions as non–Native American residents. At the same time, the government encouraged Indians to assimilate into the white world and worked to funnel Native Americans into cities, where, presumably, they would adapt themselves to the larger society and lose their cultural distinctiveness.

Despite some individual successes, the new policies were a disastrous failure on the whole. Indians themselves fought so bitterly against these policies that in 1958, the Eisenhower administration barred further terminations. In the meantime, the struggle against termination mobilized a new generation of Indian militants and breathed life into the principal Native American organization, the National Congress of American Indians, which had been created in 1944.

The Democratic administrations of the 1960s made no effort to revive termination. Instead, they made modest efforts to restore at least some degree of tribal autonomy such as funneling Office of Economic Opportunity money to tribal organizations through the Community Action programs. In the meantime, the tribes themselves began to fight for greater self-determination. The new militancy benefited from the rapid increase in the Indian population, which was growing much faster than that of the rest of the nation (nearly doubling between 1950 and 1970 to a total of about 800,000).

THE INDIAN CIVIL RIGHTS MOVEMENT

In 1961, more than 400 members from 67 tribes gathered in Chicago and issued the Declaration of Indian Purpose, which stressed the "right to choose our own way of life" and the "responsibility of preserving our precious heritage." Another example of a growing Indian self-consciousness, the National Indian Youth Council, created in the aftermath of the 1961 Chicago meeting, promoted the idea of Indian nationalism and intertribal unity. In 1968, a group of young, militant Indians established the American Indian Movement (AIM), which drew support from urban areas *American Indian Movement* and reservations alike.

The new activism produced results. In 1968, Congress passed the Indian Civil Rights Act. It guaranteed reservation Indians protections by the Bill of Rights, *Indian Civil Rights Act* but also recognized the legitimacy of tribal laws within the reservations. In 1968, Indian fishermen, citing old treaty rights, clashed with Washington State officials on the Columbia River and in Puget Sound. The following year, members of several tribes occupied the abandoned federal prison on Alcatraz Island in San Francisco Bay, claiming the site "by right of discovery."

In response, the Nixon administration appointed Louis Bruce, a Mohawk-Sioux, as commissioner of Indian affairs in 1969; and in 1970, the president promised both

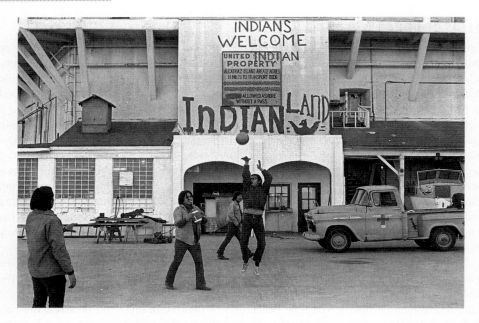

THE OCCUPATION OF ALCATRAZ Alcatraz, an island in San Francisco Bay, once housed a large federal prison that by the late 1960s had been abandoned. In 1969, a group of Indian activists occupied the island and claimed it as Indian land—precipitating a long standoff with authorities. (© AP Images)

increased tribal self-determination and an increase in federal aid. But the protests continued. In November 1972, nearly a thousand demonstrators, most of them Lakota Sioux, forcibly occupied the building of the Bureau of Indian Affairs in Washington, D.C., for six days. In February 1973, members of AIM seized the town of Wounded Knee, South Dakota, the site of the 1890 massacre of Sioux by federal troops. For two months, they occupied the town, demanding that the government honor its long-forgotten treaty obligations.

The Indian civil rights movement, like other civil rights movements of the same time, fell far short of winning full equality for Native Americans. But it helped the tribes win a series of new legal rights and protections that, together, gave them a stronger position than they had enjoyed at any previous time in the twentieth century.

Latino Activism

The fastest-growing minority group in the United States in the 1970s was Latinos, or Hispanic Americans. Large numbers of Mexicans had entered the country during World War II in response to the wartime labor shortage, and many had remained in the cities of the Southwest and the Pacific Coast. By 1960, Los Angeles had a bigger Mexican population than any place except Mexico City.

But the greatest expansion in the Latino population of the United States was yet to *Growing Latino Population* come. In 1960, the census reported slightly more than 3 million Latinos living in the United States. By 1970, that number had grown to 9 million and by 2000 to 35 million. By 2010, the number passed 50 million. Hispanics constituted more than a third of all legal immigrants to the United States after 1960.

Large numbers of Puerto Ricans (who were entitled to American citizenship by birth) migrated to eastern urban areas, particularly New York City, where they formed one of the poorest communities in the city. South Florida's substantial Cuban population began with a wave of middle-class refugees fleeing the Castro regime in the early 1960s. These first Cuban migrants quickly established themselves as a successful and highly assimilated part of Miami's middle class. In 1980, a second, much poorer wave of Cuban immigrants—the so-called Marielitos, named for the port from which they left Cuba—arrived in Florida when Castro temporarily relaxed exit restrictions. Later in the 1980s, large numbers of immigrants (both legal and illegal) began to arrive from Central and South America—from Guatemala, Nicaragua, El Salvador, Peru, and other countries.

Like African Americans and Indians, many Latinos responded to the highly charged climate of the 1960s by strengthening their ethnic identification and by organizing for political and economic power. Affluent Hispanics in Miami filled influential positions in the professions and local government; in the Southwest, Latino voters elected Mexican Americans to seats in Congress and to governorships. A Mexican American political organization, La Raza Unida, exercised influence in Southern California and elsewhere in the Southwest in the 1970s and beyond. One of the most visible efforts to organize Hispanics occurred in California, where an Arizona-born farmworker of Mexican descent, César Chávez, created an effective *César Chávez* union of largely Mexican itinerant farmworkers: the United Farm Workers (UFW).

For most Latinos, however, the path to economic and political power was more difficult. Mexican Americans and others were slow to develop political influence in proportion to their numbers. In the meantime, Latinos formed one of the poorest segments of the United States population.

KENNEDY AND CHÁVEZ César Chávez, leader of the United Farm Workers, endured a hunger strike in 1968 in the spirit of nonviolent protest against the treatment of field workers. Robert F. Kennedy, just beginning his campaign for the presidency, visited the union leader to show his support. At this point, Chávez had been fasting for several weeks. (Photo by Michael Rougier/© Time & Life Pictures/Getty Images)

GAY LIBERATION

Another important liberation movement to emerge in the 1960s was the effort by gay men and lesbians to win political and economic rights and social acceptance. Homosexuality has been a generally unacknowledged reality throughout Western civilization. Nonheterosexual men and women were forced for generations to suppress their sexual preferences, to exercise them surreptitiously, or to live within isolated and often persecuted communities. But by the late 1960s, the liberating impulses that had affected other groups helped mobilize gay men and lesbians to fight for their own rights.

On June 27, 1969, police officers raided the Stonewall Inn, a gay nightclub in New York City's Greenwich Village, and began arresting patrons simply for frequenting the place. The raid was not unusual, but the response was. Gay onlookers taunted the police and then attacked them. Someone started a blaze in the Stonewall Inn itself, almost trapping the police inside. Rioting continued throughout Greenwich Village (the center of New York's gay community) through much of the night.

The "Stonewall Riot" marked the growth of the gay liberation movement—one of the *Stonewall Riot* most controversial challenges to traditional values and assumptions of its time. New organizations—among them the Gay Liberation Front, founded in New York in 1969—sprang up around the country. Public discussion and media coverage of homosexuality, long subject to an unofficial taboo, quickly and dramatically increased. Gay activists had some success in challenging the long-standing assumption that homosexuality was aberrant behavior; many argued that no sexual preference was any more normal than another. One victory came when the American Psychiatric Association stopped categorizing homosexuality as a mental illness in 1974.

Most of all, however, the gay liberation movement transformed the outlook of many gay men and lesbians themselves. It helped them "come out," express their preferences openly and unapologetically, and demand from society a recognition that gay relationships could be as significant and worthy of respect as heterosexual ones. By the early 1980s, the gay liberation movement had made remarkable strides. Even the ravages of the AIDS epidemic, which, in the beginning at least, affected the gay community more disastrously than any other group, failed to halt the growth of gay liberation. Indeed, it not only strengthened the gay community, but it also helped Americans understand and humanize those suffering, which in turn slowly led to increased acceptance.

By the early twenty-first century, gay men and lesbians had achieved many of the same milestones that other oppressed minorities had attained in earlier decades. Openly gay politicians won election to public office. Universities established gay and lesbian studies programs. Laws prohibiting discrimination on the basis of sexual preference made slow, halting progress at the state and local levels. But gay liberation produced a powerful *Backlash against Gay Liberation* backlash as well. President Bill Clinton's 1993 effort to end the ban on gay men and lesbians serving in the military met a storm of criticism from members of Congress and within the military itself. Clinton retreated to a "Don't Ask, Don't Tell" policy and even signed the Defense of Marriage Act (DOMA) in 1996 that allowed states to refuse to recognize same-sex marriages granted under the laws of other states. Conservative voters in some cities and states approved referendum questions on their ballots outlawing civil rights protections for gay men and lesbians, and, during a bitter debate over gay rights in the 2004 presidential campaign, voted state bans on gay marriage. Antigay violence continued periodically in communities around the country.

At the same time, however, support for gay rights grew stronger in many parts of the country. In 2010, President Obama and the Congress repealed the "Don't Ask, Don't Tell" policy that forced people in the military to hide their homosexuality. And in June 2015, the Supreme Court affirmed the right of same-sex couples to wed in all 50 states.

THE NEW FEMINISM

Women constitute over 50 percent of the United States population. But during the 1960s and 1970s, many women began to identify with minority groups as they renewed demands for a liberation of their own.

THE REBIRTH

The 1963 publication of Betty Friedan's *The Feminine Mystique* is often cited as one of the first events of contemporary women's liberation. A writer for women's   *Betty Friedan* magazines in the 1950s, Friedan traveled around the country interviewing women who had graduated with her from Smith College in 1947. Most of these women were living out the dream that postwar American society had promised them: they were affluent wives and mothers living in comfortable suburbs. And yet many of them were deeply frustrated and unhappy, with no outlets for their intelligence, talent, and education. Friedan's book did not so much cause the revival of feminism as help give voice to a movement that was already stirring.

By the time *The Feminine Mystique* appeared, President Kennedy had already established the President's Commission on the Status of Women, which brought national

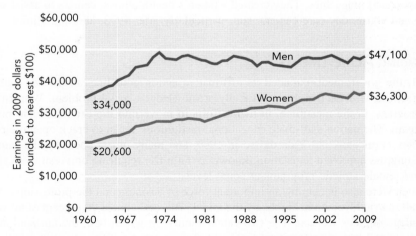

Note: People 15 years old and older beginning in 1980 and people 14 years old and older as of the following year for previous years. Before 1989, data are for civilian workers only.

MEDIAN EARNINGS BY GENDER, 1960–2009   U.S. Census Bureau data comparing the median earnings of full-time, year-round workers show changes in the gender wage gap over time. · *If the Equal Pay Act barred employers from paying women less than men for the same work, what factors might account for the differences in median earnings of men and women?* (U.S. Census Bureau, Current Population Survey, 1961 to 2009 Annual Social and Economic Supplements) attention to sexual discrimination. Also in 1963, the Kennedy administration helped win passage of the Equal Pay Act, which barred the pervasive practice of paying women less than men for the same work in some fields. A year later, Congress incorporated into the Civil Rights Act of 1964 an amendment—Title VII—that extended to women many of the same legal protections against discrimination that were being extended to African Americans and other minorities.

In 1966, Friedan joined with other feminists to create the National Organization for *NOW* Women (NOW), which was to become the nation's largest and most influential feminist organization. NOW responded to the complaints of women by demanding greater educational opportunities for women and denouncing the domestic ideal and the traditional concept of marriage. But the heart of the movement was an effort to address the needs of women in the workplace.

WOMEN'S LIBERATION

By the late 1960s, new and more radical feminist demands were also attracting a large following, especially among younger, white, educated women. Many of them drew inspiration from the New Left and the counterculture. Some were involved in the civil rights movement; others, in the antiwar crusade. Many had found that even within those movements, they faced discrimination and exclusion and were subordinated to male leaders.

In its most radical form, the new feminism rejected the whole notion of marriage, family, and even heterosexual relationships (a vehicle, some women claimed, of male domination). Few women embraced such extremes. But by the early 1970s, large numbers of women were coming to see themselves as an exploited group banding together against oppression and developing a culture of their own. In cities and towns across the country, feminists opened women's bookstores, bars, and coffee shops. They founded feminist newspapers and magazines. They created women's health clinics, centers to assist victims of rape and abuse, day-care centers, and, particularly after 1973, abortion clinics.

EXPANDING ACHIEVEMENTS

In 1971, the government extended its affirmative action guidelines to include women— linking sexism with racism as an officially acknowledged social problem. Women made rapid progress, in the meantime, in their efforts to move into the economic and political mainstream. The nation's all-male educational institutions began to crack open their doors to women. (Princeton and Yale did so in 1969, and many others soon did the same.) In 1972, Congress approved legislation (known as Title IX) requiring universities to support male and female athletic programs at equal levels.

Women were also becoming an important force in business and the professions. Nearly half of all married women held jobs by the mid-1970s, and almost 90 percent of all women with college degrees worked. The two-career family, in which both the husband and the wife maintained active professional lives, slowly became a widely accepted middle-class norm. (It had been common within much of the working class for decades.) There were also important symbolic changes, such as the refusal of many women to adopt their husbands' surnames when they married and the use of the term "Ms." in place of "Mrs." or "Miss" to signal the irrelevance of a woman's marital status in the professional world.

By the mid-1980s, women were serving in both houses of Congress, on the Supreme Court, in numerous federal cabinet positions, as governors of several states, and in many other political positions. In 1981, Ronald Reagan named the first female Supreme Court justice, Sandra Day O'Connor; in 1993, Bill Clinton named the second, Ruth Bader Ginsburg. In 1984, the Democratic Party chose a woman, Representative *Women in Government* Geraldine Ferraro of New York, as its vice presidential candidate. Madeleine Albright (under Clinton) and Condoleezza Rice (under George W. Bush) became the first women to serve as secretary of state. And in 2008, Hillary Clinton nearly became the Democratic candidate for president. She, too, became secretary of state in the Obama administration. In academia, women were expanding their presence in traditional scholarly fields; they were also creating new fields—women's and gender studies, which in the 1980s and 1990s were among the fastest-growing areas of American scholarship.

In 1972, Congress approved the Equal Rights Amendment (ERA) to the Constitution and sent it to the states. For a while, ratification seemed almost *The Equal Rights Amendment* certain. By the late 1970s, however, the momentum behind the amendment had died because of a rising chorus of objections to it from people (including many antifeminist women) who feared that it would disrupt traditional social patterns. In 1982, the ten years allotted for ratification expired.

THE ABORTION ISSUE

A major goal of American feminism since the 1920s has been the effort by women to win greater control of their own sexual and reproductive lives. In its least controversial form, this impulse helped produce an increasing awareness beginning in the 1970s of the problems of rape, sexual abuse, and domestic abuse. The dissemination of contraceptives and birth-control information became more widespread and less controversial than it had been earlier in the century. A related issue, however, stimulated as much popular controversy as any question of its time: abortion.

Abortion had once been legal in much of the United States, but by the beginning of the twentieth century, it was banned by statute in most of the country and remained so into the 1960s (although many abortions continued to be performed quietly, and often dangerously, out of sight of the law). The women's movement created strong new pressures for the legalization of abortion. Several states had abandoned restrictions on abortion by the end of the 1960s. And in 1973, the Supreme Court's decision in *Roe v. Wade* *Roe v. Wade,* based on an implied but not specified "right to privacy" first protected by the Court only a few years earlier in *Griswold v. Connecticut,* invalidated all laws prohibiting abortion during the "first trimester"—the first three months of pregnancy. But even then, the issue remained far from settled.

ENVIRONMENTALISM IN A TURBULENT SOCIETY

Like feminism, environmentalism entered the 1960s with a long history but relatively little public support. Also like feminism, environmentalism profited from the turbulence of the era and emerged by the 1970s as a powerful force in American life. The rise of this new movement was in part a result of the intensifying level of environmental degradation in advanced industrial societies of the late twentieth century. It was a result, too, of the growth of ecology, a science that provided environmentalists with new and powerful arguments.

THE NEW SCIENCE OF ECOLOGY

Until the mid-twentieth century, most people who considered themselves environmental-ists based their commitment on aesthetic or moral grounds. They wanted to preserve nature because it was too beautiful to despoil, because it was a mark of divinity on the world, or because it permitted humans a spiritual experience that would otherwise be unavailable to them. Other groups took their cue from the late President Theodore Roosevelt. These conservationists wanted to protect the environment for use in outdoor activities like camp-ing and hunting. In the course of the twentieth century, however, scientists in much of the world began to create a new rationale for environmentalism. They called it ecology.

Ecology is the science of the interrelatedness of the natural world. It addresses such problems as air and water pollution, the destruction of forests, the extinction of species, and toxic wastes, which are not separate, isolated problems. All elements of the earth's environment are intimately and delicately linked. Damaging any one of those elements, therefore, risks damaging all the others.

Among the early contributions to popular knowledge of ecology was the work of writer and naturalist Aldo Leopold. During a career in forest management, Leopold sought to apply the new scientific findings on ecology to his interactions with the natural world. And in 1949, he published a classic of environmental literature, *The Sand County Almanac,* in which he argued that humans had a responsibility to understand and maintain the balance of nature, that they should behave in the natural world according to a code that he called the "land ethic." By then, the science of ecology was spreading widely in the scientific community. Among the findings of ecologists were such now-common ideas as the "food *Rachel Carson* chain," the "ecosystem," "biodiversity," and "endangered species." Rachel Carson's sensational 1962 book, *Silent Spring,* which revealed the dangers of pesticides, was based solidly on the ideas of ecologists and did at least as much as Leopold's work to introduce those ideas to a larger public.

ENVIRONMENTAL ADVOCACY

Among the major environmental organizations were the Wilderness Society, the Sierra Club, the National Audubon Society, the Nature Conservancy, the National Wildlife Federation, and the National Parks and Conservation Association. All of these organiza-tions predated the rise of modern ecological science, but the growth of environmental threats and scientific efforts to address them kept these organizations engaged like never before. They found allies among such groups as the American Civil Liberties Union, the League of Women Voters, the National Council of Churches, and even the AFL-CIO.

Out of these organizations emerged a new generation of environmental activists able to contribute to the legal and political battles of the movement. Scientists provided the necessary data. Lawyers fought battles with government agencies and in the courts.

Many other forces contributed to what became the environmental movement. Lady Bird Johnson, the first lady, helped raise public awareness of the landscape with her energetic "beautification" campaign in the mid-1960s—a campaign unconnected to any ecological concepts, but one that reflected a growing popular dismay at the despoiling of the land-scape by rapid economic growth. Members of the counterculture contributed to environ-mental awareness with their romanticization of the natural world and their repudiation of the "technocracy."

But perhaps the greatest force behind environmentalism was the condition of the envi-ronment itself. By the 1960s, the damage to the natural world from postwar population and economic growth was becoming hard to ignore. Water pollution—which had been a problem in some areas of the country for many decades—was becoming so *Pollution* widespread that almost every major city was dealing with the unpleasant sight and odor, as well as the health risks, of polluted rivers and lakes. In Cleveland, Ohio, for example, the Cuyahoga River actually burst into flame from time to time from the petroleum waste being dumped into it; the city declared the river an official fire hazard.

Perhaps more alarming was the growing awareness that the air itself was becoming unhealthy, that toxic fumes from factories, power plants, and, most of all, automobiles were poisoning the atmosphere. Weather forecasts and official atmospheric information began to refer to "smog" levels—using a relatively new word formed from a combination of "smoke" and "fog," which became an almost perpetual fact of daily life in such cities as Los Angeles and Denver. In 1969, a damaged oil-well platform off Santa Barbara, California, spewed hundreds of thousands of gallons of crude oil into the ocean just off the popular beaches of this affluent city. This oil spill had a tremendous impact on the environmental consciousness of millions of Americans. Another, much larger spill—indeed, the largest in American history—occurred off the coast of Alaska in 1989 when the giant tanker *Exxon Valdez* hit a reef in Prince William Sound. The damage it caused to the nearby shoreline and wildlife also greatly increased environmental consciousness. In April 2010, the Deepwater Horizon oil rig exploded forty-one miles off the Louisiana coast, killing eleven. Over the next three months, chemical dispersants used to control the spill and 5 million gallons of crude oil spread into *Major Oil Spills* the Gulf of Mexico, destroying sea life and damaging the coastline. The long-term effects are still unknown.

Environmentalists brought to public attention many long-term dangers and helped create a broad and powerful movement.

EARTH DAY AND BEYOND

On April 22, 1970, people all over the United States participated in the first "Earth Day." Originally proposed by Wisconsin senator Gaylord Nelson as a series of teach-ins on college campuses, Earth Day gradually took on a much larger life. Carefully managed by people who wanted to avoid associations with the radical left, it had a less threatening quality than antiwar demonstrations and civil rights rallies seemed to have. According to some estimates, over 20 million Americans participated in Earth Day observances, making Earth Day, possibly, the largest single demonstration in the nation's history.

The cautious, centrist character of Earth Day and related efforts to popularize environmentalism helped create a movement that was for a time less divisive than other, more controversial causes. Gradually, environmentalism became more than simply a series of demonstrations and protests. It became part of the consciousness of the vast majority of Americans—absorbed into popular culture, built into primary and secondary education, and endorsed by almost all politicians (even if many of them actually opposed some environmental goals).

It also became part of the fabric of public policy. In 1970, Congress passed and President Nixon signed the National Environmental Protection Act, which created a new agency—the Environmental Protection Agency—to enforce antipollution *EPA Established* standards on businesses and consumers. The Clean Air Act, also passed in 1970, and the Clean Water Act, passed in 1972, became additional tools in the government's arsenal of weapons against environmental degradation.

Different administrations displayed varying levels of support for environmental goals, and new environmental problems continued to emerge even as older ones sometimes found solutions. Environmentalism became simultaneously a movement, a set of public policies, and a broad national ideal—and it was the combination of all those aspects that made it a powerful force in American life.

NIXON, KISSINGER, AND THE VIETNAM WAR

Richard Nixon assumed office in 1969 committed not only to restoring stability at home but to creating a new and more stable order in the world. Central to his hopes for international stability was a resolution of the stalemate in Vietnam. Yet the new president felt no freer than his predecessor to abandon the American commitment there.

VIETNAMIZATION

Despite Nixon's own deep interest in international affairs, he brought with him into government a man who at times seemed to overshadow the president himself in the *Henry Kissinger* conduct of diplomacy: Henry Kissinger, a Harvard professor whom Nixon appointed as his special assistant for national security affairs. Kissinger quickly established dominance over Secretary of State William Rogers and Secretary of Defense Melvin Laird. Together, Nixon and Kissinger set out to find an acceptable solution to the stalemate in Vietnam.

The new Vietnam policy moved along several fronts. One was the move to "Vietnamize" the conflict—that is, train and equip the South Vietnamese military to assume the burden of combat in place of American forces. In the fall of 1969, Nixon announced the withdrawal of 60,000 American ground troops from Vietnam. By the fall of 1972, relatively few American soldiers remained in Indochina. From a peak of more than 540,000 in 1969, the number had dwindled to about 60,000.

Vietnamization (and the decreased draft calls it produced) did help quiet domestic opposition to the war for a time. It did nothing, however, to break the stalemate in the negotiations with the North Vietnamese in Paris. The new administration decided that new military pressures would be necessary to do that.

ESCALATION

By the end of 1969, Nixon and Kissinger had decided that the most effective way to tip the military balance in South Vietnam's favor was to destroy bases in Cambodia and Laos that the U.S. military believed were the launching points for many North Vietnamese attacks. (Laos, Cambodia, and Vietnam are neighboring states in the peninsula of Indochina.) Very early in his presidency, Nixon secretly ordered the air force to bomb these bases; on April 30, 1970, the president announced that he was sending U.S. ground troops across the border into Cambodia to destroy them.

Literally overnight, the Cambodian invasion restored the dwindling antiwar movement to vigorous life. The first days of May saw widespread and vocal antiwar demonstrations. A mood of crisis was already mounting when, on May 4, four college students were killed and nine injured after members of the National Guard opened fire on antiwar demonstra-*Kent State and Jackson State* tors at Kent State University in Ohio. Ten days later, police killed two African American students at Jackson State University in Mississippi during a demonstration there.

The clamor against the war spread into the government and the press. Congress angrily repealed the Gulf of Tonkin Resolution in December. Then, in June 1971, first the *New York Times* and later other newspapers began publishing excerpts from a secret study of the war prepared by the Defense Department during the Johnson administration. The so-called Pentagon Papers were leaked to the press by former Defense official   *Pentagon Papers* Daniel Ellsberg. They provided evidence that the government had been dishonest, both in reporting the military progress of the war and in explaining its own motives for American involvement. The administration went to court to suppress the documents, but the Supreme Court ruled that the press had the right to publish them.

Morale and discipline among American troops in Vietnam were rapidly deteriorating in the waning years of the war. In 1971 Lieutenant William Calley was tried and convicted of overseeing a massacre of more than 100 unarmed South Vietnamese civilians in 1968 near the village of My Lai. It attracted wide public attention to the dehumanizing impact of the war on those who fought it—both Americans and Vietnamese. Less publicized were other, more widespread problems among American troops in Vietnam: desertion, drug addiction, racism, refusal to obey orders, even the killing of unpopular officers by enlisted men.

By 1971, polls indicated that nearly two-thirds of Americans supported withdrawal from Vietnam. President Nixon, however, believed that a defeat in Vietnam would cause unacceptable damage to the nation's credibility. The FBI, the CIA, the White House itself, and other federal agencies increased their efforts to discredit and harass antiwar and radical groups, often through illegal means.

In Indochina, meanwhile, the fighting raged on. American bombing in Vietnam and Cambodia increased. In March 1972, the North Vietnamese mounted their biggest offensive since 1968 (the so-called Easter offensive). American and South Vietnamese   *Easter Offensive* forces managed to halt the communist advance, but it was clear that without American support, the South Vietnamese would not have succeeded. At the same time, Nixon ordered American planes to bomb targets near Hanoi, the capital of North Vietnam, and Haiphong, its principal port, and called for the mining of seven North Vietnamese harbors.

"Peace with Honor"

As the 1972 presidential election approached, the administration stepped up its effort to produce a breakthrough in negotiations with the North Vietnamese. In April, the president dropped his longtime insistence on the removal of North Vietnamese troops from the south before any American withdrawal. Meanwhile, Henry Kissinger met privately in Paris with the North Vietnamese foreign secretary, Le Duc Tho, to work out terms for a cease-fire. On October 26, only days before the presidential election, Kissinger announced that "peace is at hand."

Several weeks later (after the election), negotiations broke down once again. Although both the American and the North Vietnamese governments were ready to accept the Kissinger–Tho plan for a cease-fire, President Nguyen Van Thieu of South Vietnam balked, still insisting on a full withdrawal of North Vietnamese forces from the south. Kissinger tried to win additional concessions from the communists to meet Thieu's objections, but on December 16 talks broke off.

The next day, December 17, American B-52s began the heaviest and most destructive air raids of the entire war on Hanoi, Haiphong, and other North Vietnamese targets.

Civilian casualties were high, and fifteen American B-52s were shot down by the North Vietnamese; in the entire war to that point, the United States had lost only one of the *"Christmas Bombing"* giant bombers. On December 30, Nixon terminated the "Christmas bombing." The United States and the North Vietnamese returned to the conference table; and on January 27, 1973, they signed an "agreement on ending the war and restoring peace in Vietnam." Nixon claimed that the Christmas bombing had forced the North Vietnamese to relent. At least equally important, however, was the enormous American pressure on Thieu to accept the cease-fire.

The terms of the Paris accords were little different from those Kissinger and Tho had accepted in principle a few months before. Nor were they much different from the peace plan Johnson had proposed in 1968. There would be an immediate cease-fire. The North Vietnamese would release several hundred American prisoners of war. The Thieu regime would survive for the moment, but North Vietnamese forces already in the south would remain there. An undefined committee would work out a permanent settlement.

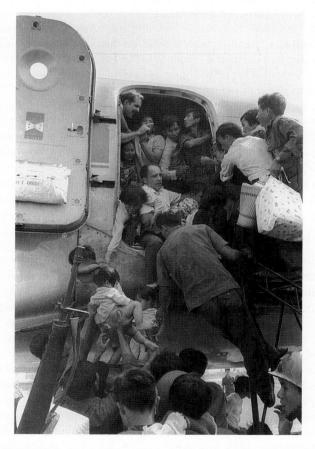

THE EVACUATION OF SAIGON A harried U.S. official struggles to keep panicking Vietnamese from boarding an already overpacked helicopter on the roof of the U.S. embassy in Saigon. The hurried evacuation of Americans took place only hours before the arrival of North Vietnamese troops, signaling the final defeat of South Vietnam. (© AP Images)

Defeat in Indochina

American forces were hardly out of Indochina before the Paris accords began to collapse. In March 1975, the North Vietnamese launched a full-scale offensive against the now greatly weakened forces of South Vietnam. Thieu appealed to Washington for assistance. The president (now Gerald Ford) appealed to Congress for additional funding; Congress refused. Late in April 1975, communist forces marched into Saigon, shortly   *Fall of Saigon* after officials of the Thieu regime and the staff of the American embassy had fled the country in humiliating disarray. The communist forces quickly occupied the capital, renamed it Ho Chi Minh City, and began the process of reuniting Vietnam under the government based in Hanoi. At about the same time, the Lon Nol regime in Cambodia fell to the murderous forces of the Khmer Rouge—whose brutal policies led to the death of more than a third of the country's people over the next several years.

Such were the dismal results of more than a decade of direct American military involvement in Vietnam. More than 1.2 million Vietnamese soldiers had died in combat, along with countless civilians throughout the region. A beautiful land had been ravaged, its agrarian economy left in ruins; until an economic revival began in the early 1990s, Vietnam remained for more than a decade one of the poorest nations in the world. The United States had paid a heavy price as well. The war had cost the nation almost $150 billion in direct costs and much more indirectly. It had resulted in the deaths of over 57,000 young Americans and the injury of 300,000 more. And the nation had suffered a blow to its confidence and self-esteem from which it did not soon recover.

NIXON, KISSINGER, AND THE WORLD

The continuing war in Vietnam provided an unhappy backdrop to what Nixon considered his larger mission in world affairs: the construction of a new international order. The president had become convinced that the old assumptions of a "bipolar" world—in which the United States and the Soviet Union were the only real great powers—were now obsolete. America must adapt to the new "multipolar" international structure, in which China, Japan, and Western Europe were becoming major, independent forces. Nixon had a considerable advantage over many other politicians in changing the assumptions behind American foreign policy. His long anticommunist record gave him credibility among many conservatives for his effort to transform American relations with communist China and the Soviet Union.

The China Initiative and Soviet–American Détente

For more than twenty years, ever since the fall of Chiang Kai-shek in 1949, the United States had treated China, the most populous nation on earth, as if it did not exist. Instead, America recognized the regime-in-exile on the small island of Taiwan as the legitimate government of China. Nixon and Kissinger wanted to forge a new relationship with the Chinese communists—in part to strengthen them as a counterbalance to the Soviet Union. The Chinese, for their part, were eager to end China's own isolation from the international arena.

In July 1971, Nixon sent Henry Kissinger on a secret mission to Beijing. When Kissinger returned, the president made the startling announcement that he would visit China himself within the next few months. That fall, with American approval, the United

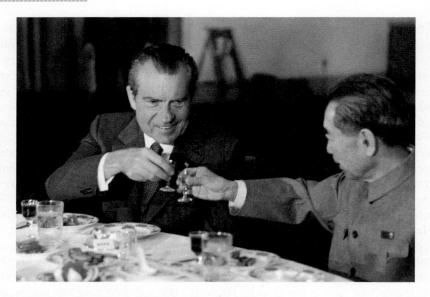

NIXON IN CHINA President Nixon's 1972 visit to China was an important step in normalizing relations between the United States and the People's Republic of China. Here, Nixon toasts the developing relationship with Prime Minister Zhou Enlai. (© Universal Images Group/Getty Images)

Nations admitted the communist government of China and expelled the representatives of the Taiwan regime. Finally, in February 1972, Nixon paid a formal visit to China. It erased much of the deep animosity between the United States and the Chinese communists. Nixon did not yet formally recognize the communist regime, but in 1972 the United States and China began low-level diplomatic relations.

The initiatives in China coincided with an effort by the Nixon administration to improve relations with the Soviet Union, an initiative known by the French word **détente.** In 1971, American and Soviet diplomats produced the first Strategic Arms Limitation Treaty (SALT I), which froze the arsenals of some nuclear missiles (ICBMs) on both sides at present levels. In May of that year, the president traveled to Moscow to sign the agreement. The next year, the Soviet premier, Leonid Brezhnev, visited Washington.

DEALING WITH THE THIRD WORLD

The policies of rapprochement with communist China and détente with the Soviet Union reflected Nixon's and Kissinger's belief in the importance of stable relationships among the great powers. But, as America's experience in Vietnam already illustrated, the so-called Third World remained the most volatile and dangerous source of international tension. Since the end of World War I, the United States and the European powers had lost or withdrawn control over former colonies. The result was a number of newly independent but economically fragile and politically unstable nations around the globe. (See "America in the World: The End of Colonialism.")

The Nixon–Kissinger policy toward the Third World tried to maintain the status quo without involving the United States too deeply in local disputes. In 1969 and 1970, the *Nixon Doctrine* president described what became known as the Nixon Doctrine, by which the United States would "participate in the defense and development of allies and friends" but would leave the "basic responsibility" for the future of those "friends" to the nations themselves. In practice, the Nixon Doctrine meant a declining American interest in contributing to Third World development. There was also a growing contempt for the United Nations, where underdeveloped nations were gaining influence through their sheer numbers. And there was increasing American support for authoritarian regimes attempting to withstand radical challenges from within.

In 1970, for example, the CIA poured substantial funds into Chile to help support the government against a communist challenge. When the Marxist candidate for president, Salvador Allende, came to power through an open election despite *Allende Overthrown* American efforts, the United States began funneling more money to opposition forces in Chile to help destabilize the new government. In 1973, a military junta seized power from Allende, who was subsequently murdered. The United States developed a friendly relationship with the new, repressive military government of General Augusto Pinochet.

In the Middle East, conditions grew more volatile in the aftermath of a 1967 war in which Israel had occupied substantial new territories, dislodging many Palestinian Arabs from their homes. The refugees were a source of considerable instability in Jordan, Lebanon, and the other surrounding countries into which they moved. In October 1973, on the Jewish high holy day of Yom Kippur, Egyptian and Syrian forces attacked Israel. For ten days, the Israelis struggled to recover from the surprise attack; finally, they launched an effective counteroffensive against Egyptian forces in the Sinai. At that point, the United States intervened, placing heavy pressure on Israel to accept a cease-fire rather than press its advantage.

The Yom Kippur War demonstrated the growing dependence of the United States and its allies on Arab oil. A brief but painful embargo in 1973–1974 by the Arab members of the Organization of the Petroleum Exporting Companies (OPEC) against *OPEC Embargo* the United States and other allies that supported Israel provided an ominous warning of the costs of dependence on foreign oil. It also prompted Congress to pass fuel economy standards, requiring automakers to raise average mileage from 13.5 miles per gallon to 27. (The standard has since been raised to 54.5 mpg by 2025.)

POLITICS AND ECONOMICS IN THE NIXON YEARS

Nixon ran for president in 1968, promising a return to more conservative social and economic policies and a restoration of law and order. Once he was in office, however, his domestic policies sometimes continued and even expanded the liberal initiatives of the previous two administrations.

Domestic Initiatives

Many of Nixon's domestic policies were a response to what he believed to be the demands of his constituency—the "silent majority" of conservative, mostly *"Silent Majority"* middle-class people who, he believed, wanted to reduce federal interference in local affairs. He tried, unsuccessfully, to persuade Congress to pass legislation prohibiting school desegregation through the use of forced busing. He forbade the Department of Health, Education, and Welfare (now called the Department of Health and Human Services) to cut off federal funds from school districts that had failed to comply with court

THE END OF COLONIALISM

On July 4, 1946, less than a year after the close of World War II, a ceremony in Manila marked what Senator Millard Tydings of Maryland called "one of the most unprecedented, most idealistic, and most far-reaching events in all recorded history." On that day, the United States voluntarily ended nearly five decades of colonial control of the Philippines, which it had acquired as part of the spoils from the 1898 Spanish-American War. Philippine independence was only a small part of a dramatic change in the political structure of the world. The close of World War II marked not only the defeat of fascism in Germany, Italy, and Japan, but also the beginning of the end of the formal system of imperialism that European powers had maintained for centuries. The repudiation of colonialism was driven in part by the heightened belief in democracy and self-determination that the war helped strengthen through much of the world. It was also driven by the weakness of the European powers after World War II and their inability to sustain control over their increasingly restive colonies. Like most great geopolitical changes, the drive for colonial independence was turbulent and often violent.

The United States had been a latecomer to the imperialist system. But even its peaceful divestiture of the Philippines reflected the challenges many imperial powers and postcolonial nations faced in renegotiating colonial relationships. America was not quite as ready to cede military presence and economic influence in the region as it was to give up political responsibility over the islands. Philippine independence came with important caveats: that the United States maintained control of Fillipino military bases and that required (through the Bell Trade Act, passed by Congress in 1946) that the Philippines not engage in any direct economic competition with the United States and that it revise its constitution to allow American interests free and unfettered access to the nation's natural resources. Many Filipinos argue that their nation did not achieve full independence until 1991, when the Philippine Senate refused to ratify a treaty that would have extended the American lease on the Subic Bay naval base (once the largest U.S. Navy installation in the Pacific). A year later, the United States closed the base and left, marking the first time in 400 years that the Philippines (once a Spanish possession) was not home to a foreign military power.

England's imperial holdings were the vastest in the world, and the existence of the British Empire was deeply embedded in England's economic life and national self-image. But it, too, withdrew from most of its colonies in the decades after World War II—beginning in 1947 with its largest and most important colony, India. The British Raj—as the colonial government was known—withdrew from South Asia in response to a growing independence movement on the subcontinent. As often happened as colonial rule ended, suppressed conflicts in the native population quickly emerged—in the case of India, between Hindus and Muslims. The price of Indian independence, therefore, was the partition of the country into India and Pakistan (and, several decades later, Bangladesh).

A year later, the British gave up its World War I mandate of Palestine (ceding the territory to the United Nations and allowing for the creation of Israel) as well as many of its holdings in Southeast Asia, including Burma and Ceylon. Malaya followed in 1957 and Singapore in 1965. In 1982, England passed the Canada Act, effectively severing Canada from the United Kingdom and culminating a move toward full Canadian self-government that had begun several decades earlier. In 1997, England returned one of its last important overseas territories, Hong Kong, to the control of China, bringing nearly to an end the era of the British Empire.

The dissolution of the British Empire did not always proceed smoothly. The Suez Crisis of 1956, in which the combined efforts of Britain, France, and Israel failed to halt Egypt's nationalization of the Suez Canal, dealt a decisive blow to England's status as a major power in the Middle East. In 1982, England's dispute over the tiny Falkland Islands erupted into war with Argentina, which claimed the islands (just off its coast) as its own. After the deaths of 258 English and 649 Argentine soldiers, England maintained its control of the Falklands, although Argentina continues to assert its right to the islands.

Despite these controversies, the dissolution of the British Empire proceeded relatively smoothly compared to the experience of the French, who became engaged in several major conflicts after 1945. In late 1946, Vietnamese nationalists rose up against the French colonial government that had recently reoccupied the region after the defeat of Japan in World War II. France's effort to return to Vietnam culminated ultimately in its defeat at Dien Bien Phu in 1954 and its subsequent withdrawal from Indochina. France also became embroiled in, and tried to suppress by force, a number of other violent colonial uprisings—in Madagascar, Cameroon, and, most notably, Algeria. The Algerian War (1954–1962) was a particularly bloody and costly conflict, taking on aspects of a civil war and involving guerrilla warfare, torture, acts of terrorism, and, eventually, the collapse of the French government in 1958. Algeria ultimately won its independence.

The end of the colonial system had its greatest impact on Africa. European powers had carved up almost all of sub-Saharan Africa in the nineteenth century. In the decades after World War II, almost all the African colonies won their independence, even if not always easily: Morocco (1956), Ghana (1957), the Congo (1960), Nigeria (1960), Uganda (1962), Kenya (1963), and Gambia (1965). African nationalism was troubled for decades by political instability and, in some countries, extreme poverty. The Caribbean also saw many new independent nations born in the postwar era, including Jamaica (1961), Trinidad and Tobago (1962), Barbados (1966), and Guyana (1966).

The most recent epicenter of independence movements has been in the lands that used to comprise the former Soviet Union. A long and costly war in Afghanistan began in the 1970s as the Soviet Union struggled to retain control of the nation in the face of powerful local insurgencies. The war was one of the principal factors in the unraveling of the Soviet Empire that began in 1991. Many of the former Soviet republics—which considered themselves colonies of Russia—soon separated from Russia and became independent nations. These included Estonia, Latvia, and Lithuania—the formerly independent Baltic nations seized by the Soviet Union during World War II. Other former Soviet possessions that became independent nations included Ukraine, Moldavia, Armenia, Georgia, Azerbaijan, Kazakhstan, Uzbekistan, Tajikistan, and Turkmenistan. Russia continues to deal with the problems of empire. A vicious conflict with Chechnya, an Islamic area of Russia insisting on independence, created terror and instability for years.

The end of colonialism was one of the most epochal global changes of the last several centuries—a change that brought to an end a system that was based on the assumption of European (and American) superiority over non-Western peoples. Despite the many problems new postcolonial nations have encountered since their independence, few, if any, such nations would choose to become colonies again. Although formal colonialism came to an end in the post–World War II era, other aspects of imperialism did not. Many former colonies, which comprise much of the nonindustrialized world, still struggle with the indirect exercise of economic power that wealthy Western nations continue to exert over them.   •

UNDERSTAND, ANALYZE, & EVALUATE

1. How did the experience of World War II contribute to the end of colonialism?
2. What have been the effects of colonialism—and the end of colonialism—on Africa? Why have the effects been so pronounced on that continent, more so than in other areas of the world?

orders to integrate. At the same time, he began to reduce or dismantle many of the social programs of the Great Society and the New Frontier. In 1973, he abolished the Office of Economic Opportunity—a centerpiece of the antipoverty program of the Johnson years.

Yet Nixon's domestic policies had progressive and creative elements as well. He signed legislation creating the Environmental Protection Agency and establishing the most stringent environmental regulations in the nation's history. He ordered the first affirmative action program for workers on federally funded projects. One of the administration's boldest efforts was an attempt to overhaul the nation's welfare system. Nixon proposed replacing the existing system with what he called the Family Assistance Plan (FAP). It would, in effect, have created a guaranteed annual income for all Americans: $1,600 in federal grants, which could be supplemented by outside earnings up to $4,000. The FAP won approval in the House in 1970, but the bill failed in the Senate. Nixon also became the first president since Truman to propose a plan for national health insurance, which likewise made no progress in Congress.

FROM THE WARREN COURT TO THE NIXON COURT

Of all the liberal institutions that aroused the enmity of the conservative silent majority in the 1950s and 1960s, none evoked more anger and bitterness than the Supreme Court

Warren Court Rulings under Chief Justice Earl Warren. The Warren Court's rulings on racial matters disrupted traditional social patterns in both the North and the South. Its defense of civil liberties directly contributed to the increase in crime, disorder, and moral decay in the eyes of many Americans. In *Engel v. Vitale* (1962), the Court ruled that prayers in public schools were unconstitutional, sparking outrage among religious fundamentalists and others. In *Roth v. United States* (1957), the Court sharply limited the authority of local governments to curb pornography. In a series of other decisions, the Court greatly strengthened the civil rights of criminal defendants and, many Americans believed, greatly weakened the power of law enforcement officials to do their jobs. For example, in *Gideon v. Wainwright* (1963), the Court ruled that every felony defendant was entitled to a lawyer, regardless of his or her ability to pay. In *Escobedo v. Illinois* (1964), it ruled that a defendant must be allowed access to a lawyer before questioning by police. In *Miranda v. Arizona* (1966), the Court confirmed the obligation of authorities to inform a criminal suspect of his or her rights. By 1968, the Warren Court had become the target of Americans who felt the United States had shifted too far toward helping poor, dispossessed, and criminal individuals at the expense of the middle class.

Nixon promised to give the Court a more conservative cast. When Chief Justice Earl Warren retired early in 1969, Nixon replaced him with a federal appeals court judge of conservative leanings, Warren Burger. At about the same time, Associate Justice Abe Fortas resigned his seat after the disclosure of a series of alleged financial improprieties. To replace him, Nixon named Clement F. Haynsworth, a respected federal circuit court judge from South Carolina. But Haynsworth came under fire from Senate liberals, black organizations, and labor unions for his conservative record on civil rights. The Senate rejected him. Nixon's next choice was G. Harrold Carswell, a Florida federal appeals court judge of little distinction. He, too, was rejected.

Nixon angrily denounced the votes. But he was careful thereafter to choose men of standing within the legal community to fill vacancies on the Supreme Court: Harry Blackmun, a moderate jurist from Minnesota; Lewis F. Powell Jr., a respected lawyer from Virginia; and William Rehnquist, a member of the Nixon Justice Department.

The new Court, however, fell far short of what the president and many conservatives had expected. Rather than retreating from its commitment to social reform, the Court in many areas actually moved further toward it. In *Swann v. Charlotte-Mecklenburg Board of Education* (1971), it ruled in favor of forced busing to achieve racial   *Burger Court Rulings* balance in schools. Despite intense and occasionally violent opposition of local communities as diverse as Boston and Louisville, Kentucky, the judicial commitment to integration was not overturned. In *Furman v. Georgia* (1972), the Court overturned existing capital punishment statutes and established strict new guidelines for such laws in the future. In *Roe v. Wade* (1973), one of the most controversial decisions in the Court's modern history, it struck down laws forbidding abortions in the first three months of pregnancy.

In other decisions, however, the Burger Court did demonstrate a more conservative temperament than the Warren Court had shown. Although the justices approved busing as a tool for achieving integration, they rejected, in *Milliken v. Bradley* (1974), a plan to transfer students across municipal lines (in this case, between Detroit and its suburbs) to achieve racial balance. While the Court upheld the principle of affirmative action in its celebrated 1978 decision, *Bakke v. Board of Regents of California,* it established restrictive new guidelines for such programs in the future. In *Stone v. Powell* (1976), the Court agreed to certain limits on the right of a defendant to appeal a state conviction to the federal judiciary.

The 1972 Landslide

Nixon entered the presidential race in 1972 with substantial strength. His energetic reelection committee had collected enormous sums of money. The president himself used the powers of incumbency to strengthen his political standing in strategic areas. And Nixon's foreign policy successes, especially his trip to China, increased his stature in the eyes of the nation.

Nixon was most fortunate in 1972, however, in his opposition. George Wallace, partly at Nixon's urging, entered the Democratic primaries and helped divide the party until a would-be assassin shot the Alabama governor during a rally at a Maryland shopping center in May. Paralyzed from the waist down, Wallace was unable to continue campaigning. In the meantime, the most liberal factions of the party succeeded in establishing their candidate, Senator George S. McGovern of South Dakota, as the   *George McGovern* front-runner for the nomination. An outspoken critic of the war and a forceful advocate of liberal positions on many social and economic issues, McGovern profited greatly from party reforms (which he himself had helped draft) that gave increased influence to women, minorities, and young people in the selection of the Democratic ticket. But in the process, the McGovern campaign came to be associated with aspects of the turbulent 1960s that many middle-class Americans were eager to reject.

On election day, Nixon won reelection by one of the largest margins in history: 60.7 percent of the popular vote to McGovern's 37.5 percent and an electoral margin of 520 to 17. The Democratic candidate carried only Massachusetts and the District of Columbia. But serious problems, some beyond the president's control and others of his own making, lurked in the wings.

The Troubled Economy

Although it was a political scandal that would ultimately destroy the Nixon presidency, the most important issue of the early 1970s was the beginning of a long-term transformation of the American economy. For three decades, that economy had been the envy of the world. In fact, however, America's prosperity rested in part on several artificial conditions that were rapidly disappearing by the late 1960s.

The most immediate change was the end of the nation's easy access to cheap raw materials, a change that became a major cause of the serious inflation that plagued the economy through much of the 1970s. For many years, OPEC had operated as an informal bargaining unit for the sale of oil by Third World nations but had seldom managed to exercise any real strength. But in the early 1970s, OPEC began to use its oil both as an economic tool and as a political weapon. In 1973, in the midst of the Yom Kippur War, Arab members of OPEC announced that they would no longer ship petroleum to nations supporting Israel—that is, to the United States and its allies in Western Europe. At about the same time, the OPEC nations agreed to raise their prices 500 percent (from $3 to $15 a barrel). These twin shocks produced momentary economic chaos in the West. The United States suffered its first fuel shortage since World War II. And although the crisis eased a few months later, the price of energy continued to rise.

Another, longer-term change in the American economy was the transformation of the nation's manufacturing sector. Ever since World War II, American industry had enjoyed relatively little competition from the rest of the world. By the end of the 1960s, however, both Western Europe and Japan had recovered from the damage their manufacturing sectors had absorbed during World War II. By the early 1970s, they were providing stiff competition to American firms in the sale of automobiles, steel, and many other products, both in world markets and within the United States. Some American corporations failed. Others restructured themselves to become more competitive again in world markets but in the process closed many older plants and eliminated hundreds of thousands of once-lucrative manufacturing jobs. The high-wage, high-employment industrial economy that had been a central fact of American life since the 1940s was gradually disappearing.

The Nixon Response

Nixon's initial answer to these mounting economic problems was a conventional anti-inflationary one. He reduced federal spending and raised taxes, producing a modest budget surplus in 1969. But when those policies proved difficult to sustain, Nixon turned increasingly to control of the currency. Placing conservative economists at the head of the Federal Reserve Board, he ensured sharply higher interest rates and a contraction of the money supply. Even so, the cost of living rose a cumulative 15 percent during Nixon's first two and a half years in office. Economic growth, in the meantime, declined.

In the summer of 1971, Nixon imposed a ninety-day freeze on all wages and prices at their existing levels. Then, in November, he launched the second phase of his economic plan: mandatory guidelines for some wage and price increases, to be administered by a federal agency. Inflation subsided temporarily, but the recession continued. Fearful that the recession would be more damaging than inflation in an election year, the administration reversed itself late in 1971: interest rates were allowed to drop sharply, and government spending increased—producing the largest budget deficit since World War II. The new tactics helped revive the economy in the short term, but inflation rose substantially. In 1973, prices rose 9 percent; in 1974, after the Arab oil embargo and the OPEC price increases, they rose 12 percent—the highest rate since shortly after World War II. The new energy crisis, in the meantime, was quickly becoming a national preoccupation. But while Nixon talked often about the need to achieve "energy independence," he offered few concrete proposals.

THE WATERGATE CRISIS

Although economic problems greatly concerned the American people in the 1970s, another stunning development preoccupied the nation beginning early in 1973: the fall of Richard Nixon. Scholars wrangle over the exact origins and legacies of Nixon's fall from grace, but they widely agree that the president's demise was in part a result of the turbulent climate of the early 1970s. It was also a result of his own reckless personality and over-powering fear that he and the nation faced grave dangers from the radicals and dissidents who were challenging his policies.

THE SCANDALS

Early on the morning of June 17, 1972, police arrested five men who had broken into the headquarters of the Democratic National Committee in the Watergate office building in Washington, D.C. Two others were seized a short time later and charged with supervising the break-in. When reporters for the *Washington Post* began researching the backgrounds of the culprits, they discovered that among those involved in the burglary were former employees of the Committee for the Re-Election of the President (CRP). One of them had worked in the White House itself. They had, moreover, been paid for the break-in from a secret fund of Nixon's reelection committee, a fund controlled by, among others, members of the White House staff.

Public interest in the disclosures grew slowly in the last months of 1972. Early in 1973, however, the Watergate burglars went on trial; and under prodding from federal judge John J. Sirica, one of the defendants, James W. McCord, agreed to cooperate both with the grand jury and with a special Senate investigating committee recently established under Senator Sam J. Ervin of North Carolina. McCord's testimony opened a floodgate of confessions, and for months a parade of White House and campaign officials exposed one illegality after another. Foremost among them was a member of the inner circle of the White House, John Dean, counsel to the president, who had warned Nixon that the Watergate cover-up was a "cancer on the presidency" and who later leveled allegations against Nixon himself.

Two different sets of scandals emerged from the investigations. One was a general pattern of abuses of power involving both the White House and the Nixon campaign committee, which included, but was not limited to, the Watergate break-in. The other scandal,   *Watergate* and the one that became the major focus of public attention for nearly two years, was the way in which the administration tried to manage the investigations of the Watergate break-in and other abuses—a pattern of behavior that became known as the "cover-up." There was never any conclusive evidence that the president had planned or approved the burglary in advance. But there was mounting evidence that he had been involved in illegal efforts to obstruct investigations of the episode. (See "Debating the Past: Watergate.")

Nixon accepted the departure of members of his administration implicated in the scandals. But the president continued to insist on his own innocence. There the matter might have rested had it not been for the disclosure during the Senate hearings of a White House taping system that had recorded virtually every conversation in the president's office during the period in question. All those investigating the scandals sought access   *Watergate Tapes* to the tapes. Nixon, pleading "executive privilege," refused to release them. A special prosecutor appointed by the president to handle the Watergate cases, Harvard law professor Archibald Cox, took Nixon to court in October 1973 in an effort to force him to relinquish the recordings. Nixon fired Cox and suffered the humiliation of watching both Attorney

WATERGATE

Forty-two years after Watergate—one of the most famous political scandals in American history—historians and others continue to argue about its causes and significance. Their interpretations tend to fall into several broad categories.

One argument emphasizes the evolution of the institution of the presidency over time and sees Watergate as the result of a much larger pattern of presidential usurpations of power that stretched back at least several decades. Arthur M. Schlesinger Jr. helped develop this argument in his 1973 book *The Imperial Presidency,* which argues that ever since World War II, Americans have believed that the nation was in a state of permanent crisis—threatened from abroad by the menace of communism, threatened from within by the danger of insufficient will. A succession of presidents believed in the urgency of this crisis, and in their duty to take whatever measures might be necessary to combat it. That led them gradually to usurp more and more power from Congress, from the courts, and from the public. Initially, this expansion of presidential power came in the realm of international affairs. It included covert and at times illegal activities overseas. Gradually, presidents began to look for ways to circumvent constraints in domestic matters as well. Nixon's actions in the Watergate crisis were, in other words, a culmination of this long and steady expansion of covert presidential power. Jonathan Schell, in *The Time of Illusion* (1975), offers a variation of this argument, tying the crisis of the presidency to the pressure that nuclear weapons place on presidents to protect the nation's—and their own—"credibility."

Another explanation of Watergate emphasizes the difficult social and political environment of the late 1960s and early 1970s. Nixon entered office, according to this view, facing an unprecedentedly radical opposition that would stop at nothing to discredit the war and destroy his authority. He found himself, therefore, drawn into taking similarly desperate measures of his own to defend himself. Nixon made this argument in his own 1978 memoirs:

> Now that this season of mindless terror has fortunately passed, it is difficult—perhaps impossible—to convey a sense of the pressures that were influencing my actions and reactions during this period, but it was this epidemic of unprecedented domestic terrorism that prompted our efforts to discover the best means by which to deal with this new phenomenon of highly organized and highly skilled revolutionaries dedicated to the violent destruction of our democratic system.*

The historian Herbert Parmet echoes parts of this argument in *Richard Nixon and His America* (1990). Stephen Ambrose offers a more muted version of the same view in *Richard Nixon* (1989).

Most of those who have written about Watergate, however, search for the explanation not in institutional or social forces but in the personalities of the people involved and, most notably, in the personality of Richard Nixon. Even many of those who have developed structural explanations (Schlesinger, Schell, and Ambrose, for example) return eventually to Nixon himself as the most important explanation for Watergate. Others begin there, perhaps most notably Stanley I. Kutler, in *The Wars of Watergate* (1990) and, later, *Abuse of Power* (1997), in which he presents extensive excerpts from conversations about Watergate taped in the Nixon White House. Kutler emphasizes Nixon's lifelong resort to vicious political tactics and his long-standing belief that he was a special target of unscrupulous enemies and had to "get" them before they got him. Watergate was rooted, Kutler argues, "in the personality and history of Nixon himself." A "corrosive hatred," he claims, "decisively shaped Nixon's own behavior, his career, and eventually his historical standing." •

UNDERSTAND, ANALYZE, & EVALUATE

1. For scholars who cite social and institutional forces as explanations for Watergate, what are these forces? How did they contribute to the Watergate scandal?
2. Most scholars see Nixon himself as the party most responsible for Watergate. How did Nixon's personality contribute to both his rise to power as president and his downfall as a result of Watergate?
3. What have been the lasting effects of Watergate on the public's perception of the presidency and the government?

General Elliot Richardson and his deputy resign in protest. This "Saturday night massacre," as it was called, made the president's predicament much worse. Not only did public pressure force him to appoint a new special prosecutor, Texas attorney Leon Jaworski, who proved just as determined as Cox to subpoena the tapes; but the episode precipitated an investigation by the House of Representatives into the possibility of impeachment.

THE FALL OF RICHARD NIXON

Nixon's situation deteriorated further in the following months. Late in 1973, Vice President Spiro Agnew became embroiled in a scandal of his own when evidence surfaced that he had accepted bribes and kickbacks while serving as governor of Maryland and even as vice president. In return for a Justice Department agreement not to press the case, Agnew pleaded no contest to a lesser charge of income-tax evasion and resigned *Ford Replaces Agnew* from the government. With the controversial Agnew no longer in line to succeed to the presidency, the prospect of removing Nixon from the White House became less worrisome to his opponents. The new vice president was House Minority Leader Gerald Ford, an amiable and popular Michigan congressman.

The impeachment investigation quickly gathered momentum. In April 1974, in an effort to head off further subpoenas of the tapes, the president released transcripts of a number of relevant conversations, claiming that they proved his innocence. Investigators and much of the public felt otherwise. Even these edited tapes seemed to suggest Nixon's complicity in the cover-up. In July, the crisis reached a climax. First the Supreme Court ruled unanimously, in *United States v. Richard M. Nixon,* that the president must relinquish the tapes to Special Prosecutor Jaworski. Days later, the House Judiciary Committee voted to recommend three articles of impeachment.

Even without additional evidence, Nixon might well have been impeached by the full House and convicted by the Senate. Early in August, however, he provided at last the "smoking gun"—the concrete proof of his guilt—that his defenders had long contended was missing from the case against him. Among the tapes that the Supreme Court compelled

NIXON'S FAREWELL Only moments before, Nixon had been in tears, saying good-bye to his staff in the East Room of the White House. But as he boarded a helicopter to begin his trip home to California shortly after resigning as president, he flashed his trademark "victory" sign to the crowd on the White House lawn. (© Bettmann/Corbis)

Nixon to relinquish were several that offered apparently incontrovertible evidence of his involvement in the Watergate cover-up. Only three days after the burglary, the recordings disclosed, the president had ordered the FBI to stop investigating the break-in. Impeachment and conviction now seemed inevitable.

Resignation   For several days, Nixon cloistered himself in the White House. Finally, on August 8, 1974, he announced his resignation—the first president in American history ever to do so. At noon the next day, while Nixon and his family flew west to their home in California, Gerald Ford took the oath of office as president.

Many Americans expressed relief and exhilaration that, as the new president put it, "our long national nightmare is over." But the wave of good feeling could not obscure the deeper and more lasting damage of the Watergate crisis. In a society in which distrust of leaders and institutions of authority was already widespread, the fall of Richard Nixon confirmed for many Americans their most cynical assumptions about the untrustworthy character of American public life.

CONCLUSION

The victory of Richard Nixon in the 1968 presidential election represented a popular repudiation of turbulence and radicalism. It was a call for a restoration of order and stability. But order and stability were not the dominant characteristics of Nixon's troubled years in office. Nixon entered office when the political left and the counterculture were approaching the peak of their influence. American culture and society in the late 1960s and early 1970s were shaped decisively by, and were deeply divided over, the challenges by young people to the prevailing social norms. These were also the years in which a host of new liberation movements joined the drive for racial equality and when, above all, women mobilized effectively to demand changes in the way society treated gender differences.

Nixon had run for office attacking the failure of his predecessor to end the war in Vietnam. But for four years under his presidency, the war—and the protests against it—continued and even in some respects escalated. The division of opinion over the war was as deep as any of the other divisions in national life. It continued to poison the nation's politics and social fabric until the American role in the conflict finally shuddered to a close in 1973.

But much of the controversy and division in the 1970s was a product of the Nixon presidency itself. Nixon was in many ways a dynamic and even visionary leader, who proposed some important domestic reforms and who made important changes in American foreign policy, most notably making overtures to communist China and forging détente with the Soviet Union. He was also, however, a devious, secretive man whose White House became engaged in a series of covert activities that produced the most dramatic political scandal in American history. Watergate, as it was called, preoccupied much of the nation for nearly two years beginning in 1972; and ultimately, in the summer of 1974, the scandal forced Richard Nixon—who had been reelected to office only two years before by one of the largest majorities in modern history—to become the first president in American history to resign. Nixon was elected to lead the nation out of a war it no longer wanted, but his shameful exit from office and the ongoing Vietnam War continued to damage the nation's self-confidence and trust in government.

KEY TERMS/PEOPLE/PLACES/EVENTS

American Indian Movement (AIM) 741

Betty Friedan 745

César Chávez 743

counterculture 739

détente 754

Earth Day 749

Free Speech Movement 738

Gerald Ford 763

Henry Kissinger 750

Indian Civil Rights Act 741

National Organization for Women (NOW) 746

New Left 737

Nixon Doctrine 754

Organization of the Petroleum Exporting Countries (OPEC) 755

Rachel Carson 748

Roe v. Wade 747

silent majority 755

Stonewall Riot 744

Students for a Democratic Society (SDS) 737

Vietnamization 750

Watergate 761

Woodstock 740

RECALL AND REFLECT

1. What was the New Left? How was it related to the counterculture?
2. How did ethnic minorities, especially Native Americans and Latinos, challenge the status quo in the 1970s?
3. What were the objectives of the new feminism of the 1970s? What gains did women achieve in this era? What setbacks did the feminist movement experience?
4. What was the "Nixon Doctrine"? How did this doctrine play out in foreign policy?
5. What was the effect of Nixon's policies on the U.S. economy? What was Nixon's response to escalating economic difficulties?

31

FROM "THE AGE OF LIMITS" TO THE AGE OF REAGAN

POLITICS AND DIPLOMACY AFTER WATERGATE

THE RISE OF THE NEW CONSERVATIVE MOVEMENT

THE "REAGAN REVOLUTION"

AMERICA AND THE WANING OF THE COLD WAR

LOOKING AHEAD

1. What economic and energy problems plagued the presidencies of Gerald Ford and Jimmy Carter? How did Ford and Carter attempt to deal with these problems?
2. What was the "New Right," and what effect did its rise have on American politics?
3. What was Reaganomics, and how did this policy affect the national economy?

THE FRUSTRATIONS OF THE EARLY 1970s—the defeat in Vietnam, the Watergate crisis, the decay of the American economy—inflicted damaging blows to the confident, optimistic nationalism that had characterized so much of the postwar era. Some Americans responded to these problems by announcing the arrival of an "age of limits," in which Americans would have to learn to live with less. By the end of the decade, however, another response was gaining strength—one that combined a steady retreat from some of the heady liberal visions of the 1960s with a reinforced commitment to traditional ideas of economic growth, international power, and American virtue.

POLITICS AND DIPLOMACY AFTER WATERGATE

In the aftermath of Richard Nixon's ignominious departure from office, many Americans wondered whether faith in the presidency, and in the government as a whole, could ever be restored. The administrations of the two presidents who succeeded Nixon did little to answer those questions.

The Ford Custodianship

Gerald Ford inherited the presidency under difficult circumstances. He had to try to rebuild confidence in government in the wake of the Watergate scandals and to restore prosperity in the face of major economic difficulties.

The new president's effort to establish himself as a symbol of political integrity suffered a setback only a month after he took office, when he granted Richard Nixon "a full, free, and absolute pardon" for any crimes he may have committed during his presidency. The pardon angered a public eager to see Nixon face criminal charges and caused a decline in Ford's popularity from which he never fully recovered. Nevertheless, most Americans considered Ford a decent man; his honesty and amiability did much to reduce the bitterness and acrimony of the Watergate years.

The Ford administration enjoyed far less success in its effort to solve the problems of the economy. To curb inflation, the president called for largely ineffective voluntary efforts. After supporting high interest rates, opposing increased federal spending (through liberal use of his veto power), and resisting pressures for a tax reduction, Ford had to deal with a confounding economic mix of rising unemployment, high inflation, and slowing economic growth in 1974 and 1975 known as "stagflation." While it occurred only during this two-year period, it was synonymous with most of the economic troubles of the seventies.

TIME LINE

1974
"Stagflation"

1976
Carter elected president

Ford pardons Nixon

1977
Panama Canal treaties signed

1978–1979
Camp David accords

Apple introduces first personal computer

American hostages in Iran

Soviet Union invades Afghanistan

U.S. and China restore relations

1980
U.S. boycotts Moscow Olympics

Three Mile Island nuclear accident

Reagan elected president

1981
American hostages in Iran released

Reagan wins tax and budget cuts

1982
Severe recession

AIDS first reported in U.S.

1983
U.S. invades Grenada

1984
Reagan reelected

1985
Reagan and Gorbachev meet

1986
Iran-contra scandal revealed

1988
George H. W. Bush elected president

1989
Berlin Wall dismantled

Communist regimes collapse

U.S. troops in Panama

1990
Iraq invades Kuwait

1991
Collapse of Soviet regime

1992
Los Angeles race riots

Persian Gulf War

Clinton elected president

Economic Problems Central to the economic problems was the continuing energy crisis. In the aftermath of the Arab oil embargo of 1973, the OPEC cartel raised the price of oil—by 400 percent in 1974 alone—one of the principal reasons why inflation reached 11 percent in 1976.

Ford retained Henry Kissinger as secretary of state and generally continued the foreign policies of the Nixon years. Late in 1974, Ford met with Leonid Brezhnev at Vladivostok in Siberia and signed an arms control accord. Meanwhile, in the Middle East, Henry Kissinger helped produce a new accord by which Israel agreed to return large portions of the occupied Sinai to Egypt. The two nations pledged not to resolve future differences by force.

As the 1976 presidential election approached, Ford's policies were coming under increasing *1976 Election* attack from both the right and the left. In the Republican primary campaign, Ford faced a powerful challenge from former California governor Ronald Reagan, leader of the party's conservative wing, who spoke for many Americans on the right who opposed any agreements with communists. The president barely survived the assault to win his party's nomination. The Democrats, in the meantime, were gradually uniting behind a new and until recently almost entirely unknown candidate: Jimmy Carter, a former governor of Georgia who appealed to the general unhappiness with Washington by offering honesty, piety, and an outsider's skepticism of the federal government. Unhappiness with the economy and a general

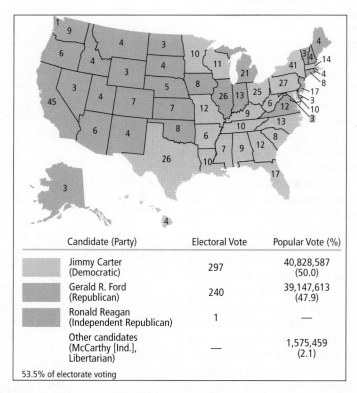

Candidate (Party)	Electoral Vote	Popular Vote (%)
Jimmy Carter (Democratic)	297	40,828,587 (50.0)
Gerald R. Ford (Republican)	240	39,147,613 (47.9)
Ronald Reagan (Independent Republican)	1	—
Other candidates (McCarthy [Ind.], Libertarian)	—	1,575,459 (2.1)

53.5% of electorate voting

THE ELECTION OF 1976 Jimmy Carter, a former governor of Georgia, swept the South in the 1976 election and carried enough of the industrial states of the Northeast and Midwest to win a narrow victory over President Gerald R. Ford. His showing indicated the importance to the Democratic Party of having a candidate capable of attracting support in the South, which was becoming increasingly Republican by the 1970s. • *What drove so many southerners into the Republican Party?*

disenchantment with Ford enabled the Democrat to win a narrow victory. Carter received 50 percent of the popular vote to Ford's 47.9 percent and 297 electoral votes to Ford's 240.

THE TRIALS OF JIMMY CARTER

Like Ford, Jimmy Carter assumed the presidency at a moment when the nation faced problems of staggering complexity and difficulty. But Carter seemed at times to make his predicament worse by a style of leadership that many Americans considered self-righteous and inflexible.

Carter devoted much of his time to the problems of energy and the economy. Entering office in the midst of a recession, he moved first to reduce unemployment by raising public spending and cutting federal taxes. Unemployment declined, but inflation soared—mostly because of the continuing, sharp increases in energy prices by OPEC. During Carter's last two years in office, retail prices rose at over a 10 percent annual rate. Like Nixon and Ford before him, Carter responded with a combination of tight money and calls for voluntary restraint. Determined to stop inflation, he appointed conservative economists to head the Federal Reserve Board, which helped push interest rates to the highest levels in American history; at times, they exceeded 20 percent.

In the summer of 1979, instability in the Middle East produced a second major fuel shortage in the United States. In the midst of the crisis, OPEC announced another major price increase. Faced with increasing pressure to act, Carter went to Camp David, the presidential retreat in the Maryland mountains. Ten days later, he emerged to deliver a remarkable television address. It included a series of proposals for resolving the energy crisis. But it was most notable for Carter's bleak assessment of the national condition and his claim that there was a "crisis of confidence" that had struck "at the very heart and soul of our national will." The address became known as the "malaise" speech (although Carter himself had never used that word), and it helped fuel charges that the president was trying to blame his own problems on the American people. Carter's sudden firing of several members of his cabinet a few days later deepened his political dilemma.

HUMAN RIGHTS AND NATIONAL INTERESTS

Among Jimmy Carter's most frequent campaign promises was a new American foreign policy based on the defense of "human rights." Carter spoke out sharply about human rights violations in many countries (including, most prominently, the Soviet Union). But the administration also focused on more traditional concerns. Carter completed negotiations begun several years earlier on a pair of treaties to turn over control of the Panama Canal to the government of Panama. After an acrimonious debate, the Senate   *Panama Canal Treaties* ratified the treaties by 68 to 32, only one vote more than the necessary two-thirds majority.

Carter's greatest success was in arranging a peace treaty between Egypt and Israel. Middle East negotiations had seemed hopelessly stalled until Egyptian president Anwar Sadat accepted an invitation in November 1977 from Prime Minister Menachem Begin to visit Israel. In Tel Aviv, he announced that Egypt was now willing to accept the state of Israel as a legitimate political entity.

When talks between Israeli and Egyptian negotiators stalled, Carter invited Sadat and Begin to a summit conference at Camp David in September 1978 and persuaded them to remain there for two weeks. On September 17, Carter escorted the two leaders into the White House to announce an agreement on a "framework" for an Egyptian–Israeli peace treaty. On March 26, 1979, Begin and Sadat returned together to the White House   *Camp David Accords* to sign a formal peace treaty between their two nations, known as the Camp David accords.

SIGNING THE CAMP DAVID ACCORDS Jimmy Carter experienced many frustrations during his presidency, but his successful efforts in 1978 to negotiate a peace treaty between Israel and Egypt were undoubtedly his finest hour. Egyptian President Anwar Sadat and Israeli Prime Minister Menachem Begin join Carter here in the East Room of the White House in March 1979 to sign the accords. (© D.B. Owen/Black Star)

In the meantime, Carter continued trying to improve relations with China and the Soviet Union. He responded eagerly to the overtures of Deng Xiaoping, the new Chinese leader attempting to open his nation to the outside world. On December 15, 1978, Washington and Beijing announced the resumption of formal diplomatic relations. A few months later, Carter traveled to Vienna to meet with the aging and ailing Brezhnev to finish drafting the new Strategic Arms Limitations Treaty II (SALT II) arms control agreement, which set limits on the number of long-range missiles, bombers, and nuclear warheads on each side. Almost immediately, however, SALT II met with fierce conservative opposition in the United States Senate. The agreement was never ratified.

THE YEAR OF THE HOSTAGES

Since the early 1950s, the United States had provided political support and, more recently, massive military assistance to the government of the shah of Iran, hoping to make his nation a bulwark against Soviet expansion in the Middle East. By 1979, however, the shah was in deep trouble with his own people. Many Iranians resented the repressive, authoritarian tactics through which the shah had maintained his autocratic rule. At the same time, Islamic clergy (and much of the fiercely religious populace) opposed his efforts to modernize and Westernize Iranian society. The combination of resentments fueled a powerful revolutionary movement, which forced the shah to flee the country in January 1979.

By late 1979, power in Iran resided with a zealous religious leader, the Ayatollah *Ayatollah Ruhollah Khomeini* Ruhollah Khomeini, who was fiercely anti-Western and anti-American. In late October 1979, the deposed shah arrived in New York to be treated for cancer. Days later, on November 4, an armed crowd stormed the American embassy in

Tehran, seized the diplomats and military personnel inside, and demanded the return of the shah to Iran in exchange for their freedom. Fifty-three Americans remained hostages in the embassy for over a year.

Only weeks after the hostage seizure, on December 27, 1979, Soviet troops invaded Afghanistan, the mountainous Islamic nation lying between the USSR and Iran. The Soviet Union had been a power in Afghanistan for years and the dominant force since April 1978; a rebellion by radical Islamic guerrilla groups threatened the new *Soviet Invasion of Afghanistan* Soviet-backed government. But while some observers claimed that the Soviet invasion was a Russian attempt to secure the status quo, Carter claimed it was a Russian "stepping stone to their possible control over much of the world's oil supplies" and the "gravest threat to world peace since World War II." Carter angrily imposed a series of economic sanctions on the Russians, canceled American participation in the 1980 summer Olympic Games in Moscow, and announced the withdrawal of SALT II from Senate consideration.

THE RISE OF THE NEW CONSERVATIVE MOVEMENT

The jarring social and economic changes in American life in the 1960s and 1970s disillusioned many liberals, caught the left off-guard and without effective responses, and provided the right with its most important opportunity in generations to recapture a dominant position of political authority in American life.

THE SUNBELT AND ITS POLITICS

One of the most widely discussed demographic phenomena of the 1970s was the rise of what became known as the **Sunbelt**—the states of the Southeast and the Southwest. By 1980, the population of the Sunbelt had risen to exceed that of the older industrial regions of the North and the East. It directly contributed to the explosive growth of the modern conservative movement.

The strong populist traditions in the South and the West helped produce opposition to the growth of government and resentment of the proliferating regulations and restrictions of the liberal state. Many of those regulations and restrictions—environmental laws, land-use restrictions, and other laws—affected the West more than any other region.

The so-called Sagebrush Rebellion, which emerged in parts of the West in the late 1970s, mobilized conservative opposition to burgeoning environmental *Sagebrush Rebellion* laws and restrictions on development. It also sought to portray the West as a victim of government control. Its members demanded that the very large amounts of land the federal government owned in western states be opened for development.

Suburbanization also fueled the rise of the right. Not all suburbs bred conservative politics, of course; but the most militantly conservative communities in America—among them Orange County in Southern California—were mostly suburbs. The seemingly tranquil life of the suburb contributed to a conservative view of the world.

RELIGIOUS REVIVALISM

In the 1960s, traditional mainstream religion experienced a conspicuous decline. But in its place began a powerful religious revival. Some of the new religious enthusiasm found expression in the rise of various popular movements and unorthodox faiths: the Church

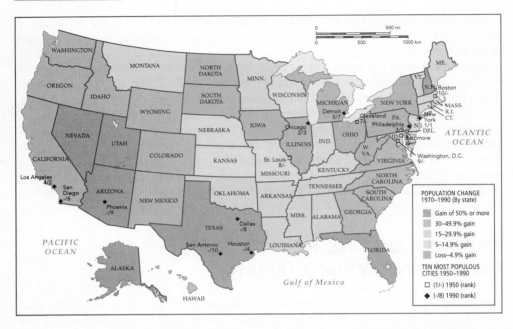

GROWTH OF THE SUNBELT, 1970–1990 One of the most important demographic changes of the last decades of the twentieth century was the shift of population out of traditional population centers in the Northeast and Midwest and toward the states of the so-called Sunbelt—most notably the Southwest and the Pacific Coast. This map gives a dramatic illustration of the changing concentration of population between 1970 and 1990. The orange states are those that lost population, while the purple and blue states are those that made significant gains (30 percent or more). • *What was the impact of this population shift on the politics of the 1980s?*

of Scientology; the Unification Church of the Reverend Sun Myung Moon; even the tragic People's Temple, whose members committed mass suicide in their jungle retreat in Guyana in 1978. But the most important impulse of the religious revival was the growth of evangelical Christianity.

Evangelicals have in common a belief in personal conversion (being "born again" *Surging Evangelicalism* through direct communication with Jesus). Evangelical religion had been the dominant form of Christianity in America through much of its history. In its modern form, it became increasingly visible during the early 1950s, when evangelicals such as Billy Graham and Pentecostals such as Oral Roberts began to attract huge national (and international) followings for their energetic revivalism.

By the late 1970s, evangelical Christians had become more visible and more politically assertive. More than 70 million Americans now described themselves as born-again Christians. Christian evangelicals owned newspapers, magazines, radio stations, and television networks. They operated their own schools and universities. Three modern presidents—Jimmy Carter, Bill Clinton, and George W. Bush—have identified themselves as evangelicals.

Some evangelical Christians supported racial and economic justice and world peace of the type espoused by civil rights leaders like Rev. Martin Luther King. But many others had a different political focus. Alarmed by what they considered the spread of immorality and disorder in American life, they were concerned about the way a secular culture was intruding into their communities, schools, and families. Many evangelical men and women, for example, feared that the growth of feminism posed a threat to the traditional family, and they resented the way in which government policies advanced the goals of the women's movement. Particularly alarming to them were Supreme Court decisions eliminating all religious observance from schools and, later, the decision guaranteeing women the right to an abortion.

By the late 1970s, the "Christian right" had become a powerful political force. Jerry Falwell, a fundamentalist minister in Virginia with a substantial television audience, launched a highly visible movement he called the Moral Majority. He founded Liberty University in Lynchburg, Virginia, to train men and women according to conservative Christian principles. The Pentecostal minister Pat Robertson began a political movement of his own and, in the 1990s, launched an organization known as the *Christian Coalition* Christian Coalition. These and other organizations of the Christian right opposed federal interference in local affairs; denounced abortion, divorce, feminism, and homosexuality; defended unrestricted free enterprise; and supported a strong American posture in the world. Some denied the scientific doctrine of evolution and instead urged the teaching in schools of the biblical story of the Creation or—beginning in the early twenty-first century—the idea of "intelligent design." Their goal was a new era in which "Christian values" once again dominated American life.

The role of religion in the growth of conservatism was not limited to evangelical Christians. In the 1970s, the Catholic Church began to make a strong case for tradition as well. The Church fought most aggressively against abortion, thus joining the evangelical right in one of the most controversial issues of the time. Not all Catholics were or are conservatives; many priests and parishioners took strong liberal positions. But in the political world, Catholics became strong allies of the right, joining evangelicals in fighting for many conservative issues.

Mormons, too, began to emerge as an important element of the right. For many years, Mormons did not publicize their conservatism. But like Catholics, many Mormons began to take openly conservative stances in the 1970s on some of the controversial battles of the time. Some of these Mormons, wealthy and successful businesspeople, became conservative political politicians in various parts of the country. (In 2012, two wealthy Mormons—Mitt Romney and Jon Huntsman, both former governors—were candidates for the presidency.)

THE EMERGENCE OF THE NEW RIGHT

Religious issues were only a part—although an important part—of what became known as the New Right—a diverse but powerful movement that enjoyed rapid growth in the 1970s and early 1980s. It had begun to take shape after the 1964 election, in which Barry Goldwater had suffered his shattering defeat. Energetic organizers responded to that disaster by building a new and powerful set of right-wing institutions to help conservatives campaign more effectively in the future. Beginning in the 1970s, largely because of these organizational advances, conservatives found themselves almost always better funded and organized than their opponents. By the late 1970s, there were right-wing think tanks, consulting firms, lobbyists, foundations, and colleges and universities. Conservatives also succeeded in building mechanisms to raise money, mobilize activists, and project their ideas to a broad audience. Building from a list compiled by Richard Viguerie after the 1964 Goldwater campaign, the right built a direct-mail operation that ultimately reached millions of conservative voters. Evangelicals such as Pat Robertson used cable television to reach the conservative faithful. Conservative radio hosts such as Rush Limbaugh created shows that attracted a vast national audience.

Another factor in the revival of the right was the emergence in the late 1960s and early *Ronald Reagan* 1970s of Ronald Reagan. Once a moderately successful actor, he had moved into politics in the early 1960s and in 1964 delivered a memorable television speech on behalf of Goldwater. After Goldwater's defeat, Reagan worked quickly to seize the leadership of the conservative wing of the party. In 1966, with the support of a group of wealthy conservatives, he won the first of two terms as governor of California.

The presidency of Gerald Ford also played an important role in the rise of conservatism. Ford, probably without realizing it, touched on some of the right's rawest nerves. He appointed as vice president Nelson Rockefeller, the liberal Republican governor of New York and an heir to one of America's great fortunes; many conservatives had been demonizing Rockefeller and his family for more than twenty years. Ford proposed an amnesty program for draft resisters, embraced the hated Nixon–Kissinger policies of détente, presided over the fall of Vietnam, and agreed to cede the Panama Canal to Panama. When Reagan challenged Ford in the 1976 Republican primaries, the president survived, barely, only by dumping Nelson Rockefeller from the ticket and replacing him with Kansas Senator Robert Dole, a steadfast conservative. He also agreed to a platform largely written by conservatives.

The Tax Revolt

At least equally important to the success of the New Right was a new and potent conservative issue: the tax revolt. It had its public beginnings in 1978, when Howard Jarvis, a conservative activist in California, launched the first successful major citizens' tax revolt with Proposition 13, *Proposition 13* a referendum question on the state ballot rolling back property tax rates. Because property taxes were the most important source of funding for schools, Proposition 13 began the slow deterioration of much of the great California education system. Similar antitax movements soon began in other states and eventually spread to national politics.

In Proposition 13 and similar initiatives, members of the right succeeded in separating the issue of taxes from the issue of what taxes supported. Instead of attacking popular programs such as Social Security, they attacked taxes themselves and argued that much of the money government raised through taxes was wasted. Virtually no one liked to pay taxes, and as the economy grew weaker and the relative burden of paying taxes grew heavier, that resentment naturally rose.

The Campaign of 1980

By the time of the crises in Iran and Afghanistan, Jimmy Carter was in desperate political trouble—his standing in popularity polls lower than that of any president in history. Senator Edward Kennedy, younger brother of John and Robert Kennedy, challenged him in the primaries. And while Carter managed to withstand the confrontation and win his party's nomination, his campaign aroused little popular enthusiasm. The stage was set for sweeping political change.

The Republican Party, in the meantime, rallied enthusiastically behind the man who, four years earlier, had nearly stolen the nomination from Gerald Ford. Ronald Reagan was a sharp critic of the excesses of the federal government. He linked his campaign to the spreading tax revolt by promising substantial tax cuts. He also championed a restoration of American "strength" and "pride" in the world.

On election day 1980, the anniversary of the seizure of the hostages in Iran, Reagan swept to victory, winning 51 percent of the vote to 41 percent for Jimmy Carter and

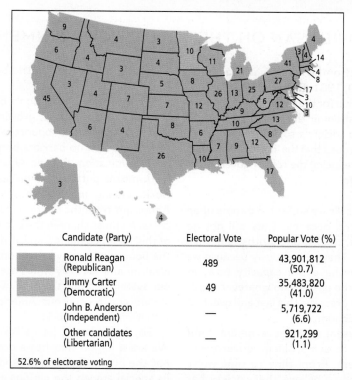

Candidate (Party)	Electoral Vote	Popular Vote (%)
Ronald Reagan (Republican)	489	43,901,812 (50.7)
Jimmy Carter (Democratic)	49	35,483,820 (41.0)
John B. Anderson (Independent)	—	5,719,722 (6.6)
Other candidates (Libertarian)	—	921,299 (1.1)

52.6% of electorate voting

THE ELECTION OF 1980 Although Ronald Reagan won only slightly more than half of the popular vote in the 1980 presidential election, his electoral majority was overwhelming—a reflection to a large degree of the deep unpopularity of President Jimmy Carter in 1980. • *What had made Carter so unpopular?*

7 percent for John Anderson—a moderate Republican congressman from Illinois who had mounted an independent campaign. The Republican Party won control of the Senate for the first time since 1952; and although the Democrats retained a modest majority in the House, the lower chamber, too, seemed firmly in the hands of conservatives.

On the day of Reagan's inauguration, the American hostages in Iran were released after their 444-day ordeal. The government of Iran, desperate for funds to support its floundering war against neighboring Iraq, had ordered the hostages freed in return for a release of billions in Iranian assets that the Carter administration had frozen in American banks. Americans welcomed the hostages home with demonstrations of joy and patriotism seldom seen since the end of World War II. But while the celebration in 1945 had marked a great American triumph, the euphoria in 1981 marked something quite different—a troubled nation grasping for reassurance. Ronald Reagan set out to provide it.

THE "REAGAN REVOLUTION"

Ronald Reagan assumed the presidency in January 1981, promising a revolution in government more fundamental than any since the New Deal of fifty years before. (See "Consider the Source: Excerpts from Reagan's First Inaugural Address.") While his eight years in office produced a significant shift in public policy, they brought nothing so

CONSIDER THE SOURCE

RONALD REAGAN ON THE ROLE OF GOVERNMENT

In this excerpt from his first inaugural address, on January 20, 1981, Ronald Reagan laid out his central vision for the role of government in society. Questioning the ability of government to solve society's social and economic ills, Reagan argued that the key to the nation's future lay in reducing the role of government in everyday life.

The economic ills we suffer have come upon us over several decades. They will not go away in days, weeks, or months, but they will go away. They will go away because we as Americans have the capacity now, as we've had in the past, to do whatever needs to be done to preserve this last and greatest bastion of freedom.

In this present crisis, government is not the solution to our problem; government is the problem. From time to time we've been tempted to believe that society has become too complex to be managed by self-rule, that government by an elite group is superior to government for, by, and of the people. Well, if no one among us is capable of governing himself, then who among us has the capacity to govern someone else? All of us together, in and out of government, must bear the burden. The solutions we seek must be equitable, with no one group singled out to pay a higher price.

We hear much of special interest groups. Well, our concern must be for a special interest group that has been too long neglected. It knows no sectional boundaries or ethnic and racial divisions, and it crosses political party lines. It is made up of men and women who raise our food, patrol our streets, man our mines and factories, teach our children, keep our homes, and heal us when we're sick—professionals, industrialists, shopkeepers, clerks, cabbies, and truck drivers.

They are, in short, "We the people," this breed called Americans.

Well, this administration's objective will be a healthy, vigorous, growing economy that provides equal opportunities for all Americans with no barriers born of bigotry or discrimination. Putting America back to work means putting all Americans back to work. Ending inflation means freeing all Americans from the terror of runaway living costs. All must share in the productive work of this "new beginning," and all must share in the bounty of a revived economy. With the idealism and fair play which are the core of our system and our strength, we can have a strong and prosperous America, at peace with itself and the world.

So, as we begin, let us take inventory. We are a nation that has a government—not the other way around. And this makes us special among the nations of the Earth. Our government has no power except that granted it by the people. It is time to check and reverse the growth of government, which shows signs of having grown beyond the consent of the governed.

It is my intention to curb the size and influence of the Federal establishment and to demand recognition of the distinction between the powers granted to the Federal Government and those reserved to the States or to the people. All of us need to be reminded that the Federal Government did not create the States; the States created the Federal Government.

Now, so there will be no misunderstanding, it's not my intention to do away with government. It is rather to make it work—work with us, not over us; to stand by our side, not ride on our back. Government can and must provide opportunity, not smother it; foster productivity, not stifle it.

If we look to the answer as to why for so many years we achieved so much, prospered as no other people on Earth, it was because here in this land we unleashed the energy and individual genius of man to a greater extent than has ever been done before. Freedom and the dignity of the individual have been more available and assured here than in any other place on Earth. The price for this freedom at times has been high, but we have never been unwilling to pay that price.

It is no coincidence that our present troubles parallel and are proportionate to the intervention and intrusion in our lives that result from unnecessary and excessive growth of government. It is time for us to realize that we're too great a nation to limit ourselves to small dreams. We're not, as some would have us believe, doomed to an inevitable decline. I do not believe in a fate that will fall on us no matter what we do. I do believe in a fate

that will fall on us if we do nothing. So, with all the creative energy at our command, let us begin an era of national renewal. Let us renew our determination, our courage, and our strength. And let us renew our faith and our hope.

UNDERSTAND, ANALYZE, & EVALUATE

1. What does Reagan mean when he says, in the opening lines of the second paragraph, that "government is the problem"?
2. Why did Reagan's call for a curb on the government's role in society and the economy strike such a popular chord in the 1980s?
3. According to Reagan, who has been treated unfairly under the previous administration? Whom are the disadvantaged?

Source: The Ronald Reagan Presidential Library, National Archives and Records Administration, www.reagan.utexas.edu/archives/speeches/1981/12081a.htm.

fundamental as many of his supporters had hoped or his opponents had feared. But Reagan succeeded brilliantly in making his own engaging personality the central fact of American politics in the 1980s. He also benefited from the power of the diverse coalition that had united behind him.

THE REAGAN COALITION

The Reagan coalition included a relatively small but highly influential group of wealthy Americans firmly committed to unfettered capitalism. They believed that the "market" offered the best solutions to most problems, and they shared a deep hostility to most (although not all) government interference in markets. Central to this group's agenda in the 1980s was opposition to what it scorned as the "redistributive" economic politics of the government (especially its highly progressive tax structure) and hostility to the rise of what they believed were "antibusiness" government regulations. Reagan courted these free-market conservatives carefully and effectively, and in the end   *Free-Market Conservatives* it was their interests his administration most effectively served.

A second element of the Reagan coalition consisted of a small but influential group of intellectuals commonly known as "neoconservatives," who gave to the   *Neoconservatives* right something it had not had in many years—a firm base among "opinion leaders," people with access to the most influential public forums of ideas. Many of these people had once been liberals and, before that, socialists. But during the turmoil of the 1960s, they had become alarmed by what they considered a dangerous and destructive radicalism.

RONALD AND NANCY REAGAN The president and the first lady greet guests at a White House social event. Nancy Reagan was committed to making the White House, and her husband's presidency, seem more glamorous than those of most recent administrations. But she also played an important, if usually quiet, policy role in the administration. (Photo by Dirck Halstead/© Time & Life Pictures/Getty Images)

Neoconservatives were sympathetic to the complaints and demands of capitalists, but their principal concern was to reassert legitimate authority and reaffirm Western democratic, anticommunist values and commitments. They considered themselves soldiers in a battle to "win back the culture"—from the crass, radical ideas that had polluted it.

Neoconservatives also strongly dissented from the new foreign policy orthodoxies of liberals and the left in the aftermath of the Vietnam War. They utterly rejected the idea that America should be a less interventionist nation, that it should work to ease tensions with the Soviet Union, and that it should tolerate radical regimes. Instead, they argued for an escalation of the Cold War as part of an effort to destabilize the Soviet Union. They insisted that the Vietnam War was an appropriate American commitment and that its abandonment was a terrible mistake. They believed that the United States had a special role to play in the world and should be willing to use military intervention to secure its vision. These ideas strongly influenced the foreign policy of the Reagan administration. The same ideas (and some of the same people) resurfaced in the early twenty-first century to help shape the international policies of the George W. Bush administration.

These groups formed an uneasy alliance with the broad grassroots conservative movement, but collectively formed the New Right. It shared a fundamental distrust of the "eastern establishment": a suspicion of its motives and goals and a sense that it exercised a dangerous, secret power in American life. These populist conservatives expressed the kinds of concerns that outsiders—non-elites—have traditionally voiced in American society: an opposition to centralized power and influence and a fear of living in a world where distant, hostile forces are controlling society and threatening individual freedom and community autonomy. It was a testament to Ronald Reagan's political skills and personal charm that he was able to generate enthusiastic support from these populist conservatives while at the same time appealing to more elite conservative groups whose concerns were in many ways antithetical to those of the New Right.

REAGAN IN THE WHITE HOUSE

Even many people who disagreed with Reagan's policies found themselves drawn to his attractive and carefully honed public image. He turned seventy years old a few weeks after taking office and was the oldest man ever to serve as president. But through most of his presidency, he appeared to be vigorous, resilient, even youthful. When wounded in an assassination attempt in 1981, he joked with doctors on his way into surgery and appeared to bounce back from the ordeal with remarkable speed. Even when things went wrong, as they often did, the blame seldom seemed to attach to Reagan himself (inspiring some Democrats to refer to him as the "Teflon president").

Reagan was not much involved in the day-to-day affairs of running the government; he surrounded himself with tough, energetic administrators who insulated him from many of the pressures of the office and who apparently relied on him largely for general guidance, not specific decisions. At times, the president revealed a startling ignorance about the nature of his own policies or the actions of his subordinates. But Reagan did make active use of his office to generate public support for his administration's programs.

"SUPPLY-SIDE" ECONOMICS

Reagan's 1980 campaign for the presidency had promised to restore the economy to health by a bold experiment that became known as "supply-side"—or, to its critics, "trickle-down"—economics. Eventually, it was called "Reaganomics." Supply-side economics *Reaganomics* operated from the assumption that the woes of the American economy were in large part a result of excessive taxation, which left inadequate capital available to investors to stimulate growth. The solution, therefore, was to reduce taxes, with particularly generous benefits to corporations and wealthy individuals, in order to encourage new investments.

In its first months in office, the new administration hastily assembled a legislative program based on the supply-side idea. It proposed $40 billion in budget reductions and managed to win congressional approval of almost all of them. In addition, the president proposed a bold three-year, 30 percent reduction on both individual and corporate *Tax Cuts* tax rates. In the summer of 1981, Congress passed it, too, after lowering the reductions to 25 percent. Reagan suceeded thanks to a disciplined Republican majority in the Senate and a Democratic majority in the House that was weak and riddled with defectors.

Reagan appointees in the executive branch of government aimed to reduce the role of government in American economic life. **Deregulation,** an idea many Democrats had begun to embrace in the Carter years, became almost a religion in the Reagan administration. Secretary of the Interior James Watt, a major figure in the antienvironmental Sagebrush Rebellion, opened up public lands and water to development and led a charge to reverse older conservationist policies. The Environmental Protection Agency (before some of its directors were indicted for corruption) relaxed or entirely eliminated enforcement of major environmental laws and regulations.

By early 1982, the nation had sunk into a severe recession. The Reagan economic program was not directly to blame for the problems, but neither did it offer a quick solution. During 1982, unemployment reached 11 percent, one of the highest levels since the 1930s. But before the recession could do great damage to Reagan, the economy recovered more rapidly and impressively than almost anyone had expected. By late 1983, unemployment had fallen to 8.2 percent, and it declined steadily for several years after that. The gross national product (GNP) grew 3.6 percent in a year, the largest increase since the mid-1970s. Inflation fell below 5 percent. The economy continued to grow, and both inflation and unemployment remained low through most of the decade.

The recovery was a result of many things. Prior years of tight money policies by the Federal Reserve Board had helped lower inflation; perhaps equally important, the Fed had lowered interest rates early in 1983 in response to the recession. A worldwide "energy glut" and the virtual collapse of the OPEC cartel had produced at least a temporary end to the inflationary pressures of spiraling fuel costs. And staggering federal budget deficits were pumping billions of dollars into the flagging economy. As a result, consumer spending and business investment both increased. The stock market rose up from its doldrums of the 1970s and began a sustained and historic boom. In August 1982, the Dow Jones Industrial Average stood at 777. Five years later it had passed 2,000. Despite a frightening crash in the fall of 1987, the market continued to grow for more than another decade. The Dow Jones average passed 18,000 in 2015.

THE FISCAL CRISIS

The economic revival did little at first to reduce the staggering, and to many Americans alarming, federal budget deficits (the gap between revenue and spending in a single year) or to slow the growth in the national debt (the debt the nation accumulates over time as a result of its annual deficits). By the mid-1980s, this growing fiscal crisis had become one of the central issues in American politics. Having entered office promising a balanced *Record Budget Deficits*   budget within four years, Reagan presided over record budget deficits and accumulated more debt in his eight years in office than the American government had accumulated in its entire previous history. Before the 1980s, the highest single-year budget deficit in American history had been $66 billion (in 1976). Throughout the 1980s, the annual budget deficit consistently exceeded $100 billion (and in 1991 peaked at $268 billion). The national debt rose from $907 billion in 1980 to nearly $3.5 trillion by 1991. Much larger deficits—and debt—were soon to come.

The enormous deficits had many causes. The budget suffered from enormous increases in the costs of "entitlement" programs (especially both Social Security and Medicare), a result of the aging of the population and dramatic increases in the cost of health care. The 1981 tax cuts, the largest in American history, also contributed to the deficit. The massive increase in military spending on which the Reagan administration insisted added much more to the federal budget than its cuts in domestic spending removed.

In the face of these deficits, the administration proposed further cuts in "discretionary" domestic spending, which included many programs aimed at the poorest (and politically weakest) Americans. By the end of Reagan's third year in office, funding for domestic programs had been cut nearly as far as Congress (and, apparently, the public) was willing to tolerate, and still no end to the rising deficit was in sight. By the late 1980s, many fiscal conservatives were calling for a constitutional amendment mandating a balanced budget—a provision the president himself claimed to support. But Congress never approved the amendment.

REAGAN AND THE WORLD

Relations with the Soviet Union, which had been steadily deteriorating in the last years of the Carter administration, grew still chillier in the first years of the Reagan presidency. The president spoke harshly of the Soviet regime (which he once called the "evil empire"), accusing it of sponsoring world terrorism and declaring that any armaments negotiations must be linked to negotiations on Soviet behavior in other areas. Although the president had long denounced the SALT II arms control treaty as unfavorable to the United States, he continued to honor its provisions. But the president proposed the most ambitious (and potentially most expensive) new military program in many years: the Strategic Defense Initiative (SDI), *Strategic Defense Initiative* widely known as "Star Wars" (after the popular movie of that name). Reagan claimed that SDI, through the use of lasers and satellites, could provide an effective shield against incoming missiles and thus make nuclear war obsolete. The Soviet Union claimed that the new program would elevate the arms race to new and more dangerous levels and insisted that any arms control agreement should begin with an American abandonment of SDI.

The escalation of Cold War tensions and the slowing of arms control initiatives helped produce an important popular movement in Europe and the United States calling for a "nuclear freeze," an agreement between the two superpowers not to expand their atomic arsenals. In what many believed was the largest mass demonstration in American history, nearly a million people rallied in New York City's Central Park in 1982 to support the freeze. Perhaps partly in response to this growing pressure, the administration began tentative efforts to revive arms control negotiations in 1983.

The administration created a new policy known as the Reagan Doctrine, designed to help resist communism and anti-Americanism in the Third World. *Reagan Doctrine* The United States sent soldiers and money to aid guerrillas and resistance movements in countries with anti-American governments—among them Grenada, El Salvador, and Nicaragua. But Reagan generally backed away from more serious warfare. In 1982, when the Israeli army invaded Lebanon, American peacekeeping forces entered Beirut to stabilize the nation. But when a terrorist bombing of a U.S. military barracks in Beirut led to the death of 241 marines, Reagan quickly withdrew the American forces. There were other terrorist events against America and other nations by attacking bombs, ships, and diplomatic buildings—the beginning of what would become a long battle against terrorism.

Reagan approached the campaign of 1984 at the head of a united Republican Party firmly committed to his candidacy. The Democrats nominated former vice president Walter Mondale. Mondale brought momentary excitement to the Democratic campaign by selecting a woman, Representative Geraldine Ferraro of New York, to be his running mate and the first female candidate ever to appear on a national ticket. But Reagan's triumphant campaign scarcely took note of his opponents and spoke instead of what he claimed was the remarkable revival of American fortunes and spirits under his leadership, *Reagan Reelected* or what he sometimes called "Morning in America." He won 59 percent of the vote and carried every state but Mondale's native Minnesota and the District of Columbia.

AMERICA AND THE WANING OF THE COLD WAR

Many factors contributed to the collapse of the Soviet Empire. The long, stalemated war in Afghanistan proved at least as disastrous to the Soviet Union as the Vietnam War had been to America. The government in Moscow failed to address a long-term economic decline in the Soviet republics and the Eastern-bloc nations. Restiveness with the heavy-handed policies of communist police states was growing throughout much of the Soviet *Mikhail Gorbachev*   Empire. But the most visible factor at the time was the emergence of Mikhail Gorbachev, who succeeded to the leadership of the Soviet Union in 1985 and, to the surprise of almost everyone (probably including himself), very quickly became the most revolutionary figure in world politics in decades.

THE FALL OF THE SOVIET UNION

Gorbachev transformed Soviet politics with two dramatic new initiatives: *glasnost* (open-ness), the dismantling of many of the repressive mechanisms that had been conspicuous *Glasnost and* Perestroika   features of Soviet life for over half a century, and *perestroika* (reform), an effort to restructure the rigid and unproductive Soviet economy by introduc-ing, among other things, such elements of capitalism as private ownership and the profit motive. He also began to transform Soviet foreign policy.

The severe economic problems at home evidently convinced Gorbachev that the Soviet Union could no longer sustain its extended commitments around the world. As early as

THE FALL OF THE BERLIN WALL   The Berlin Wall is widely considered to have "fallen" on November 9, 1989. Starting on that date and in the days and weeks that followed, people used sledgehammers and picks to tear down the wall, often keeping the broken pieces as souvenirs of this symbolic conclusion of the Cold War. (© DIZ München GmbH/Alamy)

1987, he began reducing the Soviet presence in Eastern Europe. And in 1989, in the space of a few months, every communist state in Europe—Poland, Hungary, Czechoslovakia, Bulgaria, Romania, East Germany, Yugoslavia, and Albania—either overthrew its government or forced it to transform itself into an essentially noncommunist (and in some cases, actively anticommunist) regime. Perhaps the most dramatic event of this extraordinary revolution was the tearing down of the infamous Berlin Wall.

Not all international protests against communism were so successful. In May 1989, students in China launched a mass movement calling for greater democratization. But in June, hard-line leaders seized control of the government and sent military forces to crush the uprising. The result was a bloody massacre on June 3, 1989, in Tiananmen Square in Beijing, in which an unknown number of demonstrators died. The assault *Tiananmen Square* crushed the democracy movement and restored hard-liners to power. It did not, however, stop China's efforts to modernize and even Westernize its economy.

But China was an exception to the widespread movement toward democratization. Early in 1990, the government of South Africa, long an international pariah for its rigid enforcement of "apartheid" (a system designed to protect white supremacy, much like the Jim Crow system had done in the American South) legalized the chief black party in the nation, the African National Congress (ANC), which had been banned for decades. The government also released from prison the leader of the ANC, Nelson Mandela, who had been in jail for twenty-seven years. Over the next several years, the South African government repealed its apartheid laws. And in 1994, there were national elections in which all South Africans could participate. As a result, Nelson Mandela became the first black president of South Africa.

In 1991, communism began to collapse in the Soviet Union itself. An unsuccessful coup by hard-line Soviet leaders on August 19 precipitated a dramatic unraveling of communist power. Within days, the coup itself collapsed in the face of resistance from the *Collapse of the USSR* public and crucial elements within the military. By the end of August, many of the republics of the Soviet Union had declared independence; the Soviet government was clearly powerless to stop the fragmentation. Gorbachev himself finally resigned as leader of the now virtually powerless Communist Party and Soviet government, and the Soviet Union ceased to exist.

The last years of the Reagan administration coincided with the first years of the Gorbachev regime; and while Reagan was skeptical of Gorbachev at first, he gradually became convinced that the Soviet leader was sincere in his desire for reform. In 1988, the two superpowers signed a treaty eliminating American and Soviet intermediate-range nuclear forces (INF) from Europe—the most significant arms control agreement of the nuclear age. At about the same time, Gorbachev ended the Soviet Union's long and frustrating military involvement in Afghanistan.

THE FADING OF THE REAGAN REVOLUTION

For a time, the dramatic changes around the world and Reagan's personal popularity deflected attention from a series of scandals that might well have destroyed another administration, including revelations of illegal and ethical lapses in the Environmental Protection Agency, the CIA, the Department of Defense, the Department of Labor, the Department of Justice, and the Department of Housing and Urban Development. A more serious scandal emerged within the savings and loan industry, which the Reagan administration had helped deregulate in the early 1980s. By the end of the decade, the industry was in chaos, and the government was forced to step in to prevent a complete collapse. The cost of the debacle to the public eventually ran to more than half a trillion dollars.

But the most politically damaging scandal of the Reagan years came to light in *Iran-Contra Scandal* November 1986, when the White House conceded that it had sold weapons to the revolutionary government of Iran as part of a largely unsuccessful effort to secure the release of several Americans being held hostage. Even more damaging was the revelation that some of the money from the arms deal with Iran had been covertly and illegally funneled into a fund to aid the contras, a loose group of commandos who fought against the anti-American government after the 1979 revolution in Nicaragua.

In the months that followed, aggressive reporting and a series of congressional hearings exposed a widespread pattern of covert activities orchestrated by the White House and dedicated to advancing the administration's foreign policy aims through secret and at times illegal means. The Iran-contra scandal, as it became known, did serious damage to the Reagan presidency—even though the investigations never tied the president himself to the most serious violations of the law.

THE PRESIDENCY OF GEORGE H. W. BUSH

The fraying of the Reagan administration helped the Democrats regain control of the United States Senate in 1986 and fueled hopes in the party for a presidential victory in 1988. Michael Dukakis, a three-term governor of Massachusetts, eventually captured the nomination. Vice President George H. W. Bush was the largely unopposed Republican candidate. Neither candidate succeeded in creating public enthusiasm.

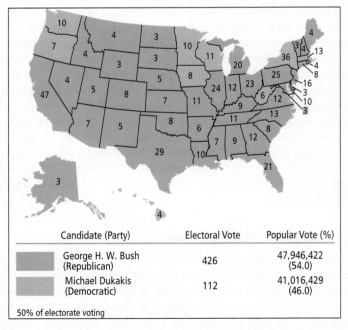

Candidate (Party)	Electoral Vote	Popular Vote (%)
George H. W. Bush (Republican)	426	47,946,422 (54.0)
Michael Dukakis (Democratic)	112	41,016,429 (46.0)

50% of electorate voting

THE ELECTION OF 1988 Democrats had high hopes going into the election of 1988, but Vice President George H. W. Bush won a decisive victory over Michael Dukakis, who did only slightly better than Walter Mondale had done four years earlier. • *What made it so difficult for a Democrat to challenge the Republicans in 1988 after eight years of a Republican administration?*

Beginning at the Republican National Convention, Bush made his campaign a long, relentless attack on Dukakis, tying him to all the unpopular social and cultural stances Americans had come to identify with "liberals." Bush won a substantial victory in November: 54 percent of the popular vote to Dukakis's 46 percent, and 426 electoral votes to Dukakis's 112. But Bush carried few Republicans into office with him; the Democrats retained secure majorities in both houses of Congress. The broad popularity Bush enjoyed during much of his first three years in office was partly a result of his subdued, unthreatening public image. But it was primarily due to the wonder and excitement with which Americans viewed the dramatic events in the rest of the world. Bush moved cautiously at first in dealing with the changes in the Soviet Union. But like Reagan, he eventually cooperated with Gorbachev and reached a series of significant arms control agreements with the Soviet Union in its waning years.

On domestic issues, the Bush administration was less successful. His administration inherited a staggering burden of debt and a federal deficit that had been growing dramatically for nearly a decade. Constantly concerned about the right wing of his own party, Bush aggressively opposed current laws governing abortion and affirmative action that damaged his ability to work with the Democratic Congress.

Despite this political stalemate, Congress and the White House managed on occasion to agree on significant measures. In 1990, the president agreed to a significant tax increase as part of a multiyear "budget package" designed to reduce the deficit—thus violating his own 1988 campaign pledge of "no new taxes."

But the most serious domestic problem facing the Bush administration was one for which neither the president nor Congress had any answer: a recession that began late in 1990 and became more serious in 1991 and 1992.

THE GULF WAR

The fall of the Soviet Union left the United States in the unanticipated position of being the only real superpower in the world. It forced the Bush administration to consider what to do with America's formidable political and military power.

The events of 1989–1991 suggested two possible answers. One was that the United States would reduce its military strength dramatically and concentrate its energies and resources on pressing domestic problems. The other was that America would continue to use its power actively, not to fight communism but to defend its regional and economic interests. The answer came quickly. In 1989, the administration ordered an invasion of Panama, which overthrew the unpopular military leader Manuel Noriega (under indictment in the United States for drug trafficking) and replaced him with an elected, pro-American regime. And in 1990, that same impulse drew the United States into the turbulent politics of the Middle East.

On August 2, 1990, the armed forces of Iraq invaded and quickly overwhelmed the emirate of Kuwait, the small oil-rich neighbor of Iraq. Saddam Hussein, *Saddam Hussein* the militaristic leader of Iraq, soon announced that he was annexing Kuwait. The Bush administration soon agreed to lead other nations in a campaign to force Iraq out of Kuwait—through the pressure of economic sanctions if possible, through military force if necessary. Within a few weeks, Bush had persuaded virtually every important government in the world, including the Soviet Union and almost all the Arab and Islamic states, to join in a United Nations–sanctioned trade embargo of Iraq.

At the same time, the United States and its allies (including the British, French, Egyptians, and Saudis) began deploying a large military force along the border between Kuwait and Saudi Arabia, a force that ultimately reached 690,000 troops (425,000 of them American). And on January 16, American and allied air forces began a massive bombardment of Iraqi troops in Kuwait and of military and industrial installations in Iraq itself.

The allied bombing continued for six weeks. On February 23, allied (primarily American) forces under the command of General Norman Schwarzkopf began a major ground offensive to the north of the Iraqi forces. The allied armies encountered almost no resistance and suffered only light casualties (141 fatalities). Estimates of Iraqi deaths in the war were 100,000 or more. On February 28, Iraq announced its acceptance of allied terms for a cease-fire, and the brief Persian Gulf War was over.

THE ELECTION OF 1992

President Bush's popularity reached a record high in the immediate aftermath of the Gulf War. But the glow of that victory faded quickly as the recession worsened in late 1991. That gave Bill Clinton, the young five-term Democratic governor of Arkansas, an opportunity to emerge as the early front-runner. Clinton survived a bruising primary campaign and a series of damaging personal controversies to win his party's nomination.

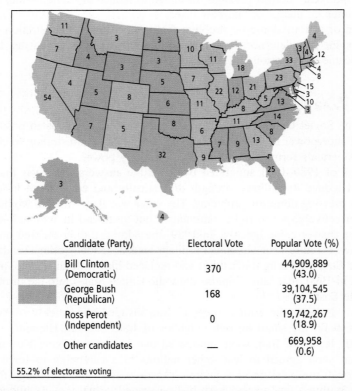

Candidate (Party)	Electoral Vote	Popular Vote (%)
Bill Clinton (Democratic)	370	44,909,889 (43.0)
George Bush (Republican)	168	39,104,545 (37.5)
Ross Perot (Independent)	0	19,742,267 (18.9)
Other candidates	—	669,958 (0.6)

55.2% of electorate voting

THE ELECTION OF 1992 In the 1992 election, for the first time since 1976, a Democrat captured the White House. And although the third-party candidacy of Ross Perot deprived Bill Clinton of an absolute majority, he nevertheless defeated George Bush by a decisive margin in both the popular and electoral votes. • *What factors had eroded President Bush's once-broad popularity by 1992? What explained the strong showing of Ross Perot?*

Complicating the campaign was the emergence of Ross Perot, a blunt, forthright Texas billionaire who became an independent candidate by tapping popular resentment of the federal bureaucracy and by promising tough, uncompromising leadership to deal with the fiscal crisis. At several moments in the spring, Perot led both Bush and Clinton in public opinion polls. But in July, as he began to face hostile scrutiny from the media, he abruptly withdrew from the race. Early in October, he reentered and soon regained much (although never all) of his early support.

After a campaign in which the economy was the principal issue, Clinton won a clear, but hardly overwhelming, victory over Bush and Perot. He received 43 percent   *Clinton Elected* of the vote in the three-way race, to the president's 38 percent and Perot's 19 percent (the best showing for a third-party or independent candidate since Theodore Roosevelt in 1912). Clinton won 370 electoral votes to Bush's 168; Perot won none. Democrats also retained control of both houses of Congress.

CONCLUSION

America in the late 1970s was, by the standards of its own recent history, an unusually troubled nation—numbed by the Watergate scandals, the fall of Vietnam, and perhaps most of all the nation's increasing economic difficulties. The unhappy presidencies of Gerald Ford and Jimmy Carter provided little relief from these accumulating problems and anxieties. Indeed, in the last year of the Carter presidency, the nation's future seemed particularly bleak in light of severe economic problems, a traumatic seizure of American hostages in Iran, and a Soviet invasion of Afghanistan.

In the midst of these problems, American conservatives slowly and steadily prepared for a political revolution. A coalition of disparate but impassioned groups on the right— including a large movement known as the "New Right," with vaguely populist impulses— gained strength from the nation's troubles and from their own success in winning support for a broad-ranging revolt against taxes. Their efforts culminated in the election of 1980, when Ronald Reagan became the most conservative man in at least sixty years to be elected president of the United States.

Reagan's first term was a dramatic contrast to the troubled presidencies that had preceded it and signaled a reversal or at least a modification of ruling economic and social policies. He won substantial victories in Congress (cutting taxes, reducing spending on domestic programs, building up the military). Perhaps equally important, he made his own engaging personality one of the central political forces in national life. Easily reelected in 1984, he seemed to have solidified the conservative grip on national political life. In his second term, however, a series of scandals and misadventures—and the president's own declining energy—limited the administration's effectiveness. Nevertheless, Reagan's personal popularity remained high, and the economy continued to prosper—factors that propelled his vice president, George H. W. Bush, to succeed him in 1989.

Bush's presidency was not as successful as Reagan's had been, and the perception of his disengagement with the nation's growing economic problems contributed to Bush's defeat in 1992. But a colossal historic event overshadowed most domestic concerns during Bush's term in office: the collapse of the Soviet Union and the fall of communist regimes all over Europe. The United States was to some degree a dazzled observer of this process. But the end of the Cold War also propelled the United States into the possession of unchallenged global preeminence—and drew it increasingly into the role of international arbiter and peacemaker. The Gulf War of 1991 was the most dramatic example of the new global role the United States would now increasingly assume as the world's only true superpower.

KEY TERMS/PEOPLE/PLACES/EVENTS

Ayatollah Ruhollah Khomeini 770
Bill Clinton 786
Camp David accords 769
Christian Coalition 773
deregulation 779
George H. W. Bush 784
Gerald Ford 774
glasnost 782

Iran-contra scandal 784
Jimmy Carter 768
Mikhail Gorbachev 782
neoconservatives 777
New Right 773
perestroika 782
Reagan Doctrine 781
Reaganomics 779
Ronald Reagan 774

Saddam Hussein 785
Sagebrush Rebellion 771
stagflation 767
Strategic Defense Initiative (SDI) 781
Sunbelt 771
Tiananmen Square 783

RECALL AND REFLECT

1. Did the Ford and Carter presidencies fail to repair the damage done to the reputation of the presidency by the Watergate scandal and Nixon's resignation? If so, why?
2. Why did the American electorate become increasingly conservative during the 1970s and 1980s? What are some examples that testify to this increasing conservatism?
3. What philosophy guided foreign policy under Reagan? How did the rise of Mikhail Gorbachev alter Reagan's foreign policy toward the Soviet Union?

32

THE AGE OF GLOBALIZATION

A RESURGENCE OF PARTISANSHIP

SCIENCE AND TECHNOLOGY IN THE NEW ECONOMY

A CHANGING SOCIETY

AMERICA IN THE WORLD

LOOKING AHEAD

1. How did increasing partisanship affect governing during the late 1900s and early 2000s? How does it continue to affect the relationship between the president and Congress?

2. How did the growth of the "new economy" affect how Americans worked and lived?

3. How was the American population changing at the turn of the century? What characterizes it, and what key challenges does it confront?

4. How did the terrorist attack of September 11, 2001, affect the United States and begin a new era in American foreign policy?

ON AN EARLY TUESDAY morning in 2001, a commercial airliner crashed into the side of one of two tallest buildings in New York, the North Tower of the World Trade Center. Within thirty minutes, another commercial airliner struck the South Tower. Before the steel girders in both towers buckled and collapsed from the tremendous heat of the burning wreckage, Americans learned of even more disasters. A plane flew into the Pentagon in Washington, D.C., and another crashed a few hundred miles away in a field not far from Pittsburgh, after passengers apparently seized the cockpit and prevented the hijackers from reaching their unknown target. In these four, almost simultaneous, catastrophes, nearly 3,000 people died.

The events of September 11 and their aftermath sparked significant changes in American life. And yet there was at least one great continuity between the world of the 1990s and the world that seemed to begin on September 11, 2001. The United States in the last years of the twentieth century and the first years of the twenty-first, more than at any other time in its history, was becoming more and more deeply entwined in a new age of globalism—an age that combined great promise with great peril.

A RESURGENCE OF PARTISANSHIP

When Bill Clinton took the presidential oath of office in January 1993, little did he or any other American realize that partisan politics would become a crippling problem. Beginning with Clinton and continuing through the administration of President Barack Obama, Democrats and Republicans regularly chose ideological purity over political compromise, effectively gumming up the machinery of the federal government and nearly bringing it to the brink of shutting down on more than one occasion. At times the political divides occurred within a party: conservative Republicans refusing the hand of negotiation to their more liberal brethren on matters of higher taxes, raising the national debt ceiling, or supporting national health insurance. Like few periods in American history, the turn of the twenty-first century showcased bitter splits between the parties that fundamentally affected how the White House and Congress functioned.

LAUNCHING THE CLINTON PRESIDENCY

Bill Clinton entered office as the first Democratic president since Jimmy Carter and the first self-proclaimed "activist" president, meaning a president seeking to expand the active role of the federal government in solving social problems, since Lyndon Johnson. Indeed, his domestic agenda was more ambitious than that of any president since the 1960s. But Clinton also had significant political weaknesses. Having won the vote of well under half the electorate, he had no powerful mandate for change.

The new administration began with a series of missteps and misfortunes in its first months. The president's effort to end the longtime ban on gay men and lesbians serving in the military met with ferocious resistance, and he was forced to settle for a compromise known as "Don't Ask, Don't Tell," which forbade recruiters to ask recruits about their sexual preferences but also forbade servicemen and servicewomen to reveal them. Several of his early appointments became so controversial he had to withdraw them. Then Vince Foster, a longtime friend of the president who served as a deputy White House counsel and previous legal partner of First Lady Hillary Rodham Clinton, committed suicide in the summer of 1993. His death sparked an escalating inquiry into some banking and real estate ventures involving the Clintons in the early 1980s, which became known as the Whitewater affair. An independent counsel began examining these issues in 1993. (The Clintons were ultimately cleared of wrongdoing in Whitewater in 2000.)

Despite its many problems, the Clinton administration had some important achievements in its first year. The president narrowly won approval of a budget that marked a significant turn away from some of the policies of the Reagan–Bush years, especially the focus on reducing personal and corporate taxes. It included a substantial tax increase on the wealthiest Americans, a sizable reduction in many areas of government spending, and a major expansion of tax credits to low-income working people.

Clinton was a committed advocate of free trade. After a long and difficult battle against, among others, Ross Perot, the AFL-CIO, and many Democrats in Congress, he secured passage of the North American Free Trade Agreement (NAFTA), which eliminated   *Free-Trade Agreements* most trade barriers among the United States, Canada, and Mexico. Later he won approval to sign a global accord that created the World Trade Organization (WTO), an international organization charged with negotiating agreements and settling disputes among its members.

The president's most notable and ambitious initiative was a major reform of the nation's health-care system. Early in 1993, he appointed a task force, chaired by the first lady. The presidential task force proposed a sweeping reform designed to guarantee coverage to every American and hold down the costs of medical care. But there was substantial opposition from those who believed the reform would transfer too much power to the government. Well-funded opposition doomed the plan. The foreign policy of the Clinton administration was at first cautious and tentative. Yugoslavia, a nation created after World War I out of a group of small Balkan countries, dissolved again into several different countries in the wake of the 1989 collapse of its communist government. Bosnia was among the new nations, and it quickly became embroiled in a bloody civil war between its two major ethnic groups: one Muslim, the other Serbian and Christian, backed by the neighboring Serbian republic. All efforts by the other European nations and the United States to negotiate an end to the struggle failed until 1995, when the American negotiator Richard Holbrooke finally brought the warring parties together and crafted an agreement to partition Bosnia.

THE REPUBLICAN RESURGENCE

The trials of the Clinton administration, and the failure of health-care reform in particular, proved damaging to the Democratic Party as it faced the congressional elections of 1994. For the first time in over forty years, Republicans gained control of both houses of Congress.

Throughout 1995, the Republican Congress, under the aggressive leadership of House Speaker Newt Gingrich, worked at a sometimes feverish pace to construct   *Newt Gingrich* what they called a "Contract with America," an ambitious and even radical legislative program. The Republicans proposed a series of measures to transfer important powers from the federal government to the states; pushed for dramatic reductions in federal spending, including a major restructuring of the Medicare program, to reduce costs; and attempted to scale back a wide range of federal regulatory functions.

President Clinton responded to the 1994 election results by shifting his own activist agenda conspicuously to the center—announcing his own plan to cut taxes and balance the budget. But the presidential politics of 1996 made compromise between the president and Congress very difficult. In November 1995 and again in January 1996, the federal government literally shut down for several days because the president and Congress could not agree on a budget. Republican leaders refused to pass a "continuing resolution" (to allow government operations to continue during negotiations) in hopes of pressuring the president to agree to their terms. That proved to be an epic political blunder. Public opinion turned quickly and powerfully against the Republican leadership and much of its agenda. Newt Gingrich emerged as one of the most unpopular political leaders in the nation, while President Clinton slowly improved his standing in public opinion polls.

By the time the 1996 campaign began in earnest, President Clinton was in a commanding position to win reelection. Unopposed for the Democratic nomination, he faced a Republican opponent—Senator Robert Dole of Kansas—who inspired little enthusiasm even within his own party. Clinton benefited from the disastrous errors by congressional Republicans in 1995 and early 1996. But his greatest strength came from the remarkable success of the American economy and the marked reduction in the federal deficit. Like Reagan in 1984, he could campaign as the champion of peace, prosperity, and national well-being.

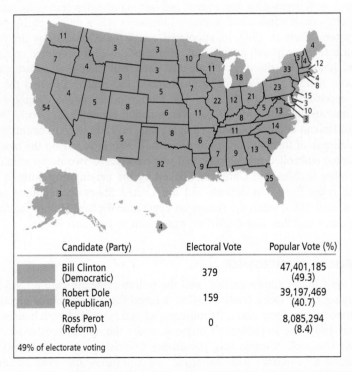

Candidate (Party)	Electoral Vote	Popular Vote (%)
Bill Clinton (Democratic)	379	47,401,185 (49.3)
Robert Dole (Republican)	159	39,197,469 (40.7)
Ross Perot (Reform)	0	8,085,294 (8.4)

49% of electorate voting

THE ELECTION OF 1996   Ross Perot received many fewer votes in 1996 than he had in 1992, and President Clinton came much closer than he had four years earlier to winning a majority of the popular vote. Once again, Clinton defeated his Republican opponent, this time Robert Dole, by a decisive margin in both the popular and electoral votes. • *After the 1994 Republican landslide in the congressional elections, Bill Clinton had seemed permanently weakened. What explains his political revival?*

In a flurry of activity in the spring and summer of 1996, Congress passed several important bills. The most dramatic was a welfare reform bill that ended the fifty-year federal guarantee of assistance to families with dependent children and turned most of the responsibility for allocating federal welfare funds to the states. Most of all, it shifted the bulk of welfare benefits away from those without jobs and toward low-wage workers.

Clinton's buoyant campaign flagged slightly in the last weeks, but the president nevertheless received just over 49 percent of the popular vote to Dole's 41 percent; Ross Perot, running now as the candidate of what he called the Reform Party, received just over 8 percent of the vote. Clinton won 379 electoral votes to Dole's 159; Perot won none, as was *Clinton Reelected* the case in the 1992 election. But the Democrats failed to regain either house of Congress.

CLINTON TRIUMPHANT AND EMBATTLED

The first Democratic president to win two terms as president since Franklin Roosevelt, Bill Clinton began his second administration with serene confidence. He proposed a relatively modest domestic agenda. He negotiated effectively with the Republican leadership on a plan for a balanced budget, which passed with much fanfare late in 1997. By the end of 1998, the federal budget was generating its first surplus in thirty years.

Clinton's renewed popularity was critical to his political survival in the turbulent year that followed, when the most serious crisis of his presidency suddenly erupted. Clinton had been the target of accusations of corruption and scandal since his first weeks in office: the investigation into Whitewater, charges of corruption against members of his cabinet and staff, accusations of illegalities in financing his 1996 campaign, and a civil suit for sexual harassment filed early in his first term by a former Arkansas state employee, Paula Jones.

In early 1998, inquiries associated with the Paula Jones case led to charges that the president had had a sexual relationship with a twenty-two-year-old White House intern, Monica Lewinsky. The most damaging charge was that he had lied about it in his deposition before Jones's attorneys. Those revelations produced a new investigation by the independent counsel in the Whitewater case, Kenneth Starr, a former judge and official in the Reagan Justice Department.

Clinton forcefully denied the charges, and a majority of the public strongly backed him. His popularity soared to record levels and remained high throughout the year that followed. In the meantime, a federal judge dismissed the Paula Jones case, which had launched the scandal.

But the scandal revived again with great force in August 1998, when Lewinsky struck a deal with the independent counsel and testified about her relationship with Clinton. Starr then subpoenaed Clinton himself, who—faced with the prospect of speaking *The Starr Report* to a grand jury—finally admitted that he and Lewinsky had had what he called an "improper relationship." A few weeks later, Starr submitted a lengthy and salacious report to Congress on the results of his investigation, recommending that Congress impeach the president.

IMPEACHMENT, ACQUITTAL, AND RESURGENCE

On December 19, 1998, the House, voting on strictly partisan lines, narrowly approved two counts of impeachment: lying to the grand jury and obstructing justice. The matter then moved to the Senate, where a trial of the president—the first since the trial of Andrew Johnson in 1868—began in early January. It ended with a decisive acquittal of the president. Neither of the charges attracted even a majority of the votes, let alone the two-thirds necessary for conviction.

Still, the trial dampened public support for the president and stiffened congressional opposition to any of his initiatives. Indeed, the last two years of the Clinton presidency were relatively quiet. The president had no real hope of major domestic achievements in the face of a hostile Republican Congress. Overseas, however, he was more active.

In 1999, the president faced another crisis in the Balkans. This time, the conflict *Kosovo* involved a province of Serbian-dominated Yugoslavia—Kosovo—most of whose residents were Albanian Muslims. A savage civil war erupted there in 1998 between Kosovo nationalists and Serbians. In May 1999, NATO forces—dominated and led by the United States—began a major bombing campaign against the Serbians, which after little more than a week led the leader of Yugoslavia, Slobodan Milosevic, to agree to a cease-fire. Serbian troops withdrew from Kosovo entirely, replaced by NATO peacekeeping forces. A precarious peace returned to the region.

Buoyed by his success overseas and a rising economy, Clinton actually finished his eight years in office with his popularity higher than it had been when he had begun. No president in the years since has experienced the same approval ratings. Indeed, despite politicians' use of new technology and polling data to connect with the public, the relationship between the elected and the voter has steadily deteriorated.

THE ELECTION OF 2000

The 2000 presidential election was one of the most extraordinary in American history—not because of the campaign that preceded it but because of the sensational controversy over its results, which preoccupied the nation for more than five weeks after the actual voting.

The two men who had been the front-runners for their parties' nominations a year before the election captured these nominations with only slight difficulty: Republican George W. Bush, son of the former president and a second-term governor of Texas, and Democrat Al Gore, former Tennessee senator and vice president under Clinton.

Both men ran cautious, centrist campaigns. In the congressional races, Republicans maintained control of the House of Representatives by a scant five seats, while the Senate split evenly between Democrats and Republicans. (Among the victors in the Senate races was First Lady Hillary Rodham Clinton, who won in New York.) In the presidential race, Gore won the national popular vote by the thin margin of about 540,000 votes out of *Florida Disputed* about 100 million cast (a difference of 0.5 percent). But on election night, both candidates remained short of the 270 electoral votes needed for victory because the Florida results were too close to call.

After a mandatory recount over the next two days, Bush led Gore in the state by fewer than 300 votes. The technology of voting soon became central to the dispute. The Gore campaign asked for hand recounts in three critical counties, which the Florida Supreme Court unanimously supported.

The battle over the ballots continued between the candidates in the news and the courts until the U.S. Supreme Court ruled on December 12. Voting 5 to 4, along ideological lines, the conservative majority ruled that the Florida Supreme Court's order for a recount was unconstitutional; insisted that according to U.S. Code any revised recount order be completed by December 12 (the same day that the ruling was issued and therefore impossible to execute); and argued that the standards for evaluating punch-card ballots were too arbitrary and unfair to withstand constitutional scrutiny. With Florida's results certified, Bush's victory in Florida—and thus nationally—stood.

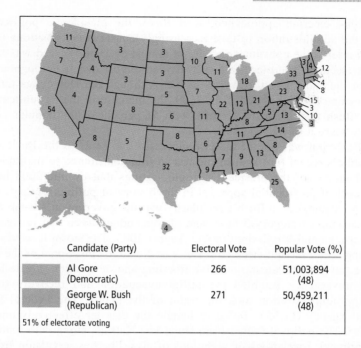

Candidate (Party)	Electoral Vote	Popular Vote (%)
Al Gore (Democratic)	266	51,003,894 (48)
George W. Bush (Republican)	271	50,459,211 (48)

51% of electorate voting

THE ELECTION OF 2000 The 2000 presidential election was one of the closest and most controversial in American history. It also starkly revealed a new pattern of party strength, which had been developing over the previous decade. Democrats swept the Northeast and most of the industrial Midwest and carried all the states of the Pacific Coast. Republicans swept the South, the plains states, and the mountain states (with the exception of New Mexico) and held on to a few traditional Republican strongholds in the Midwest. • *Compare this map to those of earlier elections, in particular the election of 1896 (Chapter 19). How did the pattern of party support change over the course of the twentieth century?*

THE PRESIDENCY OF GEORGE W. BUSH

George W. Bush assumed the presidency in January 2001 burdened by both the controversies surrounding his election and the widespread perception, even among some of his own supporters, that he was ill-prepared for the office. Nevertheless, Bush moved forcefully to enact an ambitious and controversial agenda.

Having campaigned as a moderate, Bush spent his first term as president governing as a staunch conservative and relying on the most conservative members of his party for support. He won passage of the largest tax cut in American history—$1.35 trillion. Critics noted that the massive tax cuts of 2001 went disproportionately to wealthy *Bush Tax Cuts* Americans, reflecting the view of White House economists that the best way to ensure growth was to put money into the hands of people most likely to invest.

Bush's other major domestic accomplishment was a controversial education reform bill, known as "No Child Left Behind," which tied federal funding in schools to the success of students in taking standardized tests. Still other proposals—an effort to privatize some aspects of the Social Security system, for example—never attracted significant support in Congress. Nonetheless, for most of the first three years of his presidency, George W. Bush was revered by many Americans because of his resolute stance against terrorism. Even the Iraq War, which began in 2003 and initially enjoyed widespread backing, helped sustain his popularity for a time.

As the 2004 election approached, Karl Rove, the president's political adviser, encouraged the administration to take increasingly conservative positions to mobilize the party's conservative constituency in what almost everyone agreed was likely to be a very close election. The electorate was divided almost evenly throughout the campaign, and in the end turnout proved decisive. Although the Democrats turned out in much higher numbers than they had in 2000, the increase in the Republican vote was even larger. Bush won a narrow victory, with 51 percent of the popular vote and an electoral vote margin of 35.

The 2004 election was one of the last successful moments in the Bush administration. The public's recent turn against the war in Iraq contributed to the rapidly declining approval ratings of the president himself—ratings that by mid-2008 had reached the lowest level of presidential approval in the history of polling. Perhaps even more *Hurricane Katrina* damaging to Bush's popularity was the government's weak response to Hurricane Katrina, a Category 3 hurricane of tremendous force that ravaged the Gulf Coast of Louisiana and Mississippi in late August 2005. The storm leveled many communities along the coast and crippled the city of New Orleans. Some of the levees that protected the city failed, causing massive flooding and destruction. While local, state, and federal governance fumbled the initial evacuation and recovery of southern Louisiana, the administration took the brunt of the blame. The Federal Emergency Management Agency (FEMA) failed to handle the disaster effectively and arguably made it worse. The political fallout from Hurricane Katrina, along with scandals in the Justice Department, revelations of violations of civil liberties, revulsion from aggressive interviewing tactics used against suspected terrorists, and declining economic prospects, culminating in a disastrous financial crisis beginning in early 2008—all contributed to the growing unpopularity of the president.

Bush managed some significant victories despite these setbacks. He won confirmation of two justices that he proposed for the Supreme Court: John Roberts, who succeeded William Rehnquist as chief justice; and Samuel Alito, who succeeded the retiring Sandra Day O'Connor. Both were fierce conservatives, inspiring hopes among some and fears among others that the Court would veer more sharply to the political right.

THE ELECTION OF 2008

The 2008 presidential election was the first since 1952 that did not include an incumbent president or vice president. Both parties began the campaign with large fields of candidates, but by the spring of 2008 the contest had narrowed considerably. Senator John McCain of Arizona emerged from the early primaries with his nomination ensured. In the Democratic race, the primaries quickly eliminated all but two candidates: Senator Hillary Rodham Clinton of New York, the former first lady, and Senator Barack Obama of Illinois, a young, charismatic politician and the son of an African father and a white American mother. As the first woman and the first African American to have a realistic chance of being elected president, Clinton and Obama attracted great enthusiasm. The passions driving both campaigns led to a primary contest that lasted much longer than usual. Not until the last primaries in June was it clear that Obama would be the nominee.

As the nomination campaigns were heating up, a series of financial problems erupted that imperiled the state of the economy. Indeed, by early 2008 the nation confronted its worst financial crisis since the Great Depression. The problem had several causes. For years, financial institutions had been developing new credit instruments intended to make borrowing easier and cheaper, which had lured millions of people into taking on large and risky mortgages. One such instrument, called an adjustable rate mortgage (ARM), offered homebuyers mortgages with initially low interest rates that would increase in later years. Other loans, called "jumbo loans," extended credit to people who lacked the financial means needed to pay them back. These new business practices were made possible with the repeal in 1999 of a centerpiece of New Deal legislation, the Glass-Steagall Act. Glass-Steagall had been passed in 1933 to prevent irresponsible banking practices by mandating layers of government oversight designed to catch fraud or risky investment strategies. Consumers responded to these new means of financing home purchases by snapping them up. Not surprisingly, the sale of houses, many of which were based on these risky mortgages, soared for a while, causing a "housing bubble"—a rapid rise in housing prices fueled by high demand. But the bubble eventually burst. The price of homes soon leveled off and even dipped. Those with ARMs saw them reset at much higher rates and struggled to make the higher payments. They and many owners of jumbo loans sought to sell their homes but couldn't because the market value of the home had often sunk below the value of the mortgages held, forcing some to walk away from their property and default on their loans. Foreclosures skyrocketed across the country. Many of the nation's largest banks had invested heavily in the securities that backed these risky loans; now, with the collapse of the housing market, they lost vast sums of money.

The so-called Great Recession of 2008, influenced by the loan crisis, also pushed down wages and triggered widespread job layoffs. The increased unemployment *Great Recession of 2008* rate further accelerated the downward economic spiral. Many Americans simply could not meet basic financial obligations such as the repayment of home, car, or school loans or credit card debt. There was also less money available for investing, or economic growth. Predictably, the Great Recession fueled outrage among those most affected: blue-collar and trades workers, manufacturers, and the poor. Popular anger surfaced in art, literature, and especially contemporary music. Rap, one of the newest and most successful forms of popular music, chronicled lives of despair and called for economic change. (See "Patterns of Popular Culture: Rap.")

By mid-September 2008, the financial crisis suggested an economy spinning out of control. Secretary of the Treasury Henry Paulson, supported by other economic leaders, stepped in. He proposed a massive use of federal funds to help the government bail out banks that were failing. Both the Bush administration and eventually the Obama administration won congressional support for $750 billion in the form of the Troubled Asset Relief Program (TARP) to shore up the tottering financial institutions. The bailout kept the economy from collapsing, but it remained very weak for several years, with exceptionally high unemployment rates.

This extraordinary crisis formed the backdrop against which the two presidential candidates fought out the last two months of their campaign. Neither offered clear or convincing solutions to the crisis, but most voters came to believe that Obama would likely be a better steward of the economy than McCain. Obama benefited both from the unpopularity of George W. Bush and from his success at persuading voters that McCain would continue Bush's policies. Obama held on to—and indeed increased— his lead through late September and October, helped by a heavily financed and highly disciplined campaign.

RAP

The long musical lineage of rap includes elements of the disco and street funk of the 1970s; of the fast-talking jive of black radio DJs in the 1950s; of the onstage patter of Cab Calloway and other African American stars of the first half of the twentieth century. It contains reminders of tap and break dancing—even of the boxing-ring poetry of Muhammad Ali.

Rap's most important element is its words. Rap is as much a form of language as a form of music. It bears a distant resemblance to some traditions of African American pulpit oratory, which also included forms of spoken song. It draws from some of the verbal traditions of urban black street life, including the "dozens"—a ritualized trading of insults particularly popular among young black men.

But rap is also the product of a distinctive place and time: the South Bronx in the 1970s and 1980s and the hip-hop culture that was born there and that soon dominated the appearance and public behavior of many young black males. "Hip hop is how you walk, talk, live, see, act, feel," said one Bronx hip-hopper. Some elements of hip-hop culture faded, and by the 1990s the most popular element of hip-hop culture was rap, which had by then been developing for nearly twenty years.

Beginning in the early 1970s, Bronx DJs began setting up their equipment on neighborhood streets and staging block parties, where they not only played records but also put on shows of their own—performances that featured spoken rhymes, jazzy phrases, and pointed comments about the audience, the neighborhood, and themselves. Gradually, the DJs began to bring "rappers" into shows—young men who developed the DJ style into a much more elaborate form of performance,

usually accompanied by dancing. As rap grew more popular in the inner city, record promoters began signing some of its new stars. In 1979, the Sugarhill Gang's "Rapper's Delight" became the first rap single to be played on mainstream commercial radio and the first to become a major hit. In the early 1980s, Run-DMC became the first national rap superstars. From there, rap moved quickly to become one of the most popular and commercially successful forms of popular music. In the 1990s and early 2000s, rap recordings routinely sold millions of copies.

Rap has taken many forms. There have been white rappers (Eminem, House of Pain), female rappers (Missy Elliott, Queen Latifah), even religious rappers and children's rappers. But it has always been primarily a product of the young male culture of the inner city, and some of the most successful rap has conveyed the frustration and anger that these men have felt about their lives—"a voice for the oppressed people," one rap artist said, "that in many other ways don't have a voice." In 1982, the rap group Grandmaster Flash and the Furious Five released a rap called "The Message," a searing description of the ghetto and the lack of educational and economic opportunities.

In the late 1980s, the Compton and Watts neighborhoods of Los Angeles—two of the most distressed minority communities in the city—produced their own style, known as West Coast rap, with such groups as Ice Cube, Ice-T, Tupac Shakur, and Snoop Doggy Dog. West Coast rap often had a harsh, angry character, and at its extremes (the so-called gangsta' rap), it could be strikingly violent and highly provocative. Scandals erupted over controversial lyrics—Ice-T's "Cop Killer," which some

KANYE WEST Testifying to the continued popularity of rap, as of 2014 rapper Kanye West remains one of the best-selling artists of all time, having sold well over 21 million albums and 66 million digital downloads in the United States alone. *Time* magazine has named West one of the 100 most influential people in the world. He is a rapper, songwriter, record producer, film director, entrepreneur, and fashion designer. (© Getty Images Entertainment/Getty Images)

critics believed advocated murdering police; and the sexually explicit lyrics of 2 Live Crew and other groups, which critics accused of advocating violence against women.

But it was not just the lyrics that caused the furor. Rap artists were almost all products of tough inner-city neighborhoods, and the rough-edged styles many took with them into the public eye made many people uncomfortable. Some rappers got caught up in highly publicized trouble with the law. Several—including two of rap's biggest stars, Tupac Shakur and Notorious B.I.G.—were murdered. The business of rap, particularly the confrontational business style of Death Row Records (founded by Dr. Dre, a veteran of the first major West Coast rap group NWA), was a source of public controversy as well.

These controversies at times unfairly dominated the image of rap as a whole. Some rap is angry and cruel, as are many of the realities of the world from which it comes. But much of it is explicitly positive, some of it deliberately gentle. Chuck D and other successful rappers use their music to exhort young black men to avoid drugs and crime, to take responsibility for their children, to get an education. And the form, if not the content, of the original rappers has spread widely through American culture. Rap came to dominate the music charts in America, and its styles made their way onto *Sesame Street* and other children's shows, into television commercials, Hollywood films, and the everyday language of millions of people, young and old, black and white. It became another of the arresting, innovative African American musical traditions that have shaped American culture for more than a century. •

UNDERSTAND, ANALYZE, & EVALUATE

1. What other African American musical forms have helped shape American popular culture?

2. If rap is so closely associated with the inner-city culture where it originated, what accounts for its widespread popularity and commercial success? What other forms or styles of popular music enjoy a popularity that extends far beyond its cultural origins?

3. Do you think rap's popularity will endure? Why or why not?

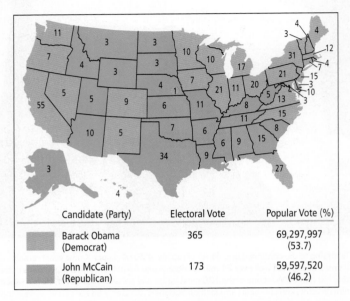

Candidate (Party)	Electoral Vote	Popular Vote (%)
Barack Obama (Democrat)	365	69,297,997 (53.7)
John McCain (Republican)	173	59,597,520 (46.2)

THE ELECTION OF 2008   The election of 2008 produced a decisive victory for Barack Obama. Democrats won majorities in both the House and the Senate, only to see the Republicans win a majority of the House two years later. • *Compare this map to the election of 2000 map. Which states did Bush win that went to Obama in 2008?*

On November 4, 2008, Barack Obama won a decisive victory, winning the popular vote 53 percent to 46 percent and the electoral vote by an even larger margin. Obama became the first Democratic candidate since Lyndon Johnson to win so large a victory.

OBAMA AND HIS OPPONENTS

The global exuberance that Obama's election created in 2008 did not linger for long. The first two years of his presidency coincided with the worst period of the economic crisis. But large supportive Democratic majorities in both houses of Congress strengthened Obama's ability to enact broad reforms. During those years, Obama passed a large stimulus package of $800 billion to support state and local budgets, public works, and other investments that he hoped would generate economic growth. He and his congressional allies also succeeded in passing significant financial regulations that were designed to avoid another crisis like the one that began in 2008. Even more important, he oversaw the passage of the Affordable *Affordable Care Act*   Care Act, a broad health-care bill that would ensure that almost all Americans would have access to insurance, regardless of their means. Yet Obama's legislation, and especially his health-care initiative, triggered fear among many Republicans about a federal government becoming too powerful and overstepping its limits. Indeed, only one Republican congressman supported the health-care bill. For Obama, who had built much of his presidential bid around the idea of bipartisanship and conciliation, the polarization of the two parties was a significant setback. Many Republican state's attorneys sued to stop the health bill. Judges were divided as to whether the bill was constitutional, and only favorable rulings by the Supreme Court in June 2012 and 2015 preserved it.

The 2010 midterm congressional campaigns were dominated by the emergence of a new *Tea Party*   social movement—the Tea Party movement, a vigorous conservative effort to reduce the national debt, lower taxes, and limit the role of government. This broad movement attracted mostly white men and women, largely from the middle class. It viewed

Obama and his peers as dangerous enemies to a stronger, more prosperous America. It helped send a large majority of anti-Obama Republicans to the House and reduced the majority of Democrats in the Senate. For the next two years, President Obama struggled to get proposals passed by Congress because nearly every Republican summarily rejected them.

In September 2011, another movement emerged—Occupy Wall Street *Occupy Wall Street* (OWS). But this movement preached a radically different agenda than the Tea Party movement. Significantly smaller and younger than the Tea Party, OWS argued for stricter financial regulation, progressive taxation, stronger support for unions, more resources to reduce unemployment, assaults on economic inequality, and the end of what it believed were unnecessary and failed wars. Its rallying cry was "We are the 99%," referring to the growing gap of income equality between the richest 1 percent and the rest of Americans. They symbolically demonstrated their grievances by camping in Zuccotti Park in the Wall Street area of lower Manhattan. Soon after, similar demonstrations took place in many other places in the United States and around the world. OWS, never a broad-based popular movement, quickly lost steam and was largely extinguished by 2013. Yet it served as an emblem of popular concern over the unsteady recent history of the economy and the ability of politicians to solve crises in general.

Obama and the Challenge of Governing

The election of 2014—the most expensive campaign in history—pitted President Obama against Mitt Romney, a former governor of Massachusetts. The campaign was not only expensive but also raucous and at times quite angry. As election day neared, the presidential debates in October became the most important part of the campaign. In the first debate, most viewers saw President Obama as tired and uninterested—a stigma that gave Romney a significant boost in the polls. But in the next two, a more energetic and commanding Obama captured support and slowly built a lead.

Still, the race was up in the air until the very end. The polls showed Obama with a persistent lead during the final weeks of the campaign, but only a razor-thin one. Enormous amounts of campaign money and effort flooded into the few states that were still up for grabs—among them Ohio, Virginia, Florida, Wisconsin, Iowa, and New Hampshire. On election night, it became clear that these states had tilted toward Obama in the last few days. He won all of them. His victory was close in popular votes, but his electoral college votes gave him a large lead with 332 votes. The Democrats also won several new senators, giving the party a majority. The House of Representatives remained Republican, but the majority was now smaller.

The political gridlock of Obama's presidency continued after his reelection. Many of his initiatives faced serious obstacles or simply did not come to pass. A major disappointment for Obama and his supporters involved the failure to enact meaningful gun control measures despite a series of horrific shootings occurring during his *Sandy Hook Shooting* terms in office, including the shooting of twenty children and six adults at the Sandy Hook Elementary School in Newtown, Connecticut, on December 14, 2012. Despite the president's promise to exert "whatever power this office holds" to generate such gun control reform, the Congress resisted enacting any such legislation. The National Rifle Association and the conservative wing of the Republican Party successfully warded off any change on the federal level of the right of Americans to buy and use guns.

The gridlock of the House also dashed any hopes President Obama had of gaining a deal on immigration. After his second inaugural, Obama and his strategists hoped to cement their gains among the Latino population revealed in the general election. Many Republicans, as well, believed that their party should reach out to this growing sector of the population by pushing through an immigration reform bill. On June 27, 2013, the Senate, in a rare show of bipartisanship, passed the Border Security, Economic Opportunity, and Immigration Modernization Act of 2013 as a comprehensive package of provisions, including a path to U.S. citizenship for illegal immigrants already in the country. But powerful conservative Republican opposition in the House, based largely on the idea that illegal immigrants should not be granted citizenship, doomed the bill and it died in Congress. Obama responded by issuing an executive order, through which he sought to implement many of the provisions of the bill over the howls of protest from House Republicans. A federal judge eventually intervened in December 2014, ruling that the president's actions were unconstitutional. This decision, along with lawsuits filed by individual states, has effectively killed the reform, at least for the immediate future.

The fate of the immigration bill embodied the challenge of governing in the early twenty-first century. President Obama had whipped up popular support for a bill tackling a pressing social issue and rallied the Senate to pass it—only to see it twist in the wind of partisan debate in the House and eventually die there. As Clinton and Bush had before him, Obama confronted the painful realities of political leadership in modern America, where fealty to political ideology often trumped any desire to compromise with a member of the opposite party or even with those in the same party.

SCIENCE AND TECHNOLOGY IN THE NEW ECONOMY

The last three decades have seen remarkable changes in American life—some a result of the end of the Cold War, some the changing character of the American population, and some a product of a rapidly evolving culture. But most of these changes were at least in part a product of the dramatic transformation of American trade and industry. Indeed, this "new economy" represented a profound shift in the nation's financial history. Throughout much of the twentieth century, manufacturing had powered the nation's economy. Making cars, rubber, steel, and airplanes, for example, had provided many workers with steady jobs and decent wages and benefits as well as entry into the middle class. But in the face of the sluggish growth and persistent inflation of the last decades of the 1900s, many American corporations began making drastic changes in the way they ran their businesses. They invested heavily in new technology to make themselves more efficient and productive and, more significantly, aggressively reduced their labor costs, which were among the highest in the world and which many economists and business leaders believed had made the United States uncompetitive against the emerging economies that relied on low-wage workers. Businesses now took a much harder line against unions. And nonunion companies became more successful in staving off unionization drives. Some companies actually moved their operations to areas of the country where unions were weak and wages low—the American South and Midwest in particular. Others simply relocated much of their production out of the United States, to such nations as Mexico and China, where there were large available pools of unorganized cheap labor.

At the same time, the digital revolution took hold. The rapid development of the personal computer and the Internet profoundly reshaped how companies operated and organized themselves, rewarding in particular college-educated workers skilled in software design and application. It also redefined how people communicated, worked, shopped, and spent their free time.

THE DIGITAL REVOLUTION

The dramatic growth in the use of computers and other digital devices was among the most significant innovations of the late twentieth century. The development of the micro-processor, first introduced in 1971 by Intel, represented a notable advance in the technology of integrated circuitry. A microprocessor miniaturized the central processing unit (CPU) of a computer, making it possible for a small machine to perform calculations that in the past only very large machines could do. Considerable technological innovation was needed before the microprocessor could actually become the basis of what was first known as a "minicomputer" and later a personal computer or "PC." In 1977, Apple launched its Apple II personal computer, the first such machine to be widely available to the public. Several years later, International Business Machines (IBM) entered the personal computer market with the first PC. So that it could focus its internal resources on developing computer hardware, IBM had engaged a small software development company, Microsoft, to design an operating system for its new computer. No PC could operate without it. The PC, and its software, made its debut in August 1981 and immediately became enormously successful. Three years later, Apple introduced its Macintosh computer. For a time, Apple could not match IBM's marketing power. By the late-1980s, the PC had established its dominance in the booming personal computer market, but IBM was replaced by Microsoft as the dominant computer company in the world. The computer revolution created thousands of new, lucrative businesses: computer manufacturers themselves, makers of the tiny silicon chips that ran the computers, and makers of software.

THE INTERNET

Out of the computer revolution emerged another dramatic source of information and communication: the Internet—a vast, geographically far-flung network of computers that allows people to communicate with others all over the world. It had its beginning in 1963, in the U.S. government's Advanced Research Projects Agency (ARPA), which funneled federal funds into scientific research projects. In the early 1960s, J. C. R. Licklider, the head of ARPA's Information Processing Techniques Office, launched a program to link together computers over large distances. It was known as ARPANET. For several years, ARPANET served mainly as a way for groups of people to exchange information and collaborate with one another through the remote use of a small handful of computer networking facilities. Gradually, however, both the size and the uses of the network expanded.

Two new important technologies made ARPANET's expansion possible. The first was a system for transmitting large quantities of data in "packets" that took advantage of ARPANET's indirect structure. The second was the development of the Transmission Control Protocol/Internet Protocol (TCP/IP), which not only provided a way to deliver addresses to machines and networks but also provided protection against lost data packets on the network.

By 1971, ARPANET linked twenty-three computers, which served mostly research labs and universities. Gradually, interest in the system began to spread and the number of devices connected to it grew. In the early 1980s, the Defense Department, an early partner in the development of ARPANET, withdrew from the project for security reasons. The network, soon renamed the Internet, was then free to develop independently. In 1989, Tim Berners-Lee, a British scientist working at a laboratory in Geneva, introduced the World Wide Web, which helped establish an orderly system for both the distribution and retrieval of electronic information over the Internet. By 2012, there were well over a

TWENTY-FOUR-HOUR NEWS CYCLE The digital revolution has contributed to a vast change in the reporting of news events and political commentary. Politicians now have much less control over how their messages are transmitted and received. (© Ian Dagnall/Alamy)

billion computers in use in the world (and many more now-obsolete ones). Virtually all of them are connected to the Internet.

The development of the Internet, along with the emergence of the computer industry and digital technology, made possible an enormous range of new products and services that quickly became central to economic life: digital music, video, and cameras; iPods, smartphones, and tablets; and Facebook, Instagram, YouTube, and Vine. These modern industries employed hundreds of thousands of people (many of them from outside the United States) and created new consumer needs and appetites.

BREAKTHROUGHS IN GENETICS

Computers helped create new scientific breakthroughs in genetics. Early discoveries in genetics by Gregor Mendel, Thomas Hunt Morgan, and others laid the groundwork for more dramatic breakthroughs—the discovery of DNA by the British scientists Oswald Avery, Colin MacLeod, and Maclyn McCarty in 1944; and in 1953, the dramatic discovery by the American biochemist James Watson and the British biophysicist Francis Crick of the double-helix structure of DNA, and thus of the key to identifying genetic codes. From these discoveries emerged the new science—and, ultimately, the new industry—of genetic engineering, through which new medical treatments and new techniques for hybridization of plants and animals have already become possible.

Scientists began to identify specific genes in humans and other living things. But the identification of genes was painfully slow; and in 1989, in an effort to accelerate the process, the federal government appropriated $3 billion to fund the National Center for *Human Genome Project*   the Human Genome. The Human Genome Project formally began its mission to identify and classify all of the more than 100,000 genes in 1990 and declared its work complete in 2003.

But genetic research was (and continues to be) a source of great controversy. Many people feared that the new science might alter aspects of human life that previously seemed beyond human control. Some critics opposed genetic research on religious grounds, seeing it as an interference with "God's plan" for human nature. Still others complained that it equipped humans with immoral powers such that, for example, parents could "design" their children and "order" certain desirable traits. And a particularly heated controversy emerged over the ways in which scientists obtained genetic material. One of the most promising sources of genetic research comes from stem cell material from human embryos, but the research deeply offends those who believe that the embryo is an early-aged human life deserving of protection from harm. In 2001, President Bush issued an executive order banning federal funding of research using new sources of human stem cells. President Obama reversed the order in 2009.

A CHANGING SOCIETY

The American population changed dramatically in the late twentieth and early twenty-first centuries. It grew larger, older, and more racially and ethnically diverse. It debated the success and scope of earlier landmark events, such as the civil rights movement and the right to an abortion. At the same time, the nation's citizenry confronted powerful new challenges, such as the spread of AIDS, the debate over gay rights and same-sex marriage, and the prospect of dwindling natural resources.

A SHIFTING POPULATION

Decreasing birthrates and growing life spans contributed to one of the most important characteristics of the American population in the early twenty-first century: its increasing agedness. The enormous "Baby-Boom" generation—people born in the first ten years after World War II—drove the median age steadily upward (from 34 in 1996 to 37 in 2011 to a projected 39 by 2035). It had important implications for the workforce. In the last twenty years of the twentieth century, the number of people aged 25–54 (known statistically as the prime workforce) grew by over 26 million. In the first ten years of the twenty-first century, the number of American-born workers in that age group did not grow at all. This combination of fewer Americans working and more of them retired put enormous stress on the Social Security and Medicare systems to continue to fulfill their financial obligations.

The slowing growth of the native-born population, and the workforce shortages it helped create, was one reason for the rapid growth of immigration. In 2011, the number of foreign-born residents of the United States was the highest in American history—more than 40 million people. These immigrants came from a wider variety of backgrounds than ever before, as a result of the 1965 Immigration Reform Act, which eliminated national origins as a criterion for admission. The growing presence of the foreign-born contributed to a significant drop in the percentage of white residents in the United States—from 90 percent in 1965 to 80 percent in 2008. (Relative to the overall population, non-Hispanic whites constituted just over 65 percent.) Latinos and Asians were by far the largest groups of immigrants in these years. But others came in significant numbers from Africa, the Middle East, Russia, and eastern Europe.

AFRICAN AMERICANS IN THE POST–CIVIL RIGHTS ERA

The civil rights movement and other liberal efforts of the 1960s had two very different effects on African Americans. On one hand, they increased opportunities for advancement to those in a position to take advantage of them. And they helped make possible the election of the first black American to the White House, an event unthinkable to all but

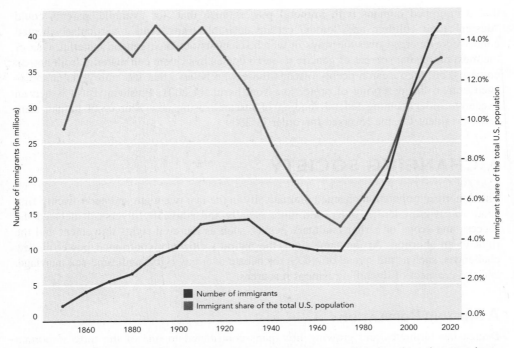

U.S. IMMIGRANT POPULATION AND SHARE OVER TIME, 1850–PRESENT This chart shows the tremendous increase in immigration to the United States in the decades since the Immigration Reform Act of 1965. • *At what point since 1850 was the immigrant share of the total U.S. population highest? When was the last time that the immigrant share was at its current level?* (Source of data: Migration Policy Institute and U.S. Census Bureau.)

the most optimistic freedom fighter during the King years. On the other hand, as the industrial economy declined and government services dwindled, there was a growing sense of helplessness and despair among large groups of poor nonwhites who continued to find themselves barred from upward mobility.

By the early twenty-first century, the black middle class constituted over half of the African *Growth of Black Middle Class* American population; progress was remarkable in the decades after the high point of the civil rights movement. Disparities between black and white professionals did not vanish, but they diminished substantially. African American families moved into more affluent urban communities and, in many cases, into suburbs—at times as neighbors of whites, more often into predominantly black communities. The percentage of black high school graduates going on to college was virtually the same as that of white high school graduates by the early twenty-first century (although a smaller proportion of blacks than whites managed to complete high school). And African Americans were making rapid strides in many professions. A generation earlier, they had been barred from many jobs because of segregation. Over half of all employed African Americans in the United States had skilled white-collar jobs in 2010. There were few areas of American life from which blacks were any longer entirely excluded.

But the rise of the black middle class also accentuated the increasingly desperate plight of less fortunate African Americans. Economic growth and the activist programs of the 1960s and beyond had never reached them. A third of the nation's black population was categorized as impoverished, often described as the "underclass." As more successful *Plight of Impoverished People* blacks moved out of the inner cities, the poor were left behind in their decaying neighborhoods. Less than half of young inner-city blacks finished high school in 2010; more than 60 percent were unemployed. The black family structure changed as well from the dislocations of urban poverty. There was a radical increase in the number of single-parent, female-headed black households. In 1970, 59 percent of all black children under eighteen years old lived with both their parents (already down from 70 percent a decade earlier). In 2010, only 35 percent of black children lived in such households, compared to 77 percent of non-Hispanic white children.

Nonwhites were also disadvantaged by many other factors in the changing social and economic climate of the late twentieth and early twenty-first centuries. Among them was Clinton's revision of federal welfare policies and a growing impatience with affirmative action. There was also a steady decline in the number of unskilled jobs in the economy. Not surprisingly, then, many blacks openly questioned the long-term successes of the civil rights movement. A steady rise in the rate of the incarceration of young black men prompted calls for better schools and intervention programs as well as a review of the justice system as a whole. Signs of popular despair surfaced during moments of racial tension, especially after the use of questionable policing tactics left black men dead, as in the case of Eric Garner in New York City in July 2014 and eighteen-year-old Michael Brown in Ferguson, Missouri, in August 2014. In these highly publicized cases, hundreds of blacks took to the streets, demanding fairer treatment by local police and decrying a lack of racial respect between Americans of different colors.

THE ABORTION DEBATE

Among the principal goals of the growing power of conservatism as it became more assertive in the late twentieth century was a challenge to feminism and its achievements. Leaders of the New Right had campaigned successfully against the proposed Equal Rights Amendment to the Constitution. And they played a central role in the most divisive issue of the late 1980s and 1990s: abortion rights.

For women who choose to terminate unwanted pregnancies, the Supreme Court's decision in *Roe v. Wade* (1973) had seemed to settle the question. By the 1980s, abortion was the most commonly performed surgical procedure in the country. But at the same time, critics of abortion began to build a powerful grassroots movement. The "right-to-life" or "pro-life" movement, as it called itself, found its most fervent supporters among Catholics; and *Right-to-Life Movement* indeed, the Catholic Church itself lent its institutional authority to the battle against legalized abortion. Religious doctrine also motivated the anti-abortion stance of Mormons, evangelical Christians, and other groups. The opposition of other anti-abortion activists had less to do with religion than with their commitment to traditional notions of family and gender relations. To them, abortion was a particularly offensive part of a much larger assault by feminists on the role of women as wives and mothers. It was also, many foes contended, a form of murder. Fetuses, they claimed, were human beings who had a "right to life" from the moment of conception.

Although the right-to-life movement was persistent in its demand for a reversal of *Roe v. Wade* or, barring that, a constitutional amendment banning abortion, it also attacked abortion in more-limited ways and at its most vulnerable points. Starting in the late 1970s, Congress and many state legislatures began barring the use of public funds to pay for abortions, thereby making them almost inaccessible for many poor women in some states. The Reagan and the two Bush administrations imposed further restrictions on federal funding and even on the right of doctors in federally funded clinics to give patients any information on abortion. Extremists in the right-to-life movement began picketing, occupying, and at rare times even bombing abortion clinics. Several anti-abortion activists murdered doctors who performed abortions; others subjected physicians to campaigns of terrorism and harassment. The shifting composition of the Supreme Court between 1981 and 2010 (during which time new conservative justices were appointed to the Court) renewed the right-to-life movement's hopes for a reversal of *Roe v. Wade*.

The changing judicial climate of the late twentieth and early twenty-first centuries mobilized defenders of abortion as never before. They called themselves the "pro-choice" *Pro-Choice Movement* movement because they were defending not so much abortion itself as every woman's right to choose whether and when to bear a child. The pro-choice movement was in many parts of the country at least as strong as, and in some areas much stronger than, the right-to-life movement.

With the election of President Clinton in 1992, a vocal supporter of "choice," the immediate threat to *Roe v. Wade* faded. Clinton's reelection in 1996 was evidence that the pro-choice movement maintained considerable political strength. But abortion rights remained highly vulnerable. Clinton's successor, George W. Bush, openly opposed abortion. Whereas Clinton had refused to sign the Partial-Birth Abortion Ban Act, Bush, to great fanfare, inked it into law in 2003. The legislation forbade physicians from performing a medical procedure called "intact dilation and extraction." The Supreme Court upheld the constitutionality of the law in *Gonzales v. Carhart* in 2007. Barack Obama supported the right to abortion when he became president, but judicial struggles over whether and to what extent society has an obligation to protect it continued. In 2007, the state of Massachusetts amended its Reproductive Health Facility Act (originally passed in 2003) to create a 35-foot buffer zone around reproductive centers that offered abortions. Its intent was to provide patients entering an abortion clinic a greater measure of safety and relief from confrontational protesters. The Supreme Court, however, declared this law unconstitutional in 2014. In *McCullen v. Coakley*, *McCullen v. Coakley* the Court ruled that the 35-foot protective zone violated the right of abortion opponents to protest peacefully and unfairly limited their free speech.

AIDS AND MODERN AMERICA

Two new and deadly epidemics ravaged many American communities beginning in the 1980s. One was a dramatic increase in drug use, which penetrated nearly every community in the nation. The enormous demand for drugs, and particularly for "crack" cocaine in the late 1980s and early 1990s, spawned what was in effect a multibillion-dollar industry. Drug use declined significantly among middle-class people beginning in the late 1980s, largely because of educational campaigns, but the epidemic declined much more slowly in the poor urban neighborhoods, where it was doing the most severe damage.

The drug epidemic was related to another scourge of the late twentieth and early twenty-first centuries: the rapid spread of a new and lethal disease first documented in 1981 and soon named AIDS (acquired immune deficiency syndrome). AIDS is the product of the human immunodeficiency virus (HIV), which is transmitted by the exchange of bodily fluids (blood or semen). The virus gradually destroys the body's immune system and makes its victims highly vulnerable to a number of diseases (particularly to various forms of cancer and pneumonia) to which they would otherwise have a natural resistance. During the early history of the disease, those infected with the virus (that is, those who identified as "HIV-positive") and became ill were almost certain to die. The first American victims of AIDS (and for many years the group among whom cases remained the most numerous) were gay men. But by the late 1980s, as the gay community began to implement aggressive education and intervention programs, the most rapid increase in the spread of the disease occurred among heterosexuals, many of them intravenous drug users who spread the virus by sharing contaminated hypodermic needles.

In the mid-1990s, AIDS researchers, after years of frustration, finally began discovering effective treatments for the disease. By taking a combination of powerful drugs on a rigorous schedule, among them a group known as protease inhibitors, even people with advanced cases of AIDS experienced dramatic improvement—so much so that in many cases there were no measurable quantities of the virus left in their bloodstreams. Currently a diagnosis of AIDS is not the near-certain death sentence it was in the late nineties; rather, new medication regimes permit those living with AIDS to successfully manage the disease and live mostly normal lives. Every president has steadily increased federal funding for AIDS research and education and for the care of individuals living with AIDS, both domestically and abroad. President George W. Bush provided $15 billion to fight AIDS in Africa, where the epidemic was rampant and the poor had little access to drugs. In the budget for 2015, President Obama has called for $30.4 billion to combat AIDS.

The Centers for Disease Control and Prevention (CDC) estimates that 1.3 million Americans currently suffer from AIDS, nearly one in seven not even realizing that they are infected. But the United States represents only a tiny proportion of the worldwide total of people afflicted with HIV, an estimated 35 million people. Over two-thirds of those cases are concentrated in Africa.

Gay Americans and Same-Sex Marriage

In the late twentieth century, inspired in part by the success of AIDS activists in winning political support and funding, many gay men and lesbians began to lobby for greater protections under the law, particularly the right to marry. Until the 1990s, the issue of same-sex marriage was not a national political issue. But in 1993, Hawaii's Supreme Court ruled in *Baehr v. Lewin* that the state needed a compelling reason to bar same-sex marriage. In response, Congress easily passed the Defense of Marriage Act (DOMA) in 1996   *DOMA* with rare bipartisan support. President Clinton signed it into law. DOMA exempted states from being required to recognize same-sex marriages from other states. It also defined marriage as being between a man and a woman and denied same-sex married couples the ability to be classified as "spouses" for federal purposes, such as the filing of joint tax returns, Social Security survivor benefit claims, adoption papers, and immigration applications. Gay rights activists identified more than 1,000 protections and responsibilities of marriage denied them by DOMA. Thirty states quickly followed suit with similar laws.

Almost immediately, gay men and lesbians and their supporters took to the courts in protest. They typically argued that DOMA and related state laws violated the Equal Protection Clause of the Fourteenth Amendment of the U.S. Constitution. They gained many victories. By 2013, eleven states had passed new legislation making same-sex marriage legal. That year as well the U.S. Supreme Court struck down the section of DOMA defining marriage as being between two people of the opposite sex, so that all married couples living in states where same-sex marriage is legal are classified as spouses by the federal government. The tide against same-sex marriage appeared to be turning. By early 2015, state and federal courts had overturned legal barriers to same-sex marriage in twenty-six states. Finally, on June 26, 2015, the Supreme Court, in a close 5-4 decision, ruled that the ability of same-sex couples to marry was a right guaranteed by the Constitution. Writing for the majority, Justice Anthony Kennedy proclaimed that "No longer may this liberty be denied."

Driving the radical change in the legal status of same-sex marriage, in addition to the guidance and political savvy of its advocates, was a profound shift in public opinion about the issue. Indeed, broad popular support for same-sex marriage grew steadily since the

SAME-SEX MARRIAGE, 2015

The debate over the right of people of the same sex to marry legally and enjoy the full range of benefits accorded to married couples under federal and state law hit a fever pitch in early January 2015.

Nearly four years earlier, Cari Searcy and Kimberly McKeand, a same-sex couple who were legally married in California under that state's laws, wanted Searcy to be able to adopt McKeand's eight-year-old biological son, under a provision of Alabama's adoption code that allows a person to adopt her "spouse's child." But Searcy's petition was denied in December 2011 based on the Alabama Sanctity of Marriage Amendment and the closely related Alabama Marriage Protection Act. Both laws declared that "Marriage is inherently a unique relationship between a man and a woman," that "No marriage license shall be issued in the State of Alabama to parties of the same sex," and that "The State of Alabama shall not recognize as valid any marriage of parties of the same sex that occurred or was alleged to have occurred as a result of the law of any jurisdiction regardless of whether a marriage license was issued." Therefore, because Alabama does not recognize the legality of same-sex plaintiffs' marriage, Searcy failed to qualify as a "spouse" for adoption purposes. Searcy appealed the denial of her adoption petition to the Alabama Court of Civil Appeals, which ruled against her and affirmed the decision of the probate court.

In federal court, Searcy sued the attorney general of Alabama, Luther Strange, and sought to declare these two Alabama state laws unconstitutional on the grounds that they violated the due-process clause and equal protection clause of the Fourteenth Amendment. Callie Granade, a federal judge for the U.S. District Court in Alabama (Southern Division), agreed in January 2015. She ordered the state to begin to issue marriage licenses to same-sex couples immediately, though the order was delayed while Attorney General Strange appealed to the U.S. Supreme Court for a stay. But once the High Court refused to hear the case, on February 9, Granade's order took effect. Some counties obliged, but others didn't, heeding the encouragement of Alabama's Supreme Court justice, Roy Moore, to ignore the federal ruling. Then, in March 2015, the state's Supreme Court ruled 7 to 1 that all probate justices (county officials officially charged with the management of marriage licenses) must cease issuing marriage licenses to same-sex couples. In June, the U.S. Supreme Court ruled that gay marriage bans such as Alabama's were unconstitutional.

In the following excerpt from Judge Granade's ruling, she clarifies why she ruled in favor of same-sex marriage.

Defendant contends that Alabama has a legitimate interest in protecting the ties between children and their biological parents and other biological kin. However, the Court finds that the laws in question are not narrowly tailored to fulfill the reported interest. The Attorney General does not explain how allowing or recognizing same-sex marriage between two consenting adults will prevent heterosexual parents or other biological kin from caring for their biological children. He proffers no justification for why it is that the provisions in question single out same-sex couples and prohibit them, and them alone, from marrying in order to meet that goal. Alabama does not exclude from marriage any other couples who are either unwilling or unable to biologically procreate. There is no law prohibiting infertile couples, elderly couples, or couples who do not wish to procreate from marrying. Nor does the state prohibit recognition of marriages between such couples from other states. The attorney general fails to demonstrate any rational, much less compelling, link between its prohibition and non-recognition of same-sex marriage and its goal of having more children raised in the biological family structure the state wishes to promote. There has been no evidence presented that these marriage laws have any effect on the choices of couples to have or raise children, whether they are same-sex couples or opposite-sex couples. In sum, the laws in question are an irrational way of promoting biological relationships in Alabama. . . .

If anything, Alabama's prohibition of same-sex marriage detracts from its goal of promoting optimal environments for children. Those children currently being raised by same-sex parents in Alabama are just as worthy of protection and recognition by the State as are the children being raised by opposite-sex parents. Yet Alabama's Sanctity laws harms the children of same-sex couples for the same reasons that the [U.S.] Supreme Court found that the Defense of Marriage Act harmed the children of same-sex couples. Such a law "humiliates . . . thousands of children now being raised by same-sex couples. The law in question makes it even more difficult for the children to understand the integrity and closeness of their own family and its concord with other families in their community and in their daily lives." [Windsor, 133 S. Ct. at 2694] Alabama's prohibition and non-recognition of same-sex marriage "also brings financial harm to children of same-sex couples," [id at 2695] because it denies the families of these children a panoply of benefits that the State

and the federal government offer to families who are legally wed. Additionally, these laws further injures those children of all couples who are themselves gay or lesbian, and who will grow up knowing that Alabama does not believe they are as capable of creating a family as their heterosexual friends.

For all of these reasons, the court finds that Alabama's marriage laws violate the Due Process Clause and Equal Protection Clause of the Fourteenth Amendment to the United States Constitution.

UNDERSTAND, ANALYZE, & EVALUATE

1. How does Judge Granade's ruling reflect—or not reflect—changing popular attitudes toward gay men and lesbians?

2. How is the definition of a "family" being redefined?

3. In what ways do the actions of Judge Roy Moore and the Alabama Supreme Court evoke tensions between the state and civil rights protesters of the 1950s and 1960s? Or are the civil rights of black Americans and gay and lesbian Americans two very different issues?

4. In his dissenting opinion in *Obergefell v. Hodges,* Supreme Court Justice John Roberts said, "The fundamental right to marry does not include a right to make a state change its definition of marriage." What does the decision in *Searcy v. Strange* have to say about the state's definition of marriage?

Source: *Searcy v. Strange*, Civil Action No. 14-0208-CG-N (S.D. Ala. Jan. 25, 2015), https://scholar.google.com/scholar_case?case=14084561318965877067&hl=en&as_sdt=6&as_vis=1&oi=scholarr (accessed March 19, 2015).

end of the twentieth century, primarily among younger generations of Americans. Still, there was no national consensus about the legality of same-sex marriage, and many southern and midwestern states had laws on the books preventing same-sex marriage or were engaged in heated legal battles over it. For example, in January 2015 in Alabama, a federal judge ruled in favor of same-sex marriage. (See "Consider the Source: Same-Sex Marriage, 2015.") But less than two months later, Alabama's Supreme Court, by a vote of 7 to 1, forbade county officials from issuing a marriage license to any same-sex couple. Ultimately the decision by the U.S. Supreme Court broke the legal stalement and compelled Alabama (and all states with gay marriage bans) to issue the licenses.

THE GLOBAL ENVIRONMENTAL MOVEMENT

An international movement for well over a century, environmentalism has grown rapidly throughout the world in the late twentieth and early twenty-first centuries. What began as a series of localized efforts to preserve wilderness sites and to clean up air and water has evolved into a broad effort to deal with concerns that affect, and threaten, the entire globe.

During the 1960s, 1970s, and 1980s, while long-standing American environmental associations such as the Wilderness Society, the Sierra Club, and the National Audubon Society were being rejuvenated, organizations elsewhere in the world sought to create an international environmental movement. The World Wildlife Fund (WWF), created in Switzerland in 1961, eventually attracted more than 5 million supporters in over 150 countries and now claims to be the world's largest independent conservation organization. Greenpeace was founded in Canada in 1971 to oppose U.S. nuclear testing off the coast of Alaska. It, too, has grown into an international organization, with 2.8 million financial supporters worldwide and a presence in forty nations.

Nongovernmental organizations (NGOs) such as Greenpeace and WWF were not the only institutions to recognize environmental concerns. In June 1972, the United Nations (UN) held its first Conference on the Human Environment in Stockholm, Sweden. Representatives of 113 countries attended the conference to discuss issues of global environmental importance—including the role of chlorofluorocarbons (CFCs), a chemical compound used in refrigerants and aerosol sprays, in depleting the ozone layer. After the conference, the UN created the United Nations Environment Programme (UNEP) to help coordinate international efforts for environmentalism and encourage sustainable development in poorer nations around the world.

The world's first "Green" parties—political parties explicitly devoted to environmental concerns (and often to other issues of social justice)—appeared in 1972, beginning in New Zealand (the Values Party) and Tasmania (the United Tasmania Group). Since then, Green parties have proliferated throughout the world, including in the United States. The most powerful Green party to date has been *Die Grünen* in Germany, founded in 1980. *Die Grünen* allied with the Social Democratic Party in a governing coalition from 1998, and in 2000, this coalition successfully passed the Nuclear Exit Law, which set a timetable of twenty years for Germany's eventual abandonment of nuclear power and a switch to renewable energy.

Large-scale ecological catastrophes have often helped galvanize the global environmental movement. Among the more significant of these events was the Bhopal disaster of 1984, in which a gas leak at a Union Carbide pesticide plant in Bhopal, India, resulted in the deaths of between 3,000 and 15,000 people. Two years later, a nuclear reactor accident in the Soviet city of Chernobyl, in Ukraine, caused fifty-six direct deaths, with predictions of many thousands more deaths to follow as a result of exposure. The area around Chernobyl itself is expected to be partially contaminated for 24,000 years, the radioactive half-life of plutonium-239. A less catastrophic nuclear accident at Three Mile Island, Pennsylvania, in 1979 heightened antinuclear sentiment in the United

States. In 1989, the oil tanker *Exxon Valdez* ran aground on Bligh Reef in Prince William Sound, Alaska, and spilled approximately 10.9 million gallons of crude oil. Eventually covering thousands of square miles of ocean water (and 1,300 miles of Alaska shoreline) in oil, the spill killed hundreds of thousands of animals instantly and devastated the fragile ecosystem of the sound. The 2010 explosion of the Deepwater Horizon well about 50 miles southeast of the Mississippi Delta caused the largest marine oil spill in history.

In developed, industrialized nations, environmental advocacy has largely focused on energy policy, conservation, clean technologies, and changing individual and social attitudes about consumption (as in the recycling movement). The growth of environmentalism is often linked to issues of human and democratic rights and freedom from First World exploitation. For example, the Green Belt Movement in Kenya, begun in 1977 by Wangari Maathai, encouraged Kenyan women to plant over 30 million trees across the nation to address the challenges of deforestation, soil erosion, and lack of water. The Green Belt Movement became an important human rights and women's rights organization, focused on reducing poverty and promoting peaceful democratic change through environmental conservation and protection. Maathai won the 2004 Nobel Peace Prize for her achievements.

Over the past two decades, the environmental movement has grown even more global in scope, with multilateral environmental treaties and worldwide summits becoming the principal strategies of advocates. In 1997, an international effort to reduce global warming by mandating the lowering of greenhouse gas emissions culminated in the Kyoto Protocol (which the United States did not join). While the George W. Bush administration rejected most efforts to limit carbon emissions, other leading Americans helped bring the issue of global warming to wide attention both in the United States and around the world. Perhaps most notable has been former vice president Al Gore, whose 2006 film *An Inconvenient Truth* may have done more to raise awareness of the threat of global warming than any other recent event—both in the United States and in many other nations. As a result of his efforts, Gore won the 2007 Nobel Peace Prize—an honor he shared with others, appropriately, given the global character of the movement he has championed. His cowinner was the Intergovernmental Panel on Climate Change, launched in Switzerland in 1988 and affiliated with the United Nations. •

UNDERSTAND, ANALYZE, & EVALUATE

1. Why are environmental movements in developing nations often linked to issues of human rights and protection from exploitation by developed nations? How do developed nations threaten the environment of developing nations?

2. What is the current status of UN initiatives to reduce carbon omissions, such as the Kyoto Protocol?

The Contemporary Environmental Movement

The environmental movement in the United States continued to expand in the decades after the 1980s. It drew inspiration from the older international environmental movement, which organized in the 1960s and steadily grew in political power. (See "America in the World: The Global Environmental Movement.") After the first Earth Day, domestic environmental issues gained increasing attention and support. Although the federal government displayed only intermittent interest in the subject, environmentalists won a series of significant battles, mostly at the local level. They blocked the construction of roads, airports, and other projects that they claimed would be ecologically dangerous, taking advantage of new legislation protecting endangered species and environmentally fragile regions.

In the late 1980s, the environmental movement began to mobilize around a new and ominous challenge—"global warming." It produced a steady rise in the earth's temperature as a result of emissions from the burning of fossil fuels (most notably coal and oil). Although considerable controversy has continued for years over the pace, and even the reality, of global warming, by the early twenty-first century a growing consensus began to emerge—in part as a result of the leadership of significant public figures, such as former vice president Al Gore, who won a Nobel Peace Prize in 2007 for his efforts to draw attention to the problem. In 1997, representatives of the major industrial nations met in Kyoto, Japan, and agreed to a broad treaty establishing steps toward reducing carbon emissions and thus slowing or reversing global warming. The Clinton administration formally signed the Kyoto Protocol, but nothing came of it. Reading the hand-writing on the wall, Clinton never even submitted it for ratification because the Senate had earlier passed the Byrd-Hagel Resolution by a vote of 95 to 0 that rejected the treaty's key tenets. President George W. Bush, while proclaiming grave concern over climate concern, refused to support the Kyoto Protocol because it excluded developing countries like China and India. Since 2009, President Obama has met with mixed success on climate change issues. While major international agreements have not materialized during his presidency, the president did champion and sign legislation raising fuel efficiency in passenger cars and trucks in 2012 and has since directed the Environmental Protection Agency to regulate coal ash, a major CO_2 emitter primarily used in creating electricity, to intense political scrutiny.

Kyoto Protocol

DEEPWATER HORIZON DISASTER In 2010, a BP (British Petroleum) offshore well, Deepwater Horizon, suffered a crippling explosion that sent approximately 5 million barrels of oil into the Gulf of Mexico. This photograph shows the attempt to cap the well. The oil leaked for months, destroying local fisheries, and the effects to the environment from the oil and the dispersants used to clean it up are still unknown. The event galvanized the global environmental movement. (© Julie Dermansky/Corbis)

AMERICA IN THE WORLD

The celebration of the beginning of a new millennium on January 1, 2000, was an important moment not just because of the change in the calendar. It was notable above all as a global event—a shared and for the most part joyous experience that united the world in its exuberance. But if the millennium celebrations suggested the bright promise of an interconnected world, other events at the dawn of the new century suggested its dark perils. Indeed, the United States' increasing role as an economic and military superpower triggered fears among many Americans about a foreign policy that was too aggressive and trade initiatives that took advantage of low-wage workers in other countries and unfairly benefited large international businesses. The rise of mass protests over America's global economic policies and terrorism painfully brought home the dangers of living in the twenty-first century.

OPPOSING THE "NEW WORLD ORDER"

In the United States and other industrial nations, opposition to globalization—or to what President George H. W. Bush once called the "new world order"—took several forms. To many Americans on both the political left and right, the nation's increasingly interventionist foreign policy was deeply troubling. Critics on the left charged that the United States was using military action to advance its economic interests—in the 1991 Gulf War and, above all, in the Iraq War that began in 2003. Critics on the right criticized humanitarian interventions in Somalia in 1993 and the Balkans in the late 1990s as too costly and risky. Others complained that the United States was ceding its sovereignty to international organizations, such as United Nations–led peacekeeping missions.

Labor unions insisted that the rapid expansion of free-trade agreements led to the export of jobs from advanced nations to less developed ones. Other groups attacked working conditions in new manufacturing countries on humanitarian grounds, arguing that the global economy was creating new classes of "slave laborers" working in conditions that few Western nations would tolerate. Environmentalists argued that globalization, in exporting industry to low-wage countries, also exported industrial pollution and toxic waste into nations that had no effective laws to control them, and contributed significantly to global warming. And still others opposed global economic arrangements on the grounds that they enriched and empowered large multinational corporations and threatened the freedom and autonomy of individuals and communities.

Varied opponents of globalization found a common enemy in the multinational institutions that policed and advanced the global economy. Among them were the World Trade Organization, which monitored the enforcement of the General Agreement on Tariffs and Trade (GATT) treaties of the 1990s; the International Monetary Fund (IMF), which controlled international credit and exchange rates; and the World Bank, which made money available for development projects in many countries. In November 1999, when leaders of leading industrial nations gathered for their annual meeting in Seattle, Washington, tens of thousands protested—most of them peacefully. But some of them clashed with police, smashed store windows, and all but paralyzed the city. A few months later, a smaller but still substantial demonstration disrupted meetings of the IMF and the World Bank in Washington, D.C. And in July 2001, at a meeting of the same leaders in Genoa, Italy, an estimated 50,000 demonstrators clashed violently with police in a melee that left one protester dead and several hundred injured. The participants in the meeting responded to the demonstrations by pledging $1.2 billion to fight the AIDS epidemic in developing countries, and by deciding to hold future meetings in remote locations far from major cities.

PROTESTING THE WTO IN SEATTLE, 1999 Thousands of demonstrators rallied at the site of the 1999 World Trade Organization meeting to protest the WTO's role in the globalization of the economy and, they believed, the exploitation of working people. They succeeded in postponing the opening of the conference. In this photograph, a protester faces Seattle police in a cloud of tear gas, waiting to be arrested. (© Andy Clark/Reuters/Corbis)

DEFENDING ORTHODOXY

Outside the industrialized West, the impact of globalization sparked other controversies. Many citizens of nonindustrialized nations resented the way the world economy had left them in poverty. In their view, the developed world exploited and oppressed them. In some parts of the nonindustrialized world—particularly in some of the Islamic nations of the Middle East—the increasing reach of globalization created additional grievances, rooted not just in economics but also in religion and culture.

The Iranian Revolution of 1979, in which orthodox Muslims ousted a despotic government, was one of the first large and visible manifestations of a phenomenon that eventually reached across much of the Islamic world. It threatened the stability of the globe. Militants used isolated incidents of violence and mayhem, designed to disrupt societies and governments and to create fear among their peoples. Such tactics are known to the world as terrorism.

THE RISE OF TERRORISM

The term **terrorism** was used first during the French Revolution in the 1790s to describe the actions of radical Jacobins against the French government. It continued to be used intermittently throughout the nineteenth and early twentieth centuries to describe the use of violence as a form of intimidation against peoples and governments. But the widespread understanding of terrorism as an important fact of modern life is largely a product of the end of the twentieth century and the beginning of the twenty-first.

Acts of what came to be called terrorism have occurred in many parts of the world. Irish revolutionaries engaged in terrorism regularly against the English through much of the twentieth century. Jews used it in Palestine against the British before the creation of Israel, and Palestinians have used it frequently against Jews in Israel—particularly in the past several decades. Revolutionary groups in Italy, Germany, Japan, and France have engaged in terrorist acts intermittently over the past several decades.

The United States, too, has experienced terrorism for many years, much of it against American targets abroad—including the bombing of the Marine barracks in Beirut in 1983; the explosion that brought down an American airliner over Lockerbie, Scotland, in 1988; the bombing of American embassies in 1998; and the assault on the U.S. naval vessel *Cole* in 2000. Terrorist incidents were relatively rare,   *Terrorist Incidents before 9/11* but not unknown, within the United States itself prior to September 11, 2001. Militants on the American left performed various acts of terror in the 1960s and early 1970s. In February 1993, a bomb exploded in the parking garage of the World Trade Center in New York, killing six people and causing serious, but not irreparable, structural damage to the towers. Several men connected with militant Islamic organizations were convicted of the crime. In April 1995, a van containing explosives blew up in front of a federal building in Oklahoma City, killing 168 people. Timothy McVeigh, a former Army soldier who had become part of a militant antigovernment movement of the American right, was convicted of the crime and eventually executed in 2001.

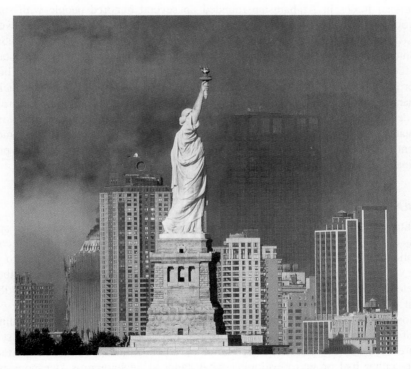

SEPTEMBER 11, 2001   A New York City symbol stands against a sky filled with the thick smoke from the destruction of another American symbol, New York City's World Trade Center towers, a few hours after terrorists crashed two planes into them. (© Daniel Hulshizer/AP Images)

Most Americans, however, considered terrorism a problem mainly confined to other nations. One of the many results of the terrible events of September 11, 2001, was to jolt the American people out of their complacency and alert them to the presence of continuing danger. Predictably, that awareness increased dramatically in the years following September 11. New security measures changed the way in which Americans traveled. New government regulations altered immigration policies and affected the character of international banking. Warnings of possible new terrorist attacks created widespread tension and uneasiness.

THE WAR ON TERROR

In the aftermath of September 11, 2001, the United States government launched what President Bush called a "war on terror." The attacks on the World Trade Center and the Pentagon, government intelligence indicated, had been planned and orchestrated by Middle Eastern agents of a powerful terrorist network known as Al Qaeda. Its leader, Osama bin Laden—until *Osama bin Laden and Al Qaeda* 2001 little known outside the Arab world—quickly became one of the most notorious figures in the world. The militant Taliban government of Afghanistan had sheltered and supported Al Qaeda previously, and most reports placed bin Laden in continued care. In 2001, NATO, led by the United States, began a sustained campaign of bombing against the regime and sent in ground troops. Afghanistan's Taliban regime quickly collapsed, and its leaders—along with the Al Qaeda fighters allied with them—fled the capital, Kabul. American and anti-Taliban Afghan troops pursued them into the mountains but failed to capture bin Laden and the other leaders of his organization.

American forces in Afghanistan rounded up several hundred people with suspected connections to the Taliban and Al Qaeda and moved these prisoners (and eventually *Guantánamo* others) to a facility at the American military base in Guantánamo, Cuba. They were among the first suspected terrorists to be handled under new standards established by the federal government in dealing with terrorism after September 11, 2001. They were held for months, and in some cases years, without access to lawyers, without facing formal charges, and were subjected to intensive interrogation, and at times torture. Many critics denounced the dangers to basic civil liberties that they believed the war on terror had created. Others argued that the new tactics were necessary to protect Americans. President Obama, in his first month in the White House, pledged to close the prison at Guantánamo. But he soon found that the promise was difficult to keep.

THE IRAQ WAR

In his State of the Union address to Congress in January 2002, President Bush spoke of an "axis of evil," which included the nations of Iraq, Iran, and North Korea—all countries with anti-American regimes that either possessed or were thought to be trying to acquire nuclear weapons. Although Bush did not say so at the time, many people around the world interpreted these words to mean that the United States would soon try to topple the government of Saddam Hussein in Iraq.

For over a year, the Bush administration slowly built a public case for invading Iraq. Much of that case rested on two claims. One was that Iraq was supporting terrorist groups that were hostile to the United States. The other, and eventually the more important, was that Iraq either had or was developing what came to be known as "weapons of mass *Weapons of Mass Destruction* destruction," which included nuclear weapons and agents of chemical and biological warfare. Less central to these arguments, at least in the United

States, was the charge that the Hussein government was responsible for major violations of human rights. Except for the last, none of these claims turned out to be accurate.

In March 2003, American troops, with support from Great Britain and several other countries and partial authorization from the United Nations, invaded Iraq and quickly toppled the Hussein regime. Hussein himself went into hiding but was eventually captured in December 2003. He was executed in Iraq on December 30, 2006. In May 2003, shortly after the American capture of Baghdad, President Bush made a dramatic appearance on an aircraft carrier off the coast of California, where he declared victory in the Battle of Iraq, praised the military and allies in the war effort, and warned, weakly, of the "difficult work to do in Iraq" while standing in front of a large sign reading "Mission Accomplished."

In the following months, however, events in Iraq suggested that the mission had only just begun. Of the more than 4,800 American soldiers killed in Iraq as of 2014, over 4,000 of them died after the "mission accomplished" speech. And despite significant efforts by the United States and its allies to hand over authority to an Iraqi government and to restore order to the country, insurgents continued to disrupt the recovery with persistent attacks and terrorist actions throughout the fragile nation.

Support for the war in the United States steadily declined in the years after the first claim of victory. The failure to find evidence of the weapons of mass destruction, whose existence the president had claimed, was a hammer blow to the war's credibility. Another blow came from reports of the torture and humiliation of Iraqi prisoners by American soldiers *Abu Ghraib* at the Abu Ghraib prison in Baghdad and other sites in Iraq and around the world.

The invasion of Iraq was the most visible evidence of a basic change in the structure of American foreign policy under the presidency of George W. Bush. Ever since the late 1940s, the containment policy had become the cornerstone of America's role in the world. The United States had worked to maintain stability in the world by containing, but not often directly threatening or attacking, its adversaries. Even after the Cold War ended, the United States continued to demonstrate a level of constraint, despite its now unchallenged military preeminence. In the administrations of George H. W. Bush and Bill Clinton, for example, American leaders worked closely with the United Nations and NATO to achieve U.S. international goals and resisted taking unilateral military action.

There had always been those who criticized these constraints. They believed that America should do more than maintain stability and should move actively to topple undemocratic regimes and destroy potential enemies of the United States. In the administration of George W. Bush, these critics took control of American foreign policy and began to reshape it. The legacy of containment was largely repudiated. Instead, the public *Bush's Foreign Policy Doctrine* stance of the American government was that the United States had the right and the responsibility to fight tyranny and spread freedom throughout the world—not just by exhortation and example but also, when necessary, by military force. In Latvia in May 2005, President Bush spoke of the decision at the end of World War II not to challenge Soviet domination of Eastern Europe. That decision had rested on the belief that such a challenge would lead the United States into another war. The controversial agreement negotiated at Yalta in 1945 by Roosevelt, Churchill, and Stalin, which failed to end the Soviet occupation of Poland and other Eastern European nations, was, the president said, part of an "unjust tradition" by which powerful governments sacrificed the interests of small nations. "This attempt to sacrifice freedom for the sake of stability," the president continued, "left a continent divided and unstable." The lesson, Bush suggested, was that the United States and other great powers should value stability less and freedom more, and should be willing to take greater risks in the world to end tyranny and oppression.

AMERICA AFTER THE IRAQ WAR

The end of the American combat role in Iraq was already under way in the last year of the Bush administration. Obama brought it to an end in 2010. At the same time, he com-

Escalation in Afghanistan   mitted significant additional troops to the war in Afghanistan, where Americans had been fighting since 2001. Obama escalated the Afghan war in 2011. For almost ten years, a major goal of American foreign policy was to find Osama bin Laden, the head of Al Qaeda, the organization behind the destruction of 9/11. In May 2011, Navy Seals found and killed bin Laden. Shortly afterward, leaders from countries of the North Atlantic Treaty Organization drafted a plan for the withdrawal of international forces from Afghanistan and facilitated peace talks between the Afghan government and the Taliban. Obama ordered nearly all American troops to leave the country and cease combat operations by the close of 2014, effectively ending American involvement in the conflict.

Despite the end of the Iraq War and the killing of bin Laden, conflict in the Middle East continued to dominate American foreign policy. Obama had appointed Hillary Clinton as his

Hillary Clinton as Secretary of State   secretary of state, and together they tried to create peace between Israel and Palestine—an effort that made little or no progress. Elsewhere they sought to improve relationships damaged by the Iraq War and to build new international trade opportunities as well. But increasing turmoil in the Middle East, and the growing power of China, created new challenges. The United States intervened in a civil war in Libya and helped end the regime of the long-standing leader Muammar Qadaffi. And in 2012, Obama and Clinton sought to stop Iran from creating nuclear weapons—an effort that remained unfinished.

DRONES Unmanned combat air vehicles (UCAVs), also known as drones, have become weapons of choice during many U.S. military engagements throughout the world. Pilots operate these vehicles from remote sites, a practice that was unimaginable when the international laws of war were last drafted in 1949. In calling for an examination of this practice, critics have cited the unintended killing of civilians in Pakistan and the targeting of three American civilians by U.S. drones in Yemen, as well as the potential for foreign governments to develop drones and follow the American precedent. (© Kirsty Wigglesworth/AP Images)

Syria, a country locked in violent civil war since 2011, experienced a new and terrifying level of bloodshed. Opponents of the Ba'ath government sought the   *Syrian Civil War* ouster of President Bashar al-Assad and his repressive regime. Assad unleashed the army in response, killing an estimated 120,000 of his own people by September 2013. The displacement of hundreds of thousands of Syrians into neighboring countries threatened to further destabilize the region. Assad's use of chemical weapons triggered a strong condemnation by the United States and its European allies. Working with Russia, a traditional ally of the Assad regime, the United States and Europe brokered a deal to remove the stockpile of chemical weapons from the country. Obama, aware of his nation's unwillingness to become involved in another ground war, resisted calls for sending troops to dislodge Assad. The violent struggle continues in 2015 with no sign of abatement in sight.

A key element in the Syrian conflict has been the rise of rebel groups committed not only to overthrowing the Assad government but also violently resisting Western backers of the ruling regime and attacking Western influence over traditional Islamic society. Most notably, ISIS (the Islamic State of Iraq and Syria), a powerful and deadly opposition force, has   *ISIS* recently embarked on campaigns of terror against Western nations, including the public execution of American and British citizens uploaded to social media websites around the world. In 2015, ISIS serves as a symbol of the persistent instability of the region and a reminder of the continuing threat of terrorism.

Turmoil in the Middle East and the threat of terrorism are not the only focal points of current American foreign policy. In a bold move that reignited memories of the Cold War, Russia, under the leadership of President Vladimir Putin, annexed the   *Vladimir Putin* Ukrainian territory of Crimea in March 2014. Putin inserted military troops to support Russian separatists and quickly established a firm grip over the local government and untrammeled access to the city and Bay of Sevastopal, home to Russia's Black Sea fleet. Ignoring a flurry of international peace initiatives and sanctions imposed by the United States, its allies, and the United Nations, Putin tightened his hold over Crimea and even implemented sanctions of his own: he eliminated most agricultural imports from countries opposing him. The relationship between Russia and America remains tense, with no resolution satisfactory to both countries over the issue of Crimea in sight. It reminds us that major conflicts between the United States and countries in central and eastern Europe did not end with the fall of the Berlin Wall or collapse of the Soviet Union but persist in the form of nations like Russia intent on aggressively expanding its sphere of international influence.

CONCLUSION

The United States in the first decade of the twenty-first century was a nation beset with many problems and anxieties. U.S. foreign policy after the attacks of September 11, 2001, had not only divided the American people but had also deeply alienated much of the world. Crises in the Middle East made it impossible to ignore the persistent threat of terrorism and extremism while conflict with Russia brought back Cold War fears of instability in eastern and central Europe. The American economy was struggling as early as 2007 and, in the fall of 2008, experienced the worst economic crisis since the Great Depression. By 2014 the economy had improved but some polls indicated a continuing sense of uncertainty about the future among many Americans. Gridlock continued at the federal level, making it difficult to achieve sweeping reform in several key areas. Political divisions—not only among politicians, but also among voters—were as great in 2015 as they had been in many years.

The United States remains the wealthiest and most powerful nation in the world, and it continues to cherish great ideals and great hopes. Moving forward into an uncertain future, Americans are burdened with serious problems and great challenges, but they are also armed with extraordinary resilience and energy that has allowed the nation—through its long and turbulent history—to endure, to flourish, and to imagine and strive for a better future.

KEY TERMS/PEOPLE/PLACES/EVENTS

Affordable Care Act 800
Afghan war 820
AIDS 808
Al Qaeda 818
Barack Obama 796
Defense of Marriage Act
  (DOMA) 809
George W. Bush 795

Great Recession
  of 2008 797
Guantánamo 818
Hillary Rodham
  Clinton 796
Human Genome
  Project 804
Iraq War 795

new world order 815
9/11 attacks 817
Occupy Wall Street
  (OWS) 801
Osama bin Laden 818
Tea Party 800
terrorism 816
Vladimir Putin 821

RECALL AND REFLECT

1. How has partisanship affected how presidents governed in the last twenty-five years?
2. How has America's relationship to the rest of the world changed as a result of the war on terror and in particular the Iraq War?
3. How did the digital revolution affect the American economy?
4. What were the key causes of the Great Recession?

APPENDIX

The Declaration of Independence
The Constitution of the United States
Presidential Elections

THE DECLARATION OF INDEPENDENCE

In Congress, July 4, 1776,

THE UNANIMOUS DECLARATION OF THE THIRTEEN UNITED STATES OF AMERICA

When, in the course of human events, it becomes necessary for one people to dissolve the political bands which have connected them with another, and to assume, among the powers of the earth, the separate and equal station to which the laws of nature and of nature's God entitle them, a decent respect to the opinions of mankind requires that they should declare the causes which impel them to the separation.

We hold these truths to be self-evident, that all men are created equal; that they are endowed by their Creator with certain unalienable rights; that among these, are life, liberty, and the pursuit of happiness. That, to secure these rights, governments are instituted among men, deriving their just powers from the consent of the governed; that, whenever any form of government becomes destructive of these ends, it is the right of the people to alter or to abolish it, and to institute a new government, laying its foundation on such principles, and organizing its powers in such form, as to them shall seem most likely to effect their safety and happiness. Prudence, indeed, will dictate that governments long established, should not be changed for light and transient causes; and, accordingly, all experience hath shown, that mankind are more disposed to suffer, while evils are sufferable, than to right themselves by abolishing the forms to which they are accustomed. But, when a long train of abuses and usurpations, pursuing invariably the same object, evinces a design to reduce them under absolute despotism, it is their right, it is their duty, to throw off such government and to provide new guards for their future security. Such has been the patient sufferance of these colonies, and such is now the necessity which constrains them to alter their former systems of government. The history of the present King of Great Britain is a history of repeated injuries and usurpations, all having, in direct object, the establishment of an absolute tyranny over these States. To prove this, let facts be submitted to a candid world:

He has refused his assent to laws the most wholesome and necessary for the public good.

He has forbidden his governors to pass laws of immediate and pressing importance, unless suspended in their operation till his assent should be obtained; and, when so suspended, he has utterly neglected to attend to them.

He has refused to pass other laws for the accommodation of large districts of people, unless those people would relinquish the right of representation in the legislature; a right inestimable to them, and formidable to tyrants only.

He has called together legislative bodies at places unusual, uncomfortable, and distant from the depository of their public records, for the sole purpose of fatiguing them into compliance with his measures.

He has dissolved representative houses repeatedly for opposing, with manly firmness, his invasions on the rights of the people.

He has refused, for a long time after such dissolutions, to cause others to be elected; whereby the legislative powers, incapable of annihilation, have returned to the people at large for their exercise; the state remaining, in the meantime, exposed to all the danger of invasion from without, and compulsions within.

He has endeavored to prevent the population of these States; for that purpose, obstructing the laws for naturalization of foreigners, refusing to pass others to encourage their migration hither, and raising the conditions of new appropriations of lands.

He has obstructed the administration of justice, by refusing his assent to laws for establishing judiciary powers.

He has made judges dependent on his will alone, for the tenure of their offices, and the amount and payment of their salaries.

He has erected a multitude of new offices, and sent hither swarms of officers to harass our people, and eat out their substance.

He has kept among us, in time of peace, standing armies, without the consent of our legislatures.

He has affected to render the military independent of, and superior to, the civil power.

He has combined, with others, to subject us to a jurisdiction foreign to our Constitution, and unacknowledged by our laws; giving his assent to their acts of pretended legislation:

For quartering large bodies of armed troops among us:

For protecting them by a mock trial, from punishment, for any murders which they should commit on the inhabitants of these States:

For cutting off our trade with all parts of the world:

For imposing taxes on us without our consent:

For depriving us, in many cases, of the benefit of trial by jury:

For transporting us beyond seas to be tried for pretended offences:

For abolishing the free system of English laws in a neighboring province, establishing therein an arbitrary government, and enlarging its boundaries, so as to render it at once an example and fit instrument for introducing the same absolute rule into these colonies:

For taking away our charters, abolishing our most valuable laws, and altering, fundamentally, the powers of our governments:

For suspending our own legislatures, and declaring themselves invested with power to legislate for us in all cases whatsoever.

He has abdicated government here, by declaring us out of his protection, and waging war against us.

He has plundered our seas, ravaged our coasts, burnt our towns, and destroyed the lives of our people.

He is, at this time, transporting large armies of foreign mercenaries to complete the works of death, desolation, and tyranny, already begun, with circumstances of cruelty and perfidy scarcely paralleled in the most barbarous ages, and totally unworthy the head of a civilized nation.

He has constrained our fellow citizens, taken captive on the high seas, to bear arms against their country, to become the executioners of their friends, and brethren, or to fall themselves by their hands.

He has excited domestic insurrections amongst us, and has endeavored to bring on the inhabitants of our frontiers, the merciless Indian savages, whose known rule of warfare is an undistinguished destruction of all ages, sexes, and conditions.

In every stage of these oppressions, we have petitioned for redress, in the most humble terms; our repeated petitions have been answered only by repeated injury. A prince, whose character is thus marked by every act which may define a tyrant, is unfit to be the ruler of a free people.

Nor have we been wanting in attention to our British brethren. We have warned them, from time to time, of attempts made by their legislature to extend an unwarrantable jurisdiction over us. We have reminded them of the circumstances of our emigration and settlement here. We have appealed to their native justice and magnanimity, and we have conjured them, by the ties of our common kindred, to disavow these usurpations, which would inevitably interrupt our connections and correspondence. They, too, have been deaf to the voice of justice and consanguinity. We must, therefore, acquiesce in the necessity which denounces our separation, and hold them as we hold the rest of mankind, enemies in war, in peace, friends.

We, therefore, the representatives of the United States of America, in general Congress assembled, appealing to the Supreme Judge of the world for the rectitude of our intentions, do, in the name, and by the authority of the good people of these colonies, solemnly publish and declare, that these united colonies are, and of right ought to be, free and independent states: that they are absolved from all allegiance to the British Crown, and that all political connection between them and the state of Great Britain is, and ought to be, totally dissolved; and that, as free and independent states, they have full power to levy war, conclude peace, contract alliances, establish commerce, and to do all other acts and things which independent states may of right do. And, for the support of this declaration, with a firm reliance on the protection of Divine Providence, we mutually pledge to each other our lives, our fortunes, and our sacred honor.

The foregoing Declaration was, by order of Congress, engrossed, and signed by the following members:

John Hancock

NEW HAMPSHIRE
Josiah Bartlett
William Whipple
Matthew Thornton

CONNECTICUT
Roger Sherman
Samuel Huntington
William Williams
Oliver Wolcott

NEW YORK
William Floyd
Philip Livingston
Francis Lewis
Lewis Morris

NEW JERSEY
Richard Stockton
John Witherspoon
Francis Hopkinson
John Hart
Abraham Clark

MASSACHUSETTS BAY
Samuel Adams
John Adams
Robert Treat Paine
Elbridge Gerry

PENNSYLVANIA
Robert Morris
Benjamin Rush
Benjamin Franklin
John Morton
George Clymer
James Smith
George Taylor
James Wilson
George Ross

DELAWARE
Caesar Rodney
George Read
Thomas M'Kean

MARYLAND
Samuel Chase
William Paca
Thomas Stone
Charles Carroll, of
  Carrollton

RHODE ISLAND
Stephen Hopkins
William Ellery

VIRGINIA
George Wythe
Richard Henry Lee
Thomas Jefferson
Benjamin Harrison
Thomas Nelson Jr.
Francis Lightfoot Lee
Carter Braxton

NORTH CAROLINA
William Hooper
Joseph Hewes
John Penn

SOUTH CAROLINA
Edward Rutledge
Thomas Heyward Jr.
Thomas Lynch Jr.
Arthur Middleton

GEORGIA
Button Gwinnett
Lyman Hall
George Walton

Resolved, That copies of the Declaration be sent to the several assemblies, conventions, and committees, or councils of safety, and to the several commanding officers of the continental troops; that it be proclaimed in each of the United States, at the head of the army.

THE CONSTITUTION
OF THE UNITED STATES[1]

We the People of the United States, in Order to form a more perfect Union, establish Justice, insure domestic Tranquility, provide for the common defence, promote the general Welfare, and secure the Blessings of Liberty to ourselves and our Posterity, do ordain and establish this CONSTITUTION for the United States of America.

Article I

Section 1.
All legislative Powers herein granted shall be vested in a Congress of the United States, which shall consist of a Senate and House of Representatives.

Section 2.
The House of Representatives shall be composed of Members chosen every second Year by the People of the several States, and the Electors in each State shall have the Qualifications requisite for Electors of the most numerous Branch of the State Legislature.

No Person shall be a Representative who shall not have attained to the Age of twenty-five Years, and been seven Years a Citizen of the United States, and who shall not, when elected, be an Inhabitant of that State in which he shall be chosen.

[Representatives and direct Taxes[2] shall be apportioned among the several States which may be included within this Union, according to their respective Numbers, which shall be determined by adding to the whole Number of free Persons, including those bound to Service for a Term of Years, and excluding Indians not taxed, three fifths of all other Persons.][3] The actual Enumeration shall be made within three Years after the first Meeting of the Congress of the United States, and within every subsequent Term of ten Years, in such Manner as they shall by Law direct. The Number of Representatives shall not exceed one for every thirty Thousand, but each State shall have at Least one Representative; and until such enumeration shall be made, the State of New Hampshire shall be entitled to chuse three, Massachusetts eight, Rhode-Island and Providence Plantations one, Connecticut five, New York six, New Jersey four, Pennsylvania eight, Delaware one, Maryland six, Virginia ten, North Carolina five, South Carolina five, and Georgia three.

When vacancies happen in the Representation from any State, the Executive Authority thereof shall issue Writs of Election to fill such Vacancies.

The House of Representatives shall chuse their Speaker and other Officers; and shall have the sole Power of Impeachment.

Section 3.
The Senate of the United States shall be composed of two Senators from each State, chosen by the Legislature thereof, for six Years; and each Senator shall have one Vote.

Immediately after they shall be assembled in Consequence of the first Election, they shall be divided as equally as may be into three Classes. The Seats of the Senators of the first

---

1 This version, which follows the original Constitution in capitalization and spelling, was published by the United States Department of the Interior, Office of Education, in 1935.
2 Altered by the Sixteenth Amendment.
3 Negated by the Fourteenth Amendment.

Class shall be vacated at the Expiration of the second Year, of the second Class at the Expiration of the fourth Year, and of the third Class at the Expiration of the sixth Year, so that one-third may be chosen every second Year; and if Vacancies happen by Resignation, or otherwise, during the Recess of the Legislature of any State, the Executive thereof may make temporary Appointments until the next Meeting of the Legislature, which shall then fill such Vacancies.

No Person shall be a Senator who shall not have attained to the Age of thirty Years, and been nine Years a Citizen of the United States, and who shall not, when elected, be an Inhabitant of that State for which he shall be chosen.

The Vice President of the United States shall be President of the Senate, but shall have no vote, unless they be equally divided.

The Senate shall chuse their other Officers, and also a President pro tempore, in the absence of the Vice President, or when he shall exercise the Office of President of the United States.

The Senate shall have the sole Power to try all Impeachments. When sitting for that purpose they shall be on Oath or Affirmation. When the President of the United States is tried, the Chief Justice shall preside: And no person shall be convicted without the Concurrence of two thirds of the Members present.

Judgment in Cases of Impeachment shall not extend further than to removal from Office, and disqualification to hold and enjoy any Office of honor, Trust, or Profit under the United States: but the Party convicted shall nevertheless be liable and subject to Indictment, Trial, Judgment, and Punishment, according to Law.

Section 4.

The Times, Places and Manner of holding Elections for Senators and Representatives, shall be prescribed in each State by the Legislature thereof; but the Congress may at any time by Law make or alter such Regulations, except as to the Places of Chusing Senators.

The Congress shall assemble at least once in every Year, and such Meeting shall be on the first Monday in December, unless they shall by Law appoint a different Day.

Section 5.

Each House shall be the Judge of the Elections, Returns and Qualifications of its own Members, and a Majority of each shall constitute a Quorum to do Business; but a smaller number may adjourn from day to day, and may be authorized to compel the Attendance of absent Members, in such Manner, and under such Penalties, as each House may provide.

Each House may determine the Rules of its Proceedings, punish its Members for disorderly Behaviour, and, with the Concurrence of two thirds, expel a Member.

Each House shall keep a Journal of its Proceedings, and from time to time publish the same, excepting such Parts as may in their Judgment require Secrecy; and the Yeas and Nays of the Members of either House on any question shall, at the Desire of one fifth of those Present, be entered on the Journal.

Neither House, during the Session of Congress, shall, without the Consent of the other, adjourn for more than three days, nor to any other Place than that in which the two Houses shall be sitting.

Section 6.

The Senators and Representatives shall receive a Compensation for their Services, to be ascertained by Law, and paid out of the Treasury of the United States. They shall in all Cases, except Treason, Felony, and Breach of the Peace, be privileged from Arrest during their Attendance at the Session of their respective Houses, and in going to and returning from the same; and for any Speech or Debate in either House, they shall not be questioned in any other Place.

No Senator or Representative shall, during the Time for which he was elected, be appointed to any civil Office under the Authority of the United States, which shall have been created, or the Emoluments whereof shall have been increased, during such time; and no Person holding any Office under the United States shall be a Member of either House during his continuance in Office.

Section 7.

All Bills for raising Revenue shall originate in the House of Representatives; but the Senate may propose or concur with Amendments as on other bills.

Every Bill which shall have passed the House of Representatives and the Senate, shall, before it become a Law, be presented to the President of the United States; If he approve he shall sign it, but if not he shall return it, with his Objections, to that House in which it shall have originated, who shall enter the Objections at large on their Journal, and proceed to reconsider it. If after such Reconsideration two thirds of that House shall agree to pass the bill, it shall be sent, together with the objections, to the other House, by which it shall likewise be reconsidered, and if approved by two thirds of that House, it shall become a Law. But in all such Cases the Votes of both Houses shall be determined by Yeas and Nays, and the Names of the Persons voting for and against the Bill shall be entered on the Journal of each House respectively. If any Bill shall not be returned by the President within ten Days (Sundays excepted) after it shall have been presented to him, the Same shall be a Law, in like Manner as if he had signed it, unless the Congress by their Adjournment prevent its Return, in which Case it shall not be a Law.

Every Order, Resolution, or Vote to which the Concurrence of the Senate and House of Representatives may be necessary (except on a question of Adjournment) shall be presented to the President of the United States; and before the Same shall take Effect, shall be approved by him, or being disapproved by him, shall be repassed by two thirds of the Senate and House of Representatives, according to the Rules and Limitations prescribed in the Case of a Bill.

Section 8.

The Congress shall have Power To lay and collect Taxes, Duties, Imposts and Excises, to pay the Debts and provide for the common Defence and general Welfare of the United States; but all Duties, Imposts and Excises shall be uniform throughout the United States;

To borrow money on the credit of the United States;

To regulate Commerce with foreign Nations, and among the several States, and with the Indian Tribes;

To establish an uniform rule of Naturalization, and uniform Laws on the subject of Bankruptcies throughout the United States;

To coin Money, regulate the Value thereof, and of foreign Coin, and fix the Standard of Weights and Measures;

To provide for the Punishment of counterfeiting the Securities and current Coin of the United States;

To establish Post Offices and post Roads;

To promote the Progress of Science and useful Arts, by securing for limited Times to Authors and Inventors the exclusive Right to their respective Writings and Discoveries;

To constitute Tribunals inferior to the Supreme Court;

To define and punish Piracies and Felonies committed on the high Seas, and Offenses against the Law of Nations;

To declare War, grant Letters of Marque and Reprisal, and make Rules concerning Captures on Land and Water;

To raise and support Armies, but no Appropriation of Money to that Use shall be for a longer Term than two Years;

To provide and maintain a Navy;

To make Rules for the Government and Regulation of the land and naval forces;

To provide for calling forth the Militia to execute the Laws of the Union, suppress Insurrections and repel Invasions;

To provide for organizing, arming, and disciplining the Militia, and for governing such Part of them as may be employed in the Service of the United States, reserving to the States respectively, the Appointment of the Officers, and the Authority of training the Militia according to the discipline prescribed by Congress;

To exercise exclusive Legislation in all Cases whatsoever, over such District (not exceeding ten Miles square) as may, by Cession of particular States, and the acceptance of Congress, become the Seat of the Government of the United States, and to exercise like Authority over all Places purchased by the Consent of the Legislature of the State in which the Same shall be, for the Erection of Forts, Magazines, Arsenals, Dock-yards, and other needful Buildings;—And

To make all Laws which shall be necessary and proper for carrying into Execution the foregoing Powers, and all other Powers vested by this Constitution in the Government of the United States, or in any Department or Officer thereof.

Section 9.

The Migration or Importation of such Persons as any of the States now existing shall think proper to admit, shall not be prohibited by the Congress prior to the Year one thousand eight hundred and eight, but a tax or duty may be imposed on such Importation, not exceeding ten dollars for each Person.

The privilege of the Writ of Habeas Corpus shall not be suspended, unless when in Cases of Rebellion or Invasion the public Safety may require it.

No bill of Attainder or ex post facto Law shall be passed.

No capitation, or other direct, Tax shall be laid unless in Proportion to the Census or Enumeration herein before directed to be taken.

No Tax or Duty shall be laid on Articles exported from any State.

No Preference shall be given by any Regulation of Commerce or Revenue to the Ports of one State over those of another: nor shall Vessels bound to, or from, one State, be obliged to enter, clear, or pay Duties in another.

No Money shall be drawn from the Treasury, but in Consequence of Appropriations made by Law; and a regular Statement and Account of the Receipts and Expenditures of all public Money shall be published from time to time.

No Title of Nobility shall be granted by the United States: And no Person holding any Office of Profit or Trust under them, shall, without the Consent of the Congress, accept of any present, Emolument, Office, or Title, of any kind whatever, from any King, Prince, or foreign State.

Section 10.

No State shall enter into any Treaty, Alliance, or Confederation; grant Letters of Marque and Reprisal; coin Money; emit Bills of Credit; make any Thing but gold and silver Coin a Tender in Payment of Debts; pass any Bill of Attainder, ex post facto Law, or Law impairing the Obligation of Contracts, or grant any Title of Nobility.

No State shall, without the Consent of the Congress, lay any Imposts or Duties on Imports or Exports, except what may be absolutely necessary for executing its inspection Laws; and the net Produce of all Duties and Imposts, laid by any State on Imports or Exports, shall be for the use of the Treasury of the United States; and all such Laws shall be subject to the Revision and Control of the Congress.

No state shall, without the Consent of Congress, lay any duty of Tonnage, keep Troops, or Ships of War in time of Peace, enter into any Agreement or Compact with another State, or with a foreign Power, or engage in War, unless actually invaded, or in such imminent Danger as will not admit of delay.

Article II

Section 1.

The executive Power shall be vested in a President of the United States of America. He shall hold his Office during the Term of four years, and, together with the Vice President, chosen for the same Term, be elected, as follows:

Each State shall appoint, in such Manner as the Legislature thereof may direct, a Number of Electors, equal to the whole Number of Senators and Representatives to which the State may be entitled in the Congress: but no Senator or Representative, or Person holding an Office of Trust or Profit under the United States, shall be appointed an Elector.

[The Electors shall meet in their respective States, and vote by Ballot for two persons, of whom one at least shall not be an Inhabitant of the same State with themselves. And they shall make a List of all the Persons voted for, and of the Number of Votes for each; which List they shall sign and certify, and transmit sealed to the Seat of the Government of the United States, directed to the President of the Senate. The President of the Senate shall, in the Presence of the Senate and House of Representatives, open all the Certificates, and the Votes shall then be counted. The Person having the greatest Number of Votes shall be the President, if such Number be a Majority of the whole Number of Electors appointed; and if there be more than one who have such Majority, and have an equal Number of Votes, then the House of Representatives shall immediately chuse by Ballot one of them for President; and if no Person have a Majority, then from the five highest on the List the said House shall in like Manner chuse the President. But in chusing the President, the Votes shall be taken by States, the Representation from each State having one Vote; a quorum for this Purpose shall consist of a Member or Members from two-thirds of the States, and a Majority of all the States shall be necessary to a Choice. In every Case, after the Choice of the President, the Person having the greatest Number of Votes of the Electors shall be the Vice President. But if there should remain two or more who have equal votes, the Senate shall chuse from them by Ballot the Vice President.][4]

The Congress may determine the Time of chusing the Electors, and the Day on which they shall give their Votes; which Day shall be the same throughout the United States.

No person except a natural-born Citizen, or a Citizen of the United States, at the time of the Adoption of this Constitution, shall be eligible to the Office of President; neither shall

4 Revised by the Twelfth Amendment.

any Person be eligible to that Office who shall not have attained to the Age of thirty-five years, and been fourteen Years a Resident within the United States.

In Case of the Removal of the President from Office, or of his Death, Resignation, or Inability to discharge the Powers and Duties of the said Office, the same shall devolve on the Vice President, and the Congress may by Law provide for the Case of Removal, Death, Resignation, or Inability, both of the President and Vice President, declaring what Officer shall then act as President, and such Officer shall act accordingly, until the disability be removed, or a President shall be elected.

The President shall, at stated Times, receive for his Services a Compensation, which shall neither be increased nor diminished during the Period for which he shall have been elected, and he shall not receive within that Period any other Emolument from the United States, or any of them.

Before he enter on the execution of his Office, he shall take the following Oath or Affirmation:—"I do solemnly swear (or affirm) that I will faithfully execute the Office of President of the United States, and will, to the best of my Ability, preserve, protect, and defend the Constitution of the United States."

Section 2.

The President shall be Commander in Chief of the Army and Navy of the United States, and of the Militia of the several States, when called into the actual Service of the United States; he may require the Opinion, in writing, of the principal Officer in each of the executive Departments, upon any subject relating to the Duties of their respective Offices, and he shall have Power to Grant Reprieves and Pardons for Offenses against the United States, except in Cases of Impeachment.

He shall have Power, by and with the Advice and Consent of the Senate, to make Treaties, provided two-thirds of the Senators present concur; and he shall nominate, and by and with the Advice and Consent of the Senate, shall appoint Ambassadors, other public Ministers and Consuls, Judges of the supreme Court, and all other Officers of the United States, whose Appointments are not herein otherwise provided for, and which shall be established by Law: but the Congress may by Law vest the Appointment of such inferior Officers, as they think proper, in the President alone, in the Courts of Law, or in the Heads of Departments.

The President shall have Power to fill up all Vacancies that may happen during the Recess of the Senate, by granting Commissions which shall expire at the End of their next Session.

Section 3.

He shall from time to time give to the Congress Information of the State of the Union, and recommend to their Consideration such Measures as he shall judge necessary and expedient; he may, on extraordinary occasions, convene both Houses, or either of them, and in Case of Disagreement between them, with respect to the Time of Adjournment, he may adjourn them to such Time as he shall think proper; he shall receive Ambassadors and other public Ministers; he shall take care that the Laws be faithfully executed, and shall Commission all the Officers of the United States.

Section 4.

The President, Vice President and all civil Officers of the United States, shall be removed from Office on Impeachment for, and Conviction of, Treason, Bribery, or other high Crimes and Misdemeanors.

Article III

Section 1.

The judicial Power of the United States, shall be vested in one supreme Court, and in such inferior Courts as the Congress may from time to time ordain and establish. The Judges, both of the supreme and inferior Courts, shall hold their Offices during good Behaviour, and shall, at stated Times, receive for their Services, a Compensation, which shall not be diminished during their Continuance in Office.

Section 2.

The judicial Power shall extend to all Cases, in Law and Equity, arising under this Constitution, the Laws of the United States, and Treaties made, or which shall be made, under their Authority;—to all Cases affecting ambassadors, other public ministers and consuls;—to all cases of admiralty and maritime Jurisdiction;—to Controversies to which the United States shall be a Party;—to Controversies between two or more States;—between a State and Citizens of another State;[5]—between Citizens of different States—between Citizens of the same State claiming Lands under Grants of different States, and between a State, or the Citizens thereof, and foreign States, Citizens, or Subjects.

In all Cases affecting Ambassadors, other public Ministers and Consuls, and those in which a State shall be Party, the supreme Court shall have original Jurisdiction. In all the other Cases before mentioned, the supreme Court shall have appellate Jurisdiction, both as to Law and Fact, with such Exceptions, and under such Regulations as the Congress shall make.

The trial of all Crimes, except in Cases of Impeachment, shall be by Jury; and such Trial shall be held in the State where the said Crimes shall have been committed; but when not committed within any State, the Trial shall be at such Place or Places as the Congress may by Law have directed.

Section 3.

Treason against the United States, shall consist only in levying War against them, or in adhering to their Enemies, giving them Aid and Comfort. No Person shall be convicted of Treason unless on the Testimony of two Witnesses to the same overt Act, or on Confession in open Court.

The Congress shall have power to declare the Punishment of Treason, but no Attainder of Treason shall work Corruption of Blood, or Forfeiture except during the Life of the Person attained.

Article IV

Section 1.

Full Faith and Credit shall be given in each State to the public Acts, Records, and judicial Proceedings of every other State. And the Congress may by general Laws prescribe the Manner in which such Acts, Records and Proceedings shall be proved, and the Effect thereof.

Section 2.

The Citizens of each State shall be entitled to all Privileges and Immunities of Citizens in the several States.

5 Qualified by the Eleventh Amendment.

A Person charged in any State with Treason, Felony, or other Crime, who shall flee from Justice, and be found in another State, shall on demand of the executive Authority of the State from which he fled, be delivered up, to be removed to the State having Jurisdiction of the crime.

No Person held to Service or Labour in one State, under the Laws thereof, escaping into another, shall, in Consequence of any Law or Regulation therein, be discharged from such Service or Labour, but shall be delivered up on Claim of the Party to whom such Service or Labour may be due.

Section 3.

New States may be admitted by the Congress into this Union; but no new State shall be formed or erected within the Jurisdiction of any other State; nor any State be formed by the Junction of two or more States, or parts of States, without the Consent of the Legislatures of the States concerned as well as of the Congress.

The Congress shall have Power to dispose of and make all needful Rules and Regulations respecting the Territory or other Property belonging to the United States; and nothing in this Constitution shall be so construed as to Prejudice any Claims of the United States, or of any particular State.

Section 4.

The United States shall guarantee to every State in this Union a Republican Form of Government, and shall protect each of them against Invasion; and on Application of the Legislature, or of the Executive (when the Legislature cannot be convened) against domestic Violence.

Article V

The Congress, whenever two-thirds of both Houses shall deem it necessary, shall propose Amendments to this Constitution, or, on the Application of the Legislatures of two-thirds of the several States, shall call a Convention for proposing Amendments, which, in either Case, shall be valid to all Intents and Purposes, as part of this Constitution, when ratified by the Legislatures of three-fourths of the several States, or by Conventions in three-fourths thereof, as the one or the other Mode of Ratification may be proposed by the Congress; Provided that no Amendment which may be made prior to the Year One thousand eight hundred and eight shall in any Manner affect the first and fourth Clauses in the Ninth Section of the first Article; and that no State, without its Consent, shall be deprived of its equal Suffrage in the Senate.

Article VI

All Debts contracted and Engagements entered into, before the Adoption of this Constitution, shall be as valid against the United States under this Constitution, as under the Confederation.

This Constitution, and the Laws of the United States which shall be made in Pursuance thereof; and all Treaties made, or which shall be made, under the Authority of the United States, shall be the supreme Law of the Land; and the Judges in every State shall be bound thereby, any Thing in the Constitution or Laws of any State to the Contrary notwithstanding.

The Senators and Representatives before mentioned, and the Members of the several State Legislatures, and all executive and judicial Officers, both of the United States and of the several States, shall be bound by Oath or Affirmation to support this Constitution; but no religious Tests shall ever be required as a qualification to any Office or public Trust under the United States.

Article VII

The Ratification of the Conventions of nine States shall be sufficient for the Establishment of this Constitution between the States so ratifying the same.

Done in Convention by the Unanimous Consent of the States present the Seventeenth Day of September in the Year of our Lord one thousand seven hundred and Eighty seven, and of the Independence of the United States of America the Twelfth. In Witness whereof We have hereunto subscribed our Names.[6]

George Washington
President and deputy from Virginia

NEW HAMPSHIRE
John Langdon
Nicholas Gilman

MASSACHUSETTS
Nathaniel Gorham
Rufus King

CONNECTICUT
William Samuel Johnson
Roger Sherman

NEW YORK
Alexander Hamilton

NEW JERSEY
William Livingston
David Brearley
William Paterson
Jonathan Dayton

PENNSYLVANIA
Benjamin Franklin
Thomas Mifflin
Robert Morris
George Clymer
Thomas FitzSimons
Jared Ingersoll
James Wilson
Gouverneur Morris

DELAWARE
George Read
Gunning Bedford Jr.
John Dickinson
Richard Bassett
Jacob Broom

MARYLAND
James McHenry
Daniel of St. Thomas Jenifer
Daniel Carroll

VIRGINIA
John Blair
James Madison Jr.

NORTH CAROLINA
William Blount
Richard Dobbs Spaight
Hugh Williamson

SOUTH CAROLINA
John Rutledge
Charles Cotesworth
   Pinckney
Charles Pinckney
Pierce Butler

GEORGIA
William Few
Abraham Baldwin

Articles in Addition to, and Amendment of, the Constitution of the United States of America, Proposed by Congress, and Ratified by the Legislatures of the Several States, Pursuant to the Fifth Article of the Original Constitution.[7]

[Article I]

Congress shall make no law respecting an establishment of religion, or prohibiting the free exercise thereof; or abridging the freedom of speech, or of the press; or the right of the people peaceably to assemble, and to petition the Government for a redress of grievances.

[Article II]

A well regulated Militia, being necessary to the security of a free State, the right of the people to keep and bear Arms shall not be infringed.

---

6 These are the full names of the signers, which in some cases are not the signatures on the document.
7 This heading appears only in the joint resolution submitting the first ten amendments.

[Article III]

No Soldier shall, in time of peace, be quartered in any house, without the consent of the Owner, nor in time of war, but in a manner to be prescribed by law.

[Article IV]

The right of the people to be secure in their persons, houses, papers, and effects, against unreasonable searches and seizures, shall not be violated, and no Warrants shall issue, but upon probable cause, supported by Oath or affirmation, and particularly describing the place to be searched, and the persons or things to be seized.

[Article V]

No person shall be held to answer for a capital or otherwise infamous crime, unless on a presentment or indictment of a Grand Jury, except in cases arising in the land or naval forces, or in the Militia, when in actual service in time of War or public danger; nor shall any person be subject for the same offence to be twice put in jeopardy of life or limb; nor shall be compelled in any criminal case to be a witness against himself, nor be deprived of life, liberty, or property, without due process of law; nor shall private property be taken for public use, without just compensation.

[Article VI]

In all criminal prosecutions, the accused shall enjoy the right to a speedy and public trial, by an impartial jury of the State and district wherein the crime shall have been committed, which district shall have been previously ascertained by law, and to be informed of the nature and cause of the accusation; to be confronted with the witnesses against him; to have compulsory process for obtaining witnesses in his favour, and to have the Assistance of Counsel for his defense.

[Article VII]

In suits at common law, where the value in controversy shall exceed twenty dollars, the right of trial by jury shall be preserved, and no fact tried by a jury, shall be otherwise reexamined in any Court of the United States, than according to the rules of the common law.

[Article VIII]

Excessive bail shall not be required, nor excessive fines imposed, nor cruel and unusual punishments inflicted.

[Article IX]

The enumeration of the Constitution, of certain rights, shall not be construed to deny or disparage others retained by the people.

[Article X]

The powers not delegated to the United States by the Constitution, nor prohibited by it to the States, are reserved to the States respectively, or to the people.

[Amendments I–X, in force 1791.]

[Article XI][8]

The Judicial power of the United States shall not be construed to extend to any suit in law or equity, commenced or prosecuted against one of the United States by Citizens of another State, or by Citizens or Subjects of any Foreign State.

[Article XII][9]

The Electors shall meet in their respective States and vote by ballot for President and Vice-President, one of whom, at least, shall not be an inhabitant of the same State with themselves; they shall name in their ballots the person voted for as President, and in distinct ballots the person voted for as Vice-President, and they shall make distinct lists of all persons voted for as President, and of all persons voted for as Vice-President, and of the number of votes for each, which lists they shall sign and certify, and transmit sealed to the seat of the government of the United States, directed to the President of the Senate;—The President of the Senate shall, in the presence of the Senate and House of Representatives, open all the certificates and the votes shall then be counted;—The person having the greatest number of votes for President, shall be the President, if such number be a majority of the whole number of Electors appointed; and if no person have such majority, then from the persons having the highest numbers not exceeding three on the list of those voted for as President, the House of Representatives shall choose immediately, by ballot, the President. But in choosing the President, the votes shall be taken by states, the representation from each state having one vote; a quorum for this purpose shall consist of a member or members from two-thirds of the states, and a majority of all the states shall be necessary to a choice. And if the House of Representatives shall not choose a President whenever the right of choice shall devolve upon them, before the fourth day of March next following, then the Vice-President shall act as President, as in the case of the death or other constitutional disability of the President.—The person having the greatest number of votes as Vice-President, shall be the Vice-President, if such number be a majority of the whole number of Electors appointed, and if no person have a majority, then from the two highest numbers on the list, the Senate shall choose the Vice-President; a quorum for the purpose shall consist of two-thirds of the whole number of Senators, and a majority of the whole number shall be necessary to a choice. But no person constitutionally ineligible to the office of President shall be eligible to that of Vice-President of the United States.

[Article XIII][10]

Section 1.
Neither slavery nor involuntary servitude, except as a punishment for crime whereof the party shall have been duly convicted, shall exist within the United States, or any place subject to their jurisdiction.

Section 2.
Congress shall have power to enforce this article by appropriate legislation.

8 Adopted in 1798.
9 Adopted in 1804.
10 Adopted in 1865.

[Article XIV][11]

Section 1.

All persons born or naturalized in the United States, and subject to the jurisdiction thereof, are citizens of the United States and of the State wherein they reside. No State shall make or enforce any law which shall abridge the privileges or immunities of citizens of the United States; nor shall any State deprive any person of life, liberty, or property, without due process of law; nor deny to any person within its jurisdiction the equal protection of the laws.

Section 2.

Representatives shall be apportioned among the several States according to their respective numbers, counting the whole number of persons in each State, excluding Indians not taxed. But when the right to vote at any election for the choice of electors for President and Vice-President of the United States, Representatives in Congress, the Executive and Judicial officers of a State, or the members of the Legislature thereof, is denied to any of the male inhabitants of such State, being twenty-one years of age, and citizens of the United States, or in any way abridged, except for participation in rebellion, or other crime, the basis of representation therein shall be reduced in the proportion which the number of such male citizens shall bear to the whole number of male citizens twenty-one years of age in such State.

Section 3.

No person shall be a Senator or Representative in Congress, or elector of President and Vice-President, or hold any office, civil or military, under the United States, or under any State, who, having previously taken an oath, as a member of Congress, or as an officer of the United States, or as a member of any State legislature, or as an executive or judicial officer of any State, to support the Constitution of the United States, shall have engaged in insurrection or rebellion against the same, or given aid or comfort to the enemies thereof. But Congress may by a vote of two-thirds of each House, remove such disability.

Section 4.

The validity of the public debt of the United States, authorized by law, including debts incurred for payment of pensions and bounties for services in suppressing insurrection or rebellion, shall not be questioned. But neither the United States nor any State shall assume or pay any debts or obligation incurred in aid of insurrection or rebellion against the United States, or any claim for the loss or emancipation of any slave; but all such debts, obligations, and claims shall be held illegal and void.

Section 5.

The Congress shall have the power to enforce, by appropriate legislation, the provisions of this article.

[Article XV][12]

Section 1.

The right of citizens of the United States to vote shall not be denied or abridged by the United States or by any State on account of race, color, or previous condition of servitude—

Section 2.

The Congress shall have power to enforce this article by appropriate legislation.

11 Adopted in 1868.
12 Adopted in 1870.

[Article XVI][13]

The Congress shall have power to lay and collect taxes on incomes, from whatever source derived, without apportionment among the several States, and without regard to any census or enumeration.

[Article XVII][14]

The Senate of the United States shall be composed of two Senators from each State, elected by the people thereof, for six years; and each Senator shall have one vote. The electors in each State shall have the qualifications requisite for electors of the most numerous branch of the State legislatures.

When vacancies happen in the representation of any State in the Senate, the executive authority of such State shall issue writs of election to fill such vacancies: *Provided,* That the legislature of any State may empower the executive thereof to make temporary appointments until the people fill the vacancies by election as the legislature may direct.

This amendment shall not be so construed as to affect the election or term of any Senator chosen before it becomes valid as part of the Constitution.

[Article XVIII][15]

Section 1.
After one year from the ratification of this article the manufacture, sale, or transportation of intoxicating liquors within, the importation thereof into, or the exportation thereof from the United States and all territory subject to the jurisdiction thereof for beverage purposes is hereby prohibited.

Section 2.
The Congress and the several States shall have concurrent power to enforce this article by appropriate legislation.

Section 3.
This article shall be inoperative unless it shall have been ratified as an amendment to the Constitution by the legislatures of the several States, as provided in the Constitution, within seven years from the date of the submission hereof to the States by the Congress.

[Article XIX][16]

The right of citizens of the United States to vote shall not be denied or abridged by the United States or by any State on account of sex.

Congress shall have power to enforce this article by appropriate legislation.

[Article XX][17]

Section 1.
The terms of the President and Vice-President shall end at noon on the 20th day of January, and the terms of Senators and Representatives at noon on the 3d day of January,

13 Adopted in 1913.
14 Adopted in 1913.
15 Adopted in 1918.
16 Adopted in 1920.
17 Adopted in 1933.

of the years in which such terms would have ended if this article had not been ratified; and the terms of their successors shall then begin.

Section 2.
The Congress shall assemble at least once in every year, and such meeting shall begin at noon on the 3d day of January, unless they shall by law appoint a different day.

Section 3.
If, at the time fixed for the beginning of the term of the President, the President elect shall have died, the Vice-President elect shall become President. If a President shall not have been chosen before the time fixed for the beginning of his term or if the President elect shall have failed to qualify, then the Vice-President elect shall act as President until a President shall have qualified; and the Congress may by law provide for the case wherein neither a President elect nor a Vice-President elect shall have qualified, declaring who shall then act as President, or the manner in which one who is to act shall be selected, and such person shall act accordingly until a President or Vice-President shall have qualified.

Section 4.
The Congress may by law provide for the case of the death of any of the persons from whom the House of Representatives may choose a President whenever the right of choice shall have devolved upon them, and for the case of the death of any of the persons from whom the Senate may choose a Vice-President whenever the right of choice shall have devolved upon them.

Section 5.
Sections 1 and 2 shall take effect on the 15th day of October following the ratification of this article.

Section 6.
This article shall be inoperative unless it shall have been ratified as an amendment to the Constitution by the legislatures of three-fourths of the several States within seven years from the date of its submission.

[Article XXI][18]

Section 1.
The eighteenth article of amendment to the Constitution of the United States is hereby repealed.

Section 2.
The transportation or importation into any State, Territory, or possession of the United States for delivery or use therein of intoxicating liquors, in violation of the laws thereof, is hereby prohibited.

Section 3.
This article shall be inoperative unless it shall have been ratified as an amendment to the Constitution by conventions in the several States, as provided in the Constitution, within seven years from the date of the submission hereof to the States by the Congress.

18 Adopted in 1933.

[Article XXII][19]

No person shall be elected to the office of the President more than twice, and no person who has held the office of President, or acted as President, for more than two years of a term to which some other person was elected President shall be elected to the office of the President more than once.

But this Article shall not apply to any person holding the office of President when this Article was proposed by the Congress, and shall not prevent any person who may be holding the office of President, or acting as President, during the term within which this Article becomes operative from holding the office of President or acting as President during the remainder of such term.

This article shall be inoperative unless it shall have been ratified as an amendment to the Constitution by the legislatures of three-fourths of the several states within seven years from the date of its submission to the states by the Congress.

[Article XXIII][20]

Section 1.

The District constituting the seat of Government of the United States shall appoint in such manner as the Congress may direct:

A number of electors of President and Vice-President equal to the whole number of Senators and Representatives in Congress to which the District would be entitled if it were a State, but in no event more than the least populous State; they shall be in addition to those appointed by the States, but they shall be considered, for the purposes of the election of President and Vice-President, to be electors appointed by a State; and they shall meet in the District and perform such duties as provided by the twelfth article of amendment.

Section 2.

The Congress shall have power to enforce this article by appropriate legislation.

[Article XXIV][21]

Section 1.

The right of citizens of the United States to vote in any primary or other election for President or Vice President, for electors for President or Vice President, or for Senator or Representative in Congress, shall not be denied or abridged by the United States or any state by reason of failure to pay any poll tax or other tax.

Section 2.

The Congress shall have the power to enforce this article by appropriate legislation.

[Article XXV][22]

Section 1.

In case of the removal of the President from office or of his death or resignation, the Vice President shall become President.

19 Adopted in 1951.
20 Adopted in 1961.
21 Adopted in 1964.
22 Adopted in 1967.

Section 2.

Whenever there is a vacancy in the office of the Vice President, the President shall nominate a Vice President who shall take office upon confirmation by a majority vote of both Houses of Congress.

Section 3.

Whenever the President transmits to the President Pro Tempore of the Senate and the Speaker of the House of Representatives his written declaration that he is unable to discharge the powers and duties of his office, and until he transmits to them a written declaration to the contrary, such powers and duties shall be discharged by the Vice President as Acting President.

Section 4.

Whenever the Vice President and a majority of either the principal officers of the executive departments or of such other body as Congress may by law provide, transmit to the President Pro Tempore of the Senate and the Speaker of the House of Representatives their written declaration that the President is unable to discharge the powers and duties of his office, the Vice President shall immediately assume the powers and duties of the office as Acting President.

Thereafter, when the President transmits to the President Pro Tempore of the Senate and the Speaker of the House of Representatives his written declaration that no inability exists, he shall resume the powers and duties of his office unless the Vice President and a majority of either the principal officers of the executive departments or of such other body as Congress may by law provide, transmit within four days to the President Pro Tempore of the Senate and the Speaker of the House of Representatives their written declaration that the President is unable to discharge the powers and duties of his office. Thereupon Congress shall decide the issue, assembling within forty-eight hours for that purpose if not in session. If the Congress, within twenty-one days after receipt of the latter written declaration, or, if Congress is not in session, within twenty-one days after Congress is required to assemble, determines by two-thirds vote of both Houses that the President is unable to discharge the powers and duties of his office, the Vice President shall continue to discharge the same as Acting President; otherwise, the President shall resume the powers and duties of his office.

[Article XXVI][23]

Section 1.

The right of citizens of the United States, who are eighteen years of age or older, to vote shall not be denied or abridged by the United States or by any State on account of age.

Section 2.

The Congress shall have power to enforce this article by appropriate legislation.

[Article XXVII][24]

No law varying the compensation for the services of the Senators and Representatives shall take effect until an election of Representatives shall have intervened.

23 Adopted in 1971.
24 Adopted in 1992.

PRESIDENTIAL ELECTIONS

Year	Candidates	Parties	Popular Vote	Percentage of Popular Vote	Electoral Vote	Percentage of Voter Participation
1789	**George Washington (Va.)***				69	
	John Adams				34	
	Others				35	
1792	**George Washington (Va.)**				132	
	John Adams				77	
	George Clinton				50	
	Others				5	
1796	**John Adams (Mass.)**	Federalist			71	
	Thomas Jefferson	Democratic-Republican			68	
	Thomas Pinckney	Federalist			59	
	Aaron Burr	Dem.-Rep.			30	
	Others				48	
1800	**Thomas Jefferson (Va.)**	Dem.-Rep.			73	
	Aaron Burr	Dem.-Rep.			73	
	John Adams	Federalist			65	
	C. C. Pinckney	Federalist			64	
	John Jay	Federalist			1	
1804	**Thomas Jefferson (Va.)**	Dem.-Rep.			162	
	C. C. Pinckney	Federalist			14	
1808	**James Madison (Va.)**	Dem.-Rep.			122	
	C. C. Pinckney	Federalist			47	
	George Clinton	Dem.-Rep.			6	

*State of residence at time of election.

(continued)

Year	Candidates	Parties	Popular Vote	% Popular Vote	Electoral Vote	% Voter Participation
1812	**James Madison (Va.)**	Dem.-Rep.			128	
	De Witt Clinton	Federalist			89	
1816	**James Monroe (Va.)**	Dem.-Rep.			183	
	Rufus King	Federalist			34	
1820	**James Monroe (Va.)**	Dem.-Rep.			231	
	John Quincy Adams	Dem.-Rep.			1	
1824	**John Q. Adams (Mass.)**	Dem.-Rep.	108,740	30.5	84	26.9
	Andrew Jackson	Dem.-Rep.	153,544	43.1	99	
	William H. Crawford	Dem.-Rep.	46,618	13.1	41	
	Henry Clay	Dem.-Rep.	47,136	13.2	37	
1828	**Andrew Jackson (Tenn.)**	Democratic	647,286	56.0	178	57.6
	John Quincy Adams	National Republican	508,064	44.0	83	
1832	**Andrew Jackson (Tenn.)**	Democratic	687,502	55.0	219	55.4
	Henry Clay	National Republican	530,189	42.4	49	
	John Floyd	Independent			11	
	William Wirt	Anti-Mason	33,108	2.6	7	
1836	**Martin Van Buren (N.Y.)**	Democratic	765,483	50.9	170	57.8
	W. H. Harrison	Whig	739,765	49.1	73	
	Hugh L. White	Whig			26	
	Daniel Webster	Whig			14	
	W. P. Magnum	Independent			11	
1840	**William H. Harrison (Ohio)**	Whig	1,274,624	53.1	234	80.2
	Martin Van Buren	Democratic	1,127,781	46.9	60	
	J. G. Birney	Liberty	7,069		—	

Year	Candidates	Parties	Popular Vote	Percentage of Popular Vote	Electoral Vote	Percentage of Voter Participation
1844	**James K. Polk (Tenn.)**	Democratic	1,338,464	49.6	170	78.9
	Henry Clay	Whig	1,300,097	48.1	105	
	J. G. Birney	Liberty	62,300	2.3	—	
1848	**Zachary Taylor (La.)**	Whig	1,360,967	47.4	163	72.7
	Lewis Cass	Democratic	1,222,342	42.5	127	
	Martin Van Buren	Free-Soil	291,263	10.1	—	
1852	**Franklin Pierce (N.H.)**	Democratic	1,601,117	50.9	254	69.6
	Winfield Scott	Whig	1,385,453	44.1	42	
	John P. Hale	Free-Soil	155,825	5.0	—	
1856	**James Buchanan (Pa.)**	Democratic	1,832,955	45.3	174	78.9
	John C. Frémont	Republican	1,339,932	33.1	114	
	Millard Fillmore	American	871,731	21.6	8	
1860	**Abraham Lincoln (Ill.)**	Republican	1,865,593	39.9	180	81.2
	Stephen A. Douglas	Democratic	1,382,713	29.4	12	
	John C. Breckinridge	Democratic	848,356	18.1	72	
	John Bell	Union	592,906	12.6	39	
1864	**Abraham Lincoln (Ill.)**	Republican	2,213,655	55.0	212	73.8
	George B. McClellan	Democratic	1,805,237	45.0	21	
1868	**Ulysses S. Grant (Ill.)**	Republican	3,012,833	52.7	214	78.1
	Horatio Seymour	Democratic	2,703,249	47.3	80	
1872	**Ulysses S. Grant (Ill.)**	Republican	3,597,132	55.6	286	71.3
	Horace Greeley	Democratic; Liberal Republican	2,834,125	43.9	66	
1876	**Rutherford B. Hayes (Ohio)**	Republican	4,036,298	48.0	185	81.8
	Samuel J. Tilden	Democratic	4,300,590	51.0	184	
1880	**James A. Garfield (Ohio)**	Republican	4,454,416	48.5	214	79.4
	Winfield S. Hancock	Democratic	4,444,952	48.1	155	

(continued)

Year	Candidate	Party	Popular Vote	% Popular	Electoral Vote	% Turnout
1884	**Grover Cleveland (N.Y.)**	Democratic	4,874,986	48.5	219	77.5
	James G. Blaine	Republican	4,851,981	48.2	182	
1888	**Benjamin Harrison (Ind.)**	Republican	5,439,853	47.9	233	79.3
	Grover Cleveland	Democratic	5,540,309	48.6	168	
1892	**Grover Cleveland (N.Y.)**	Democratic	5,556,918	46.1	277	74.7
	Benjamin Harrison	Republican	5,176,108	43.0	145	
	James B. Weaver	People's	1,041,028	8.5	22	
1896	**William McKinley (Ohio)**	Republican	7,104,779	51.1	271	79.3
	William J. Bryan	Democratic; People's	6,502,925	47.7	176	
1900	**William McKinley (Ohio)**	Republican	7,207,923	51.7	292	73.2
	William J. Bryan	Dem.-Populist	6,358,133	45.5	155	
1904	**Theodore Roosevelt (N.Y.)**	Republican	7,623,486	57.9	336	65.2
	Alton B. Parker	Democratic	5,077,911	37.6	140	
	Eugene V. Debs	Socialist	402,283	3.0	—	
1908	**William H. Taft (Ohio)**	Republican	7,678,908	51.6	321	65.4
	William J. Bryan	Democratic	6,409,104	43.1	162	
	Eugene V. Debs	Socialist	420,793	2.8	—	
1912	**Woodrow Wilson (N.J.)**	Democratic	6,293,454	41.9	435	58.8
	Theodore Roosevelt	Progressive	4,119,538	27.4	88	
	William H. Taft	Republican	3,484,980	23.2	8	
	Eugene V. Debs	Socialist	900,672	6.0	—	
1916	**Woodrow Wilson (N.J.)**	Democratic	9,129,606	49.4	277	61.6
	Charles E. Hughes	Republican	8,538,221	46.2	254	
	A. L. Benson	Socialist	585,113	3.2	—	

Year	Candidates	Parties	Popular Vote	Percentage of Popular Vote	Electoral Vote	Percentage of Voter Participation
1920	**Warren G. Harding (Ohio)**	Republican	16,152,200	60.4	404	49.2
	James M. Cox	Democratic	9,147,353	34.2	127	
	Eugene V. Debs	Socialist	919,799	3.4	—	
1924	**Calvin Coolidge (Mass.)**	Republican	15,725,016	54.0	382	48.9
	John W. Davis	Democratic	8,386,503	28.8	136	
	Robert M. La Follette	Progressive	4,822,856	16.6	13	
1928	**Herbert Hoover (Calif.)**	Republican	21,391,381	58.2	444	56.9
	Alfred E. Smith	Democratic	15,016,443	40.9	87	
	Norman Thomas	Socialist	267,835	0.7	—	
1932	**Franklin D. Roosevelt (N.Y.)**	Democratic	22,821,857	57.4	472	56.9
	Herbert Hoover	Republican	15,761,841	39.7	59	
	Norman Thomas	Socialist	881,951	2.2	—	
1936	**Franklin D. Roosevelt (N.Y.)**	Democratic	27,751,597	60.8	523	61.0
	Alfred M. Landon	Republican	16,679,583	36.5	8	
	William Lemke	Union	882,479	1.9	—	
1940	**Franklin D. Roosevelt (N.Y.)**	Democratic	27,244,160	54.8	449	62.5
	Wendell L. Willkie	Republican	22,305,198	44.8	82	
1944	**Franklin D. Roosevelt (N.Y.)**	Democratic	25,602,504	53.5	432	55.9
	Thomas E. Dewey	Republican	22,006,285	46.0	99	
1948	**Harry S. Truman (Mo.)**	Democratic	24,105,695	49.5	303	53.0
	Thomas E. Dewey	Republican	21,969,170	45.1	189	
	J. Strom Thurmond	States' Rights Democratic	1,169,021	2.4	39	
	Henry A. Wallace	Progressive	1,156,103	2.4	—	
1952	**Dwight D. Eisenhower (N.Y.)**	Republican	33,936,252	55.1	442	63.3
	Adlai E. Stevenson	Democratic	27,314,992	44.4	89	

Year	Candidate	Party	Popular Vote	%	Electoral Vote	Participation %
1956	**Dwight D. Eisenhower (N.Y.)**	Republican	35,575,420	57.6	457	60.6
	Adlai E. Stevenson	Democratic	26,033,066	42.1	73	
	Other	—	—		1	
1960	**John F. Kennedy (Mass.)**	Democratic	34,227,096	49.7	303	64.0
	Richard M. Nixon	Republican	34,108,546	49.6	219	
	Other	—	—		15	
1964	**Lyndon B. Johnson (Tex.)**	Democratic	43,126,506	61.1	486	61.7
	Barry M. Goldwater	Republican	27,176,799	38.5	52	
1968	**Richard M. Nixon (N.Y.)**	Republican	31,770,237	43.4	301	60.6
	Hubert H. Humphrey	Democratic	31,270,533	42.3	191	
	George Wallace	American Independent	9,906,141	12.9	46	
1972	**Richard M. Nixon (N.Y.)**	Republican	47,169,911	60.7	520	55.2
	George S. McGovern	Democratic	29,170,383	37.5	17	
	Other	—	—		1	
1976	**Jimmy Carter (Ga.)**	Democratic	40,828,587	50.0	297	53.5
	Gerald R. Ford	Republican	39,147,613	47.9	240	
	Other	—	1,575,459	2.1	1	
1980	**Ronald Reagan (Calif.)**	Republican	43,901,812	50.7	489	52.6
	Jimmy Carter	Democratic	35,483,820	41.0	49	
	John B. Anderson	Independent	5,719,722	6.6	—	
	Ed Clark	Libertarian	921,188	1.1	—	
1984	**Ronald Reagan (Calif.)**	Republican	54,455,075	59.0	525	53.3
	Walter Mondale	Democratic	37,577,185	41.0	13	
1988	**George H. W. Bush (Tex.)**	Republican	47,946,422	54.0	426	50.0
	Michael S. Dukakis	Democratic	41,016,429	46.0	112	
1992	**William J. Clinton (Ark.)**	Democratic	44,909,889	43.0	370	55.2
	George W. Bush	Republican	39,104,545	38.0	168	
	Ross Perot	Independent	19,742,267	19.0	0	

(continued)

Year	Candidates	Parties	Popular Vote	Percentage of Popular Vote	Electoral Vote	Percentage of Voter Participation
1996	William J. Clinton (Ark.)	Democratic	47,401,185	49.3	379	49.0
	Robert Dole	Republican	39,197,469	40.7	159	
	Ross Perot	Reform	8,085,294	8.4	—	
2000	George W. Bush (Tex.)	Republican	50,459,211	47.89	271	51.0
	Albert Gore Jr.	Democratic	51,003,894	48.41	266	
	Ralph Nader	Green	2,834,410	2.69	—	
2004	George W. Bush (Tex.)	Republican	62,028,285	50.73	286	60.0
	John Kerry	Democratic	59,028,109	48.27	251	
	Ralph Nader	Independent	463,647	0.38	0	
2008	Barack Obama (Ill.)	Democratic	69,297,997	53.7	365	61.7
	John McCain	Republican	59,597,520	46.2	173	
2012	Barack Obama (Ill.)	Democratic	65,915,796	51	332	54.9
	Mitt Romney	Republican	60,933,500	47	206	

GLOSSARY

abolitionist An advocate for the end of a state-approved practice or institution; the term is used most often in connection with the eradication of slavery.

affirmative action A policy that favors groups that historically have faced discrimination; examples include hiring, awarding contracts, and college admissions.

American System An economic plan of the early- to mid-nineteenth century designed to bolster and unify the American economy by raising protective tariffs, developing the transportation system, and establishing a strong national bank.

antebellum The period before a war; the term is commonly used to describe the pre–Civil War United States.

Antinomianism A Christian belief that salvation comes from God's grace alone and not from good works.

appeasement A foreign policy that accepts (rather than opposes) the aggressive moves of another state or actor.

artisan An independent, skilled craftsperson.

Atlantic World The peoples and empires around the Atlantic Ocean rim that became interconnected in the sixteenth century.

Baby Boom A period of increased birthrate; the term is used most often to describe such a demographic trend from 1946 to 1964.

Black Codes State laws that developed after the Civil War in the former Confederate states to limit the political power and mobility of black Americans.

black power A philosophy of racial empowerment and distinctiveness as opposed to assimilation into white culture; became popular during the Civil Rights movement of the 1960s.

brinksmanship The attempt to gain a negotiating advantage by pushing a situation to the edge of war or other disaster.

capitalist Owner of material or financial assets useful for the accumulation of additional wealth.

charter A formal order from a governmental leader or body, like the king of a court, often granting the recipient power over a body of land, a business, or a people.

checks and balances A system that grants the various branches of government the power to oversee or constrain other branches, so that no part grows too powerful.

colonization A process by which a country or territory falls, usually by force, under the control of a hostile country or territory.

conquistador A European (especially Spanish and Portuguese) conqueror of the Americas (particularly Mexico and Peru) during the fifteenth and sixteenth centuries.

conscription The practice of requiring citizens to serve in the military or other national service; the draft.

conservationist A proponent of the protection of land for carefully managed development, as opposed to a preservationist, who seeks to protect nature from development altogether.

consumerism An increased focus on purchasing goods for personal use; the protection or promotion of consumer interests.

containment The Cold War strategy that called for preventing the spread of communism, by force or by other means.

counterculture A way of life opposed to the prevailing culture; the term typically refers to the revolution in lifestyles, values, and behavior among some young people of the 1960s.

covenant A Puritan belief that an individual's relationship with God and with others rested on mutual respect, duty, and consent.

Creole A person of European or African ancestry born in the Americas; also, a person of mixed European and African ancestry.

crop-lien system A credit system widely used in the South after the Civil War in which farmers promised a portion of their future crops in exchange for supplies from local merchants.

cult of domesticity The early-nineteenth-century belief that women were the guardians of family and religious virtue within the home.

cult of honor A set of beliefs that emphasized respect, reputation, and the protection of women; often associated with white southern males in the nineteenth century.

deism The belief that God created but does not actively control the universe.

deregulation The process of removing government controls over industries such as airlines, trucking, electricity supply, and banking, with the intention of stimulating competition and innovation.

détente The easing of hostilities between countries, used especially in connection with the Cold War in the 1970s.

Dollar Diplomacy Foreign policies, especially those of the Taft administration in Latin America, that privilege American economic interests.

embargo A ban on trade with another country, especially the refusal to allow foreign ships to unload goods at port.

encomienda The right to extract tribute and labor from the natives on large tracts of land in Spanish America; also the name given to the land and village in such tracts.

eugenics The pseudo-scientific movement that attributed genetic weakness to various races and ethnicities; also describes efforts to control or isolate supposed hereditary traits through selective breeding, sterilization, immigration restriction, and other forms of social engineering.

evangelist A devout person who aims to convert others to the faith through preaching and missionary work.

factory system A method of manufacturing involving powered machinery, usually run by water, that allowed the use of unskilled labor and greater output than in the artisan tradition.

fascism A term originating with Mussolini's Fascist Party and applying to any antidemocratic regime with a supreme leader, intolerance of dissent, faith in militarism over diplomacy, and a belief in national or ethnic superiority.

federalism A political system that traditionally divides powers between state and federal governments that together constitute a federation.

globalization The process of interaction and exchange between peoples and ideas from different parts of the globe.

gospel of wealth A philosophy popularized by Andrew Carnegie that assigns moral failure to the poor and personal virtue to the wealthy, and directs the rich to devote their resources to the common good. The concept developed by Andrew Carnegie that the wealthy should use their excess resources for the good of the community.

greenbacks Paper currency not backed by gold or silver.

horizontal integration A corporate combination where a group of businesses that do the same thing are consolidated.

impeachment The process of charging a public official with misconduct, with the potential for punishment including loss of office.

imperialism The process whereby an empire or nation pursues military, political, or economic advantage by extending its rule over external territories and peoples.

impressment The act of forcing people to serve in a navy or other military operation; the term is most commonly used in connection with the actions of British fleets against American sailors in the early 1800s.

indentured servitude The condition of being bound to an employer for a specific period of time, usually in exchange for the cost of passage to a new land. The labor practice was most commonly used in Britain's American colonies.

Industrial Revolution The transformation of an economy based on increasingly mechanized production.

isolationism A foreign policy that avoids forging alliances or lending support to other nations, especially in wartime.

jeremiad A sermon of despair at society's lost moral virtue, usually warning about dire consequences in the world and the afterlife.

jingoes A term coined in the late nineteenth century to refer to advocates for expanded U.S. economic, political, and military power in the world.

long drive A journey over grasslands that allowed western cattle ranchers to deliver their animals to railroad centers.

Lowell System A factory system used to mass-produce textiles, primarily in New England, that relied on young women workers who lived in factory communities.

Manifest Destiny An ideology holding that God or fate intended the United States to expand its dominion across the North American continent.

manumission The act of freeing slaves.

McCarthyism A form of anticommunism developed by Senator Joseph McCarthy in the early 1950s that recklessly persecuted alleged communists, often without evidence.

mercantilism An economic theory popular in Europe from the sixteenth through eighteenth centuries holding that nations were in competition with one another for wealth, and that the state should maximize its wealth by limiting imports and establishing new colonies that would provide access to precious minerals, spices, and slaves.

mestizo A person of mixed European and American descent, traditionally in Spanish-speaking territories and nations.

middle grounds Places where European and Indian cultures interacted and where neither side had a military advantage.

middle passage The name given to the route used by slave ships between Africa and the Americas.

monopoly A business entity that controls an industry or market sector without competition.

muckraker A journalist who exposes scandal, corruption, and injustice; the term was especially popular during the progressive era.

nativism A belief in the superiority of native-born inhabitants over immigrants; in particular, an anti-immigrant movement that began in the early 1800s in the United States and crested with the passage of immigration restriction in 1924.

nullification A theory that individual states, as the original creators of the federal government, possess the right to invalidate federal laws if they find them unconstitutional.

Open Door The metaphor Secretary of State John Hay used in 1898 to characterize the access to Chinese markets he desired for the United States; it was later expanded to refer to a policy of granting equal trade access to all countries.

popular sovereignty A term coined by Stephen A. Douglas to adjudicate the expansion of slavery in the western territories by allowing settlers to decide the status of slavery for their territory.

Populism A reform movement of the 1890s that promoted federal government policies to redistribute wealth and power from national elites to common people; more generally, refers to a political doctrine that supports the rights of the people over the elite.

primogeniture The English system of inheritance in which estates were passed down to first-born sons.

Quasi War The name given to the undeclared war between the United States and France of 1798–1799.

Reconstruction The process by which the federal government, between 1865 and 1877, controlled the former Confederate states and set the conditions for their readmission to the Union.

Red Scare A period of intense popular fear and government repression of real or imagined leftist radicalism; usually associated with the years immediately following World War I.

republicanism A system of governance in which power derives from the people, rather than from a ruling family, aristocratic class, or some other supreme authority.

secession The act of asserting independence by withdrawing membership from a political state; it refers in particular to the South's withdrawal from the United States.

separation of powers The partitioning of authority to distinct branches of a government.

sharecropping A farming system in which large landowners rent their fields to farmers, usually families, in return for a share of the crop's production.

sit-down strike A planned labor stoppage in which workers assume their positions in a factory or other workplace but refuse to perform their duties, thus preventing the use of strike-breakers.

slave codes Laws passed in the British colonies or in American states granting white masters absolute authority over the enslaved; these included laws depriving slaves of property, free movement, and legal defenses.

Social Darwinism The belief that societies are subject to the laws of natural selection and that some societies or peoples are innately superior to others.

socialism A political theory that advocates government (rather than private) ownership and management of the means of production and distribution.

social justice A movement that seeks justice for whole groups or societies rather than individuals.

sovereignty The authority to govern; popular sovereignty refers to the idea that the source of this authority is the people, who confer authority through elections.

spoils system A process whereby elected officials give out government jobs as reward for political favors.

Sunbelt The southeastern and southwestern regions of the United States.

temperance Self-restraint, especially concerning drink; the temperance movement pushed for bans on the sale and consumption of alcohol.

terrorism The use of violence as a form of intimidation against peoples and governments.

theocracy A form of government in which political power is believed to derive from a deity, and in which religious and government structures are intertwined.

transcendentalism A philosophical and literary movement of the early nineteenth century that sought beauty and truth in nature and the individual, rather than in formalized education, politics, or religion.

triangular trade A simplified description of the complex trade networks of the Atlantic World; the triangle metaphor refers to the trade in rum, slaves, and sugar among New England, Africa, and the West Indies.

Turner thesis The theory articulated by Frederick Jackson Turner in 1893 that westward expansion into the frontier had defined and continually renewed American ideas about democracy and individualism.

vertical integration The arrangement by which a company takes ownership of businesses in various stages of production and distribution within the same industry.

virtual representation British political theory holding that members of Parliament represented all British subjects, not just those from the specific region that had elected them.

welfare capitalism A corporate strategy for discouraging labor unrest by improving working conditions, hours, wages, and other elements of workers' lives.

yellow journalism Sensationalist reporting, particularly in newspapers of the late nineteenth and early twentieth centuries, so named for the color of a character in one of the papers' comic strips.

INDEX